BURT FRANKLIN: RESEARCH & SOURCE WORKS SERIES 572
Selected Essays in History, Economics, & Social Science 187

THE ANCIENT LOWLY

The Ancient Lowly

A History of the Ancient Working People from the Earliest Known Period to the Adoption of Christianity by Constantine

VOLUME II

BY
C. OSBORNE WARD

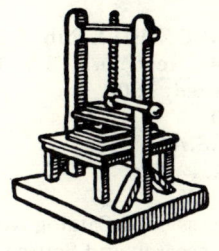

BURT FRANKLIN
NEW YORK

Published by LENOX HILL Pub. & Dist. Co. (Burt Franklin)
235 East 44th St., New York, N.Y. 10017
Originally Published: 1900
Reprinted: 1970
Printed in the U.S.A.

S.B.N. 8337-3685X
Library of Congress Card Catalog No.: 77-114817
Burt Franklin: Research and Source Works Series 572
Selected Essays in History, Economics, and Social Science 187

DEDICATED

TO ALL HONEST EFFORTS FURTHERING
THE STUDY OF TRUE HISTORY ON
LINES OF ORGANIZATION AND
DEVELOPMENT

PREFACE.

THE original ancient idea of socialism was based on the family of father, mother and children; the father and mother being endowed with the mild but positive authority and dignity of lord and lady—a loving community, changeless and eternal. They as now and forever, were to have their common table, their common industry, their common holdings, their parental and filial loves, joys, cares, prosperity, physical and spiritual salvation, all together. This is the nucleus of an undying socialism, so aged that we find no record of its origin. But so fierce and animal-like is the individual, and so graspingly covetous that this father, long before the great lawgiver came, had turned aristocrat, as explained in our first volume, converted the children to slaves, multiplied their numbers by his own law of licentiousness ruining the family microcosm, forcing the children to revolt and filling the earth with an expatriated and outcast class.

Next, and to remedy this and springing from it, came Solon's scheme. This was to enlarge the microcosm into the eranothiasos or initiated brotherhood to be composed of all such expatriated, laboring outcasts and extended by confraternity to consist of many such families united into one. These in the same manner were to be the children of a lord, master, father and mother, who, however, were always voted into place by the children themselves. Here first came into the world the great votive franchise elaborately shown in this work as the basis of scientific, practical socialism. The wording of the law handing down this mighty gift is not lost; for although not appearing in the fragment of the Twelve Tables left us, many inscriptions allude to it, among them, one or two of great value. Readers may learn this with surprise.

The law of universal suffrage was conferred upon the organized working people by both Solon and Numa Pompilius, and we have found and quoted inscriptions giving portions of it. They were not guilds like the mean and selfish non-political corporations of medieval and modern feudalism, but real, genuine voting trade unions greatly resembling the later institution called the socialist trade and labor alliance.

No new candidate or child could possibly be adopted into this enlarged family who could not prove him, or herself to be "hagios kai eusebes kai agathos"—a strictly Solonic injunction and requirement found in a large number of inscriptions of guild-like labor unions, not only of Hellenist Greeks and Asiatic Jews, but also of converted Christians of that early period and seemingly a delightful coincidence, reminding the reader of "the present reawakening of the working classes," of the modern communist Manifesto creating the International Association of Marx, which declares that "all its members shall recognize that Truth, Morality, Justice, must be the basis of the conduct toward each other and toward all men." The three Greek words of the requirement bear substantially this typical meaning. That these splendid associations were made up of a mixed membership of any and all who could, on a test or scrutiny called the "dokimasia," prove themselves to possess these three virtues, were admitted, "regardless of sex, color, creed or nationality," has been thoroughly attested by savants of our modern archæological seminaries, Dr. Foucart among many others. Under this an international scheme of political economy took root and worked with extraordinary success, until the Solonic unions spread themselves over the earth and were millions in number at the time of the Advent, notwithstanding the prodigious efforts of capitalism and its wars of conquest to suppress them.

That the scheme went farther, and under the proclamation of Jesus hazarded an open advocacy of the same socialism to embrace the world; but meeting fierce opposition, not only of the Roman gens and aristocratic, capital-controlling Jews, but later, of the church prelates themselves, who had grown to power through it and colluded with priests and kings, it sank by the cruel conspiracy canon of Laodicea to rise no more, unless this extraordinary reappearance of our own generation means its resurrection.

It was hoped that the Solonism of the combined brotherhoods, forming a microcosm, and its expansion, would have caused it to become a vast socialism with the same family tenets, elements of imperishable brotherhood and votive franchise, and be converted into a universal family association, owning and operating all the implements of labor and all the means of life, always patterning after the family nucleus wherein the government became father and mother, and the citizens the children, having, like every well-regulated family, the common table, communal ownership, management in production and distribution, and the same communal code. This was the scheme originally embodied in the memorable order to "go forth." This ancient scheme is still the longing of cheated humanity, and is the plan of salvation, and the Logos or Word of Promise. The desecration of this great original scheme becomes the more blasphemous on the discovery of a large number of ancient papyri, inscriptions and other literature proving beyond cavil that the "Word" originally, as John interpreted it, meant "Work."

Be the opinions of a prejudiced world ever so

strong, the fundamental truth remains as the prime revelation of this work, although never before brought to the light or entered upon any historical records, that the era we are living in was planted into a vast, aged labor organization, of prodigious power and influence, authorized by Solon and nurtured under his great jus coeundi, or right of combination granted the proletarian millions. This organization, in spite of every opposition of militarism and individual ambition, had spread itself over mainlands, islands and seas, and was at its best and most all-pervading, at the time of the Advent. It was densely and impenetrably secret, and consequently the initiate could go without scrip or purse, and could move under its invisible welcome and protection through a thousand villages and cities, from refuge to refuge, one of which each union is found to have possessed, and thus spread the "tidings" to the uttermost parts of the earth. They did not need to starve or falter or take thought for the morrow, for they were fed and given the password just as promised them on a certain celebrated occasion, when at Jerusalem, as we are told, three thousand joined; and though for a time silenced, leaving the economic half to linger, sorely pining under arrest, yet we need not abide in dismay; for out of it, and through that phenomenal plant, multitudes of better synagogues, temples, mosques, churches and tabernacles dot the earth to-day, which a discontented and more enlightened people desire to see thrown open to the free return and re-entrance of that original socialism which is again to give the children bread, as well as a promise in the indemonstrable beyond.

In proof of this intensely practical moiety of that

PREFACE.

ancient seed-store, we have elaborately shown that in A. D. 79, only 46 years after the pupils were ordered forth, fifteen hundred political election documents were inscribed and set up at Pompeii, beseeching the members to vote the ticket of the unions, that the workmen might have the public employment; and the old pagan temple of Isis, congregation and all, had already been converted over to the Christians, for they owned it and made its refuge their asylum and tabernacle. So again, only eighty years after the crucifixion, Pliny found them sconced among the trade unions of Asia and he had to throw them to the hungry beasts of the amphitheatres by hundreds if not thousands because, in accordance with the command of their martyred teacher, they had refused to pay tribute to Caesar.

All inscriptional, epistolary, apologetical and historical evidence, which is surprisingly voluminous, and which we have faithfully portrayed, centers down to prove that the thing we call "our era" originated in and was no other than a vast working people's movement; and the outcasts themselves understood, by a desperate effort, having for a short time for their teacher and exponent a workingman from among themselves and a carpenter by trade, to push and pry the socialism of the original family, as well as Solon's microcosm of the secret trade union, out of its occultism, and up into the open world. Had it not been suppressed it would have swept the disinherited millions into a voting cosmos or universal state, which, following the gist of things, must have swollen into a prodigious family, whose members working each for all, like a state or nation, would own and manage on a plan of equal interests, all the implements of labor, conducting all production and distribution as a family brotherhood.

Judging from the strides our modern enlightenment is making through the combined instrumentalities of the ballot and of mechanics, it is by no means too much to say that it will yet be done. But it was suppressed; and we have been so fortunate as to find the very words of the infamous edicts of suppression. We have quoted them verbatim, in the Greek and Latin texts, and have rendered them into plain English, so that future teachers may be set right on one of the most important as well as scientific and profound movements that have agitated the minds of men.

Statistics of great importance come from these inscriptions showing that by means of their eranos or union, workmen in the commonest lines of employment, receiving when unorganized only three oboles or about nine cents per long day of twelve or fourteen hours without board, got, when organized, one drachma and three oboles, or twenty-nine cents; more than three times as much per short day under government employment, with excellent food at the "prytaneum" or "mageireion" which was a public kitchen like that at Grenoble to-day. This great difference was entirely due to their being organized in the Solonic eranos or voting union. The short days are understood to mean eight hours because the law divided their day into three equal parts. Abundance of the same monumental evidence which we have elaborately set forth, shows that the workmen used their ballot with powerful energy everywhere, electing candidates to the public works who were their friends, and who almost always awarded them the government employ.

Several characters of world-wide celebrity whose

very existence has been strenuously denied because the names occur in certain standard books, are found to be historical with a certainty which places them beyond the pale of doubt and this too, through their officiating as officers of the labor unions. Among them is Luke, the doctor. Only his guild honored him. We quote the law preserved by a Roman jurist for the Digest, forbidding any dignity or social aspiration for either physicians, merchants or day laborers. Of old, they all ranked on the same social plane. We have found and fully portrayed several important inscriptions regarding him. They are entirely secular, making no reference to Luke's theological career, and totally apart from the canonical or apocryphal gospels.

One of these is a crowning or eulogium. It gives him afresh to the world; this time accompanied by a short history of his life and acts. He was honored in old age by his union of the medical fraternity, a koinon with its common table and communal code, for having been successively a manager of the Board of public works, a director of healthful gymnastics, an educator in the Schools of Tyrannus and a person of great vigor, energy and virtue. By another valuable new-found inscription we have his epitaph and know where he was placed at rest at the close of a long life of usefulness.

One of the important disclosures of this work is that of the early and vigorous co-operation of the Jews. They seem, however, not to have been Sanhedral Jews, but Semitics of Solon's guilds—a distinction as wide as the gulf separating lord from outcast—trade-unionist Jews and working people in the strictest sense. Inscriptional discovery, that elenchus of all arguments, forms our principal source of this evidence.

They are found to have existed in great numbers right where the organizations flourished, and to have joined the movement with a keen and vigorous energy. There is one strange point in their former history which we do not attempt to discuss. Certainly from the battle between Moloch and Moses which reddened the feet of Mount Sinai with the blood of three thousand Jews, there was a division and dispersion of these brilliant and tenacious people; for our main evidence rests on their firm alliance with the unions and not with the followers of Mosaism, inasmuch as they are found knitted into many guilds under the Solonic law and endorsing the patron gods and goddesses like the Gentile members, complying with the rules of the sacrifices of official paganism. When the Christians came they joined their movements with great energy and had good reasons for it; for their own mysterious priesthood had lied to them. Gentiles, Jews, Africans, Indians from beyond the Euphrates, had for seven hundred years been courting a fervid belief that the special divinity of each union they belonged to, would surely one day come in their behalf and relieve their burdens. Thus, at the time our first volume left off, the close of the conquests and the arrival of the workingman upon the scene, their condition was worse than ever known before. Conquest to destroy the unions, and to gratify the taste for blood and greed had not only ruined their once happy homes and torn them asunder, but out of their own ranks, standing armies with their wars had filled the world with innumerable heart-broken slaves.

It was a moment typical of all sorrows. But to the poor man long enjoying his peaceful union, this was more terrible than to all others. His industry had been supplanted by the labor of slaves, mostly prisoners seized in war, almost exactly as men to-day are turned out of employment by machines of their own invention. But instead of modern inanimate machines, their own flesh and blood had been ruthlessly hurled into competition against themselves and made to do for nothing the work their unions formerly coveted. Thrown out of employment by hundreds of thousands through this competition, they delved as slaves or roamed the world as tramps, and in a lingering superstition longed for a redeemer; for their Dionysus Kathegemona, their Cybele, their Osiris, their smiling, captivating Cotytto, had utterly failed them, with the boasting promises of their empty theogony—the ghastly destiny of mythical religions. They began to realize that they must solve their own problem. It may still be argued that at this very day the religion men have placed reliance in, has proved a similar failure and again they are ready to burst its bonds and get at something with a meaning; for a great complaint is abroad that the laboring elements are deserting the temples in disappointment, declaring that for them there is nothing in religion but emptiness and visionary illusion.

Of all the valuable factors entering into the era of our day this phenomenal Hebrew, be he Mosaic or Solonic, we know not, care not, was the prime, in a movement stretching from Solon to the suppression of the unions at Laodicea, about a thousand years. Like all the workers he wrote no literature, but numerous monumental relics inform us that a clause in Solon's law made the carving of the records on stone compulsory. Thus we have, along with those of Gentile races with whom he worked in marvelous harmony, thousands of epitaphs, decrees, minutes of debate, petitions, transactions of the eranos, laws, rules, sales of slaves to a patron divinity amounting to their liberation, loans of money to troops or companies from common funds of their eranos, symposiums, love-feasts, anageneses and coronations in honor of their elevation of some kurios or lord, consecration of many a pre-christian "House" or lord's temple, and funding, building and dedicating of heroons without number, all containing irrefutable history of their organization in the secret Solonic Guilds. In Asia Minor just before and during the period of the Advent they must have numbered millions. They preserved their ancient language in a corrupt form and stretched across the Syrian boundary southward into Palestine, sweeping their typical carpenter along with them as lord of the lords as they went, and were the principal quantity in the great union of over three thousand where at Jerusalem they "had all things common."

They were distinct from Jews of the Sanhedrim who taught the aristocracy of speculation. They were the true Hebrews in bulk, and represented manhood and enterprise then as now; and though in the bloody turmoils and massacres they have many times been well-nigh exterminated yet they have dared to stand out in secret or above board, for the principles underlying socialism, always opposing militarism, standing armies, and competition as the basis of political economy. This brilliant, hardworking, inextinguishable Semitic refused to die as the proud lords would have him do, and it is he who has survived the ghastly train of calamities; for his statue still shoots aloft; if not in a Jesus, in a Marx, a Lassalle or a Maimonides. The former did not write, but heralded the wonderful Word to the

PREFACE.   xvii

angles of the winds; and it is our venture that had he written he would have produced a "Capital."

In our first volume of this work we treated of the failure of irascibility and concupiscence; we had not space to tell of the marvelous antidote couched in the Solonic dispensation. The command of mutual love crops out in many inscriptions showing that there was a clause in the law requiring love among the membership. It came from the great ancient pattern and model adopted by this lawgiver. The model was the family, the purest and noblest socialism even at this day. The injunction that the members should love one another is frequently preserved in the inscriptions and crops out glaringly in a number of them. The common table of the unions was also patterned from the family; all members, once initiated, became children of it. Each, by some labor always provided by the union itself, earned his or her right to a cover at that sacred table, and all must work. It was not charity; charity was unknown. It was not a gift; it was a sacred right, as that of the child at the paternal board.

A large amount of original material used in this second volume was not in existence when the first was published. The Oxyrhynchus papyri, with words of the Logos, still lay in the moulderings of Beneseh; the amazing inscriptions of ancient written music, work of organized labor, lurked forgotten at Delphi in the pronaos of Apollo's shrine at the foot of Mount Parnassus, and nobody knew of the worth of the Briennian discovery of the Kerugma Petrou. Thousands of anaglyphs, at that time undeciphered, have been registered in documents and museums for our personal inspection and listed in the corpora Inscriptionum, while numerous savants have ranged themselves pro and contra upon this very theme. The author himself since the first publication, had to make another voyage of personal inspection, taking in Delphi, Corinth Athens, Smyrna and the Byzantine regions, to pencil numberless jottings now brought under contribution.

Able authorities and publishers have contributed their assistance toward obtaining and verifying the material in this volume. The author is under obligations to Col. Carroll D. Wright, Commissioner of the U. S. Department of Labor for courtesies in furtherance of that journey of research. A keen gratitude is also felt toward Mr. H. M. Alden, editor of Harpers' Magazine, for correct advice, and letters to the Schools of Inscriptions at Athens, and the kindest remembrance is due Mr. Wm. Dean Howells, who also furnished very valuable aid.

On the other side we were met with favors by the savants of the schools themselves. Men of great learning, and authors, like Drs. Foucart, Reinach, Cagnat, Homolle of the Academies of France and Athens, and Dr. John Oehler, of the Epigraphical Seminary of Vienna, were profuse in their attentions to our subject, contributing much inedited matter of great value, which we have faithfully reproduced in these pages.

SOURCES OF INFORMATION.

ABGARUS, Rex Edessæ Mesopotamiæ, *Epistola ad J. Christum.* Excerpt, from various works.
ÆSCHINES, *Oratio Contra Ctesiphontem.*
AM RHYN, (Otto Henne), *Mysteria.* New York, Fitzgerald Co.
Anonymous, *Supernatural Religion.* New York, 1895.
Ante-Nicine Fathers, Edited by Drs. Coxe. Riddle and various Commentators and Translators. 8 Vols., Buffalo, 1868.
Apuleius, *Metamorphosis.* Leipsic, 1850.
Aristotle, *Various Works.* Bekker, Berlin, 1831.
Arnobius, *Adversus Gentes.* Teubnerian Library, Leipsic, 1851.
Arnold, (Philipp), *Das Muenchener Bæckergewerbe.* 7th no. of Lugo Brentano's Issues. Stüttgart, J. G. Cotta.
Arrianus, (Flavius), *Indica; Commentarius Geographicus.* Lond., 1828.
Athenæus, *Deipnosophistæ.* Edited by Casaubon, Paris.
Athenagoras, *Legatio pro Christianis.*
Athenagoras, *De Resurectione.* Stephens, Paris, 1557.
Augustinus, (Aurelius), *Opera Omnia.* 11 vols., Lutitiæ Parisiorum, 1668.
Barnabas, *Epistles and repudiated Gospel.* Apocryphal N. T., London, 1728.
Baur, (Ferdinand Christian), *Die Christliche Kirche der Ersten Dreijahrhunderte.* Tübingen, 1835.
Bell, (John), *Pantheon.*
Benson, (C. E.), *In Wide World Magazine, for June,* 1899.
Blunt, (J. J.), *Dictionary of Sects, Heresies, etc.* London, 1848.
Boarius, (C. Octavius), *De Plinii Cœcilii, Dissertatio Testamentaria Inscriptionibus.* Mantua, 1775.
Böckh, (August), *Corpus Inscriptionum Græcarum.* Berlin Academy, 4 Vols., Berlin, 1824-1862.
Böckh, do. *Staatshaushaltung der Athener.* 2 vols., Berlin, 1817.
Böckh, do. *Gesammelte kleinere Schriften.* 6 vols., Berlin, 1863.
Bœhmer, (Just. Hen.), *Dissertationes II, Juris Ecclesiæ Antiquorum;* Also *De Cœtibus Antelicanis Christianorum.*
Bombardini, See Sources, in vol. I.
Bossio, (Antonio), *Roma Sotterranea.* Roma, 1789.
Bücher, (Karl), *Aufstände der Unfreien Arbeiter.* Frankfort, 1874.

Büchsenschütz, (B.), *Besitz und Erwerb im Griechischen Alterthume.* Halle, 1869.
Bunsen, (Ernest de), *On the Messiah* and other works.
Cagnat, (R.), *Les Syndicats Ouvriers à Rome.* In Vie Contemporaine, for January, 1896.
Caillemer, (E.), *Droit de Société à Athènes.* Paris, 1872.
Caillemer, (E.), *Dictionnaire des Antiquités Grecques et Romaines.* Paris, 1890.
Callistus, (Nicephorus), *Historia Ecclesiastica.*
Capitolinus, (Julius), In *Augustan Histories.*
Cedrenus, *Synopsis Historiarum.* Written about A. D. 260.
Celsus, *Logos Alethes,* or True Discourse. Ap. Origen, *Adversus Celsum.* Several old editions.
Christ, (Johann Friedrich), *Anthologia Græca Carminum.*
Chrysostom, (Dion), *Orationes.* J. J. Reiske, Altenburg, 1775.
Chrysostom, (Dion), Fragments of lost Writings. Paris, 1687.
Chrysostom, (John), *Sancti Joannis Chrysostomi, Archiepiscopi Constantinopolitani,* Opera Omnia. Parisiis, 1842.
Chrysostom, (John), *Opera et Studio Monachorum Ordinis Sancti Benedicti.* 12 vols. in all.
Cicero, (Marcus Tullius), Complete. See list of the sources of Information in vol. I.
Clement, (of Rome), *Canones Sanctorum et Venerandorum Apostolorum per Clementem a Petro.* In Corpus Juris Civilis.
Clement, (Titus Flavius Alexandrinus), *Protrepticas.* Also his *Stromateis* and *Pœdagogos.* Various excerpts.
Clinch. (George), *Anthologia Hibernica.* 3 vols., Dublin.
Cohn, (Max), *Zum Römischen Vereinswesen.* Berlin, 1873.
Corpus Juris Civilis. *Academicum Parisiense Opera et Cura* C. M. Galisset. Lutitiæ Parisiorum, 1830.
Creuzer, (Georg Friedrich), *Symbolik und Mythologie der alten Völker, besonders der Griechen.* 4 vols., Leipsic, 1810.
Crusius, (O.) *Die Delphischen Hymnen.* Goettingen, 1894.
Cumont, (Franz), *Les Inscriptions Chrétiennes de l' Asie Mineure.* Also *Archéologie avec de l' Histoire,* Paris, 1895.
Cumont, (Franz), *Monuments relatif au Culte de Mithra,* Paris, 2 vols.
Cyprianus, (Thasius Cæcilius), *Ad Rogationem.*
De Foe, (Daniel), *Political History of the Devil.* London, 1798
Demosthenes, *Pro Crorona.*
De Rossi, (Giovanni Batista), *Inscriptiones Christianæ Urbis Romæ.* 2 vols., Romæ, 1888.
De Rossi, (Giovanni Batista), *Roma Sotterannea.* 3 vols., Roma, 1864–1880.
Dietrich, (R.). *De Hymnis Orphicis, Capilula Quinque.*
Diocletianus (Imperator), *Edictum, De Pretiis Rerum venalium.*

SOURCES OF INFORMATION. xxi

Dion, (Cassius), *History of Rome.* See list of Sources of Information in vol. I.
Dion, (Chrysostom), see Chrysostom.
Dionysius, (of Halicarnassus), *Rhomaike Archæologia, vel Antiquitates Romanorum.* Frankfurt, 1586.
Dionysius, (Exiguus), *Fragmenta Epistolarum; Epistola ad Sixtum II.*
Dirksen, (Heinrich Eduard), *Kritic und Herstellung der Zwölf-Tafel-Fragmente.* Leipzig, 1824.
Doane, (T. W.), *Bible Myths,* New York, 1882.
Domaszewski, (A. von), *Cura Viarum,* in Eranos Vindobonensis. Vienna, 1895,
Donaldson, (J. W.), *History of Christian Literature.*
Donatus, (Alessandrus), *Roma Vetus et Recens,* Libri III. Paris, 1620.
Dorotheus, (Tyrius et Bibl. Patrum), *Synopsis de Vita et Morte Prophetarum, Apostolorum et Discipulorum.* Leyden, 1731.
Draper, (John W.), *Intellectual Development of Europe.* New York, 2 vols., Harpers.
Du Cange, (Charles Dufresne), *Historia Byzantina Illustrata,* Paris, 1680.
Du Cange, (Charles Dufresne), *Glossarium ad Scriptores Judæi* Halle, 1772.
Duchesne-Bayet, *Rapport sur une Mission Archéologique au Mont Athos.*
Dumont, (Alb), *Studies among the ancient Relics.* Paris, 1870.
Encyclopædia Britannica.
Eschenbachius, (Andreas Christianus), *De Scribis Veterum Romanorum.* Nuremberg, 1690.
Eschenbachius, (Andreas Christianus), *Dissertationes Academicæ.* Paris, 1705.
Eusebius, (Cæsareæ), *Demonstratio Evangelica; Historia Ecclesiastica.*
Ewald, (Georg Friederich), *Sendschreiben des Apostel Paulus.* Berlin.
Ewald, (Georg Heinrich August), *Jesus und seine Zeit.*
Foucart, (P.), *Les Associations Religieuses,* Paris, 1873.
Foucart, (P.), *De Collegiis Scenicorum apud Græcos,* Paris, 1873.
Foucart, (P.), *Mémoire sur l' Affranchissement des Esclaves,* 1867.
Fränkel, (Zacharias), *On the Eight Hour Day among the Ancients.* in Dresdener Zeitschrift, 1846.
Friedländer, (Ludwig), *De Artificibus Dionyciacis.* Königsberg, 1875.
Gaius, *Lex Duodecim Tabularum.* In Corpus Juris Civilis; Digest, XLVII., xxii.
Gfrörer, (August Friederich), *Allgemeine Kirchengeschichte,* Stuttgart, 4 vols., 1841, Also on *Philo Judæus,* 1831.

SOURCES OF INFORMATION.

Gibbon, (Edward), *History of the Decline and Fall of the Roman Empire.* 4 vols., New York.
Gildas, (Sapiens), *Historiola de Calamitate, Excidio et Conquesta Britanniæ.* London, 1684.
Giles, (Rev. Dr.), *Hebrew and Christian Records.* London.
Ginsburg, (C. D.), *The Essenes. Their History and Doctrines.* London, 1868.
Goldzieher, (F.), *Hebrew History. Heathen Mythology.*
Gorius, (Antonius Franciscus), *Monumentum sive Columbarium Libertorum et Servorum Liviæ Augustæ et Cæsarum, detectum in Via Appia.* Roma, 1728.
Granier, (Adolphe de Cassagnac), *Histoire des Classes Nobles;* also *Histoire des Classes Ouv.* Paris, 1830-1845.
Grenfell, (Bernard B.), *Oxyrhynchus Papyri.* London, 1898, with Plates.
Gruterius, (J.), *Inscriptiones Antiquæ Totius Orbis Romanorum.* Heidelberg, 1603.
Hadrian, (Imperator), *Epistola ad Servianum.* Various quotations.
Haeckel, (Ernest), *History of the Creation.* 2 vols., New York, 1887.
Harpocration, (Valerius), *Lexicon decem Oratorum Græcorum.* Berlin, 1833.
Heberdy, (R.), *Denkschrift der Wiener Akademie.*
Hefele, (Karl Joseph), *Koncilengeschichte.* 7 vols., Frieberg, 1865.
Hegesippus, *Hypomnemata.* Ap Euseb., Hist. Eccles.
Heinecius, (Johann Gottlieb), *Syntagma.* Francofurti ad Mœnum, 1841.
Hermann, (Charles Frederich), *Political Antiquities of Greece.* English trans. of Oxford, 1836.
Hermes, (Pastor), *Apocryphal Writings.* In Ante-Nicine Fathers.
Heuzy, (and Dumont), *Mission Archéologique en Macédoine.* Paris; print of the Académie des Inscriptions.
Hierocles, (Governor of Bithyma), *Logoi Philaletheis,* in Fragments as preserved.
Higgins, (Godfrey), *Anacalypsis.* 3 vols.
Higgins, (Godfrey), *The Celtic Druids.* London, 1829.
Hippolitus, (Saint), *Philosophoumena.*
Hippolitus, (Saint), *Refutatio Hœreticorum.*
Hirschfeld, (G.), *Ueber Kelainai-Apameia.* Vienna, 1875.
Hirschfeld (O.), *Römische Verwaltungeschichte.*
Homer, *Iliad* and *Odyssey.*
Hughes, (John), *Horæ Britannicæ.* 2 vols., London, 1819.
Hunt, (Arthur S.), *Logos Papiri of the Nile,* in coöperation with Grenfell, by means of London Exploration Fund.

SOURCES OF INFORMATION. xxiii

Huschke, (Georg Philipp Eduard), *Verfassung des Servius Tullius.*
    Heidelberg, 1838.
Ignatius, (Theophorus), *Epistolae.* Recens. Cotelerii, Amsterdam,
    1724; also Syriac version of Dr. Curetonius, London, 1890.
Irenæus, *Adversus Hæreticos.*
James, *Protevangelium;* likewise, *Canonical Epistle.*
Jameson, (Anne), *Sacred and Legendary Art.* London, 1874.
Jarvis, (S. F.), *Chronological History of the Church.* N Y., 1850.
Jerome, (Heironymus), *Contra Jovinianum; Letters, Homilies etc.*
Jesus, (Christ), *Epistola ad Abgarum.*
Jesus, (Christ), *Logia,* found in Ruins of Oxyrhyncus, Egypt,
    Grenfell and Hunt, Oxford, 1898.
Joannes, (Antiochensis Cognominis Malala), *Historia Chronica.*
    Oxon, 1690,
Jones, (Jeremiah), *On the Canon.* 2 vols., London, 1726.
Jovinian, *Homilies.*
Jullian, (Camille), *Inscriptions romaines de Bordeaux.* Bordeaux,
    1887.
Justinianus, (Emperor), *De Argentariorum Contractibus Edictum.*
Justinianus, (Emperor), *Omnium Legum Pandecta.* In Corpus
    Juris Civilis.
Justinus, (Martyr), *Dialogus cum Tryphone;* also *Hortatory Address to the Greeks.*
Juvenal, (Decimus Junius), *Satirae.* Leipsic, 1819.
Kaibel, (G.), *Inscriptiones Græcæ, Siciliæ, Italiæ, etc.* Berlin, 1890.
Kaibel, (G.), *Epigrammata Græca e Lapidibus Conlecta.* Berl., 1878.
King, (William), *The Gnostics and their Remains.* London.
Kirchmann, *De Funeribus Romanorum.*
Kitto, (John), *Cyclopaedia of Biblical Literature.* 2 vols., London,
    1845-1850.
Krause, (Karl Christian Friederich), *Die Drei ältesten Kunsturkunden und Freimauerbrüderschaften* Dresden, 1840.
Lactantius, (Lucius Cœlius Firminianus), *De Morte Persecutorum.*
Lactantius, (Lucius C. Firmin.), *Institutiones Divinæ.* Paris, 1783.
Lampridius (Ælius), *Alexander Severus.* Augustan Histories.
    Leipsic, 1858.
Lardner, (Nathaniel), *Credibility of Gospel History.* 5 vols.,
    London, 1757, Also *Hebrew Testimonies.*
Le Blant, (Edmond), *Etude sur les Sarcophages Crétiens de la
    Ville d' Arles.* Paris, 1878.
Le Blant, (Edmond), *Inscriptions Crétiennes de la Gaule.* Also
    Nouveau Recuil; same work. 3 vols., Paris, 1865-1895.
Lavasseur, (Emil), *Histoire des Classes Ouvrières.* 3 vols., Paris.
Liebenam, (Wilhelm), *Zur Geschichte und Oganisation der römichen Vereinswesen.* Leipzig, 1890.
Limburg-Brauwer, *Histoire de la Civilisation.*
Lingard, (J.), *Antiquities of the Anglo-Saxon Church.* Lond., 1845

SOURCES OF INFORMATION.

Livius, (Titus), *Historia Romana, Opera quœ Supersunt.* 4 vols., Lond., 1844.
Lobec, (Christian August), *Aglaophamus, siu De Theologiœ misticœ Causis.* 4 vols., Königsberg, 1827.
Logia Papyri from Oxyrhynchus, Egypt. See Grenfell, or Hunt.
Lucianus, (Samosatensis, *Apolog. pro Merc. Cond.;* and *Opera omnia quœ supersunt.* Leipsic.
Lücke, (G. Chr.), *Offenbarung Johannis.* Bonn, 1832.
Lüders, (O.), Bulletino Archæologico, Sp. 1024, 140.
Lüders, (O.), *Die Dionysischen Künstler.* Berlin, 1873.
Lycosthenes, (Wohlfahrt), *Prodigiorum Chronicon.*
Mabillon, (P.), *Etudes Monastiques.*
Macrobius, (Ambrosius Theodorus), *Opera Omnia.* Leip., 1868.
Maffeus, *Archœological Works.* Rome.
Ma-Geoghegan, (M. l' Abbé) *History of Ireland.* Paris, 1758.
Malmsbury, (William of), *Notitia Portarum, Viarum, Ecclesiarumque circa Urbem Romœ,* Rome, 1786-1799.
Manohar, (Murli), *On Government and Life in Ancient India,* In Nineteenth Century for July, 1891.
Marcellus, (Avircius), *Autobiography on Tombstone.* Hierapolis, Apostolic Age.
Mariotte, (Edme), *Vestiarium Christianum, vel Vestiarium Christianorum.*
Martialis, (Marcus Valerius), *Epigrammata,* Paris, 1825
Martyriologium Universale. Baronius, Antwerp, 1613.
Mauri, (Angelo), *Cittadini Lavatori del Attica,* Milano, 1895.
Manadier, Julius), *Qua Condicione Ephisii usi Sint,* etc.
Menger, (Anton), *Das Recht auf den Vollen Arbeitsertrag.* Stutgart, 1886.
Methodius, *Fragmenta.*
Mommsen,(Theodor), *Berichte der Sächischen Gesellschaft.*
Mommsen, (Theodor), *Römische Geschichte.*
Mommsen, (Theodor), *Corpus Inscriptionum Latinarum.* Berlin Academy, Berlin, 4 vols., folio.
Montfaucon, (Bernard), *L' Antiquité expliquée.* **Paris, 10 vols.,** folio, 1719.
Moses, *The Law.*
Mosheim, *Historia Ecclesiastica.* Also *Commentaries.*
Müller, (and Schwanbeck), *Fragmenta Historicorum Gaaecorum.*
Müller, (Friederich Max), *Origin of Religion.* Oxford, 1857,
Münter, (Friederich Chr. Karl. Heinrich), *Sinnbilder und Kunstvorstellungen der alten Christen.* Altona, 1825.
Muratorius, (Ludovicus Antonius), *Canon Muratorius.*
Muratorius, (Ludovicus Antonius), *Thesaurus Veterum Inscriptionum.* Venice, 1790.
Nardeni, *Roma Antica.*
Neander, (Augustus), *History of the Church; also The Planting.*

SOURCES OF INFORMATION. xxv

Nitzch, (Karl L.), *Observationes ad Theologiam Practicam felicius excolendam* Bonn, 1831.
Oehler, (Johann), *Das Griechische Vereinswesen, und seine Bedeutung fur das sociale und öffentfliche Leben.* Uneditd.
Oehler, (Johann), *Manuscript Excerpts to the Author.* Vienna, 1897-1898.
Oehler, (Johann), *Boulé; a Dissertation on the Athenian Political Government, and the Prytaneum.* In vol. III., of Pauly-Wissowa.
Oehler, (Johann), *Zusammenstellung der Inschriften über die dionysischen Künstler.* Excerpts.
Origen, (Chalkeus Adamainteus), *Adversus Celsum.* 8 books.
Orosius, (Paulus), *Historiarum Libri Septem.* Thorunii, 1857.
Paulus, (Roman Jurist), *Pauli Sententiarum Libri.* In Corpus Juris Civilis.
Paulus, (Apostolus), *Epistolœ.*
Perrot, (Georges), *Exploration Archéologique de la Galatie.*
Philo, (Judæus), *De Vita Contemplativa.*
Philo, (Judæus), *Quod Omnis Probis Liber.*
Philo, (Judæus), *Legatio ad Gaium.* Venice, 1822.
Philostratus, Flavius), *Vita Apollonii Tyanensis.* Paris, 1608.
Piero, *Investigation des Hieroglyphes.*
Plinius Major, (C. Secundus), *Historia Naturœ.* Venice, 1607.
Plinius Junior, (C. Cæcilus), *Epistolœ.*
Plutarch, *Apothegmata* and other works. 13 vols., Geneva, 1572.
Poland, (Dr. Prof.), *De Collegiis Artificum Dionysiacorum.* Vienna, 1895.
Pollux, (Julius), *Onomasticon.* Berlin, 1846.
Polybius, (Megalopolitanus), *Ta Sozomena Polybii Lycortœ.* 2 vols., Amstelodami, 1620.
Porphyrius, *De Mysteriis Oraculorum.* Paris, 1711.
Probst, (Akademiker), *Kirchliche Disciplin.* Leipsic, 1873.
Proclus, *Commentarii Adversus Christianos.* Paris, 1820.
Prudentius, (Aurelius Clemens), *Contra Symmachum.* Rome, 1788.
Quinn, (Daniel), *Manuscript-Information* to the author, regarding *Stone Chiselings* of *Prices* in Diocletian's Time.
Rangabé, (Directeur), *Antiquités Hell.,* Athens, Paris, 1882.
R....... ~~h. (Theodor), *Restitution des Hymnes à Apollon.* Delphi, Athens and Paris, 1895-1896.
Rheinach, (Theodor), *Explication des Inscriptions Musicales.* In Bulletin de Correspondence Héllénique. Paris, 1896.
Romanelli, (Domenico), *Viaggio a Pompeii.* Roma, 1817.
Routh, (Martin Joseph), *Dissertatio de Glossariorum Usu.* Leipsic.
Saglio, *Dictionnaire des Antiquités.*
Saniel, (Lucian), *Histories of Socialism.* In Almanac and Treasury of Facts, New York, 1899.
Savigné, (E. J.), *Guide Annuaire historique de la Ville de Vienne.* Vienne, 1876.

xxvi SOURCES OF INFORMATION.

Schömann, (G. F.), *Griechische Alterthümer:* also *Opuscula Acad.*
Seneca, (L. Annæus), *Full Works;* Editio Princeps. Naples, 1475.
Severus, (Septimius), *Rescript enforcing Lex Julia.* In Digest.
Silvester, *Silvestri Liber Martyriorum.*
Smith, (Adam), *Wealth of Nations.* Edinburgh, 1850.
Smith, (William), *Dictionary of Biblical Biography, History and Literature.* 4 vols., Boston.
Spartianus, (Ælius), *Historiæ Angustæ Scriptor.*
Stobæus, (Jonannes), *Eclogæ Physicæ et Ethicæ.* Also *Anthologium.* Meineke, 4 vols., Leipsic, 1856.
Strabo, *Geographia.* Bibliog. 3 vols., Leipsic, 1877.
Suetonius, (Tranquillus), *Vita Cæsarum* Leipsic, 1875.
Swoboda, (H), *De Griechischen Volksbeschlüsse.* Leipsic, 1880.
Tacitus, (C. Cornelius), *Annales et Historiae.* Leip., 2 vols., 1846.
Talmud, in 2 parts; *Mishna* and *Gemara.*
Targum, Aramaic Version of the *Old Testament.*
Tatianus, *Oratio ad Graecos.* Corpus Apologeticorum. Jena,1857.
Teffy, (J. B.), *Synagogue ton Attikon Nomon.* Pesth, 1868.
Tertullianus, (Quintus Septimius Florus), *Apologeticus; De Animæ Testimonio ; De Pallio.*
Theodoret, *In Vita Patrum.*
Theophilus, *Epistolae ad Autolycum.* In Ante-Nicine Fathers.
Thirwell. (Connup), *History of Greece.* 8 vols., Lond., 1852.
Thucydides, *De Bello Peloponnesiaco.* 2 vols., Leipsic, 1851,
Tillemont, (L. Sebastien), *L' Histoire Ecclesiastique.* Paris, 1717.
Tischendorf, (Lobgott Friedrich Konstantin), *Codex Sinaiticus.* Leipzic, 1862. Also *Wann Wurden,* etc.
Trajan, (Imperator), *Epistolae ad Plinium;* also *Rescripts* and inscriptional *Orders.* Various excerpts.
Ulpianus, (Roman Jurist), *Regularum Singularum Fragmenta.* In Corpus Juris Civilis.
Valens, (Imperator), *Decrees.* In Code of Theodosius.
Valentinus, *Fragmanta* app, Clementi Alexandrino. Homilies.
Van Holst, *De Eranis Veterum Graecorum.*
Venantius, (Fortunatus), *Poesis: De Itinere Suo.* Venice, 1469.
Villegardelle, (M.), *Histoire des Idées Sociales.* Paris, 1846.
Vopiscus, (Flavius), Historiae August. *In Aureliano et Saturnino.*
Wallace, (Robert), *Numbers of Mankind.* London. 175°
Wallon, (A. H.), *Histoire de l' Esclavage dans l' Antiquité.* 1848.
Waltzing, (J. P.), *Etude historique sur les Corporations professionnelles chez les Romains.* 3 vols., Louvain, 1895.
Warburton, (William), *Divine Legation.* London, 1741.
Warnkönig, (L. August), *Institutiones Juris Romani Privati.* 1819.
Welcker, (Gottlieb Friedrich), *Die Æschillische Trilogie Prometheus.* Göttengen, 1824.
Ziebart, (Erich), *Das Griechische Vereinswesen.*

CONTENTS OF THE VOLUME.

CHAPTER I.

ROMAN CONQUESTS.

THE SOLITUDO MAGISTRATUUM.

THE two deep-meaning Expressions—Forgotten but on the Return—Livy and Neander—Outworkings of the Law of Solon—Politically Organized Workmen Outnumber the Patrician Party—Voted Out—Rome Ruled by the Labor Party for five Years—A Great Victory Expunged from our Histories—Licinius Stolo's Agrarian Laws—Manlius Capitolinus—The *Jus Coeundi* of Numa Quoted—Lowering Jealousy caused by It—Plan to Exterminate the Unions—Plan of the Roman Conquest—Great Work of the Trade Unions Employed by Government—Eight Hours a Day—Reign of Saturn—Superstition that Once Heaven was on Earth—It probably Originated in those Happy Days Lost by the Conquests—Cunning Plan of the Military Conquests to delude the Unions—Story of the awful Desolation—Decimation of the Human Race—Foolish Bargain of the Unions to Secure Rome's Paternal Employ—How it Led to their Ultimate Ruin—Havoc of the Conquests Described—Important Contribution to this Knowledge, in Inscriptions—New Document Proving an Eight Hour System of the Unions—Their Existence Everywhere—Their Beautiful Government—Terrible Inroads of the Conquests—Ultimate Failure of the Roman Army to Destroy Them—Terrible Destruction of Mankind—Unionists Seized and Sold into Slavery by Millions—Did not Exterminate Them—These Slaves Became the Nationalized Tools of Labor—How Government Slaves became Machines through

xxviii CONTENTS OF CHAPTERS.

the Conquests—Their Disastrous Competition to Free Labor—Slaves as Tools like Modern Machines—Starved Millions by their Competition—Slaves secretly joined Unions which Advanced Money for their Enfranchisement—Their God himself the Buyer—How Explained—Many Inscriptions in Proof—Desperate Plan of Jesus Secretly Planted into Solon's Unions—Their Jus Coeundi—Prodigious Trade Unionism at Time of Advent—Asylums existed as Places of Refuge for Runaway Slaves, but none for Charity—Inscriptional Proof—Great Authority of the Lord of the House—The House a Temple belonging to each Guild—Comparison of the Mosaic with the Solonic Dispensation—Wonderful Evidence at Pompeii showing successful Political Activity of Unions—Conquests resulted in no Good—Left Things much Worse than Before—Could not Break up Organization—Reflections.
45

CHAPTER II.

REVOLUTIONS AMONG SEMITIC RACES.

STRIKE OF MOSES AND THE JEWS—ESCAPE FROM EGYPT.

Most Ancient and Enormous of all Strikes and Labor Rebellions—One Million Involved—The Exodus—Comparison with Eunus and Spartacus—Stinging Lash of the Slave Drivers upon the Backs of an Innocent and Enterprising People—Strange Story of the Straw and Stubble—Unreasonable Demand of a King Squeezing Them beyond Endurance—Rebellion against it of the Mildest Nature—Struck Work and Ran Away—Pharaoh and his Military Hosts in Hot Pursuit—Almost Incredible Providential Rescue—Red Sea Opens and lays bare a Path for the Hebrews but Flows back and Engulfs the Pursuers—Discovery of a Mummy of Same Pharaoh Casting Doubt—Number of the thus Emancipated Given in Exact Figures—Reflection on the Prodigious Magnitude and Effects of this Strike—Law of Moses the direct Result of it—Proof that Violent Resistance is Productive of Good—World of Labor Forced to Bow in Reverence and Respect to Moses and the Jews.   75

CHAPTER III.

MORE STRIKES IN EGYPT.

STORY TOLD IN HIEROGLYPHS.

HEBREWS not the only Egyptian Strikers—Three Thousand Years ago—Unions on Public Work at that Time—Pharaoh as a Merciless Employer—Starving the Men—It was not long after the Exodus—Birthplace of Free Masonry—Practice of Engraving Records on Stone—Queer Strike in Asia Minor—An Inscription Tells of a Mighty Strike of Bakers in Magnesia a Semitic City—All Told out on the Stone—No other Account of it Known—Great Disturbance—Cut off the Supply of Bread—A Bread Famine—Intervention of the City Council—Strikers Arrested—Their Union Broken up and its Members Forced to Furnish Bread without a Trade Union—Powerful Proof that they were under Government Employ—Great Union of the Musicians—A historic Proof that they were Employed by Governments—Music treated as a Trade—Story of an Important Strike of these Artists—Three Centuries before Christ—Like Moses and his Hebrews they Struck Work by Running Away—How they were Caught—They Ultimately Won—Full Quotations from Livy—Power of the Lord of their Union—Marching off under their Old Red Flag—The Way the Politicians Outwitted Them—Yet They Accomplished their Purpose—All under Guise of Religion though they Cared Only for their Bread and Comforts—Admitted a Pure Strike by All Commentators.   81

CHAPTER IV.

NABIS.

THE LAST OF THE EPHORI.

NABIS—A Semitic on the Rampage in Greece—How a Slave of the Conquests Overwhelmed his Oppressors—Chilon the Wise Inventor of an Unwise Measure—The Ephori—How Their Tyranny Destroyed the Laboring People—They even

Ruled and Threatened Kings—Hated by the World—Nabis the Syrian Slave Rises by his own Energy—Becomes a Cunning Military Officer—And Turns his Energies toward Extinction of the Ephori—The Ephori Described—Their Trained Assassins—How they lurked in Hedges with Sharpened Daggers—Plutarch's Account—Workingmen their Victims—Systematic Decimation of their Numbers—Working People as Tools of Labor—Nabis Swears to Exterminate the Ephori—His Wild Cruelty—Carnage among the Rich—Their Money Distributed among the Poor – Robbed Rich to Feed the Poor—Nabis Invents the Murderous Manakin—An Infernal Machine in Woman's Form—Springs fixed to Daggers that Stab the Lusty Princes who Embrace Her—Quotations from Polybius—Apega, Wife of Nabis was the Name of this Murderous Automaton—Nabis Becomes Tyrant of Sparta—Aristotle on Nationalized Tools of Labor—How Tools in Human Form were the Same Then, as Our Labor Saving Tools To-day—Fearful Competition of Such against the Free Labor Unions—The Tyrant takes their Part—His Wife and Many Ladies Work with Him—Strives to Restore the old Socialistic Form – Rings of Women who Assist him in Robbing the Rich—Imaginary Horrors and Superstition Among the People—Ghosts and Spectres Believed in—Assassinated through Intrigues of Philopæmen—Result of his Life-Work—Final Extinction of the Ephori—They Never Rose to Power again—Vengeful Life-Work of Nabis Accomplished.
89

CHAPTER V.

SOLONIC DISPENSATION.

VAST SYSTEM OF TRADE UNIONS OVER THE WORLD.

IMPORTANCE of the new Discovery of them—Their Remote Origin—Solon, Numa and Amasis the first in their Known History—Ancient Law of the Twelve Tables—Pre-Christian Christianity—Based on Mutual Help and Love—Countries where they Existed—All followed One Model—Their Common Table and Communal Code—The Prytaneum—Patterned after the City—City in Theory Modeled after the Family—Authority of Dirksen—The Competitive System Reversed—Respect for Religion—Microcosm of the Future Perfect

CONTENTS OF CHAPTERS. xxxi

State—Enmity of Wealth Against It—Herodotus Quoted—
Why the Unions had to be Secret—Took the Military Form
—Secret during a Thousand Years—Reverence to the Great
Law-Givers so Great that no Enemy Dared Molest them—
After their Amalgamation with the Christians they became
Still More Secret—Why—Sources of Information—Much
through Strabo and Arrian from Lost Works of Megasthenes, Onesicritus, Nearchus, Aristobulus, Aristotle. 99

CHAPTER VI.

INDIA'S BROTHERHOODS
EVIDENCE NEVER SEEN IN HISTORY.

The Lost Books—Handed Down to us through Strabo and Arrian
—Megasthenes—Other Men's Precious, Lost Geographical
Books—Valuable Account from B.C. 350—Theory of a Sunken Continent—Adverse Criticism of Strabo Refuted—The
Hamadryad—Story of the Modern Capture of One—Monster of Deadly Poison—King Sandrakotta—Indian Dwarfs
—Government of India—Its Labor Organizations—The IndianOlympus—Mount Nusa—Its Brotherhoods—The Colony
of Dionysus—A Cradle of the Unions—Roman Conquests
Struck them when they Struck Damascus—Blades of Damascus blocked out in India—Indian Brotherhoods Divided
into Seven Parts—Their Complete Delineation—Farmers,
Hunters and Herdsmen—Skilled Artisans and Workers on
Exchange—Great Value and Importance attached to them
—All in Government Employ—Exempt from Military Burdens—All Land Owned by the State or Society—The Useless
Military Factor—The Ephori and their Spies—The Solonic
Form of Labor Organization—It Gave Original Law and
Dominated the Career of Industry—Bartholomew Sent there
to Preach the Gospel—Peter supposed to have also Spent
Years in India. 107

CHAPTER VII.

RAGE AND HAVOC.
CONDITION AT CLOSE OF CONQUESTS.

Wrangles over the Spoils—Extent of the Havoc of Conquest—
Murderous Standing Army—Roman Generals brought Spoils
in their own Name—Countless Slaves of their Conquests—
Sulla's Massacre of 50,000—Unions fell Victims of their own

Duplicity—Judicial Murder by Crucifixion of 400 Innocents—Mostly Semitics—Story reconstructed—Heartlessness of the Senate—Plea to Save them Overruled—Savage Speech of Cassius—Law Enforced—Awful Agonies—Workers Dangerously Maddened—Longed More ardently for Promised Redeemer—The Carpenter Already Born—Endorse His Plan of Salvation—The Slave Marts—Cheap Humanity—The Poor longed for the Right of Marriage—Power of Inscriptions and Anecdotal History—Cruelties of Paulus Æmilius—Still more Secret—Seized and Thrown over Precipices—Ingratitude of Men who lived by Others' Toil—What better were Such than Brigands—Pre-Christian Martyrs—Socrates an Example—Two Persecutions of the Jews—Their Good Character made Them a Target of Hate—Great Advantage of the Common Tables—An Ancient and Revered Institution—Jews of Antioch—Roman and Pagan Hatred of them—Story of the Maccabees—Defeat of Syrian Generals—Power of the Congregation—Futile Effort to Break up the Mosaic Dispensation—Ferocious Massacre of the Hebrew Race at Jerusalem—Best Author puts Number Murdered at 1,100,000—Sanguinary Fury—Sad Loss of Arts of Damascus Steel, Crimson Dies, Imperishable Inks, Pigments and Many Inventions Ascribed to these Truculent Deeds of Savagery—They were Secrets of the Unions—Property whereby they lived and which Died with Them—World's Irredeemable Losses. 219

CHAPTER VIII.

PRE-CHRISTIAN UNIONS
NUMBERS, CHARACTER AND INFLUENCE.

ASIA the Home of Trade Organizations—Plato went with Socrates to One for the Material of His Republic—Socrates a member—Always Law Abiding—Union of Washerwomen 600 Before Christ—Typical Name Erano Thiasos, Good for all Terms—Always had Votive Franchise—Inscriptions in Proof—Ancient Eranos resembled Modern Socialistic Trade and Labor Alliance—These are the Oldest Unions on Record—Love for One Another a Command of the Law—Common Table and Communal Code Brotherly Love Stretched into the Hereafter—Burial Attachment Aided them—Rigid Examination of Candidates wishing to join—The Dokimasia—The Agnus Castus—Solonic and Christian Tenets identical—They made Slave, Freedman and Freeman Equal—Plodding Outcasts—How they loved such Tenets—Voting Unionism

CONTENTS OF CHAPTERS. xxxiii

raised them above mere Tools of Labor—Sabazios, Their Soter becomes Saviour—Serapis—Tullus Hostilius a Friend—Bridge Builders—Name Originated the Pontificate—The Pontifix a Boss Bridge Builder—Tracing Trade Unions from the Sixth Century B. C.—Manner in which they Flourished—Shielded the Poor—Eranos Loaned Means to Slaves to Buy Themselves Free—No Starvation Within the Veil—The Great Gemeinde—Stretched over All Lands—Ancient International—Hebrew Eranos—Many Jews had the Solonic Instead of the Mosaic—Unions in the Islands—Therapeutæ and Essenes were Solonic—Nazarenes a Branch—Taint of Labor—Unions of Boatmen—Of Fishermen—Merchants in those Days as low as Artisans—Longshoremen—Shippers—No Strikes, because Interests were Common—Strange Pre-Christian *Anagenesis*, or New Birth—Union of Cutters near Nazereth—Multitudes at Tyre and Sidon—Knife and Dirk Makers—Union of Gardeners at Ephesus. 147

CHAPTER IX.

SOLONISM IN OUR ERA.

THE WORLD UNDER ITS INFLUENCE.

SKETCH from A. D. 1 to 363—The Burial Attachment—Eranos at Jerusalem—The Kurios—Legalized Boss over Each Union—Peremptory Provision of Law—Was Dictator and Lord—Misunderstanding regarding Him—Plan of Salvation—Early Mutilation and Covering of Facts—When they first began to Display Secret Principles before the World—Always had Common Table—Macedonia Alive with them—Deacons—Originally only Table Waiters—Unions of Deacons or Table Waiters—Secret Common Eating Houses—Worked in the Pryteneum—Lydia of Thyateira an Officer in Dyers' Guild—How and where Converted—Gravestone of Menippus found—Therapeutæ were regular Business Guilds—Many in the Cities of the Seven Churches—Proof in their own Chiselings—Eranos and Thiasos alike—Unions of the Hetæræ—Claudius Drove them from Rome—Union of Gold-beaters—Bakers of Philadelphia—Fishers—Labor Unions Worshiped Imaginary Saviour—Ground All Mellow for One when He Came—List of various Messiahs—Karl Marx Right in Treating Religion as a Consequent and not as a Cause—Shipping Business of the unions—Degraded by Taint of Labor—Ox-drivers' Union—Lucian's Ridicule—Cotton and Linen Industry—Phrygian Bag Carriers—Called Themselves Holy Union of Bag-carriers—Sacred Union of Cotton Spinners—Of Wool Workers—Of Crimson Dye Makers—All in the Cities of the Seven Churches—Object, To better their Circumstances—Consecrations—Building Trades—Valuable Find of a Sepulchre with Glyphics of a Masons' brotherhood Converted to Christianity But Concealing the Fact for Fear of the Roman Law—Time of Paul—Celebrated C.I.G. 3857 t.—Dr. Oehler's Contribution—Splendid Find of the Shoemakers of Shoemakers' Street—Their Colony, a Church of the Temple of Cybele on the Acropolis of Kelainæ—Dr. Ramsay's Explorations—Marble Workers of Apameia—Christianized Unions of Flaviapolis in Cilicia—No Eleemosyna y Charity Existed—All under the Veil of Initiation, Furnished with Work—Beginning of Persecutions with Crippling Laws Against Them—Stretch of the Solonic Unions to Britain—Havoc of the Council of Laodicea—Canon Preserved that Suppressed the Work of Solon—Quotation—The Singing and Enjoyments Receive their Death Stroke—All Elements of Socialism Expunged by Prelates—Monastic Orders and Tyranny of Prelate Power Supervened—Ghastly Consequence in Feudal System—The World fell into a Millennial Swoon. 176

CHAPTER X.

THE GREAT GEMEINDE.

THE INTERNATIONAL OF DIONYSAN ARTISTS.

Obscurity Veils one of the Most Remarkable Facts of Antiquity—Masterly Investigation of Dr. August Böckh—Startling Curiosity—The Big Order's Make-Up—Their Tutelary Saint was the "Ennobler of Mankind and Giver of Joys"—Their Music—To gain a Living their Object—Centuries of Dense Secrecy—The Pythian Apollo—Homer—Scenic Artists—Strike of the Flutists—They Belonged to the interlinking Bond—Hated But Employed at Rome—Enormously patronized by the State—Alexander's Carnival of Hephastion—Three Thousand Musicians and Playwrights Gathered from Far and Near—Others for the Olympic Contests—Stories of Arrian, Plutarch and Athenæus Agree with Inscriptions—Wonderful Agonies—Full Description—Their Model of Pure Socialism, Father, Mother and Children—Their Common Table and Mutual Love—Microcosm of the Perfect State—Votive Franchise Substituted Father's Paternal Control—It Worked—Terrible Laodicean Canon—Eunus—The Erano-

CONTENTS OF CHAPTERS. xxxv

thiasos—The Everlasting Fakirs—How they Crawled into the Unions and Debased Principle—Menander's Desdæmona—Fakirs, Fortune-Tellers and Filter Peddlers—Aping the Official Religion to Secure Good Jobs—Emperor Hadrian patronized the Agonistic Performances—Symbol of the Serpent—Fakirs Assume Form of the Snake—A Curious Inscription—Scenic Plays at Rome—Fun Making Entertainments—Callipygian Dance—Greek Trilogy—Notwithstanding their brilliant Genius the Unions were often Poor—Sneers of Lucian—Nobler Praise by Aristotle—His Truthful Axium—The Immunes—Fishers and Hunters an Allied Branch—Billingsgate of Smyrna—Synods of Baptists—The Quingenarian Spell—Hunger of Dominion for Acts of Cruelty. 203

CHAPTER XI.

OLD INTERNATIONAL.

ITS TENETS, RULES AND METHODS.

A LIVELY Modern Inquiry—Work of the Academies—Dr. Böckh's Comprehensive Name—The Organizations' Greek and Latin Chisel-Work—Reliability of Our Authority—Secret Behind the Old Reverence for the Jus Coeundi—Their Headquarters—Trades Engrossed by it—Saint Paul the Tent-Maker. Proved to have been a Member—Their Classical Literature—Ionian Synod—Numbered Millions—Countries Occupied—The Didasculus—They had Schools and Taught the Rich—Popular with Emperors—Domitian Persecuted them—How Dr. Ramsay Found their Inscriptions—Ad Exemplum Reipublicæ—Twelve Tables—About their Temples—Theatres—Why Called Gemeinde—Cicero's Denunciation—Killed by Cruel Money Power with Aid of Standing Army. 231

CHAPTER XII.

ANCIENT MUSIC.

STONES BRINGING MELODIES BACK TO LIFE

Music of the Unions Described—Introductory Reflections—Exploded Belief That Ancient Forefathers possessed no Knowledge of Musical Notes—Discovery at Delphi in 1895—Wonderful Musical Find Chiseled on Pronaos of Temple of Pythian Apollo—Olympian Hill-Slopes—Dr. Theodor Reinach's Heliograph—Author's Visit to the Temple of Oracles—Keen Criticism of Reinach, Orusius, Welcher—Frogs of Aristophanes—Music of the Agonies—Pausanias' Treasury of the Athenians—Gevaert on Instrumental Music—Second Musical Find in 1896, still better—Valuable Illustration—Third Musical Find—A Treasure from Tralles in Asia—Influence of the Unions who possessed the Science—Outfit of the Musicians—Power of the Drama—They Sang a Doxology—Orphic Canticle—Wide Range of the Singers—The Harmostios Nomos—A Mournful Strain—The Hymnodoi—What, when at Last the Christians Came—Jealous Prelates Stabbed Genius to the Heart—Victimized by Prelate Power—Suppression at Laodicea—They Fell Forever. 239

CHAPTER XIII.

HAGIOS EUSEBES AGATHOS

COMPOSITION, HABITS, MORALS, LAWS.

THE Solonic Unions not Guilds—Neither did they resemble the Trade-Unions of to-day—Voting Trades-Brotherhoods—Meals in Common—Property in Common—Tools of Labor in Common—Question, What were They?—Categorically Answered—Best Greek Name Eranothiasos—Best Latin Name Collegium—Best Aramaic-Hebrew, was Ebionim—How this Poor Man's Name got Pilfered and Stiffened in the Schools—Love One Another a Principle—Numbers and Moral Status at Time of Advent—Determined Adherence to Marriage—Not Gnostics—Amalgamated with Christians but had to be Secret—Statistics Gleaned from the Stones—Admission Fees Known—The Dokimasia—Own Strict Rules—Charity, Beggary and Blasphemy disallowed—Initiations—Fines for the Non-Payment of Dues—Work or Starve—Contributions to Valuable Knowledge by French, Austrian, German and Athenian Academies—Author's Personal Reception by Them—Encouraged to Proceed—Scrutiny of Laws Governing the Unions—Financially helped Each Other—Revenue—Nemesis—Turned Mills of the Gods against unfair Distribution—Fines for Desecrating Graves—Cremation vs. Burial—"Sub Pretextu Religionis"—Whippers and Rhabdophores—Contortion of Word Charity—Ignominious Alms-Giving or Proffer not Tolerated—Original Prytaneum—Essenes ate in Common at Temple of Jerusalem—Coenobium at Rome. 256

CHAPTER XIV.

POLITICAL FUNCTIONS.

THE ANCIENT VOTING UNIONS.

POLITICAL Functions—The Oath of Dreros in Crete—"Dangerously Political" is Aristotle's Shibboleth—Strange Clause in Solonic Law on Corsair Trade—Rite of Baptism Originated among them—Was for Cleanliness—Members to be Pure and Clean—Against Leprosy—Tyrannos, the Pedagogue—Sabazian Thiasos—Trouble between Æschines and Demosthenes—Hadrian's Letter on the Mithraic Christians—Hierophant—Sabbath a Strictly Union Rite—Pagan Labor Year 365 Days—Love Feasts—Eight Hours Day—Synod—Congregations—Symposiums—Cremation—Cinerary Urns—Rosalia—Day of Violets—Hallelujah—Kathegemon or Forerunner—Thought to Resemble John the Baptist—The Mageireion or Common Kitchen—Public Cookshop—Resembled Grenoble—The Rule of Proxy—Functions of the Kurios or Lord-Dictator—Discovery of Dual Habits—Untwists a Curious Clause of Solon's Law—Evidence that it Stretched to Ceylon—Irrigation—System of Crowns—Crowns of Willow, Wild Olive, Tulip, Gold—The Thallou Stephanos—Crowning the Dead—Statistics of Wages from their own Inscriptions—Day's Pay for Plowmen—Cleaning—Woodwork Polishing—Hod Carriers—Mechanics—Difference between Pay of Organized and Unorganized Workmen—Dr. Maury's Researches—Statistics of Cost of Living—How Slaves as Tools of Labor Competed with Free Work—Human Machines—Pitted Slave Against Union Labor—List and Prices of Slaves—Asylums of Refuge but No Hospitals—Purchased Slaves in Order to Set them Free—Edict of Prices of Diocletion—Ideas of a Vast Workshop in the Beyond—The Demiourgos. 279

CHAPTER XV.

PRE-CHRISTIAN MARTYRS.

PRINCIPLE A CRIME PUNISHABLE WITH DEATH

A FORERUNNER the Favorite God of the Unions—Dangers of the Propaganda—Cruelty of Demosthenes—Martyrdom of

xxxviii CONTENTS OF CHAPTERS.

the Girl Ninos who Initiated New Members—Accused of Helping Slaves—Martyrdom of Theoris—Demosthenes Attacked Her—His Coarse Sensualities—Dark Rumors of another Martydom—Pitched down the Barathron—Vengence of the Kathegemon or Forerunner Goddess—Glaucothea accused and sneered by Demosthenes—Mother of Æschines—Fatal Vote by Pebbles—Gulf Separating the two Sets of Mysteries—Quenched Bloodthirst on another Woman's Veins—Fate of Neæra—Thrown off the Rocks—Neither Thiasos nor Lawyer could Save Her—Epitaph of Tryphera another Martyr—Member of a Union—Dæmon of Vengence Drives Demosthenes to Suicide—Martyrs Sneeringly Classed as Courtesans—Escape of Exquisite Phryne—Ranked with Isodaites—Baseless Slanders—Isodaites Her Angel of Equality—Athenian Snobs—She Organized an Eranos—Eloquence of Hyperides—Her Acquittal—Proofs—Socrates a Member of an Eranothiasos—Similarity to Great Later Martyr—Gathered Disciples and Apostles—Very Poor Man—Marble Cutter—His Euthanasia—Like Phryne, had his Good Angel—Billingsgate of the Piræan Fisheries—Accused of Same Crime—Prison of Socrates—Author's Visit to Grotto on the Acropolis—The Hemlock—Hour of a Great Martyr's Death.
326

CHAPTER XVI.

APOSTOLIC AGE.

THE LAW UNDER TIBERIUS, CLAUDIUS, NERO, THE FLAVII AND DOMITIAN.

PRELIMINARY OF THE CHAPTER.

PLANTING the Word—Screened at First by the Law—Emperor Tiberius Friendly—Periodicity of Man's Forward Steps—Facts which Could not be Covered—Work of our Great Archæologists—Great Events during Reign of Tiberius—Struggling to Enlarge the Microcosm into a State—An Analysis.
346

SECTION I.—TIBERIUS.

ERA Planted under this Monarch—Ever Memorial Vista—A New and Surprising Historical Sketch of Christianity—Environment of Dangers—The Poor Could not obtain Work without Organized Protection—Statement of their Influence on

CONTENTS OF CHAPTERS xxxix

Christ—Tiberius Friendly—Men at the Head of the Movement all Initiates—The Word—Hebrew History—Abgar Letters—All Known of the Circumstance—Anger of the Emperor—Pilate a Historical Character—Crucifixion Proved a Historical Event—Lynching of Stephen—His System of Common Tables Competed with Provision Rings—New Light on His Assassination—Three Thousand Members in his Union—The Murder Broke it Up—Stephen was a First Class Business Man—The Metonym.

SECTION II.,—CALIGULA—CLAUDIUS. 356

TERRIBLE Change in Treatment of Jews and Christians—Involved Thousands of Workingmen—Marvelous Discoveries—The Domus Augustalis—Caligula Began and Claudius Continued the Persecutions—Victims Secretly Organized—Discoveries of De Rossi—Underground Rome—The Columbarium—Tyrannus—Their Scholæ discovered far beneath the Surface—Driven to Such Hiding Holes at Rome—Had System and Schools in these Recesses—Caligula Murdered—Mommsen, Cagnat, Oehler and other Savants Agree that these Collegia were the Regular Solonic Unions—Full Description of School—Roma Sotterranea—Exhaustive Researches of De Rossi—Four Trades represented in the Silvani Find—Discovery that During Persecutions of Claudius, those wretched Workers Dived Down into Subterranean Abodes—Continued in Hiding Throughout Nero's Reign—Devotion for Each Other—The Strange Practice not Confined to Rome—Clement of Rome—Friend of Peter—Wrote Kerugma Petrou—Sketch of his Life—Why his Valuable Works were Suppressed—Consistency of the Term "Lord" as Manager of Business of Union—How there Came to be so Many Lords—It was a Clause in the Law of Solon—The Quinquennalis—He was also an Evangelist—Banishment by Claudius Caused Great Numbers to Escape and Colonize in Other Parts of the World—Exiles—Well Received in Asia Minor—The Gerousia turns out to be a Solonic Union—The Aventine Hill—Ægis of Diana—Colony of Shoemakers of Shoemaker Street—Evidence that the Christians Planted into and Thrived upon these Trade Organizations—Aquila and Priscilla—Other Exiles of Claudius—Episode of Demetrius—How an Important Matter is Misunderstood—His Union worked making Images for Diana at Ephesus—All tended to Madden Claudius—Supposed Quarrel of Paul, John and Peter Refuted—A perfect Harmony Agreed Upon—The Innumerable Secret Hives—Traces of Work of Joseph of Arimathea—Briennian Find of Parts of Peter's Teachings.

SECTION III.,—NERO.

NERO—Period Covering Imprisonment of Paul—Literary Evidence Burned—Accounts of the "Acts" Proved by Inscriptions to be Good History—Nazarenes a Branch—Landing of Paul at Puteoli, in Chains—Warmly Received by already Converted Brotherhoods—The Delegations—Same Unions Already Described—Centuries Old—Story of Narcissus—Nero at First Kind and Tolerant—Believed to have taken Paul with him to Spain—Grows Morose and Jealous—Employs an Able Detective, named Tigellinus—Turns Against Friends and Humanity—Closes Friendly Doors of Domus Augustalis—Seneca, Philo, Peter, Paul and a Host of Other Good Men Charged upon—Escape of Philo, Assisted by Peter—Barnabas—Nero Plots to Burn the Immortal City—Pudens, Priscilla, Claudia and the Poet Martial, all acquainted, and Friends—Story of Pudens—Was an Englishman—Organized a Union of Carpenters in England—House of the Lord—Strange Analysis of the Word—Pudens a Lord of a Union—Recent Discovery of Wonderful Inscription of Carpenters' Union at Glastonbury in Chichester—Pudens Gave the Land—Probable Gift of King Cogidubnus—Tacitus—Though Christian, it was Dedicated to Minerva—Collegium Fabrorum—Evidence Massed—Household of Claudia—All Members of Brotherhoods of Trade Guilds—Mentioned in Paul's Epistles—Also Mentioned by Martial in his Epigrammata—Recent Discovery of their Names Inscribed upon their Cinerary Urns—Nero Finds out these Things through his Spies—He is Incensed—Story of the Burning of Rome—He Swears that he will Rid Rome of the Genus Tertium, meaning the Christians—Okum, Tar, Pitch and large Quantities of Grease Gathered—Tigellinus—Spread of Fire Described—Nero Carouses on the Mæcenatian Tower—Cunning of Nero in Accusing the Hated Genus Tertium—Vast Numbers of Christians Put to Death—Fury of the Populace—Many Christians Thrown to Wild Beasts—Smeared with Tar and Grease and Set on Fire for Torches of the Nightly Carnival—Sewn up in Bags and Thrown to Rome's Hungry Dogs—Unknown Thousands Perish—Atrocious Massacre—Work of Tigellinus, Nero's Pinkerton—Statement of Tacitus, Suetonius, Orosius and Others—Paul, Seneca, Peter, Pudens and Many others murdered in Nero's Rage—Manner of Execution—Death of Nero—Celebrated Fisherman was Crucified Head Downward and the Reasons Why—His Wife also led to Execution. 512

CONTENTS OF CHAPTERS.   xli

SECTION IV.,—VESPASIAN—TITUS.

GALBA—Short Reign of Seven Months Closed by Assassin's Dagger—Vespasian—Voted to Power by Prætorian Guard—Story of Narcissus—Vespasian Friendly to the Organizations—A Moment of Safety and Rest—Flavian Amphitheatre or Coloseum—Strange Discovery of a Slab Containing Name of its Builder, a Christian—He was Guadentius, Master Workman of a Builders' Guild—Vespasian's Short Reign—Nine Years of Peace, Comfort and Prosperity—Titus, his Son—Reigned only two years—Continued Prosperity—The Celebrated Eleven Years of Happiness—Titus Continues the Kindness of his Father—Cruel in His Destruction of Jerusalem— Mild in his Government at Rome.   569

SECTION V.,—DOMITIAN.

DOMITIAN—Another Son of the Generous Vespasian—One of the most Terrible of Tyrants—An Account of his Murderous Havoc—Valuable History of Dion Cassius—Gibbon declares he means Christians though he Calls them Jews—Domitilla—Said to have Lived through Nero's Time—Atrocities of Domitian at Puteoli—Domitilla Persecuted—Her Husband Executed—Persecutions Raged at Rome—Newly Found Inscriptions Prove her a Historical Character—Inscription of Gruter—Wonderful Discoveries in Under-Ground Rome—Elegantly Ornamented Halls, School Rooms, Eating Chambers, Frescoings Sixty Feet beneath the Surface—They were Abodes of Hidden Brotherhoods during Persecutions of Domitian—Inscribed Mausoleums of Nearly all the Celebrated Martyrs Found—Peter, Paul, Domitilla, Pudens, Claudia—Innumerable Hosts of Others Unknown—Vast Revelations of the Excavation Funds—Story of Callistus and Carpophorus—Ashes of Blastus—Underground Monuments of the Via Salaria Vetus—The Catacombs of the Appian Way—Great Columbarium—End of the Tyrant Domitian.   572

CHAPTER XVII.

TRAJAN.

THE PLINY EPISODE.

PLINY and Trajan's Celebrated Persecutions—Ignatius Christophorus—Great Master Had Caressed Him When a Babe—Trajan's Sentence—Thrown to Beasts in Amphitheatre—Value of His Repudiated Epistles—One to Mary Shows She was a Member—Ancient Syriac Version Proves that Christian Eranos Emancipated Slaves—Order of Widows—

xlii   CONTENTS OF THE CHAPTERS.

Pliny appointed Governor in Asia—The Hetæræ—Pliny found them Converted Guilds—Members Refused to Buy Sacrifices—Would not Render Tribute to Cæsar—Crime Punishable with Death—Nest of such Criminals Discovered by Government Spies—Pliny's Letter to Trajan—Ordered Many to Execution—Tortured and forced Them to Curse Christ—Praised their Honesty and Virtue—Lex Julia—Trajan to Pliny—Pliny Himself Converted—Tries to Organize a Union of Firemen—Trajan Refuses, Fearing that They would Turn Christians like the Rest—Original of Letters Quoted—Frequent Mention of Words Christ and Christian—These Hetæræ had already been converted many years—Pliny in Contrition Gives Sums of Money to Children of Families he had Murdered—Inscription ad Trajanum Amisorum in Proof—The Lesson.   584

CHAPTER XVIII.

ORIGINS OF THE HOUSE OF THE LORD.

HOUSE OF THE LORD—A Phenomenal Institution—Authorized in the Twelve Tables—Secret and Invisible Union—Meetinghouse, Temple, Refuge, Public Kitchen and Hospital Combined—Mary's Grotto, the Refuge, in One—Infant Jesus Shielded in It—Proof—Herod's own Son one of the Slaughtered—Macrobius Quoted—House Took Form of the Prytaneum—Always Belonged to the Unions—Many Inscriptions as Evidence—Harmony and Success of the Centuries—Many Bible Characters Now Found to be Crowned and Garlanded Lords of Such Houses—Crescens—Narcissus—Titus—Stephen—Crispus—Tychicus, Paul's Courier—Name in Two Inscriptions—Onesimus—Ramsay on Occultism of The Secret Veil—Philemon—Epaphros—Papias' Lost Book—Explained the Economical and Ignored Paul—CIG 3865—Three Celebrated Names, Papias, Trophemus, Tychicus—MM. Ramsay and Perrot—Their Splendid Find of a Union of Masons with Tatias and Onesimus—The Union's Rules Against Quarrelling—Their Own Inscriptions Found—The Enigmatical Door of Jesus—No Quarrel of Paul With Immediate Companions of Jesus—Full and Lasting Agreement at Jerusalem—Wrangles of Imagination—Metonyms of Important Members on Conversion—Pro-Consular Spies—Luke as a Member—Important Inscription—Also Called Nicias—Taught in Schools of Tyrannus—Ashes of Both Lately Found in Columbarium—Strange Tablet—Quoted Verbatim—Cinerary Urns Preserved Deep in Hypogeum—Description of Find—Greek of Franz Quoted—Though a Hot Communist, Paul's Substantial Friend — Gerusia — Mistake about It — Now known to be Another Name for Union—Red Dyers' Heroon to Menisippus—Luke Proved to be an Ambassador from Rome—Probably Exiled—His Colony—Epitaph of Luke at Tlos—Remarkable Inscription of Philip—Law of Compulsory Inscriptions—Forced amid Dangers to Chisel Philip—Inscription Agrees with Eusebius—Hierapolis—Similar Trouvaille of Avircius Marcellus—Epitaph of the Mariner Xeuxis—His Sixty Voyages—Belonged to Union of Sailors—Avircius Speaks of the Thirteen-Years' Cessation From Persecution—This Lacuna Cleared Up—Paraphrase of the Lithoglyph The Plutonium—Complete Transcript—Jason of Thessalonica—Bridge-builders at Rome. 603

CHAPTER XIX.
CELSUS AND LUCIAN.

PAGAN Literature of Early Christian Times—Celsus the Accuser—Twits Christians of Hiding in the Secret Unions—Gynæceum—It was a School—Origen's Contra Celsum—Declaration that They were Genuine Unions—Origen His Critic Does not Deny—Belabors Christians Because Secret—Berates their Holding Love-feasts—Sneers because they were Working People—Lucian of Samosata—Pagan Wit who Lampoons the Christians—The Two were Friends—Payment of Tribute—Paschal Canon says Origen was a Brazier—Defiant Comparisons of Celsus—The Prytaneum—How the Church of St. Peter Came to be Built—The Secret Password—Temples of Refuge—Period of Columbaria—Lanuvium—Wonderful Inscription Found, 1816—Quinquennalis a Dictator—Growth in our Knowledge of the Burial Clause and Burial Attachment—Churches in Ruins of Ancient Unions—Old Temples Used as Churches—Christianized Temple of Isis at Pompeii—Old Labor Guilds—Dug Out of Lava of Vesuvius—Dr. Willens on the Labor Guilds—Pompeii—Although Christianized, at Time of Eruption, Were Still Worshiping in Temple of Isis—Owned Some of Its Property—Hated Pests Exiled—Escaping to Similar Temples of Refuge Went to Gaul, Asia Minor, Allobrogia, Vienne. 644

CHAPTER XX.
CHURCHES ON RUINS.

SCHEME of the Early Movement—Metamorphosis of the Temple into the Kuriakos—Origin of Churches—St. Peter's was from Persecuted Collegia of Diana on the Aventine—Vourkano on the Ithome—Orchomenos—Temple of Cybele at Philadelphia—The Phyles and their Guilds—Temple of Jove on Acropolis of Kelaina—Discovery at Ancona—Temple of Isis at Pompeii—How it Became Property of the Multitudes

xliv   CONTENTS OF THE CHAPTERS.

of Voting Trade Unions There—Proof that when Converted They turned it into a Church—Origin of Cathedral of Notre Dame at Paris—Remarkable Inscription Found—It was Originally a Temple of a Boatmen's Union of the River Seine.   655

CHAPTER XXI.

MASSACRE OF DIOCLETIAN.

What Became of it All—The Ancient Plan Suppressed—A Hitherto Unrecorded Murder of the Human Race—Destructive Power of the Standing Armies—The Havoc of a Traitor—Scheme of Diocletian and His Courtiers—Their Plans Against the Brotherhoods—Cruel Character of Galerius—Joint Monarchy of Four—Demand for Extermination—Formation of a League—Hierocles as their Agent—How He Passed the Dokimastirion and Slipped in—Appointed Governor—Divulged Union Secrets to the League—Rage of Galerius—Plan Determined on, was Extermination—Opinions of Drs. Ramsay, Cumont and Others—Eumeneia—Its Destruction told by Eusebius—Quotations—Governors of other Provinces Supposed to have Divulged—Evidence of Lactantius—Story of Crispins—Logos Philatheis of Hierocles—Diocletian's Edict of Prices—The Edict Quoted—The "Vilis Plebecula"—Date of the Slaughter Fixed for Feb. 22nd A. D. 303—Rancor of Mother of Galerius against the Christians—Words of Gibbon—Burning of the Book—Quoting Ramsay—Bargainers Covet their Properties—Book of Papias—Treason Against Getting of Wealth and Power—It was Burned because it Revealed the Economics of Solon's Socialism—Details of the Massacre—Porphyry—Spread over many Provinces of Proconsular Rome—Entailments of Diocletian's Atrocity—Not Until Afterwards we find Charities—Plant of Eleemosynary System—First Seeds of Feudal System—Feudal Guilds—Pauperism Appears in the World—The Orphanophulax—Laws Governing Such Institutions—Proof that they never existed Before—How Constantine took the Control of Christianity—Downfall of the Two Great Schemes of Solon and of Jesus to Redeem the World—Go Back to them, the Cry of our Strangling Race.   668

THE ANCIENT LOWLY.

CHAPTER I.

ROMAN CONQUESTS.

THE SOLITUDO MAGISTRATUUM.

THE two deep-meaning Expressions—Forgotten but on the Return—Livy and Neander—Outworkings of the Law of Solon—Politically Organized Workmen Outnumber the Patrician Party—Voted Out—Rome Ruled by the Labor Party for five Years—A Great Victory Expunged from our Histories—Licinius Stolo's Agrarian Laws—Manlius Capitolinus—The *Jus Coeundi* of Numa Quoted—Lowering Jealousy caused by It—Plan to Exterminate the Unions—Plan of the Roman Conquest—Great Work of the Trade Unions Employed by Government—Eight Hours a Day—Reign of Saturn—Superstition that Once Heaven was on Earth—It probably Originated in those Happy Days Lost by the Conquests—Cunning Plan of the Military Conquests to Delude the Unions—Story of the awful Desolation—Decimation of the Human Race—Foolish Bargain of the Unions to Secure Rome's Paternal Employ—How it Led to their Ultimate Ruin—Havoc of the Conquests Described—Important Contribution to this Knowledge, in Inscriptions—New Document Proving an Eight Hour system of the Unions—Their Existence Everywhere—Their Beautiful Government—Murderous Inroads of the Conquests—Ultimate Failure of the Roman Army to Destroy Them—Terrible Destruction of Mankind—Unioniste Seized and Sold into Slavery by Millions—Did not Exterminate Them—These Slaves Became the Nationalized Tools of Labor—How Government Slaves became Machines through the Conquests—Their Disastrous Competition to Free Labor—Slaves as Tools like Modern Machines—Starved Millions by their Competition—Slaves Secretly joined Unions which

Advanced Money for their Enfranchisement—Their God himself the Buyer—How Explained—Many Inscriptions in Proof—Desperate Plan of Jesus Secretly Planted into Solon's Unions—Their Jus Coeundi—Prodigious Trade Unionism at Time of Advent—Asylums existed as Places of Refuge for Runaway Slaves, but none for Charity—Inscriptional Proof—Great Authority of the Lord of the House—The House a Temple belonging to each Guild—Comparison of the Mosaic with the Solonic Dispensation—Wonderful Evidence at Pompeii showing successful Political Activity of Unions—Conquests resulted in no Good—Left Things much Worse than Before—Could not Break up Organization—Reflections.

Two remarkable expressions of well-known historians are recorded but as yet, little understood. The first is that of Livy, known as his *solitudo magistratuum*, B. C., 373 ; the second is that of Neander,[1] known as the "*prediction*." They prove that great events may sometimes involve the career and well-being of mankind and then drop into forgetfulness and become for a long time lost.

The expression of Livy which our historians pay no attention to, informs us that there was a time when at Rome the political power of the laboring people rose to such a stage against the dominion of wealth and aristocracy that for five years the tribunes held control and the business of the state went on without a house of lords.[2] The significance of this is that the senate was ruled out by a strong majority of the strictly working people, organized under the great law of Numa Pom-

[1] The Prediction of Neander will be occasionally referred to as we proceed. The English translation of the Prediction reads as follows: "We stand on a line between the old world and the new about to be called into being by the ever fresh energy of the Gospel. For the fourth time an epoch in the life of our church is in preparation by means of Christianity." Schaff's *Hist. of the Apostolic Church.* New York, 1851.

[2] Livy, Hist. Rome, VI. 35, fin.: Vol. I. of this work, p. 474, where Livy's remark is quoted. But as it is important we may do well to requote : " Haud irritæ cecedere minæ: comitia, præter ædilium tribunorumque plebis, nulla sunt habita. Licinius Sixtiusque tribuni plebis, refecti, nullos curules magistratus creari passi sunt: eaque solitudo magistratuum, et plebe reficiente duos tribunos, et his comitia tribunorum militum tollentibus, per quiquennium urbem tenuit." The object of the common people in these comtia or elections is here distinctly stated in the words "præter ædilium tribunorumque plebis ;" and it is plain that as the ædiles were managers of the public works and the tribunes were members of the house of representatives, the common people by the vote which elected them to office, secured their influence in being assigned the much coveted labor of the public works. In other words it was democratic socialism, for the organized trade unions in that way secured the public jobs. They were well paid and worked about eight hours per day.

THE REIGN OF SATURN. 47

pilius which was the law of Solon, being a direct result of the Solonic dispensation.

Here Livy declares that it was not possible to elect any candidate except aspirants of the plebeian race, for a period of five years ; and he makes special mention of the important fact that the men chosen were members and directors of the board of public works. This was the pure socialism which the Roman unions were carrying out, and such as is advocated with renewed and enormous energy at the present day. By voting their own candidates into the care of buildings and grounds, who in their own language were the *ædiles* or directors of public works, the very term used by Livy, workingmen, enormously organized under the celebrated statutes of Numa or rather of Solon, and afterwards enlarged and confirmed by their great statesman and King, Tullus Hostilius, are proved to have been hotly engaged in the political agitations of furnishing their unions with work from the government to an enormous extent, in building up their great city and furnishing it with those celebrated bridges, sewers and public buildings, the ruins of which are wonders of the living age, directly under government management and pay.

The celebrated Licinius Stolo, author of the agrarian law which is accounted to be the most important of ancient statutes [2] but which in reality falls in importance, far short of the great Solonic law, was, with Sixtius, a tribune of the people at that time ; and they were repeatedly elected to the tribunate, B. C. 376-357. Their combined agitation lasted ten years. When Appius Clau-

---

[2] *Encyc.* Amer., in verb. *Stolo*, where the power of this man is acknowledged. Recent researches have brought the fact to light that those tribunes and labor organizations hinted at by Livy were in close organization under the military arrangement of Numa, See E. Bormann, in *Eranos Vindobonensis*, p. 347, who gives the original tribunes as "Tribusführer" militum; but see Andrews' elaborate definition, at the close of which these tribunes are characterized as the common people, the herd, rabble, mob, etc. In fact, Livy, VI. 35, so recognizes the power of the tribunes The "rabble" held political control for five years. These words are to express the historian's contempt. In fact, the people, organized into powerful industrial unions under the ancient law of organization, had grown to be the ruling political force and strength of Rome. Bormann, already adverted to, says further : "Es bestand eine Reihe collegiastisch geordneten Functionäre mit der Bezeichnung tribuni ;" and quotes from Varro, *De Lingua Latina*, V., 55, and V., 181; also Mommsen, *St.-R.* III. sec. 110, showing that the plebs with their tribunes were all regularly organized in trade unions, and are so recorded later. B. C.128-10, by Varro.

dius was elevated to the noble office of decemvir, B. C. 451, he turned savagely against the workingmen thus organized in legalized unions, although it was their law guaranteeing them this privilege which he had the year before assisted to engrave upon one of the Twelve Tables among other early Roman statutes.[3] Involved in those great turmoils of which so little is said in history, was a noble Roman, M. Manlius Capitolinus who, B. C. 390-385, took the part of the plebs against the aristocracy. He was overcome, accused, condemned, sentenced to death and thrown from the Tarpeian Rock.[4]

In those early days Rome and most all other countries held all land as untransferable property of the state. These social commotions against the people were among the earliest to establish an aristocratic ownership by the patrician class; and they were rapidly accomplishing their purpose under a right accorded by the *lex de jure quiritio*, a law based on the assumed right to crave and demand.

The actual time of the Solitudo Magistratuum of Livy was B. C. 373, the moment of the Agrarian agitations.

There is now no doubt left in the minds of honest historians that the great event of a vacancy and interregnum of the power of the Roman house of lords, for five years of the republic, during which the lords were completely ruled out of office so that there was no senate, and the tribunes were supreme, is what caused the thus endangered grandees to organize the conquests. Working people were gaining political control.

The celebrated conquests form the principle part of the mighty events which charm, confuse, mislead all readers of history. Appius Claudius, the monster of the proud

---

[3] Dig., XLVII., tit. xxii., lex. 4; see Vol. I. of this work, pp. 346, 347 and notes and p. 217, note 87 where the law is quoted. On page 287 of Vol. I., is an account of this monster, Appius Claudius, his treachery to the workers and his swift disgrace and destruction, with a rendering from Livy of the facts.

The law recorded in the *Digest* appears under the title *De Collegiis et Corporibus*, and reads: 4, Gaius, lib. 4 *Ad legem XII Tabularum;* Sodales sunt, qui ejusdem collegii sunt; quam Graeci ἑταιρίαν vocant. His autem potestatem facit lex, pactionem, quam velint, sibi ferre, dum ne quid ex publica lege corrumpant. Sed haec lex videtur ex lege Solonis translata esse: nam illuc ita est: Ἐὰν δὲ δῆμος, ἢ φράτορες, ἢ ἱερῶν ὀργίων, ἢ ναῦται, ἢ σύνσιτοι, ἢ ὁμόταφοι, ἢ θιασῶται, ἢ ἐπὶ λίαν οἰχόμενοι, ἢ εἰς ἐμπορίαν, ὅ τι ἂν τούτων διαθῶνται πρὸς ἀλλήλους, χύριον εἶναι, ἐάν μὴ ἀπαγορεύσῃ δημόσια γράμματα.

[4] For some account of this man who reminds us of the Gracchi being martyred in the cause of agrarian laws, see Meyers, *Konversations Lexicon*, in verb. *Capitolinus*.

gens family of the Claudiæ, powerful during nearly all the stretch of republican as well as imperial Rome, was so jealous of this rising power of the poor and disinherited class of workers that he conceived the idea of exterminating them; and in collusion with many other lords of high families, advocated the idea that Rome could accomplish this purpose by flattering the organized workingman and turning their skill to the manufacture of implements of war. Every research tends to reveal evidence that there was a rising growth among the Romans, Greeks and Semitics of the working classes about the time the Solonic law was translated and engraved upon the Twelve Tables. Before the conquests, affairs of the general public were, according to Polybius and Livy, rising, on account of the ascendency of the tribunate power which came from the political organization of the plebeian or working element of the population. Civilization was everywhere prospering with a splendid outlook. The world was for the most part at peace. Grand bridges spanned the streams of Italy, Spain and Sicily. Public edifices arose in stately majesty. Architecture was at its zenith of perfection. Slavery was rapidly disappearing from the earth. Nearly all of it was the work of trade unions employed by government. After the conquests when the unions were partially throttled it was gold, power, individualism, aristocratic preference and crucifixion of the poor and downtrodden. Polybius informs us that before the conquests Rome was in the ascendant. The little acquisitions of neighboring cities and states, sometimes involving wars and strifes of short duration he does not seem to consider as classified among the great conquests. During these glorious ages there was a reign of happiness.

We strongly imagine this epoch to have been the celebrated reign of Saturn which is prehistoric and so enshrouded in mystery and historical incertitude that in another place we have ventured to regard it as mythical and untrue, although as great writers as Hesiod and Lactantius were believers. They derived their belief from tradition; and even that is generally found not to be baseless, but to be conceived from some forgotten truth.[5]

[5] Vol. I., p. 47, and note 1.

Plato and Plutarch refer to the reign of Saturn as a well-known fact. Lactantius whom we quote in this note comes out plainly with an avowal that the happy times were the results of brotherhoods which existed in vast numbers in those early ages.

We have an example of the consummate cunning of ancient military rule when directed by the rich; and the historical fact which we, for the first time venture to lay bare, is a subject for the horror and reflection of the living age; since we need but a penetrating vision to perceive that now, as the same power of the brotherhoods is again rising and a reign of Saturn is almost in sight, there appears another hideous spectre of the military and money power to use its towering genius and its magnetic forces of bribery, darkling incantations and infatuating suasion wherewith to soothe and befog its victims until it can constrict and again swallow up the human race as was done through the Roman conquests.

Much that is interesting was recorded by the poets and historians on the celebrated reign of Saturn.[6] There was a writer by the name of Aratus, whose work, before

---

[6] Hesiod, *Fragmenta Incerta*, ed. Göttling. p. 331; referring to the θίασοι, of these mysterious days of the reign of happiness:

"For common then were banquets and common were seats
Alike to immortal gods and mortal men."

Hesiod is taking this as sung by Ascra. But we have given up the search for the reign of Saturn; see I., p. 47, with note. See Plato, *Laws*, IV., 6; Bekker, Hesiod; Plutarch, *De Definitione Oraculorum*, 18; Dionysius Hal., I., 34. Lactantius was a believer that there actually once existed this reign of the "Blessed" upon the earth, for he says in his *Divine Institutions*, v. c. 6.: "Dim was the source of these evils bursting forth from the contempt of right; as those only who held too much shared their surplus. The greedy afterwards seized the works of others, clutching things as private property; and that which individuals as members had worked hard to obtain for use in common was now carried off to the houses of a few. In order to reduce people to slavery they systematically collected and accumulated life's necessaries and shut them up, making these bounties their own; not for humanity's sake, but to sweep into their own heap the makings of lust and avarice. Under the name of justice they made unequal and unjust laws to defend their plunder against the multitude." These writings of Lactantius refer to the conquests. In a further digest of this great period which he did not doubt, he calls the reign of Saturn the truly golden age of man and in the same sentence declares that this eudæmonia was the result of brotherhoods which had existed before, but which, alas, had been destroyed. There can be no doubt that this is what Polybius meant.

The *Phenomena* of Aratus, written in Greek. Cicero and Lactantius imagined it to have been the source of the belief that in the dim antiquity property was common and happiness and plentitude universal. Lust for individual gains was defined to be "black serpents, noxious with poisons, and wolves that prowl." See Virgil, *Georgics*, I., 139. Germanius Cæsar, a relative of Augustus, also translated from the lost poem of Aratus: "Nor had discord yet been known among relatives." But the legend runs: "Alas, Saturn was exiled from his throne by Jove, his mightier heir." Virgil Æneid, VIII., 320. The Latin reads:

being lost was partly translated by Cicero. It must have thrown out many hints, based upon the tradition, but so cleverly done that it charmed even Cicero, who was afterwards foremost in the efforts to suppress labor organizations. The more we study the innermost clews of this recondite history the more we are convinced that the reign of Saturn was the warming influence of the law of Solon, giving the workers full right of organization on the basis of mutual love and care. Levasseur, speaking of the misery into which the working classes fell after the suppression during the civil wars which constituted the closing struggle after the Roman conquests but a short time before the appearance of Christ, seems to hint that the good old times were those enjoyed under the working people's right of combination.

One of the main objects of their powerful organization, the right to which was given them by the great lawgivers —Solon for Greece, Amasis for Egypt, Numa for Rome —was to secure work from their various forms of government. We have now at command the newly found but abundant proof of this; and it is safe to say, judging from the evidence, that the comforts derived from this paternalism were very deep-seated and may well have been the source of the otherwise strange tradition of the reign of Saturn, the Latian god of agriculture, handicraft and civilization, and so the peace god who held the keys to the temple of Janus, muzzled the wardogs, instituted equality in theory at least, and in Greek-speaking lands was known by the name Kronos. An attempt was made to fuse the tenets of this mighty tutelary protector with those of his superior, the more powerful Jupiter; the attempt failed and the hopes of humanity were destroyed.

Long before the publication of the first volume of this work, it was discovered through exhumations at Pompeii that the Roman Collegia or trade unions were engaged

"Primus ab æthereo venit Saturnus Olympo,
Arma Jovis Fugiens, et reginis exul ademptis."
During those glorious days "The poor were admitted to share the fruits of their labor." Lactantius, *Div. Inst.*, V., 5: "Now streams of milk, now streams of nectar flowed." Ovid, *Metem.*, I., 111. Finally, after the conquests of Jupiter, the aristocrat, who presided over the gens, or patrician family races, says the muse: "Then war's indomitable rage, and greedy lust of gain succeeded." Virgil, *Æneid*, VIII., 327. Consult index to Vol. I.; also Chap. II., init.

very energetically in the political agitations to secure for themselves the appointments to do the public work. This however was not known to the world and the publication of the fact was a surprise.[7] Then followed the discovery that 450 years before Christ a powerful political contention was going on wherein men often came to blows, between the trade unions vitalized by Numa and Tullus Hostilius, and the patrician aristocracy at Rome, and which we are now setting forth under Livy's episode of the *solitudo magistratuum*. The same was also going on elsewhere, especially in Asia Minor.

These contentions between the lowly workers, descendants of slaves and children of Saturn, and the worshipers of Jove, Jupiter, Jehovah, highbloods or aristocrats claiming to be born of an inheritance of power and wealth, were by a cunning slight fused, on this very question of government employment.[8] They were so far bargained away that they consented to turn their skill and force to manufacturing on an enormous scale, the implements of warfare. By this bargain they could all be employed under government and be paid for their work, directly from the paternal treasury, and without the middleman or contractor to fleece them of their wages; thus doing the great work of the armories for the conquests. Alas, it was a deadly deal; for in the end it led to well-nigh their own destruction. When the conquests broke forth, and the doors of the temple of Janus, of which Saturn held the keys of peace and civilization, were thrown open by the aristocrat Jupiter and his war-god Mars, the retributive slaughter set in. The majority of mankind who were propertyless, and had no means except their hands and brain to live from, found themselves organized into a vast mutuality of brotherhoods.[9] Ages of contact with their masters, of whom they were formerly slaves, taught them to understand that property in trade unionism is inimical to life. Property they made common.

---

[7] *Histoire des Classes Ouverières*, I., p. 4. "Le peuple romain avait depuis longtemps perdu le sentiment de la liberté: il ne se soulevait plus à la voix d'un tribun qui lui parlait de ses droits; on lui peignait l' oppression de la noblesse; mais il était terrible quand il avait faim."

[8] I., pp. 390, 391, with notes 3, 4 and 5, containing the Latin of several: but the number since found rises to many hundreds.

[9] Report of the Nebraska State Bureau of Labor Staristics: Biennial for 1897-1898, pp. 955 sqq., on *Trade Unions Under the Solonic Law*, where their ancient principle of a common table and a common code is shown. Copied from the *Arena*, for May, 1897.

AN INSIDIOUS DEAL.

The Roman conquests destroyed tne old freedom and reduced the condition of laboring humanity to one of terrible military slavery struggling against fear, tyranny, massacre and crucifixion. Against these calamities there came many revolts, insurrections and revolutions, which we have already depicted.[10] However it may have been with the Mongolian and far eastern races of mankind the belief in the notion that there originally existed a primordial collectivism is proving itself false. Our assertion grows in force more and more. Originally the children were slaves and the most powerful was he who mauled the smaller into obedience. He mutilated or killed, or enslaved them for his selfish uses.[11] The first mutualists were the outcasts themselves and they were already enormously organized when those wisest and best of men possessing power gave an already vast combination a legal sanction; and there are growing evidences which prove that this mythic reign of Saturn who was dethroned when Jove the aristocrat tore open the portal of the temple of Janus which held the god of war, turning him loose upon his awful errand of destruction, was the veritable golden age meant in the numberless hints about the prehistoric paradise and eudæmonia of the ancient "Blessed."

An enormous resource mostly from the inscriptions, but often corroborated by coeval literature, has recently been opened to students of socialism showing that this reputed happiness which characterized those prehistoric ages, was due to the employment by the state and the municipalities, of the workers through boards of public works elected by the workers themselves. We shall quote numerous inscriptions showing this, discovered not only in Italy but in Asia Minor, Greece and Macedonia. Being voting unions they worked politically and secured the work of the public construction, guardianship and repair, which largely accounts for the excellence of the work as still exhibited in the ruins of antiquity. There are a few documents and inscriptions showing that the organizations under the Solonic law worked eight hours, dividing the day into three parts; sleep, recreation and labor.

---

[10] Vol. I,, on the insurrections, denominated *Strikes*, which they often resembled. See *index* and chapters V., VI., VII., VIII., IX., X., XI. and XII.

[11] I., pp. 84, 85 : 560; but especially pp. 68, 69, where it is seen that the learned de Laveleye admits as much regarding these Aryan races.

But this beautiful government employment was always endangered and threatened by the system of slavery; and finally almost submerged during the conquests which in millions reduced laboring people to slaves of war. There was an idea prevailing among political economists of antiquity that revenues for the expenses of the state ought to be derived from state ownership and husbandry of slaves. Why not, said Xenophon and Diophantos.[12] The slaves are property of government. Whatever their labor produces is, therefore, income for the government; slaves are tools, machinery, implements of labor, nationalized. Our evidence confirming such a condition of things covers the two centuries immediately before the conquests. It is true that the Lycurgan state of Sparta was earlier. We have already given an exhaustive description of that unparalelled iniquity,[13] namely the nationalization of the man-machine, purposely however, leaving for this second volume of the Ancient Lowly the part relating to the nationalization of slaves as tools or implements of labor.

This nationalization of slaves as implements of labor was a rasping source of competition against the organizations of freedmen or what we may call emancipated slaves, doing business for themselves under the Solonic law. These, contrary to the will of the slave owners and the slaveholding states, grew prodigious in numbers and political power, the right thereto being accorded them by some clause in that celebrated statute, which was so mutilated at the time of the conquests, both on the slab of the Prytaneum at Athens and the Tables of law at Rome, that its exact words are unknown although Gaius has

[12] Xen., *De Victigal.*; but consult Bücher, *Aufstände der unfreien Arberter*. S. 18; "Wahrscheinlich in diese Zeit, oder wenig später (B. C. 400), fählt das Projekt des Diophantos, sämmtliche Handwerke durch Staatssklaven betreiben zu lassen, wie dies zur Zeit des Aristotles in Epidamnos wirklich geschah (Aristot., *Pol.*, II., IV., 13). Da Aristot. mit Bezug auf das communistische System des Phaleas spricht so können die Worte τοὺς τὰ κοινὰ ἐργαζομένους nur so erklärt werden, wie im Textegeschehn d. h. von einer der modernen ateliers nationaux im Wesentlichen entsprechenden Einrichtung. Die öffentlichen Arbeiten blos den Sklaven zuzuweisen, wie Stark, bei Hermann, sec, 42, 8, will." etc.
One has also to read the remarkable work of Xenophon, *De Vectigal.*, passim on the Public Economies of Athens to fully understand the inhuman proposition. The state slaves were to be jobbed out to mine contractors at Laurium and the price of their daily labor some two or three oboles a day each, was to flow into the state treasury!
[13] See Vol. I., pp. 61, 69, 94, 101, sq., also pp. 527, 528, sqq., giving a review, and 559.

preserved fragments of the main form,[14] and two valuable old inscriptions confirm it.

This hideous competition of the more ancient government slaves as tools or instruments of labor, took the place, in many respects, of the modern inventions, labor-saving machines and implements, which the socialists wisely require that the public own and control in the interest of mankind to do the work now performed by wage slaves. In some countries, as in Epidamnus, the only labor performed was that of slaves, mostly belonging to the public. How could a trade union have existed there? We must conjecture that none existed. In Sparta the Helots were compelled to perform all work, while the people lounged about in easy indolence. The Helots were state property, or labor saving implements of the rich and arrogant public, and were treated as we treat inanimate machines. In cases where they became too numerous, and on account of their sufferings, sometimes causing them to become rebellious and dangerous, they were often secretly murdered.[15] In our former chapters it has been recounted how the primitive fathers possessed the right of killing their slaves, many of whom were their own children. The slaves being, according to the lex deorum or lex civilis, of the same races, the same color, the same manhood, the same natural intelligence, also possessed the same pride, the same humanity. To be ground down into the dark pit of a subjugation which made them menials of irresponsible tyrants who could at will, and without fear of arrest, plunge into their innocent hearts the deadly dagger, at any time and under any pretext, was a danger worth guarding against. As a consequence we hear of many organizations of the slaves themselves, for mutual protection and enfranchisement. Dr. Foucart, the learned academician of the school of inscription at Paris, has published a valuable work, all the evidence for which he takes from inscriptions, showing the surprising fact that these poor slaves sought the protection of their tutelary deities and actually and in great numbers sold themselves

[14] So very important is this great Solonic Dispensation, which it is now certain became the foundation of Christianity instead of the Mosaic law, that although we quote it, I., p. 127, note 87, we reproduce it as taken in the Digest, XLVII., tit. xxii., leg. 4; see *supra*, p. 48, note 3.
[15] I., pp. 87, 98; 102, 107. Systematic assassination, 107, note 46, quoting Thucydides; also I., 528, 529.

to a god, he procuring the money by a loan from his eranos, the communistic brothers of which agreed to take their pay for such loan, in the future labor of the emancipated slave who was held by them under a species of vassalage until his labor had cancelled the debt. We shall give an inscription in a note showing the legalized form of these amazing transactions, which prove to have prevailed to a vast extent, from before the conquests down to the Nicine epoch of the Christian era : Cleon, son of Cleoxenes, has sold to the Pythian Apollo, a male body the name of which is Istæus, a Syrian by birth, for the sum of four hundred francs, on the condition that Istæus is to be free, and that no man shall lay hands on him during his whole lifetime. The shrewd point is that he is sold to a god by the eranos, the mode of which we shall hereafter fully recount, proffering the money by a previous stipulation with the slave who is a member, and also with the owner. If they sold him to a human being amenable to the laws, then, under the laws of the state he would still belong to a person ; but by transferring him to a divinity, an imagined being, awful protector, presiding deity, and rendering the price to his shrine which everybody knew was the state, or if it was in some obscure place, transferring the price to the kuriakos or temple of the divinity worshiped by the eranos, then, under the law, the transfer would legalize the man's emancipation. The priest of the god handed the owner the money at the shrine.

Masters and fathers alike were feared;[16] for the law gave such an undisputed right to kill them at pleasure. During these days of constant danger the poor slaves sometimes ran away. But even in extreme cases like this they had recourse to some propitious god or goddess who took them under a grateful shelter, and no man dared invade the divinity's portals and awfully frowning environs. Foucart has made some extraordinary discoveries of this strange fact, or at least, he has written for mankind, the long dead epigraphs into the living tongues.

[16] *Digest,* I.. vi.. sec. 1. : "Igitur in potestate sunt servi dominorum. Quæ quidem potestas juris gentium est: nam apud omnes peræque gentes animadvertere possumus, dominos servos vitæ necisque potestatem fuisse." Cf. Heinecius, *Syntagm. Antiquitatum De patria potestate et de nuptiis:* Recte Imperator, sec. 2, *Inst. h, t,* ' Jus,' inquit: 'potestatis, quod in liberos habemus, *proprium est civium Romanorum.* Nulli enim alii sunt homines, qui talem in liberos habeant potestatem, qualem nos habemus.' Quamvis enim apud Persas etiam

POWER OF THE LORD-DIRECTOR.

We give in a note the newly found Andanic inscription. The meaning is as follows : " Let runaway slaves take refuge in the temples, and occupy a place set apart for them by the lords. Let no one receive such fugitives, nor nourish nor give them work. Should any one do contrary to these directions let him be held to pay the owner twice the value of the slaves besides the fine of 500 drachmas. The lord must judge on the subject and deliver to slave owners those slaves whose case is bad."

A very important question comes in here. Who was this kurios or lord? We venture to suggest that this is a most important question. The new source of historic information is crowding reluctant science into view, verifying that he was a chief and a powerful official of the unions of the ancient lowly under the law of Solon. Where seen in the myriad organizations of Rome under the law of Numa, now proved to be the same as that of Solon, he was generally called the quinquennalis. He is destined to come out of the pit of oblivion to which he was relegated and to again shine forth as the great and phenomenal power which made Christianity a success; and we shall prove in subsequent mention that he is the prime fulcrum over which is to be drawn the diametrically opposite meaning between a history of Christianity and a history of the Church. It is now established that most of the greater characters, such as Stephen, James, Paul, Peter, Luke, Zachias, John, Clement, Pudens, Titus, Phœbe, Aquila and Priscilla, Lydia, Narcissus, Apelles, Philologus, Julia, Tryhhena, Claudia, Sergius Paulus, Timotheus, Philemon, Epaphras, Tychicus, Onesimus, and many others, were kurioi or lords in the one or the other sex, having charge of the business concerns, often of rich and powerful societies. Their names are often found on inscriptions of such societies, not in a religious but, in a business sense, and identified as the self-same personages with those mentioned in the apostolic writings.

parentes in liberos imperium satis durum et fere tyrannicum exercuerint, filiis suis tanquam servis usi, teste Aristotles: *Eth.*, VIII., 12." Cf. likewise Macrob., *Saturn*, II., 5, who refers to Herod's slaughter of the infants. Dionysius of Halicarnassus confirms this, II., 26: 'Ο δὲ τῶν 'Ρωμαίων νομοθέτης ἅπασαν, ὡς εἰπεῖν, ἐδωκεν ἐξουσίαν πατρὶ καθ' υἱοῦ, καὶ παρὰ πάντα τὸν τοῦ βίου χρόνον ... . . ἐάν τὲ ἀποκτιννύναι ποοαιρῆται." And again, *Codex Just.*, VIII., tit. xlvii.,' lex 10: Patribus . . . . jus vitæ in liberos necisque potestas olim erat permissa." Josephus, *Antiqu.*, XVI., 7, in his story of Herod, Seneca, *De Clem.*, I., 17: "Quis non Vaedium Pollionem pejus oderat, quam servi sui, quod murænas sanguine humano saginabat."

In future chapters we shall give this evidence and accompany it with verbatim quotations of the original anagrams and epigraphs.

We say the whole transaction of pre-Christian emancipation, from servitude and even the protection of runaways, was under auspices of a good divinity, which the poor always claimed to possess and which the great Solonic dispensation most nobly accorded them. It is true that the public law of the state gave them no such favor; but ancient lawgivers were superstitious and dared not regard this old statute with other than reverence. It was never repealed until A. D. 363, by the Council of Laodicea.

The transfer of a slave to the tutelary god was accompanied with a regular receipt.[17] It has been shown by men of the French School of Inscriptions and the Epigraphical Seminary of Archæology attached to the University of Vienna, that a slave thus emancipated, through his sale to a god was far more secure, and his release from bondage more effective and satisfactory than his redemption, direct, from a master by will or otherwise. The solemnity of the performance ; vows before the altar; presence of the kurios or lord of the union, the presence of the senators ; majesty of the law making witnesses compulsory ; the engraving of the ceremony into stones of the temple ; the law so regulating that if the master tried any means of his re-enslavement the freedman could call help and use force ; the stipulation with the god at the portals of his gorgeous temple that he was to be free to the end of his life—all these made the transaction very

[17] Foucart, *L'Affranchissment des Esclaves, par vente à un Dieu*, p. 3, mentions an inscription (*Inscriptions recuillies à Delphes*, No. 73) : " Ἐπὶ τοῖσδε ἀπέδοτο Κλέων Κλεοξένου τῷ Ἀπόλλωνι τῷ Πυθίῳ σῶμα ἀνδρεῖον ᾧ ὄνομα 'Ιστιαῖος, τὸ γένος Σύρον, τιμᾶς ἀργυρίου μνᾶν τεσσάρων, ἐφ' ᾧτε ἐλεύθερον εἶμεν, καὶ ἀνέφαπτον ἀπὸ τὸν πάντα βίον' This was, in the years of the conquests, no fictitious sale. Formerly the formality of emancipation was fictitious; for it seemed to be rigidly severe and august, The slave had to remain actual property of the god, vested in the care of some mortal man of high rank (see account of it in Vol. I., pp. 277, 278, notes 1, 2, 3) ; λαὸς οἰκήτως θεοῦ (Euripides, *Andromed.*, V., 1089). But there came such multitudes of emancipations that the slaves, being freed from men, were likewise freed from gods : ie , were at perfect liberty and became too many to bother the gods. The slaves got this redemption money from the union to which they belonged, the name of which was the eranos. They agreed to mortgage their bodies, which really meant their labor, to the union, until the same was gradually amortized when they became free. This very fact proves that their own unions were pledged to find them work and take care of them.

MODE OF EMANCIPATING SLAVES. 59

binding and not at all easy to be forgotten. It has long been known that by some process too occult for the historian, a vast emancipation of slaves filled the world with innumerable freedmen and that this process was in vogue when Homer wrote or recited his Odyssey. We have however explained that no mention is made of freedmen in the Iliad, showing the Iliad to be the oldest.[18]

Thus from very early times we find distinct traces of two religions and two sets of gods; one favoring and the other destructive of human liberty, and two distinctly defined sytems of political economy; one peaceful, industrious, lowly, under the tutelage of Saturn, Nemesis, Dionysus, Minerva, the other warlike, arrogant pretentious, living in bloodthirst and destruction. The poor slaves in millions, protected by their good divinities, were frequently encouraged to run away and hide in the temple which in those times was always a residence,[19] and such was the law or superstition that no man or other god

[18] 1.. p. 80, where this curious if not significant conjecture is referred to Granier de Cassagnac.
[19] Foucart, *Affranchissement des Esclaves*, etc., p. 13, gives the inscription of Andanie, (vide Wallon, p. 211). It reads : Φύγαμου εἴμεν τοῖς δούλοις. Τοῖς δύλοις φύγαμον ἔστω τὸ ἱερὸν, καθὼς ἄν οἱ ἱεροὶ 'αποδείξωντι τὸν τόπον, καὶ μηδεὶς ὑποδεχέσθω τοὺς δραπέτας μήτε σιτοδοτείτω μηδὲ ἔργα παρεχέτω. Ὁ δὲ ποιῶν παρὰ τὰ γεγραμμένα, ὑπόδεικος ἔστω τῷ κυρίῳ τας τοῦ σώματος διπλασίας ἀξίας καὶ ἐπιτίμόυ δραχμᾶν πεντακοσιαν· Ὁ δὲ ἱερεὺς ἐπικρινέτω περὶ τῶν δραπετικῶν, ὅσοι κα ἤνται ἐκ τᾶς ἀμετέρας πόλεως, καὶ ὁσους κα κατακρίνει παραδότω τοῖς κυρίοις· ἄν δὲ μὴ παραδιδῷ, ἐξέστω τῷ κυρίῳ ἀποτρέχειν ἔχοντι." Many inscriptions prove it.

Foucart, *Affranch.*, p, 9, "Καὶ τὰν τιμὰν ἔχει πᾶσαν. Although every trace of the methods of these transactions does not appear in inscriptions yet some of them are more elaborate. The master, or owner, accompanied by the slave, presents himself before the great temple of Apollo at Delphi, passes the grand exterior altar, and advances toward the great portal or door, but does not cross over the threshold. Priests meet them and the slave is led up to the god. In presence of senators (political government employees) and a certain number of witnesses, they pass over to, and pay the owner, the price agreed upon, and receive the benedicton, a sort of ceremonious oratory, pronounced by the two parties, viz: "Καὶ τὸ ἀργύριον ἔλαβε εν τῳ ναῳ ἐπὶ τοῦ ὁδοῦ κατὰ τὸ μεγα θύρωμα." (No, 288, of *Inscr. Recuellies à D lphes*). It is a solemn ceremony. Soon after, the formality had to be inscribed (Nos. 345, 376, 409), winding up with : "Τοῦτα δὲ ἐγένετο ἀνὰ μέσον τοῦ βωμοῦ καὶ τοῦ ναοῦ." It was an awful solemnity in presence of the god and the prelates. Foucart, *id.*, p. 49, speaks of certain restrictions to the liberty of the persons thus sold. The lact is, Apollo and many others of these august immortals were originally living men, owning great numbers of slaves, and according with the more ancient barbarism it was customary for such despots at their death and funeral to have a certain number of slaves killed in order that they might accompany their master as servants, after death. There can be no doubt that this transier to the god was originally an awful solemnity (See I,, Chap. *Spartacus*, init.). The wretch being bought for an attendant to his majesty after death, and that originally such human sacrifices were killed so as to watch and guard the master's manes in the other or the nether world. By gradual differentiation, however, mind outgrew this barbarism. Instead of a horror, the emancipation got to be genuine liberty of the slave, and the process became a great benefaction. (Nicolaus Damascenus, in Athenæus, iv., 153; Valer. Max., *De Spectaculis*, 7. Cf. I., p. 277, note 1, on the *Tragedy of the Forum Boarium*).

dared enter this asylum to molest them. In the inscriptions, asylums of refuge but not of charity, are found at Delphi, Teos and many places where the great Dionysan artists' unions existed in Asia Minor; and it turns out that the trade unions were generally the owners of a temple, that the members used this temple to live in, or at least, for their managers and other officers to live in, and this sacred abode was made a refuge and asylum for both bond and free. These temples and seats of refuge, of business and of living economies are now proved to have been innumerable; to have operated scrupulously under the provisions, directions and specifications of the aged and revered Solonic law; and in course of time, when the master came, to have been used by, converted into, and made a refuge and asylum for, the true and original propaganda.[20] But there were no hospitals in early times because of the universal prevalence of the unions. We hear of little or no starvation through lack of employment before A. D. 300, and there was no dispensing of charities known. This was because the thriving people for the first 200 years, were self-sustaining brotherhoods of initiates. It was after the attack of the optimates upon them that we hear of hospitals. There were many asylums of refuge but they must not be mistaken for poor houses or hospitals.[21] Several inscriptions

[20] In our more recent researches upon this important fact we have gathered much corroboratory information which will be produced in proper place and form. For the present see I., pp. 147, 257, and 142 4, with note 34. There was another temple of retreat for fugitive slaves at Megara near Athens, Thucyd., III, 69, says: "'Οκοδόμησαν πρὸς τῷ Ἡραίῳ καταγώγιον διακοσίων ποδῶν, πανταχῇ κύκλῳ οἰχήματα ἔχον κάτωθεν καὶ ἄνωθεν . . . . κλίνας κατασκευάσεντας, ἀνέθεσαν τῇ "Ηρᾳ." Here in a few words, is a description of an asylum with floors above and below, beds, etc., for comfort, in a καταγώγιον or hospital dedicated to Juno. No regular hospitals however existed, because these are based on the charitable, eleemosynary system which did not come into the world until hundreds of years afterwards and are instrumentalities of feudalism. The ancient asylums we are describing were places of refuge, mostly for unfortunates, such as runaway slaves, and were protected by a god. Of the ξενῶνες, νοσοκόμιαια, πτοκοτρόφια, ὀρφανοτρόφια, βρεφοτρφόια, gerontocomia, paramonaria (Cod. Just. I., tit. III., leg. 42, sec. 6) of the, degenerate eleemosynary system, we shall later in this work give a proper account.
[21] The temple of Isis at Pompii recently exhumed, is remarkable. Formerly it was pagan and its members were socialists with a common table and a communal code of life. At the time of the catastrophe, A. D. 79, it was a Christian Church. It had a garden surrounded by walls, which was the τέμενος, or seat of the Θίασος. There was a tree, several buildings, etc. The temple of Zeus Labraundos had 5 cellæ of which we shall speak later; it was called the πρόστωον; it also had a front or ἀέιωμα, a ναός which was the residence of the divinity, οἰκετήρια, residences of the officers, larger rooms for all, οἶκος, οἰκία or τόπος. This at Pomepii was a veritable habitation for common use of the membership.

are found which are deceptive. One fragment at Rome speaks of an asylum as if it were Christian; but closer inspection proves it to have originally been a temple of Juno, although now placed to the credit of the Christians. The date is still a matter of speculation with the savants, most of whom call it a Christian find. It is to be borne in mind that at the time of Spartacus, and ages before, there were asylums which served as resorts for runaways; and of course, when the Christians came, and their terrible persecutions began, they would naturally seek these warm and kindly retreats for protection, although they were dedicated to Pagan gods.[22]

We bring these points under contribution to show the grievances of the outcasts; for all mankind deprived of the full fruits of labor in those remote ages as well as now, are treated as outcasts in this history. Under the inequitable law of entailments upon primogeniture which gave the first-born son the property, and consigned the others to beggary and dishonor, making slavery a natural result as the oldest and first of human plagues with these concomitants of scuffles, strikes and rebellions among such wretches, co-operation for escape from the wrath of the legalized patrician class was indispensable.[23]

The same grievances which held the workers, from whose labor all their tormentors lived, was also rife among the Semitic races, and their resistance through strikes, turmoils and organizations was felt in all countries and all ages, wherever and whenever the hovels of that era found them. As was stated in the first volume of this work, only the history of the working people of the great

[22] Orell., No. 1512. "Fragmentum repertum Interamniae Praetutiae.:' Orell's remarks: "Rarissima fit mentis in lapidibus, asylorum quae sub Christianismi incrementa, ac prius fortasse, ad arcendum scelerum impunitatem videntur esse sublata." He is speaking of the trag. of this *Asylum Junoni*. Cf. *Ante-Nicene Fathers*, VIII., p. 377, *Gospel* of Iseudo Matthew, Chapters 2 , 23, 24. "Jesus with Mary and Joseph wandering in Egypt without friends, went into the temple of Satrinen city, called the capital of Egypt, which was open and welcomed them." Though this story is apocaryphal the antiquity of the documents is evidence of the cust ms prevailing at the time it was written. But new and unexpected value is of late attached to them, since they are found to accord with inscriptions now and then discovered.

[23] This statement is confirmed by the learned Academician, M. Cagnat, without the slightest reserve. See Vie Contemporaine, for January, 1 96. In fact, the resistance of the working or, enslaved classes must have been great for we are informed by Athenæus, *Deipnosophistæ*, VI., 264, that there was an old law forbidding the ownership of slaves in Phocis, 499 years before Christ, It gave way to the pressure, however, so that in B. C. 360 there were some slaves there held in bondage.

Aryan blood was attempted, leaving the Semitic to be pursued in this, and consequently little mention was made of perhaps the greatest, earliest and most remarkable strike on record—that of the Hebrew race in Egypt. Of this we can here make only a brief allusion preparing the reader to better understand the causes and significance of the Roman conquests.

The whole Exodus of the Jews from the tyranny of slaveholding Pharaohs was a pure strike, beginning, so far as we have positive information, with the grievance that their cruel masters forced them to make brick without giving them the straw or other material wherewith to execute their compulsory and hateful task.

The Mosaic dispensation was one of slavery [24] whereas the Solonic dispensation is proving itself more and more, through the inscriptions recording its vast organization, to have been a veritable vehicle of emancipation of slaves and of equalization of mankind; and it will show itself to have been much the better of the two. Though the records are dim, yet the fact is at least coming to light that about one half of the Jews endorsed Mosaism and the remainder went with Solon.

The Romans early conceived a possibility of destroying their thus growing and dangerous proletarian neighbors. It required but a stroke of reason based on the purely competitory idea of the survival of the strongest and most cunning, to point out to them that in order to kill off the people whom they saw so powerfully organized in self-defense, they had but to incite their spirit of patriotism and their economic notions about working for their own government on a large scale. The plan was to inflame the whole Roman state in the direction of warfare against all the outstanding states. There were Greece, Spain, Africa, Macedonia, Epirus, Asia Minor with Syria, Sicily

---

[24] For words of Moses on the slaves, see *Levit.*, xxv., 44: "Both thy bond-men and thy bond-maids which thou shalt have, shall be of the heathen that are about you ; of them shall ye buy bond-men and bond-maids." Homer, Iliad, xxi., treats the slaves as mere animals: "Πολλούς ζωούς έχον ήδ' επέρασσα." Between 300 and 400 years before Christ, Aristotle regarded slaves as men now do inanimate labor saving machines. They were mere tools without sense ; and he declared that there could be neither common interests nor fellowship between master and slave: . . . . " Φιλία δ' ουκ έστι προς τα άψυκα ουδέ δίκαιον· αλλ' ουδέ προς ίππον ή βούν, ουδέ προς δούλον ή δούλος ουδέν γαρ κοινόν εστιν· ο γαρ δούλος έμψυχον όργανον, το δ' όργανον άψυχος δούλος. ή μεν ούν δούλος, ουκ έστι φιλία προς αυτόν, ή δ' άνθρωπος·" κ. τ. λ· (Eth. Nic., viii., 13, p. 1161).

and Palestine. The great Solonic law had organized the proletariat of all these countries. It was at that moment rapidly turning them into socialistic communities. Never were they more thrifty than on the eve of the conquests. The organizations were rapidly emancipating their slaves. A new code of political economy in the world was being inaugurated by them. A vast sympathy had been created by their brotherly love. They had learned to love and care for each other. They were strictly industrial. Their unions had become international and economically intertwined. Precisely the same principles, rules and methods prevailed in all, regardless of boundary lines. They manufactured and sold goods through a co-operative mutuality. They had agents working for these economic purposes, in every quarter; and their whole vast scheme was inculcating the most equalizing and democratizing spirit. Everywhere alike among Jews and Gentiles these excellent characteristics cropped out and were forming a noble and self-sustaining brother and sisterhood over the world.

But there was neither money, personal glory nor lordships in such a scheme of political economy. Those born to the patrician estate, the grandees, the rich and arrogant saw in the system their complete overthrow.

Under Appius Claudius the above plan was conceived of their extermination; and the indications are that it was resolved upon when the great political event ocurred which Livy designates the *solitudo magistratuum per quinquennium* through which it was tested after a five years' political conflict between the poorer people and the rich, that the patrician class, or lords were losing control, being all that time without a senate to represent them in the parliament of the nation.

The Numan unions, provided by the great law of organization, with the votive franchise, unlike the non-voting trade unions of the present day, though socially their membership was incomparably more degraded and lowly, had carefully worked their economies both from an industrial and a political point of view. As a consequence they were capable of keeping up among themselves an intense interest which for ages held them in close compact together. Their object was to so far master the

64   SOLITÚDO MAGISTRATUUM.

political situation as to obtain the public work from the
government; and we are here informed by Livy that they
held the ædiles, officers well known to be about equivalent
to our modern commissioners of public works in cities,
in power, by outnumbering their opponents at the comitia or polls.[25] This is the greatest and most important
discovery in the history of the trade unionism.[26] It being
directly coupled with that period in Roman history acknowledged by our encyclopedias to be the most critical
and important moment in that great nation's life,[27] we
cannot pass it by without a review of the circumstances.
The unions were everywhere; in city and country and
their influence was great. Levasseur assures us [28] that

[25] The ruins of Pompeii are not the only evidence recently coming to light on this political function of the organizations of the ancient workingmen. It is now proved by fresh discoveries of inscriptions with dates varying from 300 B. C. to 200 A. D., that this lever of success was enormously practiced in Greece and Asia Minor. Sometimes they got work from the state religion. But it was the same thing; since temples were state or government buildings and priests were government officers. Consult Waltzing, *Hist. Corporations Professionelles*, I., pp. 70-71: "Les collèges étaient dit-on, des corps publiques plutot que des corps industriels . . . . ils construisaient les temples, fabriquaient les ustensils et les vases sacrées; les flutistes assistaient les prêtres et les magistrats dans les sacrifices et ainsi de suite. Les collèges étaient donc destinés d' abord et surtout au service de la religion et de la cité, et c 'est précisément pourquoi on rapport leur institution à Numa." (Cf. Dirksen, p. 21). Again, Waltzing *id:* "Plusieurs de ces métiers étaient indispensable à la guerre, et suivant Dirksen, l' état n' aurait permis à l' origine que les collèges utiles au culte ou à l'armée."

[26] Dionys. Hal. IV., 17, assures us that the unions which he calls λόχοι, made arms during the conquests for the Romans : "Δύο μέν ὁπλοποιῶν τε καὶ τεκτόνων καὶ τῶν ἀλλων τῶν σκευαζόντων τὰ εἰς τὸν πόλεμον εὐχρηστα." And again, VII., 59 : "Δύο λόχοι τεκτόνων καὶ χαλκοτύπτων καὶ ὅσοι ἀλλοι πολεμικῶν ἐργων ἦσαν χειροτέχναι." Again, Oehler, *MS*; p. 3, No. 5: "Decelea—B. C. 396 : "Erwähnen möchte ich den Demoneidebeschluss, *C. I. Athenw*, IV., 2, 841 (306-5 v. Chr.), der θίασοι als stattliche Unterabtheilungen nennt, (gefunden in Dekeleia), und den Beschluss der Peiraienser gegen die Θίασοι. C. I. A. II., add., 5736." It is extremely important, showing that they were under state employ.

[27] Appleton s *Amer. Cyc. Art. Roms.* Speaking of the changes caused by the plebeian ascendency at that time says: "These changes were the most important events of Roman history."

[28] Lavasseur, *Hist. Classes Our.*, I., p. 5 sqq. According to Pliny, *Hist. Nat.* xxxiv.,I; xxx., 43; Plutarch, *Numa*, 17; Florus, I., 6; Dionys. Hal., IV., 43, the numerous colleges, or trade unions of early Rome were political fully as much as religious: and in that early time they were somewhat respected. Of this, Florus, I., 6, says: "Ab hoc populus Romanus relatus in censum, digestus in classes, curiis atque collegiis distributus. They were powerful at the time of Tarquinius Superbus; for Dionysius of Halicarnassus, IV., 43, says: "Συνόδους τε συμπάσας, ὅσαι ἐπὶ κοιγητῶν ἢ φρεατεαστῶν ἢ γειτόνων ἔν τε τῇ πόλει καὶ ἐπὶ τῶν ἀγρῶν ἐφ' ἱερὰ καὶ θυσίας πάσως κοινὰς, προσείπε μήκετι συντελεῖν, ἵνα μὴ συνιόντες εἰς τὸ αὐτὸ πολλοὶ βουλὰς ἀπορρήτους μετ' ἀλλήλων ποιῶντα περὶ καταλύσεως τῆς ἀρχῆς." They became perfect in organization. Again, through Livy, *Hist.*, IX., 30, B. C. 300, A. U. C., 443, we have a story of a model strike of the musicians, see *infra*, Ch. III. The musicians employed by the government struck work because, on account of the great expenses of the Semnite wars it was reducing her to straits. There is an inscription (Oehler, *MS.*), showing that the government employed union labor at Decelea as early as B. C 396, immediately after the Poloponnesian war. (See I., p. 134 and note 1 showing the causes). It caused jealousy and protest.

Servius Tullius overturned the old aristocratic form of government instituted by Romulus to give the liberals more privilege. He accorded to the artisans political rights, an enormous lever of power. According to this, the first voting workmen began their voting under this law, the wording of which is lost; but we know that Numa, long before, had given them the right, as well as the advice, and perhaps a demand, to organize, and that his statute is the celebrated jus coeundi, corresponding exactly with the Solonic law spread upon the Twelve Tables of Rome. As shown in the turmoils, B. C. 379-3, time of the solitudo magistratuum, this political action of the organized workers created unspeakable jealousy of the rich and hitherto dominant patricians. It was an attack on their very existence as magnates of the realm. It threatened eventually to extinguish them. Following the true instincts of labor organization, the workingmen began by voting into power those only who were pledged to secure them steady work, and these were the ædiles, or commissioners of the public work.[29] Thus they secured the work directly from the paternal government which they dearly loved. To all intents it was a vast socialist movement, its object being identical with that of the socialists of to-day. By it the people, the public, the state, became owners, managers, employers, paternal economists and care-takers of both the inhabitants and the goods of society, and this is socialism. By means of a loud noise about the impending war, like an incursion of a neighboring state, the patricians, glad of an excuse for turning a social into a bellicose scramble, worked their cajoling oratory over the unsuspecting plebeians, furnished them with abundance of government work making war implements, and accomplished their ends.

It will be claimed by those who read history in the old way as taught by our institutions of learning, that

[29] "Comitia præter aedilium tribunorumque plebis, nulla sunt habita;" Livy, VI., 35, fin. A most remarkable verification of our suspicion that war was improvised to distract the thus politico-socially organized lower classes from their powerful political hold which threatened the life and existence of the aristocracy, now follows in the next paragraph of Livy. The 35th chap. ends with the quoted statement regarding the solitudo magistratuum. The 36th begins as follows: "Alia bella opportune quievere: Veliterni coloni, gestientes otio, quod nullus exercitus Romanus esset, et agrum Romanum aliquoties incursavere, et Tusculum oppugnare adorti sunt. Eaque res, Tusculanis veteribus sociis, novis civibus, opem orantibus, verecundia maxime non patres modo, sed etiam plebem, movit. ' etc.

this startling announcement, so revolutionary of political economy based upon the competitive system, is vague and debatable. Even these reluctant ones admit the evidence of the stones. It is true that those workers never published histories of their career. They wrote in another way. If they are proven by over fifteen hundred political inscriptions on the walls of buildings, forts and fortifications of Pompeii to have done so about the time of the Apostles, they certainly must have done so at the time compassed by Livy's acknowledgment.

Again, there is the certainty that many other inscriptions have perished. Cagnat boldly declares that in all the cities it was the same. At Pompeii they could not perish because, covered by the preserving deposits of of lava,[30] they were kept dry and safe, so that to-day they come out fresh and in a state of good preservation.

Domaszewski, in an article on the public roads and thoroughfares of those times, citing two inscriptions of the time of Sulla, about B. C. 81-56, makes it appear that the colleges were well equipped and organized.[31] It must be borne in mind that we are not attempting to convey the idea that during the Roman conquests an effort was made to exterminate the organizations of labor in immediate Rome itself. The task was first to kill off the more dangerous growth of socialism in Asia Minor.

The patricians needed the organizations. Their skill in the arts was for the time transpiring, wanted to man-

[30] See I., pp. 390, 391. Orell. 4265; Momms., *De Coll. et Sodal.*, p. 59; Romanelli, *Viggio, Pompeii*, I., p. 276, who offer remarks, giving proofs positive. One election stone reads; "Marcellinum Aedilem, lignari et plostrari rogant, ut facietis;" meaning that the woodworkers and wagoners nominated Marcellinus for superintendent of public buildings and works, and want you to vote for him. For the remarkable number of inscriptions of elections, found at Pompeii and the statement that it is above fifteen hundred, see Waltzing, *Hist. Corp. Prof.*, I., p. 169: Les artisans . . . . . de Pompéi, dont le Sénat avait supprimé les collèges sous Tibère, étaient quand même restés unis et prenaient une part active aux élections. Pompéi, venait d' élire ses duumviri *jure dicundo* et ses deux édiles quelque mois avant la terrible éruption que l' englutit au mois d' Août., 79. La lutte avait été ardente, ces hautes fonctions avaient été chaudement disputées; les murs déblayés après dix-huit cents ans portent encore environ quinze cents affiches électorales, où les sociétés et les particuliers recommendaient leurs candidats. Un grand nombre de ces réclames émanent des collèges professionnels. On a trouvé celles des orfèvres *(aurifices universi)*. C. *I. L.* IV., 710);" and quotes nine other trades.

[31] *Eranos Vindobonensis*, pp. 60-64, *Cura Viarum*. Of the fury of Sulla against the unions and their membership we shall speak in future. It is certain that Cæsar during that time befriended them and that they remembered it, by voting him a superintendent of public works; for he furnished them important jobs (Plutarch *Cæsar*), repairing and constructing the Via Appiana, For more on this valuable contribution of Domazewski, see later. Consult same in *index* to Vol, II.

LURED BY PROMISES OF GOVERNMENT WORK. 67

ufacture darts, javelins, slings, swords, knives, all the footwear of the countless soldiery, clothing, bedding, tents and rams and basilisks, for battering down walls and all the accoutrements of the garrison. When bridges and war buildings were wanted these workmen were to be employed. The navy with its large equipment required large numbers of the best workmen. Such labor could not be entrusted to slaves. The oarsmen were generally slaves, but long experience had shown that free mechanics were more efficient and reliable. Rome's first requisite before setting out on her huge conquests and work of centuries, was to obtain the aid of the old unions of labor, carefully and skillfully organized under the specifications of the Solonic dispensation. If she could, by utilizing their skill, secure the mastery over the world it would then be time to turn upon these benefactors and likewise compass their extinction. The enemy to be beaten by the wars of the conquests were small kingdoms here and there, an occasional great republic like Carthage, and various peaceful, nomadic tribes. In doing this the grasping money power with its law de jure quiritare giving them a right to crave and scream for more, precisely as that hideous gorgon is doing at this day, furnished an excuse for the iniquity. Besides, the lords of the gens families who claimed to have been born possessors of the wealth which the labor of those they detested had produced, joined with the money power in the proposition to murder off the human race. But it must begin by first killing out the jus coeundi in outstanding states. Involved in this plan of internicine grasp was the idea of wheedling the home unions at Rome, by flattering them with an offer of still more government work.

But what about the similarly organized workers of the kingdoms and republics to be destroyed? They were to be conquered, killed or sold into slavery, their organizations broken up and annihilated and the wealth their labor had for ages been accumulating was to be seized and dragged to Rome; for the existence of organized labor outside was even more dangerous than that inside the city.

Such was the plan of the Roman conquests, and many a mark prompts the suspicion that to attack, insult, browbeat, rob and destroy the beautiful civilization inherent in the great Solonic dispensation, was deliberately decided upon, even though the doing of it involved the extinction of the most useful factors of mankind. This plan, and this alone would satiate the greed of screamers for nobility ; and it was the only thing that could be devised to perpetuate the false claims of lords who alleged that they were heirs to thrones, gilded trappings and the mastery over slaves. This vast and destructive work was actually carried out.

It is not our province to write a history of the conquests. Suffice it to say that it resulted in no good. It did not make the conquered governments and people better. They were in most cases thriving in organized industry and yearly improving in peaceful economies and enlightenment. Brutal attacks upon them by the great bully always ended in their apparent destruction; for wherever they survived it was by hiding in secret seclusion. In Gaul there was, before the conquests, a mowing and reaping machine which, according to several ancient writers worked well.[32] What became of it? Like the genius of the organized skilled mechanics of that fair country, it was blotted out. Many of the valuable inventions, such as that of the red and purple dyes were likewise blotted out of existence, never to be recovered. Mean jealousies instigated restricting laws against them. Besides this, the skilled artisans who held their inventions a secret and as trade unions, applied their skill and art toward producing those beautiful and useful things, were bodily seized, carried away from their happy vocations, and sold into hopeless slavery never to return. Grim war entered their peaceful homes and thriving unions and dispersed their children, prostituted their women, enslaved the representatives of skill, and the managers of myriads of secret unions, prosperous under the aged and sacred law. The vast wealth which was being accumulated by those peaceful industries was seized and transported to Rome to enrich senators and other money-getters. The immense values known to have existed before these wars were inaugurated were swept

[32] For a description of the ancient reaper, see I., p. 569, and note 109, quoting Pliny and Palladius.

away. Splendid cities were depopulated.³³ The wars raged to the death on every hand. The human race was threatened and largely destroyed. The ruinous ambition of Xerxes which, in unison with the Carthagenians a few years before the time of Appius Claudius, had aroused the spirit of warfare, likewise contributed to excite the Romans, furnishing them some excuse for their exterminatory havoc. The growth of the socialistic spirit all over the Semitic world frightened the monarchs everywhere. Kings and money-holders hated the thrifty, brilliant Jews. About the time those conquests began to rage there was a feeling of universal uneasiness among the wealth-owners and the crowned heads who went hand in hand the same as now. Xerxes the emperor of Persia, taking advantage of the great population which had for 300 years thrived under this peaceful industrialism until the brotherhoods became an organized, wealth-making factor, reciprocally working and voting for each others' good under what Dirksen denominates "a common table and communal code," conceived the idea of mustering an army large enough to conquer the world. The story is told, and excellent critics, such as Wallace and many others believe it true, that he actually mustered 3,000,000 men. They met defeat. Within a year this vast army of soldiers largely levied from the common ranks, were either dead or in the hideous captive slave pens.

Simultaneously with Xerxes and the human hyena, Appius Claudius, there was a portentous warcloud gathering at old Agrigentum in Sicily. Gelon was the Sicilian tyrant. Hamilco the Carthagenian general attacked him at Himera and the combined forces of one of the world's greatest naval battles numbered more than 600,000 men.

[33] The great city of Corinth, at that time one of the largest, most wealthy and busy in the world was almost exterminated. In the 4th century before Christ it possessed 680,000 inhabitants; I., p. 193. It is known that Rome turned her most brutal savagery against it and in B.C. 146 sacked and reduced it to ashes. An effort was made at restoration and it had regained somewhat by Paul's time. Quite a number of cities lost their existence along the Adriatic, being annihilated by these inhuman conquests. Several also in Magna Graecia, Sybaris among others, are lost and stricken from the maps of the earth. Corioli, whence the patriot Coriolanus, a thrifty and splendid place, was attacked by the conquests, destroyed, and its brilliant civilization, thrifty unions with their voting membership and rival institutions, fell into ruins and was lost from Roman geography. In fact its very site is lost: . ... "Zerstört und schon in der späteren Römerzeit spurlos verschwunden." Mayers *Konversations Lexikon*, in v. *Corioli*.

The victory was with the Aryans; and the Semitics with a supposed invincible Carthagenian prowess went down, soon to become a prey to Roman conquest.

On that same day, in a gulf of the same sea, Themistocles met the vast naval forces of Persia, numbering as many, at the renowned carnage of Salamis; and the Semitics went down by unknown thousands, never again to rise. It was the memorable battle of Salamis, B.C. 480.[34]

These two great events prepared Rome with another pretext for bloody work of ages. Lactantius[35] says that Seneca divided Rome into periods of growth: infancy and early education under Romulus, boyhood under the kings; under Tarquin it grew strong enough to burst its bonds of slavery and throw off the yoke of tyranny. When Rome had finished the Punic wars she had become fully adult. But when Carthage, long her rival in power, was destroyed she stretched out her hand by land and sea over the whole world, until, having subdued all kings and nations, the war materials failed and she abused her strength by which she destroyed herself." Thus with Polybius, Seneca thought the Roman conquests were the beginning of her downfall.[36]

As few of the cities and countries of these times took a correct census of population we can best judge of their population by the armed forces they were able to bring into the field. Sybaris in Magna Græcia, a city which in those times had a circuit of six and a quarter English

[34] Herodotus, VII., 158. It is supposed the forces of Gelon consisted of both a land army and a navy: "Γέλων δὲ πολλὸς ἐνέκειτο λέγων ; . . . . Ἀτιμίης δὲ πρὸς ὑμέων κυρήσας οὐκ ὁμοιώσομαι ὑμῖν, ἀλλ' ἑτοῖμός . . , . διηκοσίας τε τριήρεας, καὶ δισμυρίους ὁπλίτας, καὶ δισχιλίην ἵππον, καὶ δισχιλίους τοξότας, καὶ δισχιλίους σφενδονήτας, καὶ δισχιλίους ἱπποδρόμους ψιλοὺς· σῖτόν τε ἁπάσῃ τῇ Ἑλλήνων στρατιῇ." κ. τ. λ.
[35] *Divine Inst.,* VII., c. 15, He informs us that Seneca wrote these and many other things of great interest, which have been lost.
[36] Polybius, *Histories,* XVIII., 35. According to Polybius, Rome began to degenerate about B. C. 146, the year of the sacking and inexcusable extinction of the great and prosperous city of Corinth: *Encyc. Brit.,* Vol. XIX , p. 427, Stoddart, Phil. On the horrors of the conquests, Granier de Cassagnac, *Hist. Classes Ouv.,* p. 488, says: . . "soulever les esclaves. Les guerres continuelles avaient fini par épuiser la population de la race libre et par donner à la population de la race esclave une redoutable prépondérance." And repeats the following from Seneca, *De Clem.,* I., c. 24; "In senatu, dicta est, aliquando sententia, ut servos à liberis cultus distingueret. Deinde apparuit quantum periculum immeneret, si servi nostri numerare nos cœpissent." Of course this was regarding the slaves of war taken captive in the conquests. But Polybius, IV., 81, fin., speaking of the tyrant Nabis, fifty or sixty years earlier, talks of the downward tendency of Rome: " . . . . πλείστοις δ' ἐπάλαισαν ἀναδασμοῖς καὶ φυγαῖς πικροτάτης δὲ δουλείας πεῖραν ἔλαβον, ἕως τε Νάβιδις τυραννίδος· οἱ τὸ πρὶν οὐδὲ πύθομαι δυνηθέντες ἀναχέσθαι 'ῥαδίως αὑτῆς," κ. τ. λ.

miles,[37] was able to send into the field against Croton, another city not far away, likewise destroyed by the conquests, an army of 300,000 men. Croton had 100,000 soldiers. Tarentum where Spartacus careered on his memorable campaigns, had a great population at the time of its capture by the Romans; for no less than 30-000 of the brave people were taken prisoners and reduced to slavery. All this region of lower Italy had been converted to the practical socialism of Pythagoras, and the appearance is that the people were very prosperous and wealthy. One section, with a large population had no slaves ; and there is reason to believe that Croton, Sybaris and many other rich and flourishing places had well-nigh solved the social problem when the desolating wars of the conquests struck them with the blight of murder and greed, and eliminated them from the geography of the earth. Somewhat akin to the Roman conquests, and like the truculent furies of Xerxes and Hamilco, occuring as it did in the same century, was that useless 30 years conflict called the Peloponnesian war. It began its murderous ravages 20 years after the two epochal battles of Salamis and Himera, and raged 30 years, with almost unabated fury until Athens was overcome. The population of the human race was being seriously threatened when Appius Claudius tore open the gates of the temple of Janus at Rome, and spoiled all the grand peace-dreams of Numa and Tullus Hostilius.

[35] The island of Crete contained a large and thrifty population, from the days of Homer down to these conquests. Under Minos, its ancient king, who was esteemed "the wisest of legislators of antiquity," these peaceful people prospered in their enormous manufacturing industries and their commerce with the continent and the neighboring islands. Many inscriptions

---

[37] Πεντήκοντα σταδιοι Diod., XXI., c, 9; Strabo, VI., p. 405. Other large cities in this region, after flourishing for centuries, fell. Strabo, VI., p. 429. For the holocaust at Tarentum, Livy, VI., 12; xxii. 16: "Mihi miraculo fuit" Dionys. Hal, ed. Franckfurt, 1586, folio, pp. 74, 78, 79. For other mention of the conditions, see I., chap. ix., *Eunus*, init,

[38] Isocrates, *Panegyrics* and *Orations*; Wallace, *Numbers of Mankind*, p. 57, giving his own valuable remarks on statements of Athenæus, VI., 20. The island of Ægina only 180 σταδια, (20 Eng. Miles) in circumfrence, had 470,000 slaves shortly after these wars began to career. Strabo, VIII,; Plutarch, *Lycurg*. Athenæus, VI., 272, took his valuable data from Aristotle,

recently found there show them to have been well organized. The population was reduced to a few thousand disappointed and heart-broken wanderers, and their brilliant civilization went down.

The governments instituted in the place of those destroyed were inferior and contemptible. In lower Italy where the socialistic philosophy of Pythagoras had for ages prevailed, the régime of Rome caused a veritable revolution. In those countries war had been done away with so completely that when Pyrrhus entered that region with his conquering forces, he found the innocent, peaceful people so unfit for his savage and murderous habits that he disbanded the socialists and their communistic code and common table, and set up the old competitive mode of life which in the end, only served the Romans whom he was fighting. Their history presents a spectacle of degeneracy from the lofty philosophy of Plato and Socrates, down to a rehabilitation of the old competing forms.

The whole episode sums up in a recital of the most horrible series of infamies the world has known—a murderous and unprovoked assault upon, and highway robbery of, a score of innocent peoples, organized in trades of skill, living in intermutual communities, having a self-sustaining spirit, without hospitals, degrading charities or beggary; all working together for mutual happiness and comfort. We leave it to Gibbon to recount how Rome proved incapable of profiting by these acquisitions. It is true, Rome preserved the aged royalty and the false dignity of a slave-based aristocracy; but her proud gens families degenerated and lost their foothold one by one, her mighty conquests sank into murderous civil wars, her republic fell to the Cæsars; enormous wealth seized by individual army officers from the struggling conquered, and the mouldering ruins of their victims, were carried on the backs of innumerable slaves to make millionaires of generals and stock jobbers; and in A. D. 193 Rome was disgracefully sold at auction to Didius, the highest bidder, glutted with this thus gotten wealth of plunder and able to bid a thousand dollars for each man of the savage prætorian guard!

So much for a system which has proved a failure. Let us see what can be said of the parallel system of Solon

THE MOURNFUL EPISODE SUMMED UP. 73

which through these vicissitudes of carnage still lived, lives on forever, and is proving a modern success. The Roman conquest was a colossal and desperate effort to defend and perpetuate the aged competitive system which was being undermined and attacked by the great Solonic dispensation.[39] This law was engraved into stone or brazen tablets, originally in Greek, a short time after the death of Amasis, a pharaoh of Egypt, having been borrowed from him by Solon on his wide wanderings in search of the best practical methods of political economy, and later translated by a commission from Rome sent to Athens for that purpose. Its Latin paraphrase was again engraved and formed the eleventh of the celebrated Twelve Tables of Rome. During the first ages of that unparalelled masacre of humanity, the conquests, it was secretly and ruthlessly torn down; but so powerful were the sanctity and religious scruples of the Jove-worshiping Romans who dared not exterminate what they sincerely believed to be a decree of that majestic god, that there lingered several scraps, legible, but battered and outraged, which survived the havoc of the conquests so that we have to this day in the Digest of laws, immortal, sacred, glorious, the foundation rock of Christianity. Under its guardianship millions of slaves, the product of both seizure, and entailment of property upon primogeniture, were enfranchised and the poor without class distinction were made comfortable, self-supporting and happy. The conquests appear to have been a desperate attempt to destroy this vast and far-extended Solonic dispensation.

Whether the laboring classes of modern times are willing to learn wisdom by this recital of long occult facts remains a momentous question. We know that the same hatred of them still exists. Monarch, president, capitalist still views with fear all attempts of labor to organize on a political basis. "Avoid politics" has been their constant cry. Appius Claudius, 400 years before our era said to them: "don't go into politics." The duke of Arcos told Masaniello, the revolted fisherman; don't go into politics." Queen Elizabeth to her laboring subjects: "fly

[39] For our elaborately written opinions of the failure of the competitive system in the world, see *Human Aptitudes*; also Vol. I., pp. 496, 571, 573, see *index*, v. *Competition*.

politics." Kinsella, the Brooklyn editor, imploringly advised the writer of this book : "don't go into politics nor lead your people into that blind and dangerous infatuation."

But the champions of money, inheritance and prurient greed read us no lecture on how those noble fathers: Solon, the wisest of the seven wise men, Numa the incomparable king, and Moses, the father of an undying code, inscribed the votive franchise upon their laws of government. The voting clause has never failed; it can never fail; and yet in this dawn of its modern success we see on every hand millionaires growing up out of labor's earnings and amid the immoral reekings of pelf, the brigandage of a competitory civilization, the subornation of recreant evidence, the bribery of politicians, the soaring of corrupted youth to wealth and power, this political lever is threateningly used to enlarge standing armies, muzzle the press, and is insidiously preparing to again strike the workman down, fearing his socialism and his voting unions. The dangerous old weapon for their future use against him is again, as in the ages of the past, the murderous standing army.

CHAPTER II.

REVOLUTIONS AMONG SEMITIC RACES.

STRIKE OF MOSES AND THE JEWS—ESCAPE FROM EGYPT.

Most Ancient and Enormous of all Strikes and Labor Rebellions—One Million Involved—The Exodus—Comparison with Eunus and Spartacus—Stinging Lash of the Slave Drivers upon the Backs of an Innocent and Enterprising People—Strange Story of the Straw and Stubble—Unreasonable Demand of a King Squeezing Them beyond Endurance—Rebellion against it of the Mildest Nature—Struck Work and Ran Away—Pharaoh and his Military Hosts in Hot Pursuit—Almost Incredible Providential Rescue—Red Sea Opens and lays bare a Path for the Hebrews but Flows back and Engulfs the Pursuers—Discovery of a Mummy of Same Pharaoh Casting Doubt—Number of the thus Emancipated Given in Exact Figures—Reflection on the Prodigious Magnitude and Effects of this Strike—Law of Moses the direct Result of it—Proof that Violent Resistance is Productive of Good—World of Labor Forced to Bow in Reverence and Respect to Moses and the Jews.

In the first volume of this work, as plainly expressed,[1] only the great Arion races, including the populations of Europe could be considered. The scheme included ten important strikes and bloody insurrections known among the working people of antiquity, leaving for a future volume an account of the struggles of the Semitic and more eastern peoples. A skeleton of the great trade organizations was also given.

Among the labor turmoils it would be unfair not to mention the greatest and most celebrated strike and fugi-

[1] Vol. I., p. 526, *Ancient Lowly*.

tive slave episode on record, namely, the Exodus, or escape of the Hebrew families from the galling slavery to which they were condemned by slaveholders of Egypt.[2] In writing the history of labor one is often questioned regarding the construction to be put on the events, and the names given them. We have boldly and steadfastly persisted in calling things by their right names. The great wars by the gladiator Spartacus, which, the escape of the Jews from Egyptian slavery alone excepted, was the hugest on record and the greatest in the annals of the Aryan family of mankind, we designated a well defined labor strike. It was a bold venture. But the venture has been thoroughly approved by the public. If, then, the stoppage of work by the Israelites under the aggravating circumstances we are going to recount, was a historical affair of any kind it was that of a genuine strike.

The grievances causing the strike undertaken by the Hebrew race was the almost indescribable cruelty of that Pharaoh and his creatures in refusing them a mild petition made to the monarch, by two chiefs of the tribe, for permission to go to some wooded retreat where they could celebrate in honor of Jehovah, according to their beloved custom. The petition seems to have been a very mild, courteous and reasonable one. Moses and his brother Aaron were the delegates. The king granted them an interview, but evidently with much haughtiness and condescension. When they respectfully presented to him their plea on behalf of great numbers of poor and kindly desposed people, jaded to the last stage of deprivation, bad food[3] and overwork, he bluffed them with the usual mannerless guffaw and disdain in the same insulting and exasperating manner as it is done

[2] On the dates of this event there is a disagreement of authorities, as to whether it occurred in the latter part of the 14th or early in the 15th century before Chris . The *American Cyclopedia* publishes a carefully written article on "*Hebrews*," which contains the following words: . . . . nor of their exodus, which, according to some of the most celebrated Egyptological critics, Wilkinson, Bunson, Lepsius, etc., took place in the last quarter of the 14th century B. C., while according to distinct biblical passages, I., *Kings*, vi., 1, it must have happened early in the 15th." It is dated at B. C. 1455 in Meyers *Konversations Lexikon*, in verbo "*Juden*," init., and the origin of the nation, B. C. 2000, or at least, its primitive existence under Abraham.

[3] Garlic, onions. rice and a sort of peas, were the food used by the Egyptian slaves. See I., p. 446. where Herodotus *Euterpe*, 125, is quoted giving the statistics of food consumption and costs for slaves who built the Egyptian monuments.

to-day. But Moses was not a man to be turned down so easily. He mildly insisted on behalf of his countrymen. And what was the answer he got from the magnate? "Wherefore do ye lead the people from their work? Get you unto your burdens." "And Pharaoh commanded the same day the task masters of the people, and their officers, saying. 'Ye shall no more give the people straw to make brick, as heretofore. Let them go and gather straw for themselves.'"[4] The petty taskmasters or slave drivers—and we cannot understand this to mean Hebrew overseers, but rather Egyptian hirelings or government appointees, who were heartless in their pride of petty power—then drove these poor people into the desperate task of furnishing themselves with a commodity necessary for making brick. Of course the making of brick with straw as a material to cause the earth and plaster to adhere until placed in the kiln is a very natural thing, especially where the bricks are burnt or dried in the hot sun, operating in tropical regions as a brickkiln. We are suspicious that in order to make this more difficult to do, the Egyptian workmen against whom these Semitic slaves were competing, took care to gather away as much of the straw as possible so that to obtain it was an impossibility; for we are told in the same chapter that they had to ransack the country in quest of stubble, an inferior commodity, answering the same purpose. The Bible language crowds it into few words: "Let there be more work laid upon the men that they may labour therein."

On the whole it was a most cruel and barbarous mode of tyranny. The spirit of the brave rebels against such realistic spectacles of impudent and recreant power. It was too much for the manhood of the Hebrew to brook. He called the aid of the great Father to solace him in his innocence. He had done nothing to merit treatment so utterly beyond the bounds of reason and even beyond the boundary lines of the brutal slave code. He rebelled and invoked the protection of his tutelary divinity in whose gracious embraces all those credulous beings of the ancient lowly believed and supplicated themselves. Nothing could be more natural.

[4] *Exodus*, V., 4. The fifth chapter contains a complete account, giving many details.

The Book of Books now recounts and expects us to believe a long list of impossible things whether we will or not, about the descent upon earth of the mighty Jehovah, the scourge of frogs, the pestilential waters, the murrain that infected the cattle of Pharaoh and left unscathed the herds of the Hebrews;[5] the pillar of clouds by day and the streams of fire by night; the opening of the waters of the sea to let them safely pass to a land of freedom and the closing of the frowning chasm upon the chasing Egyptian host, and its extermination.[6]

This is a remarkable example of a strike in enormous proportions. The demand of the unreasonable tyrant that they should continue the manufacture without pay, as slaves, and at the same time furnish part of the materials, was a piece of heathenism so mean and rapacious as to tax our belief. Yet even now a spirit of hatred exists among the drivers of those who labor, which often exhibits itself to be as venomous and uncompromising. The Israelites could not possibly comply with such an outrageous order; for it required that they should make as many bricks as before; and a clause in the sacred history shows that a suspension of the burdensome task did not take place until they had actually scoured Egypt in search of straw and stubble wherewith to comply with this cruel and ferocious edict. When the stubborn monarch had shown by his revengeful spirit that no concessions could be expected, no lenity given, and all hope of escape was lost, they struck work in a vast mass amounting in all to considerably more than half a million.[7]

[5] *Exodus*, chapters VIII. and IX.
[6] An inscription has been recently found showing that Pharaoh himself did n it perish, or if he was drowned his body was recovered. We were unable to s e and examine this curious find for ourselves, but we quote a letter from one of the Egyptologists who are engaged by the British School of Archæology, and who send their accounts of every important discovery to London for publication. The Cairo letter appeared Aug. 8th, 1881, in the London Times and is as follows:
In a cave discovered at Deirel Bahar, near Thebes in Egypt, were found in 1881, thirty-nine mummies of royal and priestly personages. Among them was King Ramises II, the third king of the 19th dynasty, and the veritable Pharaoh of the Jewish captivity. It is very strange that he should be here among a number of other kings if he had been lost in the Red Sea. The mummy is wrapped in rose-colored and yellow linen, of a texture finer than the finest Indian muslin, upon which are strewn Lotus flowers. It is in a state of perfect preservation.
[7] *Numbers*. I., 46: "Even all that were numbered, were six hundred thousand and three thousand and five hundred and fifty;" ie. 603,550.

It is difficult for the finite mind to compass the possibility of a huge and peaceful escape from armed hosts of a wealthy and populous country, controlled by a great and frowning king whose countless warriors, armed with gleaming spears and daggers, with fiendish yells of vengeance, raging in pursuit, without feeling a submissiveness to an awful omnipotence, and collapsing back to a credulous avowal that the power which rescued them was that of God. True, the birth of science, still but a tottering infant, wraps the mind with doubt and we waft into a vortex of incredulity, while university students too narrow to probe, lecture around us and explode empiric thunders, flourishing as a certitude things windily expressed and not made positive, haggling up the conclusion that no God exists; that no miracle visits earth; that nothing unexplainable ever yet guided the hand of man; that all the stories of traditionists having done so, were traps to inveigle the silly, and sweeten the bait to capture and to devour the flesh of fools. Be it so. We are not discussing this. We are talking of the strike from work, of near a million workmen and their safe convoy by some superhuman hand, some guidance as of a wonder-god, and of the foundering of hosts of savage and hyena-like pursuers who become engulfed, while the innocent fugitives escape to a dry land of safety—a story that has come credibly down to us in the histories and the traditions of a dozen tongues.[8]

Strikes are energetically described to us as an economic failure, an all round disaster both to employers and workmen wherever they occur. Did this strike turn out a disaster to the Hebrew race? On the contrary. The very first result from it was the enactment of the law of Moses, which for the poor was the best and wisest ever written until the time of Solon. By following the same sacred record we shall find Moses pioneering his immense family to the foot of a mountain where they

[8] For the various legends, traditions and histories of this people the first is their own, which is to be found in the Old Testament and afterwards, their Gamara of the Talmud contains more points. The *Antiquities* of the Jews by Flavius Josephus, written during the last decade of the first century of the Christian era; some *Contributions* by Maimonides and a great number of modern historians and commentators. A new and unsought source of Jewish history is now cropping out from the *inscriptions* which are being gathered from every land anciently inhabited by these unconquerable and in most respects consistent and valuable people, and these inscriptions, as a general thing do nothing but corroborate and verify the written history.

rested from their fatiguing toils. The great deliverer and statesman himself, ascended the mountain and there upon tablets,[9] in an almost exactly similar manner as they afterwards chiseled the tables of Solon's law at Athens, and of the decemvirs at Rome, the Hebrew statesman and labor leader or lord, chiseled with his own or some important hand the celebrated statute which was to be the basis of the Mosaic dispensation.

We shall therefore proceed with our history of the Semitic side of the ancient lowly with the profoundest respect for the law of Moses. It is true it was a dispensation of slavery; but in those remote ages this was an all-prevailing institution, even considered just and indispensable by a large proportion of the slaves themselves. There is a vein of feeling and kindness pervading the Mosaic law.[10] It was a code too competitive and too faulty, however, to pioneer humanity into anything like a perfect and successful political economy where no hunger, inequality, or slavery could exist; but it was a magnificent forerunner of socialism already firmly begun and to our certain knowledge, legalized some eight hundred years after Moses flourished. This socialism, of which the great law of Moses was the forerunner, is to be for the most part our theme of investigation in this work.

That the law of Moses originated in a strike of working men and working women in Egypt no one will attempt to deny. That strike, and the rebellion of the Semitic family of mankind, then, was the turning point in the direction of socialism which was to redeem the world; and a foothold of the law, in spite of the chronic hatred of a murderous competitive system which has proved a failure, is now seen more and more legibly imimprinted as we study it in its steadfast growth and powerful politico-social organization all over the enlightened world.

[9] *Exodus*, xxiv., 12: "And the Lord said unto Moses, come up to me into the mount and be there and I will give thee tables of stone and a law, and commandments which I have written; that thou mayest teach them." When afterwards the tables of laws were broken into fragments another set is recorded, *Exodus*, xxxiv., 1: "And the Lord said unto Moses: hew thee two tables of stone, like unto the first: and I will write upon these tables the words that were in the first tables thou breakest."

[10] For a summarized paraphrase of the law of Moses, see I., pp. 43-46. For the full law itself see *Leviticus*, xvii—xxvi.

CHAPTER III.

MORE STRIKES IN EGYPT.

STORY TOLD IN HIEROGLYPHS.

HEBREWS not the only Egyptian Strikers—Three Thousand Years ago—Unions on Public Work at that Time—Pharaoh as a Merciless Employer—Starving the Men—It was not long after the Exodus—Birthplace of Free Masonry—Practice of Engraving Records on Stone—Queer Strike in Asia Minor—An Inscription Tells of a Mighty Strike of Bakers in Magnesia a Semitic City—All Told out on the Stone—No other Account of it Known—Great Disturbance—Cut off the Supply of Bread—A Bread Famine—Intervention of the City Council—Strikers Arrested—Their Union Broken up and its Members Forced to Furnish Bread without a Trade Union—Powerful Proof that they were under Government Employ—Great Union of the Musicians—A historic Proof that they were Employed by Governments—Music treated as a Trade—Story of an Important Strike of these Artists—Three Centuries before Christ—Like Moses and his Hebrews they Struck Work by Running Away—How they were Caught—They Ultimately Won—Full Quotations from Livy—Power of the Lord of their Union—Marching off under their Old Red Flag—The Way the Politicians Outwitted Them—Yet They Accomplished their Purpose—All under Guise of Religion though they Cared Only for their Bread and Comforts—Admitted a Pure Strike by All Commentators.

THE tendency, on the part of the laboring classes in Semitic Egypt, to strike and protest against the severity of masters was by no means confined to the Hebrews who had been reduced from peaceful agricultural pursuits, to slavery. There is an inscription, not long ago made known by Maspero, showing another important strike of workmen who were engaged on the pyramids in those days of thankless drudgery.

The Egyptologist relates that more than 3000 years ago a great and winning strike of the masons working on public works, occurred. It appears that in Egypt, under the pharaonic dynasty, the skilled artisans were organized and that, like the Romans with their collegium and the Greeks with their eranos, they were employed upon the public works. These were slaves and prove the truth of their inscriptions assuring us that slaves were organized. But even admitting that this coveted government employment was better than that to be obtained outside, which, so far as we have investigated this subject, is always the case, still nothing but a scanty pittance was given and the men had grievances amounting to starvation as is shown in this inscription.

M. Maspero, who, with his colleagues was engaged in digging up and deciphering the picture writings and hieroglyphics scrawled on the masonry of temples, pyramids and sphynxes, found an account of a pure strike of the masons. Condensed and rendered into English it gives the following curious information :

"On the tenth of the month, builders at work on the temple, rushed out, and sat down behind the chapel, exclaiming: 'We are hungry; and there are yet eighteen days before the next pay-day.' They would not work until the king agreed to hear their complaints. Two days later, Pharaoh went to the temple and ordered relief given to the masons; but on the sixteenth day they struck again. On the seventeenth and eighteenth days they also refused to work. On the nineteenth day they broke loose and raised a mob at the governor's palace and finally got their demands." The Athenian state slaves are also known to have received monthly pay in the same manner.

This is an account of a pure strike which occurred soon after the exodus of the Israelites from Egypt. Every evidence points to the probability that these masons, hod carriers, mortar mixers and laborers possessed at that early age, B. C. 1100, a powerful organization; and as men investigate the shadowy subject of free-masonry and trace this trade back to the temple-building enterprises of king Solomon, unearthing its inventions of the lost

A HUNGER STRIKE IN HIEROGLYPHICS. 83

art of brick-making at Nineveh, and probing the antiquity of pyramids and temples of ancient Egypt, they strike at the fountain head of a vast hierarchy of the masonic art stretching back beyond the dawn of recorded history, where freemasonry must have had its birth, its imperishable organization and its abiding place.

Innumerable inscriptions collected from every corner of the ancient world, Syria, Mesopotamia, Greece, Sicily and Etruria are being gathered into the museums. They bring proof that of all the ancient trades, this of the masons enjoyed primitively the highest organization, independence and enlightened power. Amasis, according to Herodotus,[1] required that workmen should be able to give an account of how they got their living on pain of death, and they had to be organized to do it. Thus it is impossible to immagine that the masons engaged at starvation wages upon the temple where this strike occurred, were not among the organized groups.

The Egyptian hieroglyphs are furnishing other strike records. There was a practice among the Semitic as well as the Aryan peoples, of engraving upon stones some record of important events. This habit which is now known to have been compulsory in many states, was especially prevalent among the ancient labor unions; and through it we now derive most of the valuable information for their history.

One such stone has recently been found in Syria, likewise a Semitic province. It shows a strike of the bakers of Magnesia, on the river Meander; and because the brief inscription which records it, does not explain the story of the grievance it is used by writers adversely, as if to prove that the labor element in those times was lawless and dangerous.

But let us relate this interesting story. The account, so far as we have it in monumental testimony, shows that at a far off date, nobody knows when, but evidently centuries before our era began, the bakers in the old

[1] *Euterpe*, c, 177. See 1,, 338, note 14, quoting Plutarch, *Solon*, showing that rganization about 900 or 1000 years before Curist was compulsory in Egypt. The words of Herodotus on the origin of the law of Solon, *Euterpe*, 177, are as follows: " νόμον δὲ Αἰγυπτίοισι τόνδε Ἄμασίς ἐστι ὁ καταστήσας ἀποδεικνύναι ἔτεος ἑκάστου τῷ νομάρχῃ πάντα τινὰ Αἰγυπτίων, ὅθεν βιοῦται· μὴ δὲ ποιεῦντα ταῦτα, μηδὲ ἀποφαίνοντα δικαίην ζόην, ἰθύνεσθαι θανάτῳ. Σόλων δὲ ὁ Ἀθηναῖος λαβὼν ἐξ Αἰγύπτου τοῦτον τὸν νόμον Ἀθηναίοισι ἔθετο· τῷ ἐκεῖνοι ἐς αἰεὶ χρέωνται ἐόντι ἀμώμῳ νόμῳ."

84 SEMITIC STRIKES OF EGYPT AND SYRIA.

cities, Magnesia and Paros, who were organized under the law of Solon, on account of some grievance not defined, struck work and refused to bake and bring to the regular market the usual supply of bread.[2] The authorities of the city, in all probability the city council which resembled a board of aldermen, being notified of the disturbance, convoked an extra session, and the *agoranomos* or clerk of the public works, as was later the case at Ephesus, when Demetrius rebelled against the preaching of Paul, delivered a speech to the people protesting against the strike; and the whole thing resulted in the ringleaders of the strikers being arrested, their trade organization being temporarily if not permanently suppressed, and the bakers being compelled by force to fur-

[2] C. I. G. 2374 e, (in Vol. 2, page 1074).
EDITOR'S REMARKS:
Pari in arce, marmor olim muro insertum; cum commentairo ed. Thierschius Comm. Acad. Bavar.), class. philos. et philol. a 1835, p. 599–632. et in tabula, quae addita est, lithographica. In sinistra paucae litterae desunt, quod lapis ibi accisus est ; praetarea foramina insunt vss. 45–49, et 65, ante vocem ultimam, unde exiguae ibi lacunae, fractusque lapis est vs. 29, quare ibi aliquot litterae tantum dimidae extant, quas lamen representavi integras. Vs. 60 ΕΠΑΓΓΑΕΛ cet, est in tabula Thierschii, sed fortasse non in marmore.

Τύχη ἀγαθή. Ἔδοξεν τῇ βουλῇ καὶ τῷ δήμῳ, Μυρμιδῶν Εἰ . . . ου εἶπεν·
5 Ἐπεὶ οὖν Κίλλος Δημητρίου ἀνὴρ ἀγαθὸς ὢν καὶ συμφέρων τῇ πόλει πρότερόν τε ἀγορανομήσας ἦρξεν τὴν ἀρχὴν καλῶς τε καὶ δικαίως καὶ ἀκολούθως τοῖς νόμοις, ἐφ' οἷς ὁ δῆμος ἐτίμησεν αὐτὸν ταῖς ἁρμοζούσαις τιμαῖς·
10 κατασταθείς τε καὶ ἐπ' ἄρχοντος Γόργου τὴν αὐτὴν ἀρχὴν ὑπερέθετο τῇ φιλοπονίᾳ, τὴν πᾶσαν σπουδὴν εἰσενεγκάμενος, ὅπως ὁ δῆμος ἐν εὐετηρίᾳ καὶ
15 δαψιλείᾳ ὑπάρχῃ χρώμενος ἄρτοις καὶ ἀλφίτοις ὡς ἀξιωτάτοις. καὶ βελτίστοις, περί τε τῶν μοσθοῦ ἐργαζομένων καὶ τῶν μισθουμένων αὐτοὺς ὅπως μηδέτεροι ἀδικῶνται ἐφρόντιζεν, ἐπαναγκάζων κατὰ τοὺς νόμους τοὺς μὲν μὴ ἀθετεῖν,
20 ἀλλὰ ἐπὶ τὸ ἔργον πορεύεσθαι, τοὺς δὲ ἀποδιδόναι τοῖς ἐργαζομένοις τὸν μισθὸν ἄνευ δίκης, τῶν τε ἄλλων τῶν κατὰ τὴν ἀρχὴν τὴν καθήκουσαν ἐπιμέλειαν ἐποιήσατο, κακοπάθειαν οὐδὲ μίαν περικάμψας, ἀκόλουθα δὲ
25 πράττων τοῖς τε νόμοις καὶ τῇ τοῦ βίου ἀναστροφῇ καὶ ταῖς ἀρχαῖς αἷς ἦρξεν πρὸ τῆς ἀγορανομίας· ὅπως οὖν καὶ ὁ δῆμος φαίνηται τὰς καταξίους τιμὰς ἀπονέμων τοῖς ὑπερτιθεμένοις πρὸςαὑτὸν τῇ φιλοτιμίᾳ, ἀγαθῇ τύχῃ,
30 δεδόχθαι ἐπαινέσαι Κίλλον Δημητρίου καὶ στεφανῶσαι αὐτὸν χρυσῷ στεφάνῳ καὶ εἰκόνι μαρμαρίνῃ ἀρετῆς ἕνεκεν καὶ φιλοτιμίας, ἧς ἔχων διατελεῖ
35 περὶ τὸν δῆμον, καὶ ἀνειπεῖν τὸν στέφανον Διονυσίων τῶν μεγάλων τραγῳδῶν τῷ ἀγῶνι, δηλοῦντας τὰς αἰτίας, δι' ἃς ἐστεφάνωκεν αὐτὸν ὁ δῆμος, τῆς τε ἀναγορεύσεως τοῦ στεφάνου ἐπιμεληθῆναι τοὺς ἄρχοντας ἐφ' ὧν ἂν πρῶτον
40 Διονύσια τὰ μεγάλα ἄγωμεν. ἐπελθὼν δὲ καὶ Δεξίοχος ἐπὶ μὲν ταῖς τιμαῖς ταῖς ψηφιζομέναις τῷ πατρὶ αὐτοῦ ἔφη εὐχαριστεῖν τῷ δήμῳ, τὸ δὲ ἀργύριον τὸ εἰς τὴν εἰκόνα καὶ τὴν ἀνάθεσιν τῆς εἰκόνος δώσειν αὐτός· ὅπως οὖν
45 καὶ ἡ εἰκὼν κατασκευασθεῖσα σταθῇ τὴν ταχίστην ἐν τῷ ἀγορανομίῳ οὗ ἂν φαίνηται αὐτοῖς μηδὲν βλάπτουσα τῶν ἀναθημάτων, καὶ τὸ ὄνομα ἀναγραφὲν εἰς στήλην λιθίνην σταθῇ παρὰ τὴν εἰκόνα, ἐπιμεληθῆναι Δεξίοχον, καθὼς ἐπαγγέλλεται.
50 Διοσκοροι. Ἔδοξεν τῇ βουλῇ καὶ τῷ δήμῳ, Εὐμένης Εὐμένους εἶπεν· Ἐπειδὴ Κίλλος Δημητρίου ἐν τε τοῖς ἔμπροσθεν χρόνοις ἀνὴρ ἀγαθὸς ὢν
55 διατελεῖ περὶ τὸν δῆμον καὶ πᾶν τὸ συμφερον πράσσων καὶ κοινῇ τῇ πόλει καὶ ἰδίᾳ τοῖς ἐντυγχάνουσιν Κίλλῳ, νῦν τε πολέμαρχος αἱρεθεὶς καὶ τυχόντος αὐτῷ τοῦ ἱεράξει τοῖς Διοσκόροις ἐν τῇ θυσίᾳ τῇ γινομένῃ τοῖς Θεοξενίοις, βουλόμενος συνεπαύξειν τοῖς θεοῖς τὴν πανήγυριν καὶ ἅπαντας μετέχειν τῶν
60 ἱερῶν, ἐπελθὼν τὸν δῆμον ἐπαγγέλλεται δημοποιήσειν ἐν τοῖς Θεοξενίοις· δεδόχθαι τῷ δήμῳ ἐπαινέσαι Κίλλον Δημητρίου ἐπί τε τῇ πρὸς τοὺς θεοὺς
65 εὐσεβίᾳ καὶ τῇ πρὸς τοὺς θεοὺς εὐσεβίᾳ, καὶ τῇ πρὸς τὸν δῆμον εὐνοίᾳ τὴν δὲ δημοθοινίαν συντελέσαι αὐτὸν ἐν τῷ γυμνασίῳ.

nish bread in future for the regular supply. This was no bread riot but a strike, such as frequently occur among the trade unions now. We give the inscription in a footnote[13] and the paraphrase of its meaning may be interesting. It is the excellent one roughed out by Dr. Waltzing: "Authors do not speak of these strikes, but epigraphy furnishes a curious example. At Magnesia, on the river Mæander, the bakers mutually agreed to cease supplying the market, and trouble broke out in consequence. At what date it occurred is unknown.[14] The Roman governor whose mame is lost, intervened and his edict, ratified at a session of the senate of Magnesia has been partly preserved. Consulting only the interests of the city, the governor did not wish to treat the strikers with rigid severity as he might have done. He hopes that his edict will suffice to render them wiser in the future. He forbids the bakers to form any more hetæræ or trade unions and orders them to regularly furnish the necessary bread. Any baker who shall associate himself with meetings, or who shall again excite sedition leading to trouble, or who shall secrete himself, or any one who shall furnish another with a hiding place, will be severely punished."

[3] *Bulletin de Correspodence Hélténique*, VII., 1883, page 504, No. 10: ". . . . . δὲ καὶ κατὰ συνθήκας . . . . . . ὥστε κινεῖν ἐνίοτε τὸν δῆμον εἰς ταραχὴν καὶ θορύβους ἐνπίπτειν διὰ τὴν σ . . . , ὀγον καὶ ἀορασίαν τῶν ἀρτοκόπων ἐπὶ τῇ ἀγορᾷ στάσεων, ἐφ' οἷς ἐχρῆν . . . . τοὺς μεταπεμφθέντας ἤδη δίχην ὑποσχεῖν.
5 Ἐπεὶ δὲ τὸ τῇ πόλει συμφέρον τῆς τούτων τιμωρίας μᾶλλον προτιμᾶν ἀναγκαῖον, ἡγησάμην διατάγματι αὐτοὺς σωφρονίσαι. Ὅθεν ἀπαγορεύω μήτε συνέρχεσθαι τοὺς ἀρτοκόπους κατ' ἑταιρίαν, μήτε προεστηκότας θρασύνεσθαι, πειθαρχεῖν δὲ πάντως τοῖς ὑπὲρ τοῦ κοινῇ σομφέροντος ἐπιταττομένοις καὶ τὴν ἀναγκαίαν τοῦ ἄρτου ἐργασίαν ἀνενδεῆ παρέχειν τῇ πόλει. Ὡς ἂν ἀλῷ
10 τις αὐτῶν τὸ ἀπὸ. τοῦδε ἢ συνιὼν παρὰ τὰ διηγορευμένα ἢ θορύβου τινὸς ἢ στάσεως ἐξάρχων, μεταπεμφθεὶς τῇ προσηκούσῃ τειμωρίᾳ κολασθήσεται· ἐὰν δέ τις τολμήσῃ τὴν πόλιν ἐνεδρεύων ἀποκρύψαι αὐτὸν , . . . δος προσσημειωθήσεται καὶ ὁ τὸν τοιοῦτον δὲ ὑποδεξάμενος τῇ αὐτῇ τιμωρίᾳ ὑπεύθυνος
15 γενήσεται. Ἐπὶ πρυτάνεως Κλ. Μοδέστου, μηνὸς Κλαρεῶνος δ', Βουλῆς ἀγομένης εἰς ἄλλο μέρος, Μαρκελλεῖνος εἶπεν, τῇδε ἀπονοίας τῶν ἐργαστηριάρχων γνω . . . . στὸν δεῖγμα χθὲς Ἑρμείας ὁ πρὸς . . . . .
[4] Waltzing, *Hist. Corp- Prof.*, p. 191, seems to think this strike of the bakers an inimical onslaught against good order because it was the plea of the governor to suppress it with a violent hand, in order that the inhabitants might be furnished their bread with regularity. We are inclined to think that the supply of bread for this city might have been a public function for there was no other source whereby to supply them. It looks very much as though the baking trade was one of the public industries and that the unions were employed as in any other of the public works. See Caguat, in *Vie Contemporaine,* Paris, Jan. 1896; "La seconde (grève) eut pour théâtre Magnesia," etc., and proceeds with the narrative. He says it was the sacred strike because he supposes it to have been very ancient. Oehler, in *Eranos Vindobonensis*, p. 280, says : "Ich verweise auf die Inschrift aus Paros, C. I. G. 2374 e. in welcher der Ἀγορανόμος (Aedile or clerk of the market), belobt wird, weil er dem Strike der Arbeiter ein Ende gemacht hatte. In dem Strike der Bäcker zu Magnesia am Maeander musste wegen der deshalb entstandenen Unruhen, der Statthalter intervenren." *Bull. Hell.*, VII., 505, 10."

The making of music is, in the sensible construction of language, a profession and a trade. Under the Solonic as well as the Numan law of labor organization, music was considered a trade, just as much as the work of the braziers or potters; and if the story of another strike details the facts, their skill was employed by the government. Another point discernible is that a remarkable amount of manhood and an amazing independence is exhibited; for these bold musicians dared face the political authorities, a thing seldom seen among government employees at the present time.

During one of the Samnite wars, in the year B. C. 309, and at the moment when the Romans wanted more money than they could collect, the censors issued a refusal to permit the collegium of musicians, or musicians' union to play at the feast of Jupiter at the expense of the city. It had been their annual custom to play at the shrine and as they had always been lavishly rewarded they took it for an unwarrantable deprivation.[5] Besides this, being voting unions, they belonged to a powerful political body of many trades who elected into power the commissioners of the public works. These in turn, appointed them to jobs under government employ. Braced by the justice of their right, they called upon their quinquennalis, or lord-master of the unions, who convoked their advisory board. On deliberation it was voted to resist the penurious demand and strike work, let the consequences be what they would. At the head of their military column, their red vexilum proudly waving at the front, they set up a march with this well-known flaming red banner to a distant town, across the Tiber. They were aware that

[5] Livy, IX., 30, *fin*. The musicians, following the regular customs of the ancient lowly, worshiped at the shrine of Minerva, not of Jupiter. He was the god of the grandees and of wealth. She was the patroness of labor and economic thrift. The cause of the strike originated in an effort of the governing powers to suppress them; and as the state was in the habit of hiring these musicians for its feasts of Jupiter, the nobles thought best to begin their tyranny at this feast. But Minerva, goddess of art, was the shrine the musicians bowed to. Festus says: "Is dies festus est tibicinum qui colunt Minervam." It was the 13th of June. Waltzing, *Hist. Corp. Prof.*, I., 201, says: "Minerve était aussi la patronne des autres collèges de musiciens." Her temple was on the Aventine Hill. Varro, speaking of them says: "Tibicines tum feriati vagantur per urbem et conveniunt ad ædem Minervæ." Waltzing, *ibid.*, p. 201: "Minerve était donc leur patronne. Ils avaient aussi, de temps immemorial, le droit de célébrer un banquet sacré au temple de Jupiter Capitolin, mais on ne nous dit pas si ce repas avait lieu pendant la même fête." Varro, *De Lingua Latina*, vi,, 16, verifies these statements.

OUTWITTED BY A POLITICIAN'S TRICK. 87

the superstitious Roman aristocracy would not dare to offend Jupiter their great protecting divinity to whose honor, not that of their own goddess, Minerva, were to be devoted these celebrations of music and praise. They judged correctly. But being straightforward and ingenuous, they knew only the honorable and manly way to win. They were not adept in the tricks of politicians, and as a consequence got outwitted just as they were outwitted on a vaster scale by similar cunning, described in our chapter on the Roman conquests. The methods of this trick, as told by the historian were as follows:

The Senate of Rome sent a commission to the neighboring town of Tibur, now Tivoli, whither the strikers had marched in a body, to ask of the political council of the place, its co-operation and intercession, with a view to induce the musicians to come out of their sulks, return to the feasts and give Jupiter the music for nothing. The reception was friendly. Negotiations were immediately opened with the strikers; but in vain. The workingmen were uncompromising. All solicitations were refused. It was now the very day before that set for the feasts. Fear that the gods would envelop them with wrath began to make Romans tremble. A stratagem was agreed upon. The musicians were to be asked to give a concert. At that pompous display they were to be inveigled into accepting potations which they seldom refused. Stuffed with wine, and when all were unconscious with inebriation they were to be taken bodily in cushioned chariots back to the eternal city and landed safely at the Roman forum, where all was in readiness for the sacrifices of the morrow. In the early dawn the sacrifices would begin. It was a cause of great sport for thousands. The multitude is a greater moral power to

6 Vexillum russeum, see Waltzing, *Hist. Corp. Prof*, I., p. 80; "Il s'agissait bien de supprimer les collèges; mais c' était une interdiction speciale émanant du pouvoir administratif, non une loi générale. Cohn raisonne *a fortiori*: le consul rappelle au peuple qu' il ne peut tenir aucune assemblée sans que le *v xillum russeum* flotte au Janicule et sans étre présidée par un magistrat; à plus forte raison d' autres réunions populaires sont défendues." He here quotes Livy, xxxix, 15, as follows: "Majores vestri ne vos quidem, nisi cum aut vexillo in arce posito comitiorum causa exercitus eductus esset . . . . forte temere coire voluerunt; et ubicunque multitudo esset, ibi et legitimum rectorem multitudinis censebant debere esset." There can be no doubt that the true grievance causing the strike was a highhanded effort of the powers to suppress the union of musicians. It certainly failed. Neither can there be any doubt that when the strikers marched in a body to Tibur, they marched under their beloved red flag.

the workingman on strike than the councils of the great. And when they awoke from their stupor and found themselves suffused with a friendly hurrah of nearly all the population of Rome gushing with flatteries around them, then they imbibed the full force of the joke by which they had been outwitted. They consented to play, but not until a stipulation was agreed to permitting them, annually in the future, to hold a jubilation, the 13th day of June, and march with their red flag and carnival uniforms through the streets, clothed with an accredited permission to solicit contributions for their benefit.

This surprising concession to them by the senate was fully equivalent to a complete success. Their strike had been won; for such a privilege accorded them in legal form was to go into practice the very next year and remain available forever, bringing them annual tribute, comfort and respect.[7]

[7] Livy, IX,, 30, 9; "Tibicines, quia prohibiti a proximis censoribus erant in æde Jovis vesci, quod traditum antiquitus erat ægre passi, Tibur uno agmine abierunt: adeo ut nemo in urbe esset qui sacrificiis præcineret. Ejus rei religio tenuit senatum: legatosque Tibur miserunt, ut darent operam, ut hi homines Romanis restituerentur. Tiburtini, benigne polliciti, primum accitos eos in curiam hortati sunt, uti reverterentur Romam: postquam perpelli nequibant, consilio, haud abhorrente ab inginiis hominum, eos adgrediuntur. Die festo alii alios per speciem celebrandarum cantu epularum causa invitant et vino, cujus avidum ferme genus est, oneratos sopiunt; atque ita in plaustra somno vinctos, conjiciunt, ac Romam deportant. Nec prius sensere, quam, plaustris in foro relictis, plenos crapulæ eos lux oppressit. Tunc concursus populi factus, impetratoque, ut manerent, datum ut triduum quotannis ornati, cum cantu atque hac, quæ nunc solemnis est licentia per urbem vagarentur, restitutumque, in æde vescendi jus iis qui sacris præcinerent. Haec inter duorum ingentium bellorum curam gerebantur." Cagnat, *Vie Contemporaine*, Jan. 1896. "La première (grève) eut lieu à Rome quand les joueurs de flute qui soutennaient de leurs monulations le chant des prêtres officiants, se retirerent, à Tibur. Ils voulaient par là protester contre un arrêt des censeurs qui leur déplaisaient." Waltzing, *Hist. Corp. Prof.*, p. 201.

CHAPTER IV.

NABIS.

THE LAST OF THE EPHORI.

N<small>ABIS</small>—A Semitic on the Rampage in Greece—How a Slave of the Conquests Overwhelmed his Oppressors—Chilon the Wise Inventor of an Unwise Measure—The Ephori—How Their Tyranny Destroyed the Laboring People—They even Ruled and Threatened Kings—Hated by the World—Nabis, the Syrian Slave Rises by his own Energy—Becomes a Cunning Military Officer—And Turns his Energies toward Extinction of the Ephori—The Ephori Described—Their Trained Assassins—How they lurked in Hedges with Sharpened Daggers—Plutarch's Account—Workingmen their Victims—Systematic Decimation of their Numbers—Working People as Tools of Labor—Nabis Swears to Exterminate the Ephori—His Wild Cruelty—Carnage among the Rich—Their Money Distributed among the Poor—Robbed Rich to Feed the Poor—Nabis Invents the Murderous Manakin—An Infernal Machine in Woman's Form—Springs fixed to Daggers that Stab the Lusty Princes who Embrace Her—Quotations from Polybius—Apega, Wife of Nabis was the Name of this Murderous Automaton—Nabis Becomes Tyrant of Sparta—Aristotle on Nationalized Tools of Labor—How Tools in Human Form were the Same Then, as Our Labor Saving Tools To-day—Fearful Competition of Such against the Free Labor Unions—The Tyrant takes their Part—His Wife and Many Ladies Work with Him—Strives to Restore the old Socialistic Form—Rings of Women who Assist him in Robbing the Rich—Imaginary Horrors, and Superstition Among the People—Ghosts and Spectres Believed in—Assassinated through Intrigues of Philopæmen—Result of his Life-Work—Final Extinction of the Ephori—They Never Rose to Power again—Vengeful Life-Work of Nabis Accomplished.

T<small>HE</small> two strikes just given, are put down by Dr. Waltzing and others as the only ones which in historic or monumental records appear as exact specimens of the modern strike. In the first volume of this work we gave the principal uprisings of freedmen and slaves, such as these of Eunus, Spartacus, Athenion and others as genuine strikes, and the response to this venture was a kind and unexpectedly appreciative one from the reading public; and as a result, to still further please, we shall mention in this volume several more, which occurred among Jews and other Semitic races in antiquity. These when mentioned at all are classed as turmoils and uprisings. We shall continue our categorical arrangement of them under the more dignified term strikes. They were not political disputes over boundary lines; they were not racial questions; they were not bursts of individual ambition. They were struggles for existence; bloody, perhaps, even terrible convulsions of physical and mental power of enslaved, overburdened and insulted workingmen, to wrench themselves loose from an otherwise hopeless destiny. It is thus that the strange story of Nabis, unworthy, though thrilling in death and devastation, comes back to us in modern history.

Away back in undatable antiquity, perhaps Lycurgus was yet living, there thrived a great character, one of the seven wise men of Greece. His name was Chilon—an oracle of a sort known now as walking cyclopedias. Many an apothegm current to-day is traced to him. It was Chilon who first said: "Man, know thyself; and it was he who died of joy on hearing of his son's victory at the Olympic games. But the kind hearted readers will falter in their admiration of one deed of Chilon He was the inventor of the slaves' tormentor, the Lacedæmonian Ephori. We cannot retouch the ephori here but refer to their work as already told in our first volume. This set of tyrants continued in southern Greece for fully 400 years, and by the appearance of such records as we possess, only met extinction through the merciless excoriation they received about B. C. 207, when Nabis, whose name, like that of Spartacus and Clodius, has been for ages covered with bitter contempt, rose against them and scoured them from the earth.[1]

Of this Nabis, unmentioned by modern historians and even by the Encyclopædia Britannica, we should know

[1] For a record of this institution, see I., in *index*, "Ephori," pointing out the pages on which we have set forth Plutarch's history of them.

nothing but for the unimpeachable authority of the historians, Polybius, Livy, and a few animadversions of the anecdotal commentators of ancient history, who lived before the reign of Constantine.[2] It is a remarkable story, very similar to that of Eunus; the more so in that there is strong evidence to prove that, like Eunus, he was a Semitic from Syria. In our opinion, after having studied the strangely recorded probabilities, this man Nabis was a member of an eranos in one of the towns of Syria; and that, like Eunus, he was forcibly taken as a military slave in chains to the Peloponnesus early in the second century before Christ. Directly or indirectly he appears the victim of the conquests: first as a slave of war and then as a rebel against the ephori who ruined the communism of Lycurgus, and was finally, like Eunus, murdered during those Roman wars.

The useless brutalities of the ephori, which Chilon attached to the system of Lycurgus are recounted to us by Plutarch.[3] A systematic method of arming young men

[2] Bücher, *Aufstände der unfreien Arbeiter*, S. 91, who takes his information principally from Polyb., IV., 81, from which we duly quote, *infra:* "Hier war nicht durch Restauration zu helfen; ja bei dem hohen Grade sittlicher Verkommenheit nicht einmal durch Revolution. Und doch führten die Verhältnisse nach dem misslungenen Versuche des Chilon eine soziale Revolution der aller entsetztlichsten Art herbei, als der Wüterich Nabis (206-192) in Sparta und Argos die Reichen tödtete, die Heiligthümer plünderte und Häuser, Aecker, Frauen und Kinder der Ermordeten an die zur Freiheit aufgerufenen Heloten und ein aus allen Enden der Welt zusammengelaufenes Gesindel vertheilte." Livy, xxxii., 38, again speaks of the work of Nabis: "Deinde, ut frequenti concione non aspernatus modo, sed abominatos etiam nomen tyranni audivit, causam se spoliandi eos nactum ratus, tradere, ubi vellet, urbem, Philoclem jussit. Nocte, ignaris omnibus, acceptus in urbem est tyrannus. Prima luce occupata omnia superiora loca, portæque clausæ. Paucis principum inter primum tumultum elapsis, eorum absentium direptæ fortunæ; præsentibus aurum atque argentum ablatum; pecuniæ imperatæ ingentes." And continues his description of the avarice and cruelty.

[3] Plutarch, *Lycurgus*. The description of the duties of the ephori, in secretly arming young men with daggers and ordering them to waylay the Helot slaves who performed the labor on which the Spartan republic, or model eudæmonia fed and luxuriated, is graphically told in I., pp. 104, 105, with an exact translation of Plutarch's words in the context. The same adhered, down to the days of Nabis who had been trained in the Lycurgan ideal, but who rebelled against it. According to Xenophon, *De Republica Lacedæmoniana*, Lycurgus was himself the founder of the ephoralty. It is probable that such cruel butchery as it produced was not intended by Lycurgus, and that this exquisite improvement was added later by Chilon, who in inventing instrumentalities of murder made himself immortal, according to the belief and wishes of the powers of individual wealth.

The ephori are known to have existed in India and to have been powerful and influential enough to be classed by Megasthenes as the sixth of the seven great classes or μέρη of that country. Strabo, from the lost work of Megasthenes, 707, 48, says. "Ἕκτοι δ' εἰσὶν οἱ ἔφοροι· τούτοις δ' ἐποπτεύειν δέδοται τὰ πραττόμενα καὶ ἀναγγέλλειν λάθρα τῷ βασιλεῖ συνεργοὺς ποιουμένοις τὰς ἑταίρας, τοῖς μὲν ἐν τῇ πόλει τὰς ἐν τῇ πόλει τοῖς δὲ ἐν στρατοπέδῳ τὰς αὐτοῦ· καθίστανται δ' οἱ ἄριστοι καὶ πιστότατοι."

with daggers, and placing them in ambush along the ways leading to, and from their labor and from these dark hiding holes, pouncing cat-like upon a man or a squad of men and women and with dæmoniac delight and gruesome legality spilling their innocent blood, may seem to some readers a just and merited scheme for obliterating the crime of poverty and punishing the affrontery of manliness. Yet this history of Nabis casts for us a dim light upon the fact that those poor Helots and slaves of the conquest long afterwards were keenly sensitive to a manhood daring to assume itself nobler than the official murderer lying in wait for their blood.

Be this as it may, the world of sympathy cannot but feel that there was a doleful excuse for Nabis and his organized legions, for cutting the throats of rich men.

Besides giving the details, a synopsis of the doings of this man, so far as obtainable, should be presented. In doing this we shall depend upon Polybius, who was born in one of the towns where Nabis careered, and at about the same time. This town was Megalopolis. We also have Livy, who wrote just at the close of the Roman conquests, Plutarch, whose authenticity is never called into question, and the Saturnalia of Macrobius. The synopsis reads about as follows: and in it we see the ferocious characteristics of nearly every one who, in those early times attempted to restore or create better conditions for the poor and oppressed by resorting to the barbarous, animal methods that lurk in the reasonless impulses of irascibility and concupiscence.

Born in Syria, of Semitic parentage, about B. C. 225; captured in the wars of the conquests by a misfortune similar to that of Eunus; dragged to Megalopolis and sold to a rich citizen, about B. C. 212; worked himself into the good graces and confidence of swarms of Helots and other surviving slaves of the Peloponnesus; and on the death of Mechanidas, succeeded through some unrecorded luck in elevating himself to be the tyrant of Sparta. He caused the young son of the deceased king to be assassinated; demanded excessive exactions from the rich, many of whom he murdered; invented diabolical engines of torture to squeeze money from the object of his hate, one of which was the celebrated automaton

SYNOPSIS OF A RECKLESS CAREER. 93

or manakin woman which in his drastic delight he called his wife Apega, that embraced her victim with human smiles and courtesy, compassed her arms about him, and drawing him to her breast loosened the tripspring which thrust a score of sharp daggers into his heart;[4] extorted money thus, with which to carry out his purposes, and therewith to secure mercenaries.

In this manner Nabis thought to restore the old, but unforgotten communism of the ancient Lycurgus by exterminating the hated ephori. Philopœmen, the Magalopolitan general forced him to a truce; he returned to the assault; great distress; Rome interferes and rushes to the aid of Philopœmen and they, with the combined armies of Greece and Rome, secure his overthrow and assassination, in B. C. 192. Total career of Nabis as a rebel and tyrant covered about 16 years.[5] The episode of Nabis, and the terrible conditions are referred to by Macrobius.[6]

Here then was a man of a high order of genius, maddened by insult which for months he had been obliged to bear, trained at his home like Eunus to the charms of

---

[4] Polybius, XIII., 4. We have at our hand the paraphrase of Casaubon from which, for facilitating the interest of the reader, we extract, rather than from the original Greek: "Idem Nabis machinam quoque, si tamen ea machina est discenda, talem struxerat Simulacrum muliebre erat, pretiosis vestibus adornatum; formæ similitudine Nabidis uxorem arte eximia referens. Quoties civium aliquos tyrannus ad se vocabat, ut pecuniis eos emungeret . . . . Equidem fortasse quod cupia persuadere tibi non valeo; Apegam vero hanc (id nomen Nabidis conjux habebat), puto tibi persuasuram simul hæc ille dicibat, et statim aderat simulacrum de quo sumus locuti. Tum autem tyrannus ubi e sede mulierem excitasset, per speciem comitatis dextram prehendens, utraque manu collocutorem amplectebatur, ac paullatim ad pectus admovebat. Erant autem illi cubiti ac brachia ferreis clavis plena, quos vestis occultabat. Similiter etiam in mammis infixos habuit clavos. Quando igitur brachia impresserat dorso mulieris, mox organis quibusdam attractum intendebat ac paullatim ad mammas adducens, eum qui premebatur omne genus voces cogebat edere. Atque hoc modo multos eorum sustulit, qui pecunia dare recusabant."

[5] "N. wurde (106-107), Tyran von Sparta, nachdem er sich mit den Gegnern der Freunde der Ephoren, warscheinlich den Heloten, vereinigt hatte, und Alles während 12-15, Jahre zerschlug, und wurde endlich (192) von Philopœmen getödtet. "Meyers Konv. Lexikon.

[6] Macrob., Saturnaliorum Libri, I., xi., 14, 15: , . . . , "Domini enim nobis animos induimus tyrannorum et non quantum decet sed quantum licet exercere volumus in servos. Nam ut cetera crudelitatis genera prætereo, sunt qui, dum se mensæ copiis et aviditate distundunt, circumstantibus servis movere labra nec in hoc quidem ut loquantur licere permittunt, virga murmur omne compescitur et ne fortuita quidem verberibus excepta sunt, tussis sternutamentum singultus magno malo luitur, Sic fit ut isti de domino loquantur quibus coram domino loqui non licet. At illi quibus non tantum præsentibus dominis sed cum ipsis erat sermo, quorum os non consuebatur, parati erant pro domino porrigere cervicem et periculum inminens in caput suum vertere." In the same dissertation he feelingly says (xi., 12, fin.): "Non potest amor cum timore miscere."

brotherhood, flowing with sympathy for the felicities of socialism, who arrives in his chains in the Peloponnesus. He finds himself surrounded by slaves who had been subjugated to be tools of the very plan of communism instituted by that ancient lawgiver.⁷ They could discuss the grievance together and through that discussion be made aware that though the idea of the original Spartan socialism as conceived by Lycurgus was good, yet its recipients, the Pericci and the Spartans or Laconians, were alone those whom that law could cover. All the Helots, three to one in proportion, were abject and detested slaves; mere labor saving machines to keep the masters alive and Aristotle hoped that shuttles, spinning wheels and quillers might some day propel themselves.⁸

Such was the terrible reminder which must have exasperated those poor men. They were three to one in numbers as compared with the "Blessed" ones who really enjoyed this socialism. They themselves were the compulsory implements which socialism of all ages required to be nationalized; and sure enough, they were nationalized—the nationalized tools of labor! Nationalizing the tools of labor is the great political demand of socialism to-day. But what of tools made of blood and bones! Implements of production and distribution of the resources of mother earth! Aristotle is the immortal who first thought of the nationalized, inanimate tool as an imple-

7For a description of this injustice, see I., pp. 101 ; 106, 526 sqq.
8Aristotle, Pol., A., IV., 4: " 'Επεὶ οὖν ἡ κτῆσις μέρος τῆς οἰκίας ἐστὶ καὶ ἡ κτητικὴ μέρος τῆς οἰκονομίας (ἄνευ γὰρ τῶν ἀναγκαίων ἀδύνατων καὶ ζῆν καὶ εὖ ζῆν), ὥσπερ δὲ ἐν ταῖς ὡρισμέναις τέχναις ἀναγκαῖον ἂν εἴη ὑπάρχειν τὰ οἰκεῖα ὄργανα, εἰ μέλλει ἀποτελεσθήσεσθαι τὸ ἔργον, οὕτω καὶ τῶν οἰκονομικῶν. Τῶν δ' ὀργάνων τὰ μὲν ἄψυχα, τὰ δ' ἔμψυχα, οἷον τῷ κυβερνήτῃ ὁ μὲν οἴαξ ἄψυχον, ὁ δὲ πρωρεὺς ἔμψυχον· ὁ γὰρ ὑπηρέτης ἐν ὀργάνου εἴδει ταῖς τέχναις ἐστίν. Οὕτω καὶ τὸ κτῆμα ὄργανον πρὸς ζωήν ἐστι, καὶ ἡ κτῆσις πλῆθος ὀργάνων ἐστί, καὶ ὁ δοῦλος κτῆμά τι ἔμψυχον, καὶ ὥσπερ ὀργάνου, πρὸ ὀργάνου, πᾶς ὁ ὑπηρέτης. Εἰ γὰρ ἠδύνατο ἕκαστον τῶν ὀργάνων κελευθὲν ἢ προαισθανόμενον ἀποτελεῖν τὸ αὐτοῦ ἔργον, ὥσπερ τὰ Δαιδάλου φασὶν ἢ τοὺς τοῦ Ἡφαίστου τρίποδας, οὕς φησὶν ὁ ποιητὴς αὐτομάτους θεῖον δύεσθαι ἀγῶνα, οὕτως αἱ κερκίδες ἐκέρκιζον αὐταὶ καὶ τὰ πλῆκτρα ἐκιθάριζεν, οὐδὲν ἂν ἔδει οὔτε τοῖς ἀρχιτέκτοσιν ὑπηρετῶν οὔτε τοῖς δεσπόταις δούλων. Τὰ μὲν οὖν λεγόμενα ὄργανα ποιητικὰ ὀργανά ἐστι, τὸ δὲ κτῆμα πρακτικόν· ἀπὸ μὲν γὰρ τῆς κερκίδος ἕτερόν τι γίνεται παρὰ τὴν χρῆσιν αὐτῆς, ἀπὸ δὲ τῆς ἐσθῆτος καὶ τῆς κλίνης ἡ χρῆσις μόνον. Ἔτι δ' ἐπεὶ διαφέρει ἡ ποίησις εἴδει καὶ ἡ πρᾶξις, δέονται δ' ἀμφότεραι ὀργάνων, ἀνάγκη καὶ ταῦτα τὴν αὐτήν ἔχειν διαφοράν. Ὁ δὲ βίος πρᾶξις, οὐ ποίησις ἐστιν· διὸ καὶ ὁ δοῦλος ὑπηρέτης τῶν πρὸς τὴν πρᾶξιν. Τὸ δὲ κτῆμα λέγεται ὥσπερ καὶ τὸ μόριον. Τό τε γὰρ μόριον οὐ μόνον ἄλλου ἐστὶ μόριον ἀλλὰ καὶ ὅλως ἄλλου· ὁμοίως δὲ καὶ κτῆμα. Διὸ ὁ μὲν δεσπότης τοῦ δούλου δεσπότης μόνον, ἐκείνου δ' οὐκ ἐστίν· ὁ δὲ δοῦλος οὐ μόνον δεσπότου δοῦλός ἐστιν, ἀλλὰ καὶ ὅλως ἐκείνου. Τίς μὲν οὖν ἡ φύσις τοῦ δούλου καὶ τίς ἡ δύναμις, ἐκ τούτων δῆλον. ὁ γὰρ μὴ αὑτοῦ φύσει ἀλλ' ἄλλου, ἄνθρωπος δὲ, οὗτος φύσει δοῦλός ἐστιν. Ἄλλου δ' ἐστὶν ἄνθρωπος, ὃς ἂν κτῆμα, ᾖ ἄνθρωπος ὤν. Κτῆμα δὲ ὄργανον πρακτικὸν καὶ χωρισόν."

ment of labor. Xenophen could not ascend so high. We of more modern ages wanted two thousand years of experience and study. Then we began to make inanimate tools. The hideous money power immediately seized and appropriated them and now we clamor for socialism; for a return to the old nationalized tools or implements of labor which Nabis raved and ravaged fair countries to set free. We are bound to drift back to the self-same beautiful communism of Sparta only with the improvement suggested by Aristotle and championed by Nabis, namely that the machines and tools be changed from the quickened human to the inanimate mechanical form, and that the three to one be exchanged for an exact proportion of equality to all.

As we study this history we are more fully informed regarding the grievances concomitant upon entailment in primogeniture, with its concentration of products upon the individual. The ephori were five secret despots, or supreme judges of the system invented and instituted by Chilon, the wise man of Greece, 400 years before, who, as Plutarch tells us,[9] trained a certain number of young men as assassins, and ordered them to be ready at any moment, with daggers, to waylay these nationalized animate tools and butcher them in sufficient numbers to keep down the labor force to a schedule tabulated at their political councils. These ephori or supreme judges were the target against which Nabis directed his relentless hatred. They were a supreme bench clothed with boundless authority.

From the description of this man at our command given by the various authors, it seems probable that he contemplated the extermination of the rich, and the restoration of the proletarian race in the same manner as promised them by Aristonicus the heliopolitan at Pergamos half a century later; but he seems to have been the most cruel and bloodthirsty of them all. The country was laid waste and the propertied people reduced to great suffering. Vast sums of money, and values of every kind were taken from the rich and given to the poor. The Roman conquests were raging and that empire, already in its youth, showed signs, by this backacting recalcitrancy of Nabis, of sure decay.[10]

[9] Plutarch, *Lycurgus*, but see I., p. 105, where Plutarch's story is repeated.

The historian Livy devotes many pages of his valuable history to a description of this strange man, and he seems to be of the same opinion with Pyrrhus that impelled him to break up the socialistic peace habits of the people of Magna Græcia on the event of his conquering invasion of Italy. There was, in those times but one idea of manhood and manliness, and it was based on the bellicose and concupiscent characteristic. The tender sympathies engendered by socialism and sober reason inherent even in the Lycurgan form of government and which had their home in the common table and the communal code attacked and destroyed by Pyrrhus, were perhaps, too fine and noble for the governments of that day. Yet they are now known to have existed to an enormous extent in the secret, organized unions flourishing under the law of Solon.

But Nabis, who knew of all these graces could only rage and rave in quest of blood, vengeance and common robbery. His particular and most successful methods were tricky schemes. In several of these he outwitted the Roman Consul, Quinctius Flaminius, in the year 197, and forced him to accept his terms. There is an account of his laying waste the valley of the Eurotas which contained the celebrated cliff, or rock of Taygetus, from whose heights the old Spartans in carrying out the law regarding race culture, used to throw their cripples, blind ones, and malborn infants, such as could not pass examination of the judges, to be jammed to jelly and a terrible death on the sharp flints below. The life of Nabis, aside from his wars and bloody incursions, is full of weird stories. Goblins and ghosts had their haunts in many a hiding hole of mountain and cave where he lurked with his doughty band, and whence he pounced upon some rich man, or other victim he hated. The shudder that is abroad, inspired by the modern resurrection of socialism, falsely conjuring up another violent division of money and goods, is believed to be a descent

[10] Polyb., IV., 81. (Paraphrase of Casaubon): "Cepitque eorum respublica magis magisque in dies retro sublabi, ac ferri in pejus; ad extremum ærumnas plurimas, seditionesque intestinas sunt experti; repetitis agrorum divisionibus atque exiliis sæpissime sunt agitati; acerbissimam denique servitutem servierunt, ad Nabidis usque tyrannidem; qui tamen olim ne nomen quidem ipsum tyrannidis ferre poterant. Sed Lacedæmoniorum res antiquitus gestas, atque adeo pleraque omnia illorum in utramque partem multi edisseruerunt: verum evidentissima omnium illa sunt, quæ post eversam funditus antiquam Rempublicam a Cleomene sunt consecuta."

VIRTUES AND VICES OF NABIS SUMMED UP. 97

of a wild old horror inspired by this great robber communist; for tradition is tenacious when ghouls and cacodemons penetrate our superstition, and wraiths and hurlothrumbos ripple our domestic peace. Down through ages of competitive havoc the proletaries, blinded by ignorance, and the wealth-owners dodging conscience, have crouched in murky niches of the earth to shudder over some baseless belief in furies, gorgons and bogies which all the time have been their friends.[11] History has left enough of the true nature of Nabis to show that beneath, and inspiring every wolfish act he perpetrated, there trembled some impulse which aimed to give the world more humanity, justice and equality.[12] While it appears true that he terrorized Greece and thrilled Rome with his schemes to kill off the rich, and aimed at the deracination of the ephori who, true to the instincts of the money and property power, had survived the original communism of Lycurgus, yet he possessed military and business ability in a large degree and had learning enough to deliver before his adversary, the Roman Quinctius, a speech so bold and able that Livy has quoted it entire.[13]

The story of this man, if we except his reported treachery and cruelty to the rich against whom, according to all the authors, he was relentlessly furious, bears some appearance of his having been another Drimakos and not very far from the same time; since the dates of their death are not more than forty or fifty years apart. It is true that the struggle of Nabis was not the first attempt at the overthrow of the ephori. It is also ascertained that the Romans, true to the purposes of property,

[11] Livy, xxxviii, 34 *fin*; "Nulla tamen res tanto erat damno quam disciplina Lycurgi, cui per septingentos annos assueverant, sublata." These words were written in connection with the story of Nabis. Consult Strabo, IV., 112.
[12] Livy, xxxii., 40, *fin*., explains the methods of his irascibility; "Et Nabis, firmato præsidio Argis, Lecedæmonem regressus, cum ipse viros spoliasset, ad feminas spoliandas uxorem Argos remisit. Ea nunc singulas illustres, nunc simul plures genere inter se junctas arcessendo, blandiendoque ac minando, non aurum modo iis, sed postremo vestem quoque mundumque omnem muliebrem ademit."
[13] Livy, xxxiv., 31: "Si ipse per me, T. Quincti, vosque, qui adestis, causam excogitare, cur mihi aut indixissetis bellum, aut inferretis, possem; tacitus eventum fortunæ meæ, expectassem. .... Nunc cum vos intueor, Romanos esse video, qui rerum divinarum fœdera, humanarum fidem socialem sanctissimam habeatis. Quum me ipse respexi, eum esse spero, cui et publice, sicut ceteris Lacedæmoniis, vobiscum vetustissmum fœdus sit, et meo nomine privatim amicitia ac societas, nuper Philipi bello renovata," And he defends himself against the aspersion that he has changed his plans.

upheld the ephori.[14] They were to the ancients what the bench is to the moderns, always ready to judge in favor of the rich. The richest man in Greece was he whom they were always ready to serve. Nabis was not the first to attempt the overthrow of the ephori and their powerful institution. Some of the kings hated them. Agis III. had already made an attempt to destroy them. Cleomenes, just before Nabis, had risen against and stifled them. But wealth is underhanded and full of secret tricks; it worked Roman influence and the ephori crawled out again.[15] Lastly came Nabis and he made a French revolution of it. He struck right and left and with a two-edged sword. As if to parry with the wit of its old enemy, he invented deathtraps and engines of devilism which throttled and jabbed with manakin and broadaxe, reddening the rivulets with blood; and on careful survey it looks as though there was neither rich man nor woman nor ephor left to rebuild the hideous institution. It sank to rise no more.

One thing however, all agree to: Nabis set free, and divided his booty with, thousands of slaves and poor freedmen in every part of his dominion, a fact recorded by the historians and commentators with ineffable disgust.[16] No matter what the pretentions of writers may be that the ephoralty after Nabis, continued to exist, it seems to have disappeared from Sparta and Argos and is lost to the pages of history.

[14] I., chap. vii., pp 163-177, where all that is known of this extraordinary emancipator, Drimakos, is carefully recounted.
[15] Myers, *Konv. Lex.* in v. *Ephori:* "Ihrer Macht erlag König Agis III., (350-330), bei seinem Versuch, die Lykurgische Verfassung wieder herzustellen; Kleomenes, III., (236-221), began seine Reform des Spartischen Staatswesens mit Aufhebung des Ephorats (223); doch ward es nach seinem Sturz (221), wieder hergestellt."
[16] Pausanias, *Discriptio Graecæ*, iv., 10, sec. 352: "Λακεδαιμονίοις δὲ ἀπηλλαγμένοις Κλεομένους ἐπανίσταται τύραννος Μαχανίδας· ἐκείνου δὲ ἀποθανόντος Νάβις ἀνέφυ σφίσιν αὖθις τύραννος. Ἄτε δὲ οὐ τὰ ἀνθρώπων ἀναρπάζοντι αὐτῷ μόνον, ἀλλὰ καὶ ἱερὰ συλῶντι, ἐν οὐ πολλῷ χρόνῳ χρήματα τε ἄφθονα καὶ ἀπ' αὐτῶν στρατιὰ συνείλεκτο. Τούτου τοῦ Νάβιδος Μεσσήνην καταλαβόντος Φιλοποίμην καὶ οἱ Μεγαλοπολῖται νυκτὸς ἀφίκοντο τῆς αὐτῆς. Καὶ ὁ μὲν Σπαρτιάτης τύραννος ἀπῆλθεν ὑπόσπονδος."

CHAPTER V.
SOLONIC DISPENSATION.

VAST SYSTEM OF TRADE UNIONS OVER THE WORLD.

IMPORTANCE of the new Discovery of them—Their Remote Origin—Solon, Numa and Amasis the first in their Known History—Ancient Law of the Twelve Tables—Pre-Christian Christianity—Based on Mutual Help and Love—Countries where they Existed—All followed One Model—Their Common Table and Communal Code—The Prytaneum—Patterned after the City—City in Theory Modeled after the Family—Authority of Dirksen—The Competitive System Reversed—Respect for Religion—Microcosm of the Future Perfect State—Enmity of Wealth Against It—Herodotus Quoted—Why the Unions had to be Secret—Took the Military Form—Secret during a Thousand Years—Reverence to the Great Law-Givers so Great that no Enemy Dared Molest them—After their Amalgamation with the Christians they became Still More Secret—Why—Sources of Information—Much through Strabo and Arrian from Lost Works of Megasthenes, Onesicritus, Nearchus, Aristobulus, Aristotle.

THERE is nothing in the history of political economy of so great importance as the new discoveries regarding the ancient jus coeundi for labor organization under the Solonic law. Though known, it has been dropped from the curriculum of college studies. There was no money in it for the individualist. It was the great incrusted diamond of future wisdom. Yet this is a phase involving a hitherto unknown side of human life.

Without a doubt this great law was but an effect, not a cause, of that organization. Labor organization has existed from remote antiquity and was powerful away back in the prehistoric ages. But with us, we know little

THE SOLONIC DISPENSATION.

or nothing of it earlier than the promulgation of the Solonic dispensation, which in our scheme, must include the almost contemporaneous one of Numa Pompilius, king of Rome. In fact, there are many things in evidence corroborating Plutarch's suggestion that the two men lived at the same time, and were agreeably acquainted with each other. We have already written abundantly regarding this, quoting the original as prescribed in the XII Tables and mentioned by Gaius,[1] and do not propose to dilate further, but proceed at once to a thorough description of its extent and influence over humanity.

The most important disclosure resulting from these investigations is the fact that there are three distinct eras or æons of Christianity, and three distinct histories— first, that of pre-Christian Christianity; second, that of the apostolic planting in the unions, exhibiting a surprising difference between a true history of Christianity and a history of the church; and third, that of the church after it struck down the Solonic unions. In this scheme of hitherto unwritten origins we write nothing of the church, being content with the more instructive study of the fundamental planting. The two are distinctly apart.

A thousand proofs, archæological and written, now attest that the strange moving power which long afterward became known as Christianity was no other than the plant or the inherent existence of that phenomenal force which swept the world and built up a new era of human civilization. It was that organization of brotherhoods under the enormous scope and influence of the Solonic dispensation.

No one will understand this amazing announcement who does not know the internal and beautiful nature of that dispensation.

There was little or no difference in the manner and objects of these organizations among the various sections and languages of the world. They very much resembled trade unions. Following the religious nature of all ancient states they almost invariably had some shrine or another to worship at, but before they endorsed the faith

---

[1] Digest, XLVII., tit. xxii., lex 4, taken for the Pandects of Justinian, from Gaius, lib. 4, ad Legem duodecim Tabularum, quoted in Vol. I., p. 127, note 87, and again in this volume.

of Christians, the gods they chose as their guardians or protectors were majesties of the lowly. They worshiped only the tutelary divinities of the outcasts of mankind; most distinctly not those of the rich. About the time of Christ the process of emancipation from slavery which we have already noticed and shall more fully describe showing it to be their own work, was so great that about one half of the homeless world were struggling as freedmen and women, entirely dependent upon their labor, manual or intellectual, for a living. They differed from present trade unions in that they were political. It is now established that they were voting unions. The law known as the jus coeundi or right of combination, gave them the ballot; and it is this privilege, legalized by Solon, which men have profited by, and are using to-day in their political progress through the world. The liberty-loving and progressive republics of the present age little understand that they are derived from the laws and practices of the ancient slaves.

In Greece, Asia Minor and the islands where Greek was spoken, these labor organizations were called eranoi, thiasoi, orgeones, hetairæ, sussitæ, synodoi, koina, and a few other terms which mean about the same thing; they are phases of the jus coeundi or right of combination recognized by Solon, Amasis and Numa, as a legitimate means of living, strictly for the laboring poor.

In Rome and Latin-speaking countries they were called collegia, sodalicia, conlegia and various other names, but their tenets and modes of procedure were almost exactly the same as those of the Greeks.

In Egypt and the Semitic countries these unions of the industrial and poorer classes are less known by name, especially in the Coptic language; although the darkness involved in this remark may yet be cleared away under the constant progress made by Egyptologists in their researches which are continually disclosing new records from the monuments. The discovery in Egypt of strikes of slaves and freedmen who bravely met and outwitted the Pharaohs, is sufficient evidence that they were very powerful. The principal name by which they were known, not Coptic but Greek, was Therapeutæ, an association closely allied to the Essenes. Later, the Egyptians had similar organizations, which under Christianity assumed a certain monastic and painfully degenerate form. They were all derived from the original jus coeundi, long existing but first promulgated through inscriptions upon the celebrated Prytaneum at Athens, and a few years later translated into Latin and honored by being engraved upon one of the Twelve Tables of Roman law.[2]

In Palestine, including old Phœnicia, the same establishments are known as essenes, ossennæ, sometimes therapeutæ, Nazarænai, Cainites and synodoi.

Throughout Gaul, Spain and Africa, and as far to the northwestward as the British Islands, and as far northeastward as Germany they generally assumed the Latin names of collegia and sodalicia, although traces are found of the German half-civilized Lupercalia.

All these various confraternities, no matter what the the name or race, possessed the same tenets and quite frequently they are found to have been linked internationally together. There are inscriptions and other records which show that in times of famine, pestilence, or war, when certain districts flourished while their distant neighbors and brothers were suffering, convoys were sent with provisions, money, medicines and social comforts for their rescue. This was done as late as the apostolic age; for several times provisions, money and comforts were conveyed from Asia Minor to the brotherhood at Jerusalem, and from Ephesus and Corinth to groups in Macedonia, showing the value of Mutual help among the poor and struggling people.[3]

Another important thing is that their plan of political organization was, by law, based on the scheme of political organization of the city of Athens. To some extent this plan followed the city in its economic scheme;[4] but as the city in ancient times, as now, was formed after

[2] See chapter II. of this volume.
[3] Acts, xi., 29; xxiv., 17; Rom,, xv., 25, 26; I. Cor., xvi., 1; II. Cor., ix., 1, 2, 5; II. Cor., viii., 3, 4; Tertullian, *Apol.*, xxxix. That such economical reciprocity was constantly going on among the unions, is shown quite profusely in the inscriptions. Mommsen, Oehler, Waltzing and several others have admitted that the one described by Tertullian was a regular collegium.
[4] The Roman state guaranteed the labor organizations the communistic form, the same as it was found in the Prytaneum of Grecian cities, as well as a common table: Dirksen, *Twölf Tafel Fragmente*, 21: "Der römische Staat vergönnte ursprünglich lediglich den Gewerben, die den Bedürfnissen des Krieges und des Gottesdienstes Zunächst fröhnten, seinen unmittelbaren Schutz und eine selbständige Communalverfassung."

NAMES OF UNIONS IN VARIOUS LANDS. 103

the competitive idea which ruled everything, the social movement could not follow it, but swung off in the direction of communism. According to this rule which was adhered to for many centuries, the trade unions formed their organizations after the model of cities of the outside world.[5]

But it must not be understood by this, that it was a political organization like that of the outside world. Far from it. The plan followed the Solonic law of labor organization and was accordingly secret, and entirely different otherwise; for it had a common table, always held property common and followed a communal code. It is true that certain parts of the ancient city permits of a common table. The Boulé at Athens, a council, like that of our boards of Aldermen in cities, was furnished with a common table, around which many a great proposition regarding the good of the city, or of the country, was discussed while partaking meals. In this respect the Solonic organization was patterned exactly after that theory of the ancient city.

But as to the communal code, it was different; and the difference was based upon the fact that a great gap yawned between the citizen and the humble class. Citizens owned all private property. Members of these organizations were not citizens; they were often slaves, but more frequently freedmen[6] struggling for a mere privilege to live on the earth. Hated by everybody, to them it was the great question of bread from day to day; and their organization was logically economical rather than religious, as some of the epigraphists would fain have us believe. Many have already discovered and confessed this error.

The great organizations of trade and labor unions, therefore, under the Solonic law, however much the enemies of human rights may argue to the contrary, were purely economic ones; in fact, the law of Solon so recognizes, and makes a specification that the workmen

---

[5] Dig., III., 4; Gaius, *libro tertio ad Edictum Provinciale*, 1: "Quibus autem permissum est corpus habere collegii societatis sive cujusque alterius eorum nomine, proprium est ad exemplum reipublicæ habere res communes, arcam communem," etc.

[6] The *Eranoi* admitted foreigners, freedmen, slaves and women. Some were composed of women entirely. On this, for full and indisputable evidence, see Foucart, *Ass. Rel.*, p. 5.

and common people who are to give an account of themselves as told by Herodotus, as to how they got their living, for purposes of the census compilation or otherwise, should be organized. Everything was economic. Religion of course, was highly respected. Indeed, everybody was religiously inclined; and they consequently believed in the powerful influence of their gods, and served them with punctilious obeisance.

A critical inspection of all evidence obtainable—and it is growing year by year—obliges us to admit that the original and ancient scheme of this organization was that of the good, pure, well regulated family;[7] that in the minds of great men, such as Cadmus, Moses, Lycurgus, Solon, Numa, Pythagoras, Socrates and his followers, and if we may suppose an incarnation of Saturn, of Dionysus, of Minerva and such tutelary powers believed to have been once living men and women before whom these lowly organizations worshiped, the state and the city themselves were modeled from the pure and holy forms of a just and loving family. This was the microcosm. It was the great pre-Christian-Christianity.[8]

Here lies the kernel of the vast phenomenon of an era of Paganism which was a failure; of an era of Christianity which is slowly proving a success. The money power or greed of property destroyed the microcosm—the city and the mutuality bearing the stamp of eternal life. They became its victim. We now know that for a thousand years it fought and struggled to destroy the great

[7] For an exhaustive discussion on this subject, see Oehler's article Βουλή in the Cyclopædia of ancient conditions and literature, entitled *Pauly-Wissowa*, Vol.III., pp. 1020-1037. The Prytaneum was the most democratical forum of the Boulé. Here, as in the council rooms of all the Solonic labor unions, we find the common table and the communal code. It may almost be compared with the microcosm of a state which took the well regulated family for its pattern. And such the pattern shows them to have been.

[8] It is a mistake to suppose the Solonic organizations to have been exclusively religious. They were economical. It does not follow, because the inscriptions constantly talk about religion of the "ἱεροποιος;" that they were necessarily religious organizations. The whole life of Socrates is proof of this. He was a member of one of these organizations and yet he was not overstocked with religion. He was an economist. All references to him by Plato and Xenophon prove this; and in Plato's Crito, Socrates, on his deathbed, doubts the existence of an immortal soul. Many of the recently discovered epigraphs make no mention of religion. Foucart, *Associations Religieuses*, pp. 29, sqq., shows three θιασοι of Sabazios at the Peireios which ı early mention Ἱεροποιος, priest or priestess. See his nos. 24, 27, 30, 32. Again, p. 31, of *id.* top, is a quote from epigraph No. 30; lines 5-19, showing that no religion of whatever sort was in their minds—only the economic good. Here is a striking illustration that what is meant by religion is only that of the economical good to the common membership.

law and its organization. But in this last effort it failed. Solon[3] and the immortals still shed their tutelary influence; the family in all its adamantine brilliancy still shines; the organization is here; and imperishable hope and economic activity survive and grow with the æons of experience.[9]

Under the Solonic dispensation, then, the family was to be the central pattern or model of the city, and the labor organization was to be patterned after the family. It was to have its common table, at the head of which sat the father or lord of the household. It was to be composed of the father, the mother and the children. All were to be treated exactly alike. Each was to have enough. Each was to do his or her share of the labor of support. None were to have things from which the others were excluded. As in the family to-day, they were to eat at the common table. All honored and loved the father and lord who in turn reciprocated; the mother and children were to love one another. Contentment, liberty, development, happiness and plenty resulted.

Another remarkable characteristic of those ancient unions was that they took the military form. They were distributed in brigades, companies and tens. This was a very early form. We hear of it first in Numa's arrangement, nearly 600 years before Christ, and the system was written up by Varro and Pliny, proving that it was exactly the plan of the military formula of the Roman army, and it was this method of military science under which the Roman conquests were carried out.

Still another peculiarity of the labor organizations was that they were secret. All through the vista of a thousand years during which time we know them, they were strictly a secret order. This habit of secrecy proved of great value during persecutions. Being legalized by a law so much revered, they were seldom molested, except when persecuted on account of their political activities. Then it was that their discipline of profound secrecy proved of greatest value. After the amalgamation of the Christians with them their secrecy was so

[9] Herodotus, "Euterpe," (II.), 177, after showing that Amasis, a Pharaoh of Egypt, nearly 600 years before Christ, instituted a law for his census which Solon reënacted at Athens, says: "Σόλον δὲ ὁ ʼΑθηναῖος λαβὼν ἐξ Αἰγύπτου τοῦτον τὸν νόμον ʼΑθηναίοισι ἔθετο· Τῷ ἐκείνοι ἐς αἰεὶ χρέωνται ἐόντι ἀμώμῳ νόμῳ."

great that for ages they maintained themselves in spite of the most searching detectives of the Roman police the world over; and the evangelizing agents continued the preaching of their original doctrines and ideas until at last they assumed the mastery and conquered the Roman world. Thus the dispensation of Solon extended through lands now known as Italy, Greece, Asia Minor, Macedonia, Palestine, Spain, Northern Africa, France, England, Ireland, Wales, Austria Hungary, Bulgaria, Servia, the countries coursed by the Danube and those of European Turkey.[10]

By our own good fortune in having the descriptive and historical geographies of Strabo and Arrian, we are in full possession of information regarding the existence of these unions in India. This information is gleaned from the histories, travels and geographies of Magasthenes, Nearchus, Aristobulus, Onesicritus, Eratosthenes and other very ancient writers who were sent out on extensive expeditions, some with Alexander the Great, and others by order of the Pergamenian kings, in the third and fourth centuries B. C. The works of these writers are themselves unfortunately lost, but Strabo and Arrian quote them. This subject of India is so little known, and yet so thoroughly explained by them that we next devote an entire chapter to it.[11]

[10] A singular example of these ancient institutions is seen in the bakers' unions of Paris, to-day, *Rapport, Office du Travail*, 1893: *Alimentation; The Bakers*. Varro, *De Lingua Latina* shows that the Roman colleges or unions of trades were so arranged; and at Paris, to-day, the boulangers, have their brigadiers or foremen of the "gang" of bakers heading the statistical schedules of wages, pp. 70-83. For a description of this, see Polybius, *Historia*, vi., c. 39, giving the arrangement of the Army. On his account of their use of the σημαία, σημεία φοινικα, vexillum, or red banner under these arangements, see Vol. I., p. 467, note 5, quoting Polybius, vi., 39.

[11] For interesting information on the origin of our term "Indo-European," consult Rudolf von Thiering's *Vorgeschichte der Indo-Europäer*, in *Die Zeit*, Vienna, Vol. II., No. 21, S. 119.

CHAPTER VI.
INDIA'S BROTHERHOODS
EVIDENCE NEVER SEEN IN HISTORY.

THE Lost Books—Handed Down to us through Strabo and Arrian—Megasthenes—Other Men's precious, Lost Geographical Books—Valuable Account from B. C. 350—Theory of a Sunken Continent—Adverse Criticism of Strabo Refuted—The Hamadryad—Story of the Modern Capture of One—Monster of Deadly Poison—King Sandrakotta—Indian Dwarfs—Government of India—Its Labor Organizations—The Indian Olympus—Mount Nusa—Its Brotherhoods—The Colony of Dionysus—A Cradle of the Unions—Roman Conquests Struck them when they Struck Damascus—Blades of Damascus blocked out in India—Indian Brotherhoods Divided into Seven Parts—Their Complete Delineation—Farmers, Hunters and Herdsmen—Skilled Artisans and Workers on Exchange—Great Value and Importance attached to them—All in Government Employ—Exempt from Military Burdens—All Land owned by the State or Society—The Useless Military Factor—The Ephori and their Spies—The Solonic Form of Labor Organization—It Gave Original Law and Dominated the Career of Industry—Bartholomew Sent there to Preach the Gospel—Peter supposed to have also Spent Years in India.

The organizations of the Solonic law and dispensation stretched beyond Asia Minor. They crossed Assyria and the Euphrates and were suffused among the populous regions of the Ganges, the Indus and the Burrempooter.

The first indications we had of this were gotten by reading, in our researches after the evidence of inscriptions and other ante-Nicine literature, of the doings of certain Christian Saints, not only those in the Testament or the Talmud, but apocryphal writings of the early Petrine period, which like the histories of Diodorus and Josephus, were held by a literary censorship in contemptuous abeyance, apparently because they were not in line with the purse-achieving ambitions behind a scheme that overthrew much of the good work of a great personage; the founder of an era which followed Solon and Numa. Like the accurate lispings of Diodorus and Pausanias these are soon to be searched after and re-read, as containing inestimable gems of truth and light.

One of these discarded records is found in the Apostolic Constitutions;[1] and is proof that, true to the words of Megasthenes and Arrian, there must have been a fine and perhaps an exalted civilization in India which still existed between three and four hundred years afterwards, when visited by Bartholomew and Paul. That these men planted the Gospel into the social orders described by Strabo, there an be little doubt. We shall prove that all the apostles and evangelists planted their faith into the already existing economic societies of laboring people in every known country of the earth, and that the task assigned to Bartholomew and a few others was in India.

Strabo, who excerpted from Megasthenes, Eratosthenes, Aristobulus, Onesicritus, Nearchus and others, whose works are unfortunately lost, gives us a complete account of the condition and influence of these societies, and more than once he comes squarely out and explains their organization, showing that they were identical with those in the west. In a few cases they even worshiped the very tutelary deity chosen by the societies of Asia Minor and the Piræus.

A few words should be said on the geography of India and its relations to the Roman conquests, which began about the time of Alexander the Great. It is believed

[1] "Ante-Nicine Fathers," Vol. VII., p. 492, note 5, "Bartholomew (a deacon) preached the Gospel according to Matthew, to the Indians, who also has been buried in India." Hippolitus, "Refutatio Hæreticorum," I., c. 22, speaks of the Brechmans (probably the Bramans) who lived on the banks of the Ganges, and were peculiar in their habits. But as high an authority as Neander, "Hist. Church," I., p. 81, Eng. trans., Boston, says Paul also went to India on one of his evangelizing tours. This is full of meaning; for he could not have penetrated those unknown regions had it not been that there were friends there. Strabo and Arrian, as we shall show, clear the mystery up. Powerful brotherhoods existed in India. They were of the Cybele and Dionysan sort, such as turn out to have been very numerous in Asia Minor, Macedonia and Greece. They held important political control; for the laws of India gave them favors and exemptions. Paul certainly went from Damascus to Arabia, which Neander conjectures, at that time stretched as far eastward as India, (p. 81). But the most astonishing verification of Paul's travels in India is the inscription of Avircius Marcellus, found at Hieropolis. See our elaborate account, pp. 638, chap. xviii., where we give the Greek in full and a running paraphrase.

by some that there was a continent stretching between southern Hindostan and Africa, and that it was sunk by an earthquake; and theorists go so far as to place the Garden of Eden there and not in Central Asia east of the Caucassus range.[2] Professor Haeckel, in his great work entitled a History of the Creation, starts out with a delineation of man, on the assumption that he originated in the land of the lemures, that branch of the simian tribe found to be the closest in physical and perhaps intellectual organism of the human race; and he even furnishes us with a set of plates exhibiting the land of the lemures, as he calls the sunken continent and places it in the Indian Ocean, between Hindostan and Africa. The opinions of this learned professor and scientist are worthy of a careful investigation. It would place the supposed Garden of Eden in the waters of the Indian Ocean! Haeckel, designating this lost continent the land of the lemures and placing it in the Indian Ocean, brings out beautiful maps of the voyages of the various tribes of men, and presumes a common origin to have been in this now sunken region. They diverge from this common center into Europe, Africa, Asia and Australasia; the tribe of Ham, going to Africa, the tribe of Japheth to Europe and the tribe of Shem to Asia. This, he believes to be the only solution to the mystery of the creation, and the Garden of Paradise. Man had been thankless and God cursed the very region of his creation and submerged it in the depths, so that the locality of the original eudæmonia is lost in the oneiromantic mists of doubt.

But our knowledge of India so far as we have it from Megasthenes and Onesicritus, and through them by the works of Strabo and Arrian who read their books before being lost, is entirely from the modern basis. The land of India when Strabo wrote was very nearly as it is now.

A few anecdotal notes may here profitably be inserted,

[2] Ezekiel, xxix., 10: "Behold, therefore, I am against thee, and against thy rivers and I will make the land of Egypt utterly waste and desolate from the tower of Syrene even unto the border of Ethiopia." For the location of this tower, see Smith's "Bible Dictionary," art. "Syrene," I., p. 657. Regarding the supposed earthquake that sank the continent, consult Prof. Haeckel of Jena, on the "Land of the Lemures." Smith puts it as the southern limit of Egypt: "From India even unto Ethiopia," "Esther," I., 1: viii., 9, mentioned by Smith, p. 658. This of itself is Bible authority that Eden is now sunk. This land was Cush, and was far south.

testing the reliability of Strabo.³ In his descriptive geography, written about the time Christ was born into the world, he speaks of a monster serpent which he denominates the ophiophage.⁴ He means the hamadryad which was said to live on trees, darting down upon and killing other snakes as well as animals and men. It was the great Cobra de Capello, the death snake of the ancient Druids. Strabo quotes as authority, Megasthenes and Nearchus. The monster is given as seventeen to nineteen feet long; an oviparous serpent only known in the dense woods and wilds of India, beyond the Ganges. It belongs to the elapines, not the vipers; it is more poisonous. It lies among the dark branches, like the anaconda. When a deer or hare or even other reptile, or a human being, ventures unsuspectingly up to the tree she noiselessly drops her whole length and weight upon him, head downward, and the first thing felt is the poisonous fangs filled with virus which far exceeds in deadliness any venom known, producing almost instantaneous death. After this she proceeds to coil like the boas about the prey, crushing its bones, and with her saliva, like the constrictor, prepares it for deglutition.

No serpent of the cobra race of such enormous size having been noted by travelers since Strabo's time, the usual criticism interposed, of doubters who not knowing all, assume to know too much, and the geographer's account was laughed at as an empiricism. After more than two thousand years from the days of Megasthenes, the French have penetrated the regions described, and a recent expedition of survey and adventure succeeded in 1890, in capturing an enormous female hamadryad about eighteen feet in length, lying in a coil upon her eggs, which it appears are incubated in the manner of fowls. An Indian boy of the wildest ledges, and darkest forests, informed the hunters of the monster's lair; but

³ Meyers, Konvers. Lexikon, in verb. *Megasthenes*: Griech. Geschichtschreiber, ging 295 v. Chr., als Gesandter des Seleukos Nikator an den indischen König Sandrokottos und sammelte dort material für sein Werk, "Indika," aus dem Arrian und Strabon entlehnt haben. Die noch vorhandenen Fragmente sammelten Schwanbeck (Bonn, 1846), und Müller, in *Fragmenta Historicorum Græcorum*, Bd. 2, (Paris, 1848).
⁴ After telling of the water monsters seen by Nearchus, he proceeds (*Geog.*, paragraph 706), to tell of the greater Cobra, 16 cubits long: "Εἰ δὲ μὴ τὸ πολὺ τοῦ πλήθους ὑπὸ τῶν ὑδάτων διεφθείρετο, κἂν ἐρημωθῆναι τὴν χώραν. Καὶ τὴν μικρότητα δ' αὐτῶν εἶναι χαλεπὴν καὶ ὑπερβολὴν τοῦ μεγέθους, τὴν μὲν διὰ τὸ δυσφύλακτον τὴν δὲ δ' ἰσχύν, ὅπου καὶ ἐκκαιδεκαπήχεις ἐχίδνας ὁρᾶσθαι."

so great was his terror that nothing could induce him to accompany them farther than a distant rock in range with their glasses, from whose top he pointed her out to them, and after taking his hire, fled in fear to his home. With great caution they crawled up to a distance within range of their rifles and although she suspected and towered to full height in her watch, the attitude but made her body a surer target and she fell pierced with bullets to the base of the ledge which formed her hiding place. The skin has been preserved.

Strabo who, like all the old anecdotal writers, tells a good story now and then, mentions the Indian pigmies, spoken of by Homer; but he gives us no assurance of the legend's truth.[5]

In connection with this falsifying depreciation of the flippant scholars and more dangerous cyclopedists we may also here pay a much deserved debt of credit to another ancient author, Orosius, whose history and geography have been very long discounted, but whose statements after centuries of contempt are now being sought as exceedingly valuable by the savants of our academies. This man knew of the great lake Victoria N'yanza, thousands of years lost but rediscovered by Speke in 1882; for he tells us in the introduction to his book against paganism that it was vast and was known as the source of the Nile.[6]

Arrian declares in his Indica that the Indians did not fight; and cites assertions from the great work of Megasthenes, which he read. He thinks the true reason was that nobody molested them. But Strabo gives the full account of the causes of this exemption and explains it sufficiently to assure us that Arrian only looked super-

[5] Strabo, *Geog.*, 711. Under Sandrokottus they were πενταστπιθάμοι, ie., 38 inches in height. Some were only τριστπιθάμοι, 23 inches tall. They waged wars on the cranes, geese, pheasants, also very large, ie: χηνομεγάθαι. These dwarfs were without noses, and breathed through two little holes above the mouth, "'ὧν τινὰς ἀμύκτηρας, ἀναπνοὰς ἔχοντας μόνον δύο ὑπὲρ τοῦ στόματος." Are these, barring the exaggerations, not the same as the modern dwarfs, of the Philippine Islands murdered by the Spaniards? There still dwells a race of pigmies in the Island of Formosa of which considerable has recently been written, much resembling those in size; Arrian, *Indica*, p. 318, (J. Gronov., Lugd.. Bat.).

[6] Orosius, *Historiarum Libri Septem Adversus Paganos*, Caput II., 17: "Fluvium Nilum, qui de litore incipientis Maris Rubri emergere videtur . . . . . Hunc aliqui auctores ferunt, haud procul ab Atlante habere fontem, et continuo arenis mergi: inde interjecto brevi spatio, vastissimo lacu exundare, atque hinc oceano tenus, orientem versus per Æthiopica Deserta prolabi, ▞▞▞ausque inflexum ad sinistram, Ægyptum descendere."

ficially upon the matter. Strabo in preserving the geographies of Megasthenes, Aristobulus, Nearchus, Onesicritus and Eratosthenes, has conferred a valuable contribution which people are now beginning to appreciate. From him Murli Manohar wrote us an article, making a pointed argument for socialism. He says that at an early period a splendid form of government existed in India whereby all the people found remunerative and guaranteed employment.[7] The workmen had it their own way. They were protected by the great king Sandrokottus, who benignantly reigned as a father governs his loving family, being exempt from all dangers and burdens of war. They were employed on public works, all land remaining the property of the state. They divided the time of labor into three parts: eight hours for labor, eight hours for recreation and instruction and eight hours for sleep.

We also possess a certain amount of monumental evidence for India, although the epigraphists seem not as yet to have extended their scientific investigations as far as India.[8] This, when accomplished, may bring corroborating evidence of our theory of the early planting in India, of trade and labor organizations, under the Solonic statute. But we already possess enough to make it certain that in some parts of India this was the case. We now proceed to the evidence of Strabo.

There was a mountain, Nusa by name, which seems to have been the Indian Olympus, honored by being the seat of the great god Dionysus, guardian and protector of the useful classes of mankind, the workers. He was a giver of joys. The city of Nusa was situated at the foot of the elevation of the same name, and is sometimes called Mount Meros, the birthplace of Bacchus. The Bacchic brotherhoods inhabited and cultivated the valleys and worked the mines and other resources of wealth which existed around about. True to the customs of

[7] See *Article in the Nineteenth Century*, for July, 1891, p. 49, No. 173. This writer extracts evidence likewise from Ælian and comes to the conclusion that the state was socialistic 400 years before Christ and employed labor on a vast scale, which he recommends.

[8] " Νῦσαν Διονύσου κτίσμα." Strabo 637, *ad fin*. For definition of Bacchus or Διόνυσος, see Liddell, *Gr. Lex.*, in verbo Βάχκος, who is honest enough, after all the defamation which was begun against this grand mythical character by the ecclesiastical writers who could not trump up any method among their schemes, by which to talk down the ancient lowly, if they adhered to a name representing a principle so sublime.

UNION COLONIES OF MOUNT NUSA.

the proletaries, they were all organized confraternities taking the thiasos of Greece as their pattern. They appear to have been a colony from some unknown part of the world, but as their organization and habits were the same as in Asia Minor, little doubt can exist that they were from the extreme west of Asia and near the Mediterranean Sea. Strabo, who was born B. C. 60 and lived 84 years, wrote about them while Christ was growing up to manhood; but as he got his information from Megasthenes who had written 300 years before, the colony was already old. He tells us of a colony of people who formed a settlement here, and had their carnivals under Dionysus, whose palace was in the mountain, and who was himself "the ennobler of mankind and giver of joys, as symbol of generation and the productive principle of nature"[9]

We are now prepared to proceed with Strabo and Arrian's beautiful descriptions of the socialism which existed during the reign of the good king Sandrokottus, at the time Megasthenes visited these regions of India.

The socialistic colony of Nusa was a Dionysan settlement of eranists of Asia Minor, who were at that age very numerous. It would appear from Strabo's paragraph, 688, that the people of India were cultivating this Dionysus, " the ennobler of mankind and the giver of joys;" and there can be no doubt that his cult was greatly furthered by the eranos, a prime organization under the Solonic code. Onesicritus, the chief pilot of Nearchus, whom Alexander sent on the celebrated sea voyage from the mouth of the Ganges to that of the Euphrates, is authority for the fact that the cult of this humanizing divinity was pursued with vigor in India.

It is thought that Nusa was the cradle, perhaps the central home of the organizations, being, as we have seen from a remark of Strabo, a colony of Dionysan unions from Greece or Asia Minor, that Nusa was but one of a thousand. Dr. Lightfoot whose authority is highly appreciated, acknowledges the brotherhoods of

[9] Strabo, 687 *fin*: "Ἐκ δὲ τῶν τοιούτων Νυσαίους δή τινας ἔθνος προσωνόμασαν καὶ πόλιν παρ' αὐτοῖς Νῦσαν Διονύσου κτίσμα, καὶ ὄρος τὸ ὑπὲρ τῆς πόλεως Μηρόν, αἰτιασάμενοι καὶ τὸν αὐτόθι κισσὸν καὶ ἄμπελον, οὐδὲ τούτην τελεσίκαρπον· Ἀπορρεῖ γὰρ ὁ Βότρυς πρὶν περκάσαι διὰ τοὺς ὄμβρους τοῦ ᾄδην Διονύσου δ' ἀπογόνους τοὺς Συδράκας ἀπὸ τῆς ἀμπέλου τῆς παρ' αὐτοῖς καὶ τῶν πολυτελῶν ἐξόδων, βαχικῶς τάς τε ἐκστρατείας ποιουμένων τῶν βασιλέων καὶ τὰς ἄλλας ἐξόδους μετὰ τυμπανισμοῦ καὶ εὐανθοῦς στολῆς ὅπερ ἐπι πολάξει καὶ παρὰ τοῖς ἄλλοις Ἰνδοῖς."

India to have been numerous and socially influential 300 years before Christ.[16] Damascus, a neighboring center of the unions of trades, especially that of cutlery, had the thiasotic and eranic method under the great law, and these are known to be very ancient. The unions manufactured blades and many varieties of cutlery out of the celebrated Damascus Steel, and it is known that the bars came from India.[11] Like the Phœnicians, they held their art a secret so that their unions might live upon and transmit it for ages and as they supposed, forever. But the Roman conquests struck Damascus with a withering blight. Modern research likewise discloses much that is valuable on ancient India in literature. One of the kings possessed a library which is said to have been so bulky that a thousand dromedaries were required to move it, and its librarian required a hundred men to place it in new quarters.

We now come to the testimony of the ancient authors already mentioned, as their works have been handed down to us through Strabo, Arrian and others.

Politically, morally, economically and socially, India was divided into seven parts.[12] These parts may be said

[10] Lightfoot, *Colossians*, p. 390, quotes from Megasthenes, admitting that he traveled through that country; but he knows nothing of the business of the κυριοι, as agents of thriving κοινα, who combined missionary work with business, now proved by inscriptions not at Lightfoot's command. Pantænus whom he mentions, p. 390, note 1, was evidently one of these; quite possibly also, Apollonius of Tyana. Lightfoot is here writing of the Essenes, an economic ass'n. Consult also Arrian, *Indica*, VIII., 1; Porphyry, *De Abst.*, IV., 17, as presented by Stobæus, *Ecl.*, III., 56, who is likewise found to have mentioned the Indians and their economic organizations. Lightfoot quotes Clement of Alex., *Strom.*, I., 18, p. 359. Speaking of the various schools of Indian thought, he brings in the Σαρμάναιοι Βάκτρων, and distinguishes two kinds of Γυμνοσοφισταί, alluding to Megasthenes. There were the Σαρμάνας or Γαράμνας, κ. τ. λ. Bardesanes also tells of brotherhoods in India. There was later a sect of Bardesan Gnostics there. But the evidence all shows that the associations were originally inspired by economic rather than sacred motives, in India as elsewhere. The practical commonsense of Strabo is of great value in disabusing our minds of this widespread error: "Καὶ οἱ νῦν δὲ ἐξ Αἰγύπτου πλέοντες ἐμπορικοὶ τῷ Νείλῳ καὶ τῷ 'Αραβίῳ κόλπῳ μέχρι τῆς 'Ινδικῆς σπάνιοι μὲν καὶ περιπεπλεύκασι μέχρι τοῦ Γάγγου, καὶ οὗτοι δ' ἰδιῶται καὶ οὐδὲν πρὸς ἱστορίαν τῶν τόπων χρήσιμοι," κ.τ.λ. Strabo, *Geog.*, 686. The Indians had an established communication with western people; but contrary to Dr. Lightfoot, who regards it as less than it really was, since it was the interacting, secret business societies that engaged in it and not the open world.

[11] See *Amer. Cyclopædia*, on *Damascus Steel*, where Niebuhr is shown to have attempted to explain the celebrated art, supposed to be lost. It was here that the early church, or original κυριακὴ, κυριοικὸς, or house of the lord was established. Damascene ornamentations, invented by Glaucus of Chios, B. C. 490, got supplies from India. A high state of trade unionism could permeate India from here very readily.

[12] Strabo, p. 703, *fin.*: "Φησὶ δὴ τὸ τῶν 'Ινδῶν πλῆθος εἰς ἑπτὰ μέρη διῃρῆσθαι."

SYSTEM OF CLASSES FOR INDIA. 115

to represent classes; for there are no indications that the undemocratical and degrading classes existed as today. People now, of one caste, will not eat at the same table with those of another; and it may be said that this was the feeling which existed at Rome among the optimates; but it is fully proved that in Rome and all cities and countries where the Solonic unions existed, the reverse is the case when their brotherly love melted away the social barriers between slaves and free men.

The first of the seven classes consisted of the philosophers.[13] They were, however, considered workers for the state, and occupied what now are called positions under the civil service. They were the educated class who worked at calculating the prospects of the government, and helped the king in his work of state. They planned the revenues, watched the process of the incomes, from planting to harvest, and the breeding of animals, and every year there was a common council held with the king on the best measures to pursue during the forthcoming year.

Under class second came the farmers or tillers; but as all the land belonged to a socialized state, the farmers worked it on shares, taking a fourth of the product and their pay in kind.[14] These farmers enjoyed complete exemption from military service and were known as immunes. There was a law by which they enjoyed protection from injury, which seems to have amounted to something like insurance against injury of health and accident.[15] While others must fight, these only plow and hoe without risk.

The third class consisted of herdsmen and hunters. These kept the cattle and other animals for the market.[16] They also freed the land from birds and beasts that destroy the seeds of the social farm lands, before being subdued by tillage. They were trustees of the common

[13] Strabo, *ibid.*, 703: "..... καί πρώτους μὲν τοὺς φιλοσόφους εἶναι κατὰ τιμήν, ἐλαχίστους δὲ κατ' ἀριθμόν· χρῆσθαι δ' αὐτοῖς ἰδίᾳ μὲν ἑκάστῳ τοὺς θύοντας ἢ τοὺς ἐναγίζοντας, κοινῇ δὲ τοὺς βασιλέας κατὰ τὴν μεγάλην λεγομένην σύνοδον, καθ' ἣν τοῦ νέου ἔτους ἅπαντες οἱ φιλόσοφοι τῷ βασιλεῖ συνελθόντες ἐπὶ θύρας ὅ τι ἂν αὐτῶν ἕκαστος συντάξῃ τῶν χρησίμων ἢ τηρήσῃ πρὸς εὐετηρίαν καρπῶν τε καὶ ζῴων καὶ περὶ πολιτείας," κ. τ. λ.

[14] Strabo, 704, *init.*: "μισθοῦ δ' αὐτὴν ἐπὶ τετάρταις ἐργάζονται τῶν καρμῶν;" *id.* 704, 40, *fin.*

[15] "Strabo, 704: "Δεύτερον δὲ μέρος εἶναι τὸ τῶν γεωργῶν, οἳ πλεῖστοί τέ εἰσι καὶ ἐπιεικέστατοι ἀστρατεῖᾳ καὶ ἀδείᾳ τοῦ ἐργάζεσθαι, πόλει μὴ προσιόντες μηδ' ἄλλῃ χρείᾳ μηδ' ὀχλήσει κοινῇ· πολλάκις γοῦν ἐν τῷ αὐτῷ χρόνῳ καὶ τόπῳ τοῖς μὲν παρατετάχθαι συμβαίνει καὶ διακινδυνεύειν πρὸς τοὺς πολεμίους," κ. τ. λ.

lands.[16] We are not definitely informed as to the exact shape of organization these hunters and herdsmen enjoyed. We know that they were combined in powerful economic unions and that they were legalized by the state and favored, as necessary to the well-being of community and of the king, and like the farmers, exempt from the burdens of war. Large numbers of hunters' unions are being found in the inscriptions of Asia Minor and the Italian provinces which will be dwelt upon later in this work. The people coming under the designation of hunters and herdsmen are said to be of the koinos, which not only means a society working in common for mutual benefit and protection, but also generally indicates the common table, judging from the language of Strabo and Arrian.

His fourth class consists of the skilled workers in the technical arts, and the dealers.[17] Singularly enough these go together according to the provisions of the Solonic law, as preserved by Gaius who took it from the XII Tables of Roman law, and wrote it down as his opinion that it was a translation from the original statute of Solon himself.[18] In other words, the artisans or skilled mechanics not only did the mechanical work of manufacture on an enormous scale, for the community under direction of the commissioner of public works, but they were credited with and performed, all the work of manufacturing implements of war. The state needed swords, darts, spears, also engines for breaking down and destroying walls, arches, and other defenses. It employed the mechanics to construct such implements and to engineer them in times of war. Thus the state employed labor. It also wisely exempted them from open combat and the burdens and dangers of war. They were too valuable to be murdered off at wholesale. Skill and genius are

[16] Strabo, 704, 41: "Τρίτον τὸ τῶν ποιμένων καὶ θηρευτῶν, οἷς μόνοις ἔξεστι θηρεύειν καὶ θρεμματοτροφεῖν ὤνιά τε παρέχειν καὶ μισθοῦ ζεύγη· ἀντὶ δὲ τοῦ τὴν γῆν ἐλευθεροῦν θηρίων καὶ τῶν σπερμολόγων ὀρνέων," κ. τ. λ.
[17] Strabo, 707, 46: "Μετὰ γὰρ τοὺς θηρευτὰς καὶ τοὺς ποιμένας τέταρτόν φησιν εἶναι μέρος τοὺς ἐργαζομένους τὰς τέχνας καὶ τοὺς καπηλικοὺς καὶ οἷς ἀπὸ τοῦ σώματος ἡ ἐργασία· ὧν οἱ μὲν φόρον τελοῦσι καὶ λειτουργίας παρέχονται τακτάς, τοῖς δ' ὁπλοποιοῖς καὶ ναυπηγοῖς μισθοὶ καὶ τροφαὶ παρὰ βασιλέως ἔκκεινται· μόνῳ γὰρ ἐργάζονται· παρέχει δὲ τὰ μὲν ὅπλα τοῖς στρατιώταις ὁ στρατοφύλαξ, τὰς δὲ ναῦς μισθοῦ τοῖς πλέουσιν ὁ ναύαρχος καὶ τοις ἐμπόροις."
[18] Digest, XLVII., Tit, xxii., lex. 4: "Sodalis sunt qui ejusdem collegii sunt; quam Græci ἑταιρίαν vocant. His autum potestatem facit lex, pactionem quam velint, sibi ferre; dum ne quid ex publica lege corrumpant. Sed hæc lex videtur ex lege Solonis translata esse," etc.

precious and it was so recognized. Thus again, precisely as told us by Murli Manohar, a state managed the labor. It operated mechanical shops and factories on a large scale. Can any one suppose for a moment that the workmen did not have a powerful political organization as in Rome, at Pompeii, in Asia Minor, composed of voting unions? It is proved by recent discoveries at Pompeii that trade unions exerted every effort at the elections to secure the choice for managers in the city's business, of those who were pledged to bestow upon them the public work. It is fortunate that we have a Strabo who so plainly exhibits the key to otherwise submerged facts of ancient socialism.

Then we are introduced to the useless factor of state, the military; and they occupy the fifth class in Strabo's enumeration. He plainly tells us that this fifth class is composed of the fighters, whose time, outside of active warfare is devoted to drill and drink.[19] There are some remnants of military organization preserved to us in the inscriptions. These will contribute, so far as they go, to the widespread influence of Solonism in another chapter, and it may be that this fifth class of the Indians possessed it, but it is doubtful. They were probably, as they have always been, simply the regular national prætorians and standing army, including the king's body-guard, as worthless as they were expensive, and like the drones consumed the products of those who formed the second, third and fourth classes of that country.

The sixth class consisted of the ephori, or king's spies and judges whose business was to watch and secretly report all current events to the king. They were clothed with power, and had a watch over the economic matters of the organizations at home, and the military affairs of the field. But their work, like the old Spartan ephori, was secret and doubtless they were as badly hated, and in the end overthrown. Nabis fought them. It was this set whom Appius Claudius of Rome organized the army and the conquests to defend; and we are awakening

[19] Strabo, 707, 47: " Πέμπτον δ' ἐστὶ τὸ τῶν πολεμιστῶν, οἷς τὸν ἄλλον χρονόν ἐν σχολῇ καὶ πότοις ὁ βίος ἐστὶν ἐκ τοῦ βασιλικοῦ διαιτωμένοις ὥστε τὰς ἐξόδους ὅταν ᾖ χρεία ταχέως ποιεῖσθαι, πλὴν τῶν σωμάτων μηδὲν ἄλλο κομίζοντας παρ' ἑαυτῶν." M. Cagnat, while working among the military remains in Africa for the French Academy, discovered evidences of a military collegium arranged in regiments, companies and decades, after the ancient plan.

now, once more to discover that the "richest" are they whom modern supreme courts are coldly handing down their august decisions to defend.[20] No matter what the justice of a Paulus, an Ulpian, or a Franklin might prescribe, the verdict of these modern ephori gages to the same occult, mephitic goddess, smiling on the "richest men" who at any moment stand ready to buy blandishments for the purblind people they cajole or auction off to the highest bidder, as did old Didius who outbade and struck off Rome to get the imperial toga. Thus it was that Rome wheeled her conquests against Nabis, and in defense of the ephori, though they were a supreme bench which at times unnumbered ordered out their trained assassins to butcher the laboring people.

Finally, we have the true aristocrats, who must not mix their precious blood in marriage, with workingmen. These were councilors and special commissioners of the king, who met at regular periods for consultation.[21]

Thus it is seen that in far off India there was a crude scheme of political socialism based upon the wise trade unionism of Solon, deeply permeating the state.

We have already shown that this vast organization followed the form of a well established municipality, the original idea of which was patterned after the family. Many cities in Greece and elsewhere had this ancient form and often possessed the prytaneum where a common table existed, at which workingmen, as well as councilors and jurists could receive food. Whether this common table was in vogue so far away as India, we have only enough evidence to form a stray suspicion; the color of the evidence points to the conclusion that it must have been so.

[20] Consult chap. iv., *supra*, p. 91, giving the uprisings of Nabis against the ephorate and for the restoration of the old Lycurgan dispensation. Note 7. *fin.*, contains Strabo's words on the ephori of India.

[21] Strabo, 707, 49: whose seventh and last class might have laid the foundation of their downfall. Such a description as Strabo gives looks bad. He says : " Ἕβδομοι οἱ σύμβουλοι καὶ σύνεδροι τοῦ βασιλέως, ἐξ ὧν τὰ ἀρχεῖα καὶ δικαστήρια καὶ ἡ διοίκησις τῶν ὅλων. Οὐκ ἔστι δ' οὔτε γαμεῖν ἐξ ἄλλου γένους οὔτ' ἐπιτήδευμα οὔτ' ἐργασίαν μεταλαμβάνειν ἄλλην ἐξ ἄλλης, οὐδὲ πλείους μεταχειρίζεσθαι τὸν αὐτὸν πλὴν εἰ τῶν φιλοσόφων τις εἴη ἐᾶσθαι γὰρ τοῦτον δ' ἀρετήν." This last, and be it said, worthless set crown the descriptions of both Strabo and Arrian who agree. Their pernicious inculcations, backed by the ephori, were alone enough to destroy the otherwise fine organizations in India.

CHAPTER VII.
RAGE AND HAVOC.
CONDITION AT CLOSE OF THE CONQUESTS.

WRANGLES over the Spoils—Extent of the Havoc of Conquest—Murderous Standing Army—Roman Generals brought Spoils in their Own Name—Countless Slaves of their Conquests—Sulla's Massacre of 50,000—Unions fell Victims of their own Duplicity—Judicial Murder by Crucifixion of 400 Innocents—Mostly Semitics—Story reconstructed—Heartlessness of the Senate—Plea to Save them Overruled—Savage Speech of Cassius—Law Enforced—Awful Agonies—Workers Dangerously Maddened—Longed More ardently for Promised Redeemer—The Carpenter Already Born—Endorse His Plan of Salvation—The Slave Marts—Cheap Humanity—The Poor longed for the Right of Marriage—Power of Inscriptions and Anecdotal History—Cruelties of Paul Æmilius—Still more Secret—Seized and Thrown over Precipices—Ingratitude of Men who lived by Others' Toil—What better were Such than Brigands—Pre-Christian Martyrs—Socrates an Example—Two Persecutions of the Jews—Their Good Character made Them a Target of Hate—Great Advantage of the Common Tables—An Ancient and Revered Institution—Jews of Antioch—Roman and Pagan Hatred of them—Story of the Maccabees—Defeat of Syrian Generals—Power of the Congregation—Futile Effort to Break up the Mosaic Dispensation—Ferocious Massacre of the Hebrew Race at Jerusalem—Best Author puts Number Murdered at 1,100,000—Sanguinary Fury—Sad Loss of Arts of Damascus Steel, Crimson Dyes, Imperishable Inks, Pigments and Many Inventions Ascribed to these Truculent Deeds of Savagery—They were Secrets of the Unions—Property whereby they lived, and which Died with Them—World's Irredeemable Losses.

WE must apprize our readers, however painful the obligation, of the terrible conditions among which the working people were suffering about the time of the appearance of the strange and extraordinary character whose name stands at the head of a new era, and whose personage is, and bids fair to remain, a prototype of the hopeful, the practical, the economical and the inspired. A name never blasphemed, and strange to record, never to this day calumniated by either friend or foe. We beg the reader's indulgence of this opportunity to outline the conditions existing during the awful swoop of those conquests which attacked and almost extinguished the fortunately indestructible Solonic dispensation. Trade unionism had been rooted into society to remain and to live. Despite the avaricious hand of the money and property power, with all its concomitant attributes of brigandage and truculent barbarity then crushing the world, it survived. It is not dead yet. The reader understanding this, may well consider our chapter on the Roman conquests, and the true intent and cunning of the old gain-getting craft.

We shall begin with the massacres of Sulla; but it is necessary to switch in certain wayside horrors along the flinty path, until we come down to the judicial murder of the four hundred which seems to have formed a trysting point, over whose sharp-angled ledge the tolerance of the oppressed staggered and swooned between a new theory of love and sympathy, and the old failure of irascibility and concupiscence.

When the great Roman conquests had been fully accomplished, having practically terminated with the subjugation of Judea and Palestine, the world fell into a phenomenal wrangle and entanglement over questions of spoil. Rome, with her scientific military equipment furnished by the trade unions as described, had gotten all, from the Spanish peninsula and the Atlantic Coast of Africa in the west, to far off India in the east, and northward even to the British Isles. All Germany, Africa, Gaul, Asia Minor, Greece, Pannonia, Macedonia, even India had fallen before her prowess and cupidity.

When all this had come to pass and mankind lay enslaved and in chains; when a thousand cities, sacked and ravaged, gave up their artisans to be bondsmen, their accumulations, a booty of conquest, their ancient governments, peaceful and prosperous, to wreckage; when all this spoil had been grasped, and conquerors were stuffed and swaggering with congestion, we find workingmen and women in millions thronging the slave marts; tearful

MASSACRE OF THE FIFTY THOUSAND. 121

humiliation of men, shocking prostitution of women, luxuriant sensualities of a sickening and loathsome nature infecting the Roman youth, demoralizing voluptuousness, exuberence of drunken passion, irredeemable moral desolation. When all was conquered, unmeasured wealth in form of booty swooped into the great city from every bleeding country of the earth; and a reeking government, crass and fumid, seethed in festering putresence and disintegration. Lost to everything but lust of lucre and lust of indulgence, an appetite abnormal in wine, amphitheatrical spectacles, bloodthirst and sexual recklessness gnawed at the heartstrings of the world. This was Rome's condition at the close of the conquests. There was many a Roman general who, having done much in bringing about this rapine and desolation to the outside world, marched victoriously back to Rome, loaded with plunder, proud of success, demanding a triumphal entry, but who was stung to the quick when he found that rivals had blocked his way to all those coveted honors. Among these disappointed aspirants was Sulla, the murderer of 50,000 workingmen in B. C. 82.

We have already seen that the working people were organized in trade unions at Rome. The conquests seem to have been originated in a purpose to undermine and destroy them. The trick had failed; for the unions were still alive and at the time of Sulla they were powerful, and still voting their tribunes into office as in the solitudo magistratuum.

Like Appius Claudius, this Sulla was an offshoot of a celebrated gens family, the Cornelian, proud, haughty, imperious; and he boasted, like Nero, that his mission on earth was to place a blight upon the aspirations of the hated workingmen so low as to have no family, no soul, and descendants only of lowborn, and contemptible slaves. Truly these were the working people. The details of this conflict we have no place to recount, but leave that horror to Sallust.[1] It is unnecessary to detail the account of this massacre. We refer our readers to the historians. It is sufficient to say that this proud gentleman, like Appius Claudius, had selected as his mission the overthrow of the voting power of the organ-

[1] Sallust, *Jugurtha*, 72, 73, says the workingmen sided with Marius, their former tribune and their constant friend.

ized proletariat with a view to crush them.² It was a prodigious work; for mechanics in great numbers were still working for the state, manufacturing quantities of arms for the army and regularly receiving their pay as government employees.

Sulla, after the battle we are going to recount, pronounced himself dictator; and historians agree that he was the first emperor of Rome, such was his dictatorial puissance. In that great battle which took place within the walls of Rome in the year 82 before Christ, Marius, the tribune, champion and friend of all the workingmen who had sided with him as patriot and friend of the proletariat generally, was overthrown by the stronger force of Sulla. Mommsen tells us that: "The army of the insurgents, for which there was no retreat, was completely extirpated." In other words as we are informed by Sallust and Appian, the entire multitude was killed. A hundred thousand men lay dead on the field. They had a general named Damasippus who commanded. He was assassinated. Corrius, another commander, and Pontus, who was wounded, and between 3,000 and 4,000 of the people—the reliable Livy says 8,000—three days after the carnage, were driven out to the Villa Publica, in the Campus Martius and there within hearing of Sulla's assembled council, and of Sulla himself, "massacred³ to

---

² We give Sallust's opinion of Sulla, written among the earliest Roman histories: "Sed, postquam L. Sulla, armis recepta Rep. bonis initiis malos eventus habuit; rapere omnes, trahere; domum alius, alius agros cupere; neque modum, neque modestiam victores habere; fœda, crudeliaque in civis facinora facere. Huc accedebat, quod L. Sulla exercitum, quem in Asia ductaverat, quo sibi fidum faceret. Loca amœna, voluptaria facile in otio ferocis militum animos molliverant. Ibi primum insuevit exercitus populi Romani amare, potare, signa, tabulas pictas, vasa cælata mirari, ea privatim ac publice rapere, delubra spoliare, sacra profanaque omnia polluere . . . Rapere, consumere; sua parvi pendere, aliena cupere; pudorem, pudicitiam divina atque humana promiscua, nihil pensi, neque moderati habere." *Bellum Catilinarium, Ex recensione* Ant. Thysii. Lugd. Patavorum, 1646, pp. 20-26.

³ Momms., *Hist. Rome*, III., p. 411. Saltus says this fearful massacre of 50,000 Roman common people by Sulla caused Lucretius, who witnessed it, to become a stoic. and prompted his spirit for the wonderful poem, *De Rerum Natura*. We quote the fragment of Livy's LXXXVIIIth book, which we are so fortunate as to find remaining, although nearly the entire book has perished. He makes the last massacre to be 8,000 instead of 3,500 as put by the unwarrantably cautious Mommsen: "Cum Samnitibus, qui soli ex Italicis populis nondum arma posuerant, juxta urbem Romanam ante portam collinam debellavit: recuperataque re publica, pulcherrimam victoriam crudelitate, quanta in nullo hominum fuit, inquinavit. Octo millia deditorum in villa publica trucidavit; tabulam proscriptionis proposuit; urbem ac totam Italiam cædibus replevit; inter quas omnes Prænestinos inermes concidi jussit. Marium, senatorii ordinis virum cruribus brachiisque fractis, auribus persectis et offossis occulis, necavit," A more horrible picture of inhumanity it were difficult to portray,

the last man, so that the clatter of arms and the groans of the dying, were distinctly heard in the neighboring temple of Bellona where Sulla was holding a meeting of the Senate."[4]

This unreasonable cruelty and almost internicine carnage was perpetrated to a large extent against the Samnites and the inhabitants of Præneste. The place had been the theatre of an earlier insurrection occurring in B. C. 198, against the exactions of the Roman rulers and rich men, and we have already fully accounted it in this work. The brave and indomitable Samnite blood[5] could not brook either degradation or slavery. They were the best mechanics Rome ever had. In the course of centuries they had broken their chains, and were free men. Intensely industrious, they were magnificently organized under the great dispensation of Numa, and at the time of the solitudo magistratuum were voting unions, numbering hundreds of thousands of prosperous members flourishing under what was exactly equivalent to the Solonic law. This tyrant Sulla, then, is to be considered an enemy of the most valuable part of the Roman public; for they never rebelled except when goaded by the grinding exactions of jealous and insatiable optimates.

Notwithstanding the desperate efforts of the rich to degrade them by means of cunning, in springing the conquests for the purpose of overthrowing the voting unions, they had maintained their organizations and political power. They had themselves become aggressive fighters. They also found sympathizers among the nobles of Rome. One of these was Marcus Livius Drusus, who, like the Gracchi, restored the old agrarian laws. The optimates murdered him as they did Gracchus a few years before.[6]

The culminating crime involved in this story is the

[4] Vol. I., pp. 150-153, and note 18, where the language of Livy, our authority, is quoted.
[5] Cicero is entirely out of patience with this ruthless cruelty of Sulla. In one place he says the sun never looked down upon a scene more unworthy: "Multa præterea commemorarem nefaria in socios, si hoc uno quidquam sol vidisset indignius." *De Officiis*, lib. II., c. viii.
[6] As a proof that the civil, or as some prefer to call them, social wars, were genuine labor turmoils, Mommsen points out the fact that leaden bullets of the date of Sulla's battles, are being picked up, on which are inscribed execrations against the low slaves and creatures whom the haughty optimates were obliged to lift their hand against.

awful and useless massacre of 50,000 Prænestians belonging to the working class, and in sympathy with brotherhoods of Rome and environing towns and districts, by the monster Sulla, who but a year or two afterwards died at Puteoli, another hive of organized working people, of a loathsome and disgusting form of putrescent venerea—a victim of morpions of the flesh.

Another shocking story is to be told. It is of the judicial murder of 399 innocent people which, under an atrocious Roman law, the senatus consultum Silenione, took place soon after the death of Christ. It was a useless massacre of innocent men, women and children because of the rash deed of one man. We shall quote the frigid words of Tacitus who delighted to recount acts of the aristocracy, as he delighted to damn the Christians to the ghastly punitions of Nero.[7] Tacitus, while he believes the Christians and Hebrews preëminently deserving of punishment, moderately objects to the exquisite refinement of Nero, in placing palanquins upon the shoulders of an enraged populace containing living bodies covered an inch thick with tar and set on fire to form flaming lights for a beastly populace, howling themselves hoarse at the exhilarating sight of a thousand such torches, each a naked man or woman, whose crime was that of loving and honoring a newly found Saviour!

Tacitus recounts to us the terrors of this other slaughter which happened under Nero just before the burning of Rome, and in words as cold.[8] A senatus consultum or law of the Roman senate had in A. D. 10, been enacted, based, as Tacitus hints, upon an old custom, which prescribed that if any slave should take the life of his owner the entire "family" as he suggestively calls them, were to be punished with death, along with the criminal himself. The man who had been murdered was a prefect of the city, Pedanius by name. He owned a large number of slaves whom he had probably, directly or in-

[7] Section *Nero* of this work, and notes: vide *index*, in verb. *Conflagration.*
[8] Tac. *Ann.*, xiv., 43-45: "Haud multo post præfectum urbis Pedanium Secundum servus ipsius interfecit, seu negata libertate cui pretium pepigerat, sive amore exoleti infensus et dominum æmulum non tolerans. Ceterum eum vetere ex more familiam omnem, quæ sub eodem tecto mansitaverat, ad supplicium agi oporteret, concursu plebis, quæ tot innoxios protegabat, usque ad seditionem ventum est senatusque obsessus, in quo ipso erant studia nimiam severitatem aspernantium, pluribus nihil mutandum censentibus. Ex quis C. Cassius sententiæ loco in hunc modum disseruit," etc. This speech of Cassius is in purport, in the text above.

JUDICIAL MURDER OF THE FOUR HUNDRED. 125

directly, seized with other plunder from the fallen victims of the conquest. Among his chattels were 400 in one family, all probably organized under one roof, and entitled to the amenities of the Domus Augustalis. They consisted of men, women and children. One of these 400 had been guilty of the crime. Goaded by insult he could not brook, he had killed Pedanius, his owner, and every one, according to this atrocious statute was to die. They were part of the war herd captured from Asia and mostly Semitics, as is duly recorded. Men, boys, girls, old women, tender infants, all must perish! But the manner of this sickening execution was the most appalling. They must be crucified. They must suffer that most painful, lingering death inherited only by the lowly and the helpless poor. Criminals of family and recognition could be punished in an honorable manner. The poor, the workingmen and women, the innocents, the little babes, the feeble, the tottering aged, with souls as cloudless as the crystal skies, were to be swooped and herded together, driven and dragged to the one Golgotha. The Roman law demanded that they be tied and nailed and hoisted upon a cross, and pierced and broken and left to die amid their shrieks and groans! It was too much. The plebeians who knew of the shocking circumstance gathered in multitudes to interfere. Rome was once more in danger. History has fixed this as one of Rome's pivotal epochs of peril. The senate was convoked and the question discussed as to whether it might not be advisable to waive for once the rigor of the harsh Silenian law.[9] But one Cassius arose and demanded the enforcement of the statute. The slaves of to-day, he argued, are more dangerous even than before. They are the booty of conquest, coming from the far-off regions of Syria, Carthage, Phœnicia; fierce Scythians, fighting Greeks, Semitics more than Europeans; and nothing but fear is capable of holding them down in their yoke of subjection. We must scare the whole race and servile herd and by this judicial triumph grind

---

[9] The assurance of Tacitus, see note 8, is important to this argument. Was this *"family"* an organization under that head? In our chapter on the Unions at Rome, section Nero, where the Conflagration is described, this judicial massacre is again brought under consideration to illustrate another statement of Tacitus; and it is there explained that a vast organization of slaves and freedmen was fostered by the emperors themselves, under title of *Domus Augustalis*.

those that remain alive down deeper into their mire of servitude and humiliation. The oration prevailed and the 399 innocents were actually killed in presence of all the plebeian hosts, that their awful supplicium might act to intimidate the world and keep them cowed through the hideous emotions of terror.

Among the poor themselves there had sprung up a new hope, and they were using their organizations and minds in many ways to accomplish some means out of their desperate condition.[10] As late as Justin Martyr the havoc was proceeding; for he says in his Discourse to the Greeks: "Do not recognize those men as heroes who slaughter whole nations;" and he denounces the high spirit of the earth's nobility.

Bishop Lightfoot assures us afresh, that a few years before the Christian era, one Claudius Isidorus left by will 4,000 slaves though he had incurred serious losses by the civil war; and he adds: "These vast masses of human beings had no protection from the Roman law." Lightfoot further admits that sometimes as many as ten and even twenty thousand slaves fell into the possession of one man.[11]

On an Etruscan tomb there has been found at Tarquinii a picture giving a representation of gladiatorial games held at the funeral wake of a wealthy man owning slaves, and ordering at his death,[12] that certain strong-bodied favorite slaves should fight and kill each other, that the Etruscan Charon might guide them to him again in the other world as a body-guard and protector. This immolation in a milder form was going on at the commencement of the Christian era, and was causing horror and fear among the Syrians and Phœnicians. These gruesome conditions, limited entirely to the poor and

---

[10] Foucart, *Affranch. des Esclaves*, p. 43, gives Delos as the greatest slave mart in the world. M. Bazaine, *Archives des Missions Scientifiques, Mém. sur l' Italie*, found an inscription showing how slaves were sold to a goddess or god, the form of the transfer producing freedom. This sort of emancipation was not confined to Apollo (see *index* of this work), nor to Delphi. In the temple of Esculapius at Stiris, and at Elatea, it appears to have prevailed; also at the temple of Serapis, at Cheronea; Serapis at Tithorea; of Bacchus at Naupactus; of Minerva Paliade at Danlis. Indeed Venus Syrienne allowed it at Phiscis. These facts are shown by the inscription which explains how many divinities acted for humanity, under the eranos, in aiding the emancipation of the slaves.

[11] Athenæus, see Bekker, *Gallus*, II., p. 113, is known to have said: "Ῥωμαίων ἕκαστος . . . . πλείστους ὅσους κεκτημένος οἰκέτας· καὶ γὰρ μυρίον καὶ δισμυρίους καί ἔτι πλείους δὲ πάμπολλοι κέκτηνται."

[12] See I., p. 279, note 5, "Waking the dead with blood."

disinherited, were every-day scenes, and are found to have been in their severest stage about the close of the Roman conquests.

The conquests were closed. The high-blooded optimates had cunningly used the credulity of trade unions, otherwise splendid and successful, and had debauched their officers as they are doing to-day, to make and man the arms and warlike equipments whereby to conquer the world; and be it said also, eventually to destroy the organizations themselves.[13] By whipping in many of the unions' head officers who as now betrayed their men for booty, they carried out their original scheming design. But no power ever yet has destroyed trade unionism.

The conquests destroyed humanity, enslaved the members in millions, curtailed progress consequent upon discussion, suspended social economies and for a time broke up the schools of their secret cult. But did the conquests destroy the unions? By no means! They went down deeper into the depths of intense secrecy. With ineffable fear and caution they lived on in darkness, but no power of optimate or ruler could break up the jus coeundi of the great Solonic dispensation. We shall proceed to further portray the sad conditions prevailing against the ancient lowly from the breaking out of the conquests to the first century of our era.

The desire of the unions, as shown by innumerable inscriptions, was to marry regularly as we now do, and raise the family. This would perpetuate the social microcosm and the common table, and be in perfect accordance with the law of organization. The family is the microcosm of the state. It is perfect socialism in essence. Alas, this the powers too well understood and thwarted from earliest written history. No law existed until centuries of the Christian era had elapsed, permitting legitimate marriage either among slaves or freed descendants of slaves. From high antiquity the children of the poor were illegitimate. This illegitimacy barred them. We search the ancient laws in vain to find a clause that made man and wife among the poor. Even as early as Isaiah it was so. In the eye of the law all

---

[13] See *Supra*, Chap. I., pp. 1-66, on the original incentive of the conquests which we have dated from the *Solitudo Magistratuum*, B C. 373, a few years after the trouble with Appius Claudius.

were illegitimate.[14] Dr. Lightfoot says: "And these vast masses of humanity had no protection from the Roman law. The slave had no relationships, no conjugal rights. Cohabitation was allowed to him at his owner's pleasure, but not marriage. His companion was sometimes assigned to him by lot. The slave was absolutely at his master's disposal; for the smallest offense he might be scourged, mutilated, crucified, thrown to the wild beasts."[15]

As a consequence, a natural warfare raged between the poor and their masters. From Plato and before, there was a constant fear of the slave. "The more slaves the more enemies" was the byword.[16] The desperate condition of the slaves was intensified by the conquests, since they broke up their organizations wherever and whenever such a result was possible. No power of violence could successfully uproot the unions, it is true; but it was accomplished without violence in another way. The Romans would invade a new territory, attack and destroy its cities, seize all men, women and children they could lay hands on,[17] run them into the slave markets to be sold, and in this manner dismember the organizations.

[14] Isaiah, LIV., 1: "More are the children of the desolate than the children of the married wife."
[15] *Epistle to Philemon, Colossians*, p. 319.
[16] Seneca, *Eph. Neor.*, 47: "Deinde ejusdem arrogantiæ proverbium jactetur 'totidem hostes esse quot servi.'" See Macrobius, I., 11, 13: "Totidem hostes nobis esse quot servis." So Testus, p. 261, Ed. Müller; "Quot servi tot hostes in proverbium est." Again, Haterias, in the older Seneca, *Controv.*, iv., *Præf.*: "Impudicia in ingenuo crimen est, *in servo necessitas*, in liberto officium." We may sum up the awful condition of the slaves of those times, just at the appearance of Christ, by quoting Wallon on *Ancient Slavery*, I., p, 332: "L'esclave appartenait au maître; par lui même, il n' était rien; il n' avait rien. Voila le principe; et tout ce qu' on en peut tirer par voie de conséquence formait aussi en fait, l'état des esclaves dans la plupart des pays. A toutes les époqués, dans toutes les situations de la vie, cette autorité souveraine plane sur aux et modifie leur destinée par ses rigeurs comme par son indifférence. Dans l' age de la force et dans la plénitude de leurs facultés, elle les vouait, à son choix, soit au travail, les natures grossières; au vice les natures les plus delicates, nouries pour les plaisirs du maître, et qui lors qu'il en était las, étaient reléguées dans la prostitution à son profit. Avant et après l' age du travail, abandonnés à leurs faiblesse ou á leurs infirmités; enfants, ils grandissaient dans le désordre, viellards, ils mouraient souvent dans la misère; morts, ils étaient quelquefois délaissés sur la voi publique.
[17] See I., p. 340, note 17, Paulus Æmilius after his victory of Pydna in Epirus, and his murder of 40,000, took a hundred and sixty thousand of the people as prisoners and had them dragged into slavery, besides robbing this fair land of ten millions in gold. Again, *id.*, p. 192-193, Gracchus saw at Sardinia 80,000 men, women and children thus sacrificed, causing the celebrated revolt of the Gracchi. But the histories of those times abound with similar horrors, as at Tarentum (*id.*, 192); Delos, where the slave shambles were, or Carthage, which actually gave up its free population to be sent to the rich plantations of Sicily.

We have great numbers of instances of this kind on record. The histories and anecdotes of that sad episode of vengeance, greed and havoc abound in appalling scenes. The old laws which during the peaceful days of the good kings had been forgotten, were scraped together against the proletarian class. The old Papyrian law, authorizing fathers to kill, enslave or sell their children engendered by their female slaves, was dug out afresh.[18] Laws forbidding marriage of the poor whether slaves or freedmen were rigidly enforced, which was an especial aggravation since the unions were in greater part moral, and religiously sworn against illegal cohabitation, as we shall thoroughly prove in our chapter on the pre-Christian period just before our era began.[19] A great calamity early struck the unions of Numa because they had manhood, and used it with their accorded right, to act politically by themselves as a new body politic. They were voting their own principles and their manhood into force, taking Plato's word as true, that the highest manhood and dignity to be had is the political; and they were making themselves a hopeful future, when, under Tarquinius Superbus, an old conspiracy law of Romulus was raked out and put into force against labor organizations on the ground that they were dangerous to the state. Dionysius says the synods, by which he means the unions, were actually suppressed, for fear that they would overthrow the government.[20] These synods, name and all, were later borrrowed by the Chris-

---

[18] *Cod. Just.*, VIII., Tit. xlvii., *lex* 10: "Patribus . . . . . jus vitæ in liberos necisque potestas olim erat permissa." Dionys. *Hal.*, II., 26, likewise quotes it. See I., p. 147, note, quoting the ancient law of Rome. See *Digest*, I., 6, for power to kill slaves, even children, which was conferred upon masters: "In potestate sunt servi dominorum. Quæ quidem potestas juris gentium est; nam apud omnes peræque gentes animadvertere possumus, dominis in servos vitæ necisque potestatem fuisse." Again, Paulus, the Roman jurist, is quoted in the *Digest*, IV., 5, preserving the law degrading the servile race: "Servile caput nullum jus habet." Likewise Ulpian's quotation, *Dig.*, IV.: "In personam servorum nulla cadit obligatio."

[19] Lightfoot, *Coloss., Philemon*, p. 319, shows inscriptions found in Asia Minor. *Gallus*, II., p. 145, proving that under the powerful unions and their moral influence the members often actually did live together as man and wife through a whole lifetime; and we shall later show by inscriptions that in Rome and various parts of Italy they did the same, overriding the law. Later, Christianity, intolerant of pagan rule, broke up the law entirely, and constituted marriage as the foundation of the family and the solidest factor of society; and it so remains. Thus the true history of Christianity antedates Christ, being always inherent in labor unions.

[20] *Dionys. Hal.*, IV., c. 43: "Συνόδους συμπάσας ἐφ' ἱερὰ καὶ θυσίας προεῖπε μηκέτε συντελεῖν, ἵνα μὴ βουλὰς ἀπορρήτους ποιῶνται περὶ καταλύσεως τῆς ἀρχῆς." Their practice of the votive franchise caused it.

tians Of course the result could be no other than to make them more secret. There is evidence that so long as they were unmolested they grew day by day more open and unsuspicious, although it appears that secrecy was the original Solonic design, following the mysteries and their ancient cult. Everything in those days was veiled mystery. It permeated the official organism of society throughout the world.

When the unions saw danger they drew back under their veil of darkness and secrecy. But they did not die. Nor did they, as Dionysius thinks, cease to exist on account of this attack of Tarquin. We are recounting unknown horrors of the conditions which prevailed against the working classes, beginning with the decrees of war of the Roman conquests, and in full vogue when Christianity began its sway. If any calm, thoughtful reader so desires, he may perceive in the contemplation of such a régime of affairs of the expatriated majority, two distinct points: the cause of that strange longing after the good old times under the reign of Saturn,[21] and the suppressed but widespread agitation for a plan of salvation. Darkly among themselves, Jew and Gentile, men and women, were meeting in their secret, forbidden scholæ or schools of discussion, all over the known world.[22] Their clubs of socialism, enormously peopled with Hebrews and Aryans alike, whose cause at that time was common, they being all brothers and sisters, met in one club-house, often underground, trembling with fear of a wolfish Roman spy. We may here quote the words of the good and much calumniated Seneca,[23] against whom,

[21] See *supra*, p. 47, note, on the *Reign of Saturn;* so also *supra*, pp. 49 sqq.
[22] De Rossi, *Roma Sotterranea*, Vol. I., gives a full account, so far as is known of these *scholæ*. Some of them were cells from fifteen to seventy steps under ground. We know their shape, of what materials they were built and to what purpose they were applied, and shall in later chapters elaborately follow De Rossi, Waltzing and other savants in bringing these wonders to the light.
[23] Seneca, *De Ira*, III., 3, 6: "Eculei, et fidiculæ et ergastula, et carceres et circumdati defossis corporibus ignes et cadavera quoque trahens uncus, varia vinculorum genera, varia pœnarum, lacerationes membrorum, inscriptiones frontis, et bestiariorum immanium caveæ." So again, Galen, the celebrated physician and surgeon who is now known to have written about Jesus Christ, notes in the line of his profession, his displeasure: " Λακτίζουσι καὶ τοὺς ὀφθαλμοὺς ἐξορύττουσι καὶ γραφείῳ κεντοῦσιν, κ. τ. λ. The laws permitting such cruelties were afterwards mollified under the influence of the Christians. See Wallon, *Röm. Alterthum*, III., p. 60. Making slaves and freedmen fight with serpents was stopped by the Petronii, *Dig.*, XLVIII., viii. Even Claudius forbade turning them into the streets to die. Dion Cass., LX., 29; Suet., *Claud.*, 25.

great and morally pure as he was, encyclopedias are using untenable invectives, perhaps because he attempted to reform Nero and his satelites and was martyred in consequence. Among the many truthful things he dared to write during those dangerous days was a detail of the horrors the poor were subjected to. Speaking of the kinds of punishment inflicted upon them, he mentions the ropes used for strangling, the horse-shaped rack, the underground workshops, the cross, and the manner of herding them into a pit, surrounded by earthwork on the rim of which, all around, they built fires of torture to blister and consume their naked bodies. In the same ghastly description Seneca pictures the method among the tyrants, of stripping these creatures and with a huge iron hook called the uncus, grabbing their bodies by the flesh, and dragging them on a run to the Tiber where they found their welcome repose beneath the waves.

All the people who fell victims in the Roman conquests as war slaves were branded, mostly by having indelible stains burned into their bodies and even, as Seneca tells us, on their foreheads. As a further example of the conditions, we may mention some laws which were afterwards transferred to the Corpus Juris Civilis, and in this manner preserved. One of these laws prescribes that workingmen must not hope to ever become higher or better in the social scale.[24] The optimates, on account of the sacredness of the aged plan of Solon, which was believed to be protected, if not created by gods and goddesses favoring labor and its fruits, dared not enact laws for its suppression until Julius Cæsar's time,

[24] The laws specify the tradesmen they apply to. For instance, in the *Codex Justinianus*, liber XI., *tit.* vii., 1, *De Murilegulis, et Gynæciariis, et Procuratoribus Gynæcii et de monetariis, et Bastagariis.* Their condition was absolutely helpless. "Monetarios in sua semper conditione durare oportet; nec dignitatis cujuscunque privilegio ab hujusmodi conditione liberari." But the same law applied to the dyers, the bakers and artisans of many other trades. The appreciation of Cicero, of the value of those who fed him is shown in his *De Officiis*, I., 42: "Illiberales et Sordidi quæstus mercenariorum, omnium quorum operæ, non quorum artes emuntur. Est enim in illis ipsa merces auctoramentum servitutis. Sordidi etiam putandi, qui mercantur a mercatoribus quod statim vendant. Nec enim quidquam ingenuum potest habere officina." Nothing noble can germinate in a mere shop! This is all the world can expect from Cicero. What of Archimides, Ericcson, Watt, Edison? As late as Seneca's time this taint continued: "Vilisimorum mancipiorum ista commenta sunt: Sapientia altius sedet, nec manus edocet animorum magistra est . . . . . Non est inguam, instrumentorum ad usus necessarios opifex." *Epist. ad Lucam,* believed to have been written to Saint Luke.

but they were mean enough to enact laws that would torment the poor people. One of these pusilanimous laws recorded in the Justinian Code, aimed at the voting dyers and members of the old fraternity called the *gynæciarii* who, during the republic and also the empire, had their shops of manufacture in the back rooms, cellars and nooks of the palaces of the rich, and manufactured all sorts of household materials. Of these we shall soon speak more fully. This cruel statute brims with peevishness and petty meanness.[25] According to it, the dyehouse and gynæceum where goods used by the nobility were manufactured and repaired, if found to turn out articles stained with spots, or when sometimes too much water was used, or negligence in their doing up was discernable by the overseer, were "blemished;" and the carelessness regarded as a capital offense. The poor criminal was, under this law, condemned to have his head struck off by one of the swordsmen who stood ready at all times to consummate such deeds.

Nor were these indignities and dangers confined to the strictly Roman realm. About this time the celebrated atimia was going on at Athens.[26] The wars of the conquests were even then raging; although at so early a period they had not yet entered Athens, yet it was their influence, and by this we mean the calamitous and baleful influence of the money power, goaded onward by the ambition of contestants for office. Men perceived the genius that was struggling under the veil of the Solonic organizations, and having also the knowledge that its innumerable members were as intelligent and as inherently noble as they themselves, might with the aid of their common table and communal code, grow into a power that would overthrow them. Let any one imag-

[25] *Cod. Just*, XI., vii., 2: "Baphii, et gynæcii, per quos, et privata nostra substantia tenuatur, et species gynæcii confectae corrumpuntur, in baphiis etiam admixta temeratio naevum adducit inquinatae alluvionis: suffragiis abstineant, per quae memoratas administrationes adipiscuntur: vel si contra hoc fecerint, gladio feriantur."

[26] For the different grades of ἀτιμία, refer to Hermann, *Pol. Antiquities*, p. 124, Oxford; also Schömann, *Asssmblies of the Athenians*, p. 67, of the Cambridge Ed. 1838, where he gives the first rank as that when a man is so completely an outlaw that any person may kill him with impunity. Fortunately for such wretches the trivial offense for which they were adjudged to this malediction was not considered the crime it was heralded to be in the open law; and the union to which the wretch belonged was powerful enough to spirit him away to some far off place of safety. The curse of the ἀτιμία applied mostly to the lowly class who were without religion or property.

ine the terrors of a man or woman outlawed, the forehead indelibly branded with the deadly word "Atimia," forever an outlaw to whom no friend but death could bring relief!

The workingman of those days was the "*sola atque unica virtus*," and might mount to the true state of nobility to which he is now rapidly rising.[27] Another and very great danger to which the worker organized under the Solonic dispensation was exposed, was the fact that his religion was a quite different thing from that of the proud official religion, and gave offense. Lactantius recounts the prevalent dangers to the common people on account of this. They were often seized, taken out to some precipice, thrown down the abyss and immolated to the heathen gods they scorned.[28] If Adam Smith found the working man the true nobility which creates the wealth of nations,[29] then the passage of Juvenal, regarding true nobility applies to them and not to those who will not work but who get their subsistance through a species of legalized brigandage, taking it all from the products of human toil which they themselves disdain to contribute. In those days the military power and the rich whom it protected could override and murder off the very class that furnished them every spoonful of food they consumed; and could pretend that the furnishers of this food, without which they must starve, were so mean that they deserved to be cast into pits, or thrown to wild animals. It is rapidly getting to be understood that such ingratitude is in reality no better than brigandage. The close of the conquests found an organized host of these earn-nothings plundering and enriching themselves upon the products of labor. Pliny informs us that half of the rich African province belonged to six persons. They had robbed the legitimate, useful grades

[27] Juvenal, *Sat.* VIII.
[28] Lactantius, *Div. Inst.*, I. He virtually admits that it was mostly the poor who thus suffered, as human sacrifices. The celebrated rock of Taygetus where babes and malborn unfortunates, used in times of Lycurgus to be cast down, to be destroyed, was in later times again used wherefrom to immolate the ancient lowly to the hideous gods of the official cult. Θυρίδες was a steep projecting crag near Taenarus, now Cape Grosso. In p. 360, Strabo likewise speaks of it.
[29] Smith, *Wealth of Nations*, Book I., Chap. v., p. 15: "Labor alone, therefore, never varying in its own value is alone, the ultimate and real standard by which the value of all commodities can at all times and places be estimated and compared."

of humanity and in a ferocious and relentless manner despoiled them of their well-earned returns.[30] The time is coming when such pillagers are to be measured according to their merit and relegated to the class of criminals.

Again, there were a considerable number of pre-Christian martyrs. Martyrdom was not begun by Christianity. We shall have an interesting list of them in a succeeding chapter. Their crime in almost every case is traceable to petulent jealousy of the aristocrats who imagined they saw in the teachings of good men like Socrates, or beautiful women like Phryne, some fault which infringed upon a narrow law of the aristocracy. Socrates had taught the Athenian youth some of the immoralities and cruelties of the official and already moribund religion, which in fact, soon afterwards died. The beautiful and intelligent mother of the orator Æschines was assailed by Demosthenes, because she was the organizer of a union of the eranos which Solon's law created. Persecutions were going on everywhere just before the Christians began their work. But the action which the rich and ruling class most deprecated was that of voting. This they hated and tried to suppress, well knowing that true, honest political action of the unions would sooner or later compass their own overthrow. Every imaginable conspiracy law which they could enact and carry out against this powerful voting propensity was vigorously tried.

There are yet in this chapter two important circumstances to be briefly recorded. They are the persecutions of the Jews in the time of the Maccabees, some 175 to 140 years before Christ; and their persecution and almost utter destruction at Jerusalem, under Titus, in the reign of the emperor Vespasian.

Of these the bare circumstances are given by historians; but the deep and fundamental causes are passed

---

[30] *Nat. Hist.*, XVIII., 25, ed. Sillig, and in book vii., 35, he further says: "Africa vero toto subacta et in deditione redacta. Magnoque nomine spolio inde capto, eques Romanus (id quod antea nemo) curru triumphali revectus est, ac statim ad solis occasum transgressus." etc; and a recent author, Dr. Anton Menger, *Recht auf den vollen Arbeitsertrag*, p. 108, says: "Niemals waren die Leiden der arbeitenden Klassen grösser als in der Zeit, wo fast jeder produktive Arbeiter ein Sklave war. Es fehlte damals auch nicht, an heftigen Kritiken des bestehenden Gesellschaftszustandes, die sich mit den besten sozialistischen Schriften der Gegenwart messen können;" and refers to Villegardelle's *Hist. des Idées Sociales*, p. 50.

over without mention. The fact is that the Jews, under the Mosaic dispensation, which was already approaching pure socialism, were set upon by the great money power and its retinue of kings, their nobility and the armies they swayed for power and protection. On this point the Jews were the wisest of people, and for this they were singled out as the target of outlawry to be cruelly exterminated. In the case of the Maccabees it seems to have been Semitic against Semitic. But in reality the Romans had their emissaries at Antioch in goodly numbers, working their influence against the Jews who swarmed with self-help organizations at that great and celebrated city. Large numbers of them were organized under the Solonic law, and combined the practical Solonic with the theoretical Mosaic law, in a harmonious blending. According to these dispensations it was the duty of every organization to protect its members and furnish them means of support and happiness. This conflicted with the pagan plan of money-getting, one of whose richest driblet-sources was the sacrifices. The Jews and the Solonic organizations were so economical that they contributed their little earnings to a common fund, preserved by a well-chosen treasurer, and at intervals they bought in provisions for the regular membership's supplies. Then all the members of each club or congregation or thiasos, appointed cooks, waiters, managers and other working forces, to prepare the meals.[31] They always provided themselves with a large dining room, utensils of cookery and the best eatables and drinkables their small means could buy, and this economy was always husbanded with vigilant discretion. A very small sum of

[31] Many recently discovered stones bear records of the amount and character of their dues or cotisations. No almsgiving and taking was allowed. Harpocration, *Lexicon*, in *verb*. Ἐρανιστής; "Μέντοι κυρίως ἐστὶν ὁ τοῦ ἐράνου μετέχων καὶ τὴν φορὰν ἣν ἑκάστου μηνὸς ἔδει καταβαλεῖν εἰσφέρων." According to this the members of an eranos paid their contributions compulsorily once a month. See Foucart, *Ass. Rel.*, pp. 42-43. The law of Solon provided for a treasurer or keeper of the funds. In nearly all the Greek inscriptions this officer is called ταμίας: Liddell, in *verb*, ταμίας. He was steward, receiver, comptroller, treasurer, as early as Herodotus. Sometimes he is called ἐπιμελητής: trustee in charge of the values. His responsibilities were great. It was a disgrace of a henious sort to appropriate or mismanage these funds inpouring from dues, fines and initiations. There is a story of Judas Iscariot, that he was the regular ταμίας of the earliest Christian brotherhood and that he protested against the use of the costly alabaster to anoint the feet of the κύριος with well-known results; and his fate for fidelity caused the formation of the society of Cainites. The Cainites remained as an organization for about two centuries and were treated as heretics. Practical eranists, they believed that Judas did right.

earnings paid in by each was sufficient to furnish abundance, always fresh and steaming at the common tables.
This common table was a mortal offense against the money power. By it the speculating market rings were at an end. Provision gamblers and intermediaries were impossible. The congregation bought supplies in gross, directly from the producer with ready money formed of the driblets from each member, flowing into the common fund. It was economic socialism.

Another offense against the money-power was the official application of this same principle—the religious incomes which before fell to the profit of the state. It was the so-called sacrifices. An inside dark lantern illumes a system of purveying robbery here, which still prevails, though the question of the ancient sacrifices is little understood and difficult to explain. It was in reality, a mixture of religion, politics and economics. A careful survey has recently revealed the fact that the cause of the great persecutions of the Christians under the emperors was more economic than religious.

The sacrifices consisted of calves, goats, sheep, oxen, heifers, sometimes choice fish and fowls, and also many lambs. The priests of the official pagan religion were themselves state officers, sometimes hereditary, and for life. The scheme was to buy up quite a number of these animals at wholesale price, or receive them as gifts. At the regular meetings, on sacred days of worship, attendance of the masses of the populace was compulsory. High prices were paid for the entertainments, and the money accruing went to the treasury of the state. This will all be explained in another chapter. If, then, on account of any heresy or rebellion in the official faith, the people refused to attend sacrifices, there was a falling off of the regular receipts of the treasury. This is why stringent laws were enacted making non-attendance a capital offense. The Jews had a religion of their own in the Mosaic dispensation, just as the pre-Christian-Christians and later the post-Christian-Christians under the Solonic dispensation, had a plan of worship of their own.

Now it was a matter of course, after the conquests began to rage in favor of paganism and its concomitant competitive system and their money and property

THE MACCABEES. 137

power, that a hatred should exist against both the Mosaic and Solonic dispensations. To worship according to the God of the Hebrews was a mortal offense against Jupiter or Jove, the immortal of the aristocracy, who drove Saturn from his temple of peace, opened the gates of Janus and loosened the dæmon of war, causing the Roman conquests to ruin the peaceful nations of the world.

Few have been able to understand the reasons for the hatred against the Jews. The truth is they were socialists. The Aryans were rank individualists. That was enough. The whole competitive world took oath to destroy the Hebrews. The conflict with the Maccabees was the consequence; and we propose to briefly relate it in order to prepare the reader for a clearer understanding of what came next, in shape of a rebellion ultimating in the overthrow of paganism and a preparatory step toward the forthcoming socialism which is now making its appearance as a science. It is an interesting episode of true history.

About the year B. C. 175, which was in the vortex of Roman conquests, Rome had her bribing emissaries in Antioch, Pergamus, Jerusalem, Ephesus, and most of the cities of Western Asia, and was working every possible intrigue to secure power and control.[32] Frequently, as at Pergamos, this was accomplished without a war. She was in the same manner secretly working her influence over the large and at that time beautiful city of Antioch. The king, Antiochus Epiphanes, thought he perceived some dreadful wrong in the prevalence of so many Jews who inhabited the city, and were conducting important industries there. This potentate began to hector and torment the Jews.

There was a man in Jerusalem, which was only about 300 miles southward from Antioch in a straight coast line, named Mattathias. He was a personage of much influence who had five sons.[33] These took oath, on the

---

[32] For an account of Rome's influence in Asia Minor, see I., chap. x., pp. 232-245. These Roman politicians worked so strong an influence over the weak Attalus, that when he died he willed his crown and state to the Romans which caused the rebellion of Aristonicus, recounted in that chapter.
[33] They were, according to the first *Book of Maccabees*, chapter ii., 1-4: "Joannan called Caddis; Simon, called Thassi; Judas, who was called Maccabeus; Eleazar, called Avaran, and Jonathan whose surname was Apphus." Just before this, Antiochus had invaded Jerusalem and virtually sacked it of its celebrated religious treasures.

death of their father Mattathias, never to surrender their Hebrew nationality. They agreed with one another and with the people to resist the Syrian incursions, and organized every musterable element to be had in all Judea, armed them as best they could and when Lysias the commander, sent by Antiochus against them, entered Judea, with about 60,000 troops Judas Maccabeus ambushed and outwitted him and drove him back, after killing about 4,000 of his men.

The next year Antiochus sent Lysias in person to Palestine, with 65,000 soldiers, some 5,000 of whom were his best cavalry. Josephus tells the story which corroborates the statement and Bible account of the Book of Maccabees.[34] The Syrian general was again outwitted by the strategic genius of Judas, a very high order of which he certainly possessed. The battle resulted in so overwhelming a crush of the Syrians that those not killed or taken prisoners escaped by flight and could not be mustered back, leaving the Jews complete masters of their beloved country, its cities, institutions and cherished traditions. Later, Jonathan, another son, carried the conquest to Antioch itself, and caused a destruction of 100,000 people.

We need but a clear philosophical vision to perceive that the animus inspiring the Syrians against the Jews was the same as that which inspired the Romans against the Solonic dispensation. There is positive and powerful evidence that in this attack on the Hebrews, the deadliest sentiment was against the "Law," and this was none other than the semi-socialistic Mosaic Dispensation.[35]

A short time before the rebellion of the Maccabees which we have just recounted, the Syrian king had taken Jerusalem with a mighty force and reduced the inhabitants to a pitiable condition and the first Book

---

[34] Josephus, *Antiquities of the Jews*, XII., c. vii., 53–5. According to Josephus, the Syrian army at the first battle was something about 60,000 strong; but that of Judas, not so great, probably about 13,000. In the next year's battle Lysias had 65,000 and Judas 10,000. Yet in both cases the victory of the Jews was complete. The last battle was fought at or near Bethsur, in Judea; that of the year before was fought at Emaus, in the north of Palestine, near the southern border of Syria.

[35] *Book of Maccabees*, I., 56: "And when they had rent in pieces the books of the law which they found, they burnt them with fire." Again, verse 57; "And wheresoever was found with any, the book of the Testament or if any consented to the law, the king's commandment was they should put him to death."

STRUGGLES TO MAINTAIN THE LAW. 139

of Maccabees in consequence begins with a wail.[36] The gigantic effort during the long centuries, to break up and destroy its organizations, even though they destroyed millions of the human race, was here manifest. What was determined upon was the extinction of social organization. It is high time to consider this momentous, but neglected truth, and at last get down to history. It was the hatred against the socialists, entertained by the competitive system. And in succeeding chapters we shall easily prove that they had a cause; for at the rate in which pure scientific socialism at that moment was growing in the correct and permanent form, the millenium would long before this have arrived on earth. The enemy took a drastic method of suppression.

The Syrians not being able to destroy the Mosaic dispensation, it was again in course of years, undertaken by the Romans. But the same animus inspired Rome which impelled Antiochus, to compass its destruction. The congregation mentioned as a potent factor[37] in those days now looks like one of the various forms of club organizations which we find among the inscriptions of the economic unions of the Solonic dispensation. The strange mention of the Nazarenes as existing at least a century and a half before the birth of Christ is certainly a worthy subject for investigation.[38]

Another fatal attack upon Jerusalem was made in A. D. 70, by the Romans under Titus. The history of this massacre, the bloodiest of the world's narratives,

---

[36] I., *verse* 51: "In the self-same manner wrote he (king Antiochus) to his whole kingdom, and appointed overseers over all the people, commanding the cities of Judea to sacrifice, city by city." And again, verses showing that the king sold the people into slavery as was done everywhere: *verse* ii, of chapter ii., reads: "And all her ointments are taken away; of the free woman she has become a slave." speaking figuratively of Jerusalem.

[37] I., *Maccabees*, chap. iii., *verse* 44; and *id.*, *verse* 49, when the Nazarites are mentioned showing them to have been an old and familiar organization. All Judea swarmed with these clubs of trades and professions. We shall show a considerable number of congregations in our future presentation of the inscriptions.

[38] I. *Maccabees*, iii., 49; "They brought also the priests' garments, and the first fruits, and tithes; and the Nazarites they stirred up," etc: This entirely agrees with Renan, who thinks that the Nazarites were a pre-Christian organization of some kind; but as this scholar had never got down to the Solonic law of economic labor organization he was unable to trace this strange club union to Nazareth or to understand that Jesus was afterwards a member and so remained during his lifetime. It was one of the innumerable progressive secret associations of those days which existed in all parts of the world.

has been accurately written out by Josephus, Tacitus and the modern authors;[39] but the animus which inspired the horrible work has been neglected both by historians and the schools of classics. Some day it will be traced to its real source—the hatred of the competitive system against socialism inherent in the old Mosaic law and dispensation. It may be somewhat true that the Jews were in a state of ferment at the time, and it cannot be denied that they were incensed at the revolt against them, of the Christian element based upon the other organic dispensation of Solon. Rome had been fighting this for centuries, and Nero swore to uproot both. Josephus distinctly informs us that the Romans made cause against the Jews on account of their murder of James the Just whom he distinctly calls the brother of Jesus. Besides, the remains of certain correspondence between Rome and king Abgar of Edessa show that a strong pretext was made out against Jerusalem based upon their treatment of Christ, who, as he claimed, had been illegally executed by Pontius Pilate. The letters of Abgar to the emperor Tiberius on the subject are history, and are as worthy of credence as the Annals of Tacitus, or the Apologies of Tertullian. In our dissertation on the evidence of Jesus as a historical personage we give all these letters verbatim with a list of splendid classic scholiasts who have contributed their unqualified sanction to their authenticity.

We may now briefly sketch the ferocious massacre of the inhabitants of the great city of Jerusalem by Titus, under his father the Roman emperor Vespasian, in the year 70–71 of our era. We leave the full account of this atrocity to Josephus, who was present and commanded troops in that conflict, and to Tacitus and other historians who confirm the account of Josephus. It appears that the Romans commenced them by a system of insupportable nagging. They knew of the pride and spirited texture of Hebrew nature. They understood its physical composition. By a scheme of goading insults, adopted as their tactics of initial assault, they expected to wrench from that proud spirit some casus prœlii leading to the cause for an attack. This scheme worked.

[39] Renan, *Life of Jesus*, Eng. *trans*, p. 309.

HORRIBLE BUTCHERY AT JERUSALEM. 141

The Hebrews were both obstinate and irascible and could not but resent even a diplomatic insult.

Ernest Renan has truthfully told us that the causes which 37 years after the crucifixion lead to the destruction of Jerusalem did not lie in infant Christianity. This is the more correct, if we speak of Christianity as it is to-day, stripped of its original socialism. But from a point of view taken by Josephus it is the reverse; for he declares expressly, and more than once, that the city was destroyed as a punishment for their terrible murder of James the Just,[40] whom he terms, in unmistakable words, the brother of Jesus, the man to whom was given the direction of the organizations of primitive socialists for whose common table and socialistic meals the proto-martyr Stephen, was stoned to death.[41] The prætorians wriggled into a pretext for bringing their murderous legions against them, and the rage began.

The Roman commander in this massacre was Titus, the youngest son of Vespasian, and brother of the cruel Domitian who afterwards became emperor. The celebrated feast of the Passover occurred annually at Jerusalem and on such occasions a large multitude was wont to gather comprising all the inhabitants, not only of the city but of the villages and country for a long distance in every direction. It was the wily scheme of the Romans to linger about with their army fully equipped, with all the necessaries for a blockade and siege. They had battering rams to knock down walls and gates in case they were closed against them. After forcing a passage into the city they commenced a systematic slaughter. It could not be dignified with the title of battle. It was more the criminal work of fiends let loose. Men, women and children were indiscriminately butchered wherever found. The Romans after forcing an entrance within the walls, guarded the breach to prevent any one from escaping. With sword and bludgeon or spear these inhuman savages ran

---

[40] The martyrdom of Κυριος 'Ιάκωβος will be elaborated in later pages.
[41] Josephus, *Antiquities*, XX., chap. ix., par. 1: "Καθίζει συνέδριον κριτῶν καὶ συνέδριον κριτῶν καὶ παραγαγὼν εἰς αὐτῶ (speaking of τὸν ἀδελφὸν 'Ιησοῦ) τοῦ λεγομένου Χριστοῦ, 'Ιάκοβος ὄνομα αὐτῷ, καὶ τινας ἐτέρους ὡς παρανομησάντων κατηγορίαν ποιησαμένους παρέδωκε λευσθησομένους ὅσοι δὲ ἐδοκοῦν ἐπιεικέστατοι τῶν κατὰ τὴν πόλιν εἶναι, καὶ τὰ περὶ τοὺς νόμους ἀκριβεῖς, 3αρέως ἤνεγκαν ἐπὶ τούτῳ." Very important! Restored by the honest and learned Neander, from the *editio princeps* of Josephus, after being expunged by Credner. Neand., *Planting*, Book IV., chap. 1, vol. 1 of Bohn's, p. 367, note.

through the streets, forced open the houses, smashed the doors leading from room to room and pillaged and murdered as they went. Not a human being was allowed to remain alive. All were slaughtered.

The details of this stupendous atrocity as told by Josephus, Tacitus and others, challenge our powers of credence. The dead lay as they fell, in windrows, throughout the city. No other massacre is on record of such gigantic proportions. The number of the killed appear in the pages of two different authors under two very different estimates. Josephus writes it down as 1,100,000, while Tacitus gives it as 600,000.[42] The probability that both are correct, we may state, upon a twofold basis of calculation. Tacitus, knowing the census tables of Jerusalem, very naturally places the massacre at 600,000; that being about the figure of the Roman census enumeration; and Tacitus knew that all or nearly all were killed. This would make the statement of the much prized historian tolerably correct. Josephus, however, has gaged his estimate from the number of people within the walls of Jerusalem at the time of the national feast of the passover, when the city was teeming with visitors in great numbers from far and near. The hideous admission alike for Tacitus and for Josephus is, that all were exterminated during the protracted and sanguinary fury. In this way Josephus could truthfully put the holocaust at 500,000 more than Tacitus, who with his usual accuracy, estimates only the population of Jerusalem. We can cite the sack of no city which was fraught with such shocking barbarity or rose to such numeric proportions, in the annals of the human race. And for what? Where lies the consistency which can parry the crime? The only answer is that it is logically consistent with the animus which drove Rome into her internecine conquests; thoroughly consistent with the reckless inhumanity which, from Appius Claudius, had been killing off the human race: —jealousy, competitive emulation, narrow hatred and a contemptible fear lest some imaginary rival take the pretentions of divine right from a hypothecated claim to blood and nobility and the wealth which was always a substance taken from unpaid labor. It is high time

---

[42] Josephus, *Wars of the Jews*, VI., ix., 3. Tacitus, *Histories*. 2, 4, 5, 9, 11.

the mind of men rise to understand the caustic advice of Lactantius, that as long as the hope of impunity favors us we should plunder and put to death,[43] a sarcasm as good to-day for the science of survival of the fittest as it was then to soothe the stings of a conscience reddened with the blood of humanity during the conquests of Rome.

There is just one short notice to make, before closing this chapter on grievances. It is that regarding the losses it entailed, many of which were irrecoverable, in the line of invention, manufacture and commerce. Just in proportion as those military ravages, systematic in nothing but carnage which decimated and robbed the race[44] were successful as engines of power to overturn a growing civilization, in that proportion were the inventions lost. It was just at that period when organized mechanics were actually inventing Aristotle's machines. Karl Marx contrasts the noble purposes and ideals animating ancient society with the lust of cruelty which capitalism breeds:

" 'If,' dreamed Aristotle, the greatest thinker of antiquity, 'if every tool, when summoned, or even of its own accord, could do the work that befits it just as the creations of Daedalus moved of themselves, or the tripods of Hephaestos went of their own accord; if the weavers' shuttles were to weave of themselves, then there would be no need either of apprentices for the master workers, or slaves for the lords.' "[45]

We have spoken of the Damascus blades, and shown that the raw steel came from India. They are so completely lost that our critical scientists are unable to find out the ancient method of their production. The skilled workmen had so far outstripped us, with all our mechanical advancement, that we cannot find the way to produce either the beautiful hues which variegated those steels and other blades of cutlery, or the temper

[43] *Divine Inst.*, III., c. 17, It was his sarcasm against those who were skeptical on immortality, but it applies here,
[44] Plutarch, *De Oraculorum Defectu*. Plutarch here admits that in his day Greece was depopulated. Consult Wallace, *Numbers of Mankind*, pp. 253-4.
[45] We have already quoted Aristotle's remarkable prediction in full; see *Supra*, p. 94, note 8. Consult Mauri, *I, Cittadini Lavoratori* p. 19, who says Aristotle's idea was thought ridiculous: "Presso i Greci invece le macchine e i motori erano sconosciuti; essi confinavano nel mondo fantastico e ridente dei sogni l' ipotesi di Aristotili, che lo strumento di lavoro potesse eseguire, presentendolo, il comando dell' operaio, e la spola corresse sulla trama del tessuto automaticamente." Aristotle, Πολιτεία, I., ii., 4.

by which one could double and redouble, and toy with them at pleasure, after which contortions they would spring back with marvelous beauty to the straight line. Wonderful hues sometimes in fantastic images characterized those blades. They cannot be reproduced. The art with the artists, was extinguished. Karsten Niebuhr and the Russian military analyst and scientist Anassoff,[46] vainly tried to find a method of their production. But the Indian and Greek mechanics were beyond them in their exquisite science and we are left behind, without a trace of the secret whereby those mechanical feats were wrought.

Again, they possessed the secret of producing inks which were never-fading. The invention reached down to the middle ages, or perhaps it were better to state that the store or stock of these indelibles lasted until the middle ages; for we find in the block prints and even in type printing an occasional book which is today as pure black and beautiful as though just done.

Of the lost reaping and mowing machines, we have already given an account.[47] It remains to be said that the senseless and bloody ravages of Julius Cæsar in the fair land of Gaul, now France, estimated to have compassed the destruction of a million human beings without fulfilling one benificent purpose or accomplishing anything but to glut ambition and stuff Rome with slaves and plunder, resulted in the final extinction of this agricultural arm. Several of the finest dyes and pigments ever possessed by the world have been lost to us in the same way. Imperishable brick and other building material were likewise lost in the same great vortex of death and desolation.

But amid the havoc of arms and the rasping besom of vengeance and rapine, one thing, be it truthfully recorded, they could not accomplish—the very thing in fact which whetted the animus of the Roman optimists, inspiring them to undertake the whole swoop of bedlam and obliteration—and that thing was the extinction of the unions under the Solonic and Numan dispensations. They could not kill trade unions nor even

[46] See *Amer. Cyc.* art. *Damascus Blades*, where it is recounted how an effort was made to analyze and restore the secret.
[47] See Vol, I., p. 569, note 109, quoting both accounts from the Latin of Pliny and Palladius.

INVENTIONS IRREDEEMABLY LOST. 145

change their voting system. By persecution, murder, and enslavement of the members and innumerable other tortures they could for a time reduce their effective force; they could drive them back into undiscernable recesses which served to hide them[48] for centuries from view; but they remained, and their influence likewise remained. It is now at last discovered that the Christians came and found the Solonic trade union principles so pure and so similar in many things to their own that they planted among and amalgamated with them. As the two were secret, and alike hated by the optimates they used each other co-operatively to shield themselves against that power and in course of time succeeded and came out of the secret chrysalis to become the foundation of a vast socialism now with all its coarseness, growing year by year into perfection.

The wonderful thing about them was the immovable solidity of the ancient law which fortified their existence. An inscription assures us that the government of Byzantium once confiscated some property of an eranos. The union brought suit and the state was obliged to make good the loss and pay dearly.[49] This one law covered the universe We give all information as yet in our possession regarding it, in our next chapter.

---

[48]De Rossi, *Roma Sotteranea*, has by a lifetime of labor unearthed the whole method of the *scholæ* which were often underground holes, sometimes grottoes and in the cities' cellars, always furnished with seats of a peculiar fashion serving as miniature amphitheatres where the unionists used to gather, take their common meal and listen to discourses on the way out of misery from living death, to salvation through their later faith.

[49] C I G. 2323; Caillemer, *Droit de Société à Athènes*, p. 11, demonstrates that they had no need of any authorization from the state; since they possessed a full autonomy of their own; and cites *The Fourth Book of Gaius*, on the *Law* of the *Twelve Tables*, in the *Digest*, XLVII., tit. 22, *De Collegiis et Corporibus* which he quotes in proof, showing that the ancient law of Solon was more powerful, more respected and revered than any statute which could be enacted at Athens, or indeed anywhere else in the world. For the text, see *Supra*, p. 48, note 3; for inscriptional references, consult our index in *verb. Laws.*

CHAPTER VIII.
PRE-CHRISTIAN UNIONS
NUMBERS, CHARACTER AND INFLUENCE.

ASIA the Home of Trade Organizations—Plato went with Socrates to One for the Material of His Republic—Socrates a member—Always Law Abiding—Union of Washerwomen 600 Before Christ—Typical Name Erano-Thiasos, Good for all Terms—Always had Votive Franchise—Inscriptions in Proof—Ancient Eranos resembled Modern Socialistic Trade and Labor Alliance—These are the Oldest Unions on Record—Love for One Another a Command of the Law—Common Table and Communal Code—Brotherly Love Stretched into the Hereafter—Burial Attachment Aided them—Rigid Examination of Candidates wishing to join—The Dokimasia—The Agnus Castus—Solonic and Christian Tenets identical—They made Slave, Freedman and Freeman Equal—Plodding Outcasts—How they loved such Tenets—Voting Unionism raised them above mere Tools of Labor—Sabazios, Their Soter becomes Saviour—Serapis—Tullus Hostilius a Friend—Bridge Builders—Name Originated the Pontificate—The Pontifix a Boss Bridge Builder—Tracing Trade Unions from the Sixth Century B.C.—Manner in which they Flourished—Shielded the Poor—Eranos Loaned Means to Slaves to Buy Themselves Free—No Starvation Within the Veil—The Great Gemeinde—Stretched over All Lands—Ancient International—Hebrew Eranos—Many Jews had the Solonic Instead of the Mosaic—Unions in the Islands—Therapeutæ and Essenes were Solonic—Nazarenes a Branch—Taint of Labor—Unions of Boatmen—Of Fishermen—Merchants in those Days as low as Artisans—Longshoremen—Shippers—No Strikes, because Interests were Common—Strange Pre-Christian *Anagenesis*, or New Birth—Union of Cutters near Nazereth—Multitudes at Tyre and Sidon—Knife and Dirk Makers—Union of Gardeners at Ephesus.

IT will naturally be asked what were these associations of the useful producing class among the ancient forefathers. The reader desires to know more of their numbers, character and principles, as well as the places they occupied.

In the first volume of this work we gave a racy and introductory statement of the facts concerning them.[1] But so enormous was the task that it was found impossible to attempt the survey of Asia Minor and the Semitic nations. Here was in fact, their home. Here it was that the true Solonic dispensation prevailed.

Very little is known of them outside of what is now being collected by archæologists researching among their inscriptions. But this is great. We find among the writings of men of letters of those times, an occasional mention of their existence. Plato, who in his Republic[2] begins the celebrated discussion by stating that they —meaning a certain small club, assuredly members of a thiasos—were parties regarded by him as most important, opens his celebrated work, the Eudæmonia, by going with Socrates down to the Piræus at the time when the eranos was holding an inauguration at the dedication of a new temple to Bendis, who, like Diana or Artemis, was called " Saviour," a daughter of Jove and Saturna, patroness of labor, and friend of the producing classes of mankind. Her father, the great Jupiter, was haughty and looked down upon laborers. She was a moon goddess, and patronized and befriended the huntsmen, agriculturists, skilled artisans and laborers. Thus, it is not a little surprising, after so long a time, to discover that the Republic of Plato was inspired and brought forth at a feast of workingmen. We have already shown that Socrates was a member; and judging from a close reading of the Republic, it becomes probable that this was one of the causes against him which not long afterwards compassed his tragic death.[3]

Although the writers say little regarding working people on account of the prevailing taint of labor, yet we find by inscriptions that they have a record of their own

[1] I., Chapters XIII., XIV., XV., XVI., XVII., XVIII., XIX., XX., XXI. These chapters relate mostly to the great trade unionism under the dispensation of Numa Pompilius, afterwards reinforced by Servius Tullius, another friend of the Roman workingmen. But they do not penetrate deeply into the Greek and Semitic unions which our second volume has charged itself to delineate.
[2] Plato, *Republic*, I., 1.
[3] Xenophon, *Convivii*, VIII., 2: " Παντες ἐσμεν τοῦ θεοῦ τούτου θιασῶται." See I., title page, and p. 553, with note, where the passage of Xenophon is quoted, and accompanied with the statement that the doctrines of Socrates were based on love, afterwards a Christian tenet.

which is reliable and old. The proofs that unions existed in the dim antiquity cannot be collected so as to make a historical train of events as we like to see them arranged in our modern times. We are consequently obliged to take up with fragmentary evidence such as is given in the inscriptions. For instance, we have pieces of stone upon which are words showing that the metal and stone workers and some of the builders had good organizations as early as the sixth century before Christ.[4] The discovery of engraved monuments carved at such an early age confirms the suspicion that there existed an enormous trade organization before the days of Numa and Solon, that they were peaceful and honest, and that the law of these sovereigns permitting organization came afterwards.

All along, from the highest dates we find the unions of trades to have had two objects as a basis of association. The first and evidently most important was that of mutual supports, and the other that of some sort of religious worship. The economical incentive was at the bottom of everything. This is clear. Six hundred years before Christ there were unions of poor washerwomen.[5] A union of washerwomen 600 years before Christ! The inscriptions show that it was to some deity; for every craft, in accordance with the early belief, had an imaginary god or goddess supposed to be looking after the interests of that special trade. Another stone slab is found at Athens, of a clothes-cleaners' union whose members likewise had an altar of consecration.

The general term designating these unions was eranos, and the functions[6] which accompany the term are spoken

[4] Oehler, *MS., Contributions to the Author*, No. 35, p. 17: "*Metall und Stein, Die Fabricate derselben wurden bereits im VI. Jahrhunderte vor Chr. aus Athen ausgeführt*: vgl. *Athen., Mittheilungen*, X., 1885, p. 156; aber ein Beweis für eine Genossenschaft in Athen noch nicht erbracht. Dagegen bestand eine solche auf Kos; dann eine συμβίωσις χαλκέων in Sigeion: CIG., 3639 und addenda; in Thyateira sind die Errichter einer Ehrenstatue die χαλκεῖς χαλκοτύποι: *Bulletin Héllénique*, X., 1886, p. 407, No. 10," But most probably the bronze referred to at Athens was manufactured by the organizations of Kos, Thyateira, etc.; or at least the rough material, as was done in India for the Damascus blades.

[5] Oehler, *MS.*, No. 16, *Contribution*, 2, p. 11: "GEWERBE. Inschriftlich ist bereits für das IV. Jahrh. v. Chr, die Genossenschaft der πλυνῆς in Athen bezeugt: CIA., II., 1327, vgl. Athen., *Mittheilung*, X., 1885, p. 77, wo eine Weihinschrift einer πλύντρια aus dem VI. Jarhh. v. Chr. mitgetheilt ist. Diesem Gewerbe nahe verwandt sind die γναφεῖς. In Athen kennen wir die Weihinschrift eines γναφεύς aus dem VI. Jahrh. v. Chr." This brings washerwomen and woolworkers' unions as early as B. C. 600; actually before Solon.

[6] Foucart, *Associations Religieuses*, p. 2; Aristotle, *Eth. Nicomachi*, **VIII.**, ix.. 7. ed. Didot; Van Holst, *De Eranis Veterum Græcorum*.

of in the earliest writings. It is spoken of by Homer, who evidently looked upon it as a little different from that assumed in later centuries. In Homer the word eranos designates a stipend paid into a common fund by a club of people, for eatables and wine at the common table, either at some special feast, or, as was more generally needful, for the poor, who worked every day and had to economize in their food by regular meals in common, such as were enormously in practice among the Greek-speaking people in all antiquity. Homer intimates that it was a part of the scheme, and approved and sanctified by the god or goddess, or whatever divinity, to have things thus enjoyed in common. But we shall come to these definitions more explicitly soon.

These associations conducted the community business, not only of eating and drinking at the common table, in fellowship with one another, but in solid business transactions; and they did it vigorously under established law.[7] They utilized the forces of their unions in exactly

THE LAW——PROOFS THAT IT WAS THE OLD STATUTE OF SOLON.
AS SHOWN IN THE FRAGMENTARY ALLUSIONS.

[7] We here give quotations as they appear in the workingmen's inscriptions, showing them all to be taken from the great original law preserved only in fragmentary form. Cf. Vol I., pp. 353-8, quoting law of the inscr. of Lanuvium, C I L., XII., No. 2112; Foucart, *Ass. Rel.*, p. 12, who also shows that this was so: " La loi des éranistes fut gravée sous les Antonins; mais elle ne fit probablement que reproduire." Now, the law is again mentioned on the stone of a θίασος, and again of an ἔρανος found at the Peirœus, *Revue Archéol.*, 1864, II, p. 399, lines 17-20: " . . . . . . γράψαντας ἐν πίνακι κατὰ τὸν νόμον, ὅπως ἂν εἶ πᾶσιν φανερὸν τοῖς βουλομένοις φιλοτιμεῖσθαι περὶ τὸ ἱερὸν ὃ τιμηθήσονται κατ' ἀξίαν," κ. τ. λ. Again, similar allusion to the great original law is seen in an inscription found at Amorgos cited by the learned Koumanoudis, in the Ἀρχαιολογικὴ 'Εφημερίς, New Series, No. 77, line 14: " . . . . κατὰ τὸν νόμον τῶν 'Ερανιστῶν." The law is referred to in an inscription of Rhodes, coronating or crowning a κυριος, C I G., 2525. It is in the museum of the Seminary of Venice; Lines 11-21, read: " . . . . . εὐεργετεῖν τὸν ἔρανον καὶ καλὰν ἀπόδειξιν ἐμ πᾶσι πεποιημένοις· τύχαι ἀγαθαι δεδόχθαι τῶν κοινῶν τῶν 'Αλιαδᾶν καὶ Ἁλιαστᾶν, κυρωθεισᾶν τῶν δε τῶν τιμῶν ἐπαινέσαι καὶ στεφανῶσαι Διονυσόδωρον 'Αλεξανδρῆ εὐεργέταν τοῦ κοινοῦ εἰς τὸ ἀεὶ χρόνον χρυσέων στεφάνων τῶν ἐκ τοῦ νόμου μεγίστων· καὶ ὁ γραμματεὺς ἀναγραψάτω τὰ δόξαντα," κ. τ. λ. C I L., Vol. vi., part 2, inscription no. 10, 234, page 1356.

THE LAW——AS SHOWN IN THE CELEBRATED ANDANIA STONE.

Corpus Inscriptionum Atticarum, Vol. III., No. 23, p. 16. We are indebted for accurate elucidations of this Law, to the remarks of the editor: "In prima parte lapidis perpauca sunt, quae intelligi possint: v. 7 ἀνδρὶ πόρεν initium ut videtur versus heroici, v. 9, νέον 16 χώρον θάρσυνεν ἄριστα? exitus hexametri, v. 19, καὶ μνήμην φθιμένοις καὶ ἀλλήλους ἀνέθηκαν, v. 20, ... ἐνιαύσιον ἐς χρόνον, ὅππως . . . . οντες ἔχοιεν . . . , v. 24-29 ἄρχων μὲν Ταυρίσκος, ἀτὰρ μὴν Μουνιχιὼν ἦν, ὀκτωκαιδεκάτῃ δ' ἔρανον σύναγον φίλοι ἄνδρες καὶ κοινῇ βουλῇ θεσμὸν φιλίης ὑπεγραψαν, v. 30-44, νόμος ἐρανιστῶν. Μηδενὶ ἐξέστω ἰσιέναι ἰς τὴν σεμνοτάτην σύνοδον τῶν ἐρανιστῶν, πρὶν ἂν δοκιμασθῇ, εἰ ἐστι ἀγνὸς καὶ εὐσεβὴς καὶ ἀγαθός. Δοκιμαζέτω δὲ ὁ προστάτης ἢ

SOCIALIST TRADE AND LABOR ALLIANCE. 151

the same manner as we do in these days. They were however infinitely superior to the modern conservative unions which refuse to coördinate themselves into a voting power; since they were voters, and according to many evidences of inscriptions and of the annals of historians, they formed themselves into what we, in these days call political parties and used all their power and influence toward electing to office the superintendents of public work, in order to secure for themselves the labor as a means of livelihood. They followed the great law of Solon, many allusions to which we here give in an elaborate note. The law itself is given on page 48.

ἀρχιερανιστὴς καὶ ὁ γραμματεὺς καὶ οἱ ταμίαι καὶ σύνδικοι· ἔστωσαν δὲ οὗτοι. κληρωτοὶ κατὰ ἔτος, χωρὶς εἴ τις προστάτης τὸ δεύτερον εἰς τὸν βίον αυτοῦ .... ἐπὶ ἐράνου καταλιφθείη. αὐξανέτω δὲ ὁ ἔρανου ἐπὶ φιλοτειμίαις· εἰ δέ τις μάχας ἢ θορύβους κεινῶν φαίνοιτο, ἐκβαλλέσθω τοῦ ἐράνου, ζημιοίμενος ταῖς διολαῖς.... κρίσεως.... ἡ πληγαῖς αἰκιζόμενος. v. 33, ἁγνός (ἅγιος Boeckh.), v. 44, αἰκιζόμενος ipse supplevi, cetera Boeckhii sunt, praeter v. 36-39, quos Keilius restituit."
Rangabé, *Antiquités Hélléniques*, Vol. II., No. 881, shows an eranos as having sued and procured judgment. The person who directed the prosecution is believed to have been the chief of the eranos. They were metics. Foucart, *Ass. Rel.*, p. 49, and note 2. Another such law process has been discovered. Rangabé's inscr., above cited, No. 881, reads. "Συνέτη ἐν Κειριάδων οἰκοῦσα, ἀποφυγοῦσα Νικόδημον Λευκονοέα καὶ κοινὸν ἐρανιστῶν, φιάλη σταθμον..... οἰκοῦσα ἀποφυγοῦσα, Here the epigraph becomes illegible. Foucart, *ibid.*, says of the same: "d'accord avec la loi de Solon."

THE LAW—AS SHOWN IN BURIAL UNION OF ÆSCULAPIUS-HYGIA.

I   LEX COLLEGI ÆSCULAPI ET HYGIAE
II   Salvia C. F. Marcellina Ob Memoriam Flavi Apolloni Procuratoris Au-
III gusti Qui Fuit A Pinacothecis, et Capitonis Aug. Liberti Adiutoris ejus
     Mariti sui optimi piissimi, donum dedit collegio Aesculapi et Hygiae
     locum aedicula cum pergula et signum Marmoreum Aesculapi et solar-
IV   ium tectum junctum, in quo populus Collegi Supra Scripti epuletur,
     quod est via Appia ad Martis intra milliarium I. et II. ab urbe euntibus
V   parte laeva inter adfines Vibium Calocaerum et populum. Item eadem
     Marcellina collegio Supra Scripto dedit donavitque sestertium quinquaginta Milia Numnium hominibus Numero sexaginta sub hac condicione, ut ne plures adlegantur quam numerus supra scriptus, et ut
VI   in locum defunctorum loco veniant et liberi adlegantur, vel si quis locum
     suum legare volet filia vel fratri vel liberto dumtaxat, ut inferat arkae
VII Nostrae partem demidiam funeratici, et ne eam pecuniam supra scriptam
     velint in alios usus convertere, sed ut ex usuris eius summae diebus
VIII infra scriptis locum confrequentarent. Ex reditu eius summae si quod
     comparaverint sportulas hominibus Numero LX ex decreto universorum
IX   quod gestum est in templo divorum in aede divi Titi con ventu pleno
     qui dies fuit V. idus Martias Bruttio Praesente et Junio Rufino consulibus uti XIII, Kalendas Octobres die felissimo Natali Antonini Augusti
X   Nostri Pii Patris patriae sportulas dividerent: in templo divorum in
     aede divi Titi c. Ofilio Hermeti quinquennali perpetno vel qui tunc erit
XI   X. III., Aelio Zenoni patri collegi X. III., Salviae Marcellinae matri collegi X. III., immunibus singulis X II. curatoribus sing. X II. populo,
     sing. X I. Item placuit pridie nonas Novembris Natali collegi dividerentex reditu supra scripta ad martis in scholam Nostram praesentibus quin-
XII quennali X VI., patri collegi X VI., matri collegi X VI , immunibus sing.
     X IIII., curatoribus sing. X IIII., panem assium III ; vinum mensuras
     quinquennali sextariorum novem, patri collegi I. immunibus sing. Sex
     curatoribus singulis Sex., populo sing. Sex. III. Item pridie nonas Jun-
XIII uarias strenuas dividerent, sicut supra scriptum est XIII. Kalendas O C

152   PRE-CHRISTIAN UNIONS.   THE LAW.

In this respect they were socialists of the manner sometimes designated the Socialistic Trade and Labor Alliance or socialistic new trade unionism. As a matter of fact, the new socialistic trade unionism is the oldest of all on record. The oldest trade unions were certainly the purest in the true philosophy and economy of scientific socialism.

Summing it all up, the inscriptional history, backed by the great law or jus coeundi of Solon, was leading the workers out and upward into Plato's highest civilization, his Eudæmonia, which was an enlightened political state wherein the workers rose from their miseries by political action through the ballot. The scheme was at first endorsed, with the wonderfully powerful movement of Jesus, but ferociously assaulted by the competitive system and finally suppressed, after a struggle of more than three hundred years.

Now, amid turbulent, disgraceful ambition of its own leaders who are catering to combinations of capital for the paltry emolument of their offerings, like the ancient fakirs, and in spite of their treachery which betrays the misled membership, the glorious Eudæmonia or state of the "Blessed" is gradually "reawaking," in the prophetic

Tobres. Item VIII. Kal. Martias die kare cognationis ad Martis eodem
XIV loco dividerent sportulas panem et vinum, sicut supra scriptum est pridie nonas Novembres. Item pridie idus Martias eodem loco cenam, quam Ofilius Hermes quinquennalis omnibus annis dandam praesentibus pro-
XV misit, vel sportulas, sicut solitus est dare. Item XI., Kal. Apriles die violari eodem loco praesentibus dividerentur sportulas vinu pane sicut diebus supra scriptis. Item V., idus Maias die rosae eodem loco prae-
XVI sentibus dividerentur sportulae vinu et pane sicut diebus supra scriptis, ea condicione qua in conventu placuit universis, ut diebus supra scriptis ii qui ad epulandum non convenissent, sportulae et pane et vinu eorum venirent et presentibus dividiretur excepto eorum qui trans mare erunt vel qui perpetua valetudine detinetur. Item P. Aeilus Augusti
XVII libertus Zenon eidem collegio supra scripto ob memoriam M. Ulpi Augusti liberti Capitonis fratris sui piissime dedit donavitque sestertium decem milia nummum, uti ex reditu eius summae in cortributione sportularum dividerentur. Quod si ae pecunia omnis, quae supra scripta est, quam dedit donavit collegio supra scripto Salvia C. F. Marcellina et P. Aelius Augusti libertus Zeno, in alios usus converterе voluerint quam in eos usus qui supra scripti sunt, quos ordo collegi nostri decrevit, et uti haec omnia, quae supra seripta sunt, suis diebus ut ita fiant dividantque quod si adversus ea quid fecerint, sive quid ita non fecerint, tunc quinquennalis vel curatores eiusdem collegi qui tunc erunt, si adversus ea quid fecerint, quinquinnalis et curatores supra scripti uti poenae nomine arkae nostrae inferant sestertium viginti milia nummum.
XVIII Hoc decretum ordini nostro placuit in conventu pleno, quod gestum est in templo divorum in aede divi Titi V. idus Martias C. Bruttio Praesente A Junio Rufino consulibus, quinquennali C. Ofilio Hermete curatoribus O. Aelio Augusti liberto Onesimo et C. Salvo Seleuco.

This Flavius Apollonius was πινακοθήκης, a member, and perhaps quinquennalis of the association of picture painters, Fab., Inscr., 724, no. 443.

language of the celebrated Manifesto of 1848, to become the vast and indeed, the only power which can prevail to supersede the curse of combinations or trusts of individuals and corporations.

Non-voting trade unions are fools. They know not and indeed refuse to know that by abjuring their manhood in refusing to strengthen their cause by the ballot, they are but wafting themselves, their cause and their hopes, backward into the feudalism of the dark ages.

But the peculiar phase of this ancient organization was the economic manner of mutually providing for each other with the things to eat, drink, wear, for shelter, and finally for sepulture after death. This accounts for the universal brotherhood in which they are known to have clung with an unflinching tenacity. They called it an "abiding faith." It was probably their table socialism and their burial attachment that inculcated the burning love for one another which has been such a marvel to the students of modern days whose task is to decipher their amazing anaglyphs. This mutual love is found to reach down far into the Christian era.

Not only did they love each other here, but they believed that after death they should all remain together—the masons with the masons; the braziers with the braziers; the potters with the potters; and thus with all the trades and professions! They made provision by means of a burial attachment to their union, that in little cinerary urns, the ashes of the members should be mixed together in order that the dead brethren be provided in the tomb with each others' society, believing that as their life-long contact in the brotherly and sisterly love had afforded so much good and such exquisite joy, so in the cinerarium, ashes would mix with ashes, affording joy in the silent and peaceful beatitudes of the long forever.[8]

There are found quite a number of slabs of marble and other stone whose grim chiselings plainly indicate that

[8] Oehler, "MSS., Contrib." II., p. 66, No. 138: "Was augeführt wurde, genügt um zu beweisen, dass die Sorge für die Bestattung der Mitgüeder, für die Erhaltung des Grabmales, und fur den Todtencultus vielfach von den Vereinen getragen wurde; dies erklärt sich aus der sakralen Grundlage aller Vereine. Die Verehrer derselben Gottheit sollen und wollen auch nach ihrem Tode vereint sein, ihnen sollen vom Vereine τὰ νομιζόμενα erwiesen. Daher erklären sich die gemeinsamen Begräbnisplätze 'einzelner' Vereine, umschlossen von einer Mauer, die Errichtung und Erhaltung der μνάματα."

love was the first moral principle while mutual care under title of economies was the first practical principle. In entering one of the numerous unions, the candidate was first carefully examined as to his or her good traits. Social standing seems not to have been much regarded. Slaves were admitted to membership.⁹ It is indeed wonderful, even amazing, after so long an interval of buried and secreted truth, to find that love, mixed with mutual economies, was the foundation rock of success and happiness for the lowly outcasts of mankind who, as now, formed four fifths of our race.

Every member must be proved by a rigid examination to be pure, clean, holy and good.¹⁰ This we positively know to have been going on 600 years before the advent of our era. Everybody knows furthermore that love, purity, goodness are the basis of our modern civilization. Foucart, who seemed, at the time M. Wescher wrote the significant words quoted in the note, not to agree, says that the word hagnos means more than holiness; it means clean; and to keep clean, pure, castus, required abstemiousness. He says it means practical, material purity; and hints that in course of time it may have crystalized into the ideal later known as agnos castus, the Lamb of God.¹¹

Another remarkable thing of these days was the general idea of what was meant by manhood. The slave, as we have seen, was nothing, had nothing and must hope for nothing. The freedman who must be carefully distinguished from the free man who could be a citizen, was the power of the organized workingmen we are discussing. The law always drew the line against him. Plato was too much of an aristocrat to recognize the work-

---

[9] Foucart, "Assoc. Rel." p. 7, shows many inscriptions which prove that slaves as well as freedmen were admitted to membership. See "Philologus, 2nd Supplement," p. 612: " Ὑπὲρ Διοσατοβυοιαςτᾶν τῶν τᾶς πόλιος δούλων Εὐαι ... ενος γραμματεὺς δαμόσιος ιερατεύσας Διὸς Ἀταβυρίου .... τῶν κυρίων Ῥοδίων ἀνέθηκε Διι Ἀταβυρίῳ...."

[10] Wescher, "Revue Archéologique," 1865, Vol. II., p. 226, comments upon these conditions, basing his remarks on the epigraph in C I G., 126, lines 31-34: "Μηδενὶ ἐξέστω εἰς τὴν σεμνοτάτην σύνοδον τῶν ἐραιιστῶν, πριν ἂν δοκιμασθῇ εἰ ἐστὶ ἅγιος καὶ εὐσεβῆς καὶ ἀγαθός." Wescher on the strength of this, adds: "Le principe de ces réunions, c'est la liberté, leur but c'est l' amélioration morale et matérielle des hommes. Les seules conditions d' admissibilité qu' elles exigent, ce sont trois vertus qu' on pourrait appeler chrétiennes: la sainteté, la piété, la bonté.

[11] As the unions were religious, or believed in supernatural aid, the idea of sacrifice is connected therewith, and has much to do with the ancient initiations. Plutarch, "De Superstitionibus," makes it mean physically clean, i. e. materially clean: "ῥυπαροὶ ἀγνεται, ἀκάθαρτοι, καθαρμοί."

ingman in his true quality as the great producing factor of the wealth and means of life, as Adam Smith so nobly argued, but he thought manhood and aristocracy had four fountains which he called sources of nobility. The first is this man's aristocracy by birth: the scond is his aristocracy by illustrious military achievement; the third springs from victories in the contests of the games, and the fourth is the preëminence of the spirit and mental powers of genius. This last, as Diogenes Lærtius who wrote a life of Plato, informs us, was the nobility he most highly prized.[12] But alas these are all counted from the citizen class. The poor expropriated descendant of the slave was totally overlooked in this estimate. He was entitled to no claims to nobility. All he had was what he earned by the hardest and this is why his organization was a boon so estimable.

To illustrate more vividly the necessity among the plodding outcasts, our ancient forefathers, of a strong and protective association of intermutual care, let us recur to the fact that for thousands of years they were regarded as not possessing souls; they were simply things, such as machines, implements of toil[13] and production.

Regarding the authority enforcing inscriptions, the wording is lost; yet everything thus far found points to a clause in the Solonic law. Several inscriptions of an early date show that it was compulsory. We have already shown that these legalized trade and labor societies were in Egypt considered by Amasis, as necessary to ascertain the manner in which the people got their living, as well as to afford the census enumerators an accurate clew to their numbers.

All the savants are now beginning to recognize and acknowledge that these unions were not only very ancient but very important factors of state. There can be no

[12] Diog. Lært. thought to be very ancient, "Vita Platonis," 31: "Διαιρεῖται δὲ ἡ εὐγένεια εἰς εἴδη τέτραρα. Ἐν μὲν, ἐὰν ὦσιν οἱ πρόγονοι καλοὶ. κἀγαθοὶ καὶ δίκαιοι, τοὺς ἐκ τούτων γεγενημένους εὐγενεῖς φασίν εἶναι. Ἄλλο δὲ ἐὰν ὦσι οἱ πρόγονοι δεδυναστευκότες καὶ ἄρχοντες γεγενημένοι," κ. τ. λ. Cf. Gran. de Cassagnac, "Histoire des Classes Nobles," p. 31.

[13] Varro, "De Re Rustica," I. 17, i: "Instrumenti genus vocale, et semivocale, et mutum: vocale, in quo sunt servi; semivocale; in quo boves; mutum, in quo plaustra." Thus the servant is a machine, like a beast, or a wagon, only that he can make a noise with his vocal organs. Again, "Digest," IV., 5: "Servile caput nullum jus habet." Taken from the great jurist Paulus; or as Ulpian puts it in "Digest," IV., 17: "In personam servilem nulla cadit obligatio." The denial of any claim to manhood or nobility or soul is also made by Plato, "Laws," VI.; Homer, "Odyssey," XVII., v. 322-323; Horace, "Sermon.," I.; "Satyr.," VI., v. 6.

doubt that the unions existed in a non-legalized form long before either Numa, Solon or Amasis and were even at this early period cutting their own inscriptions.[14]

From the earliest recorded proof of their existence obtained through their own annals 600 years before Christ, we find numbers all along of later ones and propose to occasionally sketch them as curious landmarks, as we descend the craggy steps of time. Dr. Johann Oehler, of the University of Vienna, who has given much time and travel to this subject, mentions an eranos which flourished over 400 years before Christ.[15] Natural to their miserable condition, the property and all good things of life which they had created, being taken away from them, they not only hugged their protective unionism and its common table and mutual association, but they likewise cultivated a belief in an imagined saviour. This they for centuries adhered to until He finally came. In consequence, their inscriptions teem with the mention of their god Soter or saviour, an imaginary redeemer, some day coming to deliver the world.[16] The pre-Christion saviour worshipers were among the strongest unions of labor. Their condition was made precarious by the harsh power of the wealthy, constantly speculating upon their nerve and muscle, using their female charms for beastly gratification, glutting themselves with their valuable productions and constantly talking them down. The law gave them power to slay them without process of a trial. It all quickened their longings, causing them to conjure up imaginary hopes of relief and a cherished belief in a forthcoming Saviour who was to redeem them all. This greatly whetted their habits and practice of worship and inculcated mutual love and growth of con-

---

[14] Cagnat, in "Revue Contemporaine," Jan. 1896, p. 166, says: "La tradition rapporte au roi Numa l' institution des corporations professionnelles à Rome. Pour qui ne fait point de l' existence, de Romulus et son successeur un article de foi. Cela signifie qu' elles sont aussi anciennes que la ville même."

[15] Oehler, "MSS., written to the author": "Sabazios: Die Σαβαζιασταὶ im Peireius wurden bereits oben unter den ἔρανοι erwähnt; eine in derselben Stelle gefundene Weihungsinschrift aus dem Jahre 342 v. Chr. CIA., II., 1326 wird mit Recht auf Sabazios bezogen und beweisst, dass der Cult dieses Gottes bereits im IV. Jahrh. v. Chr. im Peireius gepflegt wurde."

[16] Oehler. "MS.," I., No. 66: "In Rhodes bestand ein Διὸς Σωτηριαστᾶν Σαραπιαστᾶν κοινὸν. "Inscr." Gr. "Inscr." 162; in Lindos Διὸς Σωτηριασταί; "ibid." nr. 939i. Ζεὺς Ύέττιος. "They are recorded by the epigraphists as of about B. C. 262. It was all as their simple minds happened to imagine. The same author refers to Strabo, 606, and to the "Corpus Inscriptionum Atticarum," II., no. 616, of B.C. 300, for mention of a Zeus ϛωτηρ, and "eix Heiligthum desselben im Peireius." Dioskuros "Ad Kabiren."

science in the world. The third and fourth centuries before our era abound in saviour or messiah worship among the trade organizations. Almost all the members of the eranos built upon this hope.[17]

To be added to the above explanation of the sources of that Saviour worship which at the present day is causing vague and erroneous speculations regarding the origin of our religion, must be another well-known reason which is, that the Roman conquests based their animus largely in the ambition of individuals for gain, by plunder and the glut of vengeance. To them nothing was so delicious as the groans, sobs and dying moans of victims. Such victims must be the poor proletaires whom their aristocracy had degraded, robbed and impoverished. Let every movement of the organized modern workers beware; since the fires of that ancient hatred have never been quenched or even christianized. To rob and glut and become millionaires at the expense of the working-people is still the uppermost sentiment; and let us beware lest they, in their cunning, spring upon us another standing army with a military force, such as killed off the workers in the past. Rome by her conquests, raised the battle-axe against the useful element of the race. That same truculent money power is still here and it behooves the non-propertied majorities to take this as their warning.

Away back in the time of Numa and Tullus Hostilius there were religious congregations which were none other than labor associations worshiping a tutelary, saving deity.[18] The Arval Brothers and Sisters early assumed an aristocratic hue since they were supported by the general government and made perpetual under its sanction, in somewhat the same manner as the bridge

[17] Serapis was another of the saviour deities on whom they placed hope as a messianic power. The CIA., II., 617, has a stone showing us a προεραγίστρια, B.C. 300. In B.C. 400, ie., in that century, there was an eranos or a numerous colony of them, right in the brightest days of Socrates, who had their houses and little temples, κυριάκαι along the cliffs of the Acropolis: Oehler, "MSS. to the author": "Athen, Erwähnt wird κοιγὸν τῶν ἐρανιστῶν in den φιάλαι ἐξεχενθερικαί. Verzeichnissen, die auf der Ἀκρόπολις gefunden wurden, und dem IV. Jahrh. v. Chr. angehören C I A., II., 768; 772; 773; 775, C I A., IV²., nr. 768⁶; 772⁶; 775⁶; 775c; 775d; vergl. "American Journ. of Arch.," IV., 1888.

[18] Granier de Cassagnac, "Histoire des Classes Nobles," p. 197, sqq: "La congrégation religieuse la plus célèbre était celle des vestales, appellées Filles de Vesta," ("Vestal Virgins"). Under Numa they only numbered four. Plutarch, Numa, x.: "Πρῶτον μὲν οὖν ὑπὸ Νουμᾶ καθιερωθῆαι λέγουσι Γεγανίαν καὶ Βερηνίαν, δεύτερον δὲ Κανουληίαν καὶ Τορπηίαν."

builders. On close investigation we are astonished to find that everything in our civilization, especially our Christian religion, is derived from one or another of these innumerable trade and labor movements, legalized by Numa and Solon and employed by the state until broken up after the conquests.

But this trade unionism was originally considered a great virtue. Solon, in his law sometimes called the law of Attica, positively ordered that it be accounted honorable,[19] which at that early day proved a great triumph of craftsmanship. On obtaining this permission they began to spread over mainland and islands, until they existed everywhere.[20]

It was under this law of free organization that Pythagoras careered. Like the Gnostic in Christian times, he wanted to establish a great philosophy and totally failed. The purely economical is too practical ever to become a philosophy. Nevertheless it is known that there existed synods or communities of persons, mostly of the pedagogical, and esoteric class of mind, who, like the mechanics and laborers, had to win a living by their labor and talent. These took advantage of the great jus coeundi, and are known to have sheltered themselves from harm and hunger by means of similar unions,[21] while they went abroad to do good in the world. This is exactly what the Christians did afterwards. The Pythagorean organization, which is now known and acknowledged to have been planted into the trade and labor movement legalized by Solon, existed 600 years before Christ.

[19] Plutarch, "Solon," xx., Laws of Attica: *Ἅγιος νόμος.* "Solon, perceiving that the soil of Attica which hardly rewarded the husbandman's labor, was far from being capable of maintaining a lazy, indolent multitude, ordered that trades should be accounted honorable; that the council of Areopagos should examine into every man's means of support, and chastise the idle." Longhornes's trans.

[20] They were organized in the island of Chios long before Christ; and in Cilicia are found their relics, showing that they often dedicated to Asclepias: "Σύνοδος τῶν Ἀσκληπιαστᾶν. So in Epidamnus were the καββαδίας, "vide Feuilles d' Epidaure," no. 112; Foucart, "De Scenicis Artificibus," p. 9, who cites information from Isocrates, "Evagoras," I, 150, thus showing that the Greek unions spread to the island of Cyprus, being incited by Evagoras, B.C. 420-385, to go there and settle. This he thinks was the origin of their existence.

[21] Athenæus, "Deipnosophistæ," V., 186a, speaks of the Διογενιασταὶ, Ἀντιπατρισταὶ, Παναιτιασταὶ, as being φιλοσόφων σύνοδοι. Among the adherents of Pythagoras there was a difference between these names. In the "Anonymus" who is author of "Vita Pythagoræ apud Photium," § 1, the following distinctions are threaded out: "οἱ σὺν μὲν αὐτῷ τῷ Πυθαγόρα οἱ γενόμενοι ἐκαλοῦντο Πυθαγορικοί, οἱ δὲ τούτων μαθηταὶ Πυθαγόρειοι, οἱ δὲ ἄλλως ἔξωθεν ζηλωταὶ Πυθαγαρισταί." Compare Iamblicus; p. 80, sq. Oehler, "MSS. to the author," subjoins the remarks: "Der religiöse Mittelpunkt der Philosophenschulen war an Μουσεῖον, die Feste werden Μουσεῖα genannt; daher hat Wilh. Mollendorf die Philosophenschulen als Θίασοι Μουσῶν erklärt."

There was a union of potters at Cos which existed during the fourth century B. C. That there was a jealousy existing all along against the growth and success of these organizations is emphasized by the manner in which the crafty priests of the official or state religion captured and turned them to their own account. This was especially the fate of the union of bridgebuilders. Numa evidently had no idea that his college of pontiffs would ever become a seat of popery. Originally the college of pontiffs or union of bridgebuilders was a group of masons, carpenters and other mechanics. But they flourished because they were voting unions and obtained political control in a limited, peaceful manner. Taking advantage of some clause in the law now lost, they voted their candidates into the offices of the public works hereby securing for themselves the labor of building bridges, sewers, and public edifices for the city and state at good wages, until they worked themselves up into respectability. As all things in those days were compulsorily religious, so they also conformed with the general customs and beliefs.[22]

Another singular thing is, that as in Pontiff so in everything, the unions lend us name and all; for pontifex is bridgebuilder. Even the pope is a master bridgebuilder, though he assumes the sounding appellative of Pontiff, which translated, means boss of the union of bridgebuilders, who became celebrated legalized government Pontiffs long before the Christian era. The pontiffs were originally a trade union of bridgebuilders, working for the state on government construction. Thus everything in our modern religion is traceable for its origin to some trade organization, under the Solonic and Numan law.

Trade unions built all the great itineraries for Rome for nearly a thousand years. These unions must have been business-like concerns. An interesting account of how they so systematically worked from a very early time, is given by a recent writer, M. Domaszewski, in the Eranos Vindobonenses.[23] The manner in which trade

[22] "Plutarque rapporte en plusieurs endroits de sa "Vie de Numa," que ce roi institua le collège de pontifs et quelques autres collèges de religieux: "Ἔτι δὲ χρῆναι Μούσαις καθιερῶσαι τὸ χωρίον ἐκεῖνο, καὶ τοὺς περὶ αὐτὸ λειμῶνας." (Numa, cap. xiii.). The priests under the guise of an official religion began early to establish the pontifex maximus which lasted down through the republic and the empire and finally fixed itself permanently in the papal see.

[23] "Eran. Vindobon.," pp. 63, 64. In Greek he was called the ἐπιμελητής, in Latin, curia. The board were curatores viarum.

unions under the protective guardianship of Minerva or Diana, took the work and carried out large enterprises, is here explained. The president of each union was a sort of contractor for the state. It was the same in Asia Minor and Greece. As early as the time of Pericles, which was not long after the invasion of Xerxes and the battle of Salamis, there was a thiasos operating one of the trades on the island of Salamis. It was dedicated to Bendis, the Thracian Diana, goddess of the chase and favorite friend and patroness of the working people.

In the Greek-speaking world, the eranos not only carried out the various evolutions of performing public work, but it likewise acted as a loan society, and often loaned money toward buying slaves into their freedom. The valuable work of M. Foucart already quoted from, explains that a shrewdly practical use was made, of the god or goddess, revered by them as a tutelary saviour. It was this immortal to whom the slave was sold into liberty. We can imagine no more beautiful or efficient system of practical work for a union of working people to do. Surely, the genius of ancient labor organization must have surpassed ours of the present day. What could be more noble, more sublime than this? A strictly trade and labor organization whose members, as shown beyond question,[24] were themselves poor emancipated slaves, all, or nearly all of them having obtained their liberty in the same manner, arranges to hand over to their patron god the price of a slave, and before the awful tribunal, the august immortal delivers the thus loaned money over to a holder of human flesh, thus setting a chattel free! We have somewhat explained this ingenius and magnificent trade union function, which for shrewdness and disinterestedness surpasses anything we know of in actual existence among our labor unions.

Every qualified person unprovided with sufficient

---

[24] Foucart, *Affranchissement des Esclaves par forme de vente à une Divinité*, p. 28, has, in proof of the above astonishing facts, brought to the light a mass of inscriptions engraved under the law and at the very time the god assumed the deal in his great temple and on the consecrated altar, as we have described. See *Inscriptions Recuillies à Delphes*, Paris, Firmen, Didot, 1863, Nos. 89, 107, 126, 139, 213 and 244. The Slave borrowed his ransom money from the Ἔρανος, and the god, through the legalized and brilliant, even awe-inspiring formality of law, through his priests, paid the thus borrowed money over to the owner of the slave, who, with cringing greediness, cowering with awe and humility, took it and departed. Then the slave remained a sort of chattel to the union which was bound to support him or her and furnish work for wages, until every obole was repaid.

means wherewith to live without work could in those days, under provisions of the Solonic statute, become a member of some mutual aid society. Not only the inscriptions, from which we derive our information, but also many of the ancient writers have made contributions to establish this fact. The city of Alexandria teemed with these societies; and one is mentioned by Suidas and Athenæus which shows that they were there in the time of Ptolemy Philadelphus. There were unions of the poets, showing that it was necessary for men practicing professions to organize; since working for a living with the brain was equally as precarious as working for a living by hand. So again, Pausanias, mentions the Bactrian singers, and an inscription shows that they owned a piece of land. But we reserve for a future chapter our description of the vast international union of the ancient artists, regarding which recent finds afford incontestable proofs. A circumstance may here be mentioned which is very suggestive. They existed especially in and around the old cities of Heraclea, Trœzen, and everywhere in Cephalonia and Phrygia where the Christians settled and built up churches that for a long time practiced noble tenets in their temples.[25] The great "Gemeinde" or community and its seed of churches, which afterwards grew from it, was seated in very ancient times at Teos, Samos, Halicarnassus or Boudrum. This was an enormous congeries of associations which seemed to be bundled together into a numberless factor and to so general an extent as to seemingly engross the industrial population. It is not until within the last century, and it might be said, the last half century that this strange and countless multitude[26] of trade and professional organizations has become known to us, chiefly through their own inscriptions. They tell their

[25] Lüders. *Dionysische Künstler,* pp. 14, 15, 19, says there were 'Οργιῶνες, θίασοι and others. CIG., 522. A long inscription is found mentioning Heraclea, Cephalonia and Trœzen, which describes a crowning with a θαλλός στέφανοις, all well preserved. At Heraclea of Pontus is one given by Welcker, CIG 642f; Preller, *Gr. Mythol.,* I., 109.

[26] Lüders *Dionys. Künstler,* p. 77: "Die grosse Gesellschaft nennt sich τὸ κοινὸν τῶν περί τὸν Διόνυσον τεχνιτῶν τῶν ἀπ' Ιωνίας καὶ Ἑλλησπόντου καὶ τῶν περὶ τὸν κάθηγεμόνα Διόνυσον." They also had branches at Nemea and Isthmos, *id.,* p. 79. The same author, p. 133, devotes more than a page to an enumeration of places in these regions, including Pergamaos and Chalcedony peopled with innumerable societies about the time of Aristonicus, thus emphasizing, if not verifying our argument that Aristonicus the revolter against the treachery of Attalus III., described in chapter X., Vol. I., of this work, was a member of some powerful social organization of the proletaries,

PRE-CHRISTIAN UNIONS.

own history; and it must be said their chiselings recount it well. The German archæologists speak of it as the great "Gemeinde," with the signification of a community because of their characteristics of self-helping brotherhoods existing in thousands of clubs, each with a common table and a communal code, and yet coördinated into a sort of international union. They are found to have been very numerous 200 years before Christ and some of them are seen to be of much earlier date.

Not only Greeks and Greek-speaking people were organized in this great "Gemeinde" but we find inscriptions proving that the inhabitants of Tyre on the border of Palestine also had many organizations for aiding their trades and manufactures.[27] Even on the Island of Malta they existed; for a union is found from Tyre, of early date, whose patron god is Macod. It is an inscription of a genuine eranos, composed of the members of a Phœnician colony settled at Malta. This eranos must have been in full blast at the time Paul landed there on his way to Rome, the hints of Luke's legend proving it.

A Hebrew eranos is known to have existed at Tlos, under the Solonic law, which has been described by Mr. Hula.[28] The Jews had been driven about by the tyranny of kings, and were willing to build up new fortunes under the Solonic rather than the Mosaic dispensation. They were very popular and judging from the work of Wilhelmowitz Mollendorf, Euripides was an officer in one of these organizations.[29] The society of the eranos flourished in Cnidos, Smyrna, Tralles, Nicea and all other parts of Asia Minor; and their own inscriptions show them to have been very numerous 400

---

[27] Oehler, *Gr. Vereinswesen* ; See *infra, Index :* "Ein Verein tyrischer Hauptleute in Delos: τὸ κοινὸν τῶν Τυρίων Ἡρακλειστῶν ἐμπόρων καὶ ναυκλήρων erbittet vom athenischen Volke den Platz für einen τέμενος Ἡρακλεοῦς τοῦ Τυρίου ἀρχηγέτου τῆς πατρίδος, CIG., 2271. Zu Kos hat Diomedon eine Kultgemeinschaft zu Ehren des Herakles gestiftet."

[28] *Eranos Vindobonensis*, p. 99-102. The block containing the inscription was found by Hula who explains it. It was in a graveyard near Tlos, in Lycia. He mentions it as having been a *Judengemeinde* or Jewish congregation in Tlos. Hula has restored it, and we present the heliograph and inscription here. He adds: "Die archonten waren Beamte der Jüdischen Gemeinde, die in diesem Titel, wie auch in anderen Dingen die hellenistischen Communalverfassung adoptirte. It was, then, of course, one of the communes under the Solonic law, and so admitted.

[29] Mollendorf, *Euripides, Herakl.*, 2nd ed, p. 141, sqq : It was the Ἀπόλλων Δήλιος. The members were Δηλιασταί and Euripides officiated—a matter which honored the association. See Athenæus, X., p. 424, who calls them ὀρχησταί, the dancers.

years before Christ. One of Egyptian origin is found to have had Anubis as the patron deity. He was god of the chase. In lower Egypt are found a great number of tombstones mentioning him. He had the jackal's head, and was guardian of tombs. They also abounded in Chios and all the islands of the Ægean Sea.

Egypt was always a prolific soil for these associations. There is evidence that the Solonic organizations flourished at Alexandria from a high antiquity, and we possess a very recent acknowledgment by so high an auhority as Oehler, that a close relationship existed between all the societies of that day; which of itself blends therapeutæ, eranoi, thiasoi, essenes, nazarenes, orgeons, collegia, in fact all the various societies of this peculiar class, into one; the name alone varying with the customs and languages of the localities. All are traceable to the great paternal origin, the Solonic law, and their legible landmarks are found ranging from 600 years before our era.

Foucart, who studied them with a deep penetration, declares that these unions which in his Latin work he naturally calls collegia, frequently assumed the name of their own patron saint.[30] In Caria, a division of Asia Minor, the unions of masons are found existing from the first half of the second century before Christ. They built theatres. So also it may be put down as unwarrantable to suppose that the Therapeutic Essenes, as they are called in Judea, were a religious association, few in number and of questionable age and duration. In 278 B. C. they were strong mutual unions of workingmen and their inscriptions are found in many parts of the world. It is now admitted by scholars that they are identical with all the other prominent trade organizations, of which the thiasos or eranos was the typical example.[31]

In the fourth century before Christ there was, on the

[30] *De Scenicis Artificibus*, p. 29, "Thiasi numinis cujusdam patrocinium et cognomen assumunt, ut Serapiastæ, etc.;" and further: " in scenicis collegiis, ita in thiasis, res per magistratus et secerdotes annuos administrantur," etc.

[31] Oehler, *MSS.*: " *Therapeutæ*, Ein Θίασος in Athen, der Cult einer nicht bezeichneten Göttin pflegte, hat im Jahr 278-7 v. Chr. seine Beamten geehrt und begründet diese Ehrung auch dadurch, ἐπιμεμέληνται δὲ καὶ τῶν ἀπογενομένων καλῶς καὶ φιλοτίμως. Δελτίον, 1892, p. 100 f; CIA., no. 6156. Here follow several more inscriptions of therapeutic epitaphs all mixed up with the thiasos, which is now regarded as the type of all unions under the Solonic dispensation.

northern acclivity of the Nymph hills, a union that consecrated regularly to Zeus Philius, and its traces are found reaching back into prehistoric uncertainty. It was a genuine eranos, such as used to have the common table, which will be found accurately described in these pages. A splendid specimen of an eranos and its common table, exhibited at one of its entertainments has been found bearing date of B. C. 123,[32] and another of B. C. 119. They show the brotherly love that prevailed among the working people of those days, which were the most dangerous of the Roman conquests. A glance at the occult happiness they are enjoying affords a key to the phenomenal growth among their class which numbered three-fourths of the human race; even during that period of slaughter, they were teaching the spirit of sympathy among mankind leading to the precept that we should love our neighbors as ourselves.

The taint of labor shrouded all mankind having to work for a living. Men and women whose energies produced the riches others enjoyed, when thus left without them, were glad to find a law of liberty in the ancestral dispensation. It was as good for the merchant as for the mechanic. The merchants are discovered through the inscriptions, to have been organized in exactly the same mutual manner as mechanics and laborers. They appear to have undertaken their business methods guided by the same law and to have struggled hand in hand together upon the same social plane.

Along the banks of the Sea of Galilee are found slabs of stone upon which are engraved words showing that the boating business about 100 years B. C. flourished under a thiasos in Phœnicia, on the Sea of Galilee. This country, in those days was considered a part of Phœnicia, and in that early period there were certainly societies of fishermen and of boatmen doing the lively commerce of the lake. Mixed among them are found merchants, boat-owners, and even longshoremen organized together.[33] A Phœnician eranos dedicated to Nep-

[32] See Vol. I., plate opp. p. 451, taken from Lüders, *Dionys. Künst., fin.*; CIA., II., 1330; also CIA., II., p. 988.
[33] Oehler, *MSS. to the author;* "Kaufleute und Rhreder aus Berytos in Phœnicia," perhaps the Sea of Galilee, τὸ κοινὸν Βηρυτίων ἐπὶ ἐμπόρων καὶ ναυκλήρων καὶ ἐγδοκέων, *Bull. Héll.*, viii., p. 469, nr. 2; 474, 2; 475, 4; 472, 6. Τὸ κοινὸν Βηρυτίων Ποσειδωνιστῶν ἐμπόρων καὶ ναυκλήρων ἐγδοκέων, die unter einem ἀρχιθιασιτής standen." *Bull. Héll.*, viii., 1883, 467-1; 471-5; 475-3; Vgl. 470-5.

tune, the Hermes of Poseidon was another organization of shippers, about 90 years before Christ, and is fresh proof of the economic business life of the people prevailing everywhere under stringent organization. We find also that the longshoremen were snugly organized along with the merchants and shippers at Alexandria. Of course there could be no strikes if they were all organized into one brotherhood and we hear of none.

In passing over this monumental history of the social movement prevailing among our forefathers it is not a little strange to find them, in their paganized condition, 300 years before Christ, busy with questions of the "New birth."[34] This anagenesis is prehistoric. Many of the unions we mention inscribed the doings of their meetings, such as the consecrations, and the anagenesis, the mysteries, the baptism and even sometimes the immaculate conception or parthenogenesis, as of common occurrence, hundreds of years before the commencement of our era.

It should be constantly borne in mind that these organizations were strictly economic ones, under the law of Solon, and had nothing in common with the outside world. They were very secret, and although their outward appearance is that of religion and religious worship of one or another of the pet patron deities, yet among themselves the constant, uppermost thought was how to get a living; and we foresee a time when better scientific knowledge of them shall throw off this deceptive veil of religion which as Mommsen has already admitted, was often a cloak to shield their true object from the intolerant rigor of the law.

About B. C. 200, flourished Osiris, the great man-god, once a living, Egyptian monarch but after death an immortal, like Jupiter, floating and hovering around the superstitious and credulous minds of primitive men as the martyred saviour, or messiah resurrected and returned to save humanity. There existed at Kos a labor union known there as the synod of Osiris.[35] The Therapeutæ were also numerous at Kos, under a genuine communal association.

[34] *Corpus Inscriptionum Atticarum*, II., 610. An ὀργέων in honor of the goddess Bendis, the Thracian Diana, patroness of laborers, the chase and fructification among animal and vegetable species. It represents the new birth, 'Ἀναγένησις.

[35] Paton and Hicks, no. 54; Collitz, no. 5647. It was found on the site of the ancient Kos.

PRE-CHRISTIAN UNIONS.

Forty-seven years before Christ there was at Sidon in North Palestine, a celebrated city of the Phœnicians, a union of cutlers who manufactured knives, daggers and short swords, and the members were called machæropoioi.[36]

The dreadful system of gladiatorial games, repellent to us, in our advanced sympathies and our consequent intolerant feeling against cruelty, existed during the Roman conquests. We have sufficiently explained this in our first volume. It now only remains to exhibit the protective organizations which existed for the mutual help and solace of the victims of these gruesome sports. Unions of gladiators were very common; and judging from their numbers, it is safe to say that they were in all the municipal as well as proconsular cities of Rome where the amphitheatres existed. Fifty-eight years before Christ there was a college of gladiators in Rome.[37] It was then that great contentions were raging between the working people and money power. Conspiracy laws were that year enacted against labor organizations and Clodius was giving his life, happiness, honor and talent in their cause. Cicero was using every power of the aristocratic senate against the tribunes whose principal source of help in the conflict was the voting unions.

It is ascertained that Spartacus, whose vast revolt had occurred fourteen or fifteen years before, was also a member of a union of gladiators.

There are found unions of the sons of Vulcan, then known as the Cabiri.[38] These Samothracian cabiri or dwarf-smiths, exceedingly cunning in their art, are not a little curious. They certainly had a powerful organization at an early period, and under a secret veil protected their mysterious arts. Their union was a thiasos which practiced a cult of a messiah or saviour or at least inculcated such ideas, while they were busy at their mechanical vocations.

At an early date Rome had an organization of what were called Galloi, connected with priests of Cybele, mother of the gods. They were poor, and had to labor for a living like other working people. The author of

---

[36] These dagger makers had a feast and consecration. Their head man was ἄρχων μαχαιροποιῶν, *Revue Archeol.*, III., 1891, p. 108.

[37] Marini, *Atti.*, 2, p. 823. Some 25 others are traced to this date of B.C. 58. See Vol. I., chap. xii., *Spartacus.* Paton and Hicks found them in the name of a Σεραπιαστῶν κοινὸν, *Inscr.*, Gr. Ins., No. 162; *ibid.* no. 701, sq.; no. 371, θίασος Σεραπιαστᾶν. Also in Rhodes a Διὸς Σωτηιαστᾶν κοινόν,

[38] Oehler, in *MSS.* to the author: "KABIREN: Die Verehrer derselben

the history of the noble classes, M. Cassagnac, was surprised on investigation, to find that they differed widely from the other Arval brothers created by Romulus; for they were distinctly of the lowly class; not noble, like the priests and officers of the official religion, but that they had nothing. There was a collegium or congregation of the aristocratic priests. It consisted first of twelve members, appointed by Romulus. The number was doubled by Tullus Hostilius. After all, we are at a loss to see how the fratres arvales,[39] or even the pre-Christian college of pontiffs, can have anything to do with our work. They were aristocrats. Although known that they were, like the rest, derived from the unions of winegrowers and bridgebuilders and that they were thus descended from the lowly stock, nevertheless we find them belonging to the aristocrats.

But the other class of fratres arvales, viz, the Galloi, poor and self-abasing, and even foolish enough to descend to self-mutilation in honor of the mother of the gods, we shall include in our history; because they were the reverse to the aristocrats, and because they were from Phrygia the cradle of the great reform, producing in course of time the phenomenal era in which we live.

Finally, there was a gardener's union at Ephesus, which has lately attracted some attention.[40] There is a fragment of an inscription of another union of gardeners found at or near Smyrna. We hold, and we think we can show that all or nearly all of the pre-Christian unions presented in this chapter were economic associations under the Solonic dispensation.

Vereinen bezeichnen sich nach den Haupt-Cultusstätten, Samothrake und Lemnos sowie nach dem Attribute der Kabiren (Σωτῆρες). In Lesbos finden wir Σαμοθρακιασταί. CIG. 2167 6; *Athen. Mitth.*, xxi., 1896, p. 238; *ibid.*, p. 239, II. Jahrh v. Chr. Zu Rhodes finden wir, ein Σαμοθρακιαστῶν Μεσονέαν κοινὸν, dann ein Σαμοθρακιαστᾶν καὶ Δημιαστᾶν τῶν συνστρατευσαμένων κοινὸν." Again, Oehl., *Vereinswesen in MSS.:* "*Inschrift. Gr.*, ins., I., nr. 43: Eine Religiöse Genossenschaft, die sich aus Anlass eines Seekrieges gebildet und unter dem Schutze der Götter von Samothrake und Lemnos, die Kabiren gesellt hatten. Nr. 162, nennt uns ein Κοινὸν Σαμοθρακιασταί Σωτηριαστᾶν Ἀριστοβευλιαστᾶν Ἀπολλονιαστᾶν in Rhodes, benannt nach θεαίτητος, der es aus Anlass des Krieges begründet hatte; vgl. Nr. 75, und nach dessen Söhne 'Αστυμήδης; Vgl. Rubensohn: *Mysterienheiligthümer*, p. 234.

[39] Aulus Gellius, *Noctes Atticæ* V., viii: "Ex eo tempore collegium mansit fratrum arvalium numero duodecim. Fratres arvales appelavit (Romulus)." So, again Dionysius Hal., III., c. xxxii: "Ὁ Τυλλος εὔξατο . . . . . τὸν τῶν Σαλίων καλουμένων διπλασιάσειν ἀριθμόν." Again, Varro, *De Lingua Latina*, V., xv., 25: "Fratres arvales dicti sunt, qui sacra publica faciunt, propterea ut fruges ferant arva,"

[40] Oehl., in *MSS. to the author*: "Σύστημα κηπουρῶν ist schon erwähnt—Von Vereinen ist das Wort wohl auch zu verstehn in der Inschrift aus Ephesos, Le Bas, III., 1526—Hicks, *Manual*, nr. 205; 86 Jahr. v. Chr. Vielleicht auch in der fragmentarischen Inschrift aus Smyrna, Μουσ., Κ. Βίβλ., II., 1887, p 134, nr. 182."

As to the Christians at Rome it has been shown that they withstood the test and held out as collegia funeraticia (burial associations), and they could also possess some land and property in common.[41]

This remarkable gift to humanity seems to have applied to the working people of the whole world; for its influence stretched to India, and northward to Britain, and was officially endorsed at Rome. When, after the conquests, all the world became pro-consular Rome, the great jus coeundi, instead of being destroyed, as was the evident intention when the cunning aristocracy sprung the conquests, hooded itself under a secret veil and outlived the empire. The Solonic, then, and not the Mosaic, is the dispensation which the correct civilization and enlightenment of mankind is following; and its secret of success which has overpowered religious superstition, the intolerance of the jealous money power, with priestcraft, kingcraft, and even death itself, is its economic, self-sustaining mutualism which is gradually growing, and kneading its fibers into socialism.

The above view of the power and precedence of the Solonic dispensation over the Mosaic, is new; yet taking into consideration its scope as an economic rather than a religious factor, this view will bear inspection. The epigraphists and men of letters are beginning to admit our view. Dr. John Oehler, has sent us a special manuscript letter on the subject, points of which we translate here, in proof that the organizations existing in such vast numbers in all parts of the known world derived their right of association, or jus coeundi directly from the law of Solon, which was an economic and not a religious dispensation. He says: "The thiasoi etc., have the same objects which were possessed by the collegia funeraticia, or burial unions of Rome."[42]

[41] It is well known and admitted that in the days of scrutiny and persecution the burial attachment of the economic unions was what saved them, or shielded them from the rigors of persecution. Several scholars speak out boldly: Dr. Oehler, *MS. to the author:* "Die θίασοι, u. s. w. haben meist auch den Zweck, den bei den Römern die collegia funeraticia hatten." Again:

[42] "Die Vereinsfreiheit in Athen geht auf das von Gaius angeführte Gesetz zurück; auch in den anderen Staaten der Griechischen Welt scheint gleiche Freiheit bestanden zu haben. In den Vereinen war den Christen der ersten Jahrhunderte die Möglichkeit einer rechtlichen Existenz gegeben; für die Christen in Rom ist es erwiesen dass sie als collegia funeraticia bestanden und rechtlich anerkannt waren; also auch grundbesitz und gemeinsames Vermögen haben konnten. Dass sie auch in den Städten des Ostens in Form eines θίασος, u. s. w. auftraten, wird zwar von Ziebart geleugnet, ist aber doch anzunehmen, dass diese Abhandlung soll es beweisen. Vergl. Hatch, Edwin, *Die Gesellschaftsverfassung der Christlichen Kirchen im Alterthume,* übersetzt von Harnach. See *Supra,* Chap. I., of this work.

THEIR TOPOGRAPHY AND NUMBER. 169

It is true, Ziebarth denies that in the cities of Asia, the Christians came out in the form of a thiasos, etc., nevertheless, it is to be assumed as true and his own contribution shows it to be so."[46]

[46] Review, geographically arranged, of the ancient unions, with a statement of the Divinities they recognized before their endorsement of christianity, note!sewhere recorded in these pages but part of an extra contribution. Prepared and sent to us through the compliments of Dr. Oehler.

GREECE, ATTICA, ATHENS: 'ΟΡΓΕΩΝΕΣ.

Cities of AMYNOS, ASCLEPIOS, and DEXION; 4th-3rd century, B.C. *CIA*, Vol. *IV*, add., no. 617[c].

City of HYPODEKTES, 3rd century, B.C., *CIA*, *II*, 1061: unions of orgeones.

City of EGRETES, 306-5, B.C. Unpublished inscription, found by the *American School* at *Athens*.

City of ASCLEPIUS, 1st century, B.C. *CIA*, *II*, 990: θιασῶται devoted to 'Αρτεμις Σώτερα, ie. Diana Saviour, near DIPYLON, B.C., 267-5. *CIA*, *IV*[2], 1620, where was also found an inscr. of the Σωτηριασταί, *CIA*, *IV*[2], 1630.

City of 'ΑΘΗΝΑ, 'Εργάνη, *CIA*, 1329, 4th century, B.C.

Same place, middle of third century B.C., the Decree τῶν 'Ερανιστῶν, honoring Minerva.

City of HERACLES: *CIA*, *II*, 1111; no. 986. *CIA*, *IV*[2], 615; *II*, 1331; 1663; *IV*[2] 622[b], θίασοι representing some inferior department of the state and a φρατρια or clan that published the sworn resolution called the δημόσιον; *CIA*, *IV*[2], 841[b], 'Ερανισταί belonging to the 4th century, B.C., found on the slopes of the ACROPOLIS; see Φιάλαι ἐξελευθερικαὶ, frequently mentioning κοινὸν ἐρανιστῶν: *CIA*, *II*, 768, 772, 873, 775; *CIA*[2] 768[b], 772[b], 775[b], 775[c], 775[d].

Clump of 'ΕΡΑΝΙΣΤΑΙ, of the ὅροι, *CIA*, *III*, 1178, *IV*[2], 1138[b], found in SPARTA, 1110, PIKERMI; 1147, TATOY; 1119, MUNECHIA; *IV*[2], 1170[b] παρὰ τὴν ἱερὰν ὁδόν, and of 324-3, B.C, Here we have an ἐρανος consecrating to Zeus Φίλιος, *CIA*, *III*, 1330.

City of ATHENS; A consecration to Zeus Næus; a συνόδος, found on the ACROPOLIS: ΔΕΛΤΙΟΝ, 1890, p. 145, no. 2; middle of the 4th century, B.C. It is that of the organized washerwomen, *CIA*, *II*, 1327.

Ibid. The year B.C. 270-69, showing the officers of a κοινὸν τῶν ἐργαζομένων, *CIA*, *I*, 1332, the ἐπιμεληταί and ἱεροποιοί, for Zeus or Jupiter Σωτήρ, for 'Ηρακλῆς and the Σωτῆρες (perhaps Kabiri, dwarf mechanics), *CIA*, *III*, 616; found on the NYMPH HILLS. Two more eranists' decrees were found here, *CIA*, *II*, 615; *III*, no. 19.

At close of the 3rd century, B.C. existed an eranos with list of membership, males and females also on this hill slope, *CIA*, *II*, 988. *II*. 3208, shows an epitaph of a member of an eranos, who hailed from SELEUKEIA.

The ΣΩΤΗΡΙΑΣΤΑΙ, *CIA* *IV*[2], 630[b], show themselves to have been ἐρανισταί.

City of CYRENE on the acropolis, and belonging to the divinities of the 'Αρτεμισταί, B.C. 300, a decree of honor for Μυσαῖος. It was an ἐρανος, *CIA*, *IV*[2]. 1334[b].

Found on the same eminence an inscription with 'Ασκληπιασταί in fragmentary condition, showing evidences of both Διόνυσος and Herodes-Theater; hence 'Ασκλεπιεῖον. *CIA*, *II*, add, 617[b], 4th century B.C. Several others also appear in broken form.

Of a very interesting resolution of the Σαραπιασταί. *CIA*, *II*, 617.

Of a find of recent date of the statutes of the Tobakchen, *Athen. Mittheilungen*, *XIX*, 1894, p. 249, beb., 260, 300 B.C. Maass, *Orpheus*, p. 78[f].

PIRÆUS.

A. Schäfer, *Ass'n for Private Culture in the Piræus. Classical Annual of Philosophy*, 121, 1880, p. 417[f]; Wachsmuth, *The City of Athens in Antiquity*, *II*, p. 152 sqq.

B. 'Οργεῶνες Μητήρ Θεῶν, Magna Mater, 3rd century, B.C. *CIA*, *IV*[2], 620[b] 619; 670; 623. Magna Mater and Bendis, also Syrian Aphrodite, 'Οργεῶνες of Εὐροπίας, or unions of good living.

Γ. Θιασῶται, whose organization honored the Μητήρ τῶν Θεῶν. *CIA*, *IV*[2], 620[b], 3rd century, B.C.

170   PRE-CHRISTIAN UNIONS.

Thus we perceive that the savants of the schools of inscriptions have partly caught on to the prodigious truth that the early Christians used, and planted into

Δ. 'Ερανισταί, worshiping as Σεβαζιασταί, *CIA*, *IV*², 626ᵇ. In the same place was found a stone bearing a consecration of a ἱερρποιὸς, there was also a statue of Sabazios.

E. Organizations of tradesmen and shippers, the Κυθήριοι, emigrants.

City of CYTHERA. They had a peculiar cult in their κτίσις or settlement. They were in part wholesale merchants, and had Isis, *CIA*, *II*, 68.

City of SIDON.—Merchants. There was found at SIDON, an organization inscribed Κοινὸν τῶν Σιδωνίστων ; *CIA*, *IV*², 1335ᵇ, and dating from the 6th century, B.C. The members enjoyed may privileges. Comp, *id.*, *II*, 171.

Ibidem: Ἔμποροι καὶ ναυκλήροι. Dealers having a ναύαρχος 'Αργεῖος, *CIA*, *II*, 1339; a σύνοδος ἐμπόρων καὶ ναυκλήρων, devoted to Ζεὺς Ξένιος. They built a statue B.C. 65.

Ibidem: Ἑταιρια, to Aphrodite with a list of names of women. A mass of Ἑταιραί appear in the Piræus, known by their consecrations, resolutions, decrees, etc., and showing themselves to be unions of workmen.

Town of MARKOPULO. Mesogis or mainland near the village of Markopulo —Two inscriptions of the Eikads, Εἰκαδεῖς, of the 4th cent., B.C.. *CIA*, *II*, 1093. A lawsuit is registered for 324 B.C., showing that they were chartered organizations at that early date.

City of SUNION; slaves of the mines, organized in ἔρανοι; *Inscr.*, showing a consecration of the ἐρανισταί to Men Tyrannos.

City of LAURIUM, *CIA*, *IV*², 1326ᶜ, found at Laurium; comp. *id.*, *II.*, 1328, bet. 2nd and 3rd centuries B.C. Xanthos at Sunion, slave of Orbius, built a temple to Men Tyrannos, with money probably voted him by his eranos. This was a little after the apostolic age.

Ibidem. Artists of DIONYSOS. Large numbers found in this vicinity.

PELOPONNESUS.

At ÆGINA, ὁ θίασος φαινεμάχου. Le Bas, II, 1708.

City of CORINTH. An association of athletes, ἀθληταί, *CIG*, 110⁴, time of Hadrian.

City of Argos. Σπατοπλασταί, shoemakers, leatherworkers; 2nd century, A.D. *CIG*, 1134; δεφιδασταί, *id.*, 1135, tanners, δεεῖται. 1136, τὸ κοινὸν τῶν περὶ τὸν Διόνυσον τεχνιτῶν ἐξ Ἰσθμοῦ καὶ Νεμέας τῆς ἐν Ἄργει συνόδου Le Bas, II. 116ᵃ, B.C., 114,

City of EPIDAUROS. Σύνοδος Ἀσκληπιαστῶν ἐν Πανακείκι Καββαδίας: union of physicians; *Fouilles d' Epidaure*, no. 211.

Promontory of HERMIONE. A list of names of members of a union ded. to Demeter, *CIG*, 1207; Le Bas, *II*, 159ᶜ; *Bull. Héll.*, *III*, 1879, p. 75.

City of TRŒZEN. Initiates to the Magna Mater association, Τελεστῆρες τᾶς μεγάλας Ματρός. *Bull. Héll.*, 1889ᵇ, p. 41, B, 3rd century, B.C., *XIII*, 1889, p. 120. This last gives a list of officers.

City of SPARTA: Ἀγριππιασταί, *CIG*, 1299, *CIL*, 498, B.C. 18-12.

City of OLYMPIA. Union of acrobats, Athletes. Ἀθλετῶν κοινὸν: *Archæologische Zeitung*, *XXXIV*, 1879, p. 56, no 13; *XXXVII*, 1879, p. 133, no. 261.

CENTRAL GREECE.

City of MEGARA. Ὀργεῶνες· Dittenberger, *Inscriptiones Grœcœ Septentrionalis*, no. 33: Ποσειδώνιον καὶ κοινὸν τῶν Αἰγοσθενιτῶν, *Inscr. Gr. S.*, 43, 6th century, B.C. See also no. 109, perhaps a union of Goat-herds.

Fountains of PAGAI; *Inscr. Gr.*. p. 192: ἱερὰ σύνοδος τῶν Ἡρακλείστων.

City of TANAGRA. Ἀθαναϊσταί, *Inscr. Gr.*, p. 685, 2nd century, B.C. A society of the Immortals.

City of THESPIA: 2nd century, B.C. Συνθύται Φιλετήρειοι· *Inscr, Gr.*, σύνοδος. 1790; 2194, ἀπὸ τῶν τεχνιτῶν, Dionysan artists.

City of THEBES; Union of Dionysan Artists, 3rd century, B.C. *Inscr. Gr.*, p. 2462; τὸ κοινὸν τῶν περὶ τὸν Διόνυσον τεχνιτῶν ἐν Θηβαις, comp. 2484; 2486; 2447; 2414.

TOPOGRAPHY AND NUMBERS.

the great economic labor organizations already existing by hundreds of thousands in all parts of the world, under the Solonic dispensation. We shall now give in an extended note Dr. Oehler's MSS. kindly contributed by him to the author specially for this work. It will give the reader some idea of the immense number and spread of these societies, since every notice here recorded is a genuine chiseling from the hand of the society's own scribe.

City of CHÆRONEA. An ἔρανος whose inscription shows a decree of emancipation of a slave.
Lake of Copaïs, HALIARTOS: union of hunters; σύνοδος τῶν κυνηγῶν, *Inscr. Gr.*, p. 2850; 2nd century, B.C.
Village of Opys. Artists and tradesmen. Οἱ περὶ τὸν Διόνυσον τχνῖται οἱ ἐξ Ἰσθμοῦ καὶ Νεμέας, συντελοῦντες δὲ ἐν Ὀποῦντι, Collitz, DIALEKT. INSCHRIFTEN, 10505. They shared in common.
City of PHOCIS. Union of hunters οἱ κυναγοί vel κυνηγοί, Collitz, no. 1540; Le Bas, *II*, 988.
Mt. Parnassus, DELPHI. Ἔρανος, union of artists, κοινὸν τῶν τεχνιτῶν τῶν ἐξ Ἰσθμοῦ καὶ Νεμέας. The *inscr*. exhibits documents regarding an ordeal of emancipation, Ἐφημερὶς Ἀρχαιολογική, 1883, 161, and 1884, no. 218.
City of CHALSIS. Union of artists of Dionysus: τὸ κοινὸν τῶν περὶ τὸν Διόνυσον τεχνιτῶν τῶν ἐξ Ἰσθμοῦ καὶ Νεμέας συντελξούντων δὲ ἐγχαλκίδι, *Bull. Hell.*, *XVI*, 1892, p. 91; *XVI*, 107, 9.
City of DEMETRIAS. Longshoremen and boatmen, ἡ τῶν ὑποστόλων σύνοδος. They were therapeutæ devoted to Serapis, *Athen. Mitth.*, *VII*, 1882, p. 335. Colony of them, *Rev. Archæol.*, *III. XIV*, 1889, p. 3.
City of TEMPE LARISSA. Θιασῶται, *Athen. Mitth.*, *XVI*, 1891, p. 261, no. 1.
City of LARISSA. Union of Dionysan as attested by a gravestone. Egyptian therapeutæ, κοινόν. *Athen. Mittheilungen*, *VIII*, 1883, p. 113.
Hot Springs. THESSALONICA. Union of Dyers, Συνήθεια τῶν πορφυροβάφων. *Bull. Hell.*, *VIII*, 1884, p. 463, no, 2; Duchesne Bayet, *Mission au Mt. Athos*, p. 52, 88.
City of OLYNTHOS. Guild or Collegium, ἀρχισυναγωγὸς θεοῦ Ἡρωός καὶ τὸ κολλήγιον, *CIG*, add. 2997 f.
City of PHILIPPI. Union of playrights, *CIL*, *III*, 703; 706, Thiasi Libiri patres Tasibasteni archimimus and promistola.
Town of STOBI, Union, but trade not indicated. Foucart, *Ass. Rel.*, p. 243, no. 68, συνθιασῖται.
City of ABDERA. *Inscriptions* of 8 labor guilds.
Town of AINOS. Union of shippers, therapeutæ. Αὐρήλιος ναύκληρος θεραπευτὴς τοῦ φιλανθρώπου θεοῦ Ἀσκληπιοῦ. Dumont, *Melanges d' Archéol.*, p. 437, no. 103.
Constantinople, BYZANTIUM. Union of gardeners. Novella, *Inst. Just.*, *LXIV*, tit. xix, cap. 1, A.D. 538, Corpus hortulanorum.
City of PERINTHOS. Unions of barbers, stone-workers and rowers of boats, κουρεῖς, λιθουργῶν τεχνιτῶν; also κωπωπλῶν. Some are published, and others are yet unpublished, *Mitth. aus Oesterreich*, *XIX*, 1896, p. 12; Dumont, *Mélanges*, p. 378, no. 68.
City of PHILIPPOPOLIS. Union of hunters. Τὸ κυνηγῶν κοινόν, Dumont p. 236, no. 42.
Fortress of GANOS. A holy synod of workers of a trade not specified: ἱερά σύνοδος, Dumont, *id.*, p. 420, no. 88 c.
Isle of GALLIPOLIS. Union of hunters. Τὸ κυνεηων κοινόν. Dumont, *id.*, p. 236, no. 42.
City of NIKOPOLIS ad Istrum. A synod of presbyters, *Archæol. Epigr. Mitth.*, *XV*, 1892, y. 219, no. 47. They were θιασῶται, trade unions.
City of APOLLONIA SOZOPOLIS. Union of cowboys: Μύσται βουκόλοι. *CIG*. 2052.
City of KALLATIS. Union having both male and female members. θίασος καὶ θιασεῖται, *Archæol. Epigr. Mitth.*, *aus Oesterreich*, *VI*, 1882, p. 10, no. 16; *XI*, 1887, p. 35, no, 35; *XIV*, 1891, p. 32, no. 75.

172   TOPOGRAPHY AND NUMBERS.

In these unions it was possible during the first centuries for the Christians to have a legal right of existence given them.

City of TOMIS. House of the organized sailors. *Archæol. Epigr. Mitth.*, *XIII*, 1890, p. 93: Οἶκος τῶν ναυκλήρων, *Id.*, *VI*, 1882, p. 19, no. 39, transmitting a resolution.

Point of Land CHERONESOS TAURICA. Θιασάρκης, Latyschew. *II*, no. 19.

City of PANTICAPÆUM. Θιασεῖται, Latyschew, *II*, no. 19, B.C. 200; no. 39, 39; 60-5.

City of TANAIS. Θιασεῖται, comp. with foregoing, no. 438-60.

Isle of IMBROS. Union of Apostles of the Fulfillment, οἱ τετελεσμένοι Ἑρμεῖ, *Bull. Hell.*, *VII*, 1883, p. 166, B.C. 200. They were the dwarf blacksmiths, Cabiri.

Isle of THASOS. Union of wholesale merchants Ἔμποροί. ἀρχικεδέμπορος, dedicated to the νέον Διόνυσον. The Καθηγεμών, or Forerunner. *Journ. of Hellenic Studies*, *VIII*, 1887, p. 426, no. 32. A.D. 300.

City of LEMNOS. Union of farm laborers: Ἐργασταί, B.C. 100, *Bull. Hell.*, *IX*, 1885, p. 64, no. 8. Ὄρος τῶν ὀργεονῶν.

City of LESBOS. Mytelene. Union of Shoemakers, Οἱ τὴν σκυτικὴν τέχνην ἐργαζόμενοι. *Athen. Mitth.*, *XI*, 1886, p. 282, no. 43. Ἑρμαϊταί. *Anc. Greek Inscrs.*, *II*, 227 c. Θίασος τῶν κναφέων, shown in an epitaph.

Island of CHIOS. Union of Ferrymen. Πορθμεῖς, ἐργολάβοι, ναύκληροι, *Athen. Mytth.*, *XIII*, 1888, p. 170, no 10 a, b; no. 11, ἀρχισυνάγωγοι of a union, *CIG* add, 2227 c.

Town of KEOS. A θίασος, representing the Σαραπιασταί, Foucart, *Ass, Rel.*, no, 42.

City of TENOS. Unions of various occupations under the following patronage: Κοινὸν θιασωτῶν Δαμνιαδῶν; κοινὸν Ἀγεσιλαδων; κοινὸν θιάσωτῶν; κοινὸν Θεοξεναιαστῶν, B.C. 200, *CIG*, 2938, Συμβίωσις, φιλία; *CIG* add, 2337 b, and 6820.

Cyclade of MYCONOS. Union of earners. ἔρανος πεντακοσαι δραχμαι and εἰσφοραί. Dittenburger. *Sylloge*, no. 433.

Mart of DELOS. Unions of wholesalers, boatmen and freighters or longshoremen, storagemen, Greeks and Romans. *Bull. Hell.*, *XVI*, 1892, p. 152, no. 4; *III*, 1879, p. 151; 176, no. 3; 370, no. 12; 372, no. 13; *XVI*, 1892, p. 150, no. 1; *VIII*, 1884, p. 126; *XI*, 1877, p. 244, no. 33. Foreigners from Tyre, organized in unions, θίασος, *CIG*, 2271. *Bull. Hell.*, *III*, 1879, p. 374, no. 11. Strangers from BERYTUS, organized under an ἀρχιθιεσίτες χοινὸν Βηρυτίων ἐμπόρων καὶ ναυκλήρων καὶ ἐγδοκέων. *Bull. Hell.*, *VII*, 1883, p. 469, no. 2; 247, no. 4; 474, no. 2; 475, no. 4; 472, no. 6; κοίνὸν βηρυτίων Ποσειδωνιαστῶν ἐμπόρων καὶ ναυκλήρων καὶ ἐγδοχέων" *Bull. Hell.*, *III*, 1883, p. 467, 1; 371, 5; 473, 3. At DELOS were many Therapeutæ, who together with the wearers of black, μελανοφόροι, worked at various trades and professions. Οἱ μελανοφόροι καὶ θεραπευταί, *CIG*, 2295; *Bull. Hell.*, *VI*, 1882, p. 318, no. 3; *Monuments Grecs*, 1879, p. 40. Μελανοφόροι and ἡ σύνοδος τῶν μελανοφόροι, *Bull. Hell.*, 1892, p. 482; σύνοδος and συνοδῖται are recorded for DELOS in *Bull. Hell.*, *VIII*, 1884, p. 121; they are therapeutæ. Athenian θεραπευταί are numerously found there. Even the Roman collegia as compitalicia, see Mommsen, *De Coll. et Sodal.*, iv, abounded at this renowned slave mart, κομπεταλισταί, *Bull. Hell.*, *VII*, 1883, p. 12, no. 5. Likewise unions of the hardworking rowers and boat dredgers, ὑπερέται. *Bull. Hell.*, *III*, 1879, p. 367; ἑταῖροι. Cf. Ἀθναιον, *III*, 1873, p. 131. θιασῶται, *Rheinisches Museum*, *XXII*, 1867. p. 293, no. 283.

Cyclade City of SYROS. Union of eranists, with a κύριος or director, trade not mentioned in the *inscr*. κοινὸν τῶν ἐρανιστῶν καὶ ἀρχέρανος, *CIG* add 2347J.

City of Paros. Λιθοξόοι' marble-workers. *Athen. Mitth.*, *V*, 1876, p. 35, no. 39. *CIG*, 2396.

Town of NAXOS. Ὄρος, ἔρανος, thought to be similar to a union of surveyors. *Arch. Epigr. Mitth.*, XIII, 1890, g. 179, no. 5.

City of AMORGOS. A ὅρος, with an ἀρχέρανος and a νόμος τῶν ἐρανιστῶν, Fouc., *Ass'n. Rel.*, no. 45. Dancers of the Cordax, κορδαχίσταί τῶν περὶ τὸν Πύθον Απολλ ͻα κορδάκων, *CIG* add, 2264 a, at MINOA.

TOPOGRAPHY AND NUMBERS. 173

The right of association in Attica reaches back to, and is derived from, the law of Solon, preserved to us by Gaius. It was also the same in other states of the Grecian world, for a similar freedom appears there to

City of MELOS. Μύσται, *Athen. Mitth.*, *XV*, 1860, p. 246; *Journ. of Hell. Stud.*, *XVII*, 1897, p. 14, no. 32.
Sporade of THERA. Κοινὸν ἀνδρείον τῶν συγγενῶν, *CIG*, 2448.
City, Isle of PATMOS. Union of torch or flambeau or torch-bearers; τὸ κοινὸν τῶν Λαμπαδιστῶν. Dittenberger *Sylloge*, no. 402.
City of COS. Union of fellow journeymen purveyors: Τὸ κοινὸν τῶν συμπορνομένων πὰρ Δία Ύέττιον. Paton and Hicks, *Inscriptions of Cos*, no. 382.
City of NISYROS. Unions of self-serving plenty. Πάντα κοινία ἐν Νισύρῳ: Ἑρμαίζοντες, Ἀφροδισιασταί Σύροι, etc., *Athen. Mitth.*, *XV*, 1890, no. 134. Also a union of Breakfasters who consecrated to Hermes: Frühstückgesellschaft συναριστιόν, Hillers, *Wochenschrift für classische Philologie*, 1896, column 80.
Isle of SYME. Unions of Ἀδωνιασταί, Ἀφροδεισεασταί καὶ Ἀσκληπιασταί οἱ ἐν Αὐλαις, Ἡροείσται καὶ Οἰακιασταί. Le Bas, *III*, 301.

Island of RHODES.

Unions of Dionysan artists and playwrights: *Bull. Hell.*, *X*, 1886, p. 203 and see *index*; *Corpus Inscr. Graec.*, Insularum, I.
The labor organizations of RHODES are too numerous to mention. Among the sixty or seventy different unions known by their inscriptions to have existed in the island of RHODES, and said by Isocrates in his *Panegyric*, to have been planted there by Æschines, after his persecution at Athens by Demosthenes, are found the unions of θιασῶται at:
City of KAMIRUS. Ἐρανισταί, nos. 102, 736, 938; unions of soldiers, συνστρατευσάμενοι, *id.*, 41, 43, 75, 163, 101, 107. Also many unions of sailors, boatmen, ferrymen, longshoremen, frieght-handlers, bag-carriers, etc.

Island of CYPRUS.

Union of stowers of odures, θίασος τῆς ἀποσκευῆς; union of sweetmeats makers (doubtful), θίασος τῶν ἡδυλλίων; several others, *Athen. Mitth.*, *IX*, 1884, p. 137, no. 8; union of hunters, κυνηγοι, *CIG*, 2614.
City of SALAMIS. Union of farm laborers in Le Bas, *III*. 2757, 2786.
City of AMISOS in PAPHLIGONIA, Asia Minor, Union of ἕταιραι, mentioned by Pliny, Eranos, *X*, *Epist.*, 93, 94.
City of NICOMEDIA, BITHYNIA. Union of ἀρχιμόστης. *CIG*, 3773.
City of POMPEIIUPOLIS. Union of tool-dressers, tool-makers, and toolkeepers, θίασος ξυστων, *CIG*, 4155.
City of PRUSIAS on the Hypsios, union of Masons, ξυστικὴ καὶ θυμελικὴ σύνοδος, Perrot, *Exploration*, p. 31, no. 21.
City of CYZICUS. Union of women honoring Artemis. Union of κυνοσουρεῖται, *Monatschrift, Ber. Akad.*, 1874, p. 2, no. 1. Θεραπευταί therepeutæ in honor of Serapis and Isis, *Rev. Arch.*, *XXXVIII*, 1879, p. 258. Union of bag-carriers, σακκοφόροι, *Athen. Mitth.*, *VI*, 1881, p. 125, no. 8. Union of woolworkers, γναφεῖς, *Athen. Mitth.*, *VII*, 1882, p. 252. no, 19. Union doing business in the fisheries consisting of 15 persons, with a ξυσταρχὴς, *CIG*, 3678. *Atthen. Mitth.*, *X*. 1885, p. 205. They were connected with the tolls.
City of PANORMOS. Union of bag-carriers on the quays. σακκοφόροι λιμενῖται. Σύλλογος, *VIII*, 1873, p. 171.
City of ABYDOS. Unions of tent-makers, house-builders and farm laborers, οἱ σκηνεῖται, καί ἐργασταί. Le Bas, *III*, 1743ⁿ; δομοτέκτων, Le Bas, *III*, 1743°.
City of SIGEION. Union of brass and metal-workers, braziers, συμβίωσις τῶν χαλχεῶν, *CIG*, 3639 add.
City of PERGAMOS. Union of cattlemen, βουκόλοι, Fränkel, *Inschriften von Pergomen*, *I*, 222; *II*, 485, 486-488. Cable and cord-makers, σπεῖρα, *id.*, *II*, 319, 320, union of musicians.

have prevailed. We must here end the list of labor unions in our extended note. Only one or two could have space for mention in each town, although in some places are found as many as one hundred. The foregoing list only proves how enormously organized were the ancient working people, even as far back as Romulus. This vast trade unionism was almost as early met by another organization, the standing armies. Nor did trade unionism go down until the middle of the fourth century of our era. Early in that century it met its death-blow in the great massacre of Diocletian, and even his conspiracy against it could not have availed but for the imperial organization of a tyrant's soldiery. We give this unprecedented horror in full in our last chapter.

And yet the modern newspaper and stump speaker tell us in gross and inexcusable ignorance, if not with misleading design, that most great movements have been without organization! It is a falsehood!

Organization, mostly that of trade unionism has been at the helm of all great movements toward the enfranchisement of the laboring people of the world. Organization of kings and of men at the control of money honors and power, has always been and still is, at the helm of standing armies and other weapons of the laborers' destruction.

Another frightful record is, that when their beautiful organization was cut down by a conspiracy of monarchs, millionaires and prelates, humanity swooned away and fell into the world's dark age of feudalism.

Province of ÆOLIS.

City of Cyme. Union of inscribers, registration clerks, ἐπιγραφαί Bull Héll., XII, 1888, p. 368, no.16.
City of Smyrna. Unions of silversmiths, συνεργασία τῶν ἀργυρκόπων, CIG., 3154; also id., χρυσοχόων goldsmiths. Union of carriers or porters συμβίωσις τῶν φορτηγῶν. Amer. Journ. of Archœol., I., 1885, p. 141; union of fishermen, συνεργασία τῶν κυρτοβόλων, Le Bas, III·, 248. Union of Athletes.
A great many others are likewise registered.

CHAPTER IX.

SOLONISM IN OUR ERA.

THE WORLD UNDER ITS INFLUENCE.

SKETCH from A.D. 1 to 363—The Burial Attachment—Eranos at Jerusalem—The Kurios—Legalized Boss over Each Union—Peremptory Provision of Law—Was Dictator and Lord—Misunderstanding regarding Him—Plan of Salvation—Early Mutilation and Covering of Facts—When they first began to Display Secret Principles before the World—Always had Common Table—Macedonia Alive with them—Deacons—Originally only Table Waiters—Unions of Deacons or Table Waiters—Secret Common Eating Houses—Worked in the Prytaneum—Lydia of Thyateira an officer in Dyers' Guild—How and where Converted—Gravestone of Menippus found—Therapeutæ were Regular Business Guilds—Many in the Cities of the Seven Churches—Proof in their own Chiselings—Eranos and Thiasos alike—Unions of the Hetæræ—Claudius Drove them from Rome—Union of Gold-beaters—Bakers of Philadelphia—Fishers—Labor Unions Worshiped Imaginary Saviour—Ground All Mellow for One when He Came—List of various Messiahs—Karl Marx Right in Treating Religion as a Consequent and not as a Cause—Shipping Business of the Unions—Degraded by Taint of Labor—Ox-drivers' Union—Lucian's Ridicule—Cotton and Linen Industry—Phrygian Bag-Carriers—Called themselves Holy Union of Bag-carriers—Sacred Union of CottonSpinners—Of Wool Workers—Of Crimson Dye Makers—All in the Cities of the Seven Churches—Object, To better their Circumstances—Consecrations—Building Trades—Valuable Find of a Sepulchre with Glyphics of a Masons' Brotherhood Converted to Christianity, but Concealing the Fact for Fear of the Roman Law—Time of Paul—Celebrated C.I.G. 3857 t—Dr. Oehler's Contribution—Splendid Find of the Shoemakers of Shoemakers' Street—Their Colony, a Church of the Temple of Cybele on the Acropolis of Kelainæ—Dr. Ramsay's explorations—MarbleWorkers of Apameia—Christianized Unions of Flaviapolis in Cilicia—No Eleemosynary Charity Existed—All under the Veil of Initiation Furnished with work—Beginning of Persecutions with Crippling Laws Against Them—Stretch of the Solonic Unions to Britain—Havoc of the Council of Laodicea—Canon Preserved that Suppressed the Work of Solon—Quotation—The Singing and Enjoyment Receive their Death Stroke—All Elements of Socialism Expunged by Prelates—Monastic Orders and Tyranny of Prelate Power Supervened—Ghastly Consequence in Feudal System—The World fell into a Millennial Swoon.

IN our last chapter we gave a review of the economic associations under which the useful factor of the human race used to produce inscriptions, showing that they were organized from B. C. 600, down to the beginning of our era and that this organization had existed in all probability from a much higher antiquity than Solon, although the Solonic law which made it free under a jus coeundi, is the first source of our information.

It remains now to explain its existence and power to a considerably later date. During the earlier part of this period its influence was enormously felt, especially for the first two hundred years. As in the first long period of 700 years, covered by our last chapter, so in the succeeding period covered by this, reaching to 363, the date of the suppression by the Council of Laodicea, of the common table and the communal code on which the Solonic dispensation rested, the organizations were rather economic than religious. All traces, whether by inscriptional, or other literary record, point to this. As Mommsen says,[1] they used the guise of religion to secure to themselves the right of continuing their associations which, at about the time covered by this author, were seriously threatened; for the Senate was moved to break them up. This guise of religion answered as a cloak. Their real object was always the economic one, because they could better succeed in their terrible struggle for existence by being organized together as a mutual fraternity.

We shall begin at the year 33 or 34, with the great society at Jerusalem having a membership of 3,000 which Dr. Oehler characterizes as a species of thiasus, or perhaps an eranos having the burial attachment like a large

[1] Mommsen, *De Colligiis et Sodalicits Romanorum*, p. 87; "Ipsa illa simulata religio senatum promovit ut jus coeundi tollerat."

number he has furnished us from Asia Minor, and like the Roman collegium funeraticium,[2] the same with a burial attachment legalizing the whole business of the union. The society of Jerusalem deserves to be described from an economic point of view. This is an honor it never had. We pass over the sacred story and look at it in a plain practical way.

The fact is, that soon after the crucifixion—a hideous and cruel transaction, altogether useless and unreasonable—a reaction of the poorer common people set in. There was already a secret society of which Jesus appears to have been elected the kurios, dictator, quinquinnalis or president. That it was an economic society like thousands of others existing at that moment all over the pro-consular regions of the then vast empire, following the requirements of the Solonic law, there can be no doubt entertained by the true student of these now historical facts.

This society had resolved to bring out into the open world the principles upon which it was secretly founded, leading to the salvation of the people from the brutal cruelties of the dominant power of money, greed and royalty.

We find few if any inscriptions of this scene; what makes it historically known to us is the report of Luke, in his history of the Acts of the Apostles. Here we are fortunate enough to have a detailed account. To the increasing mass of atheists and unbelievers who, because this original and rough plan of salvation failed, now deride the whole transaction as a fiction, we can only say that it is to all outside appearances, apart from the religious gloze which is largely a subterfuge of priestcraft, as good and as reliable history as that of Thucydides, Polybius or Livy. At any rate it is ancient, disinterested and straightforward; and for this alone, deserves to be studied with sober judgment and scrutinized under the searching lens of comparative evidence; since the more it is subjected to this, the more it will be found to com-

---

[2] Oehler, *MSS. to the author*, speaking of the care of the society in regard to preservation of graves, says: "Wir finden aber Verschiedenheiten in der Art und Weise, wie die einzelnen Vereine diese Sorge bethätigen, vgl. Schiess, *Über die Römischen Collegia funeraticia*, 1, durch Beistellung des Grabes selbst .... Wir sehen auch in der ersten Christengemeinde die Sorge für die Bestattung ihrer verstorbenen Genossen: *Acta Apost.*, V., 6, Ἀναστάντες δὲ οἱ νεώτεροι συνέστειλαν αὐτόν, καὶ ἐξενέγκαντες ἔθαψαν. Cf. 9, 10.

port and harmonize with the enormous mass of hitherto unseen, but irrefutable evidence of their own chiselings upon the stones, all over the world, at that auspicious moment.

The historian who recorded this important and most interesting narrative is supposed to have been Luke, a man of culture, speaking Greek as well as Hebrew, and a member of one of these organizations. He was undoubtedly a kurios or presiding officer of much dignity for he is spoken of by other writers as having written homilies; besides he afterwards accompanied Paul in his peregrinations among distant people agitating and building up the principles, and there are found several important inscriptions touching his life.

This narrative is too little understood and valued. Ministers of religion override this important episode in our religious history. It is to the effect that the hitherto slumbering thiasos at Jerusalem, the very same Paul and Barnabas afterwards in time of famine, so generously and so bravely transported provisions and money to, from far off Asian unions of the same widespread brotherhoods, was enormously revived by the martyrdom of the master. On the day of Pentecost[3] all the members including the Twelve[4] who had been selected as the special promulgators, were gathered in their "house." The boldness of the disciples had been greatly increased by this outrage of martyrdom; besides this, large numbers of people had been converted to their plan of Salvation.

Any person who wishes may read what this plan was, although the necessary secrecy as to the doings of the initiates rendered it wise for the historian to cover his words with a religious tinge, because the law of Rome, known as the lex Licinia, required it. One must read

[3] Dr. Oehler thinks it the same as any other thiasos with funeral attachment, and refers to Acts, V., 6, 9 and 10.
[4] "$\Delta\omega\delta\epsilon\kappa a$." There can be no longer any question as to whether the unions of about this period were in the habit of sending out such delegates, independently of, and anterior to, the celebrated one at Jerusalem. We have several strange inscriptions on which are registered one point or another, of the $\delta\omega\delta\epsilon\kappa a$. Collitz, *Dialektenschrift*, No. 3051 shows a $\vartheta\iota a\sigma o\varsigma$ at Chalcedony, ($X a\lambda\chi\epsilon\delta\omega\nu$); it is an inscription referring to a $\kappa o\iota\nu\grave{o}\nu$ $N\iota\kappa o\mu\acute{a}\chi\epsilon\iota o\nu$; The reading refers to the priesthood of the "$\delta\omega\delta\epsilon\kappa a$ $\vartheta\epsilon o\acute{\iota}$." It appears to be of about the first century. No one can, as yet decipher sufficiently to know the particulars. The $\Delta\omega\delta\epsilon\kappa a$ are mentioned in quite a number of other inscriptions of purely pagan surroundings, and it is now well known that many societies had their $\epsilon\upsilon a\gamma\gamma\epsilon\lambda\iota\sigma\tau\grave{\eta}\varsigma$, or evangelist, long before Christ, as a regular officer.

between the lines. With this caution one sees that there was a common table at which all the initiated members sat. The St. James translation commits a sad error, whether intentional or not it would be difficult to say, in making a vagary of a straightforward clause of the 45th verse of the second chapter of the Acts, in saying that those who joined "sold their possesions and goods and parted them to *all* men."[5] The original of Luke did not say this at all; it said they distributed the good things among *all*—the 3,000 members he is speaking of, being most unequivocally understood. This English translation is so misleading as to spoil the reader's comprehension. He would glean, by the insidiously interpolated italicized *all*, that the historian intended to say the great world at large! Nothing could be more stupidly, we fear to say dishonestly false. The goods brought into the union were carefully distributed among the thousands who formed the membership; and we shall take the Greek Bible at its word.[6]

Such a prodigious thiasos thus proved to have an economical object at base, must, following the natural course of things, be supplied with a board of direction consisting of eminent business men.

The fact is, they soon got into trouble. They had for the first time in the whole career of the Solonic dispensation, burst their bonds of secrecy, so far as their advocacy of salvation went, and begun to parade their principles to the open world. Here, then, was a new function bursting upon the skeptical, requiring all their talent, and in another sphere. It became necessary, therefore to have a group of business men. Another trouble they encountered was the complaint that some female mem-

[5] Acts, II., 40, 41, 42, 43, 44. In the Phrygian inscriptions the mode of initiation of members into a θίασος or a κοινὸν was by baptism. The same was practiced here. In verse 40 the uninitiated were exhorted to save themselves from the bad, the dishonest, the crooks, "γενεᾶς τῆς σκολιᾶς," generation that was crooked, for they were in great danger. One of their number had been crucified by them, and there was great fear; so verse 43 assures us: "'Εγένετο δὲ πάσῃ ψυχῇ φόβος." As to the initiation it is shown by verse 41: "Οἱ μὲν οὖν ἀσμένως ἀποδεξάμενοι τὸν λόγον αὐτοῦ ἐβαπτίσθησαν," κ. τ. λ. The 44th verse plainly shows that in point of common table and community goods, the society we are here describing patterned exactly after those of Dirksen, having a common table and communal code: "Πάντες δὲ οἱ πιστεύοντες ἦσαν ἐπὶ τὸ αὐτὸ καὶ εἶχον ἅπαντα κοινά." κ. τ. λ. The unions in Phrygia and Greek-speaking regions of the world, called θίασοι, were mostly trade unions; this one at Jerusalem seems to have been one of the kind known in our times as mixed, or unions of mixed trades.

[6] *Id.*, 45, "Καὶ τὰ κτήματα καὶ τὰς ὑπάρξεις ἐπίπρασκον, καὶ διεμέριζον αὐτὰ πᾶσι, καθότι ἄν τις χρείαν εἶχε." This means plainly that the organization receiving the good things, divided them among the membership according to each one's wants.

bers from Asia Minor were being slighted or crowded aside by the others, and there arose a grievance.

They must accordingly, appoint several strictly business men who were members, and the chairman of this committee was Stephen the proto-martyr. We are fortunate in being so well informed about this episode of the life of the thiasos at Jerusalem. Stephen, a name signifying in good Greek, a crown, or a person crowned, may not at his nomination have careered under this title; for after the awful tragedy which terminated his life they honored him among their immortals with a crown of glory bought by faithful martyrdom. Stephen was an Asian Greek, with a business capacity which, with his aids, every one of whom is named in the history of Luke, soon rectified the difficulty, regulating the distribution of food at the common table. This success brought upon him and the society, the ire and vengeance of the great speculating provision ring of Jerusalem. These organized profit mongers could not make money by charging consumers high prices for goods they had gotten at a low rate. Just as a similar set of speculators recently attacked the similar organization at Rochdale in England and still undermine and freeze out co-operative provision stores everywhere, so did the speculating ringleaders of Jerusalem, burning with jealousy, energetic in their vengeance, desperate and obstinate in their greed, rave and bluster and bear down against the successful mastership of Stephen and his business-like committee. This committee with ready money flowing into a common fund could buy at wholesale from producers outside of Jerusalem all the provisions for their 3,000 members, have it conveyed directly to their co-operative kitchen without even halting at the shambles of the speculator. Without doubt this is what caused the rebellion against Stephen, and compassed his destruction. Only a short time before, the Founder of this same society, punished the iniquity of those money-grabbing speculators who had the effrontery to monopolize the sacred temple of Jerusalem. When thinkers grow in judgment and rise to the dignity of socialism and the labor problem, it will easily be seen that this celebrated attack upon the speculators in coins and doublers of values of a thousand commodities and necessaries of life whom this strange man drove from their immoral traffic, was

OPENING THE PLAN TO THE WORLD. 181

engaged in the economic task of a true political economist; and we can find nothing in the annals of that personage, or his plans and organization, disproving that he was engaged in a work of instituting an improved scheme of political economy and plan of salvation for which he suffered as Stephen suffered, and through whose suffering the deep foundations of socialism were laid.

The foregoing is here intended merely as one example in thousands of associations which existed at that moment all over Rome and her pro-consular dependencies, Judæa included.

In that very hour we find by their inscriptions, many others. In the Isle of Cyprus there was a union of agricultural laborers.[7] Recorded in the great body of Greek inscriptions there are multitudes of tablets showing that societies with a similar object existed in great numbers.[8] There is coming to light fresh evidence that Macedonia was thoroughly supplied with these societies at the time Paul was busy at Phillippi doing his celebrated evangelical work.[9]

Numberless curiosities of about these times are unearthed, among which are unions of the deacons.[10] As we understand this word it is very misleading, for deacon or diaconus was the Greek word for waiter.[11] And the original deacons at the prytanean common table of the official state were not only waiters but also menials and their work as waiters was a trade in furtherance of which they were organized.

The unions of purple dyers of the time of the Advent were numerous. As many as seventy-five slabs are already preserved in the various museums and private collections. At Hierapolis, Thyateira, Ephesus, and other cities of the Seven Churches they were especially abundant and thrifty. Lydia and Menippus, Christian char-

---

[7] Le Bas, III., 2757, 2786: Κοινὸν τῶν ὑπ' αὐτὸν τασσομένων Κρητῶν.
[8] CIG., 2529: "Ἱερὰ σύνοδος ἐς Νέμεα καὶ Πύθια" It was for a time supposed that the Roman conquests had destroyed all the organizations; but this is a mistake. No. 3308 CIG., is an epitaph to a member of an eranos.
[9] Heuzy and Daumet, *Mission Archéol.*, p. 329, no. 133: 'Ηρακλῆ θεῷ μεγίστῳ Μελέαγρος τοῖς συνθιασίταις."
[10] Oehler, *MS.*, no. 97, p. 28: "Hier anzuschliessen ist wohl auch das κοινὸν τῶν διακόνων in Ambrakia, CIGr., 1800."
[11] See Liddell, *Dict.*, in v. Διάκονος. "A servant, a waiting-man or woman. . . . . from διά κόνος, one who is dusty from running, cf., ἐγκονέω." Thus our church deacons were originally, and even at the time of Paul and Peter, waiters; and Lüder, *Donys. Künst.*, shows that some inscriptions mention them as lowly, hard working table waiters and menials, trailed in the dust by the taint of toil. This originated our deacons.

acters, of whom we reserve more elaborate mention in a future chapter, were members and influential business agents of the purple dyers' trade organization of Thyateira, one of the cities of the Seven Churches.[12]

During the early Christian period, even before the crucifixion, the Dionysan Therapeutæ are known by their mysterious and silent chiselings, to have been numerous. Recent examinations of the inscriptions have revealed that they were unions of working people organized for the purpose of helping each other in obtaining food. The story that they were confined to the island of Mœroes near Alexandria and that they were there only as philosophical cranks, with a sole purpose of mumbling religious rituals and feeding with vegetarian abstemiousness, excluding the pleasures of the world, is proved to be false. They existed not only in Egypt, but also in Jerusalem where they were hand in hand with the Essenes, and were also mysteriously numerous in many parts of Asia Minor.[13]

The hetæra[14] was a species of trade union of those times that was made celebrated by Pliny the younger in the time of the emperor Trajan, who, seeing the advantages to the hard-pressed workers in the province of Bithynia, Asia Minor where he was governor, tried to obtain permission from the emperor to organize one. This permission was refused. The society of hetæræ of those times has been much defamed. In Pliny's case it is a trade union. As governor, he had to persecute them because they had turned Christian. So everywhere we find it always to be an organization of mechanics. Although Oehler is of the opinion that the thiasos

[12] An epigraph discovered at Mount Athos, and published, Duchesne-Bayet, *Mémoire sur une Mission au Mount Athos*, p. 52, no. 83, shows that the συνήδρια τῶν πορφυροβάφων in Thessalonica honored Menippos, a purple dyer from Thyateira, with a monument at his grave. Menippos, an early Christian, is spoken of in the Apocryphal writings; Lydia was an agent for the sale of stuffs manufactured at the guild of πάρφυροβοφοι of Thyateira, the same who was converted by Paul.

[13] Oehler, *MSS.*, no. 58, 72, p. 25: "Die Gebraüchlichen Bezeichnung war: Οἱ περὶ τον Διόνυσον τεχνίται. In der Kaiserzeit wird der Kaiser als Διόνυσος hinzugefügt, wie in Inschriften von Kypros die Ægyptischen Könige neben Διόνυσος genannt werden.

[14] Very little difference existed between the Therapeutæ and the Hetæræ The θεραπευταί of Alexandria had Isis, while those of Asia Minor had Cybele for their mother protectress; but the two were about one and the same. See *Isis und Serapis—Kultus in Klein Asien*, *Wiener Numismat. Zeitschrift*, xxi., 1879, p. 1, 234; Lafarge, *Histoire du Culte des Divinités*. Oehler says: "Im Dienste dieser Gottheit stehen auch die θεραπευταί und μελανοφοροί." Therapeutæ left their inscriptions at Corcyra and Thebes, CIG., 2484. Also in Athens; Διονύσου θερσπευταί. *Mitth.*, xvii., 1892, p. 272.

IMAGE-MAKERS AND THE ICONOCLASTS. 183

was the key-word of the various trade and labor unions of those times yet we are disposed to think that this term hetæra was one which as nearly voiced the popular idea as any other.[15] As eminent an authority as Dion Cassius characterized the eranos and the hetæra as being alike.[16] It is not until recently that scholars have awakened to a knowledge of this and it is fresh proof that Oehler is right when he regards all the principal unions as one under the Solonic system.

In the building trades of Pergamus the hetæræ were organized into trades of masons with architects and bricklayers and they had a full set of officers and men. Cyprus is also found in some manner to have had unions of the building trades in a flourishing condition.[17] The towns of Attica and Macedonia, such as Megara contained unions of the hetæræ. A stone found here indicates a union of people who had regular monthly meetings at which they enjoyed a sort of banquet in common.[18] The hetæræ were working people organized into various trades and professions. Sometimes we find them as coral workers. This was their trade in Lydia and Thyateira, where just at the dawn of our era they were making little gods, goddesses and other images of coral, which had a ready sale among the pagans as ornaments for their apartments, temples, lararia and other select places; so much so that later, when Christianity planted into and captured them and protested against image worship, it caused the war of the iconoclasts The workers could not afford to lose their business and be turned into the highways to starve and they rebelled.[19] The new Testament story of Paul and Demetrius comes in here for a solution.

But the hetæræ as organized unions are celebrated

---

[15] See *infra, index* in v. *Pliny, Letters*, pointing to pages where a convincing proof is given, including the letters of Pliny to Trajan and also the emperor's answer.

[16] Dion Cassius, xxxviii., 13, says: "Τὰ ἑταιρικὰ κολλήγια ἐπιχωρίως καλούμενα." Savigny, *System des heutigen Römischen Rechts*, II., p. 260, sq. confirms it. Oehler, as we have shown *supra*, p. 296, note 46, has told us this conclusively.

[17] CIG., 3545, 3546; Fränkel, *Inschriften von Pergamon*, II., 333, of the time of Hadrian, and of course they were there at the time of Christ.

[18] In Abydos was found an inscription showing a δομοτέκτης, and his ἐργεπιίκτης, Le Bas, III., 1743. Athen, *Mitth.* IV., 1881, p. 227. A gravestone marked 'Αρισταίνετος 'Αρισταινέτου δομοτέκτων.''

[19] CIA. II., 1139; Willhelm, *Arch. Epigr. Mitth. aus Oesterreich*, xvii., 1894, p. 45; Ziebarth, p. 38. There were the 'Εικαδισταί, which we conjecture to be the image makers, although there is another and meaningless interpretation.

in the histories of the great authors. Josephus refers to them in his much studied passages, and Dion Cassius says Claudius drove them out of Rome.[20] Thus under this name they were numerous, and flourished as trade unions during the time of Christ and we now know they assisted in the evangelizing journeys of Paul, all over Asia Minor. We have two inscriptions under the name hetæra: one a union at Palmyra, of the trade of gold and silver workers; the other from Smyrna.[21] There was a union of tailors,[22] several of the shoemakers and of the bakers at Philadelphia and Thyateira, and the discovery of monumental evidence of the bakers' strike at Magnesia of which, so much as we know, we have already given in a previous chapter. It happened at or near the time of Christ.[23] Others made coral shrines.[24]

In these Asiatic cities, celebrated as being the cradle of the seven churches, teeming with organized industries of various trades, we find many highly interesting things. Numerous unions of fishermen are found in their inscriptions. Even the methods of taking members' dues and fees are shown.[25] A very Billingsgate is unearthed at Ephesus, another of the seven cities. The business of the fishery, which in this populous country was great, was conducted by unions of the fishing trade, and scenes such as are common near Blackfriers bridge were constantly going on at Ephesus, Smyrna and Antioch. At Cyzicus there was found an inscription showing a thiasos of fishermen who held a consecration to Poseidon and Aphrodite. In Pessinus a thiasos of fisher-

---

[20] Josephus, *Antiquities*, vii., 2: "'Ησαν δ' ἐκ τῶν παροίκων οὓς Δαυίδος καταλελοίπει . . . . . τῶν δὲ λατομούντων ὀκτάκις μύριοι τουτῶν δ' ἐπισάται τρίσχιλιοι καὶ τριακόσιοι." Again Dion Cassius speaks of them: LX. 6, 6: Τοὺς τε Ἰουδαίους—οὐκ ἐξήλασε μὲν, τῷ δὲ δὴ πατρίῳ νόμῳ βίῳ χρωμένους ἐκέλευσε μὴ συναθροίζεσθαι. Τάς τε ἑταιρείας ἐπαναχθείσας ὑπὸ τοῦ Γαΐου διέλυσε." This was in the time of Claudius who attacked the unions.
[21] CIG., 3154 *Smyrna*. "Συνεργασία τῶν ἀργυροκόπων καὶ χρυσοχόων." Le Bas, III,, 2602, *Palmyra*, "συνετέλεια τῶν χρυσοχόων καὶ ἀργυροκόπων." In Perinthus, another: "Μωκιανὸς ἀργυροτέχτης." *Mitth.* of Dr. Kalinkas.
[22] Ἑταιρια. Thyateira ἱματευόμενοι, CIG., 3480. The one found at Philadelphia is "Οἱ τὴν σκυτικὴν τεχνην ἐργαζόμενοι, Athen., *Mitth.*, XI., 1886, p. 282. In Philadelphia also was a ἑταιρία of shoemakers: Ἱερα φυλη τῶν σκυτέων, Le Bas, III., 656; and many others.
[23] CIG., 3495 ᵗ Ἑταιριὰ τῶν ἀρτοκόπων. Union of Bakers. See *supra*, p. 84.
[24] Κοραλλιοπλασταί. There was such a union of coral workers found in Magnesia on the Siphylos, registered in CIG., 3438. There has been some dispute among the savants regarding the coral workers. All however, agree that they were organized unionists. The coral they worked was sometimes the beautiful and rare blood red quality and very precious.
[25] Oehler, *Eranos Vindobonensis*, p. 279: "Ἐράνος κυρτοβολῶν. *Hierapolis.* Der ἀρχώνης der Genossenschaft in Hierapolis, Le Blas, III., 741, wird wohl richtig als Einnehmer der Beiträge der mitglieder erklärt."

men, manufactured fishermen's nets and baskets and probably all articles of supply for that trade.[26]

Independently of our Christianity there were hundreds of synods. A synodos in those days was a brotherhood of working people having an economical object of mutual help. At Alexandria there was found a slab showing a synod of this kind.[27] Organizations of flute players are found everywhere, not only in Asia but in Rome; and there is abundant evidence that they were largely employed by the government.[28] But these will be treated later.

The organizations of work people devoted to a saviour were innumerable. They abounded at Ephesus, Athens, Smyrna. Philippi, Thessalonica and numberless cities of Asia Minor where industries flourished. Many times they chose as their ideal presiding divinity some one or another of the mythical creatures supposed to be forever on guard watching the interests of their peculiar trade: they had Sabazios, Dionysus, Apollo, Baal, Attys, Serapis, Saturn representing the male; and Artemis, Cybele, Bona-Dea, Minerva, Isis, Nemesis, and others representing the female principle; and they adopted and adored one or another of them as their tutelary saviour. This was the ancient origin of saviours and messiahs and it lasted until superseded by the Messiah or Saviour of our era.

We have shown the terrible condition in which the laboring class was placed, in previous chapters. The worship of such an august dignitary as they believed their chosen god or goddess to be, gave great comfort and hope to their primitive minds. There was sometimes a jealous rivalry among the living dignitaries of the earth to be held in this esteem by the common people. Nero is said to have had the arrogance to assume himself a divinity and at Smyrna ordered that the people erect a shrine to him, which effrontery was treated with abhorrence.[29]

[26] Oehler, *MSS. to the author*, speaking of this, says; Es "mögen hier angefügt werden die societates welche mit der Fischerei oder der Abgabe von Fischfange zu thun hatten. In Ephesos finden wir οἱ ἐπὶ τὸ τελώνιον τῆς ἰχθυικῆς πράγματευόμενοι, Hermes, IV., 1870, p. 187."

[27] CIG. 4684ᵈ: "Σύνοδους, "Τοῖς μένουσιεντῇ συνόδῳ." Again at Athens: τῇ ἱερᾷ συνόδῳ: the holy synod. *Mitth.*, IX., 1884, p. 74. Dr. Ramsay, *Cit. and Bish. Phryg.*, points out dozens of them,

[28] Orelli, No. 1803. "Numini domus Augustorum victoriam sacram genio collegii tibicinum Romanorum Q. S. P. P. S.; ie: *qui sacris publicis praesto sunt.*" It is believed by some to be Christian.

We mention the curious facts of the saviours or soters, common in those times because their story is so frequently told in the inscriptions of the working people. There was the Phrygian Attys.[30] This whole episode of the messianic intercessor seems on a closer scrutiny to be the lugubrious wail of woe coming up from the tortured classes of mankind who were victimized and were struggling in the vortex of the compulsory devotion. Karl Marx may be right in treating of religion as a consequent and not a cause.[31] In fact, there is abundant excuse for the downtrodden, delving plodders who have peopled this earth under the dreadful circumstances of their impoverishment and degradation even if we find them groping in quest of an imagined immortal supposed in their despair to be powerful enough to rescue them. Their own suffering gave birth to a thousand saviours. Prometheus was a man-god and saviour.[32]

Dionysus was one of their most powerful saviours; and we mean by this the *Dionysos Neos*, worshiped by the entire membership of the vast international organization of artists of which so much has lately come to light that the archæologists are now busy with the study of their amazing numbers and trade organizations. This was the Dionysus *Kathegemona,* or "Forerunner." We shall devote a chapter to them as we proceed. This Dionysus we mean, is not the aristocrat referred to by Cicero,[33] although his third reference seems to be the Dionysus who was the saviour of the poor. That Cicero got hold correctly of the legend of Dionysus as descended from the Kabiri, in his third number, we have proof in the inscriptions found on the Island of Rhodes.

It is useless to attempt to numerate the unions repre-

[29] Smith, *Bible Dictionary, art. Smyrna*: "Nero appears in the inscriptions as σωτὴρ τοῦ συμπάντος ἀνθρωπείου γένους."

[30] Doane, *Bible Myths*, p. 223, "He was one of the 'slain ones' who rose to life again, on the 25th of March, or the Hilaria, or primitive Easter." See Brunswick's *Egyptian Belief*, p. 169; Higgins, *Anacalypsis*, p. 99.

[31] *Critique de la Philosophie du Droit de Hegel*, p. 2; "La religion est le soupir de la créature opprimée."

[32] Chambers' *Encyclopædia, Art. Prometheus:* "An immortal god; a friend of the human race who does not shrink from sacrificing himself for their salvation."

[33] *De Natura Deorum*, III., 23: II., 25, 5, 8; "Dionysos multos habemus: primum Jove et Prosperina natum; secundum Nilo qui Nysam dicitur condidisse; tertium Cabiro patre, eumque regem Asiæ præfuisse dicunt, cui Sabazia sunt instituta; quartum Jove et Luna, cui sacra Orphica putuntur confici, quintum Niso natum et Thyone, a quo Trieterides constitutæ putuntur." Again, Apulejus, *De Gen.*, p. 49: "Ægyptia numina guadent plangoribus, Græca choreis, barbara strepitu cymbalistarum et tympanistarum et ceraularum." Cf. Fouçart, *Ass. Rel.*, p. 69.

senting all classes of business, who in those days worshiped an imagined saviour. Their important history would be lost had they not been addicted to the custom of inscribing their doings upon blocks of stone. The messiahs and pagan saviours are thousands in number.

At Magnesia and a number of the Asiatic towns there were coral workers who had unions.[34] These may have been an element of resistance against Christianity, as was the case of Demetrius at Ephesus, who presided over the unions of image makers manufacturing trinkets which they were selling for a good living profit to the people. Luke speaks of them as the goldsmiths, at the time Paul was preaching at Ephesus. They attacked him violently, because the new faith repudiated all manner of images. The coral workers also made trinkets for the shrines of the rich who worshiped pagan gods. These corals were of the beautiful blood red variety. In the course of time this Christian interference with the unions who produced idols called forth such a powerful resistance that it became a great movement culminating in the wars of the iconoclasts.

It is very interesting to observe the shipping business as conducted by the unions under the Solonic law. There was an especial clause providing for the laboring people who obtained a living in the boating commerce.[35] We find as a consequence, great numbers of unions not only in Italy where they carried on the principal part of that class of business, but also in Greece, Macedonia, the islands, and Asia Minor. They seem to have all been directed by the same law.

Let us begin with the poorest laborers of all, the longshoremen who contracted to load and unload vessels. Upon the island of Chios have been found relics of their organizations as well as in many other places.

Egypt furnished its quota of seafaring organizations Dr. Oehler in his manuscript contributions to the author

---

[34] CIG., 3408, Κοραλλιοπλασταί, an organization of coral workers at Magnesia. Also in Smyrna these tradesmen were united into unions, Alciphron, I., 39; Herscher, *Epistolograph.*, *Græc.*, p. 44, where they are designated as κοράλλια.

[35] *Inscr. Gr. Ins.*, I., 41: "Τὸ κοινὸν τῶν μετ' αὐτῶν συνστρατευσαμένων, a consecration to the Σωτῆρες, ie: the Kabiri (old Pelasgian divinities who generated the νέος Διονυσος); No. 43, id.: "Σαμοθρακιασταί καί Λημνιασταί οἱ συνστρατευσάμενοι τὸ κοινὸν;" again, no. 75: "θιασητείων συνστρατευσάμενοι τό κοινὸν." Several others are quoted. Their saviour was this Διόνυσος no. 3, to whom they devoted their consecrations. It was just about the time of Christ's life on earth. Twenty or thirty are found at Rhodes. CIG., 3165, sqq.

has given us assurance of this, and he likewise reminds us of those at Delos. It should be remembered that Delos during the rage of the Roman conquests was the greatest slave mart of the ancient world.[36]

The evidence of the organizations of shipping, boating and carrying commerce is overwhelming. No one has with greater assiduity than Dr. Oehler, undertaken the collection of these inscriptions letting light into the true inner history of the lowly of mankind.

We now come to an enumeration of the various trades practiced strictly under the jus coeundi of Solon's dispensation, such as these frequently found in Asia Minor, including oxdrivers whom even Lucian respects.[37]

There was a society of bag-carriers, inscriptions of one of which of the age of the Apostles, have been found at Cyzicus, a city in Phrygia.

The trades in cotton and linen have, in the same manner transmitted to us some history. They are found at Hierapolis, Philadelphia, Ephesus, in Corcycus, and various places in Cilicia, Lycia, Phrygia; and the towns among whose ruins the expeditions are digging for them are Tralleis, Anazarba, Miletos, Myra and Heraclia, besides Philadelphia and the other more celebrated places already mentioned. The Body of Grecian Inscriptions contains an organization of cotton, linen and wool workers which was flourishing about the time of Christ, at Hierapolis, and another at Philadelphia, both of which afterwards became celebrated cities of the seven churches.[38] In fact nearly all of Phrygia was a hotbed of organized trades, and this is the reason for Diocletian's sweeping massacre there. Dr. Oehler, has recently mentioned an interesting find at Corcyra, which shows that their organizations extended far and wide. In Cilicia, near the old town of Corcycus, an inscription has been found, showing brotherhoods of merchants.

[36] Refer to Vol, I., p. 286, note 27; also index of that volume, in *verbo, Slavery, Slaves,* etc.

[37] Lucian, *De Saltat.*, 79: "'Η μέν γε Βακχική ὄρχησις ἐν Ἰωνίᾳ μάλιστα καὶ ἐν Πόντῳ σπουδαζομένη, καίτοι σατυρικὴ οὖσα, οὕτω κεχείρωται τοὺς ἀνθρώπους τοὺς ἐκεῖ, ὥστε κατὰ τὸν τεταγμένον ἕκαστοι καιρὸν ἁπάντων ἐπιλαθόμενοι τῶν ἄλλων κάθηνται δι' ἡμέρας Τιτᾶνας καὶ Κορύβαντας καί Σατύρους καὶ Βουκόλους ὁρῶντες· καὶ ὀρχοῦνταί γε ταῦτα οἱ εὐγενέστατοι καὶ πρωτεύοντες ἐν ἑκάστῃ τῶν πόλεων.''

[38] Oehler, *MSS. to the author*, 1897-98. EGYPT, exact place not given, but probably Alexandria: " Συνόδος ναυκληρῶν: *Bull. Héll.*, XIII., 1889, p. 239, no. 11. DELOS: Οἱ ἔμποροι καὶ ναύκληροι; *Bull. Héll.*, XI., 1887, p. 263, no. 23; 264, no. 24; XVI.; 1892,p. 150, no. 1; οἱ ἔμοόροι καὶ ναύκληροι οἱ ἐν Δήλῳ κατοικοῦντες, *Bull. Héll.*, XVI., 1892, p. 157, nos. 9, 11.''

DELOS AND ITS COMMERCE IN SLAVES. 189

This society existed during the first century and is only one of many in a large number of places, performing the labor of ordinary commerce. There is an engraving, found at Tomes, a city on the Euxine near Odessus having business communication with Alexandria, which shows a union of merchants to have existed there.[39] In those times there was as great a taint attaching to the mercantile as to the manufacturing business.[40] Merchants lived and died on the same level with mechanics. Nobody could rise who was not born to plenty and an inheritance. Mommsen speaks of a unions' "house."[41] Connected with the shipping business was the work of furnishing the people with groceries. This required an active commerce on the seas; and as a consequence we find inscriptions giving information of unions of grocers. They existed at Lemnos, Cæsaræa and Tyre. Indeed, the remains are being picked up everywhere.[42]

Oxdrivers' organizations are also found, and it appears that they were manly, as such, and held themselves in a stately and respectable posture. The oxdrivers of Pergamus were members of economic far more than religious unions.[43] We possess inscriptions showing this plentifully. Besides this, the writers are witnesses to the same thing. Many inscriptions are shown by Foucart. Lucian, who had little better language for the poor and lowly, than blackguard is here so exceptionally complacent that he speaks of the ox drivers as though they were prominent men. No doubt they were; for it often happened that their judgment was far in advance of their snobbish superiors in the pragmatics of everyday life. Archæology and history here assist each other.[44]

[39] Gaius in *Digest*, XLVIII., Tit. xxii.. 4, ad legem Duodecim Tabularum:
"'Ἐὰν δὲ δῆμος, ἢ φράτορες, ἢ ἱερῶν ὀργίων, ἢ ναῦται, ἢ σύνσιτοι, ἢ θιασῶται, ἢ ἐπὶ λίαν οἰχόμενοι, ἢ εἰς ἐμπορίαν."

[40] The union was flourishing during the Apostolic age, Athen., *Mitth.*, XVIII., 1888, p. 170, No. 10ᵃ. "Ναύκληροι καὶ ἐπὶ τοῦ λημένος λαβόντες." Also "Πορμενόντες εἰς Ἐρύθας," p. 171, 172. 11.

[41] Mommsen, *Römische Geschichte*, V., p. 284, sq. The suggestive feature of this union is, that it was called an οἶκος. Far off as it was, it is inscribed as οἶκος τῶν Ἀλεξανδρείων. Tabernacle or "house" of the Alexandrians.

[42] CIG., 2271, θίασος. The merchants and small grocers of Tyre had a σύνοδος τῶν Τυρίων ἐμπόρων καὶ ναυκλήρων, *Bull. Héllénique*, III., 1879, p. 374 Likewise: Τὸ κοινὸν τῶν Τυρίων καὶ τῶν Ἡρακλειστῶν ἐμπόρων καὶ ναυκλήρων.

[43] Curtius, *Hermes*, Vol. VII., p. 39: Cf. Fouc., p. 115, note. "Οἱ Βουκόλοι ἐτείμησαν Σωτῆρα Ἀρτεμηδώρου τὸν ἀρχιβουλόκον διὰ τοῦ εὐσεβῶς καὶ ἀξίως τοῦ Καθηγεμόνος Διόνυσου προΐστασθαι τῶν θείων μυστηρίων· Εἰσὶν δὲ βουκόλοι . . . . Ὑμνοδιδάσκολοι . . . . Σειλήνιοι . . . . Χορηγός." Then appear on the memorial, 18 names of members of the union; among them teachers of singing, a leader of the chorus and others.

[44] *Associations Religieuses*, pp. 114, 115.

At Thyateira, Hierapolis, Anazarba and Miletos, specimens of considerable interest have been recovered. At Tralleis, another city with a growing monumental history, have been found bag-carriers' associations.[45]

On careful study, it has been discovered that these associations were all organized with the one idea of bettering each others circumstances. It is true that, following the customs and practices of those days, they had their religious consecrations, some of which very much resembled those of the Christians; yet at the bottom, their scheme was to use mutual combination as a means of salvation from the multitudinous woes besetting them on every hand, in their struggle for existence.[46]

There was in those early Christian days, a great system of organized trades in the building business. We have shown in our first volume of this work, how numerous and powerful were the masons as early as Solomon and Agis I. the monster who assassinated great numbers of Helots, by taking the usual predatory advantage of his military hordes. Later, about the time of the Apostles, they appear again, splendidly, though secretly organized. Then Pisidia, celebrated, as we shall hereafter see, is where Paul was repudiated by the synagogue, but found an occult organization which opened its doors to him and his companions in some unexplained and mysterious manner. We shall moreover show that this occult intercessor in Paul's aid was none other than the trade unions we are describing. These we now refer to were unions of the building trades, well proved by the inscriptions to have been in Termessos a town of Pisidia, at that time. Several associations of masons and carpenters are found in and near the old Pisidian

---

[45] The appellation given to this union was: Ἱερὸν συνέδριον τῶν σακοφόρων τῶν ἀπὸ τοῦ μετρητοῦ, signifying the sacred association of freight bag carriers, from the weigher and measurer. Oehler, *Eranos Vindob.*, p. 279; Athen. *Mitth.*, VI., 125, 8, etc In Συλλογος, VIII., 1893, p. 1, XI., is the notice that the ἱερωτάτον συνέδριον τῶν σακκοφόρων λιμενιτῶν received 1000 drachmas from some parties, as a fine for having mutilated graves. This was also at Cyzicus, a seaport of Panormus.

[46] Oehler, *MSS. Contributions to the author:* ". . . . zeigen schon in ihem Namen dass wir es mit Vereinigungen zu thun haben, deren mitglieder gleiche Standesinterssen verfolgten und sich zur Förderung derselben zusammangeschlossen hatten. Es sind dies besonders die Genossenschaften der Kaufleute und Handwerker. Zusammenstellungen sind gegeben: Büchsenschütz, *Besitz und Erwerb*, p. 331 adm., 1; Menadier, *Qua Condictone Ephesi usi sint*, etc. p. 28 ad., 134: Wagener, *Revue Belgique*. n. s,, XI., 1869. p. 1, ff. Hermann-Blümer: *Griěch, Privateigenthümer*, p. 331 adm., 2; Liebenam, *Römisches Vereinswesen*, p. 157, Oehler, *Eranos Vindobonensis*, p. 277-78; Ziebarth. *Griech. Verinswesen*, p. 98, f., etc.

Antioch, which was the scene of the Apostle's career. But traces of unions of the building trades appear all over Asia Minor.

A very important union of the builders, now, after a large amount of wrong-reading for excusable reasons, turns out to be a Christian epitaph, chiseled on a sepulchre or mausoleum for a whole union of masons.[47] This inscription is no doubt very old, probably of the time of Paul. It adds another link to the evidence that the building trades had their unions during the Apostolic times. There was likewise a union of gardeners of Pessinus,[48] which is reported to us by the same author.

In all parts of the ancient world are found remaining monuments of secret societies. Sometimes the unions are so secret that the particular trade or profession does not appear. They go by the name of initiates, or mystic brotherhoods. This secrecy screened them so well from the rigors of outside persecution that they were able to exist for ages in form of brotherhoods in spite of the law. They were so numerous that we cannot here speak of them all individually; they deserve mention.[49 50 51 52 53 54 55]

There was a society of secret initiates at Lagina,[52] on the borders of Palestine. These initiates also left their inscriptions in Philippi; for a valuable inscription of a very early post Christian date lends us evidence. It dates

---

[47] CIG. 3857 t. Formerly it was always read as pagan; but M. Perrot, *Explor. Arch. de la Galatie*, p. 126, found the Christian cross, and also symbols of macons tools. But the text shows that it was a union of some kind of mechanics, while the names given are Christian. In this epitaph are Euphronia, Tatias, Asclepiades and Onesimus, ie: Ἐύφρων, κὲ Τατιὰς Ἀσκληηπιάδη τῷ τέκνῳ κὲ ἑαυτοῖς ζῶντες. Ὀνήσιμος [καὶ——] τοὺς ἑαυτῶν γονεῖς κὲ τὸν ἀδελφὺν ἐτείμησαν."

[48] CIG. 4082.

[49] CIG. 3422. "'Ἱερὰ φυλή τῶν ἐριουργῶν." Apparently connected with it was one of wool-washers, ἐριοπλυτοί, and its president or overseer, πρῶτος ἐργαστῆρος. This was found at Hierapolis, Le Bas. III., 648, sq.

[50] *Eranos Vindob.*, p. 277. Λινοπῶλαι which is about equivalent to the Latin lintearii, mostly linen weavers, and it is thought to have been a society for making linen goods for the market.

[51] Heberdey, *W. Retsen in Killikien, Phil. Hist. Classes*, XLIV., 1898, p. 69, No. 151. Λιναπῶλαι; also σύστημα τῶν λιμενητῶν λινοπολῶν,

[52] *Journ. Hell. Stud.*, XI., 1890, p. 240, No. 8. About the time of Hadrian. Συντελία Λινουργῶν. They erected a statue of honor to some person, CIG. 3504.

[53] I., pp. 115, 116; showing the prehistoric building trades, and a terrible massacre on account of their strike at the time of Agis I., B.C. 1055; *ibid.*, p. 373, note 2. building by them of the temple of Solomon.

[54] Oehler, *MSS*. "Gewöhnlich werden de Bauhandwerker bezeichnet als τεχνῖται. Zwei τεχνῖται aus Dokimeion haben zum Danke den τέσσερα στέμματα τῆς οἰκοδομίας und ihrem προστάτης. Hesychios, eine Weihung errichtet: Inschrift aus Ikonion, CIGr. 3995."

[55] Oehler, *MSS. id.*: "Auch in Termessos, (Pisidien), werden unter den τεχνῖται Bauhandwerker zu verestehn sein; Lauck, *Koriuski*, II., nr. 34; an Schauspieler zu denken" etc.

back to the Apostolic age. It had for its presiding officer a mystarchos and celebrated convivials to Mithras, a species of anthropotheocracy, most nearly resembling the Christian ideal.[56] The valley of the Meander, containing Magnesia as one of the important industrial cities of those early post Christian days, was replete with these democratic trade unions. They were voting in a strictly political fashion[57] at that moment on the one hand, and the emperors and their appointed state governors and other politicians were doing all in their power to prevent them from voting, on the other.[58]"

Another batch of the "initiated" where the trade practiced by the members does not plainly appear in their inscriptions, is found in the valley of the Meander, at the towns of Kyme and Klaudiapolis.[59]

We now come to the mention of the hives of organized industries that are known to have existed in Phrygia and other cities of Anatolia, at an early date. They embrace the dyers, fullers, woolworkers, lapidaries, carpet-weavers, silversmiths, tanners, and potters; and as these were principally the trades included in the law of Solon, and are more ancient than the civilization among which they are found, and as they are mostly of the age of the earliest Christianity, a corresponding importance will naturally attach to their history, enlivening the interest of the reader.

There was a trade union of the potters at Thyateira, one of the cities of the seven churches, which seems to have had a busy establishment, contributing to the immense activity of the city. At the same place thousands

---

[56] Oehler, *MSS.*, Μύσται: Verein deren Vorsteher μυστάρχαι, und ἀρχιμύσται genannt waren: In Armorion μύσται des Mithras: Feste derselben, Μιθρακαία. I., Jahrh. n. Chr.; *Rev. des Études Grecques* II., 1889, p. 18, Cumont, *Textes et Monuments figurés relatifs aux Mystères de Mithra.* I., p. 90, nr. 4." Besides these he refers to CIG. 2051 for an ἀρχιμυστής, in Sozipolis and CIA. for another, at Philippi.

[57] Professor Bendorf, *Reisen in südwestl. Kleinasien*, I., p. 156, No. 134: Ἰακχιαστί υἱεῖς, thought by some to be waiters because they kept up a shouting.

[58] Ramsey, *Churches and Bishoprics of Phrygia*, II., p. 439: "It was the policy of the emperors, alike in Rome and the provinces, to weaken the popular assemblies; and to turn the attention of the people in other directions than the exercise of political powers." He is speaking of the "popular assemblies, societies and guilds."

[59] Oehler, *MSS.:* "Dillenberger, *Sylloge*, nr. 390, endlich noch Μύσται dienen und den Kaisern etwas geweiht wurde.n *Anc. Gr. Inscr.*, III., 506, von Hicks wohl mit als Mystenverein der Demeter erklärt. In Klaudiapolis wird ein μυσταρχης CIG., 3803, in Kyme ein ἀρχιμυσητς. *Bull. Héll.*, XVII. 1893, p. 332 genannt." Konteleon, Ephesus and many other places in Asia Minor also contained the mystic associations.

SYNOPSIS OF THE BROTHERHOODS. 193

of organized workmen seem to have been busy at pottery[60] and the tanning and dressing of leather.[61]

The shoemakers of shoemaker street in Apameia will be the subject of considerable space and interest in a future chapter, it being one of those rare, precious things which add another link to the evidence that the Christians planted their gospel into the mellow soil of these almost innumerable economic unions of the ancient trades. Nevertheless, it is proper to announce them here, among the others. The author we quote from is Dr. Ramsey who had completed his scrutiny of the cities and Bishoprics of Phrygia. He finds that one quarter of that ancient city had a street called, in plain English the shoemakers' street.[62] More than this, he openly acknowledges that the shoemakers were thoroughly organized into guilds, as he thinks, although the real guilds were never created into the world until the Solonic unions were persecuted to death by the deadly Christian edicts of 363, rigorously followed until finally exterminated in 412. After this the true guilds came into the world with their petty bosses and semi-slavery. It helped to engender the feudal ages which domineered humanity for a thousand years.

All the labor unions of antiquity, wherever profiting by the jus coeundi of Solon and Numa, were invariably organized for economic means, to the end that they should assist each other in obtaining a living. Dr. Oehler mentions one of Cyzicus, in Phrygia, which was prospering in A. D. 39, about the time of the martyrdom of Stephen and the conversion of Paul. It was organized as a means to an economic end. The members were under the veil

---

[60] CIG., 3485. κεραμεῖς. It is likewise prominently mentioned by Oehler though not in his list of trade organizations; *Eranos Vindobonensis*, no. 14, p. 277.

[61] CIG. 1134, 1135, σπατολῃασταί, Βυρσοδηψαί. For the same reason ascribed to a misunderstanding, the carpet makers became mixed among these records and caused confusion.

[62] For a copy of the complete inscription, see *infra*, p. 446. Ramsay, *id.*, II., pp. 440, 461, 462, 538, gives short snatches of the important discovery. On page 440 he says: "The reference to Shoemakers' street, no. 294, suggests that the different trades were apportioned to special streets . . . . . , a guild, the head of which was called the Emporiarches Ἐμποριάρχης, is mentioned no. 309; its members were called συμβιωταί, and the term is suitable, if there was a street bearing their name." On page 461, the inscription is given entire which we copy. At the end occur the words; τῶν ἐν τῇ σκυτικῇ πλατείᾳ τεχνειτῶν." The unions of leather workers, or perhaps one great union, had a temple of Jove, see page 538, on the Acropolis called Kelainai. This author says of the same trade unions: "On a stone in the N. wall of the ruined church on the Acropolis of the Kelainai, an inscription is on the outside 'κυριε βοηθει'. It was the temple of Jove which became the κυριακή or church." Κυριε Βοηθει is admitted by all archæologists to be an invariably Christian expression.

of secrecy, and were engaged in the struggle for existence, in the same manner as a trade union at the present day.

In Italy, in and about Rome, the same thing was going on at full blast. We have evidence in abundance that the stonecutters were fully organized about that time.[63]

Then we have some valuable inscriptions showing that in Phrygia there existed thriving associations of carpet weavers. Dr. Oehler has preserved one of as early a time as A. D. 76 to 133, at Hierapolis.[64] Another union deserving attention is that of female silversmiths at Magnesia and Smyrna. We are informed by the learned professors who have worked at the meaning, that they sometimes made coins. If so, we have proof that the people engaged in the mints were organized. Some were women.

One of the most lucrative branches of business in those days of pushing manufacture and organized industry, was that of the dyers. They are commonly known as the purple dyers, although the principal colors they worked in were those of the celebrated red, in which, with the exception of dyes, their Indian competitors excelled above all others in the world. The purple dyers left valuable inscriptions in Laodicia. This is now regarded as significant even by Bible commentators, on account of the fact that Lydia, who was converted to Christianity, by Paul, at Philippi in Macedonia, was a purple dyer and a member and business agent of her union at Thyateira, one of the cities of the seven churches.[65] But the dyers of Hierapolis, Thyateira, Smyrna, and the principal towns were under a very powerful organization coming from the great Solonic law. They were an ancient factor in the industrial scheme, even as long ago as the time of Paul, who converted them to Christianity.

Dyers of Heraklea[66] and Pisidia had powerful unions at an early Christian date. The people of Phrygia were celebrated for their industry and for their love of loose

---

[63] See Vol. I., p. 369; Orelli, *Lapidarii opifices*, 4208, which was a stone cutters' union; 3246 may be a superintendent of the stone quarries; 4220, was a regular union of the lapidaries.

[64] Oehler, *Eranos Vindob.*, p. 279: Συνέδριον τῶν καιροδαπισταί, coöperative association of carpet and rug makers. It existed during Hadrian's time.

[65] *Acts*, xvi., 14. This Lydia is now recognized by the best authors and researchers to have been a member of the dyers' union at Thyateira. She was their business agent, and sold the goods.

[66] CIG., 3912 ᵃ; Le Bas, III., 741, ἀρχώνης ξυστοῦ ... τον 'Ηρακλεά—ἀνέθηκεν τῇ συνεργασία, Athen. *Mitth.*, X., p. 205; SMYRNA: CIG., 3304: δοκιμασθεὶς ... ὑπὸ τῆς συνεργασίας. These are recognized to be unions of dyers.

amusements. The world was deeply indebted to them for their enterprises, mechanical and agricultural. Of the many cities praised for these virtues, Apameia was well known to have been a hive of industries, nearly all of which were organized. There had been a political convulsion as well a seismic; for less than a century and a half B. C. the Roman conquests had overturned much of the industrial life of this and the surrounding region, and a few years after the crucifixion a terrible earthquake destroyed several cities along the Lycus and the Meander. The great dyeing business, says Oehler, was of much importance.[67] In this business also, Hierapolis in Phrygia, the celebrated city on the Lycus, comes in for an important mention.[68]

We now come to the woolworkers of Thyateira, Laodicea, Cyzicus, Flaviapolis and Ephesus, at the time of Christ, and during the Apostolic age. It may be asked why so much is here said about the Christian age. The answer is, that we are preparing the reader for some extraordinary scraps of history never yet disclosed; and though only a brief mention can be made here, yet this evidence is to be brought under consideration when we come to the chapter fitting the subject. One union of importance was at Flaviapolis in Cilicia. At this place the epigraphic schools have recently been puzzled by the discovery of inscriptions showing that the ancient trade unions took the Christians in, endorsed their tenets and turned their pagan, into Christian worship, even giving them their temples and other property for a place of meeting. While Christ was in the world Flaviapolis had a prosperous union of fullers.[69]

Laodicea, another city on the Lycus, was also a center of the woolen industry and came in for a share of that trade. Here we find inscriptions which inform us that the woolworkers were carrying on an enormous manufacture of woolen goods, even as far back as the Apos-

---

[67] Oehler, *MSS.*: SAGALASSOS, *(Ptsidien)*, be ass eine συντελεία βαφέων, Lanekronski, II., nr. 195. In Thyateira hatte die βαφείς grosse Bedeutung, gewiss auch grosses Vermögen, da sie in die Inschriften als Errichter von Ehrenstatuen, zum Theile in Auftrage des Staates genannt werden CIG., 3496, 3497, 3498, etc.

[68] See I., p. 418, on the murileguli and purple shellfish. For the unions of purple dyers, ἐργασία τῶν βαφέων for Hierapolis are recorded in Le Bas, III., 742—CIG., 3924 b, and Bull. Héll., X., 1886, p. 519, No. 16. The latter are unions at Tralles.

[69] Oehler, in *MSS.* "In Flaviapolis, Kilikien, aus Christlicher Zeit, kennen wir eine Widmung: ὑπὲρ σωτηρίας τοῦ εὐτελοῦς συνεργασίου τῶν γναφέων, Wollarbeiten,"

tolic age, when Peter, Paul and especially John, were preaching the new Gospel there.[70] The woolworkers, such as spinners, carders, weavers and fullers abounded in Ephesus. Like those of Heraclia, Laodicea and Colossæ, they were strongly organized into secret protective unions, patterned to conform to the jus coeundi.

Organizations of slaves existed in many of the Phrygian cities about this time. Their monuments are found at Laodicea, Heraclia, Ephesus and Smyrna. We have already spoken in the preceding chapter of the organization of slaves in pre-Christian ages; it is yet to be recorded that the jus coeundi of Solon was in great use long after the opening of our era. In perusing this subject of the organization of slaves which has recently been made certain by inscriptional evidence, it is naturally asked why should they form themselves into unions? It will be argued that as at present, the ancient poor were in many respects better off before, than after their era of emancipation began.[71] There was seldom any starvation, because a man looks out for his property; this vast organization offset misery by a communal framework for protection. When, afterwards, the church which was not Christianity, destroyed this organization at the council of Laodicea, the poor were obliged to feed upon charity and charitable institutions which had never before existed, and the orphanotrophia came.

But there were prodigious numbers of unions of slaves. Their unions at Delphi were mostly organized after the model of an eranos.[72] The conspiracy of Cæsar worked great damage to the success of the organizations at Delos, and the effect was that it became the most renowned of all slave marts.[73] During those fell

[70] Oehler, *MSS*; "In Laodicea am Lycus finden wir eine ἐργασία τῶν γναφέων τῶν ἀπολουργῶν d. h, von Walkern für glatte Stoffe, CIG. 3938, mit berichtigter Lesung bei Büchsenschütz, *Die Hauptstädte u. s. w.*, p. 84 adn. 14, u. p. 89; dann Blümner: *Der Maximaltarif*, p. 151, XIX., 16. In Kyzykos erhält das ἱερώτατον συνέδριον τῶν γναφέων eine Grabmult, Athen., *Mitth.*, VII., 1852, p. 252, nr. 19," Another fullers' society was in Perinthos.

[71] See *supra*. p. 160 sq., showing the method used by the eranos, for emancipating slaves through their sale to a divinity; Foucart, *Affranchissement des esclaves par vente à une divinité*, pp. 28, 47, etc.

[72] Lüders, *Dionys. Künst.*, pp. 46, 47; Wescher and Foucart, *Inscr. de Delphes*, Paris, 1863, pp. 89, 107, 139, 213, 244. The method of enfranchisement is discussed by Lüders, *id.*, p. 46 and note.

[73] Vol. I., 286. *Slave Mart of Delos*; Lüders, *Donys. Künstler*, pp. 29, 30, in an excellent explanation. The early law suppressing organizations excused the Jews according to Josephus, *Antiq.*, xiv., 10, 8: "Γαῖος Καῖσαρ ὁ ἡμέτερος στρατηγὸς καὶ ὕπατος ἐν τῷ διατάγματι κωλύων θιάσους συνάγεσθαι κατὰ πόλιν, μόνους τούτους (τοὺς Ἰουδαίους) ἐκώλουσεν οὔτε χρήματα συνεισφέρειν οὔτε συνδείπνα ποιεῖν."

conquests there was a relentless disposition to drive both slaves and freedmen to misery and death. The jealous laws followed them everywhere, crippling their primæval Solonic rights. They must have consent of their masters. They must have a curator, who in the organization, was a potent factor, being a lord on a very small scale, over them. They must, if organized, not meet oftener than twice a month.[74] M. Foucart, who was for a long time director of the archæological school of Athens, in his celebrated work on the Religious Associations, has sufficiently proved that the slaves were organized, and the opinion is growing that the organization was universal, and in strict accord with the ancient and revered statute which the combined efforts of enemies could not destroy. There was a union of slaves at Baula, near Naples,[75] and search into the resources of knowledge is revealing many more.

One thing can now be said with some assurance which a few years ago could only be surmised. It is, that the associations formerly supposed to be exclusively religious, were really economic in their object. Dr. Ramsay sees this where he shrewdly says:[76] "M. Foucart, in Associations Religieuses, appears to consider symbioseis as purely religious associations; but probably they were usually trades associated in the worship of a deity." This and succeeding words explode the idea of Foucart in our favor, since we foretold in the first volume of this work that Foucart entirely misunderstood the subject he so ably discusses, and that Wescher was right.[77] This idea must now be pushed, on so great authority. To say the least, we have enjoyed a delightful personal, and to us memorable acquaintance with this savant of the French Academy, at a session of the seminary of epig-

[74] *Dig.*, XLVII., *tit.* xxii., *leg.* 1, rescript of Severus, which is in reality the old lex Julia revived by Trajan, repeated by Hadrian, and made memorable by Septimius Severus. As preserved in the *Digest* it reads favorably only for the burial clause of the Solonic dispensation: "Sed permititur tenuioribus stipem menstruam conferre, dum tamen semel in mense coeant, ne sub prætextu hujusmodi illicitum collegium coeat, Quod non tantum in urbe, sed in Italia et in provinciis, locum habere, Divus quoque Severus rescripsit. § 1. Sed religionis causa coire non prohibentur: dum tamen per hoc non fiat contra senatusconsultum, quo illicita collegia arcentur."

[75] Mommsen, *I. N.*, 2582; the inscription is now in the Royal museum, at Naples, date wanting. For more, see Orell., 7188: "Baulano—Servorum collegium est."

[76] *Churches and Bishoprics of Phrygia*, II., 471. The page referred to in Foucart's work is 113.

[77] Vol. I., pp. 506, 507, where the difference between MM. Wescher and Foucart are discussed, our opinion balancing toward Wescher.

raphy in the palace of the Institute; besides this we
have read his magnificent work on the emancipation of
slaves through sale of their bodies to a divinity, which
is a contribution of undoubted truth, and of enormous
value for this work. It only illustrates that the wisest
of men may grope in the absence of facts, and finally
with the aid of others get themselves rightly established.

It is our desire to confine ourselves as much as possible to the Apostolic age; since it is impossible to mention one in a hundred of the inscriptions of this and the
second and third centuries. A union of engravers at
Letoon is mentioned which is important on account of
its great antiquity.[78] So the caravans of commerce between Palmyra and the west had their synods, a fact
spoken of by Mommsen in his history of Rome. These
have been figured out, deciphered and enrolled in the
Body of Greek Inscriptions, as well as the work of Le
Bas and Waddington, and in the Wolfe expedition of the
American school of archæology.

Then there were the thiasoi of the immortals, numerous enough to attract attention. They were probably
believers in a life beyond this but existed in a good organized form long before the Advent. They had a philosophy and at their reunions, when sitting in joyous association around their common table steaming with the best
of the land, their conversation used to turn to the realms
of the post-earthly unknown, and they speculated themselves into a common consciousness much akin to the
great religion of the Messiah when he came. Societies of
the immortals range all along the time also while Christ
was living; and as they were laboring people, organized
for mutual help they quickly endorsed Christianity.

Gypsies had their organization in those days. The
date of the one found in the select inscriptions of Orellius, is not known, but it is apparent that they ranged
from a high antiquity down to Constantine and that the
rag-pickers of those days were the origin of all the
gypsy tribes that have since spread over the world.

At Tyre, Sidon, Cæsarea and Joppa, all along the coast
of the Mediterranean which washed the land of Pales-

[78] Oehler, *MSS. to the author*. "Eine ἱερά ξυστικὴ σύνοδος vereint mit der θυμελικὴ wird bereits für Letoon und Prusias am Hyp. genannt; auch in Smyrna waren beide σύνοδοι vereint, wie aus der Inschrift CIG. 3173 (80–83. n. Chr.), hervorgeht, in der ξυστάρχης haben, πατρομύστης erwähnt ist; vgl. auch Nr. 3190."

tine there are monuments of the workers found. Tyre furnishes a good number.[79] Judea may, with some propriety be included in this region. The whole territory, about A. D. 5, was annexed to Syria by the emperor Augustus.

The Roman collegia, now well known to have been the same as other trade unions, are proved to have laid the foundation of our seminaries. It is at least, easily proved that they were the first to establish schools which bear any resemblance to those of the present day.

They are traced to Britain where they were early established and their influence in laying the foundation of the great Anglo-Saxon system of learning was enormous. But the instincts of greed in course of time led them in a direction of guilds, which form they assumed.[80] The collegia as guilds, were found in the Roman cities of Britain all through the Middle Ages, and from this name is to be gleaned the early history of the guilds. They were transmitted from the ancient colleges, which based their power and success upon the great law.

This old dispensation was broken up, a calamity hurled against it by an edict of the Council of Laodicea in A. D. 363, forbidding the members from enjoying their common table,[81] although the Apostolic Canon of St. Peter had three hundred years before, ordained that this economic source of mutual support, with its common table should be freely allowed.[82] This privilege of meeting together in union and enjoying the common meal was a part of the jus coeundi of Solon. It was the key to the organization without which the cohesive force or incentive blighted in a lingering dissolution. Trade union-

[79] Foucart, *Ass, Rel.*, pp, 103, 107. It has been suggested that Origen, who after his valuable lifework, was persecuted alike by Christians and pagans, was obliged to secrete himself among these mutual unions at Tyre, there to die.

[80] Gould, *Freemasonry*, I., pp. 38 and 43, with note. This was especially the case in Britain on the invasion of the German and Gallic conquerors who persecuted the colleges. See Freeman, *Origin of the English Nation*. (Macmillan's Magazine, 1870, Vol. XXI., pp. 415, 509). For the general subject, see Palgrave, *Rise and Progress of the Eng. Commonwealth*; Coote, *Romans of Britain*, pp. 336, 397; Spencer, *Inquiry into the Origin of Laws*; Pike, *History of Crime*, I., pp. 65-70.

[81] Canon 55, Vol. II.. p. 574, Mansi: "Ὅτε οὐ δεῖ ἡ ἱερατικοὺς κληρικοὺς ἐκ συμβολῆς συμπόσια ἐπετελεῖν, ἀλλ' οὐδὲ λαικούς." This was the cruel deathstroke which broke up the main economic incentive to ancient labor organization. The same Council also gave a death-stroke to their psalm singing; in fact it seems to have been the death-stroke to Christianity in favor of a grasping, jealous priestcraft and its church, greedy to devour their goods.

[82] *Corpus Legum Antiquarum; Canones S. S. Apostolorum*, 40: "Ordinavit enim lex Dei, ut qui altari inserviunt, de altari nutriantur."

ism died hard. It sank down deeper into the umbrage of secrecy. Monarchy hunted it with spies and detectives. It nevertheless so revived as to outlive persecutions; for many were the good men among the commoners and even the fathers who protested. But living in socialism with each other under the superior system of the communal code did not contribute to the wealth of provision speculators. Their diaconus or treasurer could, with the combined driblets of each member paid in once a month, buy in quantities at wholesale rates and from the producers direct. It was intolerable to the provision rings; for we know from Diocletian's edict, that it cut them off from their plans of speculation. But the hateful ban of suppression struck them yet once more in A. D. 412;[83] and this was their last; for the true trade union of the ancients was no more.

Out of its magot-breeding cadaver a horrid demidæmon grew in shape of the mediæval guilds, fit mongrel of the feudal ages. From a decent and honorable life, under the beneficent law of their unions, we find them immediately after these cruel edicts, reduced in the mental as well as pecuniary sense, so that there exists an inscription which appears to be Christian, showing a huddle of wretches in a "college of holy hut dwellers," and slum-traffickers, containing a list of 300 names of members.[84]

The result of this downfall was the creation of the guilds of the priests and petty bosses, driving the poor wretches for profit. They used to be called parabolani. It was a death-clutch of priest-power grappling at their throats.

Happy societies whose members had for a thousand years been self-sustaining and prosperous under the Solonic dispensation, now broken up by the jealous and avaricious church. Dr. Am Rhyn[85] states the facts regarding the fate of the Solonic organization when he

---

[83] Jerome, *Letters to Rusticus*, no. CXXVI., says, in proof that the Council of Laodicea had not quite extinguished the trade unions (A. D. 363), the following words: "Great numbers are unable to break from their trades they previously practiced . . . . in former days. The greed of sellers used to be kept in bounds by the action of the aediles, or, as the Greeks call them, market inspectors, ἀγορανόμοι; and men could not cheat with impunity. But now, persons who profess religion are not ashamed to seek unjust profits, and the good name of Christianity is oftener a cloak for fraud than a victim to it." Jerome then exhorts them to go back to the old community life.
[84] Orelli, 7215 ª. Romæ. Date of Honorius, "Corpus tabernariorum."
[85] **Mysteria**, Eng. *trans*, p. 162.

says: "The constitution of the trade guilds is derived partly from the collegia of artisans in ancient Rome, and partly from the monastic orders. The most elaborate of these mysteries was that of the stone masons."

So it was that the mediæval orders which broke up the ancient voting unions, seized their property, robbed them of the spirit of enterprise and success, and turned them broken and ruined over to the feudal lords.

History is now repeating itself.[86] Spasms of the same competitive system crop out even at this day. The rage of the war spirit has been felt in America; and editors have turned their columns into auxiliary batteries to aid with brag and gush the belching of murderous explosives, which modern mechanics turn against the life and limb of humanity. This was not in the scheme of the Plan of salvation of the flesh and spirit of old. It is in aid of conquest; and in these pages we have sufficiently shown that the great conquests of Rome did no good. Men are still vaunting of their puissant wit in conquering and destroying others. They did it in Rome all through the conquests. And how did it turn out? Millions exterminated; millions again impoverished and discouraged; good government overwhelmed; their wealth dragged into one putrescent center; Rome glutted by millionaires, perished of her own infections and her conquered colonies in every case went down to the bad, while the animus of organized industry, once aglow with an ascendant genius verging toward a period of rich inventions, lost hope, lost the secrets of manly arts, and sank to rise no more. So much for a once brilliant, living ingrowth which the Romans destroyed, based upon, and rooted into, a vast industrial organization well under way, and gradually lifting humanity out into a high and peaceful enlightenment.

[86] Neander, *Hist. Church*, English *trans.*, II., pp. 192, 193. The only similarity between the ancient eranos and the church of Laodician date was, that certain powers of the church stewards (οἰκονόμοι) took charge of the church property, often the great landed estates held by the church as a corporate power; and this lasted into the 12th century. Basil Cæsar, *Epistles* 285, and 237. But, says Neander: "As much as the management of the property and the protection of the poor who were supported by the church." This shows that from self-sustaining communities they had dwindled into miserable eleemosynary concerns. "The expedient," continues Neander, p. 192, was finally adopted, that the church, like other corporations, should have for its management of affairs a person skilled in law. The lawyer was called the parabolanus. *Cod. Theod.*, XVI., *tit.* ii., legg. 42. 43, providing against abuses of the arrangement. But of course, great abuses crept in.

From the foregoing it is plainly seen that the origins of socialism are intimately intertwined in the movements of to-day. Our forefathers had it in an embryonic form and struggled a thousand years to build it up and to transmit it to us in perfection, while the individualism of private ownership constantly strove to tear it down. But socialism never saw the great light of a perfected form. It could live in secret and obscurity, under cover; but the very first great master who came to proclaim it abroad to the open world was instantly met by the enemy and given but three years to advocate broadcast the long secret plan of salvation, when He met the thrilling fate of martyrdom.

Moses and Solon and the wise lawgivers could not carry socialism beyond its puerile infancy. It never assumed the majestic power inherent in complete ownership and management now demanded by the scientific co-operative commonwealth of our day, yet it taught us the mighty lesson leading to it; for the form now foreseen is no longer that of voting to power an agoranomos, who was always a mere proxy from the aristocracy, to dole out jobs of labor from the public works, but it is to wrest itself into complete ownership of all useful works, by the whole people and for the people, who are the workers and makers of all things good. Then, and never until then will the world enjoy a true democracy.

CHAPTER X.

THE GREAT GEMEINDE.

INTERNATIONAL SOCIETY OF DIONYSAN ARTISTS

OBSCURITY Veils one of the Most Remarkable Facts of Antiquity—Masterly Investigation of Dr. August Böckh—Startling Curiosity—The Big Order's Make-Up—Their Tutelary Saint was the "Ennobler of Mankind and Giver of Joys"—Their Music—To gain a Living the Object—Centuries of Dense Secrecy—The Pythian Apollo—Homer—Scenic Artists—Strike of the Flutists—They Belonged to the interlinking Bond—Hated But Employed at Rome—Enormously Patronized by the State—Alexander's Carnival of Hephastæon—Three Thousand Musicians and Playwrights Gathered from Far and Near—Others for the Olympic Contests—Stories of Arrian, Plutarch, and Athenæus Agree with Inscriptions—Wonderful Agonies—Full Description—Their Model of Pure Socialism, Father, Mother, and Children—Their Common Table and Mutual Love—Microcosm of the Perfect State—Votive Franchise Substituted Father's Paternal Control—It Worked—Terrible Laodicean Canon—Eunus—The Eranothiasos—The Everlasting Fakirs—How they Crawled into the Unions and Debased the Principle—Menander's Desdemona—Fakirs, Fortune-Tellers and Filter Peddlers—Aping the Official Religion to Secure Good Jobs—Emperor Hadrian patronized the Agonstic Performances—Symbol of the Serpent—Fakirs Assume Form of the Snake—A Curious Inscription—Scenic Plays at Rome—Fun-Making Entertainments—Callipygian Dance—Greek Trilogy—Notwithstanding their brilliant Genius the Unions were often Poor—Sneers of Lucian—Nobler Praise by Aristotle—His Truthful Axiom—The Immunes—Fishers and Hunters an Allied Branch—Billingsgate of Smyrna—Synods of Baptists—The Quingenarian Spell—Hunger of Dominion for Acts of Cruelty.

NOBODY appears to know anything about the great international amalgamated association of the ancient artists. We are indebted, first of all, to the keen and scholarly insight of Dr. August Böckh, Director of that trustworthy publication of the Berlin Academy of Science, known as the *Corpus Inscriptionum Græcarum,* for the announcement that such an organization existed among the workers of the ancient world. We are again indebted for the honest recognition of Oehler, Lüders, Foucart, Cagnat, Mauri, and many others of the schools of archæology, that this far reaching labor organization was an offshoot of the Solonic law.

But as no historian ever gave us any account of this immense curiosity of ancient civilization, we have been obliged to gather our information from scattered monuments, and in a somewhat anecdotal form. Much is derived from the stories of Lucian, from the occasional mention of Athæneus, Aristotle and others; but most of all from the racy, disconnected mention of their own inscriptions. One modern author quotes Aristotle as saying that the play-actors held greater sway with the public than the poets.[1]

We shall begin with the oldest evidence known, and follow them down to the date of the Laodicean Council when they were suppressed, seemingly through jealousy of their musical genius. Of all forms of associations of the ancient poor, the Dionysan, or Bacchic artists were most tolerated, and most patronized by the world's prominent men. They enjoyed the patronage of monarchs like Alexander, and afterwards Nero, Hadrian and Antonius Pius; and they were the authors and composers of the Delphic hymns and of the recently discovered written music, unearthing a new literature which is startling our curiosity. The scientific world is now bending its energies in the direction of all possible discovery of remains of the Dionysan artists.

A point strangely suggestive might here be subjoined for what it is worth: this Dionysus the younger, is not the aristocrat myth of pelasgic ages. He is the Dionysus Kathegemon or forerunner. Forerunner of what? Let any one pronounce the name rapidly and he will produce nearly the sound of John. Another curiosity is, that his unions were the primitive if not original bap-

---

[1] Lüders, *Die Dionysiscishen Künstler*, p. 50. His quotation is from Aristotle, Rhet., III., 1, 4: "Μείζον δύνανται νῦν τῶν ποιητῶν οἱ ὑποκριταί. Dr. Lüders regards this as a great recommendation in favor of the fine perfection to which they arrived at Athens.

tists. No member of his brotherhoods could be initiated except by the purifying application of water. This is established by thousands of inscriptions. And yet this Dion, the Forerunner was the Patron spirit at whose shrine millions, according to Dr. Böckh, were paying devotion just at the moment when that unfathomable forerunner of Palestine was receiving the homage of our own marvelous Messiah on his bended knee.

The matter of these countless associations has been so far probed as to establish that they were an important factor of ancient civilization. They were the most studious, independent, ingenious and progressive of all the ancient unions of trades and professions.

About the time of Christ's sojourn on the earth these organizations were most numerous and powerful. The love of mankind for show, entertainment and every imaginable pleasure was then at its height. Rome had conquered the world. Augustus and Tiberius were busy collecting together the broken fragments. Rich plunderers were dividing the spoils. Profligacy on the one hand and military slavery on the other formed an abyss for their reckless genius to fill. They were faithful to the specification of the Solonic dispensation, holding common interests with one another, a common table, a mutual love, a burial attachment to their secret organization, a methodical votive franchise by which they were enough shrewdly political to vote into public office the agoranomoi, or commissioners of the public works, so as to insure for themselves the appointments to perform the vast and varied labors of public entertainments which supplied them with much well-paid occupation.

Although exceeding fond of, and kind to their women, the Dionysan artists, such as singers, dancers, players, teachers, confined their personnel almost entirely to the male sex. The evidence, however, is, that woman belonged to the secret leagues, and that when their own entertainments came off, she took charge of much necessary work and was prominent and influential.

Following the discipline characterizing the Solonic dispensation, these organizations possessed a system of schools and we have a number of very important monuments which give a portrayal of their methods of teaching the youth. These we shall bring in evidence as we proceed.

The ancient poor men's god Dionysus was exactly the same as the Latin or Roman Bacchus, standing for the female Artemis for the Greek, and Diana for the Roman goddess of the poor. The best lexicographers, Liddell among them, give him the magnificent report of being the "Ennobler of mankind and the giver of joys."

A peculiarity of the Dionysan artists is that they were all worshipers of the great forthcoming soter or saviour, hundreds of years before the arrival of our accredited Messiah; and in consequence, being in expectation every moment, of his advent, were the more willing to fall in line with the Apostolic evangelism. They had a doctrine of culture of their own which was, in many respects, identical with that advocated by our Saviour. Their musical and economical organizations reach back into fathomless antiquity.[2] We should be guilty of a breach of logic by trying to trace their origin back to the time when the Chronicles were composed, because Solon is known to have given them the law of free organization, and this could not possibly have been earlier than a thousand years before Christ, although his exact date is unknown. We are reminded by some authors of the kind words regarding the artists of Dionysus, written by Arsitotle, who was employed by king Phillip in B. C. 349. Aristotle, on account of his valuable mention[3] is accredited to be the ancient who gave them their name. Considerable has been written by the epigraphists of the French, German and other scientific schools now earnestly engaged in the unearthing of monuments of antiquity, in regard to the origin of the name of this enormous organization which was spread, as we shall show, over western Asia and the whole of Europe. Among archæologists this association has come to be known simply as "The great society." This is an appellation received from Böckh, whose learning was so profound and penetrating that the living critics admit him as their authority.[4] However high their origin, all the

---

[2] *Chronicles*, XXV., 1, 2. Did the eranos have a chorister? Asaph, the Assembler, was chorister in musical services. The choir of the musical assemblies of the Dionysan musicians was fully organized and extremely ingenious and efficient.

[3] Foucart, *De Colligiis Scenicorum apud Græcos*, p. 6, says: "Vocabulum certe ipsum οἱ περὶ τὸν Δσόνυσον τεχνιταί, apud Aristotelem primum reperire est." M. Foucart, searching for the earlier records of these unions, mentions Livy, XXIV., 14, who speaks of an artist named Aristonis, as being a tragic actor at Syracuse, and thinks he must have been employed at the great theatre of Syracuse. This would make his date as early as B. C. 400.

records place them as poor, lowly, hard working people; often wandering from stage to stage and performing their popular tragedies, comedies and mimes before the people, as means of obtaining a living. They engrossed the entire field of the histrionic business;[4] made the tents, machinery, wagons, clothing, scenery and all paraphernalia of their plays, sometimes manufactured their own musical instruments, composed and wrote their own music, made and owned as a common brotherhood their temples and sometimes aped the prytanes, with their tholus, in an ambition to be genteel and respectable.[5]

The Pythian Apollo in Attica was the presiding divinity that employed these artists. In many instances this fact comes to the surface. At the temple of Delphi their music was used in chants, dirges, anthems and choruses. Several melodies have recently been found engraved on large slabs or planks of the rock with which the great edifice was built; and although the ancient musical types or characters were radically different from those of the present day, yet they have been deciphered and were even performed at the opera house in Athens in 1896, to the modern lovers of musical art.[6]

There was an eranos of this Pythian Apollo found at Amergos, in the island of Minoa, which worked for the muses and probably played the popular music for the people of the city at a very early date. Again, there has been found an eranos of these artists at Delos, the great slave mart. It commemorates a consecration. They had consecrations, agonies, camp-meetings, hallelujahs and

[4] Luders, *Die Dionysischen Künstler*, p. 77, says: "Die grosse Gesellschaft nennt sich τὸ κοινὸν τῶν περὶ τὸν Διόνυσον τεχνιτῶν τῶν ἀπ' Ἰωνίας καὶ Ἑλλησπόντου καὶ τῶν περὶ τὸν καθηγεμόνα Διόνυσον." Bœckh glaubt, dass letztere in dem Verein eine Abtheilung von solchen bildeten." Later it took the name τὸ κοινὸν τῶν συναγωνιστῶν, but Lüder suggests that these were only branches.

[5] CIG., 3160, 3190. They sometimes pretended to be important characters. They chanted hymns, and performed satyrical dances. Fouc. *id.*, p. 116, says they were prytanes; this he probably gleans from the fact that the prytanes ate at the common table at the expense of the state, cf. Oehler in the *Pauly-Wissowa*, III., pp. 1020, 1037 article Βουλή. But in all places except Attica the prytanes were no more than the Roman Pontifex maximus, and in Asia Minor, where this evidence is found, the prytanes referred to are nothing more than persons of the working class calling themselves prytanes to sound high and dignified. See Liddell, in *verb*. Πρύτανις. Once, later, when Marcus Aurelius honored them with a letter of kind greeting (A. D. 147), they were so inflated that they put up the prices of entrance to their entertainments, CIG., 3176. This letter is contained in the inscription. Their hero worship was thus carried to extravagance. CIG. 3067, 3068, 2620; Le Bas and Wadd., 93 and 2794.

[6] In the summer of 1896, the author was honored with a personal interview with M. Reinach at Paris, who principally worked the queer notes out and brought the hidden treasure to the gaze of modern men. He had no hesitancy in saying that it was the work of the artists of Dionysus and that they developed a very high degree of intelligence and skill.

many other rites suggestively similar to those of the present day.⁷ But the most surprising averment we have found regarding these Dionysan artists is that of Dr. Foucart which is to the effect that Homer was one of them.⁸ There are two mysteries hanging over this great master-poet. He is known as a wanderer through the earth, reciting his stories to the people before letters were invented. This is in accord with the erratic life of the scenic artists. Again, he was mysteriously obscure; and this, again, accords with their habits; since they were always secret organizations, studying means to please the better-to-do, and how to get themselves appointed by the ruling ones, to perform the varied popular labor of the entertainments. Homer might thus have been a secret member; and after being appointed a kurios or supreme director of the brotherhood, he could have committed his beautiful and marvelously enchanting stories to memory, assisted by a picked quota of artists who followed his majestic baton, and together they might have wandered through eastern Europe and western Asia delighting the millions who are well-known to have thronged the world centuries before the conquests came.

On the whole, judging from the prodigious magnitude and mysterious influence and genius which are coming to be known to us through their new-found inscriptions, it looks quite probable that the great poet was not alone but that he was backed up by a multitude of lesser lights.

The influence of the Bacchic artists was early felt at Rome. We have already shown their power as a factor in military and social life in the great city, as it is told to us by the historian Livy. The strike of the flutists

---

⁷ Oehler, *MSS. to the author*: "In Minoa, bei Amergos finden wir κορδακισταί τῶν περὶ τὸν Πυθον Ἀπόλλωνα κορδάκων, dancers, CIA., add. 2264.— 'Ἀπόλλων und die Musen verehrten die dionysischen Künstler, CIA,, II., 629." And again, *id.*, 3479: "Zahlrich sind die Weihungen an Apollo von den Vereinen auf Delos, was nicht auffällig ist."

⁸ Foucart, *De Scenicis Artificibus*, pp. 68, 69, sq. gives Homer as one of them. Also cites the stones and has much to say about it. On p. 70, he says that all the poets were perhaps not members of the collegium, but "plures tamen eorum participes fuisse certum est;" and shows stones to prove it. He is also quite elaborate in showing how the scenic artists mixed piety with their games. The truth, however, is, that they were economic unions, working their ingenuity through all conceivable methods to win a living; "Eleusino vera, qua civitate nulla sanctior, egregia scenicorum pietas. Quo non solum migrabant ut rem ludicram in theatro, temporeum mysteriorum, factiarent, sed etiam ut sacra sua, collegia nomine, per suos magistratus Cereri et Proserpinæ peragerent." He refers to Lenormant, *Researches at Eleusis*. 26, lines 6-11: 14: 17; and 20-28. Many κοίνα existed at that time.

recorded by him occurred B. C. 309.[9] Of course the organization which yielded to the decree of its secret council who caused this strike, had been in existence a long time, perhaps a hundred years. At any rate it proves that Rome possessed unions of the Bacchic or Dionysan artists at least 400 years before Christ.

All members were initiated into the secrets of their brotherhood, the remains of which are found everywhere. At Nemea, an old city on the Isthmes which divides the Corinthian Gulf from the Æginetan waters, a place near Corinth where the Apostle Paul labored and built a church, there was recently found an inscription remarkably well preserved. It shows a union of these artists. The slab is spoken of as: "Laudatio Philemonis." It speaks of a man from Chalcedona the ancient city standing on the heights of the Bosphorus opposite Constantinople, who was initiated by unions of Isthmes and Nemea, and whose name was Crato. He was tibicen cyclicus, one who made the rounds of the organization, performing on his flute.[10] According to the best information we can glean from their inscriptions it is manifest that these play-actors and artists of various kinds struggled very hard sometimes to obtain a living. Dr. Lüders, in his researches on their doings has shown conclusively that they were entirely of the so-called proletarian class, hard workers, vigorous, and yet with all their industry and push, could with difficulty obtain a living, although splendidly organized in self-support.[11] The strugglers were nevertheless patronized and supported in an encouraging degree by the state and by public men and institutions. Alexander the Great, who was such an admirer of them that he assembled, on the death of his much loved friend Hephaeston who died soon after his return from the conquest of India, over 3000 of their minstrels, and actors to do him honor at a protracted carnival. For several weeks they had charge of the entire festivity, performing the music as well as the dances. It appears that the em-

---

[9] See *supra*, pp. 86-88; story told by Livy, IX., 30, sq. of the strike, B. C. 309, of the musicians of Rome. What is known of the event is there given in full. It must have been an important organization, and full of plucky vigor and genius to get itself copied into the great history of Rome.

[10] Fouc., *De Scenicis Artificibus*, pp. 23, 24; Lenormant, *Researches d Eleusis.* 26, l. 25-26; *ibid.*. l. 17, et 39; l. 11-12; 21-27: l. 29-31 etc.

[11] Lüders, *Dionys. Künst,,* p. 110. " . . . . . . zur Zeit des Demosthenes durch Attica, wandernde Truppen, die nothdürftig, ihren Labensunterhalt fanden."

peror not only admired them but rewarded them magnificently for this protracted service. Plutarch and Arrian say[12] that Alexander sent for them from all the countries, far and near, and they came from the Peloponessus in Greece, and from the Euphrates in Asia, all agreeing and all being able to combine, converse and perform in concert and union at the great requiem, proving that they were expert in written music.

Chares, who is reported to us by Athenæus, gives a description of them, which accords with the information we are getting from the inscriptions;[13] and according to Arrian, whose histories, anecdotes, and incidents which have fortunately come down to us in such manner as to have escaped the havoc that has consigned to tatters so many priceless literary monuments of antiquity. Alexander patronized the artists most abundantly at the Olympic games; and on a certain occasion called together three thousand from the whole known world, to perform their so-called agonies before the public.[14] Of these agonies the origin of the familiar words, so precious and beloved by the Christian, we shall have a full dissertation as we proceed. At present we must be content with an occasional and obscure anecdote. The world was filled with the belief that a man-loving messiah, whether, Mithra, Osiris, Dionysos, Attys, Sabazios or Jesus, was persecuted to death, died in the agonies of an ignominious execution, arose and went to the beautiful elysium where he opened the gates to all the struggling and lowly denizens of earth. This wonderful transit through the veil of tears, amid writhings of torture, indescribable gloom and scowls by frowning monsters of

[12] Arrian, *Alexander the Great, Anabasis.*, in book VII., 1 4: "'Ἀγῶνά τε ἐπενόει ποιῆσαι γυμνικόν τε καὶ μουσικὸν ἠλήθει τε τῶν ἀγωνιζομένων καὶ τῇ εἰς αὐτὸν χορηγίᾳ πολύ τι τῶν ἄλλων τῶν πρόσθεν ἀριδηλότερον· τρισχιλίους γὰρ ἀγωνιστὰς τοὺς ξύμπαντας παρεκεύασε κτλ.;" see Plut. *Alex.*, 72: "Ὡς δ᾽ ἧκεν εἰς Ἐκβάτανα τῆς Μηδίας καὶ διῴκησε πάλιν ἣν ἐν θεάτροις καὶ πανηγύρεσιν, ἅτε δὴ τρισχιλίων αὐτῷ τεχνιτῶν ἀπὸ τῆς Ἑλλάδος ἀφιγμένων· ἔτυχε δὲ περὶ τὰς ἡμέρας ἐκείνας Ἡφαιστίων πυρέσσων."

[13] Lüders, *Dionys. Künstler*, p. 106, 107 reminds us of this: "Nach der Erzählung des Chares, die bei Athenäus erhalten ist, tratten, wohl in der angegebenen Reihenfolge, folgende Künstler auf: θαυματοποιοί, ῥαψῳδοί, κιθαρῳδοί, αὐλωδοί, αὐληταί μετὰ τῶν χορῶν, ψιλοκιθαρισταί· κωμῳδοί, τραγῳδοί, ψιλ[τ]; Athenæus, XII., p. 533 Casaubon.

[14] Arrian, whose early account is much esteemed; I., 11: "Τῷ τε Διῒ τῷ Ὀλυμπίῳ τὴν θυσίαν τὴν ἀπ' Ἀρχελάου ἔτι καθεστῶσαν ἔθυσε καὶ τὸν ἀγῶνα ἐν Αἰγαῖς διέθηκε τὰ Ὀλύμπια· οἱ δὲ καὶ ταῖς Μούσαις λέγουσιν ὅτι ἀγῶνα ἐποίησε. See Diod., XVII. 16: "Θυσίας μεγαλοπρεπεῖς τοῖς θεοῖς συνετέλεσεν ἐν Δίῳ τῆς Μακεδονίας καὶ σκηνικοὺς ἀγῶνας Διῒ καὶ Μούσαις οὓς Ἀρχέλαος πρῶτος κατέδειξε, τὴν δὲ πανήγυριν ἐφ' ἡμέρας ἐννέα συνετέλεσεν· Dion appears here to be confounded with Aegā. Dio Chrys., *Or.*, 5, p. 73: "Ἐν Δίῳ τῆς Πιερίας ἔθυον ταῖς Μούσαις καὶ τὸν ἀγῶνα τῶν Ὀλυμπίων ἐτίθεσαν, ὅν φασιν ἀρχαῖον εἶναι παρ' αὐτοῖς.

dæmoniac shapes and gnashing threats was the subject of their popular plays; for since humanity firmly believed in saviours and a coming redemption from the competitive calamities which beset them, it was a second nature to endorse the plays as true, and the agonies as the realistic presentation of the logic of fate long before the Christian's Saviour came. Again, the very word agony, pure Greek, was the term handed down through a millennial superstition, from long anterior to the date at which the now-known Redeemer suffered it, to save the troubled race. Thus the agony of the cross which long afterward was actually endured by a historic personage of our own era was thoroughly foreknown and had been the subject of tragedy, opera, anthem and mime for at least a thousand years; and its structure was based on salvation from persecution of the lowly who were tortured by greedy aristocrats—kings, slave drivers, traders in human flesh and labor, emperors and their privileged priests, and autocratic prelates of a sanctimonious hypocrisy and the money power.

The plan and texture of the organization was entirely socialistic. The law required them to imitate in their scheme of union, the municipal form or charter of the city in which they were organized into the unions. This was early specified by the law since registered in the Digest, but it was to be that old uncontaminated scheme supposed to have originated with Saturn, although actually from Solon and Cadmus, who instituted the prytaneum and the common table.[15]

So far as the inscriptions attest, the artists were all socialists of the sort we designate as the microcosm, or the model family. This was the prototype, and still continues the ideal. The members, like the children of the well regulated family, were to love one another; and the father and mother, together with all the children, were to live in the undivided ownership and enjoyment of their homes and means, helping each other to all the emoluments of the paternity, never coveting more than what belonged to each by right of the mutual or social bond. This model is pure socialism. The little family,

---

[15] This law of initiation ordaining that the Solonic union follow the plan of the city, reads: "Quibus autem permissum est corpus habere collegii, societatis, sive cujusque alterius eorum nomine, proprium est, ad exemplum reipublicæ habere res communes, arcam communem, et actorem sive syndicum." etc. Dig. III. iv. 1.

in the Solonic dispensation, enlarged with the hetæra and the thiasos, is what in Rome was the college. Instead of the family of one marriage it swelled so as to take in the membership of the whole union. Then the union or brotherhood, under a kurios or director, took the place of the father and mother and the initiated membership of many; all being workers, took the place of the children, and in one large fraternal bond they sought and obtained work for each other, bringing the proceeds at night, or at stated times, to the treasurer, deacon and presbyters, who bought food at wholesale for all the brethren, carefully providing a permanent residence, a common meeting house, a school, clothing, and enough of everything to fill the joys of life. Not infrequently they behaved so judiciously with themselves and the world that they were regarded, even by governments with favor.[17]

It is evident that the original design of Solon and Numa, in making this splendid arrangement conform with the plan of the city government from which, according to the law we have quoted, the organization originally sprung, was to ingraft a political economy upon the aged competitive system which, by substituting the votive franchise for the father's judgment, would give the world on a grand scale the socialism of the microcosm or in terms more simple, the socialism of the model family, where all work for each and each for all.

The plan worked for a thousand years. It was attacked twice and fought with fire and sword of extermination through the Roman Conquests, and last by the church prelates, beginning at the close of the Apostolic age, and ending in its destruction through a cruel and jealous interdict of the Council of Laodicea, A. D. 363, about thirty-eight years after the deal with Constantine.

Before they fell many were the powerful men who took their part, Servius Tullius (B. C. 560), among the rest.[18] He tried to save them because of their valuable services to the state, as well as because he admired them and restored to them the rights which Romulus had

[17] Foucart, *De Scenicis Artificibus*, p. 9: "Collegii patrocinium reciperunt Egyptii reges, tanto favore ut ipsorum nomen cum Baccho consociarent artifices."

[18] Florus, *Hist. Rom.* I., 6, 3. "Servio Tullio populus Romulus relatus in censum, digestus in classes decuriis." Tullus was the first to have the people inscribed on the public registers, the plebs being divided into colleges or brotherhoods.

pulled down. At the close of their long career of nearly a thousand years they were submerged, never in their ancient form to rise again. Nevertheless there remained glowing embers which could never be consumed, down to the present day; for a principal in justice cannot be annihilated. The date of their suppression, however, is that of Laodicea and they fell only because their common table was made a crime against the law.[19]

Among the Dionysan artists were certain agents called ergolaboi who used to go about the country bargaining for contracts for their organizations. Plato speaks of them in his second book of Politics, and their inscriptions reveal quite a number of them in Asia Minor and Macedonia. These were special agents and formed a part of the membership, proving that the artists were genuine unions of the eranoi and thiasoi of Greek-speaking countries, and collegia in the Latin countries. We have the best of evidence that they were workers organized to get a living. They have been well spoken of not only by Athenæus[20] in his celebrated Banquet of the Learned, and Hesychius, in his ancient lexicon, but also by Aristotle, the father of literary judges, in his Nicomachian Ethics.[21] Some authors have undertaken to construct a common name for the whole great institution, to answer for all the various names. Throughout the whole Greek-speaking world, the terms eranos and thiasos have a very similar meaning, and it was proposed, as shown in several inscriptions, to blend the two into one word and to call them erano-thiasos for a common term. We have authority for doing this, and it will not be original in us to make the eranothiasos subserve the pur-

---

[19] Suppressed by the Christians, A D. 363; the council interdicted the δεῖπνα ἀπὸ συμβολῆς, which stretches through antiquity, Lüders, *Dionys. Künst.*, p, 7, and note 15: "Die Sitte dieser δεῖπνα ἀπὸ συμβολῆς erstreckt sich durch das ganze Alterthum und noch in der zweiten Hälfte des vierten Jahrhunderts sah sich der Concil von Laodicea veranlasst ein darauf bezügliches Verbot zu erlassen." The words of this decree extinguishing them are: "ὅτι οὐ δεῖ ἱερατικοὺς ἢ κληρικοὺς ἐκ συμβολῆς συμπόσια ἐπιτελεῖν, ἀλλ' οὐδὲ λαϊκούς." Canon 55, Vol. II., p. 574, Mansi. The prelates and priests could have their meals at the common table, but not the people.

[20] Athenæus, VIII., 362: "'Ερανοι δέ εἰσιν αἱ ἀπὸ τῶν συμβαλλομένων εἰσαγωγαί, ἀπὸ τοῦ συνερᾷν καὶ σ...φέρειν ἕκαστον· καλεῖται δὲ ὁ αὐτὸς καὶ ἔρανος καὶ θίασος καὶ οἱ συνιόντες ἐρα...σταί και συνθιασῶται." Another definition comes from Hesychius, *Greek Dictionary*, in verbo Θίασος. H. here says: θίασος is not only an organization for democratical ends to obtain means and enjoyment, but it is also to get plenty of work. It reads as follows: "Θίασον. εὐωχίαν· καὶ πλῆθος οὐ μόνον τὸ Βακχικὸν ἀλλὰ καὶ τὸ ἐργατικόν."

[21] Aristot, *Eth. Nic.*, VIII., 11: "'Ενιοι δὲ κοινωνιῶν δι' ἡδονὴν δοκοῦσι γίνεσθαι, θιασωτῶν καὶ ἐρανιστῶν· αὗται γὰρ θυσίας ἕνεκα καὶ συνουσίας."

pose even including the Roman collegia which were the same institutions.

As a common term for the celebrated personages, many received eponyms, or names suggestive of deeds and surroundings. Eunus of Apamea, the hero of the great Sicilian revolt, in B. C. 333, had been a member of a union of Dionysan artists, and in all probability was making a living for himself and members of his brotherhood by performing tricks of legerdemain in which he was an expert, when he fell a prisoner to some band of the Roman invaders during the conquests,[22] and was sold to a wealthy citizen of Enna where he rebelled against the cruel oppression and plotted that terrible conflict, which at one time bade fair to depopulate the island of Sicily.[23] It is not a little interesting to find that very many of the names mentioned by St. Paul in his Epistles, especially his last chapter of Romans, were assumed; and there is evidence that such was the secrecy of Paul's evangelism among these organizations that when people were initiated, after conversion into the new creed which was contrary to the official religion, new names were given them. Paul himself was a member of the scene-makers branch, and when converted, his name was changed.

It may be well to speak, in a racy manner, of the range of these organizations in the various parts, basing our brief mention upon the actual inscriptions found. There was a union or eranothiasos of artists at Eleusis,[24] only a few miles from the City of Athens.[25] Many are found at Athens, others at Megara, Perinthos and Isthmus. At

---

[22] See Vol. I., chapter ix., pp. 191-231. The war of Eunus lasted ten years during which time several large consular armies of the Romans were routed and destroyed.

[23] Eunus, Greek Εὔνους, well-minded, capable. Theophilus, *Epist. to Autolicus*, cap. vii. says the Eunus of mythology was the son of Dionysus. As the unions had Dionysus for their patron divinity, nothing could be more popular for the people of enterprise and genius than to assume this bewitching name at their plays.

[24] Foucart, *De Scenicis Artif.*, p. 22, referring to Lenormant, *Recherches à Eleusis*, 26. l. 25, 26. It is an Attic inscription of an eranos and mentions its ἐπιμέλητης. It was in the time of Philip V. of Macedon. Livy, XXXI., 24. 26, speaking of his vandalism that destroyed it, says: "Quidquid sancti amoenive circa urbem erat, incensum est, dirutaque non tecta solum sed etiam sepulcra, ... ne quid inviolatum relinqueret, templa deum quæ pagatim sacrata habebant, dirui atque incendi jussit." The members who, according to Lüders were the wandering τεχνῖται, performed the Eleusinian agony.

[25] Oehler, *MSS.*: "Βακχεῖα—Athen., *Mitth.*, XIX., 1894, p. 249 f—Megara, Inschrift Gr. Soph. nr. 107. Παλαιὸν Βακχειὸν, Perinthos: Dumont, *Mélanges d'Arch.*, p. 393, nr. 72 c, τῷ Βακχειῷ Ἀσιανῶν; Rhodes, Inscr. Gr. ins. I, p. 155, Βακχείων ὑποδοχά."

Troia, during the reign of the emperor Trajan, a thiasos was in existence whose tutelary deity was Dionysus.[25] Most singular of all, after the centuries of wonder as to how the Apostle should have been whipped, imprisoned, mysteriously released and spirited off from the Roman and almost Latin city of Philippi, and after his mixture of unexplained persecution and deliverance, it turns out that the emporium was at that moment honeycombed with secret Mithraic and Dionysan societies,[26] and at least one permanent Latin troupe of histrions was stationed there.

Smyrna was alive with these organizations. Aside from the unions of porters jewelers, fishermen and other trades in this city there was an influential branch of the Dionsyan artists who performed the agonies with the object of gaining a living.[27] At Rome they were always favored. As late as Nero this favor continued; for that monarch went so far as to permanently fix them in their true Greek form.[28]

The performance of the agonies was a lucrative business with these unions. The theory of the agony was the eleusinian initiation which in fact, was the model initiatory right copied by all the secret organizations. It represented about this:—the passage through this veil of tears; the groping in darkness of the under world in crooked paths which led the wanderer into many a dark and quaggy region; the outward push, under guidance of some stalking, ethereal shade, over lurid waves of the Pyriphlegethon and other murky rivers of

[25] Μουσίκ. Βίβλιοθ., II., 1875-76, p, 118, no. 5: "αὐτοκράτορι Νέῳ, β. Τραίανῳ Καίσαρι Σεβαστῷ—τῷ καί Θιασώτῃ Διονύσου."
[26] Mommsen, *Hermes*, III., 461 ff., 1869. Inscr. from Philippi; Lüders, *Dionys. Kûnst.*, p. 97; "Wenn endlich in dem Macedonischen Philippi sogar eine ständige lateinische Truppe engagirt war." Likewise Oehler, *MSS.*, sends us word of labor unions early at Philippi.
[27] Oehler, *Eranos Vindobonensis*, p. 277, 278; list of labor organizations. Again, Oehler, *MSS:* SMYRNA: ἐυσταρχοῦστος; *Arch. Zeitung*, XXXVI., 1878, p. 94, nr. 148. Τυχοντατῆς διὰ γένους ἐυσταρχίας πάντων τῶν ἀγώνων ἐν Σμύρνῃ. CIG. 3206 τειμηθεὶς δὲ ἐυσταρχίας παρὰ τῶν κυρίων ἡμῶν.'
[28] Foucart, *De Scenicis Artif.*, p. 92, makes special mention of this event. Nero cruelly persecuted the regular labor unions but favored the Bacchic actors and musicians. Suetonius, *Nero*, XII., 13, says: "Instituit (Nero) et quinquennale certamen primus omnium Romæ, more Græco triplex, musicum, gymnicum equestre, quod appellavit Neronia." Tacitus also gives us valuable evidence: *Annales*, XIV., 20, : " Nerone quartum Cornelio Cosso consulibus, quinquennale ludicrum Romæ institutum est, ad morem Graeci certaminis, varia fama, ut cuncta ferme nova." Again, Suet., *Domitianus*, 4: "Instituit et quinquennale certamen capitolino Jove triplex, musicum, equestre gymnicum, et aliquanto plurium quam nunc est coronarum. Certabant enim et prosa oratione Græcæ Latinæque ac præter citharœdos, chorocitharistæ, et psilocitharistæ."

Hell, toward the elysian realm of eternal delights, on the "other side," "where sickness, sorrow, pain and death are felt and feared no more." These meanderings and sufferings and final joys were, in those primitive days, not only preached as now, but played to an enormous extent by the Dionysan artists, among our delighted, bewildered forefathers. What comforts us most in this retrospective sweep of imagination, is the now-known fact that thousands of agonies of different forms, and set to different music and words, were composed and sold, and their performance brought out before the rich, as a merchantable product, and for them, a living.

But the gymnastic struggles of these artists were not confined to the agonies. There was an eranos of boxers at Akroinos,[29] which is but a single specimen of the acrobats. Many more inscriptions in various places attest the existence of these pugnacious bread-winners among the Dionysan artists.

Then at Olympia, the most celebrated of all the cities of the ancient games, are some inscriptions of these enterprising artists, showing the histrionic dancers.[30] Here the athletes, in the Apostolic age, held their Œcumenical councils. This fact is proved by inscriptions of their own which seemingly the prelates of the second and third centuries would have certainly extirpated had they been farsighted enough to discern the future scrutiny of science, which was destined to lift the race into a higher enlightenment. Neglect to deface the inscriptions as they have mutilated and defaced the testimony of the earliest ecclesiastical historians, like Clement, Papias, Hegesippus and others, has given them away. The Œcumenical athletes serve in evidence.[31] This matter of the œcumenical alliance and œcumenical council turns out to be derived from the associations of the working people organized in their common household throughout all lands and among all peoples.[32]

There were great numbers of unions of wanderers,

---

[29] Oehler, *MSS.:* "'Ακροίνος;—'Αθροφόων κὲ πυκτῶν ἠϊθεών ὁπᾶς ξυστός. Athen. *Mitth.*, VII., 1882, p. 142, and others.

[30] Oehler; *id.:* OLYMPIA: ξυστάρχης. *Archaeol. Zeitung*, XXXVII., 1889, p. 133, nr. 261, Vgl. Bursiaus, *Jahresbericht*, LXIX., p. 131.

[31] Oehler, *MSS.:* "Οἱ ἀπὸ τῆς οἰκουμένης αὐληταί in Knidos: *Anc. Gr. Inscr.*, IV., no. 794, I., bis II., Jahrh. n. Chr. In Olympia wird τῶν ἀπὸ τῆς οἰκουμένης αὐλητῶν ὁ σύμπας ξυστὸς καὶ ἡ ἱερά ξυστικὴ σύνοδος erwähnt in der Inschrift, ungefähr 85, n. Chr.

[32] Οἰκουμενικός, the whole sweep of the world.

some of whom were called fakirs. Their monuments have been discovered at Tralles, Isthmus, Nemea, Delphi, Thebes in Greece, and Pergamus, Iasos, Ephesus, Pessinus, Smyrna and other places in Asia Minor. In fact the original fakirs as they are traced back to the Dionysan artists, were numerous in Rome and many an Italian municipium. They are found with their voodooism among the ragpickers of the centonarii which we have already described.[33]

Dr. Foucart, who wrote the valuable work on what he, and at that time, the entire world of epigraphy, supposed to be exclusively religious associations, though now seen to have been economic ones, likewise discusses these fakirs and wonder-workers. They are of remote antiquity and so great was the belief in their mysterious magic that they entered into the dramas of the poets[34] who wrote more than one valuable play now lost in the vortex of that most sickening syncope of humanity, the feudal ages. The ancient metragurtes was a fakir, nomad, castaway. Threatened by the dangers of the competitive world which gave him neither sympathy nor bread, he organized himself into the Dionysan brotherhoods and went about practicing sleight of hand, peddling philters and exhibiting side-splitting tricks and buffoonery. He practiced every available species of flunkyism and obsequious palaver before the rich and great with the one purpose of winning success in the struggle for existence. Dr. Am Rhyn thinks the fakirs descended from the Pythagorean school[35] of philosophy, or sect of Orphic societies, which, as the world of letters under-

[33] Vol. I., pp. 423-427; Lüders, *Dionys. Künst.*, p. 13, calls them Wunderthäter, Jongleurs, θαυματοποιοί. Spieler jeglicher Art an und producirten ihre Fertigkeit mit gleichem Erfolg neben denen der dionysischen Künstler." They used also to be called flatterers, for we have inscriptions cut by their unions mentioning them as Διονυσοκόλακες, Ἀλεξανδροκόλακες etc. Oehler in *MSS.*, also mentions them as Vereine.

[34] Foucart, *Ass'n. Rel.*, p. 176: "Plusieurs pièces, dont il ne restent malheureusement que le titre ou des fragments insignifiants, exposaient le type de ce personnage aux rires du public: 'Ἀγύρτης de Philémon, Μητραγύρτης, de Ménandre, ou Μηναγύρτης d' Antiphane. On peut rattacher à la même préoccupation de flétrir des fraudes et les désordres prevoquées par ces superstitions."

[35] Am Rhyn, *Mysteria*, p. 85, cf. Eng. *trans.*, N. Y. 1895: "Being stript of the semi-public and official character attaching to the mysteries, and of the philosophic dignity of the Pythagorean Sect, the Orphic societies became nests of swindlers and mendicants; the vagabond priests, Orpheotelestæ, admitted to their ridiculous degrees for a consideration, every credulous and marvel-gabbling postulant; for we even find victims who had themselves, with wives and children initiated every month. Other tricksters combined the Orphic cult with the Phrygian cult of Cybele, mother of the gods and with that of Sabazios, known as Μητράγυρταί, mother-beggars."

stands them, were hilarious and musical. Menander the poet, in his Hiereia and Desdæmon, admits that the wandering jugglers and fortunetellers of Cybele did all their art-work to eke out a living, under precarious and indigent circumstances. Thus they made the blind art a trade under the law. Clement of Alexandria attacks them because, by selling philters and love medicines they tended to break up marriages, which the Christians advocated. So also, in his Superstition, Menander rails upon these fakirs because their occult influence was to scare and fool the people. They worked their wiles in all directions to fashion ghosts and demons, wood-nymphs, sea urchins and centaurs, ingeniously composing plays wherein these supernatural wraiths and monsters were realistically brought before the believing hordes of playgoers and this is one reason why Plato came down with his powers against them. So great was their influence, on account of the credulity of the people, that it was firmly believed they could call up the dead to life, just as it is to-day believed of Jesus. They even claimed that they could chain up the immortal gods. Plato was much struck with their influence, and being of too high rank in the scale of correct reasoning, he was severe and pitiless against them.[36] They interfered with his state religion and political economy.

The fakir tribe of Metragurtes or beggars[37] for old mother Cybele, parent of all gods, were firmly organized under the jus coeundi of the Solonic dispensation. The principal name which they were known by, is hetæra. They often assumed the designation of congregation of religious beggars. Very little religion, however, appears to have disturbed them. It was necessary to ape the

[36] Plato, "Repub.," II., 364: " Ἐὰν τέ τις ἐχθρὸν πημῆναι ἐθέλῃ, μετὰ σμικρῶν δαπανῶν ὁμοίως δίκαιον ἀδίκῳ βλάψειν ἐπαγωγείς τισι καὶ καταδέσμοις τοὺς θεοὺς, ὥς φασι, πείθοντές σφισιν ὑπηρετεῖν." Again Laws, X., 910: " Κείσθω γὰρ νόμος οὗτος· Μὴ κεκτῆσθαι θεῶν ἐν ἰδίαις οἰκίαις ἱερά· τὸν δὲ φανέντα κεκτημένον ἕτερα καὶ ὀργιάζοντα πλὴν τὰ δημόσια."
[37] Minucius Felix, "Octavius," cap. 24: "Mendicantes vicatim deos ducunt." Tertullian, "Apol.," 42: "Non enim sufficimus . . . diis vestris mendicantibus opem ferre." Juvenal, VIII., v., 173, 175:
"Permixtum nautis et furibus ac fugitivis,
Inter carnifices et fabros sandapilarum,
Et resupinati cassantia tympani Galli."
Granier de Cassagnac, "Hist. Classes Ouvrières," 377-8, says beggars increased as emancipation did: "On les voyait se grouper tous les matins autour des temples, portant dans leurs mains des petites images des dieux. Parmi eux se mêlaient les prêtres de Cybèle, qui formaient dans le clergé païen, ou dans le collège des prêtres, une congrégation des religieux mendiants."

official religion of the countries they inhabited. Fakirs, nomads, gypsies, castaways! What else? Who else could they have been? Were these beggar-priests of Cybele the original gypsies? Let the kind reader compare them with the Roman centonarii whose innumerable organizations are found in Italy, and which we have already described.[38] Morally considered, they seem to have been no better than the ragpickers and piecepatchers of the countries farther west, and it is doubtful whether they were not internationally allied.

After the Roman conquests the amphitheatre came into existence in almost every city in pro-consular Rome. The brutal games degraded the finer sensibilities[39] of mankind which in earlier days had been cultivated by a higher status of thought, which was constrained to give way to the coarse munus officium and its ghastly infatuations, depressing the high-toned ancient gymnastic plays down to the fetid level of human athletics in the death combat with the gladium, pitted against both wild beast and fellow man.[40]

In studying the whole subject one thing is observable: the members entered the organization only by initiation. Sometimes a representative of the outside world, such as a rich man, or even in very rare cases, a king or emperor, was willing to descend to their estate and become an initiate. This occasionally happened on account of the agonies which were very alluring and fascinating. The emperor Hadrian went through the initiation of the new Dionysos, perhaps to curry favor with their power and influence.[41] The fact is, the world was in an unscientific, unsettled state, ready to believe any unnatural thing or endorse any imposition. People were in a certain sense, fetich worshipers; and to-day religion gets the better of reason; for often members of our Christian denomina-

[38] Vol. I., pp. 423-427.
[39] "Idem." p. 277, and indeed, the whole of chapter xii., giving the history of the greatest of gladiators, Spartacus, and his brilliant career.
[40] Tertullian, "De Spectaculis," cap. 12, describes the origin of the "munus officium, which was the service of men dying for their dead masters in combat. Mars and Diana were patrons of these games.
[41] Lüders, "Dionys. Künst.," p. 73, says Hadrian founded agonies at Athens, sustaining it by mention that there is an inscription in proof; CIG. 4315; "Ἡ ἱερωτάτη βουλὴ καὶ οἱ Ἀθήνησιν Ἐπικούρειοι φιλόσοφοι καὶ ἡ ἱερὰ θυμελικὴ σύνοδος;" and another as titled Ἱερὰ Ἀδριανὴ Ἀντωνείνη θυμελικὴ περιπολιστικὴ μεγάλη σύνοδος τῶν ἀπὸ τῆς οἰκουμένης περὶ τὸν Διόνυσον καὶ Αὐτοκράτορα καίσαρα Τίτον Αἴλιον Ἀδριανὸν Ἀντωνεῖνοι Σεβαστόν, Εὐσεβῆ, νέον Διόνυσον." But this Néos Dionysos or new god was certainly not meant to be the old aristocratic god revived on the Eleusinian pattern, in which Hadrian well known to have been initiated. It was a sort of Ἀδριανοκόλαξ.

tions—though of late, more rarely—when assembled at their camp meetings, run mad, howl, rave and rage during ecstasies of conversion. The ancients did the same thing except that it was almost always occultized under the veil of initiation. Intermixed with the cult of the mother-beggars or fakirs were hideous reptiles coiling around a staff of Asclepias, the bath in mud and bran and a hundred other absurdities of the Cybelian theogony. Much is found to spring from the fairy tales and songs of these brotherhoods of Dionysan artists. Thus Aristophanes describes them.[42]

The serpent was a foreign symbol.[43] They undertook at as early a date as B. C. 350, to introduce the Sabazian initiations into Athens. Many a martyr fell to the cause. The people of Attica were too far advanced for Phrygian superstitions, to carry them away upon the infatuating whirlwinds of fanaticism. The wanderers undertook their weird and dangerous task by the sly insistence of snake charming, hypnotism, oracles, fortune telling, stargazing astrology, magic, undue influence, witchery and in fact, priestcraft and cunning illusion. There is a curious inscription which has recently been discovered, showing the prevalence of the snake superstitions, a thing pushed to the front by these fakir organizations, for the purposes of winning bread for the brotherhood. It was found in Macedonia.[44]

Dr. Oehler speaks of an epicurean chorus of these entertainments in Puteoli. Of this Italian commercial city, once large and flourishing, a short distance from where Naples now stands, we shall say much in a future chapter. It was largely a Phœnician colony and the numerous

---

[42] Fragment of "Orpheus," founder of the ancient mysteries:
"But from the sacred womb Phausis begat
Another offspring, horrible and fierce:
In sight a frightful viper, on whose head were hairs; its face was
Comly; but the rest from the neck downward, bore an aspect
Dire of the dread dragon."

[43] Foucart, "Ass'ns. Rel.," pp., 8, 134, shows that the Athenians punished priests with death who introduced the Sabazian initiations: note on p. 81: "Καὶ ἐὰν παρείαν ἴδῃ ὄφιν ἐν τῇ οἰκίᾳ- Σαβάζιον καλεῖν. Theophrast., "Charact.," 16. The subject of the persecution and martyrdom of Theoris we shall consider in a more convenient place. See Foucart, "id.," p. 1:

[44] Heuzy, "Palais Grec en Macedoine," p. 30, Paris, 1892: "On y voit une femme assise, tenant enroulé et pelotonné sur les genoux un énorme serpent." Another serpent was discovered inscribed on amber; and Panofka thought it represented Jupiter in the incestuous embrace with his daughter, Proserpine. The serpent is luring her to quietude while the ferocious god accomplishes his purpose. It is read by the epigraphists to be a Phrygian mystery, and consequently must go among workingmen's monuments. It was this very Phrygian serpent that was at the bottom of Alexander's pretended immaculate conception, or assumed parthenogenesis.

unions of labor there were planted by the Phœnicians.⁴⁵ We shall mention their strange reception with the Apostle Paul on his way in chains to his trial at Rome, which resulted in his death. The Dionysan artists thronged lower Italy or what was known as Magna Græcia in the time of Brutus, for that magnate wanted to employ one of their Greek artist actors, whose skill had made him celebrated; and it shows that there were wandering troupes in Rhegium.⁴⁶ According to Tacitus, Rome introduced their plays and pedantry for the first time through Mummius, in honor of his triumphs, after the destruction of Corinth, during the conquests; a cruelty which had to be glozed over by the paltry flattery such a subterfuge afforded.⁴⁷ Like all other trade unions they strove to obtain the public work and succeeded with many magistrates. Plutarch tells us that Nero employed them, disbursing large sums of money.⁴⁸ Nero, who hated the other unions and undertook the impossible task of exterminating them by persecution, was nevertheless very favorable to the Dionysan artists.

Valuable inscriptions of these artists are found in many parts, especially at Rome and neighboring towns. One is recorded from Bovillæ, on the Appian Way, ten miles from Rome, dating from A. D. 165 and must have been there earlier. This scenic eranos was revived under Hadrian and Antoninus Pius. Their organization which flourished earlier but had met the disaster of the conquests, arose afresh. Hadrian was a friend of the mysteries, and because the societies helped him through,

⁴⁵ Oehler, "MSS.," "Eine Inschrift aus Rhodapolis, Le Bas, III., 1336 nennt; οἱ Ἀθήνισιν Ἐπικούριοι φιλόσοφοι, womit ich den Epicureius chorus in Puteoli stellen muss, CIL., X., nr. 2971. Bei Athen., VII., 298d werden die Schüler Epikurs genannt, εἰκαδισταί, weil sie in ihrem Vereine den 20 Monatstag als Gedächnisstag des Stifters feierten. Eine Inschrift aus Kyme erwähnt einen Πυρρωνιστὰς Μενεκλεῆς, Kaibel, "Epigr.," nr. 2416; Bull. Héll., XIII., 1889, p. 368, nr. 17. Der Menakles gehörte einem θίασος an, als dessen Stifter Pyrrhon angenommen ist."

⁴⁶ Plutarch, "Brutus," 21: "Καὶ τῶν περὶ τὸν Διόνυσον τεχνιτῶν αὐτὸς εἰς Νέαν πόλιν καταβὰς ἐνέτυχεν πλείστοις· περὶ δὲ Κανουννίου τινὸς εὐημεροῦντος ἐν τοῖς θεάτροις ἔγραψε πρὸς τοὺς φίλους, ὅπως πείσαντες αὐτὸν εἰσαγάγωσιν. Ἑλλήνων γὰρ οὐδένα βιασθῆναι προσήκειν."

⁴⁷ Tacitus, "Annæles," XIV., 21: "Maiores quoque non abhorruisse spectaculorum oblectamentis pro fortuna quae tum erat, eoque a Tuscis accitos histriones, a Thuriis equorum certamina; et possessa Achaia Asiaque ludos curatius editos, nec quemquam Romae honesto loco ortum ad theatrales artes degeneravisse, ducentis iam annis a L. Mummii triumpho, qui primus id genus spectaculi in urbe praebuerit."

⁴⁸ Plutarch, "Galba," 16, on which Lüders, "Dinys. Künst.," p. 95, comments as follows: "Nero endlich betrat nicht nur selbst, mit Griechischen Techniten die Bühne, sondern hatte auch stets eine ganze Schaar von ihnen in seiner Umgebung, denen er Grosse Geldsummen hinterliess."

THE GREAT GEMEINDE.

he was very favorable to them.⁴⁹ Not only Hadrian, but Marcus Aurelius, Commodus, and even Caracalla, showed them kindness. The Christians had long before planted faith enormously among these secret unions of bread-winners. This affords some measure of cause why these monarchs who were so kindly disposed to Christianity all through that prosperous period, never attacked them.⁵⁰ Car.calla took to himself the new Bacchus, which in Greek was the workingmen's Dionysus, and endorsed him and his vast organizations as the "Ennobler of mankind and the giver of joys." Foucart says that Hadrian, Antoninus Pius, and Commodus did the same.⁵¹

The Asiatic scenic artists found their way in early times as far northward into Gaul as Vienna on the Rhone, called Vienne, where, in the old pagan temple afterwards the church of the Christians, but now converted into a museum of antiquities, the author under the guidance of M. Piot, president of the Bank of Beauregard, found a dilapidated inscription of an eranos, in 1896.⁵² Very many epitaphs are found in various parts of Rhegium, now lower Italy, which are recently coming into notice. Some are brought to light from Orange, Lille-

---

⁴⁹ Orell., no. 2625. "Commune mimorum." It records a union of scenic players, "the best of that time," with their many functions and works. At the end, 60 names are inscribed, as members. This is the Boville inscr.

⁵⁰ Foucart, "De Collegiis Scenicorum," p. 93, mentions that these organizations existed at Delphi, "Inscrs. Inédites de Delphes," 468, showing the favors of Hadrian: "Imperatori Hadriano servatori qui suam ipsius Graeciam restituit et aluit, Graeci qui Plataeas conveniunt gratiae monumentum consecrarunt."

⁵¹ Gibbon, "Decline and Fall of the Roman Enpire," Vol. I., p. 47, Harpers, declares that from Trajan, in A. D. 98, to the last of the Antonines, A. D. 180, a period of 82 years, was the season selected as the most prosperous and happy in the annals of the human race. These better days are proven by Foucart, "De Coll. Scen. Artif.," who speaks of the "new Bacchus," meaning the Διονύσος καθηγεμόνος the world over; a fact which scholars of modern days cannot understand. The artists wrought for him enormous praise and profit. Slab 379, in the CIL. is a "tituli fragmentum Thyatirae repertum," CIG. 3476b. It reads: "Decretum sacrae Hadrianae, Antoninae themelicae peripolisticae magnae synodi corum qui ex toto orbe terrarum circa Bacchum et Imperatorem Caesarem, T. Ælium Hadrianum Antoninum Augustum Pium novum Bacchum, sunt, artificum."

⁵² It begins: Scenici Asiatici. Lower, on the stone, which is large, and except the lettering, well preserved, are the words: ne . . . . . . et, Qui in eodem corpore sunt vivi. Sibi fecerunt. The members had constructed the monument, probably a sepulchre for themselves. The author saw this by accident in his travels and supposed it to have been hitherto unobserved; but Lüders, "Dionys. Künst., p. 96, gives it a handsome mention, which need not be repeated, as his rendering conforms with ours. He takes them to be mimic actors. It is recorded in Orell., no. 2642, who thinks the president was the man from Asia. If so, he probably was an apostle of the "Grea' ynod," of whom we shall give more information—it being known that they sent out "Apostles." The Orellian Collection reads it as follows: "Scænici Asiaticiani et qui in oedem corpore sunt, vivi sibi fecerunt." Thus it was a scenic union like all the rest.

bonne, Arles, and elsewhere. The Roman city of Philippi in Macedonia, was well supplied with mimic artists at the time Paul established his church there.[53] These unions were commonly called svnods both in Latin and Greek. Dr. Lueders cites great authority for his statement that the organized artists enjoyed immunity throughout the whole of proconsular Rome which extended from Asia to Britain.[54] The members, like those of the collegia organized to make a living by manual labor, were at Rome excluded from the right of citizenship, sometimes temporarily, on suspicion of being seditious and dangerous. They might have been suspected of too much sympathy with the great secret trade unions we have already described. No doubt they were; for they were all struggling bread-winners together with a common cause. On this subject of comparison with the great Roman and Greek collegia, it is comforting to read inscriptions of the scenic artists showing their enjoyment of some civic rights. Probably their numbers and numeric leverage caused it.[55]

It is very interesting to note the variety of entertainment these organizations controlled. They managed the laughing, fun-making entertainments and games from the time of Aristophanes.[56] So great was the ancient passion for laughing that people would turn out in throngs to see any new joke, callipygian can-can, dance or gymnastic squirm, no matter if it was attended

---

[53] A titulus of this sort is mentioned by Foucart, "Scenic Artists," p. 10. CIG., 5762, which is that of a trade union under umbrage of the lex collegiorum funeraticiorum.

[54] "Dionys. Künst.," p. 34, "Auch diese Gesellschaften waren wie die Dionysischen Kunstler für das ganze Römische Reich concessionirt." CIG. 5907, 5913, 3500, 3501, 2931.

[55] Foucart, "De Coll. Scen. Artificum," p. 28, thus defines these skilled workmen's rights as citizens: "Quin etiam collegia suam rem apud civitates tanquam æquo jure per legationes defendebant." Two slabs from Teos show that their embassadors were sometimes admitted to a hearing before public tribunals; also one from Delos, CIG. 8067. Their own play-actors were sent as delegates: "Qua legatione funguntur poeta tragicus, citharoedus, synagonista tragicus, ita suffragiis sociorum designati ut unicuique trium partium quibus constabat collegium suus esset legatus."

[56] Oehler, "MSS.": "Die Διομειαλάζοντες bei Aristoph, "Acharn.," vs. 605, und οἱ τὰ γέγοις λέγοντες bei Athenæus, VI., 260a, können mit Lüders, "Dionys. Künst.," p. 17, in gwissen Sinne als Thiasoten des Herakles betrachtet werden. In Gewissen Sinne waren auch die ταγηνισταί (Aristophanes Komoedie deses Titels, "fragm." bei Koch, I,. p. 488-527) und die ψυχισταί des Strattis, Koch, I., p. 711, fragm. 54-59." The γελωτοποιοί, or buffoons had their eranoi. On the θίασοι καιἐράνοι carrying on the histrionic profession, see Lüders, "Dionys. Künst.," pp. 59-62, and his note 112, p. 60; Athanæus, XI., 464· Ἡμεῖς οὖν ὡς καὶ παρ᾽ Ἀθηναίοις ἐγίνετο ἅμα ἀκραώμενοι τῶν γελωτοποιῶν τούτων καὶ μίμων, ἔτι δὲ τῶν ἄλλων τεχνιτῶν ὑποτίνομεν. The old writers, unless we except large-minded men like Aristotle, can see no other thing than to run down and abuse the poor.

with some lewdness in language and display. They were likewise extremely fond of witnessing gymnastic exercises, wherever made to thoroughly conform to the expression. As a consequence we have great numbers of inscriptions of the thiastic gymnasts in all parts of the then known world.[57]

But it is now proved that for whatever industry or profession these unions were engaged the ultimate object was to get a living. They were as strictly economical as the trade unions of to-day.[58]

It has been recently advanced by some authors engaged in the analysis of this subject that the thiasos was not religious. On account of the rigid watchfulness of the law a certain devotion to the pagan gods was necesssry, but they did not feel the piety they assumed.[59] The fist-fighters of Greek-speaking countries do not appear to have been so fierce and bloody as those of Rome, except perhaps in Antioch and Ephesus where the strictly Roman games were introduced. But tragedies found their birthplace there. During the life of the younger Sophocles, B. C. 200, the tragedies of Teos, which may

[57] Oehler, *Ibid: on gymnasts, athletes, pugilists, etc.*: "*Akroinos* ἀθλοφόρων κὲ πυκτῶν ἠϊθέων ὁπᾶς ξυστός· Athen., *Mtth.*, VII., 1882, p. 142." This is sufficient proof that acrobats and pugilists, called πυκτοί or fist-fighters were included among the Dionysan artists. Again, *id*: "Σύνοδος als Bezeichnung eines Athletenvereins finden wir in dem Rescripte des Triumvir, M. Antonius, in einem Papyrus des British Museum erhalten und vom Kenyon: *The Classical Review*, VII., 1893. p. 477, veröffentlicht ist. Es wird der σύνοδος τῶν ἀπὸ τῆς οἰκουμένης ἱερονεικῶν καὶ στεφανειτῶν die Befreiung von Militärdienst und von bürgerlichen Leistungen bestätigt."

[57] Foucart *De Collegiis Scenicorum*, p. 6; "A principio scenici artifices private vitam agebant, nec nisi exercendi artificii causa, et id quidem ad tempus, convenire solebant; tandem in corpus perpetuum sese congregaverunt non actores modo sed etiam poetæ, musici et omnes quicunque Bacchi festis inserviebant." So Oehler, *MSS.*, *id.*, makes this open acknowledgment, on years of experience in the field : VEREINE DER DIONYSISCHEN KUENSTLER: Diese sind sowohl als Kultvereine des Dionysos, als auch Erwerbsgenossenschaften zu betrachten." Dr. Poland likewise says the same: *De Collegiis Artificum Dionysiacorum.* They were both artists and bread-winners.

[58] Athenæus, *Deipnosophistæ*, 20, undertakes to show that they sometimes had their drinking bouts: "Θίασον, ὅσπερ ἐστὶν ἡ ἀπὸ τοῦ πείνειν συναγωγή." But this, while at as late a date as Athenæus, may have applied to some cases, was the reverse of the record of Aristotle who said many kind things of them and gave them an excellent character. We fail to find evidence that they ever changed. At the time of Paul they had a strong business character. The eranos, thiasos and collegium were so peaceful and business-like that Hannibal on entering Italy with his conquering army suppressed them because they were not enough warlike to satisfy his vengeful blood thirst. He attacked and broke up the συσσιτοι in order to make them truculent enough to turn against and destroy one another. Strabo, *Geog.*, 250. vi. "Καμπανοῖς δὲ συνέβη διὰ τὴν τῆς χώρας εὐδαιμονίαν ἐπ' ἴσον ἀγαθῶν ἀπολαῦσαι καὶ κακῶν. Ἐπὶ τοσοῦτον γὰρ ἐξετρύφησαν ὥστ' ἐπὶ δεῖπνον ἐκάλουν πρὸς ζεύγη μονομάχων, ὁρίζοντες ἀριθμὸν κατὰ τὴν τῶν συνδείπνων ἀξίαν. Ἀννίβα δ' ἐξ' ἐνδόσεως λαβόντος αὐτούς, δεξάμενοι χειμαδίοις τὴν στρατιὰν οὕτως ἐξεθήλυσαν ταῖς ἡδοναῖς ὥσθ' ὁ Ἀννίβας ἔφη νικῶν κινδυνεύειν ἐπὶ τοῖς ἐκθροῖς γενέσθαι, γυναῖκας ἀντὶ τῶν ἀνδρῶν τοὺς στρατιώτας ἀπολαβών."

be denominated the hot-bed of the great co-operative union of Dionysan artists, existed. Gravestones to their memory are found bearing inscriptions showing that they were skilled in all the varieties of the scenic profession. They performed the Greek trilogies.[60]

The penetrating and learned Dr. Lüders reminds us in his brilliant and much quoted work on these associations, that they were often very poor and had a hard life of it even with all their skill and system. We are not entirely confined to their inscriptions for this information. Lucian considered them no better than dogs that constantly deserved a whipping. He tells us that their beautiful clothes were often seen with holes and sometimes patched up for want of earnings wherewith to buy new, and their critics on the stage were brutal to them, often hissing them out and boistrously insulting them; and it was not an uncommon thing for their manager to drive the poor fellows out into the homeless night if they failed to get the required applause.[61]

Again, we are fortunate enough to possess some remnants from the ancient pen indicating furthermore the life they led.[62] Such was the taint blighting labor in those days that they actually got the name of being too poor to be good. The great Aristotle whose records we have often quoted as kindly in their favor, is reported to have classed a certain portion of mankind, among which these organized artists are numbered, as being too poor to be good! Is not this the case with millions at this moment? Organized working men too poor to be good! Here is a most remarkable acknowledgment, and by a great authority, of the economic poverty of the poor working people at that time highly organized, B.C. 384–322, in which it is explained that the Dionysan artists as well as mechanics were so enslaved in their means

---

[60] See Welcker, on the *Greek Trilogies.*
[61] Lucian, *Apol. pro Merc. Cond.*, 5; "'Ἀλλ' οἱ μὲν, τοῖς τραγικοῖς ὑποκραταῖς εἰκάσουσιν' οἱ ἐπὶ μὲν τῆς σκηνῆς 'Ἀγαμέμνων ἕκαστος αὐτῶν ἢ κρέων, ἢ αὐτὸς 'Ηρακλῆς εἰσιν. ἔξω δὲ Πῶλος ἢ 'Αριστόδημος, ἀποθέμενοι τὰ προσωπεῖα, γίγονται ὑπόμισθοι τραγῳδοῦντες, ἐκπίπτοντες καὶ συριττόμενοι ἐνίοτε δὲ μαστιγούμενοι τινες αὐτῶν, ὡς ἂν τῷ θεάτρῳ δοκῇ,"
[62] Aulus Gellius, *Noctes Atticæ*, XX., 4, speaks of them rather kindly perhaps too dolefully, but virtually admits that the state hired and paid them for their delicious services: "Comœdos quispiam et tragœdos et tibicines dives adulescens Tauri philosophi discipulus liberos homines in deliciis atque in delectamentis habebat. Id genus autem artifices Græce appellantur "οἱ περὶ τὸν Διόνυσον τεχνῖται." Eum adulescentem Taurus a sodalitatibus convictuque hominum scænicorum abducere volens, misit ei verba hæc ex Aristotolis libro exscripta, qui προβλήματα ἐγκύκλια inscriptus est, jussitque uti ea cotidie lectitaret διὰ τί κ.τ.λ. See note 68.

of existence that they could never be good members of society!⁶³ The question which naturally arises is whether governments can afford to permit such a state of things. Is this not, after all, one of the great causes, aye the principal cause of the proverbially short life of the nations of the earth? Who ever went down so deep as Aristotle into the origin of causes as to dig up this great fact?

We make bold to venture the remark that Aristotle's averment is well based. It stands on the authority of the world's ideal philosopher and political economist. It is thus written as a Bible scripture, that when governments tolerate conditions wherein their working people are too poor, too depressed, too lowly to be good, they have arrived at the brink of the deep abyss of decomposition and death. A search into the records of a natural life shows this; and it is high time to harken to the deathless voice of Aristotle and to look up the compendious thunders of Kant whose wonderful unwinding of moral phenomena clears the intellectual sky so that we may behold his dazzling "categorical imperative" thundering to men that what they ought to do they *must* do, even though the doing require the drastic powers of individuals and of governments combined.

The ancient fishermen and huntsmen probably allied their unions likewise with the Dionysan organizations of the jus coeundi of the Solonic dispensation.

More than 300 years before our era began there were hunters regularly established in their special business, working for the Indian government under pay of the wise king Sandrakotta. They were exempt from military duty and enjoyed other immunities, which must have made them not only independent but justly proud. There are many evidences that their organization was conducted under the law of Solon.⁶⁴ Strabo not only gives us the full business of the professional hunters of India and manner in which they received their instructions and

---

⁶³ Aristotle, *Prob.*, XXX., 10; "Διὰ τί οἱ Διονυσιακοί τεχνίται ὡς ἐπὶ τὸ πολὺ πονηροί εἰσιν; ἢ ὅτι ἥκιστα λόγον σοφίας κοινωνοῦσι διὰ τὸ περὶ τὰς ἀναγκαίας τέχνας τὸ πολὺ μέρος τοῦ βίου εἰσίν, καὶ ὅτι ἐν ἀκρασίαις τόν πολιν κρόνον εἰσιν, τὰ δὲ καὶ ἐν ἀπορίαις, ἀμφότερα δέ φαυλότητος παρασκευαστικά."

⁶⁴ Strabo. *Geog.*, 704: "Τρίτον τὸ τῶν ποιμένων καὶ θηρευτῶν, οἷς μόνοις ἔξεστι θηρεύειν καὶ θρεμματοτροφεῖν ὠνιά τε παρέχειν καὶ μισθοῦ ζεύγη· ἀντὶ δὲ τοῦ τὴν γῆν ἐλευθεροῦν θηρίων καὶ τῶν σπερμολόγων ὀρνέων μετροῦνται παρὰ τοῦ βασιλέως σῖτον, πλάνητα καὶ σκηνίτην νεμόμενοι βίον. Ἵππον δὲ καί ἐλέφαντα τρέφειν οὐκ ἔξεστιν ἰδιώτῃ· βασιλικὸν δ' ἑκάτερον νενόμισται τὸ κτῆμα, καὶ εἰσὶν αὐτῶν ἐπιμεληταί."

their pay from the king, but how they used to catch and subdue the animals, and his lengthy account of this is very interesting. They thus controlled the supply of wild, fighting beasts for the amhitheatres, adding to the Dionysan amusements.

An organization of fisherman of more than ordinary numbers and importance existed at the Sea of Tiberias in the north of Palestine, at an age not far from the celebrated choice of a fisherman there, by the founder of Christianity.[65] Though the discovery is recent, it furnishes auxiliary proof regarding some of the great transactions of that day. Smyrna was a complete Billingsgate and it appears they were rigidly organized together into a powerful and judiciously conducted eranothiasos, so strong and political that they dictated by their votes on election days who should be their agoranomos or commissioner of public works, markets and provisions, thus in a certain degree, controlling the price of fish foods for the people.[66] Ephesus was also well organized in the fish business, and had a large number of unions of fishermen who plied their nets in the bays at night, and with their fishing smacks even ventured far into the sea in quest of game.[67] This was going on in a very brisk manner during the apostolic age.

Unions of fishermen are found to have existed at almost every seaport in Asia Minor, and even as far inland as Hierapolis and Thyateira. Cyzicus furnishes us with a fisherman's organization which seems to have been somewhat connected with the shipping trade. An inscription shows it to have been a consecration to Poseidon and Aphrodite. No one need be surprised on contemplating all these old and beaten paths of the ancient trade unionism under the Solonic dispensation, to find such beloved biblical words crop out, as "consecrations," "hallelujahs," "resurrections," "synods," "baptisms," "new births," love feasts, or "presbyters." Being all borrowed terms, they with their rites, were engrafted into Chris-

[65] Mention is made of it in several works. Our information is as yet, inaccurate and unreliable, because we do not possess the exact text of the slab. It may appear later.
[66] Oehler. *MSS*: "SMYRNA: eine συνεργασιά derselben wird erwähnt, welche κατὰ τὸ ψήφισμα τῆς βουλῆς irgend eine Ehrenstatue aufstellte, Μουσκ. βιβλ., I., 1878, p. 65, nr. 7; ungenau Reinach, Μυσ., XXVII., 1872, p. 464."
[67] Oehl., *ibid.*: "Es mögen hier angefügt werden die sociatates, welche mit der Fischerei oder der Abgabe von Fischfange zu thun hatten. In Ephesus finden wir: οἱ ἐπὶ τὸ τελώνιοντῆς ἰχθυϊκῆς πραγματευόμενοι, Hermes, IV., 1870, p. 187."

tianity from these unions because they were good and pure, and therefore eternal. They have from time immemorial existed and are destined to exist through time and eternity, sublime, hallowed, and though encysted in the scums of greed, yet ever the brilliant gems of justice and of truth.

A union of pearl fishers which seems to have combined its labors with those of the divers at Rome is mentioned by us in the first volume of this work.[68] But there were many unions of them stretching all along the Italian coasts wherever an estuary of the rivers existed, whether in or near large towns. In the same manner all along the Mediterranean, stretching through a coast line of nearly 3000 miles, traces of the enormous fishing business are picked up in form of unpretentious stone slabs, engraved upon by their unions, which preserved their singular but silent and modest history past the ages that have consigned all else to an eternal oblivion.

Having cursorily sketched the game hunters of the waters, let us return to those of wild animals of the land. We left this subject off with a picturesque description of Strabo and Arrian, who brought under contribution for their valuable geography, writers who about 300 years before them had seen and faithfully sketched the facts. They were Nearchus, Onesiphorus, Aristotle, Megasthenes, Nymphodorus, and others, all of whose valuable works are lost. It is possible that the science of epigraphy may find a new and charming field in India. Certainly their correct and efficient culture, now degenerated into a ghastly skeleton, has never been properly presented in literature, and what of them has been left in the vortex of revolution and disintegration is not fit to be quoted as a factor to return to.

One prominent mention of the unions of hunters is that of Haliartus. It had for its overwatching divinity the goddess Artemis, or Diana.[69] Dr. Oehler thinks it

---

[68] I., p. 113, note 62 and 389, note 1. For some account of the pearl fishers, called in Latin margaritarii, see p. 434, and note 18. It should here be admitted that the line between pearl fishers, fishermen, hunters, and the other branches of the Great Dionysan Gemeinde can be drawn with absolute certainty. It stands to reason, however, that in the case of the huntsmen who made an extensive business of catching and corralling wild beasts for amphitheatrical amusements, their alliance with this great international must have been perfectly natural.

[69] Oehler, *MSS*: "Κυνηγοί: In Παλίαρτος bestand eine σύνοδος τῶν κυνηγῶν, Inscr. Graecae, no. 2850." It was probably running the business at the time of Vespasiam and Trajan. It resembles the Italian collegium venatorum, Vol. I., p. 393, Cf. Welcker, *Gr, G.* I. 554 ; Preller, *Gr. Myth.* I. 249.

had communication with kindred organizations in Mylassa. Dr. Lüders mentions in connection with this at Haliartus, another whose inscription was found on a flag of stone at Steiris, in Phocis,[70] which contains a list of the names of members, who also were worshipers of Diana the tutelary protectrice of the huntsmen. There was in Smyrna, a thiasos of them but dedicated to the god Anubis, also a tutelary patron of the chase and Dr. Foucart believes it to have been Egyptian, because Anubis was an Egyptian divinity.[71] Dumont, in his Mix of the Archives has mentioned a similar find of what is by the archæologists, called a huntsman's union at Philippopolis, likewise a consecration to Diana.

What did the hunters do, and how came it about that they were so important? The answer is easy. After the conquests, Rome and her newly acquired dependencies fell into a quinque-centennial spell of profligacy and greed in which all the sullen and hideous appetites of the ring came forth as never before. The craze in every nook and corner of the vast empire was to bet on physical powers as exhibited in bloody and brutal combat. The blood from wounds and gashes of soldiers, prisoners and military victims could no longer be seen, to glut the scenes of torture and death; for the world was conquered and the rage of horrors had been stifled in the peace-policy of Augustus. But the hunger for acts of cruelty, whetted by a dozen generations of carnage was not to be cooled down by the languor which followed a stoppage of war. Men and women longed to behold deeds of blood and cruelty; the gladiatorial ring and its fights with wild beasts in the amphitheatre, were invented to fill the gap.[72] Great numbers of these amphitheatres were built by the ring speculators, and nearly every city of any considerable population possessed a theatre large or small, where the blood-thirsty people could assemble, pay their entrance tribute, and on tiers of stone steps, often in open skies, whether in rain or shine, feast their eyes with sights of naked men, with lions, tigers, leopards, serpents, panthers, and all the

[70] Lüders, *Dionys. Künst.*, "Weihinschrft aus Steiris in Phokis: οἱ κυνηγοί" etc.

[71] Foucart, *Ass'ns Religieuses*, p. 117: "Anubis est le dieu à tête de chacal, qui est représenté sur un grand nombre de stèles funéraires de la Basse-Égypte, amenant les âmes au tribunal d'Osiris."

[72] See I., chapter xii., p. 277 sqq. and fin., p. 332.

beasts of the world's wild forests and swamps, were huddled and starved into a condition of fury, that the multitude in their frenzy of wine, women and lust, might behold conflicts of tooth and claw and constricture, and writhing, moaning death.

The reader will now understand why so many organizations of huntsmen existed to leave their monumental history for the higher science of an advanced civilization. They were genuine workingmen, organized in protective unions, to more successfully carry out their profession in scouring forest and stream to entrap and secure the lions, tigers, panthers, serpents which were to satisfy this savage lust for sights of rage and conflict.

Dr. Waltzing, in his valuable work on the labor associations of the Romans, mentions a collegium of hunters who made the seizure of wild beasts for the amphitheatre a specialty of the chase.[73] This chase of wild beasts for the amphitheatre was especially imperative among the Romans proper, whose internecine conquests had been the cradle of every grade of cruelty, leading finally to their own downfall and extermination. From Rome the passion extended out in all directions until it compassed the known world. There is quite a numerous mention of the Roman hunters or venatores showing that there was a demand for wild animals, and no doubt the unions sometimes succeeded in securing enough to support themselves and their families well.

Dr. Oehler reminds us of such an organization at Pantopolis,[74] Egypt, whose entire business was to trap and gather wild beasts for the Pantopolan amphitheatre. In Citios, a town of Cyprus also, there was a hunters' society, with a boss hunter or manager. They also had for their regular daily business the entrapping and securing of game, not only for the table but the more royal monsters, elephants, lions and tigers, even sometimes a huge boa constrictor or other serpent to nerve the pitiless myrmidons of the sands.

---

[73] *Hist. Corp. Ches les Romains,* I., p. 198: "Collegium venatorum sacerdotum Dianæ; chasseurs de bêtes fauves dans le cirque, á Rocca d' Arce;" and cites the Corpus Inscriptionum Latinarum, Vol. X., no. 5671, by which we understand *"pour le Cirque."*

[74] *MSS:* "Pantopolis, (Aegypten), versorgten κυνηγοί unter einem ἀρχικύνιγος die städtiiche Menagerie mit dem nöthigen Futter: *Rev. des Études Greques,* IV., 1891, p. 53, nr. IV., meherere Inschriften." Again, *ibid:* "In Kition auf Kyphos finden wir κυνηγοί mit einem ἀρχικύνηγος, CIG, 2619,

CHAPTER XI.

OLD INTERNATIONAL

ITS TENETS, RULES AND METHODS.

A LIVELY Modern inquiry—Work of the Academies—Dr Böckh's Comprehensive Name—The Organizations' Greek and Latin Chisel-Work—Reliability of Our Authority—Secret Behind the Old Reverence for the Jus Coeundi—Their Headquarters—Trades Engrossed by it—Saint Paul the Tent-Maker, Proved to have been a Member—Their Classical Literature—Ionian Synod—Numbered Millions—Countries Occupied—The Didasculus—They had Schools and Taught the Rich—Popular with Emperors—Domitian Persecuted them—How Dr. Ramsay Found their Inscriptions—Ad Exemplum Reipublicæ—Twelve Tables—About their Temples—Theatres—Why Called Gemeinde—Cicero's Denunciation—Killed by Cruel Money Power with Aid of Standing Army.

WHAT is the true meaning of the inquiry now going on among our scholars in the academies of archæology? Since the prime of life of that great and accurate scholar, August Böckh, who first pronounced upon such an association among the ancients, and was so fearless as to give it a comprehensive name, great numbers of relic-hunting epigraphists, alumni from the academies of inscriptions, directors of excavations, critics in hieroglyphics and Greek and Latin chisel-work, and sometimes even business travelers and amateurs, have been alert, and on the search for more of these strange treasures which, skeleton-like, are grinning at man's ambitious wisdom and mistaken politics, ogling backward upon this grim and ghostly lore of the lost socialism.

We are safe, on the strength of such irrefutable authority, to make the startling announcement that at the time when Jesus was in the flesh teaching socialism, this organization was at its height of power and efficiency, actually numbering several millions in the various cities and districts of proconsular Rome. Secreted behind the reverence which made the jus coeundi of Solon impregnable, it had survived the attacks of the Roman conquests, outlived the war policy of suppression by extermination, gathered strength by mutual protection, sympathy and love which had become its tenets, and was at that moment blooming with a grim and occult triumph over the world. We shall show that its tenets were economic, its methods socialistic and its vitality inextinguishable.

It is now admitted that the headquarters of the so-called Great International Association of Artists were at Teos. It closely interlinked and federated with its branches in Greece, Macedonia, Palestine, Phrygia, Syria, Egypt, Italy and Gaul. Although this enormous association, stretching far and wide, was supposed to be strictly musical and histrionic, it in reality, engrossed more than a dozen trades of mechanical and professional men. Among the trades co-ordinating with the general scheme were tentmakers, of whom St. Paul is now proved to have been one; the masons, because temples, school houses and residences had to be built; gardeners and cultivators who embellished and tilled the land they owned in common; mechanics who manufactured musical instruments; engravers who chiseled the inscriptions, often illy because unlettered workingmen; clothes makers and menders, ordinary and theatrical, who kept the play actors in trim; cooks, butchers, water carriers, scene painters and decorators, and other trades too numerous to mention.

Then, as to the more strictly professional occupations, there are known to have been teachers of more than a dozen different branches of quite classical literature; for they are not only found to have furnished music and other entertainments for the people but they gave valuable instruction to the wealthy and better-to-do, to which class they could not aspire to belong.[1] Dr. Lüders has explained the schools.[2]

[1] Athenæus, *Deipnosophistæ*, XIV., 626: "Μετὰ δὲ ταῦτα τοὺς Φιλοξένου καὶ Τιμοθέου νόμους μανθάνοντες πολλῇ φιλοτιμίᾳ χορεύοσι κατ' ἐνιαυτὸν τοῖς Διονυσιακοῖς αὐλήταις ἐν τοῖς θεάτροις, οἱ μὲν παῖδες τοὺς παιδικοὺς ἀγῶνας, οἱ δὲ νεανίσκοι τοὺς τῶν ἀνδρῶν λεγομένους.

[2] Lüders, *Dionys. Künst.*, pp. 134-40 shows the manner of these schools as taken from the elaborate inscriptions containing lists of prizes, won by the boys, and the various names of the plays in which the children and others had excelled.

ORIGIN OF PUBLIC SCHOOLS.

There existed what was known as the great Ionian Synod, which came under the Ætolian Law. A synod, such as in those days was common, was a union of these artists under a statute legalizing them in great numbers, all through the Ionian towns and cities. In direct connection with them is what is known as the great synod of Teos which, away back in those days was the central city of the Dionysan union.[3] This powerful god Dionysos, protector of the products of nature, "ennobler of mankind and giver of joys," was overseer of the dramatic artists and patron of the stage. Consequently all these wandering scenic playwrights were necessarily Dionysic or Bacchic. The great federation of Teos must have numbered millions. The inscriptions show us a list of fifty-three places small and great where they were established, and where they carried on their business of public amusement, and of teaching. This list which makes no pretentions to completeness, only covers a small part of Asia Minor, Greece and Macedonia. The schools entered into competitory strife for supremacy.[4]

[3] Lüders, *Dionys. Künst.* pp. 112-132, where it is shown that in the religious point of view the members were the cultivators of the Pythian and Delphic Bacchus, or Dionysus. See Ross, *De Baccho Delphico* and Welcker, *Alte Denkmäler*, I., p. 151 sq. They worshiped the Σωτήρ or Saviour, thinking him to be Dionysus, Protector of all good in nature.

[4] Lüders, *Dionys. Künst.*, pp. 136-137 gives a list of winners who received rewards for superiority. History again, is indebted to recently found inscriptions for a knowledge of the ancient workingmen's schools. The list of prizes and of names of males of various ages and conditions winning them was found on a stone at Teos, headquarters of the great Ionian International, called by Böckh, the Great Gemeinde, a word which in German is well-known as a church community. The inscription is registered in the CIG. as 3088; see also 3059 and 3060:

ADULTS, ABOVE PRIME OF LIFE:—Πρεσβυτέρας ἡλικίας.
(This portion of the stone is illegible.)
PRIZES AWARDED
For rendering and reciting rhapsody:—ὑποβολῆς ανταποδόσεως;
    to Zoilus, son of Zoilus:
For reading and assiduity in studies:—ἀναγνώσεως;
    to Zoilus, son of Zoilus, other prizes.
PRIME OF LIFE:—Μέσης ἡλικίας;
For superiority in recitations:—ὑποβολῆς.
PRIZES AWARDED
    to Mefrodorus, son of Attalus:
For excelling in general purity of knowledge:—ἀναγνώσεως;
    to Dionysicles, son of Metrodorus:
For superiority in high attainments and varied excellence:—πολυμαθίας;
    to Athenæus, son of Apollodorus:
For skill in painting:—ζωγραφίας:
    to Dionysius, son of Dionysius,
    also to Dionysius, son of Menecratus.
Other persons whose names are too dim to be read with certainty, obtained prizes for categorically listed excellence in:
  καλλιγραφία:—beautiful penmanship and painting;
  λαμπάδος (λαμπάς); torch racing or flambeau gymnastics;
  ψαλμοῦ; psalm-singing or perhaps composition, or both;
  κιθαρισμοῦ: cithara-playing;
  κιθαρῳδίας: singing to the cithara, and others.

Judging from inscriptions and various desultory hints of the writers of those times, it is safe to state that there were thousands of them; and that, to a very large extent they were employed by the state, or municipal corporations.

In their art, schools of no very despisable size and excellence arose and flourished everywhere. Their didascalus or teacher, in many cities became so popular that wealthy families patronized them by sending their sons and sometimes, though rarely, their daughters, to be educated by them, especially in singing and amateur accomplishments, fitting them for their debut in society. The reason why they were popular with the emperors Nero and Domitian, while other communistic associations, such as the regular trade and voting unions, were persecuted and massacred by such potentates, was that they made flattery and legerdemain their business, and were obsequious and time-serving, always paying the humblest and most respectful homage to all persons in power.[5] They were called wanderers everywhere at the time of Hadrian. There is a regular title to this effect which is brought to light by the Newtonian inscription,[6] showing that the association was legalized throughout proconsular Rome.

Biographers of great men who have imagined Anacreon to have been a member of this association in its earliest days, B C. 561, may be surprised to learn that such allegiance but contributed proof to his personal or social glory. It is true, he might have known them; but it must have been a comparatively short time after Solon ordained the law. We are inclined to the opinion that the wonderful lyrics in dithyrambic verse of this great poet might have contributed a great deal toward establishing the organization and placing it on grounds of perpetuity. The monuments at Teos, Halicarnassus and in many parts of Asia Minor, are almost innumerable. So also we have a valuable notice from Dr. Ram-

---

[5] CIG. 4315. "'Η ἱερωτάτη βουλὴ καὶ οἱ 'Αθήνησιν 'Επικούρειοι φιλόσοφοι καὶ ἡ ἱερὰ θυμελικὴ σύνοδος." Again, Le Bas 1336, showing that some of them were rather Epicurean in character.

[6] *Discoveries in Halicarnassus*, II., p. 60; For more, consult CIG. 4897, 5127, 6786, 6829; Welcker, *Nachtr. z. Tril.*, p. 196; *G. G.* III., p. 311. Their compliment to Hadrian reads: "'Η ἱερὰ 'Αδριανὴ 'Αντωνείνη θυμελικὴ περιπολιστικὴ μεγάλη σύνοδος τῶν ἀπὸ τῆς οἰκουμένης περὶ τὸν Διόνυσον καὶ αὐτοκράτορα Καίσαρα Τίτον 'Αἴλιον 'Αδριανὸν 'Αντωνεῖνον Σεβαστόν, Εὐσεβῆ, νέον Διόνυσον." Lüders, p. 74, says: "Die Truppe war für den ganzen Erdkreis concessionirt, nach der Formel; ἀπὸ τῆς οἰκουμένης."

say who, to secure accurate information for his critical geography of the bishoprics and churches of Phrygia, traveled over most of the territory, and adds his personal observation to numberless quotations from learned men who preceded him in this interesting field.[7] He quotes from an eranos or thiasos—evidently not understanding the lowliness of those makers of his inscription—which if not already converted, are very near to being a full-fledged Christian church through a union of poor people who communicate their adoration of the mysterious forerunner-god who was slaughtered, and suffered martyrdom. They are proud that they could erect to him an altar out of their own means; and mention upon the epigraph that they are a thiasos. The date appears to be of the Apostolic age, and they are mithraic, the nearest pagan approach, if not already converted to Christianity. The city and district are Akmonia and Phrygia.[8]

Dr. August Böckh who edited the Body of Greek Inscriptions undertaken by the Berlin Academy, after giving the subject much time and study concludes that the Great Ionian Association of actors had for the basis of its organization the pattern of the Attic city in conformity with a clause in the original Solonic law which is lost, but fragmentarily preserved in the Roman provincial edict of Gaius. There appears nothing in the Digest containing it, which we quote in a note, to show that the law took its original form from Solon's measure; but the hint given by Böckh in various places, that this is probable, makes us feel that the comparison is the richer.[9] It is unlikely that the words in this singular edict: "*ad exemplum reipublicæ,*" were at all intended for the then existing political bodies. It is much more

[7] Ramsay, *Cities and Bishoprics of Phrygia*, II., pp. 644-645, *inscr.* no. 546: "Susuz-Keui, 'Αγ.] Τ. Διονύσῳ Καθηγεμόνι οἱ μύσται τοῦ ἱεροῦ ἁ θιάσου ἐκ τῶν ἰδίων καθιέρωσαν εἰς τὴν ἑαυτῶν χρῆσιν τήν τε ἐξέδραν καὶ τὴν προσκειμένην διαίτην." Again, on the subject of the wonderful forerunner: "The title Dionysos Kathegemon," continues the learned author, p. 644, "was used at Pergamus. He was also chief god at Teos, and in his worship the Great Association of actors, οἱ περὶ τὸν Διόνυσον τεχνῖται was united."

[8] Foucart, *De Coll. Scen. Artf.*, p. 20, speaking of the multitude of priests, mentions this, but cites CIG. 3068, 3070 to show their numbers elsewhere: "Apud Τειος, institutum fuit etiam alterum sacerdotium quum Pergamenos reges Eumenem et Attalum, quorum beneficiis collegium auctum et amplificatum fuerat, artifices, Asiatica adulatione, et vivos divinis honoribus prosequerentur et mortuos in deorum numerum referrent."

[9] *Digest*, III., 4: "GAIUS, *libro tertio ad edictum provinciale* . . . . . Quibus autem permissum est corpus habere collegii societatis sive cujusque alterius eorum nomine, proprium est ad exemplum reipublicæ habere res communes, arcam communem et actorem sive syndicum, per quem, tamquam in republica, quod communiter agi fierique oporteat, agatur fiat."

probable that Gaius had a copy either of the Solonic law containing this important provision, or a copy of the same law as translated for the Twelve Tables of Roman statutes.

Dr. Foucart published a valuable contribution in proof that these actors were numerous at Tralles in Asia Minor, and were worshipers of Hermes, the Latin Mercury, giver of good luck, and tutelary divinity who was believed to preside over skill, gymnastic arts, sciences, public business, markets and roads. In this respect, as implied by these organizations, Hermes differs little from Dionysos himself who was the Ennobler of mankind, giver of joys etc.[10] The temple of these associations was used not only for devotional exercises[11] which frequently amounted to very little, but to the practical work of their rehearsals, schools, and evening meetings, as well as their common meals and banquets. At Mitylene an inscription was found which was also the work of the great co-working organization centered at Teos. The members played dithyrambs and agonies. All over Phrygia are found their relics. At Pessinus, where the apostles Paul and Barnabas were snubbed at the synagogues and turned away, and where, through some mysterious influence of which we shall speak in a later chapter, they found ready-made brethren, a fine slab of the wandering troupes of the same body, turns up,[12] with a glaringly suggestive reminder that St. Paul, a scene maker by trade if not a member, was taken in; for somebody was there all equipped with sympathy, with a little temple, a brotherhood and means; and this somebody secretly helped them to work in a revival and establish a church at Pessinus. We shall prove that the "somebody" were unions of trade brotherhoods.

The Great Ionian Theatrical Society had powerful churches, or as they are designated by the German archæologists "Gemeinden" in a dozen cities, chief among which was Teos, and thence spreading over a large portion of the world. At Tyre there was one performing the agonies, there designated as the great Alexandrian plays. At Rome and in many parts of Italy there were

[10] Cf. any good *Lexicon*, in *verb.* Βακχος.
[11] Foucart, *Revue Archéol.*, 1865, I., p. 222; Lüders, *Dionys. Künst.*, pp. 5, 22, Also id., p. 33, gymnasts and playrights of Delos. Τὸ κοινὸν τῶν Εὐπατοριστῶν.
[12] Lüders, *Dionys. Künst.* p. 92, *inscr.* 98: Ἡ ἱερὰ μουσικῇ περιπολιστικὴ σύνοδος τῶν περὶ τόν Διόνυσον τεχνιτῶν, CIG. 4081: *id.*, pp. 93-94 and his *inscr.* 101; CIG. 5762, found at Syracuse

organizations known as the Lupercalia,[13] which became so considerable that the attention of the senate was several times called to them and they were mentioned by historians.[14] Cicero speaks of them in terms denoting contempt, regarding them as no better than wild beasts.[15] His contempt for the Germans, like a great part of his aristocratic notions brilliantly expressed in contemptuous tones, is a poor offset against the great human fact that the Germans, perhaps on this very account, have outlived Cicero and Rome, and have for some reason or another planted an immortal civilization upon the ruins of that aristocracy so boastingly upheld by the proud oratorical lawyer of Rome. The lupercalia were no other than innocent societies of the play actors, being allied to the great international association of playwrights which had their headquarters in far off Teos of Asia Minor. We strongly suspect that the trouble with Cicero was, that these "lupercalia he denounces as wild beasts, whose institutions were founded in forests and fields before the dawn of humanity and law," were on the side of Clodius, his mortal enemy, who is now well known to have defended the poor workingmen and their organizations, whom Cicero hated, persecuted and suppressed. History recounts that Clodius, to shun the vengeance of his pursuers, escaped to Bovilla whither he was chased, entering into the temple of the Bona Dea, a crime entailing death under the Roman law. Evidence now turns up that this temple was of the lower mysteries, not the great official; and that this her Dionysic habitat was one of the many asylums of retreat, in perfect accordance with usage among the poor.[16] It opened its doors freely to all persecuted persons of the fraternity to which it belonged. It was an asylum for the oppressed and persecuted. The cruel money power against which personages like Jesus, Clodius, Socrates and other mar-

[13] Böckh, CIG. 3065, Τὸ κοινὸν τῆς Ἐχίνου συμμορίας, seems to be a slight variation. Some compare it with collegia gentilicia. They are genuine θίασοι and their tombstones are numerous in Teos. They made garlanded epigraphs. Nos. 3101, and 3112 CIG. say: Οἱ θίασοι πάντες, τὸ κοινὸν τῶν Παναθηϊαστῶν: τὸ κοινὸν τῶν Διονυσϊαστῶν, showing that they had a community of economic interests. They were all busy with the means of existence, using religion to pave the way.

[14] Orell. 6010—Lanuvii, AVC. 741, B.C. 6. "Magnum Collegium Lupercorum et capitolinorum;" Referred to by Cic., see Orell., *id.*, *note*. The Capitol was the temple and is the origin of the great Lanuvian inscription.

[15] Cicero, *Pro Marco Cælio*, 11; "Fera quædam sodalitas et plane pastoritia atque agrestis Germanorum lupercorum: quorum coitio illa sylvestris ante est instituta, quam humanitas atque leges."

[16] Vol. I., *Index* in *verb*. *Asylum*, explaining this.

tyrs fought, used its low subterfuge of tergiversation, and to this day makes the encyclopedias, the histories and the rhetoricians fervid in calumnious defamation of Clodius for having invaded the secret penetralia of the Bona Dea. The least insight into facts would disabuse the encyclopedists of their error; since the Bona Dea was none other than Diana, the great protectress of the poor and provider for their fortunes, pleasures and joys. Kinship is indeed claimed for her, with Nemesis, the goddess who pursued and scourged with vengeful fury the greedy who grasped and appropriated more than their share.

CHAPTER XII.

ANCIENT MUSIC.

STONES BRINGING WRITTEN MELODIES BACK TO LIFE.

Music of the Unions Described—Introductory Reflections—Exploded Belief That Ancient Forefathers possessed no Knowledge of Musical Notes—Discovery at Delphi in 1895—Wonderful Musical Find Chiseled on Pronaos of Temple of Pythian Apollo—Olympian Hill-Slopes—Dr. Theodor Reinach's Heliograph—Author's Visit to the Temple of Oracles—Keen Criticism of Reinach, Crusius, Welcher—Frogs of Aristophanes—Music of the Agonies—Pausanias' Treasury of the Athenians—Gevaert on Instrumental Music—Second Musical Find in 1896, Still better—Valuable Illustration—Third Musical Find—A Treasure from Tralles in Asia—Influence of the Unions who possessed the Science—Outfit of the Musicians—Power of the Drama—They Sang a Doxology—Orphic Canticle—Wide Range of the Singers—The Harmostios Nomos—A Mournful Strain—The Hymnodoi—What, when at Last the Christians Came—Jealous Prelates Stabbed Genius to the Heart—Victimized by Prelate Power—Suppression at Laodicea—They Fell Forever.

So wonderful and enchanting are the fruits of investigating science which sprout and ripen out of the critical reading by our savants in the seminaries of inscription, that we are constrained from sheer amazement to ask: Are we singing to-day the identical strains that were familiarly hummed and chanted by our ancestors more than 2,000 years ago?

Such a thought reproves ridicule and assumes the serious, as we plunge down into its resources of evidence and drag up from the lugubrious literature of the forgotten workingman, the startling glyptics of his facile chisel. Not only did they compose music but they wrote it; and adapted it to beautiful verse which is preserved to us in hymns to the divinities they loved. It has long been assumed that the ancients had no musical literature; no notes by which others could read or perform on instruments the delicious strains which thrill the tasteful moderns with half of what makes life worth living. All this belittling of departed ages is giving way before the discoveries that are illuminating this brilliant science of the past. The splendid triumph of modern research is, that this cumulus of facts proving art and music and multiform learning, whose fossilized history rises from submergence into science worthy of recognition by universities of Europe, to be wholly the work of an organization of laboring people, so humble and lowly that in their own lifetime they could not regard themselves as citizens, or hardly as human beings.

The ancient musical guilds, like the burial societies, were a part of the scheme of unions whose description occupies the three preceding chapters of this work. The musical attachment was a natural adjunct which completed the whole vast business of what we have just described as the "Great Ionian Gemeinde," or church of artists and playwrights. It was not perfect without the necessary music; and as a result, this accomplishment was worked out to a state of much perfection.

We proceed immediately to a consideration of the Delphic Hymns. The analysts of the ancient music, who devoted time and talent to the subject are Welcker, Reinach, Weil, Crusius,[1] Weber, Homolle, Wessely, and others devoting their lives to the work.

In 1895 there was found in the ancient temple of Apollo, at Delphi, a small city of Antiquity situated on the little river Plistos, some miles from the Gulf of

[1] Crusius, *Die Delphischen Hymnen*, p. 90, quotes the stanzas, in his analysis of some fragments of the Glyconian hymn, with instrumental notes. In the fourth line of the second stanza occur the words: ἀπταίστους Βακχου θιάσους; and line 5: "αἰεὶ σώζετε προσπόλοις" which we take as clear proof. Weil, backed by the highly creditable Homolle, director of the excavations, believed it to be as late as B. C. 40. If true, then so much the nearer to the beginning of the Christian era, and so much the more powerful the musical argument. It proves that they actually sang into being the new Gospel; and that at Delphi the great emancipation pieces took their rise. Thus Weil and Homolle place date of hymn at B. C. 40, and Crusius, *ibid.*, p. 90, suggests that it may be so; otherwise accounting for the mention of Romans: " . . . . dass die ungesungene ἀρχά die Herrschaft der Römer sei." But Polybius who lived and wrote 100 years before, talks of the subject matter, *Histories*, II, 35: "'Ο δὲ ἀπὸ Γαλατῶν φόβος οὐ μόνον τὸ παλαιόν, ἀλλὰ καθ' ἡμᾶς ἤδη πλεονάκις ἐξέπληξε τοὺς Ἕλληνας." There was certainly a great scare among the Athenians about that time. For the κόγξ ὄμπαξ, see Lobec, *Aglaoph.*, 775 sqq.

Corinth and lying at the foot of Mount Parnassus, an extraordinary inscription engraved upon the pronaos of the once vast and magnificent temple of the Pythian Apollo. There was once an earthquake that engulfed this mountain city in catastrophe and ruin. On account of the paganism which existed in the ancient past, the Christians ascribe this seismic upheaval to the Almighty Jehovah. But curiously enough, this was after all, about the same being as the Jove of the inhabitants they condemn.

Delphi still nestles at the foot of this celebrated Mount, in a craggy dell, classic and beautiful, exquisite to the romanticist, with pocket-gulfs, flowery fragrance, gushing springs, oriental birds and crag-climbing herds, seemingly the only survivors of an ancient majesty which presided there, over the destinies of men. A purling creek still foams and tumbles past the ruins of Apollo's temple. One great mountain spring, the Castalia gurgles from the heights. It is the self-same mephetic fountain of antiquity, whose liquid, when tasted by the priest and priestess in charge of the secret work, caused them to fall into an ecstatic trance and to sing with inarticulate tones, the dirges and requiems of the great cathegemonean Apollo.

Among the recently discovered monuments of art which are fixed to the credit of the Dionysan artists, are two inscriptions of written music, of the age of B. C. 134, or as Weil and Crusius inform us, the age of Augustus. These trophies completely overthrow the aged belief that the ancients did not write music. In our recent visit to the scene of these discoveries, we received much new information through a personal conversation with M. Theodore Reinach, the critical epigraphist, whom the French Academy of Inscriptions detailed to work out the new finds at Delphi. He found the key to the musical powers of certain hitherto incomprehensible characters not belonging to the Greek alphabet. He was so kind as to present us with heliographic representations of them, taken by the artists at the excavations.

In ancient Greek music, the notes were written in a straight line and not, as with us, in a scale of ascending and descending tones. There were many characters, each of a different power and the tone was known by the shape rather than the position of the note.

SECOND HYMNE A APOLLON

MUSIC.

The experts of the Athenian school under the auspices of the French government, discovered a hymn to Apollo, which they call the first find. It was published in 1894 and is here represented, with the translation from the original heliograph. Some account of it was given in the newspapers of that time. Later, another discovery was made in the same temple, consisting of a large flag, part of the pronaos or the portal, upon which were engraved suspicious-looking letter-like characters, likewise found to be music. The old rock was so broken and worn by the convulsions of nature and the vandalism of man which had been going on since about B. C. 134, or 2160 years, that the work of reconstructing and adjusting its fragments to expose the lettering in a legible shape was at first thought impossible. Patience and skill at last prevailed. The broken fragments were toggled together and the artists succeeded in taking an indifferent heliograph such as is shown in the cuts. From this the true study of deciphering and modernizing the music was conducted, until the world is in proud possession of the precious monuments of the skill of the ancient laborer.

The scientific world had long been anticipating rich discoveries now going on under other powerful writers. Crusius brought out some new points on the Papyrus of Euripides.[2] Theodore Reinach showed us a quotation on the subject, from Dion Chrysostom,[3] referring directly to their written music. This, then was a significant hint, being from so ancient and so reliable an author. Furthermore, they found in the celebrated Frogs of Aristophanes something very significant, regarding the Delphic hymns which they afterwards discovered, as we have described.[4] Even Cicero who, like Pliny, wrote on a multitude of subjects, gives us some suggestive points which were carefully noted by the scientific experts on the track of the lost works on Dionysan artists. Crusius, perceiving the importance of all this honorable

[2] Crusius, "Delphische Hymnen," p. 92, sqq.
[3] Reinach, in "Bull. de Correspondence Héll.," 1896, p. 380, note 2, quoting Dion Chrys., "Orat.," LXVIII., p. 234; Dindorf; ‘Ὥσπερ ἐν λύρᾳ τὸν μέσον φθόγγον καταστήσαντες ἔπειτα πρὸς τοῦτον ἁρμόττονται τοὺς ἄλλους."
[4] Crusius, "Delph. Hymn.," p. 21, quotes Aristophanes, "Frogs," V. 399, ff.:
  ‘Ἴακχ’ ὦ πολυτίμοις ἐν ἕδραις ἐνθάδε ναίων,
  ‘Ἴακχ, ὦ Ἴακχε,
  ἐλθὲ τόνδ’ ἀνὰ λειμῶνα χωρεύσων
  ὁσίους ἐς θιασώτας
  πολύκαρπον μὲν τινάσσων
  περὶ κρατὶ σῷ βρύοντα
  στέφανον μύρτων," κτλ.

TREASURES OF MOUNT PARNASSUS. 245

mention, even by men elsewhere expressing the greatest contempt for their organizations, bewails the fragmentary condition of the evidence.[5] Hints from modern writers, together with their quotations, all show an acknowledgment that they are unions of the Dionysan artists.[6] Notable among those who foresaw the discoveries of written music is the great author, Dr. Welcker, whose magnificent work on the Greek trilogies surpasses all others in penetration and truthfulness to the customs and forms of the ancients. This earlier work contributed much in inspiring the French and other governments to appropriate funds with which to unearth and bring to the surface their sunken treasures.[7] The discoveries thus far at Delphi show that the agonies with the people there, were the principal attraction; and the Athenians, Corinthians, Megarians and Eleusinians during the summer, used to make pilgrimages to Mount Olympus and in the cool shades of the Delphian Parnassus, in the sacred city,[8] regale themselves in the delightful concerts and the agonies, performed by the Dionysan artists.[9]

There is a good deal of doubt as to the date of the Delphic hymns.[10] In the wording, mention is made in praise of the Romans, giving us to infer that the hymns were not written until after the conquest of Greece by the Romans which historical event took place in B. C. 146. As a consequence, Weil and Reinach are in favor

[5] Cicero, "Tusculanarum Disputatio," I., 2: "Summam eruditionem Græci sitam censebant in nervorum vocumque cantibus." And again, "Pro Muræna," 13, he says: "Ut aiunt in Græcis artificibus eos auledos esse qui citharoedi fieri non potuerunt." Similar laudations are everywhere inscribed on the stones.
[6] Crusius, "Delph. Hymn.," p. 92, regrets the "Lüchenhaftigkeit der Fragmente" found near the main inscription of the Delphic Hymn, and admits that it speaks of the Βάκχου Θιάσους, hinting that it may be a prayer for Frieden or peace; perhaps it is a prayer for Freiheit, or freedom.
[7] Lüders, "Dionys. Künst.," pp. 116, 117, speaks of there being an organized body of one bread earners. He gives an interesting account of their chorus, and its early and later uses as well as the paraphernalia in use by them on page 118; and his hints of the then unknown, show that in his mind, written music was a certainty, a fact which has been discovered since Welcker's work was published.
[8] Welcker, "Aeschyleische Trilogie;" "Griech, Tragödien."
[9] Crusius, "Delph. Hymn.," p. 64: "Auf alle Fälle aber sind attische Festgesandschaften in Delphi bei allen Agonen etwas so gewöhnliches, dass man aus ihrer Erwähnung die besondere Art des Festes kaum bestimmen kann."
[10] Crusius, "Delph. Hymn.," p. 99: "Die Hymnen mussen, nach ihrem Inhalt, wie nach ihrem poetischen und musikalischen Stil, ziemlich der gleichen Zeit, etwa der Mitte des dritten Jahrhunderts vor Chr., angehören." This would be B.C. 250, or about 100 years earlier than the estimate of the French Academy.

of placing the date at B. C. 146,[11] while Crusius suggests that it might have been composed as early as B. C. 250. Still another authority gives the date as B. C. 40. On this subject we may append some remarks indirectly from the "London Times" but directly from the "New York Sun," published at the time of the analysis of Reinach which was finished in 1896, considering it worthy of transcription into a note.[12]

Saint Saëns, an ingenious and successful musical composer first undertook to reproduce the Antigone of Æschylus, and no little interest was created regarding the outcome of the attempt.[13] At any rate the labors of Weil, Reinach and Crusius recently, have so improved upon every former work, great as is the investigation of Welcker and others and admitting that these pioneers blazed their pathway, for which we are determined that so far as lies in our power they shall receive full credit, have penetrated no less than three immortal inscriptions, and overturned the old belief that the ancients did not know how to write and teach music scientifically. There have been rehabilitations of the music of the forefathers produced in the theatres of Athens, Paris and elsewhere, in form of the modern concert; and living humanity has been regaled with the delightful strains which were composed thousands of years ago by the ancient poor man and at an age when he was regarded as little better than the dog. The whole is a triumph to his glory and honor.

[11] "Journal de Corresp. Héllénique," 1896.
[12] New York "Sun": "In their excavations at Delphi the French have unearthed the building Pausanias called the Treasury of the Athenians. They discovered the remains of two large slabs of stone, inscribed with words and music. In the first season's work they found fourteen fragments of various sizes, of which they published an account last year. Four of the fragments were distinguished from the other ten by a difference in the notation of the music, and these four made up a piece that was introduced to the public as the 'Hymn of Apollo.' They recently found another large fragment, to which the remaning ten were adjusted, and now they have a second hymn. The last line of the new hymn is followed by the first line of a decree. This shows how these compositions came to be inscribed upon the stone. The purport of both hymns is substantially the same. After the invocation of the muses the poet gives various legends of Apollo's life and works, ending with the slaughter of the Gauls at Delphi, in 179 B.C. He then imp'ored the gods for protection for Delphi and Athens and the government at Rome. The date is therefore after 146 B.C., when the Romans took possession of Greece." Yet it might have been 100 years later.
[13] New York "Musical Courier," Dec. 27, 1893: "Choruses in imitation of the ancient (music); but are they the self-same? Gevaert proves that they were rendered instrumentally by the ancients." And still again, ibid: "One brief phrase, twice repeated, of the chorus in dialogue with Antigone is given in the hypophrygian mode; but one of the choruses, the invocation to Bacchus, is written in the syntonolydian mode (fa ending on the mediant la), and has an essentially plaintive character. 'The rudimentary polyphony,' says Gevaert, 'was practiced by the ancients.' "

DISCOVERY OF MORE MUSIC. 247

The third musical find is that near Tralles in Asia Minor, known to the scientific world as the Seikilos. It is an inscription of pre-Christian antiquity, well preserved on a smooth slab of stone, and bearing the notes and also the words, composed for a wealthy citizen who, on his death-bed willed the musical branch of the Dionysan artists a sum of money out of whose use they were to commemorate his anniversary by banquet and song. The words and music are, as in the Delphic hymns, worked out into modern notes; and we are thankfully cognizant to M. Theo. Reinach who personally furnished us copies in heliograph, which we here present. This gentleman was firm in his assurance that the Delphic music, if not that of the Seikilos, which as is easily seen has not exactly the same literary system, is theirs. The monument to the Dionysan artists, from so high an authority, is certainly flattering in their favor; since M. Reinach thought that so far as he had investigated their science and aptitude, in the furtherance of the ancient civilization, he had found that they possessed high skill and efficiency.

The importance of the musical and gymnastic influence of these organizations did not escape the commentators and lexicographers of their own age. It is not generally known that there were several very good dictionaries of the Greek and Latin languages.[14] There was great rivalry in musical performances of the Dionysan artists.[15] Their skill was so great and their behavior so good that they were very popular and their music took preference to all others.[16] Mummius, Marius, Crassus, Antony, Nero, Heliogabalus, and many others of Rome's soldiers and emperors hired them to perform, and we have already recounted how Alexander at one time got three thousand from all parts of the world. That these musicians were furnished with a complete outfit, in-

[14] Pollux, "Onomasticon. III., 142: "Ἐράνος. Τῶν δὲ ἀγώγων οἱ μὲν γυμνικοὶ οἱ δὲ καλούμενοι σκηνικοὶ ὀνομασθεῖν ἄν Διονυσιακοί 'τε καὶ μυσικοί." This definition was given in the time of the emperors, and included gladiatorial entertainments occasionally.

[15] Lüders, "Dionys. Künst.," p. 116; says: "Wetteifern" between the ψιλοκιθαρισταί, who did not sing, but played; meaning their competitive rivalry. So also the same rivalry between the αὐληταὶ and the συλῳδοὶ, the latter of whom sang to the flute.

[16] They were constantly called upon to perform for rich Roman gentlemen. Tacitus, "Ann." XIV., 21, informs us that Mummius after his triumph over Corinth, engaged great numbers of these artists to perform at his protracted festivities. Polybius, XXX., 13; and Athenæus, XIV., p. 615, speak of their performances. For an account of their schools and list of prize-winners see supra, p. 233, and note 4.

cluding tents, mechanical tools and even water carriers, is made manifest by inscriptions and pictures, one of which we present as an illustration.[17] Unlike modern methods, where society is furnished with theatres, and equipments ready to receive traveling troupes, these Dionysan playwrights furnished their own paraphernalia and had means for transportation from place to place. Printing and advertising were defective, and there being no great public means of conveyance running on time like our railroads and steamers, they had to work a wandering voyage through the world, often arriving at new places unannounced, and in consequence they sometimes appeared as amateurs, although in reality they were old, practiced, professional artists.

One of the great and favorite themes which the people of those days delighted to see played and acted out was the martyrdom of their beloved god. In Phrygia, this imaginary victim was Attys, or Adonis; in Egypt he was Osiris; in Teos and its environs he was Dionysos Kathegemona; in Caucassus, he was Prometheus chained to a rock and tortured to death by ravenous birds. Each of these messiahs, while on the rack of torture, in his dying gasp gave up the ghost, feelingly imploring the Great Father to forgiv his pursuers and through his death redeem humanity. This in skeleton, as the ancient salvation, was the subject of innumerable plays, all dramatically elaborated on scenes, some of which were of highest art and perhaps, in painting and exquisite portrayal, never equalled. It is possible that they sometimes developed artistic efforts equalling if not surpassing our modern spectacular views, with weird effects, as charmingly produced by our electric and calcium beams. Thus they certainly exhibited the passion plays, including the apotheosis, while the anima of their typical man, writhing, but towering above an ignis of fiendish torture, with a benevolent omnipotence when at the triumphant pinnacle of dissolution, long before the arrival. of our

[17] Crusius, *Die Delphisch. Hymnen,* p. 31, and 42, gives a collegium of holy water-carriers which is explained: "Unter den κλυταί Δελφίδες wird ein bestimmtes collegium aus dem delphischen Priesteradel zu verstehn sein. Dem ganzen Zusammenhang nach, könnte man an Hydrophoren denken, wie sie im apollonishen Kultus bei Sühnbräuchen und bei der Orakelspendung amtirten." Again, Dr. Ramsay, *Cit. and Bish. Phryg.,* II., p. 553, found their inscriptions at Akmonia, and discovered that they sometimes owned land: "The Hymnodia were a body of persons connected with the native cultus, doubtless practicing certain ceremonies of a musical character in honor of the gods." etc.

Saviour, used to be made to cry out "Father, forgive them for they know not what they do."[18] It is known that when these plays were announced to take place, no matter in what city or locality of Greek or Latin-speaking regions of the world, the people would throng together, render in their hard-earned pittances of money to pay entrance and sit on stone steps in the open air without covering from the elements of nature, in dizzy qualms of religious delight often rising to infatuation, a chill, damp night, or a blazing afternoon, frequently contracting colds and malaria, often bringing them to the grave.[19] All along the route of their strange history we find scattering relics of these playwrights' long time existence. There was a sermon once delivered, fragments of which were picked up by the keen observers of the renaissance. It was a "Word" to the "Initiates;" and the hymn which they sang, accompanied with a doxology, comes to us in the well-known fragment attributed to Sanchuniatho, which is as much as to say that Philon was the author although he was only the translator. There was likewise a parting benediction which Warburton and Le Clerk declare to have been the *kogx ompax* which means about the same thing as watch and pray. The hymn, or Orphic canticle was attributed to the Jew Aristobulus.

There has also been found in the Columbarium at Rome, an inscription of schools where the hymns of the Asiatic artists of Dionysos, organized under the jus coeundi of the Solonic dispensation, were taught. In 1726, there was discovered, in a field at Rome near the Appian way, a large sepulchral building, so sunken in neglectful oblivion of the ages, that it was covered some seven feet under the ground. Of this strange tomb we shall have more to say in future. It is a vast edifice full of inscriptions of the life, the doings of the ancient lowly and none other. This magnificent building could not have been constructed for less than a million of dollars

[18] Miller has translated some words of the celebrated Orphic hymn: "Attis. Les Assyriens l' appellent le Trois fois regrettable Adonis." Ἄττι, σὲ καλοῦσι μὲν Ἀσσύριοι τριπόθητόν Ἄδονιν." *Philosophoumena*, ed. Miller, p. 118, showing that Attis, or Attys and Adonis were one and the same. On the *Hymnodidascales*, see Foucart, *Ass. R.l.*, p. 114. Even then the artists of Διόνυσος were writing music as well as words. Cf. Liddell in *verb.* ὕμνος.

[19] Oehler, *MSS.*, calls to mind an eranos of hymn singers at Ephesus, etc: 'Ich stelle hier die Inschriften zusammen, in welchen diese allein, oder mit den θεόλογοι genannt werden. Ὑμνῳδοί werden erwähnt in Ἀκμωνία, *Bull. Hell.*, XVIII., 1893, p. 261, nr. 44; in Νικοπολίς ad Istrum; *Archéol. Epig.; Mitth.*, aus Oesterreich, XV., 1892, 2 Inschriften, in deren einer ὑμνῳδοί."

in our own days of architectural facilities. In it we find the self-same hymn singers.[20] They existed in Rome in large numbers. They were, in fact, organized in such force that their inscriptions are found in every country of the known world, and probably numbered in the Augustian age, after human life began to recuperate under the peaceful policy of the first Cæsars which refilled the earth with population, two or three millions of initiates, all working for a living by the art of music.

There is a slab from Corcyra which shows that in the eastern Mediterranean the same struggle for existence was going on.[21] Lüders, as shown in the note below, proves a good deal regarding the personnel of the singers and accompanying musicians of the Dionysan artists' order. There is another inscription of the wandering tribe, chiseled to the memory of the burning of Delphi, showing the personnel of these workers.[22] There are monuments which show the emulatory exercises of the youth in the schools of the associations. Some of these schools were large, and judging from appearances they must have been very worthy of respect. But the real

[20] Gorius, *Monumentum sive Columbarium*, etc., p. 99, where a broken epitaph is portrayed, showing the Διδάσκαλοι τῶν Διονύσου τεχνιτῶν and proving that they existed in Rome. The fraternity extended to Pergamos, and some of its members were evidently country people even bucolic cowherds. Ramsay, *Cities and Bishop. of Phryg.*, II., p. 359: "The Βουκόλοι. worshipers of Dionysos Καθηγεμών (forerunner), the ἄξιος ταῦρος, formed a society at Pergamos which contained, besides 18 ordinary Βουκολοὶ, an archiboukolos, two hymn teachers, two Silenoi, and a Χορηγός." But these Bucolico Orphic hymns and music are very respectfully dealt with by another author Oehler, *MS*, No. 72, 22: "*Culturvereine besondere Art* Βουκόλοι—Ich habe Eranos Vindobonensis die Boukoloi in Pergamos nach Curtius (Hermes, VII., 1873 p, 39-40 nr. XII.), unrichtig als Reinderhirten erklärt, weil mir damals nur lene Publikation in Schedenapparate vorlag, was ich gegen Ziebarth's gehässige Bemerkungen feststelle. Dass darunter Diener u. Verehrer des Dionysos zu verestehn sei, hat Schöll *Satura Philologica*, p. 176, 177 erkannt. Dann haben A. Dietrich; *De Hymnis Orphicis, Capitula quinque*, p. 3-13, Reitzenstein, *Epigramm und Skolion*, p. 193. bes. p. 203 f, u. a. ausführlich darüber gehandelt. Wir finden sie inschriftlich bezeugt in Apollonia-Sozopolis CIGr. 2052; Ephesos: *Anc. Gr. Inscrs.*, III., nr. 6020; *Pergamos, Hermes*, VII., p. 39, 40, nr. 12; Fränkel, *Inschriften v. Pergamon*, II., 485; *ibid.*, nr. 72 d, 486-488; I., nr. 222 und II. p. 509: Perinthos, Dumont, *Mél. d' Arch.* p. 382.

[21] Lüders, *Dionys. Künst.*, p, 121, speaks of "Eine interessante Inschrift aus Korkyra." A wealthy citizen had bequeathed a sum of money to this Dionysan Gemeinde or church, with which annually to celebrate, by dramatic and musical performances. The inscription is well known. It stipulates that on the interest accruing from this capital the plays were to be given. The personnel is given: Three flute players, three tragedians. and three comedians had to be engaged besides the vocalists. But Dr. Lüders calculates that 3 must be accounted 3 & 3; because in other inscriptions it is proved that each foreman had 3, or a small troupe of 3, making 7. This scientific discovery comes from a debate between Böckh and Welcker.

[22] The stone which is in the ruins of the Delphic temple of Apollo, reads: "Γ ῥαψῳδοί; β κιθαρισταί; β κιθαρῳδοί; ε παῖδες χορευταί· ε ἀνδρεσχορευταί; β αὐληταί; β διδάσκαλοι αὐλητῶν; ι τραγῳδοί γ αὐληταί καὶ γ διδάσκαλοί; η χορευταί κωμικοι και γ ἱματομισθαι." These last took care of the wardrobe.

fact is, that however worthy they may have been, they got very little respect or honorable consideration, judging from the words of Demosthenes, Cicero, Lucian and Athenæus, of whom we shall give specimens as we proceed.

Near Orchomenos, Corinth, has been found an inscription showing a celebration of the Dionysan games,[23] commemorating the music of the Dionysan chorus. These organizations were not without their laws. There was a law of wills handed down to us by means of an inscription on a piece of stone, of about the time of the emperor Trajan.[24]

The musical unions were so thoroughly interlinked and organized that they acquired a habit of making pilgrimages from one part of the country to another.[25] On the march in these wanderings, the music they sang and played was the hypophrygian style, used for all dirge-like occasions, having the enharmonic rhythm and composed in accordance with their *Harmotios nomos*, a mournful and passionate strain, to which a chorus of the Orestes was set. Dr. Ramsay in his Cities and Bishoprics of Phrygia,[26] in the province of Akmonia, correctly finds that they sometimes possessed property, especially in lands; but appears ignorant of the now well-known eranothiasos and does not speak of their final extinction by the canon of the Council of Laodicea which

---

[23] Rose, *Inscriptiones Græcæ*, p. 300-301: "Ἔτι δ' ἀνδρασι χορηγῶν εἰς Διονύσια ἐνίκησα καὶ ἀνήλωσα σὺν τῇ τοῦ τρίποδος ἀναθέσει πεντακισχιλίας δραχμάς." The author adds: "Hujusmodi marmora Athenis scripta multa extant," showing that they were common throughout Greece at an early day. They are the Dionysan chorus.

[24] Foucart, *De Coll. Artf. Scenicorum*, p. 14, touching these laws, says: "Exemplum etiam legis constituendæ ex uno titulo (id est lapide) tenemus, quo tibicen Crato hereditatis suæ, cujus partem Teiis sodalibus reliquit, usum per legem, et eam quidem sacram, definivit." CIG. 3078.

[25] The name of the regularly organized band of pilgrims was "Τὸ κοινὸν τῶν συμπορευομένων πὰρ Δία Ὑέτιον,'" The rain god was connected with Zeus, the Jehovah. The object of the society in making the pilgrimages was to implore the rain governing divinity for copious showers in days of drouth. Lüders, *Diònys. Künst*. p. 27, says: "Wer von den Bürgern sich den Pilgern anschloss, wurde nach den gottesdienstlichen Ceremonien von dem Vereine empfangen."

[26] We quote the following from his recent work: "*Hymnodoi* at Akmonia, for the first time in Phrygia, we meet this body, whose existence, however, may be assumed in most Phrygian cities. The Hymnodoi were a body of persons connected with the native cults, doubtless practicing certain ceremonies of a musical character in honor of the gods, as their name denotes; but also, in all probability, having a social side, with the management of which the Ἀργυροταμίας was concerned: and this income was perhaps secured according to the method that has remained in use in Anatolia for religions, to the present century." And in note 4, he says: "The government recently took over the revenues of most foundations" (another word for society).

forbade the singing of compositions of their own, a most cruel and jealous piece of inhumanity.

Summing it all up, we shall find that when the Christians appeared upon the earth, they found in these musical, economical and peaceful societies existing in every nook and corner of the world, a rich and mellow soil to plant in; and they took to themselves the spirit of their beautiful music, some of which has undoubtedly been handed down to us from an ingenious, struggling, hymn-chanting antiquity.[27] But alas! jealousy and a malignant concupiscence of the so-called fathers but actual despoilers, finally succeeded in suppressing and uprooting all this innocence and genius. As we have shown, they had, from immemorial antiquity been growing into the possession of an occasional patch of ground, and had erected innumerable pretty little schools and temples; and it being in close harmony with their tenets, they took to their bosom this originally pure Christianity which grew to be the greedy monster of empire until they were suppressed by suffocation. The reptile coveted their little properties, and took the contemptible method of suppression to fasten its hideous coil around their holdings.[28]

It will be shown that there are reasonable grounds for believing that the original founders of Christianity, including the Master himself, were initiates into the secret penetralia of this vast order.[29] Celsus shows beyond cavil and Origen does not deny, that the Christians

---

[27] Coloss., III., 16; "Ὁ λόγος τοῦ Χριστοῦ ἐνοικείτω ἐν ὑμῖν πλουσίως· ἐν πάσῃ σοφίᾳ διδάσκοντες καὶ νουθετοῦντες ἑαυτοὺς ψαλμοῖς ὕμνοις καὶ ᾠδαῖς πνευματικαῖς ἐν χάριτι ᾄδοντες ἐν ταῖς καρδίαις ὑμῶν τῷ θεῷ. St. Paul speaks of singing psalms, hymns and spiritual songs, sing with grace in your hearts to the Lord

[28] Dionysius, *Book of Promises, Frag.*, I: "τῆς πολλῆς ψαλμοδίας. One Noëtus, or Nepos, a sort of so-called heretic, composed and delighted people, by singing psalms, which were approved. The sanctimonious priests construed this to be a sin, and watching their opportunity, waited for the Council of Laodicea, A.D. 363. Here the Dionysan artists were attacked and suppressed, a thing which could be done, because their order had become mostly Christianized. The psalm-singers were attacked by the Orthodox and exterminated. The narrow subterfuge was that psalms composed by mere laymen, were not inspired!" Argobardus, *De Ritu Canendi Psalmos in Ecclesia*, explains as follows: "Mention is made of these psalms in the epistle of the Council of Antioch, against Paul of Samostata, and in the Penthimate Canon of the Council of Laodicea, where there is a clear prohibition of the use of ψαλμοὶ ἰδιωτικοί in the church; i.e. of the psalms composed by private individuals. For this custom had obtained great prevalence, so that many persons composed psalms in honor of Christ, and had them sung in the church. It is psalms of this kind, consequently, which the Fathers of the Council of Laodicea forbade to be sung thereafter in the church, designating them ἰδιωτικοί, *id. est:* composed by unskilled men, or not dictated by the Holy Spirit."

[29] *Matth.*, XXVI.. 30: "And when they had sung an hymn, they went out into the Mount of Olives."

blended copiously with the Dionysan artists of those earlier days.[30]

Summing it all up, we find that the Dionysan artists were a part of the great economical structure of the poor and lowly races of mankind, who had organized themselves under the jus coeundi of Solon, purely for protection against the outside warring world. Being in an age of superstition, wonder-working and love of excitement, they naturally cultivated music; and as musicians and artists in rhythm and melody, branched off by themselves, although in constant concert with their congenital neighbors, the magicians, wandering tinkers, and houseless nomads who lived in tents. All worked for an economical existence; and all longed for and even worshiped a messiah whom they persistently believed to be forthcoming, with power to redeem them from their precarious condition. Their unions almost always had a burial attachment, and were at base strictly economical institutions.[31] The Dionysan experts and artists were not exclusively religious organizations. An examination of Foucart's great work, which is crowded with valuable information, reveals this clearly.[32] We were so happy as to enjoy a pleasant and instructive conversation with this savant at the Academy of Inscriptions, and remember his interest in our mention of the connection of the Solonic law with our estimate of the great orders of collegia in ancient times. Likewise we shall be a long while forgetting the delicious visits by special invitation, with MM. Cagnat, Reinach and many others connected with the Athenian Academy. Several of these men of investigation and science, were pronounced in their opinion that the religion of Jesus was originally planted into, if not an outgrowth of the organizations here described; that for the first three centuries they were shielded, protected and reared, like fledglings,

---

[30] Neander, *Hist. Church*, I., p. 161, commenting on Celsus' criticism of the Christians, taken from Origen's book, *Contra Celsum*, VI., c. 41, says that Celsus heard it from Dionysius, an Egyptian musician, that music exercised an influence over the uncultivated and profligate, but not over those who had received philosophical education."

[31] Böckh, CIG. 2834, 2845, shows members of the burial societies; Lüd., *D. K.* pp. 24, 25.

[32] Foucart, *Associations Religieuses*. After studying this celebrated work thoroughly, we cannot but arrive at the conclusion that, however foreclosed may be our prejudices, the radical fact remains, that they had at base but one great object in their vast and long-enduring organizations—that of tiding themselves through their terrible economical struggle for existence. They all had the burial attachment.

against danger, under their secret shield, until able to stand alone and assume the dignity of open Christianity. In most functions woman was prominent.[33]

But we now come to the phenomenal fact of their suppression; not by the vindictive conquests, which failed to accomplish that dismal design, but by the ungrateful church itself, whose ambitious prelates, perhaps to obtain their little properties, conspired to annihilate them under the accusation that their music was sinful because uninspired, and that their common table was criminal except for themselves and the priests.

The suppression of the unions at Laodicea sealed the doom of Christianity and its delicious music for at least 1500 years. That stroke of misjudged piety stripped off all the original economic scheme of Jesus. The plan as clearly and undisguisedly portrayed by this master, was to make of the holy family scheme, ancient, beautiful and perfect, where the babes and the fledglings and the mother and father cling around the common table and the happy threshold of the domestic home, making it a sacred sanctuary, father, mother, children and dear ones, enjoying and owning all in common. We say the plan of the great Redeemer of struggling mankind, was to burst away from the fetters of the competitive world; build wider and more wisely; substitute the brotherhood for the model family; broaden the microcosm of the original few into the cosmic hundred and thousand; so finally the government, by which, under one common interest, all mankind own the tools of manufacture and distribution, emancipating the race. This was the plan; and it worked so well that the world was being filled with millions of little loving fraternities, singing, chanting, composing, inventing, sustaining one another through the cold struggles for existence. Men and women under this scheme, co-operated in the ever purifying, ever civilizing, ennobling and mutually enfranchising jus coeundi of this dispensation. This was the famous economic scheme of that masterful and exquisite life which so sublimely descended into the pits of the brotherhoods,

[33] Foucart, *De Collegiis Scenicorum*, p. 15, says that mimic players were not found among these collegia; and adds about women: "Vix est quod moneam mulieribus nullum locum in scenicis collegiis fuisse, quum res ludicra per viros tantum honeste agi putaretur; quæcumque feminæ aut saltarent aut canerent ad tibiam citharamve, serviles et plerumque meretricum loco habitas fuisse satis est compertum." But we find her extremely useful in all the symposiums and other fields of usefulness.

and taught them to enlarge out of the fraternity into the state.

Divine wisdom, thinks Plato, is too pure and eternal to be founded on time-serving billows of mere generations and flitting centuries. It may be better for humanity on the long score, that the greedy prelates and the harpies of the money power struck the unions when they did and drove them from the earth. Perhaps so sublime a revolution, all things considered, was too early to go into effect. It may have been the ineffable foresight of omniscience that intuitively saw unwisdom in so rapid a growth of the outcasts of mankind. Aristotle had the penetration to so see what our own perception is too poor to distinguish. The fact remains that the cruel edict suppressed both the sweet music and the psalms, and their common table. All we can do is to regret the disaster. But the suppression of the Solonic law at the Council of Laodicea was the last and fatal writ of injunction, whose effects upon the world are deeply felt to this day. As we see it we must think that had the right of the syssiti been fully accorded to all instead of being restricted to the priests, the economical half of Christianity would not have been interfered with and suppressed. The money power would have given way to citizen ownership and management of all things, and labor would have long since been able to solve the problem of poverty and of lowliness.

CHAPTER XIII.

HAGIOS EUSEBES AGATHOS

COMPOSITION, HABITS, MORALS, LAWS.

The Solonic Unions not Guilds—Neither did they resemble the Trade-Unions of to-day—Voting Trades-Brotherhoods—Meals in Common—Property in Common—Tools of Labor in Common—Question, What were They?—Categorically Answered—Best Greek Name Eranothiasos—Best Latin Name Collegium—Best Aramaic-Hebrew, was Ebionim—How this Poor Man's Name got Pilfered and Stiffened in the Schools—Love One Another a Principle—Numbers and Moral Status at Time of Advent—Determined Adherence to Marriage—Not Gnostics—Amalgamated with Christians but had to be Secret—Statistics Gleaned from the Stones—Admission Fees Known—The Dokimasia—Own Strict Rules—Charity, Beggary and Blasphemy disallowed—Initiations—Fines for the Non-Payment of Dues—Work or Starve—Contributions to Valuable Knowledge by French, Austrian, German and Athenian Academies—Author's Personal Reception by Them—Encouraged to Proceed—Scrutiny of Laws Governing the Unions—Financially Helped Each other—Revenue—Nemesis—Turned Mills of the Gods Against Unfair Distribution—Fines for Desecrating Graves—Cremation vs. Burial—"Sub Prætextu Religionis"—Whippers and Rhabdophores—Contortion of Word Charity—Ignominious Alms-Giving or Proffer not Tolerated—Original Prytaneum—Essenes ate in Common at Temple of Jerusalem—Cœnobium at Rome.

Having thus far shown the existence of a hitherto unknown, but vast and wide spreading labor organization among the ancients, its attempted suppression by the Roman conquests which failed, and its final suppression by the emperors under the money power, the lords and the high-toned aspirants, the intelligent reader will ask for more about their tenets, morals and habits.

They were not guilds. Most writers, overlooking the

distinction between true trade unions and guilds of the feudal ages, treat them as no better than truckling, beggarly guilds, manipulated by petty bosses, and who so catered to feudal lords that they were suppressed by the French Revolution. It was largely this enslavement of their membership and the accumulations of their unpaid labor which built up the bourgeoisie and formed later the extremes of wealth and poverty in Europe, until suppressed in 1789.

It is a radical mistake to characterize the ancient economic organizations of the lowly workers under the jus coeundi of Solon, as no better than cringing, degenerate guilds. They were voting trade unionists; in other words, unions of men and women bereft of other means of existence, whose object in combining was to win better chances for the work of their hands, brain, their physical and mental endowments.

We are so fortunate as to possess enough of their own literature which has transcended to us, not through history or epistolary correspondence but through their own voluminous inscriptions, to prove that while the tenets and career of men and states, society and statesmen, of the great outside, competing world so graciously portrayed to us by historians, were grasping, immoral and cruel, the unheard-of men and women were all along following rules and tenets which were of the sublimest nature and replete with moral and religious lessons destined to stand as the basis of higher civilization and to abide forever.[1] They certainly understood the dignity of labor and were not ashamed to perform it. Like Adam Smith, they seemed to have known that it was they who produced the wealth of nations.[2]

In answering categorically what they were, it is very necessary to go to the bottom and bring up definitions both from their own inscriptions and from writers who

[1] Waltzing, *Hist. Corp. Prof.*, II., 161, says the object of the organizations was economic, and denies that they were like guilds of the middle ages: "Trop souvent on s' est laissé tromper par le souvenir des florissantes Ghildes du moyen age, si dégénérées sous l' ancien régime." But the old certainly possessed virtues which the more modern lacked.

[2] Mauri, I. *Cittadini Lav.*, p. 63: "Gli Ateneisi si vantavano con orgogliosa compiacenza d' essere figli di Pallade e d' Efesto. Æschilus, *Eumenides*, 12, τὸ τῶν δημιουργικῶν γένος. Plato, *Legg.*, XI., 290: Inscr. CIA. II., i., 114ᵇ, i due attivi lavoratori dell' Olympio che coll' audace ed altruista Prometeo compivano la triade divina dell' operosità manuele." sq. The Divine Triad was Pallas, Ephestos and Prometheus, who especially favored manual labor, Mauri refers to Plato's mention: "Οἴκημα κοινὸν ἐν ᾧ ἐφιλοτεχνείτην" *Protagoras*, 321. He also quotes Xenophon for similar sentiments.

lived in their times. There is scarcely any difference between the three names thiasos, eranos and collegium. This was long ago admitted by Aristotle and many others.[3] They were sometimes appropriately entitled the commonwealth of the eranists. Bekker, the Greek scholar of our own times similarly defines them.[4] Van Holst who wrote a work on this subject was of opinion that these eranist societies were strictly civil institutions and therefore different in principle from the thiasos; but his work though a valuable contribution,[5] was published before the scientific world had become thoroughly aroused regarding them.

These unions were magnificent specimens of practical mankind. They conformed to the usages of the times in which they existed. Their fundamental principle was love for one another.[6] This great precept is purely Christian, yet it was practiced a thousand years before the Advent. We are constrained to admit that the unions of love were in the world in great numbers before the birth of Christ and their strength and numbers existed at a keen height at the time the apostles were preaching the gospel of Christianity. The goodness which inspired them was often appreciated by the poets, and they gave the credit to their gods for influencing their dignity and tone.[7]

Their morality was looked upon as a pattern. They lived in days of great profligacy, but seem to have stood aloof from the temptations of the outside world. This was especially true regarding marriage. All the evidence of the monuments, from centuries before the Advent down to the close of the third century are to the effect that monogamous marriage was held very sacred. Almost everywhere we find it was firmly adhered to by the societies. Marriage was always desired by them and the slave population and their descendant freedmen and women practiced marriage in spite of the fact that there

---

[3] Foucart, *Ass. Rel.*, p. 2, cuts it off as follows: "Pour Athénée les deux termes, θίασος, ἔρανος, étaient tout á fait synomymes." And for Aristotle, he says: "Aristote employait les mots thiase et érane pour désigner des associations de nature analogue." Aristot., *Ethica Nicomach.*, VIII., ix., 7.

[4] Bekker, *Anecdota*, p. 264, 23: "Θιασώτης'—ὁ κοινωνὸς τῶν θυσιῶν δὲ καὶ οὗτοι ὀργεῶνες." *id est*: A communist who participates at the sacrifices.

[5] Van Holst, *De Eranis Veterum Graecorum*. Leyden, 1832.

[6] "Κοινὸν τῶν ἐρανιστῶν," Ross, *Inscrs. inédites Grecques*, no. 107.

[7] Euripides, *Bacchus*, 77, 549, 378, 557, 680, even when speaking of their dancing and singing in honor of the gods, carries the idea that there was the holiness of love among them

was no law permitting it. In the teeth of hostile and forbidding statutes these poor workers went unauthorized through life, in the conjugal bond; and it may be said they laid the base of marriage under the Christian regime. It was they who eventually called forth the laws of marriage among the people of the world.

Numberless inscriptions in form of epitaphs are discovered showing that a burial attachment of the unions, which alone was legalized, encouraged marriage.[8] The early Christians encouraged marriage in consequence; and there is a canon of Peter, composed by Clement of Rome, Peter's friend, afterwards bishop of Rome, which was first to make marriage a holy rite. Peter, Philip, Tertullian were married and had children. The influence of the Solonic organization was so great that in course of time there sprang up philosophies and their concomitant wranglings and dissentions, among them being Montanism which was so hypocritically pious that it denounced marriage. Gibbon, who treats celibacy of the early Christians as a monstrous offense against nature may mean one of these gnostic bodies; he certainly cannot mean the early Christians who were commanded to marry, which was in strict conformity with the practices of the unions.[9]

We now come to the more important tenets of the societies. It is made clear by the discovery of a number of inscriptions, that applicants for membership were subjected to a very strict examination before they could be admitted.[10] They must be found to be good, pious and true. The remarkable fact is here disclosed that the essenes, therapeuts, orgeons and ebionites were sub-

[8] Ramsay, *Cit. and Bish. Phryg.*, II., p. 385 no. 231 Ἀυρήλιος Γάιος Ἀπελλᾶ κατεσκεύασεν τὸ μνημεῖον ἑαυτῷ καὶ τῇ γυναικὶ αὐτοῦ κα· τῇ μητρὶ καὶ χρηστῷ φίλῳ Ὀνησίμῳ καὶ τῇ γυναικὶ αὐτοῦ· εἰ δέ τις ἐπιχειρήσει ἀνασκευάσαι τὸν τόπον, ἔστω αὐτῷ κατάρα τέκνων τέκνοις καὶ τῷ συμβουλεύσαντι. ὁ βίος ταῦτα." The συμβούλευσις here mentioned is the council of the union to which they all belonged, and it came under the Roman law of the collegia funeraticia. Numbers of epitaphs like this are found everywhere, showing marriage among working people and the endeared, self-protected families.

[9] Gibbon, *Decline and Fall*, I., pp. 549-550 Harpers, analyzes early Christian asceticism and, as if misunderstanding the great fact that the early Christians married, inveighs against celibacy as a monstrous offense against nature. On the subject, see Cleveland Coxe. in *Early Fathers*, II., p. 57, *Emendations of Similitude* 9, chap. xi. of Pastor Hermes: Euseb, *Hist. Eccles.*, III.. 30.

[10] Lüders, *Dionys. Künst.*, pp. 37-38: "Bevor er, in dem ehrwürdigen Verband, εἰς τὴν σεμνοτάτην σύνοδον aufgenommen werden durfte musste er sich ligitimiren als ein ἅγιος καὶ εὐσεβὴς καὶ ἀγαθός." Then, having established all these qualities and paid his admission fee of three drachmas, about 60 cents, and the proper dues, he. or she, is considered to have undergone the δοκιμασία or scrutiny necessary before initiation. This is the investigation of the candidate's character.

jected to the same scrutiny. Their conduct must be found to have been based upon, and consistent with, the love of God, the love of virtue and the love of man. It looks not a little strange that Neander, the powerful and penetrating historian, should discover this very principle in the power of Christian fellowship; indeed the two organizations, in the scrutiny, in baptism, in initiations and many other things, were identical.[11] An eranos is found elaborately describing the dokimasia or examination of the applicant for admission. It is given in full by Dr. Foucart, as no. 20 of his celebrated work where in line 33, occur the remarkable words. We give the entire inscription which has caused a considerable discussion among the savants.[12] More recently others have found inscriptions of the same purport. Dr. Ramsay brings a self-composed epitaph of Apameia in Phrygia which is Christian, or the work of a partly converted Christian named Gaius. This man claims to have possessed the same qualities.[13] Schömann declares that this rigid dokimasia, or scrutiny into the character of applicants was the law. This again, brings evidence that it was the Solonic law, which unfortunately was so badly mangled during the revolutions that the clause is no longer extant. The main points of the law in addition to these already given, on which admission was

[11] Neand., *Planting*, VI., chap. viii., *trans.*, says: "At these lovefeasts, the power of Christian fellowship was shown in overcoming all the differences of rank and education: rich and poor, masters and slaves, partook with one another of the same simple meal;" meaning that of the common table. Dr. Oehler in his *MSS, to the author* has given an inscription in proof, mentioning that they frequently required the words ἅγιος καὶ εὐσεβὴς καὶ ἀγαθός as a result of their δοκιμασία.

[12] For a full quotation, see *supra*, pp. 150-151; but we may here repeat a part of it, Cf, CIG. 126; Foucart, no. 20. Wescher, *Revue Archéol.*, 1865, II., p. 220 and 226; "Ἄρχων μὲν Ταύρισκος, ἀτὰρ μὴν Μουνυχιῶν ἦν ὀκτωκαιδεκάτῃ δ' ἔρανον σύναγον φίλοι ἄνδρες, καὶ κοινῇ βουλῇ θεσμὸν φιλίης ὑπέγραψαν.

Νόμος ἐρανιστῶν.

Μηδενὶ ἐξέστω ἐπιέναι εἰς τὴν σεμνοτάτην συνοδον τῶν ἐρανιστῶν, πρὶν ἂν δοκιμασθῇ εἰ ἐστι ἅγνος καὶ εὐσεβὴς καὶ ἀγαθός· δοκιμαζέτω δὲ ὁ προστάτης καὶ ὁ ἀρχιερανιστής καὶ ὁ γραμματεὺς καὶ οἱ ταμίαι καὶ σύνδικοι· ἔστωσαν δὲ οὗτοι κληρωτοὶ κατὰ ἔτος χωρὶς τοῦ προστάτου ὁμολείτωρ ? δὲ εἰς τὸν βίον αὐτοῦ ὁ ἐπὶ ἡρῴου ? καταληφθείς· αὐξανέτω δὲ ὁ ἔρανος ἐπὶ φιλοτειμίαις· εἰ δὲ τις μάχας ἢ θορύβους κεινῶν φαίνοιτο, ἐκβαλλέσθω τοῦ ἐράνου, ζημιούμενος ταῖς διπλαῖς. . . . . κρίσεως . . . πληγαῖς," Early in the imperial age of Rome.

[13] Ramsay, *Cities and Bishoprics of Phrygia*, II., p. 386, *inscr.* no 232; spoken of as the identical jurist Gaius, which perhaps is an error. It is from Eumeneia or a town near. It reads:

Γάϊος ὡς ἅγιος ὡς ἀγαθός·

Ramsay says it talks about the Christians; it certainly does, but is nevertheless skeptical regarding the Christian idea of a resurrection. Roubes defines ἅγιος a servant of the great Jehovah. It is clear that Gaius belonged to an eranos.

required was secrecy, majority ballot, 30 drachmas admission fee and the regular monthly dues.

Although this admission to the eranos was the law of Solon which demanded the rigid dokimasia we have just described, and was therefore very ancient, yet it is certain that the same virtues were required of members applying for admission to the Christian union; and the Therapeuts and Essenes followed the same rules.[14] This principle down to this day underlies the structure of the Christian religion and is likewise the basis of socialism being the physical half of the great principle of salvation.[15] Fulfilling these requirements was equivalent to being the agnus castus which in time became the figurative Lamb. This agnus castus, pure willow, was a favorite symbol of the thiasotes, used in weaving crowns, and also by their working people's unions of pre-Christian times.

To be pure, upright, respectful, lamb-like, honest and just to one another, in other words, to love neighbors as we love ourselves, were the fundamental tenets of millions of human beings of both sexes, organized under the mystically secret veil of the Solonic brotherhoods. They had been driven to the endorsement and practice of these really Christian tenets by the cruelty of their masters who held them as chattels from a time remote in antiquity; and after æons of torture and misery the good men like Solon, Numa, and Amasis had come to legalize their unions, hitherto precarious and illicit, and had given them the great coeundi so beautifully covered under their dispensation. But until a momentous Advent, their order had been hidden in an impenetrable secrecy and cowled in mysteries that darkled of doubt, and shut off the orb of publicity. Bye and bye there came another Solon who burst the bars of occultism and introduced the slow-working god of universal knowledge. He is yet proclaiming the

---

[14] Smith, *Bib. Dict.*, p. 772, speaking of the Essenes, quotes Philo, *Quod Omn. Prob. Liber*, § 12, p. 877. M. as saying that "their conduct generally was directed by their rules: Love of God, love of virtue and love of man." This conforms with the requirements chiseled upon the Athenian inscription we have quoted. These requirements are found in the Talmud.

[15] The requirements to membership everywhere were ἅγνος καὶ εὐσεβής καὶ ἀγαθός. These are fundamental. What more could be asked? So again, Clement's *Epistle to James*, cap. 3, says: "James the lord and bishop of bishops, who ruled Jerusalem." It relates that Peter at Rome, being about to die, ordained Clement as bishop, saying, among other things of Clement: "Whom I have found above all others, pious, philanthropic, pure, learned, chaste, good, upright, large-hearted and striving generally to bear ingratitude."

self-same principles until all men shall know from the least to the greatest and nations shall learn strife no more.

Next in importance after their initiation is the manner in which they paid their dues and upheld their organization. Whether these various unions had signs known only to the members is a matter which has but recently been established.[16] Some inscriptions clear it up. Fortunately we have written documents of early authorities on this point.[17] Many ancient authors have added their contributions to this information, and the same flags we have quoted as to their tenets also furnish data regarding their fees, fines and dues. Numbers of fines are found recorded upon the epitaphs. They are mostly for mutilating graves. The unions, as already seen, had a burial attachment to their order besides being shielded from molestation in the umbrage of the Roman statute known as the lex collegia funeraticia,[18] which served them for centuries as a helmet to unlimited organization, and was afterwards the law used by the Christians to shield and legalize them after they had been engrafted into the economic unions all over the world.[19] This wonderful law of the collegia licita, or legalized economic unions is that which saved Christianity from sure destruction until it had grown in abodes of darkness and secrecy, to be a vast power and became strong enough to stand and defy persecution. We are fortunate enough to know by the highest authority what the poor fellows had to pay in order to enter, and receive the benefits of the brotherhood.[20]

[16] Dumont, *De Plumbeis apud Græcos Tesseris*, p. 100; also Apuleius, *De Magnia*, 55. Foucart, *Ass. Rel.*, p. 11: "Les *signa* doivent être des emblèmes que les inities adoraient en secret."

[17] Foucart, *Ass. Rel.*, p. 141: "La cotisation était également obligatoire, et nous avons vu que la société menaçait les retardataires d' abord d' une amende, puis, de l' exclusion." He here refers to Harpocration, *Lexicon*, in *verb.* Ἔρανος as follows: 'Ἐρανιστὴς μέντοι κυρίως, ἐστὶν ὁ τοῦ ἐράνου μετέχων καὶ τὴν φορὰν ἣν ἑκάστου μηνὸς ἔδει καταβαλεῖν εἰσφέρων. On voit également par cette citation que la cotisation mensuelle était obligatoire."

[18] *Digest.* XLVII., xxii., *De Collegiis et Corporibus.*

[19] Cagnat, *Revue Contemporaine*, Jan. 1896, fin. Dr. Cagnat does not hesitate to admit with considerable earnestness that this was the case and is doubtful if Christianity without their aid and watchful care would not have been overwhelmed and lost.

[20] Lüders, *Dionys. Künst.* p. 38: "Sogleich beim Eintritt sind dreissig Drachmen zu erlegen; verlässt ein Mitglied Athen, so hat es um ferner an dem Eranos Theil zu haben, periodisch drei Drachmen als Contribution zu leisten. Dann tritt es nach seiner Rückkehr wieder in die alten Rechte ein. Der vorgeschriebene Beitrag jedoch für die an alle Versammlungen und Vortheilen participirenden einheimischen Mitglieder beträgt sechs Drachmen. Diese müssen jedesmal entrichtet werden," etc.

STATISTICS OF INITIATION.

The entrance fee was thirty drachmas, or at that time about $6.00. But first of all he must, as we have shown, undergo the dokimasia or scrutiny of high character.[21] Thus the member was compelled to contribute regularly his or her three drachmas as periodical payments, and sometimes six. If dismissed he could get back by good behavior.

Now comes the important question. What became of all these incomes into the eranos? They went to buy, in quantities and at wholesale without the usual middleman and his system of selfish profits, the food for the common table, to which all the members had an equal, democratic right. Why not? Each without exception, paid into a common fund the same sum, in form of periodical dues, sufficient to keep him or her supplied with nourishment, which under that system of the syssitoi, was furnished by the society out of these in-pouring funds; and it had a complete set of cooks, buyers, waiters[22] and officers of every kind whereby to carry out the system to perfection. Frequently as in Rhodes, they also had a periodical banquet where several societies, kindred in trade or character, enjoyed a grand reunion, accompanied by music and a variety of amusements. We give the deciding inscription in a note in full,[23] and as the subject furnishes a key to our history, we append various views regarding it, in a note bearing a close relationship to the inscription. The attendance at the meetings was compulsory, thus fixed in order to collect the dues with perfect regularity. The certainty is

[21] Lüders, *ibid.* p. 37: εἰς τὴν σεμνοτάτην σύνοδον. To get in he must prove himself ἅγνος καὶ εὐσεβὴς καὶ ἀγαθός. All of these requirements came under the unalterable law, and they carried out this law with rigid discipline.

[22] We shall soon show these waiters to be διάκονοι, deacons, who afterwards became church deacons, though from their original functions of waiters, and assistants in the "daily ministrations" (Acts VI., 1), they have sadly degenerated into their almost useless office of deacons. The διάκονος was very lively in the olden time.

[23] Foucart, *Ass'ns Religieuses*, p. 42, *inscr.* 21, and his learned opinions, subscribing a few remarks of our own on this highly important inscription, which Dr. Pittakis, 'Αρχαιολογικὴ 'Εφημερίς, no. 861, and Rangabé, *Antiqu. Héll.*, no. 811, Le Bas, *Attique*, no. 384, have already celebrated for the information of the world. It reads: 'Επὶ Διοκλέους τοῦ Διοκ. ἄρχοντος, · ταμιεύοντος 'Αρόπου τοῦ Σελεύκου Πειραιέως 'Ηροϊστῶν τῶν Διοτίμου καὶ . καὶ Παμμένου ὢν ἀρχερανιστὴς ἦν 'Αντιόχου Μαραθώνιος, ἔδοξεν τῶι κοινῶι τῶν 'Ηροϊστῶν προνοηθῆναι τῆς φορᾶς, ὅπως οἱ ἀποδημοῦντες τῶν 'Ηροϊστῶν οἷον δηποτεοῦν τρόπον διδῶσιν κατὰ μῆνα τὰς δραχμὰς τρεῖς, οἱ δὲ ἐπιδημοῦντες καὶ μὴ παραγινόμενοι ἐπαναγάγωσιν . . . . σι τὴν φοράν, τὰς ἐξ δραχμάς, ὅταν τῶν ἱερῶν ? λάβωσιν τὰ μέρη· ἐὰν δὲ μὴ διδῶσιν τὸ διπλοῦν, ἔδοξεν μὴ μετέχειν αὐτοὺς πλέον τοῦ ἐράνου, ἐὰν μὴ τινι συμβῇ ἢ διὰ πένθος ἢ διὰ ἀσθένειαν ἀπολειφθῆναι· ὁμοίως δὲ ἔδοξε ἐμβιβάζειν ἐξεῖναι τοῖς . ον δραχμῶν τριάκοντα κα . . . , τῶν ἐξ δραχμῶν καὶ μὴ π . . . , ὑπὲρ τούτων δὲ ἀναδιδόναι τὴν ψῆφον . . . .

that these meetings were regulated by law,[24] as is well known afterwards; and the members met about once a week.[25] Another inscription[26] of great importance quoted in full by Dr. Foucart and of a very early pre-Christian date, corroborates this which we have described and also shows that the laws, customs and rules changed very little from age to age. The same rules of initiation and the thirty drachmas, about five dollars and twenty-eight cents were paid by the members of the fishermen's union at Hierapolis in the first Christian century that was paid 350 years before Christ, as an entrance fee.[27] We note as proof of these collections of fees that the same practices were observed in all countries and all cities as well as among all trades and professions organized under the Solonic rule. Dr. Waltzing of the University of Louvain, who has brought out in three valuable volumes a history of these organizations as they existed in ancient Italy, shrewdly perceives their strictly economic object, in the manner of employing the income from fees, dues, and fines; and we recognize his authority as important in substantiating our own groping views, early entertained and now corroborated beyond the power of any argument which can be brought against us.[28]

[24] Foucart, *Ass. Rel.*, p. 42, shows that in the heroes' society, which, in all particulars was a typical brotherhood under the *jus coeundi* of the Solonic dispensation, the members, after passing the scrutinizing δοκιμασία, before being initiated, had to pay 30 δραχμαί entrance fee and 3 δραχμαί monthly thereafter. The littleness of this sum is astonishing when we consider the amount they realized. Three δραχμαί amount to 18 ὀβολοί. An ὀβολός was of the value of about 3 cents of our federal money. These 3 δραχμαί then, amounted to about 17 6-16, which was the amount of the dues imposed on each member, monthly, after such admission to membership. There is no direct information as to how often after; perhaps it was four times per month; though they had no weeks.

[25] This would fix the regular dues at about 52 cents per week. Harpocration, who, in about A.D. 200 wrote of them for his *Lexicon*, speaks of their compulsory payment of monthly dues: "'Ερανιστὴς μέντοι κυρίως ἐστὶν ὁ τοῦ ἐράνου μετέχων καὶ τὴν φορὰν ἣν ἑκάστου μηνὸς ἔδει καταβαλεῖν εἰσφέρων."

[26] Foucart, *id.*, p. 189. *Inscr.* no. 2, which is an important fragment found at the Peiræus, Athens, whose date is fixed at some time in the second half of the fourth century before Christ. In most particulars it agrees with the figures given in no 21, which we have just quoted.

[27] Mention is made of the 'Ερανος κυρτοβόλων—piscatores, fishermen, by Oehler, in his list of labor unions, *Eranos Vindobonensis*, p. 279: "Der αρχωνής der Genossenshaft in Hieropolis, Le Bas, III., 741, wohl richtig als Einnehmer der Beiträge der mitglieder arklärt." In another place, *MSS. to the author*, he speaks of the εἰσφερεῖν εἰς τὴν σύνοδον.

[28] Lüders, *Dionys. Künst.*, p. 24, speaks of a list of contributions of a θίασος discovered by Newton: it appears they cherished the relationship of Apollo with Cybele, the Phrygian mother of the gods. Their cult, methods of fees and otherwise were also the same in Athens, Megapolis, Laodicea and many other places; CIG. 4893; Welcker, 419; Lenormant. *Eleusis*, 106. Another somewhat defaced slab of the orgeons, Foucart, *Ass. Rel.*, p. 43, line 21, of no. 2, shows that the entrance fee was 30 drachmas 350 years B,C.

Dr. Lüders refers to the lengthy and remarkable inscription found among the ruins of the ancient theatre at Teos, maternal center of the international Gemeinde of Dionysan artists. It relates a piece of statistical history of the ancient poor. A union of playwrights at Teos in Iasos, fell into debt by some mishap; and unable to extricate itself from embarrassment alone, and being a regular branch of the international, applied to it for help. The time for this was propitious because the Dionysan festivities of the city were approaching. The cities, on account of the political influence of their voting unions and their large numbers of well organized members who worked for each other hand in hand not only as musicians and actors, but also as voters, in order to secure their choice of proper agoranomoi or commissioners of public works, employed their organizations to do all the art-work of the festivities.[29]

The petition for help from the branch that had met with "calamity," was taken up by the main synod after proper presentation of the grievance, through regular delegates, presenting the same in secret session, and complied with.[30] They then turned their influence upon the commissioners of public order for the city and induced them to select their performers from the branch in trouble, themselves lending them aid in their own way. The inscription gives a list of the experts employed. There were among them machinists for the scenic art-work, who attended to the apparatus; one tragical poet; one player of tragedy; one singer to the cithera, two flute players; two melodramists for tragedy; two comedians, an extra cithera player who had a singer for his music. In another place it is shown that such figures are to be multiplied by three, the ones mentioned being foremen of parts.[31]

[29] Waltzing, *Hist. Corp. Prof.*, 1., p. 320: "Dans les collèges païens, chacun verse sa cotisation au jour fixé, et s'il est en retard, il perd ses droits." There was no dawdling beggary, or reliance upon some "pull," or "beeler," as we see in our corrupt competitive times. Every one must work. No recognized favors because of superior means or influence: "Chez les païens," (meaning these unions) "on ne distinguit pas entre pauvres et riches; tous avaient le même droit." *Ibidem*, p. 320.

[30] See *supra*, II., pp. 203-230. chap. x., where it is frequently explained how this German word *Gemeinde* best answers to the Greek σύνοδος, afterwards becoming the synod of the Christians. The "*Great Gemeinde*" in after years was enormously planted into by Paul and other apostles, because it had the same principles.

[31] Lüders *Dionys. Künst.*, pp. 78-88, *note* 165, p. 88, reads: "Die Inschrift ist um die Mitte des zweiten Jahrhunderts vor. Chr. verfasst." Another list of artists is given by Dr. Foucart. *De Coll. Scen. Apud Græc*, p. 55.

But there was another source of revenues quite frequently brought under consideration by the old Solonic organizations, which was that of receiving donations from the outside rich[32] and sometimes even from zealous persons of means, who became members because they admired the institution and were honored by it for so doing, by receiving an annual memorial banquet after death, a thing frequent among the ancients. There is no doubt that during, and for a long time subsequent to the Roman conquests, the unions, in spite of their economic vigilance and uprightness, were often very poor and glad to get aid. Persecuted by petty traders who hated them because their wholesale purchases on socialistic principles, interfered with profits of speculating craft, such skinflints often worked their influence against the poor fellows down in the darksome secrets of communal unionism, while above they stirred up the monarchs against them. They were often so poor that the emulatory incentive among outsiders was less than the innate goodness which resides within the hearts of some rich men. M. Foucart speaks of their falling in arrears and being glad to accept occasional benefactions from the disinterestedly good but better-to-do.[33] In this class, the state was their best and principal benefactor.

Among these ancient people, ere the Christians taught them monotheism, there was a goddess, Nemesis by name, a divinity presiding over human fortunes. She was firmly believed by such strugglers to be the enemy of unjust distribution. She is represented in their engravings as riding through aerial smoke and tempest, in a fiery chariot drawn by dragons, in one hand holding a scale of justice to all men, and in the other grasping

[32] Foucart, *Ass. Rel.*, pp. 46-47: "Le plus souvent, la communauté se tirait d'affaire, grâce à la libéralité de quelques-uns de ses membres plus riches et plus zélés. Tantôt ils lui prêtaient de l' argent sans intérêt:" and refers to *inscription* no. 42 of his work; also no. 6, line 13; and no. 26, lines 10-11. The first 7 lines of no. 42, which is the nos. 2629 and 3003, of 'Αρχιολογικὴ 'Εφημερείς, read:

"Εδοξεν τοῖς Σεραπιασταῖς·
'Επειδὴ 'Επαμεινων Σωμένου
'Ανὴρ καλὸς κἀγαθὸς ὢν διατελεῖ
περὶ τὸν θίασον καὶ φιλότιμος,
χρείας τε γενομένης ἀργυρίου
εἰς 'ξυλωνίαν τῶι θιάσωι
προεισήνεγκε τὸ ἀργύριον ἄτοκον.

No. 6, lines 13-14, read: εἰς τὰς ἐπισκευὰς δὲ προαναλίσκων, καὶ τοῦ ἀργυρήρου ἀρχηγὸς γενόμενος συναχθῆναι, κτλ.

[33] *Ass. Rel.*, p. 47: "En somme, ce qui ressort de l' étude des inscriptions' c'est que ces sociétés étaient le plus souvent embarrassées, et qu' elles ne faisaient face aux dépenses que par la générosité des bienfaiteurs. '

terrible storms of pent up lightning; the whole swooping down upon millionaires, the military, the Cæsars and their standing armies, the craving sensualists whose greed for money has ever choked earth's lovely valleys with dry bones of good men robbed, starved and deprived of their just and honest dues. This fairy goddess of retribution was worshiped by the unions.[34]

Nemesis is spoken of in the writings of many authors.[35] Hers are the mills of the gods which though they grind slowly, "grind exceeding fine."[36] She is often the goddess of vengeance; also protectrice of dumb animals against the brutality of man; and did we still believe in her, she would be the divinity in charge of humane societies. She was endorsed by the trade unions of ancient Rome, among others, those of the bagpipers.

Having spoken of the methods of replenishing their common treasury it is in order to illustrate another method, that of punitive incomes. These incomes were from fines for non-attendance, awards accruing from lawsuits such as judgments, and fines for mutilating property. The latter which was far the most common, was mostly from offenders who mutilated graves and belonged to their burial attachment which was fully legalized by the Roman law. A large number of trade unions in Phrygia, Lydia, Caria, and other parts of Asia Minor have given us valuable inscriptions. We have carefully scanned Dr. Ramsay's work on the Cities and Bishoprics of Phrygia and counted no less than a hundred epitaphs, many of which were erected by unions as the context shows, and mentioning the sums forfeited in fines for mutilating graves, sepulchres, mausoleums and heroons. Specimens of these inscriptions may be interesting to the reader as curiosities, the epitaphs, being often dictated in advance by the person or persons buried. The fine in many cases is ordered to be

---

[34] Orell.. nos. 1787, 1790, 4121 and innumerable others. It is significant that working people had the boldness to organize themselves under the frowning Nemesis who guarded against the unjust and unequal distribution of their labors. The bagpipers' union of Temisvar worshiped her: Orell, no. 4121, "Deæ Nemesi Ael. Diogenes et Silia Valeria pro salute sua et Filiorum suorum mater et pater ex voto. A solo templum ex suo fecerunt. Collegio utriculariorum; Temisvarii. Mur., 551, 4."

[35] The best dictionaries mention her as an important divinity: "She brings down all immoderate good fortune and checks the presumption that attends it; being thus directly opposed to ὕβρις; and herewith she is often the punisher of extraordinary crimes." Liddell. See *supra*. Vol. I., p. 413, quoting *Cod. Theod., lib.* XIV., *Nat. et leg, tit,* VII.

[36] Plutarch, *De Sera Numinis Vindicta,* III.

paid into the tameion or receptacle which of itself, that is, this tameion, was the treasury of an association unexpressed.[37]

Sometimes it was a serious thing to meddle with the sepulchres of the sacred dead; for it will soon be explained how intense were the loves existing, after death and burial, or rather cremation, as it existed in their imagination. The fines often rose to 500 drachmas; and in several instances 1500 were collected, after due process of law.[38] Many fresh discoveries make it certain that the orgeon, thiasos and eranos were trade unions having burial attachments under the law, while at the same time they were very busy attending to the economic problems of life. In this habit of burials and cremations among the poor, half enslaved people of those days, there was a habit of burial in imagination when owners of slaves and serfs refused to grant the corpse to them for proper sepulture under their union's rules.[39] There was a fine attached in case of neglect to fulfil the rules.[40]

A very large sum of 2500[41] denarii was exacted by the bag carriers' union of Cyzicus, an organization of freight

[37] CIL., III., 1547: 'Deæ Nemesi illi templum. Pons Augusta."
[38] Rams., II., p, 392. no. 260: Ἐλπὶς Μελίτωνος τῷ ἰδίῳ ἀνδρὶ κατεσκεύασεν τὸ ἡρῷον καὶ τὸν κατ' αὐτοῦ βωμόν· ἐφ' ᾧ αὐτὴ ἡ Ἐλπὶς κηδευθήσεται καὶ Εὐτύχης καὶ Μελίτων, καὶ εἴ τινα ἄλλον βουληθῇ κηδεῦσαι ζῶσα ἡ Ἐλπ·ς· Μετὰ δὲ τὴν τελευτὴν αὐτῆς οὐδενὶ ἐξέσται τεθῆναι ἑτέρῳ χωρὶς τῶν προγεγραμμένων· ὃς δὲ ἂν ἐπιτηδεύσει, θήσει ἰς τὸ ἱερώτατον ταμεῖον δην." 5000 denarii. Perhaps Chr." The word Ἐλπὶς, according to Ramsay, p. 493, *id.*, indicates that it is Christian and the sacred treasury, ταμεῖον, shows that it was of a body of organized persons, not an individual. Like hundreds similar, now coming to light in this immediate region of Eumeneia, Phrygia. See Oehler. It in all probability is a union or guild, like R's nos. 294, 295.
[39] Oehler, *MSS.*, "In Perinthos, hat Aurelius Eutiches gegen den Verletzer seines Grabes eine Geldstrafe von je 506 zu Gunsten der συμβίωσις τῶν χαλκέων; CIG. 3636 und add. In Smyrna von 250 τοῖς φορτηγοῖς τοῖς περὶ τὸ λ βεῖκον· *American Journal of Archæology*, I., p. 141; und in Thyateira an ein κοινόν . . . . eine ihrer Höhe noch nicht bekannte Grabmult: *Monatschr., Berliner Akad.*, 1855, p. 192, no. 11." As much as 1000 danaria were paid in fines at the seaport Cyzicus, for mutilating the graves of the ἱερωτάταν συνεδριοντῶν σακκοφόρων, *vide* Συλλογος, VIII., 1873-74, p. 171. Dr. Oehler further assembles a valuable list of others who paid fines, one as high as 1500. It was a union of woolworkers who received the sum. Dr. Ramsay thinks the sign * is Christian. Dr. Ramsay says this sign to be Christian must have one of the stems vertical; otherwise it is pagan, and we notice that Oehler's *MS*. likewise makes it vertical.
[40] Mommis. *De Coll. et Sodal Rom.*, p. 101, refers to the law of the union of Lanuvium. see Vol. I., p 355; "Item placuit, quisquis ex hoc collegio servus defunctus fuerit et corpus ejus a domino, dominave, sepulturæ datum non fuerit, neque tabulas fecerit, ei funus imaginarium fiet;" and refers to Cardinalis, *Dipl. Imp.*, p. 264: "Cremabatur, scilicet imago ejus et sepeliebatur pro corpore ipso; cave cum Italis quibusdam cogites de imaginibus majorum ante funus latis."
[41] *Mith. Athen.*, VI. 1281, p 125· Κυζικος, 250 δενάρια. Ιεροσυνεδων τῶν σακκαφόρων τῶν ἀπὸ τοῦ μετρητοῦ. On the stone the figures we give are expressed in certain Greek letters.

handlers, called sackkophoroi. They sued for damaging a grave, and recovered this sum. The same methods of exacting money for mutilating graves, extended to the columbarium at Rome, and the fines were accompanied with language containing the most fearful threats.[42] An important work written by Menadier, an Italian savant, ranks the gerusiæ among the organized unions, a fact seemingly unknown to Dr. Ramsay, although we ourselves suspected, long since, that it would turn out so, after full investigation of the slabs.[43] The excavations and other resources for modern science are almost daily bringing to light from their long oblivion valuable contributions to the history of the ancient lowly. One of some moment is that of Thyateira, where certainly immense organized industries existed of many trades during the apstolic age, and into whose economic activities the religion of Jesus was planted and nurtured for the first 300 years. All the towns in the neighborhood had these unions, with the legalized burial attachment and they have left their epitaphs which tell us of the fines.[44] The synod of the society of Heroes of Akraiphia, once inflicted the heavy fine of 2000 denarii which, considering relative values, was equivalent $250, for mutilating and opening sepulchres.[45] The archæologist Mommsen declares that great numbers of colleges, or unions had this burial attachment; and the most significant of his statements is, that they used the burial clause more for the sake of holding their whole union legalized, than for the ostensible purpose of funeral benefits;[46] although he places far more to the credit of the funeral attachment, important as it was, than it ever deserved. In this burial attachment we have striking evidence that the ancient unions, on account of the severe laws, were obliged to play the makeshift of the mortuary and

[42] Gorius, *Mon. Sive Columbar.*, p. 10: "Quare eas aperire, infringere, aliud corpus superponere, obviolare, mortuos inquietare, pœnis, ac diris vetitum, summumque nefas creditum."

[43] Menadier, *Qua Condicone Ephesii*, etc., p. 59: "Ex qua natura gerusiæ pendere arbitramur, quod totiens sepulcrorum læsorum pœnas gerusiæ solvendas esse statuitur. Asiæ enim in oppidis privatorum hominum collegio, nisi omnino fallimur, nusquam hoc evenit."

[44] Oehler, *MSS*: "In Sigeion, finden wir eine Grabmult von 500 denarii, zu Gunsten der συμβίωσις τῶν χαλκέων; CIG. 3639 add."

[45] *Inscr. Græc*, Sept., 2728. It was paid to the σύνοδος τῶν ἡρψαστῶν.

[46] Momms. *De Coll. et Sodal. Rom.*, p. 97: "Omnino quidquid de singulis exemplis his certari potest casu evenire non potuit, ut leges collegiorum sacrorum omnes in urbe, in Italia, in Pannonia inventæ ea non instituta esse Deorum causa, sed ad funera curanda indicarent; ut in plerisque colligiis ex innumerabilibus quæ Deorum nomina præ se ferant eandem naturam latere facile suspicemur."

of religion, while they actually organized for economic, and social purposes."[47]

Fining members for multitudes of trivial offenses appears to have been sometimes carried to excess, and to an abuse,[48] carrying it to an extent that victims were condemned and their names were inscribed to their everlasting infamy. There is a monument of an eranos or thiasos at Trœzen showing fines paid to the goddess Cybele; but as she was a creature of ethereal imagination, the fines must have been paid to the society wherewith to defray their economic wants. The whippers of Athens enforced fines. Certain over zealous persons, in defense of the sanctity of the mysteries organized in the capacity of rhabdophores, and exacted fines from persons suspected of betraying the lictors' awful secrets, thus getting money.[49] The needs of these organizations for money as a means of existence was frequently so great, especially among the scenic actors who led a far more precarious life, that they may have sometimes abused their guaranteed powers and exacted fines out of proportion with the justice of the case.[50] Nevertheless every indication derived from their inscriptions proves that exact justice was meted out to their members and that everything was sedulously performed under the unalterable law. We now turn to the question of the ancient charity, to show how outrageously the word has been contorted.

There was no such thing as gift-giving or so-called charity recognized among the organized labor unions of the ancient lowly. The disgraceful and degrading eleemosynary scheme of proffer and alms, is the invention of church prelates but not of early Christianity. The myriad original unions into which the apostles planted Christianity wanted no charity. Each was a

[47] *Dig.*, XLVII., 11, *lex* 2. *De Extra Crim.* "Sub prætextu religionis vel sub specie solvendi voti, coetus illicitos nec a veteranis tentare oportet." The enactment of this statute shows how prone the unions were to shield themselves under the wings of any subterfuge.
[48] Foucart, *Ass. Rel.*, p. 23, cites lines 13-16, of his *inscr.* no. 4, p. 191: " Καθιστάτω δὲ ἡ ἀεὶ λανχάνουσα ἰέρεια ζάκορον ἐκ τῶν ἰερειῶν τῶν γεγενεων πρότερον. δὶς δὲ τὴν αὐτὴν μὴ ἐξεῖναι καταστῆσαι ἕως.... εἰ δέ μὴ, αἴτιος ἔστω" κτλ.
[49] Foucart, *Ass. Rel.*, p. 182: "Le γυναικόνομος, assisté de ῥαβδοφροὶ, a le droit de frapper et de punir d' une amende ceux qui causent quelque désordre ou enfreignent le réglement."
[50] Foucart, *De Scen. Artif.*, pp. 17-18: "Suffragiis designabantur ii quibus in externas civitates ad agendos senicos ludos eundum esset, mulcta mille drachmarum irrogata, si quis designatus imposito muneri deesset." *Vide* also p. 59.

microcosm of the forthcoming state which took care of the members, furnished them with work, kindness when sick, food at a common table like the typical father and mother, and burial with honors after their decease.

The good old Saint Augustine,[51] after more than 200 years of abuse of this term and of attempted malpractice against the principle, disgusted with their attendant failure, declares for the true old Christians who stuck to their first loves and tells us they were known at sight. "There is charity in their choice of diet; charity in their speech; charity in their dress; charity in their looks; at every point at which they meet, and plan, and act." It is plain by this, that the charity which, in the modern religion influencing our civilization, is made to assume the rôle of almsgiving, is not meant by St. Augustine who was disgusted. He meant and championed the word in its original and uncontorted definition, porting no such meaning as this modernized gorgon, which blights manhood and belittles labor under the ignominious proffer and recipiency of alms. The fact is, modern associated charities, so soon as it is discovered that prelates prostituting the church, are driving her paganward, out of her original economic design, will begin slowly to differentiate from the degrading eleemosynary idea, as now understood in its horrid, insulting deformity, into the ancient and honorable idea of manliness, natural to their methods of furnishing work.

The great unions we have so elaborately described were practically economical, and necessarily so under the Solonic law. This is everywhere acknowledged.[52] The eranos was not a charitable institution. Dr. Foucart, while trying to make himself believe that it was exclusively religious, seriously contradicts his own honest if not well-founded statements in showing that it was a strikingly business concern. There was no room for fakirs or loafers there. If a member without a satisfactory excuse established by law, failed to pay the sum periodically required for the common meal, he was uncompromisingly ejected.

[51] *Manichœan Heresy*, XXXIV., 73.
[52] Lüders, *Dionys. Künst.*, p. 2: " . . . . fanden sie doch in nächster Nähe eine in allen Einzelheiten ausgebildete practische Form von Vereinigungen vor, deren Hauptzüge sie nur herübernehmen und ihren Zwecken mit leichter Mühe anpassen Konnten. So verstehen wir leicht die Zusammenstellung in dem Solonischen Gesetz "

The natural outcome through the growth and spread of that vast movement, commencing in the mere microcosm, in form of the happy family and expanding into the union of many families with a tendency to become political and be the state which is the modern and correct theory of socialism, is to elevate, not to depress public dignity. It was contrary to manhood to receive any eleemosynary proffers, since labor is the source of all revenues of the family and of the wealth of nations. Charity then, is a direct blow against human dignity; and manhood cannot for a moment accept it only as a vile insult.[53] Labor creates everything and should logically have everything. To cringe to the paltry acceptance of gifts is to recognize the brigand as a factor in society. This brigand is the speculator upon labor's products. Charity therefore, is an unmanly acceptance of the rule of brigands who have gotten labor's products and thus robbed the producers of honorably created goods. To yield to this laborer, creator of all necessaries of life as the results of labor, and to punish the speculator as a common robber, was the ultimate tendency of the Solonic law. Speculation is at best but another phase of the ancient brigandage not yet outgrown. By the hand of socialism it has become stricken and is moribund.

We now come to speak of the forms of usage in vogue for the common table and the communal code of Solon. During the times in which this lawgiver lived there was a hall in Athens and in many other towns and cities in Greece where men of recognition could be offered food furnished at public expense. It was a public kitchen, supplied with the best cooks and the purest and choicest products of nature and of labor. This hall was the celebrated Prytaneum.[54] It was galaxied with statues of the great. Athens honored its marble tables containing the Solonic statutes, and it was the classic enclosure of

[53] Waltzing, *Hist. Corp. Prof.*, p. 302: ' On n' en trouve aucun example ni acune trace." This is in response to a previous remark in this same page, viz: "Ni les collèges funéraires, ni les collèges professionelles ne se proposaient un but charitable." Waltzing denies absolutely that the Roman associations practiced charity at all; and precisely the same must be said of the Greek societies.

[54] Oehler, in *Pauly Wissowa*, II., p. 1027, *sub verbo* Βουλή. "Ταμίας, des Prutaneions." He was held in close accountability and "τὰ κατὰ ψήφισματα ἀναλισκόμενα τῇ βουλῇ." These two ταμίαι are treasurers; and they also: "hatten die Kasse zu verwalten, aus der die Ausgaben für μισθὸς βουλευτικὸς, den Sold der Diener, die Kosten der Aufzeichnung der Ratsbeschlüsse und der Herrichtung gewissen Opfer bestritten wurden."

the true civilization of antiquity.[55] Thus the practice of meals in common, furnished by the state was not a new thing with the unions we are describing. It was long esteemed as a public dining hall, and thoroughly engrafted into the scheme of labor organizations, which had a house of their own, called an oikos.[56] In after years this oikos of the numberless unions became the kurioios, that is, the oikos with a presiding officer, of considerable power, crowned or garlanded for having been faithful for five years or more, and who functionated as a president of a union or guild. This officer in a great number of cases, was afterward awarded the dignity of a Christian bishop, on the absorption by the Christians; a subject remaining for another chapter.

The common table was once a great economic system of the ancient world. The celebrated plan of Lycurgus was based upon it. It is no new thing. It had been the successful plan which from time immemorial had kept the vast population of Crete alive. Cadmus had authorized it and it had succeeded. These men are still honored among the wisest lawyers the world ever produced. All was destined to succumb to the vilainous intrigues of the money power, jealous of every good which did not fill the individual's pocket or glut the ambition of monarchs.[57] Literature on this subject is not wanting, written by statesmen and philosophers of those and later times.[58] But not alone did the people enjoy the common table in Crete and Greece. It stretched to Magna Graecia in Lower Italy, especially the city of Crotona. This was a region, almost another Garden of Eden, where Pythagoras settled with his celebrated scheme, to emancipate the earth from dense ignorance and competition.[59]

In the temple of Jerusalem they had the common table,

[55] For something on this, see Foucart, *Ass. Rel.*, p. 45, quoting Hesychius, *Lexicon, in verb.* Θιασῶνες· οἶκοι ἐν οἷς συνιόντες δειπνοῦσιν οἱ θίασοι. Fouc., *id.*, says. "Des salles plus grandes destinées aux réunions de l' assemblée φιλοτίμως ὑπὲρ τοῦ οἴκου etc. Le Bas, *Attique*, no. 389; Pittakis, no. 2583.
[56] For the system pro and contra, of Lycurgus, see Vol. I., Chap. xxiv., *Final Review, Plans and Models*,
[57] Aristotle, *De Rep.*, II., 49. Bekker, Cf. Mommsen, *De Coll. et Sodal. Rom.*, p. 2: Οὐ καλῶς δ' οὐδὲ περὶ τὰ συσσίτια τὰ καλούμενα φιδίτια νενομοθέτηται (apud Lacedæmonios) τῷ καταστήσαντι πρῶτον· ἔδει γὰρ ἀπὸ κοινοῦ μᾶλλον εἶναι τὴν σύνοδον καθάπερ ἐν Κρήτῃ· παρὰ δὲ τοῖς Λάκωσιν ἕκαστον δεῖ φέρειν καὶ σφόδρα πενήτων ἐνίων ὄντων καὶ τοῦτο τὸ ἀνάλωμα οὐ δυναμένων δαπανᾶν.
[58] Am Rhyn, *Mysteria*, pp. 88-89, Eng. *trans*. "The Pythagorean League with its gymnastic exercises diligently practiced and made the cornerstone of his therapeutics, which, for the rest, was a science of dietetics. They had a common table."
[59] Josephus, *Wars*, II., viii., 5. Christianity took its earliest foothold there.

enjoyed by the Essenes and perhaps by many others.[60] This is a matter of history as any well-read scholar knows. But we doubt whether they were so well organized in the idea as the Pythagoreans, who had the syssitia with common meals and like the Numan scheme of the trade unions, were organized in companies of ten and divided into three classes: Acustici, Mathematici, Physici. They had secret, conventional symbols, by which members of the fraternity could recognize each other.[61] This interlinking of the brotherhoods was of value in carrying out commercial enterprises, and was enormously used by the Phœnicians in their colonization schemes. They could help each other in arranging and working the details of emigrations of which their wealthy colony at Putedi, near Naples is a fair example. St. Paul found a flourishing and wealthy colony in form of a genuine collegium there, on his way to Rome a prisoner bound and fettered; and we shall see that they, for some wonderful, unexplained reason, took him in, being Christians, and sent a strong delegation to escort him almost to the gates of Rome.

The societies of men and women, carrying on a trade acted differently from the trade unions of to-day. We once visited an organization of silk weavers at Valencia, Spain, which seemed to partake of the same nature as the ancients in point of common meals; for they were all interwoven so fondly, lovingly together that they had a dining hall, cooks, musicians and common entertainments. It was so in ancient Rhodes, the island in which innumerable inscriptions now prove a great movement to have once existed, but for some unaccountable reason cast off; perhaps by the Diocletian massacre or suppressed by conquest or other political convulsion. Great numbers of Rhodian inscriptions, however, are left, showing the once prosperous condition of that commercial island.

It was not an uncommon thing for boatmen and even ship owners to unite in each others interests in the same way, forming themselves into a thiasos, and have a common table, whither to assemble daily and take

---

[60] This is an extended argument for the high antiquity of Free Masonry. The signs were common to all the mysteries. Gould, *Free Masonry*, I., p. 20.
[61] Consult Vol. I., p. 169, note 10; Fou., *Ass. Rel.*, p. 43, citing no. 46. *lines* 20-24, says; "Pour les repas en commun, les members semblent avoir apporté leur part, d' abord en nature, puis en argent;" CIG. 2525 b.

meals together in common.⁶² Little difference existed between the methods of the various business or economic organizations under different names.⁶³

Then there were the "defiant comparisons" of good old Origen. He was a very thorough Greek scholar and for years of Christian prelacy, to which he was never fully admitted because of his honest doubtings, he advocated truth.⁶⁴ This great man saw the economy in the syssitia whose common table originated in the old Prytaneum of the Solonic time.

Now it is necessary to constantly recur to the fact that all these Solonic unions of trades and professions were modeled after the ancient city; and that the ancient city had its *Prytaneion* with a typical common table and common meals.⁶⁵ It was the very cœnobium, of which so much was said in ancient times.⁶⁶ The common table of the thiasos and all other ancient unions of this economic nature were borrowed from the prytaneum, instituted by Solon. Dr. Oehler's valuable article in Pauly-Wissowa, entitled "*Boule*," to which we have referred, makes it clear that there was a close relationship

---

⁶² Lüders, *Dionys. Künst.*, p. 32, cites one at Athens, where the members lived, called ἡ σύνοδος τοῦ Διὸς ξενίου τῶν ἐμπόρων καὶ ναυκλήρων, house and ship-owners or builders.

⁶³ Some light is thrown on this curious subject by Dr. Lightfoot in his work on the *Colossians*, p. 357, where thiasotes, essenes, therapeutæ and probably the collegia appear reconciled in the *Mishna Pirke Aboth*, V., 10; whence Dr. Lightfoot quotes the significant words: "He who says mine is thine and thine is mine is chasid;" ie: an initiated fellow of the brotherhood. Gratz, III., 81 and 467, makes the reading of this celebrated communistic clause to be as here stated, and it is also so admitted by Keim. It stands this way twice on one page in the *Mishna*.

⁶⁴ Origen, *Adversus Celsum*, III., 29-30, where he compares the Christian communal system with the original Athenian city, and its Prytaneum, communal code of Solon, and common meals.

⁶⁵ Oehler, in *Pauly-Wissowa*, III., p, 1026; Am Rhyn, *Mysteria*, p. 80, on the Pythagorean League: "This institution called the κοινωνίον (cœnobium, a place where people live in community), was a world in itself, and embraced all the conveniences of plain living—gardens, groves, promenades, halls, baths, etc., so that the students did not regret the hurly-burly of the outside world. Henceforth the Ἀκουσματικοί, or acustici were no longer persons of all classes and degrees but newly admitted pupils," etc.

⁶⁶ The Prytaneum of the official city was an eating house, owned and operated by the city itself; Athens especially. Dittenberger, *De Epheben Atticis*, p. 23; Lüders, *Dionys. Künst.*, p. 39; Liddell, in *verb.* Πρυτανεῖον; This last admits that earlier, the Prytaneum was a public communistic eating-house and existed in the country towns as well as Athens; "'Ἐν πρυτανείῳ ἐδείπνουν, ἐσιτοῦντο. Ar. *Pac.*, 1084; Plat. *Apol.*, 36. It was a "penetrale urbis, ubi publice, quibus is honos datus est, vescuntur." Livy, XLI., 20. From its name it is evident that the sacred fire was kept forever burning. The Prytaneum was consecrated to Vesta. At Athens it was called Θόλος, a rotunda for the common kitchen; Böckh, CIG. 3173, like εἰσηλύσιν, sacrificia introitus; see Solon, in Inscr. of Rhegium, Orell., 3838; Lüders, *Dionys. Künst.* p. 39, compares the similar εἰσιτήρια of the θίασος, with the Prytaneum. It is derived from Solon, who made it a public kitchen, or coöperative eating-house.

in the manner of initiating the system by the unions. But in doing so the society was to imagine itself the city or state in miniature. It was a microcosmic state; for inasmuch as the state supported the prytanic kitchen by levying taxes against the people, so the miniature state, the union had to levy dues from its members. It was therefore, far more democratic and just than the official or state prytanea; for it took from each alike, and fed them all, without exception, a thing which the public kitchens did not do.[67] This fact is delightfully shown by Aristotle, who has often a kind word for the poor.[68] The truth is, the grasping propensity of mankind has always stood in the way against carrying out this plan. The original prytanic system of Solon was good for the common people, especially applicable to the thiasitic organizations; but it was not long before it began to be abused. Dr. Lüders shows how this took place at Athens. They turned it into an aristocracy, making the labor of the very poor who were ruled out of its enjoyments, pay the expenses of gluttony at the common table. The aristocrats soon enacted a law excluding all but high-borns from participation at this great and economical source of public comfort.[69] The serpent of avarice and selfishness got his monstrous head into this beautiful system of the people,

It has been affirmed by many that the main pillar of Christianity rests upon that important, original promise, that the seed of woman should bruise the serpent's head. Its original plan for bruising his head was by bringing man under a communal inter-acting, inter-loving fraternity with all things common. But it lived only under the secret unions. This plan was not only spiritual but economical, which at that day had to be densely secret; and it failed temporarily in the fourth century, because it was subjected to the temptations of avaricious reptiles; men of luxury who transformed Christ's original plant-

[67] Lüders, *Dionys. Künst.*, p. 6, gives us assurance that the eranos furnished its members not only food and drink, but also "Alles andere zum Schmuck oder zur Bequemlichkeit Taugliche von den Theilnehmren zusammen getragen wurde."

[68] Ethics, VIII., 11: "Ἔνιαι δὲ τῶν κοινωνιῶν δι' ἡδονὴν δοκοῦσι γίγνεσθαι, θιασωτῶν καὶ ἐρανιστῶν· αὗται γὰρ θυσίας ἕνεκα καὶ συνουσίας," κτλ.

[69] Lüders *Dionys. Künst.*, p. 18, explains that there were twelve pure or fullblooded citizens, who "allmonatlich im Heiligthum des Herakles speisten und Parisiten genannt wurden." It became an aristocratic θίασος whose members got the privilege of partaking at this public institution, elegant and fashionable meals which were prepared and paid for by the true workers who were barred out. These were the original parasites.

ing into a hierarchy of wealth and luxury hunters. They became disgusting parasites, and in fact gave origin to the word.[70] All along the line this aristocratical grasping undermined the beautiful socialism engrafted by the law of Solon.[71] The reason so much was said about the Law of Moses being supplanted by some new, unexplained dispensation, appears to be that this Solonic dispensation which took its root in the prytanic eating house, was intended by Stephen,[72] and all the early practical economic Christians, to supplant Moses in Solon.

We have at this moment an occasional divine who has enough penetration to fully understand socialism such as was wrapped up in the secret depths of the Mosaic dispensation; but they know little or nothing about the socialism of Solon, believing that it is all in-woven into the impenetrable vortex of Mosaism. A more radical mistake cannot be comprehended. The good and pure Bishop of Durham, has expressed some living, ascendant thoughts, in saying: "Men suffering and rejoicing together when each touches all and all help each with a practical influence, teaching that as we live *by* others we can find no rest till we can live *for* others."

The system of common tables and pleasure banquets constantly shows forth in the inscriptions, and we have the great authority of Dirksen, that it was regularly endorsed and upheld by the Twelve Tables of Rome.[73] especially favoring those trade unions of Numa and Servius Tullius, who made for the Roman army the munitions of war. They were employed by the state in

[70] Lüders *Dionys. Künst.*, p. 19: "Denen die Ehre zu Theil wurde vom Staate zu solchen Parasiten gewählt zu werden, war es gestattet, auch ihre heranwachsenden Söhne am mahle Theil nehmen zu lassen." And quotes Isae., *De Astyph. Her.*, 30: 'Εἰς τοίνυν τὰ ἱερὰ ὁ πατηρ ὁ ἐμὸς τὸν 'Αστύφιλον παῖδα ἦγε μεθ' ἑαυτοῦ ὥσπερ καὶ ἐμὲ πενταχῇ, καὶ εἰς τοὺς θιάσους τοὺς Ἡρακλέους ἐκεῖνον εἰσήγαγς, ἵνα μετέχοι τῆς κοινωνίας· αὐτοὶ δ' ὑμῖν οἱ θιασῶται μαρτυρήσουσιν.

[71] Acts, Chapter VII.

[72] Ducange, *Judæa*, V. on *Socialism of the Hebrews*, attempts to show that their socialism meant, first give to kings everything and leave it to their magnanimity to distribute the goods back to the people! It went no higher than kingly power, and consequently must fall: "Judæus vero nihil proprium habere potest, quia quicquid acquirit, non sibi acqurit, sed regi, quia non vivunt sibi ipsis, sed aliis, et sic aliis acquirunt, et non sibi ipsis." Thus the Hebrew is a socialist through the Mosaic law. What kills it all is, he is infatuated with the idea of kings. Such a believer is always known by his spirit cringing before the gloze of power and majesty.

[73] Oehler, *MSS*: "Die συσσίτοι kommen als staatliche Einrichtungen zunächst nicht in Betracht; wohl aber ist zu erwähnen eine Frustück gesellschaft συνάριστων, in Nisyros. Hiller in der *Wochenschrift für Class. Philol.*, 1896, nr. 3; Sparta, 80, und eine Schmausgesellschaft χοῦς, Panormos bei Kyzikos; Ziebarth, p. 66, :'

large force, especially during the conquests as we have elaborately explained.[72]

We close this section of our chapter by reminding the reader that evidences exist proving that the great economies accruing in favor of the organized workers who adopted this system, so enraged the speculators making money by the exploiture of labor, that they mutilated, and sometimes burned the books that contained accounts of the abundance which the system yielded. One of the saddest losses to future humanity is that of the work of Papias the Apostle of Hierapolis and Laodicea and probably also of Colossæ; friend of Paul and powerful orator, who is well known to have written a valuable work now believed to be irretrievably lost. It is known by a few fragments which escaped vandalism,[73] that this good man wrote out a full schedule of the economies which come from entirely dispensing with middlemen, contractors and speculators and having the work of supply, both of production and distribution, performed by, and for, society in common.[74] We shall later speak of it again. It is sufficient here to say that, although there appears to be much secrecy and very little written record of the fate of these unions practicing the economics which flow from their system, and of course, no inscriptions to elaborate the tale, the canons of the Council of Laodicea of A.D. 363 are extant; and one of them is the fatal document which extinguished the practice, and left the ancient lowly to struggle and die, without even the privilege of longer organizing for self-sustenance and happiness.[75]

[72] We have already, I., p. 335, quoted the words of Dirksen on this subject, as given by Mommsen. Waltzing, *Hist. Corp Prof.* I., p. 163. note 1, also says: "Dirksen, disait déjà; 'Ursprünglich hat der römische Staat lediglich denjenigen Gewerben, welche den Bedürfnissen des krieges und des Gottesdienstes zunächst fröhnten, seinen unmittelbaren Schutz und eine selbstständige communalverfassung bewilligt."

[73] See *supra*, chap. I., *Solitudo Magistratuum*.

[74] Irenæus, *Adv. Hær.* V., xxxiii., 4, gives us a few fragments from this work which though written in the apostolic age, was still extant when Irenæus wrote.

[75] *Canon* 55, Vol. II., p. 574 Mansi: ὅτι οὐ δεῖ ἱερατικοὺς ἢ κληρικοὺς ἐκ συμβολῆς συμπόσια ἐπιτελεῖν, ἀλλ' οὐδὲ λαικούς. These few words signify much. By these words Christianity became a despotism.

CHAPTER XIV.

POLITICAL FUNCTIONS.

THE ANCIENT VOTING UNIONS.

POLITICAL Functions—The Oath of Dreros in Crete—"Dangerously Political" is Aristotle's Shibboleth—Strange Clause in Solonic Law on Corsair Trade—Rite of Baptism Originated among them—Was for Cleanliness—Members to be Pure and Clean—Against Leprosy—Tyrannos, the Pedagogue—Sabazian Thiasos—Trouble between Æschines and Demosthenes—Hadrian's Letter on the Mithraic Christians—Hierophant—Sabbath a Strictly Union Rite—Pagan Labor Year 365 Days—Love Feasts—Eight Hours Day—Synod—Congregations—Symposiums—Cremation—Cinerary Urns—Rosalia—Day of Violets—Hallelujah—Kathegemon or Forerunner—Thought to Resemble John the Baptist—The Mageireion or Common Kitchen—Public Cookshop—Resembled Grenoble—The Rule of Proxy—Functions of the Kurios or Lord-Dictator—Discovery of Dual Habits—Untwists a Curious Clause of Solon's Law—Evidence that it Stretched to Ceylon—Irrigation—System of Crowns—Crowns of Willow, Wild Olive, Tulip, Gold—The Thallou Stephanos—Crowning the Dead—Statistics of Wages from their own Inscriptions—Day's Pay for Plowmen—Cleaning—Woodwork Polishing—Hod Carriers—Mechanics—Difference between Pay of Organized and Unorganized Workmen—Dr. Maury's Researches—Statistics of Cost of Living—How Slaves as Tools of Labor Competed with Free Work—Human Machines—Pitted Slave Against Union Labor—List and Prices of Slaves—Asylums of Refuge but No Hospitals—Purchased Slaves in Order to Set them Free—Edict of Prices of Diocletion—Ideas of a Vast Workshop in the Beyond—The Demiourgos.

A SPECIAL chapter will now be necessary showing the political power and importance of the Solonic unions. We have already seen how political action permeated every tissue from the highest antiquity; and their enormous influence through the ballot, especially in voting into office the commisioners of public works, thus securing for the voting unions a pledge of an award of the public employment not only in towns and cities but on the great highways called itineraries or government military roads. Dr. Oehler in the appended note,[1] mentions certain inscriptions proving balloting activities which, as Aristotle hints, were "dangerously political."

The inscriptions are not only those of the unions who, promise to be good but of their enemies, who call them conspirators, and force them to swear oaths that they will abstain from political broils; as much as to say the unions were threatened against political action. Thus they were constantly girded about with lowering hostilities and afraid of assuming rights guaranteed them by the jus coeundi of Solon. All along it is observed that the wealthy opposed them; and the historians remind us of danger in the political action of these unions, and many laws were enacted for their suppression.[2]

There is a strange passage in the jus coeundi, translated, into the Latin and engraved upon one of the Twelve Tables, which has called forth a great deal of comment. It is the clause permitting the corsair business among other legitimate trades and professions, embracing brotherhoods of trade unions like orgeons, thiasotes and collegia, organized by sailors, shippers and people who live on the seas. In the corsair trade were people organized for burial purposes and those combining with one another in several crafts or professions.[3] The singular course referred to is that permitting and legalizing the privateering business; something akin to piracy, which in early times was practiced on the seas. Solon instituted the jus coeundi, as generally thought, nearly a thousand years before Christ. At the time

[1] Oehler, *MSS.;* "Aus Aristoteles, *Pol.,* VIII., (vulgo, V.) c. 6, wissen wir, dass die Mitglieder der Hetairien einen Eid leisteten. Ich möchte hier nur einige Inschriften anführen, in denen solcher politischer Vereine Erwähnung geschiet. In dem Eide von Dreros auf Kreta ist die Bestimmung enthalten: μηδὲ συνωμοσίας συναξεῖν, *Museo Italiano,* III., p. 657, no. 73ᵇ., vgl. auch ᶜ. In Itanos lesen wir in dem Eide der Bürger: οὐδὲ σύλλογον οὐδὲ συνωμοσίαν ποιησέω ἐπὶ τῷ κακίονι τᾶς πόλεως ἢ τῶν πολιτῶν, οὐδὲ ἄλλῳ συνεσσέομαι οὐδενί· Erwahnt werden συνομοσίαι in einer Inschrift aus Kythraea auf Kypros; Le Bas. III., 1212: καταλύσαντα συνωμοσίαν μεγάλην τὰ μάλιστα λυποῦσαν τὴν πόλιν.

[2] Suetonius, *Jul. Cæs..* 42, says this potentate broke up all except the older ones: "Cuncta collegia praeter antiquitus constituta, distraxit."

[3] *Digest,* XLVII., 22, 4. ἐὰν δὲ δῆμος ἢ φράτορες ἢ ἱερῶν ὀργίων ἢ ναῦται ἢ σύνσιτοι ἢ ὁμόταφοι ἢ θιασῶται ἢ ἐπὶ λίαν οἰχόμενοι ἢ εἰς ἐμπορίαν. ὅ τι ἂν τούτων διαθῶνται πρὸς ἀλλήλους, κύριον εἶναι ἐὰν μὴ ἀπαγορεύσῃ δημόσια γράμματα.

BAD LAW ALLOWING PIRACY.   281

Thucydides wrote his histories, about B.C. 398, the corsair business was still legal, and considered by many to be respectable; for he has a remarkable passage over which modern scholars are stumbling.[4] More than 200 years afterwards, from Polybius to Nero, the seas still swarmed with legalized pirates,[5] and some 70 years B.C., Rome sent Pompey the Great to destroy them. The best information at command assures us that this brigandage was originally authorized by the ancient jus coeundi; but that it was absurd and finally suppressed. Piracy or at least privateering, was certainly permitted by this clause of the Solonic law.[6]

These Solonic unions were the originators of the rite of baptism which formerly contained the idea of cleanliness embraced in "hagnos" clean, pure, "washed" standing as the first of the three cardinal words through which every candidate had to be passed in the scrutiny of the dokimasia. Although almost entirely economical, most of them being guilds, keenly business-like, and thus the providing of plentitude always uppermost in their minds, still they had religious habits and religious reverence, like all other humanity of the ancient world. One of the religio-economical rites, from time immemorial was baptism. It was originally a habit of cleanliness. This was so important as a source of health that they used it primarily as a cleansing ordeal of the body and consequently baths were the popular fixture of the unions, each of whose temples had one. For this reason more than any other the habit of copious ablutions became a part of the initiations.

It is known that early Christians could not get into the occult penetralia until they became initiates; and that baptism was the first principal rite of this initiation.[7] The ancient religion commanded cleanliness among its first requirements. The prehistoric man was a sloven; he lived in caves, grass, sod, or bamboo huts,

[4] Thucydides, *De Bello Peloponnesiaco*, I,, cap. 5: Οὐκ ἔχοντός πω αἰσχύνην τούτου τοῦ ἔργου, φέροντος δέ τι καὶ δόξης μᾶλλον· δηλοῦσί δὲ τῶν τε ἠπειρωτῶν τινες ἔτι καὶ νῦν, οἷς κόσμος καλῶς τοῦτο δρᾶν καὶ οἱ παλαιοὶ τῶν ποιητῶν, τὰς πύστεις τῶν καταπλεόντων πανταχοῦ ὁμοίως ἐρωτῶντες εἰ λησταί εἰσιν, ὡς οὔτε ὧν, κ.τ.λ.

[5] Polybius, *Histories*, II., chap. 8: Κοινῇ μὲν, ἔφη, πειρᾶσθαι φροντίζειν, ἵνα μηδὲν ἀδίκημα γίνεθαι 'Ρωμαίοις ἐξ' Ἰλλυριῶν ἰδία γε μήν, οὐ νόμιμον εἶναι τοῖς βασιλεῦσι κωλεύειν Ἰλλυριοὺς τῆς κατὰ θάλατταν ὠφιλείας.

[6] Lüders *Dionys. Künst.*, p. 5; where nearly a page is devoted to its explanation: Böckh, *Staats Havshaltung*, I , 762; Lobec. *Aglaoph.*, p. 305.

[7] For a good illustration of this, see the *Recognitions* of Clement of Rome, We shall quote from this remarkable document hereafter.

among vermin and amid indecencies and filth. Baptism and its ablutions were but an innovation of human civilization, and trade unionism as it built up the instrumentalities of advancement, naturally built baths[8] and many other fixtures of cleanliness. Search as we may, baptism did not originate with the Hebrew. It is first found as an initiatory rite of these organizations as a part of their formula of purification. Except as found among the unions or brotherhoods, as confraternities under the jus coeundi, whether Greek, Roman, essenic Hebrew, or therapeutic Egyptian, there appear to have existed no baptismal rites.[9] The rite of baptism as practiced by Christians is derived from them; and they assuredly used it early as one of the main features of initiations into their brotherhoods, at first secret, obscure and impenetrable. Originally, among the practical ancient fathers organized under the Solonic arrangement, the people used baptism as an ablution for cleanliness, and it was a principal feature of initiation into their brotherhoods. There is important evidence given in hints thrown out here and there, showing that they would not take diseased persons, affected with leprosy or other scrofulous ailments which water could not cure. Members must be pure; and purity was meant physically, spiritually. There is an important hint of this kind in the writings of Theophrast who succeeded Aristotle in the celebrated Academy at Athens and who wrote and taught at that seminary,[10] to the effect that no baptism, no lustration, and no permit to enter the temple was allowed, unless the candidate be clean. Persons afflicted with leprosy, or of another scrofulous disease supposed to be syphilis, could not be baptized.

Again, morally, no person who had committed murder could be baptized, or enter the sanctuary.[11] These restrictions are given in the inscription of Xanthos, slave

[8] Demosthenes, *Pro Corona*, § 259, speaks of the religious methods of the θιασῶται, and of course, rails at their baptism and prayer, because desiring only to defeat Æchines, his antagonist, and make a martyr of his mother, the organizer, who was an initiate. See *infra*, chap. xv.

[9] See *Encyc. Amer.*; Meyers, *Konv. Lexikon*; *Encyc. Brit.*; Chambers *Cyclopædia*; La Russe, *Dict. Universel*, on *Baptism*, regarding which there is, historically speaking, a general agreement.

[10] Theophrast., *Characters*: Κἂν ποτε ἐπίδη σκορόδῳ ἐστεμμένον τῶν ἐπι τας τριόδους ἐπελθόντων, κατὰ κεφαλῆς λουσασθαι.

[11] Le Bas and Waddington, *Inscr. d' Asie Mineure*, nos. 667-9: 680, 684, Foucart, *Ass. Rel.*, p. 126, note 1, mentions that this is not the only evidence, but that at Méonie restrictions against impurity are given in the inscription found there.

of one Orbius, who built the temple of Men Tyrannos. There is something wonderful about this Tyrannos, a sort of mystic god-pedagogue supposed of late to be connected with the Tyrannos of the Ephesian schools, and mentioned by Paul.

This baptism which was an early rite of initiation and test of purity, in later times differentiated into what is known as the ordeal of conversion of the present day.[12] The archaic pre-Christian baptists are found by consulting the inscriptions and other early literature to have originated in the Solonic communities. The rite is found among the Thracian Kotytto Baptæ, a guild at Philippi; among the Sabazian hetairæ in Asia Minor mostly Phrygian; among the essenes of Palestine, and the therapeutæ of Egypt. The allusions of Demosthenes regarding baptism cannot mean the lustrations of the official initiations of which he boasts over Æschines, who with his mother, is of poor stock. The orator means the Sabazian thiasos; and the offense is, that the mother had introduced strange, illicit practices into Athens, which were demoralizing the public ethics of the city.[13] The difference between the aristocratic gradations of mankind shown in this renowned speech, the Pro Corona, of Demosthenes, whereby we are informed of the impassable gulf separating rich from poor, exalted from lowly, and non-citizen from official life, is valuable. Æschines was a member of a thiasos and a worshiper of Eros the god of love. So was Socrates, now thought the greatest of good men Æschines was brave and eloquent, a full match for his adversary, and might have overthrown him had he had a sympathetic audience. Herein lies Demosthenes victory. His sallies against the poor man excited all the glee which wells up from prejudiced, ready-made minds. His most effective and brilliant execrations rise little above low blackguard. His vaunted mockery, imitating the cry of initiations into the lowly occultism of the secret Sabazian thiasos,

[12] *Apostolic Constitutions*, VII., 40, on the initiation of the Catechumens or Amateurs.

[13] Dübner, in the *Didot Edition* of Theophrast, calls these Asiatic ablutionists and Phrygian baptists, poor devils, in rendering into Latin Theophrast's talk about them, quoted in note 87, *supra*, as follows: "Et si quando eorum qui ad trivia accedere solent quempiam allio coronatum conspicit, aqua in caput aspersa, se lustrat;" which Dr. Foucart, p. 125, translates very freely Si par hazard, il voit manger de l' ail à un de ces pauvres diables (referring to the incident of Stilpon), qui rôdent sur les carrefours, il se burine en se versant de l eau sur la tête."

and his indecent allusions to the benevolent lady, and worse still, a purloinage from the secret ritual, were all sponged by his hired Pinkertons whom the state at his instance had fed at the prytaneum and paid with tap conjured from the poor. But Demosthenes could not deny that he himself was an initiate; and here is the point we wish to prove; that the gap separating the poor man's thiasos from the official assembly of the Greeks was as wide as the tantalizing distinction between Demosthenes and Æschines themselves. The official initiation was a great thing but the initiation into the thiasos was a crime; and it may yet come to light that this was the crime of Socrates.[14] It appears that the attack on Æschines is of more importance than generally supposed. He was a man of much education, political strength and ability and he had a philosophy embodying agitation of the socialistic principles as advocated by his thiasitic order. He had a book containing the mysteries of the "immutable law." The baptism of purification was read from this book; and the reading from it was the crime of Æschines.[15]

Connected with the Macedonian Kotytto, mother of baptism there are some curious things. It appears from Strabo that she came from Phrygia and was but another personification of Cybele, the mother of the gods.[16] It is now proved beyond contradiction that the good Christians planted in the mellow, co-sympathetic soil of these innumerable economic unions. But as their moral culture was of a purer and higher nature they found fault with certain abominations.[17] These baptists were dippers, like John who was the typical forerunner of Jesus, just as Dionysus Kathegemon was the recognized forerunner of some unknown messiah that was to come, but,

[14] Hermann, *Political Assemblies of the Greeks*, Oxford, 1836, p. 254, shows that they had similar initiations, opened the aristocratic meetings by prayer and baptized by means of lustrations: Oehler, *Pauly Wisowa*, βουλή.
[15] This book is thought to have contained the instruction on sacrifices, Foucart, *Ass. Rel.*, p. 14. There is evidence that reforms were cultivated. The thiasos always held complete control. The ἐπιμελητής convoked the assembly on the 2d day of each month to deliberate on the common interest, see *inscr.* 2, of Foucart, p. 189. Propositions for discussion had to be written out and come in proper order, and they had decrees and laws regulating them.
[16] Strabo, *Geog.*, X., 111. 16; "Ταῦτα γὰρ ἔοικε τοῖς φρυγίοις· καὶ οὐκ ἀπεικός γε, ὥσπερ αὐτοὶ οἱ φρύγες Θρακῶν ἄποικοί εἰσιν, οὕτω καὶ τὰ ἱερὰ ἐκεῖθεν μετενηνέχθαι,"
[17] These pagan immodesties clung to the habits and customs of the devotees of Cotytto; Juvenal in a *Satire* says: "Talia secreta coluerunt orgia tæda. Cecropiam soliti Baptæ lassare Cotytto." *Sat.*, II., v., 92.

as it appears, never did come unless it was in the person of our own Saviour.

Baptists of Cotytto, having their sanctuary in Macedonia, had a very powerful colony at Corinth. The trouble which the pure and virtuous Paul had with them there, will be the subject of a future disquisition in this work. Suffice it to say here that it is well-known Bible history.

We cannot break away from this theme of the lascivious baptist Cotytto, without quoting from a fragment which has escaped destruction. It was written by the early poet Æschylus, who 470 years before Christ, wrote a tetralogy now lost, but of which a few fragments remain.[18]

Another author, one of our own modern days, has looked up this subject of the baptists, and tried to penetrate all its obscurities. This is Ernest Renan, of the French Academy. Speculating on the origin of the word and the deed, Renan says: What was Sabianism? What its etymology indicates: baptism itself; that is, the religion of frequent washings and foundation of the sect still in existence, called the Christians of St. John; in other words, Mendaites, and which the Arabs call "el Mogtasila, the baptists." Renan sees such an analogy between these religions of baptism that he is confounded when he places their abode "beyond the Jordan," where the essenes lived. Did Renan know anything of the baptæ of Macedonia, of Corinth, of all the eranists, hetaeræ and therapeutæ? Or that he was dealing with a great, ancient, secret cult, embracing millions of people, covering millions of square miles? He sees a most singular problem, and there he stops! Renan knows nothing of the far-reaching Solonic scheme that was to supersede the law of Moses.

The persecution of Æschines and attempted martyrdon of Glaucothea, his mother, on account of introduc-

[18] Aeschylus, *Fragmenta,* 2, 3:—
'Ο μέν ἐν χερσὶν βόμβυκας ἔχων
τόρνου κάματον
δακτυλόδικτον πίμπλησι μέλος,
μανίας ἐπαγωγὸν ὁμολάν,
ὁ δὲ χαλκοδέτοις κοτύλαις ὀτοβεῖ.
. . . . Ψάλμος δ' ἀλαλάζει,
ταυρόφθογγοι δ' ὑπομυκῶνται
ποθὲν ἐξ ἀφανοῦς φοβεροὶ μῖμοι,
τυμπάνου δ' εἰκὼν ὥσθ' ὑπογαίου
βροντῆς φέρεται βαρυταρβής.
Juvenal, *Satyr.*, II., v., 92; quoted *supra*, note 16.

ing the baptist labor unions into Athens, form an epoch in ancient history. This was a movement involving much discussion and agitation on lines almost directly harmonious with the Christianity foretold by the great cult of the martyred Dionysus, forerunner of some saviour never mentioned and never known.[19] Of the Hemero baptists or hand-to-mouth baptists that occasionally crop out, we shall speak later. Apuleius a half Christianized pagan, is known to have been baptized and initiated into the mysteries of Isis, the Egyptian goddess of Mithraic Christianity;[20] which the emperor Hadrian in a letter to the consul Servianus, after investigating his subject with care both by himself and his agents, at Alexandria, declares to be one and identical.[21] Neander renders this growingly famous letter to read as follows: "Those who worship Serapis are Christians; and those who call themselves bishops of Christ, are worshipers of Serapis. There is no ruler of a synagogue, no Samaritan, no presbyter of the Christians who is not an astrologer or soothsayer." This letter from a great emperor shows for itself; and Neander declares it is genuine. The most prominent feature of the Sabazian and Sarapian cult, from at least 400 years before Christ was that of baptism.[22] The celebrated anecdote of what took

[19] There are two Latin inscriptions Heuzey et Daumet, *Mission Archéologique de Macedoine,* p. 152, which mention the thiasoi of the free father Tasibastinos; and Alexander Polyhister, whose work is conserved by Macrobius, *Saturnal.,* I., 18, talks of them: "In Thracia eundem haberi solem atque liberum accipimus, quem illi Sabadium nuncupantes magnifica religione celebrant, ut Alexander scribit."

[20] There are found occasional crispy notes by reliable authors, on the origin of the baptists: Dr. Oehler, *MSS.* says: "Die Originen der Kotytto waren der Vereinszweck der Βάπται, gegen die Eupolis sein gleichnamiges Stück geschrieben, Koch, I., pp. 68-69. Vgl. Lobeck, *Aglaoph.,* p. 1039." Andrews, *Lex.,* in verb. *Baptae, arum,* Priestess of the Thracian, afterwards Athenian goddess Cotytto, whose festival was celebrated in a most lewd manner. Again, Clement of Alex., who was baptized, divulges as follows: "I have eaten out of the drum, I have drunk out of the cymbal, I have carried the κέρνος ; I have slipped into the bedroom," etc. *Protrept.,* 2. Alcibiades was also an initiate.

[21] Neander, *Hist. Church,* Eng. trans., I., pp. 102, notes the Saturninus, of Flavius Vopsicus, cap. 8, who gives the letter: "Illi qui Serapem colunt Christiani sunt, et devoti sunt Serapi qui se Christi episcopos dicunt. nemo illic ἀρχισυναγώγος Judæorum, nemo Samarites, nemo Christianorum presbyter non mathematicus, non haruspex, non aleptes."

[22] Some rather indecent stories have got mixed up with this, Jove, Zeus, Jupiter, the father of Dionysos, who was Σαβάζιος, or Βάκχος, all of whom are found to be one, according to country and dialect. Jove's incest with his daughter Persephone, which was celebrated, is neatly described by Diodorus, IV., 4, as taking place at the epoptæ of the Sabazian initiation, and more fully dwelt upon by Eusebius, *Præpar. Evangel.,* II., 2, and the *Protrept* of Clement, produced Sabazios, or Dionysos, who was the patron deity of the thiasoi, eranoi and orgeons. He was the protector of the technical artists who were immensely and jealously organized. See note 23.

place once at the initiation is given by a reliable ancient writer.[23]

The gulf separating the official from the Sabazian mysteries and their baptismal rites was deep, wide and impassable. The Sabazian cult was that of the poor and lowly and established expressly for them. Why do the ante-nicene fathers talk so much about the initiations of the Sabazios? As early as Aristophanes, Diagoros of Melos, who hated the aristocratic Eleusinia, talked and wrote of the Sabazian mysteries whose principal rite was baptism and purification. His books are lost, but they were used and quoted by Clement and form to this day instructive reading.[24] We have the authority of Am Rhyn that among the fabulous personages of antiquity known to have been initiated and baptized were Orpheus, Musæus and Homer; and among the historical characters, were the lawgivers Lycurgus and Solon,[25] if not Amasis and Numa. Our valuable scientific friend Dr. Johann Oehler, who is short, crisp and practical, assures us regarding many epitaphs which have come to light showing fresh evidence regarding these historical phenomena, has sent us a MS. from his own generous pen, showing the inscriptions to abound with proofs of our foregoing statements.[26] There was something awfully mysterious and attractive about the mysteries we have described. There was the anointment by their hierophant which was applied while singing the dirge embodying the words: "Take courage O ye initiates of God whom we have saved! For to us there is deliverance from our struggling labors." In the agony, according to the cult, a god was tortured, and saved by resurrection; and this idea of the resurrection, always accompanied by that of baptism was in the world and very popular at least 400 years before Christ the anointed

---

[23] Diod., IV., 4: Μυθολογοῦσι δέ τινες καὶ ἕτερον Διόνυσον γεγονέναι πολὺ τοῖς χρόνοις προτεροῦντα τούτου. Φασὶ γὰρ ἐκ Διὸς καὶ Περσεφόνης Διόνυσον γενέσθαι τὸν ὑπό τινων Σαβάζιον ὀνομαζόμενον οὗ τήν τε γένεσιν καὶ τὰς θυσίας καὶ τιμὰς νυκτερινὰς καὶ κρυφίους παρεισάγουσι διὰ τὴν αἰσχύνην τὴν ἐκ τῆς συνουσίας ἐπακολουθοῦσαν.

[24] Firmicius, Cap. 2: Heuzey et Daumet, *Un Palais Grec en Macedoine*. p. 30; *Mission Archéologique de Macedoine;* Consult Lundy, *Monumental Christianity*, p. 385; *Anacalypsis*, II., p. 69.

[25] Am Rhyn, *Mysteria*, Eng. trans., p. 21.

[26] Oehler, *MSS*: "In Nicomedia wird ein ἀρχιμύστης διὰ βίον erwähnt, GIG. 3773; aus Ormele sind uns Vergleichnisse des Ζεὺς Σαβάζιος erhalten, Sterett, im *Epigr. Journ.* no. 44, Bis 46. Der Mysten Verein in Poimanenon begrub seine Verstorbmen Mitglieder auf gemeinsame Kosten, *Athen. Mith.*, IX., 1884, p. 35."

came to a similar torture for the salvation of mankind. In the more ancient rite of baptism and initiation, the theory which attracted the theatre goers was that of the agonies. Many efforts under the cognomen of passion plays, have been made of late years by the Roman catholics to restore the ancient agonies, but in vain. The popularity of the beautiful deaths of Dionysus, Sabazius, Attys, and Sarapis, who died to redeem mankind, have been so completely outgrown that living humanity instinctively classes it all among superstitions, for they led the mazy wanderers through the darkness of Tartarus over the lurid rivers of death and finally into the divine splendors of Elysium.[26]

Another of the humane and lasting rites which hopefully are never to pass away, was the observance of the ancient Sabbath.[27] Like baptism it was a rite of an economical sort, and was not derived from the Hebrews, who observed another day of rest. It belongs strictly to the unions of the jus coeundi of Solon. Under the the old pagan régime there was no Sunday. Labor was exacted, according to Böckh, 360 days in the year. The trade unions did better and more humanely; for they were required, by their constitution under penalty, to observe Sundays as days of rest. Neander, in his penetrating and very honest manner has tried to clear up the points of the ancient Sabbath. Admitting that they observed the day, he says of the early Christians: "They did not choose the Sabbath which the Jewish Christians celebrated."[28] In another place this accurate investigator says: "I find no evidence of a religious distinction of Sunday." It is perfectly evident that the extraordinary religious sanctity of the Sabbath is an excrescence swelling the hypocritical piety of prelates of later centuries; for at the time of Ignatius "every friend of Christ was to keep the Lord's day as a

[26] The dirge chanted by the initiates during the ordeal which was conducted with solemn and bewitching pomp by the Dionysan artists, ran:
"Θάρρεῖτε μύσται τοῦ σεσωσμένου
'Εσται γὰρ ἡμῖν ἐκ πόνων σωτηρια."
[27] Foucart, Ass'ns Religieuses, p. 169, ranks the evidence of Theophrast, the martyrdom of Glaucothea, the contest of Demosthenes and Æschines, and the words of Plutarch on superstition all together, as if their mention of the Sabbath was integral with the thiasotes: "C'était de l' Asie que venaient toutes les cérémonies expiatoires dont parle Plutarque: se frotter de l'argile, se couvrir de boue, observer le sabbat," etc., and quotes Plutarch, de Superst,, 3: Πηλώσεις, καταβορβορώσεις, σαββατισμοὺς, ῥίψεις ἐπὶ πρόσωπον, αἰσχρὰς προκαθίσεις, ἀλλοκότους προσκυνήσεις."
[28] Neand., *Planting*, Book III., chap. v. on origin of Sunday in the early church.

festival."²⁹ It was customary among the organizations we have described to hold a festival weekly. This was before the division of the year into months and weeks.³⁰ Their lovefeasts and banquets, no doubt were powerful toward influencing the emperors, in after times, in favor of the Hebrew week of seven days, but the Hebrew Sunday was not the one selected. It was decided by a number of causes to hold the festivals on the seventh day, giving the whole of one day to rest from labor. This wise provision has been handed down to us from the customs and habits of the poor workers under the Solonic dispensation, agreeing in the main with the arrangement established for the Hebrews in the law of Moses.

It is now ascertained that in addition to giving to labor the health-inspiring boon of fifty-two days of rest and recreation yearly, or one in every seventh, the noble corollary of eight hours a day was also established. While the habit of observing Sunday was preserved and handed down to us through the Christians, having endorsed it as part of the plant borrowed from the economic communes, and reducing the labor year from its ancient tædium of 360 days, was an indescribable blessing to humanity, we find that the great boon of eight hours per day was actually established, especially by the Solonic unions, although it was unfortunately discontinued and lost in the vortex of revolutions. But the unions formed through the jus coeundi of Solon were everywhere.³¹ It has been our good fortune, in ransacking the manuscripts and inscriptions to find several references on this point. We have lost the exact wording of the original law of Solon, as inscribed upon the pronaos of the old Athenian Prytaneum toward a thousand years before Christ; yet the wayside discoveries reveal that Solon, or perhaps Amasis, Solon copying, divided the day into three parts, a third to be devoted to labor, a third to study, refreshment and recreation and a third to sleep. Now, as we have just quoted from the archæologist Cagnat of the French Academy: "The

---

²⁹ Ignatius, *Epist. to the Magnesians*, IX., ad.
³⁰ Vol. 1., pp. 135, 530 explaining the long hours and the 360 days labor, with no Sundays.
³¹ Cagnat, *Vie Contemporaine*, Jan. 1896, p. 173, confirms our statement that their influence where exerted, was widespread, and that they were the same and alike in every part of the world: Les corporations professionelles n' en différaient pas beaucoup."

unions of trades and professions did not vary much from each other," so we have always held. Whether Roman collegia, Greek eranoi and thiasoi, Egyptian therapeutae or Palestinian essenes, they are found, on close inspection of their inscriptions to vary little as regards their object, habits and tenets.[32] Nothing is more certain, if these socialistic and practical economists did this, than that all the other practical organizations under the Solonic dispensation did the same thing. The essenes, therefore, furnished the typical key to the discussion,[33] and the learned disquisition of Fränkel who extracts from the Talmud, yields a fresh gem of assurance that eight hours constituted the normal day's work.

But independently of this, we yet possess the evidence of Philo. This correct and much quoted author, in his celebrated book on all goodness comes out with a plain statement for the guilds of the Egyptians which are now proved by many of their inscriptions to have been trade unions, that they divided their day into three parts, of which eight hours were devoted to labor.[34]

Many other intimations on the fact that the Greek and Roman collegia worked the eight hours normal day are coming to light through the inscriptions.

After their consistency in carrying out the scheme of economics, comes the information that among them there existed an extraordinary love for one another which is hardly accountable, and almost exceeds belief.

On initiation into a society they were to love one another. It was a requirement almost the opposite of existing conditions around them. Surrounded on all sides by hard, imperious masters, watched by the spies of the law, detested by the official religion, refused the right of

---

[32] Fränkel, in *Zeitschrift*, 1846, p 458, shows that the essenes divided their days into 3 equal parts, 8 hours of which were devoted to labor that was made both honorable and compulsory; and Smith, *Bible Dictionary*, p. 772, Bost. ed., refers to this as important. If they were all alike, their customs were alike.

[33] Josephus, *De Bell. Jud.*, V., iv., §2, speaks of the Essene Gate of Jerusalem 'Εσσηνῶν πύλη, in a way warranting us to infer that they were numerous, busy and systematic while a so-called tradition based upon facts of Josephus now lost, mentions the existence of a congregation at this πυλή who devoted "one third of the day to study, one third to prayer and one third to labor." Fränkel, *Zeitschrift*, 1846, p. 458. It was a learned Hebrew scholiast who extracted this valuable information from the Talmud, which reiterates that among Therapeutes and Essenes all things were held in common; no property being recognized, and that they refused to labor more than one third of the twenty-four hours.

[34] For a quotation, see *supra* in this vol., and refer to *index*, in verb. *Philo*, The translation of his words in *Quod Omn. Prob.*, is taken from Smith, *Bib. Dict.*, p. 772.

marriage and the family, denied the existence of a soul,[35] damned before death and afterward, the ancient workers were taught to bow before the majesty of property of their own creation, and cringe to robber barons who with military or traditional prowess deprived them of manhood and recognition exactly as they are doing today. It is thus that their oikos became not only a house to live in but a meeting house where they congregated and discussed in secret for a thousand years. It was the home of their eranothiasoi and collegia, which were one and the same among them.[36]

Beginning with our earliest records we find these organizations based upon, and carrying out, a precept of love. Even their initiations, in a crude way, point to this. In fact, the growth of love among mankind has a history, originating in some mythical personage, god or goddess; and the primeval love-cult was first breathed into those poor people by means of the ordeal of initiation into their brotherhoods.[37]

To facilitate this natural development the house or oikos was necessary; and wherever a communal property is found to have existed the inscriptions show that the first thing was a house, in which they could meet and cultivate their friendship and love. It was sometimes called a pholeterion, meaning a place of discussion and deliberation, but following the restrictions of the jus coeundi, it was also provided[38] with a common table and a plot of ground with trees and seats for ban-

[35] See *Index* of both volumes, in *verb*, "soul" pointing to pages in which this matter is discussed. It is an accorded fact that until the Christian era no lowborn of the laboring classes was thought to possess a soul.

[36] "Les Serapiastes, qui semblaient former un érane dans l' inscription Athenienne (no. 24) sont, à Cos, constitués en thiase, ce serait une preuve que les deux noms, de thiase et érane étaient devenues tout-a-fait synonymes." Foucart, *Ass. Rel.*, p. 2, *inscr.* 24.

[37] Consult Vol. I., chapter iv., p. 83-132 in which the secret initiatory cult is shown for the rich and aristocratic classes. The so-called lesser mysteries, those of the organizations we are describing, maintained a similar secrecy or occultism but were far more sympathetic. They had a Papas, of whom Attis was the type. This cult to prevent him from overdoing the love which was to prevade the soul, had him emasculated so as to exclude sexual exuberance.

[38] That the οἶκος of the eranos was a meeting house or church is now fully established and acknowledged. Cf. Webster, Standard and other *dictionaries* on origin of the word *church*. Ramsay, in *Cities and Bishoprics of Phrygia*; Foucart, *Ass. Rel.*, pp. 49, 87, where an inscription is shown: no. 2328, GIG., attesting that a thiasos superintended the construction of an οἶκος and owned the land. We have counted more than a hundred inscriptions of the Solonic order, found recently in Phrygia containing the word κυριάκον which is the English word church: Cf. Webster. Yet this was the meeting house of the ancient carpenters, woolworkers, dyers, fishermen, hunters, sailors, masons and a score of other trades!

quets and entertainments. Christianity was its noble and strikingly correct development. Nothing is now so extremely necessary as an investigation on our lines of philosophy. No substantiation can be more explicit that thiasos and eranos were labor organizations than Lüders, Oehler and others give, proving that the organizations of the jus coeundi were working for the support of their members and families.[39] They supplied themselves with all the means of comfort and plentitude, and carried on the business of individual trades with consistency and determination for centuries, until many of them accumulated a little means and sometimes considerable communal property. The council hall was often their own.[40] An important article has been published in the Pauly-Wissowa by Dr. Oehler, entitled "*Boule,*" which goes back to the distant origin of councils of this kind among the ancient Greeks, and explains the system of meals in common in the early cities, prepared in the Prytaneum, to which we have already given a definition. The unions were directed by law to pattern after this method of the public councils in cities.

It is now proven that these common meals were the celebrated lovefeasts of the ancients early grasped and followed by the Christians.[41] We find Socrates at the common table making pretty speeches on the sublime philosophy of love as embodied in the friend-making Eros, feally Dionysus; and four hundred years later[42]

---

[39] Hesychius who wrote a valuable *Dictionary* explaining the meaning of words, defines the Solonic unions in these words: "Θίασος· εὐωχίαν· καὶ πλῆθος οὐ μόνον τὸ Βακχικὸν ἀλλὰ καὶ τὸ ἐργατικόν." Originally these organizations were purely civil, not religious institutions. Lüders *D. K.*, p. 8, and this dictionary defines them as labor associations.

[40] Hesychius, *Lexicon*, in *verbo* Φωλητήρια καὶ συνόδων οἶκοι; So also Pollux, 'Ονομάστικον, VI., 7: "'Ἰθίως δὲ τοὺς τῶν θιασωτῶν οἴκους φωλητήρια ὠνόμαξον." These illustrations are quite sufficient to define the original church as a common council, or οἶκος, κύριακος etc. This word church is a derivation from Οἶκοι οἷς συνιόντες δειπνοῦσιν οἱ θίασοι. ie: houses or little churches in which the thiasotæ and eranists gathered together and took meals in common.

[41] Xenophon, *Conv.*, VIII., 1, describing a lovefeast of one of these organizations in Athens about 400 B.C., gives us valuable information showing that Eros was the love-god whom they worshiped; for Socrates in the little speech which Xenophon quotes says: Πάντες ἐσμὲν τοῦ θεοῦ τούτου θιασῶται He further makes the admission that this Eros was about identical with Dionysus. There is no question that Socrates was a member of one of these societies, at Athens, where they are known to have existed in considerable numbers.

[42] *Ante-Nicene Fathers*, VII., p. 505, Buffalo ed.: *Acts of Philip*, Athenian Hellas. Ananias accuses Philip before the Athenian philosophers, bringing charges against Jesus: "For many charges were brought in by him that he gave evil testimony: for he ate all things common and mixed with blood after the manner of the Gentiles." This strange old document must sooner or later be regarded as valuable evidence.

we find Jesus at the common table, and in the society of a similar brotherhood, enjoying a lovefeast in honor of the God of creation.

The fervency of the laboring synods, congregations and council meetings, as exhibited in their ingenious chiselings has caused a good deal of wonder among the scholars engaged in their discovery. The point of most interest is their scheme of discussion and inculcation. They all differ from the official pagan cult, although pagans themselves until the Christians came. After their rule of life they must love and take care of one another which, except in the well-regulated family, is not seen in the competitive, outside world. Wescher in one of his valuable contributions, intimates that the cult of the Greek-speaking eranothiasos was more fervent and lasting than the official institutions of state; and Dr. Foucart appears to approve this view.[43] According to the opinions of Renan, Welcher and Foucart, the reason why the state went down and the principle of the organizations went up was that the state with its religion was brutal to the laboring element, and deserved to die.

Everywhere the economical thiasotes were musical and they sang their pre-Christian hallelujahs and hymns of love.[44] The general characteristics of these unions are likewise proved to conform to their exalted culture.[45] It is in these economical labors that the females found their redeeming function. There were female officers who presided over the preparations of the banquets, and took charge of the work of preparing the common meals. We find them mentioned as deaconesses. It was largely at these repasts that the spirit of human sympathy was inculcated.

[43] *Ass. Rel.*, p. 177, approving Wescher's views; M. Renan,' *Les Apôtres*, p. 250, declares the thiasoi cultivated elevated ideas. Plutarch, *De Pith.*; *De Erroribus Oraculornm*, 20.

[44] Later the ἀναγέννησις or New Birth formed one of their themes. The ἅγιος, εὐσεβής, ἀγαθός, of which we have spoken, also formed a part of their musical praise. There was the hymn of Attis, who in a paroxysm died for mankind and rose again. See Foucart, p. 89, for the Φιλοσοφοόμενα, also Keil, *Philologos*, 1852, p. 189, all showing that the θιασῶται were cultivators of love. This, Plutarch and Xenophon both prove. Plut., *Amat.*, XIII., 5, shows that love is certainly a god : Οὐδὲ ἔπηλυς ἔκ τινος βαρβαρικῆς δεισιδαιμονίας, ὥσπερ 'Ατται τινὲς καὶ 'Αδώνιοι λεγόμενοι, δι' ἀνδρογύνων καὶ γυναικῶν παραδύεται καὶ κρύφα τιμὰς οὐ προσηκούσας καρπούμενος, ὥστε παρεισγραφῆς δίκην φεύγειν καὶ νοθείας τῆς ἐν θεοῖς.

[45] Oehler, *Eranos Vindabon.*, p. 280, speaking of their attributes and characteristics of the Zumpfte or Guilds, as he terms them, says : Das Ansehn der Genossenschaften ziet sich in den Attributen: σεμνότατος, ἱερός, ἱερώτατος, εὐγενέστατος εὐτελής, die ihnen beigelegt werden. The attribute εὐτελής here mentioned, has an especial reference to the economical care in providing for themselves the means of life.

The ancient symposiums and lovefeasts constitute one of the grandest attractions which the historian finds in a thankless desert of lowly life. They were the garden spot that nurtured the sympathy seldom found in the outside, gruesome world of which our histories speak; and although they are unmentioned and now only to be found in the skeleton-like inscriptions, which, like fossils yield ghastly records from nature's petrifactions, yet they unfold to us the deeply occult reasons why mankind, amid raging competitions did not long ago destroy itself and cease to exist. It was this phenomenal, invisible humanity, hated and maltreated by the ruling race, but closely confraternal within the veil of union, working, praying, singing, loving, providing, in inter-mutual secrecy, that perpetuated our species and held it in its physical and intellectual grandeur through the qualms of official priestcraft, kingcraft and avarice that sometimes well-nigh depopulated the earth.

This beautiful love was widespread and universal. We have already recorded in these chapters our belief that it must have been a specification of some clause now lost, of the Solonic law, of which there remains to us only a brief fragment. Love was a command. Later it was a Christian command.[46] It was love that perpetuated the fraternities until broken up and destroyed by the hideous canons of the Council of Laodicea where these unions are, above all other places, best known to have economically thrived;—a council which, backed by empire, eliminated them throughout proconsular Rome which means the world. Henceforth, love was turned to hate and wrangle and the dark and dismal feudal ages of a thousand years supervened.

To us, this love of membership which existed among the unions is phenomenal. We cannot understand it. They not only loved each other during life, but following pagan ideas of immortality, they extended this love beyond the mortal life. It was the custom among the poor to burn the bodies of the dead. Only the great, the distinguished, the men and women of recognition, could be honored by interment after the Twelve Tables which for more than four hundred years had been law,

---

[46] John, XV., 12. This is my commandment that ye love one another. Αὕτη ἐστὶν ἡ ἐντολὴ ἡ ἐμή, ἵνα ἀγαπᾶτε ἀλλήλους, καθὼς ἠγάπησα ὑμᾶς. Also John, XVIII., 34; I. John. xiii., 11; I. Thess., IV., 9; I. Peter,, IV., 8.

had been desecrated[47] through the mulitudinous calamities of the Roman conquests.

One of the first manifestations of this curious extension of love beyond this life was made in a discovery at Rome of the vast mausoleum, containing great numbers of niches for cinerary urns, all of the laboring class.[48] As is seen in his words given in the note below, the custom was already old among the Greeks, for it is mentioned in the Iliad. But our information on the application of this singular custom among the Greek trade unions has been greatly enhanced by Dr. Oehler,[49] who has lately investigated the subject with a ransacking penetration which left no stone unturned, during his recent travels. The revelations of the columbarium discovered beside the Appian Way[50] near Rome are especially interesting because it is proved that the niches contain many cinerary urns of Christians.

The well-known perentalia and rosalia of the official religion were imitated by these organizations of the more lowly ones. The living members were in common, and on a par with the dead ones. They took a sacred pleasure in bestrewing their graves with flowers. In their pagan and ante-Christian state they fervently believed that the "passing on" was a continuation of present things, to be lived and enjoyed forever and death had no dreads or pangs. Each year at the parentalia, or

[47] Cicero, *De Legibus*, ii., 23; "Hominem mortuum, inquit lex XII in Urbe ne sepulito neve urito . . . . Quid? qui post XII in Urbe sepulito sunt clari viri." See Vol. I., p. 75.
[48] On the society of the dead, see Gorius. *Mon. Sive Columbar.*, p. 142, no. CIII. The inscr. of the urn reads; ALCYONE L. ACILI. EROTIS DIV. AUG. L. CALAIS CIS VITIÆ MEIV. OSSA. IN UNO. Gorius' comments: "Commixtos simul in una olla plurimi defunctorum cineres, et in hoc columbario superius observabimus in descriptione § XI., p. 56. Nil enim amicis, et propinquis carius et optatius esse potest jucunda societate etiam post mortem. Hunc morem in unam urnam commiscendi cineres plurium defunctorum a Græcis quoque usitatum." Hom., *Iliad*. 336.
[49] Oehler, *MSS.*, *to the author*; "Was angeführt wurde, genügt um zu beweisen dass die Sorge für die Bestattung der Mitglieder, fur die Erhaltung des Grabmales, für den Todtencultus vielfach von den Vereinen getragen wurde; dies erklärt sich aus der sacralen Grundlage aller Vereine. Die Vereherer derselben Gottheit sollen und wollen auch nach ihrem Tode vereint sein; ihnen sollen vom Vereine τὰ νομιζόμενα erwiesen werden. Daher erklären sich die gemeinsamen Begräbnissplätze einzelner Vereine umschlossen von einer Mauer, die Errichtung und Erhaltung der μνάματα, u.s.w."
[50] Gorius, *Columbar.*, p. 56, showing how the ashes were found to be mixed together, again says; "Interdum etiam in una eademque urna plurium defunctorum cineres simul commixti, quod ab amicis, a pluribus affectu conjunctis factum legimus, in pristini amoris, fidelitatis, perpetuæque inter se benevolentiæ, etiam post obitum, argumentum. Ex sequentibus titulis constabit, ut videbimus, in hoc quoque monumento mixtos simul aliquando in una eademque olla plurium defunctorum cineres."

first of February, they met to appease their *manes*, these being the annual feast-days of the parentalia at Rome. Also, at the rosalia in May, they went through the same strange forms of kindred worship, bestrewing the graves with roses. In March they observed another sacred spell, bestrewing their beloved burial spots with violets. To do this task, which, like their meals, was accomplished in common, or at common expense, they accumulated the proper means by a small contribution of each member in good standing, into the union's common fund.[51] The parentalia and rosalia were strictly pagan forms but they were partly discontinued as heathenish, after the Christians took control. Abundant evidence is at hand showing that many of the so-called heathen forms and customs were endorsed and continue as sacred by the Christians to the present time.

Among such customs and habits were the hallelujahs, or ecstatic cries originating in the initiations,[52] as will be shown. The hallelujah was originally a typical shout during the ceremonies of initiation.[53] This hallelujah is again mentioned by Chrysostom six hundred years afterwards showing that the Christians engrafted it into the new religion and under them it became full of chanting melodies and so remains to this day in its non-practical, skeleton form. But the most open and telling disclosure which perhaps we have, of this rite of the initiatory feasts of the dead, from the thirteenth to the twenty-

---

[51] Cagnat, in *Vie Contemporaine*, Jan. 1896, who shows the natural reasons, why the societies always had a burial attachment.

[52] At the initiations of the Thiasos, the universal cry or shout was ὀλολυγή, the same thing as hallelujah. This was the common cry of rejoicing among the θιασῶται of Σαβάξιος. It was as early as B. C. 400-500, and is probably a term borrowed from the Central-Asians by the Hebrews, and after, by the Christians who have differentiated it from the original place, as an initiatory cry, but continue it in their camp-meetings and love-feasts, in chants and anthems. The θιασῶται always used this ecstatic shout in their initiations. See Foucart, *Ass. Rel.*, pp. 74, 75. An inscription now at the Louvre, CIG. 2771, Fouc. No. 43, and handsomely printed by the latter, on p. 223, 224, shows that the word ἐκκλησία used to-day, as an ecclesiastical term in the church, was originally a word for the councils of the initiates into the thiasos, known by the early date of this thiasos, about B.C. 196-180, to have been in constant use by the θιασῶται as a common term of their unions, and councils. Ecclesia is found in Aristophanes, *Lysistr.*, 386-390 speaking of the women of the brotherhoods; Plutarch, *Alcibiades*, 18, and others likewise mention the ecclesia of the brotherhoods.

[53] Foucart, *Ass. Rel.*, p. 75: "Pendant la cérémonie, le purificateur et les initiés poussaient l' ὀλολυγή, cri perçant, plusieurs fois répeté, et qui était usité dans les cultes d' Attis et de Sabazius." We have an ancient Greek definition also, showing what the original halleluyah was. Ὀλολυγή φωνὴ γυναικῶν ἦν ποιοῦνται ἐν τοῖς ἱεροῖς εὐχόμεναι. Harpocration, *Etimol. Magna*. Demosthenes twits Æschines where he brings out these curious things, of being a θιαώτης, and his initiations, of being those of the mean and lowly, lesser mysteries, boasting that he himself was noble enough to have been initiated into the great mysteries, along with society and kings.

first of February, is the worship of dead men; and its hallelujah is divulged by another and very reliable ancient author,[54] comporting remarkably with the mysticisms which suffused all ancient life. The god thus created amid hallelujahs and the ebulition of excessive joy was the Dionysus whom they named and worshiped as Sabazius; the forerunner, Kathegemona, veritable divinity of the vast Solonic organization, represented as "the ennobler of mankind and the giver of joys." After a full comparison, strictly scientific, of our monumental information, with other written records regarding the trouble between the working man and woman, Æschines and Glaucothea, and Demosthenes, we are unable to suppress a feeling of indignation against this eloquent defender of high-born pretention, who lampooned, and through a mere tonguey raillery caused the overthrow and martyrdom of two well-meaning and useful reformers striving to better the wretched condition of slaves and freedmen at Athens. Already it has been shown that before the time of Glaucothea and of her enemy Demosthenes, the very thiasos which the orator denounces and derides, had practiced the habit by borrowing money from the eranos, acting as a kind of bank for the common membership, to buy their people out of slavery by selling them to a god. In this way large numbers of slaves became free. Furthering this work of emancipation was the crime of the martyrs.

That the chanters of the hallelujahs were members of the societies of thiasotæ, eranoi and orgeones under the jus coeundi of Solon can no longer be denied; for they appear everywhere connected with them.

The hallelujah also has a history and function in the early church, showing that Christianity was planted into the communes already existing in great numbers and power when the Advent spread its influence in the

---

[54] Fouc., *Ass. Rel.*, p. 72, sqq., is in doubt whether they were as religious as they were economical, because they were "accessible même aux profanes." In that early, semi-barbarous time these old Sabazic initiations were, of course, somewhat brutal and savage, and their formalities partook often of the abominations of a savage life. The candidates, whether men or women, were stripped naked. The purificator, or baptizer poured on him or her, water from the crater (κρατήρ) "eau de cratère" (p. 73.) then rubbed him down with clay and bran: 'Ἀπομάττων τῶ πηλῷ καὶ τοῖς πιτύροις." This clay and bran were supposed to have a mystical effect. Harpocration, in v. Ἀπομάττων. The rite was not Greek, but borrowed from Thrace and Asia Minor. Plutarch, *De Superstitionibus*, 3: πηλωσις means wallowing in mire. The initiate then had to stand and yell: Hallelujah! I have escaped evil, I have found better things. "'Εγω γονάκον, εὑρον ἄμεινον." Demosth., *Pro Corona*, 259-260.

world.⁵⁵ The reader, then, of the remarkable and celebrated assertion of Diodorus, that they were employed by cities and states, as we have quoted in two places, should reflect that these ululations clinging to our musical religion and making it so attractive and beautiful in variety of anthems, chants and vocal quavers, which thrill alike the throngs of camp meetings, or the cavernous vaults of cathedrals, derive their exquisite harmony and far-sounding vowel explosions enchanting to all worshipers of art in aerial vibrations, to the poor workingman's protecting god who was begotten in the epoptic ecstasy of an ancient and divine initiation to become the glorious immortal that stood in watchfulness over the mechanic arts.

All these organizations were constantly working their efforts to obtain government employment. They succeeded. It may be stated positively that state ownership and control of labor was the economical outcome of the Solonic organization. We proceed to furnish proof lest our opponents file in a desire to deny it, in the interest of the competitive system. Many of the great authors, such as Aristotle, Plutarch, Lucian and Tertullian are literary evidence, while the Monumental evidence with its curious jottings corroborates their statements.

We cannot be too explicit in noting all that is proven by evidence on the subject of municipal eating-houses. There was, some 250 years before Christ, a municipal kitchen at the Piræus the seaport of Athens. It was called the *Mageireion*, and employed constantly, for at least a hundred years, a large number of butchers,

---

⁵⁵ *Ante-Nicine Fathers*, Vol. VIII., p. 539, on the Early Liturgies. Much similarity is seen in the services, suggesting that it is derived from the originals we are discussing, most of whose information comes to us through monumental proof. The scriptural reads: "Then there are read in order, the holy oracles of the Old Testaments and of the prophets; and the incarnation of the Son of God is set forth, and the sufferings and resurrection from the dead, the ascension into heaven, and His second appearing with glory; and this takes place daily in the holy and divine service." So in the monumental they had this resurrection. The liturgy is very late. The original and true functions of the deacon are now gone. Of the Christian hallelujah, John, in Revelations, xix., 1. "And after these things I heard a great voice of much people in heaven, saying: "ALLELUIA; Salvation and glory, and honor, and power unto the Lord our God." Also Psalms, (composed, at least, 1000 yrs. B.C., 1055–1015.) 106, 111; 113; 146. *Ibidem*, 3, 4, 6: "And I heard, as it were, the voice of a great multitude, and as the voice of many waters, and as the voice of mighty thunderings, saying: "Alleluia, for the Lord God Omnipotent reigneth." And this is exactly what Demosthenes derides in his far-famed blackguard of the initiations by Æschines and his mother, Glaucothea, in the Oration, *Pro Corona*.

cooks and waiters.⁵⁶ The inscription given in the note showing a common table, which undoubtedly was of so large a membership as to engross a sensible share of the population, gives a public kitchen like that at Grenoble in France, at the present day. Like the beneficent city-owned eating house at Grenoble, it employed the people direct, and they worked and furnished food at non-speculative rates for the public as a function of the public works.⁵⁷

The hymn singers of the great Dionysan unions were employed in great numbers by the state and municipal governments. Of this, we possess evidence of the stones. A thiasos, of the Thymele chorus dancers had a large membership thus employed, and exempted from military duty by the state in recognition of their musical genius and skill.⁵⁸ Diodorus tells us that thousands of the musical and play-acting fraternities of the Dionysan order were not only employed by the state official religion, which means the political state, but like those of India, they were exempted from the burden of the state tax and military services. They were workingmen, not citizens, but nevertheless appreciated. This employment by the state was very common, also at Rome for many centuries,⁵⁹ as will be seen by a glance at the index of the

---

⁵⁶ Oehler, *MSS. to the Author:* on the Μαγειρεῖον, or public cookshop, says: "Aus dem Peireius berichtet uns eine Inschrift aus dem Ende des III. Jahrhunderts v. Chr. von einem Bessclusse der Orgeonen, betreffend die Herrichtung einer Küche μαγειρεῖον zu öffentlichen Zwicken: CIA. II., 618 vgl. *Arch. Anzeiger*, 1856, p. 137, (Velsen)." This public kitchen recommended by the resolution registered on the slab of stone, by a union, and probably established and in operation for at least a hundred years, was patterned after the πρυτανεῖον in conformity with a clause of the law of Solon, and employed quite a number of the members of its own brotherhood. There is at present at least one such public kitchen, that of the city of Grenoble, France. See *Bulletin of the U. S. Dept. of Labor*, No. 12, 1897.

⁵⁷ Liddell, in *verb*, "Μαγειρεῖον, a place for cooking; a cook shop; Latin, poppina, or the place where the public cooks lived." This clause explains that it was an institution owned by the public; and it follows, as shown by the few inscriptions we have of them, that cooks engaged there, were under some sort of employment in the public work.

⁵⁸ Diodorus, *Hist. Biblioth.*, IV., 5, proves this as follows: "Καθόλου δὲ τῶν θυμελικῶν ἀγώνων φασὶν εὑρετὴν γενέσθαι (sc. Διόνυσον) καὶ θέατρα καταδεῖξαι καὶ μουσικῶν ἀκροαμάτων σύστημα ποιῆσαι· πρὸς δὲ τούτοις καὶ ἀλειτουργήτους ποιῆσαι καὶ τοὺς ἐν ταῖς στρατείαις μεταχειριζομένους τι τῆς μουσικῆς ἐπιστήμης, ἀφ' ὧν τοὺς μεταγενεστέρους μουσικὰς συνόδους συστήσασθαι τῶν περὶ τὸν Διόνυσον τεχνιτῶν καὶ ἀτελεῖς ποιῆσαι τοὺς τὰ τοιαῦτα ἐπιτηδεύοντας."

⁵⁹ Oehler, *MSS*: "In Rome erscheint als officielle Titulatur: σύνοδος ξυστικὴ τῶν περὶ τὸν Ἡρακλέα αὐλητῶν ἱεροτικῶν στεφανειτῶν. *Inscr. Gr. Itaciæ*, nr. 1054; 1055; 1107: ἱερὰ ξ. σ. u. s. w. 1105, mit dem Zusatze: ἀπὸ καταλύσεως ἐν τῇ βασιλίδι Ῥώμῃ κατοικούντων, 1109. Auf einem Siegel, dessen Fundort unbekannt ist, lesen wir ἱερὰ ξυστικὴ Ἀντωνανὴ Γορδιανὴ εὐσεβὴς Σεβαστὴ σύνοδος. CIG., 8561, Merkwürdig ist die bezeichnung Νεικήτης Ἡράκλειος· *Inscr. Gr. Ital.*, 1108 aus Rom. Neikiles soll damit wohl als Mitglied einer Athletengenossenchaft bezeichnet werden.

first volume of this work. For a long time nearly every branch of manufacture, building, public bridges and vast intineraries,[60] indeed even the food supplies with shipping commerce, and the collection of public revenues, were allotted to the various unions by the state; and evidences begin to appear showing that for five centuries at least, the unions with their innumerable members, secured this work and they divided the day's labor into three equal parts, eight hours for work, eight hours for refreshment and pleasure and eight hours for sleep. Under the Solonic dispensation those unions were non-property owners except as their goods were held in common by the membership. They were voting socialists, and they realized almost all of the immense advantages of socialism except the public recognition of their manhood, equality and citizenship, which were never achieved except by the vast and launching swoop of Christianity that has partly succeeded in putting down slavery and divine inheritance.

But it is especially refreshing to find evidence in the inscriptions of Asia Minor, Italy and Gaul that thousands of people organized in artists' unions had regular employment under the city boards of public amusement. We have already shown how careful these Solonic unions were to attend to the political end of these matters, thus voting into office their own choice of the directors of public works in order to secure their own appointment to do the task. Among many others are the musicians.[61] Allusion has already been made to the employment by Alexander the Great of these organized musicians. At the great scenic festivity, to celebrate this monarch's victory over Darius, no less than 3,000 play-actors of the organization of the Great Gemeinde were convoked. It was a musical and histrionic festiv-

[60] Domaszewksi, in *Eranos Vinodobon.*, p. 60 ff., under title, *Cura viarum*, for a correct idea of the great public and military highways of Rome and her colonies, made by the colleges.

[61] Dr. Oehler, *MSS.*, reminds us of the inscription noted by Hicks, *Anc. Gr. Inscrs.*, III., in the introduction and says: "Die ὑμνῳδοί seien eine Brüderschaft von Hymnensängern im Temple der Artemis gewesen; Levy: *Rev. des Études Grecs*, VIII., 1895, p. 247, meint die ὑμνῳδοί erscheinen als ein autonomes Corps; Ziebarth, *Vereinswesen*, p. 90, hält sie für ein Mittleglied zwischen privaten und öffentlichen Corporationen, städtliche Musikkapellen: vgl. auch, Fränkel, *Pergamon*, II., *Commentar* zu nr. 374, p. 262-270." Reference is also made to many inscrs. pointing to the same conclusions, found at Smyrna, Klaudiopolis, Ephesus, Tyre, and elsewhere. CIG., 3803, and showing them all to be in honor of Diana, protectress of labor and the chase.

VAST NUMBERS EMPLOYED BY THE STATE. 301

ity given by Chares, who was one of Alexander's generals, and who wrote stories about Alexander, most of which are lost.[62] The Dionysan artists are represented as being mostly wandering musicians and playwrights, who under the powerful direction of the Great Gemeinde wandered into many provinces and towns accepting any offer they could arrange either with cities or governments. On this we have the testimony of many authors, including Diodorus, Pliny, Plutarch, Arrian, Cleomenes, Polybius, Athenæus, Lucian and others. The nine days' festival of Alexander was enormous, where he employed these mirth makers in force.[63] Again when Hephastion, the much .oved friend of Alexander died, this monarch ordered a great funeral festivity as was the custom, lasting three days.[64] Cases of this sort were of the species of pure government, and were sporadic, disconnected and accidental; but the cases of municipal employment were carefully watched for by the unions, who had their picked political defenders at the elections, and never allowed a candidate to be nominated as agoranomos, or commissioner of public works, unless he was committed to the interests of the powerful unions and would, if elected, award the jobs to them.

Not only Alexander, but also the Cypriote kings were in the habit of engaging play-actors for their own amusement, and for their skill and genius in the public festivities and games. Stories of much interest and amusement have come down to us corroborating this.[65] A startling mention is made to the effect that after the time of Alexander who on many occasions, as we have shown, hired vast numbers, the successful generals of conquest went further than to hire and honorably pay

---

[62] Athenæus, xii., 538. The various artists employed on this occasion were "Θαυματοποιοί, Ῥαψῳδοί, Κιθαρῳδοί, Αὐλῳδοί, Αὐληταί, αὐληταὶ μετὰ τῶν χορῶν, τραγῳδοί, κομῳδοί, ψάλτης, καί Ψιλοκιθαρισταί."

[63] Diod., xvii., 16. speaking of Alexander's great nine-days' feast, says; "Θυσίας μεγαλοπρεπαῖς τοῖς θεοῖς συνετέλεσεν ἐν Δίῳ τῆς Μακεδονίας καὶ σκηνικοὺς ἀγῶνας, Διΐ καὶ Μούσαις οὓς Ἀρχέλαος πρῶτος κατέδειξε, τὴν δὲ πανηγύρεν ἐφ' ἡμέραῃ ἐννέα συνετέλεσεν." As Alexander was himself the autocrat in absolute control both of the employment by him of the minstrels, and of the monarchies it must be classed as government employ.

[64] Arrian, *Anabasis*, VII., 14: Ἀγῶνα τε ἐπενόει ποιῆσαι γυμνικόν τε καὶ μουσικὸν πλήθει τε τῶν ἀγωνιξομενῶν καὶ τῇ εἰς αὐτὸν χορηγίᾳ πολύ τε τῶν ἄλλων τῶν πρόσθεν ἀλιδηλότερον' τρισχιλίους γὰρ ἀγωνιστὰς τοὺς ξύμπαντας παρεσκεύασε, Thus 3,000 playwrights were engaged from the various unions of the Dionysan artists of different cities to perform for the great occasion. They were sumptuously treated and well paid.

[65] Plutarch, *Alexander*, 29, relates the anecdote of King Pasicrates referred to, and confirms it in *De Fort. Al.*, II., 2.

them. They took a double advantage of the popularity of the custom and cheated both the musicians and the people who rushed together in throngs to hear the agonies and witness the games.[66] On the other hand, after the commencement of the Roman conquests, they often lured or choked the play-actors themselves into making sports for them which they enormously profited upon, and in this manner debauchery went rampant at the expense of both honor and purse.

It has heretofore been alluded to that during the conquests[67] the orders of trade unions of the law of Numa were employed to do the mechanical work of the armies and navies of Rome.[68] Members did not act as soldiers, but they were formed into companies and regiments, and then set to work, making arms, machines and all the material of war, thus constituting one of the important parts of the military service. This, while it honored and remunerated them by giving direct employment at their own terms, did much more for them and for humanity; for the aristocratic soldiers in actual conflict were decimated in numbers by fighting their bold adversaries on every hand. It is well known that they sometimes died out. But these proletarian millions, organized into unions and out of danger, working for the beligerent armies, happily exempt from dangers, multiplied, throve, and grew prosperous, and in this manner, always attending to their political foothold at home, became a ruling power. The highest evidence of the archæologists has come into our possession showing that almost all the associations were habitually employed either by the army or navy, or else by the official religion and therefore by the state; and this was not confined to mechanics but included vast numbers of amusement makers who lived by these trades and professions[69] in close organization of the jus coeundi—the play artists as

---

[66] Lüders, *Dionys. Künst.*, p. 107: "Sie benutzten die Einrichtung von Spielen um das Volk für sich zu gewinnen, zuweilen auch um es auszuspländern." Much information on this is derived from *Pseudo*, Aristot., *Oecon.*, II., 30.

[67] Vol. II., *chap.*, i.

[68] Livy, I., 43: "Additæ huic classi (primæ) duæ fabrum centuriæ quæ sine armis stipendia fecerent, datum munus ut machinas in bello ferrent." Their function to make and operate the machines, was explained by Varro, *De Lingua Lat.*, from which we make extracts.

[69] Lüders, *Dionys. Künst.*, p. 61: "So bilden sich unter dem Schutze des Staates und wohl unter seiner Mitwirkung ständige Collegien mit sacralem Charakter, σύνοδοι τῶν περὶ τὸν Διόνυσον τεχνιτῶν." Plut. *Qu. Rom.*, cvii.; Tertull., *Spectacular. Artificum.*

GREAT STRIKE OF 20,000 GREEK SLAVES.

well as the image makers, tent and scene fixers and common laborers, hunters, fisherman and sellers of their products, all lived on their professions, securing each other employment just as did the bridge-builders[70] of Rome.

It is known that the government of Athens, which, during the Peloponnesian War, managed the whole public business of Attica, owned and operated silver and gold mines; and that a large share of the expenses of that tedious struggle was met by their direct yield. The state of Attica worked the mines; and after the loss of 20,000 men by the strike of B.C. 413, workingmen, to fill their places, had to be engaged from the membership of the unions. The men who struck work and escaped to Decelia, hiring themselves out to the enemy against their own country, were Athenian slaves.[71] The new men employed to take their places were in great part freedmen and well organized. The state employed them direct. In other words, they were not let to contractors, who were few in numbers at that early time.[72] Nicias and others who got a few contracts owned the slaves they employed. It was however mostly after the Roman conquests, under the hateful system. Government hired the workmen direct in almost all the earlier mining enterprises not only at Laurium, but also at its gold mines at Scopta Hyle, and its mine in the Isle of Thasos. The men, assisted by their unions, were well treated, well paid and worked only eight hours a day, thus effecting their economical enfranchisement.

Not only did the 20,000 strikers who, as state slaves, bolted the silver mines of Attica, as we have shown, effectually escape over to the Lacedæmonians and secure good government employment from that state with which their own country was at war, but we have the information that the Spartans, after their bad experience with the Helots, grew into the habit of employing large numbers, on terms arranged with the cities and the government, through the Kurios or president of the eranos. The same was done in Crete.

---

[70] For a full account, consult the *Index* of both volumes.

[71] See I., p. 134, where the story of Thucydides is quoted, and all that is known of this important event recounted; Böckh *Laurische Silberbergwerke*, shows the advantages which fell to the strikers: Drumann, *Arbeiter und Kommunisten in Griechenland und Rom*.

[72] See *Revue Socialiste*, Vol. XIII., No. 78, June, 1891, p. 659. (B. Malon).

We here come to a very important matter which has never until recenly been understood. It is the rule of proxy which is especially provided in the law of Solon and inserted into one of the Twelve Tables, to surmount the obstacles interposed by the law against the success of independent labor organization.[73]

In order to empower a union at any and all times to hire its talent with freedom, the law provides a president of the union's own choice, who is authorized to make bargains in his own individual name. What seems to have made this man's power so fixed and absolute is the fact that the organization itself took the form, or was patterned after the organization of a democratic city or state,[74] which under Solon, who had already enacted his laws creating and governing the perfect city, and had turned his attention to the best manner of governing the workers whom he seems to have considered the important factor of its inhabitants, naturally desired that their mutual unions should be patterned after the city itself. The city must have its first man in power. So also the union.

The business, therefore, of the kurios was not only to preside but to take contracts wherever possible for work, which his people should perform with the largest possible profit to themselves. Placed in this highly responsible position, with a constituency always eager to obtain state or city work, this director or president possessed a powerful influence over the board of public works; and inscriptions are found showing that they were themselves sometimes elected to fill that office.[75] The mass of evidence at command, makes it clear that the unions were recognized by the state and by the city, employed in at least a semi-official capacity, although it is evident from the inscriptions that they were at perfect liberty to hire their talent to anybody on their own account.[76]

[73] *Dig.*, xlvii., 4: ὅ τι ἂν τούτων διαθῶνται πρὸς ἀλλήλους, κύριον ἔναι, ἐὰν μὴ ἀπαγορεύσῃ δημόσια γράμματα.
[74] *Dig.* III., 4,......"proprium est ad exemplum reipublicæ," etc.
[75] Waltzing, *Hist. Corp. Prof.*, I., p. 417; "On trouve un édile dans trois collèges de juvenes et dans quelques collèges funéraires, CIL., III,, 5678. XIV., 2636, 3864 : VI., 9288. This last reads : 'Ob honorem aedilitatis titulum polivit de suo et nomina sodalium inscripsit eorum qui numera posuerunt.' It looks to us as though this ædile was a member of some powerful union, elected by it to be the aedile or agoranomos, of the city, and that he acted for them as a commissioner of public works, but likewise attended to the burial attachment, and directed the polishing and lettering of epitaphs
[76] Athenaeus, X., iv., 20, p. 482; Aristotle, *Pol.*, I., 72.

DUAL EMPLOYMENT; COUNTRY AND SELF. 305

The discovery that these trade unions practiced the dual habit of working enormously for the state while at the same moment they performed this labor, ostensibly in the name of an individual, as though the works were let by a city to an individual contractor, has untwisted a difficult thread.[77] It accounts for the mysteriously powerful kurios. It clears up the true and original meaning of the clause we have quoted in the law of Solon, requoted in the Digest. Indeed the mysticism which attaches all along, and which so frequently crops out in the inscriptions can only be made comprehensible in this way. This is why the Kurius dominus or lord is so all-powerful and held in such reverence in the New Testament.

Another important fact has been unearthed in regard to them. They were by no means so pious as has been represented.[78] Religion was only a pretext and not the initial incentive of organization. While on the one hand the unions were mostly successful in getting a living, and in some cases their guild-like rules were so happily conformed to, that they many times bought enough property to have among themselves a common house, yet they were subject to great persecution. There was once in Phrygia an uprising of some sort, which caused the artists to flee to Ephesus for safety. Attalus drove them out of their Pergamenian home to Lebados where they were re-established and in a flourishing state in the time of Diodorus.[79]

There has been much mutilation of facts regarding these important matters. While they were forming a correct nucleus for the deep-laid socialism of future generations, and while they were in the microcosmic

---

[77] Waltzing, *Hist. Corp. Prof.*, I., p. 186: "Quand les members de certains corporations se mirent au service de l' État, ce fut longtemps en leur nom privé, et non comme corporation."

[78] Julian, *Inscrs. de Bordeaux*, I., p. 209, acknowledges that religion was only a pretext: "Toutes les associations religieuses de l' empire étaient fondées en vue d' assurer à leurs membres un loculus sepulturæ et lorsque ce n' était pas le but real de ces fondateurs c' en etait au moines le but avoué et le prétexte." Thus in Julian we have an important modern author and savant without a bandage binding his eyes.

[79] Strabo, 643: "'Ενταῦθα (ἐν Δεβέδῳ) τῶν περὶ τὸν Διόνυσον τεχνιτῶν ἡ σύνοδος καὶ κατοικία τῶν ἐν 'Ιωνίᾳ μέχρι 'Ελλησπόντου, ἐν ᾗ πανήγυρίς τε καὶ ἀγῶνες κατ' ἔτος συντελοῦνται τῷ Διονύσῳ. ἐν Τέῳ δὲ ᾤκουν πρότερον τῇ ἐφεξῆς πόλει τῶν 'Ιώνων, ἐμπεσούσης δὲ στάσεως εἰς Ἔφεσον κατέφυγον. 'Αττάλου δὲ εἰς Μυόννησον αὐτοὺς καταστήσαντος μεταξὺ Τέω καὶ Λεβέδου, πρεσβεύηνται Τήιοι δεόμενοι 'Ρωμαίων, μὴ περιιδεῖν ἐπιτειχιζομένην σφίσι τὴν Μυόννησον, οἱ δέ μετέστησαν εἰς Λέβεδον δεξαμένων τῶν Λεβεδίων ἀσμένως διὰ τὴν κατέχουσαν αὐτοὺς ὀλιγανδρίαν.

state, they were yet the originals into which the Christians, soon afterward planted their higher forms. The originals of the Christian movement were simple. The tendency all through was toward an economic emancipation of the poor, no matter how great the mutilation of original accounts. The original men had a distinct plan. It was about the same as now before the world, only that at present, amidst inventions, and their concomitant complications and trusts of the wealthy, the plan is being mechanically enlarged.

According to several of the last authors preserved by Strabo, the same was going on in India.[80]

An important inscription has been found containing a certain oath of a thiasos that was written at least 396 years before Christ and preserved at Decelea, the town to which the 20,000 striking slaves from the Laurian silver mines escaped deserting over to the Lacedæmonians.[81] Another set of inscriptions pointed out by Dr. Oehler, refers to a later date, covering the age of the apostles, thence reaching down to the times of Trajan and Hadrian.[82]

There are indications that the Solonic organization at one time reached as far as Ceylon, for the earliest historic date we have, that of B.C. 316, gives evidence that the philosophy or religion of Guatama so much resembling that of Christianity was planted in that fruitful island developing a wonderful system of public works, the ruins only of which remain. It was here that ancient government works for irrigation were constructed. There still remain relics of large artificial lakes, which stand as an irrefutable proof of the excel-

---

[80] Strabo, *Geog.*, 707, 46, Meineke. They embraced: τὰς τέχνας καὶ τοὺς καπηλικοὺς, all of whom took a share in the government, λειτουργία; and they were all paid directly out of the state treasury, held by the king. See *Supra*, chap. vi., *passim*.

[81] See I., p, 134, note 1. Dr. Oehler, *MSS.*, remarks as follows: "Erwähnen möchte ich noch den Δημοθοινία Eid und Beschluss, CIA. IV.2, 841 (396 vor Chr.), der θίασοι als staatsliche Unterabtheilungen nennt, (gefunden in Dekeleia), und den Beschluss der Peiraienser, gegen θίασοι: CIA., II.add., 573 (IV. Jahrh. v. Chr)." This was very near to the times of the great strike of the 20,000. The Inscr. is valuable, as it shows that their government employ displeased the Athenians, and it furthur proves that the slaves were strongly organized; because the protest was against the θίασος, of Decelea.

[82] Le Bas, III., 1620: Ἱερὰ περιπολιστικὴ εὐσεβὲς σύνοδος καὶ σύμπας ξυστὸς τῶν περὶ Τραιανον καὶ Ἀδρίανον. It is Phrygian, a wandering, law-abiding association or synod of fully equipped choral dancers doing service for Trajan and Hadrian. Oehler shows quite a number of similar θίασοι of this sort existing during the first two centuries of our era. Athen., *Mitth.*, VII., 1882, p. 142: CIG,, 2811-2816; Athen., *Mitth.*, XIII., 1888, p, 173, No. 14; CIG, 3078, and others.

lent agricultural system of an enormous population, at that time supposed to be Buddhistic, or almost Christian. Industry was socialized and the government constructed these vast reservoirs and maintained the finest conceivable method of irrigation.[83]

We frequently have occasion to speak of the Kurios, an officer in these unions who after serving faithfully a term of at least five years, became the prime manager of a brotherhood and was endowed, under the law, with the power of managing the sub-letting of the member's labor to the state. Such power was never granted until the officer was crowned; and we now propose to emit some light on this subject of crowning. The inscriptions show that the crowns were usually laurel, ivy, gold, olive, mostly wild olive, cereals, willow, tulip, poplar and finally and sadly, thorns.

A wonderful thing about crown-honors is, that the blessing thus conferred and promulgated was not only for life but existed after death; and their belief was, just as their protecting saint assured them, that the crowning carried with it immortality and bliss—an unspeakable boon. A crowning day was a great event; and the person thus receiving it was immortalized and immensely honored. Quite surely we can trace in the humble crowning of these labor unions stretching back 400 years before Christ, the ordeal of sainthood to its origin and final melting into a tenet of the Christian religion.[84] Away back in the days of Pericles the Greek eranos was in the habit of crowning certain of its members with wreaths of wild olive. According to Dr. Foucart, the crown was always an accompaniment of the eulogium. It was most frequently formed by a simple foliage known in Greek as "thallou stephanos," and

[83] Abulfeda, (See *Encyc Brit., Article, Lake Dwellings*) gives some important facts. A. was a geographer; 13th century. Apamean lake, useful to agriculture in those times, was much outdone by the wonderful artificial reservoirs of the island of Ceylon whose immensity, strength and antiquity surpass our understanding.

[84] CIG. 2525 b, lines 30 to 38: καὶ ὁ ἐπιστάτις τοῦ κοινοῦ ἢ ὁ ἱεροκῆρυξ ἀνεγορευέτο τὸ κήρυγμα τόδε : "Τὸ κοινὸν τὸ Ἁλιαδᾶν καὶ Ἁλιαστᾶν ἐτίμασε εἰς τὸν ἀεὶ χρόνον Διονυσόδωρον Ἀλεξανδρῆ, εὐεργέταν τοῦ κοινοῦ, ἐπαίνωι, χρυσέωι στεφάνωι, διδωτι δὲ αὐτῶι τὰς τιμὰς καὶ ζῶντι καὶ μεταλλάξαντι τὸν βίον ἀρετᾶς ἕνεκα καὶ εὐνοίας, ἂν ἔχων διατελῖ εἰς τε τὰ κοινὰ καὶ τοὺς αὐτοῦ ἐρανιστάς" which means: The brother and sisterhood of the Haliades and Haliastes have honored Dionysiadorus of Alexandria for all time for the reason that he was the benefactor of the union. They have conferred upon him a eulogy, and also a crown of gold. It accords to him these honors during his entire life and after his death, as a memorial of his virtue and goodness which he never ceased to exert in the common interest of the eranists of his association.

it was very often composed of material corresponding with crowns of the peculiar divinity endorsed by the union which acted as a protector of the brotherhood. Thus the Panatheniasts made their crowns of olive for Teos, the seat of the great Gemeinde. Some made them of the lyre tulip, and others of white poplar, a tree consecrated to the sun. Some crowns were made of flowers and there are inscriptions showing that members honored by these crowns had the privilege of wearing them at occasions as long as they lived. Occasionally a crown of gold adorned one of these honored members. There was always a great feast, mostly managed by the women when a crowning was to take place raising an officer to this perpetual rank of honor.

The crowning of the dead was also of frequent occurrence,[85] and it dates from far above the second century preceding the Christian era; because Tertullian wrote a work on crowning, after he had lapsed back into the Solonic brotherhoods whence he came.[86] Tertullian, who wrote the Corona after his celebrated "lapse" into some secret society, devoted three chapters to a strong argument in favor of Christian common sense admitting that no harm could possibly come of it; and we see that crowning members in the ancient unions with honors of various sorts, is one of the remarkable features of the inscriptions. Tertullian, disgusted with the pious sanctimony of a priest-power growing up around him, lapsed back into the unions where he wrote the Corona. In connection herewith, describing crowns, we have Gorius, who mentions Tertullian with others.[87] In

[85] Oehler, *MSS.*, "Bekränzung des Grabmals durch einen Verein, Aigina, Le Bas, II., 1707, in einem Kranze: ὁ θίασος ὁ Φαινεμάχου; ausser dem χαῖρε." See also, Le Bas, III., 1743n, where there appears a crowning: οἱ σκηνετικοί καὶ ἐργασαί tent and scenic workers.

[86] Smith, *Dictionary of the Bible*, I., p. 511: "According to Pherecydes (Αὐτόχθενες, time of Herodotus), Saturn was the first to wear a crown. Diodorus says Jupiter was the first by the gods, after the conquest of the Titans; Pliny, Harpocration and others ascribe its earliest use to Bacchus who gave to Ariadus a crown of gold and Indian gems, and assumed the laurel after his conquest of India. Leo Ægyptus attributes the invention to Isis whose wreath was cereal. Tertullian, *De Corona*, argues against crowns. as unnatural and idolatrous (De Cor. Milites, cap. 7ff.). Still the ordinary and high priests wore the crown (στέφανος)" See Josephus, Ant. III. 7.

[87] Gorius, *Mon. sive Columbar*, p. xxix.: "Qui coronas conficiebant, floresque laneis floccis, et velleribus alte suspensis nectebant, et eleganter aptabant, ut clare ostendit vetustum anaglyphum quod extat in Florentino nostro Baptisterio, 'Coronarii' appellabantur; quorum fit mentio in antiquis tabulis penes Gruterum, ac Fabrettum; 'Coronarii' item dicti a Tertulliano quidem supplicis ex numero sacrificulorum; item servi qui Reipublicæ temporibus coronas in triumphis ferebant; quæ postea in manibus a quibusdam victoriolis deferebanter et triumphalibus Augustorum curribus appendebantur, quas victoriolas describit Prudentius."

course of time, after the power of the prelates had grown avaricious and haughty and succeeded in merging the socialism of the unions into the grasping claw of kings, there fell over these loving, self-help combinations a conspiracy for their extermination and they all, with their crowns and mutual care and love, went down at one fell swoop at the Council of Laodicea.

Partly allied with the crowning system of the ancient unions was the price and remuneration of labor. It is neccessary to begin with this Kurios or managing director whom we have seen crowned and honored.

The manner of rewarding service among the organizations has been quite thoroughly discussed by the archæologists. In the orgeones, eranoi, thaisoi and therapeutæ there were often two distinct methods of recompense—that of money and of the emulatory, which carried with it many priviliges. Sometimes even the magistrates were paid in this way.[88] It often happened that the magistrates received no other recompense than that of honors, which belong to the emulatory. In other words, they were paid in "recognitions." This may be easily accounted for if we consider that the eranos was a life within the veil. Every one had enough in common with the rest; and they had no use for money, or the flattering emoluments which characterize our vitiated competitive system.[89] The same may be said of the common membership. They worked for each other in working under their kurios or lord. He was not in any respect like our bosses in the management of an industry. His business was to oversee the happiness of the entire flock. They were to have each an equal share of the common product of the labor of the organization, and thus the industry of each contributed to the recompense of all.

How different was this from the wretched system going on at the same time in the outside world! We are indebted for a clear statement on this subject to an

[88] Fouc., *Ass. Rel*,. p. 33, "Afin donc que les Orgéons montrent d' une manière évidente leur reconnaissance pour les prêtresses désignées par le sort, qui ont fait preuve de zèle à l' égard de la déesse et de la communité." The Greek of the inscriptions which is no. 7 of Foucart, lines 6-8; Dumont, Essai sur la Chron. Athen., p. 46: Εὐφιλήτου ἄρχοντος, καλῶς καὶ εὐσεβῶς, τὴν ἱερωσύνην ἐξήγαγεν καὶ τὰ λοιπά.

[89] The same author, p. 30, in explanation of his notes, 30, 22, 24, 18 and 43, brings conclusive evidence that there was much zeal and rivalry in the hearts of the business managers of those days, to secure success.

Italian scholar.[90] After recounting the statistics of living for many people without the advantage of an organization, he returns to those employed by the state. We first proceed to show the wages of the unorganized; and our readers must be thankful to this tireless savant for plunging into and plodding among recondite anaglyphs and unearthing vague and cursory hints of the ancient pen.[91] The Body of Attic inscriptions presided over by Böckh and variously edited, was also ransacked by Mauri. It was soon discovered that wages of employés at the Prytaneum, or in other terms, wages paid by the government were far in excess of the pay offered by the individual concerns.[92] The difference of more than the price of board between organized and unorganized workmen as shown in the figures of our note, is remarkable. In the examples at Eleusis and the Prytaneum at the city of Athens we see the members of unions employed. With their powerful influence in securing the appointment or election of the agoranomoi and their managers of public works, their membership often got double the wages of the outside, unorganized freedmen.

We are likewise fortunate enough to have some statistics of wages for the scenic artists. M. Foucart has brought out to our notice the inscription of Le Bas and

[90] Mauri, *I Citadini Lavatori*, pp. 74–75, gives us statistics for Ancient Greece, at various dates. Aristophanes in Ἐκκλησιάζουσι, 310 (4th century B.C.), records that porters handling the waste and filth of eating houses got 3 oboles a day, 9 cents, They had no eranos or unions.
Lucian, *Timon*, 6, 12, gives Timon one-half a δράχμα, or 10 cents a day for plowing. They had no eranos.
Athenæus, *Deipnosophistæ*, iv., 168, reports that the philosophers Menedemos and Asclepiades worked nights at grinding grain at 2 δράχμαι, per night, to get money for their studies.

[91] We translate M. Mauri's *data*: In the *Corp. Inscr. Atticarum* is a fragment showing that two sawyers received 1 δραχμα each, per day, for 16 days. The same builder employed 2 roofers at 1 δρ. a day, each, for seven days, A carpenter had 5 oboles a day and board. An obolus was nearly 3 cents, so that his 5 ob. amounted to 15 cents, Federal money, see Rangabé, *Inscr.* I., p. 46. Mowers got 1 δραφμα, or 20 cents and food. Roofers are again found to receive 20 cents and table board. Mauri, p, 78, further found that wheelbarrow men without board, had their 20 cents per day. The above were all within the years B.C. 408–404.

[92] CIA, *frag*, i., 225 whole days at the Prytaneum, in 3 cases were 1 δρ. with board at the common table and full living per short day, they are found in an inscr. at Eleusis of B.C. 329–328, CIA., II., 2,834 c lines 26–28, to amount up to 2 δρ. & 3 ὀβολοι, for 3 men each, with the οἰκόσιτος or food at public table each day, the work being that of cleaning the park, scraping the columns, and working wood. In lines 28-30, of the same slab, brick, tile and hod carriers got 1 δρ. and 3 ὀβολοι each with meals at the common table, Same *inscr.*, lines 31–32, polishers and porters in the vestibule of the temple of Eleusis, with board, got 7½ oboles each. Lines 32–34, give artificers in the temple, 1 δρ., 3 oboles. Scavengers got the same. Lines, 60–62 give laborers the same price and fare for leveling and grading. But the sawyers who likewise ate at headquarters, according to lines 53–54, got each 1 and one-half δρ. which was still better.

Waddington wherein quite a list of various persons[93] is given, each receiving 100 drachmas or francs, the equivalent of one mina, for the year,[94] for those hired from Apameia and Jerusalem, and double that amount for their own brothers. It was more than a century before our era. During the time of Julius Cæsar, the playwrights of the Peloponnesus got about three-fourths of a drachma per day. But a given amount had then a higher purchasing power than now.[95] An inscription found at Athens gives one drachma per day to the artists for music and stage performance. Undoubtedly this included their food at the common table either of the prytaneum, or the mageireion of the unions themselves. At any rate they had their living in addition to the pay in money.

But the relative power of their low wages, especially of those unaided by an organization, is vividly portrayed by Dr. Mauri, who has brought the splendid disquisitions of August Böckh under contribution, in a comprehensive manner, upon the living of ancient times.[96] The interest or proceeds of money in those days was twelve percent; and it has been estimated that a well-to-do family of four persons could live and appear decently for 540 drachmas, or the interest, or other earnings of 45 minæ, at 12 percent. An estimate has been

[93] Calculating his figures from an *inscription*, CIG. 1845, lines, 15-25, Foucart, *De Coll. Scen. Art.*, p. 55, reports the stones as follows: "Mittito civitas, secundum agonothetæ legem, ad conducendos artifices et Dinoysia ex quo incipient, altero quoque anno peragat, nisi bellum obstet, differentibus senatu et concione. Conducito, e foenore trium talentorum, quinquaginta minarum Corinthiarum pretio, tres tibicines, tres tragoedos, tres comœdos (id est, tres greges tragicos et comicos)......Danto quoque artificibus e foenore victum justum, præter quinquagina minas."

[94] Le Bas, *Inscr. d' Asie Mineure*, 291, "Stephanophoro Apollinis post Antigonum Antigoni filium, agonotheta Theodoro Melanionis filio, ex eis qui prius promiserant in Dionysiis, solverunt: Agonotheta Mnesitheus Athenodori, natura vero, Menedemi filius; choragi, Menedemus Menecratis, Theophilus Anaxippi, Dionysius Menipp, Menippi, Menotimus Podonis, quisque ducentas drachmas; ex inquilinis, Agathinus Leontis Apamensis, Nicetas Iasonis Hierosolymita,, uterque centum drachmas. Foucart, *De Coll. Scenic. Artif.*, pp. 60-61,

[95] Fouc., *ibid.*, p. 55-56: "Igitur quinguaginta minæ idem valeant quod ætate nostra fere ducentæ. Illud quoquo animadvertendum, eamdem semper mercedem, quicunque futnri sint artifices, solvendam; ex quo apparet non tam artifici quam religionis observandæ studiasos fuisse Corcyrences."

[96] Mauri, *I Cittadini Lavatori*, p. 46. We render his Italian into English to facilitate the reader: "One chenice of grain per day per person; this for 4 persons cost 1 obole each day, or some 12 cents, and was a customary consumption for a poor family (famiglia più povere). For a whole year 60 δράχμαι. Böckh, *Staatshh.*, I, 141. One ὀβολος a day for boiled meat, ὄψον, cost them 240 δρ. Clothes and shoes, 15 δρ.. per person or 60 δρ. for the 4, per year. A residence used to cost 36 δρ. Total for the year, 396 δράχμαι. Time of Socrates.

made of the cost of living for a poor family of four persons during the time of Demosthenes.[97]

But there existed one horror in those days which had to be done away with before any great progress could be realized. The tools, or implements of labor were in the hands of the propertied class the same as to-day; and they were placed in competition with the labor of the unions in the same manner as is being done at the present time.

These tools of labor, so enormously used to run down the wages of human labor, were human slaves. The principal difference between then and now was that in ancient times the implements of labor were animate beings, whereas now they are coming more and more to be inanimate things. In principle, however, they were one and the same so far as their pernicious work of superseding the means of living by cheap labor product was concerned. We have shown in the first volume of this work the great numbers of slaves owned and habitually subject to employers, by rich individuals.[98]

We shall now submit a schedule of statistics of the wages of slaves, paid to the masters who sub-let their work to contractors, in a manner which may be compared to the present system of displacement of labor by machinery. If we compare the free with the ill-bargained slave labor we shall see that the poor freedman, if not sustained by the powerful organizations that constantly worked their influence politically to obtain public employment from governments and cities, were trampled to dust by outside competition. This is deemed necessary to show clearly from the very first, in order to illustrate the need of keeping themselves incessantly hedged about with strong labor unions everywhere. The weighty fact is also apparent that these unions of

[97] The above statement showing the requirements of a well-to-do family at Athens is taken from the *Oration* of Demosthenes *Contra Phœnippus*, 32, and 40, cf. Mauri, *I Citt. Lav.*, p. 78. We also have a statement of the cost of living, for the earlier date of Socrates, per year, for a poor family of 4 persons. It is: "Una Chenice (a pound and a quarter) al giorno a testa, or per person," during the year, 60 δράχμαι; for ὄψον or boiled beef once a day for the year 240 δράχμαι; for shoes and clothes, 60 δρ.; residence at 30 δράχμαι. Total, 396 δράχμαι or 90 δρ. less than was the cost of a living in the time of Demosthenes. A mina was 100 δρ. and amounted to $18,25, Amer. Federal money.

[98] Vol. II., p. 49, for members of the vernae, how slaves supplanted free, 143; how captured as prisoners of war thousands at a time, 191-195, degraded from their freedom for purposes of cheap labor, 286: 4,116 owned by Claudius, at a time and 560 owned by Crassus, and the work he hired them out to do; both p. 340; for further information see *Index* in verb. *Helots*.

trades and professions, whose members were more educated than the slaves, could throw their influence upon the boards of public works, thereby to an enormous extent receiving hope and material comfort. The displacment of their labor by slaves as human machines which in reality was very analogous to this at the present day, as the inanimate machines, was impossible where the unions controlled the public works. What wonder then, in those dire and dangerous times environing the advent of the messiah and the apostolic age, that such countless unions are found to have dappled earth in all parts where the right of combination so graciously existed under the Solonic dispensation!

But lest our own opinion on the displacement of labor by machinery be not accepted to the effect that anciently the slave or animate machine was superseded by present inanimate machines; and lest we be regarded as dreamy and untenable, we give the words and figures of living scholars.[99]

Referring to the remarkable prediction of Aristotle who in his treatise in the Nichomachian Ethics, calling such slavishness that of animate tools, he shows that this instrument was valued at only ten cents per day. In the service of contractors, a certain man paid only two oboles which were only worth three cents each, inasmuch as it took sixteen oboles to be worth a drachma, or franc of 20 cents. This shows that a poor slave's labor was constantly pitted against the free labor of the unions which existed in great numbers at that time, the third and fourth century before Christ. Miserable competition! A day's work sold at six cents! Again, where the slave was fed, the poor wretch and machine of labor only earned his three oboles per day, or nine cents! Our previous figures have shown that a freedman if organized, got his 20 to 30 oboles; and if he worked for the bureaus of public works he was also fed at the sumptuous table of the Prytanes.

Dr. Mauri, who furnishes us with the following statistics which he gathered from the works of Böckh and

[99] Mauri, *I Citt. Lav.*, pp, 83-84: "La concorrenza invece più dannosa e deleteria al lavoro dei cittadini era esercitata dagli schiavi che per la loro condizione di semplici strumenti animati (ὄργανα ἔμψυχα, Aristot., Eth. Nic., viii., 11, 6), a completa disposizione del capitalista, tenevano nell' economia antica un posto approssimabile a quello della macchina nell' industria moderna."

the Body of Attic Inscriptions, after admitting that the slave whose labor, subbed out to contractors, was in all respects similar to the machines of to-day which undermine and supersede the working people and drive them to poverty and despair, proceeds to give the low rates these human machines earned for their owners.[100]

As clearly shown by its own monuments, the eranos of the ancient Solonic organization had a specific function, long before Christ, in aiding the emancipation of humanity from slavery. The archæologists who have given this important and surprising subject an analysis do not hesitate to declare that it was undoubtedly this system which filled the world with freedmen. It was too sacred to be molested or meddled with by the enemies of the unions, even during the Roman conquests. Secret and gentle, it was allowed to go on selling men to God under the awful solemnities of the great imaginary Dionysan or Pythian Apollo, the almighty Jehovah protector of toil and its fruits and the giver of joys to man.[101]

If God bought man out of the bondage of slavery it is interesting to know what he was in the habit of paying their owners for them. Fortunately we are in possession, through the tell-tale records of inscriptions, of several accurate prices of the slaves bought and sold during those ages.[102] While the average was about one to two hundred dollars, the list, in drachmas is also given. It is interesting to know that the Jews in bondage under the ancient law, are also given in the list of prices, and thus we obtain the information that not only the Syrians, Greeks, Armenians and Phrygians

---

[100] *Ibid.*, 84; "Il nutrimento, τροφὴ, è valutato una mezza δράχμα per giorno a testa, CIA. II., 2, 834 b, lin. 4, 42–43; sono poi anche indicate le spese:

a) Del sorvegliante, un uomo per 17 schiavi, pagoto quasi 2 oboli al giorno, oltre ai 3 della pensione alimentaria, CIA. II., 2, 834 b, *linee*, 5–6, 43.

b) Dei provveditori di vivere che li recano sul luogo del lavoro due uomini a 8 δράχμαι e 2 oboli al mese ciascuno, Böckh, *Staatshaushalt.*, II., pag. 90; CIA. II., 2, 834 b, *linee* 57–58; Böckh, *Anmerkungen*, p. 33.

[101] This is the general definition given to the Διόνυσος Καθηγεμῶν, to which we have referred very frequently. He is shown by the virtue of this name, to have always been considered a forerunner, although, so long before the real Advent it is difficult to determine just what is meant.

[102] Foucart, *Affranchissement des Esclaves*, etc., p. 49: "La rançon moyenne est donc de 3 à 5 mines:" about 500 francs or $100 in Federal money, but Foucart explains that on account of certain equivocations of the laws or customs, there often occurred tormenting restrictions such as really brought prices up to 800 francs or δράχμαι; and as we have seen, p. 310, n. 90-93, of vol. II., a δρ. of that early time was worth about 2 of the present day, we find a slave selling at about $200 of our money.

got redemption from slavery by being sold to God[103] through the beneficent ministrations of the eranos of the Solonic dispensation, but also the Hebrew.[104] We shall show in the following chapter of this work, a long list of inscriptions proving that the eranos, into which the christianity was planted, and for the first hundred years nourished, was largely made up of Hebrews. The Hebrews, especially that problematic fraction of them outside of Palestine who followed the Solonic rather than the Mosaic ordeal, were strongly tinctured with the Greek mysteries and took naturally to the protective unions of the Solonic law.[105]

About 355 years before Christ a serious proposition was made by Xenophon to the Athenian government.[106]

---

[103] A leather worker brought 1,000 drachmas; a female flutist, 1,000 δρ.; an artisan, the trade not given, was sold for 600 δρ. It was found that no difference existed as to nationality. Phrygian, Athenian, Macedonian, Peloponnesian slaves, all went to the mighty Jehovah at the prices set by their owners, without inquiry regarding their place of birth or language. An Armenian brought 1,800 δράχμαι, while another brought only 300. A female Syrian, speaking Syriac who "possessed" in all probability, some extraordinary talent, like that of the woman converted by Paul, (*Acts*, xvi., 16-19.) was sold for 5,000 δρ. If women "possessed" were of such enormous profits to their owners, who can wonder at the ofttimes ridiculed story of Paul in the Acts of the Apostles? Other females from Syria brought only 200 and 300 δρ. The ordinary price of Thracian slaves was the same. A certain inscription is extant which records the price of Lacedæmonian slaves at 300 to 10,000 δράχμαι. Dr. Foucart, from whose valuable dissertation, *Mém. sur l' Affranch. des Eslaves par forme de vente a une Divinité*, p. 50, says: "La valeur ne dépendait ni du sexe ni de l' origine, mais de l' age, de la force ou de l' addresse de l' esclave." The marvel of these statistics is, that they are the registry of each slave's sale to this god, chiseled upon slabs in this divinity's own temple then and there.

[104] Fouc., *Affranch. des Esclaves*, p. 48: ......"le Juif et la Juive que nous trouvons dans nos inscriptions, ont ils été arrachés de leur patrie dans la lutte des Séleucides contre les Maccabees." On this page not all of which show Hebrew nationalities but including: "á Delphes ou dans les villes voisines Arabiques, servant à côté de Bastarnes, de Sarmates et d' Illyriens," we have the following list of prices: taken from the inscriptions: Out of 486 slaves only 25 were sold for less than 200 drachmas or francs. Sixty-two brought from 200 to 300; one hundred and seventy commanded as high a price as 300 to 400; one hundred and thirty-nine, 400; sixty brought 500; thirty sold as high as 600 francs. "Ce sont là les prix qui revienent le plus frequemmant, mais on en trouve aussi de plus élevés;" and cites one slave selling for 700 francs : eight for 800; three for 900; eight for 1,000: one for 1,500, and one for 1,800 francs or drachmans,

[105] Am Rhyn, *Mysteria*, Eng. *trans.*, p. 92: "Ever since their liberation from the Babylonian captivity by the decree of Cyrus, the Jews, even those who remained in the region of the Euphrates and native land under the Persian scepter, and therefore, after the conquest of Persia by Alexander, were exposed to the powerful influence of Grecian culture."

[106] Xen., *Revenues of Attica, De Vectigalibus*, IV., 17 ff. See also Aristot., *Pol.*, II., 4, 23, who in the words: "τοὺς τὰ κοινὰ ἐργαζομένους" is believed to mean that the nation should use its slaves as machines for manufacture and distribution in common for the plentitude of all who were free. Xenophon is more elaborate and explicit. He thought the state of Attica should let all its slaves and as many more as could be purchased, to individual contractors who were to pay a certain small sum daily for each slave's labor. This rent or hire was to go into the revenue, to defray the costs of maintaining the government.

It recommended that the Athenians hire their enormous slave population already state property, by contract to men of enterprise; the rent or hire to go for revenue. It was a most inhuman conception and would if carried out, have ruined all the trade unions of Northern Greece, and driven the entire freedman population into trampage and starvation. The proposition was met by a stormy protest from the organizations. There is an inscription found at Laurium of the date of the close of the Peloponnesian war, not far from B.C., 400, showing a protest of the organized silver miners who seem to have been extremely guarded against dangers of this kind.

They had reason to be watchful. Slaves used as mere tools of labor were property of the state and worked in large numbers as accountants, interpreters, clerks, secretaries, janitors, messengers and porters. Böckh has shown us that they were paid wages in a manner somewhat similar to the present civil service employés. But the slaves thus officiating being simple instruments of the stingy state, only received the miserable sum of three oboles for a long day's work which with rigid economy was barely enough to decently clothe them and purchase a poor pittance of food. When the state or city hired a free union man from the organizations, about double that sum was paid to him, besides, as we have just shown, he generally had good meals at the prytaneum's common tables, and he moreover, as is now for the first time made public, was allowed by a provision of the Solonic law to divide the day into three equal parts of which the hours of labor was one.[107]

As we have shown in the first volume of this work, there was found at Rome, during the apostolic age, an enormous sepulchre called a columbarium, buried in the débris of neglect and forgetfulness the roof of which was as deep as 7 feet under the surface of the ground,

---

[107] Hesiod's Έργα καὶ Ἡμέραι is perhaps the oldest written work against the hardships of slavish drudgery. The inscription protesting against the degradation of free labor by the machine labor of slaves comes later, and Macrobius, whom we have quoted in vol., I., p. 164, note 9 clearly proves that the same agitation was going on at his day. Commodianus. *Instructiones*, chap. 34, rebukes and exhorts the hard working slaves as follows: "The unsubdued neck refuses to bear the yoke of labor... O people, O man, thou brother, do not be a brutal flock. Pluck thyself forth and disengage thyself by thine own efforts. Assuredly thou art not cattle; thou art not a beast; thou art born a man." *Ante-Nicine Fathers*, IV., p. 209. Eng. trans. Date, 240 A.D.

which was restored in the year 1729 and its contents analyzed. It was the burial place of the slaves and freedmen of the early Cæsars. The practice of the unions of these people who seem to have been thoroughly organized, and into which the Christians to a remarkable extent planted their faith soon afterwards, was to burn their dead and conserve the ashes in a niche,[108] with an inscription which to this day tells us the name of the being once buried in the sacred sepulchre. Among others here laid to rest, are members of the unions of cooks, clothing cutters and tailors, bakers, sandal makers, guilders, roofers, pavers, painters, doctors and surgeons.[109]

The prevalence of countless unions in those times accounts for the strange fact that no charities were known in the ancient world. There were asylums of refuge, but no hospitals. Even in early christianity there was no such thing as charity.[110] The fearful conditions of[111] slavery prevailing everywhere was greatly relieved and assuaged by the powerful influence of the Solonic unions which held their power and popularity far down into the Christian era. "To purchase a slave and save a soul" was an injunction found in the writings of some later authors.[112] That which the eranos was enormously in the habit of doing was evidently followed by the Apostolic fathers, and it looks as if the early purchase was ordered to continue the emancipation as it found the eranos doing.

In pursuing our investigation of the prices of slaves and means of living we are indebted to Dr. Daniel Quinn, professor of Greek in the Catholic University at Washington, who for a long time resided at Athens, and

[108] See Vol. I., *plate* opposite p. 345, showing the burial niches for cinerary urns. The great columbarium has thousands of these niches for the urns, and directly under this little "pigeon hole," was cut an inscription for each person honored with burial there. Strange to say, we find among the rest several names mentioned by the Apostle Paul, of which more soon.
[109] Levasseur, *Hist. Classes Ouv.*, I., p, 11-12. De Rossi, *Roma Sotteranea*, Vol. I., *passim*.
[110] Granier, *Hist. Classes Ouv.*, p. 101, could not find any evidence of mendicancy; "Durant la période primitive de l' esclavage pur il n'y avait pas encore de mendiants."
[111] Polyb., xxxviii.. 2; xl., 2-5; xxxvii., 4, and elsewhere.
[112] *Apostolic Constitutions*, Book II., chap., 61. Provision is here made for Christians to purchase slaves for the purpose of saving them. The injunction is given as though a common thing; and it strongly suggests that it was a continuation of the old method of emancipation by sale of the slave to a god recounted in the present volume of this work, mostly the product of monumental evidence. Cf. *Index*. By recognizing them as equals they have gradually become equals.

who has kindly aided us with some valuable communications on the edicts of prices uttered by the emperors Hadrian and Diocletian.[113]

There is very little on record either of the inscriptions or of the ancient literary world to prove that unions and brotherhoods of the Solonic system ever did much in the way of philosophical agitation. They were intensely practical and business-like institutions, attending to little beyond the duty of earning a good living for the common membership and arranging and enjoying their own methods of amusements. Nevertheless they had some ideas about a vast workshop in the beyond. There was the theory of the Masterworkman or the *Demiourgos*. It was interwoven with heaven and the bliss of perfect economical conditions; a vast workshop presided over by their lord who was forever to be their demiurge and to conduct, as he had done on earth, celestial works in the realms of glory. It is believed that this was the origin of the great idea of one God who reigned in the world beyond this; and it conflicted with the pagan belief in many deities, one presiding over each of the prime necessities of mankind. The Asiatic Jews were especially defenders of this belief in a hereafter which took the form of a vast celestial workshop where all things were created by the mutual labor of the very millions who had been members in this world and who had gone to the glorious eternity, each with his hammer, or with his square and compass, to while away, in the old brotherly union the blessed days of his love-inspired, celestial forever. In the exuberent joys of this grand heavenly workshop the apprentice rose to the high honor of an efficient tradesman and amidst the delightful smiles of God in his majestic supremacy, as author and finisher over the beautiful mechanism of heaven,

---

[113] Dr. Quinn, *Personal Contribution*, writes: "The inscription on the gate of the agora at Athens refers especially to the price of olive oil. It is published in the *Corpus Inscriptionum Atticarum*, III., 38. It is an edict of the emperor Hadrian. But a more important inscription for the price of things in antiquity is the edict of Diocletian. About the year 303, A.D., the emperor Diocletian published an edict regulating the price at which commodities were to be sold. This edict was published in various parts of the empire by being inscribed on stone monuments. A Latin copy of it is to be found on the outer wall of a temple at Stratonikeia in Karia. It has been published by Mommsen in the third volume of the *Corpus Inscriptionum Latinarum* where you may find other details concerning it. The articles specified in the edict are the ordinary kinds of provisions, grain, meat, hams, sausages, fish, etc. A fragment of the same Edict was found at Plataia by the Americans when excavating there. It was published by Mommsen in *Papers* of the American School at Athens, Vol. V., pp. 302-312."

with Dionysos, whom they had worshiped below, ennobler of mankind and giver of joys, forerunner of some messiah, perhaps the pre-christian Jew's, they strongly believed they were to labor in the self-same brotherhood amid the self-same males and females who in eternity as on earth, sang pæans to the infinite and partook of the abundance at the self-same table that had nourished them in the vale of tears.

We have already, in our remarks on the extraordinary love of these unions for one another, seen that they never consented to part, but ordained that even in the grave they should be buried close to each other, and if cremated, that their ashes be mixed so that they might in the other world be in close contact and enjoy each other's society. The idea of a demiurge is but an extension of this contact. Originally the same socialism was conceived to continue in heaven as had succeeded in protecting them here; and to the primitive mind it was easy to imagine the same workshops, the same familiar Kurios, and the same great masterworkman, next in majesty to Jehovah himself, presiding and providing for the benefit of the millions who used to labor in the earthly workshops.[114] This primitive notion regarding the demiurgos or masterworkman, grew beyond the scope of the unions; for soon after the Christians were adopted into them a great and perhaps deleterious Gnostic agitation set in and caused many schisms and wranglings. It later assumed the form of what was for centuries known as angelology.[115] A curious fact[116]

[114] Δημιουργός frequently comes into the true inscriptions; also the mixture of ashes of the cinerary urns certainly does. The belief in a vast heavenly workshop presided over by a δημιουργός is but an expansion of the earthly love which makes these unions celebrated. But it bears every appearance of being later. Tertullian, arguing against Marcion, believes that the δημιουργός is the true God. Here Tertullian shows that he was an initiate; for he seems to believe in a great Master Workman of the universe. Origen, *De Principiis*, IV., c. i., § 8, makes reflections against the Demiurge whom the Jews worshipped. Irenæus, refuting Basilides, goes in a long strain against the Gnostic's "immense and innumerable multitudes of heavens always in process of being made."

[115] Irenæus, *Cont. Hær.*, II., vii., 7, argues the labor question through vague metaphor, where he shows that heaven was one vast workshop superintended by a wondrous Masterworkman who is Jesus Christ. Creation is the pleroma. So again, in the same Adv. Hær., II., vii., 2, he charges that they, the unions, would make Jesus the Δημιουργός or master-workman.

[116] See Vol. I., p. 58, note 2. Even Jupiter was originally a man. After death he was worshiped, probably first by his family and slaves, and afterwards by the tribes and nations. Almost all the great deities and immortals were once mere human beings. Mosheim, *Eccles. Hist.*, I., p. 25, 26, making reference to Creuzer, *Symbolik und Mythologie der Alten Völker*. Vossius, *Idola trie*, I., says: "The greater part of the gods of all nations were ancient heroes, famous for their achievements and their worthy deeds; such as kings, generals and founders of cities."

must here be registered: Throughout all the investigations we have been able to make, based on the science of inscriptions, as well as literary work of ancient writers, we fail to discover any officer elected or appointed for life. There was no pope during the early Apostolic age. The member went directly to God, that is, to his patron saint; and this deity, it is now known, was often a human being when in life. The member went straight to his own divinity, who was the apotheocized one once actually living on earth. But nothing appeared like a man placed in power for life until after the foothold of the greedy and ambitious gain-getters, and after their success in destroying the associations, in their own unscrupulous service of power. That they were utilized in being planted into by the early christians is proved by hundreds of inscriptions and many hints and statements of early writers, including a dozen pagan authors, many of great merit, and several of the prominent Ante-Nicene fathers of the church. These important and revolutionary disclosures are rapidly multiplying as the archæologists dig up the ruins in which they have for centuries been buried.

In closing this chapter it becomes necessary to give the statistics of their numbers and also a word more on the geography of this international Ionian Synod or great Gemeinde. Fortunately this information is at command. The epigraphists of the various schools and seminaries have secured enough of the glyptic relics to establish their positions, and list the towns, cities and country places in which their activities were felt, from about 500 B.C. to 363 A.D., or fully 800 years.[117] No less than 53 such centers of activity have been alphabetically listed. In all essential matters the scenic organizations resembled those of the other trades and professions whose sole object was to procure a living. They are reported to have employed all the various methods of the self-help organization. There was a great population at that time, and the country remained

---

[117] The more ancient plays performed were tragedies. These cover the eras of activity down to the emperors. Dion Chrisostom, the orator, who lived in the first century and had dealings with several Roman emperors, in his oration, xix., 487, says: "καὶ τὰ γε πολλὰ αὐτῶν ἀρχαῖα ἐστιν καὶ πολὺ σοφρωτερων ἀνδρῶν ἢ τῶν νυν τὰ μὲν κωμῳδιας ἅπαντα, τῆς δὲ τραγῳδίας τὰ μὲν ἰσχυρὰ ὡς ἔοικε, μένει· λέλω δὲ τὰ ἰαμβεία, καὶ τούσων μερη διεξίασιν ἐν τοῖς θιάτροις τὰ δὲ μαλακώτεα ἐξερρύηκε τὰ περὶ τὰ μέλη."

crowded with humanity until decimated and destroyed by the rage of the Roman conquests.

It was a common thing for the central direction of this great Ionian league to entertain bids from other parts desiring music. When a king, a prince or a rich man was about to give a banquet or other ceremony it was necessary to employ music and embellish the festivity with histrionic art. The Ionian artists stood ready at all times to supply this demand. Kings, emperors and nobles had only to send in their orders to the general head quarters at Teos, and the bargain was speedily arranged. The fact that this society had been engaged greatly enhanced the interest of the occasion and no doubt thousands attended on that account who would otherwise have remained absent. This worked as an inspiration, encouraging the crowds together and making a success of the entertainment. These events, on account of the skill and ardor of the artists more than any other cause, became so popular that for centuries the artists enjoyed what was almost equivalent to government recognition and pay.[118] The list of 52 places,

[118] We proceed to give the accredited list of towns and cities known to have had headquarters and to have been amalgamated with the great Gemeinde of Dionysan artists, as trade unions of the ancient Ionian league: They have been arranged alphabetically by Dr. Lüders, *Dionys. Künst.*, pp. 133-135:

1 Abdera, in Thrace; the city of the Gothamites.
2 Abydos, in Asia Minor, on the Hellespont.
3 Ægina, city and island in the Saronic Gulf.
4 Ætolia, town and country of Arcania, Greece.
5 Acarnia, neighborhood of Epirus, Greece.
6 Ambracia, colony of Corinthians, Greece.
7 Argos, city of the Pelopennesus.
8 Arkadia, a province of the Peloponnesus.
9 Athens, capital of Attic Greece.
10 Achaia, on the Corinthian Gulf.
11 Bœotia, Northern Greece.
12 Bosporus, city on the straits.
13 Byzantium, ancient Constantinople.
14 Gargorus, city of Troas, Asia Minor.
15 Herminines, territory of Hermion.
16 Ephesus, great city of Asia Minor.
17 Zakinthos, an island of the Ionian Sea.
18 Elen, city of Lucania.
19 Heracleia, in Thessaly.
20 Epiros, on the Adriatic.
21 Thronion, capital city of the Locri.
22 Histiæa, city of Attica.
23 Cassandria, City of Macedonia.
24 Cedræpolis, a city of Thrace.
25 Cephallus, a Grecian city.
26 Clitoria, a city of the Æqui.
27 Cnidas, a city of Caria.
28 Corinth, great city on the Corinthian Gulf.
29 Cynæthea, a city of Arcadia.
30 Cythera, in the island of South Laconia.

given below is sufficient to quell the wonder of readers of the life of Alexander the Great as to how he could gather so vast a musical and political force as 3,000 artists as is reported that he did on several occasions. He had only to write his order out and send it to Teos, the general headquarters of the great international league of unions, having their place of sojourn or residence in the towns and cities of the then known world, and the general Kurios or epemelites immediately dispatched to him terms and traveling agents who attended to the whole business with consummate ability.

But the 52 places cited by Dr. Lüders in 1878, have been added to since then. In fact, they are only a few of the Greek-speaking branches of the international union. Since then others have been found and enumerated; some in the old Pannonia, some in Spain and great numbers in Gaul and Britain. Many of the almost innumerable collegia of Italy frequently prove to have been members of the Dionysian artists.[119] During the time covered by these organizations, the Roman con-

31 Cyrenairea, on north coast of Africa.
32 Lacedæmon, in South Greece.
33 Milesia, city of Caria in Asia Minor.
34 Megara, great city of Attica.
35 Messenia, city of Peloponnesus.
36 Myrina, seaport of Ecelis, Asia Minor.
37 Naukratios, a seaport at the Canobic mouth of the Nile.
38 Opous, Opuntius, a town of Locris, Greece.
39 Pellene, a town on the Gulf of Corinth.
40 Rhodes, capital of Island of Rhodes.
41 Salamis, Island and town opposite Athens.
42 Samia, city of South Elis.
43 Sikyon, a city near the Isthmus of Corinth.
44 Sinopé town of Paphlagonia, or Black Sea.
45 Sosoi, a city in the Island of Cyprus.
46 Tarentum, a city on the Adriatic, Magna Græcia.
47 Tega, a city of Arcadia.
48 Tenesis, town and island in the Nile.
49 Troezen, city of Argolis, Saronic Gulf.
50 Philippi, city in Macedonia.
51 Chalcedon, city opposite Byzantium.
52 Chios, capital of Island of Chios.

Teos being this center, these 52 places were only some of the localities connected with the Great Gemeinde of the Ionian League.

[119] The author, while visiting the Museum of the old Ecclessia in the city of Vienna, in France, led by the courtesy of M. Joseph Piot, Director of the Bank of Beauregard, read a fine specimen of the Dionysan artists, and took a memoir of it, under the impression that it was a new discovery. Later, on comparison, it was found that this inscription had already been noted and analyzed. Savigny, *Guide Annuaire de Vienne*, 1876, p. 164. "Des coincidences d'Astaticus, de la corporation des Utriculaires, du dieu prudence." Delorme's, *trans*. This museum is in the old St. Peter's Church, but it was for a while in the Anc. temple Augustus Liviæ, built by Claudius in 41-43. An Inscription reads: "Con Sen Augusto,..Optimo et Divæ Augustæ." "Du consentement du Sénat: au dieu Augusti trés-bon trés grand et a la Déesse Augusta." This shows that the term Livia Augusta reached through the Apostolic Age.

quests raged with murderous fury. Their object was evidently to destroy the eranos, thiasos and collegium of the democratic dispensation of Solon, against which the competitive world raged with relentless force by war and intrigue. They sank into deeper and deeper secrecy and welded their fraternity with the great trade unions [120] into one vast economic brotherhood for sheer self-preservation. At the time of the celebrated Advent when the brutal conquests had imprisoned and sold into slavery innumerable multitudes of their membership, they were the most numerous; but had settled down into a qualm of awful secrecy which made them unknown and an indecipherable element. When taken in large numbers in Asia Minor, Rhodes and Greece and sold at Delos in slavery, they availed themselves of such opportunities as afforded, and at Rome, succeeded in earning and enjoying some protection under the Domus Augustus, or house of the Cæsars. This house of the Cæsars is one of the hitherto unriddled phenomena intimately allied with the planting of Christianity and will be exhaustively dealt with in this work, and in a manner which for the first time sheds light upon the early plant at Rome.

The socialism inherent in the Solonic dispensation and manifested in these unions which gradually grew into existence and shed light and economic influence over a large share of the human race, was in reality an evolutionary step in the direction of true political economy. It seems to have been the outcome of that primeval slavery of which we have treated in foregoing chapters of this work.[121] Slavery is there shown to have been the result of savagery, in which æon of man, the bully, who, surviving under the club-wielding force of the "fittest," pounded his way into the possession of property, and his innumerable children because his slaves and laboring machines.[122] He succeeded temporarily

[120] See chap. xvi., Sect. *Nero.*, treating of them. There should be observed a great difference between these two sets of labor organizations. Nevertheless, in the one idea of economic means of self-preservation they are one and the same.

[121] I., p. 84, *The Power of the Bully;* he was not a nomad or patriarch, but a typical Aryan property owner; See also *Index* to same vol., in *verb, slave* and *slavery.*

[122] Explained in this chapter. Vol. II., pp. 712-726. When after the great rebellions of the slaves against the masters and by means of organization, great numbers of them got their liberty, these machines became true men. Slavery began to give way to socialism. In that auspicious moment Christanity settled upon the world.

in bullying his way into possession of the property which his slaves and hirelings created. He is now being attacked afresh; and the contest that rages along the lines of civilization, is that of wages slavery against capitalism. It is the mighty principle of socialism, then, that has swept a new political economy into being and is furnishing the hope of a brilliant forth-coming enlightenment.[123] It has been proved a historical landmark that slavery, either of the vernæ or home-born quality which was the first and original, or of conquest as victims of war, did not abate the growth of population. Before the Roman conquests the indigenous, vernacular slaves so multiplied that there was a vast population, so much so that in Crete,[124] women from the time of Minos to Plato, were roaming irresponsibly along the shores of seas and paddling canoes to gain a subsistance from the gifts of the waves. Even as early as this, the poor were highly organized. During the rage of the conquests and the wars of the Greeks, Persians and Sicilians, humanity was greatly decimated by the murderous military havoc of fire, famine and sword, and millions were driven to the slavery of conquest. Great as was the desolation which resulted, we find that so soon as the peace policy of Augustus had its effect upon the generations, they again multiplied so as to be almost innumerable at Rome. The progress of emancipation however, continued and we shall soon find ourselves involved in the strange and almost subterranean story of the domus Augustus into which the Christians planted in trembling secrecy and under murderous, decimating persecutions during the reigns of Claudius,[125] Nero and Domitian.

[123] *Revue Archéologique*, 1865, II., pp. 220-326. In this article which has been severely attacked, Dr. Wescher is borne out by the discoveries of the decades which have intervened; although he might perhaps have extended the credit to cover the Roman, Egyptian and Semitic world. He says, in substance, that the Greek proletaries planted a noble and lasting civilization. See Vol. I., pp. 506-507, where a view of his opinions is given.

[124] Plato, *Laws*, vii., 11, is puzzled about what to do with them. Many of them had become emancipated at this early time, the first half of the 4th century, B.C., undoubtedly through the eranos, as shown, *Supra*, see *Index*, in verb, *Emancipation*. Women called Sauromatidæ. See I., p. 340, note 17, swarmed the sea-shore, looking for fish and shellfish, which they ate raw.

[125] Under Tiberius, who personally is an exception from this remark, the senate and lords had already begun their enmity to these people who were called Jews by the historians of that day. This monarch was deeply touched with the good report sent him by Pilate and his predecessor Lentulus, as well as by king Abgar.

It fills one with some satisfaction in these days of wear-worn literature, when as confessed by the Edinburgh Review, all subjects of value and interest are entirely exhausted, to be able to peep over the lurid river of the dead and view another side; a millennial past, of the lost Eden, Elysian park or Paradise, where the poor outcasts of a once pure microcosm, brought to the door work and plenty amidst ineffable love, faith, joy and goodly comforts. Away over the stifling miasm of competitions in which our warring ages seethed, we feel a solace as we contemplate the upwardly-towering social microcosm, already 2,000 years old, struggling against the laws of kings, ambitious despots and their rabble of ignorant majorities. We imagine them yet living in the dear old love and fellowship which beckoned to the promised one to come and lift them still more sublimely upward until their miniature socialism should burst its occult bonds and leap out into the open world, planting in the broad gaze of men the everlasting economy of life.

CHAPTER XV.

PRE-CHRISTIAN MARTYRS

PRINCIPLE A CRIME PUNISHABLE WITH DEATH

A FORERUNNER the Favorite God of the Unions—Dangers of the Propaganda—Cruelty of Demosthenes—Martyrdom of the Girl Ninos who Initiated New Members—Accused of Helping Slaves—Martyrdom of Theoris—Demosthenes Attacked Her—His Coarse Sensualities—Dark Rumors of another Martydom—Pitched down the Barathron—Vengence of the Kathegemon or Forerunner Goddess—Glaucothea accused and sneered by Demosthenes—Mother of Æschines—Fatal Vote by Pebbles—Gulf Separating the two Sets of Mysteries—Quenched Bloodthirst on another Woman's Veins—Fate of Neæra—Thrown off the Rocks—Neither Thiasos nor Lawyer could Save Her—Epitaph of Tryphera another Martyr—Member of a Union—Dæmon of Vengence Drives Demosthenes to Suicide—Martyrs Sneeringly Classed as Courtesans—Escape of Exquisite Phryne—Ranked with Isodaites—Baseless Slanders—Isodaites Her Angel of Equality—Athenian Snobs—She Organized an Eranos—Eloquence of Hyperides—Her Acquittal—Proofs—Socrates a Member of an Eranothiasos—Similarity to Great Later Martyr—Gathered Disciples and Apostles—Very Poor Man—Marble Cutter—His Euthanasia—Like Phryne, had his Good Angel—Billingsgate of the Piræan Fisheries—Accused of Same Crime—Prison of Socrates—Author's Visit to Grotto on the Acropolis—The Hemlock—Hour of a Great Martyr's Death.

THE propaganda, and the planting of new branches of this Dionysus Kathegemon, or forerunner, was a crime at Athens punishable with death. As a result of this there were a great many victims. Fortunately for our history we have quite a number of these martyrs, the details of whose deeds and punishments we propose to give in this chapter. It is no glorious feature of this record that most of these martyrs were women. For a dear little innocent woman to be stripped nude and dragged by the officers of the law to the top of a steep mountain

GIRL ORGANIZER PITCHED OFF THE CRAG. 327

crag called the Barathron, and plunged headlong into the abyss, there with broken bones to die and be devoured by beasts and vultures, may seem to modern ladies in the noble work of emancipation of their sex, a climax of brutality; yet we have some account of several such monstrous martyrdoms; and what is most terrible of all is the news that the great Demosthenes was the hideous persecutor who compassed three if not many more such sickening retributions. Every such victim was a member of a thiasos.

The first legal execution we have of this kind, that of a poor little devoted girl, for the crime of organizing a union under the new Dionysus, forerunner of something unexplained and at that time mysterious and unknown, was Ninos, a person who, because she had been born to see the miseries of the struggling poor and because poor herself, undertook to establish a self-helping cranos at Athens where the adoration of her faith could be mixed with the love of man, the workers could combine with their peers and all enjoy in common one table among the stingy fruits of toil. To be true to the Law of Solon her organization must be based upon the fundamental principles, hagios, eusebes, agathos,[1] and the members must love one another. The killing of this woman is known in history.[2] She is reported by the scholiast of Demosthenes to have vitiated the morals of the youth by selling and administering love philtres.[3] This is as silly as the similar accusation that the great poet Lucretius died of a philtre! Antiquity is as full of lies as modern ages. One other ancient apologist for Demosthenes, has likewise given us his reasons, but conflicting,[4] contradictory and untenable. The truth is, she was guilty only of the crime of being a working member of her union, and of going to Athens and there working to cary out its tenets. Few innocent women have been more egregiously slandered.[5] We are con-

[1] See *Supra, chap.* xiii., for a complete explanation of these tenets.
[2] Josephus, *Adv., Apion.*, II., 37, ascribes her guilt to the introduction of foreign and forbidden deities into Athens: Νίνον μὲν γὰρ τὴν ἱέρειαν ἀπέκτειναν, ἐπεί τις αὐτῆς κατηγόρησεν ὅτι ξένοις ἐμύει θεοῖς. Νόμῳ δ' ἦν τοῦτο παρ' αὐτοῖς κεκωλυμένον, καὶ τιμωρία κατὰ τῶν ξένον εἰσαγόντων θεὸν ὥριστο θάνατος.
[3] Schol. *Demosth.*, 431, 25: "Ἄγει δὲ τὴν Νίνον καλουμένην. Κατηγόρησε δὲ ταύτης Μενεκλῆς ὡς φίλτρα ποιούσης τοῖς νέοις." See McCauley's *Eulogy of Lucretius*. Also, Lippincott's *Biog. Dict.*, art. *Lucretius*.
[4] Schol., *Demosth.*, p. 431, 25: 'Εξ ἀρχῆς γέλωτα εἶναι καί ὕβριν κατὰ τῶν ὄντως μυστηρίων τὰ τελούμενα ταῦτα νομίζοντες, τὴν ἱέρειαν ἀπέκτειναν· μετὰ τοῦτο τοῦ θεοῦ χρήσαντος ἐᾶσαι γενέσθαι, τὴν 'Αισχίνου μητέρα μυεῖν ἐπέτρεψαν."
[5] Am Rhyn, *Mysteria*, p. 86, says she was one of the μητραγύρται.

strained to admit that Ninos was probably too poor and uninfluential to obtain permission to plant the thiasos with Dionysus the forerunner as its patron and we know from a passage of Strabo that the punishment for this was death.[6]

But we have one of the most searching and learned authorities in the German critical schools of modern days,[7] to prove that Ninos was accused for setting slaves free. This enfranchisement of slaves was going on in full force at Delphi, only about seventy miles from Athens, through the eranos,[8] and it encroached upon the terrible slave system which at Athens alone kept 400,000 human beings at that very time in bondage. If the tone of morals was such that Xenophon, without being mobbed, could propose that all the revenues of Attica should be extorted from the unpaid labor of men as machines, who can wonder that Demosthenes could with impunity have her pitched down the calcareous crags of the Barathron for her imagined offense?

But following close upon the tragedy of the girl Ninos we have a second act of valiancy by Demosthenes, the lawyer for the rich. The martyrdom of Theoris carries with it the recital of a horror. It is an execution of another beautiful and worthy maiden for the crime of being a member, active and efficient, of an eranos which garnered its overplus with desperate energy, to buy slaves and sell them into freedom to the beloved god. This practice was going on energetically at that time. She saw the terrible condition of human slavery. She lent her powers and influence to compass their relief. For this she was voted to doom by a crowd of grandee citizens of Athens, who in a vast open-air convocation, stood around the orator Demosthenes, listening in raptures to his brutal sallies against her. The trembling woman was accused of proffering an exhibit of feeling for suffering mankind ground down to the dismal misery of perpetual bondage.

[6] Strabo, *Geog.*, x., III., 18. "'Ἀθηναῖοι δ' ὥσπερ περὶ τὰ ἄλλα φιλοξενοῦντες διατελοῦσιν, οὕτω καὶ περὶ τοὺς θεούς. Πολλὰ γὰρ τῶν ξενικῶν ἱερῶν παρεδέξαντο ὥστε καὶ ἐκωμῳδήθησαν, καί δὴ καὶ τὰ Θρᾴκια καὶ τὰ Φρύγια." Nevertheless, as Josephus tells us: "The law of Athens forbade it on pain of death." *Adv. Ap.*, II., 37. The only thing to do was to leave each particular case to a general vote of the accredited citizens.

[7] Schömann, *Opuscula Academica*, III., *De Religionibus apud Athenienses.*

[8] Cf. *index* to this vol., referring to pages where the method is elaborately explained.

Plutarch in his life of Demosthenes, speaks briefly of the fact that the orator accused, and caused the condemnation of a priestess of the name of Theoris.[9] Dr. Foucart admits that she met her fate at the hands of Demosthenes, and that she was not of the official recognition, but must have opposed the legalized cult. But he does not know whence she hailed.[10]

We cannot but recall the similar treatment to-day, of many a Theoris and Ninos, by the pulpit and press, and the hate-hugging spirit of uncharitable persons who stand ready to cast the pebbles of martyrdom against noble women of our day. We have many such women ably conducting a vast and world-wide conquest for the emancipation from slavery of their race and sex. The fact is, the trend of progress is still blocked; for these slang-whangers still infest the earth and peddle out insidious innuendoes as aliment to glut the coarse sensualities of a lingering paganism. It shows the struggling despair of an idea forging a foothold upon the cliffs of greed and hate. Scarcely a day passes but we read some sneer, some animadversion, some ungenerous fling against our ladies who for many years have worked with ability to elevate their sex above the chronic inequality into which a majority are born; and many a one, so to speak, is cast off the cliffs of the Barathron through the same contemptuous word-havoc of prejudices which sent Ninos and Theoris amid the howls that made hideous the psephisma condemning people to the rocks of the Acropolis.

Before the time of Theoris, about B.C. 430, and in the lifetime of Phidias the sculptor, there appeared an organizer of these Dionysan artists at Athens. He, or she, was a so-called metragyrt or wandering priest of Cybele. The sex is doubtful, but we shall suppose this organizer a female. She was arrested, tried, condemned and thrown down the Barathron and killed. The nar-

---

[9] Plut., *Demosth.*, 14; "Κατηγόρησε δὲ καὶ τῆς ἱερείας Θεωρίδος."

[10] *Ass. Rel.*, p. 81: "Nons ignorons quels etaient le nom et le culte de la confrérie à laquelle elle appartenait." But he virtually admits that the "confrérie" was a θίασος in the next paragraph: "Nons pouvons avoir un peu plus de lumières sur le thiase que la célèbre Phryné essaya d' introduire à Athènes." The *Oration* of Demosthenes *agt. Aristogiton* throws some light on the question. But Plutarch, in addition to the line above quoted, continues: ......ὡς ἄλλα τε ῥᾳδιουργοῦστης πολλὰ καὶ τοὺς δούλους ἐξαπατᾶν διδασκούσης, καί θανάτου τιμησάμενος ἀπέκτεινε." We understand this to mean very plainly that Theoris was trying to secure the emancipation of slaves. Schömann does not admit that she was engaged in any religious affair, but rather thinks she was working at some economic problem.

rative relates that the anger of the insulted goddess was so aroused against the Athenians for this barbarous act that she caused a pest to strike them; and the calamity was so malignant that the city was obliged to erect a costly metroon to the martyred servant of the Mother of God; and her statue, a work of exquisite art, was chiseled by the great sculptor Phidias, the genius of the Parthenon and the cryselephantine Athena. Cybele having thus subdued the superstitious Athenians, caused the growth of her order to extend over all Attica. All indications at our command, however, tend to establish the point that the Athenian citizens of influence considered it an outrage, and an innovation upon their state, or official customs over which they always kept a jealous guard.

Though little is known of Theoris in the regular historic mention, yet we have some reliable hints from the story-tellers and wayside narrators among whom are Valerius Maximus, Athenæus, Harpocration and Macrobius. Harpocration gives a short notice that Theoris was tried for introducing new divinities into Athens, persecuted, denounced by Demosthenes who had her condemned.[11] M. Foucart is willing to exonerate Demosthenes from the stigma of killing a woman.[12] But he cannot penetrate the causes so deeply as the learned Schömann who has differently understood these tragedies, and logically ascribed their persecution and death to the jealous petulancy of the narrow Athenian mind. The pitching of Theoris over the cliff of the Athenian Barathron which yawned among the ledges of the Acropolis like a Tarpeian rock, and the tearing of her flesh and bones with the teeth of pitiless crags was a sight which mobs of those days would rush miles of distance, or pay a fee to behold; and when the enrapturing oratory of that genius of the bema had crammed the listeners who were to cast the pebbles for or against a wretch like poor Theoris standing under their foregone anathema, and maddened them to an enthusiam of feelingless scorn, the decision meant instantaneous death.

[11] Harpocration, *Lex.*; "Θεωρίς· μάντις ἦν ἡ Θεωρίς, καὶ ἀσεβείας κριθεῖσα ἀπέθανε, ὡς καὶ Φιλόχορος ἐν ἕκτῃ γράφει."
[12] Foucart, *Ass. Rel.*, p. 158: "Une autre prêtresse, qui Démosthène fit condamner à mort, Théoris, débitait aussi des philtres, et en même temps des poisons. Après sa condamnation, la servante qui l' avait dénoncée, continua le commerce de sa maîtresse et en communiqua les secrets au frère d' Aristogiton."

GLAUCOTHEA, MOTHER OF ÆSCHINES.

Another female martyr to the orator Demosthenes, was Glaucothea, an organizer of the eranos at Athens and the mother of the great statesman Æschines, against whom this magnetizer delivered his celebrated oration, the Pro Corona, studied to this day in our colleges, whose students are taught to overlook the contemptible theme and pay homage only to its scathing rhetoric.

Glaucothea seems to us, after having given her career a careful study, to have aided Æschines, a celebrated orator and statesman of Athens engaged in the question of the encroachment of the arms of king Philip of Macedon, upon Athenian domain. On an embassage of conciliation to the king both happened to be delegates, and they had a falling out. This in course of time grew to be bitter in personal rancor, and ended in a trial which involved the celebrated speech of Demosthenes, Pro Corona. Nearly every student of our day, who pursues a classical course, must thread parts of this much renowned among ancient orations.

In it, however, Demosthenes descends to depths of scurrility where he drags forth the family honors of Æschines. As a matter of fact the genius and career of this powerful man, Æschines, were above his birth and blood. His mother, whose name was Glaucothea, was another Ninos or Theoris. She had the temerity, with the assistance of her son, to undertake the initiation of Athenian youth into the Dionysan mysteries, and succeeded. Demosthenes who boasted that he belonged to the greater and aristocratic Eleusinian, and not to the low-born Dionysan mysteries borrowed from Phrygia, and mean and lowly,[13] was a slave owner and inherited several industries: a knife and sword factory, and a manufactory of bedsteads. The two netted him a sum of $758.10, which was at that date worth three to one of the present, making his profits equal to a regular annual income of $2,743. Several years before his trouble with Æschines, an insurrection had occurred among the slaves of Demosthenes. They rebelled against the hard treatment and murdered the director

[13] Schelling, *Philosophie u. Religion*, S, 75; The doctrine taught by the mysteries was directly in opposition to the public religion. Demosthenes in his *Pro Corona*, a speech against Æschines said: "You initiate, I was initiated." Demosthenes owned slaves and two factories. This brag shows the aristocracy of Demosthenes, a high-born, over Æschines, a low-born. He owned a knife factory and a bedstead factory, which required the labor of 52 slaves, and he owned these slaves, Cf. Vol. I., p. 548.

and perhaps partner of the orator, who managed the business. Demosthenes was so angry that he took every opportunity to enveigh against slaves, which accounts for his persecution of any and all slaves, who dared to love liberty or aid each other to a better fortune.

Among those who had dared to labor toward the alleviation of the fearfully hunted and work-driven slaves, was Glaucothea, operating with Æschines, political enemy of Demosthenes. They had initiated members and formed societies of the eranos in Athens. She was working for human emancipation and no doubt was a soothing and benevolent friend of the very slaves struggling in bondage under the tyrant Demosthenes, who hated and feared them.[14] The power of the oratory of Demosthenes against Æschines consisted in sneers.[15]

The expression of Demosthenes quoted in our note, shows that she belonged to a thiasos. She was mentioned by others as a member of a hetæra; but a hetæra is Pliny's term for a trade union of mechanics.[16] This woman was not merely the mother of the orator Æschines, so well known in history, but she was an officer of rank in the Phrygian eranothiasos, which at that date was working for the emancipation of slaves in a perfectly legal manner, by loaning money to a god, who, taking the money at his stately palace or temple, of course through a priest officiating in his mythic absence, pronounced him free.[17] Æschines was a tritagonistes or third combatant, and was consequently only a

[14] For an account of the fear of slaves in ancient times, see I., p. 141, note 33; 164; 214; 335; 75; 15. Demosth., *Pro Corona*, 259-260: "'Ἀνὴρ δὲ γενόμενος τῇ μητρὶ τελούσῃ τὰς βίβλους ἀνεγίγνωσκες καὶ τἄλλα συνεσκευωροῦ, τὴν μὲν νύκτα νεβρίζων καὶ κρατηρίζων καὶ καθαίρων τοὺς τελουμένους καὶ ἀπομάττων τῷ πηλῷ καὶ τοῖς πιτύροις καὶ ἀνιστὰς ἀπὸ τοῦ καθαρμοῦ κελεύων λέγειν. Ἔφυγον κακόν, ὕυρον ἄμεινον ἐπὶ τῷ μηδένα πώποτε τηλικοῦτ' ὀλολύξαι σεμνυνόμενος...... ἐν δὲ ταῖς ἡμέραις τοὺς καλοὺς θιάσους ἄγων διὰ τῶν ὁδῶν τοὺς ἐστεφανωμένους τῷ μαράθῳ καὶ τῇ λεύκῃ, τοὺς ὄφεις τοὺς παρείας θλίβων καὶ ὑπὲρ τῆς κεφαλῆς αἰωρῶν, καὶ βοῶν εὐοί, σαβοῖ καὶ ἐπορχούμενος ὑῆς ἄττης, ἄττης ὑῆς, ἔξαρχος καὶ προηγεμὼν καὶ κιστοφόρος καὶ λικνοφόρος καὶ τοιαῦτα ὑπὸ τῶν γραδίων προσαγορευόμενος, μισθὸν λαμβάνων τούτων ἔνθρυπτα καὶ στρεπτοὺς καὶ νεηλατα."

[15] *Oratores Attici*, II., p. 189: "Μητρὸς δ' ἦν ὁ Αἰσχίνης Γλαυκοθέας ἤ, ὡς ἔνιοι, Γλαυίδος, ἥν φασὶ τὴν πρώτην ἡλικίαν ἡταιρηκέναι κάθερομένην ἐν οἰκήματι πρὸς τῷ τοῦ καλαμίτου ἡρώῳ." So likewise Demosthenes, *Pro Corona*, § 130, speaking of the thiasotes, of which society, Æschines like Socrates, was a member, says: "Ἐκ τοῦ πάντα ποιεῖν καὶ πασχειν." This reminds us of the sneer of Cicero, when speaking of the shoemakers of Rome see Vol. I., pp. 301, 380, *note* 20. Again Harpocration, in *verb.* Ἰσοδαιτής, says the slaves were persons of the basest sort; and the scholiast of Aristophanes smites them as folls: "'Ως γυναικίας καὶ κίναιδος κωμῳδεῖται· ἐν δὲ τοῖς μυστηρίοις τῆς Ῥέας μαλακοὶ πάρεισιν." *Aves*, V., i, & 867; also 89.

[16] Pliny, *Letters*, nos. 33, 34 and 96, to the emperor Hadrian, including answers, quoted *infra*. See *index*. *Pliny*.

[17] Consult the whole Dissertation of Lüders.

third-rate actor in the plays.[18] All this was taken advantage of by the orator. The fact that the people desired such shallow arguments, being unable to comprehend the power of exact evidence as at present in a trial, was what gave him the advantage over his adversary. Demosthenes boasted that he himself had been initiated, and most royally, into the great Eleusinian Holy of Holies;[19] intimating that he himself was to be guarded by holy dæmons during his natural life and afterwards his felicity was secured for an eternity in the elysian realm. He stormed against Æschines, and in his studied terms of mockery brought the audience,[20] to whom it was unjustly given to decide, to such a pitch of pitiless enthusiasm that they cast the majority of ballots against him and he was obliged to quit Athens forever. It is known that Æschines went to Rhodes and there built up the organization enormously, besides founding a school of oratory.[21] This man is destined, when his true history and manhood shall have become disabused from the scurrility thrown over him by Demosthenes[22] and his subservient worshipers, to be made prominent among the finest geniuses of antiquity. He was the true friend and uplifter of the struggling toilers.

But it is with the mother of Æschines that we have to deal here, leaving her illustrious son and socialist orator to go to Rhodes and there build up the countless unions whose inscriptions are found more numerous perhaps than in any other place within the geography of the ancients, unless we except the Piræus. There seem to appear some dark things connecting this with the

[18] Schäfer, *Demosthenes und seine Zeit*, I., pp. 213–266. Among the wandering actors, there were πρωταγωνισταί, δευτεραγωνισταί, τριταγωνισταί, etc., in which the enemy of the orator certainly got some clues of the secrets. Thus Demosthenes, taking advantage of what he got of his secret, official detectives, poured his entire powers against him and hounded him down. Cicero once referred to these 3 parts of the plays of these actors and artists, in the following language; "Ut in auctoribus Græcis fieri videmus: sæpe illum qui est secundarum aut tertiarum partium, cum possit aliquanto clarius dicere quam ipse primarum, multum submittere, ut ille princeps quam maxime excellat."
[19] Demosth. *Pro Corona*, 259–260sqq.
[20] See Schömann *Opusc. Acad.*, III., *De Religionibus Exteris apud Atheniensses;* also his *Griechische Alterthümer*, II., p. 156; and Josephus, *Adv. Apionem*, II., 37. A vote of the recognized, that is, the property-owning and accredited people, had to be taken before any new thing could be introduced and Glaucothea failed in influence to secure this permission.
[21] Isocrates, *Panegyrikos*.
[22] Ramsay, *Cities and Bishoprics of Phrygia*, II., p. 415: "The name, (Hyagnis) is probably connected with Iyes, a name or title of Attys in rites of the great mother. Demosth., *Pro Corona*, 259–260.

great Diocletian massacre which are later to appear. Glaucothea could not have organized the eranothiasos at Athens without the initiation. To this day the secret initiation is the great attraction of Free masonry and all other similar Orders. But Demosthenes persecuted everybody who attempted such initiations except those of the great aristocratic mysteries of the official religion. Any woman who dared attempt it he called a hiereia.[23] In another place he rails at her for being the drummer to the goddess.[24]

We are destitute of full information as to the fate of Glaucothea. There is strong reason to suspect that she met the fate of Ninos and Theoris, in being like them, plunged down the precipice. Let us take advantage of this absence of positive information and hope that she lived to accompany her illustrious son to the more genial Rhodian isle of the Grecian Sea and that together they passed a happy and useful life in their chosen work. Alas! the hope is dark.

But we are not yet through with this Demosthenes. Before his haters combined and drove him to suicide his irascibile spirit was able to quench once more that prurient bloodthirst upon a woman's veins. This victim was Neæra; but the circumstance is veiled in gloom. No detailed history of the case is extant, though there is reason to suspect that the tragedy was written out by one of the ancient historians. At any rate, a certain damsel, like Ninos and Theoris, had the temerity to attempt the introduction of the eranos and its system of emancipation into Athens; and like them, she was betrayed, accused, set upon by Demosthenes, and condemned to the fatal rocks. Certain it is that she paid the penalty of death to the narrow minded laws which at length brought that city down in poverty and humiliation.[25]

In close connection with this, we find this same orator, who, to judge from the methods of modern prop-

[23] Demosth., *De Male Gesta Legatione*, § 281: "Τὸν δὲ Ἀτρομήτου τοῦ γραμματιστοῦ καὶ Γλαυκοθέας τῆς τοὺς θιάσους συναγούσης, ἐφ' οἷς ἑτέρα τέθνηκεν ἱέρεια."

[24] *Id Pro Corona*, § 284: "'Εκ ποίας γὰρ ἴσης ἡ δικαίας προφάσεως Αἰσχίνη τῷ Γλαυκοθέας τῆς τυμπανιστρίας ξένος ἢ φίλος ἢ γνώριμος ἦν Φίλιππος."

[25] She was accused, and twitted by Demosthenes, *Contra Naæar.*, of having her initiatiton paid by a certain man named Lysias. Such actions were, in those times regarded with contempt; but it is difficult to discern the basis of this dislike, unless it be that the aristocracy of Athens were narrow enough to descend to petty frivolities, so low and mean that they could not stand before the blaze of a just institution.

erty holders and their ever watchful lobbies, seems to have been no better than a corporation lawyer, we have information of another attack which he made against a certain Lysias, likewise a public speaker, whom he twits of being in love with a woman named Metaneiras. But she was so unfortunate as to be of lowly extraction. It seems to have been established that he paid the perquisites necessary to her initiation into the thiasos. But the evidence shows that the organization she joined was not that of the accredited aristocracy, but a poor people's eranos, such as Athens was hiring the oratorical talent of Demosthenes at that moment to suppress.[26]

Although the stories of these tragedies are exceedingly obscure and references rare, yet seemingly more by accident than studied mention we now and then come into possession of a fragment or an inscription which dimly discloses a wayside event. Philodemus, an epicurean, who lived during the time of Cicero, wrote a book of anthologies which contains some precious gems. Among others, is an epitaph of a beautiful girl named Tryphera, the date of whose death is not given. Judging from the reading it looks like another martyrdom. She certainly was a member of a thiasos, and like Ninos, Theoris and Glaucothea was engaged in the dangerous work of the initiation into the secret eranothiasos at Athens.

A martyr, she certainly was, and her death violent; yet the details remain mostly unrecorded. We are inclined to think the poetical epitaph which exists, an effusion from her eranos, because such glyptic literature is found only among the unions; but if so, then Philodemus plagiarized it in after days; not to praise her work for which she suffered but to gratify the more earthly impulse of sense which pictures an exquisite young form, reft of covering, trembling with terror,[27] while being dragged from the bema and the pebbles by

[26] Demosth, *Or. cont. Neœram*, says: "Λυσίας γὰρ ὁ σοφιστὴς Μετανείρας ὢν ἐραστὴς ἠβουλήθη πρὸς τοῖς ἄλλοις ἀναλώμασιν οἷς ἀνήλισκεν εἰς αὐτὴν καὶ μυῆσαι ... ἐδεήθη οὖν τῆς Νικαρέτης ἐλθεῖν εἰς τὰ μυστήρια ἄγουσαν τὴν Μετάνειραν, ἵνα μυησθῇ, καὶ αὐτὸς ὑπέσχετο μυήσειν."

[27] Foucart, *Ass. Rel.*, p. 158: "Ici gît le corps délicat de Tryphéra, petite colombe, la fleur des voluptueuses hétaires, qui brillait dans le sanctuaire de Cybèle, dans ses fêtes tumultueuses, dont les ébats et les causeries étaient pleins d'enjouement, que la Mère des Dieux chérissait, qui, plus qu'aucune autre femme, aima les orgies de Cypris, et qui eut la grâce et les charmes de Laïs. Terre sacrée, fais pousser au pied de la stèle de la bacchante, non des épines et des ronces, mais de tendres violettes."

a ferocious gang of Athenian officers, skyward, headed perhaps, by the triumphant Demosthenes, to the Acropolitan cliff, and to see her palsying form slugged down the abyss. The mangled head and trunk, and limbs, dumb in life's last quivering gasp are the horrid subject of the epitaph.

But in the cases of Ninos, Theoris, Glaucothea and Socrates, a stubborn will of the politicians refused to admit that a noble principle was the underlying incentive of their lifework, the sneers of disreputable things in their character are the most that are left us. If, then, we make bold to apply the analytical judgment of Schömann to her case we may be able to see through the scummy innuendoes and detect a high motive characterizing her tiny life.[28] Dr. Foucart to whom we are indebted for this mention, makes a serious hint sustaining our suspicion that she was another martyr, in some lines just previously given in his text, relating to this subject.[29]

False martyrs was one of the names given the poor wandering outcasts of the ancient world, and a vein of ill appreciation often amounting to ridicule is easily detected in most of the writings of commentators.[30] But they were socialists. The eranos was owner of their accumulated earnings; yet it owned property only in trust for its membership and saved individual members the worry of private holdings; so that as individuals they were rich in a common possessorship of much. They were in a position to "take no thought for the morrow." Though this was in consonance with the Solonic law, it was at loggerheads with the Athenian law and a menace to the official and competitive rules. The consequence was

---

[28] Philod., *Anthol.*, vii., 222: We give our rendering from the French, M. Dehèque's *trans:* Here lies the delicate form cf Tryphera, a little dove, a flower of the voluptuous hetæræ, that brilliantly bloomed in the sanctuary of the mother of God. In her tumultuous feasts where recreations and the conversations used to be full of enjoyment and cherished by the mother goddess, who more than any other used to love the ordeals of Venus, and who possessed the graces and the charms of Lais. O consecrated earth! Nourish the growth at the foot of this shaft, erected to the Bacchante, and crown her, not with thorns and briars, but tender violets.

[29] *Ass. Rel.*, p. 158: Speaking of the banquet to Adonis, killed by the wild boar, but changed to a flower, he says: "Cette fête était chère aux courtesans, qui se réunissaient pour la célébrer avec éclat." This is taken from Aristophanes, *Lysistrata*, p., 392-396, who gave rich talent to low ribaldry in order to be popular. It wants a Schömann to decide whether, instead of common courtesans, these females were not honest organizers.

[30] Athenæus, *Deipnosoph.*, vi., 254: "Ὁ φήσας ἐν ἄλλοιέ πλήρεις εἶναι τὰς Ἀθήνας διονυσοκοκάκων καὶ ναυτῶν καὶ λωποδυτῶν· ἔτι δὲ ψευδομαρτυρῶν καὶ συκοφαντῶν κσὶ ψἰνδοκλητήρων."

that every rich individual, every old line politician and every public priest hated the eranos; and they conspired with men of genius like Aristophanes, Demosthenes and Lucian to write and pronounce scurrilous poetry, orations and dissertations of fiction, lampooning, maltreating and slandering the devotees of socialism.

Another martyr whose supplicium must be classed with that of Domitilla of Rome is the beautiful Phryne. Domitilla did not perhaps perish, yet she is placed in the book of martyrs; neither did Phryne perish, though her escape from a yawning Barathron forges an episode as thrilling as that of the phantom ship that rode the whirling surges of the Maelstrom. Fortunately we have this history in fragmentary form, in considerable detail.

We are able to prove that this celebrated beauty and accomplished Greek woman, was not the debauch in a himation, as she has come down to us in our silly and credulous belief. That men ran crazy after her, with gifts to purchase smiles we do not deny. That she sat for Apelles to paint the fairest and most perfect form is quite probable; for she was a member of the thiasos which, as we see proved by multitudes of inscriptions, always sought to sell its talent and accomplishments to boards of public work. The exquisite sculpture of the Cnidian Venus for which Phryne sat for the great Praxiteles was public property and it was chiseled under the auspices of the public works. Her sittings then, were in virtuous keeping with the tenets of her thiasos.

This woman, like Socrates, had a betrayer. His name was Euthius and he insulted her; but receiving the repulse he deserved, was enraged and accused her of the old and much hackneyed offense against the state, of introducing new divinities and vitiating the morals of the youth. This was the threadbare accusation against Socrates.

It is not a little singular that according to his account of her, Athenæus[31] admits her escape but mentions Euthius as her pursuer. We commit no anachronism in saying there is evidence that her hater's persecutor was Demosthenes. Harpocration and Hesychius approach

---

[31] *Deipnosoph.*, xiii., § 590 b: "Ἦν δὲ ἡ Φρύνη ἐκ Θεσπιῶν. Κρινομένη δὲ ὑπὸ Εὐθίου τὴν ἐπὶ θανάτῳ ἀπέφυγε.

nearly to the facts where, in their dictionaries, they mention Isodaites as the governing spirit actuating Phryne.[32] It turns out that Isodaites was another name for Dionysus Kathegemon. Now it needs but a perceptive knowledge of Greek to understand that Isodaites is a word in common use meaning, as Liddell puts it; "Dividing equally, giving to all alike;" exactly the tenets of Nemesis. The angel called "Isodæmon, godlike, equal in fortune and happiness," which Phryne served, was a horror to the jealous Athenians who detested a socialism that would advocate the equal apportionment of the products of human labor. Yet this is precisely what this little martyr attempted to do, by organizing the eranos in Athens. In a fragment of the Greek Oration occurs this passage against Phryne: "I have shown you Phryne's blasphemy. She has devoted herself to shameless debauchery. She has introduced a new divinity. She has collected together the unlawful members of the thiasos consisting both of men and women."[33]

Notwithstanding the fact that Phryne was a member and was working all the time organizing the order, we know by popular history that many wealthy men were seized with anything but noble desires to form her acquaintance, so much so that among the more successful ones this became an open boast. It is certain that she kept right on with her secret duties amid these temptations; for this is all shown by the treachery of Euthius. He might have succeded in wheedling her far enough to discover what she was doing among the slaves and low-borns in secret and from his superabundance he may have given her money; for she was only a poor country garden girl. Certainly he could not succeed in his lascivious approaches. When defeat came, Euthius turned in jealousy, and had her arrested and the dangerous accusation brought against her that, like Socrates, Ninos, Theoris and Glaucothea, she was blaspheming the pagan divinities causing the mother of God, and Dionysus

---

[32] *Fragm. Orat. Gr.*, II., 426, *frag.*, 217: "'Ισοδαίτης· Ὑπερίδης ἐν τῷ ὑπὲρ Φρύνης· ξενικός τις δαίμων, ᾧ τὰ δημώδη γύνεικα καὶ μὴ πάνυ σπουδαῖα ἐτέλει. Every evidence accumulates to prove that these divinities, like their worshipers were of the working element. "Sacra Nyctelia quæ populus Romanus exclusit turpitudinis causa." Servius, *Ad Æneid.*, iv., v., 302.

[33] "'Ἐπέδειξα τοίνυν ὑμῖν ἀσεβῆ Φρύνην, κωμάσασαν ἀναιδῶς, καινοῦ θεοῦ εἰσηγήτεαν, θιάσους ἀνδρῶν ἐκθέσμους καὶ γυναικῶν συναγανοῦσαν. *Frag. Orat. Gr.*, II., 426.

Isodaites to establish their cult and their anti-slavery brotherhoods to take up their abode in the city of the majestic Jove. It was maddening. There now arises a question whether the Athenian council employed Demosthenes to act as prosecuting attorney. It was during this great orator's lifetime, and at a moment of political quiet when he might be supposed to act. Again, he hated the innovations of these women. Still we are wanting of his written oration, and hence the uncertainty.

But if Demosthenes did conduct the prosecution against Phryne, he was met by his peer in the criminal court. This man was not the only power in eloquence and rhetorical tactics at Athens. Hyperides was there and he espoused the trembling woman's cause. He had as a part of his rôle on that terrible day the pronouncing of the closing speech. It was magnetic with the ring and roar of select, grammatical Greek and won for him laurels of fame. As new fragments come to light it seems more and more evident that Demosthenes was his opponent at Phryne's trial. But the stubborn audience who were to decide by ballot, although convinced and overcome by this glowing presentation of her innocence, refused with a malignant prejudice to be persuaded and would have decided to have her killed had not Hyperides, who knew the chivalry of the Greeks, resorted to an act of desperation. He rushed to the frightened girl by his side, drew her violently up before the gaze of the enraged but amorous throng, and tore from her form the crimson Pallium, exhibiting beauties, such as nature had endowed her with, presenting to their gaze the exquisite original of their adorable Venus Anadyomene, and the unexcelled sculpture of the Cnidian Venus by Praxiteles, paintings and statues of immortal masters, sacred in art and true to nature; and while she stood there exposed to their enraptured gaze he roared and thundered, exploding words of eloquence in their ears with touching taunts on cruelty, reminding them that she had served their loved gods and goddesses by lending them her own exquisite contour to pattern the shapes of their sublime immortals. The story told by Athenæus and the scholiasts is that the judges, considering her beauty, cast the pebbles for her acquittal and the beautiful Phryne lived on, transmitting her exquisite qualities to the living age which in empiric wisdom keeps on screeching against this still hated girl.[34]

Before leaving this list of the agonized innocents, let us ask: what became of Demosthenes? There was some conspiracy formed in secret against him, by parties whose full history and career have never come to view; but enough is known to fix his visible enemy as Archias an officer belonging to political influences rising to power through the reverses that followed the battle of Cranon. As in the almost parallel case of Cicero, there was a secret alliance against him. Who could it be? The friends of the people he had persecuted with such malignity engaged this officer to follow him to the death. Nothing but vengeance could appease them, or mollify their chronic hate. Demosthenes was driven out of Athens in B.C. 322. Having no better retreat, he took refuge, like a runaway, in the Temple of Poseidon on the little island of Calaura. The eranos was wont to use this god's temples all of which had an asylum of refuge for slaves and others who worshiped him. Alas for the orator, Neptune had no refuge for him here. He was barred out and shut off from the holy protection the majestic god had always given the lowlier ones who organized and worshiped at his shrine.

The relentless enemies approached; and the man of renown drew from his folds the quill which had long held a dose of deadly poison; and we may imagine that, when swallowed, he bestowed the gloomy interval of his dying hour on a flitting apotheosis of a Ninos, a Tryphera, a Neæra or a Glaucothea, tumbling from the flinty crags in sequence of his eloquence of days and in doings which were gone forever.

[34] Harpocration, *Dict.*, much later has lost this idea of her sublime attributes: Διόνυσος, Yagreus, Nyctelios, Isodaites: "Ἰσοδαίτης· Ὑπερίδης ἐν τῷ ὑπὲρ Φρύνης. Ξενικός τις δαίμων, ᾧ τὰ δημώδη γύναια καὶ μὴ πάνυ σπουδαῖα ἐτέλει;" which Fouc., *Ass. Rel.* p. 81; "Divinité étrangère à laquelle se soigaient initier les femmes peu honnêttes et de la lie du people," Thus a sneer is gratuitously extended to her all along. She is called a hetaira; as if to blacken her character. But the ἑταῖραι were trade unionists. See Pliny, *Epis.; Vita*, x., Hyper., *Orat.* 20; Athen., Δειπνοσοφιστα. xiii., 590: "Ὡς εἰκὸς δὲ, καὶ δίκη Φρύνῃ τῇ ἑταίρᾳ ἀπεβεῖν κρινομένῃ συνεξητάσθή αὐτὸς γὰρ τοῦτο ἐν ἀρχῇ τοῦ λόγου· δηλοῖ· μελλούσης δ' αὐτῆς ἁλίσκεσθαι, παραγαγὼν εἰς μέσον καὶ περιρρήξας τὴν ἐσθῆτα ἐπέδειξα τὰ στέρνα τῆς γυναικὸς· καὶ τῶν δικαστῶν εἰς τὸ κάλλας ἀπιδόντων, ἀφείθη." See also *Comedy of Posidippos, the Ephes. female, Frag. Comic. Grœc.*, Ed., Didot, p. 691, where an imitation of this event takes place. A woman is threatened with capital punishment the same as in the case of Phryne and submitted to great danger of being led to execution, but is saved in the same manner, only with the greatest difficulty.

But the great martyr to the thiasos, he who surpassed all men in wisdom and power in the world, and overturned both the modes of reasoning and the creed of competition, the most useful of all the lowly, the farthest reaching friend and teacher for the suffering poor and who still stands upon the pinnacle of fame in the world, was the pre-christian Christian, Socrates.[35] Between Socrates, who flourished B.C. 486-399, and Jesus who lived A.D. 1-33, one may perceive a wonderful similarity of character. He wandered barefoot teaching the same good, and in the same way. He gathered about him disciples and apostles, who in after years continued the same doctrines and true methods of the master. Finally he died a violent death as a veritable martyr, and left a wondering world in shame and regret, to admire and follow.

The age of Socrates did not permit of many great minds. True greatness was swamped in a mean and vitiated moral atmosphere; and superstition with its millions of amulets and abracadabras hooded mind into a narrow compass. No grand moral thought could originate among people debased by centuries of despotism and accustomed to institutions that prohibited almost every exercise of social liberty, the right of free speech curtailed and the elements of true manhood stifled.

Socrates was a very poor man, and his trade was that of a stone-cutter. But his father being somewhat of a sculptor, the son was taught some of the finer niceties of the chisel and there is a story that he sculptured three small draped statues of the Graces seen at Athens as late as Pausanias. But his big head and square, rugged frame were incompatible with the taciturn motions of a shaper of stone. It was within this barefoot man of squat stature and powers of abstemiousness to lay the corner stone of a vast intellectual enlightenment; and he had it in him to block out an immortal dialectic scheme of reason and profound examination, which Plato and Aristotle and the later prodigies of progress sagaciously espoused upon which to build our

---

[35] Justin Martyr, *Apology*, chap. v.: "When Socrates endeavored by reason and examination to bring these things to light and deliver men from the demons (meaning the selfish creatures of society), then the demons themselves, evil spirits of men who rejoiced in iniquity, compassed his death as an atheist and profane person, on the charge that he was introducing new divinities."

era.[36] There were some tenets in his doctrines which will probably never be understood. He always talked to his followers about the euthanasia or the easy, happy death, and Justin Martyr tried to compare him with Plato, who believed in a Minos and Rhadamanthos who acted as judges over the just and the unjust, while Socrates had guardian spirits to warn the well-minded against error and drive evil away. Justin believed these elements of goodness were purely Christian and argued that these two teachers, together with Zeno, were pre-christian Christians.[37] Indeed, it was energetically held by several of the ante-Nicene fathers, including Irenæus and Tertullian, that Socrates was a Christian; prominent among those who held this belief was Justin.[38]

But Socrates did not follow the Mosaic dispensation. On the contrary, he followed the Solonic. He was a member of a thiasos, as we have several times shown by quoting Xenophon's convivials. He frequented the common table not only of the public Prytaneum, but also of the convivial clubs, where he would chat to the delight of the members, get hilarious, pronounce more witty toasts and guzzle more wine than any man in Athens or the Piræus. The great book, the Republic of Plato was a reminiscence of one of these convivials, at which time the brotherhood of the Athenian thiasos walked down to the Piræus, by invitation of the orgeons of the city, on the occasion of a dedication of the temple of Bendis, to the tutelary deity Pan. Old Glaukon, the beloved and long-faithful kurios, was there, Anytus, the leather man and traitor was there, Miletus, and a host of others; and it was under the inspiration of the common table, common bounties, and the rich Æginetan wine, that for days they discussed, point by point, the great problem of the best future state—the one which should bestow absolute equality and happiness to all mankind. This republic was a "crescent of promise to be rounded with the æons into the full orb of success." And it

---

[36] Justin in his second *Apology*, chap. x., argues that Socrates was a pre-christian Christian, thus: Socrates, who was more zealous in this than all of them, was accused of the very same crime as ourselves." Again, *ibid.*; "No one trusted in Socrates so as to die for this doctrine; but men died for Christ who was partially known even to Socrates; for he was and is the Word, foretelling the things that were to come to pass."

[37] Origen, *Adv. Cels.*, vii., c. 6, speaks of the Oracle calling Socrates "the wisest of men." Suidas, in *Sophocles*, quotes as follows: "Sophocles is wise, Euripides is wiser, but wiser than all mankind is Socrates."

[38] Just., **Mart. First Apolog.**, viii.

was fully concluded that in such a perfect form of government no individualism in membership could exist.

It might be interesting for the reader to ask himself why these philosophers left their great and celebrated Athenian city, based upon the finest model then known to the competitive system, and descended into the banlieues and Billingsgate of the fishy old Piræus, among the workingmen's unions, their temples, kuriakoi, common tables and hives of the provision business which fed the populations of Athens and the surrounding country. Why did Socrates not lead his pupils in philosophy to the grand temple of Magaron or the magnificent edifice of Apollo at Delphi, easily reached by the state highways and waters of the romantic Corinthian Gulf? If they were advocates of existing ideas then such a course would have been in pragmatical concord with the existing condition of things and would have harmonized with the culture of the Athenian state. But no. He ignored the arrogant, pretentious official religion of his native land. He attached himself to the great Smithian idea that labor and labor only is the source of the wealth of nations. Labor then, was at the bottom of the Republic of Plato, the celebrated admirer, pupil and mouthpiece of Socrates; and it was to the hives of labor that these immortals hied, and not to the grandiloquent priesthood of the Megaron of Athens or of Eleusis. This may seem to have expressed contempt for the official Athenian culture which was proving a disheartening failure in comparison with the beautiful littleness and humanity of industry, typified in the swarm of unions of the Piræus, some for the sea Islands, some for the Asiatic intercourse with boats, and all for Dionysus, mighty forerunner, tutelary protector of their business, the ennobler of mankind and giver of joys.

There was a creature there, son of a rich Athenian, a veritable Cacodæmon who was evidently hired to gather information from this master and like another Judas, betray him into the keeping of a jealous law. This was Anytus. Any one who reads the Republic of Plato may detect this serpent, step by step, in the thread of the discourse which delineated its structure and form. There was also Militus a probable spy from the Athenian priesthood; for angry tones are to be detected as the conversation proceeds. In course of time these slight dissentions scarcely perceptible at the Piræus developed into the celebrated accusation against Socrates which ended in his death.

It is thus seen that far from being guilty of introducing new divinities into Athens, and demoralizing the habits of the youth, for which he was accused and executed, this great man was, like Ninos, Tryphera and Glaucothea, trying to introduce the same ideas that are being advocated at this day in the open name of the labor question and the rising labor party of the world. Instead of the circumscribed sphere of the Piræus and its communes of labor, where men were shouting at every boat-landing and market-stall to sell their goods, there are now organizations numbering millions, whose voices are heard clear and ringing, at a thousand towns and cities of Germany, France, Italy, Belgium and the United States, demanding the same justice so loved by the proto-martyr Socrates and rapidly growing beyond the strength of repression which in those days of narrow-mindedness and tyranny succeeded in making a martyr of Socrates, to the shame of antiquity.[39]

It would be an entirely superfluous and unnecessary task for us to describe the martyrdom of Socrates. Any person wishing the strange details of the event may find it recorded in the encyclopedias, and in the many lives of this great man. He was put out of the way by speculators upon human toil, upon the old charge that he had apostatized from the official priesthood, and was introducing new divinities, when in reality he generally refrained from speaking against existing institutions.[40] We have ourselves visited the celebrated prison of Socrates where he was immured and where he died. It is a veritable cave, a den, unworthy the dignity of a prison and a hideous hole, to the present day unhonored with a door or portal. This gloomy vault is situated on the

[39] Am Rhyn, *Mysteria*, p. 86, of the Eng. *trans.*, speaking of the decay of popular belief in those days, says: "Many societies acted as 'links in the chain of phenomena that reached all through Grecian antiquity, indicating a reaction against the popular (official) religion, and an effort to introduce essentially different views, such as in later times were to triumph definitely, in an important form, over the Olympian gods.'"

[40] We have read Plato's accounts of the death of Socrates, both in the *Crito* and the *Phædo*, and the two disquisitions agree in the main, especially regarding the last symposium of the friends, the protracted conversation and the cup of hemlock. The *Crito* has been suspected of being spurious but there seems to be no reason for this suspicion. The *Phædo* was written in Plato's later years, whereas, the *Crito* was that of his comparative youth

THE PRISON OF SOCRATES. 345

right ascent of the Acropolis, about half way up to the summit on which stands the Parthenon, and is reached by a clumsy trail from the old market. It is not a dangerous steep although the ascent is obstructed by piles of rocks, and a dry ravine presents some difficulty to the feet. On beholding this cave once honored by an immortal philosopher and teacher, the author of this work was constrained to conclude that everything ancient —houses, walks, streets, prisons, all but public edifices, were primitive and mean in comparison with what exists to-day.

What is the bent of morals taught by these martyrdoms of old ? To-day, all efforts of that barbarous, self-hugging individualism to put down the advocates of any political movement favoring scientific socialism ; every effort of the bribe-taking lawyers and representatives in the invidious cages of legislation to increase the standing armies; every treachery of the falsified press to foist its darkling animadversions upon the unwary whereby to poison public opinion, is a trick of the hirelings of power who like the bullies of Athens derive their bread and precious existence from the humble laborer whose brotherhoods their ingratitude would exterminate.

CHAPTER XVI.

APOSTOLIC AGE.

THE LAW UNDER TIBERIUS, CLAUDIUS, NERO, THE FLAVII AND DOMITIAN.

PRELIMINARY OF THE CHAPTER.

PLANTING the Word—Screened at First by the Law—Emperor Tiberius Friendly—Periodicity of Man's Forward Steps—Facts which Could not be Covered—Work of our Great Archæologists—Great Events during Reign of Tiberius—Struggling to Enlarge the Microcosm into a State—An Analysis.

THE true history of the era we live in begins with its planting into the myriad economic unions. The germs thus planted existed in them long anterior to the Advent. These unions we have described in the preceding chapters. As the epigraphists of the schools are year by year enlarging the field, we confess that, enormous as are the proofs, they are but a handful compared with what is to yet come.

Jesus and the early Christians were all members. The general appearance is that they were screened from harm by the law of the burial attachment, called in the Digest, "*lex collegia tenuiorum*," but shrewdly improved by Dr. Mommsen into "*lex collegia funeraticia.*"

This planting was very great during the first century. It continued in the second and third, but was met and opposed with terrible resistance. It received its first death-stroke in A. D. 363, at the Council of Laodicia, at the hands of its own officers. Its haggard skeleton still stalks the earth like a darkling ghost, bereft of everything but a superstition and an ignis fatuus luring women and children into the snares of a spider-like clericity which robbed the poor of their pittances. The suicide stabbed itself as a result of the in-creeping money power originally repudiated. The claw of ambitious politicians and of kings clutched the property to get strength and individual glory. It was robbed of its great function by being bereft of one-half its usefulness, that of its original self-sustaining economies which Christ understood and included in his plan of salvation.

Knowing that this mighty accusation will be met with an iron hand, we proceed to prove our statement by an array of incontrovertible evidence, assured that with this new light, truth, sooner or later [1] will conquer, and that the era, disabused of wrong, will swing back into its old paths of victory and success.

We have already explained that the entire subject matter of this work has been intended merely as information preliminary to a great chapter on the planting of what is called Christianity. This is important, being an era of the human race.

We are quite willing to admit with the men of modern science, Hæckel, Levasseur, Darwin, Vogt and others, that the world is old, and that there have been many eras. The astute Aristotle premised all this, before concrete wisdom found a pathway into the haunts of man; and he had the profound sense to explain something of the periodicity of progressive steps in the world in struggling upward. We are told that already 20,000,000 years have elapsed since man in slimy protomorphic squalor jostled into the earth and settled; and that since then multitudes of æons have swirled past, each bringing its tittle of betterment. Each era, although contested by the selfishness begotten of individual preferment under a natural law of survival of the strongest, came, careered and finally died, outgrown and superseded by some unrecorded, prehistoric successor, which in its turn in the great rotatory play of fortune, had a career of long duration and likewise fell before the trend of the on-marching phalanx of improvement.

Among these revolutions and successions, there came in course of time, a race of men who agreed to be governed by a code of laws and rules entirely distinct from the more ancient method of brutal competition based

[1] See preface, Vol. II., of this work.

on the animal law of survival wherein the most powerful brute which could goad and exterminate opponents could live and thrive. Ants have slaves; they fence themselves about, feed, fatten, kill and eat them with all the brutish reason of this law. They are a type of the ancient pre-mosaical arrangement. They are prototypes of the competitive system. Such beings to this day, control political and social institutions. What wonder then, if our thoughts of social government are little higher than those of non-reasoning insects? Masses who feed the bully are still the slaves? Thus there have been and are within the age of letters and records, three distinct social dispensations—the competitive, the Mosiac and the Solonic. Solon gave the working people a privilege which they never before enjoyed. They took advantage of it, and organized enormously, laying the foundations of the new era in which we exist. The inscriptions which furnish us the principal information regarding this, abound in evidence, that Jewish workmen of Asia Minor threw away Mosaism and espoused the Solonic dispensation.[2]

There were two classes, perhaps two races of the Hebrews, of which history gives little account. We glean these facts mostly from inscriptions found recently. One race endorsed and followed the Mosaic, the other the Solonic dispensation. These latter were nearly all of the working class. They settled in great numbers in Asia Minor, formed themselves into trade unions, were frugal and industrious, learned the Greek and Syriac languages and appear to have been on good terms with the Hellenic Greeks among whom they lived. They engaged in no warring quarrels, easily took to the Mithric forms and mysteries which of all the various branches of polytheism most nearly resembled the Christianity of later centuries; and when the culture and faith arrived they, with many other determined working people, opened their busy unions to receive it, and it was this vast and secret power which, with the burial attachment, tided Christianity over the persecutions, making it an irresistible success. These facts will be denied; but we are setting forth an array of newly discovered

[2] Stephen, in *Acts of the Apostles*, vi., 14, accuses that the law of Moses had proved useless, in the following language: "Jesus of Nazereth shall destroy this place and shall change the customs which Moses delivered us." Ἰησοῦς ὁ Ναζωραῖος οὗτος καταλύσει τὸν τόπον τοῦτον καὶ ἀλλάξει τά ἔθη, ἃ παρέδωκεν ἡμῖν Μωϋσῆς. This prediction maddened the rich Hebrew audience.

proof which will forever establish them as truths. A later scheme however of the power of property which could not speculate and profit out of their unions, ultimately attacked the economic feature of this Christianity, and in course of time, after a struggle against their high and artistic culture, succeeded with the aid of the Roman empire, in stifling the Petrine policy of socialism and leaving it to jostle along among the rocks of the old pagan competitive system where it lingers and languishes to-day. Yet the germs never died; they are coming to life with even better roots.

At the time of Christ's stay on the earth great numbers of unions existed. As abundantly shown, they embraced nearly all the trades and professions of the population who were obliged to earn a living with labor. An old law legalized their career. Not until recently has the fact come to light that the early Christians nestled and settled among them. A prodigious effort has been made to conceal this fact; but it has at last leaked out, thanks to these recent discoveries which bring to view the otherwise unwritten history of the Solonic dispensation.

The settling of the Christians into these economic unions is mentioned a few times by the ante-Necine writers,[3] several of them pagan, inveighing against the Christians, such as Celsus and Lucian. We have already shown how enormously these unions were employed by the government.[4] They were a veritable service, for it was before the contract system got its foothold to enrich the adventurous individual and consequently was a vast economy to the nation.

[3] Socrates, *Hist. Eccles,*, V., 18, talks about the "great bakers' establishments" at Rome, of high antiquity, and admits tha. the members of the branch unions were christianized. The law permitting the bakers to organize and exist is confirmed by Gaius. *Digest*, II., iv., 1: "Item collegia Romæ certa sunt, quorum corpus senatusconsultis atque constitutionibus principalibus confirmatum est: veluti pistorum et quorundam aliorum, et naviculariorum, qui in provinciis sunt." These with the tax-gatherers, gold, silver and salt miners working for the government, enumerated in the lines above, are granted permission to organize.

[4] The words of Granier de Cassagnac, *Hist. des Classes Ouv.*, p. 308, are found on later investigation of this remarkable fact, to be replete with truth: "C'esi à l'aide des jurandes que le gouvernement organisa son service administratif, son déploiement de forces militaires et le dévelopement de son luxe architectural; il y avait des corporations qui s' étaient chargées de recueillir l' impôt; il y en avait qui approvisionnaient Rome; il y en avait qui la nourissaient: il y en avait qui pourvoyaient à ses édifices; d' autres qui habillaient ses soldats: d' autres qui les armaient; d' autres qui entretenaient les nécessités intérieures et domestiques d une ville plaine de richesses et vouée à tous les genres de plaisirs. Les jurandes étaient donc comme la charpente osseuse qui supportait ce grand corps romain."

But these large and numerous unions had another foothold of enormous importance in form of a burial attachment, stringently guaranteed by a law which has come down to us.[5] Quite recently the fact was verified that the Roman and Greek burial societies were in reality simply a name given to a full-fledged trade-union and that the union sailed under the name of the attachment, while in truth it secretly careered as an economic organization for purposes of life rather than death. This was because the burial attachment was openly legalized while the trade union part came under the law forbidding organization.[6] Through this peculiar attachment the true trade union, even in its well-known voting form actually evaded the law. Everywhere we find the unions working as modern trade-unions, for purely economic purposes. They in reality cared little for the religion they were supposed to adore. But they were almost always accompanied by two accomplishments. The most important practical one was their voting feature, whereby they secured for themselves and their membership the appointment to do the public work as an economic means of life; and the next important thing was to shield themselves by some law, from persecution. This they obtained by each union having a burial attachment. The amount of advantage this funeral attachment secured is almost incredible. Dr. R. Cagnat, with whom the author enjoyed a valuable personal interview in 1896, is fully convinced that the Christians owe their present existence to this funeral attachment of the economic trade-unions.[7] He admit-

[5] *Digest*, XLVII., xxii., 1, vide Momms., *De Coll. et Sodal.*, p. 99 sqq., who calls the coll. tenuiorum the same as coll. funeraticium, or burial society.

[6] *Digest*, III., iv., i., *init.*, Gaius, lib. 3, *Ad Edictum provinciale:* "Neque societas, neque collegium, neque hujusmodi corpus passim omnibus habere conceditur; nam et legibus, et senatusconsultis, et principalibus constitutionibus ea res coercitur," but proceeds to enumerate a few exceptions, quoted in note 3, *supra*.

[7] Cagnat, in *Revue Contemporaine* for Jan. 1896, says: "C' est pourtant en partie grâce au droit d' association et à l' insu du pouvoir que s' accomplit, à Rome et dans les provinces, la grande révolution morale et religieuse qui transforma le monde; sans lui le christianism aurait éprouvé les plus grandes difficultés, non tant á s' établir qu' à prospérer. Sans doute il sortait victorieux des ¡lus grandes persécutions; mais combien la calme qui suivait la tempête était peu sûr, combien précaire la situation fait aux fidèles ! Il fallait se cacher pour célébrer le culte, pour enterrer les martyrs, pour en honorer la mémoire, pour entendre la parole des pasteurs, C' est alors que, suivant l' illustre archéologue De Rossi, l' Église s' avisa a tourner la difficulté en prenant l' apparance d' un collége funéraire; dès lors, elle retombait sous la loi commune; elle pouvait avoir une caisse, posséder des cimitières, recevoir des dons et des legs, tenir des réunions, célébrer les fêtes des saints sur leur tombeau; ses assemblées religieuses mémes, grâce à ce subterfuge, devenaient des réunions licites."

ted that the earlier Christians planted directly into the unions.

Many other eminent Professors are alligning themselves with Drs. Rossi, Cagnat and Oehler, in the belief that the Christians were originally economic organizations for self-help, and that they planted in the societies of the Solonic dispensation.[8]

Without doubt the man who has contributed most to our knowledge of the methods by which christianity was originally planted in Italy, is De Rossi, who has given his life to the development of the under-ground Rome. He finds that the early christians were mostly either slaves or emancipated slaves, and that they were very numerous at Rome even under old Tiberius, and grew in numbers under great persecution during the reigns of Claudius, Nero, the Flavii and Domitian. The labors of De Rossi are innumerable.[9] He discovered that under the law, the members of the unions endorsing the cult of Jews, but retaining their old economic tactics[10] of earning their living, actually had to bury their dead in subterranean holes. This they did to an astonishing extent. Great under-ground cemeteries are found, some of which are five to seventy feet beneath the surface; and the excavators are constantly opening with their picks new cells, called scholæ, provided with seats of stone, scattered tools of many trades, central tables for the common meal, *thuræ theou* or doors of Jesus, secret portals of entrance and exit, wells for water and often bright and beautiful wall paintings.[11]

It will be asked why such secrecy if they possessed a legal right of organization? The answer is, that the new culture was hated, and when the police began to

[8] Am Rhyn, *Mysteria*, pp. 114-115: "In this wise was Christianism developed out of the secret associations of the ancient world."

[9] The law (lex collegia tenuiorum), is a little vague but was well understood at the time. See *Digest*, XLVII.. tit. xxii., 1. It reads: "Permititur tenuioribus stipen menstruam conferre: dum tamen semel in mense coeant, ne sub prætextu hujusmodi illicitum collegium coeat quod non tantum in Urbe, sed in Italia et in provinciis locum habere, divus quoque Severus rescrpsit."

[10] Waltzing, *Hist. Corp. Prof.*, I., p, 213, note 1, *fin:* "Les chrétiens se reunissaient aussi dans les catacombs, dans les cubicula ou chambres sepulcrales, qui prirent parfois les dimensions d' églises souterraines."

[11] De Rossi, *Roma Sotteranea*, speaking of these ancient cemeteries, the burial part of which was made legal under the law of the coll. tenuiorum, says: "Ma o di singulare natura, o anteriore alla formazione dello stile e delle fogge consuete de monumenti sepulcrali cristiani, ricorda un Eutichio prenominato Tito Flavio; nomenclatura cominciata a moltiplicarsi tra i liberti, i libertini e gli stranieri ai tempi de Flavii Augusti, ciaò alla fine del primo secolo cristiano." and cites quite a number of cemeteries. that of Lucina among others. We shall say more regarding them.

suspect that the Christians were using the unions which had the burial attachment, the old law of Julius Cæsar, of the date of B.C. 58, was hunted out and applied. It was applied as early as the time of Claudius, but Trajan's application of it about A.D. 100, comes into history so that we know.[12] Septimius Severus, even Hadrian continued this old law, and made the Christians still more secret, as has been recorded by Spartianus in the Augustan histories.[13] Why such a profound silence of literature as is revealed by these discoveries of the under-ground Rome, is a question for coming students! For our own part we are satisfied that the lowly Christians, Jews and Gentiles alike, filled with admirable love for one another in their economic brotherhoods, wisely agreed to accept the new Master for their kurios and saviour and went straight on with their work furnishing each other with employment as best they could under the sad circumstances.[14]

It was in A.D. 99 that the emperor Trajan issued the decree, based on the old lex Julia, forbidding the existence of the hetæræ or close trade organizations. It became immediately recognized that the Christians were the hated sect forming the membership. Trajan's rescript was the law used by young Pliny when governor of Bithynia. It was the deadly edict against the "collegia illicita," which are now proved to be none other than the veritable unions of the early christians. The good teacher when he taught his followers to "take no thought for the morrow, what ye shall eat or what ye shall drink, or wherewithal ye shall be clothed" was speaking, not to an outside audience in the cold competitive life of struggles for existence, such as the masses are this day enduring and starving under. No one of

---

[12] *Rescript of Trajan* carried out by Pliny. It was valid all over proconsular Rome and Rome itself. Cf. Neander, *Hist. Church*, Eng. trans., Vol. I., p. 120.

[13] *Digest, Tit.*, I., 1, § 24: Cf. Spartianus in *Augustan Hist.*, c. 17, speaking of the doings of Severus: "In itinere Palæstinis plurima jura fundavit Iudæos fieri sub gravi poena vetuit. Idem etiam de christianis sanxit. The *Rescript of Severus* reads as follows: "Divus Severus rescripsit, eos etiam qui illicitum collegium coisse dicuntur apud præfectum urbi accusandos."

[14] These sad circumstances continued amid persecutions. They had real cause for their awful secrecy; and this accounts for their habits of under-ground hiding. The law of the burial attachment legalized the ordeal of the grave; but the true object of the union was earthly, and it gave them means of existence. Under the awful rescript cf Severus, the poor fellows hugged still closer to their under-ground cells, making their cemeteries the uppermost matter of importance to ward off the brutal police. Nevertheless " many were daily burned, crucified and beheaded before our eyes." Clem., *Strom.*, II., 414; Euseb., *Hist. Eccles.*, vi., 7. So also long before.

common sense would give such counsel to anybody. No teacher is so stupid, so silly, or so infamous a liar as to give such advice; for if he were mean and false enough to attempt such wholesale deception he would be called either a hypocrite or a fool. The fact is this teacher and every one of those special pupils to whom he was teaching elements of economic, social and religious truth were members, and he told them not to be embarrassed by worry and incertitude which drive a half of mankind to failure and starvation. It was not necessary. The union in which they were all initiated members would care for them and attend to their personal wants,[15] leaving them precious time to peacefully attend to other things. It is now admitted by the greatest scholars that the economic unions mentioned by Tertullian[16] were none other than the same Roman collegia and Greek eranoi which we have explained in previous chapters.

Julius Cæsar was the first who enacted laws of supression of their organizations.[17] He was seconded by Cicero, who bitterly fought Clodius the Roman tribune, of whom we have given an account in the first volume of this work. Cicero and Demosthenes, after all our university commendations, must, in the honest story of the poor workingmen, descend to the doubtful dignity of defenders of false systems, and little if any better than our lawyers, engaged by the holders of wealth to slander and revile those honestly organized for liberty and present happiness. Both came to a violent end as a direct result of their own inhumanity and of their false system.[18]

A little later, in the terminal years of the apostolic age and during the first years of the second century, Pliny the younger, came out plainly with his celebrated

[15] *Matth.*, vi., 30-34.
[16] Tert., *Apol.*, xxxix.: "Coimus in cœtum et congregationem," etc; likewise Dr. Oehler, *MSS. to the Author*, speaks of an inscription found at Amisos in Bithynia showing an eranos of the same year that Pliny tried to persuade the emperor Trajan to permit him to organize a union of blacksmiths and firemen. We give the circumstance elsewhere. In his official letter to Trajan, he declares that these unions were innocent, and admits that they had a common table and a communal code.
[17] Momms., *De Coll. et Sodal*, p. 33; "Jus cocundi fuit, antiquis temporibus omnibus concessum." The lex Licinia, "*De Sodaliciis Supprimandis*, was one of the first conspiracy laws. It is declared by Cicero, *Pro Planc.*, 19, 46, that it applied to the Collegia. Another early conspiracy law was the Lex Gabiena; another, the Lex Cornelia; another, the Lex Porcii Latronis, see Momms., *id.*
[18] Consult Vol. I., p. 284; also 499, *note* 12.

letters. Appointed to be governor of Bithynia in the north of Asia Minor, he found that the Christians were organized in the old Solonic unions in great numbers. He was ordered by his emperor Trajan, to carry out the lex Licinia against them because they would not go to the pagan temples with their earnings and purchase at high prices, the sacrifices, or in other words, the goats, calves, ducks, chickens, or geese brought thither to be sold and eaten—a species of religious market. The explanation to this vague affair turns out to be, that the priesthood of paganism, which was a part of the Roman government, was speculating on provisions, not so much for themselves, being government-paid, as for the revenues of the empire of Rome. It reveals that large sums of money were constantly flowing into the Roman treasury through the priests and their wiles, by which the common people were kept ignorant, poor and superstitious.

The unionist cult, either of Solon or Jesus, had no commerce with this superstition and source of revenue. the Christians, while they abstained from all wrong-doing, positively refused to contribute their earnings to the Roman government through the pagan priest-power. Thus Pliny, and probably all the governors, found that the regular revenues had fallen off very greatly, and on close inquiry had discovered through their spies that the Christians were refusing to thus contribute. On investigation it was discovered that great numbers of hetæræ thiasoi, eranoi and orgeons within Pliny's jurisdiction had become christianized and had endorsed the new faith still adhering to their common table and their communal code.[19] They had turned the well-regulated family into a microcosm and enlarged it into the brotherhood of love and economics, conforming with the plan of salvation of Jesus. Each union had become a society of members, all working for one another, and economizing their incomes, keeping their money within themselves. They were no longer rushing to the so-

[19] Pliny's *Epist.* 97. See Neander, *Hist.*, I., p. 97, whose remarks show clearly that the christians under Pliny had been in close associations, long before the opening of the second century. "Trajan's rescript suppressed the hetæræ. It was the law Pliny enforced." Neander says; "These latter assemblies had been discontinued in compliance with the emperor's edict against the hetæræ." p. 120. The hetæra, temporarily suppressed by Trajan was one of the nine trade unions given in the original Solonic law.

called sacrifices to squander their earnings upon state-priests mumbling over their market speculations. This refusal to contribute to the public funds is what lay at the bottom of the persecutions; for the emperors under the Licinian law, construed it to be treason punishable with death.

This discovery of the true causes of the ancient persecutions is the more striking when we consider that said causes were not religious but economical. It has been erroneously supposed that religion was at the bottom of those terrible deeds of torture, reddening antiquity with gore. But revelations of recent times show that Rome had bruised off her veneration for the old law of Solon and Numa and become its hater. That law supplied the workers with well-paid employment, taught them economies and dignified them to a condition above the slavish payment of tribute to Cæsar, raising them higher than the craft of the ancient pagan priest and thus depriving Rome's treasury of the fleecings of her pious methods. This was the crime for which they died in millions.

CHAPTER XVI.

APOSTOLIC AGE.

THE LAW UNDER TIBERIUS, CLAUDIUS, NERO, THE FLAVII AND DOMITIAN.

SECTON I.—TIBERIUS.

ERA Planted under this Monarch—Ever Memorable Vista—A New and Surprising Historical Sketch of Christianity—Environment of Dangers—The Poor Could not obtain Work without Organized Protection—Statement of their Influence on Christ—Tiberius Friendly—Men at the Head of the Movement all Initiates—The Word—Hebrew History—Abgar Letters—All Known of the Circumstance—Anger of the Emperor—Pilate a Historical Character—Crucifixion Proved a Historical Event—Lynching of Stephen—His System of Common Tables Competed with Provision Rings—New Light on His Assassination—Three Thousand Members in his Union—The Murder Broke it Up—Stephen was a First Class Business Man—The Metonym.

IT WAS during the reign of this monarch that the era under which we exist was planted. It would be entirely out of place for us to attempt fresh history of this event. We leave this to the innumerable profane histories, and the New Testament record. But we are about to give an anecdotal account of the origins of socialism, which first appeared in form of the beautiful microcosm.

The reign of the emperor Tiberius is ever memorable as being the age of this celebrated planting; and what makes him more and more remarkable is the fresh-found long latent proof that he was kindly disposed toward that Character whom Josephus the truthful historian hardly dared to call a human being.[20] Stripped of the

[20] Josephus, *Antiq.*, XVIII., iii., 3: "Now there was about this time Jesus, a wise man, if it be lawful to call him a man; for he was a doer of wonderful works, a teacher of such men as received the truth with pleasure. He drew over to him both many of the Jews aud many of the Gentiles. He was the Christ. And when Pilate, at the suggestion of the principal men amongst us, had condemned him to the cross, those that loved him at the first did not forsake him: for he appeared to them alive again the third day as the divine prophet had foretold; these and 10,000 other wonderful things concerning him. And the tribe of Christians named from him are not extinct at this day."

sacredness we love to adore in our still ascendant culture, Jesus stands as the most perfect character the world has produced. We have, in our ingenuous casuistical and even doubting inquiry, found that all mention alike by fault-finders; by masses of the poor who will not attend church clamoring that christianity is a failure; by the Jews who believe he was an impostor because a workingman; and by Buddhists who claim that our religion is a derivative from the ancient teachings of Indian theosophists; all agree that he is stainless and without reproach. However much the critics are disposed to arraign and abuse the priesthood that succeeded, the great teacher himself stands as a faultless example of a perfect man, and is so acknowledged. A disposition to reject the evidence is overwhelmed by the fact that the old-time supposition that no mention is to be found of Christ by pagan authors is proved untrue; inasmuch as more than forty mentions were recorded of Christ and christianity by trustworthy men. There abound reliable mentions of him either historical or anecdotal by authors of early days.[21] Besides this there are inscriptions and monuments, which, after standing through the Cartesian age of doubt and ridicule, and after successive accessions of auxiliary evidence, are coming to be regarded as genuine testimony.

But the remarkable discovery of great numbers of inscriptions and other monumental proof that christianity was originally planted and had its home in the existing unions of the poor and lowly, and not in the haunts of wealth, and that it has been ruthlessly bereft of the great economic factor inherent in the Solonic organization and thus robbed of one half its usefulness, remains for this volume to set forth.

People of modern times are little aware of the fearful dangers which environed the life of the ancient poor man. Those who worked were hated and if not owned as slave property, or if not organized in close association they were in danger of being at any moment attacked and murdered. Feeling their danger they hugged each other in a manner unknown to-day. Their system of eating at a common table was enormously prevalent es-

[21] Macrob., *Saturnalia*, II., iv.: "Cum audisset inter pueros quos in Syria Herodes, rex Judæorum intra bimatum jussit interfeci, filium quoque ejus occisum, ait, 'mallem Herodis porcus esse, quam filius.'" This refers to Herod's attempt to kill him in infancy.

pecially about the time of Tiberius. It was a part of their salvation, sought after and longed for. Their system of profound secrecy covered the ancient world. To gain admission into the union the applicant must undergo a long probation and a rigid scrutiny. This scrutiny we have already given. Once in the union, the member was furnished with work. But work he must. There were no poor houses, no charities, no particular asylums but there were retreats of another kind—simply walled enclosures where the wretched, when chased, might obtain a temporary refuge; not asylums such as are now known. But the trade and labor union of the Solonic dispensation tolerated no charity. "If any will not work, neither shall he eat."[22] This is what the master said, for he was talking to a multitude of applicants who were about to join, and who did join, three thousand in number, soon after the teacher's crucifixion.[23]

There was, in those days, especially after the commencement of the ministrations of the two perfectly historical characters, John the Baptist and Jesus Christ, a branch of the great Solonic organization, called the ebionim. The members of this society were brave enough to acknowledge that they were poor mechanics, laborers, and professors; for the word which originates their name in Hebrew, the language spoken in their topographical region including Jerusalem, most of Palestine and some lower portions of Syria, signifies poor.[24] In the great scheme of the ancient labor movement praise is due the Jews for having boldly joined this organiza-

---

[22] II. *Thess.*, iii., 10: ὅτι εἴ τις οὐ θέλει ἐργάζεσθαι, μηδὲ ἐσθιέτω.

[23] *Acts*, ii., 41-42: Then they that gladly received his word were baptized; and the same day there were added unto them about three thousand souls. And they continued steadfastly in the apostle's doctrines and fellowship and in breaking of bread and in prayers." To which is to be subjoined, iv., 32: "And the multitude of them that believed were of one heart and of one soul; neither said any of them that aught of the things which he possessed was his own; but they had all things common."

[24] See Origen's definition of *Ebion*, the Hebrew for poor. *De Princip.*, IV., ch. i. Mosheim, *Eccles. Hist.*, I., 1st century, Part II., c. 5, § 17, says: "These Nazarenes are the ebionites; though commonly set down among sects of the Apostolic age, in reality belong to the 2nd century;" Hegesippus, ap. Eusebius, *Hist. Eccles.*, II., 23: "Now some people belonging to the seven sects existing among the people, which have heretofore been described by me in *Notes*," (A lost book by Hegesippus of great value); Iranæus, *Cont. Hær.*, III., xxx., quoting Theodotion and Aquila of Pontus, inveighs against the ebionites, as 'the poorer sort,' sneering them down because their name signified poor, The ebionites were fearfully attacked by Irenæus because poor *Adv. Hær.*, V., i., 1-3, and elsewhere. Justin Mart., *Diol. Cum. Tryph.*, LXXXVIII., speaking of John the Baptist makes him to have been an ebionite. Gibbon, *Decline & Fall.*, xv., note 23, admits with ineffable contempt that the organization was one of poor people. Guizot, *Commentarii de Ebioneis*, 1770, I., 8, says they were an organization of the poor.

tion in large numbers. But they were not of the sectaries and egotistic Jews of the aristocratic family of Palestinian Israelites. They were the poor working people, as much embroiled in the struggle for bread as the workingmen Jews of to-day. They took sides with the poor and famished castaways. They nobly joined their ranks.[25] The cause they espoused was that of the genuine socialism, which, in imitation of the family, swelled out into a microcosm wherein each worked for all and all for each.[26]

The great beauty of the Solonic organization is expressed in its universality; in all parts of the world with the same rules, by-laws, form of brotherhood, demand of mutual love, help and care. In all parts of the world it was patterned after the democratic city.[27] "Be ye therefore not solicitous about the maintainance, being in nothing wanting. To the artificer there is work; to the unable, commiseration; to the stranger, a home; to the hungry, food; to the thirsty, drink; to the naked, clothing; to the sick, visitation; to the prisoners, aid.[28]" But work was uppermost; being the source always provided, there was no such thing as charity, as expressed in our boards of associated charities and pitiful eleemosynary institutions. The great critic and commentator Neander, writing of those early days of the planting, admits that for a long time those people lived together at their common table,[29] providing with strange

[25] Euseb., *Hist. Eccles.*, iv., 22, quoting from the *lost book* of Hegessippus, taking it from this early author, whose work he read before it was destroyed, furnishes a great argument sustaining the belief that the Jews were at the bottom of the economic idea. This mighty association was managed for many years by James at Jerusalem. He was a Jew whom the Jews stoned to death. The whole shows that something very valuable to us now, if we could have it, has been covered up; for it shows that aristocratic, Mosaic Jews attacked and murdered James, the poor man and Solonic Jew.

[26] Waltzing, *Hist. Corp. Prof.*, I., p. 513: "Le collège était une famille, mais il était aussi une république, une cité. Citoyen de la ville, l' ouvrier n' avait pas grande chose à dire; membre du collège, il etait l' égal de ses confrères."

[27] This we have heretofore exemplified. Waltzing, Doctor of Laws, at the Louvain University in Belgium, has ably explained these social phenomena of the ancients: "Les corporations étaient l' image de la cité ou de la famille; elle constituait comme la famille, ou la cité un tout, une unité vivante"

[28] *Apostolic Constitutions*, Book IV., Sect. 1, cap. 2-4. Cap. 3, is a strong prescription against leeches, fakirs and hypocrites.

[29] Neander, *Planting*, I., ch. ii., *First Christian Community*. He declares it "formed, as it were, one family;" but acknowledges that later "it was discontinued to become the narrower communion of Christian family life." The jus cocundi of Solon under which all this was done, did not want the competitive system in business at all. Through it mankind was drifting toward socialism, and it was certainly adopted by the earliest adherents of the new faith under direct orders of the master himself.

love, for one another, taking the kindest care of families and sang, worked, prayed, feasted and worshiped in common. We have even their mode of conducting the meetings of what they called the congregation; and it is surprising to see the similarity in this respect to the meetings of the older unions of thiasoi, hetæræ and collegia, which we have previously described.[30] They appear exactly alike.

This economical institution of mutual care which was the prime incentive of the great labor organizations of the ancient world, could expect only to succeed in establishing a mere microcosm from its communal code. It had to struggle two thousand years, in terrible and often bloody vicissitudes, amid opposition by others, ignorance of its own, perversities of ambitious lusts and blind, groveling forces of opposing power. It had to undergo the retarding influences of kings and priests. These for ages swerved it often from its course; and it often well-nigh foundered on the rocks of resistance. Struggling in such tempests it is marvelous that it did not sink to rise no more. Yet it jostled into the creating of a vast church organization. Imperfect as it is, let us hope that it may yet be weaned from its despoilers who have abused and unhinged it, and come back so perfected as to re-adopt the original course pursued by the designers and planters.[31]

The similarity between these unions and those of the Greek eranos is quite surprising. They all follow the

[30] They all maintained the microcosmal form, whether Jews or Gentiles, always in apparently strict conformity with the inscription upon the eleventh of the Twelve Tables at Rome. Renan, *Life of Jesus*, Eng. trans., p. 146, gives us a complete $\vartheta\iota\alpha\sigma\sigma\varsigma$ of contemporary Ephesus, or Rhodes, where these organizations swarmed: "A Judaism outside of Jeruselem had no clergy proper; any person arose, read the lesson of the day (parasha and haphtara), and added to this a midrasch, or commentary entirely personal, in which he set forth his peculiar ideas. This was the origin of the '*Homily*' of which we find the complete model in the same treatises of Philo. The congregation had a president $\dot{\alpha}\rho\chi\iota\sigma\nu\nu\dot{\alpha}\gamma\omega\gamma\sigma\varsigma$, elders, $\pi\rho\epsilon\sigma\beta\dot{\nu}\tau\epsilon\rho\sigma\iota$, a hazzan, $\dot{\nu}\pi\eta\rho\dot{\epsilon}\tau\eta\varsigma$ or appointed reader or beadle, envoys, $\mathrm{A}\pi\dot{\sigma}\sigma\tau\sigma\lambda\sigma\iota$ or $\mathrm{A}\gamma\gamma\epsilon\lambda\sigma\iota$... and a schammarsch or sacristan, $\Delta\iota\dot{\alpha}\kappa\sigma\nu\sigma\varsigma$." This corresponds exactly with the scheme of the earlier $\vartheta\iota\alpha\sigma\sigma\varsigma$."

[31] Hermas, *Similitude*, V., 15-21, gives a few hints on what, in those early times the first planters dared to hope for. The society in this parable, is the master or lord. He owns a slave. This was a common thing even for the eranos. The father going abroad, entrusts his vineyard to the slave who is a workingman, typical of the faithful and good. This poor person though having nothing, feels an incentive to good citizenship unnatural to ordinary servants. He trims the vineyard and works so faithfully that the master on his return is delighted and makes him free and an heir with the rest of the children. Plenty of food and clothing, are given and the enfranchised bondman and his children all come into the common fold on equal footing. Thus the early church was an **emancipator, and more an economic than a religious instrument.**

model of the political state, which, as we have seen, was a regulation legalized by an early statute. M. Foucart says they were intensely secret but otherwise they were in character exactly the same as that of the outside political state.[32] By this it is safe to draw, that the poor by means of their societies were multitudinous tiny republics, or microcosms of a future great socialistic state which it is yet too early to see reproduced, because so vast a politico-economic perfection is impossible in two thousand years of individualism. But these myriad republics were nevertheless actually experienced and enjoyed not alone by the outside pagan world of proletarian outcasts using the jus coeundi but also by the early Christians. They prove on close examination of their inscriptions to have been a secret socialistic government. And Jesus had the hardihood which cost him his life, of blazing it forth to the open world. A devilish attempt, under the power of property was made to cover up facts regarding the economic half of the teachings of this good man. So much for the microcosm which is the family enlarged into the economic and inter-caring brotherhood. Based upon the state and the city governments, the theory of which was desired to be perfectly democratical, these Solonic unions throve; and when Jesus came, he attempted to burst the narrow trammels of their awful secrecy and launch their plan forth to the open world. He who dared to pronounce them public, and worthy of endorsement by government at large was immediately arrested and hung upon a cross and the secret thing of socialism cowered back into obscurity beset with contempt, and has not dared to reappear until to-day.

Leaving for a moment the all-important subject of the microcosms, we now proceed to discuss the ebionic or poor man's societies in that early time.

The typical name of this genus of Solonic unions is the essenes, although it had the various appellations of ebionim, nazarenes, hemero-baptists; and it may be well held in mind that a vast gulf exists between a history of

---

[32] Foucart, *Ass. Rel.*, p. 50: "Après avoir étudié dans le détail l' organisation des thiases, des éranes et des Orgéons, il faut maintenant apprécier leur valeur et leur influence :"

"Leur gouvernement est fondé sur le même principe que celui des républiques Grecques : assurer à la sociéte tout entière la gestion de ses affaires, soit par l' exercise du pouvoir direct, soit par un contrôle incessant de ceux auxquels il a été confié pour un temps fort restreint."

christianity and a history of the church. People ignorant of the history of christianity may with some applause of the dissatisfied moderns, claim that this institution has proved itself a disappointment to the working million who, as they learn the lie of their emasculate religion refrain in disgust from attendance at church, withered with the belief that it is "on the whole, a calamity." No one but the impervious university empiric will hereafter repeat these words. They may be true of the history of priest-power which forged out of the kuriakos the chains of Jesus, but that has little to do with the history of christianity. Christianity is the proclamation of the truths of socialism.

It is now well known that the ebionites, essenes and therapeutæ were about one and the same.[33] We are fortunately able to prove by Philo and others, including many inscriptions, that no difference exists between therapeuts, essenes and thiasoi. In fact, the two names essenes and thiasoi are derived from the same Greek word.[34] All these powerful associations being in full scope during the reign of Tiberius it is important to know more about them.[35] Dr. Oehler shows us that the therapeutæ were the same as the thiasoi.[36] Dr. Lightfoot struggling to excuse the great swindle that turned christianity over to the monopolies of money and property is suicidal enough to say: "Their simple meals are sacrifices; their refectory is their sanctuary; their president is their priest." This language of itself gives the

[33] Lüders, *Dionys. Künst.*, p. 53, note 100: "Die ganze Gesellschaft der Schauspieler habe in älteren Zeiten θίασος geheissen." The essenes and therapeutæ both are now found mixed together with the θίασος τῶν περὶ τὸν Διόνυσον τέχνιτῶν.

[34] Philo, *Quod Omn. Probus Liber*, XII., 457: "Εσσαῖοι....διαλέκτον ἑλληνικῆς παρώνυμοι ὁσιότητης." Again § 13, p. 459: τῶν Ἐσσαίων ἢ ὁσσίων, and again, *Frag*,, p. 632: "Καλοῦνται μὲν Ἐσσαῖοι, παρὰ τὴν ὁσιότητα, μοὶ δοκῶ τῆς προσηγορίας ἀξιωθέντες." This makes the derivation altogether Greek, as we proceed to show the etymons of the 3 great orders, and how by perversion of name by many dialects they are but one vast order in fact.

[35] Philo's ὁσιότητης, ie., most excellent, or holy, is from ὁσιός, hallowed. It is derived out of θίασος, by doubling the σ, for a provincial dialect, as Philo calls it. Thus we have ἐσσιος for θίασος; or, as Epiphanius writes it, 'Οσσαῖος, instead of Εσσαῖος. Some wrote it Ἐσσαηνος and Ἐσσηνος and to offset this we find in the inscriptions of Asia Minor of that date, θιασσῆνος.

[36] Oehler, *MSS.:* "Θεραπευται—Nach dem im Sarapieion auf Delos gefundenen Inschrift, *Bull. Hell.*, VIII., 1884, p. 103, haben θεραπευταί eine Weihung dargebracht für den König Mithradates Eupator, *Bull. Hell.* VI., 1882, p. 332, nr. 28, enthält eine Weihung der θεραπευταί οἱ ὑπ' αὐτῶν....ἀπόμενοι für den Antiochus, die Königen und Demetrios." In adjoined numbers, Dr. Oehler cites a dozen or more inscriptions showing the ancient therapeutæ; and all proves that as early as Antiochus, these and the essenian societies were running hand in hand, doing the trade labor and in a prosperous condition, in many cities of Asia Minor and the islands.

whole business away. He might as well admit the self-evident fact that they were pure trade and labor unions, which, living at the common table, under the communal code, and rapidly growing into a vast political power were voting for the officers who were pledged to give them the public work; and have confessed that the sanctimonious priests insidiously deprived them of this economical power and wimbled into, and finally got their holdings, degrading their pure Solonic, self-help scheme into a hideous priest-power. This comes nearer to being the history of the church.

Ebionites were hemero-baptists, a term, which translated, means hand-to-mouth initiates; but of course they conformed somewhat to the common requirements of the cotemporaneous public.[37]

Investigation reveals that the therapeutæ and the essenes were so nearly allied as to be one and the same alike in Asia Minor, Palestine and Egypt. They are now proved by several inscriptions to have worked hand in hand, during the reign of Tiberius, with the eranos, in effecting the emancipation of slaves. At Athens this eranos under the milder cognomen of the Egyptian and Syriac forms, was met with resolute and perhaps fatal resistance.[38] The inscriptions coming to light are acknowledged by the archæologist Oehler, to substantiate the supposition that they were intensely secret.

They were numerous at the time of Tiberius, and several new testimonies show them to have had the burial

---

[37] King, *Gnostics*, speaking of the Essenes, p, 1: "Their chief doctrines had been held for centuries before in many of the cities in Asia Minor. There, it is probable, they first came into existence as mystæ upon the establishment of direct intercourse with India, under the Seleucidæ and Ptolemies." This author here speaks of the "college of Essenes and Megabyzæ, high priests of Diana," at Ephesus, the Orphics of Thrace, the Curets of Crete, etc." He knows nothing of the common-place fact that the mysteries he mentions were no more nor less than the veil of secrecy, which as now, screened their actions; and still less does he know that they used these secrets to cover up their methods of furnishing each other with means of life from day to day This important fact remained hidden until the schools of the national universities with their inquisitive and patient epigraphists found it abundantly verified in the inscriptions.

[38] Oehler, *MSS.*: "Θεραπευταί. Sie werden genannt in Weihungen an die Syrische Aphrodite auf Delos, *Athen.*, IV., 1885, p. 460 f, nr. 13-15; *Bull. Hell*, VI., 1882, p. 489 nr. 4; 493, nr, 7. In den vier erstgenannten Inschriften erscheinen die ϑεραπευταί als corporation neben den Athenern und den Römern, *Bull. Hell.*, VI., 1882, p. 501, nr. 24, enthält eine Verwünschung des Theagenes gegen eine Frau, welche eine deponirte Geldsumme, die wohl für die Freilassung gegeben war, (vgl. *Serapis* bei Freilassungen in *Chaironea*) unterschlagen hat; es ist dann die Aufforderungen an die ϑεραπευταί der'Αγνῂ 'Αφροδίτη (hier Adad genannt), gestellt bei ihrer Versammlung die Verwünschung auszusprechen."

attachment legalizing all that was visible in their organization under the lex collegia tenuiorum. The penetration of Neander and Mosheim has established that the christians took refuge in them during four monarchs' reigns, and for at least a hundred years were closely allied and confounded with them. They were everywhere and were as much Greek as Egyptian or Roman; and they abounded in Phœnicia, Syria and Palestine, under one communal code but having a number of co-related names.[39] They are found to have invariably possessed the common table so popular and economical throughout the ancient world; and it was by this invaluable usage that they were able to head off the speculations of the provision rings which have been the bane of every age.[40] Renan also in his life of the Messiah several times declares that the therapeutæ of Philo were a branch of the Palestinian essenes.

We now proceed to state what is known of the influence of these organizations upon the founder of christianity. Seemingly to hide this, doubt and uncertainty have covered it. Every contamination, such as the Tübingen school has been jumbling the evidence. It is even denied that Jesus existed.[41] He is proving a strictly

[39] Neander, *Hist.*, I., p. 59 sqq., drawing all possible from Philo, who seems to have considered both orders as about alike and directly interlinked, says the therapeutic life was godly. They were Hebrews; they were composed of men and unmarried women; ascetic, contemplative; dwelt quietly on the borders of Lake Mœris; resembled anchorites; shut themselves in σεμνεία, μοναστήρια; were the same as the essenes; "evident that one was a translation of the other." I., p. 61; both repudiated slavery; and the observant and scholarly commentator joins to this that one may pre-suppose a relationship with Christian sects; sort of nominal Christians; an element of mysticism in both.

[40] Lüders, *Dionys. Künst.*, p. 12, declares that the etymon φρατρία will stand good for every other term; note 26: "In übertragener Bedeutung steht wohl auch φρατρία in weitestem Sinn für Verein; φρατρία ληστῶν, Liban, *Decl.*, IV., p. 645, τῆς τῶν πολυπραγμόνων φρατρίας. Plut., *De Kurios.*, XV., 147.... So auch συμμορία κολάκων, Liban. *Epi.*, 84, p. 46; vgl. ποιησώμεθα φρατρίας καὶ συμμορίας καὶ ὅπερ ἐπὶ συμποσίων οἱ πένητες ποιοῦσιν, ἐπειδὰν αὐτὸς ἕκαστος ἐστιάτωρ ὁλόκληρος γενέσθαι μὴ δύναται, συνελθόντες, ἅπαντες ἐξ ἐράνου τὴν εὐωχίαν εἰσφέρουσι." Joa, Chrysost., *Ad Antioch.*, Hom. XI., 122, vgl. Lobeck, *Aglaoph.*, p. 1013."

[41] Josephus, (see *index* in v. *Josephus* and *notes*, quoting his words), has been found by the scholars of very recent times to be exceedingly accurate. Several allusions of his, long denied, have lately turned out true to the inscriptions. Josephus, like Diodorus, is being searched by the scholars afresh, It has been long denied that his references to the founder were genuine. This is now no longer denied, but it turns out that he spoke of him about six times in his various works; and some of them are being quoted word for word. According to Whiston, it is found that Josephus was a member of the Essenes. Euseb., I., 11, of *Eccles. Hist.*, quotes verbatim the evidence of Josephus regarding "James, the brother of Jesus who is called the Christ." Origen, *Comm. on Matth.*, 234, says that Josephus spoke of "James the brother of Jesus, who was called the Christ." Sozomen, *Hist. Eccles.*, I., 1, gives evidence of the truthfulness of Josephus

RELIABILITY OF JOSEPHUS.

historical character and many of the best early writers have reluctantly admitted it, but their testimony has been suspiciously, not to say purposely covered up. The hawking champions of property and power, startled by a foreboding that the advocates of labor cannot longer be withheld from a knowledge of true reasons why this intellectual giant drove the money-changers out of the temple, and seeing that christianity, if realized, will also drive them to the wall, are loud against him to this day and pronounce his personality and his doctrine false. We propose to turn the light upon their blasphemy. We

and quotes his celebrated words in *Antiq.* XVIII., iii., 3. See *supra*, note, 18. Jerome is witness for the genuineness of Josephus in *De Vir. Illustr.* where the *Antiq.* of Josephus, XVIII., iii., 3, is quoted *verbatim*. Georgius Syncellus, *Chronicon*, p. 339, written, A.D. 790, quotes Josephus. Platini, *De Vitis. Pontif. in Christo*, written 1480, quotes *Antiq.*, XVIII., iii., 3, *verbatim*, adding that there was subjoined this: "And the famous name of Christians taken from him as well as the sect, do still continue in being." Photius, *Codex*, liber., XLVIII., speaks of a now unknown book of Josephus whose title was *Substance of the Universe*. In this work the Jewish historian speaks of "*The Divinity of Christ.*" Eusebius, *Hist. Eccles.*, I., 11, speaks of Josephus having in his 20th *Book of Histories*, spoken of the vengeance which fell upon the Jews who slew James the Just, who was the brother of Jesus who was called the Christ. Origen, *Comm. in Matth.*, p. 234, more than confirms it. James was murdered A.D. 62. Cassidorus, *Hist. Tripartit. e Sozomen*, about A.D. 510, gave a synopsis of Josephus' celebrated statement in *Antiq.*, XVIII., iii., 3, subscribing to its being genuine. Again Josephus mentions that "they dared put Jesus to death," written by Sozomen, A.D. 640. Theophilact., *Joan.*, *lib.* xiii., wrote about A.D. 1080, that he read from Josephus the following: "The city of the Jews was taken and the wrath of God was kindled and Josephus witnesses also, that this came upon them on account of the death of Jesus." Godfredus Viterbriensis, in his *Chron.*, p. 366 *Vers. Rufini.*, about A.D. 1240, confirms and quotes his passages. It is found that Josephus again mentions Jesus in *Antiq.*, XIX., ix., 1, in very plain terms, as follows: "So he assembled the Sanhedrim of Judges, and brought before them the brother of Jesus, who was called Christ, whose name was James." Ambrose, on Hegesippus, *De Excid. Urb. Hierosolym.*, *lib.* II. cap. 12, quotes Josephus' entire mention in *Antiq.*, XVIII., iii., 3, for genuine in A.D. 360. Nicephorus Callistus, *Hist. Eccles.*, *lib.*, I., p. 90-91, about A.D. 1360, confirms Josephus as a very reliable writer. Fourth mention: Suidas, *Voce Jesous*, wrote A.D. 980, speaking of Josephus as follows: "Jesus officiated in the temple with the priests." "This," says Whiston, in his *trans.* of Josephus, II., p. 571, "was taken from Eusebius, *Hist. Eccles.*, who says it was copied from his *Memoirs of the Captivity.*" John Malela, *Chron.*, *lib.*, X., A.D. 850; Glycas, *Annual*, p. 234, written A.D. 1120; Johann Zonaras, of Byzantium *Chronicon Annalium*, 12th century, all wrote substantiating the truthfulness of the writings of Josephus. Cedrenus, A.D. 1060, quotes Josephus, *Antiq.*, XVIII., iii., for reliable, in his work. Σύνοψις Ἱστοριῶν. Mecarius, in *Actis Sanctorum*, tom. V., p. 149, ap. Fabric, Joseph., p. 61, about A.D. 900, quotes the *Antiq.*, XVIII., iii., 3, verbatim. Both Suidas and Thophylact quoted from the *Memoirs of the Captivity of the Jews*, a book never heard of in modern times, written by Josephus, which repeatedly spoke of Jesus Christ. It must have been of great value. Gibbon, *Hist. Decl. & Fall.*, chap. xvi., note 36, says the mention of Josephus "is no vulgar forgery." Isodorus Pelusioto, pupil of Chrysostom, *lib.* iv., *Epistolarum*, 225, A.D. 410, quoted the *Antiq.*, XVIII., iii., 3, *verbatim*. But Jesus, also the christians, are mentioned—See *index* in v. incl'g. catch-words:—by Trajan, Hadrian, Pliny, Dio Chrys., Abgar, Pontius Pilate, Galen, Lentulus, Vopsicus, by four of the Augustan historians and several other Pagan writers, and indirectly, by Celsus, Lucian, Porphyry, Macrobius, and numerous inscriptional monuments, the most surprising of them being innumerable finds of under-ground Rome, all proving him a historical character.

are exhibiting proof that the socialism called christianity was cheated of its economic half. It was swindled out of the most important moiety of its usefulness and goodness; robbed of the great life-sustaining nourishment, leaving little but famishing lies which allure but do not satisfy. Awakening by their own energy, men discover that the church is far astray from the original plan of salvation. Millions refuse to longer attend the mocking ordeals of a vapid and hypocritical cant, which like the ancient official paganism despoiled the name of religion and made a history of christianity the antithesis of a history of the church.

The evidence that the ebionites, essenes, nazarenes, therapeutæ, thiasoi, hetæræ, eranoi and collegia were one and the same the world over, under the Solonic dispensation is now overwhelmingly manifest through the modern schools of science; and we shall hereafter only bring them in as occasion requires. We proceed to pen down our history of the proletarian classes then struggling under the emperor Tiberius. This powerful man after receiving the official report of Pilate, and his predecessor who wrote out the life, goodness, elevating influence and moral perfection of Jesus, which is preserved but denied, is said to have been a christian.

Matthew, the author of the book of the New Testament, says: "Now when Jesus was born in Bethlehem of Judæa in the days of Herod the king, behold there came wise men from the East to Jerusalem." It is well known and fully acknowledged that this Herod who was a brutal ruler and possessed enormous power over the province, was exceedingly jealous, and being a narrow-minded and cruel man, he caused the indiscriminate slaughter of male children, even including his own son,[42] in order to drag them all under the broadaxe at one swoop, so as to make sure the death of the prophetic Jesus among the victims of his jealous rage. But ah! there had been "wise men" there, who had taken precautions against his assassination. Something secret and extraordinary occured right here at the manger or cave which is believed to have been told in the ungarbled original history given by Matthew, written in the Hebrew-Aramaic tongue, now known to have been the

[42] See *supra*, note 19, of this chapter, quoting the anecdotal mention by Macrobius, *Saturnalia*, who gives the brutal speech of Herod, on being told that his own son was one of the victims;—"my swine rather than son."

language used by St. Matthew in his Gospel, but lost in somebody's tergiversation and ruin in after days. However, Origen, the scholar, scientist, student and recorder of facts,[43] having read the afterwards burned history of Hegesippus who wrote the story soon after the crucifixion, had in it, means of knowledge at his command. His book on the history of the doings of Jesus and his disciples, was burned because it told of the ebionitic essenes who had mellowed the field into which Jesus planted and careered, and gave an account of the escape of Joseph, Mary and the infant to Egypt. Justin, who was also very early, read it and from him we have the story.[44] But the remarkable and tell-tale point of this certainly wonderful revelation, which he traces back to a prophecy of Isaiah, is, that no distinction is made in the name of the secret order into which the three were initiated. He calls it all Mithraic, corresponding to the emperor Hadrian's letter to Servianus when in Alexandria, about A.D. 129.[45] It is known that the Mithraic mysteries were the essenic, therapeutic and eranic; and Hadrian is but one of a dozen good

[43] Origen is now admitted as the most learned of all the ancient comentators on the events recorded in the New Testament. He was attacked by the prelates and despoilers of christianity and driven to banishment and finally to a cruel death

[44] Justin, *Dial. Cum. Tryphone*, cap. lxxviii., speaks of the wise men who found the infant with Joseph and his mother in a cave. These travelers who acted very strangely after the fear and hostility to the three innocents leaked out, initiated all three into the secret order. It had to be done so that the brotherhood could spirit them away under the impenetrable umbrage of their mystic veil. Thus they could run them through the "underground railroad" as used to be said of the escape of American slaves to the free North and Canada, and land them safe in Egypt among congenital therapeutic brotherhoods who provided for their welfare: "Καὶ ἀνιστόρησα ἣν καὶ προέγραψα ἀπὸ 'Ησαίου περικοπὴν, εἰπὼν διὰ τοὺς λόγους ἐκείνους τοὺς τὰ Μίθρου μυστήρια παραδιδόντες, ἐν τόπῳ ἐπικαλουμένῳ παρ' αὐτοῖς σπηλαίῳ μυεῖσθαι ὑπ' αὐτων." κ.τ.λ.

[45] We give the statement of Flavius Vopsicus, as he quotes Hadrian's letter to his friend the consul Servianus, together with his statement, that of Phlegon the literary freedman who first wrote it in his book. Vopsicus certainly must have seen Phlegon's now lost work: after himself mentioning the Christians, in *Saturnino, Augustan Hist.*, XXIX., 7, Vopsicus says: "Ac ne quis mihi Ægyptiorum irascatur et meum esse credat quod in litteras rettuli, Hadriani epistolam ponam ex libris Phlegontis liberti ejus proditam, ex qua penitus Ægyptiorum vita detegetur: 'Hadrianus Augustus, Serviano Consuli, Salutem, Ægyptum, quam mihi laudabas, Serviane carisseme totam didici levum, pendulam et ad omnia famæ momenta volitantem. Illic qui Serapem colunt, Christiani sunt et devoti sunt Serapi, qui se Christi episcopos dicunt, nemo illic archisynagogus Judæorum, nemo Samarites, nemo Christianorum presbyter non Mathematicus, non haruspex, non aliptes. Ipse ille patriarcha cum Ægyptum venerit, ab aliis Serapidem adorare, ab aliis cogitur Christum. Genus hominum seditiossimum, vanissimum, injuriosissimum, civitas opulenta, dives, fecunda, in qua nemo vivat otiosus. Alii vitrum conflant, alii charta conficitur, alii liniñones, omnes certe cujuscumque artis et videntur et habentur. Podagrosi quod agant habent, habent caesi quod faciant ne chiragrici quidem apud eos otiosi vivunt."

writers about Christ who declares mithraism to have presented the closest resemblance to christianity of all other pre-christian secret unions or brotherhoods.

Brought up under the veil from boyhood, Jesus knew how to keep secrets.[46] Baring Gould, in his work on the Last and Hostile Gospels, charges that this Messiah did not perform his miracles as a Jewish prophet, but holds that he was brought up in Egypt as a magician and an initiate into the then heathen temples, which were those of the Mithraic and therapeutic doctrines. According to Renan, who spent money and a useful life in his research into the character, surroundings and influence of this great teacher, it seems that at best, "He was a stranger and without influence, long compelled to lock his discontent within himself and to communicate his sentiments only to the initiate society which accompanied him." According to the Ogdoad, VIII., the Decad, X., the Duodecad, XII., in all 30, the 30 æons or periods of his life are accounted for. If, as recounted in the strange averment of Irenæus, Jesus lived to be fifty years old, from the time he was initiated by the wise men, and started for Egypt, he would be a long time in Egypt learning arts, and still be thirty years in Nazareth with his father who soon returned to his home. This accounts for his powerful secret organization and possible sympathy and personal acquaintance with John the Baptist.

Search as we may, the knowledge we are able to collect of the years that elapsed between the mysterious escape from Judæa and the first intimations of him, when working at his father's trade in and about Nazareth, is extremely meager. It is acknowledged that he studied magic in Egypt. Some accounts prove him to have learned this and taught it for the economic purpose of earning a living during the danger period of his sojourn in Africa. There are some apocryphal stories about his infant precocity which are silly. He learned to be a good, intelligent member of his union; he learned to speak Greek; he had some knowledge of Syriac and Coptic; he was probably acquainted with Philo; he returned to Jerusalem and took more instructions from

---

[46] *Matth.*, xvi., 20; xvii , 9; *Mark*, viii., 30; ix., 8. "Τότε διεστείλατο τοῖς μαθηταῖς αὐτοῦ, ἵνα μηδενὶ εἴπωσιν, ὅτι αὐτός ἐστιν ὁ Χριστός." For *Mark*. viii.. 30: "Καὶ ἐπετίμησεν αὐτοῖς, ἵνα μηδενὶ λέγωσι περὶ αὐτοῦ."

Gamaliel and other learned and good rabbis of the sanhedrim, and went back to his father, an educated and accomplished young man..

He was not above work This is the everlasting glory of Jesus. Without this world-renowned attribute he is of no possible figure in a history of the ancient lowly. All commentators, all historians, all adverse critics, the Gibbons, Lucians, Porphyries, Paines, Ingersols, even the Jews unite in the unequivocal admission that he was a lowly, humble, refined, faultless, perfect workingman, against whom never a fault of movement or slip of judgment was discovered from the days he trod the earth down to this our living age.[47]

Jesus, if we must dismiss the report of Irenæus, was fourteen years old when Tiberius assumed imperial power at Rome. Jerusalem, the land of the Jordan, Nazareth, Bethlehem, belonged to Rome. This emperor, on hearing of his crucifixion which he regarded as an illegal deed, was incensed and punished the procurator Pontius Pilate severely for his part in it. Tiberius was so pleased with the good works of Christ that he wanted him enrolled among the gods of Rome.[48]

[47] Renan, *Jesus*, pp. 272, 3, 4, *trans.:* "He was probably a man of prodigious voice, eloquence, magnetism and sweetness, and knew how to make the most of them." Again p. 104: "Jesus has no visions. God does not speak to him from without, God is in Him; He lives in the bosom of God, by uninterrupted communication; he does not see Him but understands Him, without the need of thunder and the bush, like Moses; or of a revealing tempest like Job; or of an oracle like the old Greek sages; or a familiar genius like that of Socrates; or of the angel Gabriel, like Mahomet...." It is impossible to raise any question of race, or to inquire what blood flowed in his veins."

[48] Tertullian, *Apol.*, V.: "Vetus erat decretum, ne qui Deus ab imperatore consecraretur, nisi a senatu probatus.... Tiberius ergo, cujus tempore nomen christianum in saeculum intravit, annunciata sibi ex Syria Palæstina quæ illic veritatem istius divinitatis revelaverat, detulit ad senatum cum prærogativa suffragii sui. Senatus, quia non ipse probaverat, respuit." The senate in refusing was thus snubbing the emperor who is reported by more than one to have been converted. Mr. Gibbon, chap. xvi., note 105, however, thinks that the senate's refusal to place Jesus among the divinities of Rome did not raise the anger of Tiberius, who contented himself with his treating of all christians kindly during the four remaining years of his life. Eusebius and Chrysostom confirm this story of Tiberius. Ælios Lampridius, cf. Lardner, *Testimonies*, III., p. 157, testifies that Alexander Severus caused the statues of Abraham, Christ, Orpheus and others to be placed in his lararium or sanctum sanctorum, among others. Neander, II., p. 7, tells us that Constantius Chlorus, the father of Constantine, and a pagan, gave a place for Christ, by the side of the Gods of Rome. Among the Elagabulan deities is the inscription, Deæ Cyristi, in Parietinis Fregellarum, Orell, no. 1945. Gorius, *Monumentum sivi Columbarium*, p, xxiv., speaks of the tendency, at the time of Tiberius and Claudius to amalgamate the Roman deities into one: "Veluti Deam Pantheam, deorum omnium cultu et attributis honoratam fuisse." He cites the contents of the Columbarium as furnishing inscriptional evidence. In fact, it is well established by history and monumental relics that not only Tiberius but Hadrian and Heliogabulus apotheocized Him; and it looks as if Tiberius, in spite of the senate, actually set up his statue in the imperial

The archæologists inform us that while there were no baptists among the Hebrews of the Mosaic dispensation, the great Solonic organizations were baptist. This we have shown in our chapter on that subject.[49] In perfect conformity with this new discovery that Jesus founded christianity in the Solonic brotherhoods, we find him, on his return from Egypt, courting the acquaintance of John the Baptist. Commentators are confounded in this mysterious event. That there was an initiation of baptism here the whole christian world seems agreed. But nobody until now knew that thousands of genuine labor unions existed at that moment in and around those regions.[50] They thronged in Lower Syria a few leagues up from North Palestine when this occurred and the stone monuments of dozens of them are found among the ruins of Tyre, Sidon and Joppa in Phœnicia twenty-five miles away. Even fishermen's inscriptions are now being picked up on the famous bank of the Sea of Galilee. The Nazarenes were mithraic ebionites taking their name from Nazareth and nobody knows how long they had been there. There was contempt for them because they were an organization of working people. Renan has shown[51] that Nazareth was a city of contentious discussions and that its people were greatly dissatisfied with the condition of things in Judæa, about the time of Herod's reign. They were almost at a point of revolt. The miseries they were compelled to submit to galled their conscience and manhood, and they appear sad in their beautiful topographical retreat, one of the most charming in the world to this day. It is a

lararium. The much-quoted historian of the Cæsars, Ælius Lampridius, in *Alex. Severus*, XVIII., 43, brings more evidence showing that Jesus was long deified by the pagans at Rome: "Capitolium septimo quoque die, cum in urbe esset, ascendit, templa frequentavit. Christo templum facere voluit, eumque inter deos recipere. Quod et Hadrianus cogitasse fertur, qui templa in omnibus civitatibus sivi simulacris jusserat fieri, quæ hodieque idcirco, quia non habent numina dicuntur Hadriani, quæ ille ad hoc parasse dicebatur; sed prohibitus est ab is, qui consulentes sacra reppererant omnes christianos futuros, si id fecisset, et templa reliqua desecrenda." All this for the pagans who craved to have Jesus swell out of the evironment of industry to which he belonged; but on the other hand, there was at a very early time a strong opposition by the workers' organizations themselves who claimed that to inflate their master to an aristocratic realm would be blasphemy, in the interest of priests, prelates and unearned wealth.

[49] *Supra*, in the preceding chapter.
[50] Augustine's curious passage in *Joan.*, V.: "Mithra Christianus est," is explained in this discovery. Waltzing, *Hist. Corp. Prof.*, I., p. 330, refers to this astonishing confession when he says: "Les membres des collèges prefessionels et funéraires s' appelaient ordinairement *collègue;* c'est à dire membre du même collège; amici ou sodales; c' est à dire comerades et amis.
[51] *Life of Jesus*, in his beautiful topographical dissertation.

monument to their honor as men, that they had the intelligence to revolt against the oppressions they were compelled to submit to.

This personage, amid these self-help organizations, in the year A.D. 30 or before, began to teach the already developed lore of truth. He explained with wonderful powers the necessities of a universal brotherhood and the ways of salvation from the tyranny we have described. In strict conformity with the law of Solon, which was now more than ever hated by the aristocrats desiring human slavery, he worked up an opposition to existing regulations. It succeeded. He next carried his conquest into Jerusalem, seventy miles to the south. He had already worked there as a scholar. He reappeared as a teacher. It is enough to say that he attacked the economic rather than religious conditions. He discovered that there was a gang of outside traders who were using the temple of Jerusalem as a market place for gains. No one dared to disturb them because like the stock gamblers of Lombard and Wall streets, they held the shining coins. Their wealth awed the common people. The sectaries and the Sanhedrim had submitted to the infamy from immemorial time, until the interests of all were one.

But in this master they found a match. He attacked these devils of dicker and money changers and drove them from the sanctuary. It was no mere verbal suasion; he whipped them out like dogs. They had long enough blasphemed justice and honor by turning the sacred temple into shambles of mercenary greed. They had proved by their desecrations that the love of money is the root of all evil. With a powerful hand, and he must have been a giant, he seized them and violently whipped them from the place. Inexpressibly graphic and terrible is the Greek of this master-stroke of the founder of socialism.[52]

It is with reluctance that the student of human nature understands the unforgiving emotion of hate, especially when based upon the dissolute instinct of covetousness. To be interrupted from their methods of money-getting men will fortify their pretentions with a

---

[52] John, ii., 15-16: Καὶ ποιήσας φραγέλλιον ἐκ σχοινίων πάντες ἐξέβαλεν ἐκ τοῦ ἱεροῦ, τά τε πρόβατα καὶ τοὺς βόας, καὶ τῶν κολλυβιστῶν ἐξέχεε τὸ κέρμα καὶ τὰς τραπέζας ἀνέστρεψε, καὶ τοῖς τὰς περιστερὰς πωλοῦσιν εἶπεν· ἄρατε ταυτὰ ἐντεῦθεν· μὴ ποιεῖτε τὸν οἶκον τοῦ πατρός μου οἶκον ἐμπορίου.

clandestine villainy inspiring them to secret conspiracies with the officers of the law and cause them to work in secret, and form unions of their fraternities, powerful in numbers and bribing influence, such as to secure the friendship and support of fellow millionaires, prelates, politicians, kings and emperors. This was true in the case of the daring workingman who drove the ravenous corruptionists, stock gamblers and provision rings out of the temple of Jerusalem. Hatred and underhanded intrigue was soon to develop itself in the case of Stephen the proto-martyr. Jesus was a real workingman, born and raised among vigor-inspiring environments, with a feeling for the poor.[53] He went ahead, got down to the bottom, planted a vast scheme of political economy in the open world; it was secret before. True, he planted amid the mellow brotherhoods, loving, working for, and engendering sympathy among themselves, the creators and authors of sympathy, that grand and hitherto almost unknown emotion of the human breast; but they had not yet dared to lisp louder than with the still small voice that they had a soul, much less a right to herald to all the world the beautiful socialism. They had never dared to burst the trammels of contempt and danger and make of their plan an open political economy to the new salvation. No one could do this but the kathegemon, long promised to come in the spirit and the flesh. No mighty military genius, with gilded trappings and kingly pageantry; no thundering potentate or pretentious heir to proud dynasties could work the salvation of the ancient men of labor. The proud Hebrew of the Mosaic law made the mistake of his life supposing this. The poor and lowly Jews, the brilliant workingmen both of that day and of this have perceived this fundamental fact that no messiah could succeed; none but a workingman born of the flesh who in humility makes the wealth of nations, builds means of enlightenment, invents, makes and nationalizes tools of labor to solve the problem and crumble pride and arrogance into dust.

It is probable that in Egypt he learned the trade of

---

[53] Justin, *Cum. Tryph.*, 89. declares he was in the habit of working at making plows and ox-yokes: "Ταῦτα γὰρ τὰ τεκτονικὰ ἔργα εἰργάζετο ἐν ἀνθρώποις ὤν, ἄροτρα καὶ ζυγά. διὰ τούτων καὶ τὰ τῆς δικαιοσύνης σύμβολα διδάσκων καὶ ἐνεργῆ βίον. κ.τ.λ.

the dyers.⁵⁴ We have much to say in future pages about the dyers. They swarmed in Asia Minor, especially in the Phrygian Heraclia, Colossæ, Ephesus and Laodicea, and there is important Biblical mention of them in several other places.

The general teachings of Jesus were perfectly logical, and in harmony with the great words of Aristotle who told the world that men bound down to the awful miseries they were suffering in his time, could not be good citizens. That required some freedom and independence from the trammels of poverty and persecution. Under christianity, therefore, mind must be elevated to a susceptibility of good citizenship. The great trade organizations were ready. But the millions of members, all slaves or their descendants, were still too low, though now possesing some means to work out their lasting hope.

The teacher is now born. His coming business is to make the most of conditions. Economic misery must be cured.⁵⁵ Hermes Pastor, one of the earliest church fathers, proposed a cure but he was hounded down.⁵⁶ He wanted the cure, long in operation by the law and its method, celebrated as the brotherhoods, beautiful in mutual care. When the kathegemon came, he was taken in by the poor, but hunted by the aristocratic, of both Jews and Gentiles.

No shambling, floundering moon-calf could veer those centuries, unhinged by the Roman conquests, into line. Such an abnormity as a messiah to set none at liberty but Jews, and that by dint of a "conquering hero," was impossible. Another Athenion with a glittering wand

---

⁵⁴ *Apocryphal New Testament*, Lord, 1821, p. 21: "There are several stories believed of Christ, proceeding from this Gospel; as that which Mr. Sike relates out of La Brosse's *Persian Lexicon*, that Christ practiced the trade of a dyer, and his working with the colors; from whence the Persian dyers honor him as their patron, and call a dyehouse a shop of Christ." The legend tends to explain the κυριάκος of which wonder we make revelations from the archæologists; and it may be that the boy actually lived in Persia."

⁵⁵Aristotle, *Problem.*, XXX., 10, as paraphrased into Latin by Aulus Gellius, XX., 4: "Quibus causis scenici artifices plerumque pravi esse solent? Nonne quod studii sapientiæ minime participes sunt, consumpta in necessaria attificii meditatione vitæ maxima parte, et quod plerumque nunc in intemperantia, nunc in egestate degunt? Ex utroque enim pravitas oritur." Spend most of their time in extreme poverty. True! and in intemperance; just so. Then with the great Aristotle, we ask, how could they be good citizens? They could think of nothing but the lowest things.

⁵⁶ Hermes Pastor, Book III., *Similitude*, x., cap. 4· "I say that every one ought to be saved from inconveniences. Both he who is in want and he who suffereth inconveniences in daily life is in much torture and necessity. Whoever rescues a soul from physical necessity, will win for himself great joy.'

the world did not want. Another fire-spitting Eunus
with a reeking sword would have made memory shudder.
Another Spartacus could only thrill, much less convert
the dizzy race. A demokolax flunkying before Jehovah
for authority to twirl this Armageddon of Jordan into a
lake of blood and vengeance would not do. Such a return to the irascible and concupiscent champions, who
had failed, would have been a libel on the masterly prowess of a jostling movement, the only true representative of the working millions. Mosaism never taught
that labor is the highest majesty of the universe. Thus
when the teacher came to openly proclaim and redeem
the world, though meekest and humblest of the lowly,
he was "King of Kings." This Being is still fresh among
us, a factor in the science of mechanics, whether spiritual or actual we care not—a representative of progress;
an eternally evolving light, blazing down upon civilization, political economy, mutual love and care, in beams
of the old salvation. The Hebrew workingman, shrewd,
brilliant, progressive, is again to do as did great numbers of his ancient kindred. He will be swift to redis-
cover these almost demolished foundations of his own
masonry and rehabilitate the socialism he himself has
planted. If to-day there exists a race that deserves to
be proud of its record it is that of the Hebrew. We
are in possession of abundant evidence that it was the
Semitic workingmen who in Asia were foremost in planting the enormous Solonic organization which stands at
the bottom of this history. It was not the quarrelsome
aristocrats of Jerusalem whose sectaries fought for a
rich messiah, gorgeous and studded with military trappings, raging like Bar Cochbas.[57]

This species of messianism never failed to end in disaster. They wanted nothing of the kind. In Asia Minor, Babylonia, Corinth, Philippi and Greek-speaking

---

[57] Doane, *Bible Myths*, pp. 423-437, under the denomination of *Angel Messiahs*, gives a list of those he has discovered: Guatama, Simon Magus, Basilides, Menander, Manes, Appollonius and others. Bar Cochbas came last. He had an army of 25,000 men, and proposed to win by the sword, but was met and defeated by the Romans, during Hadrian's time, A.D. 130-138. General disaster attended his ravings, which ended in the second destruction of Jerusalem; see Mosheim, *Eccles. Hist.*, I., 2nd century, part I., cap. 1, § 11: "The Jews, first under Trajan, A.D. 116, and afterwards under Adrian, A.D. 132, led on by Bar Cochbas who pretended to be the messiah, laid insurrection against the Romans; and again suffered the greatest calamities. A vast number of them were put to death, and a new city, Ælia Capitolina, was erected on the site of Jerusalem, which not an individual of the miserable race was allowed to enter."

islands, as well as Palestine, the Jews prove a potent factor in the great organized industries. Their archæological remains give them their history in words more reliable than those of any historian and these words, with the crude slabs of stone which perpetuate them are in the scientific collections of many museums. Thus the ancient work of the Solonic dispensation is proved to have been largely Semitic. The Hebrews, environed by persecutions, shadowed by police, insulted and followed by proconsular spies, wisely mixed with the Gentiles for safety, and in a common bond, they all safely worked out the economical problem of life together.[58]

We are far from any wish to present a disquisition in opposition to the Mosaic dispensation. Up to that time no legal instrument of its enormous value had spread such wholesome civilization. But as it is wellknown and adhered to, alike by Jew and Gentile, and comes down to us in power and glory in the sacred writ, it stands in no need of our criticism and scarcely of our mention. It was a religion. We are not writing a religious book. Solonism was not a religion. The point in contact with a history of the strictly ancient unions is aimed only at the working people. It is seven hundred, or perhaps one thousand years more ancient than the Solonic law. It provided for slavery; the new jus coeundi emancipated slaves by buying them honorably from their masters; the jus coeundi had no king, no nationality, knew no distinction between man and man; mosaism built cities and gilded temples; the jus coeundi built only cabins of comfort and modest kuriakoi, and scholæ for business details and common tables, and had miniature groves and fountains for symposiums, banquets and communal joys. The one was proud, majestical, ambitious; the other humble, occult, undefended, except through the reverence of reigning despotism for the sacredness of lawgivers who, in almost a reign of Saturn had established it; the one paid its attentions to shrines, rites and sectaries; the other delved in industries, built up the wealth of nations, while burrowing in secret, and unknown; the one wanted its Sampsons and Solomons; the other held and hugged a code of inter-mutual love which created a vast emotional

[58] John, xiii., 29: Τινὲς γάρ ἐδόκουν, ἐπεὶ τὸ γλωσσόκομον εἶχεν ὁ Ἰούδας, ὅτι λέγει αὐτῷ ὁ Ἰησοῦς· ἀγόρασον, ὧν χρείαν ἔχομεν εἰς τὴν ἑορτήν, ἢ τοῖς πτωχοῖς ἵνα τι δῷ. See also John, xii., 6; Acts., ii., 44-45; iv., 32-34.

sympathy, with father and mother, and sweet fraternal affection—new creations which christianity made its foundation and corner-stone. Such is proved by both inscriptional and literary evidence to have constituted the difference between the Mosaic and Solonic dispensations, in the time of the emperor Tiberius.[59]

The fact can no longer be suppressed that the men at the head of this great movement were all initiates into secret orders. They were to keep secrets.[60]

Perhaps there is no more important point in this history than the discovery that the Jews of Phrygia at least the theatre of the celebrated seven churches and many others, did not follow the Mosaic, but the Solonic code. This is being elaborated by the archæologists.[61] We

[59] Smith, *Dict. of the Bible*, Bost., III., p. 2372, explains how Paul tore away from the strictly Mosaic law and discarded circumcision, which certainly would act in reconciling the brotherhoods in Asia Minor and outside of Palestine. Large numbers of the Jews left the synagogue, a purely Greek word and temple, and joined the "House of the Lord." Neander, *Planting*, chap. iii.: "It is highly probable that he was first induced by his dispositions with the Hellenists, to present the gospel on the side of the opposition to the Mosaic law." *Amer. Cyclopœdia* in verb. *Hebrews*, *Epist. to the:* "It aimed to demonstrate the preëminence of Christ over Moses and the angels of the Lord; and of the gospel over the law: and to show that the latter was typical of the former and was abolished by it." *Acta. Sanct. Theod Ancyr.*, § 3: "Paganorum atque Judæorum magnum numerum adduxit ad Ecclesiam." Max Müller, *Origin of Religion*, p. 130, thinks Mosaism and the Zend Avista one and the same. They were both heartless to the producers.

[60] Matth., xvi., 20; xvii., 9; Mark, viii., 30; ix., 8; Philo, *De Vita Contemplativa*, § 1., ii., p. 47., declares that the brotherhoods of Egypt, now proved by inscriptions found in Asia Minor to be one and the same with the industrial unions of the θίασοι, ερανοί, εταίραι and collegia, took care both of the body and the soul: "Θεραπευταὶ καὶ θεραπευτίδες καλοῦνται, ἤτοι παρ' ὅσον ἰατρικὴν ἐπαγγέλλονται κρείσσονα τῆς κατὰ πόλεις (ἡ μὲν γὰρ σώματα θεραπεύει μόνον, ἐκείνη δὲ καὶ ψυχὰς. κ.τ.λ ;) ἢ παρ' ὅσον ἐκ φύσεως καὶ τῶν ἱερῶν νόμων, ἐπαιδεύθησαν θεραπεύειν τὸ ὄν. κ.τ.λ." Thus they must have an eye on their bodily comforts, their souls and the common wealth. They were the original coöperative commonwealth. The etymological kinship of therapeutæ, essenes, θίασοι, and the rest, we have already shown. Lüders, *Dionys. Künst.*, p. 53, note 100, who in enumerating the fifty different trade unions attached to, and bound together in the Great Gemeinde, argues that they are pretty much one root-word. Renan, *Life of Jesus*, p. 206: "From this moment he takes the position no longer of the Jewish reformer but of a destroyer of Judaism."

[61] Ramsay, *Cities and Bishoprics of Phrygia*, II., p. 538, no, 399 bis: "Αὐρ. Ῥοῦφος Ἰουλιανοῦ β'. ἐποίησα τὸ ἡρῷον ἐμαυτῷ κὲ τῇ συμβίῳ μου Αὐρ. Τατιανῇ· ἰς ὁ ἕτερος οὐ τεθῇ. εἰ δέ τίς ἐπιτηδεύσι, τὸν νόμον οἶδεν τῶν Ἐιουδέων." Dr. Ramsay, substantiating his opinion by that of Rheinach, here sees that this law referred to in the inscription, though applying to the Jews, was not the law of Moses. He remarks: "This remarkable epitaph may be added here though not Christian. The law of the Jews cannot here be the law of Moses;" and farther on he says: "The phrase is suggestive of a strong Jewish element in the Apameian population." The truth seems to be, that, it being given among quite a number of unions, though undesignated in the brevity of this particular inscription, Aurelius Rhuphus was a member of a union; and it was not the Mosaic law referred to but none other than the Solonic. Ramsay, p. 638, again states, referring to this same 399: "In no. 399, bis, the law of the Jews is mentioned, and we recognize there, with S. Rheinach, not the law of Moses, but a regulation agreed upon." Of course it is the "ἢ ὁμότάφοι" clause of the Solonic law. See *Digest*, XLVII., *Tit.*, xxii., le. 4, which we have so frequently quoted.

are reminded by Strabo that the Dionysan artists in early times suffered great persecutions from the kings. Attalus drove them on account of a strike, first to Myonnesos, later to Lebedos and they had already been banished to Ephesus, where they formed great and powerful unions, retaining Teos as their central seat. As great numbers of them were Jewish working people we give his statement.[62] The learned Ramsay declares in his books on the Phrygian cities that "The Jewish community in Apameia is as old as the foundation of the city. (B.C. 280-261) The seleucid kings used the Jews as an element of the colonies which they founded to fasten their hold on Phrygia and other countries," and on the same page he adds that: "when Antiochus the great, desired to strenghten his cause in Phrygia and Lydia, about B.C. 200, he brought two thousand Jewish families from Babylonia and settled them in the strongholds granting them lands and guaranteeing them his favor in every way."[63]

Long before that they had settled throughout Asia Minor, especially in Phrygia and Syria, but the strange and difficult problem is that they do not seem to have been the real Mosaic Jews, for they came from the river Euphrates, not from Palestine. There is a legend that a great split-away occured at the Exodus.[64] We have inklings that they did not faithfully follow the law of Moses, and furthermore that these were the true proletarian Jews. Be this as it may, it has now come to the surface that those found organized so numerously in trade unions, or as the archæologist Ramsay erroneously designates them "guilds," were followers of the strictly Solonic dispensation. In our division of this chapter engrossing Sections Claudius and Nero, we

[62] Strabo, *Geog.*, 643: "'Ενταῦθα (εν Λεβέδῳ) τῶν περὶ τὸν Διόνυσον τεχνιτῶν ἡ σύνοδος καὶ κατοικία τῶν ἐν 'Ιωνίᾳ μέχρι 'Ελλησπόντου, ἐν ᾗ πανήγυρίς τε καὶ ἀγῶνες κατ' ἔτος συντελοῦνται τῷ Διονύσῳ· ἐν Τέῳ δὲ ᾤκουν πρότερον τῇ ἐφεξῆς πόλει τῶν 'Ιώνων· ἐμπεσούσης δὲ στάσεως εἰς 'Έφεσον κατέφυγον. 'Αττάλου δὲ εἰς Μυόννησον αὐτοὺς καταστήσαντος μεταξὺ Τέω καὶ Λεβέδου, πρεσβεύονται Τήιοι δεόμενοι 'Ρωμαίων, μὴ περιιδεῖν ἐπιτειχιζομένην σφίσι τὴν Μυόννησον, οἱ δὲ μετέστησαν εἰς Λέβεδον δεξάμενων τῶν Λεβεδίων ἀσμένως διὰ τὴν κατέχουσαν αὐτοὺς ὀλιγανδρίαν."

[63] Ramsay, *Cit. and Bish., Phryg.*, II., p. 668.

[64] *Exodus*, chap. xxxiii.. The story told in this chapter appears incomprehensible. There was a prodigious revolt against Moses, over the golden calf. They came to blows. No less then 3,000 of the naked creatures were slain. If there is any truth in this history it was all in regard to the law of Moses, which a large number of them refused to obey. It seems certain that a large portion of these Jews split away and left for unknown countries,

shall give the amazing discovery of the shoemakers of Shoemakers' Street in Apameia, as ably discussed by Ramsay, showing an important christian plant into an old pagan temple on the acropolis of Kelainai, in a suburb of this once great city.[65]

Driven out of Mesopotamia by the Asian kings and forced to settle in Asia Minor, the Jews flourished greatly by industry in their western homes, and existed there in large numbers under Roman domination. But they maintained their old love of kindred and were following somewhat the Mosaic law when, as reported by Cicero they sent their gold to Jerusalem.[66]

But we find that these Jews referred to are those who had traffic in proconsular Rome, as Cicero distinctly states. The Jews who really founded the unions of Laodicea and Hierapolis were from the Euphrates; and the reason we hear so little about them is that they did not write history, but like other workingmen, contented themselves with the plentitude of their industries, writing no records, except those we find on their monuments, made compulsory under the law.

Everything found on the stones tends to prove that what all the Jews of Asia Minor at that time or during the reign of Tiberius did was to get a living.[67] All goes to show that the poor were denied the right to enjoy their own religion[68] based on the salvation of the flesh. According to their business-like and correct tenets, the household was first of all, to be provided for. It was so originally with the christians.[69]

---

[65] Strabo, *Geog.*, 576: "Εἶτα Ἀπάμεια ἐ Κιθωτὸς λεγομένη καὶ Λαοδίκεια αἵπερ εἰσὶ μέγισται τῶν κατὰ τὴν φρυγίαν πόλεων,"... 577: "Ἀπάμεια δ' ἐστὶν ἐμπόριον μέγα τῆς ἰδίως λεγομένης Ἀσίας δευτερεῦον μετὰ τὴν Ἔφεσον."

[66] Cicero, *Pro Flacc.*, 28: "Sequitur auri illa invidia Judaici. Quum aurum Judæorum nomine quotannis ex Italia et ex omnibus provinciis Hierosolyma exportari soleret, Flaccus sanxit edicto ne ex Asia exportari liceret ... multitudinem Judæorum, flagrantem nonnumquam in concionibus, pro republica contemnere gravitatis summae fuit.... Apameæ manifesto comprehensum ante pedes prætoris in foro expensum est auri pondo centum pauilo minus, Laodicea viginti pondo paullo amplius." The Jews of that locality, economical and business-like, locked their gold up also in their own secret coffers. Some idea has been calculated regarding the Jews residing in these localities of Phrygia from the figures of Cicero and Josephus, wh.. make it out that they were numerous.

[67] Lüders, *Dionys. Künst.*, p. 116, cites inscriptions tending to prove tha they had no other idea than that of making a living.

[68] Tac., *Annal.*, xv., 34: "Odium generis humani." Suetonius, *Nero*, 1(, What caused the Romans to persecute the new sect of Christians was th fact that it deprived the public treasury of much income.

[69] Irenæus, *Adv. Hær.*, V., xix., 22, all through. "Unless the flesh wer.: saved, the Word would not have taken upon it the flesh. Again, quoting Paul, see *Adv. Hær.*, V., xvi. 2: "Now the final result of the spirit is th

All goes to prove that the official religion of the pagans was a tyrannical hinderance to the winning of bread. All the arguments engrossed in this study show that there was an old and deep rooted wrong forced upon the poor by the official religion everywhere. When the climax was reached the revolt arrived in form of christianity. Then the Roman persecutions began. Really they began before the Advent. When christianity was planted into the mellow ground of the secret unions, the members took it up with wonderful alacrity.

Directly adjoined to this split-away from the dispensation of Moses, of a large portion of the Semitic race calling themselves Hebrews and who in reality were the laboring and outcast class, there appear some harmonies, both historic and biographical.

The celebrated Logos of Plato, brought down by Philo, James and John, if not Matthew in his Hebrew Gospel, gives mankind a set of laws. They are being confirmed by the recent discoveries of Grenfell and Hunt in Egypt and are attributed, some to Matthew, some to Jesus.[70] But it is not the law of Moses. It is plainly something emanating indirectly from the Twelve Tables of Rome, and this logos was the basis of the collegia. Gibbon plainly tells us that Plato had the logos, and that the Alexandrian school originally Hebrew, borrowed it from Plato.[71] The author of the astute work entitled Supernatural Religion mentions what we think a fundamental but natural mistake of Justin in stating that Socrates and Plato borrowed the remark so ad-

salvation of the flesh;" and again, V., xii., 6, Irenæus argues that work of this kind was considered equal to work of procuring food and shelter. He talks about handiwork and tradesmanship, regarding them as above all other things. So Barnabas *Epist.*, chap. iii.: "To us, behold this is the fast which I have chosen, not that a man should humble himself, but that he should do away with every bond of iniquity until the fastenings of harsh agreements restore to liberty them that are bruised, tear up the unjust engagements, feed the hungry, with bread, clothe the naked, bring the homeless into the house, nor despiseth the humble."

[70] Oxyrhynchus Papyri, of Grenfell and Hunt. *Gleanings From Egypt*, (From the London Lancet.) "It is probable that no archæological literary discovery of the expiring century will in future be so celebrated as the rescue from the sands of the Egyptian Fayoum of more than 10,000 complete and fragmentary papyri by the explorers acting under the auspices of the "Graeco-Roman Branch of the Egyptian Exploration Fund," a society which, at its commencement, owed much to the late Sir Erasmus Wilson. A selection from some 1,400 documents, the greater part of which are at Oxford, and the minority at the Ghizeh Museum, has been made by Messrs. Grenfell and Hunt, who have carefully edited about 150 of them and published them with a commentary in a volume entitled "*The Oxyrhynchus Papyri: Part I, with Eight Fac-simile Plates.*" First in importance is the now famous portion of the 'Logia' or a collection of 'Sayings of our Lord.'"

[71] Gibbon, *Decl. and Fall.*, chap. xxi and note 13.

mired and studied by Justin, from Moses.⁷² But Justin was not alone in placing Plato and others among the pre-christian christian immortals.⁷³ Irenæus thought so too. A large part of the Jews, during the reign of Tiberius adopted this Logos or Word. A large part, including official Judaism repudiated it, and denounced John, Peter, the apostles and disciples. It aimed at salvation.

The recent exhumation of the so-called Logia of Egypt, about one hundred miles from Cairo up the Nile, at the site of the ancient Oxyrhynchus, brings to us long-lost evidence that he encouraged the oppressed and declared that he was with them and one of them. One Logion or Word, as John called it says: "Raise the stone and there you will find me; Cleave the wood and I am there."⁷⁴ This perfectly agrees with Origen who says he made ox-yokes and did many sorts of hard work in wood.⁷⁵

But what salvation was, is a question now rising above the pretentions of priest-power which, like that

⁷² *Supernat. Rel.*, N.Y., 28 Lafayette Place; p. 567: "Justin, who frankly admits the delight he took in the writings of Plato. *Apol* II., 12; *Dial. Cum Tryphone*, II., 2 ˢᵠᵠ, and other Greek philosophers, was well aware how Socrates and Plato had enunciated the doctrine of the Logos. *Apol.*, I., 60, although he contends that he borrowed it from the writings of Moses." The same with Theophrastus.

⁷³ Irenæus, *Adv. Hær.*, III., xxv., 5, quoting Plato, *De Leg.*, iv., 715, 716, *Timæus*, vi., 29, declaring what constitutes the Word, and says it is the beginning, the End and the Mean.

⁷⁴ We quote the new-found Oxyrhynchus Papyri containing a Word or Logion of Jesus, saved from the dry sand-dunes of the Egyptian Fayoum by Grenfell and Hunt, with their translation, who think Matthew penned it to his dictation; labled Λόγια Ἰασου, Oxyrhynchus, frontispiece, 1., plate I., p. 3: "Ἔγειρον τὸν λίθον καὶ ἐκεῖ εὑρήσεις με, σχισον τὸ ξύλον καὶ ἐγω ἐκεῖ εἰμι λέγει Ἰησοῦ." This they render as follows: "Jesus saith: Raise the stone, and there you will find me; cleave the wood and I am there." It is clear from these words that he was preaching to working people such as masons who work in stone, and carpenters, and all sorts of woodworkers, and inspiring them to take courage for he is there as one of them, and as their representative.

⁷⁵ See the preceeding note. The papyrus containing the 5th Logion says: "Δέγει Ἰησοῦς ὅπου ἐὰν ὦσιν β΄, οὐκ εἰσὶν ἄθεοι καὶ ὅπου εἰς ἔστιν μόνος, λέγω, ἐγὼ εἰμι μετ᾽ αὐτοῦ. So secret was he that a part of it was written in figures, ie; β΄. Now come the significant words of the epigraphist who found this treasure and noted it with some remarkable plates, in the Oxyrhynchus Papyri, pp. 3 ff.: and aided by valuable restorations of Prof. Blass. They write as follows: "I. We have here part of a collection of sayings, not extracts from a narrative gospel; II., that they are not heretical; III., that they were independent of the four gospels, in their present shape; IV., that they were earlier than A.D. 140 and might go back to the first century." Then they add: "These propositions especially the first, have, and it is natural, been warmly disputed. Attempts have been made to show that the Logia were extracts from the Gospels according to the Egyptians (Harneck), the Gospel according to the Hebrews (Batiffol), or the Gospel of the Ebionites (Zahn); and gnostic, mystic ebiontic or therapeutic tendencies, according to the point of view have been discovered in them. On the other hand our position has received the general support of critics such as Swete, Rendel, Harris, Heinrici and Lock."

of money and property stalks over the magnificent economic schemes of the first fathers, and consigns the salvation of Jesus to realms of reasonless etherialism; whereas, in fact he preached for the redemption of his people from the monstrous impositions and cruel brutalities of force. No doubt can longer exist that in the early apostolic age covered by Tiberius, there began a strong contention over the scope of this economic movement for the salvation of humanity.

It was the celebrated logos which the densely secret essenic and therapeutic organizations possessed. And so far they were christians, regardless of date. But in fact, the great ancient Solonic communities did not vary materially from christians.[76] There recently has been set afoot an accusation that christianity is a failure. Supposing that it was ever a part of the official religion this might be true. But it was not so. These accusers would have us understand that, if let alone, the old pagan world was rapidly achieving all that is being accomplished by christianity. True, Aristotle,[77] Dionysius of Halicarnassus, Plutarch, Strabo, and Pliny have 'presupposed this in words which they have dropped, yet not one of them all, not even modern commentators, not even Neander, can see that christianity lies undetachably on the bedrock of the labor problem. This alone, when understood in its true, economic and ethical sense, will overturn the "calamity" accusation. In truth, too much

[76] The Rev. Robert Taylor, *Diegesis*, chap. ix., in describing the therapeutic essenes, of whom he thinks Philo was a member and which recently found the inscriptions prove to be one and the same as the eranos and collegium, says: "They had, 1, parishes; 2, churches; 3, bishops, priests, and deacons; 4, they observed the grand festivals of christianity; 5, they pretended to have apostolic founders; 6, practiced the same manners which distinguished the immediate apostles of Christ; 7, used the scriptures which they believed to be divinely inspired; 8, and which Eusebius himself believed to be none other than the substance of our Gospels; 9, the same allegorical methods of interpreting these scriptures which has since obtained among christians; 10, and the self-same manner and order of performing public worship; 11, having missionary stations or colonies; 12, having missionary stations at Corinth, Galatia, Ephesus, Philippi, Colossæ and Thessalonica, precisely such circumstances as those addressed by St. Paul in his respective epistles to the Romans, Corinthians, Galatians, Ephesians. Philippians, Colossians, Thessalonians; and 13, answering to every circumstance described, of the state and discipline of the first community of the christians to the very letter; 14, and all this is nothing new in Philo's time, but of their long-established notoriety and venerable antiquity," In the *Diegesis*, p. 67, Dr. Taylor further claims that Alexandria was the cradle of christianity.

[77] Aristotle, *Eth. Nich.*, II., 3, in one of his deep thoughts, holds that the external supposes the internal and consequently nothing is hidden from omniscience, touches this closely: "$"Οτι δεῖ τὰ δίκαια πράττονας δκαίους γίνεσθαι, τὰ πράγματα δίκαια λέγεται, ὅταν ᾖ τοιαῦτα οἷα ἂν ὁ δίκαιος πράξειεν· δίκαιος δέ ἐστίν οὐχ ὁ ταῦτα πράττων, ἀλλὰ καὶ ὁ οὕτω πράττων ὡς οἱ δίκαιοι πράττουσιν."$

has been expected from, and accredited to, the pagan cult. It did not sweeten or mollify human sympathy. That was done by the myriad secret unions whose one mysterious tenet was love and care. They were labor unions. This is admitted. The labor cult, then is the original christianity. But a conspiracy forced it to at last give way and surrender the world up to the dark ages infinitely more pagan than christian.

Pursuing the discussion of Hebrew history to find the cause of these people not adhering to the law of Moses, we strike some remarkable points showing that some of them did and some did not.[78] According to the Bible this earliest refusal to conform to his law was what broke the heart of Moses in his old age.

A long period of awful revolts and massacres followed, lasting from 975 to 712 B.C. Now we have it for a certainty that the Solonic dispensation began just about this time and we are coming to a knowledge that this great branch of Hebrews adopted and made it a basis of their secret labor organizations; for we find them in the inscriptions all through that quarter of Asia. It is here that a little-known circumstance of Abgar, king of Edessa which we are about to recount, stands as a landmark in the history of christianity, though it did not begin until a few months before the crucifixion.

The conflict of the north-eastern against the Palestinian Hebrews never ended, even until the latter were destroyed; for their utter destruction may in a measure be attributed indirectly to the unquenchable rage of Abgar. We leave this for its proper place, merely remarking here that Abgar revolted against Judah for the murder of Jesus who was himself from the north, not far from Edessa, his city; and a close inspection reveals that Jesus was following, not the Mosaic, but the Solonic dispensation, its jus coeundi of labor organization and all their secret mysteries which Abgar the king certainly upheld.

[78] *Amer. Cyclop.* art. *Hebrews.* "The name Israelite applied to his (speaking of Abraham) descendants, at a much later period, about B.C. 712, at the dispersion of the ten tribes," Again: "The division of the state into two separate kingdoms was consummated B.C. 975;" and proceeds to explain that the north was settled by the tribe of Benjamin which reached east of Jordan and was called Israel, and fell to Ephraim, Manasseh as the house of Joseph. This is remarkable, since it would comprise Syria, Phrygia and in all probability Edessa and Abgar's Mesopotamia. This information is continued in words as follows: "The southern, from their chief tribe called Judah, had the advantage of possessions, the sanctuary of the old capital, and of being supported by the Levites and the priests, who gathered around it.

King Abgar a Roman subject under Tiberius, pitied, endorsed, believed in Jesus, and even prevailed upon Tiberius to avenge the crime committed on him. The letters they wrote are extant. Modern investigators are alligning themselves upon the old belief that the story is in substance true, but has been guffawed down by the bejeweled ones who could not make their methods prosper by allowing such a common sense plan of human economies to live. The story of Abgar accentuates the success of Solonism in Asia Minor as well as the thrift of christianity there, and the early christianizing of Armenia through the great Gemeinde, east and west.

It may now be said, on the dispersion of the tribes, that the re-discovery and rehabilitation into history, of the Solonic dispensation and jus coeundi account for a phenomenal hiatus in the annals of the Semitic race. It leads to the causes, inklings of which crop out of the disastrous anarchy among the idol worshipers, from the Exodus down to B.C. 920, and elucidates the Mosaic law—that greatest of all codes until Solon, and stoutly claimed to be the greatest until now. This law was so refined as to be impossible to tatterdemalion throngs of poor, uneducated working people constituting the populations. These were too simple-minded to obey, at so early an epoch, the noble and grand refinement inherent in that great rescript. The laboring, jostling majority thus wrangled and struggled under pure polytheism from B.C. 920 to 712, fighting and wallowing in obstinate self-sufficiency and failure, until there came from Athens and Rome the great law of economic organization compelling them along with everybody who had to work for a living, under penalty of death to organize in trade unions.[79]

The story of King Abgar of Edessa and his correspondence, which it is as certain as history, took place between himself and Jesus, and after the crucifixion between him and the soon afterwards murdered Emperor, must now be recounted. We have already shown that this is not a religious work, but a history of these prosy facts. It is only necessary to prove that the men who came out as champions of labor's cause were

[79] See *supra*, p. 83, and note 1, quoting the *Euterpe* of Herodotus, giving assurance that originally the organization was made compulsory on pain of death, as well as the reasons why.

historical characters. If this cannot be established, much of our history falls to the ground. As Abgar was an undoubted historical character this singular correspondence is of great importance because it helps to clear up some of the dark lacunæ making fitful and uncertain the newly discovered evidence that the Hebrews who are found in the inscriptions adopted and for ages thrived under the jus coeundi of Solon in such numbers in Asia Minor and North Phœnicia. Abgar's story therefore becomes the more important; for it helps to prove that the extreme northern and eastern Semitics, of whom this king was one, approved the Solonic rather than the Mosaic dispensation. Of course the great and all-important injunction of Moses, that which makes him immortal as a lawgiver, that which characterizes mosaism as above all other legislation, elevating mankind above competing paganism, and fully endorsed as a new commandment in the teachings of Jesus, was retained in the jus coeundi, the full text of which is lost. Solonism, then, which provided by secret labor organization for food, clothing, shelter, a place of refuge under the ægis of a god for those chased and threatened, and a method of emancipation from slavery by means of the sale of bondmen to a god, was fortified by the powerful injunction of the great law-giver Moses, that we love one another. And thus the Solonic law of the lowly was perfect.

King Abgar wrote a letter to Jesus.[80] He had a disease of some sort, difficult if not impossible to cure by the ordinary methods of the physicians. He was of a credulous turn, and living in that age of sorcery and occultism, became convinced, on hearing of the healing powers of the great master who was walking about in

[80] The letter was translated from Eusebius' *Hist. Eccles.*, I., chap. xiii., many centuries ago. It reads: "Abgarus, King of Edessa, to Jesus the good Saviour, who appeared at Jerusalem, greeting:
I have been informed concerning you and your cures, which are performed without the use of medicines and herbs.
For it is reported that you cause the blind to see, the lame to walk, do both cleanse lepers, and cast out unclean spirits and devils, and restore them to health who have long been diseased, and raise up the dead.
All which when heard, I was persuaded of one of these two, viz: either that you are God himself descended from heaven, who do these things, or the son of God.
On this account therefore, I have written to you, earnestly to desire that you would take the trouble of a journey hither, and cure a disease which I am under.
For I hear the Jews ridicule you, and intend you ill.
My city is indeed small, but neat, and large enough for us both."
(Signed,) Abgar, King of Edessa.

Judæa, performing wonderful deeds, and whose name had spread world-wide, was possessed with so strong a faith in him that in about the year 32 he sent a legate named Ananias with a letter asking Jesus to come to him, and guaranteeing him safety and comfort.[81] The messenger arrived in due time and after some waiting was ushered into the presence of Jesus, and presented the letter. This teacher on due reflection returned Abgar his answer in epistolary form. The epistle which is likewise vouched for by both Origen and Irenæus, also mentions the picture of Jesus called the Veronica which accompanies the letter. Abgar kept it. The missive was received by the king who regarded it with such veneration that he had it inscribed among the records of the

[81] Lest any person should doubt as to the dignity of this letter we quote from men of standing and literary qualities, words regarding this correspondence: Myers' *Konversations Lexikon* in verb. Abgarus: "De Unechtheit der beiden von Eusebius bewahrten Briefe wurde schon 494 vom Papste Gelasius ausgesprochen;" Gibbon, *Decl. & Fall*, chap. xlix., with note 9, refers to Lardner, *Heathen Testimonies*, I., pp. 297-309, and cites Cave, Grabe, Tillemont and the celebrated Addison as firm believers in the *Abgar Letters*. In the text, Gibbon speaks of the "*Correspondence of Christ and Abgarus*, so famous in the days of Eusebius." *Ante-Nicine Fathers*, VIII., 651-743: *Ancient Syriac Documents:* "King Abgar aided the christian plant of Thaddæus at Edessa, time of Tiberius and it flourished until Trajan. Then terrible persecutions occurred, lasting until A.D. 320. Edessa, now Orfa, was a Syriac portion of Armenia, subject to most terrible religious persecutions, iconoclastic, wars, etc. The *Syriac Documents* embrace *Letters of Abgar & Jesus; Story of King Abgar; Teaching of Addæus;* (Thaddæus), *Teaching of Simon Cephas who is Peter;* awful torture and death of *Sharbil;* awful torture and death of *Barsanna; Martyrdom* of Deacon *Habib;* of *Shamuna;* of *Guira* and vast numbers of the more common of mankind." Eusebius, *Eccles. Hist.*, I., cap., 13. The *Apocryph. N.T.*, Lond., 1721, pp. 43-44, in *Prolegomena* says: "The first writer who makes any mention of the epistles that passed between J. C. and Abgar, is Eusebius, Bishop of Cæsarea in Palestine ... For their genuineness he appeals to the public registries and records of the city of Edessa in Mesopotamia where Abgar reigned, and where he affirms that he himself found them written in the Syriac language. He published a *Greek translation* of them in his *Histories.* I., c. 13. Dr. Parker and other divines have strenuously contended for their admission into the canon of the scriptures. The Rev. Jeremiah Jones observes that the common people of England have this *Epistle* (of Jesus) in their houses in many places fixed in a frame, with a picture of Christ before it; and seriously regard it as the word of God, and a genuine letter of Christ." *The Amer. Cyc.* art. *Gnostics*, discoursing on the subject, says: "Bardasanes who flourished about A.D. 161, in the city of Edessa, now Orfa, where he was the trusted friend of King Abgar.... He was the author of hymns which remained in favor of the Eastern church, and inflexible in his hostility to paganism." The celebrated "*Syzzgies*," pairs, companionship, are the invention of Bardesanes. On the whole the evidence connects Edessa very plainly with the θίασος τῶν περὶ τὸν Διόνυσον Τεχνιτῶν. Two things are noticeable: No one doubted the genuineness of the Abgar Episode until Pope Galatius, all at once condescends to proffer us his wisdom condemning them. But he lived at the time when popes and prelates were conspiring to mutilate, burn and destroy, not this alone, but thousands of invaluable testimonies. The other point in their favor is based upon the Diocletian massacre in A.D. 303. Dr. Ramsay, *Cities & Bishoprics of Phrygia*, Vol. II., pp. 507-509, declares that the massacre utterly exterminated the Phrygian and he might have added the Syrian population: so that the whole church was killed out and no more inscriptions could be found, written after that date.

city of Edessa, in the public registers.[82] It was seen by Eusebius and entered upon the pages of his histories. It remained for centuries to be seen and consulted by all men and was well known to Bardesanes, and later in A.D. 460, to Moses Chorenensis who entered it on the pages of the celebrated ancient Syriac Documents, whence it formed a part of the history of Armenia.[83] The great Mosheim[84] is on record as admitting in a vague manner the truthfulness of this story; and Cureton, the translator, who became celebrated by his researches in ancient Syriac literature, expressed his belief that the Abgar episode is authentic.[85]

When this monarch heard of the conduct of the Jews at Jerusalem in causing the crucifixion of Jesus he was incensed. It appears that he was on some military mission with an army, and encamped on the banks of the Euphrates when the information, with its details reached him. Boiling with indignation, he wrote to the emperor Tiberius at Rome a letter, in which he demanded vengeance against the awful crime.[86] This letter is also

---

[82] *Letter of Jesus to King Abgar*, found by Eusebius inscribed in the registers and public records of the city of Edessa, in the Syriac tongue that was translated by him into Greek; Origen and Irenaeus speak believingly of it.

"Abgarus, you are happy, inasmuch as you have believed on me whom you have not seen.

For it is written concerning me, that those who have seen me should not believe in me, that they who have not seen me might believe and live.

As to that part of your letter which relates to my giving you a visit, I must inform you that I must fulfill all the ends of my mission in this country and after that be received up again to Him who sent me.

But after my ascension I will send one of my disciples, who will cure your disease and give life to you and all that are with you."

(Signed) Jesus.

[83] Abgar wrote a letter to Ardechès, also recorded by Moses Chorenensis, in his *History of Armenia* which reads in part as follows: "I know that you have heard of Jesus Christ, the son of God whom the Jews have crucified; Jesus who was raised from the dead and has sent his deciples through all the world to instruct men."

[84] Mosheim, *Eccles. Hist.*, I., First Century, Part I., chap. iii., § 7. *Letter of Christ to Abgar*: "There are respectable writers who state that Abgarus, King of Edessa, being dangerously sick, sent a letter to Christ imploring his assistance: and that Christ not only wrote an answer to the king, but also sent him his picture...... I see no very weighty reason for altogether rejecting the whole story."

[85] *Ante-Nicine Fathers, Letters of Jesus to Abgar*, and of *Abgar to Jesus*. Vol. VIII., p. 648. *Memoirs of Edessa, Introduc:* "Here the Edinburgh commentator says that Cureton firmly believed the letters to be genuine. Cureton according to Dr. Wright, was going to write down his convictions, but died. Dr. Wright says: "He (Dr. Cureton) was himself firmly persuaded of the genuineness of the Epistles attributed to Abgar, King of Edessa, and of our Lord; an opinion which he shared with such illustrious scholars as Baronius, Tillemont, Cave, R. Montague, Bishop of Norwich, and Grabe."

[86] *Letter from Abgar to Tiberius, Ante-Nicine Fathers*, VIII., p. 655: "Letter from Abgar to Tiberius, Abgar at the river Euphrates, wrote to Tiberius for vengeance on the Jews for crucifying Jesus, thus; "I have been wishing to go up to Jerusalem and lay her waste inasmuch as she has slain

extant. Tiberius who was also very deeply impressed, returned an answer.[87] Being involved in some insurrection with Spain he was temporarily prevented from comsummating the wish of Abgar to destroy Jerusalem; but he discharged from office, and disgraced the vacillating, more than half converted and christianized procurator of Judæa, Pontius Pilate, stationed at Jerusalem.[88] Abgar had actually demanded this in various letters.[89] The emperor returned to Abgar an immediate and very respectful answer.[90] In this letter the emperor confirms both the statement that he had dismissed and disgraced Pilate and that he had received the official account of that procurator on the whole affair. This report and that of Lentulus, predecessor of Pilate, both of which have been sorely discounted, are extant.[91] The Christ." Cureton and five other great scholars and critics, including Baronius and Tillemont, believe that this correspondence between Abgar and Tiberius and Abgar and Christ is reliable." It is certainly to be regretted that the death of Cureton occured before he published his statement which he had promised, since it might have revealed more on the recondite problem

[87] *Ante-Nicine Fathers*, VIII., p. 705, *Ancient Syriac Documents. Histoire d' Arménie* par Moïse de Chorène, or Moses Chorenensis, A.D. 460. Answer from Tiberius to Abgar's letter: This apparently authentic letter begins as follows: "Tiberius, emperor of the Romans, to Abgar, King of the Armenians, Greeting:" Then, after ackowledging receipt of King Abgar's letter to him he mentions Christ by name as follows: "Though we had already heard several persons relate these facts. Pilate has officially informed us of the miracles of Jesus." Again, as evidence of the allegation that Tiberius was a christian, he says, "We have commanded all those whom Jesus suits to receive him amongst the gods." In this letter the name Jesus occurs again once; and the name "christians" once.

[88] It was largely at the suggestion of Abgar who exercised a powerful influence on Tiberius, that Pilate was disgraced.

[89] A letter from Abgar to Tiberius, preserved in the *Ancient Syriac Documents* and quoted by Moses Chorenenses in his *History of Armenia*, A.D. 460, is at our command. It begins: "Abgar, king of Armenia, to my lord Tiberius, emperor of the Romans, greeting:" After a few opening platitudes he continues: "The Jews who dwell in the cantons of Palestine have crucified Jesus, after so many acts of kindness, so many wonders and miracles wrought for their good." The name Jesus occurs again in this letter and Christ, once.

[90] *Ancient Syriac Documents Teachings* of Thaddæus. *Letter* of Tiberius to King Abgar of Edessa: "And Tiberius wrote and sent to King Abgar; and thus he wrote to him." After the opening clause, Tiberius says; "Concerning what the Jews have dared to do in the matter of the cross, Pilate the governor also has written.... Because of a war with the people of Spain who have rebelled against me, which is on foot at this time, I have not been able to avenge this matter." A few lines later he says; "The Jews did not act according to the law. On this account as regards Pilate who was appointed governor there by me, I have sent another, to his disgrace, and dismissed him because he departed from the law.... For the gratification of the Jews he crucified Christ, who according to what I hear concerning Him, instead of suffering the cross of death deserved to be honored and worshiped." This is in response to another letter from Abgar to Tiberius which is also extant

[91] Meyers's *Konversation Lexicon*, in verb. Lentulus (Publius): "Angeblich der Amtsvorgänger des Pilatus soll in einem Brief (abgedruckt im ersten Bande der '*Magdeburgischen Centurien*' in Mich. Neander's '*Apocrypha*,' und in Grynäu's '*Monumenta Patrvm Orthodoxographa*; an den römischen Senat geschrieben haben, der eine Characterdarstellung Jesu enthällt."

author of the remarkable recent work on Supernatural Religion seems in doubt [92] although his ambiguous words express what we look upon as equivalent to a powerful endorsement of their authenticity since he uses an edition of the Apocrypha seventy years later than the one before us, and which we have not seen. However, the assurance of their authenticity is greatly emphasized by Cureton, who gave his life and talent to research among Arabic and Syriac literature of that quarter of the East. He was in the act of writing out his convictions on this subject when he died, 1864. It is known that during the Middle Ages the Saxons and Britons used to hang up these letters in their rooms as palladiums.[93] Cureton, Baronius, Tillemont, Cave, Montague, Grabe, according to Dr. Wright, were firm believers in the letter of Jesus, and most of them contended that it should have been preserved in the Gospel canons.

Thaddeus, one of the seventy, was commissioned, after the Pentecost to carry the tidings to Edessa.[94] There is valuable ancient history confirming this. Tacitus tells us that there was, in the Parthian kingdom governed by Abgarus, a man named Addus, now found to be Addæus, or Thaddeus, possessing great power among the people.[95] The time covered by this annal of

[92] *Supernat. Rel.*, Edition 2 vols. in one, M. G. p. 234, admitting that far from Eusebius being the first to mention the *Abgar Letters*, they were published by Irenæus and Origen centuries before Eusebius. He says half doubtingly, half believingly: "Does anyone believe the letter of Jesus to the prince of Edessa to be genuine because Eusebius inserted it in his history, as an authentic document, out of the public records of the city of Edessa?" But he mentions that the quotations of Irenæus and Origen are from the original letters, although this is averred by the *Apocryphy* of 1790. Note, In the prolegomena of the *Apocryphy* of 1721., Lond., we read: "For their genuineness he, Eusebius, appeals to the public registries and records of the city of Edessa, Mesopotamia, where Abgar reigned and where he affirms that he found them written in the Syriac." Eusebius living so near, would have hardly dared to perpetuate so self-evident a falsehood as this statement were it not true; for there were many christian as well as pagan critics at the moment he wrote and who had a grudge against him and would have detected the lie. They were inscriptions and most undoubtedly truthful.

[93] Διδαχη Θαδδαίου: "Si quis hanc epistolam secum habuerit, securus ambulabit in pace," and this is preserved as a creed in the British Museum, for the common people. It lingers even to this day in some places.

[94] *Ante-Nicine Fathers*, VIII., p. 569. Thaddeus and Abgar, *Teachings of Addæus* the Apostle. After Thaddeus had healed King Abgar, "Abgar commanded them to give to Addæus silver and gold. Addæus said to him: 'How can we receive that which is not ours? For lo! that which was ours have we forsaken as we were commanded by our lord; because without purse and without scrip, bearing the cross upon our shoulders, we were commanded to preach His Gospel in the whole creation,'"

[95] Tacitus, *Annal.*, VI., 31-32: We give his fragmentary segments for the reason that this great pagan historian certainly refers to Addeus, though he calls him Addus. What nails the suspicion fast is the secrecy he here bears witness to. It was in the old age of Tiberius and thus the time cor-

the celebrated historian, corresponds remarkably with that of his mention of Christ, recorded in his description of the conflagration of Rome.

Tiberius, soon afterwards wrote to King Abgar for whom he seems to have formed a strong attachment.[96] In this letter which may ever remain celebrated as a monument of early christianity, he mentions his attempt to prevail upon the Roman senate to allow Jesus Christ to be numbered among official divinities, a fact which is confirmed by Tertullian.[97] Neander does not consider Tertullian's statement reliable. Why not? There is everything to substantiate it. If we cannot believe history, then indeed all record of the past is founded in an opinionated incredulity and droops into chaos. The fact is, Tertullian, whose statements, like those of Diodorus, and Josephus, have forced themselves upon us through strictly scientific examination of monumental evidence, is now being researched, with care. His statements are found to agree with inscriptions and this places them beyond distrust of the merely empirical, as a careful and accurate historian.

Pilate like Jesus, becomes a historical character. After his disgrace, being endowed with riches, he wandered to Europe and settled at the old city of Vienne, twelve miles below Lyons, on the Rhone, a very ancient industrial city, at the mouth of the river Gère. There he died by his own hand.[98] We have visited a curious

responds: "Senectutem Tiberii ut inermem despiciens." Again: "Rege Artabano." Abgarus was one of the Armenian Artabani: "Parthis mittendi secretos nuntios validissimus auctor fuit Sinnaces, insigni familia ac perinde opibus, et proximus huic Addus, ademptæ virilitatis." Accustomed to secret concert, Abgar could rely on Addus, or Addeus with safety. This made him useful. But he is poisoned at last; *id.*, cap. 32: "Valuit tamen utilitas, ut Addum specie amicitiæ vocatum ad epulas lento veneno inligaret, Sinnacen disismulatione ac donis, simul per negotia moraretur." This signification here of venenum may not be deadly poison; and Thaddeus may have only been lured and deterred from consummating a purpose. But he was poisoned and gotten rid of.

[96] The letter was in answer to one of Abgar which contained these words; "If you will not be angry with me, I will say that the conduct of the senate is extremely ridiculous and absurd." And in another; "Send another governor to Jerusalem in the place of Pilate who ought to be ignominiously driven from the powerful post in which you placed him."

[97] Tert. *Apol.* V., 25: See *Index* in verb. *Tertullian.*

[98] Records published in the *Ville de Vienne*, 1876, p. 44, and frontispiece presenting a picture of the supposed Pyramid of Pilate. Delorme, *Records: "La Pyramide d' l' Aiguille."* This author mentions that there were three opinions of its antiquity, one of which, mentioned by Adon, in his *Chronicles.* "Selon l' autre, la même édifice nous offre le tombeau de Pilate, juge de Jesus-Christ qu' Adon, dans sa *Chronique*, dit avoir été exilé à Vienne par l'empereur Caius Caligula et s' y être donné la mort." Cf. Eusebius, *Chronicon:* "Anno tertio Caii Caligulæ, Pontius Pilatus, in multæ incidens calamitates, propria se manu interfecit." Jarvis, *Introduc. Hist. Church.* p. 369.

monumental proof of this. It is situated at the open crossing in the lower end of the town. M. Joseph Piot the president of the bank of Beauregard very obligingly conducted the author to this weird, towering obelisk which the authorities of that busy manufacturing city claimed to be more ancient than Romulus, have wisely preserved. The pyramid shoots up in the air nearly a hundred feet and has an archway once used by teams. There is a legend that the great stone cap surmounting the pinnacle still covers a vast sum of gold coyly sequestered thereunder, for some future accident to disclose, besides documents which may add to our knowledge of the true history of Jesus Christ.

Mosheim speaks of the Epistle of Lentulus to the Roman senate concerning which we have made a quotation from Meyers' Encyclopædia.[99] Mr. Gibbon, in his own peculiar way of assassinating credulity in words fiery hot with sarcasm and irony, also gives some opinions regarding Pilate.[100] In the Ante-Nicine Fathers, the eighth volume on the four hundred and sixtieth page, we have the correct version of the report of Pontius Pilate to Tiberius on the crucifixion, sent to that August Cæsar in Rome. This comes down to us in two Greek forms, both of which are given here. The "man named Jesus" is mentioned six times in the first, and five times in the second Greek form, which has a manuscript at the close of the fourth paragraph, naming Jesus for the sixth time. Even the letter of confession from Pilate, intended as an official report but convinced the emperor of the splendid and blemishless personage that had been ignominiously sacrificed; the more poignant to the old man because this useless, undeserved

[99] See *Supra*, note 90, of this chap. Mosheim, I., Part II., chap. 2, § 17, note 23: "The Epistle of Lentulus to the Roman senate describing the person and manners of Christ, Latin one page."

[100] *Hist. Decline & Fall.*, chap. xvi., note 105: "The testimony given by Pontius Pilate is first mentioned by Justin. The successive improvements which the story has acquired, as it passed through the hands of Tertullian, Eusebius, Epiphanius, Chrysostom, Orosius, Gregory of Tours, and the authors of several editions of the Acts of Pilate, are very fairly stated by Dom Calmet, *Dissert. sur l' Ecriture*, tom. III., p. 651, etc." Pilate certainly wrote the letter to Tiberius and Gibbon acknowledges it with a smirk couched in language like this: "We are required to believe that P. Pilate informed the emperor of the unjust sentence of death upon an innocent man and divine person....that Tiberius....conceived the design of placing the Messiah among the gods of Rome; that the servile senate disobeyed, and Tiberius protected the christians from persecution," Nothing can be truer than this latter clause; and since Gibbon, much new information substantiates the whole story. The new proofs consist in inscriptional glyptics and some of them from the excavations at Rome.

supplicium of the cross was his doom. Against this, every manly instinct revolted, because it was the official punishment of the slave and the lowly. Pilot thus unconsciously became his own accuser; and it cost him his office and his life. The document is extant. "Upon Jesus Christ," he writes, "whose case I had clearly set forth to thee in my last, at length by the will of the people, a bitter punishment has been inflicted, myself being in a manner unwilling and rather afraid—a man, by Hercules, so pious and strict, no age has had or ever will have; but wonderful were the efforts of the people......to have him crucified." This letter is certified to by Tertullian, and evidence recently discovered removes the doubts which long hovered over all the many priceless proofs, attacked as they were, and burned up, and ignored by the prelates who could not glory in power, if their darkening mists of theology should give way to honest historic records. Tertullian told the world enough to close the pratings of these later mutilators. He wrote: "All these things Pilate did to Christ, and now in fact, a christian in his own convictions, he sent word of Him to the reigning Cæsar who was at that time, Tiberius.[101] Renan, in threading the story, says Pilate was so friendly to Jesus that they had a protracted interview and that Pilate's wife interceded for him, having had a dream premonishing her to beware and allow no hurt to befall him.[102]

Nevertheless Pilate was afraid of the Jews, who were in a foment of insurrection, demanding the immediate death of the prisoner. He had not the determination of the occasion. He gave way to their importunities, signed the death warrant and took the consequences.[103]

[101] Tertull., *Apol.*, xxii., "Ea omnia super Christo Pilatus, et ipse jam pro sua conscientia Christianus, Cæsari tum Tiberio nuntiavit." But Tertullian, continuing, further declares that the Cæsars themselves were converted, as well as Pilate: " Sed et Caesares credidissent super Christo, si aut Cæsares non essent sæculo necessarii, aut si et Christiani potuissent esse Cæsæres."

[102] Renan, *Life of Jesus*, Eng. *trans.* N. Y., pp. 323-325. Cf. Matth., xxvii., 19, which is the best record of all these attestations: "Ἥιδει γὰρ, ὅτι διὰ φθόνον παρέδωκαν αὐτόν, Καθημένου δὲ αὐτοῦ ἐπὶ τοῦ βήματος ἀπέστειλε πρὸς αὐτόν, ἡ γυνὴ αὐτοῦ λεγουσα· μηδέν σοι καὶ τῷ δικαίῳ ἐκείνῳ· πολλα γὰρ ἔπαθον σήμερον κατ' ὄναρ δἰ αὐτόν,"

[103] Pilate's Sentence was recently published in the "Boletin Masonico." of Mexico. Pronounced by Pontius Pilate, the Roman Procurator. The original was discovered about the year 1380, in an iron tube, among the marble ruins of a temple in the city of Aquila, Italy, written in Hebrew characters on parchment. It is now in the custody of the keeper of the Royal and General Archives of Simancus, Spain. The original warrant, on a Hebrew parchment, reads.

Then followed the arrest, the ever memorable march of the condemned lord to Gethsemane, place of the wine press and the olive grove; the scene of Golgotha or bald hill; the prodding by fierce army officers, of unwilling, half-christian soldiers to make them do their duty; the forcing of Simon, father of Alexander and Rufus, to carry the heavy wooden cross for the condemned, by pitying soldiers, since the Roman law demanded that the culprit do it; the stripping of the master of his raiment and wrapping him in the red or scarlet robe[104] and

"In the year 17 of Tiberius Cæsar, Emperor of Rome and of all the world, unconquerable monarch; in the CXXI Olympiad; in the XXIV Iliad; and of the Creation of the World, according to the number and count of the Hebrews, four times 1157; of the propagation of the Roman Empire, the year 73; of the deliverance from slavery of Babylon, the year 430; and of the restitution of the Holy Empire, the year 497; Lucus Marius Sauricus being Consuls of Rome and Pontiff., Proconsuls of the unconquerable Tiberius; Public Governor of Judea, Regent and Governor of the City of Jerusalem, Flavius IV; its graceful president, Pontius Pilate; Regent of Lower Galilee, Herod Antipas; Pontiff of the High Priesthood—Caiphas; Ales Maelo, Master of the Temple; Rababan Ambe, Centurion of the Consuls and of the City of Jerusalem.—Quintus Cornelius Sublimius and Sextus Pompilius Rufus, on the 25th of March.

"I, Pontius Pilate, representative of the Roman Empire, in the Palace of Larchi, our residence, judge, condemn, and sentence to death, Jesus, called Christ, the Nazarene, of the multitude of Galilee, a man seditious of the Mosaic Law, against the Great Emperor Tiberius Caesar. I determine and pronounce by reason of the explained, that he shall suffer death nailed to the cross, according to the usage of criminals, because having congregated many men, rich and poor, he has not ceased to stir up tumults throughout Galilee, pretending to be the Son of God, and King of Israel, threatening the ruin of Jerusalem and the Holy Empire, and denying the tribute to Caesar; having the boldness to enter with palms, in triumph and accompanied by a multitude as King, within the City of Jerusalem in the Sacred Temple.

"I therefore command my Centurion, Quintus Cornelius, that he conduct publicly through the City of Jerusalem this Jesus Christ and that he be tied and flogged, dressed in purple and crowned with prickly thorns, with his own cross on his shoulders, so that he may serve as an example to malefactors; and to take with him two homicidal thieves; all of whom will leave by the Giarancola Gate, designated to-day Antoniana, and will proceed to the mount of the wicked, called Calvary, where, crucified and dead, the body shall remain on the cross so that it may be a spectacle and example to all criminals, and on said cross there shall be the inscription in three languages: Hebrew, Greek and Latin, In Hebrew: 'Jesu Aloi Olisidin.' In Greek : 'Ἰησοῦς Ναζαρηνός Βασιλεὺς τῶν Ἰουδαίων.' In Latin: 'Jesus Nazerenus Rex Judæorum.' We likewise command that no one of whatever class he may be, shall attempt imprudently to impede this justice by us commanded, administered and followed with all rigour, according to the decrees and laws of the Romans and Hebrews, under the penalty which those incur who rebel against the Empire."

This sentence was confirmed for the twelve tribes of Israel, by Raban, Daniel, Raban II, John Becair, Berbas, Isabel.

"For the High Priesthood: Raban, Judas, Cancasalon. Lucius, Sislili, Amasinus, Silvanus, Notary of Crime."

[104] According to Tertullian, *De Pallio*, it was the pallium which, like the himation, was red. Red was the type of the ebionites, therapeutæ, thiasoi, and the glory of all the Roman collegia, and all working people. *Apocryph.* *N.T., Epist. of Barnabas.* Tertull,, *De Pallio*, 1, written after he left the prelate power and back-slid or lapsed into the secret unions, says it was Phœnician, "punecei coloris." All agree that it was red. Lactantius, also, *Divine Instit.*, IV., 1, says: "They put upon him a scarlet robe—punecei

mocking him with the crown of thorns.[105] The being whose name and majesty stands to-day far above all others was then flogged and tied tightly to this wooden crucifix and inhumanly lifted into the air beside two real criminals, who had had their legal trial and sentence and were regularly waiting execution.[106] In the most humiliating condition, whelming ignominy, debased to the nethermost swamp of disgrace, suffering in the physical qualms which of all other torture was known to the ancient laws of vengeance [107] to reek with excruciating agony most awful, especially for a young man in full nerve and muscle writhing in this crucial climax, we say, let us pause and ask history and epistolary and monumental evidence, what was the appearance of the dying carpenter. Let us ask to be shown a photograph of Jesus.[108]

coloris—and a crown of thorns." The editor of *Ante-Nicine Fathers*, VII., p. 120; says the robe was red agreeing with Renan, and all appear to agree that it was a pallium, which being the apparel of the hives of labor found among the Greek and Asiatic inscriptions, and referred to as that of the essenes, was undoubtedly meant by the haughty non-laboring Jews whom Jesus had just before scourged as money changers and provision rings, as an expression of contempt. We have inscriptions found in the vicinity of the seven churches of Asia, registering numerous θιασοὶ τῶν ἱματοποιῶν, colleges of trade unions who made the πάλλια, and other clothing, in great quantities for commerce. See Oehler, in *Index*, Vol. II., *infra*.

[105] *Crowns* were the celebrated laurels of the unions from high antiquity, Cf. *supra*, chap. xiv.

[106] One of the clauses of the inscription of Pontius Pilate, discovered in Aquila, in 1380, reads: "Denying the tribute to Cæsar....I command.... that Jesus Christ be tied and flogged, dressed in crimson, and crowned with prickly thorns." Renan, who speaks of the inscription as genuine, declares the garment was red.

[107] The tactics of the sectaries were, like the Sacarii whom Renan's, *Life of Jesus*, Eng., p. 92 calls: pious assassins who imposed upon themselves the task of killing those who disobeyed the law in their presence, meaning the law of Moses.

[108] The actual and contemporary descriptions made by Pilate in his letter, *supra*, note to the emperor Tiberius, is our first description of this martyr. It was followed in a few days, by the report of Lentulus, Pilate's predecessor to the Roman senate, which is extant, and may be seen in Neander's *Apocrypha;* in Grynaeus' *Monumentum Patrum Orthographia*, and in *Magdeburgischer Centurien*, Vol. I. Renan thinks it genuine. Josephus, *Ant.*, XVII., III., 3, comes next with his celebrated words. Later Athenagoras says something though vaguely, in an essay Περὶ χριστιανῶν, cap. 10; "Τὸ μὲν οὖν ἄθεοι μὴ εἶναι, ἕνα τὸν ἀγένητον καὶ ἀίδιον καὶ ἀόρατον καὶ ἀπαθῆ καὶ ἀκατάληπτον καὶ ἀχώρητον, νῷ μόνῳ καὶ λόγῳ καταλαμβανόμενον, φωτὶ καὶ κάλλει καὶ πνεύματι καὶ δυνάμει ἀνεκδιηγήτῳ περιεχόμενον, ὑφ' οὗ γεγένηται τὸ πᾶν διὰ τοῦ αὐτοῦ λόγου καὶ διακεκόσμηται καὶ συγκρατεῖται, θεὸν ἄγοντες, ἐκανῶς μοι δέκειται." Neander, p. 159, quoting Lucian's *Peregrinus Proteus*, declares this adverse critic plainly says: "The christians still worship that great man who was crucified in Palestine, because it was he by whom the initiation into these new mysteries was introduced into human life. These poor creatures have persuaded themselves that they are all immortal and shall live forever." But Lucian has been misunderstood. We shall soon learn how to take him at his word. He speaks elsewhere in this same dissertation, in scurrilous language against the Dionysan artists, and of what he saw. All the initiates of that day (christian with the rest), were poor wandering creatures whom Lucian despised as deserving to be whipped. But while

A good many things are being dug up and otherwise coming to light in proof that Jesus was a genuine historical character. Something new and strange is the now wonderful Gate which used to be called the Pylé tou Theou, or door of the Lord It becomes to our disquisition more intensely interesting since it was discovered that the gate-keepers union existed in many cities, and that it is consequently probable that the one at Jerusalem where Jesus is known to have concealed himself in moments of danger and behind whose secret bars Judas betrayed him to the detectives, was none other than a social union like all the others.[109]

To be plain and fair, this work, not being a religious one in the advocacy of any particular idea, but merely a history of events, persons and characters that have

satyrizing them, Lucian gives the christians credit for being a constant brotherhood and shows their system of communism. His whole diatribe goes to show that at his time, the christians were yet working people and initiates like the other brotherhoods. Jesus was pushed forward to be the Messiah. So says Justin, *Dial.*, 191, ed. Colon, where he makes Trypho say; "He was a man distinguished above all others for piety and was therefore considered worthy to be put forward as the Messiah." Mentions "Ebionites, originally from Pella." Was he the one of whom Dionysus was the forerunner? Again, Renan, *Life of Jesus*. p. 476, sqq., is very pronounced in the belief that he was a bold revolutionist and cites the pure ebionism: "The reign of the poor is at hand, and the reign of the poor was the doctrine of Jesus." On page 179; "The name of 'poor' (ebion, 'Εβιων πτωχός), had become synonymous with 'saint' and friend of God." Renan cites Philo, *De Confusione Linguarum*, § 14; *De Migratione Abrahami*, § 1; *De Somnis*, II., § 41; *De Agric. Noe*, § 12; *De Mutatione Nominum*, § 4. The new find of Grenfell and Hunt, at Behneseh, in Egypt, of the Oxyrhynchus Papyri *supra*, note, adds to the authority for his being a historical character and a defender of the interests of labor.

[109] Κοινὸν τῶν γείτονων. See *Index* in verb. *gate*. And now we have Dr. Brüsselbach's *Papyrus*, with a plea for the oppressed, in Christ's own hand writing in Aramaic, a few lines of which are legible and which we here present, accompanied with doubts. It comes as the trophy of the Palestine Exploration society and is given as the statement of Dr. Brüsselbach, who found it and makes this description: "This manuscript is a small quarto page, written on both sides. The writing is almost entirely effaced, or so imperfect as to render a complete translation out of the question. This much, however, can be established with certainty, that it is the prayer of an oppressed and persecuted spirit, written in Aramaic. The writing is peculiar in being inscribed below instead of upon the lines.

The best preserved section is given here in fac-simile. It is signed in the name of the Savior, spelled precisely as upon the record of the gate-keeper at Jerusalem, published lately.

On the margin of the manuscript another hand using the square Galilean characters, has written the word "Savior," showing that its first owner considered this the manuscript of Jesus. The word Savior in the Galilean Aramaic of that time, is expressed Hoseach. This writing belongs to the first century, as will be admitted by all scholars.

The manuscript is very brittle. Line three of the fac-simile may be rendered, 'and still another stigma as a stain, in meekness under (persecution).' The whole is a plaint concerning persecution, that everything and every one is against him who has the divine treasure and stands alone. Every one misrepresents the word he utters; he is trodden down like dust and ashes; darkness is round about him."

We have already given numerous unions of the gate-keepers which the reader will find in their place.

operated in the development of socialism as opposed to the competitive system and their influence upon the great labor question, we propose to be irreverent enough to touch, in a concise note the desecrate phase of many doubters and show another side. We mean by this, the doubts which have prevailed as to whether Jesus was not rescued even on the cross and by some prearrangement permitted to live, through an occult complicity fixed between himself and Pilate, his wife and a secret few. Very numerous proofs have recently been adduced to the effect that he did not die; but that more tenderly treated on the cross than the two other men, he glutted the revengefulness of the Jews, being actually hanged, yet under secret orders from Pilate, he did not actually die but survived the death struggle, and lived on in secret through his natural life.[110]

The episode of Stephen, the so-called Proto-martyr, occured just at the close of the life of the Emperor Tiberius who was certainly extremely kind at that moment to the christians and must have had personally a good deal to do with them at Rome. The discovery of the first columbarium, a vast mausoleum of the christians of what now goes by the name of cemeteries and scholæ of under-ground Rome, proves that during Tiberius' reign an enormous secret plant was being estab-

---

[110] Renan, *Life of Jesus*, chap. xxiv., xxv., xxvi.; First, he was very popular, Matth., xxvi. 6 sq.; second, it was the day before the feast of the Passover, Matth., xxvi., 1, sqq; Mark xiv., 12; Luke xxii., 7; John, xlii., 29; third, and was consequently contrary to law that he should die. Jesus must be sacrificed, *Life of Jesus*, p. 324; Luke, xxii., 37. Thought of swords and defense, Luke, xxii., 26-40. The execution was against the Sanhedrim., 331-332; John, xviii., 31; Josephus, *Antiq.*, xx,, ix. Pilate was friendly to Jesus, and consequently would not kill his friend, Renan, p. 333; John, xviii., and *id.*, xviii., iv., 1, 2; Pilate's wife took a strong part for Jesus, Matth., xxvii., 19; Renan, p. 355; Pilate was right: it was going to be a juridical murder, if not headed off, pp. 336-337. Political release of a prisoner, Mark, xv., 10. Pilate tried to show that he was not a Jew, *id.*, p. 339; John xix., 12, 15. Tac., *Annales*, xv., 44: "Ergo abolendo rumori Nero subdidit reos, et quæsitissimis poenis affecit, quos per flagitia invisos vulgus christianos appellabat. Auctor nominis ejus Christus Tiberio imperitante per procuratorem Pontium Pilatum supplicio affectus erat; repressaque in præsens exitiabilis superstitio rursum erumpebat, non modo per Judaeam, originem ejus mali per urbem etiam, quo cuncta undique atrocia aut pudenda confluunt, celebranturque." Pilate tried hard to release him by the Passover; release of a prisoner, Mark, xv., 10: Pilate to show that he was not a Jew, Renan, 339; John, xix., 9; if Pilate saved him he had to do it with the utmost cunning and secrecy, Renan, 340; John, xix., 12, 15; Luke, xxiii., 2. Neither Tiberius nor Pilate condemned Jesus, Renan, 341; Doubt generally; for the Talmud says he was stoned; *Michna Sanhedrim.* vi., 4; *Talmud, Jesus, Sanhedrim*, xiv., 16; *Talmud, Bab.*, 48 a 67 a; stupifying drink offered, Renan, 346; *Talmud Bab.; Sanhedrim*; 43 a. *Prov.*, xxi., 6; Mark, xv., 23. Renan thinks he drank, *Matth.*, xxvii., 34; body was held up by a billet of wood, 346; Irenaeus, *Adv. Hær.*, II., 24; Just., *Dial. Cum Tryph.*, 91; drank posca, Matth., xxvii., 48; Mark., xv., 36; the illegal haste in taking him down caused great suspicion.

lished in the catacombs of the Appian Way, and the sepulchre of Stephen is there with an inscription.[111] We propose to relate this occurrence in the same prosy manner that belongs to any realistic history, entirely unmixed with religion; for the reason that it is a true historical event.

About the year 34 or as some think, 35 or 36, a young man from Tarsus in Asia Minor named Saul, who had been a student under Gamaliel, was a leading figure, perhaps a ringleader, as the New Testament later quotes him.[112] His face was pale with determination, for he was directing a noisy tempest of human passions like a swirling tornado of physical phenomena, in the very vortex of revolution. And such it was. It was Saul, afterwards the evangelist, pitted against Stephen, head waiter of the common tables which supplied the food for the three thousand first members of the great, first-known brotherhood and sisterhood of Jerusalem. Whether this Saul was the little blear-eyed cripple, as he is sometimes represented, is doubtful. He had some sort of chronic infirmity, it is true, but he was possessed of wonderful endurance and indomitable courage. He was a scholar of the first rank and wore the protective dignity of a Roman citizen. The trouble with this strange man was, that he was not yet converted. His large, honest, susceptible mind was at that moment in a whirlpool of the tumult he had been deputized to lead, where by an attrition of office, he was drinking in, little by little, a great principle destined, through an antipodal summersault, to make him a most celebrated and useful person. This is all that we now can say of Paul.

Let us turn to Stephen. In him we have a large, fine

[111] De Rossi, *Inscr. Christ. Urbis Romœ*, Roma, 1856, Vol. III., pp. 201,202, cap. II., *Il Testa degli atti aei martiri Greci*. "Valeriano et Lucillo Consulibus." (in note 2: fortasse sub con. Valerii et Accilii: quo anno censetur etiam Stephanus papa coronatur martirio); erat quidam vir, Hippolitus monachus, qui habitabat in cryptis, serviens domino in absconditis suis, ad quem multi Christianorum accurebant ad audiendam doctrinam apostolorum. Et dum frequenter ad eum universa turba concurreret, crescebat quotidie turba Christianorum, qui ex paganis convertebantur et babtizabantur, temporibus beati Stephani, et deducebat ad eum ex doctrina sua multos ex paganis, et babtizsbantur." It was to such secret under-ground dens that he took or pretended to have taken the body of Stephen for cremation and deposition in the urn. Of his first and actual burial at Jerusalem, we shall soon speak.

[112] *Acts*., xxiv., 5; "For we have found this man a pestilent fellow and a mover of sedition among all the Jews throughout the world and a ringleader of the sect of the Nazarenes."

young man of business. A full-blooded Hellenist Greek, probably from Ephesus. It looks as though he had been an influential kurios or lord in one of the great brotherhoods there. We have already seen that to be promoted to the degree of kurios, or as the Romans styled the office, quinquennalis,[113] he would have been high in the rank and exempt from many burdens. He was respected as a lord. Strictly, the kurios was the business manager and assumed the dignity and responsibility of president. This man was lynched. Of this, there is sufficient evidence; since the code of honor of the modern Lynch law demands a peremptory trial, wherein the accused is allowed to make a speech in self defense.

Nobody knows just how long after the crucifixion the great organization of three thousand people was formed at Jerusalem in a house of the lord. Each of the ancient unions had a house or temple, used for assemblages of deliberation, for the rooms of the common tables, the friendly refuge or home; and this was no exception, although Neander and Mosheim are in wonderment about a mere private house belonging to one of the members, as they suppose, being sufficiently capacious for so vast a membership.[114] Nevertheless, these people had the room and a sufficient auditorium, which can never be otherwise explained than that there always existed a secret society with much property, among which were capacious buildings, and that these societies resembled those of the Mithraic order.[115] But Mosheim who, through eyes blindfolded with the mystic veil wrapped around the early centuries by creatures

[113] Momms., *De Col. et Sodal.*, p. 130, and chart: "Item placuit, ut quisquis quinquennalis in hoc collegio factus fuerit, a sigillis ejus temporis, quo quinquennalis erit, immunis esse debebit, et ei ex omnibus divisionibus partes duplas dari."

[114] *Super. Rel.*, on *House of the Lord, Pentecost*, pp. 952, 953: "In the preceding chapters, *Acts*, I., 15, we learn that the number of diciples was then about 120, and the crowds which came together when the miraculous occurrence took place, must have been great, seeing that it is stated that 3,000 souls were baptized and added to the church upon the occasion. *Acta*, II., 41: Οἱ μὲν οὖν ἀσμένως ἀποδεξάμενοι τόν λόγον αὐτοῦ ἐβαπτισθησαν, καὶ προσετέθησαν τῇ ἡμέρα ἐκείνῃ ψυχαὶ ὡσεὶ τρισχίλιοι." We may ask in what house could such a multitude in Jerusalem have assembled. Apologists have exhausted their ingenuity in replying to the question."

[115] Renan, *Hibbert Lectures*, p. 35, speaking of the *Mithraic Order:* "It had its mysterious meeting, its chapels which bore a strong resemblance to little churches. It forged a very lasting bond of brotherhoods between its initiates. It had a Eucharist, a supper so like the christian mysteries that good Justin Martyr, the apologist, can find only one explanation of the apparent identity, viz: that Satan, in order to deceive the human race determined to imitate the christian ceremonies, from them."

of the property-holding power which this organization, like that of the modern socialists, threatened to extinguish, sees something which he can make out only by the greatest difficulty. He declares of Jesus, whose trouble with Judas a few days before, he is describing, that he had a regular place of refuge and retirement right then, somewhere in Jerusalem. There is no reason to believe that it varied from numerous other secret unions of the economic organizations of that day.[116] The sense of many new-found inscriptions points to a confirmation of our discovery that the "churches in our house," mentioned so frequently all through the Acts, and the Epistles were none other than these recondite establishments specially provided for under the Solonic law. They served as retreats, business places and eating houses. Here, then, we find ourselves in the delineation of the career of Stephen.

He had been appointed by Peter and other apostles, soon after the so-called glory of the members on that memorable day of Pentecost, when "suddenly there came a sound from heaven as of a rushing mighty wind and it filled all the house where they were sitting."[117] They had formed a great association patterned after the Plan of Salvation as laid out by Jesus. It varied from the ordinary collegia, thiasoi and ebionim, in that it was to both feed and otherwise economically supply the poor, and also to spread the glad tidings of salvation throughout the world.

They had but fairly got down to work when there came complaints that women members from Asia, probably ignorant of the Hebrew language and unable to make their wants intelligible on that account, were being slighted and deprived of their share of the nourishment. It was accordingly determined to appoint seven

[116] Lüders, *Dionys. Künst.*, p. 72, note 122, quoting Bursian, *Geog. Greek*, I., p. 290: "Versammlungshaus der Techniten und Handwerker," showing that the brotherhood mentioned was one of the manual workers. Mosheim, *Hist. Eccles.*, First Century, Part I., chap. iii., § 8; "His ungrateful disciple Judas, disclosing the place of his master's nocturnal retirement." Here Mosheim sees deeper than most commentators. He perceives that there was some secure, secret retreat, unknown even to the police. This was the secret Κυριακή of the brotherhood, corresponding with thousands existing at that time in Asia, Europe and everywhere. Under the protection of these initiates it was difficult to find a secluded member, unless he was betrayed by another. The hideous criminality of Judas was probably not so much in his protecting the treasury as in his divulging the secret whereabouts of the lord of the brotherhoods.

[117] Πραξεις τῶν Ἀποστόλων, II., 2: "Καὶ ἐγένετο ἄφνω ἐκ τοῦ οὐρανοῦ ἦχος ὥσπερ φερομένης πνοῆς βιαίας καὶ ἐπλήρωσεν ὅλον τὸν οἶκον, ὄν ἦσαν καθήμενοι."

thoroughly experienced business men to attend to this difficulty and rectify their grievance about the tables.[118] The names of the men who made the appointments were Peter, Barnabas, John, the three Jameses, Mathias, Andrew, Thomas, Bartholomew and Simon Jelotes. The names of the men appointed were Stephen, Philip, Prochorus, Nicanor, Timon, Parmenas and Nicholas. They appear to have all been Greeks or Asiatic Hellenists, acquainted not only with the language but their habits, manners and the organizations and mysteries they were accustomed to. Cyprian perhaps, in his fifth epistle to the Deacons, is the first to show in published form, the true business of the early deacons; but more recently numerous inscriptions of that early age are revealing fresh proofs of Cyprian's descriptions. He was faithful to the true meaning of the Greek word diaconus or deacon, a table waiter, also a person who assists in furnishing and trying on clothes, making beds to sleep on, and in fact, truck work, even menial employments where one is constantly on the run at grimy uncanny jobs. Such was the deacon until raised by prelate power under this name. The business died out with the slaughter of the economic function of the church, the employment differentiating to a high profession.[119] The whole story of this hitherto little studied but important literature is that some three thousand to five thousand plebeian or proletarian people organized by Peter and the others formed the first congregation. They were so numerous that Jewish prelates dared not attack them. They naturally had some little trouble with the economic adjustments, especially with the women and children who partook at the common tables. The Cyprian letter, written two centuries later, explains the duties of the deacons, being founded on the work of the table-

---

118 Πραξεις τῶν Ἀποστόλων, VI., 1. 'Ἐν δὲ ταῖς ἡμέραις ταύταις πληθυνόντων τῶν μαθητῶν ἐγένετο γογγυσμὸς τῶν Ἑλληνιστῶν πρὸς τοὺς Ἑβραίους, ὅτι παρεθεωροῦντο ἐν τῇ διακονίᾳ τῇ καθημερινῇ αἱ χῆραι αὐτῶν· 2. Προσκαλεσάμενοι δὲ οἱ δώδεκα τὸ πλῆθος τῶν μαθητῶν εἶπον· οὐκ ἀρεστόν ἐστιν, ἡμᾶς καταλείψαντας τὸν λόγον τοῦ θεοῦ διακονεῖν τραπέζαις· 3. Ἐπισκέψασθε οὖν, ἀδελφοί ἄνδρας ἐξ ὑμῶν μαρτυρουμένους ἑπτά, πλήρεις πνεύματος ἁγίου καὶ σοφίας, οὓς καταστήσομεν ἐπὶ τῆς χρείας ταύτης· ἡμεῖς δὲ τῇ προσευχῇ καὶ τῇ διακονίᾳ τοῦ λόγου προσκαρτερήσομεν. Acts, VI., 1-3.

119 Cyprian, Epist., V., Ad Diaconos. We prefer to give the English rendering of Ante-Nicine Fathers, Vol. V., p. 283: "If there be any who are in want of clothing or maintenance, let them be supplied with whatever is necessary." See also Acts, vi., 32. Lüders, Dionys. Künst., p. 10, says the name of the houses where the ἔρανος and the θίασος met was φωλητήρια, or φωλήτηριον, also θιασῶνος.

waiters of which Stephen the honest proto-martyr was the lord, using language of the inscriptions. But we do not have to stand entirely upon the inscriptional evidence. Considerable is furnished by the Ante-Nicine fathers,[120] regarding this lord and his household.

After the regular appointment of the seven deacons, with Stephen at their head, the work went on with regularity. An incident occured in the case of Ananias and his wife Sapphira, two Greeks living at Jerusalem, who were among the many converts and had joined the socialism which required that all, rich and poor alike; for there were no distinctions based on personal goods, should deliver their personal property to the community, a miniature state. The Acts of the Apostles inform us that all things were owned and enjoyed in common.[121] This is Bible, squarely, and the booty-getters who under cover of religion shield their individual gains in a manner recognized by the ancient Bible as brigandage, are soon to be called to account for disobedience to the great common law of christian socialism. So powerful, however, is the craving for property, that Ananias and Sapphira cheated. The result was death. We do not enter into a discussion of this event which involved their immediate dissolution. Everybody who reads the Bible knows all about it. What we desire here, is to prove that this secret organization or brotherhood was one of the collegia funeraticia or collegia tenuiorum, which were exempt under the Roman law.[122] The majesty and power of organization was undoubtedly emphasized by this event. It had an effect to madden the Jews. They considered themselves and their revered institutions attacked by this new system, which now for the first

[120] Clement's *Epistle to James*, begins with the words: "Clement to James the lord." Ignatius who wrote a half century later, and who was put down because known to favor the ebionites, recognizes the same principle. In his *Epist. to the Ephesians*, vi., he says: "Πάντα γὰρ ὃν πέμπει ὁ οἰκοδεσπότης εἰς ἰδίαν οἰκονομίαν, οὕτως δεῖ ἡμᾶς αὐτὸν δέχεσθαι, ὡς αὐτὸν τὸν πέμψαντα." And this is in reference to the brethren to whom the great κύριος, house lord, οἰκοδεσπότης Jesus the carpenter, sends a deacon to look after the household. In those days a household meant more than it means now. It was the membership of the whole cranothiasos. The *household* of Stephen, then consisted of fully 3,000 members—a very large family.

[121] Πραξεις τῶν Ἀποστόλων, IV., 32: "Τοῦ δὲ πλήθους τῶν πιστευσάντων ἦν ἡ καρδία καὶ ἡ ψυχὴ μία, καὶ οὐδὲ εἷς τι τῶν ὑπαρχόντων αὐτῷ ἔλεγεν ἴδιον εἶναι, ἀλλ' ἦν αὐτοῖς ἅπαντα κοινά."

[122] Oehler, *MSS. to the Author*: 'Ομοτάφος, referring to *Acts*, v., 6, 9, 10, positively declares there was such an organization: "Dass in der ersten Christengemeinde für die Bestattung der verstorbenen Mitglieder Sorge getragen wurde, wie die griechischen und römischen Vereinen, Sorge für Bestattung, Vereinsweck war. *Acta Apostolorum*, v., 6, 9, 10.'

in their history was being openly and boldly propagated. It contained these fundamental principles of socialism, which for ages had existed in secret practice among the Solonic unions all over the world and which was a source of economic life and welfare among the laboring poor, though it had never before attempted to sally forth from its hidden dens, its mysterious passwords [123] and its peculiar mutualism. This was the work of Jesus. He had taught his chosen few all the methods of the great law. His lifework had been that of teaching the jus coeundi; and such an unheard-of rupture of the old competitive system, with its military tactics and schools of concupiscence and irascibility, which cut off from the speculator his incentive to grasp goods, and from the priest his power to mumble deceptions or to swell in pompous pageantry, was an insufferable inroad upon the traditions and usages of immemorial ages.

But all this is just what the strange teacher and pioneer of visible socialism had actually done; and for such unspeakable temerity he had suffered the punishment of death. Stephen was the first business man who took up the work and boldly pushed it onward. Jesus had just before, and perhaps in Stephen's presence, attacked with his own hands, the gamblers in stocks at the temple, who were desecrating the faith and the economies undertaken by the master.

For this extraordinary stroke of practical rebuke, the modern socialists should be thankful. It stands to-day as a solemn argument that the doings of this brave personage were certainly in the direction of improving the economical conditions of the poor. The havoc of provision dealers whom he found speculating out of the ig-

---

[123] The password still continued. It was transmitted into the great system of Jesus and his apostles, because such was the terrific revulsion that it was found necessary to remain for centuries within the secret veil. Luke, it is now believed, speaks of this password, in his *Gospel*, x., 6: "Peace be unto this house." Any initiate hearing this would open the door of the clubhouse or temple and they would, on showing their competency, be entitled to partake at their common table and to be aided in the evangelizing work. Ramsay, *Cities and Bishoprics of Phrygia*, II., p. 548, inscription 412, has furnished us a valuable new evidence of the Christian password. It is an inscription of a purely labor union, being one of the purple or crimson dyers who, at the time of Paul's preaching were doing an enormous business at and about Hieropolis, seat of one of the seven churches of Asia. It gives the secret password of the order. The learned doctor finds it to be a converted trade-union. It is christian. The password is ΠΑΠΩΝ and unintelligible. The *inscr.* begins, "Κοινὸν τῶν Πορφυροβαφῶν" and is given in full in Ramsay's first vol., no. 28. During the time Christ was living, there were societies of "Immortals," secretly and awfully withdrawn, who had the common table and the pass. Under this pass the disciples could go without scrip, Luke, xxii., 35: "And he said unto them: 'When I sent you without purse and scrip and shoes, lacked ye anything? They said, 'Nothing.'"

norant credulity of masses, and to whom the organization of Peter, James and Stephen was so inimical, was outdone by the invasion of a nest of money-changers. Any one studying the insolence, even in our modern days, of the system of money-changing and its worldwide speculations through usury, mutilation of coins, petty peculation, and a dozen other of its mean ways, can comprehend the ratiocination of Jesus in making that celebrated raid. There are now extensive headquarters at London having branches in Paris, Amsterdam and New York, managing thousands of petty agents who fleece travelers and others by constantly pulling fluctuation wires touching hundreds of different coins, and realizing out of the disparity of silver, copper and nickel with gold. All cities and towns of the world are beset and tormented with these thieves. Scheduled values of coins and paper are furnished the money-changers every month, and they must conform or be hounded from the business. Their little tiendas, casas de cambio and broker shops are everywhere. They are the same old argentarii and numularii who had their petty, skinning traffic in Rome, Athens and Jerusalem. The author once counted nine of these little open-air stalls in one of the sea-girt marts of the Piraeus, the seaport of Athens, and found them at Gibraltar, Cadiz and Naples. Thes gangs are averse to the French metric system which would equalize the value of coins, and they have their lobbies upon the floors of every chamber of legislation especially at Washington and the palace of St. James. They are as secret as they are insidious and deceitful.

It is under these circumstances, far more economical than religious, that we find Stephen attacked by a mob of Jews. Like the modern western American, who is set upon by a mob to be lynched, he was allowed an hour or more to render in his defence. A principal charge against him was that he was opposed to the law of Moses. It indeed looks as if Stephen, like Jesus himself, might have been adverse to the Mosaic rule, since it was found to permit of corruptions such as caused Christ's celebrated attack upon the den of speculators. The Jews charged him with the crime, punishable with death, of maligning the law; [124] for they pretended to

---

[124] Πράξεις τῶν Ἀποστόλων, VI., 13. 14: Ἔστησάν τε μάρτυρας ψευδεῖς λέγοντας· ὁ ἄνθρωπος οὗτος οὐ παύεται ῥήματα λαλῶν κατὰ τοῦ τόπου τοῦ ἁγίου καὶ τοῦ νόμου· Ἀκηκόαμεν γὰρ αὐτοῦ λέγοντος· ὅτι Ἰησοῦς ὁ Ναζωραῖος οὗτος καταλύσει τὸν τόπον τοῦτον καὶ ἀλλάξει τὰ ἔθη, ἃ παρέδωκεν ἡμῖν Μωυσῆς·

arrest him because he said that the wonderful Being they had crucified had declared that he would destroy Jerusalem and change the customs which Moses delivered them. History is here to tell us that in about thirty-six years the entire population of above one million people, the best part of the great temple of Solomon, the mighty walls, arches, streets, gardens and even deep foundation stones were obliterated by the awful Roman conquest of vengeance.[125]

The most classical histories which have embellished this story admit that the life and death of Stephen form an episode in ancient history. He was a person of majesty and grandeur. While delivering his final oration he was insulted by the Jewish sectaries who had actually wimbled into a bullying and insolent mastery of the better precepts of the Sanhedrim and awed them down. Seeing that his speech was belittled and made a subject of ridicule, he "broke off from his calm address and suddenly turned upon them in an impassioned attack, which shows that he saw what was in store for him. Those heads thrown back on their unbending necks, those ears closed against any penetration of the truth, were too much for his patience. 'Ye stiff-necked and uncircumcised in heart, and ears! Ye do always resist the Holy Ghost. As your fathers did so do ye.'"[126] It was a grand spectacle. What was it all about? Like Jesus, this man had attacked their iniquitous speculations carried on even in the temples, and was, by the introduction of the co-operative commonwealth, undermining the pilfering usuries and peculations of the provision rings.[127]

[125] Josephus, "De Bell. Jud," VI., ix., 3, saw it, and as now adjudged, truthfully reported it in his histories, declaring that it was a massacre hitherto unknown to the world. The number massacred by the Roman general, Titus, was 1,150,000, according to this historian, although Tacitus, who confirms the tragedy, puts it less. See supra, p. 142. Objections have been made by some that the actual population of Jerusalem did not amount to that figure. The answer is that the massacre of Titus, took place just at the moment of the celebration of the Passover, when great numbers of the Jews were assembled from the country, filling the city with outside visitors.

[126] "As he spoke," continues Smith's "Bible. Dict.," p. 3111, "they showed by their faces that their hearts, to use the strong language of the narrative, were being sawn asunder; and they kept gnashing their teeth against him."

[127] Chrysostom, "Works," I., p. 666: "Cur Stephano viduarum cura commissa ab apostolis." This author, under the above rubric, gives some interesting theories regarding Stephen's economic mission, as head of the committee of deacons. "Stephanus diaconorum prædiscipulus." Again, ibid. XI., 553: "Diaconisse in primitivia ecclesia." XI., 454: "Diaconi munus in ecclesia." and XI., 553, "Diaconodum officia, qui mores eorum sint oportet." "Diaconi, in Ecclesia tumultum confecibant," IX., 190.

Stephen, then, is another character in the history of the ancient lowly, bearing a name mysterious, in being a metonymy, or transmutation, and in the ordinary reading he appears as an almost allegorical character. Smith says, we hear nothing of his ministrations among the poor. This is exactly the part they would rule out. It is extremely probable that he and his assistants undertook to carry out practically the work they were appointed to do, and adjust the economic design embodied in the teachings; but to assume the daring task, to bring so brilliant and enormous a scheme to the front in defiance[128] of political, religious and social institutions reigning and murdering in that cruel age of individualism and military rule, and to broadly proclaim it to the open world, as commanded by a martyred lord, was death. The man defiantly braved his peril and became the second martyr. Arraigned before an improvised tribunal he was given some minutes to express his defense. In this speech, one of the very few given in the Bible, he is admitted to have told the Hebrews that Moses was secondary and his words glowed with aggravating vehemence and were pronounced with powerful and defiant eloquence, causing them to pale with rage and gnash with anger.[129] Saul, who was the accuser, was present. With a mad rush they seized the young deacon,[130] dragged him into the suburbs of the city,

[128] Every one was killed who dared to speak for Stephen's teacher; even Tiberius. As additional evidence to that of Tertullian and the Augustan historians, that Tiberius attempted to enroll Jesus among the sacred immortals, we have Orosius, "Adv. Paganos," VII., iv.: "Tiberius cum suffragio magni favoris retulit ad senatum ut Christus Deus haberetur. Senatus indignatione motus, quod non sibi prius secundum morem delatum esset, ut de suspiciendo cultu prius ipse decerneret consecrationem Christi recusavit edictoque constituit, exterminandos esse Urbe christianos; præcipue cum et Sejanus, præfectus Tiberii, suspiciendæ religioni obstinatissime contradiceret. Tiberius tamen edicto accusatoribus christianorum mortem comminatus est." Thus they refused, threatened and afterwards murdered him.

[129] Πράξεις τῶν Ἀποστόλων, VII., 57, 58, 59: "Κράξαντες δὲ φωνῇ μεγάλῃ συνέσχον τὰ ὦτα αὐτῶν καὶ ὥρμησαν ὁμοθυμαδὸν ἐπ' αὐτὸν, καὶ ἐκβαλόντες ἔξω τῆς πόλεως ἐλιθοβόλουν· καὶ οἱ μάρτυρες ἀπέθεντο τὰ ἱμάτια αὐτῶν παρὰ τούς πόδας νεανίου καλουμένου Σαύλου, καὶ ἐλιθοβόλουν τὸν Στέφανον, ἐπικαλούμενον καὶ λέγοντα· κύριε Ιησοῦ, δέξαι τὸ πνεῦμα μοῦ."

[130] Gorius, "Mon. sive Columbar," p. 75, confirms the original function of Stephen, whose cinerary urn is inscribed under one of the ollas, of the great under-ground cemetery of Rome. The deacon was called in Latin, "Dispensator," because his early mission was to dispense the food and necessaries of life among the members. The Greeks retained or rather originated the word as διάκονος, also οἰκονόμος economist; "Dispensator is erat, qui universæ domus rationi præerat," and continues: "Suetonius in Vespas., 22 scribit: 'Admonente dispensatore quemadmodum summan rationibus vellet referri.' Dispensatores cum amanuensibus juncti, et in hoc lapide, et apud Suetonium leguntur in Nerone, c. 44." The inscr. of Gorius, which he is describing, is shown upon the same page.

TRAGIC DEATH OF STEPHEN. 405

and after the abuse they were able, in their exasperation, to heap upon him, seized stones and hurled them in tempestuous hail, breaking his bones and tearing his flesh with their cutting angles and swift flight till death rescued him from a sense of their furious rage.[835] And when the heart and tissues were quivering in dissolution they threw the clothes and probably the throbbing form at the feet of Saul.[132] This young man had steeled his conscience up to the point of vengeance and he did not flinch. He accepted a commission to persecute the brotherhoods, followed them to Asia and in some mysterious way, believing he had seen his victim Jesus, was thrown into a trance and whelmed in a wonderful conversion.

Such was the short but vigorous career and awful fate of Stephen, the proto-martyr.

[113] Smith, "Bib. Dict.," p. 3112, says of the funeral of Stephen: "His mangled body was buried by the class of Hellenist and proselytes to which he belonged, οἱ εὐσεβεῖς, with an amount of funeral state and lamentation expressed in the two words used here in the N. T., ie: συνεκόμισεν and κοπετός." The proselytes were the old, long-existing brotherhoods, converted. The word εὐσεβεῖς especially applies to them and belongs to the law of Solon as preserved in the Twelve Tables of Rome. See chap. xiii., on the fundamental requirement, Ἀγαθὸς Ἅγιος Εὐσεβής, where it is thoroughly explained as a requisite of the old pagan unions. As to the burial, the learned Dr. Oehler, in his "MSS. to the Author," speaks of the young men who took Ananias and Sapphira to burial, as performing a regular and natural rite of the burial attachment of a Solonic union. Of course then, this was the same in the burial of Stephen a few days afterwards.

[132] Πραξ. τῶν Ἀποστ. VII., 58: Καὶ ἐκβαλόντες ἔξω τῆς πόλεως ἐλιθοβόλουν Καὶ οἱ μάρτυρες ἀπέθεντο τὰ ἱμάτια αὐτῶν παρὰ τοὺς πόδας νεανέου καλουμένου Σαύλου. κ. τ. λ.

CHAPTER XVI.

CONTINUED.

THE APOSTOLIC AGE.

SECTION II.,—CALIGULA—CLAUDIUS.

TERRIBLE Change in Treatment of Jews and Christians—Involved Thousands of Workingmen—Marvelous Discoveries—The Domus Augustalis—Caligula Began and Claudius Continued the Persecutions—Victims Secretly Organized—Discoveries of De Rossi—Under-ground Rome—The Columbarium—Tyrannus—Their Scholæ discovered far beneath the Surface—Driven to Such Hiding Holes at Rome—Had System and Schools in these Recesses—Caligula Murdered—Mommsen, Cagnat, Oehler and other Savants Agree that these Collegia were the Regular Solonic Unions—Full Description of School—Roma Sotterranea—Exhaustive Researches of De Rossi—Four Trades represented in the Silvani Find—Discovery that During Persecutions of Claudius, those wretched Workers Dived Down into Subterranean Abodes—Continued in Hiding Throughout Nero's Reign—Devotion for Each Other—The Strange Practice not Confined to Rome—Clement of Rome—Friend of Peter—Wrote Kerugma Petrou—Sketch of his Life—Why his Valuable Works were Suppressed—Consistency of the Term "Lord" as Manager of Business of Union—How there Came to be so Many Lords—It was a Clause in the Law of Solon—The Quinquennalis—He was also an Evangelist—Banishment by Claudius Caused Great Numbers to Escape and Colonize in Other Parts of the World—Exiles—Well Received in Asia Minor—The Gerousia turns out to be a Solonic Union—The Aventine Hill—Ægis of Diana—Colony of Shoemakers of Shoemaker Street—Evidence that the Christians Planted into and Thrived upon these Trade Organizations—Aquila and Priscilla—Other Exiles of Claudius—Episode of Demetrius—How an Important Matter is Misunderstood—His Union worked making Images for Diana at Ephesus—All tended to Madden Claudius—Supposed Quarrel of Paul, John and Peter Refuted—A perfect Harmony Agreed Upon—The Innumerable Secret Hives—Traces of Work of Joseph of Arimathea—Briennian Find of Parts of Peter's Teachings.

The short reign of the emperor Caligula, who succeeded Tiberius, A. D. 37 to 41, lasting four years, was marked by an egregious change in the treatment of the associations' members. Recently discovered evidence establishes that immediately after the death of Stephen and Jesus an enormous christianized colony of these unions was in existence at Rome. How could this be? That there were thousands, if not a hundred thousand, there, is now ascertained to be certain. It is one of the marvels of the world. Already under Tiberius, great numbers of them in pure trade union form are found to have swarmed in palaces, courts and especially, the kitchens, wash-houses, baths and gynæciums or imperial work-shops, and now there come under contribution the newly unearthed subterranean scholæ, mausoleums and cemeteries, many inscriptions, paintings, sculptures and cinerary ollas, glaring chiselings legible and grammatical, of a vast occult christian life.[133]

How is this? The reader will say it is impossible. We shall bring forth these long-lost wonders and prove both their antiquity and truthfulness.

It was during the life-time of Augustus, Livia and Tiberius that the so-called Domus Augustalis was created for their benefit. Livia and her son were foremost in recognizing schools within the collegia.[134] The domus Augustales were homes of freedmen and slaves at the imperial courts and residences, where work was furnished them, together with the means of life. Large numbers of these people, with which Rome swarmed, were glad and sometimes even flattered to obtain this gracious protection.

So long as Augustus and Tiberius remained in power the unions, such as conformed to the laws, were unmolested and it was during their reigns that they flourished and in numbers, common goods and influence greatly increased. The vast building dug out of the earth, from

---

[133] Mr. Reber, in his ingeniously written Book, "Enigmas of Christianity," treats with contempt the idea that so early a Christian plant existed. The good friend knows nothing about the tell-tale monuments and inscriptions sleeping in an occult history. Archæology is ruled out. The vast organizations which Tiberius, the friend of Jesus, permitted to indorse this great work, constituting an era of the existence of manhood on the earth, were already in Rome, and had nothing to do but accept the truths he preached. There is evidence to show that they did this even before the crucifixion.

[134] See Vol. I., p. 365. The empress and her son gave a trade union of carpenters the privilege and also money to found a flourishing school for instructing the members and their children. Waltzing, "Hist. Corp. Prof.," I., p. 217: An inscr. C.I.L. xiv., 45. "Numini domus Augustæ dendrophori Ostienses Scholam quam sua pecunia constituerant." When all the facts are collected it will be understood that the modern colleges, name and all are developments of these ancient schools of the collegia which were trade unions of the workingmen.

a depth under the soil of seven feet, in the year 1727, near Rome on the Appian Way, was built by the unions themselves out of the common funds. The great columbarium was more than one hundred feet square. It was first supposed to have been purely a burial place; but more recent excavations show it to have been a place of many residences, and of very fine Architecture.[135]

Since the accidental discovery of this wonderful combination of graveyard and palace, the archæologist De Rossi, has given a lifetime to deeper investigation, the results of which we shall disclose as we proceed. The fact before us is, that it was originally pagan and so remained until christianity came during Tiberius, when the unions owning it, were converted to the new faith. Tiberius did not molest, but on the contrary assisted them. For this, in all appearance, he paid with his life in his old age. He was mysteriously murdered in 37. He had dared to ask the Roman senate to allow him to apotheocize the Lord of the unions. In this he met the wrath of Jupiter. The awful vengeance of Caligula Claudius and Nero, which we shall soon describe, tells how bitter was the hatred of that imperial aristocracy against a doctrine contrary to their revengeful priest-power, so soon as it was discovered that the communistic theories of a crucified carpenter were making swift head against their conscript gods.

Another strange thing about the columbariums is, that the modern schools of archæology have revealed that they did not exist before the time of Augustus, about B.C. 38 to A.D. 14, nor did they survive the days of the Flavii, or in other words, the apostolic age. That their members became completely christianized as early as Tiberius is certain.[136] The cinerary urns,

[135] Gorius, *Mon. sive Columbar.*, p. xii., xiii.: "Mirandum sane in Via Appia, olim omnium celeberrima Romanorum Mausoleis, et sepulcris ornatissima, nuper inventum est monumentum, sive columbarium libertorum, servorumque Liviæ Augustæ ac Cæsarum, quamplurimis ollarum titulis, inscriptionibus, aris, urnis, sarcophagis anaglyphico opere pereleganter sculptis, musivo opere, parergis, emblematis, monstris, quæ nos *stucchi* et *grotesche* patrio sermone appellamus, tectorio opere aliisque eximiis ornamentis valde insigne, cultorumque omnium antiquitatis aspectu dignissimum, cujus antiqua supellex sculpturæ quoque, et achitecturæ præstantissimis artibus non parum lucis conferre protest."

[136] Waltzing, *Hist. Corp. Prof.*, I., pp. 257-260: "Tels étaient les socii Columbariorum. Ces sortes de monuments semblent n'avoir existé qu' aux environs de Rome. Les plus anciens datent de la fin de la République, et les plus récents ne dépassent pas le temps des Flaviens."

also the spaces under the floors were not all in use before Nero's sweeping extinction of the christians and Jews at Rome. He murdered them all, Paul, Peter and thousands more and their remains which were carefully collected, filled them up.[137]

Gorius who wrote a full description in 1728, gives an inscription in his large illustrated work which proves that they built the great mausoleum, on the Appian Way, themselves. They paid the costs out of their own common funds and they had no other, for their life was wholly within the socialistic state.[138]

The news of the doings at Jerusalem under their own membership inspired them against the hopes of ever accomplishing anything from the aged idea of revenge through irascibility and concupiscence, as expressed in the plans of Eunus,[139] Athenion, Aristonicus and Spartacus. The meek and lowly Logos of Jesus was all that was left for them. Between the old and the new, military brutality proved more than a match for their own unscienced rebellions. They had discovered that the maxim of the new teacher, that by kindness "thou shalt heap coals of fire on their head," was true, since it worked out an exquisite refinement of vengeance, improving the old brotherhoods the world over. Besides this, it had the advantage of that dense secrecy which characterized the ancient mysteries. The church was first planted in their mellow soil. Mr. Gibbon, although he knows nothing of these great industrial unions, his lifework having transpired before the real work of archæology commenced, sees with a wonderful vision; for he

[137] Gorius, *Mon. sive Columbar.*, p. 60, § xiii.: "Ex numero ædicularum, sive Columbariorum supra quingenta, et quinquaginta, pluribus ordinibus ac lineis ubique per parietes depositorum, colligi facile potest numerus tum ollarum cinerariarum in ipsis conditarum, tum titulorum, in quibus inscripta sunt nomina, et officia libertorum, ac servorum domus Augustæ quos supra centum et mille promiscue cum feminis inlatos fuisse intelligimus in hoc commune Sepulcrum."

[138] Gorius, *Mon. sive Columbar.*, pp. 62-3. Here will be found that the magnificent monument of the Augustan family, was not the gift of emperors, but of the unions themselves, out of their common funds, whose associates furnished the necessary means. The emperors themselves, who at first were thought to have done all this for them as a gratuity, had no hand in it. They gave the unions however, their full consent. Waltzing, *Hist. Corp. Prof.*, I., p. 329, admits in his description of the symposiums of the collegia and the intense love that prevailed among them, their economic solution, their common table and their generally successful system which their socialism brought forth. He also admits that the christians early found their solace and safety there.

[139] See Vol. I., chap. vii., *Drimakos;* chap. viii., *Viriathus:* chap. ix., *Eumus;* chap. x., *Aristonicus:* chap. xi., *Athenion;* and chap. xii., *Spartacus;* all of whose revolts had failed.

says: "By a wise dispensation of Providence a mysterious veil was cast over the infancy of the church, in which the faith of the christians was matured, and their numbers multiplied, serving to protect them, not only from the malice, but even from the knowledge of the pagan world." The truth is, there had been a revolution. Their old, borrowed schemes of irascibility and concupiscence which characterized the ancient paganism, its competitive greed backed by military power, had been changed for mutual organization and mutual love and care. "Behold a new commandment I give unto you, that ye love one another."

Who built this great monument?[140] This seems to be correctly decided by Gorius. He thinks that one Tyrannus, who was an important quinquennal, under the reign of Caligula, and who had for a long time been the president of a combination of many collegia at Rome, and working under the consent and pecuniary aid of Tiberius, was overseer of the splendid architectural construction, and when it was at last finished, he dedicated it to his successor one Tiberius Claudius Veteranus, an old freedman of Augustus Tiberius, the emperor.[141]

This answers a problem which has caused much discussion among the scholars. Who was the architect and with whose money was it constructed? Who owned it afterwards? The unions, of course. Tyrannus was lord of the house, like the quinquennalis of the great collegium of Lanuvium, called by Mommsen a purely burial association, but in reality, an economic trade union with the burial attachment. He had served the unions, risen from the ranks to be a kurios or quinquennal, exempt from most of the cares and responsibilities,

---

[140] Gorius, *Mon. sive Columbar.*, p. 62, after a page of conjecture concludes: "Quare si conjecturis indulgere liceat, crederem hunc Tyrannum sociorum curatorem fuisse, et monumentum ex pecunia collata sociorum aedificasse." This is probably the truth.

[141] The *inscription* giving the words of the dedication reads: "Tyrannus Verna. Tab. Apparitor, sacris omnium immunis. Is dedit Ti. Claudio Aug. L. Veterano, Columbarium totum.

Is intullit Ianthum. Aug. L.
Fratrem suum."

Ministri:

Such are the words of the stone. Gorius further remarks and we think correctly:

"In hoc lapide eximio, cui merito principem locum damus, quod multa notatu digna contineat, Tyrannus verna dedisse legitur Tiberio Claudio Augusti liberto Veterano Columbarium totum; qui iure donationis in idem intulit Janthum Augusti libertum fratrem suum," as shown in the very instructive Lanuvian inscription. He was an immune.[142]

There is a mass of inscriptional, historical and biblical evidence serving to prove that this Tyrannus was a Mithraic demigod and emporiarch, and that he came to Rome from Asia Minor with his important system of schools, accompanied by many immigrants, and planted in the innumerable collegia that are known to have thrived under Tiberius and to have received immunities and favors through that emperor's large wealth and kindness. The early emperors well knew the value of the trade unions. Dr. Cagnat has recently portrayed this in his publications;[143] and being one of the masters of the schools of inscriptions of the French Academy, we feel doubly assured regarding these facts.

Thus, while it is proved by this inscription of the home-born slave or freedman Tyrannus, that the huge mausoleum was owned, controlled and enjoyed by the unions, it is evident that its construction was known to, and probably aided and encouraged by Augustus Tiberius. Its first calamity came with the monster Caligula. Then it met with the horrors of jealousy and vengeance throughout the reigns of Claudius, Nero and Domitian, during which time it was literally sunk into the ground, and with its many kindred cemeteries and phenomenal scholæ, is being recently unearthed from depths of seven to forty feet, to become a wonder of our age.

We now propose in our analysis of this extraordinary character, Tyrannus, who wherever found, is a slave or freedman and school master, to follow all historical, biblical and inscriptional evidence; since we find him mentioned in the New Testament, in Strabo, in Foucart,

[142] See Vol. I., p. 357: "Item placuit, ut quisquis quinquennalis in hoc collegio factus fuerit, a sigillis ejus temporis, quo quinquennalis erit immunis esse debebit;" and further the nature of this exemption or immunity. Gorius, pp. 65-66, gives a long explanation of his views on this immunity and winds up with these words, p. 66, *fin.*: "Immunitas praeterea dari potuit libertis a suis patronis sive dominis, vel tamquam beneficium, vel tamquam præmium: ut colligitur ex frequenti inscriptione quam exhibet Gruterius DCCCLXXIV., 1, et ex alia apud eumdem Gruterum MCLVI., 1, quam Fabrettus, cap. vi., p. 440, n. 60, Romæ extare dicit apud nobiles de Mignanellis."

[143] *Article* in *Vie Contemporaine*, Paris, Jan., 1896, p. 167: "Les empereurs découvrirent, vers cette époque, (about A.D: 30-130) que l'état avait tout à gagner à la prospérité des associations ouvrières à Rome, en Italie, dans les provinces. Ces réunions étant des foyers de travail, où l'administration centrale et municipale trouvait de précieux auxiliaires..C'est le moment où les syndicats paraissent le plus florissants, leurs membres sont puissants et honorés, ils sont exemptés d'impôts, et jouissent d'avantages inconnus aux simples citoyens."

Lüders, Oehler, Waltzing, most elaborately of all in Gorius, and in the great collections.[144]

The New Testament mention covers this period of the columbarium which began to be persecuted and hunted by Caligula, who, although not credited as a persecutor by Gibbon, actually murdered everybody, and for three years wallowed in the innocent blood of rich and poor alike. This celebrated mention seems rather to come into the reign of Claudius the immediate successor to Caligula. But Tyrannus' schools were going on at Ephesus, while he himself seems to be at Rome.[145] The Greek word scholæ reveals some hidden wonders connected with the early heresies.[146] The truth is, they were not heresies but genuine schools of discussion, and instruction, each with its own little membership; each with its own common table and food supply, and each with a row of seats. They were secret and generally neat, built of stone hewn smooth, often carved, and had a center table. De Rossi has dug out the one presided over by St. Peter, and it has an inscription informing us that Peter made the table with his own hands.[147]

The inscriptions show a half-pagan demigod named Men Tyrannus, a pedagogue, always connected with some manner of temple. A study of all this new-found evidence forces a concensus of points of fact, which focus upon a christian plant into a multitude of brotherhoods, invariably of plebeian blood. We know this Tyrannus to have been a Phrygian poor man's protector

[144] Strabo himself, it will be found, was under Tyrannius or Tyrannus of Pontus. Almost all the men of this name between B.C. 10 and A.D. 37, appear to have been pedagogues of the schools. It is now certain that they were the Mithraic schools; moreover the term Tyrannos is proved to be another metonym.

[145] Πραξεις των Ἀποστόλων, xix., 9: Ὡς δέτινες ἐσκληρύνοντο καὶ ἠπείθουν κακολογοῦντες τὴν ὁδὸν ἐνώπιον τοῦ πλήθους, ἀποστὰς ἀπ' αὐτῶν ἀφώρισε τοὺς μαθητάς, καθ' ἡμέραν διαλεγόμενος, ἐν τῇ σχολῇ Τυράννου τινός.

[146] Lightfoot, *Colossians*, pp. 32-34, speaks of Epaphras, Onesimus and other slavish persons and some heresies which broke out among the brotherhoods—"a combination of Judaic formulism with oriental mystic speculation, and was spreading rapidly." It was the Mithraic scholæ of Tyrannus. Tyrannus must have colonized them and thousands of people at Rome; for we find his schools or scholæ by hundreds in the pits of the columbaria.

[147] De Rossi, *Roma Sotterranea*, Vol. I., p. 182, VIA CORNELIA: "Primum Petrus in parte occidentali civitatis juxta Viam Cornelian ad miliarium primum in corpore requiescit, et pontificalis ordo, excepto numero pauco, in eodem loco in tumbis propriis requiescit.

"Ibi quoque juxta eandam Viam sedes est apostolorum, et mensa et recubitus eorum de marmore facta usque hodie apparet. Mensa quoque modo altare quam Petrus manibus suis fecit, ibidem est."

THE SCHOOLS OF TYRANNUS. 413

and teacher; that he was imported into the Piræus, and also Macedonia, particularly Philippi; that Paul had a great deal to do with his cult; that his cult was taught in the little secret temples of the thaisos and the collegium which were the original kuriakoi or churches and before, for centuries, had been the pholeteria or council chambers of the Solonic unions. The schools of Tyrannus were the movement which caused so much disturbance spoken of in the Acts of the Apostles. This system of elementary schooling, not at all averse to the system from Jerusalem, certainly was early transplanted into Rome; for the positive evidences we are digging out, all point that way.

Another undecipherable matter connected with this Tyrannus is, that a certain Xanthus often accompanies him. In Gorius, as we have just quoted, it is Ianthus.[148] Again we find this queer if not weird being at the Pisidian Antioch where Paul met a rebuff, and it looks as if his school took him in, after he had been turned out of the synagogue by the real Jews.[149]

There has been found a monument of Coloé at Philippi where many radical associations existed at the time Paul visited the place. He received imaginary information that he must go there. As a matter of fact, being an inmate of the secret unions endorsing Jesus, he had been informed through some unexplained method, that he was wanted at Philippi. There, whipped and awfully abused by the pagan official prelates, he nevertheless established this Philippian church, so celebrated in the New Testament. It was in the days either of Caligula[150] or Claudius.

A profound secrecy pervaded these columbarian organizations at an early time, presumably during the

---

[148] Foucart, *Ass. Rel.*, pp. 121-123, gives from an inscr., a valuable anecdote of a poor fellow, the slave of one Caius Orbius, about the close of the apostolic age who had to work in the Laurian mines. He found an old, deserted temple or heroon, and converted it into a sanctuary in honor of Men Tyrannus. It is probable that, feeling the need of an education, he organized a school and that it became one of the "schools of Tyrannus."

[149] It was in southwest Phrygia, right where afterwards arose the seven celebrated churches of Asia. Drs. Foucart and Oehler have proved that the Tyrannus schools and unions were baptists and they had their home in the eranos.

[150] Foucart, *Ass. Rel.*, p. 120, monument de Coloé. This Tyrannus is represented as, "vêtu d'une tunique et d'une chlamyde et coiffé du bonnet Phrygien. Il a un croissant sur les épaules, il tient à la main un thyrse, et pose le pied gauche sur une tête de taureau, Le croissant est son attribut charactéristique; il figure également dans le monument de Coloé, et sur un bas-releif de Philippi."

last two years of the reign of Caligula. He had three years. Then he was murdered by his own prætorian guard. During the first year he had been comparatively humane, but the last two were engulfed in horrors and inhumanity such as knew no distinction between rich and poor; for thousands were swept to the block, senators, prelates, jurists, blood relations, struggling christians and trade unionists; and many knew not why they had been doomed to his indescribable vengeance.

This affords us some idea of how those cringing wretches, with this great mausoleum in their possession cowering under the benign, though hideous ægis of the law of exemptions of the collegia funeraticia, went down in their secret terror under the earth, sometimes even deeper than the catacombs and there in dense darkness built their scholæ after the pattern of Tyrannus. They bore a double meaning, because so habituated to their under-ground, compulsory existence, that it got to be a second nature, and caused the catholics in after ages, even extending to our own time, to build the horrid crypts which degenerated into subterranean dungeons such as still shock the world.[151]

But the schools and influence of Men Tyrannus, and of Tyrannus, especially, where he appears as a plebeian pedagogue and extends his schools even to Pontus, beyond the city of Byzantium, went westward to the Piræus.[152]

Having shown what science is bringing to light to the effect that innumerable schools existed among those squalid slaves and freedmen, managed in the auspices

[151] All through these dangers the Roman law of the collegia tenuiorum held good, legalizing the burial attachment. Waltzing, "Hist. Corp. Prof.," I., pp. 150-151, says: "Le commandeur de Rossi a démontré que les chrétiens les imitèrent (the colleges), et que l' église, persécutée, interdite pour sa religion, fut licite comme corporation funéraire: comme telle, elle put avoir une caisse commune, posséder un cimetière, tenir des réunions, recevoir des dons et des legs." Consult "Bull. Christ.," 1864, p. 57; 1865, p. 90; 1866, pp. 11, 22; 1870, pp. 35. 36; 1877, p. 25; 1886, pp. 83, 84; also "Roma Sotterranea," I., p. 101; and 209-210.

[152] Oehler, "MSS.": "Eine Weihung der ἐρανιστῶν an Μεν Τυράννος nennt die in Laurium gefundene Inschrift, CIA, IV., p. 307, 1328, vgl. mit CIA., II., 1338." In another place, "Μὲν Τυράννος verehrt bei Sunion wahrscheinlich von den in den Bergwerken arbeitenden Sklaven: vgl. CIA., IV., 1328 e; CIA., III., 73." These associations of slaves and freedmen in the mines of Laurium and Sunion are known by various inscriptions. A great insurrectionary strike once occurred at each place. See Vol. 1., pp. 143, for Sunion; 131 for Laurium. Dr. Oehler finds traces of the Lycian Xanthos existing much later; "id. in MSS.": "Den νόμος ἐρανιστῶν aus dem zweiten Jahrhunderte n. Chr. enthält CIA., III., nr. 23, die vom Lykien Xanthos 'n Sunion, im II. und III. Jahrh. n. Chr. zu Sunion gegebenen Bestimmungen für Eranistai des Men Tyrannos, CIA., III., 75 vgl. 73 u, 75."

of this mysterious, perhaps mythical Tyrannus of whom nobody seems yet to have obtained a tangible clue, we next come to explain what thus far is known to science as exhibited by the schools of epigraphy, regarding the nature of these schools during the reigns of Caligula and Claudius, together with the known laws permitting and forbidding them.

Tertullian carefully describes the nature of his organization, such was probably in enormous use at his time, about A. D. 165, and which was at least a hundred years old when he wrote. "Our modest supper rooms" furnish us with a theme. These are being found buried from five to seventy feet under the surface of the earth. We shall describe them as they were hid away during the fury of Claudius, Nero, Domitian, and earlier without doubt under the blood-thirsty monster Caligula. At any rate they are there. Good old Tertullian, at a moment of comparative respite from the atrocious persecutions of the monarchs, speaking in his powerful apology written to them, breaks the silence of secrecy and tells men of the "fraternal stability of our community of goods, our brotherhood, how it knits, while the Roman system of individualism disintegrates. No tragedy makes a noise about our brotherhood. The family possessions which generally destroy brotherhood among you, create fraternal bonds among us. One, in mind and soul, we do not hesitate to share our earthly goods with one another. All things except our wives are common among us;" and closes his paragraph by retorting against the "sneering ado made by the persecutors of our modest supper rooms." He is describing a regular collegium, such as existed in great numbers under the law of Solon.[153]

Mommsen, who first, so far as we know, discovered the necessity of analyzing and comparing the inscriptional and Tertullianic descriptions, was at first a little in doubt, but finally concluded that the two organizations were one and the same.[154]

[153] Tert., "Apol.," xxxix. The words on this subject most attracting attention of the archæologists like Mommsen, Foucart, Waltzing, Lüders, Oehler and others are, these: "Modicam uniusquisque stipem menstrua die vel quum velit, et si modo velit, et si modo possit, apponit.; nam nemo compellitur, sed sponti confert. Hæc quasi deposita pietatis sunt. Nam inde non epulis, nec potaculis nec ingratis voratrinis," etc.

[154] Momms., "De Coll. et Sodal. Rom.," p. 91: "Erant quidem coitiones illæ illicitæ, quicquid dicit Tertullianus, sed ideo tantum, quod erant Christanorum. Non enim nego per se hæc omnia licite fieri potuisse et sæpe facta

Dr. Waltzing comes later and expresses his opinion that Tertullian's collegium was a regular thiasos with burial attachment under the law.[155] The law required that the members of a collegium should constitute their organizations a burial society. Under this distinction they might organize. It was a pretext with a loophole; and taking advantage of it, they always kept up their associations for economic and religious purposes.[156]

It is impossible to deny that the christian cult was planted into the trade unions. When Numa sanctified the Solonic law, a collegium pontificum or union of bridge-builders existed in much power. The Roman government employed them to build bridges. They included stone masons, wood workers and a variety of trades in stone, clay, brick and metals. They are known to have had master workmen. This master bridge-builder became the pontifex maximus. The title gradually took on sacerdotal power and in course of time the pontifex became the pope and is now supreme pontiff of the catholic world. Dr. Oehler squarely admits that the great Gemeinde of Dionysan artists had an object in the direction of making a living and shows that it was the principal thing.[157] Thus it is seen that all this time the unions were in quest of a living. The religion was a secondary matter. They used the burial clause of the law to shield them from the police and

esse a collegiatis. Sed collegia his nominibus omnibus licite institui ipse Tertullianus non sensit; recipi ejusmodi pias causas a collegio funeraticio, quam causam animadvertas a Tertulliano pæne primo loco collocari, nulla lex vetabat. Quod latissime patuisse et magnam partem instituorum ad pias causas, quæ postea plurima fuisse scimus, ab ejusmodi collegiis ductam esse non dubito."

[155] "Hist. Corp. Prof.," I., p. 134, note 1: "Tertullian dans son Apologétique ne dit pas expressément que la communauté chrétienne etait légale comme collège fenéraire; mais de son temps c' était généralement le cas." And again, p. 313, the professor says the collegium tenuiorum of the law, which is Mommsen's collegium funeraticium, was a regular Roman collegium; or as much as says so.

[156] Oehler, "MSS.": "Wer denkt da nicht an die christlichen Friedhöfe? Wir finden aber Verschiedenheiten in der Art und Weise, wie die einzelnen Vereine diese Sorge bethätigen, vgl. Schiess über "Die Römischen Collegia Funeraticia," 1, durch Beistellung des Grabes selbst, wenn der Verein einen gemeinsamen Begräbnissplatz hatte, durch Zahlung einer bestimmten Geldsumme ταφικό zur Bestreitung der Kosten, durch Theilnahme am Begräbnisse, u. s. w."

[157] Oehler, "MSS.": "Verein der dionysen Künstler. Diese sind sowohl als Cultvereine des Dionysos als auch als Erwerbsgenossenschaften zu betrachten. Poland hat im Programme des Weltiner Gymnasiums unter dem Titel 'De Collegiis Artificum Dionysiacorum,' 1895, darüber gehandelt, Ziebarth seine irrigen Ansichten über Κοινόν und σύνοδος berichtigt. Ich will hier nur eine Uebersicht der in den Inschriften vorkommenden Bezeichnungen der mit den theatralischen Aufführungen in Verbindung stehenden Vereine."

this made the most valuable function of the union, for working out their problem of existence.

Let us now plunge down into the under-ground recesses and with the archæologists dig out their graves and schools, such as bear the early record of Caligula and Claudius. These wonders, for ages, cherished in hideous secrecy and gloom, have been called the trophies of the apostles.[158] The columbarium which was one of the first great discoveries of the kind, and is the subject of a large folio volume in velum, elaborately illustrated, is only one of the trophies now sought by the schools of science. Nearly two hundred years old it is classic. Soon after Gorius, Antonius Bossius wrote a valued work, Roma Satterranea, or subterranean Rome but died before completing it, and Giovanni Battista de Rossi took up the subject where Bossius left off and his many works have made him famous. The combined labors of these savants, assisted by large appropriations by the government and city from time to time, have brought forth and opened to the light of day dozens of cemeteries, many of which were furnished with school rooms, called scholæ now being studied as true marvels of antiquity. We shall now attempt a description of some of them, always giving our authority in their own words, lest the facts exhumed be thrown into discredit by doubters disposed to charge us with incorrectness. It must be constantly borne in mind that these columbaria, and schools came under the law of the collegium tenuiorum, which simply means a trade union consisting of members who are of the outcast poor, and miserable. The word college was ancient and belonged to the Solonic plan, noble enough to come under the jus coeundi,[159] but its adjective was a term of contempt. At the close of the conquests, an effort was made to suppress these trade and labor unions and Cæsar, Cicero and the senate succeded in accomplishing their object only with the greatest difficulty being met by Claudius and the tribunes,[160] and were obliged to legalize the burial attachment. This burial attachment served to

[158] *Digest De Collegiis et Corporibus*, XLVII., xxii., *lib.* 4, *Ad Legem Duodecim Tabularum*.
[159] Consult Vol. I., pp. 344, 345, his law, 302, note 69; as an orator and tribune, 363.
[160] Asconius, *In Pisonem*, speaks of the law: "L. Julio C. Marcio Consulibus quos et ipse Cicero supra memoravit, Senatusconsulto collegia sub-

bring for thousands of unions the privilege of combination in a limited way. They could have a graveyard, but the conduct must be beyond suspicion; for during the commotions between Cicero and Claudius they [161] had been working politically and had elected their own tribunes and commissioners of public works to office, which, according to the persons of boasted blood, like Cicero and Cæsar, was a mortal offence. But, as shown by Cagnat and Cassagnac, the Roman government was in need of these trade organizations and their enormous and efficient labors. Accordingly the government was in some measure kind to them and employed them to do the considerable labors of the imperial court. The unions organized this into the gynæcium.[162] Thus the emperors themselves found the unions of great value to them, as well as a resource of the state, while the jealous senate circumscribed their usefulness and drove them to the wall. But these were the good emperors Augustus and Tiberius. After them came such monsters as Caligula, Claudius and Nero, and the poor wretches had nothing better to do than to dive down into the earth and immure themselves in their subterranean abodes, inapproachable by the spies of such tyrants, and hide, stifle and worship and study and perish together. In woe they thus built in secrecy their scholæ, a development of the burial attachment of the unions.

lata sunt, quæ adversus rempublicam videbantur esse." This was the year B.C. 64. The true law, preserved by Marcion is in the *Digest*, XLVII.,xxii., 3. It is only for slaves and the very poor and reads in full thus: after saying: "fuerint illicita," it proceeds: "In summa autem, nisi ex senatusconsulti auctoritate, vel Cæsaris, collegium vel quodcumque tale corpus coierit, contra senatusconsultum, et mandata et constitutiones collegium celebrat. § 2. Servos quoque licet in collegio tenuiorum recipi voluntibus dominis: ut curatores horum corporum sciant, ne invito aut ignorante domino in collegium tenuiorum reciperent, et in futurum pœna teneantur, in singulos homines aureorum centum." The law crippled the primordial Solonic rights.

[161] We are able to give quite a number of the cemeteries recently exhumed, by name, from De Rossi, *Roma Sotterranea*, Vol. I., p. 159. We find his list as follows: "Cœmeterium Calepodia ad s. Pancratium — Cœm. s. Agathæ ad Girulum — Cœm. Ursi ad Portesam — Cœm. s. Felicis, Via Portensi — Cœm. Calisti juxta Catacombas — Cœm, Prætextati inter Portam Appiam ad s. Appolinarem—Cœm. Gordianum foris Portam Latinam—Cœm. inter duas Lauros ad s. Hellenam — Cœm. ad Pileatum ad s. Bibionam — Cœm in agrum Veranum ad s. Laurentium — Cœm. s. Agnetis — Cœm. fontis sancti Petri, id est, Nymphas — Cœm. Priscillae ad Pontem Salarium — Cœm. Cucumeris — Cœm. Thrasonis ad s. Saturninum — Cœm. Feliciatis— Cœm. Hermetis — Cœm. s. Feliciatis juxta Cœm. Calisti." Many of these names occur in the *Acts*, or the *Canonical Epistles*.

[162] Levasseur, *Hist. Classe Ouv.*, I., p. 37: In Gaul dans le 4 me siècle on trouve encore six gynécés appartenant à l' état; à Arles, à Lyon, à Rheims pendant plus particulurèment les empereurs, sous autorité du comte du domaine privé, à Trèves et à Autelæ." For a description of the gynæriarius, see p. 419, Vol. I.

GREAT VALUE OF THE SCHOOLS.

These scholæ constitute one of the difficult problems of modern science. In fact we are so prejudiced and blinded that we do not desire to know the whole truth about them, seemingly because, on the outset, they show themselves to be a work of the wretchedly poor. But political science, having discovered that nations owe their wealth to labor and nothing else, there looms up a modicum of respectability and men are obliged to pay attention to the logic of truth.[163]

Even the form of these schools is known. Of course, during the peaceful days of Tiberius whose long and gentle reign lasted from A.D. 14 to A.D. 37, these poor people had their schools above ground; we even have reasons for knowing that Augustus patronized and helped them, and we know that Livia, his wife, the empress and her son and others also did.[164] It was not until the persecutions of their immediate successors began that they sank these abodes into the dark subterranean recesses. We shall only portray them in their hidden quality; and our principal object is to show that they were used by their members as a part of the burial attachment under the law of the collegium funeraticium or burial society.

Dr. Cagnat, on an investigation of this subject, found scholæ of the Roman soldiers who belonged to the unions in Africa; and we judge by his description that the general form of their edifice was about the same as at Rome.[165] Small as they were, some not being more

[163] Waltzing, *Hist. Corp. Prof.*, I., p. 217, says: "La description de ces scholæ des collèges funéraires et religieux nous sera utile pour nous faire une idée de celles des collèges professionnels, qui en différaient pourtant. D'abord, elles étaient souvent situées sur un forum de la ville, comme à Ostie, à Bénévent, à Falerio à Préneste, à Pompeii, et comme celle des scribes et peut-être des flutistes, à Rome. Souvent elles se trouvaient dans un quartier où habitaient et travaillaient les membres du collège: ainsi les marchands de vin de Lyon, avaient bien leur local dans ces canabæ qui leur servaient d'entrepôts et qui se trouvaient dans la partie N.-O. de l'isle actuelle du Tibre, entre le temple de Fors Fortuna et la porte Septimiana où etaient leur tanneries il était voisin de celui des ivoiriers et des ébénistes; en fin les tabernarii avaient leur schola au centre de la ville près du Pentheon d'Agrippa."

[164] An inscription is extant, Orell, 4088 ft, cf. Vol. I., p. 360 sq., of this work showing a school that was patronized by Livia and Augustus, who gave a sum of money to start it. It thrived. The members were carpenters who worked days for the emperor and met together to study evenings, and it stands among the very first regular schools for the working people in the world. This school in fact, may be regarded as the original of the modern college, having been an ordinary collegium or trade union such as existed in great numbers everywhere.

[165] R. Cagnat, *L' Armée Romaine d' Afrique*. pp. 540-541: "Voila ce qui les feuilles nous apprennent sur les scholæ. Les inscriptions, qui mentionnent un grand nombre de ces lieux de réunion, pourront compléter, dans une certaine mesure, ce qui précède," referring to his description too lengthy to be given here.

than eighteen feet square and only one story in height, the archæologists are unanimous in classing these scholæ as temples. But they also partook of the character of the Prytanea of Greece and Asia. An author who has searched all the evidence at command, enumerates several functions at which they must have been engaged.[166] They had the common table where all partook the common meal; some even had the triclinium, a luxury discountenanced by the christians after conversion and absorbtion of their membership into the apostolic plan. Then there was an altar at which they held their religious devotions. Several inscriptions describe the furniture. Sometimes there was a portico adorned with paintings, for they were all mechanics and laborers, and many artists in oil painting were among the members. If any one of the best painters was without employment he could be occupied for a time in a way to make the abode pleasant to the eye, and if the light of day was excluded the oil lamp took its place. De Rossi cites the circular scholæ of the union of Silvain, christianized at a very early date. It was furnished with oratories used by the christians. So deep down was it when found that it was but one grade above the catacombs. The circular shape is well relieved by several *absides* of a rectangular form, with three hemicycles. The exedra and the scholæ are similar. This find of the christian school of Sylvain has aroused a great deal of discussion and close study among the epigraphical students. Four trades are represented.[167]

[166] Waltzing, *Hist. Corp. Prof.*, 224-226, speaking of the prytanea that actually existed on a miniature scale in the scholæ, says: "Les détails épars que les inscriptions fournissent sur l' architecture des scholæ tendent même a prouver que souvent elles ne différaient en rien des temples." CIL., V. 7906. This inscription reads: "In templo ex more epularentur." VI., 10234, show that Titus harbored the christians, a little later when the rage of Domitian had ceased; and allowed their schools to crawl out of their darkness. See also CIL., X., 6483; "Ædes ut in ea semper epulentur." Thus it is constantly shown that the members always had the common table, and that their object was to furnish them economic means of life, as well as a decent burial.

[167] De Rossi, *Bull. Christ.*, 1864, pp, 25, 60; Lange, *Op.*, c., pp. 291 sqq. Huelsen, *Mitth. de l' Inst.*, 1890, p. 291, assures us that those under-ground ancient lieux of pedagogy were early christian and he has discovered that the trade of the members of this particular school was that of the eborarii or ivory-workers. They had their banquets in the tetrastyle of the exedra. The architecture is after plans and explanations of Vitruvius, V., x., 4; CI L., IX., 4112. Waltzing, *Hist. Corp. Prof.*, p. 222, says: "C' est là que les confrères se réunissaient, pendant leur loisir, pour se délasser, pour s' entretenir, pour discuter leurs intérêts, pour prendre part aux mêmes sacrifices et pour s' asseoir à la même table." Again, p. 229: "La salle à manger contenait naturellement les meubles et utensils necessaires: tables, buffet, un armoire, lits de table, cratères, amphores, vases de toutes sortes,

THE EARLY SYLVAIN BROTHERHOOD. 421

The general trend of evidence leads to the suspicion that these associations of mutual aid in Rome and the municipal cities were afraid of being accused of having joined the christians. They found, by the spirit of persecution raging against them in the outside world that their new hope was correct; they found that unless they hid away from the sweeping decrees of Caligula and Claudius, nothing awaited them but extermination; they found these monarchs jealously imagining their august family name attacked, for nothing could conceal the christian principle that all, instead of an assuming few were created equal, had souls, a right to a foothold upon the earth hitherto denied, a right to marry whom they loved, and to esteem their children as legitimate. A search of the ancient laws discloses the awful fact that the freedman and the slave had no such rights. Sometimes, by force of mere contact, they met, formed acquaintance and joined themselves in marriage. The new christianity which they were adopting stimulated them and pronounced their children legitimate, and encouraged them to feel that they had souls. But the old Roman law still admitted no marriage for the slave and the freedmen. Thus they were drawn into the new dispensation of Jesus. Being already organized in colleges they had but to endorse the new doctrines through discussion at their scholæ which we have described, and once determined to accept them, they were led to things infinitely broader, more humane and less aristocratic. They became charmed with their new faith, and would grasp it with a lifelong energy.[168] What this early Silvian union did, hundreds followed.

But we have many proofs in the inscriptions and ancient writings that these schools existed long before the arrival in the world of this new faith and hope. Under Augustus large numbers of scholæ were created by the trade unions, especially those who worked for the emperor, either in the general government works, the public works of Rome and the municipia, or in the

les uns pour conserver l' huile et le vin, les autres pour mesurer les rations, une balance pour peser celles-ci. On rencontre encore des bassins pour bains, des cadrans solaires, etc."

[168] De Rossi, *Roma Sott.*, I., p. 103, and note 1, speaking of the stipem menstruam, refers to Orell., 4073, and Henzen, l. c. pp. 9, 10: "In Fano era un locus sepulturæ convictorum, qui una epulo vesci solent." De Rossi subjoins: " E l' epulo commune potrebbero essere i Cristiani, e l' epulo commune la sacra agape." From this it may turn out that no. 4073 of **Orell. is** christian. Orelli's 4073 is a collegium.

422 THE LAW, TIME OF CALIGULA-CLAUDIUS.

gynæcium of the Augustan family.[169] This accounts for the extremely early introduction of christianity into the provinces throughout proconsular Rome, even far-off Britian. Many authors show that in the British Isles christianity had been planted as early as during the life of Joseph of Arimathea. New finds prove it.[170] We shall bring them all out in our disquisition on this subject soon, under the rubric Nero, this chapter.[171] But the extremely early planting appears to have had a literature which was laughed down by later ante-Nicine writers and these evidences perished. They were, however, seen and used in the works of other writers who are well known among the fathers.[172] It is in this second-hand manner that a good deal of valuable knowledge has transcended to us.

There is a prevalent opinion among scholars interested in these discoveries that the earlier scholæ were used as places of repose, but that after the unions were christianized they became places of retreat; and this makes the assurances very secure that as soon as the persecutions broke out, they became hiding holes. Another thing was the fact that they were always attachments to the functions of the unions and construed to be legalized. Thus the school was in almost every case a part and parcel of the funeral or burial equipment of the union and as such considered as within the pale of the law, or lex Julia, the old addendum of the lex collegia tenuiorum which we have quoted in a note. Yet to exhibit all these material trappings would be too glaring a lie and they had to be somewhat covered even before the persecutions. Dr. Ramsay, whom we shall

---

[169] CIL., VIII., 2554, speaking of the school that is in the trade union. "Pro salute Augustorum optiones scholam suam cum statuis et imaginibus domus divinae, item diis conservatoribus eorum fecerunt."

[170] Gould, *Free Masonry*, Vol. I., pp. 37, 38, 54, some time ago asseverated that as early as the time of Christ, there was a Collegium fabrorum in England, a fact confirmed by Coote, *Romans of Britain*, Lond., 1878, pp. 38, 396, 440." This has since been positively confirmed by the new and wonderful discovery of the union of carpenters to whose expenses Pudens of Paul's mention, II Timothy, iv., 21, contributed a sum of money. But this matter of so vast importance to our argument will be treated fully under the section, NERO.

[171] See *index*, in verb. *Joseph of Arimathea*.

[172] Chrysostom, *Homil.*, Tom. VI., p. 635 of ed. used by Lingard, *Hist. Anglo-Sax. Church;* Appendix, note A., 354, says: "Καὶ γὰρ αἱ Βρεττανικαι νῆσοι, αἱ τῆς θαλάττης ἐκτός κείμεναι ταύτης, καὶ ἐν αὐτῷ οὖσαι τῷ ὠκεανῷ τῆς δυνάμεως τοῦ ῥήματος ἠσθοντο· καὶ γὰρ ἐκείνη ἐκκλησίαι καὶ θυσιατήρια πεπηγασι." So again, Tertullian, *Adv. Judæos*, 189: "Britannorum inaccessa Romanis christo vero subdita....Christi nomen regnat....Christi nomen et regnum colitur."

SIGNS AND DECEPTIONS DELUDE THE SPIES. 423

quote in the proper place, has given several pages of explanation of the multitudinous and ingenious devices employed by the old unions of Phrygia, after becoming christianized, in artful escape from the military spies who shadowed them, and the police who constantly dogged them in obedience to this Roman law. But their laborious and indefatigable drudgery of descending sometimes seventy steps below the surface of the ground to build and establish themselves is amazing.[173]

Who can wonder, knowing the untiring devotion to each other, amidst the awful persecutions they were forced to suffer under such pitiless creatures as Caligula and Claudius, that they gladly obeyed the new commandment of their crucified lord to love and care for one another.[174] Entombed in the earth and enwrapped in mutual love, struggling, teaching, plying their trades, nestling, dying together, here it was that the new emotion of human sympathy found its birthplace, its cradle, its common nourishment.[175] Escape from the relentless tigers of the law became an absorbing study which did not confine itself to Rome. It stretched out in every direction.[176] It took refuge in, and enormously pros-

[173] Waltzing, *Hist. Corp. Prof.*, I., p. 223: "Schola; lieu de repos et de délassement était son nom ordinaire." On the same page, in note 1, he cites the "Augustales corporati," at Puteoli, CIL., X., 1, 888; cannophori Ostienses, XIV., 285; centonarii, at Apulum, III., 1174; dendrophori at Cemenelum; the eborarii and citriarii in Rome; fabri or carpenters in many places; clog and wooden shoemakers; fabri tignarii, fontani; and in fact, they are found everywhere.

[174] De Rossi, *Roma Sotterranea*, I., p. 177, has only reported what he saw: we give his cemeteries most of which are accompanied by the scholæ and all with altars: "Notitia portarum Viarum ecclesiarum circa Urbem Romam;" taken from the *Work* of William of Malmsbury: 1st, Via Flaminia: "Secunda Porta Flaminia quæ modo appellata s. Valentini, et Flaminia Via et cum ad pontem Molbium pervenit vocatur Via Kavenna quia ad Ravennam ducit. Ibi in primo milliario foris s. Valentinus in sua ecclesia requiescit — Via Salaria Vetus — Tertia porta Porticiana et Via eodem modo appellata... Ibi prope in eo loco qui dicitur Cucumeris, requiescunt myrtyres Festus, Johannis, Liberalis, Diogenes, Blastus, Lucina, et in uno sepulcro CCXL. Juxta Viam Salariam requiescunt, Hermas, Vasella et Protus Iacinctus, Maximilianus, Herculanus, Crispus, Panephilus, Quirinus." The last two are seventy steps below the surface.

[175] Ramsay, *Cities and Bishoprics of Phrygia*, II., p. 496: "The burial of different families in one grave was essentially opposed to the Phrygian conception, whereas it was in perfect accordance with the christian ideas of brotherhood and communion. Especially, the christians longed to be buried close to the grave of a martyr or saint." He then describes cases which are exactly the same as those given by Oehler and Gorius, concerning unions.

[176] Ramsay, *Cities and Bish. of Phrygia*, II., p. 501, based on inscriptions nos. 411, 412: "In pursuance of this policy the christians put nothing in public documents, such as their epitaphs, which could be quoted as evidence of christianity: Jewish festivals were legal, and their names could therefore be used. Benefit societies were allowed by law under certain restrictions and the communities of christians in the cities, were registered under suitable names, assimulated to those of trades or local guilds."

elyted in and built upon, the already organized secret unions at Rome, as early as Caligula, became a hive of these hiding, converted, economic unions, as shown in constantly increasing archæological finds.[177]

Having proved by unerring inscriptional evidence that the plan of salvation of the crucified carpenter was even during his life-time endorsed by the myriad economic trade unions of Rome, that they had all things common as recorded of the original organization for which Stephen lost his life, and admitting nothing as true unless credited to undeniable evidence, such as that of the penetrating Gibbon and contemporaneous chiselings of the brotherhoods themselves,[178] let us now proceed to give a few details of that remarkable plant.

There was a man named Clement who, immediately after the crucifixion had been converted at Rome by the eloquence of one of the seventy disciples. He was a noble Roman who lived at the time of the first diffusion of the new faith.[179] The disciple whose arguments converted him at Rome, was Barnabas.[180] Clement, because he was a real advocate of the pure, original economic recommendationsofthe carpenter, was ruled out of our canonical literature,[181] although what he wrote was more valuable than even the matter which has transcended to us under censorship of the prelates, in that they could make no profit out of Clement and his Petrine doctrines of communistic distribution of all things Clement, of Rome was an honest, able, consistent and unpurchasa-

[177] De Rossi, *Roma Sott.*, I., p. 106, quotes the following epitaph: "In memoriam eorum quorum corpora in hoc accubitorio sepulta sunt Alcimi caritatis Iulianæ et Rogatæ matri Victoris presbyteri qui hunc locum cunctis fratribus, feci." Every one of these names is registered with the early martyrs. Here the common table, the schola and the burial sarcophagus are one.

[178] Following such a policy to get at truth, we quote Gibbon as reliable. This historian who left nothing unscanned, and cleaned to the dregs every record, makes the followihg satisfactory statement: "Antiquity has left very few works of which the authenticity is so well established as that of the *Acts, of the Apostles*," and refers to Lardner's *Credibility of Gospel History*, Part II.

[179] For a succinct description of Clement and his conversion, see Neander, *Hist. Eccles.*, I., 32.

[180] Smith, *Bib. Dict.*, in verb. *Barnabas*, p. 247: "The Clementine Homelies make him to have been a disciple of our Lord himself; and to have preached in Rome and Alexandria, and converted Clement of Rome. The *Clementine Recognitions* make him to have preached in Rome, even during the lifetime of our Lord." The Clementine literature that was ruled out, appears to be more truthful and realistic than the gospel itself.

[181] Irenaeus, *Origins of the Episcopate*, I., (*Hist. Eccles.*, III., Sect. 3, Irenæus when he says: "This man, as he had seen the Blessed Apostles and had been conversant with them, might be said to have the preaching of the Apostles still echoing in his heart."

CLEMENT OF ROME. 425

ble man. He was converted to the economic socialism of Jesus, and was persistent in the idea and the practice until his death. His celebrated endorsement of the common table and the communal code caused the speculators to rule him out of the economical gospels where his great Epistle to the Corinthians ought to be registered. Quite a number of the modern ecclesiastical critics are now complaining[182] against his having been so shabbily treated. The eighteenth and nineteenth centuries produced many capable scholars who have been outspoken in favor of reinstating the Petrine gospel.

The probable trouble with Clement was, that unlike the great precursor who spoke in parables and indirection, he came straight out and wrote plainly. Having read and studied the writings of Plato, he was ready to endorse and assist in any practical plan based on such ideas; for Plato never made any effort to organize a single brotherhood to practically carry out his ideas. Jesus, on the contrary, did not write, but laid out all the plans and specifications for the organization and worldwide propagation of the ideas.[183] Clement heartily believed that all should labor, and that the product should accrue to all.[184] He was a man of unusual education, powerful vigor, unswerving determination and fine address. The person at Rome who converted him, said to have been Barnabas, was holding an open-air discourse as early as during the life of Tiberius, and consequently in safety and freedom from molestation by the police, but in the slummy portions of the city; and Clement, a young man or perhaps mere boy passing from school, heard it. The nearest that can be ascertained from the circumstance is that he was converted

---

[182] *Ante-Nicine Fathers*, VIII., pp. 82-84. *Recognitions of Clem.* Common Table of the Brotherhoods. Clement was seeking mental relief when he met Barnabas. Barnabas converted him at Rome. He then went, in his mental agony to Cæsarea, met Barnabas again, and Peter. Peter refused to invite him to the common meal, but himself ate, with the assembled brotherhood whose names are all chronicled. Peter, however, prayed "May the Lord grant to thee to be made like to us, in all things that receiving baptism, thou mayest be able to meet with us at the same table."

[183] Clement, *Recognitions*, as per *Trans.* of *Ante-Nicine Fath.*, Vol. VIII., p. 194: "A certain man, the wisest among the Greeks, knowing that these things are so, says that friends should have all things common... He says also, that air and the sunshine cannot be divided, so neither ought other things to be divided which are given in this world to all, to be possessed in common, but should be so possessed."

[184] Quoting *Gen.*, IV., 3-8, Clement of Rome, *First Epist.*, *Cor.* iv., says: "So God rebuked him, saying: 'If thou offerest rightly, but dost not divide rightly, hast thou not sinned?'" Here the double lesson is that the ancient sacrifice, always meant an economic contribution, generally in kind, as grain meat fruit. etc.

to socialism, and his lifework immediately opened up before him. Henceforth he was to believe and argue and teach all men that the existing competitive conditions with slaves at one end millionaires at the other were wrong. His subsequent voluminous writings, most of which have fortunately been preserved, all show it.[185] Clement was so impressed that he inquired into the meaning of such strange truths. To do this he had to descend into the abodes of the smutty unions so foul that they are characterized by M. Renan as wearing filthy gabardines, reeking with grime and smelling of an intolerable emanation of garlic and social putrescence. It is hard to believe that the highest, most correct and lasting principles, such as proved successful, anent the splendor of the directly opposite which gave way before them, should have had their birthplace and their cradle in such dens. Yet it is literally true. For the last two centuries, and most especially the last half of the nineteenth, the proofs of this have overwhelmed all opposition.[186] Even Gibbon admits it.[187]

In following the literary career of Clement of Rome, we find all through that the twit of Tertullian and Jerome that his celebrated Apostolic Constitutions and his Recognitions were suited for this "Vilis plebecula" or low-rate trash from which the movement of our era originated, were based upon the truth. It is necessary all through, to accentuate the now appreciable but anciently nauseating fact that the economic means of ex-

---

[185] Clem., *Apostolic Constitutions*, Book II., chaps. 8 and 25: The eighth chapter opens: "Those that will not work must not eat." Again: "Let young persons of the congregation endeavor to minister diligently to all necessaries." All are enjoined to work. In chap. 26, he writes: "Distribute to all those in want, with justice; and yourselves use the things that belong to the Lord; and do not abuse the privilege by eating all by yourselves." Whether this lord (κύριος) here mentioned is the one who died on the cross, or simply the lord and president of the union, which in the Greek is κύριος, is a problem.

[186] Mosheim, *First Century*, Part I., chap. iv., § 8, says: "The causes must truly have been divine which could enable men destitute of all human aid, poor and friendless, neither eloquent nor learned, fishermen and publicans, and they too, Jews, or persons considered odious, in so short a time to persuade a great part of mankind to abandon the systems of their fathers."

[187] *Decline and Fall*, Vol. I., p. 57, Harpers: "The latter were those among whom the Gospel found its most numerous recruits." Gibbon read Martial who mentions Pudens and other Bible names, and as Martial wrote some scurrility he inveighs against the whole generation found in these dives where the faith was planted. Gibbon knows nothing about the Solonic law and its labor organizations, yet perceives the cardinal fact; and then leaves us to infer that the gospel was introduced into a loathesome species of lasciviousness. He says: "poor people" are brought under contribution as examples of the most exquisite abominations.

istence was, as it is now, the highest and even noblest
aim, and that it has taken three thousand years of culture under close organization for this vilis plebecula to
grind off the ancient curse of slavery, opening the valuable discovery to view, that economic salvation is holi-
est and most difficult of all tasks in the realm of social
and political economy. Because Clement had a mind and
set himself at work with energy to carry out the plan of
salvation blocked out at Jerusalem, he was set upon by
the prelates who crawled into control, and his name so
handed down that it does not occur but once in the
New Testament. Clement wrote for Peter the apostolic canons which are preserved; and although ruled
out as canonical and Bible scripture, are in the Corpus Juris Civilis along with the Pandects of ancient
law.[188]

We now come to a recital of the manner in which
these two men became acquainted. On conversion at
Rome, Clement determined to see the apostles, the principal one of whom at that time was Peter. He had to
sell the little he had and settle up his affairs in order to
get the money to make the voyage. This accomplished,
he arrived at Cæsarea where, as it happened, the twelve
apostles were to meet, to confront the celebrated Simon
Magus in a discussion.[189] It appears that they first
met at Joppa, the seaport of Jerusalem, assembling at
the house of Simon the tanner. We mention this circumstance because it leads to an insight into a long
train of evidence proving that the apostles "met around"
in the "houses" of the unions that had been converted.
Simon, the tanner, was probably the kurios or president
of a union of leather workers at Joppa. So Dr. Oehler
thinks. There has been found at Joppa, an inscription
of the tanners' unions of the same age, which, although
it does not mention Simon, that being only the christian metonym, looks as if it might have been the same
brotherhood of tanners which welcomed Peter and en-

---

[188] He wrote the *Canons of the Church*, for Peter at a much later date at
Rome. He knew only the *Gospel of the Hebrews*, which is lost. His *Canons*
have been disallowed by the later fathers. Two letters are also extant. Peter stipulates that certain Clementine Praeceptions in eight books belong to
the *Bible*, and the rest held in mystery : "Praeceptiones quæ vobis episcopus
per me Clementem in libris octo nuncupatæ sunt, quas omnibus publicare
non oportet, ob quædam arcana quae in se continent: et *Actiones nostras
Apostolorum*."

[189] Clement, *Recognitions*. Book II., cc. 7. 8. 9. 10-18. as told by Aquila,
his former pupil.

tertained him for many days.[190] This Simon, the tanner of Joppa, had become so strong an enthusiast in the new cause, and so helpful in the practical work, that he was appointed as the twelfth apostle in the place of Judas, who committed suicide.

In passing, it may be stated that during the life of Jesus, there are seen evidences that these disciples, wandering from place to place, without homes and without money, were frequently if not constantly entertained by secret brotherhoods who fed them at their common table and out of their common substance. That christianity was originally planted in these old and long-existing communes is made plain by a critical perusal of the Gospel itself.[191]

Clement, who came out strong and bold, was the mouthpiece of Peter in after years; and the reader of the history of the ancient poor cannot but be attracted by a fair and full statement of the facts connected with his initiation into the brotherhoods under Peter's guidance.

To begin with, Clement was right. Every development of practical experience and science since Jesus who first promulgated that organization, challenges disbelief in faith, as an economic or pathological cure. A practical workingman himself, this great kurios, was a member of the brotherhoods of much judgment and sense. He organized the poor for economical salvation. Whatever interpretation priestly influence may make, this is the impregnable buttress behind which future christianity will stand. Unless restored to the prim-

[190] Oehler, *Eran. Vindob.*, p. 282. Here this archaeologist crowds many unions in a single mention, this of Simon the tanner among them: "Purpurfärbereien waren auch in Tyrus, dessen Purpur berühmt war, Strabo, XV., 2, s. 757; Plinius, *Nat. Hist.*, V., 19. Die Sidonier werden von Strabo, XV., 2, s. 757, genannt πολύτεχνοι καὶ καλλίτεχνοι, ihre Waffen waren berühmt und finden sich selbst in Sardinien; Plinius nennt Sidon, artifex vitri, *Nat. Hist.*, V., 19;—Gerber in Joppe erwähnt *Apostelg.*, x., 6." That Simon's tannery business was a union shines out in several mentions. Clement tells us this, and more. That Simon the tanner was the president, lord or κύριος of the Joppa κυριακός, is made plain by Clement's *Recognitions* when recounting in detail the story of his first acquaintance with Peter.

[191] Luke viii., 3. calls forth an acknowledgment by Neander, *Planting*, Book I., chap. 11, Vol. I., p. 26, 27. as follows: "Probably a union of this kind existed among the persons who attended the saviour, and ministered to his necessities." See Luke, viii., 3: "And Joanna, the wife of Chuza, Herod's steward, and Suzanna and many others which ministered unto him of their substance." Here is a plain and straightforward statement that Joanna, a deaconess or stewardess, and a slave or other lowly servant of one of high degree, was the officer of a secret union under the old Solonic dispensation, and that the membership, working out the hard economic problem of life, had endorsed the new plan of salvation

itive estate where Clement left it, it falls. It is in decadence now. He was a young man of sense and honesty. Seeing the unspeakable miseries of his enslaved and impoverished fellow men, he joined the good work of practically carrying it out. He joined the secret union of Peter, put his whole life into it, and wrote the valuable contributions. For doing this he was ignored a hundred and fifty years afterwards and his splendid manuscripts ruled out and nearly lost.

And Peter, the "lord;" what shall be said of this indefinable, strange friend of the Master, friend of Clement, of whom a by-word "the silence of Peter," went current for centuries? Mutilations, hitches, puzzles, quarrels with Paul, secrecy in preaching, constant stickling to baths and agapæ, loveliness of character amidst sternness of counsel, and final crucifixion head downward by Nero; these give the synopsis of this great fisherman's life. Of the silence of Peter, Origen and Tertullian assure us that like that still stranger man, Titus, nineteen years hidden away at Cæsarea, Peter was hidden at Rome for a generation, taking up the problem of salvation in what are now found to have been the Roman converted collegia; sometimes sallying forth as far as Babylon, Edessa, and back through Ephesus and Corinth to be again self-entombed among the stifling garlic and swine-eating human herd, effluvious in their clogs and gabardines, gulping in his glad tidings of great joy in the scholæ of the columbarium. The strange life-long friendship between Peter and Clement began in somewhat the following manner, if we may credit the Recognitions:

When Clement arrived in Judæa from Rome, bent on seeing the authors and founders of the plan of salvation, he was surprised to find Peter the lord almost inaccessible and as rigid against him and cold as stone. He was told to await outside and he might soon be vouchsafed an audience, expecting to see some grand, and august, monarchical personage attired in the trappings of lords. When ushered into Peter's presence he was amazed to behold a workman in plain clothes, with a face full of mildness and doubt. Though drawn together in conversation, yet Peter makes him remain outside the mystic veil; and he must not come in and eat with the brotherhood, but sends the young man to a public eating house with the benediction that he speedily become qualified to take his meals with them.[192] In the Recognitions it soon transpires that they have all things common.

Be it remembered that Peter and the eleven, Judas being dead, were for a special purpose there at Cæsarea, from Jerusalem; and had just left the struggling, earliest brotherhood whose splendid organization had recently cost them the precious life of Stephen. Simon Magus from Samaria had come down from Tyre in a raging mood against Peter who had already called him to severe account.[193] They were to meet in a great discussion. Christianity was now born, and reason and feeling were henceforward to sway against the fallacious and moribund arbitrament of steel. Amid the preparations for this event, Clement had innocently arrived. But there is one important theory of this story yet unwound—that of Peter's call at Joppa on the way to Cæsarea, and the curious occurance at the house of Simon the tanner.

Here, in the word "House," we have enough to fill a volume; for it opens up a marvelous disclosure. In Greek, the language we get everything from, the word is kuriakos or kurioikos, which when found by the archæologists engaged in deciphering numbers of inscriptions left by these unions, means a "house of the lord."[194] This lord and his responsibility to the economic union is defined in the jus coeundi of the Solonic law and kurios occurs once in the Roman ancient law of the Twelve Tables, which transcends to us in the Di-

---

[192] *Recognitions*, Book II., c. 72, Peter informs Clement that he "cannot come with us who is not permitted to take food with anyone who has not been baptized." Book II., c. 1. shows that after seven days of waiting for Simon Magus to get ready for the discussion, he must have meantime been initiated, for we find them now partaking together, under the promise, II., c. 72, that "He who wishes soon to be baptized is separated but for a little time." Then they are found in the *Recognitions*, II., c. 72, "sleeping in the same apartment, thirteen of us in all, of whom, next to Peter, Zachæus was first, then Sophronius, Joseph and Machæus, Eliesdrus, Phineas, Lazarus, and Elisæus; after these, first, Clement and Nicodemus; then Niceta and Aquila, who had formerly been disciples of Simon." etc. Again, in same sentence, "As the evening light was still lasting we all sat down." Dr. Riddle, *Ante-Nicine Fath.*, VIII., p. 97, in commenting, suggests: "The variety and correspondence point to the use of a common basis."

[193] Cf. *Acts*, viii.. 20, 21, 22, where it is clearly seen that it was all over money-getting; Simon craving for money to bribe the proselytes with. Irenæus, *Adv. Hær.*, I., xxii., 1. also tells the story.

[194] Webster, *Dict. Eng. Lang.*, in verb. *Church:* "Church: from Gr. κυριακή, κυριακόν, the Lord's house, from κυριακός, concerning a master or lord, from κυριος, master, lord." A sentence later, Webster admits it to have been "even a heathen temple."

gest,[195] where it is quite definitely stated that kurios means power or responsible authority of control; for the organization would be invalid and illegal unless guaranteed before the world to be provided with a definite or responsible manager, and in this manner such *kurios*, the translation of which is *lord*, comes to us clothed in power to administer to the welfare of the union. The law did not know the union. That was veiled; it held its lord responsible only. We have already seen that in the Roman collegia he was the quinquennalis; for he could not be a lord unless he had served faithfully at least five years.[196] In short, he was the responsible president of the union. Peter, who had been a director since before the other lord found him at the fishing nets, was now the lord Peter, according to Clement, although still a humble workingman. So Simon the tanner was a lord or director of the tanners'[197] trade union at Joppa, placing implicit reliance upon the statement of Dr. Oehler in the Eranos Vindobonensis who, accepting, with Gibbon and Guizot, that the Acts of the Apostles be good history, announces this union among the eranoi of the ancients.

These associations were no uncommon thing in Judæa and Phœnicia at that time. A purely Phœnician inscription has been found bearing date of a pagan eranos existing at Tyre, a few miles to the north of Joppa dedicated to Baal, and showing that the membership which was large, had a colony at the Piræus, the seaport of Athens.[198] Peter, on his way to Cæsarea, was invited by this Simon the tanner at Joppa to sojourn at his "House," for a few days; and it appears that while there, as recorded in the Acts, he was shad-

[195] *Dig.*, XLVII., *tit.* xxii., 4; Gaius, 4 *Ad Legem duodecim Tabularum*: "ὃ τι ἂν τούτων διαθῶνται πρὸς ἀλλήλους, κύριος εἶναι, ἐὰν μὴ ἀπαγορεύσῃ δημόσια γράμματα." For a full quotation of this law and an account of its history and translation from the original Greek law of Solon, see *supra*, p. 4 .
[196] See *supra*, pp. 5, 6 sqq with notes. Cf. *Index*, for more.
[197] *Eranos Vindobonensis*, p. 282. Here Dr. Johann Oehler, in his dissertation on the unions of Asia, ranks in his list the tanners of Joppa who are mentioned in the *Acts:* "Gerber in Joppa erwähnt *Apostoleg.*, x., 6, 17, 23, 32," this epigraphist having no doubt of its being one of the Solonic unions.
[198] Foucart, *Ass. Rel.*, p. 103; *Archæol. Zeitung*, 1872, p. 21. It was found in an old temple, built of solid marble, almost imperishable, and consequently quite well preserved. Along with it are, a Jehovah, Saviour, another a Hermes, which appears to be Greek or Hellenistic Asian. Foucart gives the inscription in his no. 26; and in his text, p. 103, he gives it as: "l' autel qu' a consacré Ben-chodesch, fils de Baaljathon, fils d' Abdeschmoun le suffète de Citium. Que son vœu soit béni par le puissant Sachoun."

owed and hounded by police from Jerusalem, bent on oversetting his plans. The cunning money rings had discovered that Simon the Magician who was evidently their tool, was being followed by Peter who had arraigned and challenged him on the money question. Simon had made money enough at his tricks to buy a slave whom he employed as a free man. He used this as an argument for his ideas, and boasted that money being the great and all important power, was needed, wherewith to emancipate all the slaves. Peter, who was ordered to travel and propagate the new salvation without money and without scrip defeated him on these very grounds, arguing like a true socialist, that Simon was an ambitious fakir, working in the interest of the money power centered at Jerusalem. Peter seems to have escaped arrest through some miraculous agency. In reality he had a powerful friend in the person of Cornelius, and another in the secret tanners' union, where he lodged for days, hidden away, and at last came out all right at Cæsarea. This accounts for Peter's suspicion and coldness to Clement, fearing that he might be another policeman on his track. The story is perfectly consistent all through, although a little romantic.

Wonderful things are now yearly springing to light to substantiate the truthfulness and the historical reliability of this whole scheme of the origins of socialism, and its plant of an ascendant civilization.

Socrates had been a member of a genuine thiasos, either at Athens or the Piræus. So likewise Clement, who imitated him, saw the cruelties which ground the slaves and other expatriated wretches whose majorities swarmed in the world, struggling, stifling, perishing everywhere without help or hope; and Socrates lived just at the moment when the eranos and its humane brotherhoods, exclusively made up of these despised sufferers themselves, was secretly lending means out of meagre dues and fees, to deal with the Pythian Apollo, a kindly god, almost identical with Dionysus, in buying here and there a slave into liberty.[199] The great and good Socrates taught against wrong and for all right by his invention of dialectic philosophy which culminated

---

[199] Foucart, *Affranchisement des Esclaves.* See *infra,* pp. 58 sqq., notes 17-19, our description of the wonderful manner in which this used to be done under the Attic law.

THE KERUGMA, OR HORN-BLAST OF PETER. 433

in his martyrdom while it prepared the mind of his young friend Plato who stood by him at his dying hour. Socrates had been too bold and outspoken. Plato continued through subtleties of letters. These Clement and Jesus, and Justin read. Jesus saw the danger of open advocacy of the principles inherent in the eranos of Socrates and taught by parable and indirection but always to the same end.

We repeat that fresh historical and archæological evidence is at this age of scientific investigation flowing in, to verify the truthfulness of the story of the early plant, and to stultify the calumnious work of the prelates who have murdered christianity and built a sweltering hierarchy they call a church. In carrying out their plan it was necessary to burn, mutilate or rule out such evidence as that given the world through the writings of Clement, whom we have momentarily left with Peter and the Twelve just enumerated apostles. Here he tells of grimy workmen, of furnishing them constant employ, of sitting around a secret common table and learning the Kerugma Petrou which he is afterwards to write as the lost Gospel of Saint Peter.

We say fresh evidence. Yes and every year. Only now there comes a find, out of Egypt, the adopted land and home of Jesus, in shape of well-preserved sayings of this master, written in Greek upon the ancient imperishable papyrus and, except those ground away by time, in letters so plain that doubt is made impossible. These finds have been dug up at Behneseh, near the River Nile and are of the stamp of official science, being the hard-won results of archæologists, sent out from London, through the Egyptian Exploration fund about January, 1897. The press, of course, puts the date of these strange writings later than they could possibly be but more than one eminent commentator makes them earlier than A.D. 60.

Let us again look at the manner in which the Logia speak: one of them reads, as interpreted by the learned archæologists; as follows: "Jesus saith: 'wherein there are' (here occurs an illegible gap) 'alone I am with him. Raise the stone and there shalt thou find Me. Cleave the wood and there am I.'" Already this astonishing fraction of lost Gospel is calling forth a wrangling discussion. The simple meaning of this expression, covered so as to be incomprehensible to outsiders, since he speaks in enigmatical sentences to the outside world or the uninitiated, is, that he represents labor; he is the champion of the stonecutter, the mason, the carpenter. Wherever these are found there he is to encourage and lift them in the hard struggles of life. Everything in those old times had a double meaning; one, the open, the epiphanious, the other beclouded and mysterious. The initiated membership understood; the uninitiated, such as spies, could not read or understand and do them harm.

Whoever travels in oriental regions to-day is surprised at the mysterious character of the architecture left in the ruins, especially of public buildings. Vast edifices, showing a superior workmanship, but mournful in dark and windowless walls; great colonnades surrounding crypts of awful, dungeon-like vaults; thick, rock-ribbed, high-climbing partitions enclosing uncanny pocket-gulfs that darkle with a dismal air of midnight— these freaks of architecture, highly technical and correct in skilled art but repellent and distasteful to the modern conception, are not the fault of workmen but simply the echoings of the genius of their age. They befitted the mysteries which formed the immemorial structure of belief. Huge gods lived upon the mountain peaks; gorgons, giants, centaurs, fates and dragons, never seen but always present, scared or exhilarated men and women, and winged immortals now angels, now monsters flapped in the air and surged in the rivers and seas, imparting mysterious mouthings inaudible except to the sacerdotal aruspex and religion-mongers who were political officers and could deceive best and make most in money and aggrandizement by keeping their doings in darkness. It explains the two-faced double-tonguing which we of a higher enlightenment cannot understand and to which Jesus, living in it, had to conform. The one audience to whom he addressed the Word or Logos was the world; the other the initiated members of his secret brotherhood.

Thus all the new discoveries are shedding light only on the evidence that the early acts of men like Clement and Peter strongly tended to solve the problem of economical salvation of the ancient lowly; and in the case of Jesus and his evangelists, it was especially so.

A very strong evidence that the teachings of Peter and Clement were inspired from the occult habits and practices of the collegia is seen in their full indorsement of marriage In the seventh chapter of Clement's epistle to James occur the duties of officers who were to preside over the brotherhoods. The words run thus: "Above all things let them join the young in marriage betimes, anticipating the entanglements of youthful passions. Neither let them neglect the marriage of those who are already old" The idea should be kept in view that Clement wrote for Peter in almost every case, and this epistle is no exception; so that it may be regarded almost as a long letter or message from Peter to James. They advised marriage while Paul discountenanced it. Now all through the list of inscriptions of the Solonic unions we find marriage. This was apparently, of all others, the dearest of rites to the poor workingman. He had no legal right to marry if a slave, and as a freedman he had none. This right to marry and have a family, which has been the foundation rock of civilization was, as we have already shown, denied the poor. The unions practiced marriage extensively as the multitude of epitaphs show, but they did it in spite of the outside official world which desired them to delve in slavery and degradation. Paul who did not want to run counter to the law, recommended celibacy. Peter and Clement came squarely out and encouraged the practice of marriage which certainly knitted the new plant into the old unions enormously.

It elevated woman to her high, sublime dignity as a human being. It cultivated her virtue so lax and susceptible under pagan institutions. It ushered her forth as an officer in the fraternities and she became highly competent and useful in managing the entertainments. Innumerable inscriptional records attest to the usefulness of woman as an excellent, methodical factor in the success of the trade unions of the ancient world. The epitaphs are rich in mention of the life-long love and honor in which she lived with her husband and children. We shall show this when we come to the Phrygian inscriptions. She found employment in the behest of the great jus coeundi of the Solonic dispensation. She assumed this management of entertainments, and often, in underground cells, inapproachable to the hateful police, dared to convene and enjoy the innocent symposium which Xenophon graphically described; and it was the married ladies, assisted by their daughters, who planned the entertainments, worked out the scheme of pleasant, mutual enjoyment, made it an economical success, and otherwise enhanced the joys of convivials.

Clement wrote the Kerugma Petrou, the lost gospel of St. Peter.[200] This, as it is known was used by Heracleon, and by Clement of Alexandria. Hilgenfeld regards these chapters of the Recognitions touching on the Kerugma Petrou, as genuine history. Prof. Riddle admits as much, and declares that they are very old. De Rossi also contributes his newly discovered inscriptional proof of Peter.[201]

Clement accompanied Peter in his travels, after the incidents in Joppa and Cæsarea which we have detailed, and continued to be his constant companion. They went to Asia and several important places in eastern Europe, and visited the islands of the sea. He wrote accounts of the adventures, portions of which are extremely romantic and thrilling in hair-breadth escapes. These diaries, jottings and reminiscences, having survived the wreck of time, are here to shed some future light upon the dark chapter of vandalism forthcoming to the eye of fairminded history and criticism.

But the most important of all the works of Clement if we perhaps except the Kerugma Petrou, or Gospel of Peter, which is lost, are the Apostolic Canons preserved in Latin,[202] and the actual basis of the rules of the

[200] *Supernat. Rel.*, p. 384, speaking of the Clementine Homilies and the Petrine writings, says: "These works, however, which are generally admitted to have emanated from the Ebionitic party of the early church are supposed to be based upon older Petrine writings, such as the Preachings of Peter, called κήρυγμα πέτρου, and the *Travels of Peter*, Περίοδοι Πέτρου." And on p. 386: "There can be little doubt that the author was a representative of ebionitic Gnosticism which had once been the purest form of christianity." The author of this celebrated work, whoever he may be, knows nothing of the great inscriptional history of this matter, or of the Solonic unions, yet sees a long distance in the right direction.

[201] De Rossi, *Roma Sott.*, I., p. 155: "Ma ciò, che, più monta, concorde a questa osservazione e la notitia registrata nel libro pontificale della stessa secensione più antica intorno al monumento del principe degli apostoli: 'Anacletus, *Memoriam beati Petri* Construxit,' et loca ubi episcopi conderentur." Lib., *Pontifical, in Anacleto.* § ii.

[202] *Corpus Juris Civilis*. We use the work supervised by C. M. Gallisset, sub-titled *Corpus Juris Civilis*, Academicum Parisiense, 1830, and shall give pages as well as sections and numbers.

church to-day. These, although strongly impregnated with the same rules which governed the more ancient unions, and which we have elaborately set forth in the previous pages of this work, as gathered from the pre-christian eranothiasos and other pagan brotherhoods of the jus coeundi of Solon, are the basis of all that is of any practical value in christianity at this day.

Let us scan some of these canons in critical comparison with the law of the Twelve Tables of Rome.[203] Canon forty ordains as a mandate that whosoever renders a service to another, that person shall return to him nourishment and means of life. Brothers recognized and received into the living rooms to enjoy the common advantages of union must be furnished with work since that is the source of their nourishment.

It was a crime punishable with expulsion, to commit self-mutilation, and Peter and the early church ranked it as a species of murder.[204] Initiation into the new brotherhood is plainly spoken of, accompanied with the command to go forth and spread the light in the new way.[205]

We have stated in our descriptions of the pagan unions that sometimes in the initiations the candidates being admitted went into ecstasy tearing, and devouring the quivering flesh of the victims of the feast. As if the new church members were understood to be the same bodies of men and women and the same unions as we there described we find that Peter feared they might commit the same ancient ferocious barbarism in the new initiations; since he decrees against such brutalities in terse and cogent words.[206] The lesson to the student is that this christianity was planted in these old barbarous unions; and this is precisely the truth. Overwhelming

---

[203] *Canones Apostolorum*, 40, *fin.*: "Ordinavit enim lex dei, ut qui altari inserviunt, de altari nutriantur." This plainly tells us that all the brothers are to be nourished; for just above, the precept is: "Percipiat autem et ipse (si modo indiget) quantum ad neccessarios suos, et hospitio exceptorum fratrum usus opus habet, ne quo modo ipse posteriore loco habeatur, quam cæteri.

[204] *Canon. Apostolorum*, 22: "Si quis quum clericus esset, virilia sibi ipsi amputaverit, deponitor; homocida etenim sui ipsius est." "Si quis episcopus aut presbyter, in una initione non tres immersiones, sed unam duntaxat quæ in mortem Domini detur, peregerit: deponitur." Canon 49.

[205] *Canon Apost.*, 49: "In una initiatione....... profecti, docite omnes gentes, baptizantes eos in nomine Patris, et Filii et Spiritus Sancti."

[206] *Canon. Apost.*, 62: "Si quis episcopus, aut presbyter, aut diaconus, aut omnino quicunque ex sacerdotali consortio, comederit carnes in sanguine animae ejus, aut a bestiis abreptum, aut suffocatum, deponitor; hoc enim lex prohibuit. Sin vero laicus fuerit, a communione excluditor."

evidence of the inscriptions is coming to light showing this, and the scholars have brought in their attestations.

Clement, of Alexandria, who lived a hundred years afterwards, in his hortatory address to the Greeks called the Protrepticon, confesses that he belonged to a secret union, known to have been one of the pagan guilds coming under the jus coeundi of Solon and protected by the law of the Twelve Tables.[207] There can be hardly a doubt entertained but that this society into which the young, vigorous Clement was early in life initiated was one of the esseno-therapeutic unions existing at that time in Egypt and Asia in much force. We shall exhibit some newly found proof in inscriptions showing that they differed very little, if any, from the eranothiasos, having the economical idea of bread-winning in mind, and were ordinarily true labor associations.[208]

The therapeutæ are found in the inscriptions in close relation with eranoi and hetæræ, first worshiping the Isis, and then among the oldest christian inscriptions. There is a passage to this effect in Eusebius.[209] The important question which we are now endeavoring to solve is, if the therapeutæ were the very early christians, whether they were among the trade and labor unions of the Solonic dispensation; for if so, and they so early joined with the christians, it must have been to better carry out their work of furnishing the members the means of life; and the greater has been the crime

[207] Eusebius, *Præpar. Evan.*, II., 2, admits this, and that Clement backslid from the secret society, divulged, and joined the more humanized, christian union; but it looks as if the whole union became converted: "Τοῦτα δὲ Κλήμης ὁ θαυμάσιος ἐν τῷ πρὸς Ἕλληνας Προτρεπτικῷ διαρρήδην ἐκκαλύπτει, πάντων μὲν διὰ πείρας ἐλθὼν ἀνήρ, θᾶττόν γε μὴν τῆς πλάνης ἀνανεύσας, ὡς ἂν πρὸς τοῦ Σωτηρίου λόγον καὶ διὰ τῆς εὐαγγελικῆς διδασκαλίας τῶν κακῶν λελυτρωμένος."

[208] Oehler, *MSS. to the author:* "Θεραπευταί· In Alexandrien finden wir den Antonius als Mitglied einer Gesellschaft aus 12 Mitgliedern die ein Wohlleben führten und sich als σύνοδος τῶν ἀμιμητοβίων, der Brüder vom unnachahmlichen Lebenswandel bezeichnen, Plutarch, *Anton*, c. 28; diese gestaltete sich nach der Schlacht bei Actium neu als συναποθανουμένων σύνοδος, c. 71; Vgl. Terent., Adelphos, 6 und 7: "Synapothnescontes Diphili Comœdiast; eam commorientis Plautis fecit fabulam." This remarkable freakishness in the reckless direction plainly shows that more than once the therapeutae indulged in extravagancies in things disreputable.

[209] Oehler, *MSS.:* "In Kyzikos die Verehrung der Isis pflegte die Therapeutai u.s.w. wie an anderen Orten die Ἰσιασταί und Σαρπισταί, über das Verhältnis der beiden Bezeichnungen lässt sich nicht sagen, da wir dieselben nicht an einem und demselben Orte nebeneinder finden. Wendland meint die bei Eusebius genannten θεραπευταί im Aegypten seien ein Jüdischer Verein gewesen, der sich nach Analogie der Cultgenossenschaften im Dienste der Aegyptischen Gottschule genannt hatte. Nach Kraus, *Real Cyclopædia der christlichen Alterthümer*, II., p. 860, fand Eusebius die ältesten Christen Alexandriens als Θεραπευταί bezeichnet."

of depriving them of their economical object thus robbing christianity of its immediate and practically valuable function, leaving it as it appears now, in this age of growing physicism, a mere skeleton of faith without works; a ghost with wan and ghastly fingers, one digit pointing to the clouds and the other to the prelate's wallet.

But we shall prove that they were economical.[210] In the rich collection of Dr. Oehler, of the Epigraphical Seminary at Vienna, which he has taken the pains to prepare and send us, we find that therepeuts wearing black were the same in object and time, with those known to Philo in Egypt. They were hard workers, dividing a day into three equal parts; eight hours for labor, eight hours for refreshment and improvement and eight hours for sleep. This was the doctrine of the Logos and of Philo.[211] We give in the foot-notes several, with this learned doctor's suggestions.[212] The melanephoroi who wore the black, the therapeutæ and the bag-carriers were all hard-working laborers who worked about the wharves, loaded and unloaded ships and boats and earned an existence as best they could in the ordinary ancient poverty and rags.[213]

Gibbon speaks of these therapeutæ who inhabited the shores of the lake Mœoris near Alexandria,[214] and as much as admits that their work was that of loading and unloading ships. Dr. Oehler, who gave considerable

---

[210] Oehler, *MSS.*, cites: "Ein Verein von Aerzten in Ephesos, ist bezeichnet als οἱ ἐν Ἐφέσῳ ἀπὸ τοῦ Μουσίου ἰάτροι. Der Verein hat ein Legat erhalten und ist mit der Aufsicht über ein Grabmal betraut. Wood, *Discov. at Ephesus*; *Inscr. from Tombs*, No. 7. Vergleichsweise führe ich auch die Gennossenschaft (therapeutic) der Medici in Benevent., CIL., IX., no. 1618; und Rom., CIL., VI., 9566."

[211] Hesiod, *Erga kai Hemerœ*, holds to this as the natural division of men's time, ordained by Jehovah. He is the first authority on ancient theogony, for the Eight-Hour day.

[212] Oehler, *MSS.*, Θεραπευτωί: "Sehen wir wohl im Dienste welcher Gottheiten wir sie finden. Οἱ μελανηφόροι καὶ θεραπευταί in Delos erscheinen als Dedikanten einer Statue an Serapis, Isis, Anubis, Harpokratos, in zwei Inscriptions, *Bull. Hell.*, VII. 1882, p. 318, nr. 3; und Monuments grecs, 1879, p. 40, während CIGr., 2295 uns eine Weihung der Priester der μελανηφόροι καὶ θεραπευταί für das Volk der Athener und der Römer an Isis, δικαιοσυνη nennt."

[213] Again, Oehler, *MSS.:* "ΜΕΔΑΝΗΦΟΡΟΙ' ΘΕΡΑΠΕΥΤΑΙ'. Auch die μελανηφόροι erklären sich am besten, dass auch sie ein Cultverein, oder vielleich eine besondere Gruppe der θεραπευταί waren nicht aber wie Lafaye will, eine Brüderschaft von Mönchen der Isis." What he means is that they were ordinary workers.

[214] Gibbon, *Decl. and Fall*, xv., and note 162: "The extensive commerce of Alexandria.... gave an early entrance to the new religion. It was at first embraced by great numbers of therapeutae, or essenes of the lake Mœeris or Moriotes, a Jewish sect which abated much of its reverence for the Mosaic ceremonies."

attention to this strange therapeutic branch of black wearers, brings under contribution more inscriptional evidence from the slabs.[215] Some very important mentions are adduced by him which now remind us that the therapeutæ were numerous at places planted into by Peter, John, Clement and perhaps Paul. They were in force at Ephesus, Antioch, Heraclea, Laodicea and other cities of the seven churches of Asia.[216] He has studied the consecrations at Christmas feasts and Greek terms found on inscriptions conveying this meaning, and although cautious about expressing an opinion, appears satisfied that the therapeuts and black clothes wearers so frequently found here must represent unions utilized by the evangelists.

But by far the most convincing specimen of these discoveries among the mossy stones which seem to be just now grinning a triumphant antithesis belying the religious idealists who want christianity not to be a growth but a miracle, is the astounding chiseling that the therapeutæ and thiasoi had apostles whom they sent out as evangelists, long before the Messiah of Judæa arrived.[217] These were strictly industrial societies, their chief object being the making of a living, but like all things ancient they assume more or less a religious phase. Having the self-same name they come down to us mixed up with our religion. They were obliged under the law to imitate the form of the political city; and as the ancient city was religious, its priests, sacrifices, sources of revenue and kuriakoi being imbued with religion, every priest, soothsayer, clerk of the oracle and army officer,

---

[215] Oehler, *MSS.*: "Θεραπευταί und μελανηφόροι. Ueber diese Cultgemeinde im Dienste der Ægyptischen Gottheiten und der Syrischen 'Αφρόδιτε sind verschiedene Ansichten ausgesprochen worden. Vgl. Lüders, *Bulletino Archæol.*, 1874, p. 105; Schäffer, *De Deli Insulæ Rebus*, p. 191f; Lafaye, *Histoire du Culte des Divinités d' Alexandrie*, u.s.w; Hauteville Regnault, im *Bull. Hell.*, VI., 1882, p. 479, etc."

[216] Oehler, *MSS.*: "Wir erfahren auch von Weihungen einzelner μελανηφόροι die deswegen interessant sind weil sie auch die Heimath der betreffenden Leute nennen, so kennen wir zwei Weihungen des Κτήσιππος Κτησίππου, Χτος μελανηφόρος an Isis, CIGr. 2294, und an Horos, 'Αθήναον, IV., 1875, p. 460, nr. 11. Dann hat Θεόφιλος Θεόφιλου 'Αντεοχεύς μελανηφόρος bedeutende Arbeiten herstellen lassen an dem Heiligthume, als Weihung an Sarapis, Isis, Anubis und Harpokrates, CIGr. 2297."

[217] Oehler, *MSS.*: "Auser Delos finden wir θεραπευταί in Demetrias; Athen., *Mitth.*, VII., 1882, p. 335, neben ἀπόστολοι, wohl des Sarapis, Kyzikoi 2 Namenlisten der θεραπευταί, *Rev. Archéol.*, n. s.. XXXVIII., 1879, p. 258, und Σύλλογος, VIII., p. 172; *Wiener Numismatische Zeitschrift*, XXII., 1889, p. 50ª. Die dabei genannte Isis ist die Isis Pelagia, die in Kyzikos verehrt wurde." He also mentions several more inscriptions found at Ephesus showing brotherhoods of the same who had apostles, and who consecrated to Diana, also two from Chios.

a paid political servant,[218] we cannot wonder that they pretended to adore their conscript gods and godesses. They were always labor societies of the Solonic type, dissatisfied with their surroundings, and when the new faith presented itself they endorsed it and built up the future civilization.

But as the Solonic unions of which these Judaic and Egyptian therapeuts[219] were a part, were closely secret, so also were the first christian brotherhoods secret, and no one but an initiate was allowed recourse to them. This is certified to by John Chrysostom in his history of the early times.[220]

We may be told that policy forbids, even at this late day, that we drag forth this fundamental fact, that christianity is the work of such hives of labor.[221] The reply is, that we are not writing a history of the ancient poor on any basis of policy. Whoever writes up the poor man must hold in contempt all allurements of policy and rise to the majesty of truth. Thus the two men, Peter and Clement, worked together, leading a secret life, and whenever they were traveling they were certainly welcomed and entertained in the mysterious "house of the lord," the inner facts of which have never before the writing of these pages been explained. Yet it is a pithy subject; and we should ourselves have remained in the dark but for the numerous disclosures coming to light through the inscriptions. There was a lord for Peter and Paul at every hand and wherever they went; and this lord of the "House" was a kurios or president of one or another of the secret trade and labor unions of Solon's jus coeundi, which at that time prove to have existed in great numbers all over the known world. We leave them at their evangelizing

[218] We have already given the law ordaining this and now give Mommsen's quote from *Coll. et Sodal. Rom.*, p. 120. The law in the *Dig.*, lib. III., iv., § 1, reads: "Quibus permissum est corpus habere collegii, societatis sive cujusque alterius eorum nomine, proprium est ad exemplum reipublicæ habere res communes, arcam communem." etc.

[219] Gibbon, speaking of the essenes and therapeutæ, says that: "It still remains probable that they changed their names, preserved their manners, and adopted some new article of faith." *Decline and Fall*, Vol I., p. 283, note 162.

[220] Chrysostom, Folio edition of the Benedictines, Vol. X., p. 347, Latin: "Qui non erant initiati, ad omnia audiendi non admittebantur." Again, IX., p. 84, their habit of sitting at the common table: "Initiati tantum sacram mensam tangere audebant." In Vol. VIII., p. 25, he disposes of their primitive methods: "Initiatorum pacta."

[221] Livy sneers down the vulgar workingmen to express the then universal contempt: "Opificum vulgus et sellularii, minime militiæ idoneum genus." *Hist.*, VIII., 20, 4.

work and proceed to unveil some of the mysteries of the "House," so frequently mentioned in the Bible and yet so little understood.

During the reign of Claudius, there was a great persecution of the christians, not only at Rome but all over pro-consular Asia, of which very little is said by the historians. Gibbon passes it by without a mention, beginning his celebrated ten persecutions with that of Nero. One good ancient author, Suetonius, adorns his life of Claudius with but an exiguous proffer of three lines.[222] His announcement, however, being the first pagan historian of note, is valuable, as it contains the first historic mention of Jesus Christ, after that of Josephus. Dion Cassius talks of them but does not say the christians, blaming it all on the Jews.

Claudius fell upon struggling unions of Rome, many of which had long enjoyed the protection of Augustus and Tiberius and for years had been employed by these emperors in their gynæcia, becoming incorporated with the Domus Augustalis, as the special servants of the first Augustan monarchs. The first calamity they encountered was instituted by Caligula who indiscriminately murdered all in sight and bemoaned the neglect of nature in forgetting to combine all Romans into a single person so that one blow of his bloody axe might sever the heads of all at a single stroke. The delight at seeing the river of blood such as Caligula's atrocious spirit conceived, made him wild with truculent disappointment, since this imperial maniac had no higher vision than to behold a lurid stream of gore. They killed the monster to rescue Rome, and the wretched empire fell into the hands of another assassin.

Claudius assumed the imperial ermine A.D. 47, and immediately began his persecutions of the christians then treated as Jews, the word christianity being at that early date unknown. They were Nazarenes. This made the poor Hebrews answerable for all the hatred against christians at Rome. But we know from the meager lines of Suetonius that Claudius expelled these

---

[222] Suet, *Claud.*, c. 25: speaking of the acts of that monarch, says: "Judæos, impulsore Christo, assidue tumultuantes Roma expulit." But Gibbon fails to understand that Claudius banished large numbers causing a great persecution, of which mention is made many times in the *New Testament*, and which accounts for some very curious things yet to be mentioned.

christians in great numbers from Rome. Probably he and his watchful police carried out the decree so far as to believe that the christians had all left Rome. Not at all. Many drooped down into the subterranean recesses of darkness and for ages lived in their communal scholæ, teaching, educating, struggling for a living, while partaking in common with one another according to plans of Jesus, carried out by Peter, Stephen and Clement, the Melancthon of Peter the lord.

We now come to the evidences of this history. Dr. Ramsay has recently explained some strange discoveries in far off Phrygia, showing a colony of these outcasts, who settled, with their industries, in Apameia. This we have fully given in the general history of Solon's unions. We now pay attention to their christianizing action. Imbued with the new, tenets, they started up their old industries at Kelænæ, a suburb of Apameia, a Phrygian city already full of trade unions, and whose inhabitants were well acquainted with the harmless manners and useful employments of these people. At Kelainæ is a high eminence called in ancient times an acropolis. On the summit of this acropolis was an old temple of Jehovah, if we are allowed to call it after the Hebrew god, or Zeus, Jove, if Greek.

Just recently there have come to light two archæological points connected with our history, to wit: the discovery of an ancient industrial street down in the town which used to be called shoemakers' street, inhabited by, and the home and shop-ground of the members of numerous trade unions of that craft.

The fact now comes to light that the temple of the old god on the summit of the acropolis was the place of worship of the shoemakers of shoemakers' street. The numerous inscriptions attesting this have been carefully collected by Dr. Ramsay and published in his work on the Cities and Bishoprics of Phrygia. The lesson conveyed by this important find is that the shoemakers, some of whom were the exiles driven from Rome by the edict of Claudius, and others, the original inhabitants of the city of Apameia and its suburbs, were early converts to the new christianity's faith, and that many of them were Jews. They attended the old temple of Jove, extended the double influence of members and means, secured a refuge from persecution, in the old vaults of the pagan asylum and in course of time the whole institution became a kuriakos or church of the christian sect.

Claudius drove great numbers of Jews and christianized Jews out of Rome about A.D. 45. This is history. Among those driven away were Aquila and Priscilla well-known to us through the writings of Paul and the Acts of the Apostles. Hundreds of hitherto useful and faithful workers in the domus Augustalis under the emperor Tiberius and consequently known to be members of the Roman collegia were thus peremptorily ordered into banishment. Aquila and Priscilla went to Corinth where they labored with Paul. Others went to Phrygia and settled, some in Apameia, some in Ephesus and many in other cities and towns. The Greek name for their colonies or settlements was ktesis. This word frequently occurs in the inscriptions. It appears that the exiles first sought a refuge in the old temple of Zeus on the acropolis of Kelænæ, and probably at first did not speak Greek; for we find bi-lingual inscriptions half Latin, half Greek, and with bad grammar in both.[223] Among the dozens of inscriptions of this group there occurs one which shows that at first these colonists were unwelcome to the people of the city and that the authorities were about to drive them away fearing that the rigor of the Claudian edict might also entangle them; but a compromise was reached whereby the refugees paid to the city a sum of money, which we suspect must have been furnished by the other similar unions in secret sympathy. At any rate they remained there for ages and went down with their leather industry to the slums of shoemaker street, prospered and in course of time were able to contribute a good sum out of the common fund of their brotherhood to bear the expense of the monument.[224] Dr. Ramsay thinks that in the shoe-

---

[223] Ramsay, *Cities and Bishoprics of Phrygia*, II., p. 474, inscription, no. 329, is a specimen. It is one of their later epitaphs. The Latin paraphrase is in CIL., III., 367, no. 7056. The Greek runs as follows: "Οὐαλέριος Ἰουλιανὸς καὶ Κασσία Κουαρτεῖνα ἡ γυνὴ αὐτοῦ ζῶντες καὶ φρονοῦντες ἑαυτοῖς ἐποίησαν τὸ ἡρῷον καὶ τὴν κατάγαιον καμάραν· εἰς ἣν ἕτερος οὐ τεθήσεται. κ.τ.λ."

[224] The epitaph which we quote in a previous note is not of the date A. D. 170, only in that the inscr. was chiseled then; for Valerius Julianus the member announced, was driven to the Apameian κτῆσις under refuge of the Kelæniae asylum by Claudius. Many years after, his successors in fond remembrance, erected the heroon to his memory, and chiseled the inscription. Ramsay himself admits in another place that this was common.

makers he has found ancient guilds. We do not think
it worth while to quarrel about this designation, but they
were not guilds such as were so numerous in the middle
ages. Guilds were degenerate successors of the trade
unions of earlier days, and were subservient creatures
of petty lords, while the trade unions were self-sustaining,
independent organizations, having no intercourse
whatever with speculating bosses, and being owners
of their own little all. Besides they had the manhood
to be voting unions and were, to a certain extent, political,
constantly on the lookout for the public work,
not only in cities, but, as proved by abundant evidence
afforded in their inscriptions which we constantly quote,
they were all over the Roman empire engaged on a
very considerable scale, in doing the national tasks of
manufacturing arms, building public edifices, constructing
military roads, furnishing music for entertainments,
public banquets and other government work in great
variety. For this work, then, they are known by many
of their writings, especially at Pompeii, to have used a
strong secret political ballot, not only for their own members,
but men of the wealthier ranks, and by this means
secured political friends at the head of such public service
who promised to give them the jobs. It was probably
in this manner that the Roman collegia got their strong
foot-hold in the Domus Augustalis or palace of the
Cæsars, which they were enjoying during the times of
Tiberius. There were great numbers of them converted
during the benign reign of this monarch, to christianity;
but they came to grief soon after his assassination by the
enemies which compassed the defeat of his movement
to recognize Jesus as a divine and wise being, and his
converts as worthy of protection.[225]

[225] Dr. Ramsay, "Cities and Bishoprics of Phrygia," II., pp. 459, 460, inscr., 290, contributes another interesting proof of the colonization of these outcasts, which we must mention. It bears date of A.D. 54-55, or persecution of Claudius. After this author, and Mommsen, have devoted two pages to it, we arrive at this conclusion: Lucius, third son of Lucius and Pamplia, Lucius Poplius, Marcus Viccius, son of Marcus, and P. Marcus Onesimus, the latter a freedman, and three others, illegitimate sons of Roman emperors, are driven from their γερουσία, or converted collegium at Rome, by Claudius. They settle in Phrygia, at the Apameian κτῆσις —See no. 305, p. 468.— At home there is money among the brotherhoods escaping banishment by hiding in the under-ground scholæ we have described. The Apameians are terrorized because of their advent and refuge at the temple. Here we think we detect a slight mistake of the learned Doctor. Our respectful suggestion is that the five Romans mentioned are not curatores conventus civium Romanorum at all,, but more probably, quinquinales collegiorum, who became by the mere change of place and language, each an ἄρχων, or

But we are not confined to the splendid work of Dr. Ramsay for this important information on the conversion of pagan hetaeræ and eranoi into economic brotherhoods of the early christians, and the mutual adoption and endorsement of the old socialism and life economies without change. Dr. Oehler has also recently contributed specimens of archæological evidence of the same character and at the same place.[226] The Apameian discoveries are all very important because this city, then a large and flourishing commercial emporium of western Asia, was full of labor unions as early as B. C. 133, when Eunus who was undoubtedly a member of one of the Phrygian associations of Dionysan artists, and a member of the Great Gemeinde, was seized as a war prisoner and carried off in slavery to become one of Rome's most powerful, desperate and successful rebels as we have fully portrayed in the first volume of this work.

We here present the entire inscription in two columns as they appear on the stone.[227] They speak of the altar being the result of the enterprise of the members' common fund and both contain the record that they were ἄρχων or ἐρανάρχος ἑταιρῶν at the Apameian Κτῆσις. With secret aid bringing it from the mother college, they offer the Apameians an ἐπιζήον "to gain the right of forming a corporate body." Many Greek-speaking shoemakers, coral workers, marble cutters and others joined, became converts, used the temple for a church, and in time, changed the old asylum on the acropolis from the temple of Jehovah or Zeus into a sanctuary of their own; "Eran. Vind.," 280, Σκυτικὴ Πλάτεια in 'Ἀπάμεια Κελαίναι "Rev. Etud. g.," II., Le Bas, III., 656: "ἡ ἱερὰ φυλὴ τῶν σκυτέων."

[226] Oehler, "MSS." 'Ἀπάμεια, Κιβοτες. "Bull. Hell., VII., 1883, p. 207, no. 29. ἐγποριάρχη........ συμπουδασαντων κὲ τῶν συμβιωτῶν καβάλλων —Maionia, CIG. 3438: ἱερὰ συμβίωσις· καὶ γεωτέρα, and refers to another, CIG, 3304 τῆ συμβιώσις τῶν Συπιγάλων, and mentions Wagener, "Rev. de l' Instruction Publique en Belgique," n. s. XI., 1869, p. 11, vermuthet συμπιλεαδείς oder Filzarbeiter." These are all Christian trade-unions. Several more are mentioned.

[227] Ramsay, "Cities and Bishoprics of Phrygia," 294, 295. (R. 1887) Mommsen, "Eph. Ep.," VII., p. 437, Weber, p. 45.

ἡ βουλὴ κ[αὶ ὁ δῆμος καὶ
οἱ] κατοικοῦ[ντες 'Ρωμαῖ-
οι ἐτείμησα[ν Τ]ιβέριον
Κλαύδιον Τιβερίου Κλαυ-
5 δίου Πείσωνος Μιθρι-
δατιανοῦ υἱὸν Κυρείνᾳ
Γρανιανὸν, γυμνασιαρ-
χοῦντα δί ἀγοραίας ἐκ
τῶν ἰδίων τῇ γλυκυτά-
10 τῇ πατρίδι δίχα τοῦ πόρου τοῦ ἐκ τοῦ δημοσίου
διδομένου· τὴν ἀνασ-
τασιν ποιησαμένων
ἐκ τῶν ἰδίων τῶν ἐν τῇ
15 Σκυτικῇ Πλατείᾳ τεχνει-
τῶ.

['Η βουλὴ καὶ ὁ δῆμος καὶ οἱ
κατοικοῦντες 'Ρωμαῖοι ἐτείμησαν]
Τι. Κλαύδιον Τι. Κλαυδίου [Μιθρι-
δάτου υὸν Κυρείνᾳ Πείσωνα
5 Μιθριδατιανόν, ἱερέα διὰ βίου
Διὸς Κελαινέως, ἐφηβαρχήσαντα
καί γυμνασιαρχήσαντα καὶ ἀγορα-
νομήσαντα διὰ ἀγοραίας καὶ ὑπεσ-
χημένον ὑπὲρ τοῦ υἱοῦ Κλαυδίου
10 Γρανιανοῦ γυμνασιαρχίαν δι' ἀγοραίας ἐκ τῶν ἰδίων δίχα πόρου τοῦ
διδομένου ἐκ τοῦ δημοσίου δηνα-
ρίων μυρίων πεντακ. χειλίων·
τὴν ἀνάστασιν ποιησαμένων
15 ἐκ τῶν ἰδίων τῶν ἐν τῇ Σκυτικῇ
Πλατείᾳ τεχνειτῶν

'Επιμεληθέντων Παπίου Δείδα τοῦ Αἰδούχου καὶ Τυράννου Μύτα καὶ Λουκίου Μουννατίου Ἄνθου καὶ Τρύφωνος Διογᾶ.

tradesmen of Shoemaker street in Kelænæ, a suburb of Apameia. We may venture to here note a running paragraph of this inscription for the convenience of the reader. An eranos, honors a workingman of this Shoemakers' street:

The council, meaning probably, council of the union, and neighbors herewith connected who are Romans, erect and dedicate a holy altar to the honor of Tiberius Claudius, son of Tiberius and Cyrena, daughter of Mithradates, for life, as a token of his faithful services. He was master of the gymnasium, and president of the board of public works in the beloved fatherland. They do this out of their own resources at an expense of 15,000 denaria. The reward and hope of resurrection springs from their own membership and from among themselves, being working people and artisans of Shoemakers' street, a suburb of Kelænæ, city of Apameia.[228] Dr. Ramsay has mentioned this very early and important collection of some twenty or more inscriptions in and around Apameia in several places of his work on Phrygia.[229]

Apameia was, as it were, a hot-bed of these organizations and presents a rich field for our explorations, especially as many of the members appear to have been victims of the Claudian persecution. We have an inscription found recently which mentions a gerousia, a word much misunderstood until Dr. Oehler brought out its true relationship to the thiasos and other unions of trade and labor. He shows in various inscriptions the folly of placing the gerousia in any other category.[230]

[228] Ramsay, "Cities and Bishoprics of Phrygia, II., p. 513, note headed "Earlier Chr. Inscr.." It may be well to quote this excellent authority: "The ruined church of very early date, which perhaps, occupies the site of the temple of Keleneus, p. 462, on the acropolis of Kelainai, has been best described by Weber, pp. 34 ff, see also my paper in "Transactions Ecclesiolog. Soc.," Aberdeen, 1880, pp. 2 ff. On one of the large blocks of which its walls are composed is engraved no. 397. Several crosses are incised in the walls. In view of probable excavation of this interesting church, a description of the ruins is unnecessary."

[229] Ramsay, "id.," p. 492. "The Zeus of the ancient city of Kelainai, beside Apameia, is known from coins with the legend, 'ΖΕΥΣ ΚΕΛΕΝΕΥΣ. The early Christian church whose ruins are still seen on the summit of the citadel, has perhaps taken the place of the temple of Zeus." His various mentions of the Apameian find will be seen on pp. 417, 440, 461, 462, 613, and 538.

[230] Ramsay, "Cit. Bish. Phryg.," II., pp. 469, 470: "Τὸ σεμνότατον συνέδριον τῶν γερόντων Τιβέριον Αἴλιον Σατουρνεῖνον Μαρεινιανὸν τὸν ἴδιον κτίστην, ἔγγονον ἀρχιερέων, καὶ ὑπατικῶν συγγενῆ. Ἐπιμεληθέντος τῆς ἀναστάσεως Μάρκου Φορβιανοῦ ἄρχοντος τῶν γερόντων, Ramsay thinks this Aelius Saturninus Marianianus was a Roman who had done some meritorious deed, favoring the Gerousia.

The number, three hundred and six, of Ramsay is another gerousia and Oehler testifies, after the close of his investigation, that it is certainly a trade union of Apameia and belongs to the same group with the shoemakers. Clearly it is a ktesis or settlement of the banished Romans, like the others, taking the name gerousia as a council of christian elders, but involved in an industry.

During those dark days of the Claudian persecution when thousands were being expelled under an accusation that they were tumultous Jews led on by one Christ to introduce insufferable heresies, establishing in the Roman city the worship of a new divinity,[231] there were many who escaped by hiding themselves under the aegis of the goddess Diana who possessed a famous temple on the Aventine Hill. The spite of the official priesthood against her culminated in the reign of Nero which we shall soon picture in our history of the great conflagration. There came to Apameia another refugee who is shown by an inscription[232] to be a Roman, and brought or organi ed a christian union there, although it is not shown that the association was in Shoemakers' street. It adds another evidence, showing that the economical incentive, leading to the furnishing of members of the brotherhoods with work and food for life's subsistence, was an important and powerful, if not the principal one in those earlier days.

The occurance of several Bible names in these inscriptions of Phrygia is causing a good deal of discussion. Apphia, a daughter of Papias and mother of Hesychius, was the kuria or president of one of these unions which dedicated a mounment with money taken from the common fund and earnings of the whole union of sixty-two people.[233] In the body of Greek Inscrip-

---

[231] See supra, chapter on Martyrs.

[232] Ramsay, "Cit. Bish. Phr.," II., p. 470, inscr. no. 307: "Γάϊον Ἀντίστιον Γαίαν υἱὸν Οὐέτερα τὸν ἑαυτῶν δικαιότατον πατρῶνα Μνησίφιλος Ἀττάλου καὶ Φίλισκος καὶ Διοκλῆς Διοκλέους Μητροπολῖται." Three natives of Metropolis place the inscription in Apameia as the meeting place of the conventus. Pliny, V., 106, to a Roman official. Consuls C. Antistius Vetus are known in B.C. 30, 36, A.D. 23, 50, 96, and L. Antistius Vetus, A.D. 55." The inscription is thus as early as Claudius.

[233] Ramsay, "Cit. Bish. Phryg.," II., p. 470, no. 309: "Ἀπφία Παπίου μήτηρ Ἡσύχῳ ἐνποριάρχῃ τέκνῳ καὶ αἰαυτῃ ἐποίησε τό ἡρῷον ἐκ τῶν ἰδίων, σπουδασάντων κὲ τῶν συμβιωτῶν κὲ λβ' ἄλλων. Ἥρως χρηστὲ χαῖρε. It is a christian mechanical συμβίωσις or economic brotherhood. Apphia the emporiarch built and dedicated this sarcophagus out of the union's funds. Paul speaks of Apphia in connection with Philip.

tions there are recorded a good many names, which have been closely investigated by modern archæologists, quite a number of which are fully ascertained to have been the same persons spoken of in the writings of Paul; and as these palæographic mentions are good history we shall give space to their presentation in the proper place.

Let us now look briefly at the coral workers and the masons of Thermal street, situated not far from Shoemaker street in the Apameian suburb, Kelænæ, and see them using the same old temple of Jove and its ancient asylum of refuge along with the shoemakers themselves. Several inscriptions of the coral workers appear.[234] The epigraphists, innocent of the labor element pervading these curious chiselings, have not conceived the true meaning of the word which in Greek expresses workers in coral. Again, a t has been cut instead of an l, or more probably age and the erosions of weather have obscured the original enough to make it resemble a t; so that the word coral was not comprehended. Dr. Oehler in his lists published in the Eranos Vindobonensis and elsewhere,[235] speaks of these coral workers in Magnesia, and we gather from him that they were image makers who made a business of manufacturing fashionable objects out of the red coral obtained from the seas.

These coral workers appear to have had their union quarters in a street where there was a thermal spring. Whether there is still a hot spring in this suburb of

[234] Ramsay, *Cit. Bish. Phr.*, II., p. 462, no. 296. We print 297 in note 227. The two are similar to 294, 295, or the shoemakers' street guild. But the inscrs. are in the under part of the epistyle and once ornamented a stoa. They talk of κουράτορας, changing λ to τ, and must have certainly been coral workers, such as Dr. Oehler finds at Laodicea and Hierapolis. They had their seat and industry in the Thermal street, Θερμαία Πλατεία. Like 394-5, they paid the expenses of the monument here commemorated, ἐκ τῶν ἰδίων τῶν ἐν τῇ Θερμαία Πλατεία τεχνειτῶν. This last word is not in 396-7, but is in 394-5 and working people are in both cases clearly meant. There is little doubt but that they were all allied to the great Gemeinde of the Dionysan artists. Though they were in all probability illegitimate offspring of the Roman Tiberii and Claudii, as their names indicate, yet they were loved and honored long after their colonization in the Phrygian home.

[235] *Eran. Vindob.*, p. 277-278: "Κοραλλιοπλάσται· nach Blümer und den Lexicis; die kleine Bilder aus Korallen machen; nach Büchsenschütz: Arbeiter welche korallen aus dem Steine coralliticus nachahmten: *Magnesia ad Sipylum:* CIG. 3408." Again, *id*, p. 279: παρόντων καὶ τῶν κοραλλιοπλαστῶν καθ' ὃ εἰς ἐκόμισεν βυβλίον διὰ Σωκράτου ἐπὶ Τ. Ἀτ. Εὐτυχιανοῦ ταμίου." And also p. 282: Die Κοραλλιοπλάσται in Magnesia....beantragen für die σύνοδος. Liebenam in his work, p. 113, thinks that the coral-workers, κοραλλιοπλάσται were constituted an association of workingmen who carved beautiful objects out of red coral and sold them as jewelry. Κοράλλιον καὶ πλάξω. They made and sold great quantities of red-coral bijous, mostly popular pagan religious ornaments.

Apameia we are not informed. Similarly to the Shoemaker street unions, the coral workers had their residences in Hot Spring street, but worshiped in the chapel all together on the mount. Dr. Ramsay thinks these guilds were a Lydian institution, which probably arises from the well-known scripture of Lydia, the woman converted by Paul, who was an officer in the sales department of a great trade union of dyers at Laodicia on the Lycus river, of which we shall treat in the proper place.

It is enough here to say that the beautiful honesty of christianity was gladly accepted by these guilds of Shoemakers' street and Warm Springs street, and that for centuries they worked for one another, partook of each others' bounties, ate in companies of many at their common table, and sang together, to the glee of the children and the joy of the communal family the hymns, some of which may in the disclosures of an inquisitive future, be found to resemble our old Methodist melodies of age untraceable, that have come down in traditional form to us from the ancient working people. So far as we are able to penetrate by the use of inscriptional evidence, the character of those unions was that of our modern Methodists who sometimes repair to the woody retreats in the mountains among the springs and the chirping birds, and sing their praises in a high key, reveling in music and in oratory, to the praise of the same Lord, and with rapturous love for the same Saviour. These joys which were later suppressed by the great massacre of Diocletian and the prelates at the council of Laodicea, did not die out. They continue to this day, imparting to the children of men a wholesome status of morals and a happy life, though in the desperate greed for individual distinction and property they have lost the fraternal common table and the ancient economic brotherhood which once made them supremely delightful.

Let us now turn our attention to the celebrated "House of the lord." In ancient days there was always a building belonging to each so-called guild which was used in common by the membership. This building, originally a temple was destined to become the typical church. The house of the lord receives a large share of mention by the apostles of the primitive church; and it now leaks out through inscriptions that it was the original temple of the converted unions, and used as an asylum or secret retreat from persecutions, and a meeting house for the propaganda.

It has been erroneously argued by many opposed to the modern christianity because it fails to bring into the world the conditions it promised and has proved a blank disappointment especially to the lowly and poor, that there is no adequate evidence extant that christianity ever had a foothold, and some defy us to prove that there ever was such a personage as Jesus Christ. Not only have great orators appeared and careered, holding these views, but such is the disappointment at the dereliction of this culture, that, among the masses countless numbers are found prone to believe it; and in the absence of a plan less disappointing, are but too willing to sink humanity back into the old pagan state.

We are not writing this work in defense of religion. Nor do we chase gossamers in quest of a solution for the problem of labor. We shall only present facts such as substantiate the authenticity of history. Unbelievers deny that this personage is a factor in history. Here only are we going to set up our protest, for the reason that persons who deny the author of the promulgation of the cult which originated socialism and mutual love and care as opposed to the paganism based on competitive antagonisms and survival of the fittest, are perfectly willing to introduce among historical personages every one else if he, or she, be honored with a record among respectable historians.

Those reading the recent archæology and topography of Phrygia; those learned enough to comprehend the new disclosures of the commander De Rossi on the diggings of under-ground Rome; those capable to read his hundred inscriptional mentions of new-found Scripture names; those fortunate enough to possess the printed and pictured labors of Le Blant in Gaul, of Foucart, Lüders, Oehler, Wagner and a dozen others in Asia Minor, Greece and Macedon, will, on their perusal, be willing to deny a paltry empiricism and except as true the seven mentions of the crucified carpenter by Josephus, the two by Suetonius, the important one by Tacitus, the nine by the early writers of the Augustan histtory, the innumerable references from Lucian, Celsus, and sharp hints by Dion Cassius, Philo and Galen, also the large number of plain mentions in letters by Trajan, Hadrian, Mark Aurelius emperors, and their appointed governors over sections of the Roman empire, like Pliny who, with Trajan's answers, early mentioned Christ and christians more than a hundred times.

But whoever is dilligent and honest enough to investigate these extant records, will soon find himself convinced of the profound secrecy which the authors of this culture endured and the absolute terror which for ages palsied the growth and stifled the knowledge of mankind regarding it.[236] For our own part, we have collected the evidences of ancient hatred against the masses who were compelled to labor, and found that whether as slaves or freedmen they were under scathing contempt on every hand, and if they attempted to raise themselves by organization to a condition even of self-respect, it had to be done with the greatest secrecy. Unorganized, the workman was but a foot-ball to be kicked about in the most horrible manner conceivable, and he was without a law. But laws for his abuse were plentiful. He could be beheaded for making a slight mistake in his work.[237] If it was so easy to inflict deadly punishment upon the lowly workingman as late as the fourth century, what should be expected if he were caught organizing as vast a system as christianity in opposition to the prevailing scheme of contempt and cruelty, contained in the ancient paganism, in the days of Caligula and Claudius? And can the modern opponents of that vast scheme with any reason wonder why it did not set the world ablaze with literature of its own or draw upon the popular sycophants who as now cur-

---

[236] Ramsay, *Cities and Bishoprics of Phrygia*, II., p. 739, devotes nearly a page of unintelligible figures and monograms, which he calls the signs by which chr. inscrs. used to be designated, by the initiated, varying only slightly from inscrs. of the outside pagan literature. These slight differences thwarted the police for generations. On pp. 489, 490, 491, 492, he gives types of these signs which long decieved the Roman authorities. Not only in Asia Minor but also all over Gaul these deceptions were practiced in order to avoid persecution. Le Blant, *Inscrs. de la Gaul*, I., p. 76 sq. See also pp. 149, 158, 402. Ramsay, II., p. 505, says; "We are therefore forced to look for meanings hidden beneath the surface in the early christian epitaphs."

[237] Levasseur, *Hist. Classes Ouv.*, I., p. 39: "La négligeance était punie des peines les plus sévères; les teinturiers qui brulaient ou tâchaient une étoffe étaient décapités. *Cod. Just.*, lib. X.. *tit.* xxii., *lex.* 4. Vel si contra hoc fecerent. gladio feriantur.'"

ried favor with monarchs and high-blooded boasters of grace and power? The trouble with these modern freethinkers who justly detest the failure of that ancient scheme to carry out its plan of salvation is, that they are ignorant of comparative history and cannot see the work of the property power or the pestilent power of ambition in men who early sidetracked the pure and splendid scheme of those ancient socialists. In blind ravings they eschew the overwhelming evidence that it had its authorship in strictly historical characters. We proceed to disentangle some of the mazy web and to bring to the light of civilization truth such as will stanch forever the tongues of our unripe orators.

We now propose to follow the evidence of anaglyphic science in proof that the christians planted and thrived during the first century, into the old trade unions; and select three well-known Biblical characters whom we have found to have been members of the ancient guilds, namely; Priscilla, Aquila and Lydia.

Saul or Paul, whom we left at the lynching of Stephen by the maddened Jews because his system of supplying the common table of the large membership of the Petrine brotherhood and the communal code, purchasing direct and at wholesale, spoiled the profit system of the provision ring, became converted to the new doctrine, and being a man of excellent education and large conscience metamorphosed and became a zealous advocate of the very thing which in comparative boyhood he had sought to destroy. In his travels and multitudinous exhortations through Asia Minor and Macedonia, and after making a celebrated speech on the Athenian Acropolis, he arrived at Corinth. Here in this great mart, the most populous of all cities except Rome, the seat of the abominations of the goddess Cotytto, who swayed at Philippi and had whipped him for daring to enter there with a higher code of morals, we find him preaching in a dubious association, invited thither by a certain Justus. Denied access to the Jewish synagogues of Corinth we shall prove that he descended into the Solonic brotherhoods, one of which had its temple and house of its lord located very near the synagogue. This man Justus was whipped and terribly abused for his kindness to Paul. Justus was not his true name; it was Titus.

But we now find two important characters coming to the front in behalf of Paul. Aquila and Priscilla, man and wife, tent-makers like him by trade, and also exiles from Rome, having been driven by the same decree of Claudius the emperor banishing Jews from Italy. They had settled at Corinth. To all appearances, like Lydia, whom we shall mention, they were members, influential officers if not sales agents of the Dionysan union of tent and scene makers, selling goods at Corinth for the histrionic profession and aiding in the musical and theatrical entertainments of this celebrated city of profligate delirium and pleasure. They had already been converted by Apollos to the new faith and turned their kind attentions to Paul. What were Aquila and Priscilla doing before their banishment from Rome? A mass of new evidence is being gathered showing that they were safely stationed in the imperial domestic establishments of Tiberius and Caligula in days of safety, and we know nothing of any positive persecution, until the edict of Claudius. But we have inklings of swarming nests of unions in the valley of the Tiber. One most valuable notice is from the great Philo, who at that very time was on a mission to this emperor on behalf of Jews or perhaps christians at the time he met Peter,[238] or the time he was on the legation to assist his fellow countrymen some of whom were massacred on account of the calumnies of Apion, which was in the time of Caligula. Aquila and Priscilla were in Rome at that time and were expelled by Claudius in the year 52. They had gone to Corinth and were in charge of some house connected with their trade of tent-making when Paul arrived.[239] The apostle first on his arrival, began teaching in a Jewish synagogue, but the doctrine of the new culture being the same which had a few years before created such an upheaval and revolt ending with the crucifixion at Jerusalem because advocated in the temple, had the same effect at Corinth, and he was soon

---

[238] Philo, *Legat. ad Caium*, § 23: "Τὴν πέραν τοῦ Τιβέρεως ποταμοῦ μεγάλην τῆς Ῥώμης ἀποτόμην κατα χομένην καὶ οἰκουμένην πρὸς Ἰουδαίων." Philo on being bitterly snubbed by the emperor, slunk into the quarter he thus describes, and inasmuch as he met and became acquainted with Peter, we know that these Jews whom he mentions as inhabiting this riverside, were christians. Baur, *Tübinger Zeitschrift, für Theol.*, 1836, Pt. III., S. 110, admits that Rome at that time had many christians, who, with the Jews, made a disturbance.

[239] *Acts*, xviii., 2, 3, and 7.

forced to leave this sanctuary and seek more congenial quarters. And here comes the interest in our history of the ancient worker. Whither did he go? It is Bible that he went to the house of one Justus, or Titus the Just.[240] One would suppose, who reads the Greek of it, that he went there to board or live. But we are not told that he had such a residence in the synagague. The facts are that he went over to an old kurioikos of the tent-makers' union presided over by a lord named Titus the Just, who, being president, and having become convinced, caused the entire brotherhood whose common affairs he conducted, to consent to allow Paul to talk to them and to the people, in their own meeting rooms at their own house of the lord.[241]

The honest and critical researcher Neander, in getting an analysis of the house of the lord so frequently mentioned in the Testament, suspected something but could not explain. He certainly mistrusted, and went so far as to admit that this house represented some association, but without the inscriptions could not quite get down to the abodes of labor and see that every trade organization under the jus coeundi of Solon, was obliged to have a responsible lord, and as a necessary corollary, a "house" of the lord; else it was not respectable; it was not even legal and might be suppressed by the police. Even as it was, they must, after the conquests, be exceedingly secret and humble.[242] But Smith, in his Bible Dictionary goes still farther than Neander.

---

[240] *Acts*, xviii., 7: After Paul had been driven from the Corinthian synagogue, says: And he departed thence, and entered into a certain man's house, named Justus, one that worshiped God, whose house joined hard to the synagogue. The revised translation admits him "Titus the Just."

[241] I *Cor.*, xvi., 19; Paul confirms this in his Epistle as above, where in A.D. 54, according to Lardner, and while in Ephesus, having left Justus at the House in Corinth, and taken Aquila and Priscilla along, says, writing to that same brotherhood: Aquila and Priscilla salute you much in the Lord, with the church that is in their House, showing that they all belonged to one brotherhood, and had all worked for at least eighteen months there at their trade together. This house, like numbers we shall presently see in the inscriptions, was an important part of the business concern of the union.

[242] *Digest*, XLVII., xxii., 4. See our quotation and full explanations, *supra*, p. 48. Neander, *Planting*, Book III., chap. v., note 1, says: "Thus it may be explained how Aquila and Priscilla, while they sojourned at Rome, Corinth or Ephesus, might have such a small society 'in their own house.' The additional evidence adduced from their own inscriptions is that 'their own house' was in all these cases a κυριακή, and that they themselves were 'not very rich persons,' as accurately supposed by Smith, *Bib. Dict.*, art. *Paul;* Ramsay, *Cit. Bish. Phryg.*, passim; Neander and Mosheim. Like Jesus, himself, they were poor workmen, who by their industry and faithfulness, had been elevated to be responsible business officers in the eranos in which they belonged. They were these responsible and substantial officers who in the collegia were known as quinquennales and in the eranoi as κύριοι, having become lords and receiving certain immunities."

In speaking of her husband's exercise under article Priscilla, this excellent cyclopedia of Biblical literature has the remark that it was in conjunction with "home duties:" "Such female ministration was of essential importance in a state of society in the midst of which the early christian communities were formed," and then refers to the American edition which considers her a deaconess. If a deaconess, she must have been one who waited on the partakers at the common table doing exactly the work which Stephen and the other six had been appointed to perform; for in the language of the Acts, in the history of Stephen, this was a necessary part of the ministrations. But every evidence whether from Clement of Rome or from the inscriptions, goes against the ministrations being charity. The members belonged to a brotherhood and it was a part of its regular business to supply them work, that they might earn a full equivalent of what they consumed; so that charity in the light of alms-giving was not allowed at that early date. Neander, in the same place says as much as this, that "Paul, if we examine his language closely, says no more than this: that every one should lay by in his own house on the first day of the week whatever he was able to save; which means that every one should bring with him the sum he had saved, to the meeting of the brotherhood, so that the individual contributions might be collected together." Of course this was for the common meals of the congregation for the week to come. This is exactly the same thing which was at that time being done by regular assessments from each, on an enormous scale.[243] As long as they did this there could be no charity about it. It was the purely economic feature of the early church which Gibbon admits but hastens to say was discontinued, taking pains to cast a slur upon it as he speaks.[244] There is some reason for imagining, if we admit that these founders were at all acquainted with Greek literature, that Peter, John, Aquila, Ignatius and such others endorsed the views of Plato, while Paul took the views of Aristotle.[245]

[243] See *supra*, in the four chapters elaborately explaining this for the pre-christian unions.
[244] Gibbon, *Decl. and Fall*, in *Hist. Christianity*, ch. ii., note 128: "The community of goods which so agreeably amused the imagination of Plato, and which subsisted, in some degree, among the austere sect of essenians, was adopted for a short time in the primitive church."
[245] Some hints touching this very interesting and important subject of the common meal in the early plant, may be had from the *Epistle of Barnabas*. The *Clementines* are especially rich in them,

THE OLD RED DYES AND DYERS. 457

The point we are substantiating is that the early church, exactly like the unions which it converted and planted into, had as its most important function the common table and the communal code of Solon,[246] and was economic, a function which it has been robbed of by speculators and the ambitious for self aggrandizement, and that this is why it has failed to solve the problem of salvation of the human race. Thus we leave Aquila and Priscilla at their work, promising in the section of this chapter on Domitian to recall them and show the reader exactly where their ashes lie in the deep subterraneous cemeteries of Rome.

We now proceed to show the strange discoveries about Lydia. According to Renan, the ancient purple was red and the garb worn by Jesus at his crucifixion was not purple but red. The red dye workers were enormously organized in western Asia. As there was at that time a large trade in stuffs dyed in these beautiful, brilliant colors, we find the purple dyers in full force and closely organized at the time of Caligula and Claudius. Dr. Oehler has contributed the supposition that Lydia,[247] the dealer in dyes belonged to the guild of purple dyers of Thyatira though Paul saw and converted her at, or near Philippi in Macedonia. But there now exists complete acknowledgment that she with the consent of the brotherhood, turned her "House" to his account, being one of the purple dyers' union at Thyatira. They were running a prosperous business and among the agents whom they sent out to work up sales of these goods was this Lydia who had quite a business center, including rooms and employees, stationed on the Strymon river near the city of Philippi.[248]

---

[246] This is admitted by Neander, *Hist. Church*, I., p. 255. *trans.*, Bost., where he says of Tertullian's aliena domus: "The care of providing for the support and maintenance of strangers, of the poor, the sick, the old, of widows and orphans, and of those in prisons on account of their faith, devolved on the whole church." He further hints that the house of the stranger is the cold, outside world; not the warm brotherhood of initiated members,

[247] Oehl., *Eran. Vindobonensis*, p. 282: "Eine Uebersicht über die Städte zeigt dass Thyateira nicht weniger als neun Genossenschaften aufweist. Ihr Purpurhandel war ausgedehnt: eine Purpurhandlerin aus Thyateira wird vom Apostel Paulus zu Philippi bekehrt; *Apostelg.*, XVI., v. 14. Berühmt sind die Färbereien von Laodicea ad Lycum gewesen, Strabo, XV., 2, § 757.

[248] Smith, *Bib. Dict.*, Bost., p, 3241, in verb., *Thyatira:* Speaking of the unions of labor there, says: "With this guild there can be no doubt that Lydia the vender of purple stuffs, πορφυροπώλις, from whom St. Paul met with the favorable reception at Philippi, *Acts*, xvi., 14, was connected."

No knowledge of any church existing as early as this at Philippi is even pretended. Nevertheless we have the true statement of Neander that Paul found a whole household and converted brotherhood [249] under charge of Lydia, of the Laodicean dyers, and this house of Lydia was capacious enough to entertain the whole group of brethren, including Paul and Silas. Now we are prepared to show that many unions or guilds of these purple dyers existed in the region of Asia Minor coursed by the river Meander and its branch, the Lycus, where were the industrial cities of Laodicea, Hierapolis and Colossæ. At Ephesus also, not far away upon the seacoast, many trade unions, the dyers among the rest, had thriving industries operated exclusively by brotherhoods firmly and powerfully organized under the ancient provisions of the Solonic dispensation. No unorganized industry could have sent out a traveling agent to dispose of dye wares, as in the case of Lydia. Such individualist factories did not exist at that time. A good sum of money appropriated and engineered by the mother guild at Laodicea to erect or rent buildings for storage, transportation,[250] a "House" of the lord who in this exceptional case was a female, had been appropriated, and they were doing a thriving business; for they must have been the principal contributors to the relief of Paul's distress soon afterwards. The same cyclopedia of Biblical literature just quoted in our note, continues by saying: "The community at Philippi distinguished itself in liberality. On the apostle's first visit, he was hospitably entertained by Lydia, and when he afterwards went to Thessalonica by the sea, the Philippians sent him supplies more than once."[251] Perhaps of

[249] *Acts*, xvi., 40: And they went out of the prison and entered into the House of Lydia; and when they had seen the brethren, they comforted them and departed. What brethren? Who else could these already organized brothers be than regular members of Lydia's union of this Macedonian branch of the Laodicean πορφυροβάφοι? Again, in the 14th and 15th verses of this chapter, she had constrained them to "come into my house and abide there."

[250] Smith, *Bib. Dict.*, p. 2490: "Lydia had an establishment in Philippi, for the reception of dyed goods which were imported from Thyatira and the neighboring towns of Asia, and were dispersed by means of pack animals among the mountain clans of Hæmus and Pangæus, the agents being doubtless in many instances her own co-religionists." This must of course be taken to mean her own confraternity, for what use would she have of religion in running her factory?

[251] *Phil.*, iv., 15; Οἴδατε δὲ καὶ ὑμεῖς, Φιλιππήσιοι, ὅτι ἐν ἀρχῇ τοῦ εὐαγγελίου, ὅτι ἐξῆλθον ἀπὸ Μακεδονίας, οὐδεμία μοι ἐκκλησία ἐκοινώνησεν εἰς λόγον, δόσεως καὶ λήψεως, εἰ μὴ ὑμεῖς μόνοι· ὅτι καὶ ἐν Θεσσαλονίκῃ καὶ ἅπαξ καὶ δὶς εἰς τὴν χρείαν μοι ἐπέμψατε."

all the trade unions of ancient times, the dyers were the most powerfully organized. They were known in inscriptions, in Scripture and in history as porphyrobaphoi²⁵² and this tenement they occupied was found by Boeckh, who conducted the first compilation of the Corpus Inscriptionum Græcarum, to possess the general name of oikos.²⁵³

Besides Lydia, thus acknowledged to have been an agent of the dyers union, we have Gaius of about the same period, also mentioned in the inscriptions of Asiatic trade unions. The Smith Cyclopædia of Biblical Knowledge, under this rubric, enumerates four men of this name, all in the apostolic age, and speaks of them as different persons. In our mode of considering the apostolic plant, however, they are all one and the same. Gaius, like Lydia, Aquila, Priscilla and many others, was the manager of a guild, and the apostles converted him, thus getting access to a "House" or kuriakos where he built up a church. Many instances of this character crop out in the sacred writ and many not thus mentioned are coming to light through tell-tale ideographs they have fortunately left.²⁵⁴

---

²⁵² Oehler, *MSS,:* Πορφυροβάφοι, THYATEIRA, contributes seven συνέδρια of these industries, several of which were represented in the inscriptions of Thyatira. Ramsay, II., p. 548, comments on the συνέδριον τοῦ 'Επισκόπου in Ignatius as though the order of πορφοροβάφοι was meant, and declares that in Phrygia they were christian societies; Oehler, *MSS.,* has an invaluable one found very recently at Mt. Athol, Thessalonica right where Paul planted with Lydia's aid; Oehler, *Eran. Vindob.,* p. 277, in the list of trade unions, CIG,, 3496 Thyateira, 3924, Hierapolis; Le Bas, III., 1867, and *American Journal of Archæology,* III., p. 348, Laodicea; again, *id.,* p. 279: συνέδρια τῶν πορφυροβάφων in Hieropolis, and other dyers unions at Ephesus; again, p. 282, at Tyre, mentioned by Strabo, 757, and Pliny, *Nat. Hist,* V., 19. So again, herewith connected: Oehler, *MS.:* "Θίασος—THESSALONICA— THIATEIRA. Interressant ist auch die Inschrift aus Thessalonika: Duchesne Bayet, *Mémoire sur une Mission au Mont Athol,* p. 52, nr. 83: die συνέδρια τῶν πορφυροβάφων hat dem Mennippos aus Thiateira ein Grabmal errichtet. Es liegt nahe auzunehmen dass auch dieser Mennipos ein πορφοροβάφος gewesen sei und zu vergleichen die Purpurhändlerin Lydia aus Thyateira welche in Philippi vom Apostel Paulus getauft wurde, *Act. Apost.,* xvi., 14."

²⁵³ Boeckh, *P. E.,* 1, 328, 2, note 199. Οίκος, according to Boeckh whose word on the Ἐράνος is authority, is the temple or lord's house of the ἐράνος. Liddell, *Greek Dict.,* in verb, Ἐράνος, says οίκος was often a house, a cave, den, place for the poor, also a place, ædes for some god. The chr. "believers dwelt κατὰ τοὺς οἴκους." The daring suggestion has been published, since the revelations made through the inscriptional contributions, that these οἶκοι or κυριάκοι of the ancient ἐράνος were the holes of the poor into which the christians planted and maintained their institution until it was able to stand alone, and the still more blasphemous and bolder hint has been held forth that the House or cave, or seclusion in which Paul was met by Jesus, accused, bedizzened and converted, was the secret οἶκος of the ἐράνος.

²⁵⁴ Ramsay, *Cit. Bish. Phryg.,* II., p. 630, note 2, speaking of the *Hymnodoi,* a musical union of the Bosphorus and in Phrygia, says: "The existence of secret societies like these made it easier for the christians to organize themselves in similar societies." Without knowing the great secret he here hits it closely.

Another of the proselytes encountered by this evangelist was Demetrius, the president or kurios of the union of image makers of Ephesus. This large manufacturing and commercial city of Phrygia possessed many trade unions of various kinds. There were tent makers of the Dionysan artists who furnished the scenes, tents and other paraphernalia of the theaters in the world of amusement; the dyers, of which we have spoken, goldsmiths, leatherers of many sorts, and not the least among all these many were the image makers who manufactured out of gold, silver, pearl, amber, coral, gems and several other precious materials, goodly quantities of images in great variety, little and large, for the ladies and for the temples of the pagan gods. Sacred bracelets, combs, beads, palladiums and golden vincula were among the saleable bijoux of their manufacture. These artists, closely organized and enjoying their profits in the usual method of community enterprise, succeeded in making a good living at Ephesus. It was, of course, for their direct advantage, in order to secure good sales and a good living, to brook no innovation of the new christian doctrine brought to Ephesus by Paul and the other evangelists which discountenanced the popularity of these ancient fads and fashions on which their existence depended. To them it was business without sentiment.

But the business of image making and selling was classed with idolatry; for all these objects they were producing were idols of the pagan divinities. There was at Ephesus a very prominent trade union character named Demetrius who was kurios, or principal in charge of the unions of image makers. The broadcast preaching of Paul, which certainly had a powerful effect, was directly against the old idolatry of the pagan worship.[255] Not understanding this we are told that a great quarrel existed between the propagators of the new salvation.

To students of the true situation and to practical thinkers this will soon appear as a far-fetched conclusion. Christianity has already been stamped by the su-

[255] Paul seems to have had a similar encounter with a man named Diotrephes, mentioned in the third Epistle of John, unfavorably. A close study of Diotrephes reveals that he was guardian of a union, like Demetrius, and would not tolerate any interference of the new missionaries, urging their doctrines into the old brotherhoods, so long as such preaching was deleterious to the business which it was their function to defend.

pervening Tübingen school as a grotesque if not comical deal in futures; for judging from the coaxing career of competition and its lordly overstriding of the originally socialistic foundation, stamping out its vitals and leaving but a skeleton, the world must at length show cause why it should not awaken from an indoctrinated superstition. Indeed it is already beginning to cry aloud with disappointment.

We have repeatedly said that it is not our province here to write up specious views. We leave this to the wranglers of gnosticism and the men of pulpit and chancel who reverberate more the mock of a hollow salary than the glow of love for their fellow men. We are groping after history; searching and unearthing the story of something called christianity; dragging forth as a result of our labors among scraps and bones and cinerary relics, a vast evidence, which warrants us in a hope that Neander's prediction is coming true.[256]

The imaginary split-away originating in the accredited trouble between Paul on the one hand and John and Peter and the immediate companions of Jesus on the other, was the self-same labor question and labor movement which we have to-day. As a matter of fact, there was no lasting quarrel, for they came to an understanding. There was a vast practical labor movement, legalized by the statute we have described, but driven into secrecy by the Roman conquests; and the immediate followers of Jesus, faithful to his teachings, pursued with consistency the tenets prescribed. Paul, a good man at heart, but a born aristocrat, at first abjured the economic factor and cast his whole life in the cause of faith, thinking only of the life beyond and believing with an intense assurance that things pertaining to the world were of little concern compared with the æons of bliss which he believed to await the denizens of earth who followed the Jesus as a post earthly God.

John and Peter, on the other hand were workingmen. They looked upon mankind as it really was; a mass of

---

[256] This remarkable prediction of a modern converted Hebrew philosopher, has been translated and reads to this effect: "We stand," said Neander, "on the line between the old world and a new, about to be called into being by the ever-fresh energy of the gospel. For a fourth time an epoch in the life of our race is in preparation by means of christianity." Schaff, *Hist. Apostolic Church*. See Lippincott, *Biog. Dict.*, art, *Neander*.

suffering humanity overcome by the sword of tyrants; ground to atoms by laws against conspiracy; reduced to a hideous slavery; bleeding with blows; intellect stifled; wives and children weeping in squalid starvation; subject at the least excuse to be hung on the awful gibbet of the crucifix and denied the right of family or the exercise of natural and honorable affections.

Which was right? Paul was a good man. We shall show in our history of his fight against the abominations that his life-work rid the world of many a den of sexual license, elevating mankind above the exuberant laxity of Cotytto and heading off the freedom of Carpocrates. But did he overreach his functions as a reformer when he ranked this iconoclasm among the abominations which he attacked?

It is here that the true labor problem comes in. Demetrius, who like the others we have mentioned, was a kurios or quinquennalis of the union of image makers of Ephesus and in appearance already converted by John, was in the act of faithfully carrying out his instructions and functions as protector and president of his union. It was a fact that Paul, in his preaching, inveighed against the worship of idols with such power that the manufacture of these images, shrines and palladiums was sensibly cut off, leaving the laboring people, members of these image makers' unions thousands in number, out of employment, to be turned out as tramps and making of Paul's christianity a sort of labor-stifling machine, like these of to-day which are intercepting human muscle and driving our artisans by millions into the roads to tramp, starve and die. John sprang at him like a tiger. Diotrephes another New Testament character apparently a director of a union similarly threatened, likewise vehemently attacked Paul.

It was a serious question. Demetrius and his unions got word from other quarters that this proto-iconoclast had worked the same arguments among them. There can be no doubt of his influence over the membership of similar unions making shrines and receiving their bread from this labor.[257] Thus the business of a multitude favored by coming under the jus coeundi, ancient, and sacredly unchangeable, held as an heirloom of anti-

---

[257] *Acts*, xix., 26. Moreover ye see and hear that not alone at Ephesus but almost throughout all Asia this Paul hath persuaded and turned away much people, saying that they be no gods, which are made with hands.

quity,[258] was all at once attacked by a Jewish reformer, a craftsman of the tentmakers and a man of no higher rights than their own Demetrius.

Another matter of utmost importance recently coming to light through inscriptional history but never before known since the days of their suppression, is that these unions of image makers defended on that memorable day by Demetrius, were actually manufacturing articles for the government.[259] We are told by the cyclopedia of Biblical literature that Demetrius was a maker of silver shrines of Artemis at Ephesus, and the *naoi argurioi* niches for models of the great temple of the Ephesian Artemis or Diana, near her statue; and that Demetrius and his fellow craftsmen, in fear of losing their trade, raised a tumult, showing in his speech before a vast out-of-door crowd how the new sect threatened to endanger their business and means of life. This is admitted by all, even Calvin.[260]

---

[258] Mommsen, *De Coll. et Sodal., Rom.*, p. 40, § 6, *in initio*, speaking of the stability of the collegium, under the jus coeundi of Solon, says: "Cum rerum ordo apud Romanos immutaretur et libera rei publicæ forma in regnum sensim abiret, Romæ quoque malorum hominum consociationes illæ, quæ turbas civiles et sequi et incitare rursus solent, sæpissime fiebant." Thus the privilege got to be exceedingly dangerous, for allusion is made to Livy's *Solitudo Magistratuum*, cf. *supra*, ch. i. Again, the traditional song so beloved by the poorer people grated against the pride of the patrician class, but this laxity, and sometimes perhaps, wantonness, were fortified in the traditional habits which did not keep pace with the splendor of urban growth. They for centuries sang their traditional songs and in Phrygia exhibited their fair ones at the Callipygian games. It is stated by Thirwell that less progress was made in 1,000 years than is being made in modern times in a hundred. In music, change was especially slow. The *Hula hula*, or, "Oh that funny feeling." is a tune believed by some to reach back into the pre-christian days. There are races now, among which no change, either of law, of fashion, or of habit and belief, transpires, and the Africans, Mongolians, Malays and Indians are some of them; whereas the true Caucasian race is exceedingly changeful.

[259] Neander, *Planting*, Book III., chap. viii., quotes *Acts*, xix., 24 sqq., and distinctly says, that "The silver shrines for Diana brought no small gains unto the craftsmen." Again, *id.*, viii.: "Small models, in gold and silver, of the proud temple of Artemis used to be made, which, being sent to distant parts as an object of devotion, brought great gains to the city." But Neander cannot see that the makers belonged to a union of silversmiths. Dr. Oehler, in his *MSS.*, sent to us, speaking of Jewish unions at Ephesus, and referring to *Acts*, xix., 24, ie., the trouble with Paul and Demetrius, seems to assure us that the union had the burial attachment, *Anc. Gr. Inscr.*, IV., no. 676: "Κήδονται οἱ Ἰουδαῖοι;" 679, "Ταύτης τῆς σόρου κήδονταί οἱ ἐν Ἐφέσῳ Ἰουδαῖοι." We expect inscriptions will yet be found proving more. Oehler, *Eran. Vindob.;* p. 281, brings this fact to mind referring to *Acts*, xix., 24, sqq., to show the, "einflussreiche Stellung der Genossenschaften im staatlichen Leben; dass sie einen grossen Einfluss auf die Masse des Volkes hatten ziegt der Aufstand, den die Silberarbeiter in Ephesos gegen den Apostel Paulus erregten: *Apostoleg.* xix., 24 f. This makes him a director of a regular union.

[260] Calvin, *In Acta Apostol.*, xix., 23 sqq., makes it plain that this trouble was entirely over the problem of bread for the workmen: "Res ipsa clamat, non tam pro aris ipsos quam pro focis pugnare, ut scilicet culinam habeant bene calentem."

Now it has not yet been explained that this Demetrius was the same man converted by John, and mentioned by him, nor that he is the Demas of the gospels, being a member of the early christian brotherhoods. Neither has it been explained that it was over him and this very trouble that the great schism occurred between Peter, John, James and Paul. This phenomenal sequestering of a great subject for nearly two thousand years will develop itself little by little as enquiry proceeds.

Let us now turn our attention to the subject of government of these people on strike. In the first place, it is well recorded that their manufacture of images, models, shrines and priestly paraphernalia was a part of the pagan worship of Diana. Next to this comes the important but well-known fact that this sort of property was largely official. The state or city owned the temple, and we are told that the sale of such things brought great gains to the city, meaning that it was public business. Without doubt the priests, who in ancient times were regular public officers, used to procure of the unions of jewelers large numbers of shrines, models and other salable trinkets, and sell them at a much higher price to the ladies of wealth, who visited the famous place, from not only the city itself but the country round about and even from the distant villages and towns. This traffic, then, with the unions, for the purchase of sacred objects, was a government function, and in the way we have described must have brought gains to the city, although it afforded the unions a sure and lucrative means of existence. The union could contract for so and so many shrines, and being paid by the city, the commerce was political and this would instigate the political incentives causing the members to organize and at the elections work and vote for the agoranomos who was willing to pledge that he would award to them the jobs rather than to any outside enterprise. As we have shown, this was done to an enormous extent at Pompeii and in many places of Asia Minor. It was in this indirect manner that the ancient unions constantly received employment, and the shrine makers of Ephesus were no exception.

Few people of our day have any idea of the importance of the temple of Diana. "Great is Diana of the

GREAT IS DIANA OF THE EPHESIANS.

Ephesians," is Bible history. It appears to have been in a good state of preservation at the time covered by our story. Few people comprehend its magnificence or its enormous proportions. The Parthenon on the Acropolis of Athens, grand as it was, sank in comparison with the size of this renowned temple of Diana. It was more than four times greater than the Parthenon, and its crumbling ruins still mark the spot where it stood for a dozen centuries, the wonder of the architectural world. Its roof was cedar and the massive entablature of marble supporting it had one hundred and twenty-eight columns sixty feet high. It was four hundred and twenty-five feet in length and two hundred and twenty feet in breadth; and in its center supported on a high pedestal stood the wonderful statue of Diana, done in costly pearls bedecked with gold to the value of millions; goddess of the moon and sister to Apollo god of the sun. She protected labor, presided over the unions of hunters and fishermen and ruled the destinies of virginity, marriage and honor. This great temple founded by the Amazons and Leleges in prehistoric antiquity, having been once destroyed by the conflagration of Erostratus, three hundred and seventy years before, and rebuilt in a splendor commensurate with the improvements of architecture, was known as one of the seven wonders of the world; the others being the colossus at Rhodes, Pyramids of Egypt, Hanging Gardens of Babylon, Statue of Jupiter at Olympus, the Pharos at Alexandria and the Mausoleum at Halicarnassas.

Of course such a vast edifice as this could not have been erected and owned by any one denominational branch of religion. It was national property. It is probable that for the most part of the twelve-hundred years it is known to have stood, it was claimed by the municipality of Ephesus. But it was government property. The very divinities, with all the scores of priests and priestesses were creatures of official religion. Piety was an official duty under the government control. Priests were paid employees of the government. The individual had no right or control over the incomes from sacrifices, [261] which as proved by the Pliny correspond-

[261] Gibbon, chap. xvi., with note 60 and elsewhere, recognized that non-attendance at the sacrifices was equivalent to non-payment of tribute to Rome basing this view on Pliny's letters, and says: "As the payment of tribute was inflexibly refused... the consideration which they, the christians, ex-

ence with the emperor Trajan, about unions converted to christianity, was the same at that time in all parts of proconsular Rome. Not only did the unions do the work of the official religion, but the members were forced under the penalty of death, to attend the sacrifices, buy the animals the farmers brought to the temples, and thus put money into the treasury of government. How fallacious then, to suppose that the artists in shrines and images manufactured by an organization presided over by Demetrius, were not indirectly working for the government.

It is equally erroneous to suppose that this great number of silversmiths and goldsmiths of Ephesus were not thoroughly organized. No wealth or good fortune or food above an exiguous pittance could be earned by an unorganized workingman at that time. Nor did Demetrius own and operate a great shrine factory, as Neander supposes.[262] It is Granier de Cassagnac who is correct regarding ancient manufacture. A rich man in those days might own slaves, and place over them a good manager, always a slave, or a freedman and thus carry on a manufactory; but this was extremely rare. Demosthenes had two factories in Athens, one for making cutlery and another for producing bedsteads. They were manned by fifty-two slaves all his own property, and his superintendent was murdered by them. He also manufactured for the state. But Demetrius did not own slaves. Those men he pleaded for were free; and the institution they subserved was a well-organized union or guild, such as Ephesus abounded in. These unions were doing business under the jus coeundi of Solon, and they had to have a kurios or president of eminent ability. This officer was Demetrius. He had a keen eye to the good of his brotherhood; hence his strong influence over the town clerk, the governor and the whole people of Ephesus. Nor was he opposed to the introduction of the reforms which had previously been brought hither by John and Peter because they did not

perienced from the Roman magistrates, will serve to explain how far these speculations are justified in facts, and will lead us to discover the true causes of the persecutions." We shall soon bring to light all that is known of the Pliny letters.

[262] Neander, *Planting*, Book III., chap. vii.: "A man named Demetrius, who had a large manufactory of such models, and a great number of workmen, began to fear, since the gospel had spread with such success....that the gains in his trade would soon be lost."

denounce the manufacture of images nor do anything
to injure the happiness of the working people. They
were not iconoclasts; for however correct the statement
that the true God was not made with hands, they were
wise enough to keep still and economical enough to let
well enough alone. They were the direct apostles and
companions of the great ebionite and Nazarene who had
come and worked as a workingman and advocate of labor, and paid his passage to immortality through the
ignominious cross. The misfortune, if it can be called a
misfortune, is that Paul should have been such an aristocrat that he cared not whether the poor workmen
were starved to death or not by his innovation which
interdicted the manufacture of idols for the salvation of
the living, so long as he gained his point for the salvation of the dead. Paul thus became the enemy of the
economical factor which Jesus had upheld in his primitive brotherhood and Peter, Apollos, James and John
were still struggling for, in their itinerancy. He sought
to kill the practical and now re-ascendant half of the
thing known as christianity. Priestcraft saw the bait
and snapped it up and the church is a whited sepulchre.
The great economic factor is ruled out.

But Dr. Lightfoot had penetration enough to see the
bottom of the schism. Demas, who is mentioned time
and again in the New Testament, proves to be Demetrius.[263] "Demetrius is no other than Demas," says Dr.
Lightfoot, especially in his[264] Introduction to the Epistle to the Thessalonians. If so, he is mentioned at least
four times over and above the full history given of the
great strike-tumult at Ephesus in the Acts, where his
name occurs twice. No word of sympathy is expressed
in the Acts of the Apostles for the working people engaged in this trouble. The original writings, including
those of Clement, the Protevangelium of James, Barnabas, the gospel of Peter, celebrated with Greeks as the
Kerugma Petrou, and many other original contributions

[263] III John, 12: *Col.*, iv., 14; *II Tim.*, iv., 10; *Philemon*, 24. The Oxford Univ. Ed., *index* Proper Names, says, Demas is contracted from Demetrius.
[264] *II Tim.*, iv., 10; but particularly *Col.*, iv., 14. In II. *Tim.*, iv., 10, ii.,
Demetrius completely forsakes Paul, "Δημᾶς γὰρ με ἐγκατέλιπεν, ἀγαπήσας τὸν
νῦν ἐαιῶνα, καὶ ἐπορεύθη εἰς Θεσσαλονίκῃ, Κρήσκης εἰς Γαλατίαν, Τίτος εἰς
Δαλματίαν, Λουκᾶς ἐστι μόνος μετ' ἐμοῦ." This shows the schism: and it
plainly began in the quarrel at Ephesus over the economic problem of the
workingmen.

including the mysteriously lost Gospel of the Hebrews, all of which are known to have gone current during the first and much of the second centuries, were ruled out and much which we have has been interpolated in their places. Great men and scholars, too numerous to mention, pronounce the early writings genuine, and admit that the reason why they were excluded is that they all advocated the plan of economies which inculcates the socialism that was being practically and uniformly carried out by the brotherhoods.

Demetrius, then, was the first open, original exponent of the purely economic plan in Asia. Stephen had tried it in Palestine and lost his life. The laborer must receive the equivalents of the products of his work, and Demetrius, John and James said Paul's condemnation of idolatry should not be allowed to interfere against it. We do not set up a disclaimer against the methods of Paul. He was not the first to protest against rushing too rapidly [265] against dangers. There are coming to

[265] GIBBON, *Decline and Fall.*, ch. xxxvii., including note 26, who seems to understand the ancient philosophy of the usefulness of lies, says: "But the operation of these religious motives, was variously determined by the temper and situation of mankind. Reason might subdue, or passion suspend their influence; but they acted more forcibly in the infirm minds of children and females."

LUKE, who was speaking to initiates behind the veil, says, viii., 10: "'Ο δὲ εἶπεν· ὑμῖν δέδοται γνῶναι τὰ μυστήρια τῆς βασιλείας τοῦ θεοῦ, τοῖς δὲ λοιποῖς ἐν παραβολαῖς ἵνα βλέποντες μὴ βλέπωσι καὶ ἀκούοντες μὴ συνιῶσιν."

ARISTOTLE, *Metaphys.* x., 8: "Religion has been handed down in mythical form from the earliest times, to posterity, that there are gods; and that things divine compass nature entire. All over and above this has been added, according to the mythical style, for the purpose of persuading the multitude, and in favor of the laws, and the good of the state. Thus men have given to the gods human forms, and have even represented them under the figure of other beings, in whose train fictions of many other things followed. But if we separate from all this the original principle, and consider that alone, we shall find that this has been divinely done; since philosophy and art have been several times found and lost, yet such doctrines or essences are preserved to us as remains of ancient wisdom."

POLYBIUS, *Histories,* VI., cap. 56, strongly hints that superstition or the inculcation among the masses of those too weak to comprehend the full truth accomplishes its realization surer and swifter than a straight attempt to teach the truth.

STRABO, *Geog.*, I., 2; "The multitude of women and the entire mass of the common people cannot be led to religion by the doctrines of philosophy; for this purpose superstition is also necessary, which must call in the aid of the myths and fables of wonder........Such things the founders of states used as bugbears to awe childish people. These myths are wanted not only for children, but for all the ignorant, who are no better than children"

HERMAS, *Vision,* Book II., c. 3, makes a prayer in accordance probably, with the above: "O Lord, I never spoke a true word in my life, but have lived in dissimulation, lying to all men, and was never contradicted. All gave credit to my words." Yet Hermas comes down to us as a man of modesty, truthfulness and wisdom.

LACTANTIUS, *Div. Inst.*, II., c, 3, says that Cicero, like Aristotle believed that good things must be taught through lies: Cicero was well aware

light strong evidences which show that Paul was wise. If our argument is true that early christianity was the original economic socialism it is believed by us to have been, he certainly was right; not in taking food from the workers but in stanching the too rapid boldness of an open advocacy into hitherto secret places. Did this man Paul not stand by and see the ghastly lynching of Stephen? Did he not stand afar and with his own eyes behold Jesus nailed to the cross? This same Paul had been an eye witness to many horrors. He had with his own eyes seen and known Jesus[266] personally and, becoming, like a good and really honest man, a convert through pure conscientiousness, he turns in their favor, and gives his life up for them.

Thus it cannot be said of this man, that he was against the Ebionitic doctrines which had as its primitive basis the salvation of man from the awful qualms of pagan slavery and the humiliation of labor from which the patrician himself drew every ounce of his sustenance. Paul saw all this, and being humbly converted to socialism, put his whole life into the cause. If, then, he varied a little from Peter, John and James, as to the details of this business, we can see no reason for condemning him at wholesale and pronouncing empty anathemas against his views. We cannot find, honestly looking at the so-called Pauline quarrel, that this man varied very materially from Peter, John and James. He was intensely and conscientiously religious. Peter and John that the deities men worshiped were false. He wanted men not to discuss things much, lest this discussion extinguish accepted doctrines which are supposed true. As a matter of fact, Aristotle, Plato, Polybius, Cicero, Strabo, Plutarch, Dion Chrisostom, for the early thinkers, and hundreds of the ante-Nicine prelates, advocated, that lies were useful, however hateful and nauseating such prevarications may now seem.

Solon, "Digest," XLVII., xx., 4, does as much in his "jus coeundi," for the much contested clause "ἐπὶ λίαν οἰκόμενοι," actually gives robbers of the sea, that is, pirates, freebooters, corsairs, the right to carry on their business as legitimate. This is worse than superstitious falsehoods.

Am Rhyn, "Mysteria," Eng. "trans.," p. 5: "Here we have men using a twofold manner of speech; for the people, they gave out communications different from those which were extended to the initiates of their secret associations."

This seemingly villainous logic of the so-called pre-christians, which was copied by later advocates, Paul not excepted, gave rise to the aphorism: The end justifies the means; and as the pagan gods universally favored lies of this sort as useful, the christians were early led away from the rigid truthfulness adhered to in the unions, and finally became worse liars than their ancestors.

[266] "II Corinth.," v., 16, reads: "But if I knew Christ personally as indeed I did know him according to the flesh— κατὰ σάρκον, in his bodily, earthly appearance, yet, now I know him so no more.

were as intensely and conscientiously practical. Paul, like the christians of to-day, had only the life beyond in view. He even had no promise for the slave. Peter and John had the hereafter not only but also the life of the living to do with; and they conscientiously preached salvation on these lines. Could they have been blamed if they instigated their powerful comrade, Demetrius, or Demas, to rebel with the large union of silversmiths, whose bread was threatened by Paul's doctrine? What had this converted union to do for or against the idol-buying customs of the official temple? We fail to see that either Demas or the artisans whose interests he controlled had anything for or against the worship of shrines in the making of which they earned a living. They simply did the work offered and got their money. Very naturally they followed the custom in this pressing emergency, like Peter who thrice denied. If they cried aloud, along with the great throng: "Great is Diana of the Ephesians," it was quite human and natural, and perhaps they did do so, but this does not accuse them.

Another matter of moment is that we commit no anachronism in these reflections. It may be asked if this incident of the strike of the image makers at Ephesus was not before John and others of the Twelve, or of the seventy, had planted at Ephesus. To this, we answer that the christian plant had been made several years before.[267] But we find a remarkably startling mention in Dr. Lightfoot's Colossian Heresy regarding Paul at Ephesus in contact with strolling wanderers, whom he imagines to be Jews because Josephus in his Jewish wars speaks of them as wandering exorcists who cast out evil spirits,[268] and brought the dead to life. Again,

[267] *Amer. Cyclopædia*, in art. *Paul:* "Struck with temporary blindness by this vision, he (Saul) was brought to Damascus, where, after three days sojourn he received his sight at the hands of a disciple named Ananias." Does this not prove that the work had been begun even before Saul's conversion? Again, *id.*, "Meanwhile, a new centre of christian influence had established itself at Antioch, the capital of Syria, and thither Paul now went at the solicitation of Barnabas." Here is ackowledgment that both Ananias and Barnabas had planted before Paul. But the accepted belief now is that John, the evangelist had been in Asia, even before either of them. He was known in the cities of the Lycus and in Ephesus. Paul had the same trouble with Diotrephes.

[268] Josephus, *De Bell. Jud.*, I., c. § 7: "Ὅρκους αὐτοῖς ὄμνυσι φρικώδεις... μήτε κρύψειν τι τοὺς αἱρετιστὰς μήτε ἑτέροις αὐτῶν τι μηνύσειν καὶ ἂν μέχρι θανάτου τις βιάζηται. Πρὸς τούτοις ὀμνύουσι μηδενὶ μὲν μεταδοῦναι τῶν δογμάτων ἑτέρως ἢ ὡς αὐτὸς μετέλαβέν ἀφέξεσθαι δὲ λῃστείας καὶ συντηρήσειν ὁμοίως τά τε τῆς αἱρέσεως αὐτῶν βίβλια καὶ τὰ τῶν ἀγγέλων ὀνόματα."

FAKIRS, AND THE BEGGAR GUILDS. 471

Lightfoot[269] speaks of essenic and similar unions on the Lycus, in Phrygia not many miles from Ephesus and almost describes the guilds.[270] And well he might; for the workingmen in the tumult against Paul were a multitude belonging to the union of shrine makers. The strolling Jews casting out devils are none other than the celebrated fakirs or Metragyrtes we have described.[271] They all belonged to the Dionysan artists. They constituted one of the most perfect trade organizations which received the benefits of, and were particularly mentioned by, the Solonic law in words that are unmistakable. This enormous, roving body is searchingly studied by the archæologists, and their numerous inscriptions compared with the descriptions of Lucian, Celsus, Julian, Porphyry and Clement of Alexandria.[272] Celsus himself, declares that the christians had a foothold in the organization of these Dionysan artists, and it is this which Dr. Lightfoot imperfectly sees and imagines to be the wandering essenians. It was very early.

Dr. Lightfoot finds that "There was an entire dislocation and discontinuity in the history of christianity in Asia Minor at a certain epoch; that the Apostle of the Gentiles was ignored and his teaching repudiated if not anathematized; and that on its ruins was created the standard of Judaism around which, with marvelous

---

[269] Lightfoot, *Coloss. Heresy*, p. 93, admits that he sees evidences of what he seems to think is essenism at Colossæ and other cities in the Lycus and even in Ephesus. He must then as a matter of course, admit that they were industrial organizations: for Foucart, Lüders and especially Oehler have found the therapeutæ which are proved to be close trade unions, involved in the bread-winning work of their trade, cf. *index* to this Vol. in verb. Therapeutæ.

[270] Lightfoot, *Coloss.*, p. 93: "Where Paul visits Ephesus, he comes in contact with certain strolling Jews, exorcists, who attempt to cast out evil spirits: *Acts*, xix., 13: 'Ἐπεχείρησαν δέ τινες ἀπὸ τῶν περιερχομένων Ἰουδαίων ἐξορκιστῶν ὀνομάζειν ἐπὶ τοὺς ἔχοντας τὰ πνεύματα τὰ πονηρὰ τὸ ὄνομα τοῦ κυρίου Ἰησοῦ, λέγοντες, ὁρκίζω ὑμᾶς τὸν Ἰησοῦν, ὃν ὁ Παῦλος κηρύσσει.

[271] Lüders, *Dionys. Künst.* Οἱ θίασοι τῶν περὶ τὸν Διόνυσον τεχνιτῶν. The particular clause which secured these roving, half-mendicant, half-preditory bands of brothers, as also the sea-rovers, or corsairs, under the *jus coeundi*, was as follows: ἡ ἐπὶ λίαν οἰχομένοι, *Dig.*, XLVII., xx., 4.

[272] Lucian, *De Morte Peregrini*, 11 sqq. We quote Middleton's paraphrase, Works. I., 19: "Lucian, who flourished during the second century, tells us that whenever any crafty juggler, an expert in his trade, who knew how to make a right use of things, went over to the christians, he was sure to grow rich immediately by making a prey of their simplicity." Again, "Celsus," in Origen, *Contra Celsum*, Book I., represents all the christian wonderworkers as mere vagabonds and common cheats, who rambled about to play their tricks at fairs and markets; not in the circles of the wiser and better sort, for among such, they never ventured to appear; but wherever they observed a set of raw young fellows, slaves, or fools, there they took care to obtrude themselves, and there they displayed all their arts."

unanimity deserters from the Pauline Gospel rallied. Of this retrograde faith St. Paul is supposed to have been the great champion, and Papias a typical and important representative.[273] The Cyclopædia of Biblical Literature of Smith is silly and aristocratic enough to say that John, the workingman, christian and bosom friend of Jesus, "was mistaken, with the others of the Twelve, in his idea of the temporal mission of the Messiah." This is a good specimen of the emissaries of wealth and property to-day, in their advocacy and their cringing subserviency to prelacy and craft setting in so early against the determined battle of Jesus to sweep the robber from the face of the earth.[274] Neander, as we here show his words in our note, boldly admits that the Pauline controversy and trouble was settled by his promising to "continue to relieve the temporal wants of the poor." Nothing can be more definite. The members of the image makers' unions were of course, the poor, for they, like all who labor, had only their hands to secure them means of life. Paul had undertaken to head this off. It being their only possible means of existence, a great tumult resulted, which the governor and the town clerk wisely and correctly pronounced to be a matter not of the public but between themselves, when he dismissed the multitude. Truly nothing can be plainer or clearer than that the whole difficulty, so tersely recorded in the nineteenth chapter of The Acts was a question of labor, and that the labor unions of Ephesus were involved. The address of Demetrius was clearly a New Testament-quoted labor speech.

This same contest against allowing christian unions to manufacture idols for heathen use, came up, long afterwards and was fought to a finish, ending in the sup-

[273] Lightfoot, *Coloss.*, 50, in addition to this strong recognition, the theory of the Tübingen school of Bauer, *Christliche Kirche der Ersten Dreijahrhunderte*, and Schwelger's *Nachapostolisches Zeitalter*.

[274] Neander, *Planting*, Book III., ix., *init.*, says: "While in this manner, christianity spread itself from Antioch, the parent church of the Gentile world . . . . a division threatened to break out between the two parent churches. It was the great crisis in the history of the church and of mankind. The question was, in fact, whether the gospel would succeed, not only then but through all future ages." Neander sees this but in his darkness attributes it all to the "spiritual fault of blessedness without circumcision," and adds to the history of Paul's journey to Jerusalem to get the matter arranged with Peter, James and John, and planning conciliation, whereby a publishing of the Gospel might go on. They did not disagree: "They agreed that Paul should continue to labor independently among the heathen making only one stipulation, namely, that as heretofore the Gentile churches should continue to relieve the temporal wants of the poor."

pression of the splendid unions by the monstrous edict of Laodicea.

Thus we have attempted to prove that this model workingman was a character in history and have shown his actual character, even so far as is known in credible and legendary record, his human side, not fearing to show his features, form and gait.[275] But all this sinks in insignificance compared with the great life-work he carried though suppressed nearly two thousand years, and now surging to the front afresh with a roar and a rush, to frighten the devotees of greed and make joyful the myriads of toil. That work was the uplifting of the secret microcosm into the majestic state.[276]

As we desire to present positive evidence on origins of socialism developed in the ancient microcosm, such as we have been able to dig up from the epitaphs and other inscriptions, we have avoided all moribund thaumatolatry possible including miracles and wonderworking, since it was these more than is supposed which created the wranglings of later periods. We have searched and recorded only that which promises to be accepted as permanent history.

Having explained all that is known regarding the turmoil at Ephesus instigated by Demas or Demetrius, Diotrephes and the artisans working in gold and silver jewelry for the goddess Diana, and having seen that no possible doubt can exist that they were a powerful branch of the Solonic organization, it is in order to fol-

[275] For something more on the *Appearance* of Jesus, see Myer's *Konv. Lex.*, in verb., *Christusbilder:* "Darnach schildert Johannes Damascenus im 8. Jahrh. das Bild Christi, womit der im 11. jahrh. bekannt gewordene Bericht des Lentulus und die byzantinischen C. harmoniren, z. B. die in Ravenna und Rom, welche Christus mit kurzem, gespaltenem Bart, langem, in der Mitte gescheiteltem Haar, und edlen Züge darstellen. Die C. in den Katakomben des Pontianus und Calixtus stammen aus dieser Zeit. So bleibt der Typus in den Mosaiken auf dem Smaragdbildnis."

[276] Mr. Reber, *Enigmas,* p. 80, might add the new Oxyrhynchus finds, the Bryennian κηρύγμα πετρού, the tell-tale points of the Clementine *Recognitions*, the Pliny *Letters*, and above all the newly-deciphered *Inscriptions*, to his list when he says: "The sacred writings of the therapeutæ, the Hebrew version of Matthew, the Epistle of James and the first of Peter, furnish the principles and doctrines which now form the life of christianity." So with equal prevision does Smith, *Biblical Dictionary,* 453, say: "The day of Pentecost is the birth-day." Every encyclopedia confirms it. Neander, *Planting*, I., c. 1, *Init.,* has it, where he says: "The Pentecost which, the disciples celebrated, soon after the crucifixion, is of great importance as marking the commencement of the Apostolic church; for here it first publicly displayed its essential character." Neander, then, knew very well that it was here that the membership was swollen from 120 to 3,000 and that they had all things common. And it all confesses that this "first plan" was the opening of the long-latent microcosm and its first outburst, into a vast future economic movement for temporal salvation.

low further this work of planting christianity among these and similar labor organizations existing at that auspicious moment in uncounted numbers, and in deep secrecy in all parts of Asia Minor. Our purpose is to show that the apostles used these unions as a welcome and genial home.[277]

The history of the early plant is involved in mystery. No one has ever explained why Peter, Titus, Thaddeus, Joseph of Arimathea and others of the companions of Jesus disappeared from view, nor whither they went. We lose track of them many years, when they reappear by some letter or quarrel, to sink back again into the recesses of obscurity, perhaps never to be seen or heard of again. These mysterious companions of Jesus are nearly all down in the Breviary of Martyriology, as having suffered death in the persecutions. One is struck with the overshadowing mystery which enshrouds Peter and his co-workers in Asia Minor, Titus in his nineteen years' hiding in Tyre and Cæsarea, John in his immense labors building up the celebrated seven churches of Asia. Into what secret dens did they creep all during those lost, untraceable years? Yet we know their time was not frittered away; for the fruits of their labor in secret cropped out all along the line in forms of splendid churches, and it was thus that the seven celebrated churches came into being.

Paul alone came out openly. But even he encountered trouble whenever he rushed himself into spheres of visable life. The truth is, Peter, Titus, John, Thaddeus and others of the original companions sequestered themselves among the unions.

These innumerable hives of labor cannot be compared with the trade unions which we have to-day. There was a vein of loving fraternity for each other, foreign from anything existing at the present time. According to the official outside world the poor who labored for a livelihood were without souls; they had no right under the law to marry and raise a family; unless covered with the legalizing veil of a burial attachment they and

---

[277] Cagnat, *Vie Contemp.*, Jan. 15, 1896, admits this: "C'est pourtant, en partie grâce au droit d' association, et à l' insu du pouvoir que s accomplit, à Rome et dans les provinces, la grande révolution morale et religieuse qui transforma le monde; sans lui (meaning trade-unionism), le christianisme aurait éprouvé les plus grandes difficultés non point tant à s' établir qu' à prospérer."

their unions were outlaws; for from the conquests, a Claudius, a Cæsar and a Cicero had crippled the hated jus coeundi of Solon and made their unions precarious. They lived at their endeared common table, a veritable institution, now so completely outgrown that it is unknown at the present age, yet was the source of their principal economy and especially delightful to them as a medium of conversation, acquaintance, sympathies and entertainments. So far as can be gleaned from literary references, generally contemptuous, and from inscriptional evidence, these meals at the common table were taken in the kuriakos of the microcosmic family, each member a worker who paid an assessment every month into a common fund. The deacon and the president bought provisions for the entire brotherhood with this money, procuring purchases at wholesale. None were allowed at the common table who did not pay the regular assessments, unless disabled by being out of work, by sickness, ald age, infancy or some other good excuse. When afterwards the christians knocked and were admitted, persecution, banishment in mines and dungeons served as an excuse. No humiliating charity, no phase of the later eleemosynary system, no beggary were ever known in these organizations. It was the law of Solon, as brought to Athens from Amasis Pharaoh of Egypt, and set up at the Prytaneum, that everyone should be able to give an honest and satisfactory account of how he or she made a living and the Solonic unions followed the law down to the suppression by the prelates in A.D. 363.

Their system of common meals was therefore no new thing. It was Pythagorean; and among aristocrats had been held in contempt as an abomination of the poor, since the abuse of it at Sybaris ages before.[278]

As shown by their anaglyphs, and especially those of the scholæ in subterranean Rome, they were allowed to believe they were gifted with a soul; a great comfort acting both ways, in inspiring both to hope and manhood. In these secret recesses, they taught themselves

[278] Chrysostom, *Works*, I., pp. 346, 697, 1034, 1040; V. 278, 654; X. 654, "Sybaritica mensa;" Vide notam, X., 654. Sybaris in Magna Græcia was sneered in antiquity, as being the city where was practiced all the wanton ease of the Pythagorean system. The meals were partaken in common, as in the Solonic unions; baths, after the idea of the licentious rich. But this was under the Pythagorean system of optimates and must by no means be confounded with the common table ceremonies of the labor unions.

to read, write, speak in public, sing, compose, forgive, and love one-another, believe in immortality, secure each other employment, and the true art of convivial enjoyment. Each union acted both socially and politically; socially, because it cultivated mutual assistance, respect, honor and love; politically, because, under the law the union itself was obliged to be framed after, and imitate the democratic city. The rules were so stringent that punishment was inflicted after death for suicide, by denying the offender the right of burial.[279] If a lazy-bones undertook to play the part of a sponge and failed to pay his monthly assessments, for the first offense he was fined and told to work, the employment being furnished him by the union; for the third offense he was expelled and the disgrace indelibly recorded against him by being inscribed upon a stone slab as minutes of the judgment before whose tribunal the sentence was pronounced.[280] It is understood that the orator Dion Chrisostom refers to these eranic rules as they were applied to the very early christians who are known to have shielded their brothers and their faith in this deep seclusion for safety, and also to have been as strict against laziness as the unions themselves of which they now formed a part.[281] There are even inscriptions discovered showing the decrees or charters on which these societies were founded, and the stipulations itemizing the various uses to which the moneys [282] of the unions

---

[279] Momms., *De Col. et Sodal.*, *Inscr. Lanuviana*, ad fin.: *Lex Collegii*: "Item placuit, quisquis ex quacumque causa mortem sibi adsciverit, ejus ratio funeris non habebitur." Cf. *supra*, Vol. I., p. 355.

[280] Foucart, *Ass. Rel.*, pp. 40, 41, 42. Fining of itself was considered a disgrace, but a severe concomitant was the exclusion or disbarring of a member from the right to vote. This severity has been discovered in three inscriptions: "Μὴ μετέστω αὐτῷ τῶν κοινῶν." One other rule was severe against immorality; "Si quelqu' un excite des batailles ou des tumultes, qu' il soit chassé de l' érane." In Asia Minor, Italy, and Greece, it was the same, Mauri, *I Cittadini Lavatori*, pp. 50-1, 'Αργίας νόμος. "Τῆς ἀργίας ἀτιμία ἔστω τὸ τίμημα, εἰ τρὶς τις ἁλώῃ.—Ἐὰν δέ τις ἁλῷ ἅπαξ, ζημιοῦσθαι δραχμὰς ἑκατόν." Id est: "La pena dell' ozio sia il disonore per chi vien tre volte convinto reo." Teffy, *Op. Cit.*, 1194; Pollux *Onomasticon*, VIII., 42. This Cyprian, *Epist.*, V., 2, confirms and declares that the agitators, even Paul, Peter, and all the others had a trade at which they labored, under the laws of the unions which forbade any person from getting something for nothing.

[281] Dion Chrysostom, *Essay on Virtue*, trans. of Gilbert Wakefield, Lond., 1800, pp., 151-160. Conversation between Diogenes and Sinapis. Here Dio gives the shirks a severe handling. This was during the lifetime of the men whose works we are now treating.

[282] Lüders, *Dion, Künst.*, p. 145: "In dem grossen Korkyräischen Decret über die Stiftung der Dionysien wird ausdrücklich der Fall vorgesehen, was mit dem Gelde zu machen sein werde: ὡσαύτως δὲ καὶ εἴ τις λίποι τὸν ἀγῶνα τῶν τεχνιτῶν, ἐγδανειζέσθω καὶ τὸ λειφθὲν ἀργύριον καὶ ὑπαρχέτω εἰς τὰν τῶν τεχνιτῶν μίσθωσιν."

EXEMPTION FROM MILITARY DUTY.

should be put. The Twelve Tables demanded it.[283] The unions when allowed to career unmolested were always the recipients of another boon. They were exempt from military duties. Dr. Gorius discovered these exemptions of the Roman collegia, as proved by important inscriptions in the Columbarium near the Appian Way, and to which we have already made reference. The scenic eranists were completely exempted in Asia Minor.[284]

Nor could the unions under the law dispose of or in any manner alienate their property which they held in common. By a far-sighted and wise jurisprudence the Solonic dispensation a thousand years before had completely recognized the gap which yawns between individual and social property, and arranged that when men combined together under its provisions, they were to be a microcosm of a perfect government, enlarged from the family, and in imitation of the ideal political government. Thus the ideal grew out of the perfect socialism which always exists in every well regulated family. This was enough. The conception was grand. It proved too sage to stand the blasts of human ambition and cupidity. Socrates gave an influential life and a pre-christian martyrdom for it; Plato, his true friend and devotee, succeeded him with his immortal Republic and Laws; Jesus came and went, like the rest, a martyred victim to this beautiful idea of social ownership, and the working millions, robbed of the possession of what their hands created, found themselves blessed with a Solonic dispensation which guaranteed them privilege and security to convert their units into mutual goods. Man in the brotherhood stands out as a family, a unit in society; common owner of the products all create. It was thus through the great Solonic dispensation, that

---

[283] Waltzing, *Hist. Corp. Prof.*, p. 64, speaking of the ancient Roman unions, says: "Ils étaient compris parmi les associations à qui les XII Tables garantirent une complète autonomie intérieure."

[284] Foucart, *De Scenicis Artificibus*, p. 41, quotes and translates from CIG, 3067, lines 14-16, as follows: "Artifices omnino immunes esse militia, quum maritima tum pedestri." And he refers us to Livy, vii., 2, and Diodorus, iv., 5, showing that theatrical people working at this trade or profession, were exempt throughout Rome, even from paying stipends. "Apud Romanos quoque provisum erat ne histriones stipendia facereni." In a former chapter we have dwelt upon the subject at length, chap. vi., *India*, giving Strabo's valuable confirmation of these immunities enjoyed among the brotherhoods of India under a great king Sandracottas.

the common property of these unions became inalienable.[285]

A profound wonder went abroad among the uninitiated, at an early date, regarding the spread of the christian culture. Writers, whose books are not lost, expressed astonishment that it could have been impregnated so early into the heathen jungles. Arnobius admires the rapidity with which the Word reached the Indians in the East and found the Britons in the North, or as he terms it, the West.[286] An astonishing sequel to his words has within recent years reached us in form of a tell-tale inscription found in the ruins of their church, built early in the apostolic age and by the men sent out. Joseph of Arimathea is a wonderful, newly discovered subject. He planted perhaps, at Glastonbury. Who else? The inscriptions recently found there, record a trade union of the carpenters, and a gift of some land for the members to erect their kuriakos, donated by Pudens, the friend of Paul, who secured permission of a British king named Cogidubnus who legalized the transaction. Pudens, who was later in Rome, lived among the Solonic collegia, married Claudia, a christian woman also mentioned in Paul's epistles, became the warm friend of the poet Martial, who was mentioned in scripture, died a martyr, and his ashes are now dug up from the under-ground cells of a collegium with a burial attachment, containing his inscription and remains of his cinerary urn. This strange find proves that the cause of the mysteriously rapid growth of the Word was none other than the secret unions existing in all

[285] These laws against disposal of common property, held good down to Valentinius and Valens. In touching upon them, we quote Granier de Cassagnac, *Hist. Class. Ouv.*, p. 349: "Leurs propriétés étaient inaliénables, ainsi que l' ont toujours été d' ailleurs les biens de toute corporation industrielle, municipale ou religieuse, en virtu des principes que nous avons établis dans le chapitre x. de cet ouvrage. L'inaliénabilité des biens des jurandes est constatée par un grand nombre de lois, entre autres, par une loi de Valentinien et de Valens: 'Patrimonia naviculariorum, quæ quo-libet genere, in extraneorum dominia demigrarant, in corporis sui jus proprietemque remeent.'" *Cod. Theod.*, lib. XIII., *tit.* vi., *leg.* 2, and *Cod. Theod.*, XIII., *tit.* vi., *leg.* 6: "Fundi omnes, ad naviculariorum dominium pertinentes, et ad aliorum jura translati....reddantur dominis." The dominus is in the same manner president or kurios which we have abundantly described, viz. the responsible individual recognized by the society, before the law. See *Digest*, XLVII., xx., p. 4.

[286] Arnob. *In Ps.*, cxlvii.: "Tam velociter currit sermo ejus, ut, cum per tot millia annorum in sola Judæa motus fuerit Deus, nunc intra paucos annos nec ipsos Indos lateat a parte Orientis, nec ipsos Brittanos a parte Occidentis."

known and accessible parts of the earth.[287] Another thing, deeply withdrawn but observed by Dr. Mauri, is that the eranos as typical for all Solonic brotherhoods, was of a dual nature, one side, the *eranikai dikai* being somewhat visible in political dealings with the state.[288] We have shown this political tendency of the eranos in its habit of loaning money to slaves desiring to buy themselves free, but we are not altogether informed whether such transactions were carried out in the mysteries with the usual secrecy or not.

We now proceed to set forth that it was these myriad occult unions of labor which were made use of during the earlier planting of the Word. The personal companions of Jesus seem to have disappeared. Nevertheless their work was most thoroughly done. When all the vast labors of this planting were accomplished there came a long period of levening, accompanied by a fierce melee of contentions; and according to the theory of the authorities we have quoted it did nothing very bad by the two centuries of wranglings. On the whole, if we be allowed to count progressive steps by æons instead of years it worked well; for although the votaries of egoism got control of the economic half of the great original plan of salvation actually for the first century carried out in miniature, such as the microcosm copying and enlarging the family, they succeeded at last in utterly ruining it, establishing the faith of Paul in a life to come while dethroning the demands of

---

[287] Lüd., *Dionys. Künst.*, begins his learned work with a description of them and an analysis of their name, as though the term ἔρανος should be typical for all the rest. He explains that they always ate at a common table "durch gemeinschaftlichen Cult, in eigenem Tempel κυριάκος, sowie durch gemeinschaftliche Mahlzeiten ihre Verwandtschaft in der Verehrung Heroen oder des Stammengottes θεὸς Πατρῷος pflegten." He quotes *Etym.*, M. 628. 23, on definition, among others also, Bekker, *Anek.*, p. 286, Harpocration, *Lex.*, Photius, and Hesych., *Lex.*, all of which define them as of a secret character, holding before christianity, sacrifices; but, all acknowledging the difficulty of getting their full record on account of their inapproachable presence.

[288] Mauri, *I Cit. Lav.*, p. 62, after instancing the contentions of Wescher, Böckh, Van Holst, Reinach, and others, says: "Gli studii più recenti tenderebbero ad assodare l' inesistenza del carattere di mutualità negli ἔρανοι, distinguendo bene i due istituti giuridicamente ed economicamente diversi, l' ἔρανος associazione e l' ἔρανος prestito, che parecchi scrittori con troppa facilità confusero insieme. Qualunque sia la vera delle due versioni, è certo però che le ἐρανικαί δίκαι di fronte al diretto publico rientravano semplicemente nel campo comune delle obligazioni civili, senza essere tutelate da speciali disposizioni da parti dei pubblici poteri." As the ἐρανικαί δίκαι, was an action arising out of the affairs of the eranos, it was often a matter referred to the civil law; but somewhat political in the emancipation of slaves through sale to a divinity.

James [289] and John that there is no salvation without works; and we have to-day the mocking skeleton of a Constantinian church instead of the warm, loving intermutual Christianity of Jesus.

We find it impossible, in fact useless, to follow these disseminators of the Word consecutively, either topograpically or chronologically; but shall for the present endeavor, so far as is known of their mysterious career, to keep within the period embracing the reigns of Caligula and Claudius, and shall notice evidences that they used to an enormous extent the kuriakoi, or houses, of these lords, who were presidents of the secret unions.

The Roman conquests were at an end. With Julius Cæsar, Cicero and the lex Julia, the Solonic unions were far from being exterminated as had been hoped by the senatorial power of the optimates. Augustus and Tiberius had lived upon the first actual imperial throne and had been too wise and prudent to molest them. Jesus, their first kurios of the "Word"[290] or Logos had come, offered a Lamb's sacrifice and gone, leaving the world his primitive diasporic brotherhood patterned exactly from the existing thousands with which pro-consular Rome more than ever teemed and had appointed trained missionaries, giving them scope to the uttermost ends of the earth. And what was that Word?[291] It was labor, work, performance of citizen duty.

Fitting these fundamental physical proofs to our work and arguing that they, with the so-called spiritual, were prominent as economic factors of their scheme,[292]

---

[289] *Epist. James*, v., 4. 'Ιδού, ὁ μισθὸς τῶν ἐργατῶν τῶν ἀμησάντων τὰς χώρας ὑμῶν, ὁ ἀπεστερημένος ἀφ ὑμῶν, κραζει. καὶ αἱ βοαὶ τῶν θερισάντων εἰς τὰ ὦτα κυρίου σαβαὼθ εἰσελήλυθασαν. Again, John. xv., 13: Greater love hath no man than this; that a man lay down his life for his friends.

[290] Neander, *Plant.*, Book V., Vol., I., says of John: "As Christ represents his Word or Words (his λόγος, his ῥήματα, his φωνήη) as the Word of God Himself, that thereby alone God reveals Himself to man the fountain of life, the word of life; so John might thereby be induced to distinguish Him or the Word which is God." This is getting very near Philo's Construction of the Logos.

[291] Adam Smith, *Wealth of Nations*, has sanctified labor with a mass of proofs never yet refuted that labor is divine power; in being the sole basis of all we have; and that which nourishes, fills us with health and spirit, lies at the bottom of home comforts, weans us away from temptation and wrong and creates plentitude and abundant treasures for family and commonwealth, is sacred. Adam Smith tells us that: "Labor is the only universal as well as accurate measure of value, or the only standard of which we may compare the values of different commodities at all times and in all places."

[292] Jerome, *Letters, Molchus, the Captive*, cap. 7, *fin.*: "I began to....long to initiate those ants and their doings, where work is for the community and common whole; and as nothing belongs to any one, all things belong to a"

we find modern commentators, who have had more than ordinary insight, expressing surprise; sometimes almost agog, always hesitating before they speak but too conscientious to deceive. Such were Mosheim, Gibbon and Neander. This latter scholar and researcher carefully, honestly and boldly prying into the origins, finds deacons, presbyters and other officers now familiar to archæologists engaged on a research of the unions, all busy in the organization which is plainly ready-made and older than the christian church. He quotes honest Mosheim, father of Ecclesiastical research, who finds the same unaccountable thing. We recommend the reader who may be in doubt, to read Neander's dissertation on the Planting, and follow this with a perusal of Mosheim's Ecclesiastical History. It is true that Neander, like Mommsen is too haughty and aristocratic in his inner soul to come down to the sublime Word of Jesus, who with ineffable humiliation and self abnegation was willing for a great and true cause, whose realization he knew to be afar off, to impersonate the truest form of the common workingman; but this only intensifies the fundamental truth that he came to save that long downtrodden factor of useful humanity. If then, he was inspired, as claimed, so much the holier and more richly inspired is the movement of labor to-day. So much the greater is the blaspheming which the modern church has committed all along the christian lines, in turning an arrogant front against the disfranchised millions on whom, like maggots and privileged paupers, it fastens and sucks and feeds, and whose solid substance its men thanklessly sap for every ounce of food and every delicious beverage without exception, that fattens them.

The Word was to be scattered to the ends of the earth. A miraculous power was bestowed upon a select few with which to accomplish it. Each and all the original companions of Jesus known to have disappeared, returned and again sequestered themselves, thus alternating between darkness and light and their lapses from the visible to the occult sometimes covered years of time and when they emerged, a new congregation always appeared.

It is known that Peter and Clement worked faithfully and harmoniously together, and that Clement wrote the last Kerugma Petrou or sermons. They were in existence when Clement of Alexandria lived, for he used them. Hegesippus the first historian of the church had Peter's Gospel. Now it is recorded that Peter, before going to Rome, traveled as far eastward as the Euphrates, taking in Constantinople and Chalcedony and was supposed to have had a copy of his teachings. But everything regarding this great journey rests in profoundest mystery. It is certain that he built up the church at Byzantium; and this fact brings us to our important inquiry.

On what principles did Peter found the Byzantine church? Regarding this we have some inscriptions and recent finds. In the year 1873, Philotheus Bryennius, head master to the higher Greek school at Constantinople, but now the ordained metropolitan of Nicomedia, discovered in the library of Jerusalem and monastery of the Most Holy Sepulchre at Constantinople, the veritable manuscript used by Peter on that journey. Peter was teaching in the far off cities, such as Byzantium and Chalcedony, and the evidence is that he must have had some assistance from secret unions who had already been located there. The MSS. found by Bryennius, we took the pains to visit and inspect in our final voyage in 1896.[293]

The theory spread itself abroad that the "Teachings" were originally written for a community of converts in some obscure locality.[294] Without the least doubt a great secret agitation was carried on among the hetaeræ

---

[293] This discovery revealed the long lost Διδάχη Πέτρου. It is none other than the celebrated teaching of Peter which was copied many times in the early ages, and was current in 1056 when this copy was taken. It is now called the "*Corex*," and was the original of Peter's *Teachings*, going current by the name "Τῶν 'Αποστόλων αἱ λεγομέναι Διδαχαί." By Rufinius, it is called "*The Judgment of Peter.*" It is acknowledged to be of the early first century. See Dr. Riddle, *Ante-Nicine Fath.*, Vol. VII., pp. 372-383. In Chalcedony directly over-against Constantinople, and in plain view, there has been found an inscription of a secret union, which was that of the Twelve; Oehler, *MSS.;* "*Nachtrag:* θιασῶται in Kalkedon bezeichnet auch als κοινόν χρέιον in einer Inschrift über das Preisterthum der δώδεκα θεοί. Collitz, *Dialektinschriften*, nr. 3051. It is a κοινὸν τῶν δώδεκα 'Αποστόλων, ie. union of the Twelve Apostles.

[294] *I. Cor.*, iv., 17, sending the brotherhoods a teacher; xi., 34: Εἴ τις πεινᾷ ἐν οἴκῳ ἐσθιέτω ἵνα μὴ εἰς κρίμα συνέρχησθε. κ.τ.λ. The words "at home" in the *trans.* are not the true rendering for οἴκῳ. That they endorsed the common table and the communal code, is shown by the otherwise incomprehensible slur cast by Paul, *Gal.*, iv., 9, twitting their old custom of being "weak and beggarly elements, whereunto ye desire to be in bondage." It is now thought by some students of the eranos of Bithynia, especially those with which Pliny, a few years later had so severely to deal, that Paul refers to their custom of the common meal, as weak and beggarly.

of the old unions in the immediate neighborhood where
this document was found, and several important inscriptions have been recently found there. But the
perfect proof afforded in the official letters which were
exchanged between Pliny and the emperor Trajan not
fifty years after the labors of Peter there, are extremely
interesting since they mention Christ and the christians
time and again showing the propagandism of Peter to
be the christianizing improvements upon a cult already
existing among a large number of unions which had the
common table of the Solonic dispensation. We shall
produce these valuable evidences, a little later in our
chapter on Trajan.

The Bryennian *Didachæ Petrou* or Teachings of Peter come squarely out in many places showing that this
itinerant ambassador used the unions. In one place it
speaks of "making churches, *kuriakæ* in the secret societies." [295] In another place the brothers were taught
to love one another and the injunction is repeated verbatim: "Thou shalt love thy neighbor as thyself;" and at
the close of this chapter is an indiscriminate commandment against charity other than so far as that word
covers its original signification which is the moral and
humane and not the economic; and warning us to kindness and sympathy for our fellow men.[296] Peter's code
of teachings likewise required the distribution of the
first fruits, another requirement of the older unions, in-
grafted into the Corpus Juris Civilis to this day.[297] The
second chapter of the Didachæ enjoins against the hea-
thenisms, which as charged by Clement of Alexandria
and abundantly shown in the inscriptions, were often
an abomination in the old unions, especially those worshiping the divinities Cybele of Phrygia, Cotytto of Ma-

---

[295] *Ante-Nicine Fath.*, Vol. VII., pp. 380-1; Euseb., *De Princtp. Præf.*, § 8, *Doct. of Peter.* Jerome found it in the gospel According to the Hebrews; and it is a part of the first and original of our Matthew, which was written in Hebrew, and garbled a century later for our use. It is known to have contained directions upon the complete economic methods, now lost and ruled out of our thus cheated christianity. The reading is "Ποιῶν εἰς μυστηριὸν κοσμικὸν ἐκκλησίας" ie. making churches in the outside or worldly secret societies. It is in the Διδαχαί τῶν 'Αποστόλων, cap. xi.

[296] These are the positive demands which we have quoted from the pre-christian unions, vide *supra* in chapter on Customs and Habits, and are father to the christian doctrine, being in the laws and regulations of the unions 300 years before Christ, and recorded in many inscriptions, as one of the qualifications of membership which candidates must submit to before admission to the κυριάκος.

[297] Διδαχαι Πετρου, τῶν δώδεκα 'Αποστόλων, cap. i., ii. Against the commission of abominations, cap. iii.

cedonia and Anubis of Egypt. These outrageous initiations, often obscene to the last degree, followed the usages of the stricter and more secret initiations of the official Eleusinian mysteries, which, so far as we can penetrate are now shown to have mixed lasciviousness with hideous cruelties and in more than one case actual cannibalism.[298] Paul fought them; and we shall explain hereby, great mistakes that are made in supposing he was fighting Peter, John and others of the personal companions of Jesus. On the contrary he was only fighting against outrageous practices which lay in the way of this higher and refined system of Jesus, which admitted all that was good, and repudiated the bad that was in them. This discovery, so long believed to be irretrievably lost, is of inestimable worth to our argument that christianity could not have succeeded had it not had the already more than half christian Word in thousands of secret unions with their arms stretched open to receive and protect them. It was the substance, economical and spiritual, in that blessed document which actually constituted the old original evangelic school.[299] Another clause of the same newly discovered document of St. Peter [300] is so valuable that we give it in the text without quoting the Greek. It deals with the labor question and shows a perfect agreement with the inscriptions already quoted: "Reception of our brethren" into the eranos: "But let every one that cometh in the name of the kurios or lord be received and afterwards ye shall prove and know him; for ye shall have understanding right and left. If he who cometh is a wayfarer, assist him as far as ye are able; but he shall not remain with you except for two or three days, if needy. But if he willeth to abide with you, being a

[298] *Canon. Apost.*, 62: "Si quis episcopus, aut presbyter, aut diaconus, aut omnino quicunque ex sacerdotali consortio, cumederit carnes in sanguine animæ ejus, aut a bestiis abreptum aut suffocatum, deponitor; Hoc enim lex prohibuit," For deeds of cannibalism, see *index*, in verb. *Abominations*. For the phallic cult, Clement of Alex. *Protrept.*, p. 76, c. 2: Ταύτης τῆς πελαγίας ἡδονῆς τεκμήριον τῆς γονῆς, ἁλῶν χόνδρος καὶ φαλλὸς τοῖς μυουμένοις τὴν τέχνην τὴν μοιχικὴν ἐπιδίδοται· νόμισμα δὲ εἰσφέρουσιν αὐτῇ οἱ μυούμενοι ὡς ἑταίρᾳ ἐρασταί."

[299] Origen, *Ad Matth.*, xiii., 54-6, in like manner makes allusion to this Gospel of Peter. It was a part of this Doctrine. It went by the name of Κηρυγμα τοῦ ἐπιγεγραμμένου κατὰ Πέτρου εὐαγγελίου, and agreed with the notions of the Jews. We refer to auxiliary evidence in Theodorus, *Hæret. Fab.* II., 2, who declares it was ebionitic in being the salvation of the proletaries, who otherwise had nothing. This Father calls it Εὐαγγελίον καθ' 'Εβραίος,

[300] Διδαχαί τῶν δώδεκα 'Αποστόλων, cap. xii., Comp. *II Thess.*. iii., 10.

tradesman, let him work and eat: and if he hath no trade according to your understanding, see to it that as a christian, he shall not live with you idle. But if he willeth not to work, he is a christmonger." Now this regulation which outlines the character of candidates for initiation into the secret society, greatly resembles many described on stone slabs where sometimes elaborate details are given. We have already explained them.[301] The fifth chapter of this document is especially interesting, as it contains a list of things and persons to be avoided. Special provision is made against admitting the wandering tramps, fakirs and deceivers who as Celsus tells us, and Lucian confirms, wandered like vagabonds over the country in quest of opportunity to crawl into the unions and sponge.

Another scripture of Peter's teachings, is: "Let no one who is at variance with his fellow, come together with you until reconciled."[302] It appears as though the *hagios, eusebes, agathos,* of the ancient unions were, in the pre-christian stage, for all the members of the koinon, direct and without an intercessor; and that in order to conform to the original wisdom they were bound to love one another, from an economic point of view if no other, that in so doing they furnish the common table, and each other with employment. But the introduction of the post-messianic period shirked the original direct self-help principle on another, viz Christ. This intermediary is Neander's buttress of hope.

Not unfrequently we come in contact with inscriptions which speak of the ex-apostles.[303] They appear to be of the purely pagan class, and a closer inspection of their remains by the archæologists reveals the fact that exapostoloi or evangelists attached to their mithraic cult were a common thing. We are only led by their tempting inscriptions into a world of wonder, and

[301] See *index* in verb. *Charity.*
[302] Here again, we find perfect conformity to the more ancient Solonic rule.
[303] Oehler, *MSS.:* "Κοινον τῶν ἐξαποστόλων," another college of the Twelve. Again· "Κοινὸν τῶν ἐξαποστόλων gefundene Inschrift. Reisen auf den Inseln des Thrakischen Meeres, p. 65, führt nach den Τηῖοι an τοῦ κοινοῦ τῶν τεχνιτῶν τῶν ἀπὸ Ἰωνίας καὶ Ἑλλήσποντου." This is another college of the Twelve, yet in the pagan stage. Dr. Oehler refers to innumerable inscriptions, found in the towns of the ancient Hellespont and the Bosphorus, as well as in the islands of these seas: "Κορκύρα, Reinach, *Mus.,* XVIII., 1863, p. 548, nr. 21 : ἱερατεύσας τῳ κοινῳ τῆς συνοδου ἀνέθηκε. Mantineia, *Athen. Mitth.,* IV., 1879, p. 146-147c : τῇ συνόδῳ, Pantakapeum, Latyschew, II., nr. 60-4 ; Μους. κ βίβλ., II 2., 1876-78, p. 51, nr. 119.

must wait for more light to dawn through them upon some perhaps astonishing trait of the history of christianity. Certain it is, that the old mithraic unions, long before the Advent, used to send out evangelizing apostles, as propagators of their cult which is known by many inscriptional and as many collateral evidences to have more than any other, resembled christianity.

Whiston and many other critical and honest writers, declared that the Doctrines of Peter "were the most sacred of the canonical books of the New Testament" and they appear to be verbatim, or as may have been believed, inspired copies of the exact language of Jesus, delivered at Jerusalem and Mount Zion, to the eleven apostles assembled there, after the resurrection. They embraced the common table, and made a demand that all labor and assist one-another as in a perfect family. They entered into the Apostolic Constitutions along with the eighty-four Petrine laws called canons of St. Peter, practically suppressed but still extant in the Latin, and used by us, as preserved in the Benedictine copies of the Corpus Juris Civilis.[304] Mr. Gibbon was in doubt whether Peter took them from some apocryphal book or an unwritten tradition; but this latter would be about equivalent to our suggestion that he committed them to memory simply by hearing them pronounced, as persons sometimes have the memory to do. Peter, it is known, spoke Greek fluently and wrote it so well that Dr. Smith declares his grammer and composition compared well with Paul's. But the ordinary reader can scarcely imagine the short distance which separates Galilee from Syria in southern Asia Minor, or the large commercial traffic from the North.

There occur many strange expressions recorded in different early writings, like the Protevangelium of James, all pointing to the universal habit of the poorer people, of eating at a common table, practicing strictly the marriage or highly virtuous social relations, instead

---

[304] *Canon. Apost.*, 40: "Præcipimus, ut episcopus res ecclesiæ in potestate habeat. Nam si prætiosæ hominum animæ fidei ejus committendæ sunt, multo utique magis oportuerit, et de pecuniis mandatum dare, ut illius arbitratu dispensentur, neque non cum timore Dei, summaque sollicitudine per presbyteros ac diaconos erogentur in pauperes. Percipiat autem et ipse (si modo indiget) quantum ad necessarios suos, et hospitio exceptorum fratum usus opus habet, ne quo modo ipse posteriore loco habeatur, quam cæteri. Ordinavit enim lex Dei, ut qui altari inserviunt de altari nutriantur; quando nec milites unquam suis stipendiis arma hostibus inferant."

of the lax and dissolute condition prevailing everywhere at that time.[305] Something was done over and beyond the merely spiritual, such as Paul is known to have exclusively taught and held to. Peter, John, James and the other personal companions of Jesus and even Jesus himself, all gave out instructions, regarding the necessity of saving the body. On this, we have many powerful passages in the writings of the earliest fathers of the movement, [306] and several strong references to the same sentiment which certainly prevailed to such a large extent that it was considered in the early organization the economical factor in christianity and indispensably necessary to the success of the spiritual.[307]

The life, adventures and martyrdom of Paul are now, after an immense adverse criticism under the Tübingen school, considered good history. But still more recent than Dr. Baur, and the literary critics, are the inscriptions of the strictly scientific age, and we are at last in possession of the archæological monuments which record the names of persons Paul used; and especially of those, who were entrusted to carry his celebrated epistles from place to place, such as Tychicus. Peter, and the other immediate companions of Jesus notably Thaddeus, Joseph of Arimathea who it is now believed went northward and planted in Britain, Philipp who hid for nineteen years in Cæsarea; all preached among and under the friendly ægis of the secret unions who endorsed, loved and protected them. This explains the phenomenal success of ancient christianity. It was economical

---

[305] *Protev.*, cap. xiii., 3: "And I (Joseph, spouse of Mary), looked down toward the earth and saw a table spread, and working people sitting around it." etc., It was this James who was the celebrated κύριος of the ebionitic poor-manism which was the foundation of the whole Solonic system of unions, although they assumed perhaps nearly a hundred names.

[306] Ignatius: "Ἐγὼ γὰρ καὶ μετὰ τὴν ἀνάστασιν ἐν σάρκι αὐτὸν οἶδα καὶ πιστεύω ἐντά, καὶ ὅτε πρὸς τοὺς περὶ Πέτρου ἦλθεν, ἔφη αὐτοῖς, λάβετε, ψυλοφησάτε μὲ, καὶ ἴδετε ὅτε οὐκ' εἰμι δαιμόνιον ἀσωμάτον· καὶ εὐθὺς αὐτοῦ ἥψαντο, καὶ ἐπίστευσαν."

[307] The *Apostolic Constitutions* are full of the care-taking spirit of the early church organizations. They show that members had to work, earn and pay their tithes. The entire sixth Book is economic and based on absolute communism. In this they resemble the Διδάχαι Πετροῦ. The *gospel* of *Works: Epistle* of James, i., 22; "Be ye doers;" i., 25; ii., 17, 20, 26; "Faith without works is dead." This, see 15, 16, had reference to the *economic* question. "If there come unto your assembly," etc., ii., 2, shows that the assembly must have been an *eranos*. "Go to, now, ye rich men. Weep and howl for your miseries that shall come upon you," v., 1. Again, v., 5, "Behold the hire of the labourers." Again, v., 14: "Is any sick among you, let him call for the elders." The same original ideas of economy as superior to everything is also seen in Irenæus. *Contra Hær.*, V., c., 2, and elsewhere, although in other places one is constrained to think he was a treacherous hireling of the enemy.

and planted among the lowly, prospered and thrived down to the disastrous days when, beautiful in musical and industrial genius, it fell a suffering victim.

In consequence we find that the lesser mysteries, those initiating the proletarian class into the thousands of self-help societies, were prone to imitate the greater or official initiations. So far as they knew and dared, they imitated the secret ceremonies of the Eleusinian rites, and we are told that it maddened the Athenians, who took affront at their presumption. A raging persecution followed the adoption of a law against the introduction into Athens of stranger divinities and the corruption of morals of the youth, under which Socrates, Ninos and Theoris suffered death and many others were persecuted.[308] But were the Athenians alone in this? After the Roman conquests and even before, it was found that large amounts of money could be made out of the gullible superstitions of the poorer classes who would pay high assessments as initiation fees, so great was their desire to become members of the unions, and to entice and wheedle them into these payments the state religion or its priests no doubt, entered into collusions with the priesthood of the lesser mysteries, as in the case of Paulina and Mundus reported by Josephus, and obtained sums of booty both for themselves and their altars, which was equivalent to the public coffers. The intrigue entered into between the man Mundus and the priests of Anubis, Egyptian dogheaded patron of the hunting-grounds, and male divinity for Diana, having at Rome his temple on the Aventine Hill in neighborship with that of Diana, was one of the most remarkable. Josephus has told it but we refrain. Suffice it to record that the emperor Tiberius, when the scandal got out, had the priests and probably also the priestesses publicly crucified, while the two principles, Paulina the victim of the trick, and Mundus the briber, who enjoyed her, escaped because of their nobler station. The reader must be here reminded that the penalty of crucifixion was confined to the lowly classes and to their representatives. Jesus was crucified because he was a workingman and his enemies recognized no aristocratic or patrician blood in him. The

[308] See *supra*, in chap. xv., pp. 347-396,

STORY OF PAULINA AND MUNDUS. 489

reputed million of slaves punished during the servile wars just ended, including the two thousand after the defeat of Spartacus, were all crucified. A little honor or even Roman citizenship, if proved, always saved the condemned one from the ignominious cross. Thus, Paul could be beheaded, while Peter, because a low-born fisherman, was hanged to the terrible cross. So the priests of Anubis were crucified. This, under the law, proves that they, with their temple on the Aventine Hill which was afterwards burned, were representatives of the same bread-winners' organizations as the inscriptions teach us, as hunters, to supply the fierce gladiatorial games.

Solon, in his law organizing the various trades, had prescribed an especial clause for the hunters and fishermen and those out in the cold, seeking a precarious living.[309] Anubis, Artemis, Diana, Isis, Sarapis and Sabazios are all related, their names and sex varying in the different countries and languages. They all represented the initiations of the lesser mysteries and had temples and altars especially for them. Besides this, they are quoted as being the protectors of laborers, artists, agriculturists and hunters, fishers and all those engaged in the work of forging a living, being the "ennoblers of mankind and the givers of joys," like Dionysus, another relation.[310]

[309] Cf. Vol. I., p. 393; also *index*, pointing to pages where we have given inscrs. of the hunters' unions. But Ramsay, *Cit. Bish. Phryg.*, II., pp. 535, 549, Apameia, under the law of the coll. tenuiorum, with the funeral attachment: συμβίωσις, κοινὸν, συνέδρια, κ.τ.λ. On account of the danger of publicity they are vague, but the epitaphs of the θιασωταί τῶν κυνηγῶν are numerous. Ramsay, II., no. 389, quotes the epitaph, still existing, of one, cited by Cumont, 213. which is puzzling the archæologists, who do not know whether the hunters are real or whether it is not a reference to the hunters and fishers of men, as a christian sign: "Αὐρήλιος Αὐξάνων δὶς ἐποίησα τὸ ἡρῷον ἐμαυτῷ καὶ τῷ ἀδελφῷ μου Δωσιτύχη δώρου χάριν σὺν τῇ γυναικὶ αὐτοῦ· εἰς ὃ ἕτερος οὐ τεθήσεται· εἰ τις δὲ ἕτερος ἐπιτηδεύσει, ἔσται αὐτῷ πρὸς τὸν θεόν· χείρετέ μοι φιλόθεοι καὶ καλοὶ νεόθηροι.'' Another similar, presents the same puzzle as to what the members are hunting: Dumont, no. 46. Dr. Oehler furnishes us with a number of valuable inscrs. of the ancient hunters, and fishermen: "Jäger—κυνηγοί. In Haliartos bestand eine σύνοδος τῶν κυνηγῶν, *Inscr. Gr.*, 9858. In Philippopolis eine κυνηγῶν κοινὸν. Dumont, *Mél d' Archéol.*, p. 33, 42. Aus Steiris ist eine Weihinschrift erhalten mit οἱ κυνηγοί. Le Bas, II., 988. Artemis, in Kition auf Kypros: κυνηγοί, CIG., 2614, In Pantopolis Egypten, κυνηγοί." The latter worked for the state and furnished the royal menageries with wild beasts.

[310] Oehler, *MSS.*, presents a number of therapeutæ who had Anubis for their tutelary divinity, engrossed in various trades, all βάπται. Lobeck *Aglaoph.*, p. 1039. Their worship was Κοτύττω. They were regular unions. "In den vier erst-genannten Inscriften, erscheinen die θεραπευταί als Corporation, neben dem Volke der Athener und der Römer, *Bull. Hell.*, VI., 1884, p. 501, nr. 24." Here it is seen that the Roman unions were frequently therapeutæ and had Isis, Anubis, Dionysos and Sabazios for their protecting powers. Hebrew unions of the same kind are also mentioned for Alexandria and Rome.

The cause of Paulina's confidence in the priests was the reputed holiness and the unspeakable reverence for Anubis. She yielded to the latter's requirements because she really believed it was a heavenly mission and had no doubt that it was an awful solemnity. She bowed to an unspeakable honor, firmly believing, as it were, that she heard the trump of Gabriel; for in the ancient belief of immaculate conceptions, angels had access to the fairest of the mortals, and no one dared to divulge an oath of initiation or question the divine sacredness of the epoptic couch.[311] On the contrary, her own husband actually consented. The date of this scandal, which threw Rome into a turmoil, was about one year after the crucifixion; for Josephus brings it in after his memorable mention of Jesus Christ; indeed, in the next paragraph, plainly telling us that it was about that time. The intermediary person who succeded in consummating the bribe and deception was Ide or Ida, a freedwoman of Mundus, the man in love with Paulina. The amount she paid the priests of Isis for accomplishing the intrigue was fifty thousand Greek drachmæ or francs; more than ten thousand dollars.

Now looking this scandal all over we find that the temple of Isis, supposed to be on the hill of the Campus Martius, was in reality in the Tiber valley, but a short distance from where now stands the church of St. Peter, and that already great numbers of christians had settled from the East among the hives of collegia and thiasoi which covered that very territory. Here were the clustering houses of the communia mimorum, Dionysan trade guilds which existed in Italy in great numbers, the identical collegia licita sub imperatoribus,[312] out of which Mommsen thinks the ordo Augus-

[311] Herodot., *Euterpe*, 61: left much of the mysteries untold because, though an initiate he dared not divulge: "Ἐν δὲ βουσίρι πόλι ὡς ἀνάλουσι τῇ Ἴσι τὴν ὀρτὴν, εἴρηται πρότερον μοι· τύπτονται μὲν γὰρ δὴ μετὰ τὴν θυσίην παντες καὶ πᾶσαι, μυριάδες κάρτα πολλαὶ ἀνθρώπων. Τὸν δὴ τύπτονται, οὔ μοι ὅστιον ἐστι λέγειν." κ.τ.λ.

[312] Mommsen, *De Col. et Sodal., Rom.*, p. 83, note 6; "Ita in communia mimorum theatri Bovillensis, Orell., 2625, commemoratur L. Acilius Eutyches omnibus corporibus ad scenam honoratus, ut in decreto colegii Serapis CI. 120: ἐπαινέσαι αὐτοὺς καὶ στεφανῶσαι θαλλοῦ στεφάνῳ ἐν Σαραπείῳ. Hæc laudatio et coronatio modo semel facta modo in tempus vitæ modo perpetua frequentissima est in collegiis Græcis CI., 109, 110, 2220, 2525ᵇ, 3065, 3066. Communia mimorum multa inveniuntur; CI., 349: 'ἡ ἱερὰ Ἀδριανή Ἀντωνείνη θυμελικὴ περιπολιστικὴ μεγάλη σύνοδος τῶν ἀπὸ τῆς οἰκουμένης περιτὸν Διονύσον καὶ Αὐτοκράτορα Καίσαρα—Ἀδρίανον—νέον Διονύσον τεχνιτῶν; ibique Böckh, CI., 2931, Trallibus: ἡ Ὀλυμπικὴ σύνοδος τῶν ἀπὸ τῆς οἰκουμένης ἱερονείκων καὶ στεφανειτῶν. Cf. 2620, 9932, 3068ᶜ; præsertim τὸ κοινὸν τῶν περὶ τὸν Διονύσον τεχνιτῶν τῶν ἐπ' Ἰωνίας καὶ Ἑλλησπόντου. Strabo, 643: CI., 2963, 3067-3072."

talis was derived. We have the best of evidence from early authors outside of the inscriptional history which is daily augmenting with the new discoveries at Rome, that the movement of the Word was rapidly spreading, at as early a date as Tiberius,[313] and what is more surprising is the frequent statements that it occupied as its most fruitful field these places of abominable practices, planting into them, says John Chrysostom, and making churches of meretricious dens.[314] These darkling, tawdry snuggeries of the Roman mine-colony from the great Gemeinde at Teos, were haunts of Osirian and Isian cult.[315] Here in the valley of the Tiber is the richest field in the world for stone monuments and epitaphs and other carvings of the early christians. We shall show much more on this subject as we proceed. It is here that Philo hid away among the therapeutic abodes to escape danger when Claudius turned him down. It was here that Peter crept when he came to preach, and in these home-stalls that Clement was converted by Barnabas in the earliest dawn of the propaganda. Later it was here that Claudius made his truculent lunge upon the Jews and christians, driving thousands into banishment. When Nero came to power he threw his most malignant spite directly upon this spot, and burned this whole region of Rome including the temple of Diana, because she befriended the poor who clustered around her temple and often sought refuge in the crypts of her asylum. This has been fully proved by the recent discovery of the phenmenal scholæ, reclining couches and sepulchral paraphernalia which sank yards underground during the persecutions that followed, and there denned and preached and suffered with the result to

[313] Chrisost., I., p. 635: "Ecclesiis brevi tempore repletus orbis." Plutarch *Symp. qa.*, VII., 3, shows that after the time of Menander, B.C. 342-291, comedies by these communia mimorum, played in Latin at Rome, and the municipia were sacred to the Διονύσος Καθηγέμων, or forerunner of a Saviour. Their hives and dens consequently offered an extremely mellow soil for converted Jews, who are well known to have been initiates in large numbers, and to have emigrated to Rome as early as Tiberius. This accounts for their persecution and exile at an early time.

[314] Chryost., III., p. 403: "Ecclesia virgo quæ prius erat meretrix." And in another place, V., p. 202, he talks of the results of the plant into this fruitful soil, mellowed by music, brotherly love, and mutual care; and for centuries hoping for the promised Saviour, in this strain: "Ecclesia olim sterilis, nunc mater est filium innumerabilium."

[315] It was this culture which Hadrian found in A.D. 122, at Alexandria, causing him to write his remarkable letter to Servianus, in which he calls them christians differing in nothing from the mithraists, and berates them all together as tricksters and frauds. See *index* in verb. *Hadrian's Letter*, pointing to where the whole letter is quoted.

bring into the world the organized Word of this era's faith.

Now the lesson of this episode of the scandal of Paulina and the priests of Isis and Anubis is, that good can sometimes come from bad. Paul and the apostles planted among the festering abominations the higher creed and the nobler thoughts, because the humanity to be saved by the new socialism lived and smothered in these lairs. Indeed, it was written that it should be so. There is a large literature left us showing this. The advocates of the new religion boasted for nearly two hundred years that they were poor, ignorant fishermen and workingmen of other trades and professions, just as was their crucified Saviour. Hundreds of documents attest this, beginning with the ancient teachings of Peter and running down to the time of Lactantius with comments of Gibbon, Mosheim and Neander; and when there came an era of wealth and pride which whetted up an unholy shame, the good men like John Chrysostom, Augustine and Jerome mourned for the return of the lost happiness, virtue and simplicity.[316]

[316] *Anc. Syriac Doc. Teachings of St. Peter:* "Moreover, because we were catchers of fish, and not skilled in books, therefore did he also say to us: 'I will send unto you the spirit,'" etc.; *I Corinth.*, 29: Διὰ τοῦ τὸ παρέδωκεν αὐτοὺς ὁ θεὸς εἰς πάθη ἀτιμίας· αἱ γὰρ θήλειαι αὐτῶν πετήλλαξεν τὴν φυσικὴν χρῆσιν εἰς τὴν παρὰ φύσιν· ὁμοίως τε καὶ οἱ ἄρρετες ἀφέντες τὴν φυσικὴν χρῆσιν τῆς θελείας ἐξανανθῆσαι ἐν τῇ ὀρέξει αὐτῶν, κ.τ.λ.; Neander, *Planting*, III., vi.: " The greater number indeed, of the persons with whom Paul came in contact at Corinth, were not, as at Athens, people of cultivated minds, but belonging to the lower class, who were destitute of the higher sentiments; Gibbon, chap. xv., over note 184: "....that the new sect of the christians was almost entirely composed of the dregs of the populace; of peasants and mechanics, of boys and women, of beggars and slaves, the last of whom might introduce the missionaries into the rich and noble families, in which they belonged." See Minucius Felix, c. viii.; Celsus ap. Origen, III., pp. 133, 144; Julian *ap.* Cyril, vi., p. 206; Mosheim, *Hist. Eccles.*, I., First Century,Pt. III., chap. 2, § 21, 22; Hermes, *On Spurious Writers:* "Celestial spirits talk more insipidly than our scavengers and porters." Again, 22: "For that a large part of the human race should have been converted by illiterate and imbecile men;" Later, after priest power set in and seized the honors, Lactantius, *Div. Inst.*, I., c. 18, complains that "smiths, potters, weavers, and all such are disallowed honors and dignity which were given by Minerva, patroness of the artificers." Lactantius further says, *id.*: "People of the lower classes were those who had hitherto been given up to the lusts that prevailed in this sink of moral corruption;" Neand., *Plant.*, Book III., ch. vii.; "a class of persons so far below themselves in numbers, respectability and political influence," etc. Tert., *Apol.*, 46, declares that a christian mechanic could readily answer such questions as had perplexed the wisest of Grecian sages." Tert., *De Anima:* "Stand forth, O soul, and give thy witness. But I call thee not as when, fashioned in schools, trained in libraries, fed in Attic Academies and porticos, thou belchest egoism. I address thee simple, rude, uncultivated, untaught, such as want thee who have thee only;—thing of the road, the street, the workshop. I want thine experience." etc. Plutarch, *Tract on Epicureanism*, c. 22, says of them sneeringly; "....and when they make offerings, they only contemplate that part of the priest's duty, which represents the slaughtering cook." Again, *De*

Probably the most remarkable and beneficent matter connected with the planting among the so-called abominations of the "vilis plebicula" of Phrygia, Macedonia, and Rome was the eventual lifting of woman up into a sphere of equality with man. It did this, and it was a thing never done before. All through antiquity we hear nothing but sneers for women. Only the one mother, the mater familias, under the great ancient law of primogeniture, could be honored and ennobled.[317] All the rest were stamped down to be used by men as mere things without dignity or honor.

The direct and immediate result of the Solonic dispensation was to furnish immense numbers of places and positions, the climbing upward into which was very similar to the modern methods of the civil employments under governments. Another lift upwards for women was marriage. The two worked together. It is mostly among the inscriptions that we find this history; and as in every case, they, or their unions for them, wrote these epitaphs, monograms and protocols, one readily sees that we have our evidence from an unquestionable source.

It was by no means unnatural that the unions of trades and labor following the original law requiring that the jus coeundi could not go outside the municipal organizations,[318] should be full of customs and habits distasteful to the refined life mapped out by the original companions of Jesus. Paul had agreed to carry out the plans of the first association organized at Jerusalem and baptized before his own eyes in the blood of the martyred Stephen. It was a solemn thing for him. He found men and women of high abilities struggling to raise from the Dionysan and Cotyttian grovelings and saw his noble mission. Now was the time to lift down-

Stoicis. Repugnantibus, c. 15: they are no better than old women, frightening children. Τὸν περὶ τῶν ὑπὸ θεοῦ κολάσεων λόγον, ὡς οὐδὲν διαφέροντα τῆς ᾿Ακκοῦς καὶ τῆς ᾿Αλφιτοῦς, δὲ ὧν τά παιδεία τοῦ κακοσχολεῖν αἱ γυναῖκες ἀνείρουσιν," and warns us that the long beard of the priest of Isis stands for little; Ramsay, *Cit, Bish. Phryg.*, II., p. 511: "Complaint of Aristidus about 'the shocking Greek used by the christians.'"

[317] See Vol. I., pp. 50-53; 72; 78, note 30, where this ancient law of the pater familias is discussed, and the cause of marriage traced to the transmission of the paternity to the first born son.

[318] *Digest*, III., iv., § 1: "Quibus autem permissum est corpus habere collegii sociatatisve sive cujusque alterius eorum nominis, proprium est ad exemplum reipublicæ habere res communes, arcam communem et actorum sive syndicum, per quem tamquam in republica, quod communiter agi flerique oporteat, agatur fiat."

trodden women out of these abominable practices. The
men, steeped in the service of their lascivious goddess,
objected and refused to be reformed. Do we hear of
the women turning a deaf ear to the innovation? We
have searched a thousand inscriptions and can find
nothing but a tendency of higher purity. In the exercise of the jus coeundi woman in the lowly unions is
known to have enormously braced and bolstered the
faltering men. These unions, whether the collegia, the
eranoi or the Dionysan Gemeinde, always treated her,
not as a menial of the patricians, but as an equal. Once
initiated, she owned her common share. She prepared
the common meal, managed the frequent banquets and
symposiums, held a noble and dignified standing, married and reared lovely children, and the countless epitaphs tell us in most delightful words that her grave
was decorated with wreaths and flowers, and that her
ebbing life was wept and mourned by more even than
is now the case in our boasted aggrandizement.[319] Ours
perish, but the slabs which were chiseled in sad lettering on her heroon is here, legible and imperishable to-
day. Dr. Foucart has done their history a service,
where he makes his important admission, speaking of
the enormous influence of the societies in those times.
He explains that woman had a powerful influence among
the secret communes,[320] and shows that in the microcosmic centers of the future socialistic state, women had
the grand and humanizing boon of the ballot, and was
at par with the men. He further exhibits the fact that
she had no such power outside the secret unions in the
Athenian or any other public assemblies. Woman was
at home only in the secret unions.[321] She had much to
do with the feasts and barbacues, such as to day are
given on the occasion of political victories.

[319] Foucart, *Ass. Rel.*, p. 6: "Les femmes jouaient un rôle important dans les thiasos de Sabazios et d' Isodaitès. Plusieurs sont nommées dans un thiase de Salamine.... Ou trouve plusieurs exemples du même fait dans les sociétés de l' île de Rhodes et des côtes voisines. Quelquefois même, la société était uniquement composée de femmes, comme le κοινὸν ἐρανισ-τριῶν de Salamine où elles formaient une section distincte, comme les θια-σίτιδες....dans les cérémonies du culte, une part considérable était accor-dée ou réservée aux femmes."

[320] Foucart, *Ass. Rel.*, pp. 181, 182 sq.

[321] Lamprid., *In Heliogab.*, 6, *Aug. Hist.*, 7: Matris Deum Sacra accepit et tauroboliatus est." The taurobolium or barbecue, cooking in state before a grand assemblage, as is done to-day, was performed at the feast of Cyb-ele. It is likewise spoken of in the inscr., vide Orell, 2351, 2326, 1899, 2327, 2323, 2328, 2303, 6147, and many others, as 2352, 2332.

The power of woman in those ancient communes was unspeakable and the rise of her influence in the world caused by this ennobling jus coeundi is seen to be very great and important. She is henceforward called the androgyne divinity.³²² It was in primitive days very different from our riper practical times in which such things are considered silly. If woman assumed dignities commensurate with her practical value in the world she was considered androgyne. In our later times she is called a crank.³²³ The ancient is somewhat more respectful.

M. Foucart's valuable notice of a slab, speaking of the unions of scenic artists whom we have all along denominated the "great Gemeinde "to distinguish them from a multitude of other unions and guilds, assures us that woman was never admitted to appear on the stage of their organization. He makes one solitary exception.³²⁴ It is a grave problem whether these higher feelings innate in woman's breast were not at the bottom of Paul's protest against the ancient abominations. But women are known to have formed an important part of the membership. In Rome and many parts of Italy there were sodalicia of young women numerous enough to offer excellent, ready-made centers for the christians to plant in.³²⁵ Freedwomen and female slaves abounded in the thiasoi and collegia of the common trade union type, whereas only freeborns are found in the scenic unions.³²⁶ This is somewhat accounted for by the fact

³²² *Ass. Rel.*, p. 107: "La conception d'une divinité androgyne était familière aux religions asiatiques, témoin de mythe d'Agdistes en Phrygie et la Vénus barbata de Cypre; Mais elle répugnait vivement aux Grecs."

³²³ Foucart, *Ass. Rel.*, nos. 21, 23, 29, woman is shown endowed with much dignity. She belongs to the θιασωται in the order of the Serapiastes. She was προιρανίστρια (nos. 21, 23, 29). These were female officers of considerable responsibility. She played an important rôle there in the several unions. Women are sometimes called θιασίτιδες. At Salamis they belonged to the κοινὸν τῶν ἐρανιστῶν, a great dignity.

³²⁴ Foucart, *De Scen. Artif.*, 58, taking it from slab of Le Bas and Wadd., *Inscr. Asie Mineure*, 257: She is the only one thus far found... "duo choragi per tres dies exhibuerunt in theatro mulierem χοροψαλτρίαν, id est, quæ simul levem citharam pulsabat et saltabat, nullo alio adhuc exemplo feminæ ingenuæ in theatro saltantis, quam con collegii scenici participem sed incolam Iasensem, artem privatim meditantem fuisse certum est."

³²⁵ Orell, 4098, Rome, date not given but early; and as these were the sodalicia, the words of Dr. Foucart, *De Scen. Artif.*, pp. 29, 30. speaking of the relative functions there, of women and men, are instructive: "Primum enim in thiasis par est mulierum et virorum ratio, sæpe etiam major mulierum, quæ aliquando sodalitatis sacerdotio funguntur; at contra scenici collegii feminam nullam participem fuisse vidimus."

³²⁶ *Ibid.*: "Insuper libertis atque etiam servis thiasi patuerunt, quum inter scenicos artifices nullum nisi ingenuum civem receptum fuisse ostendimus."

that the scenic professions required that most of their members should appear in public before aristocratic audiences; and such was the taint of slavery and of all sorts of freed labor that those not having the mark of social standing as high at least as freeborn life were to be hissed off the stage.

There is no page of history perhaps in all the world's literature on which woman so frequently or prominently appears as in the Acts of the Apostles. This history has been put to the test of a fiery crucible within the last two centuries, and might have been abandoned for imposture but for the collateral and corroborating evidence of inscriptions, more than twenty of which have been found within that time, confirming its truth. We have brought all these under contribution to prove our position. Defended by her own epitaphs, woman, who is immortalized in that document, stands forth in all her sweetness and glory. The epistle to the Romans mentions a dozen of the ancient fair, to whose truthfulness the inscriptions all stand as new and incontestable witnesses. All this proves that the reason why woman is so prominent and frequent a character in this history is because she was a noble and valuable constituent in the unions used by the christians who sought and obtained her powerful influence and practical aid in accomplishing their plant into the highly moral activities of christian unions of which she furnished an honorable moiety of the membership. De Rossi, in his excavations in under-ground Rome which are still going on, has unearthed sepulchres and other monuments containing inscriptions of a large number of their names familiar to New Testament readers and Sunday School scholars, with dates and other signs indicating beyond cavil that these inscribed urns, sarcophagi and mausoleums speak of the same Priscilla, the same Chloe, the same Domitilla and Claudia, whom Paul salutes as his co-workers in the plant.

Aside from Corinth and Philippi where the obscene goddess Cotytto held the charm and swayed the demoralization which festered among the simple-minded proletaries, Paul is known to have had trouble with his churches in Phrygia and Galatia. These people, together with the Carians, were laughing-stocks to the

Romans.³²⁷ It is among them that we have so many absurdities and ridiculous practices. The celebrated callipygian dances were seen among the susceptible maidens of Phrygia and Caria,³²⁸ but if they were organized into the order of the artists there are no evidences of it at our command. Women of unworthy character were employed by the kings and nobility to perform, not artistically, but by an alluring exposure.³²⁹ Although it probably is true, as the learned Dr. Foucart informs us, that such practices were never known in the unions of the great Gemeinde, yet there were not only at Rome but throughout pro-consular Rome, unions of lupercalian fetichs against which Cicero railed when combating Clodius who, B.C. 58, caused the repeal of a conspiracy law thus giving the workmen the right to organize their unions.³³⁰ He compared the innocent but voting unions to the lupercalia in order to intensify and heighten the oratorical effect of his sneer. These unions also came under the Solonic dispensation and were afterwards planted into and utilized by the christians, having the common table and the communal code.

The apostles were accused of introducing asceticism, which circumscribed the little of pleasure and liberty the unions enjoyed.³³¹ A long period of wrangling followed the protest of St. Paul against these practices, heightened by his other protest against the manufacture of idols by the unions as a means of earning a living. In this last he appears to have preached the doctrines of a confirmed bigot. The two protests set abroad a vast and tiresome wrangling which assumed a disrupting gnosticism and caused great splits in the whole system.

---

³²⁷ Cicero, *Pro. Flacc.*, 27: "Utrum igitur nostrum est an vestrum hoc proverbium; Phrygem plagis fieri solere meliorem? Quid de tota Caria? Nonne hoc vestra voce vulgatum est; si quid cum periculo experiri velis, in Care id potissimum esse faciendum? Quid porro in Græco sermone tam tritum est, quam si quis despicatui ducitur, ut Mysorum ultimus esse dicatur."

³²⁸ Athenaeus, 554 D.; Müller, *Archæol. der. Kunst.*, § 377, 2, Καλλιπύγος. There is a far-famed statue of Venus so-named still extant. It is at Naples, The callipygian dance was the celebrated γυνή dance of the Phrygian girls. While dancing they twisted their nude bodies around in an indecent and tempting manner.

³²⁹ Chrysostom, XI., p. 428: "In theatris nudæ mulieres comparent." These did not belong to the unions.

³³⁰ The orator's remarks are quoted in Vol. I., p. 344, note 30.

³³¹ An example of the grossness of the lupercalian unions is given by Livy, xxxix., 9, in the story of the *adolescentulus*, who in the ordeal of iniation into one was required to abstain from women for a period of ten days: "decem dierum castimonia opus esse."

Before speaking of the Gnostic schemes of philosophy which set in as early as the first century with the Carpocratian trouble, we will touch again upon the protest against the manufacture of idols forbidden by Paul. The Carpocratian philosohpy, that of free-will love between the sexes based on Plato's laws,[332] had some backing during the second century; but had not yet made its appearance at Paul's time. Tertullian declares that God continued "by probity, the artificers of idols." He says they never ought to be admitted to the House of the Lord, and spurns the excuse that they had nothing else whereon to live. But Irenæus here runs against scripture.[333]

A fact which has not yet been told from an economic standpoint is, that the trade unions worked for the state or state religion, which was the same thing. The members voted annually for the election of proper officers to influence. These officers controlled the public works; and when elected by the votes of the workmen, knew their political power and influence, and always awarded them the work by which their life and organizations were maintained. We are happy in being supplied with abundant evidence of this.

But while this was going on in proper fashion, other and more disreputable things also occupied their minds. They boasted of their ithyphallic abominations,[334] and intrigued with one another[335] and as we all know, in many

[332] Plato wanted young men of the best military powers, and highest blood, to have free and unrestricted intercourse with women, so that the bravest children should be begotten to the state, on the ground that there was need of strong children to work the protection of the state. See Plato, *Laws;* also *Republic.* Clement, *Protrept,* 4, shows that the artisans used to be occupied making all sorts of goods: "Your makers of such images and paintings, and your workers in metals and paint have introduced a motley crowd of divinities in the field of satyrs and Pans; In the woods, Nereids and Oreads and Hamadryads; in the waters, rivers and fountains, Naiads, and in the seas, Nereiads."

[333] *I Cor.*, vii., 20: "Let every man abide by the same calling wherein he was called." This may be here compared with Solon, who excused all trade unions, even that of the corsair: 'Επὶ λιαν οἰχομένος.

[334] Lüd., *Dionys. Künst.*, p. 18: "Sie trieben ihre nicht gerade züchtigen Spässe offen vor aller Welt, als ob das ein Privilegium ihres Alters sei und erklärten frei ἰϑυφαλλοί ἐσμεν οἱ συνειλεγμένοι καὶ ἐρῶντες οὓς ἂν ἡμῖν δόξῃ παίομεν καὶ ἄγχομεν." But they generally had the burial attachment; See *id.*, p. 21: "In Grabschriften aus Teos kommen in Kränzen eingeschlossen zahlreiche Erwähnungen von Thiasoten vor, als οἱ ϑίασοι πάντες CIG., 3101, 3112, τὸ κοινὸν τῶν Παναϑηναϊστῶν, τὸ κοινόν τῶν Διονυσιαστῶν, die alle den Todten durch den üblichen Kranz geehrt haben."

[335] Clement Alex., *Protept.*, c. 2. In this instance of later years, given by Clement, the christians were the iconoclasts. The prevalence of phallic worship under the Pluto and Dionysos and the vile honors to the pudenda as he terms it, together with other abominations which caused much wantonness, aggravated them to seize and destroy the idols.

cases with the higher classes, to insult Paul and drive him away. He had a similar but more romantic experience with the girl Thecla; and it turns out to have transpired in a genuine house of a lord or dictator named Onesiphorus, an epitomized account of which we give in the note below.[336]

This touching story of Paul and Thecla written in the apostolic age and believed by Baronius, Locrinus, Archbishop Wake and Grabe who edited the Septuagint, to be reliable, is a remarkable instance of such persecutions. There is nothing in the story's general outline but what might have transpired. The miraculous part regarding her escape from the jaws of wild beasts of the amphitheatre may have been overstrained. The girl lived at Lystra in a house so near the secret temple or pholeterion where the members used to snuggle together to hear the eloquent man lecture, that from her open window unseen, she could distinctly hear him. It is said that she followed Paul. This story was laughed at until recently De Rossi has discovered her ashes in the martyrs' cemetery of the Via Ostiensis at Rome.[337]

Clearing the movement of low practices at a time when paganism, after receiving its license of evil by a reaction upon the word of the great conquests, was no easy matter. The unions followed the habits of the

[336] The plot of the story shows clearly that the meeting house was a κυριακή of some secret union of lowly persons. Thecla was a high-born girl, engaged to marry a rich man she disliked, in order to please her aristocratic mother. Paul came to a secret brotherhood to preach. Thecla was of too high birth to be admitted by the sphere she circulated in, as it would be scandalous and degrading; but she overheard the voice of the Word by stealth, from the outside. She was converted and afterward eavesdropped, overhearing night after night, the new doctrine of salvation. The terrible results when her mother found it out caused her to break away from mother, betrothed and home, and her ashes of a martyr are now in Rome; see the following note 337, giving the remarks of De Rossi, who has recently discovered her epitaph. We subjoin a brief synopsis of Thecla:

It was the House of Onesiphorus; place Lystra; Thamyris, her lover; Theclia her mother; Demas and Hermoges vilify them. Thecla sat in her own home window near enough to overhear. Paul was accused before the governor. When Thecla was an outcast, Paul accompanied her to Antioch. She belonged to the royal family.

[337] De Rossi, *Roma Sott.*, I., p. 192; "VIA OSTIENSIS. Et sic vadis ad Occidentem et invenies S. Felicem Episcopum et mart....et descendis per gradus ad Corpus ejus, et sic vadis ad Paulum, Via Ostiensis, et australi parte cernis Ecclesiam Teclæ (Theclæ) supra Montem positam, in qua corpus ejus quiescit in spelunca in aquilonia parti" Again, *id.*, p. 283: "VIA OSTIENSIS: Duodecima porta et via Ostiensis dicitur modo porta S. Pauli vocatur, quia juxta eam requiescit in Ecclesia sua.

Idemque Timotheus martyr, et non longe in ecclesia, S, Teclae sunt martyres Felix et Andactus et Nemesius." Again, *id.*, p. 182; PAULUS STEPHANUS, THECLA. Prope quoque basilicae Pauli Ecclesia S. Theclae est ubi corpore jacet."

outside forms of life. Everybody believed in gods and goddesses and conformed.[338] This early attempt to stifle it was not made any too soon; for with all the precaution against it, the Carpocratian system of Gnosticism came and ruled for a long time threatening to break up the very theory of the family, and herein is attributed to a large extent the early breaking up of the agapæ, through the outrageously wanton abuses of it by the Carpocratians.[339]

The principal source of the difficulty supposed to have existed between Paul and the immediate companions of Jesus appears to have been these abominations and the contest against the manufacture by the unions, of idols through which they got a considerable portion of their living. We have already recounted the story of Paul and Demetrius at Ephesus, showing the reluctance of the unions to the introduction of any innovation against their trade. The same trouble with Diotrephes was experienced about the same time, of which we shall soon recount all we know.[340] Unfortunately these evidences are left in the dark on account of the laws establishing an espionage by the police who were shadowing them at every hand under the lex Julia, wherein all unions were forbidden except the burial attachment as already explained. Dr. Ramsay has effectively explained this in his book on Phrygia, and a perusal of this work cannot but convince the most skeptical critic of the excessive secrecy necessary to the christians when propagating their ideas among the people. For two centuries they did not dare to letter one of their numerous epitaphs except with misleading signs. The cross was a sign of christianity; consequently they dared not engrave the cross. There was

---

[338] Synes, *Enc. Calv.*, p. 185: "'Οστις λάθρα μὲν ἐστι πονηρὸς καὶ οὐδὲν ἄλλο παρέχεται γνώρισμα τοῦ θιασώτης εἶναι τῆς Κότυος, εἰ μόνον ἐν τοῦτο φανείη, περὶ πλείστου τὰς τρίχας ποιούμενος, ὡς ἐναλείφειν τε αὐτὰς καὶ βοστρυχίζειν, εὐθὺς ἅπασι πρόχειρον εἰπεῖν ὅτι τῇ Χίων θεῷ καὶ τοῖς 'Ιθυφάλοις ὠργίακε."

[339] The ἀγαπαί, or love-feasts were as early as the apostles, *I Cor.*, xi., 31, and were common in the early Greek churches, and certainly in the still earlier unions. For much on the Carpocratian system, see Clem. Alex., *Stromat.*, cap. 2, communism of women.

[340] Doane, *Bible Mith.*, p. 260, speaking of Isis, in much adoration at Rome during the time of Juvenal, and of course much before. The painters got their livelihood by picturing beautiful images. These pictures were generally of the miraculous cure, but were often obscene representations of her or of Anubis. The ἀναγέννησις and παρθενογέννεσις or virgin deliverance were extremely common pictures and paintings of this and other sorts had a lively sale. Accompanying the picture was a prayer. Horace, *Tibul.*, I., *Eleg.*, III., gives one: "Nunc Dea, nunc, securre mihi, nam posse mederi Picta docet temptes multa tabella tuis."

TRICKS AND SIGNS TO ELUDE THE DANGERS. 501

an upright, dagger-shaped sign, allowable to the unions as an indication of salvation from suffering through their patron god Dionysus, forerunner of the coming messiah, which was admissible in the epitaphs of the legalized burial attachment of the lex Julia; but it being pagan, the converted could not do otherwise than alter the blade of the dagger in a manner understood by their own initiates but never understood by the police. It succeeded; and by a later analysis we are fortunate enough to come in possession of a multitude of christian inscriptions supposed by those ancient military spies to have been pagan and to have conformed to the official religion. The same guarded language is again discernible in the account written by some unknown author of Paul and Thecla.

One acquainted with the multitudinous unions at the Pisidian Antioch into which Paul and Barnabas were received and the account given by Neander of the manner in which they were turned away from the Jewish Synagogue and were entertained by some strange secret brotherhood where they found no opposition but accomplished a splendid church organization at Lystra, can catch the inner workings of the plant. The orator dared not call this union by the real name as a collegium or eranos or hetæra or synedria or koinon, one of which it certainly was, but covered his real meaning by calling it a confraternity. Had he said hetæra which was a trade union, it would have caused a suspicion and a looking into by the governor's secret police and spies, and indeed the extinguishment of the church.

Onesiphorus who gave his "House" to the propagation of the new Gospel at Lystra, was a crowned lord of some secret union of influence. He was probably a quinquennalis with much influence in the city, though the trade he conducted is unknown. His name occurs in the Bible several times; and we may hopefully look for some additional discovery which will attest the trade he conducted at Lystra.[341]

[341] Smith, *Bib. Dict.*, in verb. "Onesiphorus—'Ονησίφορος—bringer of profit, is named twice only in the *N. T.* viz.: *II Tim.*, I., 16-18. Δώφη ἔλεος ὁ κύριος τῷ 'Ονησιφόρου οἴκῳ, ὅτι πολλάκις με ἀνέψυξε καὶ τῆς ἅλυσιν μου οὐκ ἐπησχύνθη. Again, iv.,19: Ἀσπασαι Πρίσκαν καὶ Ἀκύλαν καὶ τὸν 'Ονησιφόρου οἶκον. Further on: "And in the latter passage he singles out 'the Household of Onesiphorus" as worthy of special greeting. Then again; "But the probability is that members of the family were also active christians." His κυριακός had become an influential microcosm as is proved by the Greek original: "Δῴη ἔλεος ὁ κύριος τῷ 'Ονησιφόρου οἴκῳ."

Paul went to the Pisidian Antioch. This was a Phrygian city. It was situated in Pisidia, a subdivision of Armenia. It abounded in secret unions. There were unions of marble workers, weavers,[342] shoemakers, hymnodoi of the Dionysan artists, unions of coral workers, masons and many others. When Paul and Barnabas arrived at the Pisidian Antioch, they found a Jewish synagogue with closed doors; or as Neander has recorded the event, they were driven away and took refuge in a "House." He further admits that this experience was all among the lowly and poor who opened their little kuriakos or temple for their reception. Here in secrecy and obscurity they remained and actually succeeded in building up a prosperous church. But those who had opposed their preaching in the synagogue had among them a few "aristocratic women, belonging to the most respectable families in the city," who incited their husbands to drive them away. The same author also admits that the church thus established was composed of poor craftsmen.[343] To emphasize this we have some valuable evidence sustaining the position that Paul and Barnabas were invited to the unions that swarmed at that time throughout Phrygia. Phrygia was the home of the unions which clustered, as we have shown in our dissertation on the Apameian shoemakers of Shoemaker's street, into many busy unions under the Solonic law. Their remains are found in the Pisidian Antioch, and we have an inscription showing at least one of the very decade in the first century, when Paul and Barnabas were there. The towns not being very large nor the organization important,[344] it stands to reason that the members of this

[342] Arnobius, *Adv. Gentes*, V., § 14, with note 8, of Bishop Coxe, in *Ante-Nicine Fath.*, Vol. VI., p. 495, on the abuses practiced among the unions of Pessinus, before the arrival of Paul, who worked reforms. Girls and children of the loom, among the gentiles. Arnobius, speaking of the "horrible amusement" that prevailed there, says that even old women joined: "Do you yourselves seem to hear girls at the loom, wiling away the working hours, or old women seeking diversions for credulous children?" Then follows a dissertation too low and obscene to print. Driven to the indecences of Cybele, there were longings for something higher and better, and there is mention of their longings for a return of the reign of Saturn.

[343] Neander, *Planting*, Book III., ch. iii.; Tertull., *Apol.*, xv.. in mentioning the circumstance reminds us of Pessinus being the seat of the celebrated Phrygian worship of Cybele, mother of the gods.

[344] Oehler, *MSS.*, ANTIOCHIA PISIDIÆ ; Οἱ Θιασειται—Thiasus liberi; CIL., III., 291, Erste Jahrh. nach Chr. Like the inscrs. of Apameia. Kelainus on Acropolis, recorded by Ramsay, *supra*, see *index*. It is bi-lingual which of itself is evidence that the members are mostly exiles from Rome, driven out by Caligula, as it is too early for the edict of Claudius.

union must have known the circumstance, and would have taken a part in the planting of Paul. Another proof that this Pisidian plant was originally in a brotherhood of the jus coeundi is, that the unions here were protected by the legalized attachment of the burial clause; for near here we also find examples of this sort, very suggestive of meaning in this direction.[345]

After planting in little Antioch, they went to a place not far from there called Iconium, and from all the information we have, they met with a very similar treatment. They also visited the neighboring city of Lystra. Neander, also Smith in his Cyclopedia of Biblical Knowledge, inform us after their great research, that Lystra, possessing no synagogue or Jewish meetinghouse and there being no Jews, the only thing they could do was to make their propaganda by "entertaining into conversations."[346] This is rather laughable. But the full story reveals more. An examination shows that nearly all the ancient unions had the kuriakos or petty synagogue, such as at Rome, recently discovered by the under-ground researches of De Rossi, are called schools or scholæ in Greek, just the place to entertain conversations in the dense secret of their penetralia. They were old. Strict discipline was required by their laws, which we are in possession of through their inscriptions. Of course then, wherever Paul and Barnabas found them, they were accessible to a ready-made audience already half converted through their own discussion of miserable life and the failure of their patron goddess to rescue them.[347] Besides this, they had had apostles and evangelists of their own for centuries.

No explanation other than that these organizations abounded and welcomed Paul with a friendly embrace, can reconcile with the truth, the words of the Bible Dictionary where occurs this statement, that he sailed from Paphos to Perga in Pamphilia and went thence to Antioch in Pisidia, where they found temples: "a col-

---

[345] Oehler, *MSS.*, 'Οργεωνες: "Sorge für das Begräbniss durch Bestreitung der Kosten. Einrichtung des Denkmales, Thiasiten der Magna Mater."
[346] Neander, *Planting*, Book III., iii.; Smith, *Bib. Dict.*, III., p, 2369 sqq., Article, *Paul the Apostle.*
[347] Rams., *Cit. Bish. Phryg.*, Vol., II., p. 534, *inscr.* 388, under heading of *Christian Inscriptions of S. W. Phrygia*, describes a christian epitaph of the butchers of this section. The words "καί τοίς τέκνοις" we read as referring to his many children, ie: the flock of which Αύρ. 'Αρτεμάς, was the lord or κύριος. In other words, it was a brotherhood of the butchers, and shows that later the plant of the evangelists became prosperous and populous,

ony," said to be of Jews. Here too, Paul speaks out boldly. He is among the non-Jew pagans. This is not the great Antioch. There seems not to be the slightest doubt that the apostles found many eranoi and thiasoi, or that there was a hot-bed within which to plant the Gentile church.³⁴⁸

Neander, who is loth to acknowledge anything favoring the plant among the poor, is forced out and obliged to speak plainly regarding their habit of participating at a common table.³⁴⁹ He makes a clear acknowledgment that the first organization was a microcosm of the forth-coming universal condition of prime if not uppermost importance.

Neander who groped about for years among old manuscripts, arrives at the conclusion that Paul and Barnabas found other help than that of Jews. He hates to admit that the Word dived into labor's dens in a land covered by the works of these earnest apostles; so like several other commentators when they run across such instances, he leaves his riper opinion somewhat obscured by an allusion to them, without apparently recognizing that they are one and the same society. The existence of societies like these made it easier for the christians to organize themselves in similar associations.³⁵⁰ Though this is not a positive statement that the Phrygian hymnodoi were actually converted to the new faith, yet it amounts to the same thing. The regular epigraphical reports of the expert linguists and palæographists sent out on exploring and excavating labors from the schools of archæology are beginning to use terms which are unmistakable. When an old trade union a few years ago was found completely christianized at Flaviopolis, they said:³⁵¹ It is interesting to see these trade guilds, so common under the empire in Asia

---
³⁴⁸ In proof of this, see Smith, *Bib. Dict.*, p. 2372, where it is recorded that; "The two went together through Syria and Galatia, visiting the churches." What churches? How could there be churches in this hostile pagan land, never before visited by an evangelist! The answer is that they found the κυριακοί in numbers organized under the ancient jus coeundi as their ready-made foothold.
³⁴⁹ Neander, *Planting*, Book III., ch. v.: "The celebration of the Holy Supper continued to be connected with the common meal, in which all as members of one family, joined."
³⁵⁰ *Cit. Bish. Phryg,*, Vol., II., p. 630, note 2.
³⁵¹ *Journ. of Hellenic Study*, XI., 1890, p. 236, no. 1. The date of this Phrygian inscription is placed later, but it only shows that the plant had thrived from a much earlier time. Oehler, in a *letter to the author*, says: "Es wird nötig zu untersuchen in wie weit Christen in Vereinen und gewerblichen Genossenschaften vertreten sind."

Minor, passing unchanged into the church."[352] We have hinted that these christian unions, many of which were allied to Dionysan artists who had their home in and around the two Antiochs and became known of late to the German scholars as the great Gemeinde, began, after waiting, hoping and discussing for hundreds of years in their scholæ and their symposiums, to look for a more promising messiah to relieve their miseries than their long honored Attis, Dionysus and Cybele. In fact they were cultivating a divinity known as the forerunner, at the time Paul visited this region. The Greek name of this divinity was Dionysus Kathegemon. He was the avant-courier. Spoken rapidly, this first name sounds somewhat like John, and as all the Phrygian brotherhoods were baptists, we may imagine that they at least would take graciously to our celebrated pioneer who, like Dionysus when in the flesh as the forerunner heralding the messiah, suffered martyrdom.[353] Dr. Foucart who admits that Pessinus, a part of Galatia, was the center of this religion, proves that the ancient Pa or Papas used as the familiar names for this deity, is the origin of the name pope; and cites the inscription recorded in the Greek body, as evidence.[354]

These were the cities and countries in which Paul and Barnabas planted the first christian churches, and the celebrated epistle to the Galatians was written to these people. They were organized hives of industry. The union just quoted was an organization of wool workers. We find almost every trade represented. We find them prosperous, happy, sitting at a common table with deacons and deaconesses attending to the daily [355] minis-

[352] *Journ. Hell. Stud.*, XI., 1890, p. 236. The Greek of this christianized trade union of woolworkers, reads as follows: "Ὑπὲρ σωτηρίας του εὐτελοῦς συνέργειου τῶν γναφέων τὴν μετερίαν ἡμῶν ταύτην καρποφορίαν δέχου Δέσποτα παρὰ τῶν ἀρχίων σου δούλων, παρέχων ἄφεσιν ἁμαρτιῶν ταῖς ἡμετέραις ψυχαῖς καὶ καλὴν, ἀπαλογίαν."

[353] Ramsay, *Cit. Bish. Phryg.*, II., p. 375, discussing the relationship of the above-mentioned Σωτὴρ and Μὲν Ἀγαθαίμων, says: "In illustration of the complex priesthood, a Roman epitaph may be quoted (Kaibel, 1449): "Κεῖμαι Αὐρήλιος Ἀντώνιος ὁ καὶ ἱερεὺς τῶν τε θεῶν πάντων, πρῶτον Βοναδίης, εἶτα μητρὸς θεῶν καὶ Διονύσου Καθηγεμόνος τούτοις ἐκτελέσας μυστήρια, κ.τ.λ. We are very suspicious that as the distance between Galilee and Pisidia was but a few miles, there was some relationship here, in Phrygian imagination.

[354] CIG., 3817. The city of Pessinus or Galatia was celebrated for this worship. Strabo, 567 has given us the best statement: "Πεσσινοῦς δ' ἐστὶν ἐμπόριον τῶν ταύτῃ μέγιστον, ἱερὸν ἔχον τῆς μητρὸς τῶν θεῶν σεβασμοῦ μεγάλου τυγχάνον· καλοῦσι δ' αὐτὴν Ἀγδιστιν."

[355] Chrysostom reverts to those early times with a sigh. Vol. IX., 94: 'Christianorum priscorum vita communis."

trations. They were manufacturers. They had all things common. When they took on the faith in the Saviour they made the church their old kuriakos over into a temple of christian love and kept their economical habits. Such churches were bound to prosper. Hardly indeed was the transition from paganism perceptible.[356] Differing in one point from old official methods they would not pay tribute to the heathen cæsarism. This brought them into frequent troubles. Because they refused to attend the regular official worship and refused to buy the pagan sacrifices they were persecuted. It was the money question. To attend the pagan service and buy the lambs, beeves, poultry and other eatables of the so-called sacrifices at a ruinous price would heap large profits into the pagan temple which was an instrument of the official religion and a part of the state; it would make their earnings a considerable factor of the national incomes. The persecutions were a natural political result. For this reason it was necessary to belong to a brotherhood in which they could have their own common table, their own common sacrifices independently of the old official duty, because if they could escape with a clear conscience from the outrageous prices demanded for these sacrifices by the priests at the temples, at best no better than speculating market stalls, they added not only a boon of freedom but a large economical advantage; because by their own plan they could buy with combined monthly dues, sufficient for the whole brotherhood at wholesale prices, without this speculating middleman at all. This economy was a good half of their revenue, and it must be acknowledged that christianity which struck out for independence was a great economical as well as religious reform. We ought to be profiting by it to-day. But we have gone back to the ancient provision speculator and nothing is so needful as a Jesus to go into the infamous temples of speculation and tear down the altars of greed and whip out the priests and money changers who, as before, still infest the sanctuaries of mankind.

[356] Ramsay, *Cit. Bish. Phryg.*, II., p. 609, no. 506, describes a θίασος of this vicinity: "On a marble stele, with the relief of Μέν, with Phrygian cap and crescent on the shoulders; 'Αγαθῇ τύχῃ. ἔτους σνδ'. Μηνὶ 'Ασκαηνῷ φράτρα 'Ηλιοφῶντος 'Αντιόχου καὶ Ποπείου Μάρκου ἀνέθηκαν." Dr. Oehler has demonstrated that the φράτρα was a regular union under the Solonic dispensation.

All over this land of Galatia which was really a section of Phrygia including the Pisidian Antioch, Apameia, Akmonia and other marts, the christian culture found a warm welcome among the numberless unions, who had a right to expect that their great, all-powerful Cybele, mother of the gods, and her son Dionysus, patron of economical prosperity and giver of joys to men, would come down from the vaulted dome of heaven and rescue them from want and danger. But they came not and at last a lowly, crucified Jesus appeared in infinite humility, to tell them to persevere, build their socialism higher, hold good their common table and communal love and fight free of Cæsar's exacting tribute.

Previously to A.D. 54, Paul lived a long time at Antioch, supposed by most commentators to be the greater capital city, but more probably both. From these centers he made excursions, often hiding away mysteriously, and once for a term of several years.[357] Whither he disappeared to again emerge rested and robust nobody knows. He was a craftsman engaged in furnishing scenic outfits for the artists. It is a new discovery that this region abounded in secret unions, including those of the Dionysan artists known by at least thirty fine instances which we have collected, to have endorsed the teachings of the evangelists in full and taken them in, shielding them from danger, legalizing their Word through the burial clause of the jus coeundi, hearing it in the dense secret of these lovely refuges, and when thoroughly rested and refreshed, letting them go under their benign ægis, often with an attendant who was no other than one of their own kurioi or quinquennial lords, who acted as courier for their post office and carried the Epistles "to all the churches." We are soon to astonish our readers with an adduction from the great Corpus Inscriptionum Græcarum of the Berlin Academy, quoting many inscriptions as a new historical resource wherein occur, among thousands of pagan ideographs the names of some old proselytes to Paul, Peter and John, such as Tychicus, Onesimus, Philemon and others mentioned in the canonical New Testament books. But this evidence must be deferred for a later chapter of this work.

[357] *Acts*, xiv., 28; xviii., 23; xii., 25; Smith, *Bib. Dict.*, *Paul at Antioch*, p. 2363; 2396; worked as a σκηνοποιός, *Acts*, xviii., 3.

The burial attachment or lex collegium funeraticium, and tenuiorum is found quite repeatedly in this section,[358] but although it was lawful to organize and hold a burial society, yet the law evidently understood that funerals were the only object of such unions. So when, as in almost every case, the main object of protection of industry, economy of the common table, joys of the entertainments and the general advantages of a trade union were combined, leaving the funeral as a mere toy under cover of which to shield the whole; when, we say, this was by any want of secrecy discovered by the police, they were attacked by the pro-consul's spies and severely dealt with. Dr. Lightfoot discovers this in his dissertation on Paul's Epistles and shows us how dangerous it was to attempt to distribute them "to all the churches," great care being necessary to prevent their suppression. If caught, the epistles must not contain one word about the unions having anything to do with the brotherhoods or the brethren they mention. There was a strict censorship, under the military management and if Paul had dared to speak of the unions it would have caused his celebrated canonical books to be condemned and burned.

But the evidences are too numerous and too strong to longer admit a quibble. In his thorough investigation, Dr. Ramsay found several unions which he interprets as christian societies the apostles modeled after, and shows them to be benefit unions; but in name and outward appearance trade unions or trade guilds, such as existed at that time at Hieropolis in great numbers. The one at Akmonia was a christian protopyleiton,[359] or

[358] Oehl., *Eran. Vindob.*, *Genossenschaften.* Again, Oehl., *MSS.*: "PISIDIEN: Ἐταιραί Vereinen. Athen., xiii., 5856, berichtet dass Gnathaina einen νόμος συσσιτικός festgestellt habe; Alkiphron, I., 39, nennt θυσία συμπόσιον und gemeinsames Mahl der Hetairen an den Adonien. *Anthol. Palat.*, VIII., 728, *Kallim. Epigr.*, xi., vom welchen wir lernen: πολλῶν προστασίη νέων γυναικῶν kennen, 722 und 723." All of the ἐταιραί we have seen that were found in Phrygia had the burial attachment. Dr. Ramsay, *Cit. Bish. Phryg.*, II., p. 720, no. 655, remarks: "The salutation given in earlier inscrs. is now confined to the brother." Here we have another collegium funeraticium, the burial attachment of which was permitted a brotherhood, who take their right to hold themselves organized from Sept. Severus who perpetuated the lex coll. fun. and the union is consequently as late as the 3d century. It is a trade bearing the name of κοινὸν, and had been christianized.

[359] Ramsay, *Cit. Bish. Phry.*, II., pp., 562-3. no. 455-7. Here we have a christian gate keepers' union, with the burial attachment at the town of Karamon Agora. Dr. Ramsay, p. 563, speaking of the bequest on the epitaph, says: "We must understand that the society to which he gave his bequest was a christian benefit and burial society." The *inscr*, itself shows it to have been a gate keepers' union: B., no. 456: "Ὑποσχόμενος τῇ γειτοσύνῃ

gate keepers' union found in a town not far from Pisidia. There was a brotherhood of the gatekeepers at Jerusalem already mentioned and explained. Everything tends to prove that the original idea of universal christianity was toward a socialism in which all things were had in common. In a note[360] we here allude to a multitude of evidences scattered variously among the inscriptions and especially among the scriptures of the good, honest old fathers like Lactantius, Jerome, Chrysostom and Epiphanius. There are found quite a number of inscriptions, some of which are epitaphs, on which are engraved, with dates of their birth, marriage and initiations, words recording the "incomparable love" of each others' associations; and the early fathers have left us statements expressing regrets that

τῶν πρωτοπυλειτῶν ἄρμενα δικέλλατα δύο κατὰ μῆνα καὶ ἀγωγὸν ὀρυκτόν ἔδωκεν ἐφ' ᾧκατὰ ἔτος ῥοδίσωσιν τὴν σύμβιον μου 'Αυρηλίαν." There is a group of these inscriptions of the gate keepers' unions in this town. Dr. Oehler has also contributed several: vide *index* in verb. crucifixion and other catchwords. A gate union was at Jerusalem and it is almost certain that a γειτοσύνη προτοπυλειτῶν was the γερουσία or brotherhood which secreted Jesus at Jerusalem and the retreat that was divulged by the treachery of Judas securing to the police his whereabouts, arrest and crucifixion. See *index* in catchword, *gate-keepers*. Dr. Oehler, referring to *Revue des Études Grecques*, II., 1889, pp. 24-5, says: "Die γειτοσύνη των προτοπυλετῶν wird erklärt als association crétienne." They were numerous and prove to have been a species of guild. They were "neighborhoods." Lüders, *Dionys. Künst.*, p. 34, CIG., 3931. Ehrenbeschluss aus Tralles; "Ἡ φιλοσεβάστη γερουσία καὶ οἱ γέοι καὶ ἡ Ὀλυμπική σύνοδος τῶν ἀπὸ τῆς οἰκομένης ἱερονείκων ἐτίμησαν, κ.τ.λ. Hadrian begünstigte eine σύνοδος ξυστικὴ τῶν περὶ τὸν Ἡρακλέα ἀθλητῶν."

[360] Irenœus, *Adversus Hær.*, III., xxiii., 8; IV., vi., 4. Tatian wanted all things common so that there might be a perfect economy in provisioning the members. Cf. *Amer. Cycl.*, art, *Tatian.* Tatian was hard on robbers. Orell, 2182, Arretii showing an intense secrecy everywhere: "Nemini se arcana enunciaturum;" Clem. Alex., *Strom.*, II., xix., says of the contract system, which jobbed the work rightly belonging to the working unions out to speculating contractors, as now, saying they were "caravanserai, filthy and filled with dung, because belonging to others;" Jerome, *Adv. Jovinianum*, bib. II., c. 6, from *Matth.*, x., 9; xix., 21, shows that Jovinian discussed this subject though his work is lost. "All are commanded to have but one coat, no food or money, no staff, neither shoes on their feet." It of course refers to the providing of all these things by the secret commune into which they are initiated, which plainly shows that those ordered out were under the secret ægis of the loving brotherhood which, on showing of passports and giving the password, were to be fully supplied, The process of initiation is hinted at by Chrysostom, VII., 151; Sacrificium iniatorum quæ.," etc. It is a hint on the early initiation necessary to admission to the cœna communis, or common meal; the economical question of bread. So Chrysost., again, III., 257; "Mensa communis priscæ Acclesiæ temporibus." But bewails that all is now gone. *Id.*, IX., 84: "Mensam sacram communem tangere audebant initiati tantum." All, high and low were originally equal; II., 426, 437: "In mysterium participatione nulla exceptio personarum; una mensa imperatori et pauperi." Polycarp, *Epist. Phil.*, vi., on duties: "Let the presbyters be compassionate and merciful to all, bringing back those that wander, visiting all the sick and not neglecting the widow, the orphan, or the poor, but always providing that which is becoming in sight of God and man." Rom., xii., 17; Cor., viii., 31. Again, chap. xi., expressing grief on account of Valens, Polycarp says; "I am greatly grieved for Valens....I exhort you therefore that you abstain from covetousness, πλεονέξια." etc. This fellow had robbed the social fund.

all at their later time was lost, and exhorting brethren to return to their old communal fold.[361] Jerome, who wrote about the old primitive brotherhoods long afterwards, attests that they followed the Roman law of centurions, forming themselves into divisions or companies of one hundred and then into brigades of a thousand, and frequently a union was a thousand in number.[362] St. Augustine, one of the purest of the early fathers, writing on morals, throws broad hints out regarding the unions of brotherhoods of all kinds and speaks of "their living together in a most chaste and holy society.... No one possesses anything of his own; no one is a burden to another. They work with their hands in such occupations as may feed their bodies......... The products of their labor they give to their deacons so that no one is worried with the care of his body, either in food or clothes, or in anything else required for daily use or for the common wants and ailments. They assemble from their work-shops before they take the common meal, to hear their lord president, sometimes in numbers of three thousand or more; for indeed one society may have many above three thousand." And again: "Much more is created by their frugal industry than they can use; and they distribute it about for the general welfare."[363]

The early teachings of all the immediate companions of Jesus are backed up by innumerable allusions of ante-Nicine fathers in declaring that the messiah who

[361] Lüders, *Dionys. Kunst.*, p. 37. gives an account—vide *supra*, ch. xiii., of the inscriptions containing the law believed to have been a clause in Solon's *jus coeundi*, requiring that the candidate for admission should be found under examination of the δοκιμασία to be ἅγιος, καὶ εὐσεβὴς καὶ ἀγαθός, else he or she could not be elected to membership. In the Diatessaron of Tatian, discovered in 1877, we find that to be a member good and pure one must give up to the whole congregation all worldly goods, to be managed by the διάκονος, for the common good.

[362] Jerome. *Epistles*, xxii., 35; "After this, the meeting breaks up and each company of ten goes with its lord, or κύριος, to its own table to partake of the common meal."

[363] *Acta Sanct., Mens. Maj.*, Tome III., App., § 77, gives some strong information concerning one Actas, whose works are lost, and whose acts suppressed. He organized unions during the first century. They are supposed by some to have been imitated by Pachomius who formed the great cœnobia upon an island in the Nile near Thebes. These latter were very populous, but intolerably sanctimonious, amounting to a pious tyranny, such as can never be tolerated by free men. We are however, inclined to think that those organized by Actas resembled those of the regular trade and labor unions of Solon. Anthony, in *Ancient Life*, § 77, speaks of Pachomius as the founder of the monks, and though they were of little value to the world, we quote: "Κατὰ τὴν ἀρχὴν ὅτε μοναχός γένονα, οὐκ ἦν κοινόβιον, ἀλλ' ἕκαστος τῶν ἀρχαίων μοναχῶν μετὰ τὸν διωγμὸν κατὰ μόνας ἠσκείτο, καὶ μετὰ ταῦτω πατὴς ἡμῶν ἐπιήσε ταυτο ἀγαθὸν παρὰ κυρίου."

was to come and did come, was in every respect a workingman; and there are many stories among the contemporaneous writers, of the hard life he had to eke out long before he assumed the rôle of his exalted messianic functions. Thus Justin, in his celebrated colloquy with Tryphon, declares that even after his return from Egypt to his father's home in Galilee, he worked at the carpenter's trade and also made plows and yokes, being not ashamed of his occupation, but on the contrary obtaining praise for his industry as an honorable example before the economic world.[364] "Be at work," said Jerome, "doing something, that the devil may always find thee busy."[365]

It has been already explained that the mithraic colleges of purely pagan origin and nature, were in their teachings the nearest of all to the plan of salvation of the christian cult, and it may be added that not a few believe that Christ, while in Egypt working for a living when a boy, was a member of this peculiar sect. The associations of Mithra, however, were exempt from the persecutions suffered by the christians [366] for the reason that they were supposed to be pagan, not christian and to pay tribute by attending the sacrifices and otherwise conforming to the law.

[364] Justin, *Dial.*, 78: "Καὶ τέκτονος νομιζομένου ταῦτα γὰρ τὰ τεκτονικὰ ἔργα εἰργάζετο ἐν ἀνθρώποις ὤν, ἄροτα καὶ ζυγά· διὰ τούτων καὶ τὰ τῆς δικαιοσύνης σύμβολα διδάσκων, καὶ ἐνεργῆ βίον."

[365] Jerome, *Coll.*, 773, Pt. II., Vol. IV.: "Facito aliquid ut te semper diabolus inveniat occupatum." *Epist. ad Rust.*, so Paul's system declares that christianity never tolerated idleness.

[366] De Rossi, *Roma Sott.*, III., p. 509: "L' iniquitò del rigore contra i Cristiani consisteva in ciò, che moltissima società religiosa d' origine greca, asiatica, egizia—furono generalmente tolerate ed anche permesse nel imperio Romano;" and Waltzing, *Hist. Corp. Prof.*, I., p. 139, remarks that the christians were supposed to be iniquitous while the mithraic associations were tolerated. He further thinks that the mithraic fraternities were the hetæræ, probably meaning before their conversion to christianity.

CHAPTER XVI.
CONTINUED.
THE APOSTOLIC AGE.
SECTION III.,—NERO.

NERO—Period Covering Imprisonment of Paul—Literary Evidence Burned—Accounts of the "Acts" Proved by Inscriptions to be Good History—Nazarenes a Branch—Landing of Paul at Puteoli, in Chains—Warmly Received by already Converted Brotherhoods—The Delegation—Same Unions Already Described—Centuries Old—Story of Narcissus—Nero at First Kind and Tolerant—Believed to have taken Paul with him to Spain—Grows Morose and Jealous—Employs an Able Detective, named Tigellinus—Turns Against Friends and Humanity—Closes Friendly Doors of Domus Augustalis—Seneca, Philo, Peter, Paul and a Host of Other Good Men Charged upon—Escape of Philo, Assisted by Peter—Barnabas—Nero Plots to Burn the Immortal City—Pudens, Priscilla, Claudia and the Poet Martial, all acquainted, and Friends—Story of Pudens—Was an Englishman—Organized a Union of Carpenters in England—House of the Lord—Strange Analysis of the Word—Pudens a Lord of a Union—Recent Discovery of Wonderful Inscription of Carpenters' Union at Glastonbury in Chichester—Pudens Gave the Land—Probable Gift of King Cogidubnu—Tacitus—Though Christian, it was Dedicated to Minerva—Collegium Fabrorum—Evidence Massed—Household of Claudia—All Members of Brotherhoods of Trade Guilds—Mentioned in Paul's Epistles—Also Mentioned by Martial in his Epigrammata—Recent Discovery of their Names Inscribed upon their Cinerary Urns—Nero Finds out these Things through his Spies—He is Incensed—Story of the Burning of Rome—He Swears that he will Rid Rome of the Genus Tertium, meaning the Christians—Oakum, Tar, Pitch and large Quantities of Grease Gathered—Tigellinus—Spread of Fire Described—Nero Carouses on the Mæcenatian Tower—Cunning of Nero in Accusing the Hated Genus Tertium—Vast Numbers of Christians Put to Death—Fury of the Populace—Many Christians Thrown to Wild Beasts—Smeared with Tar and Grease and Set on Fire for Torches of the Nightly Carnival—Sewn up in Bags and Thrown to Rome's Hungry Dogs—Unknown Thousands Perish—Atrocious Massacre—Work of Tigellinus, Nero's Pinkerton—Statement of Tacitus, Suetonius, Orosius and Others—Paul, Seneca, Peter, Pudens and Many Others Murdered in Nero's Rage—Manner of Execution—Death of Nero—Celebrated Fisherman was Crucified Head Downward—His Wife also Led to the Cross.

THE most important period in the history of the ancient lowly, if we are allowed to except the reigns of Tiberius and Claudius covered in the preceding section of this chapter, is the imprisonment and execution of Paul, Peter and thousands of converted workers, including the celebrated burning of Rome. It is a story never rightly understood, and covers tragedies instigated by jealousies attendent upon the tremendous growth of socialism planted at a phenominally early stage of the movement we are trying to portray.

It must be taken fully into consideration that an enormous trade organization already existed at Rome, of which history makes no mention; and we are consequently recording these facts in defiance of history which caters to the mighty for favors and drops the unrecorded power of the lowly in treacherous, cruel oblivion.

We have dared to take issues against this humiliating ingratitude and come out with the truth on the origins of socialism, the great plant, which the property power tried with an energy worthy of better things, to drive into defeat and destruction. They did not succeed. They burned much literary testimony, but could not destroy the evidence of the stones.

We have already noted the enormous early christian plant at Rome. Many strange side lights regarding this appear in the data, apparently spurned by history. These we shall collect and bring to the broad glare of light, leaving to future analysis their place in the fate of human records.

It will be remembered, because fully recorded in the Acts of the Apostles, that Paul went, under arrest, to Rome, perferring to be tried for his alleged crimes before the emperor himself, to being the victim of his irascible and prejudiced tormentors at Jerusalem who accused him of being a "pestilent fellow, a mover of sedition among all the Jews throughout the world, and a ringleader of the sect of the Nazarenes."[367] This is significant talk, if we take into consideration the new testimony established by Oehler and the scholars of the Berlin Academy, regarding the conclusion that these

[367] *Acts*, xxiv., 5: Εὑρόντες γὰρ τὸν ἄνδρα τοῦτον λοιμὸν καὶ κινοῦντα στάσιν πᾶσι τοῖς Ἰουδαίοις τοῖς κατὰ τὴν οἰκουμένην, πρωτοστάτην τε τῆς τῶν Ναζωραίων αἱρέσεως.

Nazarenes were none other than branches of the organization of laborers and outcasts, under the benign Solonic dispensation. It was the origin of socialism which has ever since been honestly striving to establish itself in the world.

Paul had the foresight to demand a trial before the emperor at Rome. The Jews would gladly have applied "Lynch-law" upon him and he knew it, and saved his life by demanding that his trial take place before that majesty at Rome—a rather desperate decision, since both Claudius and Nero turned out to be terrible enemies and persecutors of the early christians.

The whole story is told in the Acts of the Apostles; and this succinct account is regarded by Guizot as good and well-substantiated history, and as it is not denied by Gibbon, we refer the reader to that valuable document.[368] Few narrations of sea voyages exceed Luke's in romantic interest, as they cover shipwreck, an episode with a poisonous viper, strange legends of sailors and a final landing at Puteoli where the extraordinary incident occured. We shall leave the history of this whole sea voyage from Palestine to Italy, to the reader's free perusal in other books.

But from the moment he set foot upon the land at Puteoli the history is ours. It is that of the ancient lowly; and we lay claim to no originality in our version except that our evidence is mostly new and that it has never before been rendered to the open world.

No city among all those where the labor unions organized under the Solonic dispensation abounded, is found possessing a greater number than Puteoli. It was in ancient times an excellent commercial harbor of Campania in Italy, only about seven miles from the present site of Naples. Cumæ, the place where Blossius was born, was a suburb or sister town. Of this noble character who espoused the cause of Tiberius Gracchus in the interest of the oppressed, we have already made a full statement.[369] The remarkable feature of this seaport was that its workingmen's organizations were

[368] *Acts,* xxiv., to xxviii., inclusive, wherein the story of Paul's incarceration under Felix is told, and the manner in which Drusilla came more than once to his rescue. The slow-working law permitting him to lie two years and more in confinement at Cæsaræa, is painful; since they were two of the most valuable years of this bold agitator's life.
[369] See Vol. I., *Aristonicus,* chap. x., pp. 239-242.

colonies from parts of Palestine. One large union of
the crimson cloth makers and sellers was from Tyre.[370]
They were a colony which had been settled by the Phœnicians at Puteoli for a long time. Dr. Lüders gives an
account of it in the second century. The parent union
at Tyre assessed an exhorbitant tax of ten thousand denaria against the union in Italy which it could not pay.
An inscription explains it.[371] As at this time all Palestine was Roman, it was a Roman collegium. In Puteoli in very early times there was a collegium of christian tradesmen engaged at some kind of carpentering
work, probably ship-building. The union had received
the Word from the missionaries of Palestine and it was
strong at the time of Paul's landing there en route for
Rome.[372]

A large number of inscriptions are left to the archæologists conveying proof that Puteoli was alive with labor unions at the time of Paul's visit in the spring of
the year 61. "We came," says Luke, "to Puteoli, where
we found brethren and were desired to stay seven days;
and so we went toward Rome; and from thence, when
the brethren heard of us, they came to meet us as far as
Appii Forum and the three taverns."[373] Here Paul met
the brotherhoods again.[374]

They were dined and wined and persuaded to sojourn
with the friends for seven days. There is no mistaking
the language. They were fellow brothers, fellow christians! Who had been there at this early date in the
midst of the reigns of the tyrants Nero and Claudius,
to convert these unions to christianity? All the com-

[370] Origen, a brazier by trade, when persecuted by prelates years afterwards, fled from Caesarea to Tyre, and sought safety and solace, like good
old Tertullian, among the secret mysteries of his youth and under their protecting aegis ended his valuable life in quiet security.
[371] Orell., "Henzen," no. 6082. It was a θίασος Placidianos; Momms., Beitrag der Sächsischen Gesellschaft, "Phil. Hist.," 57-62; Oehler, "MSS.":
"Puteoli, CIL., x., 1585, Vergl. Thiasus Juventutis in Nerona, CIL., 1828.
[372] Orell, 2385: "Ex S. C., Dendrophori curati qui sunt sub cura xv., vir
S. F. virorum clarrissimorum patron. L. Ampius Stephanus Sac. M. Deum
quinquennalis Dendrophorum. Dedicationi hujus panem, vinum et sportulas
dedit." Then follows a list of eighty-six names of members of the union.
[373] "Acts," xxviii, 13: Καὶ μετὰ μίαν ἡμέραν ἐπιγενομένου νότου δευτεραῖοι
ἤλθομεν εἰς Ποτιόλους, οὗ εὑρόντες ἀδελφοὺς παρεκλήθημεν ἐπ' αὐτοῖς ἐπιμεῖναι
ἡμέρας ἑπτά· καὶ οὕτως εἰς τὴν Ῥώμην ἤλθομεν. κ.τ λ.
[374] Smith, "Bib. Dict.," Vol. III., p. 2392. Not less than twenty inscriptions of about this date adorn our sources of information. They point to a
great number of unions, collegia, sodalicia, and other fraternities, right here
in Puteoli; Henzen—Orellius, III., p. 524, noting a new one, more recen-t
dug up, no. 7206. Many were dedicated to Minerva and Diana; III., pp. 524-5.
They are coll. scabellariorum, musicians.

mentators are puzzled. The fact is, there was a plant there of long standing. Even while Jesus was preaching in Judæa missionaries had come to this important place and had established the new Word. It was their Word of life and hope.[375]

Judging from the number found to have been doing business at the town of Puteoli for a period of about three hundred years before and after the Advent, we have arrived at the conclusion that the population consisted mainly of organized unions. There were few others there. Some fine gentlemen's seats and a few villas are on record for the vicinity; but this was entirely due to the exquisite beauty of the bays including the Bay of Naples visible in the distance, to the romantic rocks and forest-clothed crags, the heights of Vesuvius to the south, to the many gushing springs of pure, healthful water which adorned the vicinity, and to the exquisite climate; all in rebuke of the report that its name Puteoli, stink-pots, coming from stagnant waters that in reality never existed. The cognomen of putridity took its origin in the fact that it was a labor hive filled almost exclusively with what were long supposed to be foul and contemptible working people,[376] and the epithet had gone abroad as far as Rome and Athens that it was a stinking place and accordingly deserved to be changed from the old name of the stink-pots to Puteoli, by which name it was ever afterwards known at Rome. We point out in footnotes some of the multitude of these trade and labor organizations which have thus far been brought to the light through their own inscriptions. They range from regular old Numan collegia to the Dionysan artists, several of which are found to have been allied with the great international Gemeinde with its headquarters at Teos.[377] They are also

---

[375] Neander, "Plant.," Book III., chap. ix: "But the Roman christians had already, even before he arrived at Rome, evinced their sympathy; since several of their numbers traveled a day's journey, as far as the town of Forum Appii, and some of them a shorter distance to a place called Tres Tabernæ, in order to meet him. In the "Epist. to the Philippians" he sends a salutation to the whole church πάντες οἱ ἅγιοι, which is proof of the close connection in which he stood with them."

[376] Waltzing, "Hist. Corp. Prof.," I., 162: "Dans l' antiquité l' homme qui n' avait que ses bras et son métier pour vivre, celui qui, même riche se livrait à un travail manuel, était méprisé."

[377] See "supra" in chap. xi., where will be found an explanation of what we term "The Great Gemeinde," using the German word, because it embraces a happy expression of the full meaning of the συνόδοι τῶν περὶ τὸν Διόνυσον τεχνιτῶν. For many collegia found here, see "Notizia degli Scave," 1891,

known to have been unions organized under the jus coeundi and colonized from the mother unions at Tyre, Sidon, Cæsarea and cities of Asia Minor in the same manner as that resorted to by bees when overcrowded by the pack of population, as it were, they "swarm" to distant hives and set up business by themselves. The Puteolanian collegia escaped the notice of the archæological inscriptions until Mommsen and Lüders called them to notice, since which they are attracting more attention to the extent of their true historical value in shaping the origins of christian socialism.[378] Before proceeding with Paul to Rome let us tarry with him on his seven days' sojourn, and imagine that we ourselves, accept the heartfelt invitation of these interwoven, mutually self-supporting, loving and banqueting unions at Puteoli. We shall find in the anaglyphs of their vernacular chisel enough to wonder at.[379] We find that not only here in the maritime city itself where an extensive and commodius harbor shielding the vessels of the Italians and Phœnicians, made traffic in the far-famed dyes as well as in all other merchandise, a source of wealth, such unions existed, but also at Cumæ and Pompeii, extending to Capua and even to Rome. The organizations were countless. We shall follow for the present their traces only at Puteoli itself and the environing towns within sight, like Cumæ, Naples and the populations that fringed the great volcano about

p. 167; it is placed at A.D. 78 but of course was in existence before that time. Cf. "Inscr. Gr. Ital. Sic.," no. 830, which is conjecturally placed later. A Πολίτευμα Φρυγῶν in Puteoli worshiping the Ζεὺς Φρυγὸς before conversion. "Bull. Hell.," XIII., 1889, p. 239f., 11; Oehler, "MSS.": "Noch ein Κοινὸν derselben Art wird hier erwähnt." This is very important, being as is believed the identical union into which the christians were first received at this place as early as the plant at Jerusalem, and supposed to be the one which welcomed Paul. It was terribly persecuted by Domitian, vide infra, Section "Domitian."

[378] Henzen, in "index, Geographica," Vol. III., Orell., p. 17. "Coll. Puteolanorum," 1694; "id.," 6315; "Col. Put.," 4124; 3652 which is a colony, classed here as a collegium; Cf. Orell., 3698. Coll. Flavia Augusta; 5504, 5518, a coll.; 6519, a coll.; 4430, Coll. Puteolanum and Colonia Puteolana. These seem to have been all linked together and are of the first century.

[379] Waltzing, "Hist. Corp. Prof.," I., p. 125, mentions the dendrophori, cf. CIL., X., 3699, 3700, for Cumæ, a suburb of Puteoli, which possessed a villa of Cicero and the estates of the reformer Blossius; CIL., X., 1642; XIV., 168, 169, 256; X., 1647; Lüders, "Dionys. Künst.," p. 30, 31, cf. "supra," note 295; Livy xxxii., 29, xxxiv., 45, mentions these great colonies; Tac., "Ann.," xiv., 27; Orell., 3697, 3698. All these testify to their early dates. Muratorius, 524,2; the collegium juvenum is recorded in Henzen, Vol. III., of Orell., nos. 4101, 3976, 6065, 2168, See "Index, Collegia Sacra, publica privataque." Juvenum Sutrii Tiburtini, Trebulæ, Veronæ. During Hadrian's time there flourished more than one θίασος, and ἔρανος. Momms., "De Coll. et Sodal, Rom.," p. 6, from Spartianus, "Hadrian," c. 27, A.D. 76-136.

the time it exploded, engulfing its walls, arches, roofs, its two thousand voting unions and its busy and turbulent humanity.

But one thing must be here explicitly noted: If the movement of Pompeii on the day of the eruption of Vesuvius contained such a vast number of these politico-socialistic trade unions that over fifteen hundred inscriptions at this later date are seen grinning their tell-tale history which reveal more glaringly than the words of a Sallust, the certitude that they controlled important elections in their interest and with their superior vote secured for themselves the public works of the city, doing it by electing candidates of their choice to the boards of aldermen and of the public works; if, we say, the unions are proved by such irrefutable witnesses as this, so also did the unions of all other municipia of this region and of Rome. It may be hard to believe, but the crust must be swallowed. Dr. Cagnat affirms it in unmistakable terms.[380]

The silent, grimy testimony of fifteen hundred dodgers, hand-bills and posters indelibly blazed upon the inside of the walls of a city and found after a lapse of two thousand years, must bear a solemn weight to the extraordinary power of evidence which it is our duty to drag forth in proof of the vast and long-mellowed field which christianity planted. Dr. Cagnat gives his evidence that Pompeii was not alone. Puteoli, bespecked with these organizations,[381] must, as he declares, have

[380] Cagnat, a member of the French Academy, of Inscriptions, in "Vie Contemporaine," Jan. 1896, pp. 175-6: "Quelques mois avant la terrible éruption du Vésuve qui l' engloutit, Pompéi venait de nommer ses magistrats annuels, duumvirs et édiles. La lutte avait été ardente; du moins avait-on multiplé les affiches électorales ou les inscriptions murales qui en tenaient lieu; on en a retrouvé plus de quinze cents en déblayant les ruines. Un grand nombre des proclamations émane des corporations; les cuisiniers, les marchands de bois; les boulangers, les pâtissiers, les carbaretiérs, les joueurs de balle même, etc. . . . . Ce qui se passait à Pompéi avait lieu aussi ailleurs assurément: et tant qu' une vie municipale quelque peu active subsista dans l' empire Romain, on peut être assuré que les corporations professionelles y prirent part." See Vol. I., pp. 390-1, of this work.

[381] Waltzing, "Hist. Corp. Prof.," I., p. 212, speaking of mausola preserved at Puteoli, says: "Les monuments communs des sociétés et collèges funéraires étaient construits sur le même plan." This correctly shows that an upper hall was for the union's business and meetings. Again, ibid., p. 336: "Les collèges de cultores Jovis Heliopolitani de Pouzzoles—Puteoli—possédaient un champ de sept arpents avec une citerne et des Tabernae, et ceux là souls en avaient la jouissance qui ne contrevenait pas au reglement: "Hic ager—corum possessorum juris est qui in cultu corporis Heliopolitanorum sunt cruntve, atqui ita is accessus jusque esto per januas itineraque, ejus agri, qui nihil adversus lecem et conventionem ejus corporis facere perseveraverint." CIL., X., 1579.

PUTEOLI SWARMED WITH VOTING GUILDS. 519

been a city of voting trade-unions in the same manner. All these associations appear to have come under the old lex Julia and its modification regarding burial regulations, and they followed strictly the law of Solon demanding that the principles on which cities of ancient times were based should be held as the pattern of their organization.[382]

The same contempt which enveloped the actual workman whether at a trade or at common labor, also contaminated those engaged in mercantile business or in commerce of any kind. As a result we find many unions of merchants everywhere, and not a few at Puteoli. They all come under the old Solonic dispensation. The colonies from Tyre, in Phœnicia, had an especial object in furthering their large trade in the celebrated brilliant red and purple dyes, when they established the branches at Puteoli.[383] Some surprise is caused by the discovery at Puteoli, and among these unions, of the fact that many Hebrews were also there; and as this accounts for a celebrated paragraph in the Dion Cassius, we cannot refrain from noting it here. What adds to the interest regarding this is the now ascertained certainty that these Hebrews were the very christians who befriended Paul on his arrival,[384] and invited him to sojourn with them for seven days, or a time long enough for them to send a herald to Rome to acquaint the similar brotherhoods of his forthcoming arrival that they might send a delegation of their numbers to meet him at Forum Appii and Tres Tabernæ. Now Dion Cassius, in his history of Domitian who succeeded Nero after the two short years of Titus and consequently only about thirty years after the visit of Paul, recites the story of Domitilla, her persecution and banishment and

[382] Waltzing, "Hist. Corp. Prof.," I., p. 513: Tous les collèges suivirent un modèle commun, a savoir, la cité. Ils jouissaient tous d' une complète autonomie intérieure; l' Etat qui, depuis l' an 7 avant notre ère ne reconnaissait plus le droit d' exister qu' aux collèges autorisés . . . . . et cette constitution est modelée sur celle de la cité dans laquelle ils sont établis; 'ad exemplum reipublicæ. "Dig.," III., iv., 1.' " already quoted.

[383] Waltzing, "Hist. Corp. Prof.," p. 235: "A Pouzzoles la corporation des marchands tyriens parle des dépenses que lui occasionnent les jours de fête de l' empereur." Mommsen, "I. N.," 2479, Orell., 6082. It is a thiasus that had survived the persecution of Domitian.

[384] Smith, "Bib. Dict.," p. 2648, says, discussing Paul: "We should also notice the fact that there were Jewish residents at Puteoli. We might be sure of this from its mercantile importance; but we are positively informed of it by Josephus, "Antiq.," XVII., xii., § 1, in his account of the pretended Herod Alexander to Augustus; and the circumstance shows how natural it was, that the apostles should find 'brethren' there, immediately on landing."

the murder of many Jews at Puteoli and confiscation of their property. Gibbon, with great insight and fairness, in referring to this, declares that Dion actually meant the christians. His remarks are now proved by the cumulative evidence of the monuments to be absolutely correct. Many trade guilds are found to have been already christianized at this place and to have industriously chiseled their history as such. Among the unions of these brotherhoods that sheltered Paul is the one numbered 4124 of the old archæological work of Orell. It secretly screened him from harm, and was temporarily suppressed and its members killed by Domitian a few years later. Long before this and indeed before his landing at Puteoli, the emperor Claudius banished large numbers of Jews from Rome, sweeping them all together especially the christians and Jews under one fell ban; and Suetonius, in his life of Claudius, makes his record of this edict in a few lines which have become celebrated.[385]

These unions and guilds were very early christianized. This fact also receives powerful proof in the inscriptions. There are the remains of a pagan kuriakos, which had become a church as early as the last days of Tiberius. It was a union of dyers. When a child of the quinquennalis or president died he was sepulchred in a niche called an ædicula, as the words explain.[386]

Notwithstanding the furious efforts of the emperor Domitian to deracinate them they continued down to A. D. 260 at least, which again shows how impossible it was to suppress the ancient unions. When better times came, Hadrian, who was their friend, established a thiasus at the town of Naples six or seven miles down the bay,[387] now a great city. Here occurred the wonderful stroke of Masaniello, manager of the fishermens' union, which produced a law that never has been repealed. A story told by Philostratus the biographer of Apollonius of Tyana, tends to illustrate the numbers and influ-

[385] Suet., "Claud.," 25: "Judæos, impulsore Chresto." etc.
[386] Orell., 7373—Puteolis—C. Nonius Flavianus Plurimis annis orationibus petitus Natus. Vixit anno uno. Mensibus xi. In cujus honorem Basilica, Hæc a Parentibus adquisita contectaque est, requievit in pace. To which the learned editor subjoins: "In inscriptione christiana in ruderibus antiqæ ecclesiæ cathedralis Puteolanæ reperta aedicula sepulcralis basilica videtur appellata esse." The ecclesia noticed by Jerome, "Epist., was a κυριακή.
[387] CIG., 5804, cf. Lüders, "Dionys. Künst.," p. 35: " ἡ φιλοσέβασος καὶ φιλορώμαιος Ἀλεξανδρέων περιπολιστικὴ εὐσεβὴς σύνοδος.

ence of the brotherhoods at the seaport of Puteoli during Domitian's time. This philosopher and magician was arrested and miraculously escaped. In an hour, if we are to believe the impossible story, he was at Puteoli among the "brethren."[388]

Another proof of the very early plant there, of the Word and to all appearance even long before the arrival of Paul at Puteoli, is the legend of Patrobas, one of the seventy who are listed in the Breviary of original men. Patrobas was a real character and is mentioned by Paul in his salutation to the Romans, in connection with Asyncritus, Phlegon, Hermas and Hermes; and he is said to have been appointed to be the bishop of a church at Puteoli, probably the same aged temple of whose basilica we have just given the inscription of the infant son of the president of the union of dyers. He, with Philologus, suffered martyrdom probably under Domitian.[389] Still another wonderful discovery, by the diggers, is the ancient temple of Isis at Pompeii, almost in sight of Puteoli, where is found a church in ruins. Nobody knows how long before the great eruption which swallowed a populous city this church was converted to christianity; but as the volcanic convulsion which was witnessed by Pliny the naturalist, occurred only eighteen years after Paul's visit to Puteoli, the closely neighboring town, we have a right to rank all such organizations together[390] and may cite the newly discovered temple at Pompeii but recently unearthed. It was a habitation, therefore a home. In this the members originally performed labor from which they derived their daily bread and when christianized the economic methods were retained, showing its economic character. The place possessed the common livings, shape and style of architecture and all the paraphernalia of the ancient kuriakos.

Among all these friendly officers of the brotherhoods Paul passed at Puteoli his seven days of sojourn. There

---

[388] Apollonius, when triumphantly told by Domitian that he now was fast-bound and secure, leaped from his chains and disappeared in mist. In an hour he was at Puteoli a hundred miles away, with Damus his faithful friend and all the rejoicing brotherhoods. Doane, "Bib. Myths," p. 261.

[389] Wolf, "Cur Philolog."; Smith, "Bib. Dict.," p. 2362, where Patrobas is treated as a proselyte, and appropriate mention of these points, is made.

[390] Fouc., "Ass. Rel.," 45: "Le temple d'Isis a Pompéii donne une idée assez exacte d' un de ces sanctuaires; on pourra se les représenter encore mieux, en voyant quelques-uns des monastères helléniques, en particulier celui de Vourkano sur l' Ithome ou celui d' Orchomène, élevé sur les ruines du temple des Charités."

was the old fashioned common table and communal code. There the thrifty membership knew no want. If he desired, he could work at his trade of tent and also scene making, for the Dionysan artists were also there; and judging from the economic grandeur of the man's character it should surprise no one to hear that he turned his art to the work which offset the expenses of his daily keeping. On bidding the dear ones good-bye the cortege set out for Rome. Hitherto the journey from Cæsarea had been by sea; now it was by land and it is no small distance from Naples to Rome.

But at the Forum Appianum they were met by a delegation of the "brethren," from Rome. These were also christians. How came they converted and how happens it that such a fine escort met them so fortunately to conduct them to the gates of the great city? But they had not traveled from this place farther than to a village known as the Three Taverns when they were again met by a third escort. It was from Rome; from the Aventine, and temple of Diana. All these complimentary brotherhoods now joined their numbers and escorted him to Rome to be tried before the emperor. Arrived in Rome, we find that Paul was treated with great courtesy and comparative respect for a political suspect and criminal. We are informed that he was allowed to occupy a house rented by himself and there held meetings undisturbed for a period of two years.[391]

In view of the fact that the monarch on the throne at this time was the blood-thirsty Nero who soon afterwards burst upon these people and almost exterminated them, we cannot understand this leniency, except that there was a strong influence exerted upon him, not so much from the Jews as from the Romans and Greeks. We have some remarkable side evidences on the great influence exerted upon the house of the Cæsars by the freedmen or enfranchised slaves and sometimes even by the slaves themselves. The remarkable unions of the domus Augustalis prove this. It is now known that the columbaria were built by them, for they had powerful unions of their trades organized with the tacit consent of the imperial families and in the case of Tiberius,

---

[391] *Acts*, xxviii., 30: ʿΈμεινε δὲ ὁ Παῦλος διετίαν ὅλην ἐν ἰδίῳ μισθώματι· καὶ ἀπεδέχετο πάντας τοὺς εἰσπορευομένους πρὸς αὐτόν, κηρύσσων τὴν βασιλείαν τοῦ θεοῦ καὶ διδάσκων τὰ περὶ τοῦ κυρίου Ἰησοῦ Χριστοῦ μετὰ πάσης παρρησίας ἀκολύτως.

enormously assisted by the imperial household.[392] Their workshops were the gynæcia, in which the manufacture of all articles of clothing of the imperial family, and all the washing and other laundry work was done. These collegia came under the lex Julia and had the funeral attachment, under which, for centuries they flourished with the consent of the imperial and the opulent families who were in need of their labor.

Occasionly there arose men of great genius of this class. We may point to Narcissus who flourished during the days of Claudius and probably was a well-known character under Tiberius and Caligula. He is mentioned by Paul as a christian.[393] Narcissus was one of the very early christians. He was a Greek slave of the Roman conquests, a man of powerful genius and extraordinary composition. He had the address to ingratiate himself into the confidence of the emperor Claudius. By the consent of this monarch and while his private secretary, he took contracts of the Roman governments to build bridges, public buildings and other government works, and wound up by taking the contract to pierce the tunnel of Fucino,[394] not many miles from Rome, to let out the poisonous waters from a lake, as a sanitary measure. Claudius employed Narcissus to do this vast work by contract and during the eleven years he was doing the work, employing thirty thousand workmen out of whose unremitting toil he enlarged his wealth so as to reach the sum of four hundred million sesterces or about thirteen million five hundred thousand dollars, making him one of the richest men in Rome.[395] Any one desirous of the truth about this man

[392] Waltzing, *Hist. Corp. Prof.*, I., p. 264: "La maison impériale et beaucoup de familles opulentes possédaient des légions d' esclaves et d' affranchis. Tous ces serviteurs d' une même maison formaient un ou plusieurs collèges funéraires, qui se disent adorateurs des lares de leurs maîtres. A Rome, l' un des plus connus est le collegium quod est in domu Sergiae Paullinae. CIL., VI., 9148, 9149, 10260-10264."

[393] Narcissus was certainly the quinquennalis of a great household. This means that he was another president, or κύριος of a powerful union of the domus Augustalis. *Romans*, xvi., 11: Greet them that be of the household of Narcissus, which are in the lord. The Greek original does not say "household": 'Ασπάσασθε τοὺς ἐκ τῶν Ναρκίσσου, τοὺς ὄντας ἐν κυρίῳ.

[394] Suetonius, *Claudius*, 22: "Fucinum aggressus est.....per tria autem millia passuum, partim effossa monte, partim exciso, canalem absolvit aegre; et post undecem annos, quamvis continuis trigenta hominum millibus sine intermissione operantibus," etc.

[395] Suet., *Claudius*, 28: "Sed ante omnis Narcissum ab epistolis, et Pallantem a rationibus, quos decreto quoque senatus non præmiis modo ingentibus, sed et quaestoriis praetoriisque ornamantis honorari libens passus est." For a fine short dissertation on Narcissus, see Smith, *Bib. Dict.*, p. 2067.

whose almost unlimited influence with the house of the Augusti, an influence which survived him and caused much of the lenity of Nero towards Paul, will have difficulty in getting down to an extended view. The Cyclopedia of Biblical Literature is in doubt about his being the same person Paul mentions in the sixteenth chapter of his epistle to the Romans. But there can be no mistake because the names, general circumstances and dates agree exactly, and we hear of no other Narcissus.[396] Thus the indications are that there were not only many influential converts, all of the proletarian class, organized into secret unions and with the consent and assistance of the imperial house, but that many times the first of them exerted their influence to succor them from harm. The case of Narcissus is but a single instance; but it may serve to illustrate the causes of the phenomenal progress of the primitive plant.

But Paul being a secret member and initiate, dared not divulge; and we must not expect him to go into any extended explanations in his mention of those who helped him during his confinement. The "household" which he mentions is the very place called in Asia the kuriakos, which is meant in the words " his own hired house." The truth is, Paul went to one of the many households, and lived with the brethren as a two-years' guest. It may have been the very one formerly presided over by the powerful Narcissus. This letter to the Romans from Corinth was written according to Lardner, in the year 58. Many households[397] are mentioned more at this early date, than afterwards. There can now no longer exist any doubt but that here is the

[396] *Bib. Dict.*, p. 2067: "NARCISSUS, Νάρκισσος, *daffodil;* — A dweller at Rome, *Romans*, xvi., 11, some members of whose household were known to St. Paul as christians. Some persons assume the identity of this Narcissus with the secretary of Emperor Claudius: Sueton., *Claudius*, 28; but that wealthy and powerful freedman satisfied the revenge of Agrippina by a miserable death. Tac., *Ann.*, xiii., 1. It was three years before this Epistle of Paul to the Romans was written, A.D, 54-5." But this stands for little since there is great strife as to the date of both the Epistle and the death of Narcissus. On the death of Narcissus, Tac., *Ann.*, xiii., 1: " Ab his proconsuli venenum inter epulas datum est apertius quam ut fallerent, nec minus properato Narcissus Claudii libertus, de cujus jurgiis adversus Agrippinam rettuli aspera custodia et necesitate extrema ad mortem agitur...." Under close comparison, the dates agree with Paul's letter.

[397] *Romans*, xvi., 11., *Household of Narcissus; id.*, xvi., 3, 4, 5, church in house of Priscilla and Aquila; verse 10, household of Aristobulus. These and many other households mentioned continually by Paul and the *Acts*, were the κυριακαί where they served the common tables.

kuriakos of the common tables, which is not only explicitly provided for by the law of the Twelve Tables of Rome and the older Solonic Statute from which it was translated, but engrafted into the rules and regulations of the primitive church of Jerusalem by Jesus and followed by Peter, James, John and Stephen, as we have abundantly shown, and in every inscription, especially those of the under-ground Rome brought to light by De Rossi and the epigraphical academies.

It was under the guardian care and protection of the numerous secret old unions which had already been converted, that Paul worked for two years unmolested. He went down into the slummy places of the Gentile colleges and brought them to receive the Word. Peter was also there much of the time. Their work was secret. There are indications that the language mostly used was Greek, although Paul could probably write Latin, else he could not have so easily maintained his acquaintance with Seneca; for we have a fine set of epistles written in Latin which were passed between Paul and Seneca, the celebrated statesman and champion of letters. There are many who believe Seneca died a christian. He certainly was a martyr.

It is impossible to follow the two great apostles consecutively in their career at Rome. No written history is left us even by Luke who is supposed to have written the Acts. It is probable that he actually wrote more, but as his pen-picture is believed to have been accomplished in 63, and as Paul arrived in Rome in 61, he could not have carried it farther. Everything remains in mist, and we must pick up our testimony on the great and wonderful plant from the gravestones of martyrs. Let us then be systematic, doing nothing which science will not approve by its irrefutable stamp of certitude.

Leaving Narcissus and his household, let us turn to a still more diaphonous character, Sergius Paulus, also mentioned by Luke.[398] Dr. Lightfoot, convinced by his critical examination, declares that the early christians had no other churches at all than the old temples of the unions. "The christians," said he, "were first rec-

[398] *Acts*, xiii., 7: Ὅς ἦν σὺν τῷ ἀνθυπάτῳ Σεργίῳ Παύλῳ, ἀνδρὶ συνετῷ. Οὗτος πρὸς καλεσάμενος Βαρνάβαν καὶ Σαῦλον ἐπεζήτησεν ἀκοῦσαι τὸν λόγον τοῦ θεοῦ. For more, consult De Rossi, *Roma Sotterranea*, I., p. 209.

526   *NERO.*

cognized"⁹⁹ by the Roman government as collegia."
Neander in his history of the planting, speaks in the
third book, of this Sergius Paulus, a proconsul of Paphos, who was converted by Paul and Barnabas on the
first evangelical journey. This Paulus, he says, had
been led astray by Simon Magus, the itinerant Jewish
Goës, from Samaria, who was the Barjesus and a "virulent opposer of christianity which threatened to 'deprive him of his domination over the minds of men.'"
Some subtle mystery attaches to the history of this
man whose name occurs in the thirteenth chapter of the
Acts; but it is certain that he afterwards figured at
Rome, and being another personage of commanding
presence he became a quinquennalis, and thus a responsible manager, as required by the special clause in the
law of the Twelve Tables, which the most virulent of
the Roman government dared not meddle with.⁴⁰⁰ Sergius Paulus is known so little that had we not the positive evidence of several lettered mausolea, sepulchers,
common gravestones and cinerary urns bearing his name
in adjective form, we should have only the meagre mention in the Acts of the Apostles. But these have come
to unearth his history and give their positive evidence
that he was a quinquennalis of great power and influence, like Narcissus, Pudens and Priscilla. He presided
over the genuine working people's trade unions and
aided in the conversion of the members to a knowledge
of the Word.⁴⁰¹ The evidence is too positive to admit of
any mistake.

Everything touching the early plant was necessarily
veiled in profound mystery, a fact recognized long afterwards by many of the pre-Nicine fathers, after the

³⁹⁹ Lightfoot, *Coloss.*, p. 241, note quoting on the suggestion of Probst.,
Kirchliche Disciplin, p. 182, 1873; *Rom.*, xvi.. 14, 15: τοὺς σὺν αὐτοῖς ἀδελφούς,
τοὺς σὺν αὐτοῖς πάντας ἀγίους. κ.τ.λ. And subjoins: "Of the same kind
must have been the 'collegium quod est in domu Sergiae Paulinae,' De
Rossi, *Rom. Sott.*, Vol. I., p. 209, stating that the christians were by the
Roman government first recognized as trade unions, and as such were protected by reason of the burial attachment."

⁴⁰⁰ Waltz., *Hist. Corp. Prof.*, I., p. 215, note 2, speaking of the collegia
domestica, and the collegium Numinis dominorum quod est sup templo
divi Claudi, CIL., VI., 10241. Another the collegium domus Augustalis,
which we have already mentioned, see *supra*, SECTION Caligula-Claudius,
note 310; again, CIL., VI., 9404, 10,251.

⁴⁰¹ Maffeus, *Mus. Ver.*, 256, 4, gives the very remarkable union found in
Rome; "Hermeroti Arcario, V., A XXXIIII, Collegum quod est in domu
Sergiae Paullinae fecerunt Agathemur et Chreste Arescon fratri piisimo Bo-
næ memoriæ." In the preceding note of Orellius, 2413 is a remark signifying the editor's classification of several *inscrs.* here grouped as collegia
compatilicia. If this be true, the one we quote is a genuine labor union.

WORDS OF DIONYSIUS STIGMATIZING LABOR. 527

conquest of liberty was achieved.[402] M. Granier de Cassagnac whose well-based opinions we have frequently brought under contribution in this work, recognizes that the early christian plant was in the trade unions, in some significant words.[403] But it must here be taken into consideration that at this date of the early dawn when Sergius Paulus gave up his high commission as pro-consul of Paphros and went back into the slummy colleges of the working people reeking with filth and in "garlic and gabardines," a convert to the Word, at a time when such wretched creatures were not believed to possess a soul, and that their touch was a stain to persons of any position; we say it is natural that de Cassagnac should use this as an argument to prove how men outgrew their humility.[404] It was especially in sinks, inhabited for centuries by these people who had no laws to protect them, that women were subjected to insult and abuse; for licentiousness went hand in hand with starvation, nakedness and cruelty.[405] We are reminded in a passage of the eminent scholar, Levasseur, of the words of Dionysius of Halicarnassus, which is a bold assertion, that a stigma attached to labor, both mercantile and mechanical, so pungent that it was forbidden the Roman citizen to exist that way. In other words, labor was a forbidden crime.[406]

[402] Chrysostom, *Works*, Vol., VIII., p. 426: "Christiani in mysteriis se mutuo amplectebantur."
[403] *Hist. Classes Ouv.*, p. 335; Ou peut dire que le corps des bateliers etc. était dans 1 empire ce qu' a été 1' ordre de Saint Benoit dans la chrétienté:" and quotes the *Code*, Theod., xiv., tit. iii., leg. 4, as follows: "Optio concessa est his qui e pistoribus facti sunt senatores;" also the law of Valentinian and Valens of the year 371, and another of Gratian, of the year 379. It had an elevating tendency; but at this late date it must be considered as a christian regulation, *Cod.*, Theod., XIII., tit. v., legg. 14, 15.
[404] Homer, Iliad, II., v., 201-2:
"... Σὺ δ᾽ ἀπτόλεμος καὶ ἄναλκις,
Οὔτε ποτ᾽ ἐν πολέμῳ ἐναρίθμιος, οὔτ᾽ ἐνὶ βουλῇ;'
But the modern Levasseur and Cagnat tell us that it was the unions which elevated these people from their misery. Cagnat, *Vie Contemporaine*, Jan. 1896. p. 170: "Le commerçant et 1' ouvrier étaient, chez les Romains, assez méprisés; unis ils grandissaint à leurs yeux." He further states that they were honorable and existed: "Dans toute 1' étendue de 1' empire;" and declares that the christian unions described by Tertullian were one and the same with these.
[405] Seneca, *Controv.*, iv., Praef., speaking of the saying of Haterius: "Impudicia in ingenuo crimen est, in servo necessitas, in liberto officium."
[406] Dionys. Hal., *Archœol.*, ix., 25: " Οὐδενὶ ἐξῆν Ῥωμαίων οὔτε κάπηλον, οὔτε χειροτέχνην ἔχειν βίον." so Euripides in *Phœniss.*, V., 408: "Πένης γὰρ οὐδὲν εὐγενὴς ἀνήρ." No laborer is a well-born man. See *O. T. Apocryph.*, *Ecclesiasticus*, chap. xxxviii., 33; *Cod. Just.*, iv., tit. lxiii., leg. 3: "Nobiliores natalibus, et honorum luce conspicuos, et patrimonio ditiores, pernicio**ᵇ**ᵐ urbibus mercimonium exercere prohibemus, ut inter plebeios et negotia᷄ᵣres fecilius sit emendi vendendique commercium."

Returning to the kind of collegia to which this of Sergius Paulus belonged, we have the decision of the scholars that the words and surroundings of the inscription show it to be an old collegium compatilicium, one of the lowest and meanest designated by Cicero as the brand of unions, dangerous, made up of the dregs of the city and infested by thieves.[407] The truth is that this Cicero, boasted in our colleges as the great founder of Latin literature, was the arrant enemy of the poor, and in fighting them in the interest of his buccaneer class who lived on the robber baron idea of "something for nothing," he at last lost his contemptible life by the violent opposition of these very unions he so virulently attempted to destroy. The kind-hearted Dr. Levasseur, in his history of the ancient workers declares that after the conquests under the Roman law and during the time covered by the conspiracy laws of Cicero and Julius Cæsar, the working people were veritable serfs of the shops.[408]

Such was the wretched condition of things at the time Sergius Paulus left his high appointments in Paphos, island of Cyprus, a convert to christianity and the despised but correct socialism of the poor and went back to Rome a lord of many unions, a kurios, which was to him, a greater honor and a more lasting glory than to be a hypocritical creature of officialism. Dr. Lightfoot, speaking of the proselyte Theophilus, who was converted in a similar manner and also went to Rome, makes his astonishing admission that: "The christians were first recognized by the Roman government as collegia," and thinks they were originally burial societies. This is true; for most of the old unions possessed the burial attachment, and thus in a manner, secured their legalization.[409] But Dr. Lightfoot con-

[407] Mommsen, *De Coll. et Sodal. Rom.*, p. 59: "Ita Cicero, *Pro Mil.*, 9, 22, de Ambitu Clodii sequestris consulum qui erant futuri 'Collinam novam delectu perditissimorum hominum conscribebat.'" Here Cicero is speaking of the Collegium opificum. Again, same page: "Collegia enim a Clodio ex fæce urbana constituta sunt ut asseclas fideles et validam latronum manum sibi compararet, si fides Ciceroni." This remark of Mommsen is preceded in the same paragraph thus: "Collegia triburia a compatiliciis quæ Clodius restituit." thus certifying that it was the compatilicia to which colleges Sergius Paulus attached himself.

[408] Levass., *Hist. Cl. Ouv.*, Tom. I., p. 39: " Veritable serfs de l' atelier, ces ouvriers ne pouvaient se soustraire à leur misérable condition. On leᵃ marquait au bras avec un fer rouge." *Cod. Theod.*, lib. X., tit. xxii., leg. 4.

[409] Clem., *Recog.*, x., 71: "Theophilus....domus suæ ingentem Basilicam ecclesiæ nomine consecraret." Lightfoot seems to regard the cases of Theophilus and of Sergius Paulus as similar.

tinues his statement, citing De Rossi's Under-ground Rome, in the following significant words: "Of the same kind must have been the collegium quod est in domu Sergiæ Paullinæ, for the christians were first recognized by the Roman government as collegia, or burial societies or clubs and protected by this recognition, held their meetings for religious worship within the limits of the Roman empire."

Nothing can be clearer than that Sergius Paulus, whatever his office under the Roman government might have been before his conversion, went down among the common people and abode with them, and was crowned for his business gifts, a kurios or manager of a powerful union operating an industry under the lex Julia.

We say there is left us no historical statement showing the doings of Paul while imprisoned at Rome, and that our information is confined to inscriptional evidence. One of the most remarkable under this class is Pudens—a strange history of the plant into the densely secret unions, which has never before risen to the surface.

Our next historical character then, will be Pudens. Through him, we can illustrate, not only that the early christians used the old economic unions as ready-made seed-beds with their mellow soil to plant and cultivate an undying socialism in, but we find him an excellent fulcrum over which to pry up from deep obscurity the strange mysticism of the "house of the lord." We have already seen with what frequency this expression occurs in the New Testament, with its variants such as "household," and "church that is in his house," and the frequency of its repetitions, in the pre-christian as well as the post-christian inscriptions.

We have seen that this house was the aged kuriakos which Webster and all the lexicographers declare to be the original for "church." Before the Advent the word was of common occurence in thousands of guilds and unions of labor, and when the Word of the teachings on which our era is based, was set upon by the enemy of proletarian mankind and its life threatened, it crept into the good old kuriakos, the house of the lord, or church, was greedily taken in, nurtured in secret, screened for centuries, fostered under the communal code, blessed with the beaming smiles of love and goodness and family honor, and made to grow in sympathy, humility, enlightenment, until it could live and develop in peace. Now let us analyze this ancient house in which the christians found rest in socialism. In doing this we first run squarely against a clause in the Solonic law as it was engraved into one of the Twelve Tables of Rome after first being translated from the more ancient slab that stood in the old Prytaneum of Athens: *kurion einai*. Nobody until now has been able to tell just what this meant. The solution remained for the epigraphists themselves. This term kuriakos is in reality two words. Kurios was in Greek a common term, meaning master, manager, lord, overseer, in fact a person in charge of an affair. It meant one responsible for the business in hand; one to whom the police or the officers of the law could always refer, as a responsible unit of many; and this he always was. Therefore, speaking figuratively, the responsible individual, the father, president or lord, acted by authority of the union or unions he managed, in all cases where authority was required. This was the kurios. He it was, not the union, who took contracts from the governments to build roads, canals, perform the public works, do the managing in the household of the Cæsars, furnish music for the royal entertainments and even feed the cities. The members did the work.[410] Here is the key to Solon's trade unionism. The second half of the word, akos or oikos is in Greek a house. It stood for a residence, a mansion or a temple. When ruled over by the kurios the two words compounded became the kuriakos or kurioikos, a house of the lord; and this arrangement was compulsory under the law which we repeat below, in a note in full, or all that is left of the law.[411] This term was transferred from Greece and Asia Minor to Italy and appears in

[410] Waltzing, *Hist. Corp. Prof.*, I., p. 185: "Selon Choisy, les collèges se divisaient en groupes qui entreprenaient des travaux sous la conduite et la responsabilité pécuniaire d' un ouvrier plus habile ou plus riche; celui-ci traitait avec les magistrats et jouait le rôle d' entrepreneur."

[411] *Digest*, XLVII.. xxii., 4: "We here repeat only the passage over which so much haggling has occured: "'Ἐὰν δὲ δῆμος, ἢ φράτορες, ἢ ἱερῶν ὀργίων, ἢ ναῦται, ἢ σύνσιτοι, ἢ ὁμόταφοι, ἢ θιασῶται. ἢ ἐπὶ λίαν οἰχόμενοι, ἢ εἰς ἐμπορίαν. ὅ τι ἂν τούτων διαθῶνται πρὸς ἀλλήλους, κύριον εἶναι, ἐὰν μὴ ἀπαγορεύσῃ δημόσια γράμμανα.'' Κύριον, appointed, or as substantive the appointed, ie.: κύριον εἶναι must be understood in phrase form, and to signify that any and all the unions of fellowship doing for one-another are to have some κύριος or lord of household whom the law, which is protected by another clause, may hold responsible."

PUDENS' WONDERFUL GUILD OF CARPENTERS.

great numbers of inscriptions modified into cyriacus, queriacus, hyracius and several other terms all of which according to Ramsay, are known as christian signs.[412] Thus under the law, every plebeian union or guild was obliged to have a responsible master or lord who stood for all the members and their actions. But he himself was responsible to the members of the union for everything he did. We have already seen in our chapter on crowning, how the unions often exalted and garlanded their brilliant men. There is evidence to prove that Tychicus, Narcissus, Pudens and nearly all the principal men mentioned so obliquely and almost mysteriously in the New Testament were none other than these garlanded and crowned lords.

Pudens, an Englishman, is mentioned by Paul in the New Testament. This fixes the date in which he flourished, to which we shall soon recur. But the happy discovery of a tablet in Britain or ancient England, showing that he was an Englishman and that he organized a trade union of carpenters at Glastonbury is one of the very important things we have been able to discover in our research for evidence on these revelations proving that the christians planted in the economic labor unions, among the ancient lowly. After nineteen centuries we now appear able to develop the scientific evidence that Pudens is a true historical character flourishing under Claudius and Nero. He appears at home, being sent back to England by Claudius, and there, at Glastonbury, to have organized the carpenters' union or guild which built the once great temple or cathedral whose ruins are a wonder of the modern world.[413] We now come to the strange find of a "Neptuno et Minervæ

[412] Ramsay, *Cit. Bish. Phryg.*, II., p. 493. This researcher like M. Le Blant, has worked out the christian signs such as were used and understood by the members in secret, but were incomprehensible to the outside world. See pp. 491-496, and 502, with *inscrs.*, and full explanations.
[413] Smith, *Bib. Dict.*, p. 2638-9: "Pudens, Πουδης, a christian, friend of Timothy at Rome. St. Paul, writing about A.D. 58, says: "Eubulus greeteth thee, and Pudens and Linus and Claudia." *II Timothy*, iv., 21. He should have finished the verse, viz: "and all the brethren," for it is remarkable that this Pudens had to do with a collegium or guild of carpenters, in Britain, and undoubtedly another at Rome. Again, Smith, *id.*, 2d column, p. 2638, quotes: (see our note 385) "A Latin inscription found in 1723, at Chichester, connects a Pudens with Britain and with the Claudian name. It commemorates the erection of a temple by a guild of carpenters with the sanction of King Tiberius Claudius Cogidubnus, the site being the gift of Pudens, the son of Pudentinus. Cogidubnus was a native king appointed and supported by Rome (Tac., Agric., 14). He reigned with delegated power probably from A.D. 52 to 76."

532   LAW UNDER NERO.

Templum." This temple at Glastonbury was probably constructed by the members of the above union for the benefit of which, according to the inscription recently found at Glastonbury in Chichester, England, Pudens contributed a lot of land.[414] This is proved to be the same Pudens who is mentioned by Paul; and the analysis summed up fixes the inscription at about A.D. 52 to 76.[415] In this we have another charming and genuine inscription showing that the christians planted into the economic labor unions known at that time to have been not only numerous but to have generally possessed the burial attachment, thus securing them against the conspiracy clauses of the lex Julia. The great weight which this adds to our argument is augmented by the numerous mentions of Pudens, his wife Claudia and Linus, all the household and all his personal acquaintances.[416] Pudens must have made the acquaintance of Claudia in Britain, for the episode of Martial's acquaintance with them was not long before the conflagration and the execution of Paul, about A.D. 64, whereas the contribution of Pudens in favor of building for the carpenters of Chichester in England a kuriakos of the collegium to be dedicated to Minerva, goddess of the technical arts, was in 57.[417] The Cyclopedia of Biblical Literature,

[414] Smith, *Bib. Dict.*, p. 2638 and note, quoting the inscription as follows: "Neptuno et Minervae templum pro salute domus divinae, auctoritate Tiberii Claudii Cogidubni regis, legati Augusti in Brit., Collegium fabrorum et qui in eo a sacris sunt de suo dedicaverunt, donanti aream Pudenti, Pudentini filio."
[415] *Timothy*, iv., 21: "'Ασπάζεταί σε Εὔβουλος καί Πούδης καί Λίνος καί Κλαυδία καί οἱ ἀδελφοί πάντες."
[416] Martial, *Epig.*, iv., 13; again, in I., 32; iv., 29; v., 48; vi., 58; vii., 11, 97. Martial connects the household with Pudens, Claudia and Linus, in viii., 60, and ix., 53; and he knew them personally while they were at Rome. It is the same Claudia mentioned by Paul. *II Tim.*, iv., 21, in connection with the three men. Martial's Claudia was a beautiful woman altogether too young for the "flourishing family." This makes it now evident that she was a deaconess, and her husband, Pudens, was a kurios, or president of the kuriakos or κυριοικός, sometimes also written κυριακή, making Pudens a lord of the house now proved by abundant pre-christian inscriptions to be the θίασος, ἔρανος, or ἐταιρα, according to the usage of the province where they are found.
[417] Tac., *Annal.*, XII., 32: "Ceterum clade Icenorum compositi qui bellum inter et pacem dubitabant; et ductus inde Cangos exercitus. vastati agri, praedae passim actae, non ausis aciem hostibus, vel si ex occulto carpere agmen temptarent, punito dolo. iamque ventum haud procul mari quod Hiberniam insulam aspectat, cum ortae apud Brigantas discordiae retraxere ducem, destinationis certum, ne nova moliretur nisi prioribus firmatis. et Brigantes quidem, paucis qui arma coeptabant interfectis, in reliquos data venia, resedere: Silurum gens non atrocitate, non clementia mutabatur, quin bellum excerceret castrisque legionem premenda foret, id quo promptius veniret, colonia Camulodunum valida veteranorum manu deducitur in agros captivos, subsidium adversus rebelles et inbuendis sociis ad officia legum." The Silurus mentioned is that of the Chichester region.

speaking of Claudia says, she was a female christian mentioned by Paul in his letter to Timothy and that there is reason for supposing that she was a British maiden, daughter of King Cogidubnus an ally of Rome. It is the general opinion that Pudens soon became a senator at Rome which is a mistake; also that Claudia, whom he married, was of noble stock, which is likewise a mistake.[418] The facts turn out that this Pudens, like Narcissus, was a favorite with the emperor at Rome, being a shrewd and successful business manager. He was some great lord of a college household working secretly for the unions of carpenters at Rome and abroad. All the inscriptions show that he was a freedman; for his ashes are registered in a cinerary urn of the columbarium on the Appian Way, which shows him to have been of plebeian birth.[419]

This opens to our new discovery, which is being verified by a mass of newly dug up inscriptions, that almost all the persons engaged in that early movement were of lowly-born stock. Claudia's very name as given in the Chichester inscription shows her to have been, though a daughter, yet a daughter of a king by a slave mother. Martial referring in his poems, to the christians, though he does not quite mention the name, calls Claudia Rufina, showing that she was a freedwoman of the gens Rufus; and the indications are that the pair were both of freedman stock. Pudens is commemorated in the Byzantine church on April 14, and in the Roman church May 19. Hippolytus, who wrote out the names of the disciples with a short account of each, declares Pudens to have been one of the seventy disciples. We find the "collegia Pudentiana, whose house, in the valley between the Viminal Hill and the Esquiline, served during his life-time for the assembly of the Roman christians and afterwards gave place to a church now

[418] Tac., *Agric.*, 14: "Quaedam civitates Cogidubno regi donatae (is ad nostram usque memoriam fidissimus mansit), ut viteri ac jam pridem recepta populi Romani consuetudine, haberet instrumenta servitutis et reges."

[419] Smith, *Bib. Dict.*, p. 2638 sq., Art, *Pudens*, says: "Modern researches among the columbaria at Rome, appropriated to members of the imperial household, have brought to light an inscription in which the name of Pudens occurs, as that of the servant of Tiberius or Claudius." *Journ. of Classical and Sacred Philolog.*, IV., 76; Orell.. 1184 and 5024, shows the Pudens inscription as follows: "Nardu poeta Pudens hoc tegitur tumulo;" Gruter, 1118. 6; Lupulus, p. 17. Orelli's 5024 reads: "Ad nostrum n. 1184: 'Nardu poeta Pudens hoc tegitur tumulo.' vide Osann, in *Jahrbücher*, VIII., i., p. 65 refert M\artialis, lib, 4, *Epist.* 13: 'Claudia Rufe meo nubit peregrina Pudenti.' Tum., *Ibid.*, 9, 2, p. 232: 'L. Valerium L. F. Pudentem,' Gauteri, 332, 3."

known as that of S. Pudentiana, a short distance back of the Basilica of St. Maria Maggiore." The same authority informs us that early writers declare that there was but one Pudens.[420]

We next come to the collateral evidence of Lingard. "We are told," he says, "that history has preserved the names of two British females, Claudia and Pomponia Græcina, both of them christians, and both living in the first century of our era."[421] The Scripture informs us that Claudia, the wife of Pudens at Rome, was a christian." On the second page he says, "she was a Briton, and it must be acknowledged that the coincidence is striking and the inference probable." We may safely sum up the evidence of Martial in a few words. He comes to the front at an early date having arrived from Spain somewhere between A.D. 60 and 66, and writes about the christian community at Rome, telling us of Linus, Pudens, Claudia and her household, speaking of them as his friends. If he was admitted to their common table he must have himself been a member. He proves that they were not people of high rank but descendents of slaves. Again, the scurrility of his writings is nothing against this argument; for all the original unions planted into were at that time low and many of them even lewd, just like Martial himself. It was later that the improvements came. Paul had a severe time trying to clean out the vagabondage and the obscenities which existed in the early plant, especially at Corinth. This we have already shown.

But much that has been said regarding Pudens, Narcissus and Claudia might be repeated of Eubulus, Crescens, Titus, Onesiphorus, Linus and many others. The economic functions of their lives are veiled in mystery. What they did, their history could not set forth for two reasons: they were initiates and their secret life-work could not be divulged; and if they had divulged they would have been subjected to persecution. The old members were often adroitly worked over from members of a secret collegium or eranos, and sometimes re-initiated among the christians. Dionysius relates, in

[420] Smith, *Bib. Dict.*, p. 2638-9.
[421] Lingard, *Hist. Anglo-Saxon Church*, 141, 145, referring to *II Tim*., iv., 21, strengthened by Martial's *Epigrammatica*, iv., 13, vi., 53: Claudia, Rufe, meo nubit pregrina Pudenti, Claudia cæruliis cum sit Rufina Britannis Edita."

one of the fragments of his lost epistles, to one of the brethren of his episcopate, the procedure by which he made the change. He was in a thiasos, apparently of the collegium frumentariorum, one of the grain provisioners' legalized unions. "He had been a partaker in the assembly of the faithful: Throwing himself at my feet he began to confess and protest that his former formula of baptism by which he had been initiated into the non-christian congregation was not of the right kind, being full of blasphemy and impurity. He had been initiated by wicked words and deeds. He was so afraid of divulging that he dared not look up or speak distinctly." Dionysius worked him over by slow gradations. It is a clear case among thousands, of conversion after first being initiated into a collegium. Other similar cases are given by Eusebius.[422]

Thus we find by closely scanning the life and career of Pudens that Paul in mentioning him was treating a historical character. But his name occurs yet more, as history; for recent scientific labors have disclosed his sarcophagus and inscriptions which mark it. Pudens sleeps in the necropolis of Priscilla, in one of the deep under-ground vaults in the Via Salaria Nova. Gorius, about the year 1728, mentioned some traces of Pudens as though his ashes were inscribed in the suburban museum of Strozius;[423] but further knowledge lay in darkness until De Rossi and his coadjutors carried their investigations to an ultimate conclusion.[424] They have found Pudens in the same cemetery with Priscilla whose resting place has already become celebrated, and it appears that the ashes of Rufa, likewise mentioned by Martial, and those of Novella, are there. De Rossi[425]

[422] Dionys, *Frag. Epist.*, ix., x.; for other such tell-tale information, see Euseb., *Hist. Eccles.*, VI., 40; VII., 11. The *Epist. of Dionys.*, x., agt. *German.*, reveals a similar case.
[423] *Mon. sive Columb.*, text, p. 105.
[424] De Rossi, *Roma Sotterranea*, I., p. 188: "Vengo al cemetero di Priscilla sulla Via Salaria nuova. Molto dovrei dire intorno a questo cemetero; ma poiche io qui attendo alla somma possibile brevità, rimetto per ora il lettore a quel poco, che ni ho scritto nel dichiarare le imagine scelte della B. Vergine Maria trata delle catacombe romane p. 15-19. Ivi ho riepilogato aliquanti degli argomenti dimonstranti la somma antichità della regione di quel cemetero, nel cui centro è la così detta cappella greca; regione, che ho dichiarato essere la primitiva ed originaria, quella ov' ebbero sepolturai prima Pudenti ed i martiri insigni, onde tanta rinomanza venne alla necropoli di Priscilla."
[425] *Idem.*, p. 171: "'Incerto anche rimasi sul' acclamazione 'NAVIGI VIVAS IN CHRISTO,'" (this last word being the well-known sign). And continues: "che se legge nella così detta cappella greca del cemetero di Priscilla, la quale mi pareva senza dubbio un istorica cripta."

lays stress upon these being all, without doubt histori‑
cal and of earliest christian antiquity.

The emperor Nero, who reigned A.D. 54 to 69, was at first well disposed toward the Roman collegia. Tiberius had been kind to them and certainly furthered the planting of christianity among them by lending his powerful assistance in giving the members work. The method of doing this was that of Augustus and Livia, who had founded the celebrated Domus Augustalis for their protection. We have seen in the first volume of this work that the Roman trade unions, unlike these of to-day, were genuine voting organizations of labor. They carried out the theory of the socialist trade and labor alliance. They were possessed of their ballots which they used enormously in the municipalities, as shown by the recent discoveries at Pompeii, at Rome and in Asia, not only in electing their own choice of ediles, agoranomoi or commissioners of public works, but even the powerful tribunes, who constituted the house of representatives, and in the making of the laws stood next to the senate. We have also seen that but a few years before the mild reign of Augustus began, Cicero, Cæsar, Clodius, Mark Antony and many other historical characters were having fearful and indeed bloody times with these trade unions, because they would not be suppressed, but grew in political power to the ineffable disgust of the great and august senators who had long denied that working people had either rights or souls. What these trade unions wanted was an opportunity to labor for a living. Centuries before, and all through the Roman conquests, they had been working on an enormous scale for the government in doing the national work. They did it direct without the skinning contractor. The conquests had ruined these good old days of their prosperity and happiness by creating millions of competing slaves of war, whom the grasping generals, like Crassus, had brought to Rome. These men, formerly freedmen largely organized into unions under the old law, now slaves of war, stocked the labor market. Their owners were eager to find remunerative work for them, and jobbed them out for a small sum per day to do work, not only for the ordinary people but also for the government. This com‑

petition threatened the bread-winning hopes of the multitudinous trade unions, old and fully established, under the Solonic law.

Terrible strifes were the result. Cicero espoused the cause of the aristocrats who had imported the competing slave labor, and Clodius took sides with labor.

They all lost their lives in these fearful contests. We regard them as the most momentous days in history. When Augustus assumed the reins of government he saw the necessity of conciliatory measures which would appease the contending forces. He invented the domus Augustalis. The scheme and plan of the domus Augustalis was to favor the collegia or trade unions. In it was the gynæcium, a sort of manufacturing, cleansing and repairing business. Those doing this labor were doing government work, for what was the emperor and his imperial family but the government? Thousands upon thousands of freedmen and women were thus mustered in and given employment.

Meantime, the violent seizure of slaves of war had ceased. No more were brought into the great city. Those who had already been dragged thither sought to join the collegia and obtain some crumbs of comfort by blending with the great masses of labor organizations at Rome. This explains the otherwise unaccountable condition of things at Rome just at the moment when Paul and Peter were propagating the new Word of hope and promise. Contrary to general opinion, the domus Augustalis or household of the Cæsars was a vast concern. There were constantly many thousands kept at work of some kind. They had departments, with a variety of shops. A regularly organized college or union worked each trade. The shoemakers had their place; the clothing-makers for the imperial family were very numerous. They ostensibly did only the work of the imperial family, but in reality, for hundreds of wealthy families, in touch with the nobility, either by blood, or friendship all over the city, making the work enormous. The same is to be said of all the other branches of labor.

Claudius, as we have seen in the case of the freedman Narcissus, had utilized this establishment of the domus Augustalis, and we have no evidence that he ever antagonized it. What he did was to drive and persecute and banish the christians whom he naturally treated as Jews; for these had planted into and nearly captured all of the trade unions obtaining and enjoying government employ as collegia in the domus Augustalis. This is what maddened Claudius and Nero. The old unions still smarting under the insulting laws of Cæsar and Cicero, who might be denominated the Pinkerton advocates of their hated and abusive masters, could not be suppressed. They sank into a sullen secrecy. They met in their wretched abodes and discussed their economic future. Their general desire was very similar to that of the christians already appearing at Rome from Jerusalem. The slaves of conquest were also of their opinion. They all wanted freedom. They were unanimous that as they were the creators of all good things, they ought to be awarded their share. The spies of Claudius and Nero were lurking in their unions to hear and report their language.

Claudius, in this manner discovered that the bold doctrines of a certain contemptible carpenter who had been crucified at Jerusalem, and consequently a Jew, was to a large extent the cause of the dangerous dissatisfaction becoming widespread. This caused him to issue the edict of expulsion of the Jews. It was an edict of expulsion of the christians as well. We have already remembered it.

Let this suffice for Claudius. We now come to Nero and his burning of Rome. Ebionism, nazarenism and christianity had allied themselves with the unions of the Solonic dispensation to permanently rid the world of the pest of the money-power and kingcraft. The fight was on Nero, who boasted of an ancient greatness in a family of the gens Claudia, and held a very shortsighted opinion that he represented a glorious, eternal dynasty. Luke, on the other hand, a socialist, was at that very moment writing a history of the Acts. The reverse of that tyrant: "He was an exalted democrat and ebionite, thoroughly opposed to property, and persuaded that the day of the poor is at hand."[426] What else could be expected than a clash? This Cæsar, the most profligate, virulent, bloodthirsty and destructive of all known monarch brigands, against a meek and lowly guild of carpenters!

[426] Renan, *Life of Jesus*, Introduc., p. 36.

GLADIATORIAL HUNTSMEN. 539

There were at Rome two or three great temples of the female divinities who, for centuries, were supposed to have been protecting or tutelary goddesses of the various trades and arts. These great divinities were Minerva, goddess of spinning, weaving[427] and the manufacture of woolen textile goods. Minerva was the great protecting friend of labor and of the laboring people. She was the goddess to whom the union of carpenters at Glastonbury, near London, in A.D. 4, had dedicated their wonderful christian temple for which Paul's friend Pudens, had contributed an area of land. She was also under the Greek appellative of Athena, the principal tutelary divinity for the great Gemeinde next to Dionysus, the forerunner, great and venerated "protector of man." In fact, they merged together.

After Minerva, came Diana the renowned Artemis of the Greeks and sister of Apollo, god of the red dyers, of flaming beauties, of bows, arrows, hunting equipments and of archery. She is the goddess of the hunters, and in those days of the gladiatorial combats, the chase was no small affair, for the unions of hunters had to be international. To carry on the great work of furnishing live animals for the amphitheatres it was necessary to have powerful men constantly on watch in many a remote jungle risking their lives with thongs, snares, nets and lassoes, wherewith to seize and convey uninjured to Rome the savagest wild beasts of forest, river and sea. We have already mentioned some of the inscriptions portraying the hunters.[428] They were always organized in powerful unions with Diana as their protecting divinity.

Again, there was the temple of Isis. She was the same for Egypt as Demeter was for the Greeks, or Ceres for the Romans. In the ancient superstition she was the wife of Osiris the great Egyptian martyr god, and closely related to Anubis,[429] the dog-headed god of the hunting. Such was the inconsistency of the ancient

---
[427] And,, *Lat. Dict.*, in verb. MINERVA; "Goddess of wisdom, sense, reflection, arts and sciences, poetry, spinning and weaving." She is the same for Rome as the Pallas Athena was for Greece. During these times in question she was a protectrice of the woolen manufacture: Virgil, *Æneid*, VIII., 409: "Tolerare colo vitam tenuique Minerva."
[428] For much on the inscrs. of Hunters under the Solonic dispensation, see *index* to each volume of this work, using proper catchwords.
[429] Vide *supra*, pp. 488 sq. Story of Josephus regarding a scandal on her account.

theogony that a veritable jumble existed in the minds of men regarding their divinities. But the lower mysteries brought to the producers and distributors of all labor products a far more consistent promise in setting particular functions as the task of particular divinities, according to the place and language. Thus Isis, Demeter, Ceres and Cybele were believed to protect the fruit of the land and were consequently chosen by the unions of farmers, grain grinders, furnishers of hemp, flax and producers of vegetable raw stock, and likewise all products of manufacture; while Anubis, Diana and Artemis took care of the unions of hunters, fishermen and even of the mollusks from the inks of which the red, purple and other dyes were made.

Peter was probably a member of a union; and if so, then, following the ancient superstition, he would have been before conversion, on bended knees to Artemis. Nor is there anything surprising in this. Several suggestive inscriptions have been recently discovered about the Sea of Galilee, of fishermen's unions. The monuments are known to be very ancient. There were certainly a good many fishermen's societies in the north part of Palestine. A few miles farther north in Syria, there were many unions both of fishers and hunters, and their careful mention has been paid attention to. [430] Renan assures us that most if not all of the immediate companions of Jesus were closely and secretly organized.[431]

Vast numbers of the poor fellows, splendidly organized, had placed their faith in these tutelary divinities at Rome, firmly believing that their favorite gods and goddesses would come to rescue them from their miserable condition. But they came not. About the time of Nero they were in a wretched and worse sunken condition than ever before. The great scheme of the Pagan religion had proved a dismal failure. God and goddess had neglected them. The crypts of the temples of Isis, Diana, and Minerva could be used by them as places of refuge, but these beloved deities themselves never came. They were, at the time of Christ's advent very despondent. The awful conquests had rolled by without an offer of a helping hand. They were ready to shake off

[430] See *index*, in words, *Hunters*, *Fishermen*, etc.
[431] Renan, *Life of Jesus*.

OLD GODS NEVER CAME TO THE RESCUE. 541

the deception which for lucre the priests of the old theogony had from immemorial time imposed upon them. When Jesus came and really, practically, fleshly, humbly as one of them, mounted the cross and died before their eyes for them, they wheeled as by a stroke of magnetism and grasped hold of his plan of salvation, the Word of promise.

But what made their conviction more ready and pronounced, a conviction based upon the failure of their gods to protect them in desperate troubles and danger, was undoubtedly the terrible crucifixion within their memory and before their eyes of the fated four-hundred slaves. This horrible judicial massacre, which we have fully related,[432] was perpetrated near Rome, about the first year of Paul's sojourn there, A.D. 61. A lord of the patricians, probably on account of some cruel treatment of the slaves of his household, had been killed by one of them who could not sink his manhood so low as to bear the outrage. Tacitus alleges that he was refused permission to buy himself free. The dire and relentless vengeance of law which the senate seized upon was consummated and the adorable honor of a member of a gens family, vindicated and avenged by this judicial crucifixion of the one perpetrator of the deed and of all the other servants of the murdered prefect's "family," three hundred and ninety-nine in number.

During the conquests the grasping army officers had dragged thousands of families in Greece, Asia Minor, Epirus and Macedonia to Rome, to be the menials of drunken, arrogant lords of the Roman world. The three hundred and ninety-nine were paraded in chains before the public, all other slaves forced to behold, and mercilessly crucified.

Such was the hideous condition of things at Rome at the time Paul arrived. So great was the danger that he had to be cautious. He is known to have preached in secret and to have converted thousands. The spread of the new doctrine excited attention. Nero had his spies. They were everywhere. Under pretense of true penitence, they secretly joined the new christian brotherhoods, overheard what was going on and went back to their royal master with the news. But the curious fact remains to be told that the christians had their

[432] See *supra*, in chap. vii., *Rage and Havoc*, pp. 124-125.

headquarters in the temples of Minerva, Isis and Diana. This was especially true of Diana on the Aventine Hill. Her great edifice was the resort of thousands of trade unionists all over Rome. The city, long before Nero came to power, was being rapidly converted to the christian faith. These converts were not from the ranks of the revengeful rich, but from the lowly slave classes, great numbers of whom inhabited the abodes contiguous to Diana's temple, and they had free access to it.

Nero, through his spies, saw the growth of the new culture and had the penetration to understand that it meant the overthrow of a long-time theogony of his ancestral god-head. With christianity there would exist no longer a competitory survival of the fittest, a bully, a brute. Her mild powers of reason and brotherly love had no province in Nero's brain. He craved only for vengeance and destruction. He was a profligate.[433] History refuses to give us the bottom truths regarding the incentives which urged this ferocious creature whom a false system had clothed with power. These fundamental causes lurked in an unspeakable hatred by the aristocracy against the poor and laboring element. Their particular offense under Nero was the same with that which caused his predecessors, Caligula and Claudius, to persecute and drive from Rome the christians on the anti-Semitic plea that they were Jews. But they had begun to dig and cover themselves in the pre-mortuary graves of under-ground Rome, where even the spies and police and emissaries of the prætorian guard dared not enter. They had availed themselves of the burial clause of the Julian law and though alive and eating at the common table in the deep-sunk cells of their scholæ, embracing each other with their ineffable love and sympathy, they were chanting the same hymns [434] they bor-

[433] Gran. de Cass., *Hist. Class. Ouv.*, p. 368: "Voulait il voir une bataille navale, il faisait creuser un lac assez vaste et assez profond pour y faire manœuvrer deux flottes." Suet., *Nero*, xi.: "Exhibuit et naumachiam marina aqua, innantibus belluis." Again, *id.*: "Toujours vêtu de soie et d' étoffes d' Orient, il ne portait jamais deux fois le même habit, Suet., *Nero*, xxii.

[434] See *supra*, in chap. *Music*. The hope of the future is that other and more complete inscriptions may yet be discovered revealing the airs. As we have suggested, there may be in store for us astonishing disclosures of tunes containing scraps of our own melodies, sung and chanted by those poor, weeping workers, sequestered among the catacombs too deep for the torch of Nero. It was the thousands of poor fellows above ground whom he burned alive. There was a vast humanity below who were to survive.

rowed from the musical artists of Dionysus and perhaps many of the identical tunes we hear at our camp meetings and jubilees to-day. Accompanying these sunless symposiums was the hope, almost denied by Plato, half accorded by Homer, doubted by Socrates,[435] reasoned into oblivion by Lucretius, reprobated in furious contempt by Nero, but promised with a brilliancy that dazzled their minds in a coma of exuberance by their own beloved, meek, messianic Jesus, that they all had souls and were men and women—no longer dogs and beasts of the field, forest and swamp. Neither Diana, Isis nor Minerva really guaranteed them immortality. The mysteries of a classic eleusinium could promise the wealthy aristocrat life on the other side; but we have little, if any assurance that by initiation into the lesser mysteries there was really promised a life beyond. The general purport of the inscriptions is dark on this great point; but when an inscription is found with words about a hope grounded in eternity, we have the assurance that it is christian and archæologists class such words on trade-union graves as signs of the christian life.

Thus armed with a soul, darkling and trembling in self-dug dungeons, going stealthily up at dawn to their dangerous, ill-paid labor, crawling back in secrecy, and after a sober repast, meeting brothers and sisters by the dim oil lamp in the miniature schola of their crypt, these wretched "little groups," lived and sang and died.

It is twitted that they "smelled of garlic, these ancestors of Roman prelates; that they were poor proletaries dirty and clownish, clothed in filthy gabardines, having the bad odor and breath of people living badly. Their retreats breathed an odor of wretchedness exhaled by persons meanly clothed and fed, and collected in a little room."[436]

Such was the condition of things at the time of the great conflagration. We now turn our attention to this celebrated historical event. This monarch, endowed with absolute, despotic power, early exhibited symptoms of a dangerous mania, although in the beginning of his sixteen-years' reign, he was passably tolerant to his supjects. A sickness, thought to have proceeded from ven-

[435] Plato, *Crito.*
[436] Renan, *Life of Christ*, p. 96.

eria, turned his mind in a direction of wantonness and cruelty, and there were thousands of the common people of the old unconverted line of pagans ready to fight against[437] the new developments in and around the temple of Diana on the Aventine. After a number of extraordinary feats of squandering the public money, he determined to root out the christians and compass their annihilation.

Mr. Gibbon is of the opinion that the burning of Rome did not occur until A.D. 69, but the usual calculations put it some five or six years earlier.[438] The history of the great conflagration of Rome lies to this day in a state of much obscurity. Dion Cassius declares that Nero himself set fire to it and was responsible partly for the crime.[439] Tacitus, another historian of much accuracy, does as much. The accurate and careful Suetonius likewise declares without hesitancy that Nero perpetrated the crime of burning Rome on purpose.

But some four years at least elasped between the arrival of the apostle in Rome in 61 and the incendiarism. Though a prisoner, he was allowed a liberty which seems to have been nearly equivalent to being at large. We know that Nero was very fond of music and that he greatly favored the Dionysan artists many of whom enjoyed his patronage at Rome, and others, especially the mimic actors, were from Asia Minor as members of the great Gemeinde. Very many side evidences induce us to believe that Paul was a member and that he turned his trade as scene and tent maker to aid these unions in furnishing their shows with the necessary paraphernalia of the histronic art. In this case he would be able

---

[437] Neander, *Planting*, Book III., ch. vii.: "Moreover, in the Neronian persecution, the christian church appears as a new sect, much hated by the people, a genus tertium, of whom the people were disposed to credit the worst reports, because they were opposed to all the forms of religion hitherto in existence."

[438] Gibbon, *Decline and Fall*, ch. xvi.. with note 44: "The capital was burnt during the civil war between Vitellius and Vespasian, the 19th of December, A.D. 69; on the 10th of Aug., A.D. 70, the temple of Jerusalem was destroyed by the hands of the Jews themselves, rather than by those of the Romans." This would make the time beween the two dates, only 222 days,—a proposition which cannot be sustained.

[439] Gibbon, *Decline and Fall*, ch. xvi., note, gives the principal authorities for Nero's conflagration as Tacitus, *Ann.*, xv., 38-44; Suetonius, *In Neronem*, 38; Dion. Cassius, LXII., p. 1014; Orosius, *Adv. Paganos*, VII., 7. Dion Cassius, LXII., 16, init., starts out with the words: "Μετὰ δὲ ταῦτα ἐπεθύμησεν (ὅπερ που ἀεὶ ηὔχετο) τήν τε πόλιν ὅλην καὶ τὴν βασιλείαν ζῶν ἀναλῶσαι."

to touch a very tender spot in Nero's heart, for the monarch was passionately fond of the mimes which they brought into Rome. We hear nothing definite of the apostle, but there is a legend strongly set forth, that he was allowed to go to Spain by consent, if not the request of Nero, and that while there he planted the Spanish branch of the church. What is still more surprising is that Nero is actually said to have gone with him. He is known to have made himself one of the buffoons[440] in the mimic shows. He made the playwrights concessions of large sums of money,[441] for their mimes and pantomimes were a great charm to him. But while he was friendly to the Solonic unions on the one hand, he despised their tendency to endorse the worship of the new messiah. The christians were preaching at Rome just then, a promise to the laboring millions that they had bodies and immortal spirits as worthy of salvation as any of the great wealth owners. The christians in Rome were propagating the fundamental idea of socialism two thousand years before its possible realization. They knew not the vast expanse of time necessary to prepare the world for such an immense transition. They knew not that earth and humanity are great, and ideas are met with repugnance. Christianity had invaded the unions that Nero loved.

The thought of such a change threw this monarch into a spasm of angry revengefulness. He had in his shallow egotism worked himself to believe that he was descended from a line of immortals, stretching back to Romulus.[442] Dion Cassius testifies in strong words to

[440] Lüders, *Dionys. Künst.*, p. 95: "Cäsar liess nach seinen Siegen in Spanien Schauspieler in allen Sprachen auftreten. Nero endlich betrat nicht nur selbst mit griechischen Techniten die Bühne, sondern hatte auch stets eine ganze Schar von ihnen in seiner nächsten Umgebung, denen er grosse Geldsummen hinterliess." Suetonius, *Octav.*, 43: "Ludos fecit nonnumquam vicatim ac pluribus scenis per omnium linguarum histriones." For a remark on *Nero* see Plutarch, *Galba.*, 16.

[441] *Idem*, p. 95: "Dass es in Rom eine andauernd ansaässige Gesellschaft Griechischer Künstler gab in derKaiserzeit, bezeugt eine Inschrift aus Gallien, in der 'die heilige Synodos in Rom' genannt wird.'"

[442] Dion. Cass., LXII., 18: "Ἔσχατος Αἰνεαδῶν μητροκτόνος ἡγεμονεύσει" Dion thinks the mother murderer was beset by the evil spirit, to "clean the place." "Τὰ παρόντα θειασθέν," ie.: Θειάω, fumigate, to clean and purify, and thus restore to the gods. Nero imagined that as the city had become polluted by the christians it was his natural function as a descendant of Æneas, to fumigate, purify, cleanse and restore it to the gods by a hallowing purification; and all this to the end that the Julian line with its origin in Æneas become supreme, should assume its former majesty. "Τελευταῖος γὰρ τῶν Ἰουλίων τῶν ἀπὸ Αἰνείου γενομένων ἐμονάρχησε," This is certainly a strong light clearing up the argument that Dio thinks Nero set Rome on fire purposely, in order to purify the city.

this. Nothing can be more probable than that, as Gibbon most definitely affirms, in a similar case of Domitian's persecution at Puteoli, the careful Cassius, not knowing the secret christians, but thinking with everybody else, that it was all the work of Jews, says Nero burned Rome for the purpose of killing out the nests of christians from the low quarters among the communes. Again, Suetonius whose birth took place almost at the hour the flames were raging, has no hesitation in saying that Rome was set on fire purposely.[443] He gathered oakum and pine knots from the manor houses of his own and sang songs of the capture of Troy, from a pinnacle of the Mæcenatian tower, in joyful transports. The popular legend runs, that " Nero fiddled for Rome to burn." The fact more accurately stated is that he had gathered many loose women and profligate men of the aristocratic families, and invited a number of the wandering, dissolute fakirs from among the musicians, to ascend the tower to a flat stand large enough to accomodate them and there in security and at a commanding elevation, they all had a boisterous jolification, the emperor himself playing upon a cithera while they sang and danced ditties of the Trojan war.

The object of Nero was to cast contempt and hatred on the christians. The great mass of the common people do not come into this crime. It was the *genus tertium* described by Neander, who were to be attacked. They had early settled in Rome. Christians had been at work among the thousands of collegia from before the crucifixion. These facts come to us through the inscriptions and monumental relics of their activity. The idea here to be conveyed by a genus tertium[444] or a third element is almost exactly the same as that which caused the persecution and martyrdom of members of the thiasos at Athens. It was jealousy. They called it

---

[443] Suetonius, *Nero*, 38-40, declares Nero burnt Rome on purpose, after a thorough determination, on account of the: "Deformitate veterum ædificiorum et angustiis flexurisque vicorum." This is prefaced with the words: "planeque ita fecit." He then resumes his discourse with the words: "incendit urbem tam palam, ut plerique consulares cubicularios ejus, cum stuppa tædaque in prædiis suis deprehensos, non attigerint; et quædam horrea circa domum Auream, quorum spatium maxime desiderabat, ut bellicis machinis labefacta atque inflammata sint quod saxeo muro constructa erant."

[444] Neander, *Hist. Chr. Church*, I., pp. 92-5. Neander here speaks of the communities and the "secret sect to which these enemies of the gods abandoned themselves," Nero, he says, tried to fix the guilt of the conflagration upon a genus tertium.

the introduction of new and foreign divinites into Attica, a crime under the law punishable with death. In every case at Athens, including those in which Demosthenes was involved the offenders found to have introduced a foreign religion, were members of the secret unions.[445] So, also in Rome, it had long been the immigrants, as either slaves of war dragged thither by force, or business agents as at Puteoli, or evangelists sent out from the primitive brotherhood which Jesus had organized at Jerusalem, who introduced the new gospel of the Word, and they introduced it first among the collegia. But we should here call to mind the conversion of Tiberius the emperor, who actually tried to secure the consent of the senate to proclaim Jesus openly and legally as one of the gods in the galaxy of the Roman pantheon. Few stop to think that the mysterious assassination of Tiberius may reasonably have been inspired by this jealous conservatism of the old theogony in whose purple and ermine of the great gens families and princely bloods strode and pretentiously assumed dignity under the awful mysticism of priest-power and an overbrooding divinity.

We say we are assured from the variety of fragments and squibs of evidence that are being collected, that Paul was allowed by Nero to go to Spain, and that the conflagration and execution of the two greatest apostles followed immediately in its trail. It was in the year of our era, sixty-four.

On July 18, A.D. 64, there suddenly burst forth a flame of fire, first kindled among some old wooden booths used as stalls of the poorest of the people. It was at the southeast end of the Circus Maximus and not more than one or two blocks away from it. Here were wont to congregate the hucksters having unions of their trade, and their members sold certain eatables to the throngs. In one direction the fire rapidly spread over the Palatine and Velia, up to the cliffs of the Esquiline Hill. The fire also started off in another course. It struck the Aventine. Here was the great temple of Diana, goddess of the huntsmen and the poor. The Forum Boarium was next invaded by the flames. This is where the first gladiatorial combat took place in B. C. 264,

---

[445] See *supra*, chap. xv., pp. 327-345., on *Pre-christian Martyrs*.

through the aristocrats Marcus and Decimus Brutus, a couple of lords who on the death of their father forced his favorite slaves to fight each other to the death in order that the deceased parent might have the assistance of these, his favorite servants, in ghost-form, in the after world.[446]

The fire spread toward the Tiber. There were no modern fire-extinquishing engines then. After consuming the Velabrum and licking unhindered, its lingering vestiges, it ran down into the river Tiber, and was finally stopped by the huge masonry of the Servian Wall. After fiercely burning for six days and seven nights, and its fury had apparently become exhausted, it suddenly broke out afresh in the northern quarter of the city desolating two regions of the Circus Flaminius and the Via Lata. There being no adequate mechanical appliances in existence, little could be done. Of course thousands of people turned out against the ruinous heats, but in vain; and when it came to a manageable standstill, only four of fourteen regions of Rome remained. Three had been completely destroyed, and seven others were now in ruins. Thirty-thousand corpses were registered.[447]

No sooner were the flames exhausted for want of aliment than Nero came down from his tower and in loudmouthed invectives charged the whole iniquity against the christians.[448] Although the Encyclopædia Britannica in its article on Nero fails to charge this monarch with the intentional deed, yet nearly all others are emphatic in their accusation, that he worked up the whole

[446] Valer. Max., *De Spect.*. 7: "Gladiatorium munus primum Romæ datum est in foro Boario, Appio Claudio M. Fulvio Coss., dederunt M. et D. Bruti, funebri memoria patris cineres honorando. Athletarum certamen a M. Scauri tractum est munificentia."

[447] Suetonius, *Nero*, 38: "Per six dies septemque noctes ea clade sævitum est ad monumentorum bustorumqne diversoria plebe compulsa: Tunc præter immensum numerum insularum domus priscorum ducum arserunt hostilibus adhuc spoliis adornatae, deorumque ædes ab regibus ac deinde Punicis et Gallicis bellis votæ dedicatæque et quidquid visendum atque memoribile ex antiquitate duraverat. Hoc incendium e turre Mæcentiana prospectans lætusqne flammæ ut aibat, pulchritudine Halosin Ilii in illo suo scænico habitu decantavit. Ac ne non hinc quoque quantum posset prædæ et manubiarum invaderet, pollicitus cadaverum et ruderum gratuitam egestionem, nemini ad reliquias rerum suarum adire permisit; conlationibusque non receptis modo verum et efflagitatis provincias privatorumque census prope exhausit. Accesserunt tantis ex principe malis probrisque quædam et fortuita; pestilentia unius autumni, quo triginta funerum milia in rationem Libitinæ venerunt.

[448] Meyers, *Konv. Lex.* in v. *Nero*: "... dass er 64, nach dem grossen Brande, durch dem ein grosser Theil der Stadt zerstört wurde die in Rom anwesenden Christen als angebliche Urheber desselben unter den grausamsten Martiren tödten liess."

NERO'S MASSACRE OF THIRTY-THOUSAND. 549

plot, stood over it and nurtured it, and even prevented the fire department from doing anything toward putting it out. Under his abject and absolute power it was doubtless pronounced by him a treason punishable with immediate death. This we know by inference. The expressed abhorrence of Seneca.[449] The discovery of a conspiracy against Nero, in which Seneca, C. Calpernius Piso, Plautius Lateranus, the poet Lucanus and others were suspected of being concerned as a junta to rid the world of this monster, caused their immediate death.[450]

We are now coming to one of the most atrocious massacres ever recorded of human beings: Nero's vengeance against the christians.

The greater part of the quarter consumed in this conflagration was inhabited by the communes and collegia, and before proceeding, it behooves us to give all that is known in relation to their lowliness and misery in the abodes and especially such as shows them to have been members of the collegia.[451] Donatus, an antiquarian of the eighteenth century, describes the conflagration and certifies to its having taken place in the year 64.[452] Levasseur, who wrote a valuable history[453] of the working

---

[449] Seneca, *Epist.*, denouncing the monster to St. Paul; cf. Jerome, *Catalog:* "Senecam non ponerem in Catalogo Sanctorum nisi me illae epistolae provocarent, quae leguntur a plurimis Pauli ad Senecam et Senecae ad Paulum." And August, *Epist. ad Maced.*, LIII.: "Omnes odit qui male odit." Seneca is now revealed to have been converted by Paul, and to have humbled himself to the collegiate ranks; Guizot, in note to *trans.* of Gibbon, in ch. xvi., note 42, *fin.:* "Moreover the name of christians had long been given in Rome to the disciples of Jesus, and Tacitus affirms too positively, refers too distinctly to its etymology, to allow us to suspect any mistake on his part.

[450] *Amer. Cyc.*, art. *Nero*, announcing their deaths, says: "The discovery of a conspiracy against him served to develop his ferocity;" and speaking of his brutal triumph in the murder of these celebrated men: "The senate was induced to receive the intelligence of their fate as the news of a great victory, and the infamous Tigellinus, the emperor's principal instrument, was decreed triumphal honors." This of itself, quite clearly shows, that it was a case of Nero's incendiarism.

[451] Suetonius, *Nero*, 16, certainly places the christians down among the lowest strata, at Rome. The short sentence usually quoted is not enough of this significant paragraph. Immediately in front of, and succeeding the words so commonly used by commentators, are words fully as significant: "Publicae coenae ad sportulas redactae. Interdictum ne quid in popinis cocti praeter legumina aut holera veniret, cum antea nullum non obsonii genus proponeretur. Afflicti suppliciis Christiani, genus hominum superstitionis novae ac maleficae. Vetiti quadrigariorum lusus, quibus inveterata licentia passim vagantibus fallere ac furari per locum jus erat. Pantomimorum factiones cum ipsis simul relegatae."

[452] *De Roma Antiqua*, lib. III., p. 449; Nardini. *Roma Antica*, p. 487.

[453] Levass., *Hist. Cl, Ouv.*, I., pp. 14, 15, 16. On p. 16, with note 3, reference is made to Dion Cassius, LX., 6, touching the suppression of the unions. Most authors understand Dion Cass. to mean here the christians. But they are all treated as ἑταιραί, which is the borrowed term for collegia.

classes of northern Europe, in giving the origin of their trade organizations, about the time of the crucifixion and a little later, attributes much of the success of the great movement to them.

From a careful survey of the sources of information, the organizations which he had to do with in this affair, were the collegium juvenum, a society which he aided and fostered in his younger days;[454] the collegia mimorum toward whom he also felt a strong affection; the lupercalia, another gaming union, pronounced by Mommsen to be harmless;[455] the collegia vectigalariorum; collegia vinariorum; collegia vini fumatorum; collegia lenunculariorum of the coasting boats; collegia naviculariorum, collegia compatilicia and a host of the more common sort, such as the cobblers, rag-pickers and patch-piecers.

When this tyrant's rage, however, turned against these unions, which was not until his spies, like Tigellinus brought him news that they were all rapidly adopting the christian faith,[456] his wrath knew no bounds. They were immediately given the appellation of "burners" and the great calamity was charged to their account. The burners must be punished. The burners were the innocent christians, too innocent to deny their love of Jesus. The great historian Tacitus, commended in all our colleges, a pagan who hated the christians with a cruel conscience, excused Nero's indescribable torture of these poor beings; moreover he declared that their punishment was just and well deserved.

The recent discovery of the columbaria and of the ancient christian cemeteries discloses the fact that not only the dead, but the living went down into the subterranean abodes. During the persecutions of Claudius they dug themselves great caverns. It is presumable that in them very many thus escaped the fury of Nero.

[454] Mommsen, *De Coll. el Sodal. Rom.*, p. 83: "Collegia juvenum quae a Nerone instituta creduntur propter ludos juvenales."

[455] Suetonius, *Aug.*, 31: "Sacrum Lupercale paulatim aboletum, restituit."

[456] To show that Nero well comprehended that this new element threatened the existence of the reign of Jupiter and his gens aristocracy, see Orell., 5229, an *inscr.*, Romae, Gori, *Symbol, Lit.*, T. 4, Praef., p. xii. It reads: "JOVI OPTIMO MAXIMO SANCTI MARTYRES DOMINIque SANCTI successerunt SANCTIS MARTURIBUS etc." No doubt can exist as to this being purely christian; since they always claimed to have succeeded Jove,

While the flames were raging overhead all was quiet in the secret under-ground abodes. Amid the turmoils of persecution, which during the reign of Claudius, had driven thousands from Rome, all was quiet in these netherworlds. Each union had its scholæ, a part of a basilica, and the members were all initiates. They were thus screened from the search of Tigellinus and eluded Nero's charge that they were the burners of Rome. If, then, they suffered to a large extent we are not made aware of it. Our great source of information is Tacitus;[457] but Suetonius[458] followed and fully confirmed by

[457] Suetonius, *Nero*, 38: The very commencement of this fine passage is sufficient to show that Suetonius had no doubts that Nero was the incendiary; he quotes Nero's own Greek: "Dicente quodam in sermone communi.

'Εμοῦ θανόντος γαῖα μιχθήτω πυρί!

Immo, inquit, ἐμοῦ ζῶντος! Planeque ita feci. Nam quasi offensus deformitate veterum aedificiorum et angustiis flexurisque vicorum, incendit urbem tam palam, ut plerique consulares cubicularios ei‿s, cum stuppa taedaque in praediis suis deprehensos, non attigerint; et quaedam horrea circa domum Auream, quorum spatium maxime desiderabat, ut bellicis machinis labefacta atque inflammata sint, quod saxeo muro constructa erant. Per sex dies septemque noctes ea clade saevitum est, ad monumentorum bustorumque diversoria plebe compulsa. Tunc praeter immensum numerum insularum domus priscorum ducum arserunt hostilibus adhuc spoliis adornatae, deorumque aedes ab regibus ac deinde Punicis et Gallicis bellis votae dedicataeque, et quidquid visendum atque memorabile ex antiquitate duraverat. Hoc incendium e turre Maecenatiana prospectans laetusque *flammae*, ut aiebat, *pulchritudine* Halosin Ilii in illo suo scaenico habitu decantavit. Ac ne non hinc quoque quantum posset praedae et manubiarum iuvaderet, pollicitus cadaverum et ruderum gratuitam egestionem, nemini ad reliquias rerum suarum adhire permisit; conlationibusque non receptis modo verum et efflagitatis provincias privatorumque census prope exhausit. Accesserunt tantis ex principe malis probrisque quaedam et fortuita: pestilentia unius autumni, quo triginta funerum milia in rationem Libitinae venerunt.

[458] Tacit., *Annal.*, xv., 38: "Sequitur clades, forte an dolo principis incertum (nam utrumque auctores prodidere), sed omnibus quae huic urbi per violentiam ignium acciderunt gravior atque atrocior. Initium in ea parte circi ortum, quae Palatino Caelioque montibus contigua est ubi per tabernas, quibus id mercimonium inerat quo flamma alitur, simul coeptus ignis et statim validus ac vento citus longitudinem circi corripuit. Neque enim domus munimentis saeptae vel templa muris cincta aut quid aliud morae interiacebat. Impetu pervagatum incendium plana primum, deinde in edita adsurgens, et rursus inferiora populando, anteiit remedia velocitate mali et obnoxia urbe artis itineribus huc que et illuc flexis, atque enormibus vicis, qualis vetus Roma fuit. Ad hoc lamenta paventium feminarum, fessa [aetate] aut rudis puritiae aetas, quique sibi quique alliis consulebant dum trahunt invalidos aut opperiuntur, pars mora, pars festinans, cuncta impediebant. et saepe, dum in tergum respectant, lateribus aut fronte circumveniebantur; vel si in proxima evaserant, illis quoque igni correptis, etiam quae longinqua crediderant in eodem casu reperiebant. Postremo, quid vitarent quid peterent ambigui, complere vias, sterni per agros; quidam amissis omnibus fortunis, diurni quoque victus, alii caritate suorum, quos eripere nequiverant, quamvis patente effugio interiere, nec quisquam defendere audebat, crebris multorum minis restinguere prohibentibus, et quia alii palam faces iaciebant atque esse sibi auctorem vociferabantur, sive ut raptus licentius exercerent, seu iussu.

39. Eo in tempore Nero Antii agens non ante in urbem regressus est quam domui eius, qua Palatium et Maecenatis hortos continuavarat ignis propinqueret. Neque tamen sisti potuit, quin et Palatium et domus et cuncta circum haurirentur. Sed solatium populo exturbato ac profugo campum

the astute Orosius,[459] gave us a quite lengthy and valuable statement which covers a number of facts omitted by Tacitus. Orosius, later attributes a well edited confirmation, having evidently obtained his information [460] from Suetonius and the public records of the city undertaking department, to furnish posterity an idea of the numbers perishing in the terrible massacre.[461]

Martis ac monumenta Agrippae, hortos quin etiam suos patefecit, et subitaria aedificia extruxit quae multitudinem inopem acciperent; subvectaque utensilia ab Ostia et propinquis municipiis, pretiumque frumenti minutum usque ad ternos nummos. quae quamquam popularia in irritum cadebant, quia pervaserat rumor ipso tempore flagrantis urbis inisse eum domesticam scenam et cecinisse Troianum excidium, praesentia mala vetustis cladibus adsimulantem.
40. Sexto demum die apud imas Esquilias finis incendio factus, proruptis per immensum aedificiis, ut continuae violentiae campus et velut vacuum caelum occurreret. necdum positus metus, cum rediit haud levius rursum grassatus ignis, patulis magis urbis locis; eoque strages hominum minor, delubra deum et porticus amoenitati dicatae latius procidere. plusque infamiae id incendium habuit, quia praediis Tigellini Aemilianis proruperat; videbaturque Nero condendae urbis novae et cognomento suo appellandae gloriam quaerere. quippe in regiones quattuordecim Roma dividitur, quarum quattuor integrae manebant. tres solo tenus dejectae: septum reliquis pauca tectorum vestigia supererant, lacera et semusta.
[459] Orosius, *Adversus Paganos*, VII., 7: "Luxuriae vero tam effrenatae fuit, ut retibus aureis piscaretur, quae purpureis funibus extrahebantur. frigidis et calidis lavaret unguentis. Qui etiam nunquam minus mille carrucis confecisse iter traditur. Denique Urbis Romae incendium voluptatis suae spectaculum fecit. Per sex enim dies septemque noctes ardens civitas regios pavit adspectus. Horrea quadro structa lapide, magnaeque illae veterum insulae, quas discurrens adire flamma non poterat. magnis machinis, quondam ad externa bella praeparatis, labefactatae atque inflammatae sunt; ad monumentorum bustorumque diversoria infelici plebe compulsa. Quod ipse ex altissima illa Maecenatiana turre prospectans, laetusque flammae (ut ajebat) pulchritudine, tragico habitu Iliadem decantabat. Avaritiae autem tam praeruptae exstitit, ut post hoc incendium Urbis, quam se Augustus ex lateritia marmoream reddidisse jactaverat, neminem ad reliquias rerum suarum adire permiserit, cuncta, quae flammae quoquo modo superfuerant, ipse abstulit. Centies centena millia sestertium annua ad expensas a senatu sibi conferri imperavit.
[460] Oros., *Adv. Pag.*, VII., 7, 473, after telling of Peter's crucifixion and Paul's decapitation subjoins statistics of the enregistered numbers who perished, taken the following year: "........tanta Urbi pestilentia incubuit, ut triginta millia funerum in rationem Libitinae venirent." Of course, this does not include thousands of christians taken down in the secret crypts of under-ground Rome by the hiding brotherhoods. The 30.000 corpses he mentions were regularly registered in the records of undertaking establishments.
[461] Dion. Cassius, *Nero.*, LXII., 16-18: "Μετὰ δὲ ταῦτα ἐπεθύμησεν (ὅπερ που ἀεὶ ηὔχετο) τὴν τε πόλιν ὅλην καὶ τὴν βασιλείαν ζῶν ἀναλῶσαι. τὸν γοῦν Πρίαμον καὶ αὐτὸς θαυμαστῶς ἐμακάρισεν, ὅτι καὶ τὴν πατρίδα ἅμα καὶ τὴν ἀρχὴν ἀπολομένας εἶδεν. Λάθρα γὰρ τινας, ὡς καὶ μεθύοντας, ἢ καὶ κακουργοῦντάς τι ἄλλως, διαπέμπων, τὸ μὲν πρῶτον, ἕν που καὶ δύο καὶ πλείονα, ἀλλὰ ἀλλοθι ὑπεμπίμπρα, ὥστε τοὺς ἀνθρώπους ἐν παντὶ ἀπορίας γενέσθαι, μήτ' ἀρχὴν τοῦ κακοῦ ἐξευρεῖν, μήτε τέλος ἐπαγαγεῖν δυναμένους, ἀλλὰ πολλὰ μὲν ὁρῶντας, πολλὰ δὲ ἀκούοντας ἄτοπα. οὔτε γὰρ θεάσασθαι ἄλλο τι ἦν ἢ πυρὰ πολλὰ, ὥσπερ ἐν στρατοπέδῳ· οὔτε ἀκοῦσαι λεγόντων τινῶν, ἢ ὅτι "τὸ καὶ τὸ καίεται· ποῦ; πῶς; ὑπὸ τίνος; βοηθεῖτε." θόρυβός τε οὖν ἐξαίσιος πανταχοῦ πάντας κατελάμβανε, καὶ διέτρεχον, οἱ μὲν, τῇ, οἱ δὲ, τῇ, ὥσπερ ἔμπληκτοι. καὶ ἄλλοις τινὲς ἐπαμύνοντες, ἐπυνθάνοντο τὰ οἴκοι καιόμενα. καὶ ἕτεροι πρὶν καὶ ἀκοῦσαι ὅτι τῶν σφετέρων τὶ ἐμπέπρησται, ἐμάνθανον ὅτι ἀπόλωλεν. Οἵ τε ἐκ τῶν οἰκιῶν ἐς τοὺς στενωποὺς ἐξέτρεχον, ὡς καὶ ἔξωθεν αὐταῖς βοηθήσοντες, καὶ οἱ ἐκ τῶν ὁδῶν εἴσω ἐσέθεον, ὡς καὶ ἔνδον τι ἀνύσοντες. Καὶ ἦν ἡ τε κραυγὴ καὶ ὀλολυγὴ παίδων ὁμοῦ, γυναικῶν, ἀνδρῶν, γερόντων, ἄπλετος,

THE INFAMOUS TIGELLINUS. 553

Having, with the underdealing agency of his detective Tigillinus, whom he held as a protégé of the domus Augustalis, and who had such aptness both for cunning and ability to subserve his purposes that Nero submitted to him the burning of Rome, the plan went forward. The Roman city, frightened by the growth of a new sect, and warned by a partial eruption of Vesuvius, was in a state of superstitious trepidation. On such occasions, under the pagan theogony, mankind, whether at Rome or Athens, rushed promiscuously into a credulous tremor, ready to ascribe such things to the wrath of Jove. The great boa, mentioned by Pliny, which measured seventy-five feet in length ventured from the neighboring jungles, crawled into the city and climbing the Vatican Hill, struck out right and left at man, woman and child. After much labor of all the hunters, and great

ὥστε μήτε συνιδεῖν μήτε συνεῖναί τι ὑπὸ τοῦ καπνοῦ καὶ τῆς κραυγῆς δύνασθαι. καὶ διὰ ταῦθ᾽ ὁρᾶν ἦν τινας ἀφώνους ἑστῶτας, ὥσπερ ἐνεοὺς ὄντας. κἂν τούτῳ πολλοὶ μὲν καὶ τὰ σφέτερα ἐκκομιζόμενοι, πολλοὶ δὲ καὶ τὰ ἀλλότρια ἁρπάζοντες, ἀλλήλιος τε ἐνεπλάζοντο, καὶ περὶ τοῖς σκεύεσιν ἐσφάλλοντο. Καὶ οὔτε προϊέναι ποῖ, οὔθ᾽ ἑστάναι εἶχον ἀλλ᾽ ὤθουν, ὠθοῦντο· ἀνέτρεπον, ἀνετρέποντο· καὶ συχνοὶ μὲν ἀπεπνίγοντο, συχνοὶ δὲ συνετρίβοντο, ὥστε σφίσι μηδὲν ὅ, τι τῶν δυναμένων, ἀνθρώποις ἐν τῷ τοιούτῳ πάθει κακῶν συμβῆναι, μὴ συνενεχθῆναι· οὐδὲ γάρ οὔτ᾽ ἀποφυγεῖν που ῥᾳδίως ἠδύναντο· κἂν ἐκ τοῦ παρόντος τις περιεσώθη, εἰς ἕτερον ἐμπεσὼν ἐφθείρετο.

17. Καὶ ταῦτα οὐκ ἐν μιᾷ μόνον, ἀλλ᾽ ἐπὶ πλείους καὶ ἡμέρας καὶ νύκτας ὁμοίως ἐγένετο. Καὶ παλλοὶ μὲν οἶκοι ἔρημοι τοῦ βοηθήσοντος σφίσι ἀπώλοντο, πολλοὶ δὲ καὶ ὑπ᾽ αὐτῶν τῶν ἐπικουρούντων προσκατεπρήσθησαν. οἱ γὰρ στρατιῶται, οἵ τε ἄλλοι, καὶ οἱ νυκτοφύλακες, πρὸς τὰς ἁρπαγὰς ἀφορῶντες, οὐχ ὅσον οὐ κατεσβέννυσάν τινα, ἀλλὰ καὶ προσεξέκαιον. τοιούτων δὲ δὴ ἄλλων ἀλλοθι συμβαινόντων, ὑπέλαβέ ποτε τὸ πῦρ ἄνεμος, καὶ ἐπὶ τὰ λοιπὰ ὁμοῦ πάντα ἤγαγεν· ὥστε σκευῶν μὲν περὶ ἢ οἰκιῶν μηδένα μηδὲν ἔτι φροντίσαι, πάντας δὲ τοὺς λοιποὺς ἑστῶτάς που ἐν ἀσφαλεῖ τινι ὁρᾶν ὥσπερ νήσους τινὰς καὶ πολεῖς ἅμα πολλὰς φλεγομένας· καὶ ἐπὶ μὲν τοῖς σφετέροις μηδὲν ἔτι λυπεῖσθαι, τὸ δὲ δημόσιον ὀδυρομένους, ἀναμιμνήσκεσθαι ὅτι καὶ πρότερόν ποτε οὕτως ὑπὸ τῶν Γαλατῶν τὸ πλεῖον τῆς πόλεως διεφθάρη.

18. Πάντων δὲ δὴ τῶν ἄλλων οὕτω διακειμένων, καὶ πολλῶν καὶ ἐς αὐτὸ τὸ πῦρ ὑπὸ τοῦ πάθους ἐμπηδώντων, ὁ Νέρων ἔς τε τὸ ἄκρον τοῦ παλατίου (ὅθεν μάλιστα σύνοπτα τὰ πολλὰ τῶν καιομένων ἦν) ἀνῆλθε, καὶ τὴν σκευὴν τὴν κιθαρῳδικὴν λαβών, ᾖσεν ἅλωσιν, ὡς μὲν αὐτὸς ἔλεγεν, Ἰλίου ὡς δὲ ἑωρᾶτο, Ῥώμης. Τοιούτῳ μὲν δὴ πάθει τότε ἡ πόλις ἐχρήσατο, οἵῳ οὔτε πρότερόν ποτε, οὔθ᾽ ὕστερον, πλὴν τοῦ Γαλατικοῦ. Τό, τε γὰρ Παλατῖνον ὄρος σύμπαν, καὶ τὸ θέατρον τοῦ Ταύρου, τῆς τε λοιπῆς πόλεως τὰ δύο που μέρη ἐκαύθη· καὶ ἀνθρώποι ἀναρίθμητοι διεφθάρησαν. ὁ μέντοι δῆμος οὐκ ἔστιν ὅτε οὐ κατὰ τοῦ Νέρωνος ἤρατο, τὸ μὲν ὄνομα αὐτοῦ μὴ ὑπολέγων, ἄλλως δὲ δὴ τοῖς τὴν πόλιν ἐμπρήσασι καταρώμενοι, καὶ μάλισθ᾽ ὅτι αὐτοὺς ἡ μνήμη τοῦ λογίου τοῦ κατὰ τὸν Τιβέριόν ποτε ἀσθέντος ἐθορύβει. ἦν δὲ τοῦτο.

Τρὶς δὲ τριηκοσίων περιτελλομένων ἐνιαυτῶν,
Ῥωμαίους ἔμφυλος ὀλεῖ στάσις.

Ἐπειδὴ τε ὁ Νέρων, παραμυθούμενος αὐτούς, οὐ δαμοῦ ταῦτα τὰ ἔπη εὕρασθαι ἔλεγε, μεταβαλόντες ἕτερον λόγιον, ὡς καὶ Σιβύλλειον ὄντως ὄν, ᾖδον. ἔστι δὲ τοῦτο.

Ἔσχατος Αἰναδῶν μητροκτόνος ἡγεμονεύσει.

Καὶ ἔσχεν οὕτως, εἴτε καὶ ὡς ἀληθῶς θεομαντείᾳ τινὶ πολεχθέν, εἴτε καὶ τότε ὑπὸ τοῦ ὁμίλου πρὸς τὰ παρόντα θειασθέν. τελευταῖος γὰρ τῶν Ἰουλίων τῶν ἀπὸ Αἰνείου γενομένων ἐμονάρχησε. Χρήματα δὲ ὁ Νέρων παμπληθῆ καὶ παρὰ τῶν ἰδιωτῶν καὶ παρὰ τῶν δήμων, τὰ μὲν βίᾳ ἐπὶ τῇ προφάσει τοῦ ἐμπρησμοῦ, τὰ δὲ παρ᾽ ἑκόντων δῆθεν ἠργυρολόγησε, καὶ τῶν Ῥωμαίων αὐτῶν τὸ σιτηρέσιον παρεσπάσατο.

struggles, there being then no firearms, the monster was killed and when cut open, the dead bodies of children it had swallowed were found. This cast abroad a lugubrious shudder and whetted the belief that the Almighty had sent him to foreknell some wonderful event. The time of this serpent story on close inspection seems to correspond. Tacitus relates, of the same time, that a fearful collapse and conflagration occured at Placentia, a neighboring town, of an enormous amphitheatre, and that in its flames fifty-seven thousand persons [462] were crushed and burned; and the report on reaching the capital terrified the inhabitants and frenzied them with a desire to appease the gods supposed to be raging with wrath in the dome-vaults of heaven, even if it cost the lives of the detested rabble infesting the Aventine, Esquiline and Vatican hollows and hills. This was the more aggravating when it was found that the Aventine had been invaded by the christians, and that the goddess Diana, with her famous temple, protecting great numbers of trade unions,[463] had flagitiously turned against all mankind by endowing the lowly-born with property and souls, thus giving her temple on the Aventine up to desecration. In spite of the mighty men of blood and property and souls she had wilfully pronounced for the detested workingmen!

The idea once worked up in the imaginative mind of Nero, he wreaked dire vengeance. Says Tacitus, "he inflicted the most exquisite tortures. While the fires were raging he published to the Roman world that it was the work of the horrible 'burners,' the christians, who had invaded Rome, seized the sanctuaries of the gods and in the atrocious frenzy of their enthusiasm and infatuation had wheedlingly persuaded Minerva and Diana to accept them as men born with souls! All these under the vulgar appellation of christians, he says, Nero

---

[462] Tac., *Hist.*, II., 21. The work of building the amphitheatre had been let out on contract and as in most cases of contract work the jobbers thought of nothing but profit, they neglected to give it the necessary strength and it fell with the great weight of so vast a multitude, crashing down with tremendous force to the bottom. Before the people could escape the structure took fire and burned to death those who were not crushed in the ruins.

[463] Momms., *De Coll. et Sodal. Rom.*, p. 113: "Notabiles sunt natales Dianæ, Antinoi, collegii in hac tabula et in ordine cenarum nominati. Natalis collegii memoratur quoque in lege coll. Æsculapii." The college at Lanuvium was also one of Diana, and we have inscriptions of nearly one hundred others; see *index* in verb. *Hunters, Kunegoi, Venatores, Fishermen*.

THE BOOK OF DAMNATION. 555

"branded with most deserved infamy. They derived their name and origin from Christ, who, in the reign of Tiberius, had suffered death by the sentence of Pontius Pilate." Referring to the presumed persecution by Caligula, as we have already explained, and to the well verified actions of Claudius amounting to a great persecution against them, we have sufficient evidence to see that Nero knew their history when he marked them on his book of damnation. But, continues Tacitus, who recognized that the work of the christians was not checked by Caligula and Claudius; "it again burst forth and not only spread over Judæa, the first seat of this mischievous sect, but was even introduced into Rome, the common asylum which receives and protects whatever is impure, and outrageous."[463] Whiston in substance, renders: "broke out in the city of Rome whither there run from every quarter, noisily, all flagrant and shameful enormities. At first, then, those who confessed were seized, after a vast multitude had been detected through their testimony, and were convicted; not so much as really guilty of setting the city on fire, but as hating all mankind; nay, they made a mock of them as they perished, and destroyed them by putting them into the skins of wild beasts and setting dogs on them to tear them to pieces; some were nailed to the cross and others burned to death. They were also used in the night time instead of torches for illumination. Nero had offered his own garden for this spectacle. He also gave them over to the wild circensian games, and dressed himself like a driver of a chariot (quadrigarius) sometimes appearing among the common people, sometimes in the circle itself; whence a commiseration arose, though the punishments were lauded at the guilty persons, and such as deserved to be made the most flagrant examples, as if these people were destroyed, not for the public advantage, but to satisfy the barbarous humor of one man."

From the descriptions which we quote both in the translation and original, from four celebrated and reli-

[464] Gibbon, *Dec. & Fall*, ch. xvi., over note 28. Gibbon's *trans.*, has undergone the criticism of eminent men, some of whom were critically adverse to him; and has been pronounced faultless. We therefore follow it in our paraphrase, expanding only on our own account to heighten but not to impair the information for our special argument. The exact translation is given in our *analysis*, and the Latin original, we here give in note 467.

able ancient authors, Tacitus, Suetonius, Dion Cassius and Orosius, we may profitably compile a modernized statement of one of the most disgraceful, bloody and destructive atrocities in the annals of events. Such a statement would run like this:

Rome, to begin with, was full of trade and labor unions struggling for bread under the old Solonic jus coeundi, its primitive rights shorn by the conspiracy laws which followed Appius Claudius and the Roman conquests. These unions are disappointed by failure of the old divinities to work out a realization of their promise to emancipate and save; Advent of a new Messiah of their own flesh, blood and craftsmanship; early ingrafting of his Word of promise and plan of salvation into these unions through evangelists who were in Rome in less than a year from the crucifixion;[465] the guild of St. Matthew is there at work around the great friendly temple of Diana on the Aventine, and in the booths of the circus maximus, with Joseph of Arimathea at their head and Pudens, Blastus and Crescens, and a host of the seventy, working by consent of these trammeled divinities, Dionysus, Diana, and Bacchus,[466] who were never allowed by the human property-power to do as they agreed; a friend in Tiberius who is assassinated; an enemy in Caligula who ogles at an impending horror; an enemy in Claudius who drives the Jew christions into exile; a hideous burlesque of human nature in the maniac Nero, who in a qualm of jealousy hires

[465] At Rome was found a tablet (see Gruter. 946, 6,) believed to be that of Joseph of Arimathea, entered in the *Orellian Collection*, as no. 4424. An empty tomb "in quam nemo antea fuerat illatus, ut Josephi Arimathaei." It is of a union of the bridge builders, Collegium pontificum. It was a mausoleum-like building, with a schóla, and vault for burial. Usual fines are stated, under the lex coll. tenuiorum, or funeraticium, for any person using the temple as a salesroom. Fabr., p. 53, It is of the date of the virgin, and hints that Joseph of Arimathea went to Rome and planted in a bridge-builders' union. It is in the columbarium. It is after this that Joseph must have gone to England. There is an inscr. at Jerusalem showing that he might have later returned to his native country and died there. In this case, like Stephen and several others the remains were in after years taken back to Rome, Oehler is in doubt: "Cf. Inscrift worauf er (Joseph) in der Kirche des heiligen Grabes in Jerusalem begraben ist." The absence of Joseph's ashes mentioned in the above passage: "In quam nemo antea fuerat illatus" ut Josephi Arimathæi may be accounted for by the failure of an effort to find the tomb at Jerusalem which has more recently come to light.

[466] Bacchus and Dionysus are one. Renan. *Apôtres.* p. 250: "Quelques-uns de ces thiases" (meaning the trade unions worshipping Bacchus or Dionysus) "surtout ceux de Bacchus, avaient des doctrines relevées, et cherchaient a donner aux hommes de bonne volonté quelque consolation. Si il restait encore dans le monde Grec un peu d' amour, de piété, de morale relgieuse, c' était grace à la liberte, de pareils cultes privés." This agrees with Böckh's good opinion of Bacchus.

Tigillinus, to carry out his plans for burning Rome. Such is the truthful synopsis of the greatest historical event of christianity, if we except the crucifixion.

Following the unmistakable statement of Tacitus we are able to particularize somewhat upon the details of this tragedy. The first punishment mentioned is that of the cross. As the flames were raging for seven days it is supposable that those of the multitude who could not escape, who failed to descend into the depths of under-ground Rome and like the badger hide in the tangling sinuosities of subterranean trails, were first caught; and we know how they perished. It was by the old crucifix. A law existed at Rome making this horrible supplicium the only death allowable for the ancient lowly. A citizen of Rome could not be crucified. A working man, on the contrary, could not be executed in any other way. Thus Tacitus in saying that they suffered on the cross admits that they were the lowly workers. But they perished on the cross in multitudes. Furthermore, in the seven days in which this conflagration raged it is more than supposable that great numbers, nailed to the cross and hung betwixt heaven and earth, were left these seven days to suffer indescribable agonies unattended, unpitied, in summer's sun, amid the blaze and smoke and desolation. till death brought them their welcome anæsthetic. But the shrieks of crucifixion did not bring Nero sufficient satisfaction. Tigellinus, cunning in invention, thought of the skin-bag torture. Thousands were wrapped naked, in the skins of wild beasts that had been slain in the combats of the amphitheatre. Prowling, famished dogs that always ranged as friendless tramps of cities, were corralled into the Neronian garden, and these sad, skin-wrapped christians, floundering in resemblance of savage beasts that once wore their shaggy pelts, presented a toothsome morsel for the quadrupeds and as they attacked the weaponless workers, tearing flesh and causing wails and groans, the heartless populace and parasitical co-adjutors yelled with jeers and derision. The third and last contingent of the "ingens multitudo," mentioned by Tacitus, suffered a still more terrible death. Rome was lighted at night, if at all, only with oil lamps whose stingy glare shed but a faint flicker compared with our electric street illuminations.

Sometimes, at the triumphal entry of a powerful military conqueror these meager lamps gave place to torchlights of oil and pine knots, which glared upon the dingy bricks and mortar their hideous power. Nero and his henchmen bethought themselves of a species of triumphal display probably to wind up the spectacle.

We are not told the number that suffered in this last and third method of torture; but considering that it was the prime cause of the monarch's joy, that he dressed himself in the regalia of a chorister, centered the death march into the gardens and the esplanade of the circus maximus, called a city full of spectators to view it, seemingly for amusement at beholding the ghastly consequence and capped the climax with its lugubrious enchantment of torch-lights and shrieks of agony, we must conclude on measuring the possibilities with the man's gift in deeds of atrocity, that it again mounted to the number of many thousands; for both Tacitus and Orosius say that thirty thousand corpses were registered at the morgue.

What, then, was this crowning supplicium? The murder of thousands more! On this the testimony is complete. They were seized by the police of Nero and under explicit orders, men, women and children were wrapped in bags which had first been saturated with grease and an asphaltic turpentine which exudes from the Appenine pines. These high combustibles were mixed with the greasy products of the pork business, in great quantities, and once all melted together, the liquid was poured hot, an inch thick on the bags which were made to enshroud the naked forms. When all was ready and night had come, a thousand palanquins were ordered and each was loaded with the melancholy bundle of inflamable asphalt and grease, with several victims, fat and lean to fill each one. These were then mounted on the palanquins, eight of Nero's stout carriers at the handles, and all were ignited in flames. Nature knows no favoritism and will not interfere against the most horrible events. The wretches thus shrouded in bags of grease, inflamable turpentines, asphalts and fats, were fired! Crack, burst out the conflagration afresh; this time no longer the tumbling buildings and booths. Those were all consumed. It was the human torch, darting crackling tongues of flame; a lurid glare to illumine the Neronian procession. And the monster sat in his chariot, gloating in realized vengeance at the agony of christians who had dared to circumvent the long-time glory of derelict ancient gods!

The historic torchlight pageant now began. With thousands of christians tied in bags of grease and petroleum, blazing with the flames of hell, the procession of palanquins marched, in a ghostly hour at the close of the seven-nights' conflagration, down the Via Appia through the Forum Boarium, into the gardens of Nero at the foot of the Quirinal Hill. Thundering bursts of joy from small boys of the families of Roman gentlemen and howls from the throats of a million haters of the new philosophy of the Word; female turbulence betwixt sympathy and repudiation of the half-converted; prowling dogs, wild with famine in the city of monopolized plenty; raging tramps, self-emancipated from the slavery of conquest—in all a ghastly cortège thronged into the gardens of Nero, some to worship the emperor of cruelties, some to shout acquiescence to the torch-lit scene some to thunder in the general roar of acclaim, and yell in horrid mockery of the writhing fuel which helped the petroleum and the fish-oil to scare away the night with their reflecting gleam from the walls of the dark, gloomy city. Unnumbered, quivering bodies of burning, shrieking, human torches, yielded as they proceeded on the course, their dismal moans, adding to the general melancholy of the historic occasion.

There is no history that relates farther the results of this holocaust. When the agony was over, in the desolate subterranean cubicules, the mournful requiem and the Te Deum were chanted and trembling survivors gathered, as best they could the charred bones and melted crosses from the public morgue, and in secret crypts and niches of their columbarii deposited them with their ashes, daring even to inscribe on the footstone of each olla and cinerary urn the correct legend of their personality and their death; and thus it is that we at last have their history. The life labors of Bossius, Gorius, Muratorius, Marini, De Rossi, and the later scholars of the academies are disclosing the truth of these statements. Tacitus talks coldly of these martyrs.[467]

[467] Tacitus, *Annales*, XV., 44: "Sed non ope humana, non largitionibus principis aut deum placamentis decedebat infamia, quin iussum incendium crederetur. ergo abolendo rumori Nero subdidit reos, et quaesitissimis pœnis affecit, quos per flagitia invisos vulgus Christianos appellabat. auctor nominis eius Christus Tiberio imperitante per p͞ r͞uratorem Pontium Pila-

What in that vortex of angry revolutions and demolitions, became of Peter and Paul? Knowing that at the time of the great conflagration they were in Rome, what became of them? They suffered with the rest; but as they were the great and recognized exponents of the new faith and Word, the manner of their destruction is especially interesting. We have some points.[468] Terrible as was their tribulation, they were inspired with a belief in the immediate realization of an angelic republic.[469] They were, in our opinion, after carefully scrutinizing the evidence, both members of the prevailing Solonic organizations springing from the jus coeundi, multitudes of which were being converted to christianity, and as converts, shielded under the veil of their secrecy. Until now the Cæsars had been kind and with the exception of Caligula and Claudius' momentary fits of jealousy, they had been protected. As the great labor organization of antiquity they had built Rome and were proud of it. We know positively that both Peter and Paul belonged to them. This knowledge is by induction, but probing denials only reveal new points of its certainty. Paul and perhaps Peter had become personally acquainted with the celebrated Seneca, who at that moment was serving at the court of Nero. Many letters between Paul and this good optimate were inter-

tum supplicio affectus erat; repressaque in praesens exitiabilis superstitio rursum erumpebat, non modo per Iudaeam, originem eius mali, sed per urbem etiam, quo cuncta undique atrocia aut pudenda confluunt celebranturque. Igitur primum correpti qui fatebantur, deinde indicio eorum multitudo ingens, haud perinde in crimine incendii quam odio humani generis convicti sunt. Et pereuntibus addita ludibria, ut ferarum tergis contecti laniatu canum interirent, aut crucibus affixi, aut flammandi, atque ubi defecisset dies, in usum nocturni luminis urerentur. Hortus suos ei spectaculo Nero obtulerat, et circense ludicrum edebat, habitu aurigae permixtus plebi vel curriculo insistens. Unde quamquam adversus sontes et novissima exempla meritos miseratio oriebatur, tamquam non utititate publica, sed in saevitiam unius absumerentur.

[468] Clement of Rome, *Epist. to James.* c. 8: "Peter, just before martyrdom, and about to die, gave instructions to presbyters 'Love all your brethren with grave and compassionate eyes; be to orphans the same as parents; to widows be humane like husbands; affording to them their means of existence in all kindness, arranging marriages for those in their prime and for those without a trade assist with the necessary support through such work as they can do; and for the tradesman find employment'" In cap. 9, Peter continues, by exhorting them to brotherly love, and the mutual partaking of food at the common table, so that they may "be each others' guests." This is in accord with Canon 25, *Ap. Const:* "Ex hic qui caelibes in cenum pervenerunt jubemus, ut lectores, tantum et cantores, si velint, nuptiis contrahant."

[469] Chrysost, IX., p. 66, showing the happiness of the pentecostal and early christians: "Christiani prisci angelica Republica erant." He seems to mean that they formed a politico-economic state for earthly as well as post-mortem existence, which, on account of its perfect communism he calls the Angel republic.

changed and we are so fortunate as to have them all.
But Paul being a Roman citizen was accorded citizenship and honored with what was denied to Peter who was at best, in the opinion of those aristocrats, nothing but a workingman. As such he was their organizer unto the new life.

That Peter was hanged upon the cross of his beloved master is history;[470] yet the evidence is mostly confined to the mention found in the scriptural writings and the historians of the early church. Tertullian is authority for the proof that Peter was one of the victims of Nero's rage, at the burning of Rome.[471] Peter was a married man. We have some account though meagre, of his wife; and it may add to the interest and value of our narrative, as they both met martyrdom, to carry their annals along together. Neander turned his scrutinizing search to getting all the testimony extant and found that both Peter and his wife suffered martyrdom at Rome during the Neronian persecutions.[472] Tacitus,[473] Suetonius, Dion Cassius and Orosius have given us a solid general basis to work on which makes the filling-in contributions of Clement, Tertullian, Chrysostom and the archæological discoveries of recent days more interesting. There is one thing very instructive connected with their deaths. They were cremated, not buried in the flesh,[474] like Paul; and their death was by crucifixion; whereas Paul was honored with a noble execution, and the same is said of Justin Martyr.

This is because Peter, like Jesus himself, was a workingman. So great was his power as the successor of

---

[470] Smith, *Dict. Bib.*, p. 2454: "The fact, however, of St. Peter's martyrdom at Rome rests upon very different grounds. The evidence for it is complete, while there is a total absence of any contrary statement in the writings of the early Fathers. We have, in the first place, the certainty of his martyrdom, in our Lord's prediction: John xxi., 18, 19: 'Ἀμὴν, ἀμὴν λέγω σοι, ὅτε ἦς νεώτερος ἐζώννυες σεαυτὸν καὶ περιεπάτεις, ὅπου ἤθελες· ὅταν δὲ γηράσῃς ἐκτενεῖς τὰς χεῖράς σου καὶ ἄλλος σε ζώσει καὶ οἴσει, ὅπου οὐ θέλεις. Τοῦτο δὲ εἶπε σημαίνων, ποίῳ θανάτῳ δοξάσει τὸν θεόν.

[471] Tert., *De Scorpiaco*, cap. 12: "At Rome Nero was the first who stained with blood the rising faith. Then is Peter girt by another, when made fast to the cross. John, xxi., 18, 19, which 18th verse foretells to Peter by Christ himself, the manner of his death."

[472] *Planting*, Book IV., chap. i.

[473] On this celebrated page of history, Renan, *Hibbert Lectures*, p. 70, of trans., says: "The authenticity of this passage cannot be disputed."

[474] The demand for cremation at Rome was a law of the Twelve Tables. For Cicero's mention of it, see Vol. I., p. 75, note 19, and he says noblemen only could be buried; Gorius, *Mon., Sive. Columb.*, p. 2: "Quum Lege XII Tabularum defunctorum corpora in Urbe urere, aut sepelire vetitum esset; de quo More Kirchmannus, *De Funere, Rom.*, Lib., II., cap. 22."

Jesus, recognized agent or head evangelist, the "rock' of the whole movement that christians of the early apostolic age were extremely proud of the fact that he was the fisherman, as Jesus had been the carpenter. Peter was the great apostle of economies. We know from Clement, his friend, that the common table with him and his brotherhoods was considered of the utmost importance.

This common table was not only an economic resource for a brother and sisterhood composed of poor people who lived by their toil, but it being the climax of the last supper of their beloved master, was a veritable "cœna sacra," on all devotional occasions. Socrates the great martyr and pre-christian-christian hallowed the cœna sacra in the symposiums of many a thiasos.[475] It seems not a little strange that Rome, a vast city, at that time estimated to have contained two million inhabitants[476] should have been so sensibly influenced by these organizations.

But, the real fact is, that the conquests, by which it had been hoped the unions, members and all, should be exterminated, actually concentrated still more; coming as they did from organized regions, dragged ruthlessly thither as prisoners of war. Before those wars Greek was little spoken at Rome. Only the polite and wealthy knew it and that mainly as an accomplishment. At the time we are describing Greek was the common vernacular; and what made it humiliating to the rich and great was that it was used by slaves and freedmen, already accustomed to a first-class unionism in far off Greek-speaking lands, huddling together their old loves and rebuilding their old organizations to Nero's horror and disgust.

Peter, though not, like Paul, a prisoner, was a Greek-speaking unionist. The old unions of the Greek-speaking East had for centuries the *anagenesis* or new birth— a striking instance of the manner in which old tenets clung to the christian plant. Many societies having the new birth, whatever it was, introduced the name of

---

[475] *Plato, Pol.*, 1; Xenoph., *Convers.*, 8; where Socrates describing love and mutual fellowship is heard to say: "Πάντες ἐσμέν τοῦ θεοῦ τούτου διασώται."

[476] Consult Chamb. *Encyc.*, art. *Rome*. This is the number estimated for the time of Vespasian.

OLD OSTIAN WAY STUDDED WITH UNIONS. 563

the new anagenesis into old Solonic unions.[477] Spain had the kuriakos, or if transplanted and set up in Rome, the name is found changed to Cyriacus. Peter and his wife lived in one of these at Rome, in the Via Ostiensis.[478] The most credible evidence we have regarding Peter's wife shows her to have been a deaconess of this miniature union, in the old road or street leading down the Tiber to Ostia the port of Rome. This great road teemed with trade organizations.[479] Hundreds of inscriptions showing this are discovered. The cemetery of Peter is on this road. The vast trade union system along the Ostian Way just about this time was one of the wonderful points of neglected history. That Peter and his family were prominent in one of these large unions there can never exist a doubt. Until persecution struck them they could live, preach and prosper; for under the veil there was no poverty and all were equal.[480] Of course, then, this peculiar family would become the butt of Nero's special wrath. They had introduced a new divinity; they preached and worked and organized, in Greek and Hebrew tongues; they were too prominent to escape the spies of the Roman guard. Indeed they may have been doomed like Seneca before the incendiary struck the flints which fired the city.[481]

Unable to find a detailed history of the martyrdom of this pair we can only clutch, in passing, the scintillæ which occasionally fly from the pen of cursory writers. One of these informs us that Peter's wife suffered first. Clement of Alexandria enriches these desultory mentions

[477] Oehler. *MSS.*, says: "Ὀργεῶνες. Athen., Peiraeus, CIA. II., 610; ein νόμος der ὀργεώνων zu Ehren der Bendis, IV Jahrh. vor Chr.—Die Thraker besonders concessionirt als ὀργεῶνες der Bendis in Peiraeus: Inschrift des IV oder III Jahrh. vor Chr., ungenau publicirt. Ἀναγένησις, 1896. For more of these, see *Index*, catchword, *Anagenesis*. There were many of these orgeons whose members believed in and subscribed to the new Birth, ἀναγένησις, which is still a tenet in the Petrine part of the church.
[478] De Rossi, *Roma Sott.*, I , p. 583: "Κυριακὸς Πέτρου or Cyriacus Petri Cœmeterium S. Cyriaci via Ostiensis—Petrus Mallius addit ubi est ecclesia S. Cyriaci." Peter was a lord as we have explained; and so he was κυριος over this "House of the Lord."
[479] See Vol. I., pp. 382-4 and 440-2.
[480] Lactantius, *Div. Inst.*, V., 14, 15: " Nemo Deo pauper est, nisi qui justitia indiget.........nemo Clarissimus nisi qui opera miseracordiæ largitur fecerit........apud nos inter pauperes et divltes, servos et dominos interest nihil ; nec alia causa est cur nobis invicem fratrum nomen imperitamus, nisi qui pares esse nos credimus."
[481] Seneca, *Epist. to Paul*, just after the conflagration: "The christians and Jews are indeed commonly punished for the burning of the city; but that impious miscreant who delights in murders and butcheries, and disguises his villainies with lies, is appointed to, or reserved for his proper time.

in his Hortatory dissertation.[482] The fine details of these sufferings are covered in darkness, but the main facts have in a wonderful manner come down. We may with precision assume that Peter was married to a kind, sympathetic woman and mother and that she was high in office, performing the practical duties of a motherly manager, and that while her husband was disseminating the Word she was waiting on the common table and making happy the hungry who flocked in those times of danger, to her motherly retreat and were fed and comforted; for such was the early christianity.

The drama here closes to again open upon a death scene. We now hear of Peter's wife that she fell a victim to the merciless rage of Nero. She was led to execution. Her husband was also under arrest. Peter saw her on the march toward the Roman Golgotha, and in his agony cried out to the dying woman words of cheer.[483] There were probably also many other women dragged to execution with her and dying on the same gibbet.

And now for Peter himself. In the light of a christian father he was, in the opinion of Nero and his creatures a ringleader; pronounced worthy of death he was led up to the cross. It is well known that this apostle had on the eve of similar suffering denied his master, which seems to have affixed itself upon his mind. He thought it worthy of himself to die on the cross, but when the hour came he doubtless thought that he was unworthy of following him on equal footing, and chose to be executed head downward.

As already observed, the poor and those among the ancient lowly who were obliged to earn their living as they went, were not buried within the city of Rome. Their bodies were usually burned. The burnt cinders of millions of the more wretched were cast out to mix with the dusts of dirty streets. But those belonging to a union with the burial attachment were always pro-

---

[482] *Strom.*, VII., Vol. III., p. 253, ed. Klotz, Leipz., 1832; "Φασί γ' οὖν τὸν μακάρεον θεάσαμενον τὴν αὐτοῦ γυναῖκα ἀγομένην τὴν ἐπὶ θάνατον, ἡσθῆναι μὲν τῆς κλήσεως χάριν καὶ τῆς εἰς οἶκον ἀνακομιδῆς ἐπιφωνῆσαι δὴ εὖ μάλα προστεπτικῶς τε καὶ παρακλητικῶς ἐξ ὀνόματος προσειπόντα. μεμνήθω αὐτὴ τοῦ κυρίου."

[483] Clem Alex., *Strom.*, VII. Neander, *Plant.*, Book V., chap. i., calls to mind the words of Clement who hands us down the tradition that when Peter saw her being led to martyrdom, he cried out: "O remember the Lord."

vided with an olla or *cinerarium* and niche or miniature vault for its reception.[484] This accounts for the construction of the columbaria,[485] the first of which was discovered in 1827, near the Appian Way, and is in a good state of preservation and of prodigious size. The unearthing of the great columbarium so excited the attention of the epigraphical schools that money was appropriated for continuing the research, and Bossius and De Rossi, with Gorius before them, devoted their lives to a strictly scientific investigation with the result that a mass of evidence is exhumed proving the truth of the New Testament writings and also of many hitherto doubtful statements contained in the apochryphal contributions and hitherto unfathomable allusions of the profane writers in poetry and prose.[486] De Rossi declares that the epigraphs and monuments are traced with precision to as early an age as the Flavii, who began their power and influence as emperors and high military leaders in the year 69, while the apostles were yet living. In fact this date fixes the chiselings discovered in the under-ground cemeteries in the days of Claudius and Nero.

After tracing Peter, the beloved and trusted companion of Jesus, to the cross which stretched out his arms as truthfully predicted by his messianic master, and amid his dying wails and those of his dear and innocent wife, we turn from the mournful scene to Paul. What became of him? Here again we are cowled in the precarious scraps and darklings of an aggravating incompleteness. Some say he went to Spain, planting there

---

[484] Chrysost., III., p. 109: " Petrus qui Christum negaverat, post ressurrectionem pro illo mortuus est, cruce capite in terram verso affixus." Again in Vol. VIII., p. 494: "Petro inverso capite crucifixus." Benedictine, *Trans.* Again, Orosius, VII., 7: "Nam primus Romæ Christianos suppliciis et mortibus adfecit, ac per omnes provincias pari persecutione excruciari imperavit: ipsumque nomen extipare conatus beatissimos Christi Apostolos Petrum cruce Paulum gladio occidit.

[485] For an account of the columbaria, see *Index*, in verb. *Columbarium*, pointing to pages containing our elaborate information, with illustrations.

[486] De Rossi, *Roma Sott.*, Tome I., p. 186, thinks there can no longer exist any doubt as to the accuracy of the information derived from these finds: "L' esame dei tituli istorichi citata dal Bossio in favore de documenti ignoti al Bossio illustrianti l' esistenza e la storia di questi cemeteri medesimi dovranno a poco a poco essere accuratamente compiuti ai debiti luoghi lungo tutta l'opera della Roma sotterranea. Appunto nei cemeteri. cui la storia o la traditione assegna l' origine apostolica al lume della più essata critica archæologica io veggio, per così dire, gli incunabuli e dei cristiani ipogei, e dell' arte cristiana e della christiana epigrafia; ivi io trovo memorie de persone, che sembrano de tempi de Flavii a de Trajano e per fino dato precise di quegli anni."

the Word, and it is strongly hinted that Nero who seems at first to have fancied him and excused him from trial, actually accompanied him. But if so, he returned before the conflagration. Again, it is told to us by later writers that he was also in Britain and built up the church,[487] perhaps with Joseph of Arimathea, at Glastonbury.[488] Although it looks very doubtful whether the apostle could in so short a time have made his voyage with the slow modes of travel of those days, and gotten back as early as the year 64, yet he was a man of prodigious energy and unflinching determination, always full of enthusiasm and practical ideas. The episode of Joseph of Arimathea is going to bear inspection. It is about certain that whether Paul went or not, Joseph must have planted the church at Glastonbury not far from London, and that it was then that the union of carpenters was created, which Pudens planned and helped to organize by presenting them a plot of land, shown by the recent discovery of an inscription among its ruins.[489] It is recounted of many of these evangelists that they traveled great distances and organized their Word as if by magic, the result of their labors being permanent. So Crescens went northward as far as Lyons and Vienne.[490] But the fact must be known that a great number of trade unions existed at Vienne as early as Appius Claudius; and Crescens must have been

---

[487] Lingard, quoting Theodoret in the *Hist. Anglo-Saxon Church*, App. note A., p. 350, speaking of "Our fishermen, publicans, tent-makers, etc., quotes Theodoret: Περὶ νόμων, on the Attendance unto the suffering Greeks: "Ἑλλήνικων Θεριπευτικὴ Παθημάτων." Theodoret here discusses the great evangelizing work of "Our Fishermen, publicans and tent-makers, who brought the law of the Gospel to all men, and persuaded not Romans only and the subjects of Rome, but the Scythians and Sauromatæ, and the Indians and the Seres, and the Hircanians and Bactrians and the Britons, and Cimbrians and Germans and in a word every nation and race of men to adopt the laws of him who died upon the cross. The original of Theodoret runs as follows: "Οἱ δὲ ἡμέτεροι ἁλιεῖς καὶ οἱ τελῶναι καὶ οἱ σκυτοτόμοι ἅπασιν ἀνθρώποις τοὺς εὐαγγελικοὺς προσενήνοχασι νόμους· καί οὐ μόνον 'Ρωμαίους καὶ ὑπὸ τούτοις τελοῦντας, ἀλλὰ καὶ τὰ Σκυθικὰ καὶ τὰ Σαυροματικὰ ἔθνη, καὶ 'Ινδοὺς καὶ Αἰθίοπας, καὶ Πέρσας καὶ Σῆρας, καὶ Ὑρκανοὺς, Βακτριανοὺς, καὶ Βρεττανοὺς, καί Κιμβροὺς, καὶ Γερμανοὺς, καὶ ἁπαξαπλῶς παν ἔθνος καὶ γένος ἀνθρώπων δέξασθαι τοῦ σταυρωθέντος τοὺς νόμους ἀνέπεισαν."

[488] Lingard, *Hist. Antiqu., Anglo-Saxon Church*, app., note A., pp. 354-5: "There remains but one more testimony, that of Venantius Fortunatus, a poet of the sixth century, who in the following lines is supposed to state that St. Paul actually visited Britain:
"Transit et oceanum, vel qua fecit insula portum,
Quasque Britannus habit terras, quasque ultima Thule."

[489] See *Index*, in verb. *Glastonbury*, referring to where its Latin is quoted.

[490] Smith, *Bib. Dict.*, p. 506, refers to Paul's mention, *II. Tim.*, iv., 40, that he went to Dalmatia and admits that he may have been the founder of the church in Vienne.

THE WAY PAUL MET HIS DEATH.   567

assisted by their milling industries on the river Gère. They were certainly a very active and tireless force of workers.
   There is, however, but one assured point regarding Paul after about A.D. 64. He was condemned and suffered death. The manner of his execution was by decapitation.[491] The indications are that Nero, so long as he knew nothing more against him than that he was connected with the Dionysan unions, which furnished him so many entertainments, was favorable; but when, through his spies, he discovered that he was one of the great advocates of the new religion, he became very much enraged and after a mock trial ordered his execution. Being a Roman citizen, he had the honor, however, of being beheaded, rather than crucified.[492] This unbridled and frightful monster — an undoubted maniac, continued in power for five years his senseless destruction of the human race, proving the absurdity of imperial government, and was at last killed by a conspiracy of his own friends.
   There was a rumor current for nearly a half century, that Nero, who had threatened to return and finish his work of assasination, would again emerge from his assumed hiding and come back to resume sway from beyond the Euphrates.[493]

   [491] Chrysost., Vol., IX., p. 407: " Neronis jusu, Paulus capite truncatus est;" *id.*, xi., p. 186: "Nero imperatore in Paulum sæviabat." Smith, *Bib. Dict.*, in verb. *Peter:* "The time and manner of the Apostle's martyrdom are less certain. The early writers imply, or distinctly state, that he suffered at, or about the same time (with Paul), Dionys. Areop., *Opera; "κατὰ τὸν καιρόν,"* with Paul, in the Neronian persecution. All agree that he was crucified, a point sufficiently determined by our Lord's prophecy. Origen, ap. Euseb., *Hist. Eccles.*, III., 1. who could easily ascertain the fact, and ....is not inaccurate in historical matters, says that at his own request he was crucified with his head downwards. This statement was generally received by christian antiquity.
   [492] *Ante-Nicine Fathers*, VII., 494, note 7. It is one of the two Vienna *MSS.*, and reads: "Paul, the teacher of the Gentiles, having proclaimed the Gospel of Christ to the Gentiles from Jerusalem even to Illyricum, was cut off in Rome while teaching the truth, by Nero and King Agrippa, being beheaded, and has been buried in Rome itself;" Meyers, *Konversations Lexicon,* in verb. *Paulus:* "Endlich wieder in Rom verhaftet und unter Nero zugleich mit Petrus hingerichtet und zwar enthauptet worden sein. Warscheinlicher schlossen schon die zwei Jarhre der Apostelgeschichte mit Process und hinrichtung ab. Die Kirche hat ihm zugleich mit Petrus den 25 Jan. als Pauli Bekehrungstag gewidmet.
   [493] Neander, *Plant.*, Book V., and *Hist. Church*, I., p. 137, orig., telling the story written afresh by Lücke, *Einleitung* i. d., *Offenb, Johannis,* that Nero, was believed by John the Evangelist at the time he wrote the *Revelations,* not to be dead, but escaped to a retreat beyond the Euphrates to save himself from the wrath of the people. *Rev.*, xiii., 3, where Nero is meant, as one of the beasts. He is thought by many to have been the monster of the bottomless pit.

On the spot near where stood the temple of Diana and exactly the area covered by the low dens of workingmen along the Tiber, a temple has been built by the irrepressible christians far surpassing the glories of the ancient edifice, who, says Gibbon, "derive their claim of universal dominion from a humble fisherman of Galilee."

History uses its low subterfuge of tergiversation, and makes the encyclopedias to this day, like Cicero of old, fervid in calumnious defamation of Clodius. This champion of labor they accuse of invading the shrine of the Bona Dea. The least insight into facts would disabuse the encyclopedists of their error; since the Bona Dea was none other than Diana, like Clodius protector of the poor and provider for their fortunes, pleasures and joys. Kinship is indeed claimed for her, with Nemesis, the goddess who pursued and scourged with vengeful fury the greedy who grasped and appropriated more than their share. Such is the foundation and origin of the great Vatican cathedral of Rome.

CHAPTER XVI.

CONTINUED.

THE APOSTOLIC AGE.

SECTION IV.,—VESPASIAN—TITUS.

GALBA—Short Reign of Seven Months Closed by Assassin's Dagger—Vespasian—Voted to Power by Prætorian Guard —Story of Narcissus—Vespasian Friendly to the Organizations—A Moment of Safety and Rest—Flavian Amphitheatre or Coloseum—Strange Discovery of a Slab Containing Name of its Builder, a Christian—He was Guadentius, Master Workman of a Builders' Guild—Vespasian's Short Reign— Nine Years of Peace, Comfort and Prosperity—Titus, his Son—Reigned only two years—Continued Prosperity—The Celebrated Eleven Years of Happiness—Titus Continues the Kindness of his Father—Cruel in His Destruction of Jerusalem—Mild in his Government at Rome.

ON the death of Nero, the scepter fell for the space of seven months to Galba when, like Tiberius, Claudius and Nero, he fell by the assassin's dagger.

Vespasian, a soldier without the prestige or power of a great gens family, but extremely popular, was chosen mostly at the instance of the army, to be emperor; and he was raised to that high station in 69, the same year Nero fell. Here comes again into history the strange double-functioned character, Narcissus, the same powerful freedman, who as a favorite of the freedmen of the domus Augustalis and business genius under Claudius, took the contract of cutting the tunnel for letting out the unwholesome waters of Lake Fucino.[495] Paul mentions him in one of his Epistles as a christian. In back years when both were young, Narcissus, working his influence on the emperor Claudius, secured Vespasian's appointment to go to Germany as legatus legionis and in A.D. 43, this future monarch even went to Britain on a similar mission. Thus Vespasian not only knew the christians and was under great obligations to them for their acts of kindness, but he may have been a convert, like Seneca.

The results were natural. Vespasian treated the new sect with much respect and favor, but was an enemy to the Jews. He repealed the cruel rescripts of Nero, rebuilt the temples burned in the fire, restored the influence of the domus Augustalis and reopened the gynæcia, and the booths where so many thousands in the umbrage of the old collegia had earned a living.

Among other things this emperor did was to build the great Flavian amphitheatre, the ruins of which are still a landmark for curiosity seekers at Rome. There is an inscription in form of an epitaph to the architect, Guadens by name, who built this colosseum and who was a genuine christian.[496] His name and works are inscribed upon a stone which, as an epitaph, is recorded in the archæological records, and has been commented upon with much interest at the epigraphical seminaries. He certainly worked for Vespasian and Titus, being an architect of merit, else he could not have constructed so vast and famous an edifice. But Vespasian was so relentlessly inimical to the Jews that he forced twelve thousand of them to work as war prisoners on its con-

---

[495] The prodigious amount of work is told to us by Suetonius, *Claudius*, 20: "Fucinum aggressus est .... per tria autum millia passuum, partim ecfosso monte, partim exciso, canalem absolvit ægre, et post undecim annos, quamvis continuis triginta hominum millibus sine intermissione operantibus." After eleven years working night and day the tunnel was opened but the water would not flow. Agrippina, Nero's mother, wife of Claudius was so angry that she caused the murder of Narcissus.

[496] Orell., 4955—Romæ. The date is that of Vespasian. — *Epitaph of the Man who Built the Coliseum.* Its last few lines read: "Tue Autori promisit iste. Dat. Kristus." *Id est Christus*, "Omnia tibi qui Alium parabit Theatrum in Celo." meaning that Christ has promised thee the author all things who shall design, prepare and construct another theatre in heaven. The editor's note runs: "Hunc putant architechtum fuisse Amphitheatri Flaviani, a Vespasiano propter Christiana sacra, quibus nomen dederit, supplicis affectum. Sermone barbaro minimeque Vespasiani seculum referenti difficultatem aliquam creari nemo infitiabitur." This man was certainly a member of the Dionysan artists and a κύριος or quinquennalis; but he probably outlived Vespasian and Titus and was executed by Domitian. The great Coliseum was dedicated in A.D. 80. See note 498.

struction. Two testimonies prove him to have been a christian; first the epitaph reads explicitly that he died in Christ; again Vespasian was very favorable to the christianized unions of Dionysan artists and awarded them the appointments to perform public work on a large scale. The inference therefore is that Guadentius and his union of skilled masons built the Flavian Ampitheatre; he, as quinquennalis or responsible director, presiding over the architectural work up to its completion in A.D. 80. Following the rule given us by Dr. Ramsay, to the effect that the date of an epitaph is by no means the date of the interment, but that in many cases it was chiseled much later, we have the latter part of the note of explanation in the Orellian collection disentangled: Guadens or Guadentius, the architect, as we have seen, was not executed by Vespasian, but years later by Domitian, who murdered thousands. Those objecting to the statement[497] in the inscription on account of the "barbarous language not conforming with the politer Latin of Vespasian's time, will find themselves nonplussed by Ramsay's discovery that the epitaph was not chiseled before the death of Domitian, who discouraged letters and whelmed all such artistic work in degeneracy and ruin.

Titus, his son, on the death of Vespasian in 97, took the control of government, and during his two years' reign the same friendship continued toward the christians at Rome. For our history these two reigns are uneventful. They are the celebrated Eleven Years of peace and happiness.

[497] Ramsay, *Cities and Bishoprics Phryg.*, commenting on his no. 366: "The dates of this and many other inscriptions is not to be understood as the date of the death of the person buried in the tomb. It was only in the developed christian epitaphic system that the day of death was engraved on the tomb." This very important fact pointed out by Dr. Ramsay is especially true of the early inscrs., and in another place he admits that secrecy on account of dangers was the cause.

[498] Orell., no. 4955, note *ad fin.*: "Fieri tamen potest, ut diu post Vespasiani tempora Guadentio tunc jam pro Martyre culto positus sit titulus." The inscription is in the present church of S. Martina at Rome; see Venuti, *Deser.*, T. I., p. 51. *Romæ Sotterranea della Chiese de S. Martina.*

CHAPTER XVI.

CONCLUDED.

THE APOSTOLIC AGE.

SECTION V.,—DOMITIAN.

DOMITIAN—Another Son of the Generous Vespasian—One of the most Terrible of Tyrants—An Account of his Murderous Havoc—Valuable History of Dion Cassius—Gibbon declares he means Christians though he Calls them Jews—Domitilla —Said to have Lived through Nero's Time—Atrocities of Domitian at Puteoli—Domitilla Persecuted—Her Husband Executed—Persecutions Raged at Rome—Newly Found Inscriptions Prove her a Historical Character—Inscription of Gruter—Wonderful Discoveries in Under-Ground Rome— Elegantly Ornamented Halls, School Rooms, Eating Chambers, Frescoings Sixty Feet beneath the Surface—They were Abodes of Hidden Brotherhoods during Persecutions of Domitian—Inscribed Mausoleums of Nearly all the Celebrated Martyrs Found—Peter, Paul, Domitilla, Pudens, Claudia— Innumerable Hosts of Others Unknown—Vast Revelations of the Excavation Funds—Story of Callistus and Carpophorus—Ashes of Blastus—Under-ground Monuments of the Via Salaria Vetus—The Catacombs of the Appian Way— Great Columbarium—End of the Tyrant Domitian.

NOT so, with the monster Domitian, Vespasian's younger son. He blasted the good name of the Flavian stock. Dion Cassius and Tacitus are our principal chroniclers of this creature's career. For some reason he became incensed against the unions of Puteoli. There is no historical reason given for his especial hatred of the christians of this place. We have, in section Nero of this chapter and elsewhere, shown that there existed many organizations at Puteoli. It was left for Domitian to sysmatically persecute them, giving as his reasons that their moral methods did not conform with the established paganism.[499] On the character and career of this monarch, who reigned A.D. 81-96, every authority is agreed that he terribly persecuted the christians.[500] It was Domitian who banished John the evangelist, to the Isle of Patmos and about the same time he commenced the persecution of the Jews. Dion Cassius, as Gibbon avers, means the christians, where he recounts Domitian's frightful persecution of the Jews on account of *atheotes* or conversion to christianity;[501] for he certainly could not have meant atheism, although he might have had reference to the perversion of morals, such as christianity used to excite against pagan ethics.

We will now turn back, as we have promised, to Puteoli, the place celebrated by the landing of Paul and his phenomenal reception and entertainment by brothers, on his way to Rome and death. There is a lapse of twenty years. Domitian, another cruel monarch, like Nero, has determined upon rooting out the new "pests." On this we have the fortunate history of Dion Cassius. At the commercial Mediterranean port of Puteoli, once celebrated for its shipping, great numbers of trade organizations existed. A very large contingent of the population of this city was Hebrew-Phœnician, speaking a lingo of the Greek. The Phœnicians had colonized the place with branch unions as positively shown by inscriptions. This was all acceptable enough to the Romans so long as they remained pagan and conformed to the state religion; but the moment it was discovered

---

[499] Dion Cassius, LXVII., c. 14: "Ἔγκλημα ἀθεότμτος, ὑφ' ἧς καὶ ἄλλοι ἐς τὰ τῶν Ἰουδαίων ἔθη ἐξοκέλλοντες πολλοὶ κατεδικάσθησαν."
[500] Meyers, *Kon. Lex.*, in verb. *Domitianus:* "Vorzugsweise ersah er sich die ausgesehnsten und bedeutendsten Männern zu opfern seiner Grausamkeit: aber auch Juden und Christen wurden verfolgt, und drei-und-neunzig wurden mit einmal alle Philosophen aus Rom vertrieben."
[501] Neander, *Plant.*, Book V.; *Hist. Chr. Rel.*, I., p. 96, *trans.*, note 3, is the historian who confirms the statement. Again, he says: "The words of Dion Cass., LXVII., cap. 14: 'Ἔγκλημα ἀθεότητος, ὑφ' ἧς καὶ ἄλλοι ἐς τὰ τῶν Ἰουδαίων ἔθη ἐξοκέλλοντες πολλοὶ κατεδικάσθησαν.' The uniting of the charge of ἀθεότης with that of an inclination toward Jewish customs, may have allusion to christianity, if ἀθεότης is not to be understood as barely referring to the denial of the gods of the state religion....... the charge of ἀθεότης........could, a fortiori, be brought against the conversion to christianity."

574   THE LAW UNDER DOMITIAN.

that they had become allies with the hated christians who introduced a new divinity in the worship of Christ, there was a great deal of trouble.[502]

Domitian, through his spies discovered this, and now the history of Dion Cassius avails us. It appears from this author, who begins the fourteenth chapter of his sixty-seventh book with a description of the environs of Puteoli and the neighboring island of Pandataria, where Domitilla was banished, that people here meant as those persecuted, are the same Puteolenses, who, about twenty years before had feasted and favored Paul, and escorted him to Rome. We have already shown abundant evidence proving that they were the membership of a large number of trade and labor unions colonized from Phœnicia, close by Cæsarea, where Paul was tried and where he shipped to meet the sentence of the emperor.

Although not of the noblest Roman stock, like his predecessors Galba and all before Vespasian, still he took upon himself in contradistinction to his father and brother, to wage war on the christians. There is a jumble of meanings caused by the failure of Dion Cassius to mention the name of christians, but calling them all Jews, then the general term by which in Rome the Semitic race was known; and it will be necessary to clear this up by quoting the well-expressed judgment of Gibbon;[503] who speaking of the outbreak of this great persecution which seems to have burst forth at Puteoli, says; "Domitilla was banished to a desolate island, on the coast of Campania; and sentences, either of death or confiscation were pronounced against a great number of persons who were involved in the sad accusation. The guilt imputed to their charge was that of atheism and Jewish manners—a singular association of ideas which *cannot with propriety be applied except to the christians.*" Continuing on the same subject the honest historian speaks of this imputation as an " honorable crime," and

---

[502] Milman, *as editor of Gibbon*, ch. xvi., note 117: "Dion Cassius must have known the christians; they must have been the subject of his particular attention: since this author, Gibbon, supposes that Dion wishes his master to profit by these 'councils of persecution.'" Guizot in a note to his *Translation of Gibbon*, says: "It is probable that Dion Cassius has often designated the christians by the name of Jews."

[503] *Decl. and Fall*, ch. xvi., with notes 51, 52, 53, 54, 55, and taking his information from Dion Cass., LXVII., Xiphilin, who brings in the celebrated christian, Saint Domitilla.

adds: "The church has placed both Clemens and Domitilla among its first martyrs, and has branded the cruelties of Domitian with the name of the second persecution. It was in fact, the third.

Domitilla, although she is canonized among the martyrs, certainly did not loose her life in this banishment, but must have been put to death later probably as an outcome of the conspiracy which worked the assassination of the monarch fifteen years later. The name of the assassin was Stephen, Domitilla's freedman.[504]

The acknowledgment of Gibbon and Guizot is, that the property of those not executed outright was confiscated. It is well established that the unions located at Puteoli were guilds possessing assets in common which amounted to large sums of money.[505] The disappearance of these associations for about half a century and the non-mention of Puteoli either by the christians or by profane history is proof that they, together with the churches, went out of history, because they were almost completely extinguished. It had been a vast hive of organizations and most of their faithful inscriptions, like those of Rhodes, which met the same fate, were of an earlier date than Nerva. Everything was sunk into oblivion by the inhuman act of Domitian and his truculent military cronies.[506]

Let us now proceed to the real history of this and the other persecutions of this despot.[507] They also raged at Rome. It looks certain that Dio means Peter's friend.

The best we can do here, is to paraphrase Dion's account in a running form; he says, speaking of Domitian's cruelties a short time before his assassination by Stephen who was Domitilla's household servant that:

[504] Suetonius, *In Domit.*, 17, where considerable is given of the tragedy. An array of conspirators is mentioned, making it appear that it was connected with gladiatorial games "quidam e gladiatorio ludo vulneribus septem contrucidarunt." See Philostratus, *Vita Apollon.*, I., 8.

[505] Dion Cass., *id.:* "Οἱ δὲ, τῶν γοῦν οὐσιῶν ἐστερήθησαν," clearly explains that it was their property that was seized.

[506] See the *Inscr.*, Orell., no. 1246, of the date A.D. 117, showing that at Puteoli they had all gone back to the old pagan worship.

[507] Dion Cass., LXVII., xii. 14: "Ἐν τουτῷ τῷ χρόνῳ ἡ ὁδὸς ἡ ἀπὸ Σινοέσσης ἐς πουτεόλους ἄγουσα λίθοις ἐστορέσθη. κἂν τῷ αὐτῷ ἔτει ἄλλους τε πολλοὺς καὶ τὸν Φλάβιον Κλήμεντα ὑπατεύοντα, καίπερ ἀνεψιὸν ὄντα, καὶ γυναῖκα καὶ αὐτὴν συγγενῆ ἑαυτοῦ Φλαβίαν Δομιτίλλαν ἔχοντα κατέσφαξεν ὁ Δομιτιανός. ἐπηνέχθη δὲ ἀμφοῖν ἔγκλημα ἀθεότητος, ὑφ' ἧς καὶ ἄλλοι ἐς τὰ τῶν Ἰουδαίων ἤθη ἐξοκέλλοντες πολλοὶ κατεδικάσθησαν. καὶ οἱ μὲν, ἀπέθανον, οἱ δὲ, τῶν γοῦν οὐσιῶν εστερηθήσαν. Ἡ δὲ Δομιτίλλα ὑπερωρίσθη μόνον εἰς Πανδατερείαν· Τὸν δὲ δὴ Γλαβρίωνα τὸν μετὰ τοῦ Τραιανοῦ ἄρξαντα, κατηγορηθέντα τὰ τε ἄλλα, καὶ οἷα οἱ πολλοὶ καὶ ὅτι καὶ θηρίοις ἐμάχετο, ἀπέκτεινεν."

"About this time the road which leads from Sinuessa to Puteoli was bestrewn with stones,[508] for the same year Flavius Clemens a consul and relative, the son of Flavius Sabinus, who was married to Domitilla, Domitian's niece, was arrested and executed, together with a great many others. The crimes charged against these persons was treason or blasphemy against the official religion; and on account of this, many others were also pursued and condemned, Domitilla among them. Some of them were punished with death, and others had their property seized and confiscated. Domitilla herself was banished to the isle of Pandataria, off the coast. Glabrio, who had been an archon for a certain Trajan, and many others, were informed against, hunted down, forced to enter the ring as gladiators with wild beasts, and killed."

This, literally rendered, is about the substance of Dion's short-cut but significant words. Now who was this Glabrio and who was Trajan for whom and whose he had served. It would be interesting to know who this Glabrio was. He could not have been a military commander for Trajan, afterwards emperor, for he was of too low a birth—a thing shown by his being condemned in the arena, although Trajan was a grown man at the time. The more probable truth is that the Trajan here meant, was some powerful kurios or archon of the unions, for indeed, Dion as much as says so, and that Glabrio was their business man in charge. Domitian and his greedy creatures were swift to seize and profit by their property. It resolves itself into another of those terrible massacres of the christians where they were flung naked and unarmed, like good old Ignatius, to the fierce beasts on the sands of the amphitheatre.

History is silent, but there is an inscription upon a slab of this date, which is accredited to Naples, about seven miles from the city of Puteoli, showing that those poor wretches, such as were left of them, having lost their manhood in these persecutions, resorted to a flattery of Domitian in order to appease his official hounds during the bloody work and terror at Puteoli, where he persecuted his christian relations, Domitilla and Clem-

[508] This appears to be an epigrammatical expression; it was a moment of cruelties and great suffering.

ens and thousands of the unnumbered poor.[509] The archæological records of Flavia Domitilla are numerous and not only establish her as a historical character, but dispel every doubt that she was a directress to a kuriakos at Puteoli. It is the same Domitilla mentioned by Dion and is counted among the martyrs as having been a christian, persecuted and some think put to death at this maritime city of Campania.[510] Little has been made public regarding this remarkable character. An effort has been made to deny her race as one of the proletarians, and to establish her as a noble. It has been strongly argued that the Clemens connected with the story of Dion Cassius quoted by us, who was put to death by Domitian at Puteoli, was in reality no other than Peter's friend. One thing is certain. He was a christian. According to Dion he was married to Domitilla. But an inscription which we have just quoted shows two Domitillas, and one, if not both, were freedwomen. This woman was Domitian's niece, but only by a morganatic alliance so frequent in those times. Flavius Sabinus was of real gens family stock;[511] but the inscription which we quote,[512] gives evidence that these characters are over-strained.

The early christians did not plant their Word of promise among the rich and great but among the poor and lowly who really needed the promised salvation, and that salvation had the economical as well as the spiritual promise. Nevertheless Domitilla, either directly or indirectly came in for considerable sums of money or other goods for in her name we find the most sumptous equipments of under-ground Rome.[513] It ap-

[509] Orell., 1246, A.D. 117. The inscription simply mentions Nerva, but is of little value to our purpose. Much better *.* Orelli's no 763; it speaks of both Sabina and Domitilla. It reads: "Sal'na Aug., Sabina clere. Ser. T. Caes. Aug. ab ornamento sui fecit.—DOMITANUS DOMITIA FLAVIA DOMITILLA." Romæ in urnula. This is a very suggestive one; date of Domitian, since it speaks of Flavia Domitilla.
[510] Gruter, 245, 5: "Flavia Domitilla, filia Flaviæ Domitillæ, Imp. Cæsaris....Ani neptis fecit Glyceræ I., et libertis libertabusque, posterisque eorum, curante T. Flavio Onesimo conjugi. Benemer." Found at Rome in an ear-shaped crypt, and bearing the evidences of being a memento of a college of christians.
[511] Gibbon, ch. xvi., note 51.
[512] See *Index*, in verb., *Domitilla*, for our note quoting the *insc.*, of Orell., no. 763, where they are clericals, and mere servants. In the no. 245 of Gruter the Domitillas are freedwomen.
[513] Waltzing, *Hist. Corp. Prof.*, I., pp. 212, 213, says: "De Rossi, *Bull. Crist.*, 1865, p. 95, Renan, *Marc Aurèle*, p. 537, a découvert à Saint Domitille une vaste salle, ornée de peintures et entourée de bancs en pièrres; à côté. on remarque un puits et une citerne c'était la schola où les chrétiens

pears that Domitilla in those dangerous times was a great power. She must have been of considerable consequence, for there have been found many suggestive inscriptions pointing to her influence and support and it is history that a man named Stephen, who was either a slave or freedman of Domitilla and who had recourse to the palace, crawled into Domitian's private presence and murdered him, whether with the knowledge of his mistress or not is not positively known. There is an inscription, found near Puteoli, which exhibits Domitilla as a priestess, proving that she was a great kuria, or mistress of a kuriake at that place.[514]

Although this once important benefactress and comforter of the persecuted unions is made prominent mention of at Puteoli, yet she survived her banishment in the isle of Pandataria and when she returned to her work at the town and found naught but desolation, the members all dead or scattered and the property in the hands of their enemies she must have returned to Rome. So fierce had been the persecution here, likewise in the city, that whatever she did to restore happiness and order is unknown except through recently discovered inscriptions. But the fact that she is on the Breviary of martyrs at Rome, gives us a very strong and darkling hint that she must actually have suffered a violent death under Nerva or Trajan.[515]

In the words of De Rossi given in our notes in this

s' assemblaient leurs agapes." De Rossi, *Roma Sotterranea*, I., pp. 184-185, found her in the Via Ardeatina: "Cœmeterium s. s. Hermetis et Domitillæ (Petrus Mallius addit: est foris portam Pincianam, ubi est ecclesia s. Hermetis martyris). Urbis Romæ cœmiteriorum mirabilium." *id.*, p. 177. Callistus and Peter are in the same cemetery, Via Ardeatina. As to the secrets of this cemetery, he says, p. 168: "In uno di quali vidi nella volta le imagini de martiri istorici di quel cemetero, designate dai lori nomi, Pietro Marcellino, Tiburzio, Gorgonio," He further states that more excavations may show other valuable things and that, to prove that the cemeteries were not unknown in the 2nd century, pictures of the 2nd century were found there. The despoilers did work of years as late as A.D. 150. But every appearance proves the great secrecy that was kept up.

[514] Orell., 740, 741, 742, 743, 744. The number 740, speaks of the House of eternal peace. It was during Domitian's frightful reign, when it is known nearly all the christians were murdered. The fine inscriptions are christian. Some of the poor fellows belonged, or had belonged to the emperors as slaves or freedmen. They were mostly christianized collegia. The legends show this. No. 747 speaks of Domitilla and is christian.

[515] Orell., 2231: "C. Asconio C. F. Fab. Sardo. IIII., Vir. I. D. Præf. Fabr. fratri Cusiniæ M. F. SARDI MATRI ET SIBI ASCONIA C. F. AUGURINI SACERDOS DIVÆ DOMITILLÆ."

[516] De Rossi, *Rom. Sotteran.*, I., p. 186, has established that Domitilla, together with her κυριακη are in the cemetery of the Via Ardeatina; "Fatte queste osservazioni sui pochi monumenti che oggi conociamo del cemetero di Lucina passo a quello di Domitilla sulla Via Ardeatina, e che questo cemetero sia la necropoli, cui il Bossio con i Suoi seguaci quasi per auton-

chapter, mention is made of an extra **pagan inscription** found in the interior of the ciriacus or in Greek **kuriakos** or chapel of this under-ground Mausoleum of Domitian and this "una lapide profana contemporanea," is held by a geologist who was engaged in the excavations of the spot in 1860, to be proof positive that **this** is the burial place of Domitilla.[516, 517]

It appears, that the excavations presided over by **De** Rossi and others have uncovered from a great depth a huge ciriacus, or kuriakos or subteranean church. All customs and habits have a legitimate origin, and the origin of a graveyard around a church lies in the burial clause of the ancient law of the collegium funeraticium, or collegium tenuiorum, the meaning of which was a society of the poor and degraded. Solon gave those the right to organize for mutual help knowing the great power of socialism as a purely economic means; that right during the Roman conquests was stripped from them by the pusilanimous aristocrats, with the exception of the clause permitting organization for burial purposes. The unions then, hid their economic phase while they sedulously kept it in spite of all attempts to put them down, and continued to all outside appearance under the legalized burial clause, sanctifying their confraternity with a temple and placing their graveyard around it. Here we have the chapel and churchyard and it is so to-day. There were no such institutions known to earlier pagan times.

But during the fierce attacks of Claudius, Nero and Domitian, even the law permitting this ambiguous association did not enough shield them from the grip of Roman law, and they then dived under ground, maintaining still, and according to law, a graveyard around their chapel. As the ground for many feet in depth

omassia ha dato il nome di Callisto, lo domostrerò con ogni certezza in questo volume. Ma preverò anche un altro punto assai più importante, che cioè il nome di Domitilla datogli nei documenti ecclesiastici è autenticato da una lapide profana contemporanea a Flavia Domitilla. Qui adunque le origini del sepolcreto contemporaneo al primo seculo dal solo nome di Domitilla sono a bastanza certificate."

[517] This curious tablet reads: "M. Antonius restitutus felicit Ypo gev. sibi et suis fidenti. in Domino." It reads like an epitaph speaking in very strong language of the faithful brotherhood in the Lord. The remarks of De Rossi, *Rôm. Sott.*, I., p, 109, are: "........ed assai più antico è ll seguente prezioso titoletto rinvenuto nel 1853 dentro il cemetero di Domitilla, (See above just quoted.) La bella formula '*fidentibus in Domino*' in questo latissimo titulo aggiunta al '*suis*' ci spiega, che il '*sibi et suis*' nelle epigrafi cristiane non può averi quel largo sensa, che ha nello pagano."

is planed away, these otherwise phenomenal sepultures appear. So Domitilla had her kuriake or in Latin cyriacus, with her chapel.

But in her case it was a splendid abode, Hades-like, though it was.[518] De Rossi, as we have shown, described a vast hall ornamented with paintings and surrounded with stone seats. On one side there is a well and also a cistern. This is the schola, a large room the christians used in secret, to assemble and enjoy their love-feasts, listen to sermons, deliberate upon and arrange for the economical means of the day and the morrow, and enjoy the common meals together. So they had not only this of Domitilla, which so fortunately answers as a splendid and undeniable specimen, but many others, some of which we shall be able to show. De Rossi [519] has been able, partly with his own labor and partly through the aid of his brother, Michele Stefano, a geologist engaged in these excavations, to bring to light two other important specimens of historical characters of the time of Paul, buried or conserved in two different under-ground cemeteries; those of the Agro Verano, and of San Valentino.

One of the martyrs whose ashes now lie in the underground Rome, is Callistus. This is another strange double-dealing character of these tempestuous and dangerous times when a dense secrecy was an absolute necessity. He is recorded in the Ante-Nicine Breviary of Martyrs, and his name appears in connection with a strange story. He first appears as a christian slave of a man named Carpophorus at Rome, and probably a heartless slave driver who thought of nothing beyond making profit out of the labor of his wretched chattels.

[518] De Rossi, *Rom. Sott.*, Vol. I., p. 168: "Con le piante del Bossio in mano tentai de retrovare e riconoscere il sito d'uno di principali ingressi e delle principali cripte del cemetero, che allora si chiamava di Callisto, e che vedremo essere di Domitilla. Nel labirinto di quella spaventosa necropoli in' inaltrai attraverso gl' interramenti e le rovine rinvenni el punto indicato nella pianta del Bossio," etc., and he cites his note 3 (Rossi): "Vedi la pianta dell' ordine inferiore dell cemetero di Callisto, no. 3.

[519] See *supra*, note 513.

[520] *Roma Sott.*, I., p. 60, of *Analysis* of his brother Michele Stephano de Rossi, a geologist detailed in the excavations at Rome: "........ora accenneró soltanto tre esempli assai dimonstrativi, che mi sono fortuiti dall' agro Verano, dal cemetero di S. Valentino e da una regione del cemetero di Domitilla. Sulla Via Tiburtina presso l' agro Verano il colle, ov' è il vasto cemetero di Ciriaca, negli ultimi anni naturalmente, brano nella sua ultima lacinia merèdionale.......... che quelle gallerie e cubicoli secondano perfino la sinuosità dell' esterna costa dell colle. Nel cemetero di S. Valentino sulla Flaminia si accede ora ai piani diversi, non per scale interne, ma per apertura orizzontali," etc.

But in Callistus he found one not so easily handled; he was indeed outwitted by him, for the slave wimbled himself into his master's confidence and soon became private secretary and treasurer. Here the scale turns against him, for the next we hear is that he is in a pistrinum or treadmill, having been sent there by Carpophorus for the alleged crime of embezzlement. This, it is charged, was a fraudis pia, by his many friends in the guild of the house of the Cæsars, secretly christian. Their influence secured his freedom. After he had manifested his ability in the secret union, we find him again arrested by the Roman police and sent to far-off Sardinia as a public convict, to work in the mines. But the christians had by this time a regular discipline established in their unions, to cover such cases.[521] Callistus was a second time assisted by some secret means, which is however, explained by Tertullian a century later in his apology, declaring that his union or corpus collected money for such purposes. The next we hear, is that Callistus is made a bishop and finally we have him recorded as a martyr in the Roman Catholic Breviary. So we have Saint Callistus.

Examining the subterranean inscriptions exhumed by the epigraphical seminaries, we find this same Callistus to have been cremated and his ashes preserved in the same cemetery along with many others in the Via Appia at Rome, now protected under cover of the church of San Sebastiano which we visited on a memorable occasion, in the year 1869.[522]

Another New Testament character is exhumed and rises to the surface, in the name and person of Blastus, a christian Phœnician, who was chamberlain to King Herod at Tyre and Sidon.[523] This is interesting to those

[521] Tert., *Apol.*, xxxix., later, and as soon as it was safe to divulge, lets out the whole method, and Mommsen, Waltzing, and Oehler admit that it was a regular collegium or trade union: "corpus sumus de conscientia religionis et disciplinæ........modicam unusquisque stipem menstrua die.... apponit....... Nam inde non epulis, nec potaculis, nec ingratiis voratrinis dispensatur, sed egenis alendis humandisque, et pueris et puellis re ac parentibus destitutis, jamque domesticis senibus, item naufragis, et si qui in metallis, et si qui in insulis vel in custodiis, duntaxat ex cause dei sectæ, alumni confessionis suæ fiunt."

[522] De Rossi, *Rom. Sott.*, I., pp. 184-5. Relics of two apostles in the Via Appiana deposited a short time after their death: "E fosse anche il cemetero di Callisto appellato altresse di Lucina." and again in his *Index Itinerarius*, p. 180: "Cœmeterius Callisti ad S. Xystum, Via Appia" and much of value on p. 232 "*Callisto—San Sebastiano*—Via Appia."

[523] *Acts*, xii., 20: "Ἦν δὲ ὁ Ἡρώδης θυμομαχῶν Τυρίοις καὶ Σιδωνίοις· ὁμοθυμαδὸν δὲ παρῆσαν πρὸς αὐτόν, καὶ πείσαντες Βλάστον, τὸν ἐπὶ τοῦ κοιτῶνος τοῦ βασιλέως, ᾐτοῦντο εἰρήνην διὰ τὸ τρέφεσθαι αὐτῶν τὴν χώραν ἀπὸ τῆς βασιλικῆς.

wishing to know why so many Phœnicians flourished among the early christian unions. The story of Blastus connecting him with the escape of Peter from prison, and his influence with Herod at Tyre and Sidon, is told us in the twelfth chapter of the Acts. But our interest is aroused by the evidence it furnished that the Phœnicians, who possessed such powerful colonies at Puteoli, were so early converted to the Word of promise.

Blastus went to Rome; for his ashes are preserved among the martyrs with an unmistakable inscription in the ecclesia Johannis, Via Salaria Vetus.[524]

Priscilla was a great character. She died the martyr's death like all the others under circumstances long unknown, but recently coming to light. The discoveries of under-ground Rome much resemble those of Pompeii. They are both products of government conducted excavations of the repositories holding human remains deposited by accident or purpose at about the same period, in the same necropolis. Urns, catafalques, funeral sites and many evidences of ancient custom evince themselves through these modern exhumations. Both sets of labors also bring forth objects of common living, and are means of instruction for those seeking the knowledge of how men once lived.

Priscilla or Prisca, as she is called in Paul's Epistle[525] to Timothy, though boldly appearing several times in the Testament, is nevertheless very obscure, being unmentioned in many of our great cyclopedias. Since the exhumation of a large basilica with a magnificent cubiculum in under-ground researches at Rome, it is probable that this neglect will be rectified in future editions

[524] De Rossi, *Roma Sott.*, I., p. 176: "Deinde vadis ad orientem donec venias ad ecclesiam Johannis martyris Via Salinaria; ibi requiescit Diogenus martyr sub terra; sub terre quoque Blastus martyr; deinde Johannis martyr; postea Longinus martyr, etc.; Gorius, *Mon. sive Columb.*, p. 139: An inscr. shows that he is in an olla of the columbarium, having been a bondman of Nero who probably killed him at the conflagration: "Hujus pariter nominis in Florentino Ceppulo Musei Suburbani Strozii, p. 371, no. 122, ubi legitur 'Blastus Cæsaris servus Neronianus et in Actis Apostolorum cap. XII., 20, Blastus præpositus Cubiculo regis Herodis.'" The inscr. is broken but enough remains to show that Blastus was by trade a lampendias or wool-weigher, of course engaged in the imperial gynæceum which is to say, a member of the collegium Domus Augustalis and furnishing the spinning and weaving for Nero's household. See the inscr. itself, under the niche receiving the cinerary urn. De Rossi, *id.*, p. 177: "Tertia porta Porticiana,........ibi prope in loco qui dicitur Cucumeris requiescunt martyres Festus, Johannis, Liberalis Diogenes, Blastus, Lucina et in uno sepulcreo CCLX., et in altero, XXX."

[525] *II Tim.*, iv., 19; *Romans*, xvi., 3; *I. Cor.*, xvi., 19; Cf. Smith, *Bib. Dict.*, p. 2588.

as the results of our modern study become gradually understood.[526] De Rossi is by no means the only investigator of these revelations. She is mentioned by several others.[527] Gorius, and after him Bossius, William of Malmsbury, Gruterius and the Berlin Academy have all entered valuable data upon their pages. De Rossi enters more elaborately into the subject than any other author whose works we have consulted.[598] This strange subterranean basilica or cathedral of Priscilla is not only occupied by her, but the urns with their unmistakable epitaphs in Latin or Greek, containing many others mentioned in the New Testament, are also there. The ashes of Pudens are among others.[529] His career and historical acquaintance with Seneca, Paul and the poet Martial, we have given in our account of Nero's conflagration of Rome.

[526] De Rossi, *Rom. Sott.*, I., p. 189: "In fatto, a quella distanzia medesima ci è additato il celebre cemetero di Priscilla, ottimamente reconosciuto dai prime autori della Roma sotterranea, alla sinistra della via sotto la vigna de Cuppis." But she is not alone; *id.*: "Ivi stesso sotto una vigna alla destra, il Bossio vide un altro cemetero separato da quello di Priscilla. Oggi ambedue sono collegati per moderne cave di pozzolana; ma l' antica esistenza dell' uno independentemente dall' altro, mentre ambedue sono posti alla distanza medesima dalla città, fe argumentare al Bossio, che se il prime dee essere chiarmento di Priscilla, il secundo lo dee essere di Novella."

[527] Bossius, *Roma Sott.*, from which all the more modern hypogeists are extracting, on p. 438, says: "Senza lume di candela si vede una gran nicchia a modo di tribuna lavorata di stucco a fagliami, e intorna alla nicchia si vedono alcune lettere rosse che per essere quasi affatto scancellate non si sino potuto leggere, quelle poche però che vi rimangono, sono benissime fatte, sotto la qual nicchia doveva essere anticamente l' altare, essendo il luogo assai spazioso." The color of the ink or material with which these niches were decorated is an indelible red. De Rossi, p. 191, says he saw Priscilla's in the Via Salaria Nova and that it was exactly similar. Bossius, perhaps, did not know that it was Priscilla.

[528] De Rossi, *Roma Sott.*, I., 171: "Nelle cripte del cemetero de santi Pietro e Marcellino e in quelle de Pretestato vidi qualche graffito, ma non me sembrarano della classe, di che ora tratto. Incerto anche rimasi sul' acclamazione NAVIGI VIVAS IN che se legge nella così detta cappella greca del cemetero di Priscilla, la quale mi pareva senza dubbio un istorica cripta."

[529] De Rossi, *Roma Sott.*, I., p. 188. PUDENS, Priscilla, *Via Salaria Nova*: "Vengo al cemetero di Priscilla sulla Via Salaria nuova. Molto dovrei dire intorno a questo cometero; ma poichè lo qui attendo alla somma possibile brevità, rimetta per ora il lettore a quel poco, che ne ho scritto nel dichearare Imagini scelte della B. Virgine Maria trata dalla catacombe romane, p. 15-9. Ivi ho reipilogato aliquanti degli argomenti dimostranti la somma antichità della regione di quel cemetero, nel cui centro è la casi detta *cappela greca;* regione, che ho diciarato essere la primitiva ed originaria, quella ov' ebbero sepoltura i prima Pudenti ed i martiri insigni, onde tanta rinomanza venne alla necropoli di Priscilla." Pudens is in the necropolis of Priscilla.

CHAPTER XVII.

TRAJAN.

THE PLINY EPISODE.

PLINY and Trajan's Celebrated Persecutions—Ignatius Christophorus—Great Master Had Caressed Him When a Babe—Trajan's Sentence—Thrown to Beasts in Amphitheatre—Value of His Repudiated Epistles—One to Mary Shows She was a Member—Ancient Syriac Version Proves that Christian Eranos Emancipated Slaves—Order of Widows—Pliny appointed Governor in Asia—The Hetæræ—Pliny found them Converted Guilds—Members Refused to Buy Sacrifices—Would not Render Tribute to Cæsar—Crime Punishable with Death—Nest of such Criminals Discovered by Government Spies—Pliny's Letter to Trajan—Ordered Many to Execution—Tortured and forced Them to Curse Christ—Praised their Honesty and Virtue—Lex Julia—Trajan to Pliny—Pliny Himself Converted—Tries to Organize a Union of Firemen—Trajan Refuses, Fearing that They would Turn Christians like the Rest—Original of Letters Quoted—Frequent Mention of Words Christ and Christian—These Hetæræ had already been converted many years—Pliny in Contrition Gives Sums of Money to Children of Families he had Murdered—Inscription ad Trajanum Amisorum in Proof—The Lesson.

THE REIGN of Trajan is signalized in the history of socialism through the remarkable episode of the Plinian persecutions and judicial massacres of the ancient poor. We are fortunate enough, secret as were the wretched members below, and niggardly of news as was the great Roman state above, to have a considerable amount of monumental and literary evidence which the cringing historians never brought to the front, but which now serves our purpose in proving that just at the close of the apostolic age, even before the last companion of Jesus was gone, the pure trade union, or, so to speak, socialistic trade and labor alliance, was flourishing in Asia Minor, enjoying in common many comforts at the common table, in the shops of their co-operative commonwealth and in their mutual protection under the secret veil; and that they had endorsed and were practicing the plan of salvation as laid down by the great master in the Word of promise.

Before entering upon the Pliny episode let us first mention the martyrdom of Ignatius, the Christophorus, or the man who, when a babe, Jesus had lovingly caressed and kissed in Palestine, saying, "suffer little children to come unto me, for of such is the kingdom of God.[1]" Little is known of this man who had evidently devoted his life-time to preaching the Word of promise in and around Smyrna, when the emperor Trajan arrived here on a flying visit through the various sections of his enormous realm. Ignatius was preaching in a loud voice at Smyrna where he was faithfully presiding over the flock. Through his spies, Trajan received information against him and had him ordered into his presence. Here the emperor questioned him regarding the work he was doing, which the old man did not deny, but most courageously acknowledged. Hearing the bold language of Ignatius, already about eighty years old, Trajan became enraged and on the spot sentenced him to be transported in chains, between a guard of about a dozen soldiers, to Rome and thrown to the raging wild animals in the enclosure of games during a gala function of the great Flavian amphitheatre.

On the way thither, escorted, as he writes, by ten leopards,[2] he wrote the celebrated epistles, which for many centuries were spurned as spurious by the prelates, who for toward two thousand years have rendered the original socialism of christianity useless by their greed and subserviency to kings. Their hiding of the truth of the Ignatian letters through multifarious Latin and Greek interpolations, however, proved futile on a long-time estimate, for the recent discovery by Cureton, of the lost Syriac originals in an old Armenian convent restores them as true. Ignatius was the follower of the

[1] Gibbon, *Decl. and Fall, Vindication:* "According to the tradition of the modern Greeks, Ignatius was the child whom Jesus received into his arms." See Tillemont, *Mém., Eccles.,* tom. II., part ii., p. 43.
[2] Ignatius, *Epist. to the Romans,* chap. ii., 8: "From Syria even unto Rome, I fight with beasts both of sea and land, both night and day; being bound to ten leopards, which is to say, such a band of soldiers," etc.

ebionitic socialism of Jesus.[3] On the way to execution, after a tedious journey, the escort arrived at the old town of Puteoli[4] in Southern Italy, but to his chagrin could not land, owing to a storm which kept them at sea. They kept on northward to the Port of Ostia, seven miles from Rome, and to one of the gates, there to meet a detachment of the old prætorian guard which escorted them to the amphitheatre at Rome, where were gathered and in breathless waiting, sixty thousand betting, gambling, wine bibbing debauchees and lovers of blood-spilling scenes and sights of horror and suffering. No time was lost for the expedition was late and Rome had turned out to behold another martyrdom.[5]

This man, of all others whose writings were not destroyed, has best described the true nature of the ancient church and its resemblance to the original unions into which it planted. In his epistles, he portrays the true position of the deacons, who, as we have shown, were waiters on the common tables. Ignatius speaks of them as a factor of the economic department which had always existed during the early christianity. The modernized church has transformed the deacon of the good old times into a mere official of the spiritual formula, obliterating his functions. He is nothing. In the old times he was a waiter, and his labor was helping to prepare the meals, and when prepared, he assisted the partakers as his proper calling. Ignatius, in his letter to the Trallians, treats the waiters with the utmost courtesy, but ascribes them to their place.[6]

This old martyr recognized also the prime factor of love among the brothers and sisters together with the

[3] In a manuscript of an earlier date, Ignatius in his *epistle to John*, speaks of: "Many of our women here who are desirous to see Mary the mother of Jesus, and wish day by day to run off from us to you, that they may meet with her and touch those breasts of hers which nourished the Lord Jesus, and inquire of her respecting some rather secret matters." In other words, they dared not write openly for fear of the spies of the emperor. This confesses that everything was behind the densely secret veil.
[4] See *Ante-Nicine Fathers*, Vol. IV., p. 130. He desired to land and see what was left by Domitian, of the brethren, but was prevented by a heavy storm. Regarding the plant at Puteoli, its treatment of Paul, *vide* Chap. xvi., Section *Nero* and Section *Domitian*, for great persecutions.
[5] Chrysostom, Vol. II., p, 593: "Ignatius........in medio theatro feris objectus, martyrum obit."
[6] *Epistle to the Trallians*, c. I., 7: "The deacons, also, as being the ministers of the mysteries, must by all means place all. For they are not only deacons of meat and drink, but of the church." In verse 8, he writes: "In like manner, let all reverence the deacons.........bishops........presbyters....as the college of the apostles. Without them there is no church." In this letter the genuine ancient college is recognized.

great necessity of mutual aid and especially providing each other jobs whereby to earn the driblets of money to be paid by each member in the form of assessments, exactly as was the case in the old Solonic unions.[7] This old preacher was constantly talking and writing of the economies derivable through his organized brotherhoods, both for the flesh and spirit.[8] In his epistle to Mary, strong mention is made of her secret order, so dark and obscure that she dared not speak. One gathers that the "secrets" were within the veil and that they had no right to convey their thoughts from one to another by means of letters; in fact, it was, as Ramsay has remarked, "very dangerous." In one of the best letters to Polycarp, Ignatius speaks out plainly regarding the unions or brotherhoods. The commonly known versions evidently garbled the meaning, but the newly found Syriac version brought to light by Dr. Cureton, conforms with the ancient conditions. Here the "commume" is the old eranos.[9] There were, as in the more ancient unions at Delphi where the eranos used to purchase the liberty of slaves by their sale to a god, many bondmen in the Ignatian brotherhood and it was a common thing; but he seems to imagine it was too much for the christian unions to purchase their liberty through loans by the society for the purpose, fearing lest it might exhaust their funds.[10] Thus our assertion is verified that the christians first planted among the economic unions existing under the law of Solon, following their methods of emancipating slaves and otherwise doing good during the whole of the first century.

[7] *Apocryph. N. T.*, Lond. ed., 1728; *Epist.*, Ignat., *Phillippians*, ch. iii., 10, 11, 12: "Stand, therefore in these things... be immutable in the faith, lovers of the brotherhood, lovers of one-another, companions together, kind, gentle to each other, despising none." Verse 12: "Be all of you subject to one-another."

[8] *Epistle to the Trallians*, ch. xii. His Eucharist had the common table.

[9] Ignat., *Epist to Polycarp*, IV., Syriac version: " Assemble together often. Keep an account of all the members by name. Despise not the slaves, male or female. Do not encourage their desire to obtain their freedom at the expense of the commune." This shows that, like the old eranists, they were unionists.

[10] It is reluctantly admitted that emancipation of the slave members was one of the functions of the early church. Ignatius, *Polycarp*, 4, wrote: "Μὴ ἐράτωσαν ἀπὸ τοῦ κοινοῦ ἐλευθεροῦσθαι." Dr. Ramsay, *Cities and Bishoprics of Phrygia*, II., p. 546, notices this, and quotes the *Apostolic Constitutions*, IV., 9: "Τὰ ἐξ αὐτῶν, ὡς προειρήκαμεν, ἀφοριζόμενα χρήματα διατάσσετε διακούντες εἰς ἀγορασμοὺς τῶν ἁγίων, ῥυόμενοι δούλους καὶ αἰχμαλώτους, δεσμίους." κ.τ.λ. So Lightfoot, *Coloss. Phil.*, p. 324: "One of the earliest forms which christian benevolence took, was the contribution of funds for the liberation of slaves."

Again, Ignatius speaks of the order of Widows, and there is evidence that a society existed composed of poor women who had lost in the wars their husbands and friends. The mention of this company of widows also appears elsewhere; and it was an important part of the early organization.[11] After the death of Paul, Ignatius declares that this evangelist of the Gentiles was an initiate into the mysteries, made so because he had been chosen. Many suggestive remarks come to us from his pen, tending to clear up things mysterious. Among others, is one in the letter to the Smyrnians who had refreshed him, soul and body, referring to the friendly meals in the communal brotherhood. While reminding them of his personal gratitude, he touches upon the duties of deacons. They with the elders are to be "compassionate and merciful toward all, turning them from their errors, seeking those that are weak, not forgetting little ones, but always providing for them what is good." All are to refrain from covetousness. Such was old man Ignatius, who was thrown to the starved wild animals in the amphitheatre as one of the early martyrs of Trajan's persecutions, to die an awful death.

About the time this terrible judicial cruelty occurred, A.D. 107, according to Gibbon, who discredits Pagi's Chronicon and stands by Baronius, this same emperor Trajan, appointed the celebrated Pliny, a nephew of the great scientific author, C. Plinius Secundus,[12] to a high position of power in Asia. The Plinys were of an optimist family, owning estates at Como. This Pliny was naturally a benevolent and thoughtful gentleman and the world has gladly given him credit for it. Made governor of Bithynia, he came in contact with a most saddening duty. It was no less than that of torturing and killing great numbers of christianized trade unionists, who as we have already shown, swarmed, like a republic in miniature, right in this part of Asia Minor,

[11] Ignac., *Epist. Phillippians, Company of Widows,* chap. xv. Salutation to the Company of Virgins and Widows, Order of Widows.
[12] Baronius places it in the year 102, which would be years before the martyrdom of Ignatius. We quote Gibbon. *Decline and Fall,* ch. xvi., note 157: "Pliny was sent into Bithynia, according to Pagi, in the year 110. Now that accurate chronologer (meaning Baronius) places it in the year 102." See the fact recorded in his *Critica Historica Chronologica;* but in *Annales,* C Baronii, A.D. 102, p. 99, Sect. II., § 3. The words of Pagi, tome I., p. 100, are : "Plinius igitur anno Christi centesimo decimo Bithyniam intravit." Quite likely Baronius is right. This would make the Plinian epistles still more valuable.

BITHYNIA AND BYZANTIUM DESCRIBED. 589

at the very time, and as the Plinian letters prove, even many years anterior to Pliny's appointment.[13]

Bithynia was a strip of a rich, well watered, densely populated country, covered with towns and rich in agriculture, manufactures and trade.[14] It was flanked on the north by the Byzantine Europe and stretched along the Bosphorus from the Sea of Marmora and along the Black Sea, with that magnificent stream skirting its whole length on the north, facing in plain view of what is now Constantinople, its beautiful green hills and valleys the joy and glory of Anatolia. As we proceed with this almost marvelous Plinian episode, the reader will ripen an acquaintance with the number and value of the Solonic unions which were precisely the factors this almost converted governor was dealing with, their christianized temples, their mutual loves, their communal table and their prosperous though secret ranks.

We have already abundantly shown that the hetæræ were genuine trade unions. The union of firemen which Pliny asked Trajan's permission to organize was to be a hetæra. Trajan refused fearing they might, if organized, be too prone to christianize and thus make trouble. But they were already numerous, as their inscriptions show.[15] The trouble with them was that they refused to pay tribute after their conversion. This stopped the buying of lambs at the sacrifice, throttling the provision rings. The true cause of the Roman persecutions was seen by Gibbon, though he knew nothing of the sources of information furnished by the inscriptions. Yet he was right in charging against the christians that after conversion they refused to attend pagan worship. Pagan worship was at that time reduced to a groveling subserviency to the money power. The priests, answering to our modern lobbyists and representatives favored with special advantages, and idly reveling in the interests of certain rich people, principally army officers and others who amassed fat fortunes out of the Roman conquests,

[13] Walizing, *Hist. Corp. Prof.*, I., p. 514: "Pline le Jeune, ne dit il pas que pour les esclaves la maison ell-meme est comme une république et comme une cité: 'Servis respublica quædam, et quasi civitas domus est.'" *Epist.*, VIII., 16.
[14] Bithynia was a Satrapy of Phrygia. Its chief river was the Sangarius. It was bounded N. by the Euxine, S. by Phrygia and Galatia, E. by Paphlagonia, W. by the Propontis or Sea of Marmora and Mysia.
[15] Oehler. *MSS.*: "Bithynia, Bryllion, jetzt Triglia; Θιασωται, durch die Relief-darstellung als Thiasoten des Zeus erklärt, *Bull. Hell.*, XVII., 1893, p. 573, no. 32, Unions of Jehovah!

worked hand in hand with the emperors in building up splendid establishments.

Among other supposed duties of the people was a strict attendance at the pagan worship. In the official temples there were fixed days of assembling, although they had no Sunday. On such occasions it was common for the priests to give banquets. As all, rich or poor, bond or free, were invited to partake and pay, it served as a revenue to the state, because the officers of the law collected a tithe of the incomes. Then again, these meetings answered as a sort of public market. The priests obtained lambs, sheep, poultry, calves, fish and other provisions and the worshipers at the shrines purchased them and took them home to their own families, after paying therefor an exorbitant price. According to the teachings of the priests, these prices were but a sacred contribution to the great official religion.

When, however, the christians made their appearance and refused to buy the high priced luxuries from such markets because they were poor and could not afford it, and because they had their own common table which they furnished with cash through their monthly assessments[16] then the Roman laws struck them a deadly blow. The accusation against them was that they refused to pay tribute to Cæsar. Of course it was true as we may well imagine, that the priests working with the provision rings which were thus extorting enormous prices from the poor through their credulity and blind faith, being intercepted in their profit-making career by the growing faith in the new Word of promise, were so incensed that their rage knew no bounds. They combined their influence with every other, including that of the profit incentive, brought it as a grievance before the emperors, on the plea that these sects were an outrageous, blasphemous, unheard-of innovation against the Roman state, and argued that they should be treated with the utmost rigors of the law.[17] This had also been exactly the case on their first public appearance at Jeru-

[16] See *supra*, pp. indicated in our *index*. The sacrifices are already quite fully explained; but the Pliny episode is the most remarkable history of this on record, which makes repetition necessary.
[17] It was the old *lex Julia:* Waltzing, *Hist. Corp. Prof.*, I., p. 160, quoting Pliny, *Epist.*, 96: "Quod ipsum facere desisse post edictum meum quo secundum mandata tua hetærias esse vetueram." Here it is shown: "first that the christian ecclesiæ and the Asiatic hetæræ were one and the same; second that Pliny suppressed them, under the lex Julia, revived by Trajan as "suspected."

salem. Jesus, who was kurios or lord, not only refused tribute, but he went boldly into the booths in the great temple which had been desecrated by these gamblers in stocks, adulterated foods, chipped coins, jewels of the sectaries, animals of the sacrifice, paraphernalia of the priesthood and all the bric-a-brac and abracadabra of their profit-yielding trade. In both cases the craving for accumulating profit by means of the vantage-lever of religious superstition lay at the bottom of the whole trouble.

There was a temple at Nicomedia, as well as at Chalcedon, Astacus, and every other town and village in Bithynia. Under the usages of the old official religion, each temple was dedicated to some one of the recognized divinities, and each had its set of priests and mysteries. The people in their so-called pagan state of mind, were taught by those priests to save up their earnings as sacrificial tribute "to the holy altar of their god." What of these incomes not filched by the priests, went to the public treasury. Attendance was compulsory and dereliction punished.[18] Struggling against the law compelling them to attend these feast days and religious occasions to be fleeced of their hard savings, the christians, when persecutions came, slunk back into the secret recesses behind their veil.

Pliny made a research into their condition and after finding them innocent and correct, he wrote to the emperor whose personal friendliness he enjoyed, for instructions. The letter is extant and we produce Whiston's rendering in which it is shown that, among other things, the christians were already numerous and had been so for years. Pliny mentions Christ three times and calls the christians by name ten times; while Trajan's answer mentions the christians twice. We here reproduce both:

[18] Gibbon, *Decl. and Fall.*, ch. xvi., over note 14, setting aside the sentiment and principle involved in socialism, pronounces the christians guilty, and like Tacitus, wants to see them punished: "The personal guilt which every christian had contracted in thus preferring his private sentiments to the national religion was aggravated in a very high degree by the number and union of the criminals. It is well-known and has been already observed that the Roman policy viewed with the utmost jealousy and distrust any association among its subjects; and that the privileges of private corporations, though formed for the most beneficial and harmless purpose, were bestowed with a very sparing hand. The religious assemblies of the christians who had separated themselves from the public worship appeared of a much less innocent nature." Here Gibbon sees the Solonic union as an innocent corporation: but when it became christianized it lost its innocence.

Pliny's letter to the emperor Trajan.

"Sir:—

It is my constant method to apply myself to you for the resolution of all my doubts; for who can better govern my dilatory way of proceeding, or instruct my ignorance? I have never been present at the examination of the christians, on which account, I am unacquainted with the points to be inquired into, and what, and how far, they are to be punished; nor are my doubts small, whether there is not a distinction to be made between the ages of the accused and, whether tender youth ought to have the same punishment with strong men; whether there be not room for pardon upon repentance, or whether it may not be an advantage to one who had been a christian, that he hath forsaken christianity; whether the bare name without any crimes, or the crimes adhering to that name, are to be punished. In the meantime I have taken this course about those who have been brought before me as christians. I asked them whether they were christians or not. If they confessed that they were christians, I asked them again and a third time, intermixing threats with the questions. If they persevered in their confession I ordered them to be executed;[19] for I did not but doubt, let their confession be of any sort whatever, that this positiveness and inflexible obstinacy deserved to be punished. There have been some of this mad sect whom I took notice of in particular as Roman citizens, that they might be sent to that city. After some time, as is usual in such examinations, the crime spread itself, and many more cases came before me. A libel was sent to me, though without an author, containing the names of many persons accused. These denied that they were christians now, or ever had been. They called upon the gods, and supplicated to your image which I caused to be brought to me for that purpose, with frankincense and wine; they also cursed Christ; none of which things as it is said can any of those who are really christians be compelled to do; so I thought it fit to let them go. Others of them who were named in the libel, said they were once christians but had ceased to be so; some

[19] The humane translator here remarks in a note: "Amazing doctrine! that a firm and fixed resolution of keeping a good conscience should be thought, without dispute, to deserve death."

three years, some many more and one there was that said that he had not been so these twenty years. All these worshiped your image and the images of your gods; these also cursed Christ. However they assured me that the main of their fault, or of their mistake, was this, that they were wont, on a stated day, to meet together before it was light and to sing a hymn to Christ, as to a god, alternately; and to oblige themselves by a sacrament or oath not to do anything that was ill, but that they would commit no theft, or pilfering, or adultery; that they would not break their promises, or deny what was deposited with them when it was required back again. After this it was their custom to depart and to meet again at a common but innocent meal which they had left off doing upon that edict which I published at your command and wherein I had forbidden any such conventicles.[20] These examinations made me think it necessary to inquire by torments what the truth was, which I did of two servant maids who were called deaconesses; but still I discovered no more than that they were addicted to a bad and extravagant superstition.[21] Hereupon I have put off further examination and have recourse to you, for the affair seems to be well worth consideration, especially on account of the number of those that are in danger; for these are many of every age, of every rank, and of both sexes, who are now and are hereafter likely to be called to account, and to be in danger; since this superstition is spread like a contagion, not only in cities and towns, but into country villages also, which there is still reason to hope may yet be stopped and corrected. To be sure, the temples which were almost forsaken begin already to be fre-

[20] Here Dr. Whiston, not understanding the meaning of the exact text "hetærias," which is precisely the trade union we are energetically proving that the christians planted into, makes the dismal and misleading blunder of calling them conventicles. The original of Pliny reads: "Quod ipsum facere desisse post edictum meum, quo secundum mandata tua hetærias esse vetueram." This mandate of Trajan was the revival of the old conspiracy law of Julius Cæsar. The hetæras were regular trade unions, as we have abundantly shown.

[21] The reader will here easily perceive that Pliny is giving Trajan the tenets of the regular eranos then flourishing throughout Asia Minor, especially numerous in Phrygia, and its satrapies, Bithynia and Pontus; the secret veil, the ἀγάπη, the high honor and truthfulness, the cœna sacra, the approved character, the ἀγαθός, εὐσεβής, ἅγιος, (See ch. vii.) and finally the office of deacon and deaconess through whom as humble waiters, the common tables were served Some of their secret membership, after conversion, had ceased to be christians, but they remained in the unions as before.

quented; and the holy solemnities which were long intermitted begin to be revived. The sacrifices begin to sell well everywhere, of which very few purchasers had of late appeared; whereby it is easy to suppose how great a multitude of men might be amended if place for repentance be admitted.[22]"

Now the national statute under which Pliny "ordered them to be executed," was none other than the old lex Julia which Trajan had revived to fit these cases. The punishment was either crucifixion or throwing them naked to famished wild beasts of the amphitheatre and invariably in the presence of a great crowd of sightseers who, if there was such a terrible scene announced, would pay large fees for admission, thus filling the pockets of the men who furnished the people with amusements. The craze for gratifying this inhuman and pitiless frenzy grew more and more insatiable until Honorius, a christian emperor, suppressed it by an edict.[23] The law Pliny and Trajan enforced was that of Julius Cæsar against the trade unions. This is borne out by Asconius,[24] Mommsen[25] and De Rossi,[26] also by Suetonius and Tacitus and it may be necessary to give some account of the origin and career of this early conspiracy law called the lex Julia.

Julius Cæsar's law against Solon's great scheme of organized labor, generally called Cæsar's conspiracy law, was enacted and went into force B.C. 58. It extended to Delos and indeed throughout pro-consular Rome.[27] It was particularly severe against the collegia, the thiasoi and the eranoi.[28] After restitutions by Clodius and his memorable conflict with Cicero, the law remained a dead letter until Trajan, who re-issued it in the rescript that

[22] Pliny, *Epist.*, X., no. 97.
[23] *Cod. Just.*, xi., tit, xliii., 1: "Cruenta spectacula in otio civili, et quiete domestica non placent quaproper omnino gladiatores esse prohibemus."
[24] Ascon., *In Cornel.*, p., 75: "Frequenter tum etiam cœtus factiosorum hominum, sine publica auctoritate malo publico fiebant........propter quod postea collegia sancta et pluribus legibus, sublata sunt." Vide Vol. I., p. 347.
[25] Momms., *De Coll. et Sodal, Rom.*, pp. 93-5.
[26] De Rossi, *Roma Sotterranea*, I., p. 102: "Plinio nella celebre epistola a Trajano tra gl' illegittimi convegnni de Cristiani prohibiti dalle antiche leggi e dai recenti editti contra le eterei non annouverà i loro funebre riti." etc. Here De Rossi fully admits, as he does later, that the trade unions called by the Greeks, ἑταιραι, were christianized organizations.
[27] Josephus, *Antiquities of the Jews*, XIV., x., 8, shows that the Hebrews were excepted.
[28] Suet., *In J. Cæs.*, 42: "Cæsar cuncta collegia praeter antiquitus constituta distraxit." " ...... ut sodaltates decuriative discederent." Vide Momms., *De Coll. et Sodal. Rom.*, p. 50, and his explanation.

Pliny obeyed, when he executed all the christians he could lay hands on if they would not curse Christ. Hadrian revived it again under a rescript of his own and caused the death of many more christians. But the most celebrated resuscitation of the lex Julia on record, that which caused it to be registered in the Digest, is in form of the well-known rescript of Septimius Severus.[29]

It appears that the subject of suppressing the unions had been brought to the attention of the Roman senate before this law of Cæsar was enacted; for it is certain that as early as B.C. 64 a measure was passed crippling them which Mommsen discusses as being motived by the propensity of the unions to become a political power by the votive franchise, which we think was a right and privilege accorded in the wording, now lost, of the original Solonic law.[30] This old law, on account of the secrecy of the poor strugglers, often temporarily fell into disuse only to be revived as a last pretext and we find Augustus, with all his mildness, issuing the earliest rescript.[31]

Having touched upon the old conspiracy law powerfully defended by Cicero and as valiantly fought by Clodius, which statute seems to have been the outcome if not the triumph of the Roman conquests, and shown the ground-work of the various rescripts which subsequent monarchs of Rome issued to drive the voting unions to the wall, we may return to the momentous letters.[32]

Trajan's epistle to Pliny, in reply:

"My Pliny;— You have taken the method which you ought in examining the causes of those that had been

[29] *Digest*, XLVII., *Tit.* xxii., i,. 1: "Mandatis principalibus praecipitur praesidibus provinciarum, ne patiantur esse (collegia) sodalitia, neve milites collegia in castris habeant; sed permittitur tenuioribus stipem menstruam conferre: dum tamen semel in mense coeant, ne sub praetextu hujusmodi illicitum collegium coeat; quod non tantum in urbe sed in Italia et in provinciis, locum habere, divus quoque Severus rescripsit.'

[30] Waltzing, *Hist. Corp. Prof.*, I., p. 177: "Aussi pensons-nous que la plupart des collêges d' artisans furent supprimés en l' an 64 comme contraires à la sûreté publique." and cites Mommsen, *De Col. et Sodal. Rom.*, p. 75; Drumann, *Arbeiter und Kommunisten*, etc., p. 155; Wallon, *Esclavage*, III., 97, and 460-1.

[31] Suet., *Aug.*, 32: "Plurimae factiones titulo collegii novi ad nullius non facinoris societatem coibant; igitur collegia praeter antiqua et legitima dissolvit."

[32] For a full account of Cicero and his war with Clodius, the powerful tribune who took sides with the unions and restored them to a temporary right to organize, and for the manner in which both lost their lives in the struggle, see Vol. I., pp. 422, 344, 363, 474.

accused as christians; for indeed no certain and general form of judging can be ordained in this case. These people are not to be sought, but if they are accused and convicted they are to be punished; but with caution, that he who denies himself to be a christian and makes plain that he is not, by supplicating to our gods, although he has been one formerly, may be allowed pardon on repentance. As for the libels sent without an author, they ought to have no place in any accusation whatever; for that would be a thing of very ill example and not agreeable to my reign." [33]

Almost at the same moment that Pliny received this rescript contained in the above letter from Trajan a fire broke out in the city of Nicomedia, which for want of a proper fire extinguishing department could not be repressed until great damage was done. Such work, controlled by the agoranomion or ædilship, a sort of board of public works under the official, political control, was nevertheless almost always performed by the trade unions. The law of the Twelve Tables held good in Rome, through the law of Solon, as well as at Athens, Asia Minor and Macedonia. Its old trade unions were largely employed by the state and by municipalities to do the public work, and this made them, in a certain degree, political; since they were, even in those early times, endowed with the right to vote. By referring to these statements the reader will readily perceive that the system redounded copiously, not only to the advantage of these workmen, but to the state direct; because the then organized mechanics and workmen scientifically and practically carried out the great system of government life.

Again, they were paid for all this under the general proverb that the government is the better boss, and so it is.[34] In Rome, Pompeii, as shown by great numbers of newly-found inscriptions, and in Asia Minor, especially the provinces of Bithynia and Pontus where Pliny was, this system prevailed; but doubtless owing to the previous persecutions, this Nicomedia was without the

---

[33] Whiston, in his *Translation of Josephus*, Lond., Chatto & Windus, Vol. II., pp. 604-6, *App.*, *Dissertation*, III.

[34] See Vol. I., pp. 381, 416, 495, 536, showing how municipal and government labor in vast amount was given over to the unions, and even the provisioning of the population. Indeed the supply of the great cities of provisions as well as the making of bridges was always done by them.

system, and in consequence suffered a great loss by the fire.

Pliny who had a practical insight, perceived that what was wanted was a union of firemen. There were great numbers of workmen desirous of joining the firemen's union and anxious to fall into line for the public good, as well as their own. The old conspiracy law of Julius Cæsar, however, stood in the way, and it was necessary to obtain permission for Pliny to organize such a union or hetæra by special word from the emperor.

Accordingly Pliny wrote a letter to Trajan asking permission to organize a needed union of firemen. He represented that only smiths, and other skilled workmen should be chosen as members and that he would himself see to it, that not more than a hundred and fifty be initiated.[35]

Mr. Danziger, who has recently written a valuable article for the Cosmopolitan on Ancient Trade Unions, mentions this circumstance, and we shall prefer his translations to our own. The letter of Pliny runs as follows:

"While traveling in a remote part of the province, I witnessed a conflagration at Nicomedia that destroyed many private residences and two public buildings, the Gerusi and the Isson, although a long square ran between the private and public buildings. The fire gained in destructiveness, partly on account of the strong wind and partly because of the inactivity of the populace. But the people could have done nothing had they desired to be of any assistance, there being no fire engine or buckets or any other of the utensils necessary to extinguish the flames.

"I have at once given orders for the purchase of fire engines and all other implements needed in a similar emergency. I now beg leave to suggest to you, my lord, the advisability of organizing a fire company, to consist of about a hundred and fifty members of the carpenters' guild. I would make it my business that none but artificers should be eligible as members, and that no one

[35] Pliny, *Epistle ad Trajan*, x., no. 33 *ap* Waltzing, *Hist. Corp. Prof.*, I., p. 159: "Aprés avoir parlé d' un incendie qui avait causé de grands ravages à Nicomédie, Pline ajoute ‘Tu, domine, dispice, an instituendum putes collegium fabrorum dumtaxat hominum CL. Ego attendam ne quis nisi faber recipiatur neve jure concesso in aliud utantur; nec erit difficile custodire tam paucos.'"

should misuse his membership. I think that such a small number of men, could easily be kept in order and in service."

The emperor Trajan replied:

"You have conceived an idea that we could organize a fire company in Nicomedia, the men to be of the carpenters' guild; you have seen similar organizations in other cities. We must bear in mind, however, that frequent disturbances in said cities caused by such corporations, have led some to regret their existence. Whatever might be the cause, aim or name of such unions, the danger of political agitation is always near. I should consider it, therefore, far better to spare no cost in ordering fire engines and such things as are necessary to quench a conflagration, and to remind the inhabitants of houses to lend a helping hand in time of need, and if necessary to compel the populace to assist rather than organize a guild with political possibilities."

Pliny, on reading this letter, appears to have at first considered it favorably, but on reflection he was reminded of the trouble which the christian hetæræ or unions had already caused and in it saw a monarch's refusal to allow such a society to be organized. His language is respectful, but terse and decided.[36] In terminating this letter which always amounted to something equivalent to a ukase, he advises Pliny to impress firemen into the service, but not to organize a trade union, intimating as his reason that they would "briefly" fall into the christian rut, dissent from paying tribute, cease to attend the sacrifices as before, and thus become rebels against the state, making themselves criminals liable to be punished by persecution and death. This accords with the wisdom of Gibbon who declares that at heart the emperors were kind in their reluctance to permit these bloody deeds; but that refusal to pay tribute as Jesus indirectly and ambiguously advised[37] and as, there-

---

[36] The original answer of Trajan to Pliny, *Epist.*, x., no. 34, runs: "Tibi quidem, secundum exempla complurium in mentem venit posse collegium fabrorum apud Nicomedenses constitui. Sed meminerimus provinciam istam et præcipue eas civitates ejusmodi factionibus esse vexatas. Quodcumque nomen ex quacumque causa dederimus iis qui in idem contracti fuerint... ....hetæriæque brevi fient. Satius itaque est comparari ea quæ ad coercendos ignes auxilio esse possint," etc. Here he plainly refers to christians who torment the unions with vexatious factions.

[37] Matth., xvii., 24: Jesus prevented Peter from paying tribute, meaning apparently the membership, on the ground that the children were free; xxii., 17; Luke, xxiii., 2: Τοῦτον εὕρομεν διαστρέφοντα τὸ ἔθνος καὶ κωλύοντα

fore, the christian tenets upheld, was a crime punishable with death under the law; and the duty of an emperor was to carry out the laws of the nation. This was all in perfect accord with the old pagan scheme of justice. Pliny's wisely projected organization of firemen for the city of Nicomedia was nipped in the bud, by the short-sighted jealousy of the monarch on the throne. Christianized or not, his society of skilled workmen, splendidly organized as they knew how to be, would have made their city safe from the ravages of fire. But the jealous Trajan, afraid of the christians and fearing that the members might not pay tribute to Cæsar, refused. Much that is otherwise bedimmed, is cleared up by these letters.

But there is still another statement among the Plinian letters which we have not yet seen — that of the "Amisos erani." The name eranos, like thiasos, is the type of the ancient Greek trade union. Wherever it occurs the archæologists concede that a true union existed under terms of the Solonic law of labor organization, and it is unmistakable. The city of Amisos was situated in Pontus, a division of the satrapy of Phrygia, being attached to Bithynia and was included in Pliny's jurisdiction as governor of Bithynia. Dr. Oehler cites an inscription, a fragment of which is legible, which appears to be the source of this veritable Plinian letter to Trajan. It is therefore of great importance, verifying our wonderful discovery that those early, indeed apostolic christians planted into the eranos.[38] Those reading the letter, which we have already quoted, informing the emperor that he had sent many christians to execution, perhaps thousands, will perceive that he speaks of some when put to the torture to force confession, admitted that they had been members twenty years before. This was confessing that this country had been peopled by christians from the middle of the reign of Domitian; but probably no doubt they had been there as early as Claudius and Peter, Paul and John.

Now the inscription cited by Dr. John Oehler is found

Καὶσαρι φόρους διδόναι, λέγοντα ἑαυτὸν Χριστὸν βασιλέα εἶναι. The general inculcations of Jesus were against carrying out the law demanding the payment of tribute.

[38] Oehler, *MSS.*, Amisos erani. Pliny, *Epist.*, 93 und 94, I. Jahrh. n. Chr.. "Eranos, Amisos." Source not given; see Orell., no. 1172.

to be as early as the first century. The eranos mentioned is likely to have been formed by the people expelled from Rome by Claudius, and had flourished for more than half a century. Under the cruel edict sent to Pliny by Trajan, which he acknowledges he had carried out thus disbanding the eranos to destroy the christians, he had produced fearful havoc among many innocently organized people who depended for their living upon their mutual reciprocity and support. To deprive them of the economies derived from union and mutual brother and sisterhood was in those days of terrible persecution almost coequal with starvation. From reading the letter Pliny wrote to Trajan almost begging him to let them reorganize, one sees that this officer's heart was touched. He beheld, especially at Amisos, little children in rags, their fathers and mothers thrown to wild beasts, their endeared association suppressed and no asylum or orphanage, whither to flee to find refuge.[39]

The rather grateful answer of Trajan sparingly gave him permission to reorganize them,[40] but evidently he felt that although this might ultimately heal some of the ghastly wounds he had been compelled to inflict, yet this was not quick enough to save the poor little ones already cast out to die; for he made them a bequest of a sum of money out of his private purse.

We quote this telling inscription[41] from Pontus reg-

[39] Pliny, *Epist.*, x., 92: ad Trajanum: "Amisenorum civitas libera et fœderata beneficio indulgentiæ tuæ legibus suis utitur. In hac datum mihi libellum ad eranos pertinentem his litteris subjeci, ut tu, domine, dispiceres quid et quatenus aut permittendum aut prohibendum putares."
[40] Pliny, *Epist.*, x., 93, Traj. ad Plinium: "Amisenos, quorum libellum epistolæ tuæ junxeras, si legibus istorum, quibus de officio fœderis utuntur, concessum est eranum habere, possumus quominus habeant non impedire, eo facilius, si tali conlatione non ad turbas et ad inlicitos cœtus, sed ad sustinendam tenuiorum inopiam utuntur. In ceteris civitatibus, quæ nostro jure obstrictæ sunt, res hujusmodi prohibenda est."
[41] Orell., *Inscr. Lat. Select.*. I., pp., 255-256, *Historia Literaria*, No. 1172: C. PLINIUS L. F. O. V. F. CAECILIUS ‖ AUGUR. LEGAT. PROC. PR. 1) PROVINCIAE PONT ....2) ‖ CONSULARI POTESTATE IN EAM PROVINCIAM ET 3) ...... ‖ IMP. CAESAR, NERVA TRAIANO. AUG. GERMAN 4) ....‖ CURATOR ALVEI TIBERIS ET RIPARUM. . ET ‖ PRAEF. AERARI. SATURNI. PRAEF. AERARI, MIL. ‖ QUAESTOR. IMP. SEVIR. EQUITUM . . ‖ TRIB. MILIT. LEG. III. GALLICAE ‖ X. VIR. STLITIB. IUDICAND. THERM. . . ‖ ADIECTIS IN ORNATUM HS CCC. AMPLIUS IN TUTELA HS CC T. F. I. . . ‖ — E. LIBERTOR. SUORUM NOMIN. HS. ‖ XVIII. LXVI. DCLVI. REI. . . ‖ INCREMENT. POSTEA AD EPULUM PLEB. URBAN. VOLVIT PERTIN . . . ‖ AMPLIUS DEDIT IN ALIMENT. PUEROR. ET PUELLAR. PLEB. URB. HS ‖ CCC. IN TUTELAM BYBLIOTHECAE HS C. — Mediolani. Grut. 454, 5. 1028, 3. Murat. 732, 1. accuratius ap. Zachar. *Exc. litt.,*

istering this gift, which speaks of the boys and girls of the poor families who were in want and showing that the good man was touched by the disastrous work of his own hand. So important is this inscription regarded that an author of the eighteenth century wrote a dissertation upon it which was published at Mantua in 1773, and contains all collectable information regarding it. The name of this author was C. Octavius Boarius.

"If they persevered in their confession, I ordered them to be executed." This is the significant statement of Pliny's celebrated letter to Trajan. We have preferred to give Whiston's rendering because he is the translator of Josephus, so calm, long-tried and classical that no one will question its glowing words.

How many did he order to execution, and what was the nature of that death? We have already seen that under the Roman law the punishment of death for the lowly and poor was either the ignominious cross or the still more hideous one of being stripped, on days of the public festivities and thrown to the starved lions, tigers and serpents of the amphitheatre. Pliny is silent regarding these horrors.

But the actual numbers thus killed by him is a subject which has caused no little speculation among thoughtful people. Pliny is also silent here. On the massacre of Diocletian for the same crime in the same country, Lactantius stingily says, "great numbers." Now comes the profound archæologist Dr. Ramsay, who, searching for their stone monuments there, traces the mementos of a vast population with epitaphs and chiselings of a multitude of forms down to the fatal date of that massacre, and strikes an end of them so definitively, that he is forced to the shocking conclusion that on that fatal night the whole population, embracing a large portion of Asia Minor met a horrible and violent death.

Who knows then, but that Pliny's cold executions covered a population. Certain it is that he was him-

p. 98., cuius typum exhibemus.   Omnes celebratissimae huius inscript. recensiones collegit C. Oct. Boarius: *De Plinii Secundi Testamentaria Inscript.*
— *Dissertatio.* Mantuae 1773, 4. nunquam mihi visa.
1) PRO. PR. Murat. melius.   Paullo ante O. V. F. est; OV-*Fentina tribu.*   2) Supple: Ponti *et Bithyniae*, Marini *Atti.* p. 758.   3) et *in Thraciam ab.* id.   3) Germanico *Dacico missus.* id,

self deeply distressed; and it all proves that it was possible in those days of unscrupulous tyranny, to cover the earth with blood, while the historians, glad to shield themselves behind the buttress of acquiescence, obsequiousness and flattery, allowed their pen to perjure itself as a suborned instrument of darkness and falsehood.

But the striking and remarkable point to be here recorded is the fact that Pliny's conscience forced him to be the originator of the great system of asylums, charities and orphanages. Before this bloody persecution which took place at the early beginning of the second century, there were no charitable institutions of any kind. Under the great Solonic law, on which those christians planted, everybody had work and plenty, and no begging, no charity, no want existed. Pliny had killed out and cut down those staunch elements of self-support and his wretched conscience constrained him to make the original proffer of money from his private purse, which proved the foundation of the vast eleemosynary and beggarly system of charitable institutions, which now cover the earth with shame.

CHAPTER XVIII.

ORIGINS OF THE HOUSE OF THE LORD.

HOUSE OF THE LORD—A Phenomenal Institution—Authorized in the Twelve Tables—Secret and Invisible Union—Meetinghouse, Temple, Refuge, Public Kitchen and Hospital Combined—Mary's Grotto, the Refuge, in One—Infant Jesus Shielded in It—Proof—Herod's own Son one of the Slaughtered—Macrobius Quoted—House Took Form of the Prytaneum—Always Belonged to the Unions—Many Inscriptions as Evidence—Harmony and Success of the Centuries—Many Bible Characters Now Found to be Crowned and Garlanded Lords of Such Houses— Crescens—Narcissus—Titus—Stephen—Crispus—Tychicus, Paul's Courier—Name in Two Inscriptions—Onesimus—Ramsay on Occultism of The Secret Veil—Philemon—Epaphros—Papias' Lost Book—Explained the Economical and Ignored Paul—CIG 3865—Three Celebrated Names, Papias, Trophemus, Tychicus—MM. Ramsay and Perrot—Their Splendid Find of a Union of Masons with Tatias and Onesimus—The Union's Rules Against Quarrelling—Their Own Inscriptions Found—The Enigmatical Door of Jesus—No Quarrel of Paul With Immediate Companions of Jesus—Full and Lasting Agreement at Jerusalem —Wrangles of Imagination—Metonyms of Important Members on Conversion—Pro-Consular Spies—Luke as a Member—Important Inscription—Also Called Nicias—Taught in Schools of Tyrannus—Ashes of Both Lately Found in Columbarium—Strange Tablet—Quoted Verbatim—Cinerary Urns Preserved Deep in Hypogeum—Description of Find— Greek of Franz Quoted—Though a Hot Communist, Paul's Substantial Friend — Gerusia — Mistake about It—Now known to be Another Name for Union—Red Dyers' Heroon to Menisippus—Luke Proved to be an Ambassador from Rome—Probably Exiled—His Colony—Epitaph of Luke at Tlos—Remarkable Inscription of Philip—Law of Compulsory Inscriptions—Forced amid Dangers to Chisel Philip— Inscription Agrees with Eusebius — Hierapolis — Similar Trouvaille of Avircius Marcellus—Epitaph of the Mariner Xeuxis—His Sixty Voyages—Belonged to Union of Sailors —Avircius Speaks of the Thirteen-Years' Cessation From Persecution—This Lacuna Cleared Up—Paraphrase of the Lithoglyph—The Plutonium—Complete Transcript—Jason of Thessalonica—Bridge-builders at Rome.

WE have hitherto given an occasional mention, but no adequate analysis of the phenomenal House of the

Lord. Long before the Advent this institution existed among the ancient lowly. It was the direct outcome of the great law. That itself, ordained it. This great ancient statute, destined to live forever, holy, religious and just, distinctly specifies in one of its fragmental clauses,[1] in which *kurion einai* occurs, that in each trade union there should be one responsible person who was to be answerable for the whole brotherhood. The outside public law knew nothing of the deftly invisible brotherhood secretly organized in an inapproachable nook. It specified that one individual representing the members alone having the direction within and without should be ever visible, and personally responsible for the whole. Should a riot or turmoil occur, the officers of the law did not immediately arrest the rioters themselves, but they approached the kurios, who was obliged to call a council of the inner brotherhood, and work with the official authorities of the state as a representative of the secret and invisible union. This man was the kurios. In the Roman tongue he was the quinquennalis. But we are now in the Greek-speaking world. Here he was the kurios, cure, high priest or lord.

The little temple, such as each trade union owned as a possession, situated on a plot of land, which we know by the inscriptions contained a graveyard, was at once a shrine with its altar, a school house and a church. As a church, it was not only a place of worship of their tutelary divinities, but a place of amusement and entertainment. Here were enjoyed the frequent communal meals, to which the entire membership resorted to partake of the plentiful, common bounties. No want, no suffering, no starvation, no charity of the eleemosynary order existed, whereat the deserving are humiliated to the degradation of accepting proffers of the compassionate. The Solonic dispensation knew no charities. Every member was furnished with work. Every one *must* work, otherwise go without. Every member was especially employed for this object, and if he or she secured by this labor more or less, so long as it covered the monthly assessment, it made no difference; they were all alike in this elysian abode, and all enjoyed freely together.

[1] *Digest*, LXVII., xxii., 4.

A SPECIAL PROVISION OF SOLON'S LAW.   605

The House of the Lord, then was the poor man's temple of ancient times, and was the natural result of the old, original law of Solon, which had been sanctioned by Numa, and stipulated the functions and responsibilities of the lord or kurios.

Now what sort of an establishment was the House of the Lord?[2] In addition to its being a meeting house, a retreat for fugitives,[3] a cœnobium for the common meals and a large home-hall in general for the brothers, it was also a pharmacopœia and sometimes furnished with beds and accomodations for the sick. The humble grotto-like appartment for Mary's accouchment was one of these in its crude and ancient form, being both a stall and booth, and it had a brotherhood; for Origin's plausible story of the secret initiation of the three by the wise men makes this certain. Nothing would do but this quick initiation into the secret brotherhood so that they could take them off to Egypt by night, as it were, on the "under-ground railroad;" for the edict issued to assassinate the babes was all-sweeping and so unexceptionally carried out that it even cut the innocent throat of Herod's own son![4]

This curative function was adopted by the christians in the very earliest times. They did not follow a highly ethical plan of life laid down by some of the gnostics afterwards. They simply endorsed the modes and practices of the Solonic unions. They converted the unions to their own Jesus or Messiah; were taken body and soul into their temple and into the membership, and en-

  [2] Ramsay, *Cities and Bishoprics of Phrygia*, II., p. 357, in addition to our own descriptions assures us that it had a medical attachment: "At Dionysopolis we saw abundant proof that Asklepias, Dionysos and Apollos types on coins like these express merely different aspects of one ultimate divinity, not different gods. In ordinary life the medical power of the god was naturally the one most frequently appealed to; and we may feel certain that, as at the hieron of Men Karou, a medical establishment was attached to the temple." etc.
  [3] See Vol. I., pp. 247, asylum of refuge of the Palikoi; 143-4, note 34, asylum of the castle of Sunion where the runaway slaves received succor; 257: "Forest asylum amid the roar of waters and the gloom and fumes of sulphur." Such a refuge for the poor in distress appears to have been peculiar to the Solonic institution and we know that the law provided for this refuge, in the shape of the ancient temple; for as it was dedicated to one of the protecting goddesses or gods who held tutelage over the inmates no one ever dared to touch a refugee so long as he remained within the enclosure.
  [4] See *Index* referring to note quoting Macrobius. This remarkable statement of Macrobius—short and irrelevant as it is; merely anecdotal and in ilustration of another trifling matter—is an invaluable coincidence to prove the rescue of Jesus a historical event. Macrobius is known as high authority.

606   THE HOUSE OF THE LORD.

dorsed and all agreed to conform to the aged rules of the revered statute of the Prytaneion. This is fully acknowledged by the accurate Mosheim,[5] and we now proceed to give the reader an overwhelming array of proof, believing it best for this purpose not to adhere too closely to consecutive and chronological arrangement, but to choose such examples from a large mass before us as well as secure the best effect, and borrowing our statements from every geographical source in pro-consular Rome, in anecdotal form, from A.D. 33 to 300. This includes the story of the Crispins.

An almost invaluable evidence for our argument that the early christians planted into, and owed their phenomenal success to their great and all-prevailing labor brotherhoods, is found in an inscription for which we are indebted to Dr. Ramsay, and which we here quote in a note, together with its sister inscription confirming that both are purely christian, although much disagreement exists.[6]

The learned Dr. Ramsay, on page 549, fully admits that this is a trade union; that it was christian; that it is from near the city of Laodicia, accredited to Heropolis, and that it was one of the benefit associations under the lex collegia tenuiorum, which, though he can seemingly understand nothing of what we are proving, and what he himself is inadvertently proving, yet it is exceedingly probable that it is the very union to which Lydia belonged and for which she was acting agent in the sale of its wares at Philippi, when Paul converted her.

The few terminal lines, of No. 411, here quoted, show that the carpet-weavers likewise were connected, in the

[5] Mosheim, II. Cent., Pt. ii., Sect. 5, confesses that the christians adopted heathen forms of organization, including initiations and mysteries. Dr. Cagnat, *Vie Contempor.*, Jan. 1896, goes farther and declares these organizations were none other than the unions.
[6] Ramsay. *Cit. Bish. Phryg.*, I., p. 545, no. 411; ref. to Wagner, *Revue de l' Instruction Publique en Belgique, Nouv., Série.* xi., pp. 1 f; *Philologus*, xxxii., p. 379. The inscr. reads: "Ποπλίου Αἰλίου Γλύκωνος ——— Ἀμιανοῦ τοῦ Σελεύκου· ἐν ᾗ κηδευθήσονται αὐτὸς καὶ γυνὴ αὐτοῦ......... καὶ τὰ τεκνα αὐτῶν· ἑτέρῳ δὲ οὐδενὶ ἐξέσται κηδευθῆναι· κατέδωκεν δὲ καὶ τῇ σεμνοτάτῃ προεδρίᾳ τῶν πορφυροβάφων στεφανωτικοῦ δὴν· διακόσια πρὸς τὸ δίδοσθαι ὑπὸ τῶν τόκων ἑκάστῳ. NMZ ἐν τῇ ἑορτῇ τῶν Ἀζύμων· ὁμοίως κατέλιπεν καὶ τω συνεδρίῳ τῶν καιροδαπιστῶν στεφανωτικοῦ δὴν. ρ´ ἑκατὸν πεννήκοντα ἀπὸ....a line lost....ἐν τῇ ἑορτῇ Πεντηκοστῆς. No. 412, which we need not give proves 411 to be a christian union of dyers and carpet-makers. It is in vol. I., and is no. 58, p. 119
[7] See Oehler, *Eranos Vindobonensis* pp. 277, 279: "So hat die προέδρια der πορφυροβάφοι in Hieropolis von M. Aur. Diodorus 300 Denare erhalten mit bestimmter Widmung, Le Bas, III., 1687."

same brotherhood with dyers. A large number of these unions existed there on the Lycus River, in what was called the Pentapolis. This was a tract of territory coursed by the Meander and its tributary, the Lycus, and on which stood five celebrated cities, three of which were in sight of each other—Hierapolis, Laodicia and Colossæ. Laodicia was one of the cities of the seven churches. As the epigraphical critics advance in a scientific conception of these stone relics they open up surprising words of acknowledgment that the presbyters of the Ignatian epistles are none other than presbyters of the unions.[8] And so indeed, it will be easily seen that all the officers and all the members were alike in name and function; the unions holding tenaciously to their old plan of mutual economies while the evangelists of the Word of promise labored for the spiritual. Under this arrangement there was perfect harmony and amazing growth and success for a period of three centuries.

Archæologists discover that the celebrated Crescens, founder of the church at Vienne, a few miles below Lyons, on the Rhone, was one of these Greek "responsible and crowned directors." He was merely a slave who by a remarkable natural ability exercised in an intelligent way, became a freedman, in which social estate we know him. Paul[9] mentions him as the man sent to Gaul while Titus went to Dalmatia, and Demas, now known to have been Democrates,[10] forsook him entirely. But let us follow Crescens. This strange character appears in the inscriptions, and the excavations of De Rossi, and the researches into the columbarium at Rome. Crescens must have been a distinguished and accomplished personage. He was a Hellenistic Greek and

---

[8] Ramsay, *Cit. Bish. Phryg.*, II., p. 548: "The συνέδριον τῆς γερουσίας, or τῶν πρεσβυτέρων, CIG, 3912, 3916, 3417, 3222, is analagous to the συνέδριον τῆς προεδρίας τῶν πορφυροβάφων—a unique expression which seems to mean 'the Council of Presidence,' ie., Proedroi of the society of Porphyrobaphoi. The term πρόεδρος τῆς ἐκκλησίας was used of the Bishop; and the Council of Presbyters, συνέδριον τοῦ ἐπισκόπου, Ignatius, Philad., 8, might be termed προεδρία." Dr. Ramsay here appends the following suggestive words in note 2: "Compare *Magn.*, 6, συνέδριον τῶν ἀποστόλων, *Magn.*, 13, στεφάνου τοῦ πρεσβυτέριου. In *Apostolic Constitutions*, II., 28, presbyters are σύμβουλοι τοῦ ἐπισκόπου καὶ τῆς ἐκκλησίας στέφανος." Thus the old crowned κύριος or responsible overseer directing this union of dyers provided for in the Solonic law, holds good in the church without change of name, degree or form.

[9] *II Tim.*, iv., 10: Δημᾶς γὰρ με ἐγκατέλιπεν, ἀγαπήσας τὸν νῦν αἰῶνα, καὶ ἐπορεύθη εἰς Θεσσαλονίκην· Κρήσκης εἰς Γαλατίαν, Τίτος εἰς Δαλματίαν. κ.τ.λ.

[10] See our account of the affair, *supra*, Chap. xvi., Section *Tiberius*.

hailed from Phrygia in the Pentapolis.¹⁰ The inscription given below plainly shows that Crescens was an official of the emperor at Lugdunum, now Lyons. Whatever the date of the inscription, this man was as early as Claudius and he must have been sent to Lyons on duty as a public officer and in this was like Narcissus, who, because of his abilities, acted in a political capacity for the emperor, while at the same time working for the membership of his kuriakos or church. Prof. O. Hirschfeld correctly finds that Crescens was an important member of the domus Augustalis. This clears up the whole mystery and is proven by a number of inscriptions besides this which we quote for Phrygia, in under-ground Rome.

Now while in Phrygia, Crescens was a steward at the military camps. So says the inscription; he was in a similar capacity at Lyons and Vienne,¹² and he became procurator castrensis, "doing duty in fit measure, administering to our affairs. And we erect this statue, in the faith of final resurrection, to said Crescens, the emancipated slave of Zosimus."¹³ These mentions and those of De Rossi and Gorius are not of the Crescens who later suffered under Decius, but the same Crescens living under Claudius, mentioned by Paul.

The fact that Crescens was attached to the domus Augustalis settles all cavil as to his being a member of a union, for these were the unions themselves; and as he was a courier who like Tychicus, carried letters, he may have worked for Paul in that capacity. Crescens, according to De Rossi, was buried near Pudens in the cemetery of Priscilla, which is in the Via Salaria Nova.

¹¹ Ramsay, *Cit. Bish. Phryg.*, II., p. 704, no. 641, reads: "'Η Β. καὶ ὁ δ. ἐτείμασεν, Μ, Αὐρ. Σεβαστῶν ἀπελεύθερον Κρήσκεντο, ἐπίτροπον φρυγίας καὶ ἐπίτροπον Καστρῆσιν, ἐν παντὶ καιρῷ εὐεργετήσαντα τὴν πόλιν ἡμῶν. τοῦ ἀνδριάντος τὴν ἀνάστασιν ποιησαμένου. Μ. Αὐρ. Σεβαστῶν ἀπελευθέρου Σωσίμου." CIG, 3888.

¹² *II Tim.*, iv., 10: ....ἐπορεύθη εἰς Θεσσαλονίκην· Κρήσκης εἰς Γαλατίαν, Τίτος εἰς Δαλματίαν.

¹³ De Rossi, *Rom. Sott.*, I., p. 192, giving the inscription found in the Cœmeteria Priscillæ. Clodia γ Ispes γ Clodi γ Crescens. Apostolic Age. The letters are colored with the never-fading red minium or Cinnabar. Again: "L. Clodius Crescens, Clodiæ Victoriæ, Conjugi incomparabili," showing that these freedmen married in spite of the law. But Gorius, *Mon. Sive. Columbar.*, p, 168, *epitaph*, cxliv., finds that he might have been a courier, and adjoins Tiberius Claudius, which was not his name, only his title, because a servant of the emperor: "Ti. Claudius Crescens dicitur cursor. Actes Libertæ, id est Claudiæ." etc. Fabretti, p. 350, no, 33; 333, no. 497; Gor., 107, show an *epitaph* of the same Crescens, in the Columbarium, remarking: "Ita quoque Creses legitur in alio lapide, in memoriam liberti Claudii," and explains the variation in the spelling.

There appear evidences that these masters of unions who were, in Rome the crowned quinquennales, and in the Hellenic countries the crowned and honored kurioi or responsible agents under the law were known as the lords of the business house for the conduct of manufacture in the unions; and thus Crescens was another lord of the House.

Titus was another and similar crowned lord and he is made historic by the mentions of him in the New Testament and several corroboratory inscriptions. Any person reading the Second Epistle to the Corinthians, eighth chapter, eleventh to the twenty-fourth verses, will perceive that what is here spoken of Titus is to the effect that he was a member and that, like Stephen, he was engaged in transporting supplies of provisions from one place to another. The doctrine inculcated in these significant verses is that of socialism. Titus, though faithful and influential, was a very mysterious character. It is consistent with our scheme to assume that he was another lord of the House. There can be no doubt of it, as we study the evidence. He is acknowledged to be the Justus, who at Corinth, gave Paul his "House," when the synagogue was refused him.[14]

The Cyclopedia of Biblical literature unwittingly proves Titus to have been an officer whose mission was to work out the economic functions of this evangelical work in which Paul was engaged. The English translation, for some reason, neglects to give the true name of Titus to the episode of Paul's plant in the little House "joined hard to the synagogue," after he had been refused admission to it. This convenient House was the temple of one of the many unions at Corinth, then a hive of organized industries. Paul took up his abode in this kuriakos, worked and preached there, and the same became the church of Corinth. The church could not have been the synagogue referred to because

---

[14] *Acta Apost.*, xviii., 7: Καὶ μεταβὰς ἐκεῖθεν ἦλθεν εἰς οἰκίαν τινὸς ὀνόματι Ἰούστου, σεβομένου τὸν θεόν, οὗ ἡ οἰκία ἦν συνομοροῦσα τῇ συναγωγῇ. Κρίσπος δὲ ὁ ἀρχισυνάγωνος ἐπίστευσε τῷ κυρίῳ σὺν ὅλῳ τῷ οἴκῳ αὐτοῦ, καὶ πολλοὶ τῶν Κορινθίων ἀκούοντες ἐπίστευον καὶ ἐβαπτίζοντο. But in this St. James rendering there appears a seemingly dishonest tergiversation; for the new translation rectifies this statement from the original Greek Manuscript, which reads: ἦλθεν εἰς οἰκίαν τινὸς ὀνόματι Τίτου Ἰουστοῦ, κ.τ.λ. clearly showing that Justus was Titus, ie., Titus the Just.

its membership was Gentile, while that of the synagogue was Jew, and they persecuted and would have overwhelmed and driven him and the band of brothers from Corinth, had Seneca's brother, the major, not interfered. The Crispus, who took Paul into the little House hard by, was Titus himself, and the reported name, Justus, was only an adjective qualifying him as Titus the Just.[15]

This Titus was a Hellenistic Greek and not a Jew. He was very active in the spread of the Word of promise and is supposed to have traveled a good deal for the cause. The rational view is that he was one of the crowned lords or responsible managers for a guild, doing business in those parts and that he used his influence wisely in the spread of the new doctrine among the converted unions. He is now supposed to have ended his life in Crete.[16]

This senseless tergiversation which should rank with the pious frauds, and is excused only in the "harmonistic renderings," which mollify a lie into a policy, is outdone in several places where the lord is turned into a God.[17] This is precisely what we should have looked for, coming as it did, from the prelates who had ruled out Clement, and the Logia of Matthew, because they treated the real, original, economic christianity.

From a point of view of our argument the name Tychicus is one of the most remarkable as evidence of the christian plant into the Solonic brotherhoods and the economical uses to which christianity turned the kurios and the House of the Lord. We have just seen

---

[15] "Τιτοῦ 'Ιουστοῦ." Cf. Smith, Bib. Dict., pp. 3266-3270, who, for some unseen cause, fails to admit this, though, at the same time, showing that he is endorsing a bad or perhaps dishonest translation from the original, which has Τιτοῦ. It should read: "And he departed and went into a certain man's house named Titus the Just, one who had been converted." Titus was not a Jew, but a Hellenistic Greek; both parents being Gentiles. He was an advocate and doer of the economic. He was a worker. He sided with Paul afterwards in putting down the Corinthian abominations. See our careful statement pointed to in index. Titus made it his great mission to relieve wants; Smith, Bib. Dict., p. 3267, and managed most of the contributory labor, lending aid to Judea, etc.

[16] Paskley, Travels in Crete, I., 6, 175 "On the old site of Gortyna is a ruined church of ancient and solid masonry, which bears the name of St. Titus, and where service is yet celebrated." Titus was in close organization with Paul and Barnabas.

[17] Critical readers, such as scholarly ministers, may find plenty of instances where κύριος is rendered by θεός. The tergiversation is harmonistic with the church but not with christianity, for often the word κύριος is thus changed from its original meaning as a man directing the union and actually has no reference to God whatever.

that Crescens, instead of being as some commentators imagine, a personage of high estate and an officer in the optimist ranks, was a slave or freedman and also a courier for the army of Rome; but at the same time a man of high estate in the plebeian fraternities. Exactly the same can be said of both Tychicus and his friend Onesimus who acted as carriers for Paul's letters. The three men worked together. Onesimus was the slave of Philemon. He procured his emancipation probably through the coöperation of the guild or union over which Philemon presided, in compliance with the aged methods of such organizations.

To Tychicus is accredited the work of distributing, and even of helping to write the Pauline epistles.[18] As a matter of fact, however, he did not write them. The particular one here meant is the epistle to the Ephesians. We begin by referring to the correct estimate made by Dr. Ramsay regarding the danger of attending to such work. All through pro-consular Rome there were at that time military spies ferreting out the christians of whom the Romans were becoming very jealous. Many had already been driven out of Rome and it was known that such exiles were settling down among the unions of Asia Minor.[19] M. Le Blant has also seen with a keen insight that in order to avoid the searching espionage both the unions and the christians had to live under a set of signs and a system of occultism or they might at any moment be arrested. To read their inscriptions correctly, as they are still found, the epigraphists have worked out a full set of their signs and symbols whereby to analytically do it and thus distinguish whether they were christian or pagan. A fine illustration of this tendency on the part of the christians to outwit the spies, is recorded in the Body of Greek Inscriptions of the Berlin Academy of Sciences,[20]

[18] *Coloss., ad fin.:* " Πρὸς Κολοσσαεῖς ἐγράφη ἀπὸ 'Ρώμης δια Τυχικοῦ καὶ 'Ονησίμου." On this, see Lightfoot, *Coloss.,* pp. 37 and 231-2, text and note.
[19] Ramsay, *Cit. Bish. Phryg.,* II., pp., 488-90, and in many other places; CIG., 3857 t. "'Ο δεῖνα ἢ οἱ δεῖνες τῷ δεῖν. καί Δόμνῃ γονεῦσι γλυκοτάτοις μνήμης χαριν." This epitaph wants to hide from the police and the outside world, the fact that its tablet stands for a membership of some brotherhood, whose trade and whose list of names, together with their beloved manager, a female, no person is permitted to know except the survivors themselves.
[20] CIG. 2857 t. Ramsay, *Cit. Bish. Phryg.,* II., p. 489, in showing their secret and hiding propensities, cites CIG. 3857 t, L.W. 780, which appears to be an ordinary inscription as at first published. It reads: Εὔφρων κε Τατ

and admirably exhibited by Dr. Ramsay, who explains that they resorted to the occultism of the secret veil and splendidly succeeded in fooling the sneaking spies. The statement bearing such information as is given in our note is unsatisfactory; but fortunately M. Perrot made a more searching examination of the stone and observed a cross at the top marking the religion of the deceased, while masons' tools lay inscribed at the bottom of the stone, indicating the occupation. We then observe that Euphron and Onesimus are christian names; while Tatias and Asclepiades, though only ordinary pagan names, are often used by christians. In Gaul, M. Le Blant mentions a number of slabs[21] and endeavors with a good deal of success, to work out their system of hiding, both in life and death.[22] In further illustration of this hiding, necessitated by great dangers attending and always threatening these poor downtrodden people, we may here give as examples, the styles of monogram and other blinds which the christianized unions used.

With our description of Tychicus the news and letter carrier, we shall have to carry with us Onesimus, the runaway slave. He had left Philemon of Colossæ, escaped to Rome, had fallen in with the now imprisoned Paul which is A.D. 62, during the reign of Nero. Their province of a post office function was Asia Minor. Phœbe, a woman, carried his letter to the Romans from Cenchrea near Corinth: Titus and Luke did it for the Corinthians and Epaphroditus did the work for his letter to the Philippians. The utmost secrcy was especially necessary at this moment.[23] Paul, who for a

ιὰς Ἀσκληπιάδῃ τῷ τέκνῳ κὲ ἑαυτοῖς ζῶντες. Ὀνήσιμος [καὶ ....] this lacuna included the names of the members of which we are unfortunately deprived. There was fear of the police. Then the inscription continues: τοὺς ἑαυτῶν γονεῖς κὲ τὸν ἀδελφὸν ἐτείμησαν. So again in the CIG., 3857ʳ, Δάδας φιλέρωτος καὶ ἡ δεῖνα αὐτοῖς ἔτι ζώντες καὶ Τυχικὸς καὶ Ἀμμιὰ τὰ τέκνα αὐτῶν· καὶ Δημήτριος ἀδελφῷ, καὶ Ζωτικὴ καὶ Ἀταλάντη τέκνῳ μνήμης χάριν· Ἥλιος λατύπος, Τυχικὸν ἀδελφὸν ἐτεημησε. In the same Book of Greek Inscriptions, no. 3857ᶜ: Τατιὰς Τυχικοῦ τῷ δεῖνι ἀνδρί. It has about the same explanation as for 3857ᵇ, ie., it belongs in the same place.
[21] Le Blant, *Inscr. de la Gaule*, Vol., II., pp. 197, 255, 146 283, 211; Vol. I., p. 365, showing his scrutiny in working out these secrets.
[22] CIG., 3857ᵗ, reads: "a. Εὔφρων καὶ Τατιὰς Ἀσκληπιάδῃ τῷ τέκνῳ καὶ ἑαυτοῖς ζῶντας· b. Ὀνήσιμος .... τοὺς ἑαυτῶν γονεῖς καὶ τὸν ἀδελφὸν ἐτείμησαν."
[23] We cannot better illustrate this significant though little known method of covering the agitators' propaganda and screening them from danger, than by presenting Dr. Ramsay's carefully elaborated explanation in a full page plate. *Cities and Bishoprics of Phrygia*, Vol. II., pp. 526-7: 371. (S. 1882 1887). Ishekli. CIG. 3902⁰, Cumont, 137. Ἀυρ. Μηνόφιλος β´ τοῦ Ἀσκληπιάδου

HOW THEY OUTWITTED THE ROMAN SPIES. 613

short time enjoyed some favor with Nero, had made friendship with the great and gifted Seneca destined to die under this monarch's jealous rage, was at this moment losing hope and had but a few more weeks to live. The two letter carriers performed their work faithfully.

But how did they do it? This is the important question. They could not have gone forth boldly on the high roads with a considerable bundle of papyrus or of pergamen in their hands which written in plain Greek, would have cost them dearly if detected. Even to this day such a carrier in that same part would be arrested unless furnished with a strong passport. How did they get their passports? They were both of lowly degree, Onesimus, nothing but a runaway slave; the government rangers were constantly looking for and arresting such. Nothing of the kind. Under the great Solonic statute there was, as we have abundantly shown, one powerful officer representing each trade union, eight of which were enumerated, and each one so specified having a number of kindred trades. Those men represented the valuable industries of the country and each of them was honored with splendid crowns, and exempt from most of the manual work, but legally responsible before the police and the law for everything his union did. They were the celebrated immunes of the ancient world.[24] It is thoroughly recorded that the immunes under the great Solonic dispensation were exempt from military duty and that they were accorded many privileges.

Dr. Lightfoot, after remarking that Tychicus was charged by Paul to deliver his messages in Asia Minor

βουλευτὴς κατεσκεύασα τὸ ἔμπροσθεν σύνκρουστον ἑαυτῷ κὲ Ἀπολλωνίῳ υἱῷ, κὲ γυναικὶ αὐτοῦ Μελτίνῃ, κὲ Μηνοφίλῳ κέ Ἀσκληπιάδῃ ἐγγόνοις, κὲ οἷς αὐτὸς περιὼν Βουληθῇ. Εἰ δέ τις ἐπιχειρήσει θεῖναι ἕτερον, ἔσται αὐτῷ πρὸς τὸν Ἰησοῦν χριστόν.

[24] Gorius, *Mon. sive Columb.*, p. 65, in quoting the inscription of Tyrannus, the emancipated slave who during the reign of Claudius was an immune who gave and dedicated the columbarium: "Tyrannus Verna. Tab. apparitor sacris omnium immunis." etc. On the quality of the immune, Gorius remarks: " ... . ac propria significatio hujus vocis immunis afferatur. Neque enim ea nunc primum prodit in lucem; quum in vetustis inscriptis saxis, plures immunes facti legantur verum in quo consistat immunitas libertis data, de qua hactenus viri docti siluere, profecto haud facile dictu est. Immunitas igitur duplici modo considerari potest; vel in quantum ad rem civilem; vel ad rem sacram; plures vero sunt causæ quibus variis personis dari potuit....... Immunitas quoque dabatur non modo Provinciis, municipiis, coloniis, magistratibus, collegiis, verum etiam viris optime de iisdem meritis; vel pro aliquo temporis spatio, vel perpetuo."

or proconsular Asia, says: "The two names, Tychicus and Onesimus occur in proximity in the Phrygian inscriptions found at Altentash, Benisoa."[25] Now, if the churches of proconsular Asia were planted in the eranoi as claimed, Tychicus, as well as Onesimus after his enfranchisement, could have been very important and responsible kurioi, not only at Colossæ and the towns on the Lycus, but all over Asia Minor, and so come into the inscriptions of the masons, dyers and others.

Our suspicion that the House of Philemon, the reputed owner of the slave Onesimus was not a private one but the temple of a guild, is strongly borne out by the fact that he had been converted under some occult circumstances by Paul; but as this apostle refused to have anything whatever to do with the economic side of the movement, carefully confining himself to the spiritual although obliged to use, plant into and receive sustenance from these unions, we are left quite in the dark. It has been shown that these secret societies, besides furnishing their members, male and female, bond and free with food at a common table, clothing, work, housing and entertainment, likewise secured the enfranchisement of their slave members, long before and long after the Advent. Philemon was a responsible director of some powerful guild or union at Colossæ. He was lord of a household,[26] and certainly in the capacity in which we find him, a great man. Nothing can be plainer than that he was invested with this power by the law, making his dignity, "kuriou," under the Solonic dispensation as seen in the fragment preserved in the Digest.

Another great character who must likewise necessarily go along with us is the celebrated Papias, whose book, the Expositio Oraculorum, is completely lost. Every evidence extant shows that this lost work must

---

[25] Böck., CIG., 3857 r, "Δάδας Φιλέρωτος καὶ ἡ δεῖνα αὐτοῖς ἐτὶ ζῶντες καὶ Τυχικὸς καὶ Ἀμμία τὰ τέκνα αὐτῶν· Καὶ Δημήτριος ἀδελφῷ, καὶ Σωτικῇ καὶ Ἀταπάντη τέκνῳ μνήμης χάριν. Ἥλιος λατύπος, Τυχικὸν ἀδελφὸν ἐτείμησε," More than a dozen inscriptions already found at Altentash Benisoa, all representing unions, show that this place was a hive of industry.

[26] Lightfoot, Colloss.: τῃ κατ' οἶκον σοῦ ἐκκλησίᾳ. "Philemon had placed his house," ie. οἰκία, honored and enlarged in the N. T. with the title of ἐκκλησία, "at the disposal of the christians at Colossæ for their religious and social gatherings." But this very House was standing and also probably the temple and out-houses and the grave-yard, when Theodoret wrote, about A.D. 440: "Πόλιν δὲ εἶκε (ὁ Φιλήμων) τὰς Κολόσσας. Καὶ ἡ οἰκία δὲ αὐτοῦ μέχρι τοῦ παρόντος μεμένηκε."

LOST BOOK OF PAPIAS. 615

have expounded the full economic scheme of the early christianity as originally formulated in the plan of salvation of Jesus. A fragment of this book attributed to Epaphros, or as some say Papias, comes down to us through Eusebius, who quoted the passage relating to the great advantages of socialism over competing individualism.[27] The valuable book of Epaphros gave the rules of socialism as laid down by Peter and John, and which we are afraid Paul suppressed or if not Paul himself, the prelates who afterwards came and drove out and burned the vestiges of that grand culture planted by the early fathers.

This Epaphros or Epaphroditus was a christian orator at Colossæ, under Philemon and his church was a union of the brotherhood. It is believed that he converted the freedman Epictetus who gave philosophical dissertations which, for a time, seemed to make of this cluster of manufacturing cities on the Lycus, another Athens. However, it is not certain that the great lame orator was ever converted. Epaphros is credited with the dangerous but honored task of carrying Paul's letter to the Philippians, and thus, like Tychicus, of being another post office messenger for the early movement.[28] An inscription has been found, and is much commented on of late years, which is recorded in the body of Greek inscriptions under number 3865i. It was discovered at Trajanapolis, is very aged and winterworn, but legible enough to exhibit three important names, two of which are in our canonical scriptures and the other apocryphal. These names are Papias, Trophymus and Tychicus.[29]

[27] Epaphros, *Lost Book, Fragment*, iv., *trans. of Ante Nicine Fathers*. Fragment, iv., speaks of the good time coming in which "vines shall grow having each 10,000 branches, and each branch 10,000 twigs; and each true twig 10,000 shoots; and every one of the shoots 10,000 clusters; and on every cluster, 10,000 grapes: and every grape when pressed will give 25 metres of wine. In like manner a grain of wheat will produce 10,000 grains, and every grain 10,000 more. The whole is intended as a wild and exaggerated estimate of the immense fruits of socialism as compared with the stingy things the workman now realizes.

[28] Philippians, Epaphroditus carried this message from Rome, A.D. 62 "Πρὸς Φιλιππησίους ἐγράφη ἀπὸ ῾Ρώμης δι᾽ Ἐπαφροδίτου.

[29] CIG., 3865i: "Παππίας Τροφίμου και Τυχικῆς." Waddington, in Le Bas, *Inscr.*, 718, tells us that it is from Trajanapolis. and belongs to the year 199; but according to Ramsay, this by no means implies that the heroes of the epitaph we. of that date. On the contrary, this inscription set up in A.D. 69 or 70, m., have caused the arrest and crucifixion of the whole brotherhood. But the calm of 199 just before the persecution of Severus broke out in 202, gave the unions boldness to set up the epitaph.

616   THE HOUSE OF THE LORD.

Tychicus, as we have seen, was Paul's letter carrier, and journeyed the distance from Rome to Ephesus for that purpose. Trophemus is a well-known name in the Bible, being mentioned repeatedly. He traveled with Tychicus and Paul on long journeyings. He was in Jerusalem at the time of the great riot when Paul was denounced as a ring-leader of the sect of the Nazarenes. It is now as much as proved that the two names occurring on the inscription 3865i are no other than genuine mentions of these men. Furthermore, they blindly bring out the information that they represent a guild of the dyers.[30] We shall now bring in evidence as proof of the dense mist under which these labor organizations were befogged, the already celebrated and much debated inscription of one which is described by Dr. Ramsay.

This is No. 3857t in the Body of Greek Inscriptions. Similar specimens have been found by M. Le Blant in Italy and Gaul. There was found at Altentash Benisoa the ancient ruin in southwest Phrygia, near Palestine and not far from the sea, in what we have distinguished as a hive of christianized trade and labor unions all destroyed and annihilated as we shall show, by the terrible massacre of Diocletian, a stone, whose lettering from outside appearance was read as a strictly pagan inscription.[31] Closer inspection, however, showed that it had a cross on the top, proving it to be christian and certain mason's tools such as the trowel which lay at the bottom, proved likewise that the Euphron, Tatias and Onesimus it mentioned were not only masons but represented the masons' trade organization in considerable numbers. Thus the christians were glad to find refuge and a pleasant, congenial and inviting nest among the old Solonic unions, driving at that time the industries

[30] It has been found that CIG., nos. 3857 ^{c}, 3857 ^{r}, 3865 ^{i}, 2918, 3665, 1625, 3495, 3173, 3304, dyers, 3846, 3846 ^{z}, 3847, 3827, 3846 ^{p}, 3879. 3983, 3902, 3962, 3962, as well as Muratorius, pp. DCCCCXIII., MCCCXCIV., MMLV., are all unions under the Solonic law. The archæologists err a trifle in denominating them guilds. The term should be trade union.

[31] CIG. 3857^t: "Εὔφρων κὲ Τατιὰς Ἀσκληπιάδῃ τῷ τέκνῳ ζῶντες. Ὀνήσιμος καὶ ――― τοὺς ἑαυτῶν γονεῖς κὲ ἀδελφὸν ἐτείμησαν. "At first," says Ramsay, Cit. Bish. Phryg., Il., p. 489, no. 366, "it was passed off as in ordinary pagan inscription." But fortunately, M. Perrot., Exploratio Arch. de la Galatie, p. 125, made a fresh copy, and observed the cross at the top, marking the religion of the deceased, while mason's tools at the bottom, indicate the occupation. In id., 3857 ^{c}, Τατεὶς or Τατιὰς is the son of Tychicus. This makes the family to have been masons by trade. The union which honors them in this epitaph was a masons' union.

of the world and living in a perfect socialism, which after two thousand years, is destined, as Jesus intimated, to swell out and cover and engross political economy and end in the perfect political state. These beautiful specimens show the true origin of socialism in our vale of tears.

Thus we have, in bringing to the front this one man Tychicus, accompanied by Onesimus the post office officals of primitive life, an epimelites or trade union manager of that great power recognized under the Roman law as authority working in an occult function with christianity, for the spread of its doctrine that no man or woman who joined its scheme of salvation need suffer if he would work, earn, feed and be happy at the common board.

In our dissertation on Tychicus, we must therefore train such Biblical characters as Trophemus,[32] Apphias, Onesimus and Philemon into line because they were in a certain respect, all associated together. We are leaping into no wild conclusion when we argue that these men had each his functions mapped out to him by the business union over whose economical interests he presided, and that when that warm, thrifty, nest-like brotherhood became converted to the new Word of promise and undertook the unctious work of culture, in addition to their regular old-time habits, they were more than ever obliged to avail themselves of their burial clause in the law and present in their visible phases of life only the sepulchral drapery of death and the tomb. Dr. Lightfoot has deftly told us that: "the christians were first recognized by the Roman government as colleges of burial, and protected by this recognition, doubtless held their meetings for religious worship." And he clearly recognizes in the same sentence that they held these meetings in their own temples with which they were invariably provided, when he adjoins, that: "there is no clear example of a separate building set apart for christian worship within the limits of the Roman empire before the third century."[33]

[32] See *index* to this Vol. Trophemus etc., for inscriptions found mentioning these names as officers in trade unions. They are now regarded by several of the most penetrating inscription readers, as the very same mentioned in the Bible.

[33] We cannot do better for our argument than to here repeat this author's own illustration substantiating this: *Acts*, xii., 72: Συνιδών τὲ ἦλθεν ἐπί τὴν οἰκίαν τῆς Μαρίας........ οὐ ἦσαν ἱκανοὶ συνηθροισμένοι. κ.τ.λ. and

The new word of promise had one of its principal and greatest charms, in that it gave all the down-trodden branch of mankind a soul, a right to marry and have a family, and a right to aspire to full man and womanhood—great thoughts, fraught with hopes and blessedness. The old gods and godesses adorned by these Solonic unions from early ages down, and subscribed to as divinities, had never offered them this. They had dared to hope for the advent of their long-expected pagan messiah, but alas, he or she had never come and their condition, especially just at the close of the conquests, was getting worse instead of better. They were disappointed. They were reasonable and listened to the glad tidings of great joy, and endorsed the new Word of promise which Cybele, Minerva, Kotytto and Dionysus never gave Thus it was the poor and lowly and not the high-born and wealthy class who constituted the original christianity. It was not in finely built churches they planted, but in the old, omnipresent pre-christian kuriakæ, one of which, as thousands of their chiseled monuments testify, belonged to each of the brotherhoods under the Solonic law.

But, as it was extremely difficult to find entrance into a Solonic eranos, and impossible, unless the candidates, after a veritable dokimasia or scrutiny, proved, that, he or she was hagios, eusebes, and agathos,[34] or morally pure, honest, not covetous, but good, he could not enter any more than a camel could enter through the eye of a needle. But fortunately for the aspirant there was a door. In the union this door was the thura tou kuriou, passage to the lord. In the later initiation it was the thura tou kuriou, the door of Jesus.[35] Until this

Rom., xvi., 14, 15: τοὺς σὺν αὐτοῖς ἀδελφοὺς, τοὺς σὺν αὐτοῖς πάντας ἁγιους. Here the ἁγιος of the old pre-christian unions comes in. See Chap. XIII., passim. And yet again, Clement, Recogn., x., 71: "Theophilus..domus suæ ingentem basilicam ecclesiæ nomine consecraret." These basilicæ are now coming to light from under-ground Rome, as the secret school rooms of these very burial unions, a thing made possible by the above-mentioned burial clause already described.

[34] " Ἁγιος καὶ εὐσεβὴς καὶ ἀγαθός." This law of the unions, was discovered on the now celebrated stone, Rangabé, Antiquités Hélléniques, no. 881, lines 9, 24. Supra, p. 260; CIG., 126, It is the great Νόμος ἐρανιστῶν, Fouc., Ass. Rel., no. 20, p. 202. It reads: "Ὁ ἀρχιερανιστὴς καὶ ὁ γραμματεὺς καὶ οἱ ταμίαι καὶ σύνδικοι· ἔστωσαν δὲ οὗτοι κληρωτοὶ κατὰ ἔτος χωρὶς τοῦ προστάτου ὁμολειτωρ δε εἰς τὸν βίον αὐτοῦ ὁ ἐπὶ ἡρῴου καταληφείς· αὐξανέτω δὲ ὁ ἔρανος ἐπὶ φιλοτειμίαις· εἰ δὲ τις μάχας ἢ θορύβους κεινῶν φαίνοιτο, ἐκβαλλέσθω τοῦ ἐράνου, ζημιούμενος ταῖς διπλαῖς. κ.τ.λ. The stone is here broken and illegible.

[35] Ignatius to the Philippians, chap. II., 23: "He is the door of the Father: Θυρα τοῦ πατρος ἐστιν."

memorable revolution in human ethics the poor had no Father. The Roman gens law of primogeniture was opposed to it. It would lead to equalization. The touch of a workman was regarded as a taint. He had not even a promise of immortality. He was cursed. Jesus, the new and last messiah, was his first promise and it yielded the socially submerged millions a mighty comfort.

Uprightness was the prerequisite as in contrast with our present political thieves and legalized rascals. Legalized under the common generalities of Solonism, they tended toward purity. They had laws of their own; were governed by rules of their own; and even had strict laws against immorality, conspiracy, all forms of wrong doing and were growing to be self-ruling and correct.[36] Their celebrated thura tou theou, door of Jesus, as it was later known in christian times, meant in reality, nothing other than this leaping the rigid and to some, impassable bar of initiation;[37] and it is now known only in the spiritual sense as conversion and joining the church. In the days of Tychicus, Philemon, Trophemus and Epaphros it meant more; it meant the economic membership as well; for those who were so fortunate as to succeed in passing the dokimasia were ushered into the presence of the brotherhood, furnished immediately with something to do, and invited to the common table and all the bounties of fraternity. This

[36] We have several inscriptions which lay down their inside law against disorders. They were willing under the original terms of the Solonic law, to follow that statute; they followed the civil and political existing forms; they used νόμος for law or rule; ἀγορά for meeting; ψηφίσματα for decisions and resolutions; managers and rulers were ἄρχοντες. Demosth., *Pro Corona*, § 259. Dr. Oehler has kindly furnished us, in his manuscript, the following references:

In der Itanos lesen wir im Eide der Bürger: οὐδὲ σύλλογον οὐδὲ συνωμοίσαν ποίησεω ἐπὶ τῷ κακίωνι τᾶς πολέος ἢ τῶν πολιτῶν, οὐθὲ ἄλλῳ συνεσσέομαι οὐδενί." But this must have been some resolution against them or prescribing for them by outside citizens. For the one of their own, regarding political action, see *supra*, p. 617, note 78. For an inscription of an eranos, giving its self-constituted rules against riot, see Foucart, *Ass. Rel.*, p. 42: "Si quelqu' un excite des batailles ou des tumultes, qu' il soit chassé de l' érane." For the Greek text of this important find, see *id.*, no. 20, lines 40-2: "Εἰ δέ τις μάχας ἢ θορύβους κεινῶν φαίνοιτο, ἐκβαλλέσθω τοῦ ἐράνου." The same severe rule of the Roman collegia appears in the typical inscription of Lanuvium: "Si quis autem in opprobrium alteralterius dixerit, aut tumultuatus fuerit ei multa esto, HS. N." and considerable more. See Vol. I., p. 357. Again, Oehler, *MSS.:* "Erwähnt werden: συνωμοσίαι in einer Inschrift aus Kythræa auf Kypros: Le Bas, III., 2767, dann in Kibyra: Le Bas, III., 1212: Καταλύσαντα συνωμοσίαν μεγάλην τὰ μάλιστα λυποῦσαν τὴν πόλιν."

[37] It meant what it said; θύρα τοῦ κυρίου, ie., the door to the lord, way to the man at the helm of the union where plenty was, and dangers were past.

great economy, was, carried out as afterwards agreed upon by Peter, James, Paul and Titus at Jerusalem.[38] There they all agreed, after the experience with Demetrius and the silversmiths whose unions had protested against the narrow and bigoted preaching of Paul, threatening to throw the multitudes of workmen out of employment. They agreed and Paul dropped it. The episode of Diotrephes belongs here. At that moment there was started a great wrangle about the gnostic homoousian or which in fact was little other than a discussion protracted for more than a hundred years, over this word. It meant equal distribution of property; for ousia is the Greek for possessions or property, and homos, also homoios prefixed makes this remarkable word which caused a discussion lasting centuries with the Gnostics. It was a compound, born at that very time; for though we have the two words in common use in the classics, we fail to find the compound in use before the wrangling over it set in. The whole Gnostic embroglio was fallacious, misleading, useless and not worthy of our consideration.

The old Solonic law which centuries before had created and legalized the unions, made a special provision that the property belonging to them should be held in common and should belong to no one person but to all alike. It was ratified at Rome and occupied a line of statutory scripture in the Twelve Tables.[39] When probed down it will be found that about this time the guilds of the Solonic and Numan dispensation were possessed of much property. Dion Cassius has told us that Domitian and Nerva [40] killed the members, as we have proved, and confiscated their ousia or property.

[38] *Acts*, xv., 19, 29. The Epistle of James touches strongly upon this celebrated agreement and reconciliation.
[39] Dirksen, *Zwölf Tafeln*. "Der Römische Staat vergönnte urspringlich lediglich den Gewerben, die den Bedürfnissen des Krieges und des Gottesdienstes zunächst fröhnten, seinen unmittelbaren Schutz und eine selbsständige Communalverfassung."
[40] Dion Cass., LXVIII., 1. The modern writers are all agreed that he means the chr. It was immediately after Domitian's persecution quoted in Section *Domitian*, from Dion, LXVII., 14. and shows that Nerva also persecuted, or at least, killed many chr. In the quotation referred to, plain mention is made of their property, Dion calls οὐσια: "Καὶ ὁ Νερούας τοὺς τε κρινομένους ἐπ' ἀσεβείᾳ ἀφῆκε, καὶ τοὺς φεύγοντας κατήγαγε· τοὺς τι δούλους καὶ τοὺς ἐξελευθέρους, τοὺς τοῖς δεσπόταις σφῶν ἐπιβουλεύσαντας, πάντας ἀπέκτεινε. Καὶ τοῖς μὲν τοιούτοις οὐδ' ἄλλο τι ἔγκλημα ἐπιφέρειν ἐπὶ τοὺς δεσπότας ἐφῆκε τοῖς δὲ δὴ ἄλλοις οὔτ' ἀσιβείας, οὔτ' Ἰουδαϊκοῦ βίου καταιτιᾶσθαί τινας συνεχώρησε πολλοὶ δὲ καὶ τῶν συκοφαντησάντων, θάνατον καταδικάσθησαν· ἐν ᾧς καὶ Σέρας ἦν ὁ φιλοσόφος.

FALSE NAMES AS DECOYS AGAINST DANGER. 621

So here in Asia Minor they owned many small properties because there were many organizations. The sum of these petty, innocent properties was an immense property which the grasping potentates got. A principal office of the deacons was to hold sacred this property belonging to each union.[41] Emile Levasseur hints to us that the Roman trade unions were planted into by the christians down to the days of Gratian and Honoius. He further thinks it was enormous, and quotes the law, suppressing the yet remaining paganism in the unions of wood-workers, and others still paying homage to pagan divinities.[42]

Philemon was a metonym for play-actor and occurs quite frequently in the inscriptions, so that only one or two are recognized belonging to this individual character now being considered.[43] The opening of Paul's noted letter to Philemon.[44] A short distance from the old and now demolished city of Colossæ, in a town called Aphrodisias where these pleasurable unions were plentiful is found an inscription containing the name of Philemon as well as Onesimus, and it is considered suggestive of the former influence of these men in that region. In the same manner, these ancient records occur, bearing the names of Epaphros, Trophemus, Tychicus, and some of them are quoted by the epigraphical critics of our seminaries as having been the identical characters of Bible mention. Their children and their childrens' children who, more tenderly than is usual, loved the precious names of the original founders, come like-

---

[41] Origen, *In Matth.*, tom. xvi., § 22, speaking of the functions of the διάκονος, says: "'Οἱ διάκονοι διακοῦντες τὰ τῆς ἐκκλησίας χρήματα." This was the same hundreds of years before the christians began to plant into them; and the same names were used. The deacons had charge of the property.

[42] Levass., *Hist. Class. Ouv.*, I., p. 57: "Il est certain que les collèges possédaient des temples et des terrains consacrés au culte d' une grande étendue puisque Gratian et Honorius eurent soin de les mentionner en ordonnant la confiscation de propriétés qui servaient encore à la religion païenne: "*Cod Theod.*, xvi., tit. x., l. 20, ann. 415: "Omnia loca quae frediani, quae dendrophori, quæ singula quaeque nomina et professiones gentilitiae tenuerunt epholis (epulis) vel sumptibus deputata, fas est, hoc errore submota, compendia nostrae domus sullivare." Cicero distinguishes between the gentile and the slave races as follows: "Gentiles sunt qui inter se eodem nomine sunt, qui ab ingenuis oriundi sunt, quorum majorum nemo servitutem servivit, qui capite non sunt diminuti." Cic., *Top.*, vi., 29.

[43] Φιλήμων in Greek was a play-actor. Aristot., *Rhet.*, III., 42.

[44] Lightfoot. *Coloss.*, p. 331, Greek text, reveals that Philemon's House was no other than an ἐκκλησία of the old initiates, apparently Dionysan, of which Philemon was an archon or bishop. CIG., 2782: "ΟΛ. 'Απφίας ἀρχιερείης Ἀσίας, μητρὸς καὶ ἀδελφῆς καὶ μάμμης συνκλητικῶν, φιλοπάτριδος." κ. τ.λ. Apphias was chief priestess of the union, at first a strictly pagan, business concern, but afterwards christianized.

wise later, in the tombs prepared for them. It is a strange history of departed socialism.

In winding up our notes on Tychicus and his celebrated companions, we must again refer to Epictetus the cripple and emancipated slave of Colossæ. Epaphras, his christianized friend, was a fellow prisoner of Paul at Rome, though he planted christianity among the unions of Hierapolis. In A.D. 66 he was again with Epictetus the moralist, who approached very nearly to christianity. Though a native of Hierapolis, only seven miles from Colossæ, they often met and knew each other. It looks as if they were both fellow initiates of Cybele. They both underwent long suffering for their almost similar faith; in such sad, struggling advocates we find these origins of socialism always in the poor, the unrecognized, the lowly. All are seen to have been low, poor and mean, though they announced the revolution. Many other very suggestive inscriptions[45] occur which are being lately pointed out by the epigraphists as containing scripture names and are listed as guilds or unions.

Let us now undertake a synthetic analysis and history of Luke. Were it not for the late discovery of much monumental evidence, and had we nothing more than what has come down to us through the New Testament with comments by the early fathers and historians, we should be unable to tell this story. But fortunately for us, there have sprung into light several statements about him, which tell in epitaphic fashion much to excite interest. Ernest Renan obtained for his researches enough to cause his remark that Luke was an ebionite who thoroughly opposed the holding of individual property. He also says that he was a full-blood Jew.[46] Paul called him his fellow-laborer; indeed they must have been together, and none could have been more intimate with the apostles.[47] He knew all the details regarding the work of the immediate companions of Jesus and so

[45] CIG., 3857 u : '' Ονήσιμος Φιλέρωτατος ἐτὶ ζῶν σὺν τοὶς παιδίοις μοῦ Φιλήτῳ καὶ Καλλιγενεία καὶ Ονησίμη, σὺν τῷ γαμβρῷ Εὐτυχίῳ, μετὰ τοῦ ἐγγόνου Βασιλίου ἐποιήσαμεν μνήμης χάριν.'' On one apparently very valuable reference to Luke, if we read aright, See Dion Chrysostom, quoted by Th. Reinach, in *Bull. de Cor. Hélénique*, 1896, p. 380.
[46] Renan, *Life of Jesus*, p. 36, of Eng. trans.
[47] *Epist. Phil.*, 24: Μάρκος, 'Αρίσταρχος, Δημᾶς. Λουκᾶς, οἱ συνεργοί μοῦ. *Coloss.*, iv., 11, where he is spoken of as the "beioved physician." That Luke was quinquennal to the order of medical doctors, we now proceed to prove by the ancient carvings on the stone

likewise of Paul, being able as their historian to write
an account which has been declared by eminent critics,
Guizot among the rest, to be a compend of true history.

But although Hebrew, speaking that tongue, he was
a native of Asia Minor and probably of Tlos, in Cilicia
and possessed a good knowledge of at least three languages which he constantly used; the Greek, Syriac and
Hebrew. In the Acts of the Apostles he often speaks in
the second person, showing that on the voyage through
Macedonia he must have seen and known Lydia, the
member of the dyers' union [48] and traveled with the
evangelist party to Troas. If Demas was Demetrius, as
critics say, then Luke knew him; and the great length
and care devoted to the story of the strike of the image
makers at Ephesus under the direction of Demetrius,
shows that he in all probability was present, and lent
his influence in a wise direction, rescuing his friends
from harm. But being with John and Peter in sympathy, he must have sided with Demetrius against Paul's
bigotry and in favor of upholding the workmen of the
image makers' society in maintaining their means of
earning a living.

But we have other remarkable proof of Luke being
not only a friend and co-worker with Paul, but an otherwise historical character. One epigraph recorded in the
Body of Greek Inscriptions brings this out. But in addition to this we have two others, and no two of all anaglyphs are recorded by the same archæologist. Before
proceeding to a reproduction of these three gems of history in the corroboration of our argument that true
christianity was planted in the ancient Solonic unions,
it is well to remind the reader that on account of the
dangers from ever-present spies of the proconsuls and
their police, the poor fellows were constantly obliged to
hide their names and identity under the veil proffered
by a studied occultism. Thus Luke had many names.
He went as Loukos, Loukios, Lucanus, Leukas, Nicias,
and several other metonyms to suit various immediate
necessities.[49]

[48] See *supra*, by referring to *index*, where an account is given of her, together with inscriptional evidences.

[49] Lightfoot, *Coloss.*, p. 239: "Lucas, meaning St Luke, is doubtless a contraction of Lucanus. Several old Latin *MSS*. write out the name Lucanus in the superscription, just as elsewhere Apollos is written Apollonius. On the frequent occurrence of this name, see *Ephem. Epigr.*. II., p. 28. 1874."

This is one of five inscriptions memorialized by Dr. Franz in a monogram on Five Inscriptions and Five Cities. Dr. Wolf discovered it in the Anatolian town of Ahatkoi, once Trajanopolis, where many interesting ruins are being studied. The rubric of this great inscription reads *agathe tyche*, and is an invariable christian sign. Again, it introduces Luke as Nicias the conqueror, meaning it perhaps in a spiritual sense. Before giving the full inscription in our note a running paraphrase is necessary, leaving our more correct translation for the appendix:

The members in general and council or synod of the koinon hereby honor Nicias the adopted of Esculapius, god of medicine and surgery, and whose Latin name is Luke, with the gift of an altar, under the august emperial care; the same to be a testimonial of ours during his whole lifetime. For a long time he has ministered in charge of the public works, governing with integrity and efficiency. He was during two quinquennalian terms, master of the gymnastic schools and excercises being connected with the schools of Tyrannus.[50] He also acted faithfully in the capacity of secretary, and was useful in other work.

The reference made in this inscription to the resurrection is a sure proof that it is christian; the word being anastasis, which is unmistakable. Besides, the fact that he is president of the body to which he belongs and which he serves, points to that body as being a thiasos or koinon. The great activity of a life-time of Luke here acknowledged, together with the date, his being one of the physicians, and all other harmonies combined, show the recipient of the honors to be Saint Luke of the Gospel.

Now one more word in regard to the schools of Tyrannus[51] mentioned in this inscription and then we will produce in a foot-note the exact original of the tablet itself. This Tyrannus, whoever he was, appears in a mul-

---

[50] This remarkable fact brings forth additional proof of what we have already said regarding the *Schools of Tyrannus*. See our *Index*, catchwords, *Tyrannus, schools*, etc. There is a fund of curious information in this school of Tyrannus, mentioned in the *Acts*, made still more important by the recent discovery in the Columbarium that Tyrannus rendered a great service to Rome.

[51] *Acts*, xix., 9: "'Ὡς δὲ τινες ἐσκληρύνοντο καὶ ἠπείθουν, κακολογοῦντες τὴν ὁδὸν ἐνώπιον τοῦ πλήθους, ἀποστὰς ἀπ' αὐτῶν ἀφώρισε τοὺς μαθητὰς. καθ' ἡμέραν διαλεγόμενος ἐν τῇ σχολῇ Τυράννου τινός,

TYRANNUS, IMMUNE OF THE COLUMBARIUM 625

tiform manner throughout the Greek epigraphs and is at the head of a great columbarium at Rome as the man who dedicated, if he did not build the structure. As many scholæ are found by De Rossi in under-ground Rome, known to have been the secret retreats where the hiding unionists, deep in subterranean vaults, had schools, occult meetings, and even common meals, so also are similar scholæ found in some of the deepest recesses or hypogea of this columbarium over whose main portal is inscribed the dedication of Tyrannus. It is reasonable therefore, to suppose that he is the same Tyrannus whose schools Luke mentions in his history of the Acts of the Apostles.[52] He was himself a freedman of the emperor Claudius. He might have been so at Ephesus where the Asian school of Tyrannus was. The time agrees in all the inscriptions and in the Bible mention as being the second half of the first century,[53] and it must have extended, at least from the days of Tiberius, during whose reign, Jesus had lived and labored, down to the reign of Trajan. Luke, though a communist was so intimate with Paul that he accompanied him for years and it was he who, in company with Titus, acted as post messenger, carrying the second epistle to the Corinthians, from Philippi to Corinth, as early as the year A.D. 57.[54]

We now come to our account of the second archæological tablet containing the name of Luke. For this we are indebted to Dr. Ramsay who first put us on the inspection. In the first inscription which we have just

---

[52] Gorius, "Mon. sive Columb.," p. 65. The inscription reads:
"Tyrannus, verna Tab. Apparitor.
  Sacris omnium immunis.
  Is dedit. Ti. Claudio Aug. L. Veterano.
    Columbarium totum.
    Is intulit Zanthum. Aug. L.
  Fratrum suum.
    ˉMinistri."

[53] CIG, 3858: "Ὁ δῆμας καὶ ἡ βουλὴ ἐτείμησεν Νικίαν Ἀσκληπιαδώρου τὸν καὶ Λούκιον, ἱερέα Σεβαστῆς Εὐβοσίας διὰ βίου, ἀγορανομήσαντά πολυτελῶς καὶ στρατηγήσαντα ἀγνῶς καὶ γυμνισιαρχήσαντα τοδέ πεντετηρικοὺς ἀγῶνας ἐπὶ Ἰουλίας Ξενουήρας καὶ Ξερουηνίου Κλαπίτωνας, καὶ γραμματεύσαντα πιστῶς· τὴν ἐπιμελειαν ποιησαμένου τῆς ἀναστάσεως Συμμάχου. ἐφηβάρχου καὶ ἱερέως, τοῦ ἀδελφοῦ αὐτοῦ. Collected by Böckh. The Latin remarks of the editor, Dr. Frazier are to the effect that this Nicias called also Lucias meaning Lucas, was priest to Agrippina, wife of Claudius; and refers to coins of Akmonia. "Est igitur sacerdos Augustæ cujusdam. Jam quum in nummis quos diximus Acmonensum Agrippinæ fuisse sacerdotem." Place where found: "In vico Ahatkoi, in cœmetero repperit Baro Wolfius Russus. See Franz Fünf Inschriften und Fünf Städte in Klein Asien, p. 6.

[54] "II Epist. Cor.," at close: Πρὸς κορινθίους δευτέρα ἐγράφη ἀπὸ Φιλίππων τῆς Μακεδονίας διὰ Τίτου καὶ Λευκᾶ.

given, it will be remarked that the actual parent was not mentioned, but in lieu of this, his tutelary divinity the god of medical professions. Agreeing with Paul's mention, Luke was a physician. In the second epigraph his father's name was also Luke. We can agree perfectly with Dr. Ramsay in his suggestion that the circumstance belongs to the middle of the first century. The work of chiseling it, however, was not under Claudius; for that would have been very dangerous. But this author fails to understand the true Phrygian meaning of the word gerousia which occurs twice in the inscription. He wants it to mean some sort of council of elders or great men. It means nothing of the sort. It means a trade guild, as Dr. Oehler found by close inspection; a body of associates conducted the details of a considerable industry that had employed Luke as a business agent, just as the red dyers of Laodicea employed Lydia, or the dyers of the same place employed, honored and crowned Menippus,[55] whose christian inscription has recently been discovered at Mount Athos. Dr. Oehler who visited them in various parts of Asia Minor, found, as he informs us through valuable epistolary correspondence, that the word gerousia had the full import of a union or thiasos; and he justly complains of the misconstruction put by excellent savants upon the term, not comprehending that it is a corporate body of workingmen.[56] The gerousia, twice mentioned in this inscription chiseled to the honor of Luke, is a labor union[57] and certainly one of those most venerated, frequently met with among the thousands of multiform

---

[55] Oehler, "MSS.": "Interressant ist auch die Inschrift aus Thessalonike: Duchesne-Bayet, "Mémoir sur une Mission au Mont Athos," p. 52, n. 83: die συνήθεια τῶν πορφυροβάφων hat den Menippos aus Thiateira ein Grabmal errichtet; es liegt nahe auszunehmen, dass auch dieser Menippos ein Πορφυροβάφος gewesen sein und zu vergleichen die Purpurhändlerin Lydia aus Thyateira, welche in Philippi vom Apostel Paulus getauft wurde. "Act. Apost.," xvi., 14."

[56] Oehler, "MSS." "Grabmulten d. h. Geldbussen, welche wegen Verletzung eines Grabes zu zahlen sind (Menadier, "Qua Condicione Ephesei," u.s.w., p. 59), behauptet unrichtig: ' Ex qua natura gerusiæ pendere arbitramur, quod toticus sepulcrorum læsorum pœnas gerusiæ solvendas esse statuitur. Asia enim in oppidis privatorum hominum collegio, nisi omnino fallimur, nunquam hoc evenit.' " It is here seen that Dr. Oehler, on the contrary, believes that the Gerusia in Asia Minor, was a collegium, and he has elsewhere cited a dozen specimens.

[57] This is admitted by Lévy, "Revue Et. Gr.," 1895, p. 249, who says of the συνήγορον occurring in same inscr, that the συνήγορος was a "sorte d' ambassadeur chargé d' aller défendre au dèhors les intérêts de la corporation." In French, the word corporation is understood to be trade union. Thus the συνήγορον τῆς γερουσίας, the terminal words of the inscription, must be understood to mean agent of the union.

palæoglyphics which research is gradually bringing to the light of science.

Luke, the dominant character in this inscription, is recognized, as in the other one, to be a priest of the Augustan lord's house and engaged in the colonization scheme which transplanted thousands of Roman christians from their unions in Rome over to Asia Minor, where they could better breathe the air of freedom. The ktisis mentioned is a colony of unionists driven from Rome by the ukase of Claudius. They went over in large numbers, to Phrygia. We have already found them at Apameia and have shown the colony of shoemakers of Shoemakers' street in Kelainos. It was a ktisis or colony from Rome. This of our inscription is another. The exact place where they settled is Apameia, perhaps Kelainos. Among the progonoi, the fathers or founders, was Luke without doubt; for he was a big man in those dangerous, troublous times. They were working at some manufactory at the time this inscription was chiseled.[58] Not Dr. Oehler only, but others, now seem to think that the word gerousia is simply another of the many names by which the Solonic unions were known.

We may pharaphrase this inscription in words about as follows: The elders of the gerousia hereby honor Luke or Atilios, whose father's name is also Luke. He was priest to some one of the Augustan princes. He was a lover of good management, admired the fatherland, acting as ambassador and taking precedence as an elder, always in gracious comity with the Cæsars. They honor him with a gift; since he is ranked above the others in the city and union who have striven to establish a colony; and he is above the other founders, working in a statesmanlike manner, well and reverently, for the business interests of this guild.

It is important to state that Luke was sent from Asia Minor to Rome to see Paul just at the time of his execution by Nero, A.D. 64, and the embassy mentioned may have reference to this. Certain it is that the inscrip-

[58] Ramsay, *Cities Bish. Phrig.*, II., pp. 468-9: "Οἱ Γέροντες ἐτίμησαν Λού͂κιον Ἀτίλιον Λουκίου υἱὸν Παλατίνᾳ Πρόκλον νεώτερον, ἱερέα τῶν σεβαστῶν φιλογέροντα καὶ φιλόπατριν, πρεσβεύσαντα πρὸς τοὺς σεβαστοὺς, δωρεᾷ ὑπὲρ τῶν εἰς τὴν κτίσιν διαφερόντων, ἔν τε ταῖς λοιπαῖς τῆς πόλεως καὶ τῆς γερουσίας χρείας ἁγνῶς καὶ δικαίως ἐκ προγόνων πολιτευόμενον, συνήγορον τῆς γερουσίας." Legrand et Chamonanard, *Bull. Corresp. Hellenique*, 1893, p. 247.

tion could not have been chiseled before the peaceful season under Vespasian and this would bear out the remark of Dr. Ramsay putting its date at A.D. 70-79, a space covering the reign of Vespasian. What makes the names so blind is just what we have all along been endeavoring to explain. The original cause was danger. If they did not conceal name, identity and literary documents, including epitaphs, they were exposed to persecutions.[59]

We now come to the third inscription which is an epitaph and records Luke's death. It is not very clear. It appears that in the ancient cemetery of Teos, a town in Lycia, not far from the Phrygian scenes we have described, there has recently been found an epitaph bearing very boldly the name of Luke. It is entirely Jewish but nothing appears to stand in the way of his having been a christian. A running paraphrase of this monument would read something as follows:

Ptolemy, the son of Luke, being an inhabitant of Tlos, has himself constructed this sepulchre or sepulchral chapel from foundation to roof, out of the funds of the union,[60] and also for the son of Ptolomy, that is, Ptolomy number two, son of Luke, who has fulfilled the term of his archontate or presidency of the union among us Hebrews, so that this sepulchral chapel is for all the Jews; and no other person from outside is permitted to obtrude himself within. Any one found encroaching shall pay to the plebeian members owning this enclosure a fine of......drachmas.

That this monument is of a family of Lukes, is conjectured, apparently, by Hula himself; for he brings as testimonies in this article, a passage from Chrysos-

---

[59] Ramsay, *Cit. Bish. Phryg.*, II., pp. 491 "........it s certain that the christians at baptism commonly took an additional name." Again p. 501: "......The christians put nothing in public documents, such as their epitaphs, which could be quoted as evidence of christianity." On many other pages, this astute observer, who drew his conclusions from the stones he analyzed in their distant abodes, shows many deceptive signs, only understood by the initiates, and that for centuries they evaded the spies.

[60] Lines 2, 3: ἐκ τῶν ἰδίων. Nothing proves more definitely than this expression, that an eranos is always understood by this mention. It is a specification in the Solonic *jus coeundi*, *Dig.*, III., iv., 1, § 1, "arcam communem." *Dig.*, XXXVII., 3, § 4: "bonorum possesio societas et corporibus adgnosci potest." Oehler, *Eran. Vindob.*, p. 279: "Die genossenschaften haben ......eine gemeinsame Casse: τὰ ἴδια, aus der Ausgaben in dem Namen der Genossenschaft bestritten werden und können Schenkungen, Grabmulten, u.s.w. erhalten. So hat die προεδρία der παρφυροβάφοι, in Hierapolis von M. Aur. Diodoros 300 Denare ἐκ τῶν ἰδίων mit bestimmter Widmung, Le Bas. III., 1687."

tom where in the old Paris edition of 1687 is a reference to the fact that Luke wrote a homily,[61] as if it were a conceded fact that the two stories were written of one man.

But there is another reason for not discrediting the probability that this heroon belonged to Luke of Bible celebrity. He was a Jew, and so communistical, that Renan declares he belonged to the ebionitic branch and this would make the socialistic donation of his Gemeinde or union of a common sum out of its treasury in perfect accord with the Solonic dispensation. Again the learned Hula admits, drawing his conclusion from the general appearance and diction of the epitaph, that it was erected in the first century, or in the apostolic age, and and cites Salomon Reinach's rule that about the time of Claudius, Luke was always found spelled exactly as in this inscription.

Thus Luke, all through his valuable life was lord of a great eranos and indeed a great character. It has already been shown that a union's manager arose in quinquennalian civil service to be an immune, and received his crown of honors under the Law; he was an apostolos, even in pagan times, and he often went vibrating from place to place carrying, wherever the unions of labor were, the glad tidings that at last, the great Saviour had arrived on earth, fully believing in Jesus, as the promised messiah. Luke, in accordance with this statute, rose as an ambassador, the highest honor conferable through the law, to be an apostle; and of prechristian apostles there were many. Luke was one and being an educated gentleman in the medicinal art, won the favors of all mankind. He associated with Paul, traveled as an evangelist with him, wrote the Acts of the Apostles for him, which were canonized as Holy Writ; and in his declining years, went back to Tlos, the town of his nativity to die and be greatly honored by the se-

[61] In a note, p. 101, it appears that the Chrysostom quoted may be the one who lived in Rome during the first century. At any rate this author and orator was the only Chrysostom who, though Greek, could write Latin; and he certainly mentioned the christians. Dr. Hula says: "Auf meine Bitte hat Fl. Weigel die Ausgabe in Paris eingesehen und die Stelle in Tom. II. derselben, S. 521 in einer "Homilie" gefunden, welche als erste einer gemeinsamen Gruppe steht mit dem gemeinsamen Titel: "Homiliae in loca quædam S. Lucæ." Sie beginnt mit den Worten: 'De solsitiis et aequinoctiis et nativitate domini nostri Jesu Christi et Johannis Baptistae nescio an quisquam ausus sit arcanum, fratres, ante Christi nativitatem intelligere,' " **cf.** Wesseling. "De Judæorum Archontibus."

cret communistic association to which he had[62] hitherto belonged.

There is a remarkable monumental history of Philip, the founder of the church of Hierapolis, on the Lycus, in the close neighborhood of Thyateira, one of the celebrated seven churches of Asia. These two cities, Thyateira and Hierapolis, were hot-beds of the Solonic unions, swarming with innumerable organized industries. Of these unions are red dye manufacturers, the woolworkers, great numbers of carders, carpet makers, organizations of grocers, fishermen who had probably, in addition to the catch in the small River Lycus, flowing past Hierapolis, extended their nets, lines and seines to the Meander and thence down to the sea. Then there are slabs indicating the existence in this vicinity, of cotton manufacture, huntsmen's unions, masons, and other builders in abundance, quite a number of which cite the time of their highest activity as the apostolic age.[63]

We have two, or perhaps we might better say two sets of wonderful inscriptions from the ancient church

[62] "Eran. Vindob.," E. Hula, "Eine Judengemeinde in Tlos.," p. 101:

Πτολεμαῖος [Λ]ε[υ-
κίου Τλωεὺς κατεσκεύασεν ἐκ
τῶν ἰδίων τό ἡρῷον ᾁσό θεμελίων αὐτὸς καὶ ὑπὲρ τοῦ υἱοῦ αὐτοῦ Πτολεμαίου β′
5 τοῦ Λευκίου ὑπὲρ ἀρχοντείας τελου-
μένας παρ' ἡμεῖν Ἰουδαίοις ἅστε αὐ-
τό εἶναι πάντων τῶν Ἰουδαίων καὶ
μηδένα ἐξὸν εἶναι ἕτερον τεθῆναι
ἐν αὐτῷ· ἐὰν δέ τις εὑρεθείη τινὰ
10 τι[θ]ῶν. ὀφειλέσει Τλ[ω]έων τῷ δήμῳ
[δραχμ]ὰς.

Der Name Λεύκιος Z. 5, der Schriftcharakter, orthographische und lautliche Erscheinungen (ἡρῷον Z. 3, αὐτῷ Z. 9, τῷ δήμῳ Z. 10, ἡμεῖν Z. 6, ὀφειλέσει Z. 10, —— eine Form, die auf lykischen Inschriften öfters begegnet —— τιθῶν Z. 10) wohl auch der dem römischen "a fundamentis" nachgebildete Ausdruck ἀπὸ θεμελίων Z. 3, weisen die Inschrift in römische Zeit, in das Ende des ersten Jahrhunderts nach Christus. Ueber dieses hinauszugehen hält die Sorgfalt ab, mit der die ganze Inschrift geschrieben ist, vielleicht auch die Form Λεύκιος statt Λούκιος. Freilich findet sich die Form Λεύκιος noch in christlichen Inschriften: C. I. Gr., 9165, 9423; im Allgemeinen aber scheint für die Länder mit regerem römischen Verkehr Salomon R e i n a c h Recht zu haben, wenn er "Traité d' épigr.," S. 520 die Regel aufstellt: "vers l' époque de Claude, la transcription Λουκιος predomine de plus en plus en dehors d' Athenes." Vergl. Michel O l e r c, "Bull. corr. hell." X S. 401; V i e r e c k, "Sermo Græcus," S. 49.

[63] Oehler, "Eranos Vindob.," pp. 277, 278, 279, 280, 281, 282; "id., MSS." "In Laodicea am Lycus finden wir eine ἐργασία τῶλ γναέφων τῶν ἀπγουρῶν (fullers,) für glatte Stoffe CIG. 3938." Again; "In Hierapolis in Phrygien bekränzt die ἐργασίά τῶν καφέων ein Grab: Le Bas, III., 742., CIG., 3924. In Thyateira hatten die βαφεῖς grosse Bedeutung, gewiss auch grosses Vermögen. "In Thyateira werden wir οἱ τοῦ στρατάρχου ἐργασταὶ καὶ προξενηταὶ σωμάτων genannt, "Athen. Mitth.," xxi., 1896, p. 262. In Philadelphia ist eine ἱερὰ φυλὴ τῶν ἐριουργῶν bezeugt, CIG., 3422, Wüscher, ἐριοπλυτοὶ mit ihrem Werkmeister, πρῶτος ἐργάτηγος, lehrt uns eine Inschrift aus Hierapolis in Phrygien kennen; ihre Vereinigung wird als ἐργασία bezeichnet: Μουσικ βιβ., V., 1884-5, p. 79."

of Hierapolis. But inasmuch as three celebrated cities in Bible mention stand within sight of each other, all on the Lycus a few miles above the mouth of that stream into the Meander, we shall see that so far as their monuments are concerned they are all blended together by their proximity and the thick population along these beautiful banks.

In introducing the inscription commemorating the apostle Philip, the same who was made a deacon at Jerusalem by the pentecostal brotherhood along with the proto-martyr Stephen, to manage the common table or "daily ministrations,"[64] it is necessary to give the eranist law and rule making the chiseling of inscriptions compulsory even in very dangerous times.[65] It had to be done to conform with the law which the unions through six hundred vicissitudinal years, sedulously complied with; and when the dangers attending the obnoxious christian plant set in, they still observed the old law as far as they dared. This must account for the exceptional inscriptions we are going to produce. But an element of political power existed in these unions of the Lycus, even in the early ages. They voted and controlled elections, and were political. Herein lay much power and dignity. But in later years the christians took footing among them,[66] and contrary to the ethics of the old unions, refused to pay tribute, incurring the capital penalty. Pliny found that they would not go to

[64] *Acts*, vi., 1: Ἐν δὲ ταῖς ἡμέραις ταύταις πληθυνόντων τῶν μαθητῶν ἐγένετο γογγυσμὸς τῶν Ἑλληνιστῶν πρὸς τοὺς Ἑβραίους, ὅτι παρεθεωροῦντο ἐν τῇ διακονίᾳ τῇ καθημερινῇ αἱ χῆραι αὐτῶν........διακονεῖν τραπέζαις. κ.τ.λ. and in verse 5, Stephen, Philip, and five others are chosen as deacons "to serve the tables,"

[65] Foucart, *Ass. Rel.*, p. 13, His no. 7, gives the rule, lines 19-21: "στεφανοῦν δὲ καὶ εἰς τὸν ἔπειτα χρόνον κατ' ἐνιαυτὸν καθ' ἑκάστην θυσίαν καὶ ἀναγορεύειν ἀναγραφὲν τὸν στέφανον αὐτῆς τοὺς ἐπιμελητάς· ἀναγράψαι δὲ τόδε τὸ ψήφισμα τοὺς ὀργεῶνας ἐν στήλει λιθίνει καὶ στῆσαι ἐν τῶι τεμένει." Again Foucart, p. 25: "Ils étaient chargés de la gravure des décrets honorifiques et de l' exposition de la stèle etc.; no. 6, line 26: 'Ἀναγράψαι δὲ τόδε τὸ ψήφισμα ἐν στήλει λιθίνει τοὺς ἐπιμελητὰς καὶ στῆσαι ἐν τῶι Μητρώων." κ.τ.λ. Archæol. Anzeiger, 1855, p. 83; Le Bas, *Attique*, no. 382. Found at Moulins du Pirée in 1862; now in the Petit Musée du Pirée. Dumont, *Essai sur la Chronologie des Archontes athéniens*, p. 46.

[66] Oehler, *MSS.:* Πορφυροβάφοι. Eine Innung derselben in Hierapolis ist bezeugt durch eine Inschrift, welche vielfach behandelt ist; Le Bas, III., 1687, las: τῷ συνεδρίῳ τῆς προεδρίας τῶν πορφυροβάφων, was als Unterstützungskasse für die ärmeren Mitglieder der Gennossenschaft erklärt und dem Einflusse des Christenthums zugeschrieben wurde: Vgl. auch Wagener, *Revue de l' Instruction publ. en Belgique*, n. s, XI., 1869, p. 348, die richtige Lesung; τῆς προεδρίας und Erklärung gegeben; vgl. *Journal of Philol.*, xix., p. 100; Ramsay, *Amer. Journ. of Archæol.*, III., 1887, p. 343 eine richtige Lesung: τῆς προεδρίας etc. Here Oehler complains that Menadier has misconceived the true import of this important monument, the προεδρία being a christian council

the pagan sacrifice and buy sheep, lambs, beeves, poultry and vegetables of the old provision dealers, but followed the tactics of their master and drove them out of their temples by practicing against them a sort of boycott. It was then that the unions were in great danger. There is an inscription showing how they used politics and even as christians secured favor thereby. By this means, and on a large scale, they were performing government work under their individual name. This recognized name was that of their legalized kurios, governor or president.

One of these names at Hierapolis was Philip. Another one at the same place was Avircius Marcellus, for both of whom splendid inscriptional history has come to light.[67] Waltzing failed to understand that this is from the direct specification, comprehensible in the kurion einai of the law of Solon. This one individual alone was recognized for nearly a thousand years, while the membership under the secret veil, and out of sight, did the work and their secret proedria stood behind this one man who alone was in sight of the open world, elected him, crowned him, performed the government work from all outward appearances, for him, and when he died, built for him an honorary heroon out of the common fund. There is sufficient assurance that at Hierapolis and Thyateira these guilds possessed extensive accumulations which they held and enjoyed in common.

Behind the sacred veil of these secret unions there was no mendicancy, no charity, no lack of plentitude, no prostitution.[68] Woman, enfranchised from the economic horrors which in our days of boastful christianity drive her to despair, rose to the grandeur of her nature and stood above taint. She will do it again if this pure

[67] Waltzing, *Hist. Corp. Prof.*, II., p. 195. Krauze is right; Waltzing, 164, says: "On a voulu faire aussi des collèges....des associations industrielles, constituées pour exércer leur métier en commun sous la direction de leur chefs... à tel point que quand les membres de certaines corporations se mirent au service de l' État; ce fut longtemps en leur nom privé, et non comme corporations."

[68] Jullian, *Inscr. de Bordeaux*, p. 950: "La création des collèges eut une assez grande conséquence dans l'histoire de la plèbe, où ils se recrutaient exclusivement. Les plébéiens étaient, d' après le droit ancien, des hommes qui n' avaient ni famille ni religion; ils ne formaient aucune société, ni religieuse, ni civile, ni politique. L' institution attribuée à Numa fit précisement de la plèbe une société, en les groupant en collèges, sous la protection d' une même divinité elle donna aux plébéiens l' unité religieuse que leur manquait........cette institution de Numa établit entre les plébéiens un premier lien politique."

PHILIP OF HIERAPOLIS. 633

and ennobling socialism shall ever be brought back to the light of its true and beneficent civilization.

Such was the true condition of things at the time Philip was managing one of those influential unions at Hierapolis. The danger of inditing the inscription we are about to adduce was greatly softened by the wealth and dignity of the brotherhood. But there is a strong probability that it was not actually chiseled until the peaceful and safer days of Vespasian, as Dr. Ramsay has pointed out. Some instances are known where even a hundred years elapsed before the union dared to erect and expose such a monument.

Smith affirms this in his biblical literature.[69] Notwithstanding his long, dark sequestration in Cæsarea, where he continually taught the Gospel among the secret unions, converting and building among them, the potters, dyers, tanners, as in the case of Simon recently found to have been the kurios of the tanners' guild at Cæsarea, he is likewise found at Colossæ and with his daughters; two of whom remained with him in this city while one went to Ephesus. While Philip was building up the new faith he had a foothold also upon the great church of Hierapolis, the closely neighboring town, and he died in the embrace of that renowned and pioneer church.[70]

Dr. Ramsay who brings some history of Philip to view, remarks: "In this inscription we have a clear proof that a church (doubtless *the* church) of Hierapolis was dedicated to St. Philip."[71] Here and in this vicin-

[69] Smith, *Bib. Dict.*, p. 2488, gives us a synopsis of PHILIP: From the city of Samaria; *Acts*, viii; Samaritans' Messianic hope, John, iv., 25; iv., 40; went down from Samaria to Cæsarea, p. 2488; lost for nineteen years at Cæsarea; Saul of Tarsus saw him after his conversion, *Acts*, ix., 30; Cæsarea the center of his activities; Paul visits him at his House in Jerusalem. as one of the Seven, *idem;* had four daughters, *Acts*, xxi., 8, 9; died bishop of Tralles, Acta Sanctorum, June 6. The House where he and his daughters lived, seen by travelers as late as the time of Jerome, A.D. 400; Epist. Paulae, §8; Ewald, Geschichtliche, IV., pp, 175, 208-14: Baumgarten, *Apostelgeschichte*, § 15, 16. Smith does not speak of the inscription.

[70] The wonderful recently deciphered inscription on the tomb of Philip at Hierapolis, CIG, 8779; Ramsay, *Cit. Bish. Phryg.*, II., p. 552, no. 419; Cockrell, J.H.S., 1885, p. 346: Cumont, 131, reads:
Εὐγένιος ὁ ἐλάχιστος ἀρχιδιάκονος κὲ ἐφιστὼς τοῦ ἁγίου κὲ ἐνδόξου ἀποστόλου κὲ θεολόγου Φιλίππου.

Under this is a garland, with the monogram: Χριστός, almost and purposely concealed, written between Alpha and Omega, the initial and terminal of the Greek alphabet, "A καὶ Ω," which is known to be an unerring christian sign,

[71] Here Dr. Ramsay refers to Lightfoot, *Coloss.*, p. 45, who quotes Polycrates, *ap.*, Eusebius, *Hist. Eccles.*, III., 31; V., 24: "Φίλιππον τὸν τῶν δώδεκα ἀποστόλων ὃς κεκοίμηται ἐν Ἱεραπόλει, καὶ δύο θυγατέρες αὐτοῦ γεγηρακυῖαι παρθένοι, καὶ ἡ ἑτέρα αὐτοῦ θυγάτηρ ἐν ἁγίῳ πνεύματι πολετευσαμένη, ἡ ἐν Ἐφέσῳ ἀναπαύεται."

ity, under protection of the secret brotherhood he labored during the remainder of his life. Three, or at least two, of his devoted daughters remained with him to the end; one having gone to Ephesus, but as the distance between the two cities is not great, she may have visited her father and sisters at Colossæ and Hierapolis at least once a year. Notwithstanding the discovery of a fragment of the ancient Solonic Statute making these anaglyphs compulsory for the sake of reference in cases where the public laws and the inspection of the police required it, the day came when they were obliged to practice intense secrecy, sometimes through ambiguities and sometimes through deception. These days covered the actual period of Philip's residence in Asia Minor. It was during the time of the persecutions of Claudius and Nero, when on account of the edicts of Caligula and Claudius they were exiled from Rome in great unmbers and went over to the old brotherhoods of weavers, spinners, shoemakers as·at Akmonia, dyers as at Thyatira, woolworkers as at Hierapolis, and settled the Romano-Hellenistic colonies called the ktises. Those poor evangelists well understood the injunction of the master: "let not thy left hand know what thy right hand doeth."[72] They engaged in the hazardous work of turning the old establishments with their numerous membership over to the new plan of salvation through the hated Logos or Word of Jesus. At that trysting moment such a command was quickened in pithy meaning; in the later days of christian degeneracy the meaning is lost. He was talking to the initiates who stood around him, and it looks as if Philip might have been one of them. He was teaching them how to go forth and plant. All seem to admit that this has now no meaning. The modern world has lost it. At the time it was uttered a large percentage of the poor of the earth were under secret pledges with their unions and brotherhoods as initiates, safely ensconced behind the mysterious veil. The world was a valley of mystery. To divulge was not only treachery and disgrace, it was often death. To divulge or, in fact, not to hide and cozen by tergiversation, or veer away suspicion and arrest by ambidextrous guile, would have brought a legion

---

[72] *Matth.*, vi., 3,

of Roman spies and pro-consular satelytes into their camp and broken up the mysterious individuality of ancient brotherhood. It would have sent, as in Pliny's case, "many to execution." It was during those frightfully dangerous days of the early planting that the habit of pious fraud came into the world and humanity has not yet outgrown it. Men like Philip and Avircius whom we are now going to introduce to the reader. were in two worlds at once—the outside and the penetralia. They could be true and faithful to each other under cover of brotherhood, and co-operate for protection; but what they said and did and how they lived, they dared not divulge. In the safe umbrage of this loving retreat, after a long life of hard work and usefulness, we leave Philip the good old apostle and companion of the originals to wax aged and die, and his loving friends and brethren to vote him a heroon with a garland and secret password cozily entwined between the Alpha and Omega, which was to be used to secure his admission, past the roaring pyriphlegethon, through the shining portals of hope, into Elysium.

A running paraphrase of this historical palæograph may be useful to readers too busy to turn to the appendix or to trust to their own classics for a more tasteful rendering. It is short and simple.

"PHILIP, the select, large-minded chief waiter and arch-deacon, of high standing in authority, devoted and famous as an apostle and champion of the divine nature."

In introducing to the reader the celebrated inscription of Avircius Marcellus, a Roman-Greek, who, like the others, had suffered on account of the edict of Claudius driving the trade unions out of Rome over to Apameia, Ephesus and Hierapolis, we feel obliged to present as a parallel illustration, the case of the old man Zeuxis, who, in a similar manner, prescribed his own epitaph long before his death.

Flavius Zeuxis, a ship's captain, belonged to the order of the Collegia Nautiorum. We give in a note[73] the epitaph, and in our text a paraphrase of the general meaning, leaving to the more critical reader our translation

[73] Rams., *Cit. Bish. Phryg.*, II., p. 553, no. 420: "Φλαούιος Ζεῦξις ἐργαστὴς πλεύσας ὑπὲρ Μαλέαν εἰς Ἰταλίαν πλοᾶς ἑβδομήκοντα δύο κατεσκεύασεν τὸ μνημεῖον ἑαυτῷ καὶ τοῖς τέκνοις φλαουίῳ Θεοδώρῳ καὶ φλαουίῳ Θεύδᾳ καὶ ᾧ ἂν ἐκεῖνοι συνχωρήσωσιν."

in the appendix. Flavius Zeuxis, a man loving hard toil at his trade, engaged, in the good business of mariner between Malea the dangerous Cape Mary and Italy, having made in his lifetime seventy-two voyages, causes the erection of this memorial sepulchre. It is to be the tomb of himself and his children, by name, Flavius Theodore, and Flavius Theuda; and indeed, when the time comes, also for the comrades united in the brotherhood with him.

Here we have an old man who is combined with many associates of the union or unions of mariners with headquarters at Hierapolis. After seventy-two voyages over the dangerous cape, always feared by the ancient sailor on account of the treacherous storms; having braved and out-lived them all, in his old age he has come back to Hierapolis to die. The monument which has outlived the political and meteorological vicissitudes of nearly two thousand years must have been solidly built and costly.

Not far from this, about three miles to the southward in the old bath-house at the hot springs there was until recently, another singular monument. As we interpret it, an old man named Avircius Marcellus, whose name shows him to have been a Roman, but who claims to be a citizen of this town, had a still more elaborate sepulchre made for himself and his.

Now when we hold this curious and wonderful find as only one of thousands of the same sort chiseled in those days, we can treat with no lightness the opinions of several learned doctors who are puzzled with it. We are obliged to vary from them however as to the date. The inscription of Avircius is indeed blind in its diction and misleading; but it is certainly detailing history of the age of Paul; and Dr. Ramsay admits that this disciple saw and journeyed with Paul. What is perhaps invaluable as a point in history is that it reads as though this acquaintance was in Babylon and the region of the Euphrates—a revelation which would help to clear up the literary statements of several Ante-Nicine fathers, who also declare that Paul in the interval between his two imprisonments visited Babylon. So it is strenuously declared of Peter; but all records of the circumstances are shrouded in dense mystery. More light is needed and Avircius may shed a first sight glimmer.

But what we think not so marvelous about Avircius is the commonplace reading for a very commonplace thing. The old man had been a weaver or knitter, evidently during the most of his life. If he was one of those driven by Claudius out of Rome by that edict of banishment and went over when young to Hierapolis, as some did to Kelainæ and others did to Ephesus, there should be nothing surprising if they settled a Roman ktisis early among the brotherhoods; since this of itself would have established christianity in the kuriakos of the old guilds. Nor would this interfere with Prof. Ficker's theory that he was a priest of Cybele; for Hadrian, a few years afterwards discovered that at Alexandria, right among the working people whom he mentions as skilled, such were nothing other than organizations turning their name from pagan to christian. So in the Phrygian Pentapolis it was the same christian converts who were innumerable,[74] and they were so secret that they had to employ illusions of various sorts to evade the ogling eyes of the police lest they be arrested.

But another proof that Avircius lived and labored during the apostolic age is his acknowledgment in glaring terms upon the stone, that it was at the close of the thirteen years' cessation from persecution.[75] Now Claudius, and Caligula before him, were the two first persecutors. Nero followed and continued the tragedy until his assassination in 69. Vespasian's whole reign was one of peace and kindness, and also that of his son Titus who reigned until 81. Thus from 69 to 81, and a year before Domitian began his furious murders, were just thirteen years; and what makes this a coincidence corroborating our estimate of this stone's apostolic date is Dr. Ramsay's own statement that the valley was early

---

[74] A christian roofers' association is discovered and recorded in CIG 3877: Κύριε βοήθει· περὶ εὐχῆς Εὐνομίου κὲ παντὸς τοῦ οἴκου αὐτοῦ....στρώσεως. The first glance shows that it is christian, since κυριε βοηθει are strictly christian. See Ramsay, *Cit. Bish. Phryg.*, II., p. 736, no. 671. Παντὸς τοῦ οἴκου shows that the person here understood is a lord of a House as usual, in other words, a president of a union of roofers.

[75] Lightfoot, *Coloss.*, pp. 54. 66. He rightly thought Avircius to have been very early, and makes a statement, based on his better and original judgment before being confused by Ramsay's suspicion that Avircius came late, to the effect that Avircius followed Papias, who knew Paul. "In the earlier editions, I had given a place to Avircius, Bishop of Hierapolis, between Papias and Claudius Apollinaris following the extant *Acts of Avircius*" and refers to his further discussion of the subject in his *Ignatius and Polycarp*. I., ᴛ 477 sq.

christianized; he speaks of Bartholomew and his work, being near that of Paul, as though hinting his partly formed opinion that Avircius might have aided in the work. He admits that Avircius helped to build the Hierapolitan church as the history centers round the name of Avircius only; the date he assigns as fixed by the thirteen years of profound peace, but overlooks the great fact that these thirteen years were during the benign reigns of Vespasian and Titus.

Dr. Ramsay[76] is anxious that Avircius should disclaim against Montanism, but there is not a word in the inscription about it; he admits in support of this absurdity an interpolation in the form of the word *phaneros* in place of the original and comprehensible word *kairos* showing him to have practiced the quills and shuttle for a living, and to have worked in the thrums and threads of woof and warp. A kairos was a weaver, and the word sometimes had a terminal omega as in this case; he admits that Avircius wrote for this epitaph: "In Rome, I saw the emperor and empress:" In another place: "I met and traveled with Paul." He compares (p. 729) a passage in Reinach *eis to erarion demou Rhomaion* favorably with a passage in this; yet such a sentence would mean that the fine was to be paid into the eranos—erarion being a corruption of eranion which is good Greek for eranos—of the Romans, the poor people, plebeians. Evident secrecy shows him an initiate. The spelling shows it as an early inscription of the time of Claudius.

[76] Ramsay, *Cit. Bish, Phryg.*, II., pp. 722-3:

Ἐκλεκτῆς πόλεως ὁ πολείτης τοῦτ' ἐποίησα
  ζῶν, ἵν' ἔχω καιρῷ [φανερῶς] σώματος ἔνθα θέσιν,
οὔνομ' Ἀουίρκιος ὤν, ὁ μαθητὴς Ποιμένος ἁγνοῦ,
4 ὃς βόσκει προβάτων ἀγέλας ὄρεσιν πεδίοις τε,
  ὀφθαλμοὺς ὃς ἔχει μεγάλους καὶ πάνθ' ὁρόωντας·
  οὗτος γάρ μ' ἐδίδαξε .... γράμματα πιστά,
  εἰς Ῥώμην ὃς ἔπεμψεν ἐμὲν βασιλῆαν ἀθρῆσαι,
8 καὶ βασίλισσαν ἰδεῖν χρυσόστολον χρυσοπέδιλον·
  λαὸν δ' εἶδον ἐκεῖ λαμπρὰν σφραγεῖδαν ἔχοντα·
  καὶ Συρίης πέδον εἶδα καὶ ἄστεα πάντα, Νίσιβιν,
  Εὐφράτην διαβάς· πάντη δ' ἔσχον συνομήθεις.
12 Παῦλον ἔχων ἐπόμην, Πίστις πάντη δὲ προῆγε
  καὶ παρέθηκε τροφὴν πάντη, Ἰχθὺν ἀπὸ πηγῆς,
  παμμεγέθη, καθαρόν, ὃν ἐδράξατο Παρθένος ἁγνή,
  καὶ τοῦτον ἐπέδωκε φίλοις ἔσθειν διὰ παντός,
16 οἶνον χρηστὸν ἔχουσα, κέρασμα διδοῦσα μετ' ἄρτου.
  ταῦτα παρεστὼς εἶπον Ἀουίρκιος ὧδε γραφῆναι.
  ἑβδομηκοστὸν ἔτος καὶ δεύτερον ἦγον ἀληθῶς.
  ταῦθ' ὁ νοῶν εὔξαιθ' ὑπὲρ αὐτοῦ πᾶς ὁ συνῳδός.
20 οὐ μέντοι τύμβῳ τις ἐμῷ ἕτερόν τινα θήσει·
  εἰ δ' οὖν, Ῥωμαίων ταμείῳ θήσει δισχείλια χρυσᾶ,
  καὶ χρηστῇ πατρίδι Ἱεράπολι χείλια χρυσᾶ.
We restore καιρῷς for φανερῶς, as it makes sense, see Hesych., ii.. 110

All these are acknowledgments of our point that this inscription relates of a certain disciple who came to or was born at Hierapolis, worked at his trade in textile weaving, worked with Paul, John and the others as an apostle, and being a lord of the house of weavers, grew old in good works, and was loved and remembered in after ages.

Of all the superstructural, predetermined efforts to relegate this honest old saint who had worked for Paul, to the degenerate wranglings of gnosticism, this senseless talk of professors, looks to us most absurd The modest little inscription, per se, hardly talks that way.

We paraphrase it conscientiously to our own interpretation:

"I, a citizen of this town and one of the chosen, hereby and while living, construct and ordain, being a weaver at the loom while in the flesh, under the name *Avircius* a disciple for the holy Ghost, was one who fed sheep and flocks at the foot of the mountains, having my eyes open to the great, rushing progress ahead and taught the words and writings of faith. We were in Rome where the crowds are collected, and saw the emperor and empress, golden-sandaled, arrayed in royal robes; saw the people having a brilliant butchery. And the land of Syria I saw and all its towns and cities, including Nisibis across the Euphrates. The brothers, all gathered together; having Paul they were busy with him and followed him. They provided every delicacy, fish from the fountain; mixed beverages for the crowd, and co-sympathy the chaste and holy maiden won and grasped; and of all that there was, he gave to the brothers to eat;—wine, the purest to be had, mixed beverages, he gave us with bread. All this on the friendly hearth Avircius saw, so that in this wise he might write it down. Two and seventy years have I thus righteously accomplished in the sense of fellow-sharing and enjoyment.

Let no one then, obtrude himself upon my tomb or allow another to enter; but should it be done, a fine of two thousand pieces of gold shall be paid into the treasury of the eranos on account of the Roman members, and a fine of one thousand pieces of gold into the treasury of the eranos on account of the good and serviceable city of my nativity, Hierapolis."

Dr. Ramsey says the inscription was for centuries at the hot springs in the old bath-house, a short distance south of Hierapolis. This was near the mephitic Plutonium, spoken of by Dr. Lightfoot, as known to the superstitious during the time of Paul.[77]

After carefully fanning the chaff from the wheat, and sifting the legendary from the solid fact, we are prepared with sufficient evidence from the stone itself, to place Avircius Marcellus as one of the earliest fathers, like Ignatius who actually lived and whose name, like this, does not occur in the canonical writings. He probably worked with Bartholomew; and very certainly with Paul, if we can believe the stone. If he was mentioned in the Epistles the name has been suppressed or overlooked. Like Ignatius, he was fond of being known and recognized, commemorating himself by means of this composition and epitome, chiseled upon his tomb — a thing especially frequent, and also in constant usage among the collegia and eranoi everywhere.[78] We have many wills, both Latin and Greek, bequeathing money to them in considerable sums, the only remuneration being that the unions appropriate annually to the deceased donor a memorial feast. Avircius had become so emboldened by thirteen years of the two delightful reigns of Vespasian and Titus, who, though severe with the Jews, were, like Tiberius, friendly, almost fatherly to the christians, that he ventured boldly to try his fortune in this modest bit of literary history of himself. He was, to all appearances, another father or president; a kurios or lord of an important guild — a union of textile workers owning a house, or as they would call it before conversion, a temple; and this, if he was a recognized

---

[77] Lightfoot, "Coloss.," p. 12: "At Hierapolis was a spot called the Plutonium, a hot well or spring, from whose narrow mouth issued a mephitic vapor immediately fatal to those who stood over the opening and inhaled its fumes. To the mutilated priests of Cybele, alone, so it was believed, an immunity was given from heaven, which freed them from its deadly effects. Indeed, this city appears to have been a chief centre of the passionate mystical devotion of ancient Phrygia."

[78] Oehler, on "Wills, MSS.": "In Thessalonike hat eine Priesterin εἰς μνίας χάριν αἰωνίας 2 Plethren Weinbirge hinterlassen damit die Mystem jährlich an ihrem Grabe ein Fest feiern, wohl die Rosalia, Duchesne-Bayet, "Mission au Mont Athos," p. 35, nr. 44.". Again: "In Thera erfahren wir ausser der grossen Stiftung der Epikteta von dem Legate einer gewissen Argea: diese hat einem κοινόν fünf hundert δράχμαι versprochen ὥστε ἐπάγεσθαι ἀνά πᾶσαν ἑβδόμαν αὐτάς τε καὶ τὰς θυγατρὸς Ἰσθμῶς καταβ'. Lüders, "Dionys. Künst.," p. 25 und nr. 48." A woman wills 500 drachmas, to be repaid in annual banquets in her own and her daughter's honor, at the periodical meeting IG. 2469; Rangabé, 893, 1208; Ross, 423. Many others are noticeable.

magistrate and responsible president, head or director would make him a cure, a father and lord. Thus the temple, following the scheme of the law of Solon, under provisions of that aged statute, would be a house of the lord. Paul, several times is seen to have disappeared and he probably hid himself away in these delightful, congenial, but inapproachably occult retreats.

Dion Chrysostom and Josephus who lived at the same time, could write well, but Avircius could not. Dr. Ramsay complains bitterly at the shabby Greek in the inscriptions, and the frequent bad spelling met with, but does not seem to comprehend the standing excuse. Wherever these learned and very critical epigraphists think they are dealing with an important character, a gerusiarch, a quinquennalis, or even sometimes an Asiarch and are judging him from outward appearances, they are in reality dealing with one or another of these kurioi or epimelites who were sure to be self-made men, who by an inborn aptitude or happy capacity for business, had worked themselves by years of toil, care and fidility to the position of quinquennalis or kurios, and been crowned, though often descendants of slaves, and in many cases actual slaves without any education except what they had picked up. The outside world treated all such with scathing contempt as Lucian tells us the men in the secret unions could never obtain the slightest contact with them. Yet if we believe Origen, Celsus and Lucian, these were the secret hives which the early christians had built our era and civilization into.

How then could we expect this faithful old Roman, Avircius Marcellus, to scratch down a chapter in Dion or Paul's beautiful Greek upon his sepulchre?

Quite an extended apocryphal literature has come down to us through this inscription of Avircius, the old original who wrote his epitaph at Hierapolis. It is all legendary and hypothetical, trumped up to suit the whims and the caprices of the post apostolic priestcraft.[79] There is, however, one inscription marking the grave of

[79] We recommend the reader's attention on the subject of the later conceptions regarding it, to Dr. Ramsay's invaluable work, *Cit. Bish. Phryg.*, Vol. II., pp. 722-9. This eminent researcher has himself conceived the date of the original Avircian or Abircian inscription, to be as late as Severus, which is, however, impossible and untenable.

a certain Avircius Porphurius, which it is worth our while to make mention of and quote,[80] on account of the beautiful engraving of the child Jesus upon the stone, giving the epitaph. The date of this monument is without doubt correctly stated by Dr. Ramsay at about A.D. 300. He is perhaps a descendant of the old man at Hierapolis, although it was common at that time to give to new converts another name at the baptism, or the initiation.

But the original stone of the first Avircius who was the disciple, as he names himself, and became so celebrated on account of the celebrity of the church at this place that many legends have come down, even to this day, and still wilder tales and imitations filled the more primitive mind. There are indeed twenty or thirty inscriptions showing this, all of a later period by some two hundred years, and we shall pass them by without further notice.

Paul was once lost from Ephesus in some mysterious manner for two years, and we are disposed to think that he may have sequestered himself here under the friendly care and secret protection of this union of warm-hearted brothers all busy weaving the textiles for the tents and bedding and other artistic paraphernalia he knew how to make for the Dionysan artists, and loved so much to do as real recreation from his exhausting evangelistic labors; also perhaps to recover from his known, chronic malady.

In the same manner we might trace many New Testament names back to the unions over which they presided. Among them, besides those already enumerated, we could single out Phœbe, Nymphas, Jason of Thessalonica, Barnabas, Bartholomew and a host of others. They each had an unexplained power and influence and performed their work well. The Breviary of the martyrs and apostles gives us vague assurance and data as to how long each lived, to what functions they rose, and when, where and how they died; but this is legendary and so late in after years that they should be accepted with caution.

[80] Ramsay, *Cit. Bish. Phryg.*, Vol. II., p, 736, no. 672; Cumont, 190; Le grand and Chamonard, BCH. 1893, p. 290; It reads: "'Αβίρκιος Πορφυρίου διάκων κατεσκεύασα τὸ μεπόριον ἑαυτῷ καὶ τῇ συμβίῳ μου Θρευπρεπίῃ κὲ τοῖς τέκνοις."

We have brought these illustrations forward to explain the phenomena of the early plant. The dangers attending a revelation of what those unions did to the outside world must now be plain to the reader. The house of the lord of the Solonic law was legitimate and kindly treated under Tiberius, and after Nero, by the Flavian emperors for about thirteen years; but it was terribly handled by Claudius, Nero and Domitian. The domus Augustalis had its industries within the building of the imperial family, each department of the labor being worked by a specially organized trade and each of these sections of the business was called a gynæceum. Following the proclivities of all the Solonic unions, each was supplied with a school called schola. The method continued to the time of Celsus who hated them because they had become christians; and there is a scrap quoted from his last book, by Origen which sheds so much new light upon our argument that we cannot but quote the English translation.

Apparently assuming that he is one of them, Celsus mockingly taunts the christians: "We are indeed in private houses, as workers in wool and leather, and fullers and persons of the most uninstructed and rustic character, not venturing to utter a word in the presence of their elders and wiser masters; but when they get hold of the children privately, and certain women as ignorant as themselves, they pour forth wonderful statements to the effect that they ought not to heed their fathers and teachers......but must leave them and go with the women and their playfellows, to the women's apartments, or to the leather shop, or to the fuller's shop, that they may attain perfection." Celsus is sneering at, and accusing the christian communes of poverty and other things which he considers vile. Origen, in defense of them quotes, quibbles and does not deny.

CHAPTER XIX.

CELSUS AND LUCIAN.

PAGAN Literature of Early Christian Times—Celsus the Accuser—Twits Christians of Hiding in the Secret Unions—Gynæceum—It was a School—Origen's Contra Celsum—Declaration that They were Genuine Unions—Origen His Critic, Does not Deny—Belabors Christians Because Secret—Berates their Holding Love-feasts—Sneers because they were Working People—Lucian of Samosata—Pagan Wit who Lampoons the Christians—The Two were Friends—Payment of Tribute—Paschal Canon says Origen was a Brazier—Defiant Comparisons of Celsus—The Prytaneum—How the Church of St. Peter Came to be Built—The Secret Password—Temples of Refuge—Period of Columbaria—Lanuvium—Wonderful Inscription Found in 1816—Quinquenalis a Dictator—Growth in our Knowledge of the Burial Clause and Burial Attachment—Churches in Ruins of Ancient Unions—Old Temples Used as Churches—Christianized Temple of Isis at Pompeii—Old Labor Guilds—Dug Out of Lava of Vesuvius—Dr. Willens on the Labor Guilds—Pompeii—Although Christanized, at Time of Eruption, Were Still Worshiping in Temple of Isis—Owned Some of Its Property—Hated Pests Exiled—Escaping to Similar Temples of Refuge—Went to Gaul, Asia Minor, Allobrogia, Vienne.

THERE was a considerable literature at a very early time written by the members of the unions, the early historians and a number of able and brilliant pagan writers, before the middle of the second century. That of Clement we have already given. One valuable book, that of Epictetus, called the *Enchiridion,* was written by Arrian at the close of the apostolic age, according to his pupil, probably at Hierapolis. He may be yet discovered to have actually written information of great value to our subject, and undoubtedly gave hints in his lectures regarding the plant of the christians into the old brotherhoods. Another valuable and very early

A BRAZEN LITERARY STATEMENT. 645

book was the Expositio Oraculorum of Papias a friend and companion of St. Philip, and undoubtedly of Paul. It appears that he was martyred, perhaps in the time of Domitian. It is very sad to reflect that this work was destroyed. It contained rules of life among the brotherhoods and was suppressed because it told just what we greatly want to know. To all appearances, much that was written in his book confirmed what Celsus charged and Origen did not deny.

Then Hegesippus wrote another very valuable work, which is known to have recorded much concerning the Nazarene, the ebionites and the eranists; all of which associations are now put by our investigators among genuine unions and labor guilds. But this invaluable book of Hegesippus is also lost.

It was early in the second century, only a few years after Pliny had undergone his disagreeable experiences with the christians who had planted among the trade unions of Bithynia that Celsus came out with his significant book, against the christians entitled "Logos Alethes" or The Word of Truth. This work was so completely suppressed that no copy is supposed to exist to-day. Fortunately for the world, however, Origen in attempting a refutation of what Celsus wrote, has left us in his "Contra Celsum," many of its important verbatim statements and a large number of lengthy quotations from it, so that for our particular purpose in this argument, the book is preserved.

Here in a brazen statement written at an early age is the wonderful disclosure which we have announced and are attempting to verify by every literary and inscriptional evidence to be found; namely that the christians planted into and for the first two hundred years derived their sustenance, support, legalization, and economical life from labor unions of the ancient world. The evidence of Celsus is overwhelming.[1] Celsus was born in A. D. 112, or as some think, A. D. 120, and he afterwards wrote of what he had seen in his early boyhood. He bitterly accuses the christians of entering into secret

[1] Origen, "Contra Celsum," I., says: Πρώτῳ Κέλσῳ κεφαλαιόν ἐστι διαβαλεῖν χριστιανισμόν, ὡς συνθήκας κρύβδην πρὸς ἀλλήλους ποιουμένων χριστιανῶν παρὰ τὰ νεμομισμένα." The συνθήκη was a secret association of workingmen, a trade union, for so says Pliny. Origen seems to acquiesce in these allegations for he goes on to state the reasons why this was so, without denying it.

associations, with the object to discredit their agapæ or lovefeasts, and is opposed to them, evidently because he knew that the old unions existing all around him, had been enjoying such legal rights from time immemorial, and being himself a pagan, was angry because the new sect had adopted these symposiums of true love and virtue.

Celsus belabors the christians in his book, because they resorted to the utmost secrecy during the persecutions,[2] hiding away in occult brotherhoods. He declares that they were secret societies contrary to law and had their lovefeasts or agapæ, which included the common table. The great Origen, quoting this, makes no effort at refutation; he is glad that the accusation is true and proceeds to rejoice at their success, declaring that they first planted in the mass of the uneducated. He boasts of the phenomenal growth of the new plant, especially as the way was "beset with opposition from princes, chiefs, captains, guards and all, to speak generally, who were possessed of the smallest influence; and in addition to these, the rulers of the different cities, the soldiers and the people." Celsus held that the poor, the wretched who had to work for a living, the outcasts who were not allowed to be enumerated in the census of population and the artists and mechanics, were the element planted into.[3] Celsus seriously charged that they were composed of barbarian elements. Yet these were powerfully organized at that time.

Lucian, the celebrated sarcastic writer, lived and flourished during the same years with Celsus and we now know positively that the two ingenious men were acquaintances. But while Celsus appears to have composed his book to curry favors with the influential in order to obtain some appointment, Lucian squarely acknowledges that he wrote to make a living by selling his productions. Of the two we should admire this last exquisite blackguard most.

But Lucian, although he does not often mention the name of the christians, gives us some powerful points tending to prove our discovery that christianity had for

---

[2] Origen, *Contra Celsum*, VIII., c. 41: "'Ἤτοι φεύγοντες καὶ κρυπτόμενοι ἢ ἀλισκόμενοι χαὶ ἀπυλλύμενοι." Cf. Neander, *Hist. Eccles.*, I., p. 108, note 1.
[3] Origen, *Cont. Cels.*. VIII., c, 27. Consult *Ante-Nicine Fathers*, Vol. IV., pp. 397 and 408. The admissions of both Celsus and Origen are complete.

its early cradle the unions of laboring people. In one place he speaks of them directly in connection with the Dionysan artists and indeed the wandering fakirs belonging to their vast organization, and shows how these metragyrtes, vagabonds, wonderworkers and jugglers, cunningly took advantage of christian credulity, wimbled themselves into their brotherly embraces and swindled them of their means.[4] The celebrated Conyers Middleton, a university professor at Cambridge during the seventeenth century, speaks of the intercourse between christians and this branch of the great Gemeinde as follows: "In the performance of their miracles, they were always charged with fraud and imposture by adversaries. Lucian who flourished during the second century, tells us that whenever any crafty juggler, expert in his trade, and who knew how to make a right use of things went over to the christians, he was sure to grow rich immediately by making a prey of their simplicity; and Celsus represents all the christian wondermakers as mere vagabonds and common cheats, who rambled all about to play their tricks at fairs and markets; not in the circles of the wiser and better sort, for among such they never ventured to appear, but whenever they observed a set of raw young fellows, slaves or fools, there they took care to intrude themselves and so display all of their arts." Here we have a metragyrte, christianized. Of all the many branches of the great Gemeinde, to an analysis of which many archæologists are devoting time and learning, these metragyrtes were the falsest and meanest in the whole international union. Quite a number of pagan writers and bitter adversaries of the christians gave vent to their hatred of them during the ante-Nicine age and an immense literary warfare followed against Celsus, Porphyry, and the emperor Julian,[5] because they all lampooned the fakirs. These metragyrtes were the typical fakirs of the ancient and modern world. Not one was there who was not an initiate into

[4] See *Index*, in verb. *Lucian*, pointing to a full description of this organization. The above quotation given in our text is from *Middleton's Works*, I., p. 19.
[5] Jerom., *Adv. Jovinianum, Apolog.* II., p. 135: "Origenes, Methodius, Eusebius, Appollinaris, multis versuum millibus scribunt adversus Celsum et Porphyrium, Considerate quibus argumentis et quam lubricis problematibus diaboli spiritu contexta subvertunt; et quia interdum coguntur loqui, non quod sentiunt sed quod necesse est dicunt adversus ea quæ dicunt Gentiles."

some union of the great international order.⁶ Under umbrage of such a power they worked their wiles to get influence, wherewith to fleece the christians who succeeded in converting membership after membership and they often penetrated the dingy grottoes, mud-hovels, and tents of the wandering wonderworkers and fakirs. Celsus says the element which the christians preferred, was the ignorant, the unintelligent, the foolish, "by which words acknowledging that such individuals are worthy of their God; manifestly showing that they desire, and are able to gain over only the silly workmen, the mean, the stupid, along with their women and children."⁷

Celsus who certainly knew of the trouble which Pliny encountered with the christianized unions in Bithynia and Pontus, was aware that these unions, christian members and all, had left paganism which he loved to bow down to and extol, accuses that: "The cause which led to the new state of things was their rebellion against the state." And he takes the clue that both the Jews and the Romans considered the innovation of christianity to be a rebellion. The new Word of promise, with its refusal to allow its communicants to pay into the temples the accustomed tribute, or buy the sacrifices, was robbery of the government's treasury. Celsus carried his accusation farther and attacked Jesus' life in Egypt,⁸ declaring, on account of his wretched penury while there, that he was obliged to hire himself to perform tricks of legerdemain and thus work out a scanty living by cheating. He accuses the christians, in his third chapter, of barbarism, twitting that Jews and Gentiles were mixed and confounded, keeping up their false teachings in secret. Origen does not deny a word of the accusations, but waives the straight forward discourse of Celsus, which undoubtedly let much light into their communal origin and economic life.

⁶ *Digest*, XLVII., xxii., 4: "ἢ ἐπὶ λίαν οἰχόμενοι." This clause in the law of Solon under which the μητραγυρτες were organized carried out the letter of its text, legalizing wandering vagabonds, the fakirs, gypsies and as Dr. August Böckh maintained, it likewise covered pirates and corsairs.
⁷ Celsus, Λόγος 'Αληθῆς, *ap.* Orig., *Adv. Cels.*, III., c. 44.
⁸ Neander, *Hist. Eccles.*, I.. p. 152, note 1. quoting Celsus, Lucian's friend, *ap.* Orig., *Adv. Christianos*, which is the same Λόγος 'Αληθῆς, where he accuses that Jesus on account of his poverty was obliged to hire himself out to the same cheat and deception. "Ὅτι οὗτος διὰ πένιαν εἰς Αἴγυπτον μισθαρνήσας κἀκεῖ δυνάμεων τινῶν πειραθείς, ἐφ' εἷς Αἰγύπτιοί σεμνύνονται, ἐπανῆλθεν, ἐν δυνάμεσι μέγα φθορω δὲ καὶ αὐταῖς θεὸν αὐτὸν ἀνηγόρευσιν."

The eminent Mosheim, in discussing this subject of the phenomenal success of the early plant, while he knows nothing of the secret unions and their influence to secure food, shelter, protection in their secret abodes and permanency of the Word of promise, after once being converted, makes the admission of the truth of Celsus' slurring,[9] that the first christians were no better than mere plebeian slaves and paltry laborers delving in fields and workshops; and argues that virtue and self-denial of the apostles would not of itself have converted great numbers to christianity. He brings in the testimony of such pagan writers as follows: "Others, following the example of Celsus, Julian, Porphyry and other enemies, bid us consider that the churches gathered by the apostles, were composed of plebeian characters, servants, laborers in the field and shop, together with their women."

We have abundant proof that all these were closely organized into economic guilds and unions. Indeed, the second accusation of Celsus against the christians was as much as to say that the plant was in the Solonic brotherhoods already established.

Origen was himself a tradesman and had to work at his profession as brazier while teaching the youth at Alexandria because the four oboles a day which he reluctantly took as a recompense for his work were not enough to sustain life. Alexandria being full of therapeutic, mithraic and essenic societies, branches of the great Solonic compact as we are now told by the inscription-readers of the seminaries, and there being unions of braziers doing business in that town during this sage's time, it is quite likely that he was a member. This probability is the more reasonable when we reflect that while teaching at Cæsarea, years afterwards, when persecuted by the arrogance of the already ambitious and intolerant prelates, he disappeared in Tyre and lived out the remainder of his life under the veil of some secret brotherhood, for particulars of which we are left in the dark. Anatolicus, in his Paschal Canon, declares "Origen, the most erudite of all, and the acutest in making calculations — a man too, to whom the

---

[9] Mosheim. *Die Rebus Christ*, pp. 90-2; *Hist. Eccles.*, I., First Century, pt. I., ch. iv., § 10,

epithet Chalkeutes or brazier is given."[10] Outside of this he is known to have been a mechanic. Yet Origen, in his celebrated effort to refute the diatribes of Celsus, virtually acknowledges a great deal to be true. He says: "Celsus compares inconsiderate believers with metragyrtæ, soothsayers, mithræ and sabbadians," giving out that the christians went hand in hand with, and were a part of them; but he does not deny that it was so. Upon this we might call the readers' attention to the fact that mithræ were invariably organized into unions and are so classed in the most recent books and papers of the archæologists. The mithræ approached nearest to christians in their belief, line of life and their brotherly affiliations, of all ancient organizations known; yet they are pronounced to be trade guilds.

We have now come to the most convincing argument of Celsus, that of the "defiant comparisons." To introduce this we must drop our modern plan of reasoning, based upon things as we see them to-day. We must contemplate mankind, divided into two great hemispheres, the one visible, the other veiled in mystery; the one open and official, the other lowly and unrecognized. We must look upon the vast, secret organizations compelled by law to follow and be patterned after the plan of organization forming the best democratic cities, they in turn being patterned after the socialism of the well regulated family. The trade union, therefore, was a microcosm of the state; having the common table because that is the economic socialism of the family. The plan was adopted by the disciples of Jesus in accordance with his special teachings. The first objection the modern critic would raise to this is that the model city of the ancients did not have the common table. The answer is: "Go back to the higher antiquity of Solon and Lycurgus and Numa Pompilius and you will find it. You will find it in the Prytaneum of Athens,[11] and

[10] Anatol., *Paschal Canon*, 1; See *Ante-Nicene Fathers*, Vol., VI., p. 146, where the above *trans.* stands. The χαλκευταὶ were included in the original list of Solonic and Numan unions. *Dig.*, XLVII., tit. xxii., lex. 4. The unions of braziers were very important and influential in Rome. They were extensively employed by the government after the commencement of the conquests, making armor for the use of the troops. Plutarch, *Numa*, 17, tells us that Numa placed it as one of the unions of the great Numan law: "'Ην δὲ ἡ διανομὴ κατὰ τὰς τέχνας αὐλητῶν, χρυσοχόων, τεκτόνων, βαφέων, σκυτοτόμων, σκυτοδεψῶν, χαλκέων, κεραμέων."

[11] Oehler, *Pauly-Wissowa*, Vol. III., p. 1026: "Die Prytanen bildeten gleichfalls eine politische Körperschaft. Sie erwählten für die Dauer der

FINE STATE AND MUNICIPAL KITCHENS. 651

Dr. Oehler has shown that it was also in many of the cities.

In the great outside official, political world of Athens and many other cities there was an enormous state kitchen, where was cooked and served, the very best that could be procured for the members of the Prytaneum, for visitors from different lands, and on certain occasions for the common people, the workingmen, especially, when they assembled here to give evidence which they had a right to do under the law.

The Prytaneum of Athens, adopted by a great many cities, carried out the plan of the common table, practically. It expanded the microscosm of the well regulated family out into the perfect political state, and so far as it went, carried out the principles of socialism. But it was imperfect since those crowned were all it cared for.[12]

That the Prytaneum, a part of the political council of government, had a common table and a communal code, and that the model at Athens was copied into hundreds of other cities, is an established fact. Thousands of people received there, their meals at the common expense of the state all through antiquity, and it was the scheme of their democratic government; but spoiled by the whimsical idea of class.

Thanks to christianity which turned its engines against class and boldly extinguished it, actually planting itself among the poor and ignorant and deriving its support for centuries from the laboring man, the source of all wealth and the fountain of every mouth full of food! The socialism of to-day is basing upon this its vast organization soon to oversweep the arrogance of such privileged and fawning sycophants, and assert and demand its righteous claims. This is the christianity which Celsus hates.

Prytanie einen Schreiber und einen Schatzmeister, CIA. II., 431, 440, 454, 869, 872. Die Prytanen hatten ein Amtslokal in der Nähe des βουλεστήριον, wo sie gemeinsam auf Staatskosten speisten θόλος und σκίας genannt. Aristot., 'Αθ'. πολ., 48, 3, 62, 2: Harpokration, s. θόλος. Ph. s. οἰκίας; Dem., xix., 190; Andok, 112, 45; Poll., VIII., 155; Paus. I., 5, 1; οκοίς CIA, II., 476, u.ö. Sie hatten das Recht Leute, die sich um sie verdient gemacht, zu bekränzen, wie sie selbs oft vom Rate und Volke bekränzt wurden, CIA, II., 190. u.ö. Ueber die Thätigkeit der Prytanen, vgl., Plato. leg. II., 758, B-D. Aristot., 'Αθ' πολ. 43, 3, 6; Aristoph., Equit., 300. An die Prytanen wendeten sich die fremden Gesandten."

[12] Oehler, βουλή in *Pauly-Wissowa*. III., p. 1025: "Νόμος δὲ ἦν τὴν βουλὴν τὴν δόξασαν τῷ δήμῳ καλῶς βεβουλευκέναι στεφανοῦσθαι, Dem., xxii., 12, 36: Aristot.. 'Αθ' πολ, 46, 1."

Celsus in twitting the secret brotherhoods, against whom he claims to make new disclosures based on their meanness in that they belonged to nothing noble and were nothing but low dregs of humanity such as Cato had pronounced that the very contact with was a taint that could not be washed off except by purification in presence of a god, strikes his typical argument, which he calls a *defiant comparison*.

The defiant comparison of Celsus was this: The Prytaneum, ancient, sacred, honorable under legalized form in antiquity, gift to mankind forever, by the wisest of lawgivers, had been smirched through the ineffable daring of the meanest of the human race, the christian brotherhoods of labor, in that they imitated its hallowed economies of the common table and communal code! Celsus did not know of the trade union clause of this ancient statute specifying nearly a dozen trades for these very workers he accuses; or if he did he is not so clear as was Tertullian regarding their settlement among the unions. He only knew that they were found imbedded into and among the occult brotherhoods.[13] This, he and Lucian could perceive without joining; but Hierocles, in the time of Diocletian, was perfidious enough to join and become initiated into their penetralia for no other purpose than to play the spy, and upon his fell perfidy the great massacre was perpetrated, which Dr. Ramsay thinks annihilated them in Phrygia.

Of this, we shall give the reader all that is obtainable, later. Origen, deriving his conclusions from Celsus, calls to mind the fact that the council of the Athenian Prytaneum, where was inscribed for centuries, the original Law of Solon upon a stone slab in the council chamber, was always known as the "*ecclesia*," and what seemingly exasperated Celsus, being a Greek, was that the low-born creatures should use this very word as the name of their temples of worship, the kuriakos, church or house of the Lord. He forgets that clause chiseled upon this stone requiring that each union should imi-

---

[13] Tertullian, *Apolog.*, xxxix., comes out in unmistakable words, in admission that the christian and Solonic brotherhoods were one and the same. See our *index*. In catchwords pointing to pages where it is quoted and where also the acknowledgment of this *is* made by Mommsen, Foucart Oehler, etc. But the remarkable secret to Tertullian's bravery, culminates in his lapsing back into his old and beloved collegium, where he lived to a very old age.

tate the plan and scheme of the city and the perfect state, the model for which was supposed by the Athenians to be the sublimest, stretching toward perfection. The Boulé or council with its Prytaneum, included, as Dr. Oehler shows in the learned article which we have quoted, the common table and communal code.

But while Origen pretends to refute the charges of Celsus, he acknowledges the truth of his "defiant comparisons;" and this is perhaps the most conclusive point we have yet uncovered, showing the christian plant to have been into the ancient unions of potters, braziers, dyers, spinners, weavers and others, all of whose plans of organization were compulsory, under that great law, obliging them to follow the plan of the ecclesia or council of city and state. Ecclesia, then, being the name originally used on the slab in the pronaos of the ancient Prytaneum, we find the comparison of Celsus [14] to be perfectly correct; for the church became the ecclesia on the one hand, speaking in classical generalities; and the kuriakos or house of the union's lord became the church speaking in the commonest every day terms; and it remains so to this day.

But it is to the inscriptions recently being found in many parts that we see a complete verification of the truths of this history. The word ècclesia occurs in almost innumerable inscriptions throughout Greece, Macedonia, and Asia Minor. But not alone for trade unions; the word ecclesia is derived from the ancient boulé with its sub-council at the Prytaneum, and the word diocese also.[16]

The diocese then, is also derived from the ancient trade-union of the Solonic dispensation. Christianity, of which we for the first time give a true history, endorsed the diocese, word, import and all. The prelates

[14] Origen, *Cont. Cels.*, III., cc. 29, 30. So likewise, Origen admits that the defiant comparison consists in the fact that his own church of God was the assembly or ecclesia of Athens, and hundreds of other cities having the Prytaneum with its common table.

[15] Oehler, *Pauly-Wissowa*, art. βουλή: speaking of the functions and province of the secretary: "Der ὑπογραμματεὺς τῆς βουλῆς diente zur regelmässigen Unterstützung des Ratsschreibers, CIA, II., 329, 363, 431, 441. Poll., VIII., 98, erwähnt noch den ἀντιγραφεύς, von dem es heisst πρότερον μὲν αἱρετός, αὖθις δὲ κληρωτὸς ἦν, καὶ πάντα ἀντεγράφετο παρακαθήμενος τῇ βουλῇ: Harpokration, sub verbo βουλή hat die weitere Angabe διττοὶ δὲ ἦσαν ἀντιγραφεῖς, οἱ μὲν τῆς διοικήσεως, ὥς φησι Φιλόχρος ὁ δὲ τῆς βουλῆς, ὡς Ἀριστοτέλης ἐν Ἀθηναίων πολιτείᾳ. In der That wird es derselbe Beamte gewesen sein der Gegenschreiber, welcher als Buchhalter oder Controler des Rates alle die Geldverwaltung des Rates betreffenden Verhandlungen zu beaufsichtigen hatte."

of later ages in collusion with the sycophant falsifiers of their aged competitive system working as they still do in abeyance to monarchs and manipulators, endeavored to suppress these facts.

The works of Porphyry, Celsus, Hierocles and perhaps Zosimus, would furnish much new evidence, if they had not been publicly burned by Theodosius, in A.D, 435.

We know that Zeus is a myth of the past. No more honor is devoted on him. He has lost his aerial throne in the vault of heaven and become obsolete. No one worships him any more. The Greek Jehovah was a deception and a fraud. Yet Porphyry, his worshiper, another pagan like Celsus, wrote a book against the christians, lampooning them in the vilest terms for that which Celsus accused them of, but protesting against any calumniation of the great Jesus whom he declared ought never to be spoken of except in kindest terms. "That pious soul who ascended into heaven, had by a certain fatality become a stumbling block of error to those destined to no share in the gift of the gods and in the knowledge of the eternal Zeus."[16]

Hierocles' work,[17] Logoi Philalethes, regarding christians recounts a great deal which Celsus, Hadrian, Porphyry had already said against Christ and christianity. But it all fell to naught as soon as christianity had aroused the mind of man above the superstitious ratiocinations based on the untenable Jove who, with his palatial structures in the vaulted dome of heaven, proved to be but a ghostly invention arising from the superstitions of simple-minded antiquity. The immense follies of priest-power, which so long had swayed the human mind, began now seriously to crumble; but it did not fall without an overwhelming landslide.

[16] *Fragments*, of Porphyry's Περὶ τῆς ἐκ Λογίων φιλοσοφίας, see Neander, I., p. 170, where he canvasses the moribund theogony of paganism.
[17] Ramsay, *Cit. Bish. Phryg.*, II., p. 507, believes from the evidence of Lactantius who lived about that time, and of Eusebius, that the whole, or nearly the whole of the christian population of southwest Phrygia were massacred. See Gibbon in his sixteenth chapter. Judging from a former use of the word conventicle, we are disposed to think that "conventiculum," in the above quotation, was intended by Lactantius to mean the unions or brotherhoods of that country. We know they were exterminated.

CHAPTER XX.

CHURCHES ON RUINS.

SCHEME of the Early Movement—Metamorphosis of the Temple into the Kuriakos—Origin of Churches—St. Peter's was from Persecuted Collegia of Diana on the Aventine—Vourkano on the Ithome—Orchomenos—Temple of Cybele at Philadelphia—The Phyles and their Guilds—Temple of Jove on Acropolis of Kelaina—Discovery at Ancona—Temple of Isis at Pompeii—How it Became Property of the Multitudes of Voting Trade Unions There—Proof that when Converted They turned it into a Church—Origin of Cathedral of Nôtre Dame at Paris—Remarkable Inscription Found—It was Originally a Temple of a Boatman's Union of the River Seine.

CONSISTENT with the laws which we have carefully explained, nearly all the established pre-christian trade unions possessed their temple as common property, around which were the graveyard, the grove and many fixtures for meetings, discussions, entertainments and comforts of every kind. These, after the crucifixion, and the celebrated enlargement or expansion proposed and carried out by the messiah under his plan of salvation, gradually developed into churches.

There are many monuments and ruins lately being noted, which attest this and we now proceed to point out a few of them.

From Tiberius, who befriended this arrangement, through the short reigns of Vespasian and Titus, there elapsed a period of about sixty years and this constituted the era of the Roman Columbaria; for it was during this time that the christians with their swarms of converted trade and labor unions descended into the earth and hid themselves, sometimes seventy feet below the surface. The period thus engrossed was the one in which the burial colleges took their foothold and developed such specimens of large and model guilds as that of Lanuvium.[1]

During this time, and under the protecting law of the collegium funeraticium, or tenuiorum—a word whose import gave still greater latitude to organization than the purely burial phrase of Mommsen, circumscribed by his word funeraticium which does not appear in the Digest—the christians began to recover from the terrible disaster and it was not long before they were planning the restoration of the temple of Minerva, not far from the ancient site on the Aventine Hill. The cathedral of St. Peter at Rome, therefore, may be considered as originally a church on ruins, as was also that of Paris; and it may be truthfully assumed that both of the now grand and imposing structures are developments from old guild temples of the time of Tiberius and perhaps ages before.

With our former descriptions of the so-called burial union of Lanuvium we may proceed to the union itself and a word on the church built from its ruins. Lanuvium, or as it is now called Citta Lavinia, is at a distance of only eighteen miles from Rome, on the Appian Way. The inscription was discovered in 1816. It has been thoroughly analyzed by Rattius, Cardinali and Mommsen, and is admitted to be the most perfectly preserved union of the burial type.[2] It has been a subject of much mention of late, by most of the great archæologists. Dr. Waltzing speaks of its president called in the tablet the quinquennalis, as the "dictator," and his great importance in this one instance is but an example of the almost supreme power held by every kurios or director in all the unions of the world alike. They were veritable dictators or lords having a temple

[1] Waltzing, *Hist. Corp. Prof,*, p. 261. True collegia tenuiorum or funeraticium. Dr. Waltzing holds these to be trade unions, and to have been the immediate successors of the columbaria, purely Roman institutions, having few imitations outside of the capital city: "Les plus fameux sont, le collegium Æsculapi et Hygiæ, à Rome; les cultores colegii Silvani de Philippes; le collegium Jovis Cernani d' Alburnus Major en Dacie, et un Collegium Silvani de Lucanie, qui nous out lessé de belles inscriptiones."

[2] See Vol. I., pp. 353-8, where the entire inscription is given, including the law of the union. As to its size and shape, see Mommsen, *De Coll. et Sodal. Rom.*, p. 130: "Inventa est Lanuvii (città Lavinia) a. 1816, sub ruderibus balnei publici, cum ipsis, quibus adfixa fuerat ferramentis, in tabula marmorea sæpe fracta, longa septem palmas cum tribus unciis; alta tres palmas unciasque decem ex hodierna mensura Romana. Inscriptio ipsa supra sex palmas uncias octo, infra sex palmas cum una uncia occupat."

FUNCTIONS OF TEMPLE EXPLAINED. 657

under their management,³ and this house, or in Greek, kuriakos, was the New Testament "house of the Lord," after the christians began to convert their membership to the new Word of promise.

This large and numerous guild was not, as Mommsen and others half a century ago, held, confined to the single function of the burial of their own dead. This can be proved by closely consulting the words of its law. But the more recent researches among similar inscriptions of similar date, in Asia Minor, are convincing the epigraphists that they were all trade unions of the genuine sort, only possessing in later times the legalization of the burial attachment under which they covertly careered.⁴ We are not clearly informed regarding the church after the conversion of this great guild. Sooner or later it was converted and the temple of Diana, on whose tetrastyl the marble inscription was chiseled, became one of the christian shrines.

At Pompeii another remarkable church on the ruins of the ancient temples of gods and goddesses is found, through the excavations, among the lava beds, and which is another proof of the falsity of historians, prone to cater to their monarchs, desirous only for self-preferment and working among falsehoods for the glory of individuals. A great temple of Isis is found to have been completely converted to christianity. The earthquake which overwhelmed the city took place in A.D. 79. Jupiter, who controlled the destinies of time and events was believed to be angry. Pompeii had been sunk, Rome burned, Jerusalem massacred, pythons of enormous size had entered the eternal city swallowing children alive; an amphitheatre, the work of contract jobbers had collapsed, destroying fifty-seven thousand innocents, and many awful casualties had come to pass, which were regarded by superstitious men and women as premonitions of many still more serious and dreadful events.

---

³ Waltzing, *Hist. Corp. Prof.*, I., p. 211: "À Lanuvium, A.D. 136, le dictateur fait tenir une assemblée générale du collège de Diane et Antinoüs dans le temple de ce dieu, pour voter les statuts, et ces statuts sont affichés par son ordre sous le tetrastyl ou pronaon de ce temple, CIL. XII., 2112, lines 1-3, 7.

⁴ The inscription itself speaks of being dependent for their thrift upon their labor; "Bene adque industrie contraxerimus ut exitu defunctorum honeste prosequamur." They certainly worked for their own emancipation from slavery.

As in Rome, so in Pompeii, this temple of Isis, like the goddess herself commanded the respect and veneration of mechanics and the working people generally. Connected with Anubis, Isis was regarded as the patron divinity of the chase and her functions were in many other respects akin to those of the great Roman Diana and Greek Artemis. She also presided over the destinies of fishermen whose guilds were numerous and powerful at Pompeii. We have already shown the influence of these and of the other collegia that swarmed in that old Campanian city. Near this place clustered the numerous guilds of Puteoli, which could easily be seen on the coast to the north. These places have already been distinguished for their trade organizations. In Pompeii and as we are assured by Profs. Waltzing and Cagnat, in many and probably all the towns and cities, these trade unions were voting for their choice in officers of the boards of public works and having great contentions at the elections and their political power was strongly felt in their interests; for they desired, and by political means obtained, the appointment to do the work of the public building, street cleaning, fire department, and fulsome quantities of other tasks by which they were enabled to work but eight hours a day and receive excellent pay. It was on the eve of one of these elections that the awful volcanic eruption occured which engulfed the whole population, probably one hundred thousand or more and it is declared to have been the most all-sweeping and disastrous ever known in the world.

Among the immense and often wonderful ruins which have recently been taken from the beds of lava and debris covering the city is the skeleton of this identical temple of Isis. At the moment the earthquake occured this temple was a christian house of worship; but the metamorphosis from a strictly pagan temple to a brotherhood of the new faith had been recent. It might have commenced during the reign of Claudius or even Tiberius, but must have been very secret, if not entirely suspended and covered up at the time of Nero and the

[5] See *Index*, catchwords referring to pp. where will be found a review of this subject and an account of the pending election showing by the inscriptions of the voting unions themselves, that a great political contest of the unions was going on at the moment the city was overwhelmed.

later years of Claudius. But the most interesting feature of this discovery, judging from the surroundings and general appearance is the evidence of many guilds belonging to the industrial movement then in a prosperous condition. There are some strong proofs that it was the temple and headquarters of these organizations, perhaps their property. At any rate, many of the best writers class this find among the corporations of labor under the law of Solon.⁶ In the note which we here append, are some of forty or fifty unions of various trades and professions taking part in the election which was about to come off, when the disaster came and made a vast and ghastly grave of Pompeii.⁷ They worshiped at the shrine of Isis; but as this goddess was proving a myth by never carrying out promises as hoped for from such divinities and in earlier ages strictly believed in, the unions which understood nothing but things practical were the first to forsake things barren of profits to them and this is why they endorsed the Word of promise, preached by the evangelists. So, from adorers of Isis, a myth and an invention of the infatuated imagination, they easily became believers in christianity and the evidences are that the temple of Isis had already become a shrine of the converted unions when the eruption came.

The scheme of the early christianity was based on the Solonic method of salvation from poverty. Priestcraft of the pagan sort, such as made payments to provision rings, buying of sacrifices to fatten pagan priests compulsory and the refusal, punishable with death if caught in the act, because it was a high treason against the state.

Economical religion then, of Jesus, was the foundation rock of the era we are at this day struggling to carry out. Poverty was to be buried forever. The in-

⁶ Waltzing, *Hist. Corp. Prof.*, I., pp. 169-70, gives a list of the unions of Pompeii as indicated by the inscriptions that were posted just before this election; and speaks cf them as "les fidèles de l' Isis et les adorateurs de Venus, patronne de Pompeii." They are as follows: "Lignarii universi, truck sellers, IV., 851, 960; lignarii plostrari, CIL. IV., 486; pomari universi, fruit sellers, IV., 149, 180, 183, 202, 206; caupones, shopkeepers, IV., 336, 1838; culinari, cooks, IV., 373; pistores, bakers, IV., 886; pastry cooks, libari, IV., 1768, clibanari, cooks on a large scale, IV., 677; they made beautiful loaves of bread; poultry dealers, gallinari, IV., 241, 373; fishermen, piscicapi, IV., 826; dyers, offlectores, IV., 864; fullones, fullers, IV., 816; saccari, bag makers, IV., 274, 497; sagari, blouse makers, IV., 753; tonsores, barbers, IV., 713; unguentari, perfumers, IV., 609."

⁷ See Vol. I., pp. 390, 391 and note 5. 416.

dividual was to be furnished through powerful organization or co-operate power, with the means of life. There was to be no eleemosynary charity. Every human being must work and be furnished by his union with work; and the wretched charity which still prevails was to be spurned in disgust as unworthy of the noble manhood of nations. All men were recognized as being created equal, and in theory, wages like chattel slavery was to be no more.

On these salutary ideas the new faith in the workingman messiah rose. It planted itself in temples of the old gods and godesses who had for ages been promising much for the laboring poor they pretended to emancipate, but never did.

We could enumerate many evidences of this absorption of the old temple of Isis by the converted unions collected from the tell-tale ruins of Vesuvius. The Isians prove to have held the college or union of the faithful of Isis and there were the adorers of Venus, patron goddess of Pompeii.[8] Every one of the forty or fifty unions mentioned on the chiselings, etchings, paintings and scrawls which have been uncovered thus far proves to have been a guild of some kind, and the object of the political contention was to secure the election of the ædiles, who were the same as the agoranomi of the Greek unions whose similar political contentions were to secure the same object, namely to elect their own candidates to the boards of public work, so that their own memberships of unions might secure the award of doing the work of the city.

Dr. Willems took much interest in the ancient labor movement as developed to our knowledge through preserves of this great eruption, and has written out a lengthy explanation of the part taken by the unions of all sorts engaged in the election, but particularly the mechanics.[9] According to him, the colleges were intimately connected with the temple of Isis which was a christian sanctuary and schola at the moment of the

[8] CIL, IV., 1146: Venerii; see Waltzing, *id.*, p. 170: "Il y avait aussi des cercles, d' amusement portant les sobriquets de tard-buveurs, larronneaux et dormeurs, et une société des joueurs de balle, CIL. IV., 1147, Enfin, on trouve des sodales, dont le nom spécial est inconnu. Toutes ces associations soutiennent avec ardeur le candidat de leur choix," a making of the election coming off the moment of the eruption.

[9] Willems, *Election Municipale de Pompeii*, pp. 26 sqq; see also CIL *Preface*; G. Boissier, *Relig. Rom.*, II., p. 295.

disaster. It needs but a small stretch of imagination to perceive that these labor guilds which had been suppressed by Tiberius on the event of the historic turmoil or strike in the year A. D. 13, finding they were stifled by the law of conspiracy, sequestered themselves in the asylum or refuge of the motherly temple and were thus converted.

In the same manner, and after an imperial edict from Rome which compassed the exile of thousands of these "hated pests," settlements were made in many distant cities and towns of proconsular Rome. The plan was to convert and occupy either little temples of the unions as was done in innumerable cases, or to cluster in and around the larger sanctuaries of the gods and goddesses as in the case of the Isis of Pompeii. Several of these later specimens may be traced to a desire to escape from danger. It was with this for a principal reason, without doubt, that the ancient temple of Zeus on the old acropolis of Kelainai, a suburb of Apameia in Phrygia was colonized into by the shoemakers and their guilds of Shoemakers' street.[10] A more perfect example of a church on ruins would be difficult to find among all the testimonials of antiquity; but we have given the epigraph itself and its thorough description in another place.

At Vienne, in France, archaic capital of the Allobrogians, there are to be seen many evidences of a similar transformation by the converted labor unions of ancient Dionysan temples, to the church.[11] All correct history has been covered up by the ruins, many of which are as ancient as the persecutions which occured there and at Lyons, twelve miles up the river Rhone from this place. They are recently coming out as historical.

At Puteoli there are ruins of another temple which became a church after serving for ages as a refuge for the unions. We possess inscriptions establishing this as a permanent argument in proof of our assertions

[10] See *supra*, pp. 445-7, note 227, where we have laid stress on these inscriptions, quoting one of them in full.
[11] Savigny, *Guide de Vienne*, 98. Rue Capriens de Vienne: "C'est là qu' existait le superbe palais des empereurs romains." "Le splendide jardin était evironné de fortes murailles dont les murs épaisses avaient cinq pieds." This became a church after falling into ruins. The city was permeated with industrial unions of a dozen trades.

regarding the ancients having planted and established the new Word into already existing institutions.[12]

There are also strong reasons for believing a capture occurred so to speak, of the ancient temple of Cybele at Philadelphia in Lydia, one of the Phrygian subdivisions of Asia Minor, first and from a time unknown, by the trade unions, and then through them, after conversion, by the christians. This would have made the celebrated city of the seven, a veritable church on ruins. The basis of this theory is very deep. It is similar to the capturing by the same converted unions of the temple of Isis at Pompeii. We suspect that an effort was made by the enemies of organized trades to suppress them here in somewhat the same manner, and about the same time as their suppression at Pompeii, where we find them by no means suppressed, but flourishing in secret under the ægis of the holy mother.

Mommsen has had the penetration to discover something here, in his investigation of the law of their votive franchise, although he does not appear to have seized the full application. He points to a multitude of trade unions or guilds at Philadelphia. We have an inscription which speaks of seven phyles or sacred tribes existing there. Dr. August Böckh thought these phyles were subdivisions of the people, but they were genuine trade unions, as now ascertained; and it has been suggested that some unaccountable event, perhaps that of a terrible eruption which occured there, scared away all except the working population, too poor to escape. This would have left the tribal guilds in possession of the place, temple and all, and being already organized, they stayed and continued their industries, shoemaking, cotton spinning and weaving, also dyeing of the celebrated crimson. Wagener[13] cites Strabo who almost

---

[12] CIL, Vol. X., no. 1579: "Hic ager—eorum posessorum juris est qui in cultu corporis Heliopolitanorum sunt eruntve, atqua ita is accessus jusque esto per januas itineraque ejus agri. qui nihil adversus lecem et conventionem ejus corporis facere perseveraverunt." These "cultores" in addition to the pagan temple which became a christian asylum, had seven arpents of land,

[13] Waltzing, *Hist. Corp. Prof.*, p. 173, 174 : "... particularité vraiment curieuse que nous trouvons à Philadelphie, en Lydie. Les ouvriers en laine et les cordonniers y portent les noms de ἱερὰ φυλὴ τῶν ἐριουργῶν, et ἱερὰ φυλὴ τῶν σκυτέων. Le Bas, 648, 656; CIG, 3422; Une inscription parle de sept φυλαί ou tribus sacrées existant dans la ville, CIG 3422: "... ......C'est la βουλή qui décrète la statue et confie à un collège le soin de l'ériger, *Bull. de Cor. Héléniques*, II., 593. no. 1: " ...... à Philadelphie les tribus génétiques se confondaient avec les corporations d'artisans."

confirms this and fixes the time to cover the event. But by far greater is the probability that during the reign of Caligula, an edict came, banishing all the converts called by Suetonius Jews, followed by another in the reign of Claudius, which drove many thousands over into Asia Minor where they settled into numerous colonies, carrying the evangelism of the new Word of promise with them; and being themselves broken fragments of the Roman unions, easily mixed with the old guilds at Philadelphia, colonizing around the sympathetic and mellow mithraism of the mother duly fusing with, converted her priests and used her temple for their kuriakos or church. What fortifies this argument is the fact that all the imperial hosts were tinted with a grudge against all newly converted temples and finally their hatred rose so high that under Diocletian they were exterminated by the great massacre.

We have spoken of the capture by the christians, of strongholds of Solon's unions. There are many positive proofs of it. During the reign of Alexander Severus, A.D. 239, there was a union of pagan cooks at Rome who owned in their own home a lot of land. It was precious to them, being the place where stood the temple dedicated to their goddess of nourishment. They had never been converted, and when their retreat was encroached upon by the christians they objected with so strong a resistance that it became a heated contention. The dispute was over the possessorship of the land. After much wrangling, amounting at times to an altercation between the two factions, it was finally left for the emperor himself to decide. Alexander Severus was a mild, humane monarch. Many commentators declare that he was virtually a christian. He bought pictures of many of the great and good. In his lararium he had images of Jesus, of Apollonius of Tyana, of Orpheus and others not admitted by the censorious senators, such as had refused to permit the emperor Tiberius to deify Jesus just after his crucifixion. In fact, he seems to have carried out the plan of Tiberius, two hundred years before, of admitting the master as one of the gods of the people of Rome.[14]

[14] Neander, *Hist. Eccles.*, I., p. 127. The story of the dispute between the christians and the pagan cooks is likewise here related, *id.*, p. 125.

After a prolonged contention as to who should own the property, the cooks or the christians, the question went to this emperor. On giving it due consideration, Alexander Severus decided that it was the property of the christians, and transferred it to them. The only redress was for the union of cooks (pastillariorum collegium) to themselves renounce the faith of the pantheists and endorse the new Word of promise forming the scheme, or half economical half spritual advocacy of the early christians involving conversion of the cooks to christianity.

Several suggestive discoveries have been made at Ancona in Italy, on the Adriatic sea. An old cathedral is there which was once a House of a lord or dictator, who in the Greek inscription recently deciphered was a kurios. It has been proved that this officer was synonymous with the Roman quinquennalis. The inscription speaks of a thiasos, and also of a koinon.[15] The whole shows a pagan temple, once a shrine of a union of working people with their communal code but converted over to the christians.

The Vourkano, on the Ithome Mount, or Ithone according to Liddell, was a sort of sacred position of the god Jupiter in those times, situated in Thessaly, more anciently the Pelasgiotis, near Metropolis.[16] Here on the craggy heights and mountain steeps existed a temple of Jupiter which was metamorphosed to an institution for christian worship. Furthermore it was largely influenced by the converted unions.

Another of the same kind is that of the Orchomenos,

---

[15] De Rossi, *Roma Sott.*, Vol. I., p. 107. Εἰς τηνδε τὸ ἡρῷον κοινὸν τῶν ἀδελφῶν. It appears to have had some relations with Heraclea: "In Eraclea nel porto il famoso Ciriaco (κυριακὸς) d' Ancona lesse la sequente izcrizione, che dalle preziose memoria de viaggi de lui me studiosamenta raccolte era trazzo per la prima volte alla luce. The epitaph reads:
Αὐρ. φιλιππιάνος. χ, ἐποιησα ἐμου Τῳ καὶ τῃ γυναίκι μοῦ Αὐρ. Δενιανη χ καὶ τῳ πατρι μοῦ Αὐρ. Νεόφυτῳ χ. Εἰ δε τις τολμησε ἑτερον βάλειν δωσει τοις ἀδελφοις χ. φ'.
The reading and the signs evince that it must have been some sort of christianized union. The ruins of the temple which became the church, are still to be seen.

[16] *Iliad*, II., 729. Foucart, *Ass. Rel.*: "Le temple d' Isis à Pompéii donne une idée assex exacte de l' un de ces sanctuaires; on pourra se les répresenter ancore mieux, en voyant quelques-uns des monastères Hélléniques, en particulière celui de Vourkano sur l' Ithome, ou celui d' Orchomène, elevé sur les ruines du temple de charités. La construction du temple et de ses dépendences était la première affaire et la plus importante pour la société;" Liddell, in verb. Ἰθωμη; "A fortress in Thessaly, the Pelasgiotis, near Metropolis, *Iliad*, II., 729. A stronghold of Messina, on Mt. Ithome, with a temple of Jupiter," Herodotus, IX., 34.

one of several cities of Greece, on the site of which are the evidences of a church built upon the ruins of an ancient temple. It was for a long time actuated by the unions of the Solonic system. They held sway and controlled its destinies under christian auspices.

We begin another astonishing revelation by the announcement that the church of Saint Peter was a direct result of the great conflagration of Rome by Nero in the year A.D. 64. This particular hatred and spite was turned against the christian collegia clustered in and around the goddesses Diana and Minerva, supreme among the tatterdemalian throngs of the Vatican and Aventine Hills and of the valley below.[17] Thither it was that the wrath and vengeance of Nero were especially directed. He raged and tore about this quarter like a madman. He pushed his spies and obsequious lieutenants into their dark alleys and lanes, some of them of the feminine sex often worse and more truckling flunkies for imperial favors than the obsequious harpies of the male sex, even Tigellinus himself. They all bent their subservient energies toward the frightful massacre and many of them were speedily repaid by being awarded the fatal judgment from Nero to banishment or the axe.

The great church of Saint Peter at Rome arose out of this renowned experience, and is positive proof that christianity took its actual origin in the poor workingmen's unions. No other claim whether of opulent individual now stationed there, or of the obsequious millions, can be historically insisted upon. Saint Peter's is derived from the great temple of Minerva, goddess of labor and of her who blessed the fruits of toil. Let others think as they may, this is the fact; and the colleges which clustered around her standard were very numerous.[18]

The discovery of the origin of the celebrated église

[17] See *supra*, Section NERO, *fin.*, where this great conflagration and the awful destruction of the trade unions and christians by fire and torture are recounted.

[18] Waltzing, *Hist. Corp. Prof.*. I., p. 199: "Avant d, s'associer, les artisans avaient deja leur patron. C' était naturellment le dieu dont les attributs approachaient le plus du métier. C' est ainsi que Minerve trouva tant d' adorateurs. Déesse de l' intelligence, elle fit invoquée pour tous ceux qui s' occupaient d' art, de sciences et d' industrie. C'est la divinité protectrice de mille gendres d' ouvrages de l' esprit et de la main, dit Ovide: 'Mille dea est operum.'"

of Notre Dame and that it was originally and as early as Tiberius, a little huntsmen, fishermen and lumbermens' temple in the Seine and a veritable trade union of Solon's pattern may be a little surprising. Such is nevertheless the truth.

In the metamorphosis of the temple into the kuriakos of the christian régime there is something marvelous. Hundreds of such temples were taken by the christians from the crumbling, moribund pagans, and converted into houses of worship. Of course this was done by slow degrees, but we find them everywhere and have devoted the chapter to a review only of some of the remarkable instances when the ancient guild became the christian church.

In Paris, on the present site of the church of Notre Dame, and in the crypt of the choir, was found in 1711, an inscription,[19] which will conclusively prove that Notre Dame is none other than an improved temple of the guild of such boatmen, doing trade business on the river Seine.

It is inscribed to Tiberius, who reigned from A.D. 14 to 37 and all through the active life of Jesus. During his time there was a large population on the whole length of the river. Paris, Rouen and what is now Havre were flourishing commercial places and agriculture was in a thrifty condition. There was needed a line of boats running from the sea to Paris and this need was perhaps supplied by the collegium nautarum or boatmen's union, very much as was the case on the Tiber.[20] This union of boatmen was discovered in a dark and long neglected crypt under the choir of Notre Dame which stands on an island in the Seine near the center of the city. M. Le Roi,[21] in Félibien's history of

---

[19] M. B. Le Roi, *Sur l' Origine de l' Hôtel de Ville,* dans l' *Histoire de Paris,* de Félibien,
The inscription reads:
"TIBERIO CÆSARI,
AUG. JOVI. OPTIMO,
MAXIMO MONUMENTUM,
NAUTÆ PARISIACI,
PUBLICE POSUERUNT."

[20] See Vol. I., Chapters xv, xvi., where the vast commerce as well as the provisionment of Rome, is shown to have been conducted by the coll. Nautarum.

[21] Granier, *Hist. Class. Ouv.,* p. 374, was the first to bring this notable case of a Gallic collegium to our view. He says: "Ceci résulte clairement de l' histoire du commerce primitif de Paris, et de l' inscription suivante trouvée dans les feuilles faites en 1711, sous le choeur de Notre Dame." M. Le Roi, *Origine de l' Hôtel-de-Ville; Hist. Paris,* par Félibien,

the commerce of Paris, has given us what is known of the origin of the monument.

There is nothing unnatural in this case. The unions almost always possessed a plat of land, a little graveyard and a house of their lord. This we have abundantly shown, together with the Roman law governing their action. The union of boatmen originally possessed this islet in the river, built their house or kuriakos upon the piece, making of it probably a rough and primitive affair. Their graveyard was the islet itself. Here they used to hold their meetings and here they met in their schola or main room of the little temple, dedicated to their tutelary divinity, and enjoyed their common meal. When a holiday came they met and threw open the whole establishment with its garden full of trees, and held an entertainment in the manner of the true symposium. In due course of time the christians came and converted the membership, after which the temple became a church and later developed into one of the most celebrated houses of worship in the world.

We paraphrase this inscription in our usual manner, leaving the reader his time for a more critical rendering from the original Latin.

"The union of boatmen of Paris, publicly establish and dedicate this monument of their temple, to the august, Tiberius Cæsar, the great and best, under Jupiter, protecting god of Rome."

CHAPTER XXI.

MASSACRE OF DIOCLETIAN,

WHAT Became of it All—The Ancient Plan Suppressed—A Hitherto Unrecorded Murder of the Human Race—Destructive Power of the Standing Armies—The Havoc of a Traitor—Scheme of Diocletian and His Courtiers—Their Plot Against the Brotherhoods—Cruel Character of Galerius—Joint Monarchy of Four—Demand for Extermination—Formation of a League—Hierocles as their Agent—How He Passed the Dokimastirion and Slipped in—Appointed Governor—Divulged Union Secrets to the League—Rage of Galerius—Plan Determined on, was Extermination—Opinions of Drs. Ramsay, Cumont and Others—Eumeneia—Its Destruction told by Eusebius—Quotations—Governors of other Provinces Supposed to have Divulged—Evidence of Lactantius—Story of Crispins—Logos Philaletheis of Hierocles—Diocletian's Edict of Prices—The Edict Quoted—The "Vilis Plebecula"—Date of the Slaughter Fixed for Feb. 22nd A.D. 303—Rancor of Mother of Galerius against the Christians—Words of Gibbon—Burning of the Book—Quoting Ramsay—Bargainers Covet their Properties—Book of Papias—Treason Against Getting of Wealth and Power—It was Burned because it Revealed the Economics of Solon's Socialism—Details of the Massacre—Porphyry—Spread over many Provinces of Proconsular Rome—Entailments of Diocletian's Atrocity—Not Until Afterwards we find Charities—Plant of Eleemosynary System—First Seeds of Feudal System—Feudal Guilds—Pauperism Appears in the World—The Orphanophulax—Laws Governing Such Institutions—Proof that they never existed Before—How Constantine took the Control of Christianity—Downfall of the Two Great Schemes of Solon and of Jesus to Redeem the World—Go Back, the Cry of our Strangled Race.

WE have thus brought down the history of the ancient lowly from the highest antiquity until we arrive at the fatal year A.D. 303, when an awful massacre occured, known as that of Diocletian, whereby the populations of many of the regions we have described, who had survived the persecutions and were beginning to expand, grow perfect and thrive, were swept in a moment from the earth.

Something has already been said regarding a certain recreant member of the unions named Hierocles who turned spy and betrayer after receiving initiation into the brotherhoods' mysteries, divulging to the monarch and his officers all the secret doings, in order to secure an appointment as governor of Bithynia. This traitor worked the ruin of the men he had sworn to befriend.

The scheme of Diocletian, his courtiers and some of the prelates now forming an element which at last succeeded, was to destroy the great jus coeundi. Being regarded with reverence as the behest of Solon, this had for nine centuries withstood the inimical powers of the aristocratic world.[1]

In all our researches into the causes of great events in the history of labor, we have been unable to discover any signs of decay in the rising organization and gradual forward trend under this great statute, until we come to this massacre of Diocletian. From that fell moment, A.D. 302, or as some report, 303, the trade and labor unions appear to be stricken, and cease to carve their records. From that gloomy date charities of the eleemosynary sort began to arise, filling the moral and social atmosphere with their loathsome and sickening ethics. Always before this had the unions and brotherhoods been self-sustaining; always hitherto had they refused to permit of alms-giving hospitals, or even beggars, except when organized under a clause of the law. The massacre of Diocletian was the true beginning of the end of the renowned jus coeundi of Solon and Numa Pompilius. Let us first recount what is known of this egregious atrocity.

When in A.D. 284, Diocletian, a promising soldier of the Roman army drove his dagger through the body of Aper, the "hated boar," for killing Numerian, the other soldiers around him in orgies of enthusiasm, arose to the dignity of law as had been done many times before,

[1] Lactantius, *Divine Institutes*, V., 11, in his account of it, brings in the law of Diocletian regarding the prices of provisions which we have already discussed. See *index*, in verb. *Prices*. We quote this law more fully *infra*, note 12, of this chapter.

and ushered or ran him unexpectedly into the mighty office of emperor of the now vast dominion of Rome. This new monarch felt that he was incompetent to cope with the duties of such an enormous task and appointed three more Cæsars to assume the purple with him, apportioning to each of them a defined territory, himself retaining Africa and the Asian and other Greek-speaking provinces. Their names were Maximian, Constantius and Galerius.

Galerius, who received Macedonia for his share, after military reverses, gained a victory in Persia where in the proconsulates, on the march through Phrygia and Edessa he had seen the christians in great numbers. He was a pagan of a ferocious and cruel nature, and became greatly enraged against their numbers and success as builders of their new scheme of civilization, so contrary to his own. His whole influence was immediately exerted upon Diocletian, on his triumphant return, against them. He is known to have demanded their extermination.

Diocletian, himself friendly, almost a christian, refused. The wiles of Galerius were exerted and as the empire was full of those like himself who hated them, it was not long before they formed a secret league to gather all sorts of evidence against them.[2] Into this league was drawn the man named Hierocles who became the arch spy and traitor.

This man worked an underhand intrigue to secure admission into one of the guilds of Nicomedia that had become christianized. He had succeeded, probably under guize of a mechanic, and a residence and acquaintance among the toilers, in familiarizing and perhaps endearing himself to the extent that when he applied for admission there were those on the dokimasterion or board of examination, who were willing to report him *hagios, eusebes, agathos*.[3] The incident of this treachery shows the enormous power and influence of trade unionism over the world.

[2] Meyers, *Konv. Lexikon*, in verb. *Diocletianus:* "Seine für das alternde Reiche überaus wohltätige Regierung ist von christlichen Schriftstellern deswegen schwer verunglimft worden, weil er, seit 303, ungewiss aus welcher Veranlassung, eine blutige, besonders von Galerius' grosser Grausamkeit geübte Verfolgung über die Christen verhängte."

[3] For this stringent requirement of the Solonic law testing candidates, consult *supra*, ch. xlii., where all that is known, including the facts found in an inscription is explaned in full.

Hierocles, on consultation with another secret association having the opposite object of discussing, detecting and destroying the hated guilds who had turned their secret power toward protecting the christians and had endorsed them together with their tenets, began systematically to divulge to them that which he was able to discover of the inner doings of the great trade union system throughout Asia Minor. Drawn into this latter conventicle, were the three beings, Constantius, Maximian and Galerius, and the great emperor over them all, Diocletian himself, though he reluctantly consented to join. Galerius is supposed to have been the prime mover of the conspiracy. Hierocles was made governor of Bithynia and in this capacity, having the double function of the political power on the one hand, and the hidden sources of knowledge from behind the unions' secret veil on the other, he oscillated to and fro between them, industriously and punctiliously meeting at the sittings of both, and insidiously receiving and reporting all information. The courage, determination and growth of the now populous christian movement was in this manner accurately made known.

The rage of Galerius knew no bounds. He was heartily encouraged by all the lesser members of the league. Diocletian, however, who was at heart a conscientious man and adverse to giving his consent to their cruel demands was reluctant for some time, until he detected some lurking conspiracy abrew, which would probably have resulted in his own assassination. He at last gave up and subscribed to the worst.

The plan determined on appears to have been that of a sudden extermination of the whole organized population of these regions, far and near. It was to be done by using the standing army of the imperial power. Exact details of this awful event are wanting, as every document daring to mention the calamity except that of Lactanius, has been burned, and the history of it a few years later by Eusebius is purposely guarded and vague. The most remarkable evidence is this which is now coming to view by the discovery of modern researchers in quest of inscriptions, that nothing more of that style of literature is to be found since the date of the awful massacre.

Dr. Ramsay, who served science for years searching palæographic remains in Phrygia, sums up these three sources of information in proof of the magnitude of this exterminatory massacre, and we should err in attempting to give our own rather than his bold conclusions:[4]

"As an example of what took place in Phrygia, Eusebius mentions that the christian city" (he is here speaking of Eumeneia), "which was alluded to in paragraph eight, was burned to the ground with its people, even women and children."

On the same page this author continues:

"Moreover, to one who has by the patient toil of years tracked out these christian communities by their formula of appealing to 'the god,' it comes as one of those startling and convincing details of real life and truth, that the one recorded about the destroyed people is that they died appealing to the god over all. Unconsciously Eusebius writes as the epitaph over the ashes of the destroyed people the words by which we have recognized the epitaphs which they themselves habitually composed."[5]

The same author adds that another governor who engaged himself to Galerius and his bloody work, named Theotecnus, who ruled the province of Galatia at the same moment that Hierocles was making his treacherous plot in divulging the secret which he had in a most sacred promise sworn to defend. Indeed the reading of Eusebius explains that cities in Phrygia, Eumeneia with them, were suddenly surrounded by military force, and that all who did not retract were destroyed.

As a matter of fact, there was a governor for every province in all proconsular Rome. These were but two of the dozen for Asia Minor alone; and it would be difficult, on account of the care taken by four great rulers who waged this startling massacre to cover up all clues leading to a knowledge of it, to even form an adequate conjecture as to its general extent. It might have swept over Spain, Italy, North Africa, Macedonia, Gaul, and even the islands of Rhodes and Britain.

[4] Ramsay, "Cities and Bishoprics of Phrygia," Vol. II., pp. 507-8.
[5] The words of Euseb., "H. E.," VIII., 11, are: Ὅλην Χριστιανῶν πολίχνην αὔτανδρον ἀμφὶ τὴν Φρυγίαν ἐν κύκλῳ περιβαλόντες ὁπλῖται, πῦρ τε ὑφάψαντες, κατέφλεξεν αὐτοὺς ἅμα νηπίοις καὶ γυνάξι, τὸν ἐπὶ πάντων θεὸν ἐπιβοωμένοις· ὅτι δὴ πανδημοὶ, πάντες οἱ τὴν πόλιν οἰκοῦντες, λογιστής τε αὐτὸς καὶ στρατηγὸς σὺν τοῖς ἐν τέλει πᾶσι φαὶ ὅλῳ δήμῳ Χριστιανοὺς σφᾶς ὁμολογοῦντες, οὐδ' ὁπωστιοῦν τοῖς προστάτουσιν εἰδωλολατρεῖν ἐπειθάρχουν."

We are certainly very fortunate in having two so reliable and scholarly writers as Lactantius and Eusebius, and especially the former, who was a bold, classical author, living at the very moment when the holocaust occurred. His testimony, given regarding the similar destruction of another population completely fortifies that of Eusebius for Eumeneia. The splendid writer is probably describing the destruction of Nicomedia, the capital of Bithynia, ruled by Hierocles, and the chosen city of Diocletian himself. But he alludes in one place to that gory tempest in Phrygia.[6]

In connection with the great persecutions of Diocletian we must not fail to bring in the episode of the Crispinian union of Shoemakers in what is now Soissons, France. The dates of this part of the massacre vary but a little from that of the great holocaust of Anatolia.

The massacres at Soissons and vicinity are known to have been committed about the time Hierocles was writing his Logos Philaletheis, or some time before being appointed governor of Bithynia. It circulated among the enemies of the unions, stirring up the old pagan hatred against the christians, and was mostly intended to stop the influx of christianity into these organizations. That this work, afterwards suppressed and burned, was translated into Latin and used by the enemies of the Crispinian community of shoemakers in France, is certain. While it fiercely attacked the idea of the unions for shielding the christians, it is said to have contained passages apologizing in favor of the christians, as originally existing and he would hear to nothing against the excellence of Jesus Christ as a great and good man.[7]

The story of Crispin and his brother Crispianus may be read in many current books and is honorably men-

[6] Lactantius, *Div. Inst.*, V., 11, is probably referring to either the same described by Eusebius, quoted in our preceding note or some other similar diaster in Phrygia.; "Sicut unus in Phrygia qui universum populum cum ipso pariter conventiculo concremavit." Lactantius, *De Morte Persecutorum*, cc. vii-xix., gives a lucid recital of the entire horror.

[7] Lact,, *Div. Inst.*, V., 2, admits this, and thinks that the book afterward worked as an apology for his fierce and bloody persecutions. He speaks as though some chapters of it "were at variance with themselves, enumerating so many and such secret things," that he appears to have been one of the same sect. Cf. Dr. Coxe, in *Ante-Nicine Fathers*, VII., p. 137. Lactantius reviles Hierocles for his perfidy in betraying the secret order, by divulging that which he had sworn to keep.

tioned in the encyclopædias. We have ourselves given a small account of them in our first volume of this work. Some time near the close of the third century the governor of the district, Rictius Verus, actuated by Diocletian or perhaps Galerius, had them arrested and thrown headlong into a huge cauldron nearly full of melted lead.[8] It was they who created the order of shoemakers, which came down through ten centuries, latterly with the name of Frères Cordonniers, and was still in full vigor at the breaking out of the French revolution in 1789, when it was suppressed, and its history stands as another irrefutable proof of our discovery that it was the trade unions which endorsed, protected and formed for the first three centuries the bone and sinew of christianity.

We are indebted to M. Le Blant for some valuable information regarding the sepulchre and place of burial of these Crispins of the shoemakers' guild. The church of Soissons erected during the early ages has a basilica and a crypt where their ashes are encased, and it is thought to be one of the most venerated tombs in Europe.[9]

This persecution, involving the deaths of the Crispins and the temporary suppression of the union of shoemakers because they shielded the christians, was begun some years before the bloody culminus which we have described on the evidence of Lactantius and Eusebius. The more we study these fragmentary proofs the less certain we become as to the reputed compassion of Diocletian; since the murders were going on fifteen years before the final blast.

The suppression of the union methods of buying and distributing provisions caused so much protest that the

[8] Meyers, *Kon. Lex.*, "CRISPINUS, *Heiliger und Martyrer*, aus einer vornehmen römischen Familie flüchtete mit seinem Bruder Crispianus, wegen der Christen Verfolgung des Kaisars Diocletian nach Soissons, wo beide das Schuhmach-handwerk trieben, aber um 287 vom Landpfleger Richtius Verus verhaftet und in einen mit geschmolzenem Blei angefüllten Kessel geworfen wurden. Sie sind die Patrone des Schuhmach-handwerks. Bekannt ist die Sage, dass sie das Leder Stahlen, um den Armen, unentgeldlich Schuhe zu verfertigen, weshalb man Wohltaten, die auf andere Kosten erzeigt werden, Crispinaden nennt. Tag; 25 Okt."

[9] Le Blant, *Inscriptions Crétiennes*, I.. p. 439. Here some effort is made to cast light on the Crispins. An inscription, called that of Dagobert and Chlodobert, quotes Gregory of Tours, *Historia Francorum*, V., xxxv., to show that they are buried "dans la basilique de Saint Crépinien"........ une des tombes les plus vénérées." Gregory wrote: "Voverunt vota pro eo; sed media nocte, anhelus jam et tenuis spiritum exhalavit; quem in basilica sanctorum Crispini et Crispiniani martyrum sepelierunt."

emperor conceived, about A.D. 300, the idea of his now celebrated law regulating the sale of almost all articles of common necessity which we have already described,[10] though it is here necessary to revert to. The effect of this edict regulating prices appears to have been the reverse of anything one could have suspected.[11]

We imagine that the shedding of much blood complained of by Lactantius may have been caused by the shuffles which a violent change in methods of competition would produce, causing scuffles and battles with the officers struggling to enforce the unwelcome law. This is one of the very few laws in antiquity to be found arbitrarily regulating prices of every day commodities. It is certain that the unions themselves who had always enjoyed the communal code with the privilege of choosing their market would be greatly disturbed by such a measure.[12] There is a good deal of doubt to this day as to the causes of the bloody results of this law. It is now established that the failure of the monarch's petted edict caused his assent to the murders.

One remarkable thing in connection with the great

[10] Compare our remarks on this subject, *supra*, pp. 317-318, note 113. For other remarks, consult *Index* in catchwords, *Prices, Diocletian*, etc.

[11] Our authority is Lactantius, who lived at the time and could not be mistaken. He says, *De Morte Persecutorum*, 7: vide *Ante-Nicine Fathers*, VII., p. 302, where a rendering is given which we prefer: "He (Diocletian) also when by various extortions he had made all things exceedingly dear, attempted by an ordinance to limit their prices. Then much blood was shed for the veriest trifles. Men were afraid to expose aught for sale, and the scarcity became more excessive and grievous than ever, until, in the end the ordinance, after having proved destructive to multitudes, was from mere necessity abrogated." The exact words of this authority run: "Tunc, ob exigua et vilia multus sanguis effusus, nec venale quidquam metu apparebat et caritas multo deterius exarsit, donec lex necessitate ipsa post multorum exitium solveretur."

[12] It was called EDICTUM DIOCLETIANUM DE PRETIIS RERUM VENALIUM. The edict ran as follows:

EDICT. DIOCL., I. Placet igitur ea pretia, quae subditi brevis scriptura (der in dem Gesetz enthaltene umfassende Tarif) designat, ita totius orbis nostri observantia contineri, ut omnes intelligant egrediendi eadem licentiam sibi esse præcisam. The parinthesis is Menger's remark; cf., *fin*.

EDICT. DIOCL., II. Placet, ut, siquis contra formam statuti huius conixus fuerit audentia, capitali periculo subigetur.

EDICT. DIOCL., III. Idem autem periculo etiam ille subdetur, qui conparandi cupiditate avaritiæ distrahentis contra statuta consenserit

EDICT. DIOCL., IV. Ab eius modi noxa immunis nec ille præstauitur, qui habens species victui atque usui necessarias post hoc sivi temperamentum existimaverit subtrahendas; cum pœna vel gravior esse debeat inferentis paenuriam quam contra statuta quatientis.

Dr. Anton Menger, *Recht auf den vollen Arbeitsertrag*, pp. 88-9, has discussed the results of this law, and states on authority of Mommsen, *Verhandlungen der Königlichen Sächsischen Gesellschaft der Wissenschaften*, 1856, that it was first uttered in A.D. 301, just before the outbreak of the persecution.

Diocletian massacre is that its history points only to the so-called "vilis plebecula" as the element against which Galerius and his co-adjutors directed their special attention. There is no disputing that this was the main pillar of the early plant. On scanning the whole source of testimony it is found that christianity as a whole was formed of men and women who were barred out of the spheres of society and respectability. But the original promoters gloried in and boasted of this fact. It was not individual trappings that was wanted. The first advocates were all carpenters, fishermen, clerks and men and women of a variety of trades and professions totally repudiated by the citizen class.[13] The higher classes, including the nobility, who thought they saw in it a rising heresy against their conscript gods, were about the time of Diocletian's two fatal edicts, intensely inflamed. The ultimatum of extermination, was truculently championed by Galerius. Diocletian gave the order. He excused the severity on the pretext that the christians, taking advantage of their hiding places in the unions were working out a dangerous heresy against the state.[14]

The exact time at which the butchery at Nicomedia began, was day-break, February 22, A.D. 303, the day of the Roman festival of the Terminalia. It is reasonable to suppose this also to be the date of the tragedy elsewhere. Gibbon thinks the mother of Galerius incited the authorities to fix the slaughter on this day but he does not conceive that this was far from accidental. Numa, who had sanctioned the great law whose consequences Galerius feared and hated, had even put bounds to the fields which the wealthy coveted and had consecrated this wisdom by erecting a temple to

[13] Jerome, *Comm, in Epist. ad Galat.*, cap. v.: "Ecclesia Christiana.... ....de vili plebecula congregata est;" Tertull,, *Apol.*, III., "Omnem sexum, ætatem, conditionem, et jam dignitatem........Servorum jam fidelem dominus olim mites ab occulis relegavit."

[14] The Roman jurist Paulus, lib, V., tit. xxi., declared that whoever introduced new religions whose tendency and character were secret and which disturb the minds of men, "De quibus animi hominum moventur," should be banished if belonging to the higher rank, or punished with death if belonging to the low. This was because sacred caeremoniae Romanae were entangled and interrupted by christianity; ergo cause of the persecutions. It attacked and ruptured the state religion—an old offense like that of the brotherhoods of Rome. Celsus on same grounds accuses the christians of attacking the "religiones licitæ" or state worship: "Ὣς συνθήκας κρύβδην παρά τὰ νενομισμένα ποιουμένων." l. I., c. 1. The Roman law expressly forbade it as a crime, according to Neander, *Hist. Church*, I., p. 7 sq.

the god Terminus, whose feast-day was February the twenty-second.[15] Diocletian and the league probably ruled that as this was the beginning of liberty, so now it was to be the terminal day of liberty, the day on which Numa and Solon's great movement must die.

At early dawn the prætorian præfect marched in company with a large force of the likewise maddened army, the generals with their regulars, their captains and lieutenants, and all accompanied by the tribunes and officers of the revenue, marched up the steep, to the Nicomedian church. With large bludgeons and rams they smashed in the door and made a rush for the sanctuary. Finding nobody here to kill, they seized all the copies to be found of the Christian Bible and hymn book and taking them to a place out side burned them to cinders. The beautiful building was then attacked and though strong to resist the frenzy, the work of demolition was persevered in until it lay a mass of ruins.

A regular edict against the christians was now set forth and their bodily torments systematically began on the twenty-fourth. This enactment read that all churches should be violently consumed by fire, and this was to be extended throughout the entire vast empire. "It was enacted that their churches, in all the provinces of the empire should be demolished to their foundations and the punishment of death was pronounced against all who should presume to hold any secret assemblies for the purpose of religious worship."[16] We see by this statement confirmed by Lactantius, Eusebius, and many other good authors, most of whose books however, were burned under ban, that the persecution exterminated both the secret communities and their property. We have for this the direct statements of ancient and modern authors of great merit, that two large cities were exterminated and may hence infer that thousands fell.

The suppression of valuable works of friends and enemies of this great movement, such as Papias' Instructions, the celebrated Logos Alethes, or Word of veritable truth, written by Celsus, the book of Porphyry[17] en-

[15] Perhaps rightly, gleaning it from Lactantius. *De Mort. Persecut.*, c. 11, who says: "Dapibus sacrificabat pœne quotidie, ac vicariis suis epulis exhibebat. Christiani abstinebant, et illa cum gentibus epulante, jejuniis hi et orationibus isistebant; hinc concepti odium adversus eos."
[16] Gibbon, *Decl. and Fall*, Chap. xvi., text above note 152.
[17] Porphyry's Περὶ τῆς ἐκ Λογίων Φιλοσοφίας, was written about A.D. 271.

tirely lost, that of the perfidious traitor Hierocles entitled Logoi Philalethes, those of Zosimus and of the Emperor Julian, has bereft us of much evidence regarding the plant of the christians into the ancient economic unions, and of many details of this great final massacre —a heavy loss, over which we can now do nothing but mourn. It is very probable that they wrote much on the massacre. They were mostly destroyed[18] by fire. Dr. Ramsay is of the opinion that the cause of the arrest of inscriptions, noticeable from about A.D. 300, in Phrygia was this cruel massacre of Diocletian and his helpmeets Galerius and others.

Having jostled and stumbled across a dark chasm of fragmentary literature and arrived at the certainty that all proconsular Rome came under the condemnatory edict of Diocletian, and having seen that at least two large cities were actually blotted out, let us feel ourselves prepared with the more interest in the astounding words of Dr. Ramsay,[19] who in his personal research for the relics of those people discovers all at once at an unexpected moment answering to the exact period of this massacre that their inscriptions are no more to be found and that a sad and sickening degeneracy of mankind in those regions prevails.

Dr. Ramsay, in basing the belief entirely upon his own discovery of the archæological monuments, unhesitatingly declares that the people were exterminated, all meeting a terrible death. But as he is investigating Phrygia only, he speaks only for Eumeneia. Cumont also speaks in the same strain for a much larger territory. Cumulative evidence now verifies the tragedy.

[18] A work by Dionysius, commented on by Tischendorf, and later by the author of *Supernatural Religion*, pp. 481-92, shows that there was much literature afloat at the time he wrote, which was afterwards lost. A fragment of Dionysius' *Epistle to the Romans*, is preserved by Eusebius, *Hist. Eccles.*, iv., 23, and reads: "Ἐπιστολὰς γὰρ ἀδελφῶν ἀξιωσάντων με γράψαι, ἔγραψα. Καὶ ταύτας οἱ τοῦ διαβόλου ἀπόστολοι ζιζανίων γεγένικαν, ἃ μὲν ἐξαιροῦντες ἃ δὲ προστιθέντες. Οἷς τὸ οὐαὶ κεῖται. Οὐ θαυμαστὸν ἄρα εἰ καὶ τῶν κυριακῶν ῥαδιουργῆσαι τινες ἐπιβέβληνται γραφῶν, ὁπότε καὶ ταῖς οἱ τοιούταις ἐπιβεβούκασι."

[19] We have taken the pains to enumerate the genuine θίασοι, ἑταίραι and ἔρανοι, all unions or trade guilds coming under this appellation of "communities," and find some fifty interspersed among his large collections. They range from the date of the crucifixion down to A.D. 300. For authority that this investigator is correct, see Böckh, CIG., 3857, 3857[d], 3857[u], 3857[k], 3857[a], 3857[n], 3857[q], 3857[g], 3857[h], 3857[i], 3857[l], 3857[f], 3857[p], 3857[m], 3857[b], 3857[w], 3957[t], 3980, 3938, 3857[a], alpha, 3857 γ and many others. Nearly all of them have been settled upon as christianized trade organizations of various kinds.

But let us follow Ramsay farther. On another page in the same book he continues:

"Lactantius mentions that this was done by a governor and no governor could have ventured on such an act, unless he had a full commission to exterminate the christians.[20] A general massacre, evidently, was deliberately planned by the central government and carried out by suitable agents. While this case has been selected as an extreme example of barbarity on the one side, and of steadfastness on the other, it may be taken as indicative of the policy carried out everywhere...... We may confidently say that historical and archæological evidence is agreed as to the fate of Eumeneia, the active and courageous element of the population was annihilated by fire, and sword in the years following, A.D. 303 and the development of the city was suddenly terminated."

Again: "To this end was directed all the power of a highly organized government, moved by a single will, commanding almost unlimited resources, for the space of ten years."

As to the results of a catastrophe of such enormous dimensions, he says:

"Even a mere casual glance over the list of christian inscriptions in the Appendix must suggest the question. Where are the post Constantian inscriptions? ......The contrast between the rich intellectual and political life of the third century and the inarticulate monotony of the many centuries that succeeded, is painful; one recognizes in the numbers of our catalogue the signs of a great misfortune to the human race, the destruction of a vigorous and varied life."

As M. Cumont has pointed out, the reason for the change must lie in the great massacre of Diocletian and his co-adjutors and successors, A.D. 303-313."

The above are words of calmness and wisdom. This great disaster to the human race was allowed to pass in

---

[20] The governor for Bithynia, Hierocles, we have just described. There can be no doubt that he had unlimited power. A similar governor had a hundred years before not only had unlimited power to kill them but Trajan expected him to do it. This was the kind-hearted Pliny, who succeeded in moving that emperor to some measure of kindness. We have fully recounted this history in our 17th chapter. All of his letters show that the object of this imperial rage was the christianized unions of labor. But Ramsay gives additional hints to the effect that the governor with unlimited powers for Galatia was Theotecnus, *ibid.*, p. 507.

oblivion where it remained for many centuries. As by it the opposition against it by a conspiracy of bargainers at that moment busy incubating their scheme to make themselves owners of the numerous social properties. Whoever peruses the elaborate description of them which we have given in foregoing chapters of this work may understand that though small, taken apart, they were enormous in the aggregate. A covetous few had long seen that they could fall into possession of millions if by fair means or by foul, they could get them. Inasmuch as the whole christian institution, including innumerable properties of the unions holding it under its powerful care suddenly disappear and all at once we see vast estates of prelates taking their place[21] within twenty-five years from the massacre, we may naturally suppose that these ambitious persons conspired with Diocletian and the league, of which Constantius, Maximian and Galerius were members, to compass the almost total extermination of both the name and the membership of the Solonic organization. Once dead, their property was easily confiscated and they could go and take possession.[22] Virtually, Solonism was dead from the day the axe of Diocletian fell. What followed is but a ghastly spectacle of degeneracy.

Before giving an account of the degeneracy caused by this calamity we may dwell a moment upon the geographical extent which it reached eastward and in the islands of the archipelago. As was stated, Bartholomew was sent to Edessa. Little is heard from this place ex-

[21] Long before this, the same craving was rife, and the incipient prelates were on tiptoe to possess themselves of these little fortunes which the hard-working communists had by centuries of consistency collected. Origen, whom they hated and persecuted, understood this, *De Principiis*, II., c. 9, § 5: "...... to grant them a higher and more honorable position; to favor others with the grant of principalities; bestow powers upon some, dominion upon others; confer on some the honorable seats in tribunal; enable some to shine with more resplendent glory, and glitter with starry brightness; give some the glory of the sun, others of the moon, others of the stars."

[22] The book written by Papias of Colossæ, called *Christi Sermonum Expositio*, is known to have been popular in Asia, especially Phrygia, Pontus, and Cappadocia and so, of course, Byzantium, at the moment this persecution broke loose. As it gave a glowing description of the enormous economics and other advantages of the socialistic over the prevailing competitions, it was hated by that class of people we are describing and all the copies to be found were soon after burned. It has been thought that this work was used by the league to inflame Diocletian, and bring his reluctant mind to consent to the massacre. Methodius, one of the true and unflinching, who had been influenced by this book of Papias, was martyred along with the rest. Fragments still exist of his *Essays on the Martyrs*, some of which are preserved by Eusebius.

cept what comes to us in apocryphal form. We are informed that under protection of Abgar, the movement thrived. Especial attention was paid to music. It is now believed that the "gnosticism" advocated there by Bardesanes, was little other than the peculiar ideas of the Dionysan artists, including their charming music.[23] Bardesanes was himself a musician and a composer of great merit and for his devotion to these noble traits which distinguished the good and the accomplished, he was set upon by the Roman persecutions and thus died a violent death. Bartholomew had long before met the same fate. Although most of the literature written during the lifetime of Diocletian and Galerius has perished, considerable remains from the pen of later writers attesting the extent to which the sudden acquisition of these properties inflated the prelates and others into whose hands they fell.[24] Lactantius, whose sad fate it was to live during the awful conflicts of Diocletian's persecution, mourns for a return of the reign of Saturn.[25] Thus from an earlier time than that of Galerius, even as early as Cyprian and Origen, we detect this grasping tendency which finally ruined the beautiful scheme of Jesus.[26] Dr. Ramsay attempts to explain the terrible degeneracy and ignorance which fell over the world from the days of Diocletian to A.D. 412, attributing it to this massacre. But as he is investigating the special territory of Phrygia and the particular city of Eumeneia, we may imagine the extent of his convictions as to the wider sweep of this calamitous

[23] Foucart, *De Coll. Scenicorum*, 52, shows that they worked to make the musical displays as magnificent as possible: "Tanti momenti videbatur ludos sacros quam splendidissime peragi, quum ad augendam certaminum laudem, tum maxime ad conciliandam civitati per magnificentiam apparatus deorum benevolentiam."

[24] Gibbon, *Decl. and Fall*, chap. xxv, note 37, after a dissertation of his own on this subject, refers to Gregory Nazianzen, *Orat.*, xxxii., 526 and says: Gregory Nazianzen describes the "pride and luxury of the prelates who reigned in the imperial cities; their gilt car, fiery steeds, numerous train, etc. The crowd gave way as to a wild beast." Here in note 42, *id.*, Gibbon quotes Jerome (tome I., p. 13) who is ashamed: Pudet dicere, sacerdotes idolorum mimi et aurigæ, et scorta, hæreditates. There came a law against it, and Jerome regrets that there should be cause for such a law: "Nec de lege queror; sed doleo cur meruimus hanc legem." Amenianus, xxvii., 3, 9, exclaims: "When I view the splendor of the capital, I am not astonished that so valuable a prize should inflame the desires of the ambitious." Though they never had popes in Tertullian's time, yet he says, *De Jejuniis*, c. 13, 711: "Aguntur præterea per Græcias, illa certis in locis Concilia ex universis ecclesiis, per sua et aliora quaeque in Commune tractantur, et ipsa representatio totio nominis christiani magna veneratione celebratur."

[25] Lactantius, *Divine Institutions*, V., c. vi.

cause of degeneracy. He states that: "There seems to be no adequate explanation to the obvious facts except in some great calamity which destroyed the active, progressive section of the population and gave play to forces that were making for stagnation and ignorance.[26]" These well-chosen words "making for stagnation," clearly explain our own statement that the degeneracy and ignorance had been gnawing against the pure and thrifty unions that took them in, fed and sheltered them on the solid foundation of their great law, protecting the right of combination.

But these tendencies to corruption and degeneracy were by no means unheeded by powerful men of that time. Porphyry, one of the brightest pagan writers, is supposed to have written his greatest suppressed work against them and even John Chrysostom thought so.[27] The thoughtful Ramsay bemoans the downfall of learning, which he declares was very progressive from A. D. 47 to 303. He says, citing Elias of Hadrianapolis, that bishops were so ignorant as not to be able to write their names.[28] What wonder, then that the vast and thriving scheme of the original founders fell into the ruthless hands of a Constantine to become a pillar of Monarchy!

[26] We quote Gibbon's rendering of Cyprian, "De Lapsis," p. 89; "Epist.," 65: who appends in a note that "the charge is confirmed by the nineteenth and twentieth canons of the council of Illiberis. Cyprian wrote that "there were too many among the African brethren who, in the execution of their charge violated every precept, not only of the evangelic perfection, but even of moral virtue. By some of these unfaithful stewards, the riches of the church were lavished in sensual pleasures, by others they were perverted to the purposes of private gains, of fraudulent purchases and of rapacious usury." Ramsay, "Cit. Bish. Phryg.," II., p. 506.

[27] Chrysost., VI., 488; "Porphyrius Deo inimicus, adversus christianos scripsit;" Gran. de Cassagn., "Hist. Classes Nobles," p. 283: "Les diverses et immenses propriétés du clergé païen portaient dans les lois romaines, le nom de loca templorum" and cites Libanius,"Orat. Pro Temp.,"" § 3: Πολλαὶ μὲν ὑπωρίαις, πολλαὶ δὲ ἐν πεδίοις ἐφάνησαν." The work of Porphyry, "Adversus Christianos," destroyed by the emperor Theodosius, was not adverse to the pure original movement but dealt terrible blows against these corruptions of kings and prelates and it was the insidious money power that compassed its public burning. This misery was fastened upon humanity by a law of Honorius, "Cod. Theod.," X., tit. xxx., c. vi, making mere priests the lords of the land: "Eaque de jure temporum..........sub perpetua conductione, salvo dumtaxit canone." Thus having robbed the true old unions of their thousands of temples as we have elaborately described, they obtained imperial authority to own them as feudal lords.

[28] Ramsay, "Ib.," p. 509; "From being the champion of education it became more and more markedly the opponent of education, and looked on culture and literature and art, with glowing disfavor; its bishops were worse educated, till in 448, we find a Phrygian bishop unable to sign his name, Elias of Hadrianople, "Hist. Geog.," p. 92, but able to frame canons to bind the whole christian world at the Council of Constantinople." Elias quotes him as having confessed: "Eo quod nesciam literas."

VAST SUBMERGED UNIONISM OF RHODES. 683

Not only Edessa suffered, but also the island of Rhodes, which as we have already seen in our chapter on the pre-christian martyrs, was, according to the celebrated Isocrates, enormously organized and planted with Solonic unions and schools, by Æschines after his defeat by the orator Demosthenes. What became of the innumerable unions of Rhodes? When, and by what catastrophe were they destroyed? This is one of the unanswerable problems causing modern archæologists to stumble; since it is here that the greatest number of valuable monuments of antiquity are found. Thousands of epitaphs and other inscriptions found there reveal the most valuable information we have of the Solonic unions. From about Diocletian's time no new chiselings are to be found. It looks as though the whole population of that prosperous and busy island had been suddenly swept from the earth.

The massacre struck the old Asiatic city of Altentash, where remains in quantities of these christian unions are now attracting special attention. Quite a showing in the addenda numbers, to three thousand eight hundred and fifty-seven of the Body of Greek Inscriptions, is printed from this heap of christianized industrial unions.[29] So valuable was the discovery, that archæological schools have given no little labor and search towards unearthing the monuments which the victims left, to be lost for ages in these ruins. Altentash, in southwest Phrygia, near the sea, was another city which many evidences demonstrate to have been striken from the earth by the massacre.

Let us now pay attention to another hideous entailment of this Diocletian Disaster. It is that of the creation and growth of alms houses, eleemosynary retreats, proffering charities, and all such beggarly institutions which never existed before.

The archæologists have searched in vain for these establishments among the inscriptions of earlier times. They were the very natural outcome of several great catastrophes which stopped the Solonic dispensation from its course; for under its more ennobling and humane career, such charity was forbidden and unknown.

---
[29] See supra, p. 616, where the subject is discussed. The wonderful inscr. CIG., 3867t is from Altentash. With the aid of Perrot and Ramsay we have there shown all points known.

We have our first glimpse at one, in the case of Pliny who, after he had forced many to execution, broken up the self-supporting unions and been the compulsory witness of the dreadful sufferings of widows and orphans of his own murderous hand, endowed with his private money a primitive hospital in which these wretched sufferers might wrestle with poverty through his charitable act. This had happened almost exactly[30] a hundred years before. Being a natural result of such a calamity, the instance of Pliny prepares our understanding for the consequences of the far greater destruction of Diocletian.

The vast amount of misery and pauperism which fell over the world was added to by the canons of Nice in 325, and was completed by the final stroke of the canon of Laodicia in 363. It is almost certain that the endowment of Pliny became the basis of the first charitable asylum. There were under the law thousands of asylums or temples of refuge, but they were not charities as we understand the word. Charity in ancient Greek, before becoming contaminated by the poverty and want under which laboring humanity after the massacres cringed, was a word of quite another meaning. Charity until the persecutions had an ennobling power. It meant kind will toward one another. It is now, in its degenerate transformation, an indignity, and its recipient is degraded to beggary. There were no such beggars in the ancient civilization; and we have produced abundant proof that the Solonic unions did not tolerate it. Neither were the christians of the first century allowed to ask for charity. The whole vast eleemosynary system as we see it, was brought into the world by the violent suppression of the poor people's right of combination. It may accurately be stated to have had its origin in the massacres.

It was soon endorsed as one of the natural entailments of human property. Furthermore, it could be used by those in power to enormously bolster the assumption of divine rights in property and to restore the ancient pagan law of entailment upon primogeniture

[30] See supra, ch. xvii., fin. We should remain without knowledge of this but for the fortunate inscr. of Pontus, which of itself gives the history of the sad affair. Unlike Hierocles, Pliny was possessed of a kind nature and though the sullen edict of Trajan was unbending, he could thus retrieve an injured conscience.

and heredity in kings. The consequent of this breaking up of the unions of labor was the feudal system.

From the date of Diocletian we find hospitals, poorhouses, orphanages and alms-proffering asylums. A very few are represented in the inscriptions.[31] They are now known to have yielded to these degrading conditions with reluctance.[32] Dr. Waltzing, who strenuously denies that charity in the earlier unions was practiced, admits that in later centuries they so far lost their independence that this species of degeneracy became common.[33]

We search in vain among the great authors and likewise among their own monuments for any traces of the purely eleemosynary institutions. Mommsen speaks of Tertullian's thirty-ninth apology containing the celebrated statement of his unions' functions, but is obliged to admit that this great father is describing a union or college like the rest, and is constrained to recognize the orphanage as an institution of later christian days.[34]

Only a little more than twenty years from the time the Diocletian atrocity was committed, the celebrated Nicine council was called and was presided over by the emperor Constantine. What sort of a man was

[31] The first ὀρφανοφύλαξ we have found dates a little later than the year 300. We are indebted for several at the mouth of the Don, to Dr. Oehler "MS. to the author," citing Latyschew, "Inscr. Pont. Eux.," II., nrs. 438, 539, 442, 443, 546, bis 449, 451, 455, 460; III., Jahrh. nach Chr.; Latyschew, "Griech. Inscr.," 1892-8, p. 64, no. 1; p. 65, no. 2, mit ὀρφανοφύλαξ." Some of these latter are very near the labors of Pliny, and those, dating 220, are thought to have originated in Pliny's persecution, and his remorse fund.

[32] Levas., "Hist. Class. Ouv.," I., p. 134, is authority for our assumption that the colleges were firmly based on the non-charity economical and self-supporting clause, quoting St. Jerome as follows: "Fratres ejusdem artis in unum domum, sub uno praeposito (foreman) congregantur: verbi gratia ut qui texunt lina, sint pariter, qui mattas, in unam reputantur familiam; sarcinatores, carpentarii, fullones, gallicarii (shoemakers), seorsum a suis praepositis gubernantur; et per singulas hebdomadas ratiocinia operum suorum ad patrem monasterii referunt." Praef St. Hier., ad reg. St. Pacomium "Codex," reg. tom. I., p. 25.

[33] "Hist. Corp. Prof.," I., p. 321: "Pour soulager toutes les misères, la religion chrétienne créa des institutions speciales qui recurent, dès Constantin, la personification civile sous le nom de brephotrophia, xenochia, or. phanotrophia, ptochotrophia." In the "Cod. Just." I., ii., 23, a Juliano is the law: "Inter divinum publicumque jus et privata commoda, competens discretio sit, sancimus .... sive venerabilibus xenonibus, vel ptochotrophiis, vel monasteriis masculorum vel virginum, vel orphanotrophiis, vel bephotrophiis, vel gerontocomiis, necnon juri civitatum vel donatorum," etc. Again, "idem.," I., iii., p. 35 and 46, the laws regulating charitable institutions are given in detail.

[34] Quae enim a senatu maxime...videbatur collegia ad eos usus instituta quibus postea christianis temporibus inserviebant orphanotrophia, ptochotrophia, aliaque similia nulla inveniuntur. "De Coll. et Sodal. Rom." p. 90.

this? We are indebted to Zosimus for some hints regarding him, for although the work of this pagan is lost, a fragment has been preserved by one of the fathers conveying to us the facts.[35] Constantine stands as the pivot over which for ages the two great parallel schemes of religion balanced and still balances. Nearly all the noble, original thought, sentiment, humanity, economical democracy and socialism were wiped out, under him and his immediate predecessor. The great plan of salvation of the true ancient lowly endorsed, completed and promulgated by the carpenter of Nazareth and accepted, furthered, sheltered and protected for centuries by the countless labor unions of Solon was through these two powerful monarchs stricken as if with palsy, never to rise again, unless the second coming is this which we to-day behold rolling up in the dusty whirlwinds of our modern labor movement with its ultimatum once more fixed as of old, in economic freedom.

Go back is the cry of the millions still in distress. Go back has been the moan of the great and good all along through the centuries, when they beheld the people stifling in the qualms of the same old monster of competition, guarded and abetted by his police watching his divine right of property, and laying all things under havoc which are opposed to individualism, kingcraft, standing armies and the power of gold.

We are now about to close this volume and we do it repeating the eloquent plea of the ante-Nicine fathers, to go back. There is evidently coming a great and mighty struggle based on this demand. It is the demand of the labor movement for the twentieth century. Go back to that pure, sweet, loving, self-supporting socialism outlined by the great law of Solon.[36]

[35] Socrates, "Hist. Eccles.," III. c. xi., taking the story from Zosimus, "Hist. Romaika." Good encyclopedias declare that this author "cannot be accused of a deliberate misrepresentation of facts." We here get the information that Constantine was ambitious, unscrupulous and cruel, and that it was through his cunning plots, even to the extent of murdering his own family, that he step by step rose to the full control of the empire. Zosimus remarks that Constantine's crimes were so great that when he applied to the pagan priesthood for forgiveness and absolution, those clericals refused to grant forgiveness. This forced him to make his supplication to the christian priests who forgave him, took him in with all of his load of sins and henceforward christianity was adopted. We may perhaps state that this was the real basis of the Constantinian deal which at once legalized and paganized christianity.

[36] It was demanded by good old Cyprian, "Epist.," 73: "...ut si aliquo mutaverit et vacillaverit veritas, ad originem dominicam et evangelicam traditionem revertamur;" A canon of the Council of Nice, read: Τὰ ἀρχαῖα ἔδη κρατείτω. See supra, in the title page of this volume. This shows that

We have given in this volume, the second of the Ancient Lowly, a voluminous and faithfully prepared history of the great Solonic dispensation, which for about a thousand years gave working people of all races occupations and phases the right of combination into unions of trades and professions for their own aggrandizement. We have traced this wonderful and long revered and honored statute through the vicissitudes of persecution, intrigues of enemies, exterminatory wars for its overthrow and finally the awful massacre which opened a way for its complete suppression, a tragedy which was not complete until the enactment of the canon at the council of Laodicea in A.D. 363.[37] It then fell away and the spirit of trade unionism gradually and strugglingly developed into a sickly feudalism which hovered over and ruled the dark ages of another thousand years.

It is true that the immediate system of that vast organization cannot be rehabilitated—only the principle involved. For the close association there will come an enormous public ownership. For the employment by the trade unions, of the personal membership themselves, there will come government employ. For the little collegiate schools there will be the great socialistic common school system, already under way and in a splendid condition. Everything will be on a vaster scale commensurate with the improvements of to-day's enlightenment.

In all this the principle of the old Solonic plan remains unscathed and the overgrown institution now known as the church, with its immense common property and its countless numbers, when reconverted to its original functions and duties may easily and with consistency go back to Jesus and again lend a hand in the forth-coming resuscitation of a strangled race.

however, subdued by the presence of so fearful and mighty an autocrat as Constantine the Great, who presided and watched over the proceedings, yet honest and conscientious men were there in great force who were determined to see the true precepts of the original champions of the great movement for enfranchisement of humanity, finally carried out. And this is the still small voice that never dies.

[37] We may be excused for repeating this canon, given *supra*, page 213: "The words of this decree extinguishing them are. "Ὅτι οὐ δεῖ ἱερατικοὺς ἢ κληρικοὺς ἐκ ἐπιτελεῖν, ἀλλ' οὐδὲ λαικούς. This powerful religious rescript might have been issued by the emperor of Rome; for few as are its words it annihilated their common table upon which their all was based; and to break up this ancient boon of support was equivalent to their extermination. But the same jealous council also killed out their long-time hymns and anthems on the pretense that their composers were not ordained by divine providence.

INDEX.

A

Abgar, King of Edessa, 140; wrote letters to Rome, 140; wrote a letter to Jesus, 384; letter quoted, note 80; wrote letters to Tiberius, 386; quoted, notes 83 & 86; demanded punishment of Pontius Pilate, 387, note 89: thriving Solonic organization at Edessa, 681.
Abiding faith, lasting after death, 153.
Abraham, Roman emperors honored his statue, 369, note 48.
Academy of France, xviii.
Acts of the Apostles, great union described, 178.
Actors, cruel treatment of by the ancients, 225; great society of, in Ionia, 233sq; led a hard life, 270.
Advent, unions at time of, IX; vast labor organizations then existing, X.
Adonis or Attys, 249, note 18.

Ædiles, directors of public works, 47; commissioners of city work, 64.
Æschylus, quotation, 285, note 18.
Æschines, a union member, 283; quarrel with Demosthenes, 296, 297, notes; story recounted, 331; splendid genius, 333; founded school of oratory and wonderful unions at Rhodes, 333.
Africanus, belief of, XIV.
Agis I, monster who assasinated great numbers of helots, 190; Agis III, hated the ephori, 98.
Agonies, how played in ancient times, 215, 216, 211, 245, 288.
Agrarian agitation, 48.
Alexander, 106, 108, 112; patronized musicians, 204; employed 3,000 at a funeral, 209, 247; his pretense to the immaculate conception, 220, note; great festival, 300;

other mention, 210, 322.
Alexandria, mutual aid societies, 161.
Altentash, remarkable remains of its trade guilds, 683 ; destroyed by the massacre, 683.
Amasis, 73, 101 ; census as pharaoh, 105, note; found on inscriptions, 155 ; legalized the unions, 261 ; his eight-hour law, 289.
America, war spirit in, 201.
Amphitheatres, Christians butchered in, XI ; origin of, 219.
Anagenesis. (new birth). on Hebrew stone tablets, XVI ; same, see Oehler.
Anacreon, believed a member of the artists' guild, 234.
Anaglyphs deciphered, XVIII; see inscriptions.
Ananias, story of, 400.
Anatolicus, quotation from, 649-50.
Ancona, inscription found at, 664.
Andanie, inscription of, 59, note 19; protection to run away slaves, 57.
Angtus, traitor to Socrates, 343.
Apameia, important discoveries from, 445.
Apelles, painted Phryne, 337.
Apocryphal gospels, XIII; writings, 107.
Apollo, shrine where written music was found, XVIII; friend of slaves, 126; hymns to, 241.
Apollonius, miraculous escape of, 521.
Apostolic constitutions. 108.
Apostles, in India, 108. entertained by secret unions, 428; mysterious disappearance accounted for, 474, 507 ; Acts of the, women prominent, 496.
Appius Claudius, made a decemvir, 48; his spies, 117-8.
Aquila, driven from Rome, 444; biblical character, 454.
Aratus, Phenomena of, what it taught, 50, note 6.
Argos, 98.
Aristobulus, lost writings, 106, 108, 112 ; a hymn atrributed to him, 249.
Aristonicus, his promises, 95, 161.
Arisitophanes, enemy of the unions, 337 ; on the artists, 220.
Aristotle, his prophecy as to his tools of labor, 94-5, note 8; on machines, 143, 313 ; on play-actors, 204, note 1 ; says workers are too poor to be good, 225, notes ; speaks kindly of them, 276 ; his ideas endorsed by Paul, 456 ; gave the greatest of labor organizations their name, 206 ; Jesus followed some of his teachings, 373 ; his views on religion, 468.
Arnobius, on growth of Christianity, 478
Armories, Rome's bargain with the unions, 52.
Arrian, on Indian civilization, 106-11, 210.
Arsenals, unions emyloyed to manufacture arms, 67.
Artists, great International association of, 232.
Arvales, brothers and sisters, 157 : order was created by Romulus, 167.
Asia, unions of, XI; Asia Minor, great numbers of organized Hebrews, VIII, XVI ; trade unions, 101 ; were voting guilds, 117 ; pre-christian trade associations, 162.

INDEX.

Assasination, systematic, 55, note 15; see massacre of Diocletion, 668-87.
Athenæus, on musicians, 210.
Athenion, strike against oppression, 90.
Athens, modern schools of inscriptions, author's visit, XVIII; boulé, common tables of, 103; cruelties to slaves, 133; repudiated the Phrygian cult, 220.
Athletes at the Olympian games, 216.
Atimia, how it branded workers, 133.
Attalus. a weak king, 137, and note.
Attys, a protecting messiah, 210, 248, 288; was the same as Adonis, 249.
Auction, Rome bid off to Didius, 72.
Augustus, protected the poor, 407; aided the unions, 536-537; earliest rescript against some of them during reign of, 595.
Avircius Marcellus, great inscription at Hierapolis, 636sqq.; facts regarding him, 640-1; text of his epitaph, 638, 639, notes quoting it.

B

Bacchus, wrongly interpreted by us, 112; identical with Dionysus, 206.
Bakers, strike at Magnesia, 84, 85, notes 2 and 3; again, 184 laws applying to, 131.
Ballot, XII, XIII; possessed through the jus coeundi, 101.
Banner, flaming red, 86.
Baptism, practiced in the cult of the unions, 281, 370.
Baptists, the original, 204, 205; hand-to-mouth Baptists, 363; schools of Tyrannus all Baptists, 413, note 149.
Barathrom, crag of, girl thrown from, 327.
Bar Cochbas, pretended messiah, defeated, 374, note 57.
Bardesanes, a musician of Edessa, 681.
Barnabas, with Paul at Antioch, 502.
Bartholomew, visited India, 108; died in the persecutions, 681.
Battle between Moloch and Moses, XIV.
Bendis, a goddess, 148.
Beneseh, the same as Oxyrhynchus; papyri from, XVIII.
Bible, gospels of Clement, Peter and James ruled out, 467-468.
Blastus, a biblical martyr, 582; see lists of De Rossi.
Board of Public Works, XIII.
Boatmen's union of Paris, 666, note 20.
Böckh, on Dionysan artists, 235.
Bossius, unfinished work on underground Rome, 417.
Boxers of Greece and Rome, 224.
Brahmins, habits of, 108, note 1.
Brick making in Egypt, 77; without straw, 77-9; at Nineveh, 83.
Bridge builders, unions of, founded by Numa, 159, 416.
Briennial discovery, XVIII; a manuscript, 482-3.
Brigandage, forms of, 422.
Britain, early schools in, 199; Christian plant, 422.
British Islands, ancient unions of, 102.
Brotherhood, patterned after the true family, XII; Solonic, IX, 100; in India, 108, note; their influence, 113-4,

692   INDEX.

Brutus, patronized Dionysan artists, 221.
Building trades, unions of, 190-191.
Burial unions, of Christians, 168; in Asia Minor, 199; laws regulating, 253, 262, 268; rites among, 295-6; attachment, 348-50; how it screened the early Christians, 352; Stephen was buried by them, 405, note; the attachment affixed to great numbers, 417, 418, 500, 501, 579; common in the time of Caligula, 414, and notes.

C

Cabiri, or dwarf smiths, 166.
Cadmus, originated the idea of the model family, 104; authorized the common table, 166.
Cæsar, conspiracy of, 196.
Cainites, their origin, 135, note.
Caligula, fate of, 408; his character, 411; murderous havoc, 414; his river of blood, 442.
Caltistus, first known as a slave 580; his ashes discovered, 581.
Calvin on Paul and Demetrius, 463.
Canon of Laodicia, suppressing the unions, 213, note 19.
Capitalism, its efforts to suppress the unions, IX.
Caracalla, endorsed Dionysus, 222.
Carpenter, the typical Hebrew, XVI.
Carpocration, school, 500.
Catholics, origin of their crypts and dungeons, 414.
Cato, hated the poor, 525.
Cave of Deirel Bahar, mummies of Pharaoh, 78.
Celsus, lost book of, 645; scathing quotation from, 643; his defiant comparison, 652; his work suppressed, 677.
Cemeteries, the new-found underground graves of Rome, 417sqq., see De Rossi.
Ceylon, Solonic unions unearthed in, 306.
Chares, lost works of, 210.
Charities, as alms-giving unknown, 60.
Charity, in eleemosynary form disallowed in the unions, XVII; cannot find its traces among the inscriptions, 317; Peter's commandment against, 486; Pliny's thought to have been the earliest gift, 602; beginning of the modern system of, 669, 683.
Chilon, one of the seven wise men of Greece, 90; inventor of the ephorate, 90; the man who first established this system of public officials, 91, 95.
Christ, strikes in his time, 184; Rome would have avenged him, 140; endorsed socialism, 152; an initiate, 252; like a second Solon, 261; suffered under the money power, 237; how he escaped Herod's order, 366-7; declared a fakir in Egypt, 648; door of Jesus, 619; received a letter from Abgar, 642; name mentioned by Lampridius, 370, note 47; a perfect character, 356, 357; like Socrates, 341; economic side of his teachings, 361; Josephus on, 365; how he escaped Herod, 366, 367, note 44; a perfect workingman, 369, note 47, 510;

educated as a magician, 368;
list of very ancient authors
who mentioned him, 365,
note 41; learned the dyers'
trade, 372,373; King Abgar's
letter to, note quoting it, 80;
Pilate to Tiberius, 389-91;
text of Pilate's sentence, 391,
note 103; had some secret
refuge in Jerusalem, 398;
Lentulus, 393, 394, note 108;
punishment of Pilate, 386,
387; his recently found sayings on Oxyrhynchus papyri,
433, 434; his "Word," 480;
admitted as a Roman god, by
Tiberius, 547; by Serverus,
663; his plan destroyed by
Nicene Council, 686.
Christianity, early endorsed by
the unions, 198; death blow
to, 199, 254, note 83,
quoting the Canon of Laodicea; how baptism originated,
281: how Christian marri-
ages originated, 259; saved
by Rome's laws of burial,
262; went with the early
communes, 298, 364; it was
adversely defined by Hadrian
286; planted in dens of vice,
347, 491; gave marriage rites
to all, 421; vast growth in
Rome, 407; in Asia,470; decadence of, 506; took its
first root in labor unions,645,
656sq; lost books on, 654.
Christians, owned Temple of
Isis, thrown to wild beasts,
X1; unions in Egypt, 101;
their secrecy during persecutions, 105; pre-christian,
104; burned and tortured by
Nero, 124; why persecuted,
136; caused the troubles
with the iconoclasts, 187;
their nomenclature borrowed
from the unions, 227; how
we have cor torted and spoiled

their word charity, 271;
mentioned by Spartianus,
352, note 13; mentioned by
Hadrian, in famous letter,
367, note 45; mentioned by
Vopsicus, id., note 45; by
Trajan, 352; mentioned in
lost books of Josephus, 363;
refused to pay tribute, 354;
had no pope, 320; Nero's
massacre of, 549sqq.; their
sufferings and death, 555;
Tiberius, Vespasian and Titus
friendly to, 571; Pliny's letters regarding, 593; secret
signs used by, 611spq.; the
lowest of humanity were the
first, 618.
Chrysostom, writings about
Luke, 628, 629.
Cicero, translates the socialism
of Aratos, 51; his words on
Sulla's massacre, 123, notes
5, 6; fought the unions, 166;
on workingmen, 131, note;
contempt for their schools,
251; quarrel with Clodius,
497.
Cinerary rites, mixing of ashes
of many members of
both sexes, 295, note 18.
Citizenship, too poor to be
good, 55.
Claudia, wife of Pudens, 532.
Claudius, Appius, made a decemvir, 48.
Claudius, Emperor, persecutes
Christians, 442; also the
Jews, 520.
Clement of Alexandria,attacked
the professional magicians,
218; member of a union, 693.
Clement of Rome, works of,
cast out, 216, 425; Peter's
tribute to, 261; converted
by Barnabas, 424; list of his
works, 427, note 188; traveled with Peter, 436; wrote
Canons of Peter, 437.

694   INDEX.

Cleomenes, attacked the ephori, 98.
Cleon, sold Istaeus to a god, 56.
Clodius, friend of poor man, bitter contempt for, 166, 537; railed at by modern writers, 568; facts regarding his death, 237, note 16; was bitterly denounced by Cicero, 353.
Cogidubnus, early British king, 531.
College, origin of the modern, 419.
Collegia, were the Roman trade unions, 101, 199, 407; Dionysan artists, 213; its love feasts, 192; fostered by Tiberius, 411; their burial clause in the law, 416; as burial societies, 529; lists of, 169-73, note 46; list of, in Nero's time, 550.
Columbarium, slaves' burial place and mausoleum, 295, 316; also place of residence, 408; who built it, 410; persecution, 412; date of its discovery, 464, 565.
Common table, in pre-christian unions, 164; among the Dionysan artists, 205; originated by Solon and Cadmus, 211, 650; in Luke's union, 178sq; where they discussed, 198; part of great ancient economic system, 273, how supported, 263, 456; in Athens, 372; in the prytaneum, 273; Neander on, 504; in the scholæ, 420; treatment at Laodicea, 199, 213; called criminal 254; enmity of the merchants, 266, 646; Socrates ate there, 342-3; seven deacons to control it, 398-9; Stephen its head waiter, 396; the last supper, 562.
Communal Code, XIII, 103;
found to be a pillar of the prytaneum 104. note; existed in medical fraternities, see Luke.
Communism of Lycurgus, 91.
Communist, manifesto, VIII.
Competition, of slaves against workmen, XV; Hebrews opposed it, XVII; man against man, 55.
Competitive system against Socialism, 139, 140; against the unions, 323, 348.
Concupiscence, its failure, XVII.
Conflagration, Nero's human torch-lights, 124, 558; roasting men in pits, 131; account of Rome's burning, 547sqq.; of Amphitheatre at Placentia 555; at Nicomedia, 596, 597.
Conquests, the Roman, 45-74.
Constantine, 91; destroyer of Solonism, 663.
Cooks, union of, captured by Christians, 685sqq.; crimes of 686, note.
Constantius, with Galerius against the unions, 671.
Coral workers, unions of, 189, 449, 450.
Cotytto, mother of baptism, 284; abominations of, 462, see Paul.
Corinth, destroyed by Mummius, 221.
Council of Laodicea, 213, note 19.
Crato, flute-player, 209,
Creation, Haeckel's idea of, 109.
Crescens, slave, and friend of Paul, 607-9
Crete, early population of, 71.
Crispin, founded shoemakers' union, 673-4.
Crucifixion, 53, 488; was the legal mode of punishment for

the lowly born, 488, 557.
Cumont, on Diocletian's massacre, 677sqq.
Cutters, union of, at Sidon, 166.
Cybele, in unions of India, 108; beggars of, 218 ; how she took revenge on Athens,329, 330.
Cyprian, on degeneracy, 682, note 260.

D

Damascus, cutlery of, 114, note 11; steel, a lost art, 114, 143.
Dance, Callipygian, 497, note 328.
Dancers, Dionysan, 208.
Danziger, on the unions, 597.
Deacons, waiters in the unions, 181, 263 ; their true business 399 ; Ignatius on, 586, see Stephen.
Delos, the slave mart, 126, 196; shipping trade there, 187 ; musical union at.
Delphi, author's journey to, xviii ; inscription of music found, 239, 255; hymns, in the ancient notes, 241, 246, true notation interpreted 207; slaves had their unions at. 196.
Demetrius, president of the image makers' union, 460 ; defended them, 463 ; a powerful leader, 466 ; his labor speech quoted in the Acts, 472.
Demiourgos, a heavenly master workman, 318.
Demosthenes, attacked Glaucothea, 134 ; sneered at the schools of the poor, 251, 283, 327 ; struggle against Æschines, 296, 297, 331, note 53; caused the death of Ninos and Theoris, 328, notes ; was a lawyer, 335 ; systems which he defended, 353 ; story of his death, 340, owned two factories, 466.
De Rossi, valuable works, 351 ; his discovery of Peter's table, 412 ; took up work left by Bossius, 417; on graves of biblical persons, 580 ; his vast excavations of underground Rome, see Nero.
Diaconus, how changed, 263.
Diagoras, lost work of, 289.
Diana, her temple at Ephesus, 465; was the goddess of hunting, 539 ; endowed the poor with souls, 554, note 463.
Didius, bought Rome at auction, 72.
Diocese, a word derived from Solon's law, 653.
Diocletian, his massacre in Phrygia, 188, 601, 652; edict against the unioms, 200 ; remarkable statement of, 298 ; edict regulating prices, 318 ; made emperor for committing a murder, 569.
Diodorus, censorship of, his works, 109 ; on unions of Puteoli, 575, note 507.
Dion. Cassius, on unions, 183, 184; wrote description of burning of Rome, 545, note 442 ; again 552, note 461.
Dionysan Artists, most progressive of the ancient unions, 205; tried to be respectable, 207 ; their œcumenical council at Olympia, 216, 253 ; suppressed at Laodicea, 252, notes; sad poverty of, 225 ; catered for favors of nobility, 234 ; Teos, headquarters of, 224, thronged lower Italy, 221 ; story of their unions of playwrights, 265 ; **Hadrian**

696   INDEX.

initiated into, 219; god of fishermen and hunters, 227-229; they wrote music, 245; their skill and efficiency, 247; a dirge chanted by, 288, note; employed by the state, 299; see Alexander; list of cities where they flourished, 320-1; their organization treated as a crime, 328-30; blamed as fakirs, 471, 647.

Dionysus Kathegemon, or forerunner, xv, 284, 505; forerunner and saviour, 186; loving messiah, 210, 224, 288; son of Jove and Persephone, 286, note 22; ennobler of mankind, 113; god of Indian unions, 108, note 1; therapeutæ under him, 182; endorsed by Roman emperors, 222; patron of the stage, 233; was the Sabazius, 297; his mysteries were for the lowly born, 331, 332, was the same as Bacchus, 206.

Diophantos, wanted state slaves, 54.

Diotrephes, a biblical character 462.

Dispensations, the three great, 348.

Dokimasia, the test of, and its rigidity, 263, note 21.

Domitian, persecuted the Christians, 519, 573sqq.

Domitilla, a Roman martyr, 337; persecuted by Domitian, 519-20; a Christian initiate, 574; niece of Domitian, 577; violent death, 578, notes; her burial place, in the Via Ardeatina, 578, note 516.

Domus Augustalis, explained, 324, 407, 445, 536.

Drimakos, compared with Nabis, 97.

Druids, their death snake, 110.
Drusus, murder of, 123.

E

Earthquake, in Phrygia, 195.
Ebionites, hand-to-mouth baptists, 363, unions of the poor. 358, 359, note 24.
Ecclesia, word derived from Solon's law, 653.
Eden, surmised to have been on a since sunken continent, 109.
Edicts of suppression, xii.
Egypt, eight hour day in, 290; inscriptions found, 379; sayings of Jesus, 433.
Eight-hour day of therapeutæ, 439; proof of inscriptions, 53.
Eleusinian mysteries, 214, note 287, 331-2, 484, 543.
Emancipation, through sale of slave to god, 56, 58, note 17, 314, 315; women punished for buying slave into freedom, 328, system under Christianity, 587.
Emens, battle of, 138, note 64.
Epaphros, Epaphroditas, see Papias.
Ephorate, an institution of the rich, 97; five despots, 91, 95; first created by Chilon, 90; risings against, 98; in in India, 117; for more, see Nabis.
Epidamnos, slave labor there only, 55.
Epictatus, 616, 622.
Epistles, bearers of 610sqq.; original of Ignatius, 585-6
Eratosthenes, lost writings of, 106, 108, 112.
Eranos, 101; mentioned in Homer, 150; members hoped for a messiah, 157; in Isle of Malta, 162; same as thia-

INDEX.   697

sos, 213; did the public work, 160; law of admission to, 260-5, notes 11-31; more on the law, 476-7; opposition at Athens, 335.
Ergolaboi, job bargainers, 213.
Essenes, allied to therapeutæ, 363.
Eudæmonia, or blessed state, 53.
Eunus, compared to Nabis, 91; rebel slave, uprising, 214, 446.
Euripides, as member,-162.
Eurotas, goblins of, 96.
Exodus, strike of the Jews, 76.

F

Fakirs, nomads, gypsies, castaways, 219; the early Ephesian, 471, play upon Christian credulity, 647.
Family, was the model for ancient unions, xvii; Claudian power of, 49; was the model of the city, 105.
Fees, laws of, and contributions, 263, note 23.
Feudal ages, sickening swoon of humanity, 217.
Feudalism, selfish corporations of, viii.
Feudal system, origin of, 193; took growth on destruction of the unions, 685.
Firemen, union of, 589.
Fishermen, their organizations in Asia Minor, 184; allied to Dionysan artists, 226; unions at Smyrna, 227.
Forerunner, of socialism, 80.
Freedmen, struggles to obtain work, 312, see slaves.
Freemasonry, antiquity of, 274, 334.
French revolution, something like it in Sparta, 98; suppressed the feudal guilds, 258.
Frogs of Aristophanes, 244, note 3.

G

Galerius, conspired in the massacre, 670.
Garden of Eden, 109.
Gardeners, union of, at Ephesus, 167.
Gate keepers' unions, 394, 508.
Gaul, unions in, 102.
Gelon and Hamilco, battle of, 69.
Gemeinde, what it was, 161, 204. see chapter of that title.
Gentiles, in harmony, xvi.
Germanius Cæsar, translated book of Aratus, 50, note 6.
Germany, aged ruius of, 102.
Gerousia, was a labor union, 626.
Gibbon, on celibacy, 259; on usefulness of lies, 468, notes 25, 26; on the massacre, 676.
Gladiators, organized in unions, 166; their games, Roman craving to witness, 229, 230.
Glastonbury, unions of carpenters, 531, 532, note 414.
Glaucothea, mother of Æschines, 285, 286; a probable martyr of Demosthenes, 297; story of her persecution, 331sqq.; her fate, 334.
Government, as father and mother, xii; its employment, 54; ownership of temples of Diana, 465.
Gould, Baring, believed Jesus a magician, 368.
Gracchus, 48, 123.
Greece, seven wise men of, 90; terrorized by Nabis,97; trade unions of, 101; its mutual aid societies, 161, 162; list of unions in, 169; musical

INDEX.

notation, 209; sort of written characters, 241; cremation in, 295.
Grenfell and Hunt, in Egyptian archæology, 379, note 70; sayings of Jesus, 380, note 74.
Grenoble, public kitchen, xiii, 279.
Grocers, unions of, 189.
Guadens, architect builder of Flavian amphitheatre, 570, note 496.
Guatama, influence in Island of Ceylon, 306-7, note 86.
Guilds, mediæval, 200; general characteristics, 257; a degeneracy from early trade unions, 445.

H

Hadrian, famous letter on Christians, 296, note 21; 367 note 43, 491, note 316; friendly to the unions, 221; an initiated member, 219; edict on prices,318; mentions Jesus, 365, note 41.
Häckel, Prof. on lost continent 109.
Hæphastion, 209, 301.
Hagios, a test requisite, 670.
Ham, tribe of, 109.
Hamadryad, cobra, snake of India, 110, 111.
Hannibal, how he treated the socialists, 224.
Hebrews, in the trade unions, 130; did not originate baptism, 282; keeping the sabbath, 289-90; persecuted along with Christians, 442; two classes of, 348; regarding the messiah, 372; their proud record, 374; some broke away from Mosaic law, 376, 377, notes; received Paul at Puteoli, 519-20; edict of Claudius against, 538; Vespasian's enmity, 570.
Hegesippus, lost work of, 359, note 25; 645, 367.
Helots, 55, 92, 94.
Hermas, prayer on falsehood, 468.
Herod, on massacre of the infants, 357, note 21; jealousy, 366; his own son one of the infants victimized, 605.
Heroes, society of, 269.
Hesiod, quoting Ascra, 50; on reign of Saturn, 49.
Hetæra, form of trade union, 182, sometimes as fakirs, were the unions mentioned by Pliny, see chap. xvii.
Hieræa and Desdæmona of Menander, 218.
Hierapolis, hot spring, 640,note 77; see Avircius.
Hierocles, a Christian spy, 652, his book, 654, 673; treachery of, 669sqq.; suppression of his works, 677-8.
Homer, on the pigmies, 111; mentions the eranos, 150; thought a Dionysan artist, 208; was baptized, 287.
Homolle,director of archæological excavations, xviii.
Honorius, suppressed gladiators 594.
Hospital, not known in early days, 60, 317.
House of the Lord, 529-30; origin of, in the unions, 657; see subject in full, chap. xviii.
Hunters' unions, in India, 115-116; their business, 539; allied to the Dionysan artists, 226.
Hyperides, secured acquittal of Phryne, 339.

I

Ignatius, death of, 385, note 2.
Illiad, older than Odyssey, 59.
Image makers, 183, see Demetrius.
Immortals, societies of the, 198.
India, ephori in, 91, note 3; Solon's unions in, 106; lost histories of, 107; lost continent, 109; its deadly hamadryad, 110; vast library in, 114; seven classes of Strabo, 114sqq. and many notes; eight hour day, 112; the voting unions of, 117; hunters of, 227, 228, 229, note 64; mechanics of, 144; exempted workers from war duty, 299.
Infernal machine, 92, 93, note 4.
Initiation, of Jesus in a cave, 367, note 42.
Inks, the non-fading, a lost art, 144.
Inscriptions, recording Hebrew debates, petitions, sales, loans, etc., xvi; of Avircius Marcellus, 108, note 1; of hunters' unions, 116; based on law, 150, 152, note 7; quoting it, compulsory, 155; a list of, 169; on St. Luke, 178, note 4, 624sqq., note 23; of Dionysan artists, 211; showing snake superstition, 220; showing prizes on school exercises, 233, note 4; of society of actors, 236; of ancient music, 245-7; of schools in the columbarium, 249; source of our knowledge, 257; showing examination of applicant to admission. 260; of epitaphs, 267, 268, notes; relation of unions to each other, 265; of great movement in Rhodes, 274, 333; as to baptism, 282, note 9; showing that unions were employed by the state, 300; giving statistics of wages, 410, notes 91 to 96; showing sale of slaves to god 314, 315, notes 102. 103; regarding fees of members, 263, notes; Pontius Pilate's sentence of Jesus, 393; note quoting it in full, 106; found in underground vaults, 407, notes; on Peter's table, 412; of Christian therapeuts, 440; a memorial tablet, 449; secret signs in. 500; of the carpenters' union at Glastonbury, 532, note 419; one showing Pliny's gift to girls and boys, 599-600, note 41; showing Christians in the trade unions, 606sq; showing how unions shielded Christians 615sq; from Pompeii, 659; found at Nôtre Dame, 666, note 19; none found of later date than Diocletian, 682.
Instruments of torture, 131.
Inventions, Nabis' diabolical, 92, 93, note 4; many lost in Roman conquests, 143.
Irascibility and concupiscence a failure, xvii.
Isis, her temple owned by Christians, see Pompeii; paintings for the goddess, 500, note 340; she was the same as Ceres and Demeter, 539; goddess of the workers, 658.
Ivory workers, school of, 420, note 167.

J

James the Just, his death, 140, note 39; called the brother

of Jesus, 141; the tragedy described by Josephus, 365, note 41; stoned, 359, note 25.

Janus, temple of, 52.

Japheth, tribe of, 109.

Jerome, wrote on the old unions 510.

Jerusalem, labor organizations at, 102 ; its destruction by Titus, 134, 139sqq.; 142, note 42; sacked by the Syrians, 138 ; a great communistic society in, 177, note 2; the common table, 273-4, notes; Stephen's prophecy of its destruction, 403.

Jesus, high officer in an association, 177; review of his martyrdom, see chap. xvi, § Tiberius; his death caused the revival of association,178; how he attacked the speculators, 180-1; worked on lines of the economies, 181.

Jews, strikes among, 90; in the Solonic unions, 135; were socialists, loved their common tables and communal code, 135, 136, 137 ; how Rome nagged them, 140; how some of them prefered the Solonic to the Mosaic dispensation, 162; their belief in the heavenly workshops, 318 ; how they bore slavery, 215, notes, 103, 104; Sanhedrim had Christ killed because a lowly workingman.

John, unions existing at the time of, 196; the Baptists, 204-5, 284; identical with Dionysus, 505 ; the apostle was a laborer, 461.

Jonathan, the Maccabee, 138.

Joppa, Peter's adventure there among the tanners, 431, note 197.

Joseph of Arimathea, early plant in Britain, 478.

Josephus, censorship of his works, 107 ; wrote on account of the Maccabees, 138; a commander at destruction of Jerusalem, 140; his accuracy proven. 364, note; lost works, 365, note 41; Mundus scandal, 488.

Jove, Jupiter, Jehovah, aristocrats, 52.

Jubilation of striking musicians of Rome, 88, note 7.

Judas Iscariot, 135, note 31 ; criminality of, 398, note 116.

Judas Maccabeus, defeated the Syrians, 138.

Judea, date of annexation to Rome, 199

Julian, emperor, suppression of his works, 677.

Julius Cæsar, wars of, 144 ; the first who attacked the unions 353.

Jupiter, originally a man, 319, note 116.

Jus coeundi, of Solon, new discoveries regarding it, 99.

Justice, basis of true conduct among men, viii.

Justin Martyr, on the nobility, 126; what he thought of Socrates, 341, note 35, 342 ; preserves the story of the story of the flight into Egypt, 367.

K

Kant, powerful socialistic thesis, 226.

Kelainai, shoemakers of, 661.

Kerugma, of Peter, xviii, see Clement.

Kinsella, 74.

Kitchen, at Grenoble, 299 ; at the Piræus, 295, see prytaneum, mageireion.

Kogx ompax, sound of falling

INDEX. 701

pebbles, 240, note 1.
Ktisis, colony, of exiled Romans, 634.
Kurioikos, House of the Lord, 441.
Kurios, lord, the qninquennalis, 57, 397; president of a union, 304-5; crowning ceremony of a, 307; also kurioikos, their meaning, 430-1; what he was, 530; duties, 604.

L

Labor, instruments of, owned by the state. xii; organized in antiquity, 99; its tools nationalized, 94; the taint of, 225; os a divine power, 480, note 291; made a crime,527, note 406.
Lactantius, on reign of Saturn, 49; his sarcasm, 243; on Diocletian's massacre, 654, note 17; says he burnt up an entire people, 673, note 6; on the book of Hierocles, 673, note 7; his valuable information on labor law regulating prices, 675, notes 11, 12.
Lanuvium, burial associations of, 656.
Laodicea, council of, 58; killed out the unions, 199, note 81, quoting canon; a memorable cruelty, 251-2, note 28; crushing edict of, 473.
Laurium, strike in silver mine, 414.
Lawgivers, the three, Amasis, Numa, Solon, 51.
Laws, that of Moses, 79, 80; of Solon, 83, note 1, quoting Herodotus; de jure quiritio, 48; of the scrutiny, 260, note 12; inscriptions revealing, 152, note; harsh to slaves, 129, 131; Solonic, suppressed at Laodicea, 212, 255; against voting unions, 132, 134, 166.
Le Blant, on early Christian dangers, 611.
Lemures, monkeys, 109.
Levasseur, on miseries of ancient workers, 51.
Lex de Jure Quiritare, 67; lex Julia against unions, 594; Licinii, 47; Solonis, see Twelve Tables.
List of places containing unions 169-73, note 46; of prizes awarded by unionist schools, 233; of 52 known headquarters of the Dionysan unions, 321-2, note 118; of burial places of martyrs, 423, note 174.
Livy, 49, on Nabis, 92, 96, 97, notes 11, 12, 13; on Sulla, 122, note 3; deprecated the workers, 441; account of strike, 208, also 88, note 7, giving strike in full.
Logos, Word of Promise, x; new found logon of the Oxyrhynchus, xviii, see Papyri, 433-4; see Grenfell and Hunt.
Lost statements of Josephus,regarding Jesus, 141; consult Josephus in this index.
Love, the first principle of the unions, 154.
Lucian, despised the lowly, 189; stories of, 204; sneers down the occupation as mean, 225; also their schools, 251; scurrilous literature, 337; said artists deserved to be whipped, 393, note 108; an exquisite blackguard, 646-7.
Lucretius, did he die of a philtre? 327.
Luke, epitaph of, xiii; the doctor, inscriptions on, by his

union, 178; reliability of his writings, 177; believed in common property, 538, 622; inscriptions mentioning, 625, note 53; head of the order of medical doctors, 622; wrote story of Demetrius and Paul, 623.

Lupercalia, unions in Italy, 237. see same in index in Vol. I.

Lycurgus, 90; communism of, 91, 97; his species of socialism, 94, 104; plan based on common table, 273, 650, 651; was initiated by baptism, 287.

Lydia, a purple dyer, 194; agent of her unions, 457, 458, 606.

M

Maccabees, 134.

Machines, of labor, Aristotle on 62, note 24; -man, nationalized, 54; reaping, 144; inanimate displace the animate, 313.

Macrobius, his account of Nabis, 93, note 6, speaking with sympathy of slaves; statement regarding the murder of the infants, 605, note 4.

Mageireion, xii.

Magnesia, strike of the bakers at, 84, note 2, 184; coral workers at, 187.

Maimonides, xvii.

Malta, unions of, 162.

Marcellus, Avircius, inscriptional epitaph, 108, note 1; see Avircius.

Marcus Aurelius, his kind letter to the artists and playwrights, 207, note 5.

Marius, battle with Sulla, 122; friendly to the working people, 121.

Marriage, originated among the lowly born, 259; was denied the freedmen, 435.

Martial, wrote epigrams about Paul's friends, 534.

Martyrs, Theoris, through Demosthenes, 328; some were officers for Cybele, 329-30; one was Ninos, the girl organizer, 328; another was Tryphera, at Athens, 336; tried to kill Phryne, 327; another, Næra, thrown from the cliff, 334; another, Socrates, by poison, 341sq; another was Stephen, 402-405; another, Seneca, proven to have been a Christian, 525, see Seneca; others were Callistus, Blastus, 580-3, and a thousand more, see Nero; another was Ignatius, thrown to wild beasts, 586.

Marx, International Association, see preface; quoted on Aristotle, 143; aphorism regarding religion, 186.

Masaniello, head of the fishermen's union, 520-1.

Masons, powerful in Solomon's time, 190.

Maspero, hieroglyplics deciphered, showing strike, 81, 82.

Massacre, of the Jews, xvi; of the 50,000, by Sulla, 120-4; of the 400 in Rome, 124-5, 541; at Jerusalem, 139, 601, 142, note 42, 403, note 125; of Diocletion, 601, 668-87, 188; of workingmen, by Agis I, 191, note; of the infants, Herod's words, 357, note 21; by Nero, 549sqq.; of the labor unions, 670sqq.

Mattathias, of the Maccabees, 137.

Matthew, his Hebrew gospel lost, 483, note.

Maximian, conspired with Ga-

INDEX. 703

lerius against the unions, 671.
Mechanics, strides made in, xii.
Mechanidas, 92.
Medical attachment to the unions, 605, note 2.
Megalopolis, birthplace of Polybius, 92.
Megasthenes, lost works of, 106, 108, 109, 110, 112, 228; how he found civilization in India, 108; his story of the monster cobra, 110; on the ephori, 91, note 3.
Menander, on the wandering jugglers, 218.
Men Tyrannus, a teacher, 412, 414.
Merchants, forbidden social aspirations, xiii; organized like mechanics, 164; on same level with, 189; for the law, see index, "taint" of labor.
Messiah, those worshipped before Christ, 185; Attys, Dionysus, 186; extended belief in a, 210; was a favorite theme for the plays, 245; list of pretenders, 374, note 57.
Methodists, resemble more than others the ancient unions, 450.
Metragyrtes, original fakirs and wonder-workers, 674.
Microcosm, family a nucleus of a state, vii; social formula, 105; was hated by the money power, 104; was the ideal of Cadmus and Solon, 211.
Middleton, Conyers, on Dionysan artists, 647.
Military, a dangerous factor, 117, 118; power of, 133, 157; its destructiveness during the conquests, 46-74.
Minerva, protectrice of musicians, 86; a tutelary power, 104, note 8; patronized labor 539.
Ministrations, the daily, 263.
Minos, King of Crete, 71.
Mithraic unions, almost Christian, 511, 649, 650.
Moloch, battle with Moses, xiv.
Money power, destroyed the microcosm, 104; its martyrs, 237.
Money changers, as they were organized, 401sqq.
Mortar mixers, Egyptian, 82.
Mosaic law, originated in a strike, 80; almost a socialism 135; dispensation, 136-137; how it differed from Solonism, 375-6; Hebrews broke away, 376-7, notes 59-64; some abandoned it for that of Solon, 348, note 2.
Moses, Strike, 77; story of the Exodus, 75-80, with notes; a tutelary power, 104; his law partly supplanted by that of Solon, 277, 348, 376, 377; his important injunction, 384.
Mount Sinai, battle with Moloch, xiv; Nusa, see India.
Mowing machine, 68.
Mummius, destroyed Corinth, 221; engaged musicians for festivals, 247.
Mundus and Paulina, story of, 488-90.
Municipal employ, 53.
Murli Manohar, on India, 112, 117.
Music, a trade and profession both, 86; unions of flute players, 185; Delphic hymns found, 204; aged musical unions, 206, 207; their choristers, 206; skill of Dionysan artists, 207; strike of the flutists, 208; Crato, a flutist, 209; expert in reading it, 210; Nero charmed, 215; the great International Asso-

ciation, 232; teachers of singing, 234; notation, 240; the ancient, recently performed, 246; the Seikilos, 247; methods of traveling in performance of, 248; inscriptions of hymn singers, 249-250; personnel of a company 250; chorus, 251; suppression of, 252, note 28; its effect on the uneducated, 253; its doom, 254; list of musicians at a festival, 265; hymns at the feasts, 293, note 44; the hallelujah, 296-7; reflection, 298, 299; traditional song, 463, note; did the ancients compose some of our own melodies? 542, note; thrived at Edessa, 681.

Mutualists, first outcasts, 53.

N

Nabis, full account of, chap. iv, 89.113; destroyed the ephorate, 90; resembled Eunus, 91; was a military slave, 91; rose to be tyrant of Sparta, 92; his genius, 93; duration of his career, 93; infernal machine, 93, note 4; his hatred of the ephors, 95; his tricks, 96; his aim was high though bloody, 97; speech before Quinctius, 97; set slaves free, 98, 117; synopsis of him, 92.

Narcissus, a rich Roman trade-unionist, 523, note 394; dug the tunnel of Fucino, 523; his powerful influence, 524; knew Paul, 524, note 396; assasinated by Agrippina, note 396; his wealth, 523; more on, 569-70, note 495.

Nationalization of slaves as tools of labor, 54.

Nazarines, an early sect, 139;

an organization of working people, 370.

Neæra, martyred by Demosthenes, 334.

Neander, speaks of the common tables, 504; his prediction, 461.

Nearchus, story of poisinous serpent, 110; lost writings of 106 8; geographer, 228.

Nero, burned the populace alive, 124; his killing of Seneca, 131; thought himself a god, 185; patronized the playwrights, 204, 215, note 28; persecuted the unions, 221, note 28, 545-6; employed large numbers, 221; note 48; his revenge, 408; burned quarters of the poor, 491; his blood-thirstiness, 538; hilarious during the conflagration, 545-6; his massacre of the Christians, 549sqq.; made torches of them with grease, 558sq; results of his rage, 665.

Nicomedia, massacre at, 676-7; Pliny's account of a fire at, 596-7, notes 35, 36.

Ninos, martyred girl-organizer, 327-8, notes 2, 3, 4.

Nôtre Dame, church of, originated in a union of the boatmen, 665-6, note 19.

Numa, was probably acquainted with Solon, 100; gave the workers the jus coeundi, 101, 261; his military system, 105; information regarding, 104, 108, 123, 149, 156, 227; was baptized, 287; his great dispensation, 148, 212; common table in his day, 650-1.

Numbers, of Jews that escaped from Egypt, 78, note 7.

Nusa, the Indian Olympus, 112, 113, notes 8, 9.

Nymphodorus, lost geography,

INDEX. 705

228, see Vol. I, chapter on Drimakos.

O

Oath, of Dreros, 280, note 1.
Occultism, in Solon's dispensation, xii.
Odyssey, not as old as Iliad, 59.
Œcumenical councils known in the meetings of the Dionysan unions, 216, note 32, explaining.
Oehler, Dr. John, his assistance given the author, xviii; manuscript on the inscriptions, 156, 292, 416; his authority, 163; on character of the ancient unions used by Christians, 168, note 42; extensive list of their habitat, 169-73, note 46; on the therapeutæ, 440; on the inscription revealing Pliny's gift, 599-600, note 38,
Oikos, as a House of the Lord, 457, note 253; see House.
Olympic games, 90; artists patronized by Alexander, in great numbers at, 210, note 14.
Onesecritus, lost books of, 106, 108, 109, 112; listed by Strabo among his authorities 228.
Onesimus, slave and friend of Paul, 611.
Onesiphorus, 501.
Origen, 275; valuable work burned, 367; flight and seclusion, 515, note 370; a brazier by trade, 515, 649, note 370; preserved the work of Celsus, 645-6; did not deny some of its statements, 648.
Orosius, 111; his testimony regarding the source of the Nile being a great lake, 111, note 6; on Nero, 552, note 469.
Orpheus accredited founder of the mysteries, 220; was initiated by baptism, 289.
Osirus, Egypt's god, 165; a man-loving messiah, 248.
Ovid, socialistic quotation from his sayings, 50, 51, note 6.
Ox drivers, unions of, 188-189, notes 37, 43.
Oxyrhynchus papyri, 380, note 75.

P

Paganism, as a failure, 104.
Painting, a scenic, 248.
Palestine, unions of, 102.
Pantomimes, common in Ionia and Pontus, 188.
Papias, lost work of, 278, 645; a work on socialism, 614-616; it expounded the plan advocated by Jesus, 615; effects of its suppression, 677-678; its full name known, 680, note 22.
Papyri, Oxyrhynchus, 380, note 75sqq.
Parabolani, what they were, 200.
Paros, strike of bakers at, 84, note 2.
Parnassus, shrine of Apollo, see Music.
Passion play, pre-christian, 248; modern agonies the same thing, 288, note 26, showing how chanted.
Password, of the ancient unions 401, note 128.
Paternalism, comforts derived from, 51.
Paul, his travels, 108, 178, note; did he visit India? 108; at Malta, 162; his trouble with Demetrius, 183, 187; how

assisted, 184; unions and their influence at time of, 196; repudiated at Pisidia, 190, 236; organized a mission at Corinth, 209, 285; secrecy of, 214; escape from Philippi, 215; befriended 274; a tentmaker by trade, 232; in chains, 221; story of a woman, 315, note 103; his earlier career, 396; caused Stephen's death, 404; great change, 453; an aristocrat, 461; thought to have met Jesus at an oikos, 459, note; hurt business of the imagemakers, 462; was for the dead, not the living, 467; sent out as a teacher, 487; story of Thecla, 499, note 336; preaching caused wranglings, 497-8; adventures at Antioch, 502; letters 508; prefered trial by the emperor, 513-14; prison fare at Rome, 522; conditions there, 542; did he go with Nero to Spain? 544; death of, 561-2; beheaded, not crucified, 567, note 491; who carried his epistles, 609sqq.; where he spent two years unaccounted for, 642; thought to have visited Babylon, 636.

Pausanius, accurate description of, 108.

Pergamenian kings, 106.

Periœci, a people of Sparta, 94.

Persecutions, pre-christian, 134; real cause of, 355; of Christians under Claudius, 442; under Nero, see Conflagration; of Domitilla and the Jews at Puteoli, 519-20; the 13 years of, 637; Diocletian's 673.

Pestilence, in Egypt, 78.

Peter, unions at time of, 196; his tribute to Clement, 261, note 15; ordained marriage, 259; Petrine socialism stifled 349; founded a great congregation, 399; a marble table hewn by him, 412; patronized the common table and communal code, 425, note 183; synopsis of his career, 429; his argument with Simon Magus, 431-2; lost gospel of, 433; canons of, written for him by Clement, 437-8; endorsed the theory of Plato, 456; how Paul was less practical, 461; and the Byzantine church, 482; existing copy of his teachings, 483-4; was crucified head downward, 564, 565, note 484; his wife suffered also. 561 562, 563, 564, note 482; did he visit Babylon? 636.

Phaleas, his slaves for government workshops, 54.

Pharaoh, inscription suggesting that he did not perish 78, note 6; outwitted by the strikers, 101.

Philadelphia, unions at, 188; Christian growth at, 662.

Phidias, 329-30.

Philemon, a slave owner, 614; the house of, 621, note 44.

Philip, apostle and lord, 632; was a manager at Hierapolis, 633; wonderful inscription and epitaph, 633, 635, note 70.

Phillipines and Formosans, pigmies of, 111.

Philo, on eight hour day, 290, note 32; was snubbed at Rome by the emperor, 454; slunk into the unions for safety and became acquainted with Peter, 454, note 238.

Philopœmen, rose against Nabis 93.

Phlegon, preserves Hadrian's

INDEX. 707

letter about the Christians, 367, note 43.
Phrygia, trade unions of, 179, note 5; Diocletian's massacre in, 188, 655, 656; causing the extermination of the people, 678, 679, see entire chapter, 668-87, with notes; relics of the actors' societies, 236; Christian unions of, 443.
Phryne, 134; accused, 337; story of her escape, 339, notes 31, 32, 33, 34
Phyles, unions of Philadelphia, 662, 663.
Physicians, forbidden social aspirations, xiii.
Piræus, 108, see Unions at.
Plato, on reign of Saturn, 50; on politics, 129; republic, how inspired, 148, 342; his highest civilization, 152; his four sources of aristocracy, 155; against Dionysan fakirs, 218; on divine wisdom, 255; and Socrates compared, 342; his logos, 379, 425; somewhat endorsed by John and Peter, 456.
Plays, tragedies the more ancient, 320.
Playwrights, account of unions of, 265; see chapter on the Great Gemeinde, 203-30.
Pliny, Cæcilius, found Christians were the members of the unions of Asia, xi, 182, note 15; on Christian unions, 465; mentions Jesus, 365, note 41, 452, 465, 466; letters on the Christian trade organization, 464, 466, note 261; his numerous mentions of Christ, 452; a benevolent man, 588; letter to Trajan, 591-593, notes 20, 21; his trouble about the firemen. 597, 598, note 35; Trajan's answer,
597, note 36; extent of his execution of Christians, 601; his unlimited power to kill them, 601, 602; his charitable gift, 684.
Pliny, Cæcilius Secundus, on the Roman army, 105; what he pre-supposed, 381; saw the eruption that destroyed Pompeii, 521; his evidence regarding the enormous serpent, 553-4.
Plutarch, on reign of Saturn, 50; on the ephori, 91, note 3; reliability of, 92; on the trained assassins, 95, note 9; says Numa and Solon knew each other, 100; on Dionysan artists, 210; his evidence that the unions were political to get government work, 298; on the Logos, 381.
Poets, on the reign of Saturn, 50; inscriptions at Pompeii, xi, 66, note 30, 117; control by workers, 48; warned against, 74.
Pollux, on gymnasts, 247, note 14.
Polybius, on good times before the conquests, 49; on the infernal machine of Nabis, 92, 93, note 4.
Pompeii, voting unions at, 66, note 30, 117; their power and numbers, 518; strike at, caused their suppression, A.D. 37; its newly found temple of Isis. 521, note 390; this temple now dug out of the lava, 657, notes 3, 4.
Pontiff, pontifex the once bridgebuilder, 159, 416, see Pope.
Pontius Pilate, Abgar's vengeance, 140; degraded after crucifixion, 386, 387; his death and obelisk, 389-90, note 98; wrote a report re-

garding Christ to Tiberius, 390-91, notes 101, 102;text of his order condemning Jesus, 391, 394, note 103; did he rescue Christ from the cross? 395, note 110.
Pope, originally a master bridgebuilder, 159, 505.
Potters, early unions of, 159.
Praxiteles, Phryne a model for 337.
Prediction, Neander's, 46, note 1, 461, note 256.
Prelates, did they conspire to kill Solonism? 680, notes 21, 22; their ignorance, 682, note 28.
Prices of slaves, see Slaves, statistics, 310, note 91; Diocletian, edict of, 669, note 1, 675, quoted in note 12.
Priests of Cybele, 166.
Priscilla, a bible character,454; her ashes found, 582, note 524.
Prisoners, made slaves, xv.
Prometheus, a messiah, 186, note 32; theme for plays, 248.
Prytaneum, inscription, 102; a democratic forum, 104; had a public kitchen. 272; its good qualities, 275-6; attachment of the boulé, 292; its common table, 316, 650.
Psalms, ruled out of the church 253, see canon of Laodicea.
Pudens, known to Paul and Martial, 478; a strange character, 529; an Englishman, 531; one of the 70, 533-4; founded the carpenters' guild at Chichester, see Glastonbury; his remains found at Rome, 522, 535,583, notes 414, 424, 529.
Puteoli, ancient chorus at, 220, 221, note 44; a hive of unions 514sq; a "stinking place," 516, note 376; massacre at, 576-7; pagan temple there, 661-2.
Pyriphlegethon, 215.
Pyrrhus, opposed to socialism, 72; his invasion of Italy, 96.
Pythagorus, 104, scheme failed 158; his league, 273, notes 58, 59; his system used at Sybaris, 475, note 278

Q

Quinquennalis, see kurios, 57, 397, 307, 604,and chap. xviii, 602-43.
Quinctius, Roman commander, tricked by Nabis, 96; hears speech of Nabis, 97, note 13.

R

Ramsay, English archæologist on Phrygian unions, 637-38, notes 74, 76; on extermination of Phrygians, 678-9; on the degeneracy caused by Diocletian's destructive work 681-2, note 28.
Reaper, mower, the ancient lost invention of France, 68, note 32.
Red vexillum, flag or banner of the musicians on strike, 86, note 6.
Redeemer, the longing of the poor, xv, see Messiah, Dionysus, Jesus.
Reinach, his personal assistance 207, note 6; found the key to the written music, 241.
Renan, on causes of destruction of Jerusalem, 141; on baptism, 285; on relationship of the essenes and therapeuts, 364; on the nature of Jesus, 368.

Rescript, of Severus, 352, note 13; of Trajan to Pliny, 600, see whole of chap. xvii, 584-602; edict or rescript of Diocletian, regarding prices of food, 675, note 12; ordering his great massacre, 668-87.
Rhodes, ruins of, 274; unions planted in, and nurtured by Æschines, 282.
Right to kill children, 55; law given, 56, note 16.
Rochdale, coöperators attacked by speculators, 180.
Roman conquests, what they resembled, 123; victims branded, 131; basic causes of, 157; attacked socialism, 212; disastrous results, 201; true causes of, 589.
Rome, put down the work of Nabis, 93, 97; early signs of its decay, 95, note 10, quoting Polybius; unions at, 101; traffic in slaves, 120; profligacy of, 205; origin of system in its army, 105; secret unions, 106; voting unions of, 117; economic unions after the conquests, 181; its butchery of the Jews, 140, 142; its Dionysan artists, 209, 215; its laws against labor organization, 212-13; craze for gladiatorial games, 230; columbarium found at 249-50, note 20; its burial rites for the unions, 295-96; exempted the unions from war duty as immunes, 299-300; its conquest aimed to kill the unions, 323; its revenues from pagan sacrifices, 354; its under-ground Christian sepulchres, 395sqq.; with notes of De Rossi; destruction of Jerusalem by, 403; fruitful field for research, 491; condition of labor at, 536sqq.; Nero's destruction of, by fire, 544sqq.

S

Sabazios, a martyred Saviour, 288.
Sacrifices, incomes from, compulsory attendance at, 465, 466; their object to fill the government treasury, 589; non-attendance, the cause of the persecutions, 589-91, notes 16, 17, 18.
Saint Augustine, on charity, 271; on communism of the old unions, 510, note 363.
Saint Matthew, his Hebrew gospel, 366-67.
Saint Peter's Church, on ruins of Diana's temple, 656, 665.
Saint Saëns, attempts to restore the Greek music, 246, note 13.
Salamis, battle of, 70; see Himera, Gelon, Themistocles.
Salvation, the ancient idea of, 248.
Samnites, wars, strike of the musicians, 86-8, notes 5, 6, 7; mechanics of Rome, 123.
Sandrokottus, 110, 112, 113; his hunters, 226.
Saturn, reign of, 49; 104.
Saviour, antiquity of belief in a, 156, 157, notes 16, 17; Dionysan artists worshiped him, 206, 207, notes 3, 4, 5.
Scene makers' unions, Paul a member, 214.
Scenic artists, unions of, Homer a member, 208, note 8; their unions in Gaul, 222, note 52.
Scholæ, secret meeting in the 130; shape described, 130, note 22; in Greece, 412, notes 144, 146; origin of, 418, 419, note 163

Schools, list of prizes awarded at contests. 233, note 4; the Dionysan, 250, 251; of Tyrannus, 412, notes 144, 146; see Demetrius; and Paul's trouble at Ephesus, 413; transplanted to Rome, 413, notes 148, 149, 150; under plebeian schoolmasters teaching everywhere, 414, note 152; of Sylvain, 420, note 167.

Scrutiny, of the dokimasia, 260, note 12.

Sea, of Galilee. fishers' and boatmen's unions, 164.

Seikilos, an inscription of music, 247.

Semitic races defeated, 70; see Jews, Hebrews.

Seneca, strangled by Nero, 130; his words on Roman cruelties 131, note 24; a friend of Paul, 613; his letters to Paul 525, see Letters.

Septimius Severus, rescript against the unions, 595, note 29.

Serapis, a martyred saviour, 288.

Sergius Paulus, a powerful kurios, 525-26, notes 399-401.

Serpent, boa, story of, 553-54.

Servianus, letter of Hadrian to, 269, note 21; 367, note 43; 491, note 316.

Severus, Alexander, a humane emperor, 663-64.

Servius Tullius, friend of the unions, 146, 212.

Seven churches, cities of the, 181-82.

Seven Wonders, 465.

Shem, tribe of, 109.

Shoemakers, their street, in Apameia, 443; settled in temple of Zeus, Kelainai, 661, note 10; Crispin, unions in France, 673-74, note 9.

Silurus, a province of Britain, 532, note 414.

Silvain, Christian school of, 420, note 167.

Simon Magus, his debate with Peter, 429.

Simon, the tanner, took the place of Judas, as twelfth apostle, 428; shielded Peter in his brotherhood, 427; an apostle and kurios at Joppa, of the union of tanners, 633.

Slaves, freed by being sold to a god, 56, 101, 126, 160, 297, 314, 363, 432; the ephori their tormentors, 90; ambushed and butchered, 92; as labor saving machines, 94, 312; tools which Aristotle said might be superseded by inanimate machines, 94, note 8; murdered to keep down their number, 95; set free by Nabis, 98; vast numbers at Rome, 126; forbidden to marry, 129, 421; branded on forehead, 133; cast off the precipices, 133; admitted into the unions, 154; great mart of, at Delos, 186; organized in Phrygia, practiced marriage despite its illegality, 258-59; refused burial, 268; great strike of, near Athens, 303; Xenophon's inhuman proposition, 315; prices paid for their labor, 313, 314, note 100; Roman burial place of, 316; vast numbers in Athens, 328; bloody mutiny of, in workshops of Demosthenes, 331, 332; how one founded a school, 413, note; great influence on the emperors, 523; bought into freedom by Christian unions, 587.

Smith, Adam, his great statement regarding labor, 157.

INDEX. 711

Socialism, of Sparta, 94; the modern demand for, 95, 96; was discussed by the slaves, 130, of the Mosaic law, 135; conflict against the Jews was because they were born socialists, 137; recent regrowth of, 139, 152; ancient 151, 152; a sprout from abused labor, 168; that of Jesus and Stephen, 180,181; origins of, 202, 473; sprang from the model family, 211, 212; a martyr of the money power, 239; correct theory of, 272; how being undermined, 277; deep and indestructible, 305-6; wages under it, paid unions by the state, 309, 310, notes 90, 91, 96, quoting Mauri; slavery gave way to, 323; it was half of original Christianity, 363; was the teaching of Jesus, 359, 361, 401; the ideal life, 477-78; original idea of Christianity, 509; in Second Epistle to the Corinthians, 609; in older Athens, 336, 651; go back to get it, 686-687.

Socrates, an economist, 104, note 8; a martyr, 134; belonged in a union, note 3; one of the best of good men, 283; at the common table, 292; accusation against, 337; in what respect he resembled Jesus, 341; at the feast of Piræus, 342; taught openly to the world, 342, 433; growth of his ideas, 344; his dingy prison, 344-45.

Soissons, seat of Crispinian shoemakers, 673-74.

Solomon, 82.

Solon, evidence that he knew Numa Pompilius, 100; gave the right of the ballot, 101; his unions more economical than religious, imitating the family, 104, 165; his influence still felt, 105; was followed by a great personage, 108, 140; protected the poor, 131; his unions survived the conquests, 144; labor organization before him, 149, 156; exalted trade-unionism, 158, 261; planted seed of socialism, 202, 206; originated idea of imitating model family, 211; aimed to elevate laborers; baptism an influence in establishing the Sabbath, 288; his system involved the eight-hour day, 289; paterned after the city, 304; privileges granted the laboring class, 348; legalized the corsair business, 469, note 265; common table, 650-51.

Solonic law, 55, note 14; 96; list of countries over which it prevailed, 106, note 10; recognizes the unions, 103; made the unions secret, 103; its extent into India, 107; in the Christian era, 196; it enumerated nine trades, 188sqq., including notes; was a basis of modern civilization, 168; killed by the edict of Diocletian, 199; and Council of Laodicea, 255; permitted piracy, 280-81; how it differed from the Mosaic, 375-376; as an established dispensation, no charity in the, 604; Diocletian's scheme to destroy it, 669, 680sqq.

Solonism, killed by Diocletian, 680; go back to it again, is the admonition, 686, 687.

Sophocles, his tragedies were played by the unionist actors, 224.

712   INDEX.

Soter, the same as Saviour, 156.
Soul, the poor denied a, 291, note 35, referring to index Vol. I, catchword "soul."
Spain, unions in ancient, 102; belief that Paul accompanied Nero to, 512, 545, note 440.
Sparta, Nabis, tyrant of, 92, see Nabis.
Spartacus, 76; the great strike of, 90, 166; further accounts of, 219, note 39, see Vol. I, chap. xii, on Spartacus.
Spartans, their socialism, 94; hurled poor cripples from the cliffs, 96.
Stephen, proto-martyr, 141, 395-96; his practical, prytanic eating house, 277, note 76; large household, 400, note 120; made chairman of committee of managing deacons, 180; martyred for socialism, 181; was lynched, 397; stoned to death in a hurried manner, 402-5; splendid organization, 430; why he suffered their rage, 453.
Stolo, Licinius, 47.
Strabo, valuable geography of, 106; opinionated by modern critics, 110, 111; on the monster cobra, 110, note 4; on the pigmies of India, 111, note 5; on hunters of India, 226, note 64; date of his birth, 113; his opinion, 381; his interpretation of the great geographers whose works he read, see India; his opinion, with others, on the value of lies and prevarications, 468, note 265.
Straw, Hebrews obliged to make bricks, without, 77.
Strikes, in Egypt, 81; of the bakers at Magnesia, 85, note 4, 184; economic failure of, not at all certain, 79; of the Roman musicians, 86-8, 208, 209, notes 5, 6, 7; specimens of modern, 89; seldom mentioned in history, 90; of other slaves and freedmen in Egypt 101; at Athens of 20,000 slaves, 303, note 71, Vol. I, 134; at Laurium and Sunion, 414; of the image makers, 623, see Demetrius.
Suetonius, on the burning of Rome, 546, note 443.
Sulla, his unrelenting massacres and destruction, 120; slaughter of 50,000 defenceless people, 121, 124; details of his butchery of 8,000, 122, note 3; an enemy of progress, 123; horrible death of, 124.
Sunion, strikes of the trade unions of, 414.
Suppression of the unions at Laodicea, 213, note 19, see Canon, Council, Laodicea.
Sybaris, its size and military power, 70, note 37; held in detestation, 475, note 278.
Synod, a union of tradesmen, 185, 198; that known as the Great Ionian, 233, notes 3, 4; a name given to many unions in Greece and all proconsular Rome, 223, notes 53, 54, 55.
Syrene, tower of, and location, 109, note 2.

T

Tables, the common, in Homer, 150.
Tacitus, statement regarding the execution of the four hundred, 124, note 8; on the fall of Jerusalem, 140, 142, note 42; on Thaddeus at

INDEX. 713

Edessa, 388, note 95; on the serpent and the catastrophe at Placentia, 554, note 462; his description of the conflagration, 551, 552, note 458; more on same, 556, 557, 559; his words regarding Christ, 559, note 467; Whiston's translation of, 555.

Talmud on early Petrine period, 107.

Tanners, union of, at Joppa, 427, 428, note 190, see Simon the Tanner.

Tarquin, enemy to labor movement, 129.

Taygetus, precipice whence malformed infants were thrown, 96; death place for common people stamped with the atimia, 133, note 28.

Temples, description of, 60, notes 20, 21; later they became the Christian churches, 660sq.

Teos, general headquarters of the Dionysan unions, 224-25; interlinked and federated internationally, 232-33; its vast schooling system, 233, note 4, giving list of prizes to winners; inscription found at, 265, note 29.

Tertullian, Apologies of, 140; was married, 259; reliable as a literary evidence, 298; his works now being more closely scanned, 389; Gibbon's rail against, 390, note 100; describes an almost perfect form of ancient union, 415, note 153; on Christian and Solonic unions, 652, note; Mommsen's opinion of it, 685.

Thaddeus, sent out as one of the Seventy, 388, note 95.

Thecla, story of Paul and, 499, note 336; where she was buried, 499, note 337.

Theodosius, publicly burned the books, 654.

Theotecnus, governor in Galatia during massacre, 679, note 20.

Themistocles, 70.

Therapeutæ, allied to the essenes, the type of all the Greek unions, 163.

Thiasos, 363; early joined the Christians, 438; were a branch of the great family of trade unions, 182, 438-39, notes 208, 209, 210; wearers of black, 438sq.

Thucydides, mentioned the pirates as privileged under the law, 281.

Tiberius, the emperor, 324; believed to have been converted, 366, 547; was pleased with Christ, and asked the senate to have him enrolled among the Roman divinities, 369, note 48; punished Pilate, 366, 386-87; was probably assassinated for his devotion, 404, note 128; protected the poor, 407; a gentle monarch, 418, 445.

Tigellinus, Nero's spy, 550-51, notes 457, 458.

Titus, 134; his destruction of Jerusalem, 139sqq., 429; when emperor, was friendly to the Christians, 571.

Titus, a kurios of Bible fame, 609-10.

Tools, human beings as, 54.

Trade unions, power and work of, 49, 100; purely economical, 103; of steel workers in India, 114; how firmly rooted. 120; on their death blow, 200.

Trajan, rescript against the

Christians, 352; mentions Christ in his letters, 591-92; his letter to Pliny, 596, 597, notes 35, 36.
Tralles, an ancient city now being investigated for its inscriptions, 190.
Tripsprings, of Nabis' infernal machine, 92-4.
Tryphera, a pre-christian martyr, 336.
Tullus Hostilius, favored voting unions, 47, 52.
Twelve Tables, Solon's labor law in, and quoted in the Digest, 48, note 3; a work partly of Appius Claudius, 48, 525-26; insertion of law into Digest from the work of Gaius, 100, 102, 116; the law quoted, 189, note 39; upheld common table and communal code, 277; specified cremation and burial regulations, 294-95, note 47; had in them the important law of proxy, 304; had the Logos, as basis of the labor organization; mention the kurion, 430-31.
Tychicus, courier of Paul, 608; labored hard in spreading good works, 611-13.
Tyrannus, builder of the columbarium, 410, 625, notes 52, 53.
Tyrannus, school teacher in Asia, the schools were baptists, 413, notes 148, 149, 150; numerously mentioned, also in the Bible, 411, 412, 625; founder of the schools, 625.

U

Under-ground Rome, see De Rossi, Roma Sotteranea.
Unions, era of apostles, 100; ancient voting, 101; political plan of, 102, 151, 280sqq.; international, 102; struggles for existence, 103; modeled after city, 103, note 5, 304; their common tables, 103, 212, 620; economic more than religious, 104. note 8, 165; imitated well-regulated family, 104; their secrecy, 105, 130, 276, 634; took military form, 105; of Bakers in Paris, 106, note; not entirely destroyed by Roman conquests, 121, 144; their political functions suppressed 129; existed before Solon and Numa, 149, 156; examination for membership, 154, notes 10, 11; of various trades, 183, 184; of pontiffs or bridge-builders, 159; of poets and singers, 161; of dwarf smiths, 166, see Cabiri; of seafarers, 187; of washerwomen, 149; of woolworkers, 195, 196; of artists, 204-205, see Great Gemeinde; of wandering fakirs, 217; of wonderworkers, 217-218, notes 33, 34, 35; of beggars, gypsies, 218; of image makers, 464; of musicians, 250; of Crispin Shoemakers, 673-674; of hunters for the amphitheatres, 230; list of, in Asia Minor, 630; happiness among, 164; list of pre-christian, 169; mentioned in Acts of the Apostles, 178-80; exterminated at last, 193; of slaves, 197; very progressive, 205; how befriended by Tullius, 212, 213; economies of, 224; great headquarters at Teos, 224; how they helped Paul at Pessinus, 236; shielded Christians, 252-53, 349; tenets, 257; their strict

morality, 258-59; initiations, 259-60, 286, note; symbol, 261; entrance fees, 263-64; were business-like, 271; baptists, 281; authorized the Sabbath, 288-89; their eight hour laws, 289-90; common meeting house, 291; exempt from taxes and war duty, 299-300; crownings, 307; employed by the state, 309-310, note; bought their slave members free out of common fund, 314; belief in a workshop in eternity, 319; protected in the Domus Augustalis, 323; burial places, 351; had no charities, 358; aided Christ's flight into Egypt, 367-68; their favorite color was red, 392, note; the great one at Jerusalem, 396-97; driven into under-ground cells by persecution, 414; caused rapid growth of Christianity, 407, 656sqq.; efforts to suppress, 417; sent out evangelists, 440; were not strictly guilds, 445; advanced the Word, 479; Paul with them in Asia, 503-4; some of them full of abominations, 516; worked for the state, 596; all had a lord's house, 605; manner of initiation into, 618-19; owned property in common, 620; reviled by Celsus and Lucian 645sq; the phyles, 662-63.

V

Varro, on the Roman army, 105.
Vespasian, was kind to the Christians, 570-71.
Victoria Nyanza, lake, Orosius calls the source of the Nile, 111, note 6.
Vienne, ancient inscription there, 222, note 52, 661.
Vopsicus, preserved Hadrian's letter to Servianus, 367, note 45.
Voting unions of trades and professions, secure their own commissioners of public work, 65, note 29; a menace to tyrants, 134; Cicero against, 166; attempt to break them up, 201; socialistic inculcations of, 212; persecuted by Nero and Domitian, 234; at Pompeii, 518, note 380; power of, 536; election managed by, at Pompeii, 659, sqq.

W

War, of the iconoclasts, 183; the Peloponnesian, 303.
Washerwomen, organized 600 years B. C., 149, note 5.
Wealth owners dodging conscience, 97, note 11.
Wescher, on economic unions, 197.
Widows, ancient order of, 588.
Woman, beginnings of her uplifting, 435-36, 493-97.
Wonderworkers, unions of, 217, 218, notes 33, 34, 35.
Woolworkers, unions of, 195.
Workingmen, as Roman slaves, 120-121; the 50,000 massacred by Sulla, 121-122; low social position of, 131; too poor to be good, 225, 226, note 63; produce all the wealth of nations, 257; no laws to protect, 452; Jesus a thorough workingman, 369, note 47, 511, note 364; in constant danger, 357.

X

Xenophon, his proposed system of revenues of Attica, 54, note 12, 95, 315, note 106, 328; on the Ephori, 91, note 3; his words in the Convivials, showing that Socrates was a member, 342.

Xerxes, his greatest of all armies, 69.

Z

Zeus, temple of at Kelainai, 661 see Jupiter.

Zeuxis, Flavius, sea captain, inscriptional history of, 635, note 73; his epitaph written by himself, 636.

Zosimus, the suppression of his works, 677-78.